Third Edition

INTERNATIONAL
BUSINESS

A MANAGERIAL PERSPECTIVE

Brief Contents

Contents

Maps

Preface

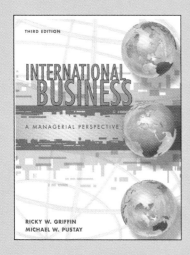

With real cases,
real companies,
real events, real issues . . .

The new *International Business: A Managerial Perspective* is engaging and user-friendly for students and instructors alike!

Are your students prepared to operate in the new international marketplace? Do they understand how traditional business functions are influenced by culture, geography, and technology?

Let Griffin and Pustay show them how!

In the third edition of their internationally popular text, Ricky W. Griffin and Michael W. Pustay illustrate how successful managers must function in a competitive world. *International Business: A Managerial Perspective* is packed with current examples that reflect the vibrancy of the field of international business. This student-friendly text offers a managerial approach to international business—with an emphasis on skills development, e-business, and an excellent map program, which you'll find outlined and fully described on the following pages of this Preview.

The many new features, exercises, and cases in the third edition reflect the changing world of international business and make this the essential book for your course.

This preview will show you why!

New features, cases, and exercises help students understand global issues . . .

> **THE THIRD EDITION IS THOROUGHLY UP-TO-DATE AND TECHNOLOGICALLY WIRED!**

Authors Ricky Griffin and Mike Pustay encourage students to attain 'cultural literacy' in international business—for example, to be able to talk knowledge-ably with a visiting executive from a French multinational corporation or to understand and analyze the impact on themselves and their firms of trade negotiations with Mexico. With that in mind, the third edition now features **a greater emphasis on cases** and other tools to help students become familiar with the international marketplace.

Now, with 48 cases—including chapter opening cases, chapter closing cases, and two comprehensive cases at the end of each part—integrated throughout the text, students work with tangible examples of the concepts discussed in each chapter.

E-Culture [1]

The rise of the Internet is altering the world's business cultures. It is affecting attitudes toward risk tak-ing, decision making, organizational hierarchy, compensation, and education. For example, compared to their U.S. counterparts, many Asian and European firms are much more risk adverse. One British manager argues that U.S. dot-com compa-nies "see more value in trying and failing, and therefore learning, than getting it right before implementing" e-commerce ven-tures. This may be due to a greater accept-ance of failure in the United States relative to Europe and Asia. Notes one European manager, "If you've been bankrupt in the United States, it shows you're entrepreneurial and take risks. Over here, if you're bankrupt, it's still seen as evidence of moral turpitude."

Moreover, many European and Asian firms are very hierarchical and make decisions slowly and methodically. Although this approach has served them well over the decades, it may not be suited to competing in the fast-moving Internet economy. Conversely, the culture of many U.S. companies seems better adapted to the Internet's quick pace. Such is also the case for Danish companies, which tend to be open and nonhierarchical. Notes one Dane, "You could call us rebels. We do not do as we

> "The rise of the **Internet** is altering the world's **business cultures.**"

120

CLOSING CASE

The Benefits of Foreign Exchange

The Athenaeum Hotel and Apartments in London's Piccadilly is a small privately owned hotel which has business travellers from the U.S. as the majority of its guests. Sally Bulloch, general manager, says one way of finding out if the hotel was giving customers what they wanted was to compare it with what they are offered in the U.S.

She suggested swapping jobs for a week with Valerie Ferguson, general manager of the Ritz-Carlton in Atlanta, Georgia, and secretary of the American Hotel and Motel Association. . . .

Ferguson decided to take up Bulloch's offer and go ahead with the swap. She says: "I had no idea what I would get out of it but I saw it was an opportunity to gain an insight into how I could further develop my product. About 35 percent to 40 percent of our guests are international and I wanted to walk away with a better idea of how to service that business and how to build it up."

Business travel is increasingly based on the notion of servici global travellers with similar wants and needs. Ms. Ferguson sa however, that there can be enormous differences.

"One thing that has left an indelible impression is that Europe travellers are not as vocal as Americans—you have to take more tin to pull the information out. In America, a guest might go to the fro desk and say 'my breakfast was terrible,' but the British are just n going to do that. We've got to find a way of getting that feedba rather than make the assumption that everything is OK."

One way might be to contact visitors after they have left the ho "I don't think they will speak to you unless something major happe but once they get home or to the office, they might," she says.

Guests with limited English could be inhibited by language dif culties, and Ms. Ferguson believes one of her achievements over t past five years at the Ritz-Carlton is to ensure that staff speaking number of languages are available at all times.

... and learn how to succeed in the international marketplace

To give students greater insights into international business, the third edition now includes three new content boxes entitled, *Wiring the World*, *Venturing Abroad* and *Bringing the World into Focus*, which highlight coverage of current issues related to technology, entrepreneurship, and doing business with a global perspective.

The *Wiring the World* boxes provide insights into the impact of e-commerce on how business is conducted internationally.

Wiring the World
THE INTERNET, NATIONAL COMPETITIVENESS, AND CULTURE

What does it take to succeed in the Internet age? According to some experts, a country needs "superliquid and vast capital markets, venture-capital networks, world-class universities, risk-taking culture, restructuring ethos, and high-tech talent pools."[2] The Internet, however, threatens to upset numerous culture norms. As you read this chapter, think about the requirements for success in the Internet age and the various elements of culture that are discussed. For example, you might consider the following questions:

• In some business cultures, pay is linked to seniority. Dot-com businesses, however, rely heavily on stock options to compensate their employees, and younger workers often have greater technical skills than older workers. How can such cultures reconcile these conflicting norms?

• Can group-oriented cultures that promote a slow, consensus-building style of decision making act quickly enough to compete in the fast-moving e-commerce environment?

• Some cultures dislike uncertainty and risk taking. How can they thrive in the Internet age, which to date has been characterized by high levels of uncertainty and risk?

• Some business cultures stress conducting business with those persons with whom you or your company has developed a long-term, trusting relationship. Is such an approach outmoded in the Internet age?

VENTURING *Abroad*
ENTREPRENEURSHIP

Let's briefly review some key elements of Japanese culture and how the culture affects Japanese business practices. Note how this culture is learned, interrelated, and shared and how it defines group membership. The first cultural element that plays a major role in Japanese business practices is the hierarchical structure of Japanese society. The social hierarchy strictly defines how people deal with each other. In fact, speaking the Japanese language requires that one know one's position relative to the person to whom one is talking. Different forms of language are used depending on whether one is conversing with a superior or a subordinate. Thus, when two Japanese businesspeople meet, they immediately exchange business cards, in part to determine their relative status so that they can know which form of address to use.

A second cultural element is groupism. A person is identified as a member of a group rather than as an individual. This group identity is ingrained in Japanese children at an early age. Watching the differences between children in a U.S. preschool and those in a Japanese preschool is interesting. The U.S. school focuses on nurturing the individual by praising individual accomplishments and working to raise the child's self-esteem. The Japanese school concentrates on transforming spoiled preschoolers.

The *Venturing Abroad* boxes expose students to the opportunities and challenges of conducting business outside their home country.

The *Bringing the World into Focus* boxes helps students to understand the context—historical, cultural, political—of international business.

Bringing the World into FOCUS
THE IMPACT OF JAPANESE CULTURE ON BUSINESS

Let us briefly review some key elements of Japanese culture and how it affects Japanese business practices. Note how this culture is learned, interrelated, and shared, and how it defines group membership.

The first cultural element that plays a major role in Japanese business practices is the *hierarchical structure* of Japanese society. The social hierarchy strictly defines how people deal with each other. In fact, speaking Japanese requires that you know your position relative to the person to whom you are talking. Different forms of language are used depending on whether you are conversing with a superior or a subordinate. Thus, when two Japanese businesspeople meet, they immediately exchange business cards, partly to determine their relative status so they can know which form of address to use.

A second cultural element is *groupism*. A person is identified as a member of a group rather than as an individual. This group iden-

> Mom-and-pop stores like this liquor retailer have been a mainstay of the Japanese economy. International pressures to open the Japanese economy to foreign retailers threaten a society that highly values harmony and loyalty.

until consensus is reached. The need to preserve *wa* is one reason many Japanese firms encourage after-work socializing and partying by Japanese salarymen. These parties are a means of building

Ongoing features that help students grasp concepts . . .

BUILDING GLOBAL SKILLS

This exercise will help give you insights into how cultural and social factors affect international business decisions. Your instructor will divide the class into groups of four or five people. Each group then picks any three products from the first column of the following list and any three countries from the second column. (Or, your instructor may assign each group three products and three countries.)

Products	Countries
swimsuits	France
CD players	Singapore
desks and bookcases	Poland
men's neckties	Saudi Arabia
women's purses	Taiwan
throat lozenges	Italy
film	South Africa
shoes	Russia

Assume that your firm already markets its three products in your home country. It has a well-known trademark and slogan for each product, and each product is among the market leaders. Assume further that your firm has decided to begin exporting each product to each of the three countries. Research the cultures of those three countries to determine how, if at all, you may need to adjust packaging, promotion, advertising, and so forth in order to maximize your firm's potential for success. Do not worry too much about whether a market truly exists (assume that market research has already determined one does). Focus instead on how your product will be received in each country given that country's culture.

Follow-Up Questions

1. What were your primary sources of information about the three countries? How easy or difficult was it to find information?
2. Can you think of specific products that are in high demand in your home country that would simply not work in specific other countries because of cultural factors?
3. How do you think foreign firms assess your home culture as they contemplate introducing their products into your market?

Building Global Skills exercises get students involved with skills-oriented exercises.

Working with the Web exercises tie the book to the vast learning potential of the Internet.

WORKING WITH THE WEB:
BUILDING GLOBAL INTERNET SKILLS

Learning about Cultural Values

A variety of Internet sites provide useful information about cultural differences among countries. (Check out the textbook's Web site for linkages to some of the most interesting ones.) Pick three countries that Hofstede studied. Visit several of these Web sites and review the material provided for your three countries. Relate the material you find to Hofstede's work. For example, does the material about each country on the Web site seem consistent or inconsistent with Hofstede's findings about that country? If relationships between the Web site and Hofstede's analysis are not obvious, can you speculate as to why this is true?

Also at the end of each chapter, you'll find the *In The News* feature, an exercise that helps students stay on top of changing events in international business and allows them to comprehend how the theories and concepts they have learned in the chapter are incorporated into the everyday decision making of international business.

IN THE NEWS

1. Visit the *Financial Times* Website at www.ft.com and click on "News." Then click on "Country Surveys." Scroll down and click on "Work-Life Balance," and research sums of the feature articles under that heading. Compare the issues that arise in various countries and cultures. What can you learn about their differences and similarities?
2. Compare the U.S., U.K., and global editions of the *Financial Times* homepage. What differences can you find? Why do you think they exist?

. . . focus on technology, and achieve success

To help students see an issue from different perspectives, the *Point/Counterpoint* features provide opposing viewpoints on controversial business topics and serve as a launch pad for student discussion and research. No right answers are provided—instead, the basic pros and cons of each side are highlighted and discussed, and where appropriate, the authors discuss the ethical implications of these debates.

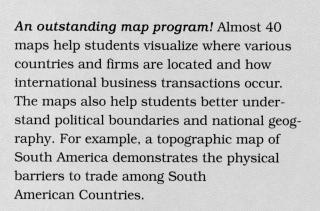

An outstanding map program! Almost 40 maps help students visualize where various countries and firms are located and how international business transactions occur. The maps also help students better understand political boundaries and national geography. For example, a topographic map of South America demonstrates the physical barriers to trade among South American Countries.

Teaching and learning tools for instructors and students . . .

Order the text packaged with a subscription to

> *Financial Times*

For daily updates that help students understand subjects ranging from economics to IT, a 15-week subscription to one of the world's leading business publications is the answer! The **Financial Times** has numerous features that help students understand the rapidly changing world of international business. The accompanying FT.com Web site gives students an archive of not only the **Financial Times**, but also 3,000 other publications—an invaluable research tool!

> *myPhlip*

www.prenhall.com/griffin

Prentice Hall's Learning on the Internet Partnership/Companion Web site is the most advanced text-specific site available on the Web! Developed *by professors for professors and their students*, the new myPHLIP provides professors with a customized course Web site, including new communication tools, one-click navigation of chapter content, and great PHLIP resources such as current events and Internet exercises. It also features an interactive and exciting online student study guide.

. . . Everything you need for a course that gets students excited and involved!

› INSTRUCTOR'S RESOURCE CD-ROM

This helpful CD-ROM includes the Instructor's Manual, PowerPoint slides, and the Win/PH Test Manager. Containing all of the questions in the printed Test Item File, Test Manager is a comprehensive suite of tools for testing and assessment and allows educators to create and distribute tests for their courses easily.

› INSTRUCTOR'S MANUAL

The helpful Instructor's Manual includes sample syllabi, lecture outlines, and answers to all end-of-chapter and case questions.

› TEST ITEM FILE

Over 100 questions per chapter, including multiple choice, true/false, short answer and essays.

› WINPH CUSTOM TEST MANAGER

This electronic version of the Test Item File includes the Test Manager program.

› POWERPOINTS

Available on the IRCD-ROM and the myPHLIP Web site, adopters will receive more than 20 slides per chapter, including maps and figures from the text, in addition to highlights of key chapter material.

› TRANSPARENCIES

100 of the most important PowerPoints are available to adopters in the form of four-color acetates.

› INTERNET GUIDE TO INTERNATIONAL BUSINESS

This helpful guide provides students with the Internet resources available for International Business topics.

› ONLOCATION VIDEOS

Four part-ending video segments in VHS format are available for professors.

❯ STANDARD ONLINE COURSES

(WebCT, Blackboard, Course Compass)

Premium Web CT, an online course from Prentice Hall features Companion Web Site and Test Item File content in an easy-to-use system. Developed by educators for educators and their students, this online content and tools feature the most advanced educational technology and instructional design available today. The rich set of materials, communication tools, and course management resources can be easily customized to either enhance a traditional course or create the entire course online.

❯ GLOBE CD-ROM

Atlas and exercises for International Business. Includes political and physical maps, exercises based on cultural and economic geography, as well as "Geo Concepts," which focus on regional issues and their impact on International Business.

Acknowledgments

The cover of this book identifies two authors by name. In reality, *International Business: A Managerial Perspective* represents a true team effort involving literally dozens of skilled professionals. While any and all errors of fact, omission, and emphasis are solely our responsibility, we would be remiss if we did not acknowledge those who contributed to this and earlier editions of this book.

First of all, thanks to our editors at Prentice Hall: John Sisson, Melissa Steffens, Theresa Festa, Ron Librach, and Elisa Adams. Working with them has been an absolute pleasure, given their graciousness and professionalism. Thanks also to our marketing manager Michael Campbell, supplements editor Jessica Sabloff, art director Cheryl Asherman, and everyone else at Prentice Hall who had a hand in bringing the third edition to press.

Next, we gratefully acknowledge the contributions of Martin Meznar of Arizona State University, who wrote the instructor's manual, and Andrew Yap of Florida International University, who wrote the test item file.

Thanks also to our colleagues at other universities who reviewed the manuscript, contributed suggestions, and helped us make this edition the best international business textbook for students and teachers:

Anke Arnaud
University of Central Florida

Allan Ellstrand
California State University Long Beach

Tao Gao
Hofstra University

Basil J. Janavaras
Mankato State University

Sara L. Keck
Pace University

John A. Lehman
University of Alaska Fairbanks

Roderick J. Matthews
University of Wisconsin

Claudio Milman
Rollins College

Peter Ping Li
California State University Stanislaus

Jaime Ortiz
Florida Atlantic University

Christopher J. Robertson
Northeastern University

Carol Sanchez
Grand Valley State University

Michael Shaner
Saint Louis University

Gregory K. Stephens
Texas Christian University

At Texas A&M University, we have had the good fortune to work with one of the finest groups of professional colleagues anyone could imagine. We also appreciate the support of other colleagues, past and present, whose expertise and insights have been incorporated into this manuscript.

Finally, we would also like to acknowledge the contributions made by our families—Glenda, Dustin, and Ashley Griffin and Zandy, Scott, and Katie Pustay. They didn't write a single word of the book or draw any of the maps or artwork, but their imprint can be found on everything we do. They support us, encourage us, and inspire us. They give our work—and our lives—meaning. It is with all our love and affection that we thank them.

About the Authors

About the Authors

Ricky W. Griffin holds the Blocker Chair in Business Administration at Texas A&M University. He serves as Executive Associate Dean of the Mays College of Business and as professor of management at Texas A&M University. After receiving his Ph.D. from the University of Houston in 1978, he joined the faculty at the University of Missouri-Columbia before moving to Texas A&M University in 1981.

Professor Griffin teaches international management, organizational behavior, human resource management, and general management. He has taught both undergraduate and graduate students, participated in numerous executive training programs, and taught in Europe. A member of the Academy of Management, he has served as division chair of that group's Organizational Behavior division.

Professor Griffin has written several successful textbooks, including *Management, Organizational Behavior* (with Greg Moorhead), and *Business* (with Ron Ebert). He is currently conducting research on workplace violence in Canada and job design differences and similarities among firms in Japan, Europe, and the United States.

Michael Pustay is professor of management at Texas A&M University. He currently serves as associate director of the Center for International Business Studies and as associate director of the Center for International Business Education and Research at Texas A&M. He is the North American editor of the British journal *Transport Reviews*. Professor Pustay received his B.A. in economics *summa cum laude* from Washington and Lee University in 1969 and his Ph.D. in economics from Yale University in 1973. He taught at Purdue University and Bowling Green State University prior to joining Texas A&M's business school faculty.

Professor Pustay, who has taught international business for 12 years, focuses his teaching and research efforts on international business and business-government relations. His work has appeared in such professional journals as the *Journal of Management, Southern Economic Journal, Land Economics*, and *Transportation Journal*. He is currently researching the role of regional trading blocs on the world economy and the impact of domestic economic policies on international competition.

Professor Pustay is a member of numerous professional organizations, including the Academy of International Business, the American Economic Association, the Association for Canadian Studies in the United States, and the Transportation Research Forum. He has served as a consultant for a variety of public and private organizations, including the U.S. Department of Transportation, the Small Business Administration, the Civil Aeronautics Board, and Reliant Energy.

CHAPTER

The Business of the Olympics

Every two years, the world's attention turns to the Olympic Games. Given that international business and the global economy play such a dominant role in the world today, it should come as no surprise that the Olympics have come to reflect international business at its most intense. The games are governed by the International Olympic Committee (IOC), which is based in Switzerland. The IOC decides where the games will be held and which sports will be represented, and it oversees the selection of judges and referees. Each country wanting to send athletes to compete in the games establishes a national committee to organize its Olympic effort. These committees are supervised by and report to the IOC.

"The **Olympics** reflect international business at its **most intense**."

Potential host cities must give elaborate presentations to the IOC and make substantial commitments in terms of facilities, a volunteer workforce, and related organizational support. For example, as part of its winning bid to host the 1998 winter Olympics, Japan promised to build a new high-speed rail line between Tokyo and Nagano, the site of the games. Further, the infighting to be selected is vicious. China threatened a trade war with the United States after the U.S. Senate passed a resolution that hurt Beijing's chances to host the summer Olympics in 2000, a prize eventually seized by Sydney,

1

An Overview of International Business

OBJECTIVES

After studying this chapter, you should be able to:

〉 Discuss the meaning of international business.

〉 Explain the importance of understanding international business.

〉 Identify and describe the basic forms of international business activities.

〉 Discuss the causes of globalization.

Australia. After Salt Lake City lost its bid for the 1998 games, the city's local organizing committee launched a massive undertaking to lure the 2002 games. Unfortunately, its efforts included widespread gift giving and lavish entertaining of IOC delegates that crossed ethical boundaries. As these facts became public, they triggered a worldwide cry for reforming the IOC.

Why would a city want to host the Olympic Games? Most compete for the privilege because the games would thrust them into the international spotlight and promote economic growth. Further, the tourism benefits are long lived; for example, skiers, skaters, and snowboarders continue to enjoy the facilities at previous Olympic sites such as Nagano, Lillehammer, Calgary, Albertville, and Lake Placid, pouring money into the local economies long after the Olympic torch has been extinguished. The games also are frequently a catalyst for improving a city's infrastructure. For example, the high-speed rail line between Tokyo and Nagano halves the travel time between the two cities—a benefit that continues for local residents and for future visitors.

Because of the high cost of running the Olympics, both the IOC and national Olympic committees are always alert for ways to generate revenue. Television coverage provides one significant source of revenue. NBC paid

$1.27 billion for the U.S. broadcast rights for the 2000 Sydney summer games and the 2002 Salt Lake City winter games. It then shelled out an additional $2.3 billion to lock up the U.S. broadcast rights for the 2004, 2006, and 2008 games—even though their sites had not yet been determined. Broadcast rights for Europe, Australia, Asia, and the rest of the Americas will sell for smaller but still breathtaking amounts to local broadcasters. NBC and these broadcasters, in turn, will sell advertising time to companies eager to market their goods to Olympic fans throughout the world. For example, in July 1997—three years before its first ad would run—General Motors contracted with NBC to be the exclusive advertiser of automotive products for the 2000, 2002, 2004, 2006, and 2008 Olympics, a package worth over half a billion dollars.

Another important source of revenue for the IOC and for national committees is corporate sponsors, who wish to capture the prestige and visibility of being associated with the games. The highest-profile level—and, at $55 million, the most expensive—is that of worldwide partner, a designation valuable to firms that market their products to consumers throughout the world, such as Coca-Cola, Kodak, Panasonic, and Samsung. The primary benefit of worldwide partnership is that the partners get priority advertising space during Olympic broadcasts, if they choose to buy it. For example, Coca-Cola paid $60 million above and beyond its partnership fee for television advertising during the 1996 and 2000 games.[1]

The millions of dollars spent on the Olympics by television networks and corporate advertisers reflect the internationalization of business—the result of the desire of firms such as Coca-Cola, Panasonic, and Samsung to market their products to consumers worldwide. The forces that have made the Olympics a growing international business are the same forces that affect firms worldwide as they compete in domestic and foreign markets. Changes in communications, transportation, and information technology not only facilitate domestic firms' foreign expansion but also aid foreign firms in their invasion of the domestic market. These trends have accelerated during the past decade due to the explosive growth of e-commerce and the reduction in trade and investment barriers sponsored by organizations such as the World Trade Organization and the European Union. Indeed, these changes are so profound that many futurists now talk about the "boundaryless" global economy—an economy in which national borders are irrelevant.

The global economy profoundly affects your daily life, from the products you buy to the prices you pay to the interest rates you are charged to the kind of job you hold. By writing this book, we hope to help you become more comfortable and effective in this burgeoning international business environment. To operate comfortably in this environment, you need to learn the basic ideas and concepts—the common body of knowledge—of international business. Further, you must understand how these ideas and concepts affect managers as they make decisions, develop strategies, and direct the efforts of others. You also need to be conversant with the fundamental mechanics and ingredients of the global economy and how they affect people, businesses, and industries. You need to understand the evolution of the global economy and the complex commercial and political relationships among Asia, Europe, North America, and the rest of the world.

To help ensure your future effectiveness in the international business world, we plan to equip you with the knowledge, insights, and skills that are critical to your functioning in a global economy. To that end, we have included hundreds of examples to help demonstrate how international businesses succeed—and how sometimes they fail. You also will read tips and extended examples about global companies in special features called "Bringing the World into Focus," "Venturing

Abroad," and "Wiring the World," and you will have the chance to practice your growing skills in end-of-chapter exercises, "Building Global Skills," "Working with the Web," and "In the News."

International business consists of business transactions between parties from more than one country. Examples of international business transactions include buying materials in one country and shipping them to another for processing or assembly, shipping finished products from one country to another for retail sale, building a plant in a foreign country to capitalize on lower labor costs, or borrowing money from a bank in one country to finance operations in another. The parties involved in such transactions may include private individuals, individual companies, groups of companies, and/or governmental agencies.

How does international business differ from domestic business? Simply put, domestic business involves transactions occurring within the boundaries of a single country, while international business transactions cross national boundaries. International business can differ from domestic business for a number of other reasons, including the following:

- The countries involved may use different currencies, forcing at least one party to convert its currency into another.
- The legal systems of the countries may differ, forcing one or more parties to adjust their practices to comply with local law. Occasionally, the mandates of the legal systems may be incompatible, creating major headaches for international managers.
- The cultures of the countries may differ, forcing each party to adjust its behavior to meet the expectations of the other.
- The availability of resources differs by country. One country may be rich in natural resources but poor in skilled labor, while another may enjoy a productive, well-trained workforce but lack natural resources. Thus, the way products are produced and the types of products that are produced vary among countries.

In most cases the basic skills and knowledge needed to be successful are conceptually similar whether one is conducting business domestically or internationally. For example, the need for marketing managers to analyze the wants and desires of target audiences is the same regardless of whether the managers are engaged in international business or domestic business. Although the concepts may be the same, however, there is little doubt that the complexity of skills and knowledge needed for success is far greater for international business than for domestic business. International businesspeople must be knowledgeable about cultural, legal, political, and social differences among countries. They must choose the countries in which to sell their goods and from which to buy inputs. International businesses also must coordinate the activities of their foreign subsidiaries, while dealing with the taxing and regulatory authorities of their home country and all the other countries in which they do business.

There are many different reasons why students today need to learn more about international business. First, almost any large organization you work for will have international operations or be affected by the global economy. You need to understand this increasingly important area to better assess career opportunities and to interact effectively with other managers. For example, in your first job assignment, you could be part of a project team that includes members from Mexico, Uruguay,

Canada, and the United States. A basic grasp of international business would help you understand more fully why the team was formed, what the company expects it to accomplish, and how you might most effectively interact with your colleagues. You also need to study international business because you may eventually work for a firm that is owned by a corporation headquartered in another country. For example, 5.2 million U.S. citizens work for U.S. affiliates of foreign-owned corporations, while foreign subsidiaries of U.S. corporations employ 8 million Europeans, Asians, Africans, Australians, Canadians, and Latin Americans.[2]

Small businesses also are becoming more involved in international business. If one day you start your own business, you may find yourself using foreign-made materials or equipment, competing with foreign firms, and perhaps even selling in foreign markets. The growth of e-commerce has also opened up new opportunities for small businesses. Previously, to enter foreign markets, firms often needed to painstakingly build distribution networks and brand recognition country by country, a process that often favored large firms over small ones. Today, a well-developed Web site can draw the business of consumers throughout the world without the need to establish a physical presence in each country, making it easier for small businesses to participate in the international marketplace. "Wiring the World" presents an example of how the Internet has presented opportunities for a small entrepreneur.

Another reason for you to study international business is to keep pace with your future competitors. Business students in Europe have traditionally learned multiple languages, traveled widely, and had job experiences in different countries. More European universities are launching business programs, many of which require students to spend one or more semesters in different countries. Asian students, too, are actively working to learn more about foreign markets and cultures, especially those of North American and European countries. These students, training to become managers, will soon be in direct competition with you, either in jobs with competing companies or in positions within your own company. You need to ensure that your global skills and knowledge will aid your career, rather than allowing their absence to hinder it.

Wiring the World

MOLDOVA'S PRESCRIPTION FOR INTERNET SUCCESS

The growth of the Internet is providing unexpected business opportunities for firms large and small. One Florida entrepreneur, John Harris, noticed that Moldova (see Map 1.1), a new country created when the Soviet Union collapsed in the early 1990s, was assigned the domain suffix *md* for its Web addresses by an international agreement governing the Internet. While *md* may not mean much in Moldovan, Harris recognized that it has a very specific connotation in the United States, the world's biggest Internet user.

Harris negotiated a 25-year contract with Moldova's Republican Center for Informatics. He markets Web addresses to medical organizations, pharmaceutical companies, and others who want *md* in their Web address, paying Moldova $20 a year for each sale. After 18 months, he has sold rights to 8,000 *md* addresses at $299 a year.

Source: "Moldova Gains as Cybername Nets Doctors," *Financial Times*, January 20, 2000, p. 4.

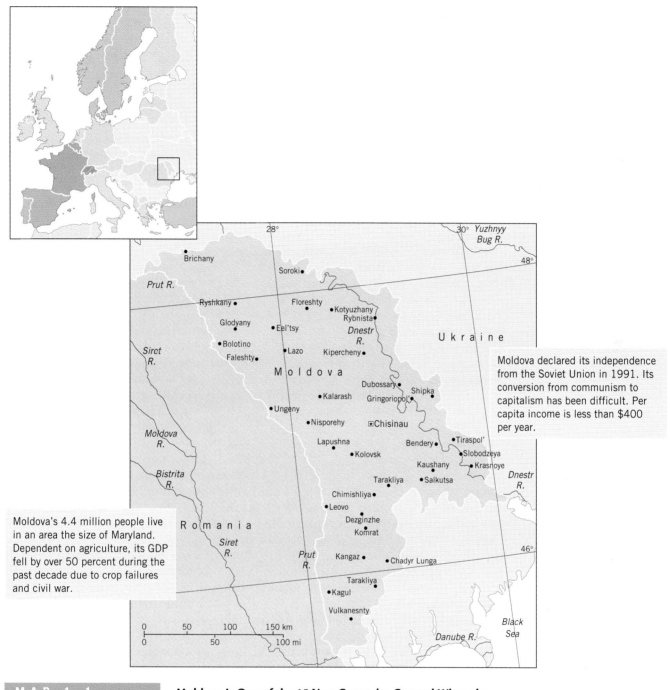

Moldova declared its independence from the Soviet Union in 1991. Its conversion from communism to capitalism has been difficult. Per capita income is less than $400 per year.

Moldova's 4.4 million people live in an area the size of Maryland. Dependent on agriculture, its GDP fell by over 50 percent during the past decade due to crop failures and civil war.

MAP 1.1

Moldova Is One of the 15 New Countries Created When the Soviet Union Disintegrated

You also need to study international business to stay abreast of the latest business techniques and tools, many of which are developed outside North America. For example, Japanese firms have pioneered inventory management techniques such as **just-in-time (JIT) systems**. Under JIT, suppliers are expected to deliver necessary inputs just as they are needed. Similarly, European firms such as Volvo and Japanese firms such as Honda were among the first to experiment with such labor practices as empowerment, quality circles, autonomous work groups, and cross-functional teams to raise the productivity and satisfaction of their work-

VENTURING *Abroad*

A ROSE BY ANY OTHER NAME . . .

All entrepreneurs need to have a basic understanding of standard business, legal, and financial terminology. For an entrepreneur doing business internationally, this terminology takes on additional complexity because different phrases and terms are likely to be used in different countries. Consider, for example, the different terms used to connote business liability in various countries.

Most people in the United States are familiar with the abbreviation **Inc.** and are accustomed to seeing business names such as Southwest Airlines, Inc. and Lands' End, Inc. The term, of course, stands for *incorporated* and means that the financial liability of the company's owners is limited to the extent of their investments if the company fails or encounters financial or legal difficulties. Other countries have different terminology when dealing with this concept of *limited liability*.

For example, Germany uses three different terms to reflect different forms of limited liability. **Aktiengesellschaft (AG)** is used for a large, publicly held firm that must have a management board and a board of directors. Examples include Deutsche Bank AG

and Volkswagen AG. **Kommanditgesellschaft auf Aktien (KGaA)** is used for a firm that is owned by limited partners but has at least one shareholder with unlimited liability. Henkel KGaA, a German chemicals manufacturer, is an example. Finally, **Gesellschaft mit beschränkter Haftung (GmbH)** applies to smaller, privately held companies.

In Japan **kabuskiki kaisha (KK)** is used for all limited-liability companies. In the Netherlands **BV (besloten vennootschap)** refers to a privately held, limited-liability firm, and **NV (naamloze vennootschap)** refers to a publicly held, limited-liability firm, such as Philips NV. The United Kingdom also distinguishes between privately held and publicly held limited-liability companies, using **Ltd.** for the former and **PLC** for the latter. Examples are Swire Pacific Ltd. and Glaxo Wellcome PLC. Italy uses **SpA (la società per azioni)** to denote a limited-liability firm, such as Benetton Group SpA and Fiat SpA. France uses **SA (société anonyme)** for the same purpose, as in Carrefour SA and Hachette SA.

forces. Managers who remain ignorant of the innovations of their international competitors are doomed to fail in the global marketplace.

Finally, you need to study international business to obtain cultural literacy. As global cultures and political systems become even more intertwined than they are now, understanding and appreciating the similarities and differences of the world's peoples will become increasingly important. You will more often encounter colleagues, customers, suppliers, and competitors from different countries and cultural backgrounds. Knowing something about how and where their countries and companies fit into the global economy can help you earn their respect and confidence as well as give you a competitive edge in dealing with them (see "Venturing Abroad"). Conversely, if you know little or nothing about the rest of the world, you may come across as provincial, arrogant, or simply inept. This holds true regardless of whether you are a manager, a consumer, or just an observer of world events.

> INTERNATIONAL BUSINESS ACTIVITIES

Historically, international business activity first took the form of exporting and importing (see "Bringing the World into Focus"). However, in today's complex world of international commerce, numerous other forms of international business activity are also common.

Exporting and Importing

Exporting is the selling of products made in one's own country for use or resale in other countries. **Importing** is the buying of products made in other countries for use or resale in one's own country. Exporting and importing activities often are

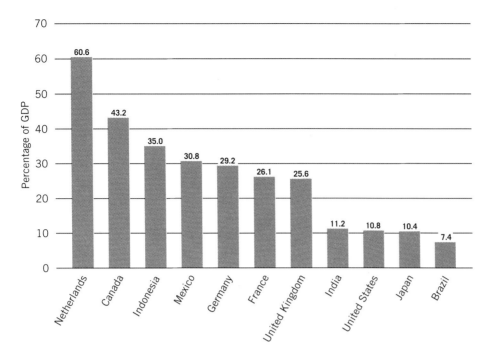

FIGURE 1.1

Exports of Goods and Services as a Percentage of GDP for Some Key Countries (1999 Data)

Source: International Monetary Fund, *International Financial Statistics*, August 2000.

subdivided into two groups. One group of activities is trade in goods—tangible products such as clothing, computers, and raw materials. Official U.S. government publications call this type of trade **merchandise exports and imports**; the British call it *visible trade*. The other group of activities is trade in services—intangible products such as banking, travel, and accounting activities. In the United States this type of trade is called **service exports and imports**; in the United Kingdom it is called *invisible trade*.

Exports are often critical to a firm's financial health. For example, about 53 percent of Boeing's commercial aircraft sales are to foreign customers, creating tens of thousands of jobs at the company and thousands more at the factories of its parts suppliers. International sales often are equally important to smaller firms. For example, exports generate half of the revenues of Weather Modification, Inc., a small North Dakota weather monitoring and cloud seeding company. Trade is important to countries as well. As Figure 1.1 shows, exporting accounts for over 60 percent of the Netherlands' gross domestic product (GDP), and over a quarter of the GDPs of Canada, Germany, France, and the United Kingdom.

International Investments

The second major form of international business activity is **international investments**—capital supplied by residents of one country to residents of another. Traditionally, such investments are divided into two categories: foreign direct investments and portfolio investments. **Foreign direct investments (FDI)** are investments made for the purpose of actively controlling property, assets, or companies located in host countries. (The country in which the parent company's headquarters is located is called the **home country**; any other country in which the company operates is known as a **host country**.) An example of an FDI is the purchase of all the common stock of Sweden's Volvo Corporation by Ford Motor Company. After the purchase Ford installed its own executives to oversee Volvo's operations and integrate them into Ford's global procurement and marketing programs.

Bringing the World into FOCUS

THE EARLY ERA OF INTERNATIONAL BUSINESS

International business originally consisted of international trade. Trade between nations can be traced back as far as 2000 B.C., when tribes in northern Africa took dates and clothing to Babylonia and Assyria in the Middle East and traded them for spices and olive oil. This trade continued to expand over the years, encompassing more regions and a growing list of resources and products. Even the Olympic Games have their roots in this early era, with the first games being held in Greece in 776 B.C. By 500 B.C. Chinese merchants were actively exporting silk and jade to India and Europe, and common trade routes were being established.

Success in international trade often led to political and military power. First Greece and then the Roman Empire prospered in part because of exploitation of international trade. Ancient wars were fought to maintain trade dominance. For example, the North African city of Carthage became an international business center that rivaled Rome in the third century B.C., as merchants from Europe brought precious metals and glass to trade for the grains, ivory, and textiles offered by African merchants. Over a period of 100 years, Rome fought three bloody wars with Carthage to maintain its trade supremacy, finally beating the Carthaginians in 146 B.C. The victorious Romans burned the city and plowed salt into the soil so that crops could not grow to ensure that Carthage would never again rise as a rival.

During the Middle Ages, Italy became a focal point for international business because of its central location in what was then the world market. The political and military strength of Venice, Genoa, and Florence reflected their roles as major centers of international commerce and banking that linked trade routes between Europe and China.[3] In 1453 these trade routes were severed when the Turks conquered Constantinople (now Istanbul) and gained control of the Middle East. Europe's trade with China had been particularly profitable, so European governments became interested in finding new ocean routes to the Far East. Backed by the Spanish government, Christopher Columbus sailed west from Europe looking for such routes. His landing in the Caribbean islands served instead to identify an important new source of resources and, eventually, led to the colonization of the Americas by European countries.

As European countries colonized the Americas, new avenues of trade opened. Settlers throughout the Americas sold raw materials, precious metals, and grains to Europe in exchange for tea, manufactured goods, and other commodities. Most of the American territories eventually became independent countries and important contributors to the world economy.

Another phenomenon of great importance to international business developed during the colonial period and the subsequent Age of Imperialism: the growth of FDI and multinational corporations (MNCs), both of which involve foreigners supplying and controlling investments in a host country. European capitalists from such imperialist powers as the United Kingdom, France, the Netherlands, Spain, Belgium, and Portugal nurtured new businesses in their colonial empires in the Americas, Asia, and Africa, establishing networks of banking, transportation, and trade that persist to this day. The earliest of these firms include the Dutch East India Company (established in 1600), the British East India Company (1602), and the Hudson's Bay Company (1670). These and latter-day trading companies, such as Jardine Matheson Holdings, Ltd., owned copper mines, tea and coffee estates, jute and cotton mills, rubber plantations, and the like as part of their global trading empires.[4]

During the nineteenth century the invention and perfection of the steam engine, coupled with the spread of railroads, dramatically lowered the cost of transporting goods over land and thereby made larger factories more economical. This development in turn broadened the extent of FDI. The forerunners of such large contemporary MNCs as Unilever, Ericsson, and Royal Dutch/Shell took their first steps on the path to becoming international giants by investing in facilities throughout Asia, Europe, and the Americas during this period. New inventions promoting technological change further stimulated FDI. For example, in 1852 Samuel Colt built a factory in Great Britain to produce his famous firearms, and later in the century Dunlop built factories in Belgium, France, and Japan to exploit its tire-making expertise.[5]

Portfolio investments are purchases of foreign financial assets (stocks, bonds, and certificates of deposit) for a purpose other than control. An example of a portfolio investment is the purchase of 1,000 shares of Sony's common stock by a Danish pension fund. With this investment the pension fund is trying to raise the rate of return on its asset portfolio rather than to control Sony's decision making.

For the same reason many investors in recent years have bought shares of mutual funds that specialize in foreign stocks and bonds.

Other Forms of International Business Activity

International business activity can also take other forms. Licensing, franchising, and management contracts are among the most important. **Licensing** is a legal arrangement whereby a firm in one country licenses the use of its intellectual property (patents, trademarks, brand names, copyrights, or trade secrets) to a firm in a second country in return for a royalty payment. For example, The Walt Disney Company may permit a German clothing manufacturer to market children's pajamas embroidered with Mickey Mouse's smiling face in return for a percentage of the company's sales. **Franchising**, a specialized form of licensing, occurs when a firm in one country (the franchisor) authorizes a firm in a second country (the franchisee) to utilize its operating systems as well as its brand names, trademarks, and logos in return for a royalty payment. For example, McDonald's Corporation franchises its fast-food restaurants worldwide. Finally, a **management contract** is an arrangement wherein a firm in one country agrees to operate facilities or provide other management services to a firm in another country for an agreed-upon fee. Management contracts are common, for example, in the upper end of the international hotel industry. Hoteliers such as Marriott and Hilton often do not own the expensive hotels that bear their brand names throughout the world but rather operate them under management contracts.

A firm that engages in any of these types of transactions can be labeled an international business. More formally, we can define an **international business** as any organization that engages in cross-border commercial transactions with individuals, private firms, and/or public-sector organizations. But note that we have also used the term *international business* to mean cross-border commercial transactions. Whenever you see this term, you need to determine, from the context in which it is being used, whether it is referring to a general process involving transactions across borders or to a single organization engaging in specific transactions across borders.

The term **multinational corporation (MNC)** is used to identify firms that have extensive involvement in international business. A more precise definition of a multinational corporation is a firm "that engages in foreign direct investment and owns or controls value-adding activities in more than one country."[6] In addition to owning and controlling foreign assets, MNCs typically buy resources in a variety of countries, create goods and/or services in a variety of countries, and then sell those goods and services in a variety of countries. MNCs generally coordinate their activities from a central headquarters but may also allow their affiliates or subsidiaries in foreign markets considerable latitude in adjusting their operations to local circumstances. Table 1.1 lists the world's largest MNCs.

Because some large MNCs, such as accounting partnerships and Lloyd's of London, are not true corporations, some writers distinguish between multinational corporations and **multinational enterprises (MNEs)**. Further, not-for-profit organizations, such as the IOC and the International Red Cross, are not true enterprises, so the term **multinational organization (MNO)** can be used when one wants to refer to both not-for-profit and profit-seeking organizations. Because of the common use of *multinational corporation* in the business press, however, we use it in this book, even though technically its use should be restricted to businesses that are legal corporations.

⟩ International business is extremely important to Boeing. In 1999, 53 percent of its aircraft sales were to foreign airlines. Boeing sells aircraft to virtually every major airline in the world. Its biggest competitor is Airbus, which is controlled by a consortium of European aerospace firms.

TABLE 1.1

The World's Largest Corporations

Rank 1999	1998			REVENUES $Mil.	PROFITS $Mil.	Rank	ASSETS $Mil.	Rank	EMPLOYEES Number	Rank
1	1	General Motors	U.S.	176,558.0	6,002.0	14	273,921.0	49	388,000	11
2	4	Wal-Mart Stores	U.S.	166,809.0	5,377.0	19	70,245.0	142	1,140,000	3
3	8	Exxon Mobil	U.S.	163,881.0	7,910.0	5	144,521.0	97	106,000	121
4	3	Ford Motor	U.S.	162,558.0	7,237.0	12	276,229.0	48	364,550	13
5	2	DaimlerChrysler	Germany	159,985.7	6,129.1	13	175,068.8	81	466,938	8
6	5	Mitsui	Japan	118,555.2	320.5	330	62,360.0	154	38,454	321
7	7	Mitsubishi	Japan	117,765.6	233.7	367	78,949.2	133	42,050	302
8	10	Toyota Motor	Japan	115,670.9	3,653.4	39	160,571.6	90	214,631	38
9	9	General Electric	U.S.	111,630.0	10,717.0	1	405,200.0	28	340,000	15
10	6	Itochu	Japan	109,068.9	(792.8)	484	59,153.9	160	5,306	483
11	11	Royal Dutch/Shell Group	Brit./Neth.	105,366.0	8,584.0	3	113,883.0	109	96,000	137
12	13	Sumitomo	Japan	95,701.6	314.9	331	47,819.8	182	33,057	344
13	18	Nippon Telegraph & Telephone	Japan	93,591.7	(609.0)	483	179,512.2	79	223,954	35
14	12	Marubeni	Japan	91,807.4	18.5	444	54,446.9	171	32,000	351
15	15	AXA	France	87,645.7	2,155.8	86	508,647.3	11	92,008	144
16	14	International Business Machines	U.S.	87,548.0	7,712.0	8	87,495.0	125	307,401	18
17	19	BP Amoco	Britain	83,566.0	5,008.0	23	89,561.0	123	80,400	170
18	16	Citigroup	U.S.	82,005.0	9,867.0	2	716,900.0	3	176,900	56
19	17	Volkswagen	Germany	80,072.7	874.7	199	67,275.9	147	306,275	19
20	21	Nippon Life Insurance	Japan	78,515.1	3,405.4	45	423,281.5	22	71,434	195

Source: Fortune, July 24, 2000, p. F-1.

› THE CONTEMPORARY CAUSES OF GLOBALIZATION

The growth of international business in recent years has been clear and dramatic. But why has this growth occurred? And why is international business activity likely to continue to skyrocket during the next decade? There are two broad reasons: strategic imperatives, which motivate globalization, and environmental changes, which facilitate it.

Strategic Imperatives

Several basic motives have compelled firms to become more global in both their orientation and actions. These strategic imperatives include leveraging a firm's core competencies, acquiring resources at low cost, expanding into new markets, and competing with industry rivals.

To Leverage Core Competencies. One major motive for globalization is the opportunity to leverage a core competency that a firm has developed in its home market. A **core competency** is a distinctive strength or advantage that is central to a firm's operations. By utilizing its core competency in new markets, the firm is able to increase its revenues and profits. Nokia, for example, developed cutting edge cellular phone technology that was eagerly adopted by domestic consumers in Finland. Nokia's managers quickly recognized that the firm could increase its revenues and profits by expanding its operations and sales in other countries. Similarly, since its birth in 1972, Singapore Airlines has worked hard to develop award-winning standards of customer satisfaction and reliability that have wooed millions of Asian passengers to its flights. Believing that travelers in other markets would welcome the tender loving care the carrier is renown for, Singapore Airlines has deftly expanded its services to 90 cities in over 40 countries throughout the world.

To Acquire Resources and Supplies.   Another important reason for going international is to acquire resources such as materials, labor, capital, or technology. In some cases organizations must go to foreign sources because certain products or services are either scarce or unavailable locally. For example, North American grocery wholesalers buy coffee and bananas from South America; Japanese firms buy forest products from Canada; and firms worldwide buy oil from the Middle East and Africa. In other cases firms simply find it easier and/or more economical to buy from other countries. As a result, many firms have located facilities in less developed countries to lower the firms' production costs. For example, Compaq constructs the chassis for its personal computers at its plant in China. Lower labor costs there enable the firm to make a chassis and ship it to Houston for final assembly for $57 less than it would cost to build it in Houston.[7]

To Seek New Markets.   Seeking new markets is also a common motive for international expansion. When a firm's domestic market matures, it becomes increasingly difficult to generate high revenue and profit growth. For example, the market for toothpaste in Canada, the United States, and the European Union can be classified as mature—most people there understand the value of oral hygiene and have the financial resources to regularly purchase toothpaste. Thus firms like Procter & Gamble, Unilever, and Colgate-Palmolive cannot expect to achieve significant growth in sales from their toothpaste products in these markets and have aggressively moved into emerging markets like China, India, and Indonesia to seek expanded sales. Expansion into new markets carries with it two other benefits. First, a firm may be able to achieve economies of scale, lowering its average costs as its production increases. Second, such expansion diversifies a firm's revenue stream. As it serves more countries, the firm becomes less dependent on its sales in any one country, thereby protecting itself should that country's economy turn sour.

To Better Compete with Rivals.   Finally, businesses sometimes enter foreign markets to better compete with industry rivals. For example, as Coca-Cola expands aggressively around the world, rival Pepsi-Cola has little choice but to follow and try to keep up. Should Pepsi allow Coca-Cola to dominate important markets, Coca-Cola could use profits from those markets to finance attacks on Pepsi in still other markets. Such thinking permeates industries such as earth-moving equipment and photographic films, where the leading firms continually attack and counterattack each other in every region of the world to prevent their rivals from getting a stranglehold in any country.

Environmental Change and Globalization

These strategic imperatives provide firms with the motivation to internationalize their operations. However, firms would not have been able to expand their international activities to the extent we have observed during the post-World War II period without significant changes in two key areas: the political environment and the technological environment. ◢

> Technological changes greatly affect international business. The emergence of the Internet is one of the most significant technological changes in recent years. Laurie McCartney, owner of eStyle, an online retailer, is typical of the thousands of dot-com entrepreneurs who plan to use the Internet to expand their businesses internationally.

Changes in the Political Environment. During the first half of the twentieth century, firms wishing to enter new markets were often frustrated by barriers against foreign trade and investment erected by national governments. For example, after World War I many countries, including the United States, France, the United Kingdom, and Germany, imposed tariffs and quotas on imported goods and favored local firms on government supply contracts. As a result, international trade and investment declined throughout the 1930s. However, after World War II these policies were reversed. The major trading powers negotiated reductions in tariffs and quotas and eliminated barriers to FDI within their borders. Many of the reductions were negotiated through the General Agreement on Tariffs and Trade (GATT) and its successor, the World Trade Organization (WTO). Regional accords, such as the European Union, the Mercosur Accord, and the North American Free Trade Agreement, also have relaxed trade and investment barriers among their members.

Technological Changes. Changes in governmental policies encouraged international business activity. Improvements in technology—particularly in communications, transportation, and information processing—made international business more feasible and more profitable. Think about the difficulties of conducting business internationally when the primary form of transportation was the sailing ship, the primary form of data processing was pencil and paper, and the primary form of communication was the letter delivered by a postman on horseback. Transportation improvements during the past 150 years—from sailing ship to steamship to seaplane to jet airliner—mean that a manager in London no longer needs to spend weeks traveling in order to confer with colleagues in New Delhi, Toronto, or New York. Advances in transportation also have stimulated growth in international tourism, which is the largest component of international trade in services. (See "Bringing the World into Focus" for an example of the impact of international tourism on a local economy.) The increasing ability of computers to rapidly process vast quantities of information allows firms to manage offices and factories located in every corner of the globe. Exxon Mobil, for example, relies on its computers to adjust continuously the output of its refineries and the sailings of its tankers to meet changes in worldwide demand for its products. Changes in communications technology, such as the advent of facsimile transmission and electronic mail, enable a manager in Tokyo to receive reports from colleagues in Amsterdam, Abidjan, and Auckland in minutes rather than days. These technological advances make managing distant businesses far easier today than executives would have dreamed possible just a few decades ago and so have facilitated expansion into international markets.

2000 and Beyond: The Challenges of the Internet Age. The impact of technology on international business activity has accelerated during the past decade due to the introduction and rapid exploitation of the Internet. Its advent is redefining the global marketplace. Managers in every country and in every industry are struggling to analyze the impact of e-commerce on their firms and ways of doing business.

Bringing the World into FOCUS

ANNE OF RED HAIR

What was Yoshiko Nishimura's reaction when she arrived at Cavendish on Prince Edward Island? "I cried for happiness upon arrival. Every Japanese girl dreams of one day paying respect to the land of Anne of Red Hair. She is much beloved."

Prince Edward Island (PEI), the smallest of Canada's maritime provinces, routinely attracts summer visitors from Central Canada and the Northeastern United States. Although they enjoy PEI's rural scenery and charming towns and villages, few North Americans share, let alone understand, Nishimura's intense reaction to the island. Yet she is not alone. Thousands of her countrywomen annually make the trek—maybe a better word would be pilgrimage—to visit an old farmhouse in Cavendish that supposedly served as the model for the home where Anne Shirley, the fictional heroine of Lucy Maud Montgomery's *Anne of Green Gables*, grew up. One Japanese travel magazine found that among its female readers Cavendish was the fourth most popular foreign city they wished to visit, being topped only by New York, Paris, and London, even though it is not an easy trip. It takes at least 20 hours to fly from Tokyo to Toronto, catch a connecting flight to Halifax, another connecting flight to Charlottetown, PEI's capital, and then travel the last 30 miles or so by road to Cavendish.

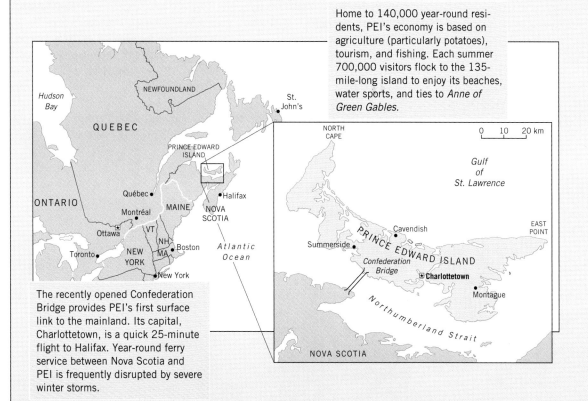

Home to 140,000 year-round residents, PEI's economy is based on agriculture (particularly potatoes), tourism, and fishing. Each summer 700,000 visitors flock to the 135-mile-long island to enjoy its beaches, water sports, and ties to *Anne of Green Gables*.

The recently opened Confederation Bridge provides PEI's first surface link to the mainland. Its capital, Charlottetown, is a quick 25-minute flight to Halifax. Year-round ferry service between Nova Scotia and PEI is frequently disrupted by severe winter storms.

MAP 1.2 **Prince Edward Island Is Home to Anne of Green Gables and a Vibrant Tourism Industry**

(continues)

Montgomery's book has long been a favorite of preteens in Canada and the United States. It has been translated into numerous languages and sells well in many markets. In Japan, however, the book has achieved cultlike status subsequent to its publication in 1952 under the title *Anne of Red Hair*. Today, thousands of Japanese girls subscribe to "Anne" magazines that explore in loving detail the lives of L. M. Montgomery, Anne, and her fictional family and friends. Thousands more journey to Cavendish to visit sites associated with Anne and her creator. Some wear red pigtail wigs and paint freckles on their faces to better honor their idol. They spend millions of dollars purchasing Anne place mats, Anne key chains, and other Anne memorabilia that PEI merchants are only too happy to sell them. Some enroll in classes taught by the L. M. Montgomery Institute at the University of Prince Edward Island. The truly dedicated Anneophiles even drag their fiancés to PEI so they can be married in the same front parlor of the farmhouse where Montgomery was wed in 1911.

Why is *Anne of Red Hair* so popular among Japanese women? No one really knows. Perhaps Anne's rebelliousness and frankness appeal to Japanese women who are expected to conform to the restrictive roles laid out for them by their culture, or maybe Anne's love of nature and her loyalty to her family are the keys to her allure. Whatever the reason, it is obvious that Lucy Maud Montgomery's spunky little heroine—whether she is known as Anne of Green Gables or as Anne of Red Hair—has touched the hearts of young readers around the globe. She has also linked the merchants of PEI to the largest component of the $1.3 trillion trade in international services—tourism.

Sources: "Green Gables Books a Crowd," *Boston Globe*, August 10, 1997, p. A1; Calvin Trillin, "Anne of Red Hair," *The New Yorker*, August 5, 1996, pp. 56–61.

Some experts believe that the stunning performance of the U.S. economy in the 1990s was at least partially attributable to its aggressive integration of information technology into home and office. For much of the post-World War II era Western Europe and Japan had slowly gained ground on the United States by simultaneously adopting U.S. technologies and nurturing their own innovations. U.S. per capita income was 31 percent higher than that of other major industrialized countries in 1970, but that gap had been narrowed to only 10 percent by 1990. During the 1990s, however, the gap began to widen again, reaching 22 percent by the end of 1999. Although several factors no doubt interacted to cause this turnaround, the increased investment in and use of information technology by U.S. firms and consumers certainly played a significant role.[8]

Figure 1.2 depicts differences in historical and projected Internet usage for selected regions. Usage in North America grew from about 100 users per 1,000

FIGURE 1.2

Internet Usage Takes Off: Internet Users per Thousand People, by Region

Source: *Business Week*, January 31, 2000, p. 75.

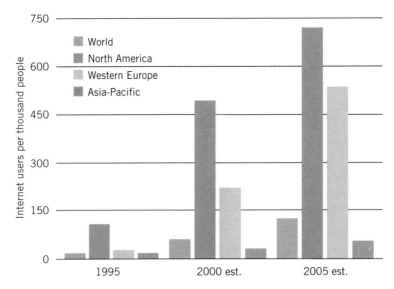

Data: Computer Industry Almanac

people in 1995 to over 450 users per 1,000 people in 2000. This figure is projected to grow to almost 750 users per 1,000 people by 2005. Current Western European and Asian Pacific usage of the Internet lags behind that of North America, although the gap between North America and Western Europe is projected to shrink dramatically by 2005. A similar story is presented in Figure 1.3, which suggests that the United States leads the world in spending on information technology as a proportion of gross domestic product, with Sweden a very close second.

The growth of the Internet and other information technologies affects international business in at least three different ways. First, the Internet and associated technologies facilitate international trade in services, including such diverse industries as banking, consulting, education, retailing, and even gambling. For example, many Canadian and U.S. companies have shifted their customer service and data entry operations to areas with lower labor costs in and outside North America. As long as the transaction can be performed electronically, the physical location of the facility is of little importance. India, for example, has a growing call center business, providing customer care and trouble-shooting services for customers of numerous MNCs throughout the world. The chapter's closing case, "The Brave New World of Global E-Commerce," provides several other examples of how the Internet is contributing to growth in international services trade.

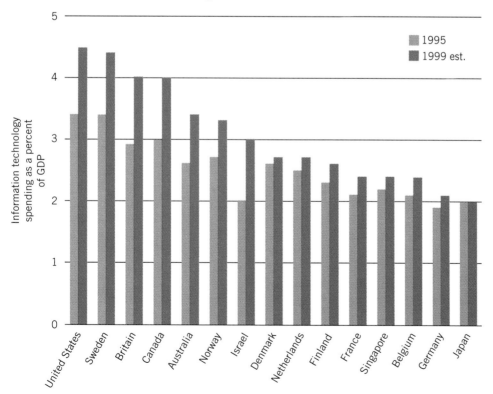

Data: International Data Corp.

FIGURE 1.3

Who's Ahead?

Source: "The New Economy," *Business Week*, January 31, 2000, p. 77. Based on data from International Data Corp.

Second, the Internet serves to level the playing field, at least to some extent, between larger and smaller enterprises regardless of what products or services they sell. In the past a substantial investment was often needed to expand into foreign markets, but the Internet potentially changes this. For example, a small business based in western Missouri, southern Italy, eastern Malaysia, or northern Brazil can create an effective Web site and compete with much larger businesses from around the world.

Third, the Internet holds considerable potential as an efficient networking mechanism among businesses. So-called business-to-business networks can link global businesses with their suppliers, customers, and strategic partners in ways that make it faster and easier for them to do business together. For example, manufacturers have traditionally procured necessary parts and supplies by having a purchasing agent prepare paper forms in duplicate and mail them to the supplier. Once received, the order has to be processed, entered into production, and then shipped back to the manufacturer—a process that could take weeks. With network linkages, the manufacturer can place the order online much faster and more efficiently. In a truly integrated system, the supplier will be able to monitor the manufacturer's inventory, anticipate the need for additional parts, and start making them before the order is even sent. The potential savings are enormous. GM, for example, estimates that preparing a purchase order costs the company $100; by switching to online purchasing, GM believes it can cut these costs by 90 percent.[9]

› AN OVERVIEW OF THE CONTENTS OF THIS BOOK

In writing this book, we have started with the assumption that most readers will eventually work for or own a firm that is affected by international business activity. Our goal is to help them become more comfortable and effective managers in the competitive global marketplace. To do so, we provide our readers with the knowledge and skills necessary to succeed in international business.

We have structured the contents of the book to move from relatively macro, or general, issues to increasingly micro, or specific, issues that managers deal with regularly. Our rationale is that managers must fully understand the context of international business to work effectively within that context. This broad, general context provides the backdrop within which all international business occurs. At each increasingly specific level within that context, the international manager is faced with more specific and operational issues, problems, challenges, and opportunities.

Part One comprises Chapters 1, 2, 3, and 4. It provides an overview of the world's marketplaces. Chapter 1 has supplied some background definitions and discussed the contemporary global business environment. Chapter 2 provides a wealth of economic and geographical information about the world's major economies and business centers. Chapters 3 and 4 describe the national environments of international business—the more specific country-level environmental context that affects and impacts business activity and opportunities.

Parts Two through Four follow a logical progression of topics, moving from the broad, general issues confronting international business to increasingly more specific, focused issues that managers face daily (see Figure 1.4). Part Two discusses the international environment in more detail, addressing the overall con-

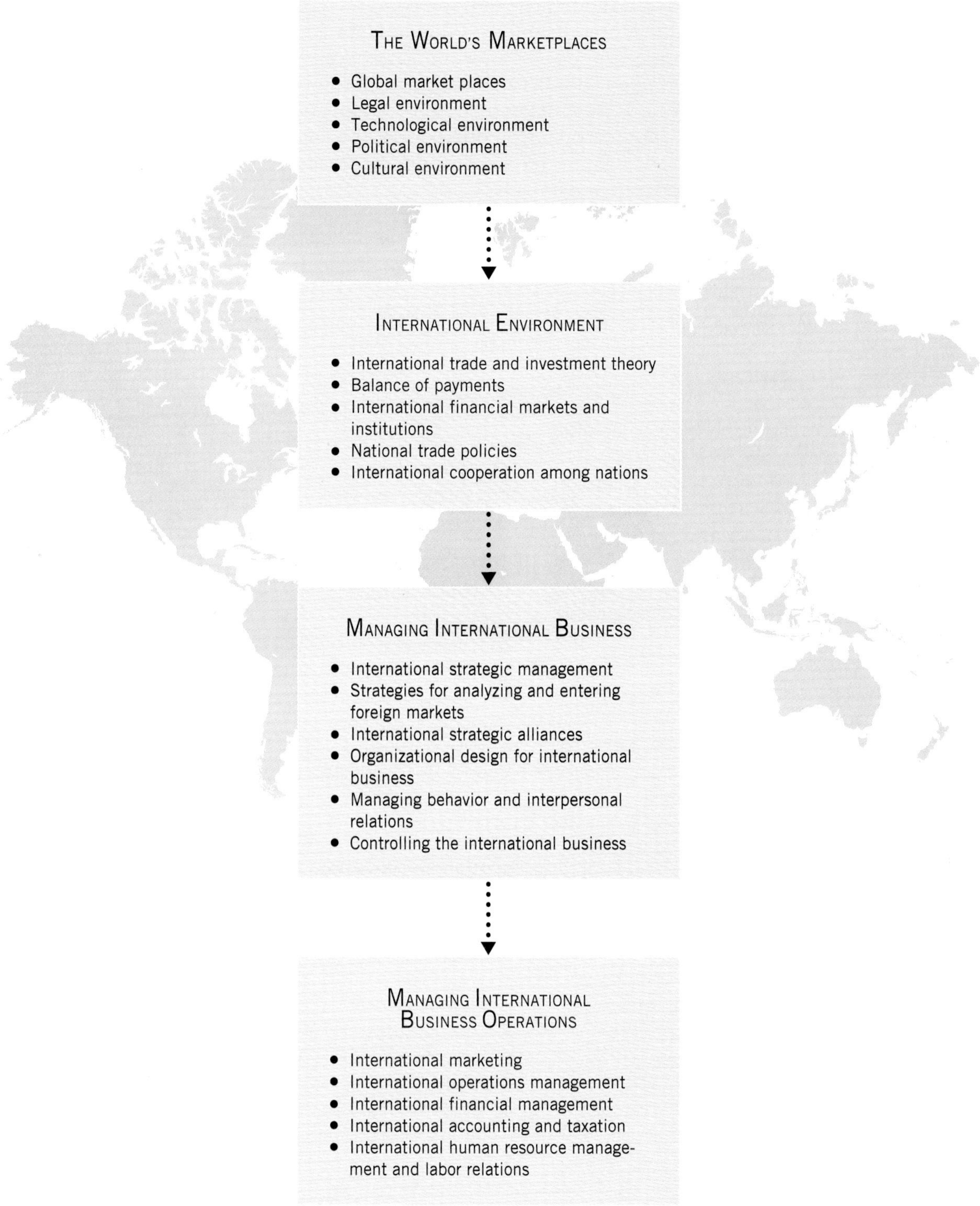

THE WORLD'S MARKETPLACES

- Global market places
- Legal environment
- Technological environment
- Political environment
- Cultural environment

INTERNATIONAL ENVIRONMENT

- International trade and investment theory
- Balance of payments
- International financial markets and institutions
- National trade policies
- International cooperation among nations

MANAGING INTERNATIONAL BUSINESS

- International strategic management
- Strategies for analyzing and entering foreign markets
- International strategic alliances
- Organizational design for international business
- Managing behavior and interpersonal relations
- Controlling the international business

MANAGING INTERNATIONAL BUSINESS OPERATIONS

- International marketing
- International operations management
- International financial management
- International accounting and taxation
- International human resource management and labor relations

FIGURE 1.4 **Framework for This Book**

text of international business and introducing many of the global forces and conditions that affect organizations and managers. Part Three adopts the perspective of a specific organization, focusing on general management issues such as international strategies, modes of entry into foreign markets, joint ventures and strategic alliances, organization design, organizational behavior, and control in international business. Part Four covers the management of specific international business functions: marketing, operations, finance, accounting, and human resource management.

CHAPTER REVIEW

Summary

International business encompasses any business transaction that involves parties from more than one country. These transactions can take various forms and can involve individual companies, groups of companies, and/or government agencies. International business can differ from domestic business because of differences in currencies, legal systems, cultures, and resource availability.

Studying international business is important for several reasons. First, any organization you work for, even if small, is likely to be affected by the global economy. Someday you may work for a foreign-owned firm. Further, you need to keep pace with other managers who are learning to function in international settings. Finally, you need to be culturally literate in today's world.

International business activity can take various forms. Exporting involves selling products made in one's own country for use or resale in another country. Importing involves buying products made in other countries for use or resale in one's own country. Foreign direct investments are investments made for the purpose of controlling property, assets, or companies located in foreign countries. Other common forms of international business activity include licensing, franchising, and management contracts.

An international business is one that engages in commercial transactions with individuals, private firms, and/or public sector organizations that cross national boundaries. Firms with extensive international involvement are called multinational corporations, or MNCs.

International business has grown dramatically in recent years because of strategic imperatives and environmental changes. Strategic imperatives include the need to leverage core competencies, acquire resources, seek new markets, and match the actions of rivals. Although strategic imperatives indicate why firms wish to internationalize their operations, significant changes in the political

and technological environments have no doubt facilitated the explosive growth in international business activity that has occurred since World War II. The growth of the Internet and other information technologies is likely to redefine global competition and ways of doing international business once again.

Review Questions

1. What is international business? How does it differ from domestic business?
2. Why is it important for you to study international business?
3. What are the basic forms of international business activity?
4. How do merchandise exports and imports differ from service exports and imports?
5. What is portfolio investment?
6. What are the basic reasons for the recent growth of international business activity?

Questions for Discussion

1. Why do some industries become global while others remain local or regional?
2. What is the impact of the Internet on international business? Which companies and which countries will gain as Internet usage increases throughout the world? Which will lose?
3. Does your college or university have any international programs? Does this make the institution an international business? Why or why not?
4. What are some of the differences in skills that may exist between managers in a domestic firm and those in an international firm?
5. Would you want to work for a foreign-owned firm? Why or why not?

BUILDING GLOBAL SKILLS

List different products you use on a regular basis, such as your alarm clock, camera, car, coffee maker, computer, sneakers, telephone, television, VCR—perhaps even your favorite CD, shirt, fruit juice, or type of recording tape. Determine which firms made these items. After you have developed your list, go to the library and research the following for each item:

1. In which country is the firm headquartered?
2. What percentage of the firm's annual sales comes from its home market? What percentage comes from other countries?
3. Where was the item most likely manufactured?
4. Why do you think it was manufactured there?

Follow up by meeting with a small group of your classmates and completing these activities:

1. Discuss the relative impact of international business on your daily lives.

2. Compile a combined list of the 10 most common products the average college student might use.
3. Try to identify the brands of each product that are made by domestic firms.
4. Try to identify the brands of each product that are made by foreign firms.
5. Does either of your lists of 10 products include items that have components that are both domestic made and foreign made?

WORKING WITH THE WEB: BUILDING GLOBAL INTERNET SKILLS

Marketing Tourism in Prince Edward Island

Let us go back to "Bringing the World into Focus" on pages 15 and 16, which discussed the growing market of Japanese tourists—primarily young adult females—visiting Prince Edward Island (PEI). The World Wide Web is becoming an important mechanism for selling goods and services internationally. Visit the Web site of the PEI government. Suppose you were thinking about visiting PEI. What information would you like to have to plan your visit? Does this Web site provide that information? Now put yourself in the shoes of a young Japanese woman who is an ardent admirer of

Anne of Red Hair. Does the Web site meet the young fan's needs? What changes would you recommend in the government's Web site to cater to this market?

Now examine how the private sector deals with some of these questions. Do a Web search on *Anne of Green Gables* and a search on tourist accommodations and attractions on PEI. Which Web sites are of most value to prospective tourists?

Each chapter of this book contains a "Working with the Web" skill-building exercise. The book's Web site contains linkages to some Web sites that may be of use in doing this assignment and those found in later chapters.

WE INVITE YOU TO VISIT THIS BOOK'S COMPANION WEB SITE AT www.prenhall.com/griffin

IN THE NEWS

1. Visit the homepage of the *Financial Times* (*www.ft.com*), and use the search feature to locate recent articles about franchises. Try searching for "franchise expansion" or "franchise acquisition." Select several articles from within the last two or three weeks, and note the names of the franchising compa-

nies, the country in which they are headquartered, and the amounts of money involved in the transaction. What can you conclude about the status of franchising as a form of international business?

2. On the *Financial Times* homepage refer to the list of articles under the heading "Business News." (You may need to click on "news" first.) What is the core competency of each company in

today's news? If you do not know, do a little research on the company to find out.

Scan the articles you located in question 2 to find out whether the firms are making headlines for leveraging their core competencies, acquiring new resources, seeking new markets, or matching the actions of their rivals. If none of these, characterize the company's recent actions as best you can. Do they have implications for the firm's international operations?

CLOSING CASE

The Brave New World of Global E-Commerce

The rapid development of the Internet during the past decade is reshaping the global economy. Firms large and small are busily developing innovative ways of harnessing this technology to cut their costs, expand their market reach, and develop new products. For example, Ford, GM, and DaimlerChrysler recently announced plans to create an electronic trade exchange to purchase automotive parts and supplies online. Nissan and Renault quickly joined the partnership, and Toyota indicated that it, too, was very interested in participating. Company officials estimate that together they could shave off more than $20 billion of the more than $250 billion the companies spend annually on parts procurement. Sears and Carrefour announced a similar business-to-business online exchange geared to the needs of retailers.

Such cost-cutting opportunities are also available to much smaller businesses. The Lee Hung Fat Garment Factory, a family-owned Hong Kong manufacturer, slashed its costs of communicating with its foreign customers by one-third by relying on the Internet rather than faxes and telephone calls. Instead of express mailing product samples to its customers, the company now uses a Web camera to transmit photos of garment mock-ups over the Internet. Company managers estimate they save 15 to 20 percent in design costs using this technology.

Companies can also use the Internet to expand their reach into new markets. Venezuela's Loquesea.com (the Spanish equivalent of "whatever") is marketing a Web site designed to meet the needs of cyber-savvy teenagers throughout Latin America. After five months of operations, Loquesea was already drawing 15 million "hits" a month, attracting the advertising dollars of MNCs such as Coca-Cola eager to target this market.

The growth of the Internet offers consumers many benefits as well. For example, Europeloan is Europe's first mortgage lender to rely solely on the Internet. This Belgian company can offer low-cost mortgages to homeowners throughout Europe while competing against local banks because it has no expensive "bricks and mortar" investments in branch banking facilities. For example, in early 2000 it was able to offer Swedish borrowers five-year fixed loans at 6.86 percent, easily beating the 7.4 percent rate demanded by local Swedish bankers. Similarly, Primus Online is providing discounts to European consumers by pooling orders from them and then obtaining discount prices from suppliers by buying in bulk. Further, numerous universities have launched or are planning to launch online MBA programs to train managers around the world to meet the challenges of the brave new world of global e-commerce.

The boundaryless activities of the Internet also create substantial challenges for government policy makers, businesspersons, and consumers. One question is which country's laws apply when international transactions occur over the Internet. For example, gambling is legal on the Caribbean island country of Antigua. However, a 40-year-old U.S. law prohibits gambling across state or federal borders using telephone lines. The U.S. government has filed suit against World Sports Exchange, an Antigua-based company that offers online sports gambling, claiming that the company violates the law when it allows U.S. citizens to use its services. The controversy has yet to be resolved by the courts. Another issue is who is responsible for Internet content. The head of CompuServe's German office narrowly avoided a prison term after a Bavarian court determined that the company failed to block access by German Web surfers to pornographic sites on the Internet. Another open question is who will protect consumers from international cyberfraud.

Other impediments have arisen. For example, consumers purchasing products from foreign suppliers over the Internet still have to deal with their local customs services. One hard-luck British consumer was delighted to purchase a $110 CD-ROM from a U.S. Internet-based software company, a price substantially less than British retailers were demanding. However, Her Majesty's revenue officers demanded an additional $159 in customs duties before they would release the goods, thereby turning a bargain into a fiasco.

Case Questions

1. As the Internet becomes increasingly prevalent in international business, are there some industries that will be more affected than others? Why?
2. Are certain kinds of firms (varying by size, industry, age, and/or other characteristics) more likely than others to be affected by the growth of international e-commerce? Why?
3. In your opinion should anyone govern Internet content? Should countries be allowed to impose their own legal and political standards regarding appropriate content on the Internet?

4. Some experts believe that the eventual winners in the global e-commerce arena will be the large, powerful multinationals of today—Ford, Royal Dutch/Shell, Sony, and similar firms—that have name recognition and the financial resources to do whatever it takes to win. Other experts, however, think that the dominant firms in an electronic world will be the new start-ups—firms like Amazon.com, America Online, and so forth—that are not bound by traditional ways of doing things and that really see themselves as Internet businesses as opposed to businesses that have started using the Internet. What is your opinion? Why?

Source: "Europe Internet Mortgage Lender Opens in Sweden, *Financial Times*, February 18, 2000, p. 13; "Land of Laptops and Lederhosen," *Financial Times*, February 17, 2000, p 14; "Cross-Border Regulations Create Hurdle for Cybershoppers, *Financial Times*, February 16, 2000, p 7; "U.S. Prosecution to Challenge Lawless World of Cyberspace," *Financial Times*, February 14, 2000, p. 1; "Web Site Aims to Attract Latin American Teens," *Wall Street Journal*, February 9, 2000, p. A22; "Open Door to Career Success," *Financial Times*, February 7, 2000, p. 9; "Family Garment Business in Hong Kong Uses Internet to Gain Access to Global Customer Pool, *Wall Street Journal*, November 24, 1999, p. B11B.

CHAPTER

The First Rule: Know the Territory

When Victor Cardenas, a Cuban expatriate employed by a British joint venture, opened his pizza parlor in Minsk, the capital of Belarus, he knew he faced many challenges. What he didn't anticipate, however, was having his restaurant closed by the local authorities for selling lasagna. It seems that lasagna was not included in the official Belarussian cookbook, a holdover from the Soviet era which prescribed to the letter the recipes to be followed in all of the country's restaurants. Fortunately, the Belarussian Department of Public Nutrition allowed Cardenas to reopen 10 days later, after he secured special licenses that let him sell exotic house specialties like ravioli and lasagna.

"... to sell **exotic** house specialties like ravioli and **lasagna**."

Advertisements for the Energizer bunny were spectacular failures when they were run on Hungarian television. Most viewers there assumed that the ads were for toy bunnies. One U.S. company that makes baby care products tried to boost sales in Hungary by featuring a mother warmly embracing her baby. Unfortunately, the model in the ad was wearing a ring on her left hand; Hungarians wear their wedding ring on their right hand. Noted one Hungarian advertising executive, "It was so obvious to viewers that this woman was telling everyone in Hungary that she wasn't married. And then Western marketers wonder why people here won't buy their products."

Global Marketplaces and Business Centers

OBJECTIVES

After studying this chapter, you should be able to:

❯ Evaluate the impact on business of the political and economic characteristics of the world's various marketplaces.

❯ Appreciate the uses of national income data in making business decisions.

❯ Discuss North America as a major marketplace and business center in the world economy.

❯ Describe Western Europe as a major marketplace and business center in the world economy.

❯ Discuss the problems facing the economies of the former communist countries of Eastern and Central Europe.

❯ Discuss Asia as a major marketplace and business center in the world economy.

❯ Assess the development challenges facing African, Middle Eastern, and South American countries.

Rich farmland has made Ukraine one of the world's premier granaries. In the early 1990s Monsanto targeted this market, selling $38 million worth of fertilizers and herbicides to the agricultural ministry. However, it took Monsanto a year to receive payment, and then only after the U.S. State Department interceded on its behalf with the newly elected president, Leonid Kuchma. Burned by this experience, Monsanto decided to bypass the agricultural ministry and sell directly to private distributors and collective farms. This did not prove to be a wise move because it enraged apparatchiks (a Soviet era term for bureaucrats), who disliked any attempt to reduce their power. Ukrainian prosecutors, acting on behalf of the agricultural ministry, began harassing Monsanto's customers, asking why they were buying foreign products. Ukrainian courts declared Monsanto's chemicals unsafe, even though they had passed strict U.S. regulatory requirements. In addition, farmers using Monsanto products were denied licenses needed to export their crops.[1]

Businesses trying to internationalize their operations often blunder because they fail to obtain information vital to their success. Ignorance of basic geography, market characteristics, culture, and politics may lead to lost profits or, in the extreme, doom a venture to failure. Linguistic and cultural ties, past political associations, and military alliances play significant roles in the world pattern of trade and investment and in shaping the opportunities available for businesses today. For example, London's contemporary importance as a world financial center arises from the political and military power of the British Empire in the nineteenth century. Similarly, Austria serves as a bridge between Western and Eastern Europe because of transportation, educational, and cultural linkages that remain from the 600-year reign of the Hapsburg dynasty over the Austro-Hungarian Empire.

Providing an overview of the world economy is a challenge because of its vast size. Much of the world's current economic activity is concentrated in a group of countries called the **Triad** (Japan, the European Union, and the United States) or the **Quad** (the Triad plus Canada). Together the 807 million residents of the Quad countries produce 73 percent of the world's gross domestic product (GDP), as Figure 2.1 indicates. Many business gurus, such as Kenichi Ohmae, the former managing director of McKinsey & Company's Tokyo office, believe that major corporations must be competitive throughout the Quad if they wish to keep pace with their industry rivals. Many multinational corporations (MNCs) have operationalized Ohmae's warning and recognized the importance of competing globally to expand their customer bases. Global strategic thinking typifies industries such as airlines, banking, securities, automobiles, computers, and accounting services.

This is not to suggest that international managers can ignore markets outside the Quad; during the past two decades many of these markets have been growing much faster than those of the Quad countries. Indeed, because astute international managers increasingly need a thorough and sophisticated understanding of the opportunities available in each of the six inhabited continents, we provide a brief overview of all the world's marketplaces in this chapter.

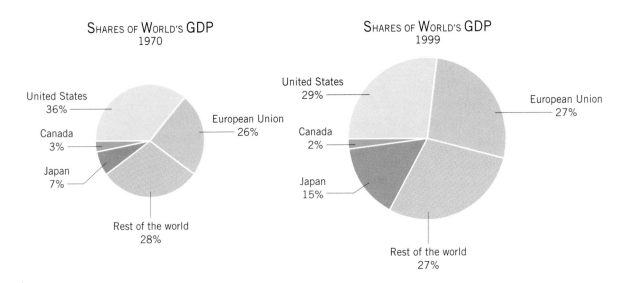

SHARES OF WORLD'S GDP
1970

United States 36%
Canada 3%
Japan 7%
Rest of the world 28%
European Union 26%

SHARES OF WORLD'S GDP
1999

United States 29%
Canada 2%
Japan 15%
Rest of the world 27%
European Union 27%

FIGURE 2.1   **The World Economy: 1970 and 1999**

Source: World Bank Web site (*www.worldbank.org*).

THE MARKETPLACES OF NORTH AMERICA ‹

North America includes the United States, Canada, Mexico, Greenland, and the countries of Central America and the Caribbean. Home to 473 million people, these countries produce approximately 33 percent of the world's output.

The United States

The United States has only the world's third largest population and fourth largest land mass, yet it possesses the largest economy. With a 1999 GDP of $8.7 trillion, it accounts for more than one-quarter of the world's GDP. As Map 2.1 shows, the United States enjoys the highest per capita income of the North American countries.[2] The United States occupies a unique position in the world economy because of its size and political stability, accounting for about one-seventh of world trade in goods and services. It is the prime market for lower-income countries trying to raise their standards of living through export-oriented economic development strategies. It is also the prime market for firms from higher-income countries trying to attract business from its large, well-educated middle class. (See Venturing Abroad.)

VENTURING *Abroad*

CLASSIFYING COUNTRIES BY INCOME LEVELS

Often the single most important piece of information needed by international businesspeople about a country is its income level. Income levels provide clues to the purchasing power of residents, the technological sophistication of local production processes, and the status of the public infrastructure.

One important source of income statistics is the World Bank, which divides the world's countries into high-income, middle-income, and low-income categories. High-income countries are those that enjoy annual per capita incomes of at least $9,266. (**Per capita income** is usually measured by dividing a country's **gross domestic product [GDP]** by its population. GDP is the total market value of all goods and services produced in a country during some time period, such as a year.) The high-income group comprises three clusters of countries. The first cluster is drawn from the **Organization for Economic Cooperation and Development (OECD)**, a group of 30 market-oriented democracies formed to promote economic growth. The OECD includes 23 Western European countries (the European Union plus the Czech Republic, Hungary, Iceland, Norway, Poland, the Slovak Republic, Switzerland, and Turkey), four Pacific Rim countries (Australia, Japan, New Zealand, and South Korea), and Canada, Mexico, and the United States. Twenty-three of the OECD's 30 members fall in the high-income category. (The remaining members—the Czech Republic, Greece, Hungary, Mexico, Poland, the Slovak Republic, and Turkey—are classified as middle income.) The second cluster comprises oil-rich Kuwait and the United Arab Emirates. The third cluster consists of smaller industrialized countries—Hong Kong, Israel, Singapore, and Taiwan.

Middle-income countries have per capita incomes of more than $755 but less than $9,625. This category includes most of the former Soviet bloc, which generally enjoyed high levels of development in the 1930s but fell behind the western economies economically after World War II. Other countries in this category, such as Argentina, Slovenia, and Uruguay, have been undergoing successful industrialization and economic growth and may be elevated to the high-income category by the end of this decade.

Lower-income countries, often called developing countries, have per capita incomes of $755 or less. This category includes some countries, such as China and Sri Lanka, whose economies are growing substantially because of external aid, sound domestic economic policies, foreign direct investment (FDI), and/or exploitation of valuable natural resources. Officially labeled "underdeveloped" by the United Nations General Assembly in 1971, these countries have the potential for above-average economic growth. Other countries, designated "undeveloped" and "least developed" by the United Nations, have low literacy rates, per capita incomes, and economic growth. They are less attractive to international businesses because they offer less consumer demand and lack the public infrastructure necessary for reliable production and distribution of goods and services. A prime example of this latter category is Somalia, an East African country wracked by drought, civil war, and starvation.

Sources: World Bank, World Development Report 1999/2000 (Washington, D.C.: World Bank, 2000) and the bank's Web site (*www.worldbank.org*).

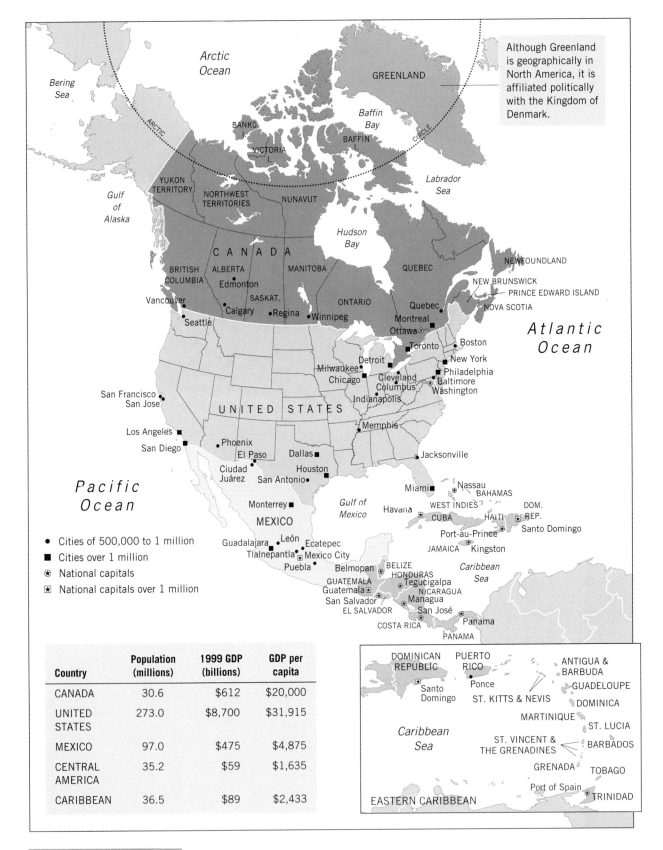

Although Greenland is geographically in North America, it is affiliated politically with the Kingdom of Denmark.

- ● Cities of 500,000 to 1 million
- ■ Cities over 1 million
- ⊛ National capitals
- ⊠ National capitals over 1 million

Country	Population (millions)	1999 GDP (billions)	GDP per capita
CANADA	30.6	$612	$20,000
UNITED STATES	273.0	$8,700	$31,915
MEXICO	97.0	$475	$4,875
CENTRAL AMERICA	35.2	$59	$1,635
CARIBBEAN	36.5	$89	$2,433

MAP 2.1 **North America**

The U.S. dollar serves as the **invoicing currency**—the currency in which the sale of goods and services is denominated—for about half of all international transactions and is an important component of foreign-currency reserves worldwide. Because of its political stability and military strength, the United States also attracts **flight capital**—money sent out of a politically or economically unstable country to one perceived as a safe haven. Citizens unsure of the value of their home country's currency often choose to keep their wealth in dollars. The United States also is an important recipient of long-term foreign investment. Foreigners have invested nearly $1 trillion in U.S. factories, equipment, and property.

Although international trade has become increasingly more important during the past decade, it is a relatively small component of the U.S. economy. U.S. exports of goods and services in 1999 totaled $956 billion but were only 11 percent of U.S. GDP. However, this figure is somewhat misleading. Because of the country's large size, trade that might be counted as international in smaller countries is considered domestic in the United States. For example, the money spent for a hotel room in neighboring Belgium by a Dutch motorist trapped in a thunderstorm 50 miles from home late at night is counted in the international trade statistics of both Belgium and the Netherlands. A similar expenditure by a Connecticut motorist stuck in New Jersey after watching a football game at the Meadowlands is a purely domestic transaction.

As discussed throughout this book, MNCs heavily influence international trade and investment. In 1999 the world's 500 largest corporations had total sales of $12.7 trillion. Given the importance of the United States in the world economy, it should come as no surprise that 179 of these corporations, or about 36 percent, are headquartered in the United States, including 36 of the largest 100 (see Figure 2.2). General Motors is currently the world's largest company, with sales of $177 billion in 1999.

Canada

Canada has the world's second largest land mass, although its population is only 30.6 million. Eighty percent of the population is concentrated within a 100-mile band along the country's southern border with the United States. Exports are vital to the Canadian economy, accounting for 43 percent of its 1999 GDP of $612 billion.

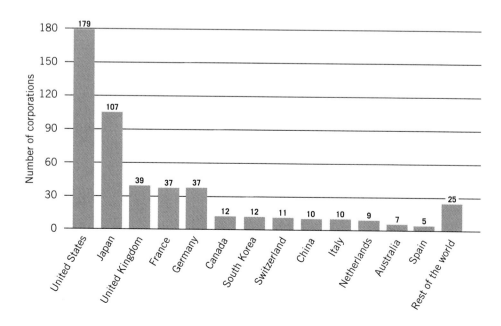

FIGURE 2.2

Headquarters of the World's Largest Corporations in 1999 by Country

Source: *Fortune*, July 24, 2000, pp. F-1ff.

〉 Exports of natural resources are an important component of the Canadian economy. This $200-million drilling vessel will pump 100,000 barrels of oil a day destined for the U.S. market once it is positioned off the coast of Newfoundland.

Canada's most important exports reflect its rich natural resources: forest products, petroleum, minerals, and grain. The United States is the dominant market for Canadian goods, receiving over three-quarters of Canada's exports in a typical year. Two-way trade between the United States and Canada forms the single largest bilateral trading relationship in the world.

International investors have long been attracted to Canada because of its proximity to the huge U.S. market and the stability of its political and legal systems. Canada's excellent infrastructure and educational systems also contribute to the performance of its economy. However, a major threat to Canada's political stability—and to its ability to attract foreign investment—is the long-standing conflict between French-speaking Canadians (many of whom live in the province of Quebec) and English-speaking Canadians. A strong separatist movement has existed in Quebec since the 1960s, and English-speaking Canada has been pressured to adopt policies to diffuse separatism. This conflict has affected domestic and international businesses in many ways. For example, firms exporting products to Canada must be aware of the country's bilingual labeling laws. Also, the riskiness of loans to Quebec firms would increase substantially, at least in the short run, if the province were to become a separate nation, as the 40-year-old separatist movement desires.

Mexico

Now the world's largest Spanish-speaking nation, Mexico declared independence from its Spanish conquerors in 1810. Like the United States, Mexico is a federal system but one whose head of government, a president, is elected by popular vote every six years. Mexican politics have been dominated by the Institutional Revolutionary Party (PRI), which has lost only one presidential election (in July 2000) since its founding in 1929. For over half a century the PRI promoted a program of economic nationalism under which Mexico discouraged foreign investment and erected high tariff walls to protect its domestic industries. During the past two decades, however, Mexico abandoned these policies and opened its markets to foreign goods and investors. Mexico also reduced the government's role in its economy by selling off many publicly owned firms, such as Aeromexico and Telefonos de Mexico. In 1994 Canada, Mexico, and the United States initiated the North American Free Trade Agreement (NAFTA), which is reducing barriers to trade among the three countries over a 15-year period. Thousands of foreign companies have established new factories in Mexico to take advantage of NAFTA, generating hundreds of thousands of new jobs in the process. In 1999 Mexico signed a similar agreement with the European Union, hoping to create additional benefits for its citizens.

Central America and the Caribbean

Besides the United States, Canada, and Mexico, the North American continent is occupied by 20 other countries that are divided geographically into two groups: Central America and the island states of the Caribbean. Collectively their population equals 72 million—more than twice the population of Canada. However, their total GDP of $148 billion is far less than Canada's $612 billion. With a few exceptions (notably Costa Rica), the economic development of these countries has suffered from a variety of problems, including political instability, chronic U.S. mili-

INFRASTRUCTURE FOR E-COMMERCE

In analyzing e-commerce opportunities around the world, dot-com entrepreneurs need to recognize the close relationship between a country's ability to embrace the Internet and its existing infrastructure. Figure 2.3 indicates the strong relationship between telecommunications infrastructures and Internet hosts per capita. These data, coupled with those in Figures 1.2 and 1.3, suggest that the combination of well-developed telephone infra-

structures and widespread access to the Internet put Canada, the United States, and the Scandinavian countries at the leading edge of emerging information technologies and thus are prime markets for electronic commerce.

Source: World Bank, World Development Report 1999/2000 (Washington, D.C.: World Bank, 2000), pp. 22–23.

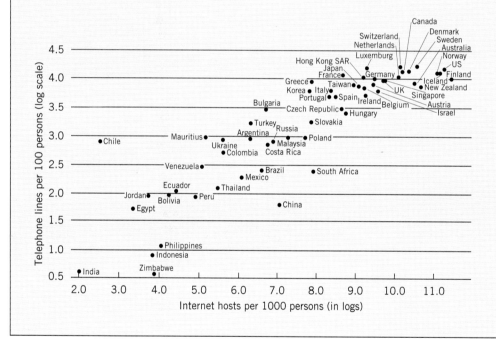

FIGURE 2.3

The Extent of the Phone Network and Internet Usage

Source: The World Economic Forum, *The Global Competitiveness Report: 1999*, Oxford University Press,1999, p. 23.

tary intervention, inadequate educational systems, a weak middle class, economic policies that have created large pockets of poverty, and import limitations by the United States and other developed countries on Central American and Caribbean goods, such as sugar and clothing.

THE MARKETPLACES OF WESTERN EUROPE ❮

Western European countries are among the world's most prosperous, attracting the attention of businesses eager to market their products to the region's wealthy consumers. These countries can be divided into two groups: members of the European Union (EU) and other countries in the region (see Map 2.2).

As the EU's leading voice favoring free trade, the United Kingdom provides a strong counterweight to France's protectionist tendencies.

As the political leader of the EU, France has long been a strong advocate of increasing the EU's power.

The German central bank had de facto control over the monetary policies of EU members, but its role was taken over by the European Central Bank (ECB) in 1999. The ECB now controls monetary policy for countries using the euro.

Greece and Austria are geographically in Central Europe, but economically in Western Europe.

Arctic Ocean

Denmark Strait

Reykjavik · ⊕ ICELAND

Norwegian Sea

Murmansk

SWEDEN

FINLAND

FAEROE ISLANDS
🏴(Denmark)

SHETLAND ISLANDS
(U.K.)

NORWAY

Helsinki

ORKNEY
ISLANDS

Oslo

Stockholm

SCOTLAND

Glasgow · ⊕Edinburgh

Baltic
Sea

DENMARK

North
Sea

Copenhagen

Atlantic
Ocean

N.
IRELAND

UNITED
KINGDOM

Dublin ⊕

IRELAND

WALES · Birmingham

ENGLAND

The
Hague ⊕

NETH.

■Hamburg

■Berlin

Amsterdam

London ⊕

Brussels⊕

GERMANY

Cologne

BELGIUM

⊕Bonn

LUX.

■Frankfurt

Paris ⊕

Munich■

Vienna⊕

FRANCE

Zurich

Bern⊕

SWITZ.

LIECH.

AUSTRIA

Geneva

Milan■

Bay of
Biscay

Bordeaux

Turin■

Marseille

MONACO

ITALY

Adriatic Sea

ANDORRA

CORSICA

Rome
⊕

PORTUGAL

Madrid
⊕

Barcelona

Naples■

GREECE

Aegean Sea

SPAIN

Valencia

Lisbon ⊕

SARDINIA

Ionian
Sea

Athens

Seville

Palermo

Strait of Gibraltar

SICILY

MALTA ⊕ Valletta

CRETE

Mediterranean
Sea

Powerful, rich EU members
Less powerful, rich EU members
Relatively poor EU members
New EU members, 1995
Other Western European nations
■ Cities over 1 million
⊕ Capitals over 1 million

MAP 2.2   **Western Europe**

The EU, which we discuss in greater detail in Chapter 9, comprises 15 countries that are seeking to promote European peace and prosperity by reducing mutual barriers to trade and investment. During the past decade the EU has made tremendous strides in achieving this objective. With a 1999 GDP of $8.3 trillion and a population of 377 million, it is one of the world's richest markets. EU members are free-market-oriented, parliamentary democracies. However, government intervention and ownership generally play a more important role in these countries' economies than in that of the United States. In 1999, 11 EU members created a new common currency known as the euro; Greece joined this currency bloc in 2001. By the middle of 2002 these 12 countries will eliminate their own national currencies and rely only on the euro for legal tender.

From an economic perspective Germany is the EU's most important member. With a 1999 GDP of $2.1 trillion it possesses the world's third largest economy, after Japan and the United States. It is a major player in international business; in most years it is the world's second largest exporter, trailing only the United States. Because of the strength of the German economy and the government's strict anti-inflation policies, Germany has played a major role in formulating the economic policies of the EU.

Politically, France exerts strong leadership within the EU. The French government has been a leading proponent of increased political, economic, and military union within Europe and of strengthening the powers of the EU's government. France also has advocated restricting free trade in commodities important to its economy, such as agricultural goods, automobiles, fish, and semiconductor chips.

France's positions have not gone unchallenged, however. The United Kingdom has steadfastly resisted French initiatives to strengthen the EU's powers and, as a traditionally strong supporter of free trade, has provided an important counterweight to French protectionist tendencies. The U.K.'s capital city, London, is a major international finance center, employing over 300,000 in its financial services sector. The United Kingdom is also a major exporter and importer of goods, an important destination for and source of foreign investment, and home to the headquarters or regional divisions of numerous MNCs.

Western European countries that are not EU members include Iceland, Malta, Norway, and Switzerland, plus several "postage stamp" countries such as Andorra, Monaco, and Liechtenstein. Classified as high income by the World Bank, these free-market-oriented countries collectively account for 2 percent of the world's GDP.

THE MARKETPLACES OF EASTERN EUROPE AND CENTRAL EUROPE ‹

No regions of the world are undergoing as much economic change as Eastern Europe and Central Europe, which are in the midst of the painful process of converting from communism to capitalism. Soviet leader Mikhail Gorbachev's 1986 reform initiatives of glasnost (openness) and perestroika (economic restructuring) triggered the region's political, economic, and social revolutions. Eastern Europe includes the 15 separate countries that resulted from the disintegration of the Soviet Union in 1991 (see Map 2.3). (Geographically, several of these countries are in Asia, but because they share economic problems with their European counterparts, they are discussed in this section.) Central Europe is composed of Albania, Austria, and the former Soviet satellite states of Bulgaria, Czechoslovakia (now divided into the Czech Republic and the Slovak Republic), Hungary, Poland, and Romania. Central Europe also includes Bosnia-Herzegovina, Croatia, Macedonia, and Slovenia, which were carved out of Yugoslavia (see Map 2.4).

The three Baltic republics were conquered by Soviet troops in 1940. They were among the first of the republics to claim their independence and are the only ones that did not join the Commonwealth of Independent States.

The five Central Asian republics are populated largely by Muslims, whose cultural heritage is very different from that of their former countrymen in Russia, Belarus, and Ukraine. The area is rich in natural resources such as oil and gas.

The Caucasus republics have suffered much political instability. Armenia and Azerbaijan have fought over their regional boundary; rebels have tried to topple the government of Georgia. That portion of Russia lying in the Caucasus (the land between the Black and the Caspian Seas) has had similar problems, most notably in Chechnya.

RUSSIA

Legend:
Baltic republics
Caucasus republics
Central Asian republics
• Cities of 650,000 to 1 million
■ Cities over 1 million
⊛ Capitals
⊞ Capitals over 1 million

CHINA

Alma-Ata ⊞
Bishkek ⊛
KYRGYZ REPUBLIC

TAJIKISTAN
Dushanbe ⊛

AFGHANISTAN

Tashkent ⊞
UZBEKISTAN

TURKMENISTAN
Ashgabat ⊛

IRAN

Aral Sea

KAZAKHSTAN

RUSSIA

Yekaterinburg ■

Perm' ■

Ufa ■

Kazan' ■
Tol'yatti ● Samara
Nizhniy Novgorod ■

Saratov ●

Moscow ⊞

Voronezh ●

Volgograd ■

Caspian Sea
Baku ⊞
AZERBAIJAN
GEORGIA Tbilisi ⊛
ARMENIA Yerevan ⊛
AZER.

St. Petersburg ■

Rostov ■

Dnipropetrovs'k ■
Donets'k ■
Kharkiv ■

Kryvyy Rih ● Zaporizhzhya ■

ESTONIA
Riga ⊛ LATVIA
Vilnius ⊛
LITHUANIA
RUS.

Minsk ⊞
BELARUS

Kiev ⊞
UKRAINE

L'viv ●

MOLDOVA
Chisinau ⊛
Odesa ■

Baltic Sea

POLAND

SLOVAKIA

HUNGARY

ROMANIA

BULGARIA

SERBIA

Black Sea

Aegean Sea

M A P   2 . 3   **Eastern Europe**

The Former Soviet Union

The Union of Soviet Socialist Republics (Soviet Union or U.S.S.R.) emerged from the disintegration of the Russian empire that followed its defeat in World War I. In the chaos that ensued from the 1917 abdication of Czar Nicholas II, the Communist Party seized control of the Russian government and established the Soviet Union in the name of the workers and peasants. The communists outlawed the market system, abolished private property, and collectivized the country's vast rich farmlands. By doing so, they succeeded in reducing the enormous income inequalities that had existed under czarist rule. Despite this success, the population's standard of living increasingly fell behind that of the Western democracies.

Gorbachev's economic and political reforms led to the Soviet Union's collapse in 1991 and subsequent declarations of independence by the 15 Soviet republics, which are now often referred to as the **Newly Independent States**, or **NIS**. In 1992, 12 of the NIS (all but the Baltic countries of Estonia, Latvia, and Lithuania) formed the **Commonwealth of Independent States (CIS)** as a forum to discuss issues of mutual concern. Members of the CIS established a free trade area, which means that their exports to one another are free of tariffs. The most important of these new countries is the Russian Federation (Russia), which was the dominant republic within the former Soviet Union. As an independent state, Russia is the world's largest country in land mass (6.5 million square miles) and the sixth largest in population (147 million people). The country is well endowed with natural resources, including gold, oil, natural gas, minerals, diamonds, and fertile farmland.

The transformation of the economies of Russia and some of the other NIS from communism to a free-market system has not been easy, to say the least. Boris Yeltsin, Russia's first democratically elected president, tried to privatize many of Russia's state-owned firms. Although some newly privatized firms improved their productivity, many fell into the hands of individuals who were more concerned with looting corporate assets than in restoring the companies' economic health and performance. Under Yeltsin's administration, Russia's central government staggered from one financial crisis to another, burdened by an inability to collect taxes and a political need to subsidize the inefficient state-owned enterprises that it was unable to sell to private interests. Russia's second president, Vladimir Putin, faces many challenges in restoring Russia to economic health, not the least of which is reassuring foreign investors who have largely adopted a wait-and-see attitude because of their concerns about the country's government.

❯ Russia's efforts to privatize state-owned enterprises have met with mixed success. This aging Siberian aluminum smelter is the world's largest. After it was privatized in the mid-1990s, the speculators who purchased it did little to modernize its operations.

Central Europe

Central European countries that were aligned with the former Soviet Union also face serious challenges (see Map 2.4). With the collapse of the region's communist governments, the regional trading system established by the Soviet Union broke down, and the former Soviet satellite states had to adjust to the loss of guaranteed export markets. The Central European countries also had to restructure their economies from centrally planned communist systems to decentralized market systems.

NORWAY

SWEDEN

FINLAND

DENMARK

ESTONIA

Communist support of heavy industry and indifference to pollution contributed to environmental havoc throughout much of Central Europe. One particularly devastated region is the industrial triangle between Dresden, Katowice, and Mlada Boleslav.

LATVIA

LITHUANIA

Following the revolutions of the 1980s, four of Yugoslavia's six republics broke away to become independent nations. The status of the two remaining republics, Serbia and Montenegro, remains uncertain. While some blood was shed when Macedonia, Slovenia, and Croatia separated from Yugoslavia, several hundred thousand lives were lost in Bosnia-Herzegovina and Kosovo's quest for independence. At issue is the extent of Serbia's control over the Balkan peninsula.

GERMANY

Gdànsk

RUS.

Bydgoszcz

BELARUS

Dresden

Poznan

Warsaw

POLAND

Mlada Boleslav

Wroclaw

Łódź

Prague

Lublin

Katowice

CZECH REP.

Cracow

Brno

SWITZ.

Vienna

SLOVAK REPUBLIC

UKRAINE

FRANCE

AUSTRIA

Bratislava

Budapest

Ljubljana

SLOVENIA

HUNGARY

MOLDOVA

Zagreb

CROATIA

BOSNIA-HERZEGOVINA

Belgrade

ROMANIA

ITALY

Sarajevo

SERBIA

Bucharest

Albania is Europe's poorest country, the result of its Stalinist-style economy, which eliminated the private sector. Albania split from the Soviet bloc in 1961, believing the bloc's policies were insufficiently Marxist. Today, about one-fifth of its labor force works abroad, sending home funds vital to Albania's survival.

MONTENEGRO

Titograd

Sofia

Black Sea

Tirane

Skopje

BULGARIA

Plovdiv

ALBANIA

MACEDONIA

GREECE

Aegean Sea

Ionian Sea

TURKEY

▨ Former Yugoslavia
● Cities of 350,000 to 1 million
✪ Capitals
⊞ Capitals over 1 million

MAP 2.4

Central Europe

The Czech Republic, Hungary, and Poland—all of which are now classified as upper middle-income countries by the World Bank—are further along in restructuring their economies than other Central European countries, although the three have followed different paths. They have attracted more FDI than their neighbors, as Table 2.1 indicates, and have become members of the OECD.

The Czech Republic's transformation to capitalism got off to a fast start. Czech Prime Minister Vaclav Klaus enjoyed strong support for his efforts to build a society based on democracy and a free market. He initiated a privatization scheme that was highly praised at the time. Klaus's privatization program utilized vouchers, which were sold to Czech citizens for a nominal 1,000 Czech crowns (about $34) and which gave them the right to purchase shares in state-owned industries. Most Czechs used their vouchers to buy shares in investment funds controlled by Czech banks, which in turn bought shares in state-owned companies being privatized. However, this approach brought neither new capital nor new management to these companies. As a result, many of them ignored the painful process of cutting payrolls and improving efficiency. The Czech Republic now faces the onerous task, initially deferred by its privatization approach, of improving the efficiency of its formerly state-owned firms.[3]

In contrast, Poland's first post-communist government adopted a policy of "shock therapy" to reform its economy. It opened the country to imported goods, provided tax breaks to new companies, and relaxed price controls on basic goods. Another key initiative was the encouragement of entrepreneurship. The Polish government cut red tape, designing its company registration form to fit on a single page. As a result of these measures, 2 million new businesses were created, approximately one new business per 19 Poles. Poland's policies have attracted FDI from a "who's who" list of MNCs, such as Daewoo, Nestlé, General Motors, and ABB Asea Brown Boveri.[4]

Hungary was the least communistic of the communist countries. In 1968 it instituted market-oriented reforms within the context of communism, known as **market socialism** or, more colorfully, "goulash communism." After the Berlin Wall fell, Hungary passed new laws covering bankruptcy, accounting practices, and banking, which forced Hungarian firms to be profitable or go out of business. Over 30,000 bankruptcies resulted. Although this sink-or-swim approach caused hardships for the average Hungarian, it swept the deadwood out of the economy and

TABLE 2.1

Foreign Direct Investment in Central Europe

	POPULATION (IN MILLIONS)	FDI (IN MILLIONS OF DOLLARS)							
		1993	1994	1995	1996	1979	1998	1999	1993–1999
Albania	3.4	58	53	70	90	48	45	41	405
Croatia	4.5	120	117	115	506	515	893	1384	3650
Czech Republic	10.3	654	878	2568	1435	1286	2734	5093	14648
Hungary	10.1	2350	1144	4519	2274	2167	2037	1951	16442
Poland	38.7	1715	1875	3659	4498	4908	6365	7270	30290
Romania	22.5	94	341	419	263	1215	2031	1041	5404
Slovak Republic	5.4	199	270	236	351	174	562	354	2146
Slovenia	2.0	113	128	177	194	375	248	181	1416

Source: International Monetary Fund, *International Financial Statistics*, November 2000.

encouraged foreign firms to invest in the country. On a per capita basis Hungary has received more FDI than any other country in the region, as Table 2.1 shows. Particularly notable are investments by foreign automobile manufacturers. Ford, General Motors, Suzuki, and Volkswagen have all built new factories in Hungary, employing thousands of the country's skilled workers.[5]

Economic reforms are less advanced in Albania, Bulgaria, and Romania because these countries were slower to develop a political consensus about the direction they wanted their economies to take. The situation is far worse in parts of what was Yugoslavia. Slovenia avoided almost all the chaos that surrounded the disintegration of Yugoslavia. This was true to a lesser extent in Croatia and Macedonia. However, the economies of Serbia, Montenegro, and Bosnia were devastated by the brutal war over control of Bosnia in the early 1990s and over Kosovo in the late 1990s. These conflicts, needless to say, discouraged most MNCs from investing there.

❯ THE MARKETPLACES OF ASIA

Asia is home to over half the world's population, yet it produces only 25 percent of the world's GDP (see Map 2.5). Asia's importance to international business cannot be minimized. The region is a source of both high-quality and low-quality products and of both skilled and unskilled labor. Asia is both a major destination for foreign investments by MNCs and a major supplier of capital to non-Asian countries. More important, its aggressive, efficient entrepreneurs have increasingly put competitive pressure on European and North American firms to improve their productivity and the quality of their products.

Japan

Japan, an island country of 127 million people, rose from the ashes of World War II to become the world's second largest economy (with a GDP of $4.4 trillion in 1999) and an important member of the Quad. (See "Bringing the World into Focus.") Japan's rapid growth during the past 50 years is due in part to the partnership between its Ministry of International Trade and Investment (MITI) and its industrial sector. MITI has used its formal and informal powers to guide the production and investment strategies of the country's corporate elite. For example, immediately after World War II, MITI encouraged Japanese firms to concentrate their efforts on such basic industries as steel and shipbuilding. As other countries entered these industries, MITI and Japan's MNCs shifted their focus to producing automobiles, consumer electronics, and machinery.

MITI has been aided by Japan's concentrated industrial structure. Japanese industry is controlled by large families of interrelated companies, called **keiretsu**, that are typically centered around a major Japanese bank. The bank takes primary responsibility for meeting the keiretsu's financing needs. The members often act as suppliers to each other, thus making it more difficult for outsiders to penetrate Japanese markets. Members are also protected from hostile takeovers by an elaborate system of cross-ownership of shares by which members of a keiretsu own shares in each other's companies. Toyota Motors, for example, owns 19 percent of the common stock of Koito Manufacturing, and other members of Toyota's keiretsu own 40 percent of Koito's stock. Koito in turn is the primary supplier for Toyota's automotive lighting needs. Keiretsu members often rely on a **sogo sosha**, an export trading company, to market their exports worldwide. Typically the sogo sosha is also a keiretsu member.

Japan's economic growth slowed in the 1990s, however. Its GDP grew at an annual rate of 1.3 percent, compared to 2.9 percent for the United States and 2.2 percent for Canada. Many experts are concerned that the Japanese political and economic systems have not been able to adjust quickly enough to the changes in

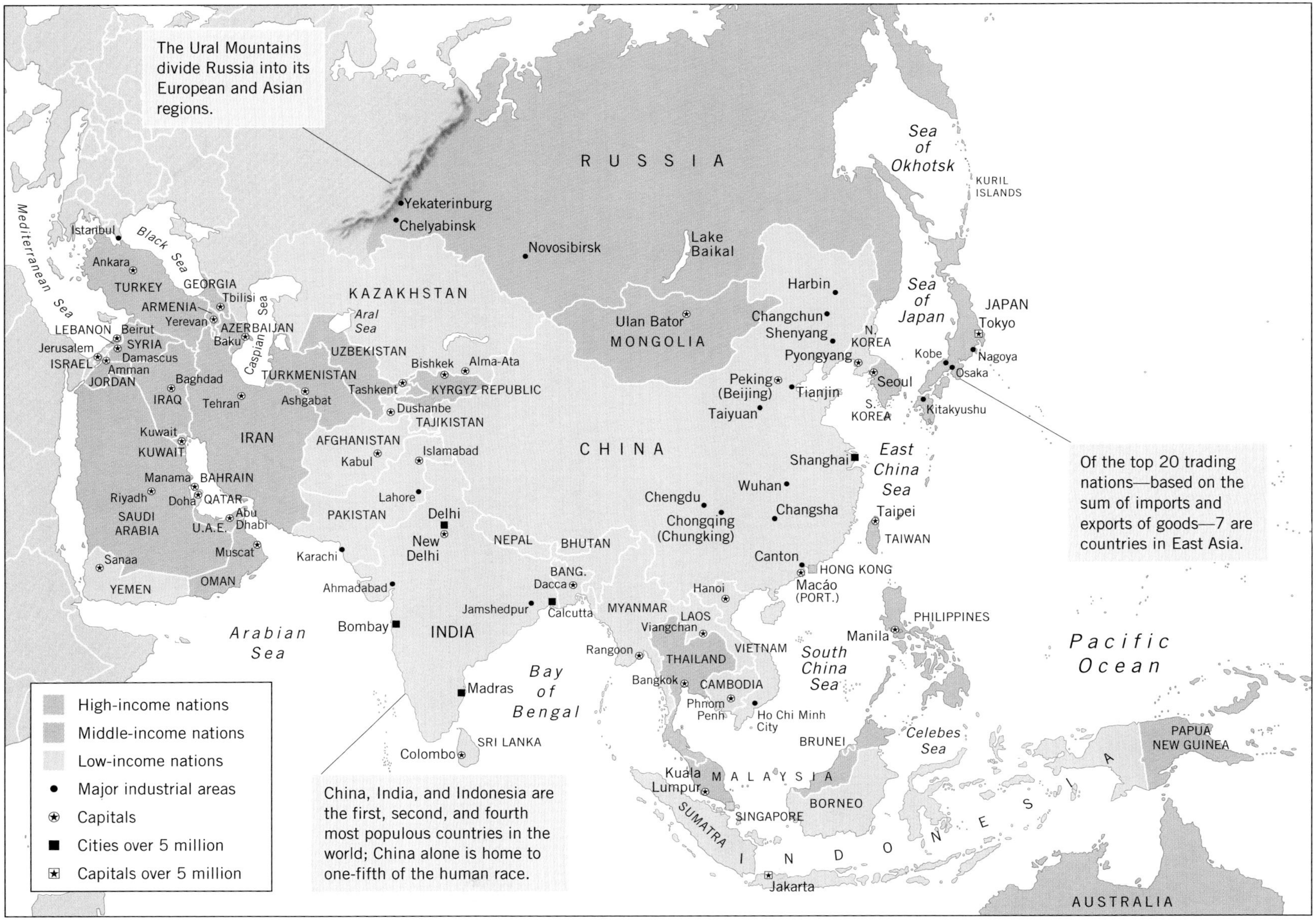

Of the top 20 trading nations—based on the sum of imports and exports of goods—7 are countries in East Asia.

The Ural Mountains divide Russia into its European and Asian regions.

China, India, and Indonesia are the first, second, and fourth most populous countries in the world; China alone is home to one-fifth of the human race.

Pacific Ocean

Sea of Okhotsk

KURIL ISLANDS

JAPAN
Tokyo
Nagoya
Osaka
Kobe
Kitakyushu

Sea of Japan

PAPUA NEW GUINEA

AUSTRALIA

N. KOREA
Seoul
Pyongyang
S. KOREA

East China Sea
Taipei
TAIWAN

PHILIPPINES
Manila

Celebes Sea

Harbin
Changchun
Shenyang
Tianjin
Shanghai
Changsha

Peking (Beijing)
Taiyuan

Wuhan

HONG KONG
Macão (PORT.)
Canton

South China Sea

BRUNEI
BORNEO

R U S S I A

Lake Baikal

Ulan Bator
MONGOLIA

Novosibirsk

C H I N A

Chengdu
Chongqing (Chungking)

Hanoi
LAOS
Viangchan

VIETNAM
CAMBODIA
Phnom Penh
Ho Chi Minh City

THAILAND
Bangkok

MYANMAR
Rangoon

Kuala Lumpur
M A L A Y S I A
SINGAPORE
SUMATRA

Jakarta

I N D O N E S I A

Yekaterinburg
Chelyabinsk

KAZAKHSTAN
Aral Sea

Alma-Ata
Bishkek
KYRGYZ REPUBLIC
Dushanbe
TAJIKISTAN

UZBEKISTAN
Tashkent
TURKMENISTAN
Ashgabat

Islamabad

NEPAL
BHUTAN

BANG.
Dacca
Calcutta

Jamshedpur

INDIA
Madras

SRI LANKA
Colombo

Bay of Bengal

Delhi
New Delhi

Lahore

AFGHANISTAN
Kabul
PAKISTAN
Karachi

Ahmadabad
Bombay

Caspian Sea

GEORGIA
Tbilisi
ARMENIA
Yerevan
AZERBAIJAN
Baku

IRAN
Tehran

Baghdad
IRAQ

Kuwait
KUWAIT
BAHRAIN
Manama
QATAR
Doha
U.A.E.
Abu Dhabi

Muscat
OMAN

Arabian Sea

Istanbul
Ankara
TURKEY
Black Sea

LEBANON
Beirut
SYRIA
Damascus
ISRAEL
Jerusalem
Amman
JORDAN

Riyadh
SAUDI ARABIA

Sanaa
YEMEN

Mediterranean Sea

Asia

	High-income nations
	Middle-income nations
	Low-income nations
●	Major industrial areas
⊛	Capitals
■	Cities over 5 million
⊛	Capitals over 5 million

MAP 2.5

39

Bringing the World into FOCUS

WHO'S NUMBER TWO?

By all measures, the economy of the United States is the world's largest. Who's number two depends on how you measure size. Most sources of such data compare sizes by taking a country's gross domestic product (GDP) measured in its home currency and converting that figure to a standard currency (for example, the U.S. dollar) using existing exchange rates. However, some experts believe that to make meaningful comparisons one must adjust the original GDP figures for purchasing power parity—that is, differences in purchasing power among the local currencies. Figure 2.4(a) shows the world's seven largest economies when adjustments for purchasing power are not made; Figure 2.4(b) shows the seven largest economies when purchasing power adjustments are made. Note that China jumps from the seventh to the second largest economy, and India leaps from the twelfth to the fourth when adjustments for purchasing power are made.

FIGURE 2.4

Source: Based on data provided by The World Bank Group, *http://www.worldbank.org/*.

GDP UNADJUSTED FOR PURCHASING POWER (1999)

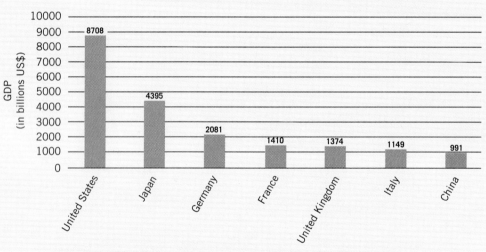

GDP ADJUSTED FOR PURCHASING POWER (1999)

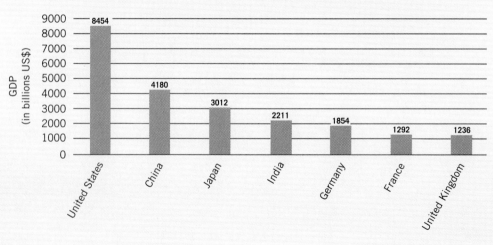

the world economy created by the growth of e-commerce. Moreover, it has received much international criticism because of the perception that it employs unfair trading practices to market its exports while using numerous nontariff barriers to restrict imports to its domestic market (we will discuss this further in Chapter 8).

Australia and New Zealand

Australia and New Zealand are the other traditional economic powers in Pacific Asia. Although they share a common cultural heritage, significant differences exist between the two countries, which are separated by 1,200 miles of ocean (see Map 2.6). Australia's 19 million people live in an area of 2.97 million square miles. Because much of the continent is arid, most of the population is concentrated in the wetter coastal regions, with approximately 40 percent living in either Sydney or Melbourne. Australia is rich in natural resources but has a relatively small workforce. As a result, its exports, which in 1999 accounted for 19 percent of its $390-billion GDP, are concentrated in natural resource industries (such as gold, iron ore, and coal) and in land-intensive agricultural goods (such as wool, beef, and wheat).

New Zealand's 4 million people live on two main islands—the more populous North Island and the more scenic but less temperate South Island. After systemat-

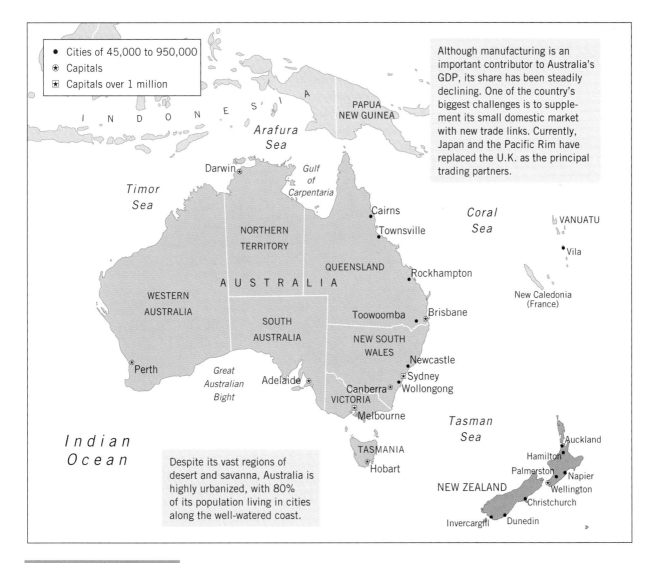

Although manufacturing is an important contributor to Australia's GDP, its share has been steadily declining. One of the country's biggest challenges is to supplement its small domestic market with new trade links. Currently, Japan and the Pacific Rim have replaced the U.K. as the principal trading partners.

Despite its vast regions of desert and savanna, Australia is highly urbanized, with 80% of its population living in cities along the well-watered coast.

MAP 2.6   **Australia and New Zealand**

› The contrast between the economic performance of communist North Korea (bottom) and that of capitalist South Korea (top) has been dramatic. After the Korean War ended in 1953, both countries ranked among the world's poorest. Housing, food, and other consumer goods are still scarce in North Korea, and its per capita income has fallen below $1,000. The export-oriented economic policies of South Korea have generated an economic boom. The country's per capita income is $10,155, and it is a major force in the world economy.

ically deregulating and privatizing its economy in the 1980s, New Zealand gained an international reputation as being in the forefront of the worldwide shift toward greater reliance on market-based policies. Trade is extremely important to the country; in 1999 exports constituted 31 percent of its $54-billion GDP. Over half of New Zealand's exports are attributable to its extensive pasture lands—these exports include dairy products, meat, and wool. Australia, Japan, and the United States purchase approximately half of New Zealand's exports and imports.

The Four Tigers

Pacific Asia is one of the world's most rapidly industrializing regions. South Korea, Taiwan, Singapore, and Hong Kong in particular have made such rapid strides since 1945 that they are collectively known as the "Four Tigers," a reference to the Chinese heritage that three of the four countries share. They are also referred to as the newly industrialized countries (NICs) or the newly industrialized economies (NIEs). The Four Tigers are the only countries once categorized as less developed by the World Bank that have subsequently achieved high-income status.

South Korea. The Republic of Korea, more commonly known as South Korea, was born of the Cold War, which left the Korean peninsula divided into communist North Korea and capitalist South Korea. Since the end of the Korean War in 1953, South Korea has been one of the world's fastest growing economies. Exporting accounted for 42 percent of its 1999 GDP of $407 billion. To promote economic development, Korea has relied on tight cooperation between the government and 30 or so large, privately owned, and family-centered conglomerates that dominate the Korean economy. The most important of these conglomerates, or **chaebol**, are Samsung, Hyundai, Daewoo Group, and LG (formerly Lucky-Goldstar). In many ways the Korean government has tried to follow the economic path established by the Japanese: discouragement of imports, governmental leadership of the economy, and reliance on large economic combines for industrialization.

Unfortunately, Korea's growth came to a screeching halt as a result of the 1997–1998 Asian currency crisis, and many of the chaebol were plunged into financial difficulties. Some observers argued that their problems were due to overexpansion and the poor lending practices of Korean banks. Many of the chaebol seemed to be more interested in size than profitability and borrowed money to enter industries already burdened by overcapacity, such as automobiles. A primary problem facing the Korean government is what to do with the financially weakened chaebol. One option is to let them fall into bankruptcy or be taken over by foreign companies. Another option is for the government to bail out the wobbly chaebol through low interest loans. International agencies such as the International Monetary Fund favor the former course of action, while the leaders of the politically powerful chaebol are lobbying for the latter.

Taiwan. Taiwan, as the Republic of China is commonly known, is a small island country off the coast of mainland China that is home to 22.2 million people. It was born in the aftermath of the civil war between the nationalist forces led by General Chiang Kai-Shek and the Chinese communists led by Mao Tse-Tung. After their defeat on the mainland in 1949, Chiang's army and government fled to Taiwan. Declaring the island "the Republic of China" and himself the rightful governor of the mainland, Chiang set about developing the Taiwanese economy to support a promised invasion of the mainland. Redistribution of land from large estate holders to peasants increased agricultural productivity. Reliance on family-owned private businesses and export-oriented trade policies has made Taiwan one of the world's fastest growing economies during the past three decades, with a real growth rate averaging over 8 percent annually over that time span. Exports were $122 billion in 1999, or 34 percent of the country's GDP of $357 billion.

Taiwan's economic development has been so fast paced that it can no longer compete as a low-wage manufacturing center. Consequently, Taiwanese businesses more recently have focused on high-value-added industries such as electronics and automotive products. However, the businesses still need low-wage workers. Despite the lack of diplomatic relations between Taiwan and China, Taiwanese businesses increasingly are investing in factories and assembly plants in China to access the low-wage workers they need.

Singapore.　　The Republic of Singapore is a former British colony and a small island country off the southern tip of the Malay peninsula. To combat the chronic unemployment that plagued the country when it became independent in 1965, Singapore's government initially emphasized development of labor-intensive industries such as textiles. This economic policy proved so successful that Singapore shifted to higher-value-added activities, such as oil refining and chemical processing, and high-tech industries, such as computers and biotechnology. With a population of only 3.2 million, Singapore now suffers from a labor shortage. It can no longer compete with such countries as Honduras and Indonesia in the production of price-sensitive, labor-intensive manufactured goods.

In 1999 Singapore's per capita income was $26,356 and its exports totaled $139 billion, or *164 percent* of its GDP of $85 billion. That figure is not a misprint. Singapore thrives on **reexporting**. Singapore's firms take advantage of the country's excellent port facilities to import foreign goods and then reexport them to other countries (particularly neighboring Malaysia). Besides being an important port and center for oil refining, Singapore provides sophisticated communications and financial services for firms in Pacific Asia and is well on its way to becoming the region's high-technology center.

Hong Kong.　　Hong Kong was born of the "opium war" (1839–1842) fought between the United Kingdom and China. As a consequence of this war, Hong Kong was ceded to the British. In 1860 the British obtained possession of Kowloon on the Chinese mainland, and in 1898 they were granted a 99-year lease on an area of the mainland known as the New Territories. The lease expired on July 1, 1997. On that date China again assumed political control of Hong Kong and designated it a special administrative region (SAR). As an SAR, Hong Kong enjoys a fair degree of autonomy. It has its own legislature, economic freedom, free port status, and a separate taxation system. Hong Kong will enjoy these privileges until 2047. However, China has made it clear that it will impose its own political will on Hong Kong.

Hong Kong's attractiveness to international businesses lies in its deep, sheltered harbor and its role as an entry point to mainland China. Almost 7 million people are packed into Hong Kong's small land area. Hong Kong offers highly educated, highly productive labor for industries such as textiles and electronics and provides banking and financial services for much of East Asia. As a result of common culture and geography, Hong Kong entrepreneurs often act as intermediaries for companies around the world that want to do business with China. Hong Kong has also traditionally served as a bridge between Taiwan and its political enemy, China. Accordingly, Hong Kong has thrived as an entrepôt for China, receiving goods from it and preparing the goods for shipment to the rest of the world, and vice versa. Export statistics for Hong Kong reflect its role as a reexporter. Hong Kong exported $210 billion worth of goods in 1999, or 132 percent of its $159 billion GDP.

China

With over 1.2 billion people, China is the world's most populous country. It also is one of the world's oldest, ruled by a series of emperors from 2000 B.C. until the early 1900s, when a republic was founded. A chaotic civil war facilitated a Japanese invasion in 1931. After the Japanese were expelled at the end of World

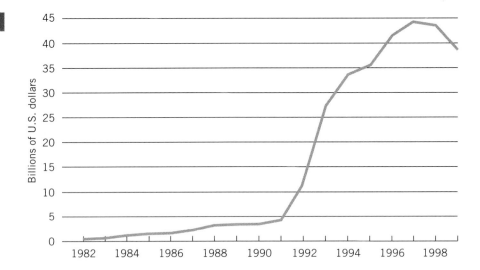

FIGURE 2.5

**Annual FDI Flows to China,
1982–1999**

Source: Data from International
Monetary Fund, *International
Financial Statistics Yearbook* and
International Financial Statistics,
August 2000.

War II, the civil war resumed. Finally, in 1949 the communist forces of Mao Tse-Tung defeated the nationalist army led by General Chiang Kai-Shek.

Communism in China under Mao Tse-Tung went through several stages. The Great Leap Forward was a program undertaken from 1958 to 1960 to force industrialization through the growth of small labor-intensive factories. The program's failure led eventually to the Cultural Revolution in 1966, during which youthful communist cadres indiscriminately purged Communist Party members suspected of deviating from Mao's doctrines. The political chaos that followed set back the country's economic progress, as many of its most productive and educated members were exiled to the countryside to repent their ideological sins.

After Mao's death in 1976 the government adopted limited free-market policies. Agriculture was returned to the private sector, and entrepreneurs were allowed to start small businesses such as restaurants and light manufacturing. Foreign companies were permitted to establish joint ventures with Chinese firms. As a result, FDI and economic growth soared, as did hopes for increased political freedom. However, Communist Party leaders were unwilling to relinquish their powers. The massacre of several thousand pro-democracy demonstrators in Beijing's Tiananmen Square in June 1989 chilled economic and political relations between China and the Quad countries for several years.

Nonetheless, China is following a unique path. It continues to adopt market-oriented economic policies under the Communist Party's watchful eye. As a result, China's economy is becoming increasingly schizophrenic. Half the country's output is produced by state enterprises noted for their low productivity and shoddy products; the remainder is produced by private firms. Private-sector development has attracted the attention of firms worldwide. FDI in China has exploded since 1992, as Figure. 2.5 indicates. Of particular note are the increased investments by overseas Chinese investors living in Taiwan, Hong Kong, and Singapore, who see China as a source of hard-working, low-cost labor, an increasingly scarce commodity in their own communities.

India

India is the world's second most populous country, having reached the one billion mark in 2000. It also is one of the poorest countries, with a per capita GDP of only $460. India was part of the British Empire until 1947, when the Indian subcontinent was partitioned along religious lines into India, where Hindus were in the majority, and Pakistan, where Muslims were dominant. The eastern part of Pakistan became the independent nation of Bangladesh in 1971. The new country of India adopted many aspects of British government, including the parliamentary system, a strong independent judiciary, and a professional bureaucracy. For most of its post-World War II history, the country has relied on state ownership of key industries—including power, transportation, and heavy industry—as a critical element of its economic development efforts.

India's bureaucracy can be cumbersome and slow to provide documents necessary to do business in the country. Until 1991 India discouraged foreign investment, limiting foreign owners to minority positions in Indian enterprises and imposing other onerous requirements. For example, as a condition for remaining in the country, the Coca-Cola Company was retroactively required in the 1970s to divulge its secret soft drink formula. Coca-Cola refused and chose to leave the market. Coca-Cola subsequently reentered the Indian market as a result of Prime Minister Rao's 1991 market-opening reforms, which reduced trade barriers, opened the doors to increased FDI, and modernized the country's financial sector.

These reforms have begun to pay off. India has attracted much FDI from MNCs based in the Quad countries, and its real GDP growth has averaged 6 percent annually since the reforms began. (See the chapter's closing case, "A Boom in Bangalore," for a discussion of one industry that has thrived as a result of these reforms.) However, problems remain. A lack of clarity in government policy has created enormous confusion for some foreign investors. The World Bank has warned that failure to trim red tape may threaten the flow of foreign capital into sectors crucial for India's economic growth.

Southeast Asian Countries

Asia is home to numerous other countries at various stages of economic development. Of particular note are Thailand, Malaysia, and Indonesia, countries with low labor costs that have been recipients of significant FDI during the 1980s and 1990s. As labor costs have risen in their homeland, many Japanese MNCs have built satellite plants in these three countries to supply low-cost parts to parent factories in Japan. U.S. and European MNCs have used these countries as production platforms as well. The Thai, Malaysian, and Indonesian economies boomed as a result of exports generated by FDI. Their GDPs enjoyed annual growth rates averaging over 7 percent from 1980 to 1995. However, the currency crisis of 1997 and 1998 damaged these three countries badly, with Indonesia bearing the heaviest blows.

THE MARKETPLACES OF AFRICA AND THE MIDDLE EAST ❮

Africa covers approximately 22 percent of the world's total land area and is rich in natural resources. Egypt occupies the northeastern tip of the African continent and represents the western boundary of what is commonly known as the Middle East.

Africa

The African continent, shown in Map 2.7, is home to 796 million people and 55 countries. Most of Africa was colonized in the late nineteenth century by the major European powers (Belgium, France, Germany, Italy, Portugal, Spain, and the United Kingdom) for strategic military purposes or to meet domestic political demands. The tide of colonialism began to reverse in the mid-1950s, as one by one the European powers surrendered control of their colonies. Vestiges of colonialism remain in today's Africa, affecting opportunities available to international businesses. For example, Chad, Niger, and the Côte d'Ivoire (Ivory Coast) retain close economic and cultural ties to France. They link their currencies to the French franc and follow French legal, educational, and governmental procedures. Because of these ties, French manufacturers, financial institutions, and service-sector firms

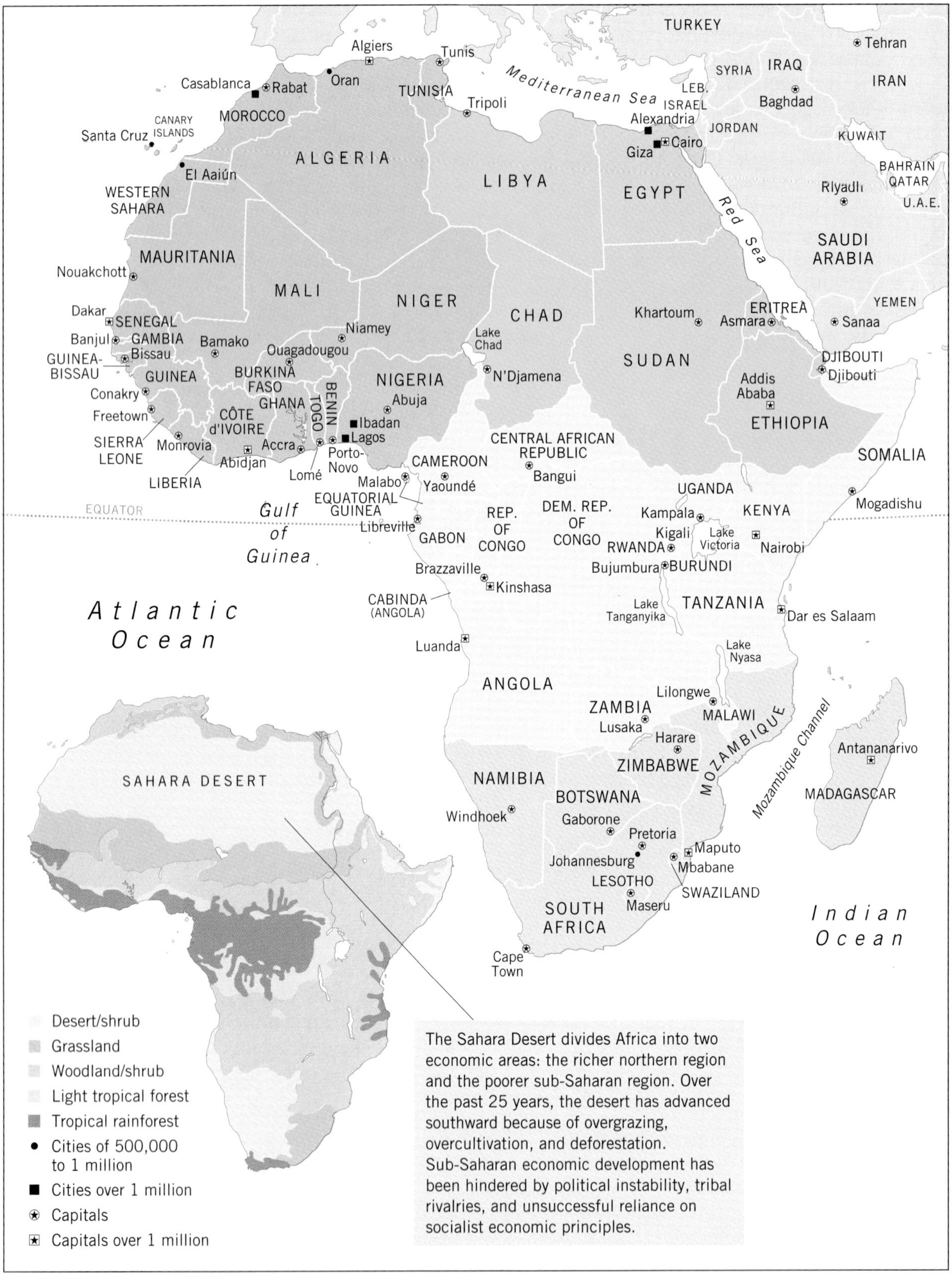

TURKEY

Algiers Tunis

Casablanca Rabat Oran TUNISIA Tripoli

Santa Cruz CANARY
ISLANDS MOROCCO

El Aaiún

WESTERN
SAHARA

MAURITANIA

Nouakchott

Dakar

SENEGAL

Banjul GAMBIA

GUINEA-
BISSAU Bissau

Conakry

GUINEA

Freetown

SIERRA
LEONE Monrovia

LIBERIA

Abidjan

CÔTE
d'IVOIRE

GHANA

Accra

Bamako

Ouagadougou

BURKINA
FASO

BENIN

TOGO

Lomé

Porto-
Novo

Niamey

NIGERIA

Abuja

Ibadan

Lagos

ALGERIA

MALI

NIGER

Lake
Chad

N'Djamena

LIBYA

CHAD

SYRIA

IRAQ

Tehran

IRAN

LEB.
ISRAEL
JORDAN

Baghdad

KUWAIT

Mediterranean Sea

Alexandria

Giza Cairo

EGYPT

Red Sea

SAUDI
ARABIA

BAHRAIN
QATAR

Riyadh

U.A.E.

YEMEN

Khartoum

SUDAN

ERITREA

Asmara

Sanaa

DJIBOUTI

Djibouti

Addis
Ababa

ETHIOPIA

SOMALIA

Atlantic
Ocean

EQUATOR

Gulf
of
Guinea

CAMEROON

Malabo

Yaoundé

EQUATORIAL
GUINEA

Libreville

GABON

CABINDA
(ANGOLA)

Brazzaville

REP.
OF
CONGO

Kinshasa

Luanda

CENTRAL AFRICAN
REPUBLIC

Bangui

DEM. REP.
OF
CONGO

UGANDA

Kampala

RWANDA

Kigali

Bujumbura

BURUNDI

Lake
Victoria

KENYA

Nairobi

Mogadishu

Lake
Tanganyika

TANZANIA

Dar es Salaam

Mozambique Channel

ANGOLA

Lake
Nyasa

Lilongwe

ZAMBIA

Lusaka

MALAWI

MOZAMBIQUE

Antananarivo

NAMIBIA

Windhoek

Harare

ZIMBABWE

BOTSWANA

Gaborone

Pretoria

Johannesburg

Maputo

Mbabane

SWAZILAND

MADAGASCAR

LESOTHO

Maseru

SOUTH
AFRICA

Cape
Town

Indian
Ocean

SAHARA DESERT

- Desert/shrub
- Grassland
- Woodland/shrub
- Light tropical forest
- Tropical rainforest
- • Cities of 500,000
  to 1 million
- ■ Cities over 1 million
- ⊛ Capitals
- ⊞ Capitals over 1 million

The Sahara Desert divides Africa into two
economic areas: the richer northern region
and the poorer sub-Saharan region. Over
the past 25 years, the desert has advanced
southward because of overgrazing,
overcultivation, and deforestation.
Sub-Saharan economic development has
been hindered by political instability, tribal
rivalries, and unsuccessful reliance on
socialist economic principles.

MAP 2.7   **Africa and the Middle East**

often dominate international commerce with these countries. Similarly, the public institutions of Kenya, Zimbabwe, and the Republic of South Africa are modeled along British lines, giving British firms a competitive advantage in these countries.

Much of Africa's economy is tied to its natural resources. Libya enjoys the continent's highest per capita income—$7,900 in 1999—because of its substantial oil reserves. Crude oil production also accounts for one-half the GDPs of Angola, Gabon, and Nigeria and one-quarter that of Algeria. Agriculture also is important to many African countries. For some, agricultural products are their major exports. For example, coffee, cocoa, and palm oil account for 80 percent of Côte d'Ivoire's exports, and coffee and tea comprised 80 percent of Rwanda's exports prior to the eruption of tribal conflict in that country. Unfortunately, the population in many African countries is largely employed in subsistence farming; these countries include Gambia, Mozambique, Sierra Leone, Tanzania, and Zambia.

Many experts believe South Africa will be the dominant economic power and the continent's growth engine during the twenty-first century. South Africa possesses fertile farmland and rich deposits of gold, diamonds, chromium, and platinum. Many MNCs used South Africa as the base for their African operations until the 1970s, when the United Nations imposed trade sanctions against the country because of the government's apartheid policies, which called for the separation of blacks, whites, and Asians. As a result of these external pressures, the government extended voting rights to all its citizens in 1994. Nobel Peace Prize winner Nelson Mandela was elected president in May 1994 in the country's first multiracial elections. In 1999 South Africa's exports—primarily minerals—accounted for 25 percent of its $131-billion GDP.

Middle East

The Middle East includes the region between southwestern Asia and northeastern Africa (see Map 2.8). This area is called the "cradle of civilization" because the world's earliest farms, cities, governments, legal codes, and alphabets originated there. The region was also the birthplace of several of the world's major religions,

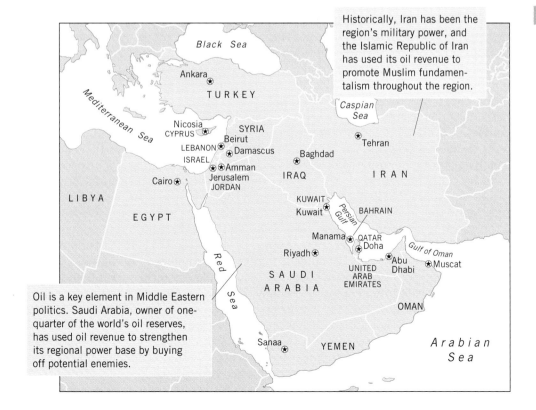

Historically, Iran has been the region's military power, and the Islamic Republic of Iran has used its oil revenue to promote Muslim fundamentalism throughout the region.

Oil is a key element in Middle Eastern politics. Saudi Arabia, owner of one-quarter of the world's oil reserves, has used oil revenue to strengthen its regional power base by buying off potential enemies.

MAP 2.8

The Middle East

including Judaism, Christianity, and Islam. The Middle East has had a history of conflict and political unrest; during the latter half of the twentieth century it saw the Arab-Israeli wars, the Iran-Iraq war, and the Persian Gulf war, all of which raised the risk of doing business in the region.

In 1999 Saudi Arabia, with a GDP of $129 billion, had the largest economy in the Middle East, but Israel enjoyed the highest per capita income at $16,260 per annum. The region is home to many oil-rich countries. In Saudi Arabia, for example, oil accounts for 40 percent of GDP and 90 percent of total export earnings. The oil-rich nations of the Middle East are attempting to diversify their economies for "life after oil." Kuwait has used its oil revenues to develop an impressive portfolio of investments; Dubai, which is one of the seven United Arab Emirates, offers foreign investors all the benefits of a foreign-trade zone (discussed in Chapter 8), an excellent infrastructure, and an entry point for exports to the region.

› THE MARKETPLACES OF SOUTH AMERICA

South America's 13 countries, shown in Map 2.9, share a common political history as well as many economic and social problems. A 1494 papal decree divided colonization privileges between Portugal, which got Brazil, and Spain, which got the rest of the continent. Spanish and Portuguese explorers subjugated the native populations, exploited their gold and silver mines, and converted their fields to sugar cane, tobacco, and cacao plantations. By the end of the eighteenth century, the hold of the two European powers on their South American colonies had weakened. Led by such patriots as Simon Bolivar, one colony after another won its independence. By 1825 the Spanish flag was flying over Cuba and Puerto Rico only. However, independence did not cure the continent's problems. Many South American countries suffer from huge income disparities and widespread poverty among their peoples, leading to political instability and continual cries for reform.

For much of the post-World War II period the majority of South American countries followed what international economists call **import substitution policies** as a means of promoting economic development. With this approach, a country attempts to stimulate the development of local industry by discouraging imports via high tariffs and nontariff barriers. (The opposite of import substitution is **export promotion**, whereby a country pursues economic growth by expanding its exports. This is the developmental approach successfully adopted by Taiwan, Hong Kong, and Singapore, as discussed earlier in this chapter.) For most South American industries, however, the domestic market is too small to enable domestic producers to gain economies of scale through mass production techniques or to permit much competition among local producers. Thus prices of domestically produced goods tend to rise above prices in other markets. These policies benefit domestic firms that face import competition. However, they cripple the ability of a country's exporters to compete in world markets because the companies must pay higher prices for domestically produced inputs than do their foreign competitors. Inevitably, the government must subsidize these firms and often nationalize them to preserve urban jobs. The high costs of doing this are passed on to taxpayers and to consumers through higher prices, but over time the government runs a budget deficit. The result is inflation and destruction of middle-class savings.

Many major South American countries—including Argentina, Brazil, and Chile—adopted these well-intended but ultimately destructive import substitution policies. In the late 1980s, however, the countries began to reverse their policies. They lowered tariff barriers, sought free-trade agreements with their neighbors, privatized their industries, and positioned their economies to compete internationally. Chile, for example, is now one of the most free-market-oriented economies in the world. These policy shifts are expanding South America's role in world trade, attracting foreign capital to the continent, and increasing productivity and per capita incomes.

During the late 1980s, many South American governments stimulated economic growth by adopting policies promoting free trade and private enterprise, thereby increasing the continent's appeal to U.S., European, and Asian MNCs. Chile now has one of the most free-market economies in the world.

International business in South America is affected by its physical geography. The Andes Mountains make it difficult to transport goods between Pacific Coast countries and their inland neighbors. Other mountain ranges, as well as the dense forests of the Amazon River Basin, similarly limit transport of goods.

- Cities of 350,000 to 1 million
- Cities over 1 million
- Capitals
- Capitals over 1 million

MAP 2.9   **South America**

CHAPTER REVIEW

Summary

To compete successfully in the international marketplace, managers need a basic understanding of the world's markets and their interrelationships. Managers also need to assess opportunities available in these markets. For example, a key indicator of a country's desirability to international businesses is its per capita income, which provides information about its consumers and its value as a production site.

The Quad countries—Japan, members of the EU, the United States, and Canada—are of particular importance to MNCs. Some experts believe that firms cannot succeed in the global economy unless they have a significant presence throughout the Quad.

The North American market—Canada, Mexico, the United States, Central America, and the island countries of the Caribbean—is one of the world's largest and richest markets. The United States and Canada have the largest bilateral trading relationship in the world. Mexico's economic reforms, initiated in 1982, have made it a more important force in the world economy.

Another large, rich market for international businesses is Western Europe, particularly the 15-member EU. The EU members are free-market-oriented, parliamentary democracies. With the 1989 collapse of European communism, Eastern European and Central European countries are undergoing a transition from communism to capitalism. Most have adopted market-oriented policies to stimulate economic growth. Their growth prospects and unmet consumer demand are attractive to many Asian, North American, and European MNCs.

Asia is home to several of the fastest growing economies of the post-World War II period. Japan and the Four Tigers—South Korea, Hong Kong, Singapore, and Taiwan—have grown dramatically because of economic policies that focus on export promotion. Because of the economic successes of Japan and the Four Tigers, other countries such as India and China have begun to reverse their inward looking economic policies. Australia and New Zealand are also important economies in this region.

Many African countries regained their independence during the 1950s and 1960s. Their economies primarily rely on natural resources and agriculture. Middle Eastern countries have played an important role in the world economy thanks to their oil wealth.

The South American countries have been independent since the early nineteenth century. Although many of them are rich in natural resources and farmlands, the continent's economic development since World War II has been hindered by chronic political unrest and import substitution policies. During the 1980s, however, key South American nations—including Argentina, Brazil, and Chile—shifted toward more market-oriented, export promotion growth strategies. Privatization and reduced governmental regulation have prompted renewed interest from international businesses in the continent.

Review Questions

1. What is the Triad? What is the Quad? Why are they important to international businesses?
2. How do differences in income levels and income distribution among countries affect international businesses?
3. Describe the U.S. role in the world economy.
4. What role did MITI serve in the Japanese economy?
5. What is a keiretsu?
6. Who are the Four Tigers? Why are they important to international businesses?
7. What is a chaebol?
8. Discuss the role of natural resources and agriculture in Africa's economy.
9. How did import substitution policies affect the economies of Brazil and Argentina?

Questions for Discussion

1. Regional trading blocs, such as the EU and NAFTA, are growing in importance. What are the implications of these trading blocs for international businesses? Are they helpful or harmful? How may they affect a firm's investment decisions?
2. Discuss the problems facing Central European and Eastern European countries in the 1990s. What opportunities are available to international businesses in these countries?
3. Many American and European businesspeople argue that the keiretsu system in Japan acts as a barrier to foreign companies entering the Japanese market. Why do you think they believe this?
4. Ethnic ties, old colonial alliances, and shared languages appear to affect international trade. Why might this be so? If true, how does this affect international businesses' strategies regarding which markets to enter?
5. What can African countries do to encourage more foreign investment in their economies?

BUILDING GLOBAL SKILLS

Success in international business often depends on a firm obtaining information about foreign markets so that it can make exporting, importing, and investment decisions. Among the most useful sources are the following:

Survey of Current Business, published monthly by the U.S. Department of Commerce, is a basic source of statistical data on the U.S. economy. It provides detailed analyses of international trade and investment activities affecting the United States.

The World Factbook provides basic geographic, ethnic, religious, political, and economic information on all countries. It is put out by the U.S. Central Intelligence Agency and is particularly useful because it compiles data about small, obscure, and politically controversial areas. For example, if you were an executive for Crestone Energy Corporation, which was hired by China's government to hunt for oil and gas around the Spratly Islands, *The World Factbook* is one of the few sources in which you could learn that the islands, many of which are under water at high tide, have no permanent population yet are claimed and garrisoned by five different countries—China, Malaysia, the Philippines, Taiwan, and Vietnam. Armed with this information, you would realize that Crestone's explorations would be extremely sensitive and possibly the target of political conflict.

Background Notes, a U.S. State Department series, provides 10-to-14-page profiles of individual countries. Each profile is intended to give a quick overview of a country's geography, culture, living conditions, political orientation, economic policies, and trading patterns. *Background Notes* are particularly useful for briefing employees who are given temporary assignments in a foreign country.

Country Commercial Guides is another U.S. State Department series. It provides detailed information about laws, regulations, economic conditions, and so forth about the world's major commercial marketplaces.

World Development Report, published annually by the World Bank, presents numerous tables detailing information about World Bank members, including population, income and income distribution, infrastructure, government expenditures, trade, production, living standards, health, education, and urbanization.

Commodity Trade Statistics is an annual United Nations report that provides detailed data on each country's exports and imports, which are classified by commodity and by country of destination or origin. The report is an excellent source of minutia—for example, the value of pork exports from Denmark to Portugal in 2001. However, it is rather clumsy to use when time-series information is required—for example, Denmark's total exports from 1983 to 2000.

Balance of Payments Statistics, International Financial Statistics, and **Direction of Trade Statistics** are reports published by the International Monetary Fund (IMF). *Balance of Payments Statistics*, issued annually, contains data about balance of payments performances of IMF members. The monthly *International Financial Statistics* offers international and domestic financial data on members' domestic interest rates, money and banking indicators, prices, exports, and exchange rates. *Direction of Trade Statistics* details the exports and imports of each IMF member on a quarterly basis.

National Trade Data Bank (NTDB) is distributed monthly by the U.S. Department of Commerce. The NTDB is available at many college libraries and at all federal depositories. It is packed with information assembled from other data sources, including some of those listed here. The NTDB also contains databases not readily available elsewhere. Suppose, for example, that your company produces mountain bikes and is looking for a German distributor. The NTDB provides information on whether any German distributors are interested in distributing foreign made mountain bikes. The NTDB also contains *A Basic Guide to Exporting*, a step-by-step guidebook developed by the U.S. Department of Commerce to assist first-time exporters. This guide contains an extensive list of sources of information often used by international businesses.

Assignment

Go to your library and examine each of these standard references. Then answer the following questions:

1. What was the total value of U.S. imports from Belgium last year? Of U.S. exports to Belgium?
2. What is the total level of U.S. investments in Belgium? Of Belgian investments in the United States?
3. Profile the economy of Belgium: What is its GDP? What is its per capita income? How fast is its economy growing? What are its major exports and imports? Who are its major trading partners?
4. Profile the people of Belgium: What languages do they speak? What is their average educational level? What is their life expectancy? How fast is the population growing?

After answering the questions using the printed sources, try to obtain the same information using the Internet. (The textbook's Web site provides linkages to some Web sites that may be helpful, although you should search out other sites as well.) Which questions were easier to answer using the printed material? Which were easier to answer using the Internet?

WORKING WITH THE WEB: BUILDING GLOBAL INTERNET SKILLS

Traveling the Globe

Assume you are responsible for planning business trips for five of your company's managers. Travel for each manager will originate in St. Louis, Missouri. The destinations are as follows:

- London, United Kingdom
- Ho Chi Minh City, Vietnam
- Moscow, Russia
- Cairo, Egypt
- Warsaw, Poland

Use the Internet to locate answers to the following questions:

1. What is the best way for each manager to get from St. Louis to her or his destination?
2. What are the likely transportation costs for each trip?
3. Assuming a three-day stay for each manager, what additional travel costs are likely to be incurred?

4. Assuming the trip is in January, what weather conditions might be anticipated? What if the trip is in July?

5. What travel documents are required for each trip?

6. Are there any health or safety warnings currently applicable to each destination city?

7. What is the local language and currency?

WE INVITE YOU TO VISIT THIS BOOK'S COMPANION WEB SITE AT www.prenhall.com/griffin

---

IN THE NEWS

1. Use the "Global Archives" on the homepage of the *Financial Times* (*www.ft.com*) to search for recent articles about trading blocs in two global marketplaces. Based on your reading, decide which bloc seems to present better opportunities for companies seeking to venture abroad. Why did you choose this bloc?

2. Use the *Financial Times* Web page to research information about the political stability of one of the global marketplaces discussed in this chapter. Find out as much as you can about the region's past history. What historical factors have contributed to the region's political stability?

CLOSING CASE

A Boom in Bangalore

What is the fastest growing industry in India? Software, by far. The software industry serves as a poster child for the success of India's economic reforms and the benefits of opening up its economy. For decades India's universities annually graduated tens of thousands of well-trained engineers, but India's inward-looking economic policies often failed to utilize the engineers' talents. The government's economic reforms, coupled with the blossoming of the Internet, have made the Indian software industry a powerful force for modernizing India's economy. Since the reforms were initiated in 1991, the industry has grown by an estimated 50 percent annually. Software is rapidly becoming India's primary export. For the year ending March 2000, software accounted for $3.8 billion in export earnings; one government agency believes this figure will rise to $50 billion by 2008. The industry is also a magnet for FDI. In 1999 over $300 million of foreign venture capital flowed into the industry, double that of 1998. Experts estimate that by 2008 the industry will annually attract $10 billion in venture capital from foreign firms eager to access the knowledge of India's best and brightest students.

Bangalore is the epicenter of India's software industry; Bombay, New Delhi, and Hyderabad also house many software and information technology firms. Bangalore is home to Wipro Ltd. and Infosys Technologies Ltd., which are now India's third and fourth largest companies when measured by market capitalization. Both companies have tapped into India's large pool of highly trained English-speaking workers. Although occupying different market niches, both companies have stressed quality and the need for a global approach. For example, each qualifies for a high-quality rating from the Software Engineering Institute, a certification program sponsored by the U.S. Department of Defense. Infosys pioneered in India the use of stock options to win the loyalty and commitment of its professional staff. It was also the first Indian company to list its shares on a U.S. stock exchange. About a third of the company's 4,000 workers are now rupee millionaires, while over 100 are dollar millionaires, an unheard of level of wealth creation in a less-developed country. Observing its rival's success, Wipro has introduced a stock option program of its own.

There are some dark clouds, however. The Indian software industry has thrived because of its labor cost advantage: U.S. programmers are paid about three times as much as those in India. However, salaries of Indian programmers are rising as much as 25 to 30 percent a year because of heightened demand for their talents, so India's labor cost advantage is likely to erode somewhat. Moreover, in many areas of the country the telecommunications infrastructure and electrical grid are overburdened. Although savvy software executives invest in portable generators so work can continue should electrical brownouts occur, this is obviously a short-term solution. Indian software executives are lobbying their government to continue to deregulate, privatize, and encourage FDI in the country's infrastructure so they can better compete against rivals in the Quad countries.

More troublesome is the potential acceleration of the country's "brain drain." By some estimates more than half the 100,000 engineers produced annually by India's universities and technical institutes emigrate to the United States each year. Very few of these talented individuals make their way back home—less than 1 percent, claim government experts. This exodus of India's precious human capital may worsen, harming the country's development prospects, because the United States and Europe are contemplating reducing their immigration barriers for skilled foreigners.[6]

Case Questions

1. Why has India been able to build a thriving software industry? What are the country's advantages in this market? What are the country's disadvantages?

2. How important is it for India to stem the flow of skilled engineers to countries like Canada, the United States and those in the EU?

3. What can India do to slow down its "brain drain"? Should the government sponsor programs like India Venture 2000 (discussed in "Wiring the World" on page 69.)

Helping Developing Nations: Aid or Trade?

Aid from the richer countries of North America, Western Europe, and Asia helps build roads, generate electricity, shelter families, and feed hungry children in developing countries.

Aid is better than trade.

Many people throughout the world are concerned about improving living standards in developing countries. Some of this concern is prompted by humanitarian reasons, a desire to enrich the lives of poorer people. Some is based on a security rationale: Improving living standards in poorer countries makes them less likely to threaten the lives and property of their neighbors. Some is based on economics: Raising the income levels of these countries broadens the markets available to firms based in richer countries. Regardless of the motivation, what is the best means of accomplishing this task: aid or trade? That is, should the developed countries give developing countries resources (aid) or provide markets for their goods instead (trade)?

Many experts believe that the development of the less developed countries is dependent on aid. Richer nations annually provide some $60 billion in aid to poorer countries. Much of this aid is destined for infrastructure projects such as electrical generation, new roads, and telecommunications systems. A strong correlation exists between per capita income and infrastructure. Adequate infrastructure is often a requirement for a multinational corporation in deciding where to locate a factory or distribution facility. But private investors may be unwilling to lend funds for such public projects because of the financial weakness of a country's government. Therefore, aid may be the only way in which necessary improvements to the infrastructure can be financed. For example, $63 million of U.S. aid went to build roads in the southern Philippine island of Mindanao. This infrastructure improvement was a critical element in the development of the area's fishing industry.

Other aid may be used to alleviate human suffering directly. Gifts of food, medicines, and building materials help feed, heal, and house millions of people. Such aid is particularly beneficial when civil strife, such as the civil wars that have plagued Rwanda, Somalia, and Sudan, causes farmers to flee their homes, leaving crops rotting in the fields.

Aid also may be preferable to trade because it creates fewer political problems in the donor's country. Developing nations that successfully export often discover that importing countries raise barriers to their goods. For example, the developed nations willingly contribute $1 billion in aid to Bangladesh annually but slap tariffs and import quotas on 80 percent of its exports.

Trade is preferable to aid.

An old Chinese proverb notes: "Give a man a fish and you feed him for a day. Teach a man to fish and you feed him for a lifetime." In line with this ancient wisdom many development experts believe that it is better to base economic development on trade than on aid. Trade provides jobs for residents of less developed countries. The wages provided by these jobs get spent in the local economy, generating demand for local businesses and employment opportunities for local residents.

More important, as domestic firms expand their exports, their managers and employees learn new skills and techniques for producing and marketing these goods. They make contacts with foreign distributors, earn goodwill with foreign customers, develop credible reputations with foreign lenders, and learn the ins-and-outs of dealing with the customs services of foreign countries. This improvement in a country's stock of human capital inevitably gets transferred to other firms and industries as employees leave to start their own companies or get lured away by domestic competitors. The aggregate effect is to raise the competitiveness, productivity, and efficiency of the economy as a whole. The postwar economic successes of countries such as Singapore, Hong Kong, and Taiwan are based on this pattern of export-driven economic development. Other experts support trade-based economic development because of the failures of aid programs. Long-term food aid, for example, often depresses local crop prices so that farmers cannot make a living, forcing them to abandon their fields and seek work in urban areas. When U.S. and UN troops entered Somalia in 1992, for example, they brought so much food to feed the local population that Somalian farmers were unable to raise crops profitably. In the next growing season fields remained unplanted, thereby making the country more dependent on outsiders. And far too often aid takes the form of large, ill-planned projects that do little to improve a country's living standard. For example, international donors, including the World Bank and Denmark, Norway, and Sweden, donated over $16 billion to Tanzania between 1961 and 1987. Much of this money was used to finance nationalization of the country's industries and relocation of 14 million peasants and their families to newly collectivized farms. Because of inefficiencies of the state-owned industrial sector and reductions in agricultural productivity at the collective farms, the net result of the aid was a halving of Tanzania's per capita income between 1980 and 1993.

The job of this Indonesian textile worker—and the continued economic development of her country—is dependent on access to the markets of the Quad countries.

Wrap-up

1. In your judgment which is better, trade or aid?
2. What alternatives, other than aid, are available to improve the infrastructures of developing countries?
3. Which should determine how foreign aid is spent, the donor countries or the recipient countries?

Sources: "Food Crisis for 34m Africans," *Financial Times*, August 5, 1994, p. 3; "World Bank Attacked for Backing Nyerere," *Financial Times*, July 27, 1994, p. 12; "World Bank Laments Its Tanzania Role," *Financial Times*, July 27, 1994, p. 3; "Empty Promises," *The Economist*, May 7, 1994, pp. 11–12; "The Kindness of Strangers," *The Economist*, May 7, 1994, pp. 19–22; "Developed Nations Want Poor Countries to Succeed on Trade, But Not Too Much," *Wall Street Journal*, September 20, 1993, p. A10.

CHAPTER

The Second Cultural Revolution

The explosive growth of the Internet has unleashed opportunities and challenges everywhere. New industries are being established before our very eyes. The traditional ways of buying and selling, purchasing and distributing, and disseminating and acquiring information are being subjected to the Darwinian imperative: Adapt or die. The Internet revolution has created even more challenges for public policy makers, who must reconcile existing laws designed for the "old economy" with changes needed to accommodate the demands of e-commerce and the "new economy." The boundaryless nature of the Internet presents additional quandaries for those governments that would like to maintain walls between their citizens and the rest of the world.

"The **Internet** presents a **threat** to the state's **commercial** interests."

The Internet challenges no government more than that of the People's Republic of China. For the past 30 years the ruling Communist Party has navigated a tricky path in promoting China's economic growth. The party has struggled to maintain its political hold on the country while continually increasing the economic freedom allowed to its people. China's leaders recognize that the country must embrace the Internet and master its underlying technologies if China is to continue on its upward economic trajectory.

Legal, Technological, and Political Forces

3

OBJECTIVES

After studying this chapter, you should be able to:

› Describe the major types of legal systems confronting international businesses.

› Explain how domestic laws affect the ability of firms to conduct international business.

› List the ways firms can resolve international business disputes.

› Describe the impact of the host country's technological environment on international business.

› Explain how firms can protect themselves from political risk.

› Analyze the risks facing international firms doing business in emerging market economies.

The Internet is growing in popularity. China's Web surfers totaled some 17 million in mid-2000, a number that has quadrupled in less than two years. A recent survey suggests that the Chinese primarily use the Internet to acquire information and news. Therein lies the rub. To stimulate domestic development of Internet technology, China's leaders need to encourage Web surfing. However, they also wish to maintain political control of the populace by reducing the influence of outsiders and limiting political debate among the citizenry. The Chinese government fully recognizes the power of the Internet as a political weapon and as an independent source of information. In 1999, for example, the Falun Gong, a million-person spiritual movement that was banned by the Beijing government, used the Internet to organize and coordinate nationwide protests against the government's policy toward the movement. The Internet presents a threat to the government's commercial interests as well, particularly state-owned telecommunications and publishing monopolies. Millions of Chinese citizens have switched to Internet-based telephone service, thereby avoiding the high long-distance prices charged by the state-owned telephone monopoly, China Telecom.

The Chinese government has adopted a variety of measures to protect state-owned enterprises, suppress foreign influences, and maintain its political power. In 1999 it verbally banned foreign investment in Chinese Internet service providers (ISPs), Internet content providers, and other dot-com ventures, after hundreds of millions of dollars of foreign venture capital had already flowed into private dot-com start-ups. It tried to protect state-owned news media by restricting the development of private online news media. Online broadcasters must receive permission from the State Administration for Radio, Film, and Television. Only accredited reporters are allowed to report news in China, but the government has not yet accredited any reporters working for online companies. Any firm wishing to sell publications over the Internet must similarly receive permission from the Press and Publications Administration.

The Chinese government has also proclaimed that its harsh laws against disseminating state secrets apply to the Internet as well. The State Bureau of Secrecy issued rules prohibiting the use of chat rooms, Internet bulletin boards, or e-mail to disseminate state secrets. To enforce these rules, the secrecy bureau required that any ISP or Internet content provider must pass a "security certification" before it can operate. The secrecy bureau also established the Internet Information Management Bureau to eliminate "harmful" information from the Internet. Although this may sound reasonable, recognize that a state secret is often defined as any information that has not yet been officially released to the public. Indeed, prior to the passage of these regulations, chat rooms played a major role in uncovering corruption in Fujian province and in the port city of Xiamen.

Another approach Chinese officials have adopted to reduce Western influence on China's Internet sector is to promote Linux- instead of Microsoft-based programs. State agencies are being encouraged to use Red Flag, a Linux-based operating system developed by the state, and discouraged from using Windows 2000. Other domestic dot-com entrepreneurs are receiving funding from state agencies, such as the post office and the army, to develop Chinese-language software using Linux.

The government's often hostile and sometimes contradictory policies toward foreign presence on the Internet have had some negative consequences. Several foreign companies have chosen to steer clear of the country for the time being. Intel, for example, decided to locate its Internet data-service center in Hong Kong to avoid any political problems with the Beijing government. Unfortunately, such actions slow the transfer of technology to China's dot-com industries.[1]

Virtually all decisions facing international managers—who to hire, how to market their company's goods in the host market, which technologies to adopt, and so forth—are affected by the national environment of the country in which the transaction occurs. For example, as the opening case indicated, foreign Internet firms wishing to establish operations in China must surmount many legal and political barriers. Foreign managers working in China who assume the rules of the game are the same as in their home country are asking for trouble. The goal of this and the next chapter is to understand the impact of the various dimensions of a country's environment on the management of a firm's international business. This chapter discusses the legal, technological, and political dimensions, while Chapter 4 focuses on the cultural.

› THE LEGAL ENVIRONMENT

A domestic firm must follow the laws and customs of its home country. An international business faces a more complex task: It must obey the laws not only of its home country but also the laws of all the host countries in which it operates. Both home and host country laws can critically affect the way international firms con-

Wiring the World

LAW AND THE INTERNET

Most existing laws predate the World Wide Web. Adjusting these laws to the needs of the Internet age is a massive undertaking, to say the least. One basic issue is deciding which country's laws should oversee e-commerce transactions. Activities sponsored by a Web site may be legal in its home country yet violate the laws of other countries. Yahoo! Inc., for example, was found guilty in 2000 of allowing neo-Nazi paraphernalia to be sold on its Web sites in violation of a French law that prohibits the sale of anything that incites racism. While Yahoo! had carefully excluded such goods from its French portal, it had not done so for its U.S. sites. Because French citizens had access to the U.S. Web sites over the Internet, Yahoo! was fined $2,800 and given two months to make the site inaccessible to French Internet users.

National policies toward consumer privacy also need to be adjusted. Many U.S. companies routinely collect information from their customers which the companies then use internally to cross-sell other products, or the companies sell the information to third parties. Similarly, many Web sites produce "cookies" that help facilitate repeat online transactions. For example, the cookies allow an online travel vendor to remember customers frequent flyer numbers, whether the customers prefer an aisle or a window seat, and the billing addresses of their credit cards. However, European laws provide consumers with stronger privacy protection than do U.S.

laws. Under European law any information collected from a consumer for one purpose cannot be used for another purpose without the express permission of that person. U.S.-based Web companies must thus alter their marketing and information-gathering practices to accommodate European privacy laws.

Another issue is what to do with "cybersquatters"—people or firms who try to register domain names of established organizations or famous people and then sell back the names to their owners at inflated prices. The World Intellectual Property Organization operates an arbitration program to reduce this problem. Although successful, it has not totally eliminated cybersquatting.

Sources: "Court Setback for French Buyers at Web Auctions," *Financial Times*, May 4, 2000, p. 3; "U.S. in Tentative Pact Protecting Europeans' Privacy," *Wall Street Journal*, February 24, 2000, p. B6; "'Cybersquatters' Squeezed as Internet Arbitration Takes Off," *Financial Times*, February 23, 2000, p. 18; "Land of Laptops and Lederhosen," *Financial Times*, February 17, 2000, p. 14; "Cross-Border Regulations Create Hurdle for Cybershoppers," *Financial Times*, February 16, 2000, p. 7; "Border Crossings," *Wall Street Journal*, November 22, 1999, p. R41; "In Europe, Surfing a Web of Red Tape," *Wall Street Journal*, October 29, 1999, p. B1. "Judge Fines Yahoo! for Neo-Nazi Auction," *Houston Chronicle*, May 23, 2000, p. A4.

duct their business. These laws determine the markets firms may serve, the prices they can charge for their goods, and the cost of necessary inputs such as labor, raw materials, and technology. The laws may also affect the location of economic activity. For example, as the opening case indicated, some Internet companies have chosen to base their operations outside the People's Republic of China because of the seemingly arbitrary rules imposed by its government. "Wiring the World" discusses some additional effects the rapid growth of the Internet has had on the legal systems of various countries.

Differences in Legal Systems

National legal systems vary dramatically for historical, cultural, political, and religious reasons. The rule of law, the role of lawyers, the burden of proof, the right to judicial review, and, of course, the laws themselves differ from country to country. In the United States, for example, in times of economic distress firms can lay off workers with minimal notice and severance pay. In Belgium, however, firms wishing to trim their white-collar workforces must provide each worker with three months' notice, three months' severance pay, or some combination of the two for every five years (or fraction of five years) the employee has worked for the firm. Access to the legal system also may vary from country to country, as suggested by Figure 3.1. In the United States, for example, easy availability of lawyers and nondiscriminatory access to its legal system are helpful to international businesses wishing to settle disputes with suppliers and customers. South Korea, in contrast, suffers from a shortage of lawyers because of its tough bar exam—only 2 percent of the candidates taking it pass. Thus many international businesses are forced to resolve disputes privately rather than utilize South Korea's courts. Because the Indian court system has a backlog of over three million cases, many attorneys advise their business clients to settle conflicts out of court rather than wait as long as 10 years to be heard in a court of law. The situation is worse in Portugal, where civil suits can take 12 years to traverse its courts.[2]

Common Law.   Common law is the foundation of the legal systems in the United Kingdom and its former colonies, including the United States, Canada, Australia, India, New Zealand, Barbados, Saint Kitts and Nevis, and Malaysia. **Common law** is based on the cumulative wisdom of judges' decisions on individual cases through history. These cases create legal precedents, which other judges use to decide similar cases.

Common law has evolved differently in each common law country. Thus laws affecting business practices vary somewhat among these countries, creating potential problems for the uninformed international businessperson. For example, manufacturers of defective products are more vulnerable to lawsuits in the United States than in the United Kingdom as a result of evolutionary differences in the two countries' case law.

In addition to evolutionary differences in case law, **statutory laws**—those enacted by legislative action—also vary among the common law countries. For example, many business transactions between firms and the British government are shielded from public scrutiny—and the prying eyes of competitors—by Britain's Official Secrets Act. In contrast, more information about transactions between firms and the U.S. federal government is publicly available because of the U.S. Freedom of Information Act. Even the administration of law may vary. For example, in the United States the plaintiff and the defendant in a lawsuit generally pay their

FIGURE 3.1

Lawyers per 100,000 Population

Source: University of Wisconsin, Institute for Legal Studies, from *The Economist*, March 5, 1994, p. 36. © The Economist Newspaper Group, Inc. Reprinted with permission. Further reproduction prohibited.

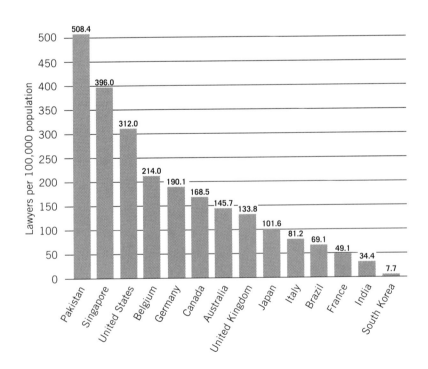

own legal fees. Often, defendants agree to quick settlements regardless of the strength of their cases to avoid expensive litigation. In the United Kingdom, the losers in trials pay the legal expenses of both parties. Thus the British have less incentive to file frivolous lawsuits.

Civil Law.   The world's most common form of legal system, **civil law**, is based on a codification, or detailed listing, of what is and is not permissible. The civil law system originated in biblical times with the Romans, who spread it throughout the Western world. Its dominance was reinforced by the imposition of the civil-law-based Napoleonic Code on territories conquered by French emperor Napoleon Bonaparte during the early nineteenth century.

One important difference between common law and civil law systems is apparent in the roles of judges and lawyers. In a common law system the judge serves as a neutral referee, ruling on various motions by the opposing parties' lawyers. These lawyers are responsible for developing their clients' cases and choosing which evidence to submit on their clients' behalf. In a civil law system, the judge takes on many of the tasks of the lawyers, determining, for example, the scope of evidence to be collected and presented to the court.

Religious Law.   **Religious law** is based on the officially established rules governing the faith and practice of a particular religion. A country that applies religious law to civil and criminal conduct is called a **theocracy**. In Iran, for example, a group of mullahs, or holy men, determine legality or illegality through their interpretation of the Koran, the holy book of Islam.

Religious laws can create interesting problems for firms. The Koran, for example, denounces charging interest on loans as an unfair exploitation of the poor; thus Muslim firms and financial institutions have had to develop alternative financing arrangements. Muslim businesses often rely on leasing arrangements, rather than borrowing money, to obtain long-term assets. In Iran banks often charge up-front fees that act as a substitute for loan interest payments, and owners of bank deposits receive shares of the bank's profits rather than interest payments. Pakistani banks are in the process of adopting similar policies—often referred to as Islamic banking—because Pakistan's Supreme Court issued a ruling in December 1999 declaring all interest-bearing transactions to be contrary to Islamic law. The ruling gave the government, bankers, and investors two years to revise laws, rewrite existing loans, and eliminate interest payments.[3] Family-owned firms are often influential in countries where legal systems are based on the Koran because members of an owner's extended family may be the best available source of capital, given the costs of circumventing the prohibition on interest.

Countries relying on religious law often have other features, such as an absence of due process and appeals procedures, that should make outsiders cautious. In Saudi Arabia, for example, all foreign firms must have a local representative or sponsor, typically a government agency or a person well connected to the royal family. Should a commercial dispute arise between a foreign businessperson and the local representative, the local representative can have the foreigner detained by the local police. Because no independent judiciary exists in the country to protect the foreigner's rights, the foreigner is in a weak bargaining position.

Bureaucratic Law.   The legal system in communist countries and in dictatorships is often described as bureaucratic law. **Bureaucratic law** is whatever the country's bureaucrats say it is, regardless of the formal law of the land. Contracts can be made or broken at the whim of those in power. The collapse of Zairean dictator Mobutu Sese Seko's government in 1997, for example, threatened the viability of all existing contracts signed by foreign companies and triggered a mad scramble to revalidate old contracts and negotiate new ones with the government of his successor, Laurent Kabila.[4] Protections that may appear in the country's constitution—such as the right to an attorney and the right to hear witnesses against one—

may be ignored if government officials find them inconvenient. For example, the formalities of Ugandan law afforded Ugandans and foreigners little protection under dictator Idi Amin's regime of terror during the 1970s. Similarly, the elaborate protections detailed in the constitution of the former Soviet Union offered little solace to the victims of Joseph Stalin's political purges during the 1930s.

In countries relying on bureaucratic law, the ability of a multinational corporation (MNC) to manage its operations is often compromised by bureaucrats. International managers are often confronted with arbitrary rules or decisions that have the force of law. Western investors, for example, first learned that foreign investments in China's Internet industry were illegal when the minister of information technology, Wu Jichuan, answered a reporter's question to that effect at a press conference in September 1999. Yet foreign firms like America Online, Goldman Sachs, and News Corp. had already invested an estimated $100 million in Chinese dot-com companies without any indication that the investments were inappropriate. Because the minister's announcement was made without any notice, the foreigners had no inkling whether their investments would be grandfathered or confiscated. They learned that an unfortunate by-product of bureaucratic law is the lack of consistency, predictability, and appeal procedures.

International businesspeople must be aware of these general differences in legal systems to avoid costly misunderstandings. They should also rely on the expertise of local lawyers in each country in which the businesspeople operate to help them comply with the specific requirements of local laws and to counsel them on substantive differences in due process, legal liabilities, and procedural safeguards.

Domestically Oriented Laws

The laws of the countries in which an international business operates play a major role in shaping the opportunities available to that firm. Some of these laws are primarily designed to regulate the domestic economic environment. Such laws affect all facets of a firm's domestic operations: managing its workforce (recruitment, compensation, and labor relations laws); financing its operations (securities, banking, and credit laws); marketing its products (advertising, distribution, and consumer protection laws); and developing and utilizing technology (patent, copyright, and trademark laws). Although such laws are primarily focused on the domestic marketplace, they may indirectly affect the ability of domestic firms to compete internationally by increasing their costs, thus reducing their price competitiveness relative to foreign firms. For example, labor costs for manufacturers in Germany, France, and Belgium are among the world's highest as a result of government-mandated benefits packages. These manufacturers, therefore, find that their products are less price competitive in export markets; many of them that compete internationally stress their products' quality rather than their price.

Domestically oriented laws may also inadvertently affect the business practices of foreign firms operating outside the country's borders. Often firms whose products are geared to the export market alter their production techniques to meet the regulations of the importing countries, even though the firms' operations are legal within their home country. For example, Grupo Herdez chose to alter its production processes in Mexico in order to sell its goods in the U.S. market. Grupo Herdez is one of Mexico's largest producers of mole, a spicy but sweet sauce made from chocolate and chili peppers. The firm's traditional way of preparing the chilies for production—laying them out to dry in the sun for several days—failed to meet hygiene standards of the U.S. Food and Drug Administration (FDA). To receive the necessary FDA approval and benefit from the growing U.S. market for Mexican foods, Grupo Herdez had to develop a new technology that uses electronic dryers to prepare the chilies for mole production.[5]

Laws Directly Affecting International Business Transactions

Other national laws are explicitly designed to regulate international business activities. Such laws are often politically motivated and designed to promote the country's foreign policy or military objectives. A country may attempt to induce a second country to change an undesirable policy by imposing **sanctions**—restraints against commerce with that country. Sanctions may take many forms, such as restricting access to high-technology goods, withdrawing preferential tariff treatment, boycotting the country's goods, and denying new loans. For example, the United States imposed sanctions against India and Pakistan after they conducted underground nuclear testing in violation of U.S. nuclear nonproliferation laws.

An **embargo**—a comprehensive sanction against all commerce with a given country—may be imposed by countries acting in unison or alone. For example, the United Nations embargoed all trade with Iraq after Iraq's 1990 invasion of Kuwait. Most countries embargoed goods to or from South Africa during the 1980s to protest its apartheid policies. The United States has unilaterally embargoed trade with Cuba since 1961, when the attempted U.S.-supported overthrow of Fidel Castro died on the beaches of the Bay of Pigs. Similarly, India acted alone during the early 1990s when it embargoed trade with Nepal because it believed Nepal's prime minister was favoring China's interests over India's (see Map 3.1).

A particularly important form of sanction is export controls on high-technology goods. Many technologically advanced countries control the export of so-called **dual use** products that may be used for both civilian and military purposes. For example, McDonnell Douglas ran afoul of U.S. dual use controls when it sold sophisticated machine tools to the China National Aero-Technology Import and Export Company (Catic), which claimed that the equipment would be used to build civilian aircraft. However, the tools were instead shipped to a military factory that builds ballistic and cruise missiles.[6]

Countries may also attempt to regulate business activities that are conducted outside their borders, a practice known as **extraterritoriality**. For example, firms are vulnerable to U.S. antitrust lawsuits if they engage in activities outside the United States that diminish competition in the U.S. market. In one such case the

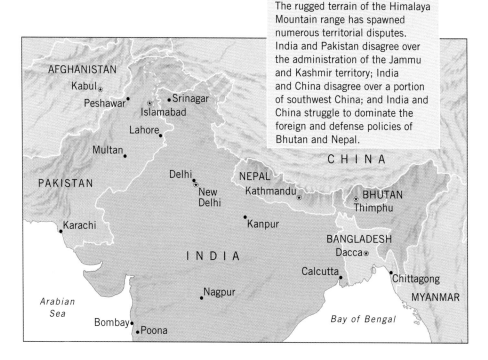

The rugged terrain of the Himalaya Mountain range has spawned numerous territorial disputes. India and Pakistan disagree over the administration of the Jammu and Kashmir territory; India and China disagree over a portion of southwest China; and India and China struggle to dominate the foreign and defense policies of Bhutan and Nepal.

MAP 3.1

Northern India and Neighboring Countries

United States successfully sued Pilkington PLC, the British owner of the most important patents for producing flat glass, for limiting the ability of its U.S. licensees to use the technology in international markets. U.S. authorities claimed that Pilkington's policies hurt U.S. exports and reduced the incentive of U.S. flat glass producers to invest in research and development, thereby lessening competition.[7]

Antiboycott provisions in U.S. trade law also have extraterritorial reach. U.S. antiboycott law prohibits U.S. firms from complying with any boycott ordered by a foreign country that prohibits trade with a country friendly to the United States. This law is primarily directed against a 1954 resolution adopted by the League of Arab States that calls for a boycott of any firm that does business with Israel. Baxter International found itself in deep trouble after a U.S. grand jury investigated it for selling discounted hospital supplies to Syria, allegedly as a bribe for the Arab states terminating their boycott of the company. Baxter pleaded guilty to violating the antiboycott law and paid a fine of $6.6 million.[8]

The Helms-Burton Act is probably the most controversial application of extraterritoriality affecting international business today. This act is directed against international firms that "traffic" in the assets of U.S. companies that were confiscated by the Cuban government when Fidel Castro assumed control in 1959. Over time the Cuban government has leased or sold many of these confiscated assets to foreign companies. The Helms-Burton Act authorizes the U.S. government and the former U.S. owners of the confiscated assets to take action against their new foreign owners. The U.S. government can deny entrance to the United States of officers of companies that benefit from the use of these confiscated assets; such a fate has befallen executives of Canada's Sherritt Corporation, which is producing nickel and cobalt from a mine formerly owned by Freeport McMoRan, a New Orleans-based natural resources company.

In the eyes of the U.S. government the Helms-Burton Act is simply designed to ensure that foreign companies do not profit from Cuban property that was stolen from U.S. owners. In the view of many other countries, such as Canada and the European Union, the Helms-Burton Act is an ill-conceived policy of trying to bludgeon them into joining the U.S. anti-Castro crusade. By some estimates 85 percent of all foreign-owned private property in pre-Castro Cuba was owned by U.S. interests, so it is easy to see why the disposition of confiscated property in Cuba is more important to the United States than to other countries.[9] Another important example of extraterritoriality is the Foreign Corrupt Practices Act, the purpose of which is explained in "Bringing the World into Focus."

Laws Directed Against Foreign Firms

On other occasions countries may pass laws that are explicitly directed against foreign-owned firms. Ownership issues are a particular area of concern. In most countries there is ongoing debate between the political left and right regarding the appropriate balance between governmental control of the economy and reliance on market forces to allocate resources. Often when leftist governments obtain power, they choose to transfer ownership of resources from the private to the public sector, a process known as **nationalization**. Most vulnerable to such actions are industries that lack mobility: natural resource industries such as crude oil production and mining and capital-intensive industries such as steel, chemicals, and oil refining. When the host government compensates the private owners for their losses, the transfer is called **expropriation**. When the host government offers no compensation, the transfer is called **confiscation**. Most governments, including that of the United States, recognize the right of other national governments to mandate the transfer of private property within their borders to the public sector, although non-host governments do expect that foreign owners will receive suitable compensation for their lost property. For example, many Arab oil-producing countries nationalized the properties of Western oil firms after 1973. These countries, however,

Bringing the World into FOCUS

SHOULD BRIBES BE A COMPETITIVE WEAPON?

In many countries a small payment to government officials such as customs officers, immigration authorities, and building inspectors is an accepted part of doing business. If they want to succeed in these countries, international businesspeople are often faced with the ethical problem of whether to make such payments or face long delays in clearing customs, obtaining work permits, or completing building inspections and telephone installations. These payments are often justified on the basis that civil servants are underpaid, that "this is the way things are done here," or that the payments do not affect government policy. Less benign by any ethical standard, however, are large payments—often on the order of 10 to 20 percent of the contract amount—made to well-connected politicians and government officials to allow a firm to win major contracts.

The U.S. Congress, in another application of the principle of extraterritoriality, passed the **Foreign Corrupt Practices Act (FCPA)** in 1977 to regulate payments to government officials in other countries. The FCPA prohibits U.S. firms, their employees, and agents acting on their behalf from paying or offering to pay bribes to any foreign government official in order to influence the official actions or policies of that official to gain or retain business. This prohibition applies even if the transaction occurs entirely outside U.S. borders. However, the FCPA does not outlaw routine payments, regardless of their size, made to government officials to expedite normal commercial transactions, such as issuance of customs documents or permits, inspection of goods, or provision of police services.

After the FCPA was passed, many U.S. MNCs argued that this law would put them at a substantial disadvantage in competing for international sales because at the time many of their rivals in other Quad countries were not burdened by similar antibribery laws. One U.S. Department of Commerce study suggested that U.S. firms lost $20 billion in international sales in a typical year to foreign companies that were able to pay bribes.

The damage bribery does to the global economy extends far beyond the loss of sales by U.S. businesses. For example, official corruption has destroyed the infrastructure and economy of developing countries such as Zaire (now renamed the Democratic Republic of the Congo), while the economic development of many other countries has been slowed by the inefficiencies created by choosing suppliers based on the size of the bribe rather than on the quality of the product or the price being charged.

Leaders of the world economic community have begun to acknowledge the seriousness of the problem. The World Bank and the International Monetary Fund have threatened to cut off aid and loans to countries unwilling to battle official corruption. Perhaps more important—because bribery takes both a briber and a bribee—in 1997 members of the Organization for Economic Cooperation and Development (OECD) agreed to a bribery ban that would apply to firms headquartered or located in member states. The annual reports of Transparency International, a Berlin-based anticorruption group, rank the Nordic countries of Denmark, Finland, Sweden, and Norway among the least corrupt countries, with Australia, Canada, the Netherlands, and New Zealand close behind.

Sources: "Momentum Builds for Corporate-Bribery Ban," *Wall Street Journal*, September 23, 1997, p. A16; "Nigeria Seen as Most Corrupt Nation," *Financial Times*, August 1, 1997, p. 4; "Germany Says Business Bribes on the Rise," *Wall Street Journal*, April 14, 1997, p. A12; "Corruption Destroys Zaire's Infrastructure," *Houston Chronicle*, April 3, 1997, p. 24A; "Anticorruption Drive Starts to Show Results," *Wall Street Journal*, January 27, 1997, p. A1; "Commercial Corruption," *Wall Street Journal*, January 2, 1997, p. 6; "Kantor Calls for Bribery Action," *Financial Times*, July 26, 1996, p. 3; "Foreigners Use Bribes to Beat U.S. Rivals in Many Deals, New Report Concludes," *Wall Street Journal*, October 12, 1995, p. A3.

offered the Western firms a combination of compensation, continuing operating agreements, and future drilling rights which the firms found acceptable. Conversely, a key element in the U.S. conflict with Cuba is Cuba's lack of compensation for assets seized from U.S. firms.

Privatization. The conversion of state-owned property to privately owned property is called **privatization**. Although not strictly an issue of host country control, privatization is the opposite of nationalization and creates opportunities for international businesses. Most state-owned enterprises sold to the private sector are unprofitable, undercapitalized, and overstaffed. Nevertheless, they are often attractive to international businesses seeking to expand their operations into new markets located in key sectors of a national economy, such as telecommunications, transportation, and manufacturing.

Privatization, which gained momentum in the 1980s, stems from two primary forces: political ideology and economic pressure. Political ideology prompted Margaret Thatcher, the prime minister of the United Kingdom from 1979 to 1990, to call for diminishing the role of the state in the economy. During the 1980s the British government sold its interests in British Airways, British Telecom, the British Airport Authority, and British Petroleum. Brian Mulroney, head of Canada's Progressive Conservative Party, followed a similar agenda during his tenure as Canada's prime minister from 1984 to 1993, as have the leaders of Argentina, Brazil, Chile, Mexico, and many other countries during the past decade.

Privatization has also resulted from competitive pressures that firms face in global markets. The telecommunications industry provides a perfect example of this phenomenon. That industry has benefited from rapid technological change, yet many national governments, facing enormous budgetary pressures and deficits, have found it difficult to raise the capital required to upgrade and expand state-owned telecommunications systems. As a result, countries such as Argentina, Mexico, Chile, Venezuela, and the United Kingdom have privatized telecommunications services.

Constraints on Foreign Ownership.   Many governments limit foreign ownership of domestic firms to avoid having their economies or key industries controlled by foreigners. For example, Mexico restricts foreign ownership in its energy industry, believing that the benefits of its oil reserves, which it views as part of its "national patrimony," should accrue only to its citizens. Canada effectively limits foreign ownership of newspapers to 25 percent as part of its program to protect the country's culture from being inundated by its neighbor to the south. Foreign firms are often excluded from the radio and television broadcasting industries. For example, the United States limits foreigners to 25 percent ownership of U.S. television and radio stations. Similar rules exist in Europe.

Countries can also constrain foreign MNCs by imposing restrictions on their ability to **repatriate**, or return to their home countries, profits earned in the host country. Such restrictions were common in the 1980s, but many countries, such as Botswana and Ethiopia, abolished their repatriation controls during the 1990s as they adopted more free-market-oriented policies.

The Impacts of MNCs on Host Countries

Firms establishing operations beyond the borders of their home country affect and are affected by the political, economic, social, and cultural environments of the host countries in which the firms operate. To compete effectively in these markets and maintain productive relationships with the governments of the host countries, managers of MNCs must recognize how they and their firms should interact with the national and local environments.

Economic and Political Impacts.   MNCs affect every local economy in which they compete and operate. Many of their effects are positive. They may make direct investments in new plants and factories, thereby creating local jobs. Such investments provide work for local contractors, builders, and suppliers. MNCs also pay taxes, which benefit the local economy, helping to improve educational, transportation, and other municipal services. For example, when Toyota began operating in Georgetown, Kentucky, the $1.5 million it paid in property taxes represented almost one-quarter of the town's municipal budget. Technology transfer can also have positive local effects. An important benefit to the Beijing municipal government of its joint venture with American Motors was access to the latest U.S.

automotive technology. General Electric raised the productivity of Hungary's largest light bulb manufacturer by transferring technological knowledge to the Hungarian firm.

MNCs may also have negative effects on the local economy. To the extent MNCs compete directly with local firms, the MNCs may cause these firms to lose both jobs and profits. Also, as a local economy becomes more dependent on the economic health of an MNC, the financial fortunes of the firm take on increasing significance. When retrenchment by an MNC is accompanied by layoffs, cutbacks, or a total shutdown of local operations, the effects can be devastating to a local economy. For example, in 2000 BMW announced that it would liquidate its ownership of Rover by selling part of its interests to Ford Motor Company and the rest to a small British buy-out specialist. Many U.K. politicians immediately raised concerns that BMW's decision would devastate the local Oxford economy, a region long dependent on Rover's factories and jobs.

MNCs also may have a significant political impact, either intentionally or unintentionally. Their sheer size often gives them tremendous power in each country in which they operate. Furthermore there is always the possibility that this power may be misused. Even when it is not, MNCs are often able to counter efforts by host governments to restrict their activities. The MNCs simply threaten to shift production and jobs to other locations. For example, when Spain passed new laws in the early 1990s that raised labor costs, MNCs such as Colgate-Palmolive, S.C. Johnson & Son, Kubota, and Volkswagen closed some of their Spanish factories and/or slashed payrolls. The result was soaring unemployment that reached 24.5 percent in the mid-1990s.[10]

Cultural Impacts. MNCs also can exert a major influence on the cultures in which the companies operate. As they raise local standards of living and introduce new products and services previously unavailable, people in the host cultures develop new norms, standards, and behaviors. Some of these changes are positive, such as the introduction of safer equipment and machinery, better health care and pharmaceuticals, and purer and more sanitary food products. Other changes are not positive. Nestlé, for example, has received much criticism for its promotion of infant formula in the world's developing countries. Mothers in these countries were allegedly enticed into buying the formula but were not trained in its proper use. The mothers diluted the formula to make it go further and often were unable to follow adequate sanitation procedures. As a result, critics argue, infant mortality in these countries increased significantly.

Dispute Resolution in International Business

Disputes in international commerce can be very complicated. Typically, four questions must be answered for an international dispute to be resolved:

1. Which country's law applies?
2. In which country should the issue be resolved?
3. Which technique should be used to resolve the conflict: litigation, arbitration, mediation, or negotiation?
4. How will the settlement be enforced?

Many international business contracts specify answers to these questions to reduce uncertainty and expense in resolving disputes. The courts of most major trading countries will honor and enforce the provisions of these contracts, as long as they are not contrary to other aspects of the country's public policy.

If a contract does not contain answers to the first two questions, each party to the transaction may seek to hear the case in the court system most favorable to its own interests, a process known as **forum shopping**. Forum shopping allegedly places U.S. manufacturers at a disadvantage in international markets. Monetary awards are higher in U.S. courts, so many plaintiffs' lawyers attempt to use these courts to adjudicate foreign lawsuits for product defects in U.S.-made goods sold internationally. In contrast, a foreign manufacturer of a good sold outside the United States would not face the threat of having to defend its product in a U.S. court because the manufacturer lacked a tie to that forum.

Whether a foreign court order is enforced is determined by the principle of comity. The **principle of comity** provides that a country will honor and enforce within its own territory the judgments and decisions of foreign courts, with certain limitations. For the principle to apply, countries commonly require three conditions to be met:

1. Reciprocity is extended between the countries; that is, country A and country B mutually agree to honor each other's court decisions.

2. Proper notice is given the defendant.

3. The foreign court judgment does not violate domestic statutes or treaty obligations.[11]

Because of the costs and uncertainties of litigation, many international businesses seek less expensive means of settling disputes over international transactions. Often business conflicts will be resolved through alternative dispute resolution techniques, such as arbitration. **Arbitration** is the process by which both parties to a conflict agree to submit their cases to a private individual or body whose decision they will honor. Because of the speed, privacy, and informality of such proceedings, disputes can often be resolved more cheaply than through the court system. For example, a five-year-old conflict between IBM and Fujitsu over the latter's unauthorized use of proprietary IBM software that was moving slowly through the U.S. judicial system was settled quickly with the help of two neutral arbitrators from the American Arbitration Association.[12] Similarly, 16 francophone African nations have established a regional commercial arbitration court in Abidjan, Côte d'Ivoire. By providing a site for resolving commercial disputes independent of behind-the-scenes politicking or pressures from a host government, this court should encourage more international trade and investment in the 16 countries.[13]

Another set of issues arises when an international business is in a dispute with a national government. The legal recourse available to international businesses in such disputes is often limited. For example, the U.S. **Foreign Sovereign Immunities Act of 1976** provides that the actions of foreign governments against U.S. firms are generally beyond the jurisdiction of U.S. courts. Thus if France chose to nationalize IBM's French operations or to impose arbitrary taxes on IBM computers, IBM could not use U.S. courts to seek redress against the sovereign nation of France. However, the Foreign Sovereign Immunities Act does not grant immunity for the commercial activities of a sovereign state. For example, if the French government contracted to purchase 2,000 personal computers from IBM and then repudiated the contract, IBM could sue France in U.S. courts.

Countries, including the United States, often negotiate bilateral treaties to protect their firms from arbitrary actions by host country governments. These treaties commonly require the host country to agree to arbitrate investment disputes involving the host country and citizens of the other country. The United States and Jamaica have such a treaty. When the Jamaican government announced a tax increase on Alcoa's aluminum refining plant despite a contract between the two parties that prohibited such an increase, Alcoa was able to force the Jamaican government to submit its decision to arbitration.[14]

› THE TECHNOLOGICAL ENVIRONMENT

Another important dimension of a country is its technological environment. The foundation of a country's technological environment is its resource base. Some countries, such as Australia, Argentina, and Thailand, are blessed with much fertile agricultural land. Other countries, such as Saudia Arabia, South Africa, and Russia, are endowed with rich natural resources like oil, gold, and diamonds.

Countries such as China and Indonesia have abundant labor supplies, while other countries, such as Iceland and New Zealand, do not. The availability or unavailability of resources affects what products are made in a given country. Because of their abundance of fertile land, Australia, Argentina, and Thailand are major exporters of agricultural goods. Similarly, the easy availability of low-cost labor allows firms in China and Indonesia to produce labor-intensive products for the world market. Conversely, firms in Iceland and New Zealand are net importers of such products because these firms lack low-cost labor which hinders their ability to manufacture labor-intensive goods profitably.

Countries may change or shape their technological environments through investments. Many countries, such as Canada, Germany, and Japan, have invested heavily in their infrastructures—highways, communications systems, waterworks, and so forth—to make producing and distributing products easier. Similarly, many countries have invested heavily in human capital (see "Venturing Abroad"). By improving the knowledge and skills of their citizens, countries improve the productivity and efficiency of their workforces. Investments in infrastructure and human capital have allowed developed countries to continue prospering in world markets despite the high wages paid to workers in those countries.

Another means for altering a country's technological environment is **technology transfer**, the transmittal of technology from one country to another. Some countries have promoted technology transfer by encouraging foreign direct investment (FDI). For example, Hungary and Poland jump-started their transition from communism to capitalism by using tax and other incentives to entice firms like General Electric and General Motors to build new factories there. Other countries have improved their technological base by requiring companies eager to access a country's resources or consumers to transfer technology as a condition for operating in that country. Saudi Arabia, for example, mandated that oil companies wishing to extract its crude oil hire and train Saudi petroleum engineers, who then learned state-of-the-art exploration and extraction methods on the job. Similarly, the Chinese government approved General Motors' request to build Buicks in Shanghai only after GM agreed to establish five research institutes in China that would train

VENTURING *Abroad* — TAPPING INDIA'S HUMAN CAPITAL

India is now the world's second largest exporter of software, thanks to the thousands of well-trained engineers its colleges and universities produce each year. Companies around the world, including venture capitalists, are eager to tap into this vast pool of talent. The giant management consulting firm McKinsey and Company hit upon an innovative way to uncover budding dot-com entrepreneurs. It sponsored India Venture 2000, a contest to solicit new information technology business ideas. The response to the contest was overwhelming—more than 4,000 proposals. After careful reviews by teams of its top consultants, McKinsey invited 67 finalists to the fanciest hotel in Bombay, where McKinsey had rented an entire floor. The finalists pitched their ideas to groups of venture capitalists, strategic investors, and seed money specialists assembled by McKinsey.

McKinsey's managers believe 20 to 30 of these proposals will turn into real businesses.

Members of India's business establishment are following similar strategies. Hindustan Lever, the country's largest consumer goods manufacturer, offers to fund new venture ideas generated by its current employees. Blue chip Indian conglomerates like Tata and Mahindra & Mahindra have established their own venture capital subsidiaries. Given the enormous pool of homegrown talent and the burgeoning worldwide demand for information technology services, India is likely to remain an important hunting ground for the world's venture capitalists.

Sources: "Bombay Dotcoms Arise," *Financial Times*, May 25, 2000, p. 27; "India Wired," *Business Week*, March 6, 2000, pp. 82ff.

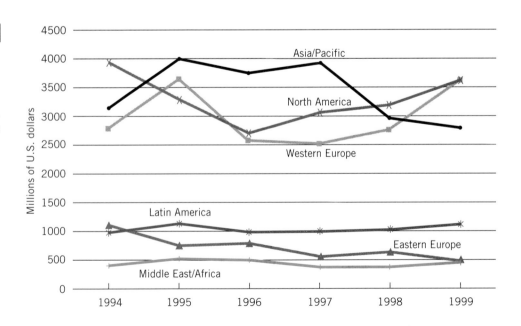

Chinese engineers and advance China's technological know-how in such areas as fuel injection systems and power trains.

An important determinant of a country's technological environment—and the willingness of foreign firms to transfer technology to the country—is the degree of protection that its laws offer intellectual property rights. Intellectual property—patents, copyrights, trademarks, brand names, and so forth—is an important asset of most MNCs. It often forms the basis of a firm's competitive advantage/core competency in the global marketplace. The value of intellectual property can quickly be damaged unless countries enforce ownership rights of firms. Countries that provide weak protection for intellectual property are less likely to attract technology-intensive foreign investments. Weak intellectual property protection also discourages local firms from developing intellectual property of their own.

Most countries have passed laws protecting intellectual property rights. Protection of such rights has also been promoted by numerous international treaties. Among these are the International Convention for the Protection of Industrial Property Rights (more commonly known as the Paris Convention), the Berne Convention for the Protection of Literary and Artistic Works, the Universal Copyright Convention, and the Trade-Related Intellectual Property Rights agreement (part of the Uruguay Round). On paper these laws and treaties would appear to provide adequate protection to owners of intellectual property. However, not all countries have signed the treaties. Further, their enforcement by many signatories is lax.

Weak protection for intellectual property rights can have high costs for international businesses. According to the Business Software Alliance, piracy of computer software cost its members $12 billion in revenues in 1999. As Figure 3.2 indicates,

› Protection of intellectual property rights is an important concern to international businesses, which lose over $3 billion a year to sellers of pirated videos and CDs like this one in Jakarta, Indonesia. The copyright holder receives no income from such sales and may experience damage to its reputation if the copies are of poor quality.

FIGURE 3.2

Software Revenue Lost to Piracy

Source: Based on data from the 1999 Global Software Piracy Report, conducted by the Business Software Alliance and the Software & Information Industry Association, May 2000.

Western Europe and North America account for more than half this total, but piracy rates are highest in Eastern Europe and the Middle East. Music and movie companies estimate that their losses due to illegal duplication of cassettes, CDs, and videos exceed $3 billion annually. Unfortunately for these companies, technology is allowing pirates to move faster than ever. For example, bootleg copies of *Star Wars Episode 1: The Phantom Menace* were on sale in the streets of Malaysia, Indonesia, and Hong Kong two days after the movie was released in the United States—and two months before Queen Amidala and Jar Jar Binks were to make their Asian debuts.[15]

International conflicts often develop because intellectual property laws are not consistent. For example, the United States follows a "first to invent" patent policy, as do Canada and the Philippines.[16] This system focuses on protecting the rights of the "true" inventor. Unfortunately, it also encourages much litigation as competing patent applicants attempt to prove they were the first to invent the product. The "first to file" system adopted by other countries avoids this litigation by unambiguously assigning rights to the first patent applicant. However, it also puts a premium on speed in applying and favors larger firms with deeper pockets.

Differences in patent practices can also lead to conflicts. For example, Japanese firms tend to file numerous patents, each of which may reflect only a minor modification of an existing patent. Conversely, U.S. patent law requires that patentable inventions be new, useful, and nonobvious. Accordingly, U.S. firms tend to file far fewer patents than Japanese companies. This has led to trade disputes between the United States and Japan over the use of so-called patent flooding by Japanese firms. With patent flooding, a company files a series of patent applications protecting narrow, minor technical improvements to a competitor's existing patents. Patent flooding makes it difficult for the competitor to improve its own technology without infringing on the intellectual property of the patent flooder. CyberOptics, the small Minneapolis developer of LaserAlign (a software and laser-based technology that helps robots position miniature components on circuit boards), provides an example of a firm that believes it has been harmed by patent flooding by a much larger company. CyberOptics had worked closely with Yamaha for five years to incorporate CyberOptics technology on the pick-and-place robots Yamaha used to produce its motorcycles and other products. Both companies agreed that, without each other's consent, neither would file for patent protection for technology they had developed jointly. However, CyberOptics discovered that Yamaha had filed 26 patent applications in Japan, Europe, and the United States for technology that CyberOptics believed was developed collaboratively based on the LaserAlign system. CyberOptics further discovered that Yamaha was allegedly warning potential CyberOptics customers that they might be in violation of Yamaha's patents if they purchased CyberOptics' services. Consequently, the Minneapolis firm sued Yamaha for breach of contract and infringement of its patents.[17]

Registration of trademarks and brand names can also cause problems for international businesses. Generally, most countries follow a "first to file" approach, which often lends itself to abuses against foreigners. A firm may popularize a brand name or trademark in its home market, only to find, when it attempts to export its product to a second country, that an opportunistic entrepreneur has already applied for the intellectual property rights in that country. For example, J.C. Penney, which had registered its trademark in most markets to avoid such problems, lost the rights to its name in Singapore to a small entrepreneur who adopted the name "J C Penney Collections" for her two clothing stores. The High Court of Singapore, while acknowledging that J.C. Penney had validly registered its trademark in that country, determined that the U.S. firm had lost the right to its company name for failure to exercise its use in Singapore.[18]

Administrative delays may also hurt the rights of intellectual property owners. In Japan approval of a trademark application often takes four times as long for a foreign firm as for a Japanese firm. Approval of foreign patent applications may also take a long time. For example, three decades elapsed before Japanese courts in 1989 recognized Texas Instruments' (TI) original patents on integrated circuits, substantially reducing TI's royalty payments from Japanese licensees. Some firms, such as Fujitsu, have been able to avoid paying TI any royalties, arguing that Fujitsu's circuit designs rely on newer, more improved technology rather than on TI's original patents. In essence the slowness of Japan's judicial process allowed companies like Fujitsu to benefit from TI's technology during the early days of the semiconductor industry without having to compensate TI for its intellectual property.[19]

› THE POLITICAL ENVIRONMENT

An important part of any business decision is assessing the political environment in which a firm operates. Laws and regulations passed by any level of government can affect the viability of a firm's operations in the host country. For example, minimum wage laws affect the price a firm must pay for labor; zoning regulations affect the way it can use its property; and environmental protection laws affect the production technology it can use as well as the costs of disposing of waste materials. Adverse changes in tax laws can slowly destroy a firm's profitability. Civil wars, assassinations, or kidnappings of foreign businesspeople and expropriation of a firm's property are equally dangerous to the viability of a firm's foreign operations.

Political Risk

Most firms are comfortable assessing the political climates in their home countries. However, assessing the political climates in other countries is far more problematic. Experienced international businesses engage in **political risk assessment**, a systematic analysis of the political risks they face in foreign countries. **Political risks** are any changes in the political environment that may adversely affect the value of a firm's business activities. Most political risks can be divided into three categories:

- Ownership risk, in which the property of a firm is threatened through confiscation or expropriation
- Operating risk, in which the ongoing operations of a firm and/or the safety of its employees are threatened through changes in laws, environmental standards, tax codes, terrorism, armed insurrection, and so forth
- Transfer risk, in which the government interferes with a firm's ability to shift funds into and out of the country

As Table 3.1 shows, political risks may result from governmental actions, such as passage of laws that expropriate private property, raise operating costs, devalue the currency, or constrain the repatriation of profits. Political risks may also arise from nongovernmental actions, such as kidnappings, extortion, and acts of terrorism.

Political risks may affect all firms equally or focus on only a handful. A **macropolitical risk** affects all firms in a country; examples are the civil wars that tore apart Sierra Leone, Zaire, Bosnia, and Rwanda in the 1990s. A **micropolitical risk** affects only a specific firm or firms within a specific industry. Saudia Arabia's nationalization of its oil industry in the 1970s is an example of a governmentally imposed micropolitical risk. Nongovernmental micropolitical risks are also important. For example, Disneyland Paris and McDonald's have been the target of numerous symbolic protests by French farmers, who view them as a convenient target for venting their disgust with U.S. international agricultural policies.

Any firm contemplating entering a new market should acquire basic knowledge of that country, learning, for example, about its political and economic structures

TYPE	IMPACT ON FIRMS
Expropriation	Loss of future profits
Confiscation	Loss of assets
	Loss of future profits
Campaigns against foreign goods	Loss of sales
	Increased costs of public relations efforts to improve public image
Mandatory labor benefits legislation	Increased operating costs
Kidnappings, terrorist threats, and other forms of violence	Disrupted production
	Increased security costs
	Increased managerial costs
	Lower productivity
Civil wars	Destruction of property
	Lost sales
	Disruption of production
	Increased security costs
	Lower productivity
Inflation	Higher operating costs
Repatriation	Inability to transfer funds freely
Currency devaluations	Reduced value of repatriated earnings
Increased taxation	Lower after-tax profits

TABLE 3.1

Examples of Political Risks

in order to control the firm's political risks. The firm needs answers to such questions as:

- Is the country a democracy or a dictatorship? Is power concentrated in the hands of one person or one political party?

- Does the country normally rely on the free market or on government controls to allocate resources? How much of a contribution is the private sector expected to make in helping the government achieve its overall economic objectives? Does the government view foreign firms as a means of promoting or hindering its economic goals?

- Are the firm's customers in the public or private sector? If public, does the government favor domestic suppliers? Are the firm's competitors in the public or private sector? If public, will the government allow foreigners to compete with the public firms on even terms?

- When making changes in its policies, does the government act arbitrarily or does it rely on the rule of law?

- How stable is the existing government? If it leaves office, will there be drastic changes in the economic policies of the new government?

Most MNCs continually monitor the countries in which they do business for changes in political risk. Often the best sources of information are employees. Whether they are citizens of the home country or of the host country, employees possess firsthand knowledge of the local political environment and are a valuable source of political risk information. The views of local staff should be supplemented by the views of outsiders. Embassy officials and international chambers of commerce are often rich sources of information. Governments themselves can supply vital information. Most governments signal their economic and political agendas during the political campaigns that lead to their elections or during the military campaigns that lead to the overthrow of their opponents; once in office,

› Deterioration of diplomatic relationships between Iran and the United States following the seizure of the U.S. embassy in Tehran by student revolutionaries raised the level of political risk faced by U.S. firms operating there.

the governments continue to provide useful information about their current and future plans. Moreover, numerous consulting firms specialize in political risk assessment to help firms evaluate the risks of doing business in a particular country. Several international business publications annually print surveys of political risk around the world. Map 3.2 depicts the results of one such survey published in *Euromoney* magazine.

What and how much information a firm needs to assess political risk will depend on the type of business it is and how long it is likely to be in the host country. The greater and longer lived a firm's investment, the broader its risk assessment should be. A Singapore toy manufacturer that subcontracts with a Chinese firm to assemble toy trucks needs to know about politically influenced factors such as trends in exchange rates, reliability of customs procedures, and the legal recourse available to it should the Chinese subcontractor fail to deliver products that meet contract specifications and deadlines. If the Singapore toy manufacturer wants to build and operate its own toy factory in China, its political risk assessment must be broadened. It needs to scrutinize its vulnerability to changes in laws dealing with labor relations, environmental protection, currency controls, and profit repatriation. It also needs to weigh the likelihood of the Chinese government nationalizing foreigners' property or splitting into warring factions and triggering a civil war.

Some degree of political risk exists in every country, although the nature and importance of these risks vary. The French farmers' protests merely inconvenienced the managers of Disneyland Paris and McDonald's, whereas the ethnic cleansing conducted by Serbian nationalists in Kosovo destroyed the economic viability of firms operating there. In political risk assessment, as in most business decisions, it is a matter of balancing risks and rewards. If a firm is considering an investment in a politically risky environment, it should be sure that it can obtain rates of return that are high enough to offset the risks of entering that market. Firms already operating in a high-risk country may choose to take steps to reduce their vulnerability. For example, a firm can reduce its financial exposure by reducing its net investment in the local subsidiary, perhaps by repatriating the subsidiary's profits to the parent company through dividend payments, by selling shares in the subsidiary to host country citizens, or by utilizing short-term leases to acquire new capital equipment rather than purchasing it outright. Alternatively, a firm might build domestic political support in the host country by being a good corporate citizen; for example, the firm might purchase inputs from local suppliers where possible, employ host country citizens in key management and administrative positions, and support local charities.

To reduce the risk of foreign operations, most developed countries have created government-owned or government-sponsored organizations to insure firms against political risks. For example, the **Overseas Private Investment Corporation (OPIC)** insures U.S. overseas investments against nationalization, insurrections or revolutions, and foreign-exchange inconvertibility. In 1999 OPIC sold Enron $62 million worth of insurance to cover its investment in a Brazilian energy pipeline.[20] However, OPIC insurance is limited to firms operating in countries with which the United States has signed bilateral investment treaties. The **Multilateral Investment Guarantee Agency (MIGA)**, a subsidiary of the World Bank, provides similar insurance against political risks. Private insurance firms, such as Lloyd's of London, also underwrite political risk insurance.[21]

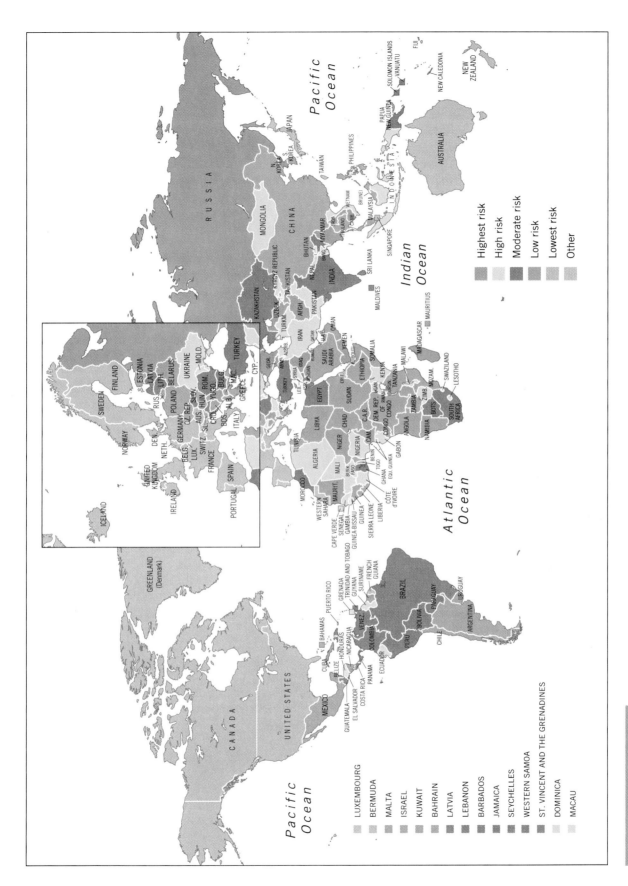

MAP 3.2 **Countries' Relative Political Riskiness, 2000**

Source: Euromoney's Annual Survey of Country Risk, *Euromoney*, September 1999, pp. 251ff.

Legend (map key):
- Highest risk
- High risk
- Moderate risk
- Low risk
- Lowest risk
- Other

Inset legend:
- LUXEMBOURG
- BERMUDA
- MALTA
- ISRAEL
- KUWAIT
- BAHRAIN
- LATVIA
- LEBANON
- BARBADOS
- JAMAICA
- SEYCHELLES
- WESTERN SAMOA
- ST. VINCENT AND THE GRENADINES
- DOMINICA
- MACAU

The Emerging Market Economies

Political risk assessment is particularly important when a country is undergoing substantial political, economic, and legal changes. This is the case in the former centrally planned economies of Eastern Europe and Central Europe. (A **centrally planned economy** (CPE) is one in which government planners determine prices and production levels for individual firms.) Creating a modern market economy from the remains of a centrally planned system is an enormous and complex challenge. It produces concomitant micropolitical and macropolitical risks for international businesses.

A primary source of political risk in most of these countries is the instability of their political systems. Democratic traditions are weakly rooted in many of the countries of Central Europe and Eastern Europe, particularly those that emerged from the former Soviet Union and its czarist history of one-person rule. Although some former Soviet bloc countries, such as the Czech Republic, Hungary, and Poland, have quickly established functioning democracies, others, such as Azerbaijan, Belarus, and Kazakhstan, have not. Ethnic conflicts also permeate the region. For example, the province of Chechnya has fought two well-publicized, bloody wars of independence from Russia. A similar struggle has allowed ethnic Armenians to carve out their homeland of Nagorno-Karabakh from Azerbaijan.

Government unpredictability is another cause of political risk in these countries. One source is the continued employment of Soviet-era bureaucrats, who often use their control over required licenses and permits to frustrate the plans of private businesses. For example, Motorola spent $2 million on feasibility studies for establishing a mobile-phone network after receiving assurances from the Ukrainian Ministry of Communication that no fees would be charged to obtain an exclusive frequency for its service. Later the ministry changed its mind, proposing to assess a fee of $65 million annually, jeopardizing the $500 million project. Similarly, Monsanto found itself under investigation by a branch of the Ukrainian Ministry of Agriculture after the company began to sell its agricultural chemicals to private distributors and farmers directly, instead of through another branch of the Ministry of Agriculture.[22]

Another problem faced by these countries is establishing tax codes and tax collection systems that raise necessary revenues but still encourage economic growth. Such a problem has plagued Russia. By some estimates it collected only 50 to 60 percent of the taxes due it during Boris Yeltsin's administration. This creates several difficulties. First, low collection rates discourage many firms and individuals from paying their taxes, in the belief that if nobody else is paying taxes, then why should I? Facing shortages of tax revenues, the government then imposes new taxes to make up the revenue shortfall. The cumulative burden of these taxes would likely bankrupt any firm that tried to pay them all. IBM, for example, announced that it would pull out of a joint production venture for just this reason.[23] The net effect is that the tax code discourages many firms, both domestic and foreign, from investing in Russia.

Second, shortfalls in tax collections mean that the government is late in paying its employees, military forces, and pensioners, which in turn makes it difficult for them to obtain goods or repay their creditors. This in turn increases the prevalence of small bribes as a means of paying for the bureaucracy. Government agencies are expected to generate "nonbudget" funds, such as arbitrarily imposed fines that may look like bribes to the cynical, to fund the salaries that the central government is unable to pay. At least one Russian entrepreneur has received a request from a government agency, faxed on its letterhead, for a bribe to allow her restaurant to open. The breakdown in public services also allows organized crime to thrive. Rather than deal with criminal groups, many foreign companies resort to hiring security services, often operated by former KGB or police officials, to protect their interests and steer them out of sticky situations.[24] Not surprisingly, one of the first actions taken by Russian President Putin after his election in 2000 was to propose reforms in Russia's tax laws and their enforcement.

Foreign firms participating in the transition of former communist economies to a free-market system have also encountered operational difficulties. The public infrastructures of these countries have been neglected for the past 40 years. Highways, airports, and distribution systems for electricity, water, and natural gas are often overtaxed and unreliable. Deficiencies in communications systems have proven to be particularly troublesome to Western firms used to telephone conference calls and overnight package deliveries—remember, the communist governments wanted to control communication among their populations, not encourage it.

The executive education and management training needs of these countries are also huge. Under the communist system capital was allocated to businesses according to a central plan. Production quotas were assigned to factories, whose output was distributed to state-owned retail stores. Given the scarcity of consumer goods, the stores quickly sold whatever was given them to sell. Under this system there was no need for entrepreneurs or for specialists in finance or marketing. Accounting and management information systems were designed to monitor production, not costs or sales or inventory levels. As a result, multiple layers of managers must be trained in the skills needed to run a business in a competitive market economy.

These training needs extend below the managerial level. Many communist factories were plagued by low production levels. Workers' attitudes could be summed up by this remark: "They pretend to pay us and we pretend to work." Attitudes in service industries were anything but service oriented. Because of the lack of consumer goods, most sales personnel treated customers as beggars pleading for the right to buy what few goods were available. As a result, international businesses beginning operations in these countries must thoroughly train their employees in the behaviors and attitudes required in a competitive market economy.

Despite these difficulties, many foreign firms have recognized the potentially rich market the emerging market economies offer. The consumer goods market is particularly attractive because of the poor quality and scarcity of such goods under state control. As one businessperson noted, "The late Soviet Union could awe the world by putting men in space, but it couldn't make decent detergents, soaps, and shampoos."[25] Although the risks are high, so are the potential rewards because the market is indeed huge and underdeveloped.

CHAPTER REVIEW

Summary

The legal systems used by the world's countries vary dramatically. The former British colonies follow the common law tradition of the United Kingdom, while most other Western countries use the civil law system that originated with the Romans. A few countries, such as Iran and Saudia Arabia, use religious law, while centrally planned economies use bureaucratic law.

Laws adopted by national governments can influence the global marketplace in many ways. A country can impose restrictions on the ability of firms to conduct business internationally and can indirectly affect their competitiveness by raising their costs of doing business. A country's laws may also have extraterritorial reach, affecting transactions conducted beyond the country's borders.

MNCs operating in a host country can influence the country's economic, political, and cultural environments. Often these changes are positive. For example, FDI generates new employment opportunities and raises the productivity of local workers. MNCs can also impact the host country negatively by increasing competition for workers or by introducing products or practices incompatible with the local culture.

Resolution of international disputes is an important dimension of the legal environment. Because of the costliness of international litigation, firms often attempt to resolve disputes through dispute resolution techniques such as arbitration. When U.S. MNCs are dealing with sovereign countries, however, their ability to resolve conflicts is often hindered by the terms of the Foreign Sovereign Immunities Act.

The technological environment is an important facet of the national environment. A country's natural resources, as well as its investments in physical and human capital, affect the country's attractiveness as a location for international business activities. A country's willingness (or unwillingness) to enforce intellectual property rights of foreign firms often plays a major role in their location decisions.

International businesses operating in foreign environments are subject to political risks. To protect themselves from changes in the political environment, firms should continually monitor the political situations in the countries in which they operate by consulting with local staff, embassy officials, and, where appropriate, firms specializing in political risk assessment.

Firms doing business in the emerging market economies of the former Soviet bloc countries face particularly high levels of political risk. In many of these countries democratic traditions are weakly rooted or nonexistent. Ethnic conflicts still plague the area. The political leaders of these countries often fail to understand the importance of designing stable economic policies and have not yet developed sound tax codes. The lack of skills necessary to operate a business in a free-market economy is also an impediment to the revitalization of these emerging economies, as are deficiencies in public infrastructures.

Review Questions

1. Describe the four different types of legal systems with which international businesses must deal.
2. What is extraterritoriality?
3. How can an MNC affect its host country?
4. How do expropriation and confiscation differ?
5. Why do countries impose restrictions on foreign ownership of domestic firms?
6. What is the difference between "first to invent" and "first to file" patent systems?

7. How do restrictions on repatriation of profits affect MNCs?
8. What is political risk? What forms can it take?
9. What is OPIC's role in promoting international business activity?
10. What difficulties do countries with centrally planned economies have in transforming them into free-market economies?

Questions for Discussion

1. What options do firms have when caught in conflicts between home country and host country laws?
2. What is the impact of vigorous enforcement of intellectual property rights on the world economy? Who gains and who loses from strict enforcement of these laws?
3. Consider the following transactions. Which of them would you consider to be bribes that should be outlawed by international agreements?
   a. A payment to a customs inspector to allow your goods to clear customs more quickly
   b. Hiring a law firm that employs the son of the president of the country
   c. Making a $10,000 donation of equipment to the local university, one of whose alumni is an important government minister (would your answer change if the amount were $10 million?)
   d. Creating a joint venture with a local company controlled by a close relative of the country's president
   e. Donating 2 percent of your company's profits to a private charity controlled by the country's president
4. Do you agree with the U.S. government's policies restricting the export of dual-use goods? Why or why not? (You may wish to check out the Bureau of Export Administration's Web site, which details how the bureau operates.)
5. Map 3.2 presents the relative political riskiness of countries at the beginning of 2000. For which countries has political riskiness changed significantly since then?

BUILDING GLOBAL SKILLS

This exercise will help you better understand the influence of legal and political forces on a firm that is entering a foreign market. Your instructor will divide the class into groups of four or five members each and then assign a different type of firm to each group. Types of firms include food retailers, general merchandisers, auto parts makers, steel producers, paper recyclers, computer manufacturers, beer producers, cigarette makers, filmmakers, and petroleum refineries.

Assume your group is a top management team of a foreign firm. The firm has decided to expand into the United States and has selected the local community as its first point of entry. Your task is to find out what legal and political barriers the firm may encounter and to develop a general strategy for dealing with them. Use whatever resources are available. For example, you could interview a member of the city council or a representative from the area's economic development committee. You could also identify potential competitors and discuss what strategies they might adopt to block your entry. As

you identify potential barriers, try to determine if they are industry specific or applicable only to foreign firms.

Finally, carefully assess each potential political or legal barrier and determine how difficult or easy it might be to address it.

Follow-Up Questions

1. How easy or difficult was it to identify political or legal forces affecting your firm's proposed entry?
2. What political or legal barriers might exist that you were unable to identify?
3. Are the potential barriers so great as to keep your firm out altogether? Why or why not?
4. Do different levels of government (city, state, and federal) pose different political and legal barriers to your firm? If so, describe these differences.

WORKING WITH THE WEB:
BUILDING GLOBAL INTERNET SKILLS

Assessing Political Risks

As this chapter amply illustrates, firms are confronted with assessing political risks in any market in which the firms operate, although some markets are riskier than others. Suppose you are employed by a pension fund that has been asked to lend $100 million to build one of the pipelines discussed in the closing case, "A Job for 007." The project sponsors are willing to pay an interest rate 8 percent above the rate currently being paid by U.S. treasury bills, so your boss is definitely interested in examining the proposal. Your boss assigns you the task of conducting a political risk assessment of the project. (For purposes of this assignment, pick one of the pipeline routes discussed in the closing case.)

You may wish to begin this assignment by listing all types of political risks that could possibly affect the ability of your pension fund to receive interest payments and the return of its principal in a timely fashion. Having developed this list, you then need to assess the likelihood that the risks will arise and affect the pipeline route you have selected.

 WE INVITE YOU TO VISIT THIS BOOK'S COMPANION WEB SITE AT www.prenhall.com/griffin

IN THE NEWS

Visit the *Financial Times* Web site at *www.ft.com* to answer the following questions:

1. The *Financial Times* provides current news about political and economic events occurring in countries around the world. To access this information, click on "News" on the *Financial Times's* Web site. Next click on "Country Surveys" from the list that appears on the left. Click on several of the countries mentioned in the chapter and investigate what's happening there. What industries are likely to benefit from these events? Which ones are likely to be hurt?

2. Use the search function to find recent articles about intellectual property law. Read one or two of the most relevant articles (concerning different countries if possible) and identify the issues facing firms and lawmakers, as well as any progress or proposed solutions mentioned.

CLOSING CASE

A Job for 007

During the winter of 2000 millions of people around the world watched Pierce Brosnan play James Bond, 007, in *The World Is Not Enough*. The movie's plot centered on the destruction of an existing pipeline bringing oil from the Caspian Sea to Western markets. The pipeline's destruction would make the value of a new pipeline owned by the movie's villainess skyrocket. Although Hollywood producers are often accused of playing fast and loose with the truth, *The World Is Not Enough* focuses on a real world problem: There's a lot of oil in the Caspian region, but it has to be brought to market. Moreover, if you are looking for a perfect example of the importance of political risk analysis, you cannot find a better one than the conundrum facing oil companies trying to exploit the rich oil and gas reserves of the Caspian Sea and the Central Asian Republics.

Baku, the capital of Azerbaijan, is the center of the oil industry operating in the Caspian Sea region. Home to nearly 40 percent of Azerbaijan's 7.5 million citizens, Baku is also the Caspian's main port (see Map 3.3). The Caspian Sea sits on a sea of oil, which virtually every oil company in the world is eager to exploit. The companies know where the oil is; they know how to get it out of the ground. There's just one catch: They need to get the oil to market, and all the possible transportation routes traverse territory marked by political instability.

The problem is most acutely felt by the Azerbaijan International Operating Company (AIOC), which is owned by a consortium of oil companies, including British Petroleum, Exxon, Unocal, Pennzoil, and Russia's Lukoil. AIOC expects to spend $8 to $10 billion over the next three decades to develop and produce 4 billion barrels of Caspian Sea oil. AIOC can ship the oil to Western markets through two pipelines from Baku to the Black Sea. The first route, which is 850 miles long, goes from Baku to Russia and thence to the Black Sea port of Novorossiysk. The second route goes from Baku through Georgia to the Black Sea port of Supsa, a mere 550-mile journey. Unfortunately, the first route goes through Grozny, the capital of the breakaway Russian province Chechnya. Chechnyian rebels fought the Russian army to a standstill during a bloody revolt from 1994 to 1996 and proclaimed their independence from Moscow's control. Russian troops reseized most of the province in early 2000 in a bitter struggle that horrified foreign human rights observers. Armed conflict could break out again at any time. The second route, which bypasses Russia, goes through rough mountainous terrain where security is difficult. Local residents routinely tap into an existing pipeline in the area, siphoning off oil to heat their homes. Moreover, some Russian politicians have indicated their displeasure with the second route, claiming that it threatens the "energy security" of Russia. (A less charitable interpretation is that Russia does not wish to lose its monopoly over the transportation of Caspian Sea oil and the lucrative transit fees that it generates.) The Yeltsin and Putin administrations have not blocked the pipeline's development, but if Russian nationalists capture control of the government in the next election, they might

adopt a more bellicose policy. Turkish officials, concerned about traffic jams and possible collisions of oil tankers going through the narrow Straits of Bosporus (which separate the continents of Europe and Asia at Istanbul) on their way to Western markets, prefer a new pipeline from Baku to Ceyhan. Although this 1,236-mile route would be very expensive—an estimated $2.9 billion—Turkish officials fear that one collision between loaded tankers at the Bosporus would make the *Exxon Valdez* disaster seem like a minor slipup.

Azerbaijan has problems of its own. Although business is thriving at bars like the Ragin' Cajun and Margaritaville that cater to slaking the thirst of free-spending American oilfield workers, the oil boom has not yet benefited the average citizen: Annual per capita income is only $420. The country is run, Soviet style, by a former KGB general, Geidar Aliev, who is not a poster boy for democracy. After taking office in a 1993 coup, Aliev suppressed political dissent, stifled freedom of the press, and imposed a blockade on neighboring Armenia. Moreover, after Azerbaijan declared its independence from the Soviet Union, the ethnic Armenians of the Nagorno-Karabakh province declared their independence from Azerbaijan. A bloody, still unresolved civil war ensued, sending hundreds of thousands of refugees to Baku and other cities.

Meanwhile, oil companies operating on the other side of the Caspian Sea in Turkmenistan and Kazakhstan face similar problems. California-based Unocal, which owns production rights in Turkmenistan, is proposing to build an oil pipeline and a gas pipeline from Turkmenistan to Pakistan. The only problem is that the proposed route goes through Afghanistan, which has been ripped apart

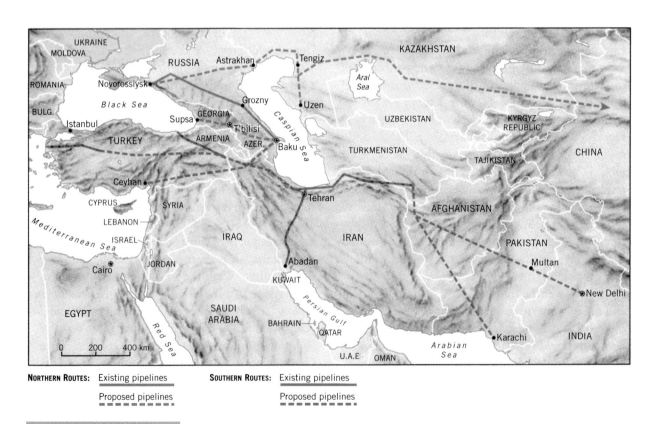

NORTHERN ROUTES:	Existing pipelines	SOUTHERN ROUTES:	Existing pipelines
	Proposed pipelines		Proposed pipelines

MAP 3.3   **Possible Pipeline Routes**

by insurrections and civil wars since the mid-1970s. Even Sylvester Stallone (remember *Rambo III*?) has been unable to bring political stability and peace to the Afghanis. Another possible pipeline route for Turkmen oil is through Iran to the Persian Gulf or through Iran and Turkey to the Black Sea. However, the United States has exerted diplomatic pressure to discourage companies from doing business with Iran. The volatility in diplomatic relations between the United States and Iran should make company executives think twice about this project. Moreover, Russian companies like Gazprom are unhappy that such a route would limit their access to Turkmen reserves.

Kazakh oil has a similar set of options and a similar set of problems. One potential pipeline route is to go around the northern coast of the Caspian Sea to Novorossiysk. Although avoiding Chechnya, the Kazakhs would be at the mercy of a Russian government that has a reputation for imposing new tax burdens on foreign companies whenever it faces a revenue shortfall. Alternatively, Kazakh oil could tap into the Turkmen pipelines to Pakistan or Iran.

A route through China is another possibility. In 1997 the Chinese National Petroleum Company purchased a 60 percent stake in Aktobemunaigazs, a leading Kazakh oil company, which controls reserves containing 1 billion barrels of high-quality crude oil and 220 billion cubic meters of natural gas. In conjunction with Korean and Japanese firms China also agreed to finance and construct a new 1,800-mile pipeline to Karamay in the western Chinese province of Xinjiang, which would then tap into China's existing pipeline grid and allow Kazakh oil access to the Chinese, Japanese, and Korean markets and generate huge transit fees for China's government. Unfortunately, Xinjiang, a vast desert province, is the subject of a small but tense rebellion by native Uighur separatists. The Uighurs, who are ethnic cousins to the Turkic populations of the Central Asian republics, resent the growing influx of the Han Chinese to the province. Today the Han Chinese comprise 38 percent of Xinjiang's population, whereas in 1949 they comprised only 5 percent. The Uighurs claim that the Han (the main ethnic group in China) have flooded the province and reserved the best jobs for themselves. So far the attacks of the poorly trained and poorly armed separatists have had little impact on Chinese control of the province, although local residents fear the situation could worsen. During 1997 riots in the border city of Gulja, the army had to escort 1,200 Han settlers out of town to safety.

Needless to say, each of these choices poses problems for the oil companies operating in the region. Nonetheless, they are ready for the challenge, mostly because the potential rewards are so large. Proven oil reserves in the region are estimated to reach 15 to 20 billion barrels; based on the area's geology, some experts believe as much as 160 billion barrels lie underground waiting to be discovered.[26]

Case Questions

1. Characterize the types of investments that are most vulnerable to political risk. Characterize those that are least vulnerable. Oil and natural gas pipelines are immobile and long lived. They are also very expensive. On a scale of 1 to 10, with 10 being highest, how vulnerable are they to political risks?

2. Which of the pipeline routes discussed in the case offers the least political risk? Which offers the greatest political risk? (You may want to refer to the "Working with the Web" exercise for help in answering this question.)

3. In his novel *Kim*, Rudyard Kipling introduced the phrase "The Great Game" to describe the struggle between the Russian czars and the British Empire to control the wealth of Central Asia and the Caspian Sea. Clearly, the great game is being replayed as countries fight to control access to the area's oil and natural gas reserves. What can international businesses do to protect themselves from the geopolitical struggles of Russia, China, Iran, the United States, and other nations that are taking place in this region?

CHAPTER

E - C u l t u r e

The rise of the Internet is altering the world's business cultures. It is affecting attitudes toward risk taking, decision making, organizational hierarchy, compensation, and education. For example, compared to their U.S. counterparts, many Asian and European firms are much more risk adverse. One British manager argues that U.S. dot-com companies "see more value in trying and failing, and therefore learning, than getting it right before implementing" e-commerce ventures. This may be due to a greater acceptance of failure in the United States relative to Europe and Asia. Notes one European manager, "If you've been bankrupt in the United States, it shows you're entrepreneurial and take risks. Over here, if you're bankrupt, it's still seen as evidence of moral turpitude."

> ## "Many European and Asian firms make decisions slowly and methodically."

Moreover, many European and Asian firms are very hierarchical and make decisions slowly and methodically. Although this approach has served them well over the decades, it may not be suited to competing in the fast-moving Internet economy. Conversely, the culture of many U.S. companies seems better adapted to the Internet's quick pace. Such is also the case for Danish companies, which tend to be open and nonhierarchical. Notes one Dane, "You could call us rebels. We do not do as we

4

The Role of Culture

OBJECTIVES

After studying this chapter, you should be able to:

> Discuss the primary characteristics of culture.

> Describe the various elements of culture and provide examples of how they influence international business.

> Identify the means by which members of a culture communicate with each other.

> Discuss how religious and other values affect the domestic environments in which international businesses operate.

> Describe the major cultural clusters and their usefulness for international managers.

> Explain Hofstede's primary findings about differences in cultural values.

> Explain how ethical conflicts may arise in international business.

are told but what we think is right, and we talk to anybody we feel like in the organization without going through the official hierarchy. This . . . means there is a strong chance that ideas dreamt up lower down in a company will be taken on by management."

Compensation practices create further difficulties. U.S. dot-com companies are famous for showering stock options on their employees, from the CEO down to the secretarial staff. Many European companies abhor compensating lower-level employees with equity. For example, German software giant SAP refused to provide stock options to its U.S. employees for fear of upsetting its German staff at company headquarters. By the time the company reconsidered its policy, it had lost dozens of its top U.S. managers to other software companies. Conversely, when InterX, a British computer hardware company, decided to enter the online information services business, it offered stock options to all the employees hired to staff the operation. Another approach is that taken by CCR Inc., a Korean Internet software company. Each quarter the CEO doubles the salaries of the two workers he believes have excelled during that time span. Such a policy is a major departure from the seniority-based pay programs of most Korean companies.

Educational systems may also create advantages in certain countries. One British business professor believes that educational approaches like those favored in Denmark and the United States are well suited to the Internet age. She gives Danish education high marks in fostering technical excellence and understanding the needs of the marketplace. More importantly, she notes that "the Danish education system trains people to ask questions instead of learning facts by heart." Because the Internet age rests on rethinking and restructuring the ways firms, suppliers, and customers interact with each other, "thinking outside the box" confers competitive advantages to people with that ability. Conversely, educational systems that focus on memorization of facts, such as those of many Asian countries, may be left behind. Some countries are responding to this challenge. Hong Kong's secretary of education has proposed that Hong Kong abandon its emphasis on rote learning, arguing that the "traditional oriental education system is not conducive to creativity. In the new technology world, there's a certain part of the brain we have forgotten about and we need to open it up and we need to change the system in order to do that."[1]

Firms and businesspeople venturing beyond their familiar domestic markets soon recognize that foreign business customs, values, and definitions of ethical behavior differ vastly from their own. Firms that rely on their familiar home culture to compete in a new market can jeopardize their international success, as SAP's unwillingness to alter its compensation policies in the U.S. market demonstrated. (See "Wiring the World" for additional insights into this problem.) Indeed, virtually all facets of an international firm's business—including contract negotiations, production operations, marketing decisions, and human resource

Wiring the World

THE INTERNET, NATIONAL COMPETITIVENESS, AND CULTURE

What does it take to succeed in the Internet age? According to some experts, a country needs "superliquid and vast capital markets, venture-capital networks, world-class universities, risk-taking culture, restructuring ethos, and high-tech talent pools."[2] The Internet, however, threatens to upset numerous culture norms. As you read this chapter, think about the requirements for success in the Internet age and the various elements of culture that are discussed. For example, you might consider the following questions:

- In some business cultures, pay is linked to seniority. Dot-com businesses, however, rely heavily on stock options to compensate their employees, and younger workers often have greater technical skills than older workers. How can such cultures reconcile these conflicting norms?

- Can group-oriented cultures that promote a slow, consensus-building style of decision making act quickly enough to compete in the fast-moving e-commerce environment?

- Some cultures dislike uncertainty and risk taking. How can they thrive in the Internet age, which to date has been characterized by high levels of uncertainty and risk?

- Some business cultures stress conducting business with those persons with whom you or your company has developed a long-term, trusting relationship. Is such an approach outmoded in the Internet age?

management policies—may be affected by cultural variations. This chapter high-lights some of the cultural differences among countries and explains how under-standing those differences is invaluable for international businesspeople.

CHARACTERISTICS OF CULTURE ‹

Business, like all other human activities, is conducted within the context of society. **Culture** is the collection of values, beliefs, behaviors, customs, and attitudes that distinguish one society from another. A society's culture determines the rules that govern how firms operate in the society. Several characteristics of culture are worth noting for their relevance to international business:

- Culture reflects *learned behavior* that is transmitted from one member of a soci-ety to another. Some elements of culture are transmitted intergenerationally, as when parents teach their child table manners. Other elements are transmitted intragenerationally, as when seniors educate incoming freshmen about a school's traditions.

- The elements of culture are *interrelated*. For example, Japan's group-oriented, hierarchical society stresses harmony and loyalty, which has historically trans-lated into lifetime employment and minimal job switching.

- Because culture is learned behavior, it is *adaptive*; that is, the culture changes in response to external forces that affect the society. For example, after World War II, Germany was divided into free-market-oriented West Germany and communist-controlled East Germany. Despite their having a common heritage developed over centuries, this division created large cultural differences between *Ossis* (East Germans) and *Wessis* (West Germans). The differences resulted from adaptations of the East German culture to the dictates of com-munist ideology regarding attitudes toward work, risk taking, and fairness of reward systems.

- Culture is *shared* by members of the society and indeed defines the membership of the society. Individuals who share a culture are members of a society; those who do not are outside the boundaries of the society.

ELEMENTS OF CULTURE ‹

A society's culture determines how its members communicate and interact with each other. The basic elements of culture (see Figure 4.1) are social structure, lan-guage, communication, religion, and values and attitudes. The interaction of these elements affects the local environment in which international businesses operate.

Social Structure

Basic to every society is its social structure, the overall framework that determines the roles of individuals within the society, the stratification of the society, and indi-viduals' mobility within the society.

Individuals, Families, and Groups.   All human societies involve individuals living in family units and working with each other in groups. Societies differ, how-ever, in the way they define family and in the relative importance they place on the individual's role within groups. The U.S. view of family ties and responsibilities focuses on the nuclear family (father, mother, and offspring). In other cultures, the extended family is far more important. Arabs, for example, consider uncles, broth-ers, cousins, and in-laws as parts of their family unit to whom they owe obligations of support and assistance. Other societies utilize an even broader definition of fam-ily. For example, Somalia's society is organized in clans, each of which comprises individuals of the same tribe who share a common ancestor.

FIGURE 4.1

Elements of Culture

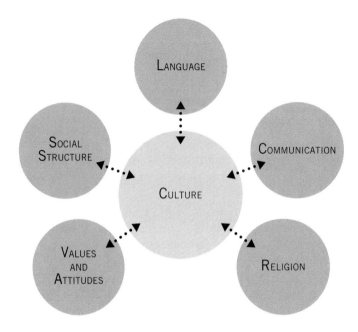

These differing social attitudes are reflected in the importance of the family to business. In the United States, firms discourage nepotism, and the competence of a man who married the boss's daughter is routinely questioned by coworkers. In Arab-owned firms, however, family ties are crucial, and hiring relatives is a common, accepted practice. Similarly, in Chinese-owned firms, family members fill critical management positions and supply capital from personal savings to ensure the firms' growth.[3]

Cultures also differ in the importance of the individual relative to the group. U.S. culture, for example, promotes individualism. Schools try to raise the self-esteem of each child and encourage each one to develop individual talents. Because respect for individual authority and responsibility is so strong in the United States, children are trained to believe that their destinies lie in their own hands. Conversely, in group-focused societies such as China and Japan and in Israel's kibbutzim, children are taught that their role is to serve the group (see "Bringing the World into Focus"). Virtues such as unity, loyalty, and harmony are highly valued in such societies. These characteristics often are more important in hiring decisions than are personal accomplishments or abilities.[4]

Social Stratification.   Societies differ in their degree of **social stratification**. All societies categorize people to some extent on the basis of their birth, occupation, educational achievements, and/or other attributes. However, the importance of these categories in defining how individuals interact with each other within and between these groups varies by society. In medieval Europe, for example, the roles and obligations of peasants, craftsmen, tradesmen, and nobles were carefully delineated by custom and law. The British class structure and the Indian caste system provide more recent examples of the same phenomenon, in which one's social position affects all facets of one's dealings with other people. In other societies, social stratification is less important. For example, a U.S. bank president may haughtily bark orders at the janitorial staff when on the job yet willingly take orders from those same individuals when cleaning up after a church fund-raiser.

Multinational corporations (MNCs) operating in highly stratified societies often must adjust their hiring and promotion procedures to take into account class or clan differences among supervisors and workers. Hiring members of one group to do jobs traditionally performed by members of another group may lower workplace morale and productivity. In less stratified societies, firms are freer to seek out the

Bringing the World into FOCUS

THE IMPACT OF JAPANESE CULTURE ON BUSINESS

Let us briefly review some key elements of Japanese culture and how it affects Japanese business practices. Note how this culture is learned, interrelated, and shared, and how it defines group membership.

The first cultural element that plays a major role in Japanese business practices is the *hierarchical structure* of Japanese society. The social hierarchy strictly defines how people deal with each other. In fact, speaking Japanese requires that you know your position relative to the person to whom you are talking. Different forms of language are used depending on whether you are conversing with a superior or a subordinate. Thus, when two Japanese businesspeople meet, they immediately exchange business cards, partly to determine their relative status so they can know which form of address to use.

❯ Mom-and-pop stores like this liquor retailer have been a mainstay of the Japanese economy. International pressures to open the Japanese economy to foreign retailers threaten a society that highly values harmony and loyalty.

A second cultural element is *groupism*. A person is identified as a member of a group rather than as an individual. This group identity is ingrained in Japanese children at an early age. Watching the differences between children in a U.S. preschool and those in a Japanese preschool is interesting. The U.S. school focuses on nurturing the individual by praising individual accomplishments and working to raise a child's self-esteem. The Japanese school concentrates on transforming spoiled preschoolers, whose every wish to date has been met by their doting mothers, into members of a cohesive group. Strong group identity is reinforced by Japan's ethnic homogeneity and its relative isolation from the rest of the world until the 1850s.

A third element of Japanese culture is *wa*, or social harmony. The goal of each group member is to promote harmony, or consensus, within the group. Decisions are not made within Japanese organizations by upper-management fiat because that would upset the *wa*. Rather, group members must discuss and negotiate until consensus is reached. The need to preserve *wa* is one reason many Japanese firms encourage after-work socializing and partying by Japanese salarymen. These parties are a means of building trust among group members and allowing them to develop consensus on issues facing their firm. Similarly, many firms compensate their employees based on seniority, rather than individual performance, to preserve *wa*.

A fourth cultural element is *obligation*, or duty. The individual, once hired, becomes indebted to the firm. The debt owed the firm for agreeing to employ the person is so great that the person can never repay it. The person owes everything to the firm, and the firm's needs come first, even before personal and familial needs. The strong cultural disapproval of an employee moving to another firm stems from this facet of Japanese culture. At the same time, the firm accepts certain responsibilities toward the employee, much as a feudal lord accepted the obligation to protect the peasants, serfs, craftsmen, and merchants in the lord's

(continues)

realm. The traditional lifetime (until age 55) employment prac- down of the Japanese economy in the 1990s. Fujitsu, for example, tices of many major Japanese firms stem from this cultural ele- announced in 1998 that it would abandon its seniority-oriented ment, which in turn affects other Japanese business practices. compensation approach and adopt a merit-based pay and per- Because of the lifetime employment relationship, Japanese firms formance philosophy. Other firms have quietly trimmed their take considerable care in selecting employees and force job appli- commitment to lifetime employment. Nonetheless, these tradi- cants to undergo rigorous testing and interviewing prior to being tional practices remain the norm in most large Japanese firms. hired. Once hired, employees recognize that their jobs depend on the long-term survival of their employer and that their jobs are secure as long as the firm is secure.

A handful of Japanese firms are beginning to scrap some of these culturally based business practices in response to the slow-

Sources: Richard G. Newman and K. Anthony Rhee, "Self-Styled Barriers Inhibit Transferring Management Methods," *Business Horizons*, May–June 1989, pp. 17–21; "Fujitsu to Institute Merit-Based Pay for All Employees," *Wall Street Journal*, March 26, 1998, p. B5.

most qualified employee, regardless of whether that person went to the right school, goes to the proper church, or belongs to all the best clubs. In highly stratified societies, advertisers must tailor their messages more carefully to ensure that they reach only the targeted audience and do not spill over to another audience that may be offended by receiving a message intended for the first group. In less stratified societies, such concerns may be less important.

Social mobility is the ability of individuals to move from one stratum of society to another. Social mobility tends to be higher in less stratified societies. It is higher in the United States, for example, than in the United Kingdom or India. Social mobility (or the lack thereof) often affects individuals' attitudes and behaviors toward such factors as labor relations, human capital formation, risk taking, and entrepreneurship. The U.K.'s formerly rigid class system and relatively low social mobility created an "us versus them" attitude among many British industrial workers, causing them to eye suspiciously any management efforts to promote workplace cooperation. Until relatively recently, some British working-class youth dropped out of school, believing that their role in society was preordained and thus investment in education a waste of time. In more socially mobile societies, such as those of the United States, Singapore, and Canada, individuals are more willing to seek higher education or to engage in entrepreneurial activities, knowing that if they are successful, they and their families are free to rise in society.

Language

Language is a primary delineator of cultural groups because it is an important means by which a society's members communicate with each other. Experts have identified some 3,000 different languages and as many as 10,000 distinct dialects worldwide (see Map 4.1).[5]

Language organizes the way members of a society think about the world. It filters observations and perceptions and thus affects unpredictably the messages that are sent when two individuals try to communicate. In one famous experiment in Hong Kong, 153 undergraduate students, bilingual in English and Chinese, were divided into two groups. One group was given a class assignment written in English; the other was given the same assignment written in Chinese. The professor in charge of the experiment took every precaution to ensure that the translations were perfect, yet the answers given by the two groups differed significantly, indicating that the language itself altered the nature of the information being conveyed.[6]

In addition to shaping one's perceptions of the world, language provides important clues about the cultural values of the society and aids acculturation. For example, many languages, including French, German, and Spanish, have informal and formal forms of the word *you*, the use of which depends on the relationship between the speaker and the person addressed.[7] Existence of these language forms

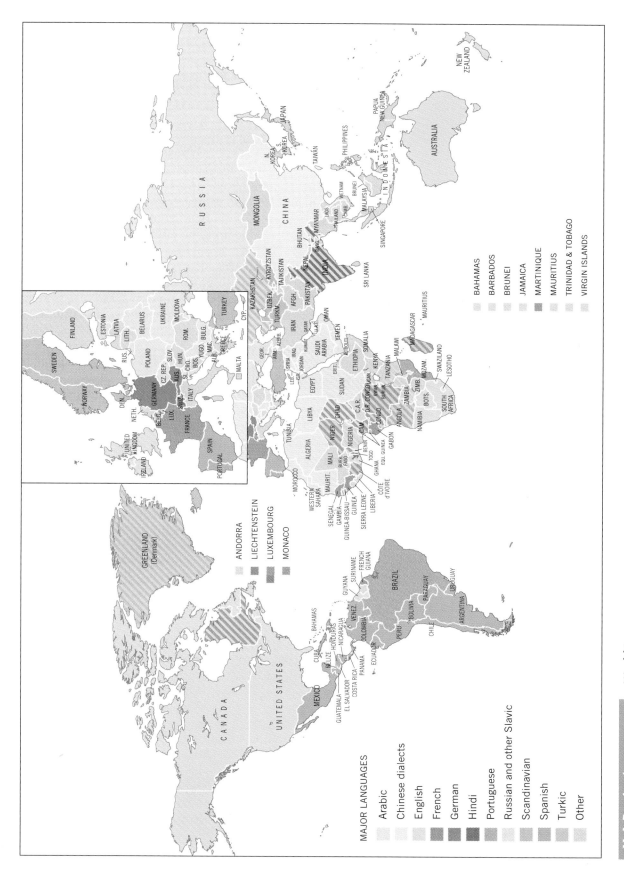

World Languages

MAP 4.1

MAJOR LANGUAGES

- Arabic
- Chinese dialects
- English
- French
- German
- Hindi
- Portuguese
- Russian and other Slavic
- Scandinavian
- Spanish
- Turkic
- Other

ANDORRA
LIECHTENSTEIN
LUXEMBOURG
MONACO

BAHAMAS
BARBADOS
BRUNEI
JAMAICA
MARTINIQUE
MAURITIUS
TRINIDAD & TOBAGO
VIRGIN ISLANDS

provides a strong hint that one should take care in maintaining an appropriate level of formality when dealing with businesspeople from countries in which those languages predominate.

The presence of more than one language group is an important signal about the diversity of a country's population and suggests that there may also be differences in income, work ethic, and/or educational achievement. For example, India recognizes 16 official languages, and approximately 3,000 dialects are spoken within its boundaries, a reflection of the heterogeneity of its society. In several mountainous countries of South America, including Bolivia and Paraguay, most of the poor rural population speaks local Indian dialects and has trouble communicating with the Spanish-speaking urban elites. Generally, countries dominated by one language group tend to have a homogeneous society, in which nationhood defines the society. Countries with multiple language groups tend to be heterogeneous, with language providing an important means of identifying cultural differences within the country.

Savvy businesspeople operating in heterogeneous societies adapt their marketing and business practices along linguistic lines to account for cultural differences among their prospective customers. For example, market researchers discovered that English Canadians favor soaps that promise cleanliness, while French Canadians prefer pleasant- or sweet-smelling soaps. Thus Procter & Gamble's English language Canadian ads for Irish Spring soap stress the soap's deodorant value, while its French language ads focus on the soap's pleasant aroma.[8] Generally, advertisers should seek out the media—newspapers, radio, cable television, and magazines—that allow them to customize their marketing messages to individual linguistic groups. For example, in the United States the development of Spanish language cable television channels such as Univision has allowed advertisers to more easily customize their advertisements to reach the Hispanic market, without confusing their marketing messages to the larger English-speaking audience.

Language as a Competitive Weapon.   Linguistic ties often create important competitive advantages because the ability to communicate is so important in conducting business transactions. Commerce among Australia, Canada, New Zealand, the United Kingdom, and the United States is facilitated by their common use of English. For example, when Giro Sport Design, a Soquel, California, manufacturer of bicycle helmets, decided to manufacture its products in Europe rather than export from the United States, the firm told its location consultants to find a plant site in an English-speaking country. William Hanneman, Giro's president, noted, "With all the problems you have in running a business abroad, we didn't want to be bothered by language."[9] The firm located its European production facilities in Ireland, where it enjoyed a plentiful supply of well-trained English-speaking labor, economic development incentives, and tax benefits.

Similarly, Spain's Telefonica SA moved aggressively into Latin America as part of its internationalization strategy. Benefiting from the region's privatization programs, it has bought controlling interests in the formerly state-owned telephone monopolies of Argentina, Chile, and Peru. Spanish banks such as Banco Santander, Banco Bilbao Vizcaya, and Banco Central Hispano adopted a comparable approach, investing heavily in Argentina, Chile, Mexico, Peru, Puerto Rico, and Uruguay.[10] Turkey is fast becoming the jumping-off point to do business in the Turkic areas of the former Soviet Union, such as Azerbaijan, Kazakhstan, and Turkmenistan. The linguistic legacy of colonialism also affects international business, as Map 4.2 indicates.

Lingua Franca.   To conduct business, international businesspeople must be able to communicate. As a result of British economic and military dominance in the nineteenth century and U.S. dominance since World War II, English has emerged as the predominant common language, or **lingua franca**, of international business.

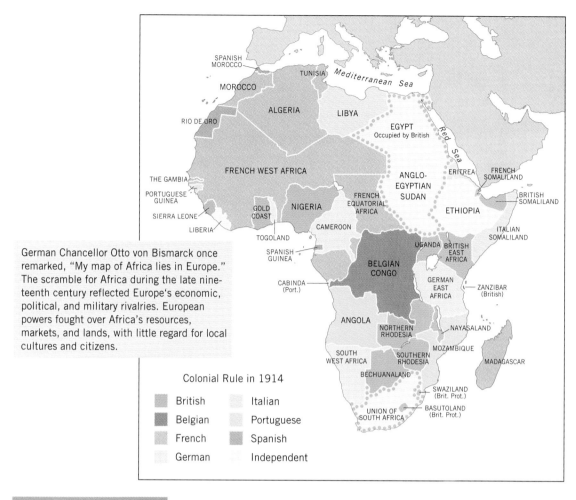

German Chancellor Otto von Bismarck once remarked, "My map of Africa lies in Europe." The scramble for Africa during the late nineteenth century reflected Europe's economic, political, and military rivalries. European powers fought over Africa's resources, markets, and lands, with little regard for local cultures and citizens.

Colonial Rule in 1914

British
Belgian
French
German
Italian
Portuguese
Spanish
Independent

MAP 4.2   **Africa's Colonial Heritage**

Most European and Japanese public school students study English for many years. Some countries that have many linguistic groups, such as India and Singapore, have adopted English as an official language to facilitate communication among the diverse groups. Similarly, firms with managers from many different countries may use English as the official corporate language. For example, Philips, the Dutch-based electronics MNC, has used English for intracorporate communications since 1983. Switzerland's Brown Boveri and Sweden's Asea adopted English as their corporate language after their merger in 1987. The board of directors of SKF, a Swedish ball bearing manufacturer, conducts its meetings in English because the board is composed of 11 Swedes, one Italian, one German, and one Swiss.[11] As "Wiring the World" notes, the adoption of English as a lingua franca creates problems for countries, such as France, that wish to maintain the purity of their language.

The dominance of English seemingly gives an advantage in international commerce to people whose native language is English, particularly when transactions are done in Canada, the United Kingdom, or the United States. However, failure by native English speakers to learn a second language puts them and their firms at a decided disadvantage when negotiating or operating on foreign turf. For example, a few years ago Lionel Train Company moved its manufacturing facilities to Mexico to take advantage of lower labor costs, but it could not find enough bilingual managers to run the plant. As a result, the firm eventually shut down the plant and moved its operations back to the United States.[12]

Wiring the World

FRENCH LANGUAGE EXPERTS COIN NEW WEB WORDS

As the Internet revolution sweeps the world, the Académie Française is fighting to maintain the purity of the French language by coining uniquely French words and phrases for well-known Internet buzzwords. The World Wide Web, which hip Parisian Netizens call "le Web," is officially known as "la toile," which translates into "the spider web." Similarly, the academy's official phrase for e-mail is "message électronique."

Subtle differences, perhaps, but the writers who serve on the academy are determined to keep foreign words out of the language by providing French substitutes for use in government documents and schools. Ordinary citizens are not required to use the terms offered by the academy, although officials hope people will adopt suggested French phrases such as "causette" instead of chattering on about online chat sessions.

Sometimes the drive to use French words makes for unusual designations. The academy calls hackers—programmers who break into computer systems and Web sites—"les fouineurs," meaning "the nosy people." Other substitutes are fairly close, such as "localisateur universal," which translates into "universal locator," the official French term for URL (universal resource locator), a Web address.

Since the Académie Française was founded by Cardinal Richelieu in 1635, it has made considerable headway in persuading the French to adopt its substitutes for non-French words. Nobody talks about a computer in France; instead, they talk about an "ordinateur," a word the academy proposed. On the other hand, many Internet entrepreneurs resist the official French phrases. They prefer to say "le start-up" instead of "la jeune pousse," which means "young sapling." Although the popular press continues to mix French and Web terms in headlines, such as "Surfez le Web," the academy is pressing on with its mission to keep non-French buzzwords out of the language.

Source: Vivienne Walt, "E-Words Are Tough for France to Swallow," *USA Today,* May 1, 2000, pp. 1A–2A. Used with permission.

Because language serves as a window on the culture of a society, many international business experts argue that students should be exposed to foreign languages, even if they are unable to master them. Although mastery is best, even modest levels of language training provide students with clues about cultural norms and attitudes that prove helpful in international business.

Translation.   Of course, some linguistic differences may be overcome through translation. The process, however, requires more than merely substituting words of one language for those of another. Translators must be sensitive to subtleties in the connotations of words and focus on translating ideas, not the words themselves. Far too often, translation problems create marketing disasters. A classic case is KFC's initial translation of "Finger Lickin' Good" into Chinese, which came out as the far less appetizing "Eat Your Fingers Off." Similarly, the original translation of Pillsbury's Jolly Green Giant for the Saudi Arabian market was "intimidating green ogre"—a very different image from what the firm intended (although it still might encourage children to eat their peas).

Firms can reduce the chances that they are sending the wrong message to their customers by using a technique known as backtranslation. With **backtranslation**, one person translates a document, then a second person translates the translated version back into the original language. This technique provides a check that the intended message is actually being sent, thus avoiding communication mistakes.

When communications to nonnative speakers must be made in the home country's language, speakers and writers should use common words, use the most common meanings of those words, and try to avoid idiomatic phrases. Caterpillar is faced with the problem of communicating with the diverse international users of its products. It developed its own language instruction program called Caterpillar Fundamental English (CFE), which it uses in its overseas repair and service manuals. CFE is a simplified, condensed version of English that can be taught to non-English-speaking people in 30 lessons. It consists of 800 words that are necessary to repair Cat's equipment: 450 nouns, 70 verbs, 100 prepositions, and 180 other words.[13] "Bringing the World into Focus" presents other hints for communicating internationally.

Bringing the World into FOCUS

INTERNATIONAL COMMUNICATION: A PRIMER

Conversational Principle #1: Recognize that many cultures need to know as much as possible about you and the firm you represent. Always remember when you are in Latin America, Asia, and parts of Western Europe that even the most seemingly casual, insignificant conversations have a level of significance far beyond that dictated by the content being discussed. Conversations about your family, your firm, or current events are used to "warm up relationships," just as one might warm a car engine on a cold day. You should also give your hosts insights into you as a person and recognize their need to find out what makes you "tick." . . .

Conversational Principle #2: Speak slowly, clearly, and simply. Avoid jargon, slang, clichés, and idiomatic usage. When foreigners learn English, they learn a "correct" version of formal English. When they listen to people from the United States (or Australia, Canada, or the United Kingdom) lapsing into slang or idiom, they become confused. We must realize that even an everyday expression such as "Let's get rolling" or "I'm all ears" can be perplexing if the foreigner tries to translate it literally. . . .

Conversational Principle #3: Sprinkle your conversation with at least some words and phrases in the language of your listeners. It is regarded as "good manners" to make at least an attempt to learn a few phrases in your host's language. . . .

Conversational Principle #4: Be careful about what your body language and your tone of voice communicate. When listeners cannot follow what is being said, they will pay far greater attention to body language. And if they do understand English, they will look for contradictions between what is said and how it is said. . . . Tone of voice also plays an important role when communicating internationally. There are vast cultural differences at play here: notice, for example, how softly people from most Asian cultures speak. People from the United States often seem loud and aggressive in negotiations and vigorous in arguments. And negotiations in Latin American, Mediterranean, and Central European countries are far louder, often including heated, arm-waving exchanges of opinion that rarely mean anything personal. . . .

Presentation Principle #1: Respect many foreign audiences' desire for greater formality of presentation. U.S. businesspeople generally like presentations that seem natural and spontaneous, not "canned" or overly rehearsed. Most other countries . . . expect more formality. "Natural" presentations . . . give the impression that the speaker has not respected the audience sufficiently. . . .

Presentation Principle #2: Allow for differences in behavior of foreign audiences. . . . Japanese audiences, for example, usually sit and nod their heads (which means they understand, not that they agree) and say nothing. However, on some occasions, they may start frenzied talking among themselves. Or, in open discussions, they may suddenly become evasive. What this usually means is that something said is disturbing to them. . . .

Presentation Principle #3: Have patience; design your presentation's length, completeness, and "interruptability" with the audience's culture in mind. U.S. businesspeople are impatient and are used to fast-paced, efficient presentations. Most foreigners, with the probable exceptions of Germans and the Swiss, prefer slower, more deliberate efforts. . . . Japanese, Latin American, and Arabic audiences expect a presentation to be in short, separate segments that allow time for questions and digestion of what has been presented. . . .

Presentation Principle #4: Match rank and age of presenter to rank and age of important members of foreign audiences. In many American companies, meritocracy is dominant and fairly young executives rise rapidly to powerful positions early in their career. In other cultures, however, age (or seniority) is a major indicator of status. Therefore, sending young executives, regardless of their rank, to negotiate important contracts with businesspeople in those cultures can be a disaster.

Sources: Ronald E. Dulek, John S. Fielden, and John S. Hill, "International Communication: An Executive Primer." Reprinted from *Business Horizons*, January–February 1991. Copyright © 1991 by the Board of Trustees at Indiana University, Kelly School of Business. Used with permission.

Saying No. Another cultural difficulty international businesspeople face is that words may have different meanings to persons with diverse cultural backgrounds. North Americans typically translate the Spanish word *mañana* literally to mean "tomorrow," but in parts of Latin America, the word is used to mean "some other day—not today."

Even the use of *yes* and *no* differs across cultures. In contract negotiations, Japanese businesspeople often use *yes* to mean "Yes, I understand what is being said." Foreign negotiators often assume that their Japanese counterparts are using *yes* to mean "Yes, I agree with you" and are disappointed when the Japanese later fail to accept contract terms that the foreigners had assumed were agreed to. Misunderstandings can be compounded because directly uttering "no" is considered very impolite in Japan. Japanese negotiators who find a proposal unacceptable will, in order to be polite, suggest that it "presents many difficulties" or requires "further study."[14] Foreigners waiting for a definitive "no" may have to wait a long time. Such behavior may be considered evasive in U.S. business culture, but it is the essence of politeness in Japanese business culture.

Communication

Communicating across cultural boundaries, whether verbally or nonverbally, is a particularly important skill for international managers. Although communication can often go awry between people who share a culture, the chances of miscommunication increase substantially when the people are from different cultures. In such cases, the senders encode messages using their cultural filters and the receivers decode the same messages using their filters. The result of using different cultural filters is often a misunderstanding that is expensive to resolve. For example, a contract between Boeing and a Japanese supplier called for the fuselage panels for Boeing's 767 aircraft to have a "mirror finish." Labor costs for the part were higher than expected because the Japanese supplier polished and polished the panels to achieve what it believed to be the desired finish, when all Boeing wanted was a shiny surface.[15]

Nonverbal Communication. Members of a society communicate with each other using more than words. In fact, some researchers believe 80 to 90 percent of all information is transmitted among members of a culture by means other than language.[16] This nonverbal communication includes facial expressions, hand gestures, intonation, eye contact, body positioning, and body posture. Although most members of a society quickly understand nonverbal forms of communication common to their society, outsiders may find the nonverbal communication difficult to comprehend. Table 4.1 lists some of the many common forms of nonverbal communication.

Because of cultural differences, nonverbal forms of communication often can lead to misunderstandings. For example, in the United States, people discussing business at a party typically stand 20 inches from each other. In Saudi Arabia, the normal conversational distance is 9 to 10 inches. A U.S. businessperson conversing with a Saudi counterpart at a party will respond to the Saudi's polite attempts to move in closer by politely moving back. Each is acting politely within the context of his or her own culture—and insulting the other in the context of that person's culture.[17]

Differences in the meanings of hand gestures and facial expressions also exist among cultures. Nodding one's head means "yes" in the United States but "no" in Bulgaria. Joining the thumb and forefinger in a circle while extending the remaining three fingers is the signal for "okay" in the United States; however, it symbolizes money to the Japanese, worthlessness to the French, male homosexuals to the Maltese, and a vulgarity in many parts of Eastern Europe.[18] Needless to say, international businesspeople should avoid gesturing in a foreign culture unless they are sure of a gesture's meaning in that culture.

TABLE 4.1

Forms of Nonverbal
Communication

Hand gestures, both intended and self-directed, such as nervous rubbing of hands

Facial expressions, such as smiles, frowns, and yawns

Posture and stance

Clothing and hair styles (hair being more like clothes than like skin, both subject to the fashion of the day)

Walking behavior

Interpersonal distance

Touching

Eye contact and direction of gaze, particularly in "listening behavior"

Architecture and interior design

"Artifacts" and nonverbal symbols, such as lapel pins, walking sticks, and jewelry

Graphic symbols, such as pictures to indicate "men's room" or "handle with care"

Art and rhetorical forms, including wedding dances and political parades

Smell (olfaction), including body odors, perfumes, and incense

Speech rate, pitch, inflection, and volume

Color symbolism

Synchronization of speech and movement

Taste, including symbolism of food and the communication function of chatting over coffee or tea; oral gratification, such as smoking or gum chewing

Cosmetics: temporary, such as powder and lipstick; permanent, such as tattoos

Drum signals, smoke signals, factory whistles, police sirens

Time symbolism: what is too late or too early a time to telephone or visit a friend or too long or too short to make a speech or stay for dinner

Timing and pauses within verbal behavior

Silence

Source: Reprinted with permission of Simon & Schuster Inc. from the Macmillan College text *An Introduction to Intercultural Communication* by John C. Condon and Fathi Yousef, Copyright © 1975 by Macmillan College Publishing Company, Inc.

Even silence has meaning. People in the United States tend to abhor silence at meetings or in private conversation, believing that silence reflects an inability to communicate or to empathize. In Japan silence may indicate nothing more than that the individual is thinking or that additional conversation would be disharmonious. U.S. negotiators have often misinterpreted the silence of their Japanese counterparts and offered contract concessions when none were needed, simply to end a lull in the discussion.[19] Attitudes toward silence also affect management styles. In the United States good managers solve problems. Thus U.S. managers often attempt to dominate group discussions to signal their competence and leadership abilities. In Japan good managers encourage their subordinates to seek solutions that are acceptable to all involved parties. A Japanese manager therefore will demonstrate leadership by silence, thereby encouraging full participation by subordinates attending a meeting and promoting group consensus.[20]

Gift Giving and Hospitality. Gift giving and hospitality are important means of communication in many business cultures. Japanese business etiquette requires solicitous hospitality. Elaborate meals and after-hours entertainment serve to build personal bonds and group harmony among the participants. These personal bonds are strengthened by the exchange of gifts, which vary according to the occasion and the status of the giver and the recipient. However, business gifts are opened in private so as not to cause the giver to lose face should the gift be too expensive or too cheap relative to the gift offered in return.[21] Because the rules for gift giving can be quite complicated, even to native Japanese, etiquette books that detail the appropriate gift for each circumstance are available.[22]

Arab businesspeople, like the Japanese, are very concerned about their ability to work with their proposed business partners; the quality of the people one deals with is just as important as the quality of the project. Thus the business culture of Arab countries also includes gift giving and elaborate and gracious hospitality as a means of assessing these qualities. Unlike in Japan, however, business gifts are opened in public so that all may be aware of the giver's generosity.[23]

Norms of hospitality even affect the way bad news is delivered in various cultures. In the United States bad news is typically delivered as soon as it is known. In Korea it is delivered at day's end so it will not ruin the recipient's whole day. Further, in order not to disrupt personal relationships, the bad news is often only hinted at. In Japan maintaining harmony among participants in a project is emphasized, so bad news often is communicated informally from a junior member of one negotiating team to a junior member of the other team. Even better, a third party may be used to deliver the message to preserve harmony within the group.[24]

Religion

Religion is an important aspect of most societies. It affects the ways in which members of a society relate to each other and to outsiders. It shapes the attitudes its adherents have toward work, consumption, individual responsibility, and planning for the future. Sociologist Max Weber, for example, has attributed the rise of capitalism in Western Europe to the **Protestant ethic**, which stresses individual hard work, frugality, and achievement as means of glorifying God. The Protestant ethic makes a virtue of high savings rates, constant striving for efficiency, and reinvestment of profits to improve future productivity, all of which are necessary for the smooth functioning of a capitalist economy.

In contrast, Hinduism emphasizes spiritual accomplishment rather than economic success. The goal of a Hindu is to achieve union with Brahma, the universal spirit, by leading progressively more ascetic and pure lives as one's reincarnated soul goes through cycles of death and rebirth. The quest for material possessions may delay one's spiritual journey. Thus Hinduism provides little support for capitalistic activities such as investment, wealth accumulation, and the constant quest for higher productivity and efficiency.

Islam, while supportive of capitalism, places more emphasis on the individual's obligation to society. According to Islam, profits earned in fair business dealings are justified, but a firm's profits may not result from exploitation or deceit, for example, and all Muslims are expected to act charitably, justly, and humbly in their dealings with others. The Islamic prohibition against payment or receipt of interest noted in Chapter 3 results from a belief that the practice represents exploitation of the less fortunate.

Religion affects the business environment in other important ways. Often religions impose constraints on the roles of individuals in society. For example, the caste system of Hinduism traditionally has restricted the jobs individuals may perform, thereby affecting the labor market and foreclosing business opportunities.[25] Countries dominated by strict adherents to Islam, such as Saudi Arabia and Iran, limit job opportunities for women, in the belief that their contact with adult males should be restricted to relatives.

The impact of religion on international businesses varies from country to country, depending on the country's legal system, its homogeneity of religious beliefs, and its toleration of other religious viewpoints. Consider Saudi Arabia, home of the holy city of Mecca, to which all Muslims are supposed to make a

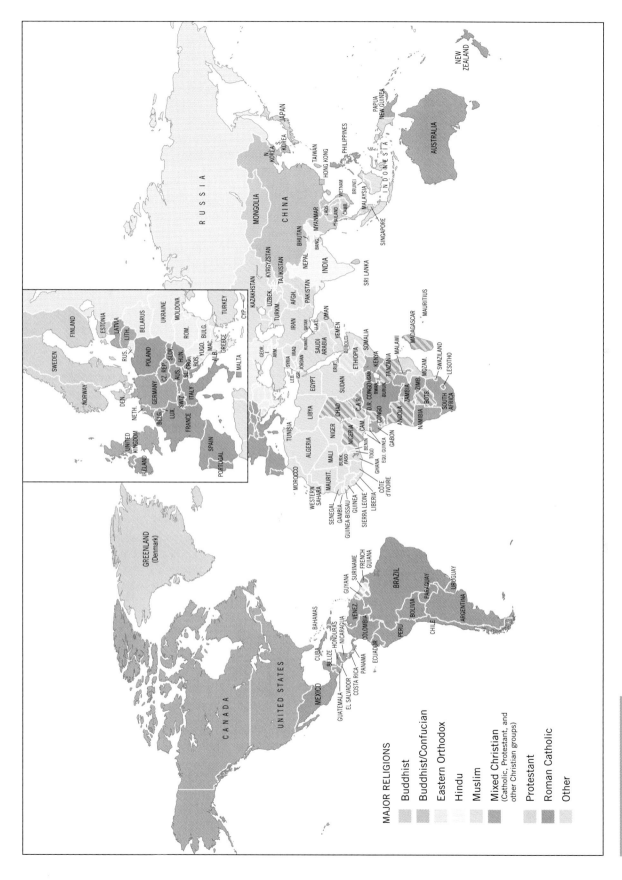

MAJOR RELIGIONS

Buddhist

Buddhist/Confucian

Eastern Orthodox

Hindu

Muslim

Mixed Christian
(Catholic, Protestant, and
other Christian groups)

Protestant

Roman Catholic

Other

M A P   4 . 3   **Major World Religions**

> Religion often plays an important role in shaping cultural values and business behavior. This pioneering Irani filmmaker must walk a fine line between her artistic vision and the dictates of Iran's Islam-based law.

pilgrimage sometime in their lives. The teachings of the Koran form the basis of the country's theocratic legal system, and 99 percent of the Saudi population is Muslim. Strong political pressure exists within the country to preserve its religious traditions. It is impossible to overstate the importance to foreign businesspeople of understanding the tenets of Islam as they apply to exporting, producing, marketing, or financing goods in the Saudi market. For example, work stops five times a day when the faithful are called to pray to Allah. A non-Muslim manager would be foolish to object to the practice even though it seemingly leads to lost production. Foreigners must also be considerate of their Saudi hosts during the holy month of Ramadan, when the Muslim faithful fast from sunrise to sunset. Female executives of Western firms face additional obstacles because of Saudi attitudes toward the appropriate roles for women, attitudes which stem from their religion. Even actions taken outside Saudi borders may affect commercial relations with the country. For example, McDonald's made a major faux pas when it printed the flags of the 24 soccer teams participating in the World Cup finals, including that of Saudi Arabia, on its paper takeout bags. The Saudi flag includes a sacred inscription that reads, "There is no God but Allah, and Mohammed is His Prophet." Muslims in Saudi Arabia and other countries were outraged, believing that Islam had been insulted by including the name of Allah on a container that would be thrown into garbage cans. McDonald's quickly apologized and pledged to stop using the bags, thereby diffusing a controversy that would have affected its business in Saudi Arabia and other Muslim countries.

Values and Attitudes

Culture also affects and reflects the secular values and attitudes of the members of a society. Values are the principles and standards accepted by the members; attitudes encompass the actions, feelings, and thoughts that result from those values. Cultural values often stem from deep-seated beliefs about the individual's position in relation to his or her deity, the family, and the social hierarchy that we discussed earlier. Cultural attitudes about such factors as time, age, education, and status reflect these values and in turn shape the behavior of and opportunities available to international businesses operating in a given culture.

Time.   Attitudes about time differ dramatically across cultures. In Anglo-Saxon cultures, the prevailing attitude is "time is money." Time represents the opportunity to produce more and to raise one's income, so it is not to be wasted. Underlying this attitude is the Protestant ethic, which encourages people to better their positions in life through hard work, and the puritanical belief that "idle hands are the Devil's workshop." As a result, U.S. and Canadian businesspeople expect meetings to start on time, and keeping a person waiting is considered extremely rude.

In Latin American cultures, however, few participants would think it unusual if a meeting began 45 minutes after the appointed time.[26] In Arab cultures, meetings not only often start later than the stated time, but they also may be interrupted by family and friends who wander in to exchange pleasantries. Westerners may interpret their host's willingness to talk to these unscheduled visitors as a sign of rudeness and as a subtle device to undermine the Westerners' dignity. Nothing could be further from the truth. This open-door policy reflects the hospitality of the host and the respect the host offers to all guests—just the sort of person with whom the Arab presumes the Westerners want to do business.[27]

Even the content of business meetings can vary by country. If a meeting is scheduled for 2:00 P.M., U.S., Canadian, and British businesspeople arrive at 1:55 P.M. and expect the meeting to start promptly at 2:00 P.M. After exchanging a few pleasantries, they then get down to business, following a well-planned agenda that has been distributed in advance to the participants. At the meeting the positions of the parties are set forth and disagreement is common. In contrast, in Japan or Saudi Arabia the initial meeting often focuses on determining whether the parties can trust each other and work together comfortably, rather than on the details of the proposed business. This time, however, is not being wasted. Because these cultures value personal relationships so highly, time is being utilized for an important purpose—assessing the qualities of potential business partners.

Age. Important cultural differences exist in attitudes toward age. Youthfulness is considered a virtue in the United States. Many U.S. firms devote much time and energy to identifying young "fast-trackers" and providing them with important, tough assignments, such as negotiating joint ventures with international partners. However, in Asian and Arab cultures, age is respected and a manager's stature is correlated with age. These cultural differences can lead to problems. For example, many foreign firms mistakenly send young, fast-track executives to negotiate with government officials of China. The Chinese, however, prefer to deal with older and more senior members of a firm, and thus may be offended by this approach.

In Japan's corporate culture, age and rank are highly correlated, but senior (and by definition, older) managers will not grant approval to a project until they have achieved a consensus among junior managers. Many foreign firms mistakenly focus their attention in negotiations on the senior Japanese managers, failing to realize that the goal should be to persuade the junior managers. Once the junior managers consent to a project, the senior managers will grant their approval as well.

Education. A country's formal system of public and private education is an important transmitter and reflection of the cultural values of its society. For example, U.S. primary and secondary schools emphasize the role of the individual and stress the development of self-reliance, creativity, and self-esteem. The United States prides itself on providing widespread access to higher education. Research universities, liberal arts colleges, and community colleges coexist to meet the educational needs of students with disparate incomes and intellectual talents. In contrast, the United Kingdom, reflecting its past class system, has historically provided an elite education to a relatively small number of students. Germany has well-developed apprenticeship programs that train new generations of skilled craftspeople and machinists for its manufacturing sector. The Japanese and French educational systems share a different focus. Their primary and secondary schools concentrate on rote memorization to prepare students to take a nationwide college entrance exam. The top-scoring students gain entry to a handful of prestigious universities—such as Tokyo University or Kyoto University in Japan and the five *grandes écoles* in France—which virtually guarantee their graduates placement in the most important corporate and governmental jobs in their societies.[28]

Status. The means by which status is achieved also vary across cultures. In some societies status is inherited as a result of the wealth or rank of one's ancestors. In others it is earned by the individual through personal accomplishments or professional achievements. In some European countries, for example, membership in the nobility ensures higher status than does mere personal achievement, and persons who inherited their wealth look down their noses at the nouveau riche. In the United States, however, hard-working entrepreneurs are honored, and their children are often disdained if they fail to match their parents' accomplishments.

In Japan a person's status depends on the status of the group to which he or she belongs. Thus Japanese businesspeople often introduce themselves by announcing not only their name but also their corporate affiliation. Attendance at elite universities such as Tokyo University or employment in elite organizations such as Toyota Motor Corporation or the Ministry of Finance grant one high status in Japanese society.

In India status is determined by one's caste. The caste system, on which much of India's social hierarchy is based, divides society into various groups including Brahmins (priests and intellectuals), Kshatriyas (soldiers and political leaders), Vaishyas (businesspeople), Sudras (farmers and workers), and untouchables, who perform the dirtiest and most unpleasant jobs. According to Hinduism, one's caste reflects the virtue (or lack of virtue) that one exhibited in a previous life. Particularly in rural areas, caste affects every facet of life, from the way a man shapes his mustache to the food the family eats to the job a person may hold.[29]

❯ SEEING THE FOREST, NOT THE TREES

These elements of national culture affect the behavior and expectations of managers and employees in the workplace. International businesspeople, who face the challenge of managing and motivating employees with different cultural backgrounds, need to understand these cultural elements if they are to be effective managers. To a beginning student in international business, however, this discussion of the elements of culture can be very confusing. Moreover, many students and businesspeople panic at the thought of memorizing a bunch of rules—the French do this, the Arabs do that, and so on. Fortunately, numerous scholars have tried to make sense of the various elements of culture. Their efforts make it easier for international managers to understand the big picture regarding a country's culture and how it affects their ability to manage their firms. In this section, we present the work of several of these scholars.

Hall's Low-Context–High-Context Approach

One useful way of characterizing differences in cultures is the low-context–high-context approach developed by Edmund and Mildred Hall.[30] In a **low-context culture** the words used by the speaker explicitly convey the speaker's message to the listener. Anglo-Saxon countries, such as Canada, the United Kingdom, and the United States, and Germanic countries are good examples of low-context cultures (see Figure 4.2). In a **high-context culture** the context in which a conversation occurs is just as important as the words that are actually spoken, and cultural clues are important in understanding what is being communicated. Examples are Arab countries and Japan.

Business behaviors in high-context cultures often differ from those in low-context cultures. For example, German advertising is typically fact oriented, while Japanese advertising is more emotion oriented.[31] High-context cultures place higher value on interpersonal relations in deciding whether to enter into a business arrangement. In such cultures preliminary meetings are often held to determine whether the parties can trust each other and work together comfortably. Low-context cultures place more importance on the specific terms of a transaction.[32] In low-context cultures such as Canada, the United Kingdom, and the United States, lawyers are often present at negotiations to ensure that their clients' interests are protected. Conversely, in high-context cultures such as Saudi Arabia, Japan, and Egypt, the presence of a lawyer, particularly at the

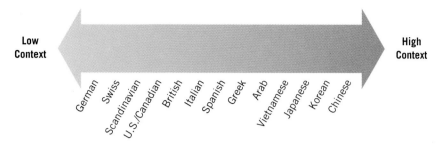

Low Context

High Context

German · Swiss · Scandinavian · U.S./Canadian · British · Italian · Spanish · Greek · Arab · Vietnamese · Japanese · Korean · Chinese

FIGURE 4.2

High- and Low-Context Cultures

Source: From Edward T. Hall, "How Cultures Collide," *Psychology Today*, July 1976, pp. 67–74. Reprinted with permission from *Psychology Today* Magazine, Copyright © 1976 (Sussex Publishers, Inc.).

initial meeting of the participants, would be viewed as a sign of distrust. Because these cultures value long-term relationships, an assumption by a potential partner that one cannot be trusted may be sufficient grounds to end the negotiations. Table 4.2 provides additional information about differences in negotiating styles across cultures.

The Cultural Cluster Approach

The cultural cluster approach is another technique for classifying and making sense of national cultures. Similarities exist among many cultures, thereby reducing some of the need to customize business practices to meet the demands of local cultures. Anthropologists, sociologists, and international business scholars have analyzed such factors as job satisfaction, work roles, and interpersonal work relations in an attempt to identify clusters of countries that share similar cultural values that can affect business practices. Map 4.4 shows the eight country clusters developed by one such team of researchers, Ronen and Shenkar. (In their study, four countries—Brazil, India, Israel, and Japan—were not placed in any cluster.) A **cultural cluster** comprises countries that share many cultural similarities, although differences do remain. Many clusters are based on language similarities, as is apparent in the Anglo, Germanic, Latin American, and Arab clusters and, to a lesser extent, in the Nordic and Latin European clusters. Of course, one can disagree with some placements of countries within clusters. Spain and the countries of Latin America share many culture values, as do Israel and the United States.

Many international businesses instinctively utilize the cultural cluster approach in formulating their internationalization strategies. Many U.S. firms' first exporting efforts focus on Canada and the United Kingdom. Hong Kong and Taiwanese firms have been very successful in exploiting China's markets. As we noted earlier in the chapter, many Spanish firms have chosen to focus their international expansion efforts on Spanish-speaking areas in the Americas.

Closeness of culture may affect the form that firms use to enter foreign markets. Researchers have found, for example, that Canadian firms are more likely to enter the British market by establishing joint ventures with British firms, while Japanese firms are more likely to enter the British market via a **greenfield investment**, that is, a brand-new investment. The likely reason for the difference? Because of the relative closeness of their national cultures, Canadian firms are more comfortable working with British partners than are Japanese firms.[33]

TABLE 4.2

Differences in Negotiating Styles across Cultures

JAPANESE	NORTH AMERICAN	LATIN AMERICAN
Emotional sensitivity highly valued.	Emotional sensitivity not highly valued.	Emotional sensitivity valued.
Hiding of emotions.	Dealing straightforwardly or impersonally.	Emotionally passionate.
Subtle power plays; conciliation.	Litigation not as much as conciliation.	Great power plays; use of weakness.
Loyalty to employer. Employer takes care of its employees.	Lack of commitment to employer. Breaking of ties by either if necessary.	Loyalty to employer (who is often family).
Group decision-making consensus.	Teamwork provides input to a decision maker.	Decisions come down from one individual.
Face-saving crucial. Decisions often made on basis of saving someone from embarrassment.	Decisions made on a cost-benefit basis. Face-saving does not always matter.	Face-saving crucial in decision making to preserve honor, dignity.
Decision makers openly influenced by special interests.	Decision makers influenced by special interests but this often not considered ethical.	Execution of special interests of decision maker expected, condoned.
Not argumentative. Quiet when right.	Argumentative when right or wrong, but impersonal.	Argumentative when right or wrong; passionate.
What is down in writing must be accurate, valid.	Great importance given to documentation as evidential proof.	Impatient with documentation as obstacle to understanding general principles.
Step-by-step approach to decision making.	Methodically organized decision making.	Impulsive, spontaneous decision making.
Good of group is the ultimate aim.	Profit motive or good of individual ultimate aim.	What is good for the group is good for the individual.
Cultivate a good emotional social setting for decision making. Get to know decision makers.	Decision making impersonal. Avoid involvements, conflicts of interest.	Personalism necessary for good decision making.

Source: From Pierre Casse, *Training for the Multicultural Manager: A Practical and Cross-Cultural Approach to the Management of People*. Washington, D.C.: SIETAR International, © 1982. Reprinted with permission of the author.

Hofstede's Five Dimensions

The most influential studies analyzing cultural differences and synthesizing cultural similarities are those performed by Geert Hofstede, a Dutch researcher who studied 116,000 people working in dozens of different countries.[34] Although Hofstede's work has been criticized for methodological weaknesses and his own cultural biases, it remains the largest and most comprehensive work of its kind. Hofstede's work identified five important dimensions along which people seem to differ across cultures. These dimensions are shown in Figure 4.3. Note that these dimensions reflect tendencies within cultures, not absolutes. Within any given culture, there are likely to be people at every point on each dimension.

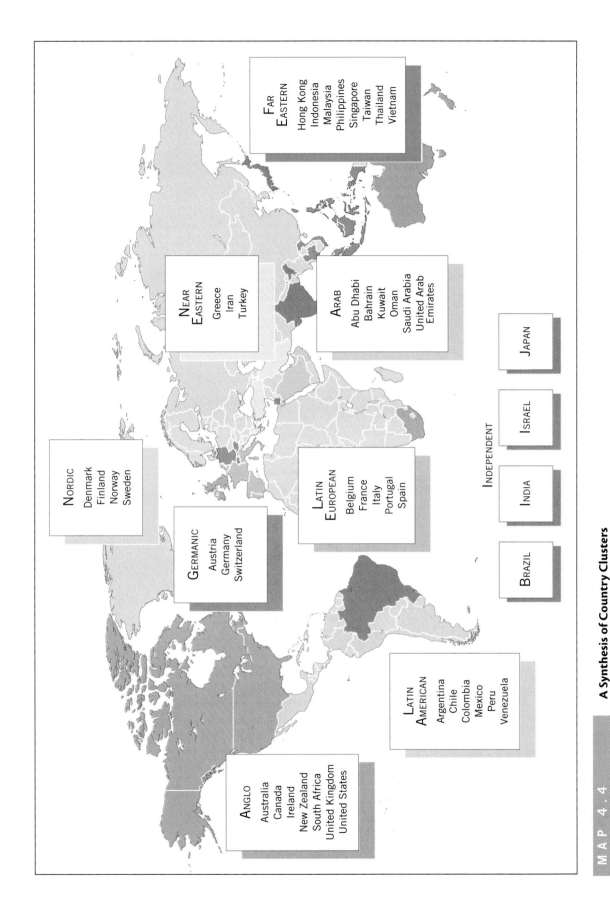

MAP 4.4   **A Synthesis of Country Clusters**

FAR EASTERN
Hong Kong
Indonesia
Malaysia
Philippines
Singapore
Taiwan
Thailand
Vietnam

NEAR EASTERN
Greece
Iran
Turkey

ARAB
Abu Dhabi
Bahrain
Kuwait
Oman
Saudi Arabia
United Arab Emirates

NORDIC
Denmark
Finland
Norway
Sweden

GERMANIC
Austria
Germany
Switzerland

LATIN EUROPEAN
Belgium
France
Italy
Portugal
Spain

INDEPENDENT

JAPAN

ISRAEL

INDIA

BRAZIL

LATIN AMERICAN
Argentina
Chile
Colombia
Mexico
Peru
Venezuela

ANGLO
Australia
Canada
Ireland
New Zealand
South Africa
United Kingdom
United States

Source: From Simcha Ronen and Oded Shenkar, "Clustering Countries on Attitudinal Dimensions: A Review and Synthesis," *Academy of Management Review*, Vol. 10, No. 3 (1985), p. 449. Reprinted with permission.

FIGURE 4.3

Hofstede's Five Dimensions of National Culture

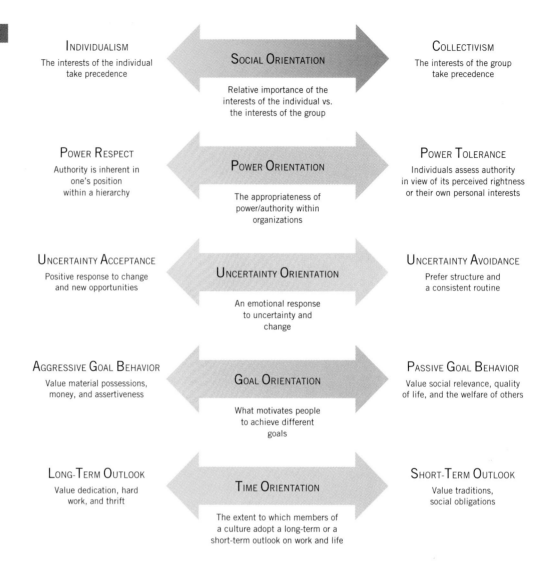

INDIVIDUALISM
The interests of the individual take precedence

SOCIAL ORIENTATION

Relative importance of the interests of the individual vs. the interests of the group

COLLECTIVISM
The interests of the group take precedence

POWER RESPECT
Authority is inherent in one's position within a hierarchy

POWER ORIENTATION

The appropriateness of power/authority within organizations

POWER TOLERANCE
Individuals assess authority in view of its perceived rightness or their own personal interests

UNCERTAINTY ACCEPTANCE
Positive response to change and new opportunities

UNCERTAINTY ORIENTATION

An emotional response to uncertainty and change

UNCERTAINTY AVOIDANCE
Prefer structure and a consistent routine

AGGRESSIVE GOAL BEHAVIOR
Value material possessions, money, and assertiveness

GOAL ORIENTATION

What motivates people to achieve different goals

PASSIVE GOAL BEHAVIOR
Value social relevance, quality of life, and the welfare of others

LONG-TERM OUTLOOK
Value dedication, hard work, and thrift

TIME ORIENTATION

The extent to which members of a culture adopt a long-term or a short-term outlook on work and life

SHORT-TERM OUTLOOK
Value traditions, social obligations

Social Orientation

The first dimension identified by Hofstede is social orientation.[35] **Social orientation** is a person's beliefs about the relative importance of the individual and the groups to which that person belongs. The two extremes of social orientation, summarized in Table 4.3, are individualism and collectivism. *Individualism* is the cultural belief that the person comes first. Key values of individualistic people include a high degree of self-respect and independence. These people often put their own career interests before the good of their organizations, and they tend to assess decisions in terms of how those decisions affect them as individuals. Hofstede's research suggested that people in the United States, the United Kingdom, Australia, Canada, New Zealand, and the Netherlands tend to be relatively individualistic.

Collectivism, the opposite of individualism, is the belief that the group comes first. Societies that tend to be collectivistic are usually characterized by well-defined social networks, including extended families, tribes, and coworkers. People are expected to put the good of the group ahead of their own personal welfare, interests, or success. Individual behavior in such cultures is strongly influenced by the emotion of shame; when a group fails, its members take the failure very personally and experience shame. In addition, group members try to fit into their

	COLLECTIVISM	INDIVIDUALISM
In the family	Education toward "we" consciousness	Education toward "I" consciousness
	Opinions predetermined by group	Private opinion expected
	Obligations to family or in-group: • Harmony • Respect • Shame	Obligations to self: • Self-interest • Self-actualization • Guilt
At school	Learning is for the young only	Continuing education
	Learn how to do	Learn how to learn
At the workplace	Value standards differ for in-group and out-groups; particularism	Same value standards apply to all: universalism
	Other people seen as members of their group	Other people seen as potential resources
	Relationship prevails over task	Task prevails over relationship
	Moral model of employer-employee relationship	Calculative model of employer-employee relationship

TABLE 4.3

Extremes of Social Orientation

Source: Reprinted from Geert Hofstede, "The Business of International Business Is Culture," *International Business Review*, Copyright 1994, page 3, with kind permission from Elsevier Science Ltd., The Boulevard, Langford Lane, Kidlington OX5 1GB, UK.

group harmoniously, with a minimum of conflict or tension. Hofstede found that people from Mexico, Greece, Hong Kong, Taiwan, Peru, Singapore, Colombia, and Pakistan tend to be relatively collectivistic in their values.

International firms must be aware of differences in the social orientations of countries. Nepotism is often frowned on in individualistic cultures but may be a normal hiring practice in collectivist cultures. In countries such as the United States, where individualism is a cultural norm, many workers believe they should be compensated according to their individual achievements. They judge the fairness of any compensation system by whether it achieves this objective. U.S. firms thus spend much time and resources assessing individual performance in order to link pay and performance. A firm that fails to do this will likely lose its more productive employees to firms that do.

Because of its group-oriented culture, prevailing compensation practices in Japan are very different. In most Japanese corporations a person's compensation reflects the group to which he or she belongs, not personal achievements. For example, all individuals who join Toshiba's engineering staff in 2001 receive the same compensation, regardless of their individual talents, insights, and efforts. The salaries received by each cohort within the corporation reflect seniority: Engineers who join Toshiba in 2001 receive higher salaries than engineers who join the firm in 2002 but lower salaries than engineers who start in 2000. This compensation structure, which lasts for the first six to eight years the employee works for the firm, encourages employees to focus on group goals. Although a handful of Japanese corporations have begun to abandon these group-oriented approaches in favor of more merit-oriented ones, individual-oriented approaches remain the exception, not the rule.

These cultural differences help explain the widely publicized differences in CEO pay between the United States and Japan. In group-oriented Japan the CEO's pay symbolically reflects the performance of the group. In the United States the CEO's pay is presumed to measure the CEO's contribution to the firm. Even the way the issue is framed reflects the cultural values of the United States: The question "How can President Smith of the XYZ Corporation be worth $10 million?" implicitly assumes that the CEO's pay should measure his or her individual contribution to the organization.

A similar pattern characterizes the career progression and job mobility of employees. In individualistic societies a person's career path often involves switching employers in search of higher-paying and more challenging jobs so that the person can prove his or her capabilities in new and changing circumstances. Indeed, in the United States a person's failure to accept a better paying job at another firm raises suspicions about the person's ambition, motivation, and dedication to his or her career. However, in collectivistic cultures, such as Japan, changing jobs is often interpreted as reflecting disloyalty to the collective good (the firm) and may brand the person as unworthy of trust.[36] Because of this stigma, job switchers traditionally have had difficulties finding appropriate jobs in other Japanese companies. Although this norm is changing because of the economic stresses Japan underwent in the 1990s, job mobility is much lower in Japan than in the United States.

Power Orientation

The second dimension Hofstede proposed is power orientation. **Power orientation** refers to the beliefs that people in a culture hold about the appropriateness of power and authority differences in hierarchies such as business organizations. The extremes of the dimension of power orientation are summarized in Table 4.4.

Some cultures are characterized by **power respect**. This means that people in a culture tend to accept the power and authority of their superiors simply on the basis of the superiors' positions in the hierarchy. These same people also tend to respect the superiors' right to that power. People at all levels in a firm accept the decisions and mandates of those above them because of the implicit belief that higher-level positions carry the right to make decisions and issue mandates. Hofstede found people in France, Spain, Mexico, Japan, Brazil, Indonesia, and Singapore to be relatively power respecting.

In contrast, people in cultures characterized by **power tolerance** attach much less significance to a person's position in the hierarchy. These people are more willing to question a decision or mandate from someone at a higher level or perhaps even refuse to accept it. They are willing to follow a leader when that

TABLE 4.4

Extremes of Power Orientation

	POWER TOLERANCE	POWER RESPECT
In the family	Children encouraged to have a will of their own	Children educated toward obedience to parents
	Parents treated as equals	Parents treated as superiors
At school	Student-centered education (initiative)	Teacher-centered education (order)
	Learning represents impersonal "truth"	Learning represents personal "wisdom" from teacher (guru)
At the workplace	Hierarchy means an inequality of roles, established for convenience	Hierarchy means existential inequality
	Subordinates expect to be consulted	Subordinates expect to be told what to do
	Ideal boss is resourceful democrat	Ideal boss is benevolent autocrat (good father)

Source: Reprinted from Geert Hofstede, "The Business of International Business Is Culture," *International Business Review*, Copyright 1994, page 3, with kind permission from Elsevier Science Ltd., The Boulevard, Langford Lane, Kidlington, OX5 1GB, UK.

leader is perceived to be right or when it seems to be in their own self-interest to do so but not because of the leader's intangible right to issue orders. Hofstede's work suggested that people in the United States, Israel, Austria, Denmark, Ireland, Norway, Germany, and New Zealand tend to be more power tolerant.

Persons from power-tolerant cultures believe that hierarchies exist to solve problems and organize tasks within organizations. Power-respecting business cultures, such as those in Indonesia and Italy, assume that hierarchies are developed so that everyone knows who has authority over whom. In approaching a new project, power-tolerating Americans would first define the tasks at hand and then assemble the project team. Conversely, power-respecting Indonesians would first determine who would be in charge and then assess whether the project would be feasible under that manager's leadership. Such attitudes obviously have important consequences for international businesses. As the opening case noted, a power-tolerant culture may be more suited to the needs of dot-com startups than a power-respecting culture.

These cultural differences regarding the role of hierarchies were highlighted in a survey that asked international managers to respond to the following statement: "In order to have efficient work relationships, it is often necessary to bypass the hierarchical line." Swedish, British, and U.S. managers agreed with the statement. They believed that superiors do not necessarily have all the information subordinates need to make decisions and that it is efficient for a subordinate to seek out the person who has the relevant information regardless of the firm's formal hierarchy. Italian managers, on the other hand, disagreed: Bypassing a superior is a sign of insubordination, not efficiency, in the Italian business culture.[37]

Differing cultural attitudes toward power orientation can lead to misunderstandings in business. For example, when firms are negotiating with each other, a firm from a power-tolerant country will often send a team composed of experts on the subject, without concern for rank or seniority. However, a team composed of junior employees, no matter how knowledgeable they are about the problem at hand, may be taken as an insult by managers from a power-respecting culture, who expect to deal with persons of rank equal to their own. Also, the use of informalities by U.S. managers—for example, calling a counterpart by that person's first name—may be misinterpreted by managers from power-respecting cultures as an insulting attempt to diminish another's authority. Similarly, the willingness of U.S. managers to roll up their sleeves and pitch in on the factory floor during an emergency is likely to win praise from U.S. production workers. Conversely, Indian managers would find performing such menial tasks beneath their dignity. Worse, managers so lacking in self-respect would be deemed unworthy of respect or obedience from their peers and subordinates.[38]

At other times such cultural norms may lead to tragedy. During the late 1990s, for example, Korean Airlines (KAL) suffered an abnormally high number of fatal accidents. Some aviation safety experts attributed the problem to the power-respecting norms of Korean culture. Behavioral scientists found that KAL first officers (the second-in-command pilots) were often unwilling to suggest to their captains that the captain might be making a mistake even if the mistake was putting the aircraft in danger. KAL's reliance on ex-military pilots exacerbated the problem because military pilots have been trained to obey the orders issued by the chain of command. To remedy this problem, KAL changed its cockpit recruitment strategies, focusing on hiring foreign pilots and nonmilitary pilots who would be more likely to question the captain in case of emergency.[39]

We can gain additional perspectives on Hofstede's dimensions by viewing them in combinations. For example, when social orientation and power orientation are superimposed, individualistic and power-tolerant countries seem to cluster, as do collectivistic and power-respecting countries (see Figure 4.4).

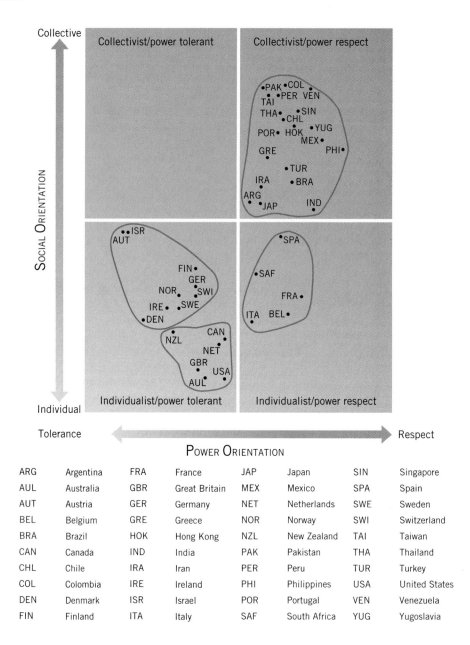

ARG	Argentina	FRA	France	JAP	Japan	SIN	Singapore
AUL	Australia	GBR	Great Britain	MEX	Mexico	SPA	Spain
AUT	Austria	GER	Germany	NET	Netherlands	SWE	Sweden
BEL	Belgium	GRE	Greece	NOR	Norway	SWI	Switzerland
BRA	Brazil	HOK	Hong Kong	NZL	New Zealand	TAI	Taiwan
CAN	Canada	IND	India	PAK	Pakistan	THA	Thailand
CHL	Chile	IRA	Iran	PER	Peru	TUR	Turkey
COL	Colombia	IRE	Ireland	PHI	Philippines	USA	United States
DEN	Denmark	ISR	Israel	POR	Portugal	VEN	Venezuela
FIN	Finland	ITA	Italy	SAF	South Africa	YUG	Yugoslavia

Uncertainty Orientation

The third basic dimension of individual differences Hofstede studied is uncertainty orientation. **Uncertainty orientation** is the feeling people have regarding uncertain and ambiguous situations. The extremes of this dimension are summarized in Table 4.5.

People in cultures characterized by **uncertainty acceptance** are stimulated by change and thrive on new opportunities. Ambiguity is seen as a context within which an individual can grow, develop, and carve out new opportunities. In these cultures certainty carries with it a sense of monotony, routineness, and overbearing structure. Hofstede suggested that many people from the United States, Denmark, Sweden, Canada, Singapore, Hong Kong, and Australia are uncertainty accepting.

In contrast, people in cultures characterized by **uncertainty avoidance** dislike ambiguity and will avoid it whenever possible. Ambiguity and change are seen as undesirable. These people tend to prefer a structured and routine, even bureaucratic, way of doing things. Hofstede found that many people in Israel, Austria, Japan, Italy, Colombia, France, Peru, and Germany tend to avoid uncertainty whenever possible.

	UNCERTAINTY ACCEPTANCE	UNCERTAINTY AVOIDANCE
In the family	What is different is ridiculous or curious	What is different is dangerous
	Ease, indolence, low stress	Higher anxiety and stress
	Aggression and emotions not shown	Showing of aggression and emotions accepted
At school	Students comfortable with • Unstructured learning situations • Vague objectives • Broad assignments • No timetables Teachers may say "I don't know"	Students comfortable with • Structured learning situations • Precise objectives • Detailed assignments • Strict timetables Teachers should have all the answers
At the workplace	Dislike of rules, written or unwritten	Emotional need for rules, written or unwritten
	Less formalization and standardization	More formalization and standardization

TABLE 4.5

Extremes of Uncertainty Orientation

Source: Reprinted from Geert Hofstede, "The Business of International Business Is Culture," *International Business Review*, Copyright 1994, page 3, with kind permission from Elsevier Science Ltd., The Boulevard, Langford Lane, Kidlington OX5 1GB, UK.

Uncertainty orientation affects many aspects of managing international firms. Those operating in uncertainty-avoiding countries, for example, tend to adopt more rigid hierarchies and more elaborate rules and procedures for doing business. Conversely, uncertainty-accepting cultures are more tolerant of flexible hierarchies, rules, and procedures. Risk taking ("nothing ventured, nothing gained") is highly valued in uncertainty-accepting countries such as the United States and Hong Kong, whereas preserving the status and prestige of the firm through conservative, low-risk strategies is more important in uncertainty-avoiding countries such as Spain, Belgium, and Argentina. As the opening case indicated, uncertainty-accepting cultures may be more attuned with the needs of the new e-commerce economy.

The second-guessing that followed the 1998 crash of Swissair 111 off the coast of Nova Scotia provides a dramatic example of how uncertainty orientation influences business practices. As you may remember, smoke suddenly filled the cabin of the plane as it was enroute from New York to Geneva. The Swissair pilot swung the troubled aircraft out to sea in order to dump excess fuel before landing. Unfortunately, the plane plunged into the sea before it could reach safety. A controversy broke out over whether the pilot's decision to circle and dump fuel before landing was correct. Some U.S. airline pilots interviewed by the media suggested that the pilot should have landed the plane as soon as possible once smoke was detected. Swissair officials defended their pilot, noting that the captain followed Swissair's emergency procedures published in the carrier's operating manual. The U.S. pilots retorted that in such emergencies pilots should exercise their independent judgment, regardless of what is contained in the company manual. Swissair officials countered that the procedures detailed in the manual reflected the state-of-the-art understanding of what to do in an emergency, and thus its pilots did the right thing in adhering to the manual. The "rules are there to be obeyed" viewpoint of Swissair's officials reflects their country's uncertainty-avoiding culture, while the "rules are made to be broken" attitude of U.S. pilots reflects America's uncertainty-accepting norms.

It is interesting to consider uncertainty orientation along with the social orientation dimension. Job mobility is likely to be higher in uncertainty-accepting countries than in those characterized by uncertainty avoidance. Some Japanese firms have traditionally used lifetime employment practices partly in response to the uncertainty-avoiding and collectivistic tendencies of the Japanese culture. However, lifetime employment—as well as the seniority-based pay and promotion policies traditionally used by Japanese firms—may not be an effective policy when transplanted to individualistic and uncertainty-accepting countries. For example, Japanese firms operating in uncertainty-accepting Canada and the United States have been forced to modify their pay and promotion policies because North American workers are more oriented toward an individualistic "pay me what I'm worth" attitude and are less worried about job security than are their counterparts in Japan. Similarly, as the opening case indicated, SAP's unwillingness to grant its U.S. employees stock options caused the German software company to lose many of its best American employees.

Goal Orientation

Hofstede's fourth dimension, **goal orientation**, is the manner in which people are motivated to work toward different kinds of goals. One extreme on the goal orientation continuum is aggressive goal behavior (see Table 4.6). People who exhibit **aggressive goal behavior** tend to place a high premium on material possessions, money, and assertiveness. At the other extreme, people who adopt **passive goal behavior** place a higher value on social relationships, quality of life, and concern for others.

According to Hofstede, cultures that value aggressive goal behavior also tend to define gender-based roles somewhat rigidly, whereas cultures that emphasize passive goal behavior do not. For example, in cultures characterized by extremely aggressive goal behavior, men are expected to work and to focus their careers in traditionally male occupations; women are generally expected not to work outside the home and to focus on their families. If they do work outside the home, they are usually expected to pursue work in areas traditionally dominated by women. According to Hofstede's research, many people in Japan tend to exhibit relatively aggressive goal behavior, whereas many people in Germany, Mexico, Italy, and the United States exhibit moderately aggressive goal behavior. Men and women in passive goal behavior cultures are more likely both to pursue diverse careers and to be well represented within any given occupation. People from the Netherlands, Norway, Sweden, Denmark, and Finland tend to exhibit relatively passive goal behavior.

TABLE 4.6

Extremes of Goal Orientation

	PASSIVE GOAL BEHAVIOR	AGGRESSIVE GOAL BEHAVIOR
In the family	Stress on relationships	Stress on achievement
	Solidarity	Competition
	Resolution of conflicts by compromise and negotiation	Resolution of conflicts by fighting them out
At school	Average student is norm	Best students are norm
	System rewards students' social adaptation	System rewards students' academic performance
	Student's failure at school is relatively minor problem	Student's failure at school is disaster; may lead to suicide
At the workplace	Assertiveness ridiculed	Assertiveness appreciated
	Undersell yourself	Oversell yourself
	Stress on life quality	Stress on careers
	Intuition	Decisiveness

Source: Reprinted from Geert Hofstede, "The Business of International Business Is Culture," *International Business Review*, Copyright 1994, page 3, with kind permission from Elsevier Science Ltd., The Boulevard, Langford Lane, Kidlington OX5 1GB, UK.

These cultural attitudes affect international business practices in many ways. For example, one study showed that decisions made by Danish managers (a passive goal behavior culture) incorporate societal concerns to a greater extent than decisions made by more profit-oriented U.S., British, and German executives (from more aggressive goal behavior cultures).[40] Similarly, studies of the Swedish workforce indicate that the country's egalitarian traditions, as well as workers' desires to maintain comfortable work schedules, often make promotions less desirable than in other countries. Many Swedish workers prefer more fringe benefits rather than higher salaries.[41] Or consider the impact of the role of women in business. In Sweden the high proportion of dual-career families makes it difficult for many workers to accept a promotion if it entails moving. Not surprisingly, Swedish firms are among the world's leaders in providing fringe benefits such as maternity and paternity leave and company-sponsored child care.

Time Orientation

Hofstede's fifth dimension, **time orientation**, is the extent to which members of a culture adopt a long-term versus a short-term outlook on work, life, and other aspects of society. Some cultures, such as those of Japan, Hong Kong, Taiwan, and South Korea, have a long-term, future orientation that values dedication, hard work, perseverance, and thrift. Other cultures, including those of Pakistan and West Africa, tend to focus on the past and present, emphasizing respect for traditions and fulfillment of social obligations. Hofstede's work suggests that the United States and Germany tend to have an intermediate time orientation.

INTERNATIONAL MANAGEMENT AND CULTURAL DIFFERENCES ‹

Some experts believe the world's cultures are growing more similar as a result of improvements in communication and transportation. Thanks to MTV and CNN, teenagers worldwide have been able to enjoy the wit and wisdom of Beavis and Butthead, while their parents can learn about politics, scandals, disasters, and culture in other countries. Lower airfares generated by increased airline competition mean that more tourists can learn about other cultures firsthand. MNCs facilitate this process of **cultural convergence**, for better or worse, through their advertisements that define appropriate lifestyles, attitudes, and goals and by bringing new management techniques, technologies, and cultural values to the countries in which they operate.

Understanding New Cultures

Nonetheless, cultural differences do exist. When dealing with a new culture, many international businesspeople make the mistake of relying on the **self-reference criterion**, the unconscious use of one's own culture to help assess new surroundings. For example, a U.S. salesperson who calls on a German customer in Frankfurt and asks about the customer's family is acting politely according to U.S. culture—the salesperson's reference point—but rudely according to German culture, thereby generating ill will and the potential loss of a customer.[42] In behaving as expected in the United States, the salesperson forgot the answer to a critical question: "Who is the foreigner?"

Successful international businesspeople traveling abroad must remember that they are the foreigners and must attempt to behave according to the rules of the culture at hand. There are numerous ways to obtain knowledge about other cultures to achieve **cross-cultural literacy**. The best and most common means, not surprisingly, is personal experience that results from conducting business abroad—as part of either a business trip or a long-term assignment—or from nonbusiness travel.[43] Many firms, such as Motorola, offer cross-cultural training programs to their employees headed for foreign assignments.[44] Information about spe-

cific cultures can also be obtained from various published sources. For example, Brigham Young University publishes a series of highly regarded *Culturegrams* on more than 175 countries, and the U.S. government publishes detailed descriptions and analyses of the economies, political systems, natural resources, and cultures of the world's countries in a series of volumes called *Country Studies.*

Cross-cultural literacy is the first step in **acculturation**, the process by which people not only understand a foreign culture but also modify and adapt their behavior to make it compatible with that culture. Acculturation is of particular importance to home country managers who frequently interact with host country nationals—for example, a plant manager from the home country or a marketing director working overseas at a foreign subsidiary.

To complicate matters further, many countries have more than one culture, although the level of such cultural diversity varies by country. Japan, with a population consisting of 99.4 percent ethnic Japanese, is extremely homogeneous. Conversely, the United States is culturally heterogeneous, with significant Caribbean, Latin American, Middle Eastern, Hispanic, African, and Asian communities complementing the dominant Anglo-Saxon culture. Successful international businesspeople must recognize the attributes of the primary national culture as well as any important subcultures in culturally heterogeneous societies.

› Rapid changes in telecommunications technologies have accelerated the process of cultural convergence and opened up new opportunities for international businesses. Nortel has targeted Latin America as a prime market for its wireless services.

Cultural Differences and Ethics

Cultural differences often create ethical problems. Acceptable behavior in one culture may be viewed as immoral in another. For example, in many poorer countries low-paid workers often expect a small payment in return for stamping a passport or finding a "lost" hotel reservation. Such behavior may appear inappropriate to members of richer countries like the United States or Germany, where such a payment would be considered a bribe.

Consider the following scenarios:

- To assist the sale of your products in a particular foreign market, it is suggested that you pay a 10 percent commission to a "go-between" who has access to high-ranking government officials in that market. You suspect, but do not know, that the go-between will split the commission with the government officials who decide which goods to buy. Should you do it? Does it make a difference if your competitors routinely pay such commissions?

- You have a long-standing client in a country that imposes foreign exchange controls. The client asks you to pad your invoices by 25 percent. For example, you would ship the client $100,000 worth of goods but would invoice the client for $125,000. On the basis of your invoice, the client would obtain the $125,000 from the country's central bank. The client then would pay you $100,000 and have you put the remaining $25,000 in a Swiss bank account in the client's name. Should you do it? Would it make a difference if your client is a member of a politically unpopular minority and may have to flee the country at a moment's notice?

Needless to say, your answers to these questions will reflect your culture as well as your personal circumstances.

CHAPTER REVIEW

Summary

Understanding cultural differences is critical to the success of firms engaging in international business. A society's culture affects the political, economic, social, and ethical rules a firm must follow in its business dealings within that society.

A society's culture also reflects its values, beliefs, behaviors, customs, and attitudes. Culture is learned behavior that is transmitted from one member of a society to another. The elements of culture are interrelated and reinforce each other. These elements are adaptive, changing as outside forces affect the society. Culture not only is shared by the society's members but also defines the society's membership.

A society's culture comprises numerous elements. The social structure reflects the culture's beliefs about the individual's role in society and the importance of mobility within that society.

Language is another important cultural element because it allows members of the society to communicate with each other. Communication can also take nonverbal forms, such as facial expressions, hand gestures, voice intonation, and use of space. These nonverbal forms of communication are often difficult for outsiders to master.

Approximately 80 percent of the world's population claims some religious affiliation. Religion influences attitudes toward work, investment, consumption, and responsibility for one's behavior. Religion may also influence the formulation of a country's laws.

A society's culture reflects and shapes its values and attitudes, including those toward time, age, status, and education. These affect business operations in numerous ways, such as in hiring practices, job turnover, and the design of compensation programs.

Researchers have grouped countries according to common cultural characteristics. Hall and Hall developed the low-context–high-context classification scheme, which focuses on the importance of context within a culture. To some extent the existence of cultural clusters eases the difficulties of doing business internationally. Researchers have discovered that many countries share similar attitudes toward work roles, job satisfaction, and other work-related aspects of life. Often countries within a cultural cluster share a common language.

The pioneering research of Geert Hofstede has identified five basic cultural dimensions along which people may differ: social orientation, power orientation, uncertainty orientation, goal orientation, and time orientation. These differences affect business behavior in numerous ways and often lead to cross-cultural misunderstandings.

Cultural differences often create ethical dilemmas for international businesspeople. Behaviors that are acceptable in the home country culture may be deemed inappropriate by the host country culture. Such cultural conflicts commonly arise among persons from different cultural backgrounds, and international businesspeople must be prepared to deal with any ethical conflicts that result.

Review Questions

1. What is culture?
2. What are the primary characteristics of culture?
3. What is a lingua franca? Why has English become a lingua franca?
4. What is backtranslation? What problem is it designed to solve?
5. Describe the difference between high-context and low-context cultures.
6. What are cultural clusters?
7. What are individualism and collectivism? How do they differ?
8. Discuss the differences in pay systems between U.S. and Japanese firms. To what extent are these differences culturally determined?
9. What is power orientation?
10. What is uncertainty orientation?
11. What are aggressive and passive goal behaviors? How do they differ?
12. What is the self-reference criterion?

Questions for Discussion

1. How can international businesspeople avoid relying on the self-reference criterion when dealing with people from other cultures?
2. How important is it for native English-speaking people to learn a second language? Should all business students whose native tongue is English be required to learn another language? Why or why not?
3. U.S. law protects women from job discrimination, but many countries do not offer women such protection. Suppose several important job opportunities arise at overseas factories owned by your firm. These factories, however, are located in countries that severely restrict the working rights of women, and you fear that female managers will be ineffective there. Should you adopt gender-blind selection policies for these positions? Does it make a difference if you have good reason to fear for the physical safety of your female managers? Does it make a difference if the restrictions are cultural rather than legal in nature?
4. Under what circumstances should international businesspeople impose the ethics of their culture on foreigners with whom they do business? Does it make a difference if the activity is conducted in the home or the host country?
5. Is nonverbal communication more important or less important when two people speak different languages? What are the pitfalls of trying to use only nonverbal communication to "talk" to someone from another country?
6. How would you evaluate yourself on each of Hofstede's dimensions?
7. Assume you have just been transferred by your firm to a new facility in a foreign location. How would you go about assessing the country's culture along Hofstede's dimensions? How would you incorporate your findings into conducting business there?

BUILDING GLOBAL SKILLS

This exercise will help give you insights into how cultural and social factors affect international business decisions. Your instructor will divide the class into groups of four or five people. Each group then picks any three products from the first column of the following list and any three countries from the second column. (Or, your instructor may assign each group three products and three countries.)

Products	Countries
swimsuits	France
CD players	Singapore
desks and bookcases	Poland
men's neckties	Saudi Arabia
women's purses	Taiwan
throat lozenges	Italy
film	South Africa
shoes	Russia

Assume that your firm already markets its three products in your home country. It has a well-known trademark and slogan for each product, and each product is among the market leaders. Assume further that your firm has decided to begin exporting each product to each of the three countries. Research the cultures of those three countries to determine how, if at all, you may need to adjust packaging, promotion, advertising, and so forth in order to maximize your firm's potential for success. Do not worry too much about whether a market truly exists (assume that market research has already determined one does). Focus instead on how your product will be received in each country given that country's culture.

Follow-Up Questions

1. What were your primary sources of information about the three countries? How easy or difficult was it to find information?
2. Can you think of specific products that are in high demand in your home country that would simply not work in specific other countries because of cultural factors?
3. How do you think foreign firms assess your home culture as they contemplate introducing their products into your market?

WORKING WITH THE WEB: BUILDING GLOBAL INTERNET SKILLS

Learning About Cultural Values

A variety of Internet sites provide useful information about cultural differences among countries. (Check out the textbook's Web site for linkages to some of the most interesting ones.) Pick three countries that Hofstede studied. Visit several of these Web sites and review the material provided for your three countries. Relate the material you find to Hofstede's work. For example, does the material about each country on the Web site seem consistent or inconsistent with Hofstede's findings about that country? If relationships between the Web site and Hofstede's analysis are not obvious, can you speculate as to why this is true?

 WE INVITE YOU TO VISIT THIS BOOK'S COMPANION WEB SITE AT www.prenhall.com/griffin

IN THE NEWS

1. Visit the *Financial Times* Web site at *www.ft.com* and click on "News." Then click on "Country Surveys." Scroll down and click on "Work-Life Balance," and research some of the feature articles under that heading. Compare the issues that arise in various countries and cultures. What can you learn about their differences and similarities?

2. Compare the U.S., U.K., and global editions of the *Financial Times* homepage. What differences can you find? Why do you think they exist?

CLOSING CASE

The Benefits of Foreign Exchange

The Athenaeum Hotel and Apartments in London's Piccadilly is a small privately owned hotel which has business travellers from the U.S. as the majority of its guests. Sally Bulloch, general manager, says one way of finding out if the hotel was giving customers what they wanted was to compare it with what they are offered in the U.S.

She suggested swapping jobs for a week with Valerie Ferguson, general manager of the Ritz-Carlton in Atlanta, Georgia, and secretary of the American Hotel and Motel Association. . . .

Ferguson decided to take up Bulloch's offer and go ahead with the swap. She says: "I had no idea what I would get out of it but I saw it was an opportunity to gain an insight into how I could further develop my product. About 35 percent to 40 percent of our guests are international and I wanted to walk away with a better idea of how to service that business and how to build it up."

Business travel is increasingly based on the notion of servicing global travellers with similar wants and needs. Ms. Ferguson says, however, that there can be enormous differences.

"One thing that has left an indelible impression is that European travellers are not as vocal as Americans—you have to take more time to pull the information out. In America, a guest might go to the front desk and say 'my breakfast was terrible,' but the British are just not going to do that. We've got to find a way of getting that feedback, rather than make the assumption that everything is OK."

One way might be to contact visitors after they have left the hotel. "I don't think they will speak to you unless something major happens but once they get home or to the office, they might," she says.

Guests with limited English could be inhibited by language difficulties, and Ms. Ferguson believes one of her achievements over the past five years at the Ritz-Carlton is to ensure that staff speaking a number of languages are available at all times.

She is impressed by the efforts made at the Athenaeum to make guests feel at home. "There are all these reminders that you are at home—whether it's a bowl of apples or wonderful nick-nacks in the lobby. We like to think you can get a homey atmosphere in a Ritz-Carlton—we have afternoon teas and a special breakfast for Japanese guests—but customers don't want it so comfortable that it's like an old pair of shoes."

For her part, Sally Bulloch of the Athenaeum believes there is a difference in attention to detail. "It's higher over here. For instance, I've often found that if there is a bowl of fruit in an American hotel, it tends to stay there all week, whereas we change it every day." But she admires the informality of U.S. hospitality, and would like to incorporate more of it in the hotel. "We can sometimes be too British," says Ms. Bulloch. "It took me 10 years to get a hamburger on our room-service menu. I kept suggesting that was what our guests wanted but kept being told 'that is not what we do at the Athenaeum.'"

She adds: "Many travellers want a quick tea or coffee but do not want to sit at a table. At the Ritz-Carlton outside the breakfast room they had this wonderful silver urn and attractive cups, not paper cups, so people could just have some coffee. It's very American but then why not give our American guests what they want rather than . . . what we think they should have?"

Despite the difference in size between the two hotels—the Ritz-Carlton has 457 rooms and the Athenaeum has 157—Ms. Ferguson says the day-to-day management is very similar. "It's the same, except for the British accent." But decisions can be made more quickly in a smaller hotel, she says. "Product development is managed quite differently in an independent hotel than from a chain. While our standards are very similar and our company is decentralized with a lot of decisions made at the hotel, the decision-making process here is faster—we're trying to regain that entrepreneurial spirit."

Ms. Bulloch says she has been struck by the amount of time spent by senior staff in U.S. hotels on administration. "My impression has always been that senior staff tend to be in meetings or handling paperwork. But you don't know what's going on unless you are on the floor, and guests often want to meet the managers," she says.

Ms. Ferguson says she is going back to Atlanta with "an increased awareness of the importance of face-to-face contact. Each employee here tries to establish a relationship with the guest; they try and remember the guest's name."

Both would like to extend the swap to other staff. "I would eventually like some of our housekeepers and reception staff to do the swap and to experience what it's like to travel as a guest—especially when you are jetlagged," says Ms. Bulloch. "There's nothing worse than arriving at 7:30 A.M. and a smiling girl at reception says, 'Sorry, your room won't be ready till 11' and you want to kill her. Since lots of people leave early, we get the maids to start at 6 A.M. instead of at 8 A.M. With three maids, a room can be ready in eight minutes."

She goes on: "We ought to be able to understand our guests' needs. For example, when you are in the U.S., you notice how people will give detailed orders in a restaurant. I don't want our staff not to know what a guest is talking about if they ask for a low-sodium meal."

Ms. Ferguson would like to use the idea of a swap as an incentive to staff by offering it to the hotel's employee of the year. "A lot of our people don't get to travel."

Case Questions

1. What lesson might an international manager learn from this case?
2. What business characteristics lend themselves most to organizational learning from using this practice? What characteristics are least conducive to learning from this practice?
3. What are the advantages and disadvantages of using the method described in the case?

Source: "The Benefits of Foreign Exchange," *Financial Times*, January 15, 1996, p. 12. Reprinted with permission.

Considering Cultural and Political Forces: MTV Europe and Yahoo!

Background

This video shows how MTV Europe and Yahoo! have taken into consideration sociocultural and political factors in penetrating markets abroad. In essence the message from both companies is, "When in Rome, do as the Romans do." Both companies have been very sensitive to the various countries' cultures, social structures, and political climates. They have customized their products and services accordingly to satisfy local demands. The companies also looked at the long traditions and histories of the countries they wanted to do business in, including China, France, Denmark, Sweden, and Mexico.

MTV Europe

Since it was launched in 1981, MTV has become an international player, especially in Europe, by "thinking globally and acting locally." Peter Einstein, president of MTV Europe, led the charge when he said, "Be there, give them what they want, in whatever form." MTV Europe, which currently reaches 77 million homes, has adopted a European strategy—it offers local versions of its satellite/cable TV network programming to compete in individual European countries. These more-focused offerings have gradually been replacing MTV Europe's wider regional programming, and versions for the Netherlands, Spain, and Eastern European countries are now being considered. When the network launched MTV Central Germany, it added 11.2 million homes to its customer base. Regional advertisers still make up the largest share of the network's ad revenues, but the number of advertisers has increased to 600 (local and regional) from 235 (mostly regional) advertisers in 1995.

YAHOO! Inc.

Yahoo! is an Internet search engine headquartered in Santa Clara, California, that helps people navigate the World Wide Web. The company's principal product is an ad-supported Internet directory that links users to millions of Web pages. The site leads the field in traffic (95 million pages viewed each day) and is second only to Netscape in online advertising revenues. Yahoo! has targeted guides for geographic audiences (such as Yahoo! Travel), demographic audiences (see Yahooligans!, a Web guide for children), special-interest audiences (Yahoo! Finance), and community services (Yahoo! Chat).

The company is moving into the Internet access market through an alliance with AT&T and has agreed to acquire fellow Internet player, GeoCities. Japan's SOFTBANK, the largest shareholder in Yahoo!, has 15 international Web properties outside the United States. Yahoo! now has offices in Europe, Pacific Asia, and Canada—and has a global network of 22 world properties. Although the company's stock price dropped considerably in 2000—along with other dot-coms—Yahoo!'s net income in the first three quarters of 2000 was $168.6 million, a big increase over the $10 million earned during the same period in 1999.

Questions

1. What do you think would have happened had MTV Europe not localized its content in each foreign market? How would changing have helped MTV Europe? What might be the costs of not changing?
2. How did MTV Europe approach penetrating the cultures of the various countries it had dealings with? Give details. What approach did Yahoo! take? Give details.
3. Pick a country where Yahoo! or MTV do not have a presence. If you were an executive for one of these companies, what cultural, political, or technological issues would you need to address before venturing into that country?

The Ethics of Global Tobacco Marketing

Cigarette smoking was once considered to be elegant and glamorous. Movie stars, athletes, politicians, and other public figures were often photographed holding or smoking a cigarette, and tobacco companies aggressively pushed their products as a basic commodity in the same way firms today market soft drinks and fast foods. Driven in part by the allure of fashion and in part by this aggressive marketing, the annual consumption of cigarettes by U.S. smokers increased steadily from 54 per person in 1900 to a high of 4,345 in 1963.

In 1964, however, things began to change. The U.S. Surgeon General released a report that demonstrated a clear link between cigarettes and lung cancer. During subsequent years numerous reforms were put in place that affected the ability of tobacco firms to market their products in the United States. Among the most stringent were bans on television and radio advertising, mandatory warning labels on cigarette packages, high sales taxes, and age restrictions for the legal purchase of cigarettes. These measures, combined with increased public awareness, caused the annual consumption of cigarettes by U.S. smokers to drop to less than 2,500 in 1999.

There are three major international cigarette makers today. Philip Morris, the world's largest, is a U.S. firm that manufactures such brands as Marlboro, Benson & Hedges, Parliament, and Virginia Slims. R.J. Reynolds, also a U.S. firm, markets Camel, Doral, Salem, Winston, and other brands. British American tobacco (BAT), a British firm, sells such brands as Kool, Raleigh, and Viceroy (BAT's U.S. operation is called Brown & Williamson).

As pressures to curb cigarette smoking in the United States increased during the 1970s and 1980s, the big three sought to diversify their tobacco sales geographically by focusing their efforts on markets other than Western Europe or North America. These new markets offer two major advantages. First, many of them place few restrictions on tobacco sales. Second, growth prospects in these markets are higher because of rising incomes and reductions in trade restrictions.

Central and Eastern Europe offer significant opportunities. Communist government officials actively promoted the use of cigarettes and vodka. These commodities were cheap to make, and their addictive character helped maintain order and discipline in society. Indeed, after the collapse of communism and the move toward an open market in Russia, cigarette shortages caused riots in Moscow. Not surprisingly, then, cigarette makers rushed to enter the former Soviet bloc countries, where total annual cigarette consumption is estimated to be as high as 700 billion, compared to 500 billion in the United States.

Philip Morris, R.J. Reynolds, and British American Tobacco have discovered that consumers in this region crave affordable, high-quality, Western-style products. Cigarettes seem to fill at least part of the bill. The three firms have plastered cities throughout Central and Eastern Europe with billboards featuring the Marlboro Man—an icon of America, the West, and freedom—or symbols of other Western brands. Not surprisingly, the number of smokers in Central and Eastern Europe continues to escalate. Philip Morris is perhaps the most successful firm in this region so far, partly because it was able to buy the Czech cigarette monopoly, Tabak, in 1992 during that country's privatization program. Philip Morris also has purchased majority interests in formerly state-owned cigarette factories in Hungary, Kazakhstan, Russia, and Ukraine. The other major producers also have staked out positions in the region. R.J. Reynolds operates two joint ventures in Ukraine with local companies, and BAT bought a controlling interest in Uzbekistan's leading cigarette producer.

Asia is another major battlefield. The Japanese have long been heavy smokers. The Japanese market was essentially closed to foreign firms until the Bush administration in the late 1980s pressured the Japanese to reduce their high tariffs on imported cigarettes and end Japan Tobacco's monopoly over the domestic market. Because Japanese consumers have long been interested in products they strongly associate with the United States (such as Levi Strauss jeans, McDonald's restaurants, and Disney films), U.S. cigarette makers are now finding Japan a fertile market for their brands.

The story is similar in the Philippines, China, Taiwan, Korea, Vietnam, Malaysia, Hong Kong, and Indonesia. Aggressive advertising, often targeted at young consumers and women, is inducing more and more people to become smokers. For example, a 1985 survey of high school students in Taiwan found that only 26 percent of males and 1 percent of females had ever smoked a cigarette. Six years later, a similar survey found 48 percent of males and 20 percent of females had smoked.

These efforts and strategies have been very controversial, raising ethical concerns about the behavior of the firms and the U.S. government. Critics argue, for example, that the tobacco giants are being socially irresponsible by taking advantage of uninformed, impressionable consumers who do not fully understand the health risks of smoking.

The tobacco companies respond that they are doing nothing wrong. They point out that local governments, especially in Central and Eastern Europe, have encouraged their investments. They also note that they are simply taking advantage of legal market opportunities that already exist. Indeed, failing to do just what they are doing might seem to be a disservice to their stockholders and employees.

Among the most controversial issues are the marketing practices international tobacco companies employ. China provides a good case in point. That country has a law that prohibits the advertising of cigarettes, but the law bans only the display of and actual mention of a cigarette. Philip Morris actively promotes its Marlboro brand without ever showing a picture of or mentioning cigarettes. One of its radio commercials, for example, proclaims, "This is the world of Marlboro. Ride through the rivers and mountains with courage. Be called a hero throughout the thousand miles. This is the world of Marlboro." Philip Morris's efforts appear to be paying off: Its brand recognition is high among Chinese consumers. One Canton factory manager, when asked by an interviewer why he smokes Marlboro, replied, "Marlboro shows my superior position to others. I'm more privileged."

More controversial has been the role of the U.S. government. Although it discourages cigarette usage at home, it played an active role in opening foreign markets to U.S. tobacco firms. In the 1980s the U.S. Trade Representative (USTR) (the government agency in charge of international trade negotiations) successfully hammered out agreements with Japan, South Korea, Taiwan, and Thailand to end their restrictions on the sale of foreign cigarettes. The USTR attacked foreign countries for utilizing public policies the U.S. government itself had adopted. Taiwan, for example, previously disallowed all cigarette advertising as a means of discouraging cigarette consumption. As a result, most cigarettes were consumed by adult males. In 1986, however, the U.S. government exerted pressure on the Taiwanese government to allow greater access to its market by U.S. firms. Bowing to this pressure, Taiwan not only opened its market to Philip Morris and R.J. Reynolds but also relaxed its regulations on cigarette advertising. These Western firms have focused their marketing efforts on teenagers and females, believing older males will continue to smoke domestic brands. U.S. brands now sell well among those targeted audiences. When Taiwanese health officials tried to strengthen the warning labels on cigarette packages, ban smoking by those under 18, and prohibit vending machine cigarette sales, the USTR counterattacked, claiming these efforts would hurt U.S. tobacco companies. The USTR took similar stances in trade negotiations with Japan, South Korea, and Thailand, threatening these countries with Super 301 retaliation if they did not open their markets to U.S. cigarettes.

All in all, the international marketing efforts of U.S. cigarette makers seem to be working. Exports account for about 30 percent of U.S. cigarette production, and the firms' primary target markets—teenagers, females, and the affluent—are purchasing U.S. cigarettes in record numbers. But the controversy over such marketing practices intensified in 2000, with the initiation of a major effort by the World Health Organization (WHO), a Geneva-based branch of the United Nations, to curb tobacco products. WHO estimates that if current consumption trends continue, 500 million people currently alive will die from tobacco use. It is proposing that all UN members raise tobacco taxes, eliminate cigarette smuggling, and ban tobacco advertising and sponsoring of sporting and music events.

Questions

1. Summarize the basic ethical and social responsibility issues that this case illustrates.

2. If you managed an international tobacco firm, what actions would you take today to protect your market opportunities abroad?

3. Do you think other foreign cigarette makers, such as those in Japan, will ever be able to crack the U.S. market? Why or why not?

4. In most Asian cultures cigarette smoking is restricted to males. Should foreign cigarette makers respect the cultural values of these countries and restrict their marketing efforts to males? Should females be targeted for marketing as well?

5. In February 1998 the U.S. State Department changed its tobacco policy, instructing all U.S. embassies to stop promoting sales of U.S. tobacco products. U.S. embassy personnel also are directed "to support, rather than challenge, local antismoking laws and regulations that may reduce U.S. tobacco company sales, as long as they are applied in a nondiscriminatory manner to both imported and domestic tobacco products." Do you agree with this policy change? More generally, what is the appropriate role of the U.S. government in foreign tobacco marketing?

6. What policy should the U.S. government adopt regarding WHO's plan to reduce tobacco use globally? What position should Philip Morris, R.J. Reynolds, and British American Tobacco adopt?

Sources: "Tobacco Sector Accused of 'Invisible' Anti-WHO Campaign," *Financial Times*, August 3, 2000, p. 3; "U.S. Embassies Stop Assisting Tobacco Firms," *Wall Street Journal*, May 14, 1998, p. B1; "Getting Acquainted," *Business Eastern Europe*, October 20, 1997, p. 4; "Smoke Signals," *Business Eastern Europe*, April 22, 1996, p. 17; Stan Sesser, "Opium War Redux," *The New Yorker*, September 13, 1993, pp. 78–79; "Smoking Level Lowest in 50 Years," *USA Today*, November 17, 1994, p. D1; "Cigarettes May Find New Foe in Trade Rep," *Wall Street Journal*, August 1, 1994, p. B1; "Tobacco Companies Race for Advantage in Eastern Europe While Critics Fume," *Wall Street Journal*, December 28, 1992, pp. B1, B4; "U.S. Cigarette Firms are Battling Taiwan's Bid to Stiffen Ad Curbs Like Other Asian Nations," *Wall Street Journal*, May 5, 1992, p. C25; "Opiate of the Masses," *Forbes*, April 11, 1994, pp. 74–75.

A Rat in My Soup

Looking for the best-tasting rodent in town.

BY PETER HESSLER

"Do you want a big rat or a small rat?" the waitress asked.

I was getting used to making difficult decisions in Luogang, a small village in southern China's Guangdong Province. I'd come here on a whim, having heard that Luogang had a famous restaurant that specialized in the preparation of rats. Upon arrival, however, I discovered that there were two celebrated restaurants—the Highest Ranking Wild Flavor Restaurant and the New Eight Sceneries Wild Flavor Food City. They were next door to each other, and they had virtually identical bamboo-and-wood decors. Moreover, their owners were both named Zhong—but, then everybody in Luogang seemed to be named Zhong. The two Zhongs were not related, and competition between them was keen. As a foreign journalist, I'd been cajoled to such an extent that, in an effort to please both Zhongs, I agreed to eat two lunches, one at each restaurant.

The waitress at the Highest Ranking Wild Flavor Restaurant, who was also named Zhong (in Chinese, it means "bell"), asked again, "Do you want a big rat or a small rat?"

"What's the difference?" I said.

"The big rats eat grass stems, and the small ones eat fruit."

I tried a more direct tack. "Which tastes better?"

"Both of them taste good."

"Which do you recommend?"

"Either one."

I glanced at the table next to mine. Two parents, a grandmother, and a little boy were having lunch. The boy was gnawing on a rat drumstick. I couldn't tell if the drumstick had belonged to a big rat or a small rat. The boy ate quickly. It was a warm afternoon. The sun was shining. I made my decision. "Small rat," I said.

The Chinese say that people in Guangdong will eat anything. Besides rat, a customer at the Highest Ranking Wild Flavor Restaurant can order turtledove, fox, cat, python, and an assortment of strange-looking local animals whose names do not translate into English. All of them are kept live in pens at the back of the restaurant and are killed only when a customer orders one of them. Choosing among them involves considerations beyond flavor or texture. You order cat not just because you enjoy the taste of cat but because cats are said to impart a lively *jingshen* (spirit). You eat deer penis to improve virility. Snakes make you stronger. And rat? "It keeps you from going bald," Zhong Shaocong, the daughter of the owner of the Highest Ranking Wild Flavor Restaurant, told me. Zhong Qingjiang, the owner of the New Eight Sceneries Wild Flavor Food City, went further. "If you have white hair and eat rat regularly, it will turn black," she said. "And if you're going bald and you eat rat every day your hair will stop falling out. A lot of the parents around here feed rat to a small child who doesn't have much hair, and the hair grows better."

Earlier this year, Luogang opened a "restaurant street" in the newly developed Luogang Economic Open Zone, a parkland and restaurant district designed to draw visitors from nearby Guangzhou City. The government invested $1,200,000 in the project, which enabled the two rat restaurants to move from their old, cramped quarters in a local park into new, greatly expanded spaces—about 1,800 square feet for each establishment. The Highest Ranking Wild Flavor Restaurant, which cost $42,000 to build, opened in early March. Six days later, the New Eight Sceneries Wild Flavor Food City opened, on an investment of $54,000. A third restaurant—a massive, air-conditioned facility, which is expected to cost $72,000—will open soon. A fourth is in the planning stages.

On the morning of my initiation into rat cuisine, I visited the construction site of the third facility, whose owner, Deng Ximing, was the only local restaurateur not named Zhong. He was married to a Zhong, however, and he had the fast-talking confidence of a successful entrepreneur. I also noticed that he had a good head of hair. He spoke of the village's culinary tradition with pride. "It's more than a thousand years old," he said. "And it's always been rats from the mountains—we're not eating city rats. The mountain rats are clean because up there they aren't eating anything dirty. Mostly, they eat fruit—oranges, plums, jackfruit. People from the government hygiene department have been here to examine the rats. They took them to the laboratory and checked them out thoroughly to see if they had any diseases, and they found nothing. Not even the slightest problem."

Luogang's restaurant street has been a resounding success. Newspapers and television stations have reported extensively on the benefits of the local specialty, and an increasing number of customers are making the half-hour trip from Guangzhou City. Both the Highest Ranking Wild Flavor Restaurant and the New Eight Sceneries Wild Flavor Food City serve, on average, 3,000 rats every Saturday and Sunday, which are the peak dining days. "Many people come from faraway places," Zhong Qingjiang told me. "They come from Guangzhou, Shenzhen, Hong Kong, Macao. One customer came all the way from America with her son. They were visiting relatives in

Luogang, and the family brought them here to eat. She said you couldn't find this kind of food in America."

In America, needless to say, you would be hard-pressed to find 12,000 fruit-fed rats anywhere on any weekend, but this isn't a problem in Luogang. On my first morning in the village, I watched dozens of peasants come down from the hills, looking to get a piece of the rat business. They came on mopeds, on bicycles, and on foot. All of them carried burlap sacks of squirming rats that had been trapped on their farms.

"Last year, I sold my oranges for 15¢ a pound," a farmer named Zhong Senji told me. "But this year the price has dropped to less than 10¢." Like many other peasants, Zhong decided that he could do a lot better with rats. Today, he had nine rats in his sack. When the sack was put on a scale in the rear of the Highest Ranking Wild Flavor Restaurant, it shook and squeaked. It weighed in at just under 3 pounds, and Zhong received the equivalent in yuan of $1.45 per pound, for a total of $3.87. In Luogang, rats are more expensive than pork or chicken. A pound of rat costs nearly twice as much as a pound of beef.

At the Highest Ranking Wild Flavor Restaurant, I began with a dish called Simmered Mountain Rat with Black Beans. There were plenty of other options on the menu—among them, Mountain Rat Soup, Steamed Mountain Rat, Simmered Mountain Rat, Roasted Mountain Rat, Mountain Rat Curry, and Spicy and Salty Mountain Rat—but the waitress had enthusiastically recommended the Simmered Mountain Rat with Black Beans, which arrived in a clay pot.

I ate the beans first. They tasted fine. I poked at the rat meat. It was clearly well done, and it was attractively garnished with onions, leeks, and ginger. Nestled in a light sauce were skinny rat thighs, short strips of rat flank, and delicate, toylike rat ribs. I started with a thigh, put a chunk of it into my mouth, and reached for a glass of beer. The beer helped.

The restaurant's owner, Zhong Dieqin, came over and sat down. "What do you think?" she asked.

"I think it tastes good."

"You know it's good for your health."

"I've heard that."

"It's good for your hair and skin," she said. "It's also good for your kidneys."

Zhong Dieqin watched me intently. "Are you sure you like it?" she asked.

"Yes," I said, tentatively. In fact, it wasn't bad. The meat was lean and white, without a hint a gaminess. Gradually, my squeamishness faded, and I tried to decide what, exactly, the flavor of rat reminded me of. But nothing came to mind. It simply tasted like rat.

Next door, at the New Eight Sceneries Wild Flavor Food City, the Zhongs were more media-savvy. They asked if I had brought along a television crew. They looked disappointed when I said that I hadn't. Then the floor manager brightened and asked me how I'd liked their competition.

"It was fine," I said.

"What did you eat?"

"Simmered Mountain Rat with Black Beans."

"You'll like ours better," she said. "Our cook is better, the service is quicker, and the waitresses are more polite."

I decided to order the Spicy and Salty Mountain Rat. This time, when the waitress asked about my preference in sizes, I said, pleased with my boldness, "Big rat."

"Come and choose it."

"What?"

"Pick out the rat you want."

I followed one of the kitchen workers to a shed behind the restaurant, where cages were stacked atop one another. Each cage contained more than 30 rats. The shed did not smell good. The worker pointed at a rat.

"How about this one?" he said.

"Um, sure."

He put on a glove, opened the cage, and picked up the chosen rat. It was about the size of a softball. "Is it O.K.?" he said.

"Yes."

"Are you certain?"

The rat gazed at me with beady eyes. I nodded.

Suddenly, the worker flipped his wrist, swung the rat into the air by the tail, and let go. The rat made a neat arc. There was a soft thud when its head struck the cement floor. There wasn't much blood. The worker grinned. "You can go back to the dining room now," he said. "We'll bring it out to you soon."

"O.K.," I said.

Less than 15 minutes later, the dish was at my table, garnished with carrots and leeks. The chef came out of the kitchen to join the owner, Zhong Qingjiang, the floor manager, and a cousin of the owner to watch me eat. "How is it?" the chef asked.

"Good."

"Is it too tough?"

"No," I said. "It's fine."

In truth, I was trying hard not to taste anything. I had lost my appetite in the shed, and now I ate quickly, washing every bit down with beer. I did my best to put on a good show, gnawing on the bones as enthusiastically as possible. When I finished, I sat back and managed a smile. The chef and the others nodded with approval.

The owner's cousin said, "Next time you should try the Longfu Soup, because it contains tiger, dragon, and phoenix."

"What do you mean by 'tiger, dragon, and phoenix'?" I asked warily. I didn't want to make another trip to the shed.

"It's not real tigers, dragons, and phoenixes," he assured me. "They're represented by other animals—cat for the tiger, snake for the dragon, and chicken for the phoenix. When you mix them together, there are all kinds of health benefits. And they taste good, too."

Questions

1. Although the American who wrote this story visited Luogang's restaurants voluntarily, many international business practitioners working abroad involuntarily confront things they find odd or offensive. Suppose you had been invited by a very important customer to the New Eight Sceneries Wild Flavor Food City restaurant. What would you have done, if, like the author, you had been invited to pick out your dinner in the shed behind the restaurant?

2. Cultural values play an enormous role in shaping attitudes toward food. Are there any foreign foods commonly available in your home country that you or your friends simply will not eat?

3. Are there any aspects of your home culture that foreign visitors might find offensive? If so, what are they?

4. What measures can you take to protect your foreign guests from aspects of your home culture they might find offensive?

Source: Reprinted with permission of Peter Hessler. This article first appeared in *The New Yorker*, July 24, 2000, pp. 38ff.

CHAPTER

Caterpillar: Making Money by Moving Mountains

Caterpillar, Inc., headquartered in Peoria, Illinois, is the world's largest producer of heavy earth-moving and construction equipment, with a 30 percent share of the global market. The company's complex involvement in international business is typical of most major firms today. Cat, as the company is widely known, manufactures engines and earth-moving, construction, and materials-handling equipment at 61 factories spread over five continents. About 40 percent of its 66,896 employees work outside the United States. Almost half of its 1999 output of $19.7 billion was purchased by foreign customers: $5.2 billion as exports from the United States and the remainder as output from Cat's 29 overseas factories. Caterpillar is no newcomer to international production. It established its first overseas factory in the United Kingdom in 1951. Its 1963 joint venture with Mitsubishi Heavy Industries was one of the first such investments by a U.S. firm in Japan. In 1998 it purchased Perkins Engines, a British producer of small-to-medium size diesel engines, which had been a primary supplier of such engines to Cat. Caterpillar plans to leverage the Perkins acquisition to develop new products for the small and compact construction equipment market and for the agricultural market.

"**Exchange rate** changes continually affect price **competitiveness**."

After studying this chapter, you should be able to:

〉 Understand the motivation for international trade.

〉 Summarize and discuss the differences among the classical country-based theories of international trade.

〉 Use the modern firm-based theories of international trade to describe global strategies adopted by businesses.

〉 Describe and categorize the different forms of international investment.

〉 Explain the reasons for foreign direct investment.

〉 Summarize how supply, demand, and political factors influence foreign direct investment.

International Trade and Investment Theory

Because downtime of a critical piece of equipment can halt construction, success in this industry depends on equipment reliability and after-sales support. Caterpillar has two competitive advantages that have enabled it to dominate the international heavy-equipment market:

1. A commitment to quality that makes the Caterpillar brand name a symbol of tough, reliable products

2. An effective network of 207 dealers worldwide who sell and service Caterpillar's products

The importance of these two elements has been summed up by John Bibby, a typical Cat customer, who runs John Bibby Backhoe Hire, an excavating firm in a Melbourne, Australia suburb. Bibby is a small operator—he owns only one piece of equipment—so when his backhoe is not operating, his business is essentially shut down:

It was embarrassing before I got my Cat machine because something would break down every week. Now, that kind of thing just doesn't happen very often . . . and when it does, they send somebody out straight away and the blokes fix it right up. I'm happy with the parts you can get and the availability of them. And I know a lot of the boys now. You know, once you're in a good thing, you don't want to get out of it.[1]

Caterpillar engages in many forms of international business. It is an exporter, sending its well-known yellow earth-moving equipment to virtually every country in the world. It is an importer, purchasing parts from Asian, European, and North American suppliers. Cat is an international investor, owning and operating factories in 22 countries. It also is an international borrower, seeking short-term and long-term capital from investors and banks throughout the world. The company is involved in the international licensing of technology, both in purchasing the right to use innovative technologies developed by foreign firms and in selling the use of its own technologies to other foreign firms. It also franchises the rights to sell its equipment to 63 U.S. dealers and 144 foreign dealers.

Of course, given the fierceness of international competition, Caterpillar's future is no more assured than that of any other global enterprise. Its archrival, Komatsu Ltd., enjoyed lower labor costs during the 1980s and a reputation for producing innovative, high-quality products. In the early 1980s Komatsu undercut Cat's prices to U.S. customers by as much as 40 percent, causing an 11 percent erosion in Cat's domestic market share. Slashing its own prices, Cat stopped the market-share losses, although its profitability suffered. The rise in the value of the yen from 1985 to 1995—it reached a peak of 80 yen to the dollar in April 1995—helped Cat by eroding Komatsu's cost advantage. Unfortunately for Cat, the yen fell 44 percent in value over the next 40 months, reaching a low of 144 yen to the dollar in August 1998. Since that time, the yen has recovered some of its value. In April 2001 it was trading in the range of 120 to 125 yen to the dollar, making Japanese exports some 33 to 36 percent cheaper than they were in the spring of 1995. Because these exchange rate changes continually affect the price competitiveness of Cat's products, Cat's managers know they must accelerate their drive to become more cost efficient.

The company has responded to this challenge. In the past five years Cat invested $3.5 billion in plant modernization to improve manufacturing quality. During the same time span, it sank another $2.6 billion into research and development, which yielded 296 new or improved products and over 2,100 patents. Cat also worked with its 4,000 suppliers to improve the quality of parts and supplies.

Cat also aggressively reined in its labor costs, although this effort came at a high price. In 1992 it fought a bitter five-month strike by the United Auto Workers in order to slow down wage increases, relax productivity-robbing work rules, and shrink its labor force. After the union called off the strike, the company suffered through 11 more union walkouts and 440 unfair labor practice complaints filed before the National Labor Relations Board. The 1992 strike was finally settled in 1998, and, clearly, not all the wounds from that struggle have been healed. Caterpillar faces the challenge of improving its labor relations because it must rely on these same workers to improve productivity and the quality of its output in the face of Komatsu's competition.[2]

Caterpillar is a microcosm of the complex business relationships that bind firms and countries in the contemporary global marketplace. In this chapter we analyze the underlying economic forces that shape and structure the international business transactions conducted by Caterpillar and thousands of other firms. We discuss the major theories that explain and predict international trade and investment activity. These theories help firms sharpen their global business strategies, identify promising export and investment opportunities, and react to threats posed by foreign competitors. As they introduce you to the economic environment in which firms compete, the theories help you understand why a firm like Caterpillar can be simultaneously an exporter, importer, international investor, international borrower, franchiser, and licensor and licensee of technology.

INTERNATIONAL TRADE AND THE WORLD ECONOMY ‹

Trade is the voluntary exchange of goods, services, assets, or money between one person or organization and another. Because it is voluntary, both parties to the transaction must believe they will gain from the exchange or else they would not complete it. **International trade** is trade between residents of two countries. The residents may be individuals, firms, nonprofit organizations, or other forms of associations.

Why does international trade occur? The answer follows directly from our definition of trade: Both parties to the transaction, who happen to reside in two different countries, believe they benefit from the voluntary exchange. Behind this simple truth lies much economic theory, business practice, government policy, and international conflict—topics we cover in this and the next four chapters.

As Figure 5.1 indicates, world trade has grown dramatically in the half century since the end of World War II. Total international merchandise trade in 1999 was $5.6 trillion, or approximately 19 percent of the world's $30 trillion gross domestic product (GDP); trade in services that year amounted to $1.3 trillion. The Quad countries accounted for over 60 percent of the world's merchandise exports (see Figure 5.2). Such international trade has important direct and indirect effects on national economies. On the one hand, exports spark additional economic activity in the domestic economy. Caterpillar's $5.2 billion in exports generate orders for its U.S. suppliers, wages for its U.S. workers, and dividend payments for its U.S. shareholders, all of which then create income for local automobile dealers, grocery stores, and others, which in turn add to their own payrolls. On the other hand, imports can pressure domestic suppliers to cut their prices and improve their competitiveness. Failure to respond to foreign competition may lead to closed factories and unemployed workers.

Because of international trade's obvious significance to businesses, consumers, and workers, scholars have attempted to develop theories to explain and predict the forces that motivate such trade. Governments use these theories when they design policies they hope will benefit their countries' industries and citizens. Managers use them to identify promising markets and profitable internationalization strategies.

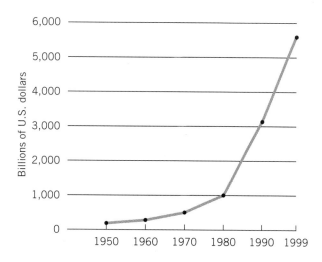

FIGURE 5.1

The Growth of World Merchandise Exports Since 1950

Sources: *International Monetary Fund Supplement on Trade Statistics* (International Monetary Fund, Washington, D.C.: 1990); World Trade Organization Web site (*www.wto.org*), August 2000.

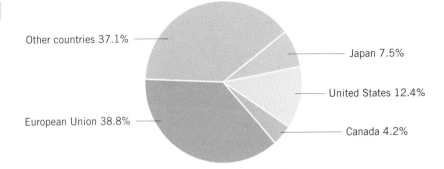

FIGURE 5.2

Sources of the World's Merchandise Exports, 1999

Source: World Trade Organization, Annual Report 2000.

› CLASSICAL COUNTRY-BASED TRADE THEORIES

The first theories of international trade developed with the rise of the great European nation-states during the sixteenth century. Not surprisingly, these early theories focused on the individual country in examining patterns of exports and imports. As we discuss in more detail later in the chapter, these country-based theories are particularly useful for describing trade in commodities—standardized, undifferentiated goods such as oil, sugar, or lumber that are typically bought on the basis of price rather than brand name. However, as multinational corporations (MNCs) rose to power in the middle of the twentieth century, scholars shifted their attention to the firm's role in promoting international trade. The firm-based theories developed after World War II are useful in describing patterns of trade in differentiated goods—those such as automobiles, consumer electronics, and personal care products, for which brand name is an important component of the customer's purchase decision. In this section we examine the classical country-based theories of international trade; in the next section we explore the more modern firm-based theories.

Mercantilism

Mercantilism is a sixteenth-century economic philosophy which maintains that a country's wealth is measured by its holdings of gold and silver. According to mercantilists, a country's goal should be to enlarge these holdings. To do this, the country should strive to maximize the difference between its exports and its imports by promoting exports and discouraging imports. The logic was transparent to sixteenth-century policy makers: If foreigners buy more goods from you than you buy from them, then the foreigners have to pay you the difference in gold and silver, enabling you to amass more treasure. Mercantilist terminology is still used today, for example, when television commentators and newspaper headlines report that a country suffered an "unfavorable" balance of trade—that is, its exports were less than its imports.

At the time mercantilism seemed to be sound economic policy, at least to the reigning monarchs. Large gold and silver holdings meant they could afford to hire armies to fight other countries and thereby expand their realms. Politically, mercantilism was popular with many manufacturers and their workers. Export-oriented manufacturers favored mercantilist trade policies, such as those establishing subsidies or tax rebates, that stimulated sales to foreigners. Domestic manufacturers threatened by foreign imports endorsed mercantilist trade policies, such as those imposing tariffs or quotas, that protected the manufacturers from foreign competition. These businesses, their workers, their suppliers, and the local politicians representing the communities in which the manufacturers had production facilities all praised the wisdom of the monarchs' mercantilist policies.

However, most members of society are hurt by such policies. Governmental subsidies of the exports of certain industries are paid by taxpayers in the form of higher taxes. Governmental import restrictions are paid for by consumers in the form of higher prices because domestic firms face less competition from foreign producers. During the Age of Imperialism governments often shifted the burden of mercantilist policies onto their colonies. For example, under the Navigation Act of 1660 all European goods imported by the American colonies had to be shipped from Great Britain. The British prohibited colonial firms from exporting certain goods that might compete with those from British factories, such as hats, finished iron goods, and woolens. To ensure adequate supplies of low-cost inputs for British merchants, the British required some colonial industries to sell their output only to British firms. This output included rice, tobacco, and naval stores (forest products used in shipbuilding).[3] This particular mercantilist strategy ultimately backfired—it contributed to the grievances that led to the overthrow of the British Crown in the American colonies.

Because mercantilism does benefit certain members of society, mercantilist policies are still politically attractive to some firms and their workers. Modern supporters of such policies, called **neomercantilists** or **protectionists**, include such diverse U.S. groups as the American Federation of Labor-Congress of Industrial Organizations, textile manufacturers, steel companies, sugar growers, and peanut farmers.

Protectionist attitudes are not limited to the United States. North Americans and Europeans have long complained that Japan limits the access of foreign goods to its market. For example, it took 40 years of negotiations before Japan grudgingly agreed in the 1990s to allow the importation of foreign rice, and even then it limited rice imports to less than 10 percent of its market. Asian and North American firms criticize the Europeans for imposing barriers against imported goods such as beef, automobiles, and videocassette recorders. Such finger-pointing is amply justified: Nearly every country has adopted some neomercantilist policies to protect key industries in its economy.

> One of Japan's competitive strengths lies in its utilization of technology to lower production costs. The robots at this Honda plant can be reprogrammed quickly and inexpensively, thereby lowering the cost of model changeovers.

Absolute Advantage

Neomercantilism has superficial appeal, particularly to patriots who want to strengthen their country's economy. Why shouldn't a country try to maximize its holdings of gold and silver? According to Adam Smith, the Scottish economist who is viewed as the father of free-market economics, mercantilism's basic problem is that it confuses the acquisition of treasure with the acquisition of wealth. In *An Inquiry into the Nature and Causes of the Wealth of Nations* (1776), Smith attacked the intellectual basis of mercantilism and demonstrated that mercantilism actually weakens a country. In Smith's view mercantilism robs individuals of the ability to trade freely and to benefit from voluntary exchanges. Moreover, in the process of avoiding imports at all costs, a country must squander its resources producing goods it is not suited to produce. The inefficiencies caused by mercantilism reduce the wealth of the country as a whole, even though certain special-interest groups may benefit.

Smith advocated free trade among countries as a means of enlarging a country's wealth. Free trade enables a country to expand the amount of goods and services available to it by specializing in the production of some goods and services and trading for others. But which goods and services should a country export and which should it import? To answer this question, Smith developed the **theory of**

TABLE 5.1	OUTPUT PER HOUR OF LABOR		
		France	Japan
	Wine	2	1
	Clock radios	3	5

The Theory of Absolute Advantage: An Example

absolute advantage, which suggests that a country should export those goods and services for which it is more productive than other countries are and import those goods and services for which other countries are more productive than it is.

Absolute advantage can be demonstrated through a numerical example. Assume, for the sake of simplicity, that there are only two countries in the world, France and Japan; only two goods, wine and clock radios; and only one factor of production, labor. Table 5.1 shows the output of the two goods per hour of labor for the two countries. In France 1 hour of labor can produce either 2 bottles of wine or 3 clock radios. In Japan 1 hour of labor can produce either 1 bottle of wine or 5 clock radios. France has an absolute advantage in the production of wine: One hour of labor produces 2 bottles in France but only 1 in Japan. Japan has an absolute advantage in the production of clock radios: One hour of labor produces 5 clock radios in Japan but only 3 in France.

If France and Japan are able to trade with one another, both will be better off. Suppose France agrees to exchange 2 bottles of wine for 4 clock radios. Only 1 hour of French labor is needed to produce the 2 bottles of wine bound for Japan. In return France will get 4 clock radios from Japan. These 4 clock radios would have required 1.33 hours of French labor had France produced them rather than buy them from Japan. By trading with Japan rather than producing the clock radios itself, France saves 0.33 hour of labor. France can use this freed-up labor to produce more wine, which in turn can be consumed by French citizens or traded to Japan for more clock radios. By allocating its scarce labor to produce goods for which it is more productive than Japan and then trading them to Japan, France can consume more goods than it could have done in the absence of trade.

Japan is similarly better off. Japan uses 0.8 hour of labor to produce the 4 clock radios to exchange for the 2 bottles of French wine. Producing the 2 bottles of wine itself would have required 2 hours of labor. By producing clock radios and then trading them to France, Japan saves 1.2 hours of labor, which can be used to produce more clock radios that the Japanese can consume themselves or trade to France for more wine.

Comparative Advantage

The theory of absolute advantage makes intuitive sense. Unfortunately, the theory is flawed. What happens to trade if one country has an absolute advantage in both products? The theory of absolute advantage incorrectly suggests that no trade would occur. David Ricardo, an early nineteenth-century British economist, solved this problem by developing the **theory of comparative advantage**, which states that a country should produce and export those goods and services for which it is *relatively* more productive than other countries are and import those goods and services for which other countries are *relatively* more productive than it is.[4]

The difference between the two theories is subtle: Absolute advantage looks at *absolute* productivity differences; comparative advantage looks at *relative* productivity differences. The distinction occurs because comparative advantage incorporates the concept of opportunity cost in determining which good a country should produce. The **opportunity cost** of a good is the value of what is given up to get the good. Most of us apply the principles of comparative advantage and opportunity cost without realizing it. For example, a brain surgeon may be better at both brain surgery and lawn mowing than her neighbor's teenaged son is. However, if the surgeon is comparatively better at surgery than at lawn mowing, she will spend most of her time at the operating table and pay the teenager to mow her lawn. The brain surgeon behaves this way because the opportunity cost of mowing the lawn is too high: Time spent mowing is time unavailable for surgery.

Let us return to the example in Table 5.1 to contrast absolute and comparative advantage. Recall that France has an absolute advantage in wine and Japan has an absolute advantage in clock radios. The theory of absolute advantage says that France should export wine to Japan and Japan should export clock radios to France. As Table 5.1 shows, France also has a comparative advantage in wine: With 1 hour of labor it produces 2 times as much wine as Japan does but only 0.6 times as many clock radios. Thus France is *relatively* more productive in wine. Japan has a comparative advantage in clock radios: With 1 hour of labor it produces 1.67 times as many clock radios as France does but only 0.5 times as much wine. So Japan is *relatively* more productive in clock radios. The theory of comparative advantage says that France should export wine to Japan and Japan should export clock radios to France. For the example in Table 5.1, the theory of absolute advantage and the theory of comparative advantage both yield the same outcome.

Now let us change the facts some. Suppose productivity stays the same in Japan but doubles in France as the result of new job training programs. Table 5.2 shows this new situation. France now can produce 4 bottles of wine or 6 clock radios per hour of labor. France now has an absolute advantage in *both* wine and clock radios: For each hour of labor France can produce 3 more bottles of wine (4 minus 1) or 1 more clock radio (6 minus 5) than Japan can. According to the theory of absolute advantage, no trade should occur because France is more productive than Japan in producing both goods.

The theory of comparative advantage, on the other hand, indicates that trade should still occur. France is 4 times better than Japan is in wine production but only 1.2 times better in clock radio production. (Alternatively, Japan is only 0.25 as good as France in wine production but 0.83 as good in clock radio production.) France is comparatively better than Japan in wine production, while Japan is comparatively better than France in clock radio production.

By the theory of comparative advantage France should export wine to Japan and Japan should export clock radios to France. If they do so, both will be better off. In the absence of trade 1 bottle of wine will sell for 1.5 clock radios in France and for 5 clock radios in Japan. If Japan offers to trade 2 clock radios for 1 bottle of wine, France will be better off—*even though France has an absolute advantage in clock radio production.* Without trade sacrificing 1 bottle of wine domestically would yield France only 1.5 clock radios in increased production. With trade France could get 2 clock radios by giving up 1 bottle of wine to Japan. France gets more clock radios per bottle of wine given up by trading with Japan than by producing the clock radios domestically.

Japan also gains. Without trade Japan has to give up 5 clock radios to get 1 more bottle of wine. With trade Japan has to give up only 2 clock radios to obtain 1 more bottle. Japan gets more wine per clock radio given up by trading with France than by producing the wine domestically. Even though France has an absolute advantage in both wine and clock radio production, both countries gain from this trade. It is comparative advantage that motivates trade, not absolute advantage. For another insight into comparative advantage and the problems inherent in neomercantilism, see "Bringing the World into Focus."

OUTPUT PER HOUR OF LABOR		
	France	Japan
Wine	4	1
Clock radios	6	5

TABLE 5.2

The Theory of Comparative Advantage: An Example

Bringing the World into FOCUS

THE LINCOLN FALLACY

For centuries professors and politicians have debated the wisdom of allowing foreign producers to sell their goods on equal footing with domestic producers. To free-trade advocates limiting consumer choice to domestically produced goods is a violation of free-market principles and the spirit of competition. Many other groups, however, see free trade as selling out our fellow citizens. According to these groups, buying foreign goods sends our jobs and hard-earned money to foreign nations, building their economies by tearing down ours. This timeless argument is as common today as it was when Abraham Lincoln endorsed it in his characteristically direct fashion: "I know this much. When we buy manufactured goods abroad, we get the goods and the foreigner gets the money. When we buy the manufactured goods at home, we get both the goods and the money."

To the trained eye Lincoln's argument is conspicuously and dangerously flawed. But how many people disagree with his logic or understand why they should? Like most misleading arguments, Lincoln's case against free trade is true in and of itself, but it is also incomplete. It is true that buying domestic goods keeps our money in the country whereas buying foreign goods sends our money abroad, but this is only part of the story. What we also need to consider are the resources needed to produce goods. When we buy goods produced domestically, some local resources must be used: labor, materials, and a physical location. When we buy goods from abroad, however, foreign resources are used, leaving the domestic resources free to be used to make something else. In other words, buying from abroad frees up domestic resources that can be used in a more productive manner, leading to greater wealth for our country.

Adding this part of the story to Lincoln's argument renders a more complete comparison between buying domestic goods and buying foreign goods. The complete comparison could be phrased like this: "When we buy goods made at home, we get the goods and the money but have to use up resources that could have been used to make other goods. When we buy manufactured goods abroad, the foreigner gets the money, but we get the goods and get to keep the resources which then can be used to make other goods." If those freed resources are used in more productive industries, we will have more goods to consume when we are open to international trade than we would if we were not open to trade. The same logic holds for our foreign trade partners, and so this argument implies that free trade makes all countries better off.

The idea that free trade is better for everyone boils down to an argument for specialization that is similar to the commonsense notions we use in our daily lives. Most of us buy almost everything we consume. We buy our food from markets, our clothes from stores, and our cars from automobile manufacturers. It is certainly true that when we buy our clothes from a store, we get the clothes and the store owner gets the money, but this is a good thing, isn't it? After all, buying our clothes from a store rather than making them ourselves frees up the time it would have taken us to make our own clothes. Most of us use this time to specialize in our own productive specialty, whether it is carpentry or computer programming. We then trade our services in what we do best for those that others do better than us. By specializing and trading, rather than producing everything ourselves, we channel production to the most efficient producers, thereby ensuring more production overall and more goods and services for everyone to consume. This principle holds for nations just as it does for individuals. By specializing in what they do best and trading freely, countries are able to produce more of everything and, consequently, their citizens have more to consume than they would if trade was limited by tariffs, quotas, or other barriers.

Source: We are grateful to our colleague Peter Rodriguez for allowing us to reproduce his analysis here. Reproduced with permission from *The Legal Environment of Business*, (third edition), Bierman et al., Eddie Bower Publishing, Dubuque, Iowa, 2000.

Comparative Advantage with Money

The lesson of the theory of comparative advantage is simple but powerful: *You are better off specializing in what you do relatively best. Produce (and export) those goods and services you are relatively best able to produce, and buy other goods and services from people who are relatively better at producing them than you are.*

TABLE 5.3

The Theory of Comparative Advantage with Money: An Example

	COST OF GOODS IN FRANCE		COST OF GOODS IN JAPAN	
	French Made	Japanese Made	French Made	Japanese Made
Wine	Fr 18	Fr 40	¥450	¥1,000
Clock radios	Fr 12	Fr 8	¥300	¥200

Note: For example, 1 hour's worth of French labor can produce 4 bottles of wine at a total cost of Fr 72, or an average cost of Fr 18 per bottle. At an exchange rate of 25 yen per franc, a bottle of French-made wine will cost ¥450 (450 = 18 × 25).

Of course, Tables 5.1 and 5.2 are both simplistic and artificial. The world economy produces more than two goods and services and is made up of more than two countries. Barriers to trade may exist, someone must pay to transport goods between markets, and inputs other than labor are necessary to produce goods. Even more important, the world economy uses money as a medium of exchange. Table 5.3 introduces money into our discussion of trade and incorporates the following assumptions:

1. The output per hour of labor in France and Japan for clock radios and wine is as shown in Table 5.2.
2. The hourly wage rate in France is 72 francs (Fr).
3. The hourly wage rate in Japan is 1,000 yen (¥).
4. One French franc is worth 25 yen.

Given these assumptions, in the absence of trade, a bottle of wine in France costs Fr 18, the equivalent of ¥450, and clock radios cost Fr 12, the equivalent of ¥300. In Japan a bottle of wine costs ¥1,000 (Fr 40), and clock radios cost ¥200 (Fr 8).

In this case trade will occur because of the self-interest of individual entrepreneurs (or the opportunity to make a profit) in France and Japan. For example, buyers for Galeries Lafayette, a major Paris department store, observe that clock radios cost Fr 12 in France and the equivalent of only Fr 8 in Japan. To keep their cost of goods low, these buyers will order clock radios in Japan, where they are cheap, and sell them in France, where they are expensive. Accordingly, clock radios will be exported by Japan and imported by France, just as the law of comparative advantage predicts. Similarly, wine distributors in Japan observe that a bottle of wine costs ¥1,000 in Japan but the equivalent of only ¥450 in France. To keep their cost of goods as low as possible, buyers for Japanese wine distributors will buy wine in France, where it is cheap, and sell it in Japan, where it is expensive. Wine will be exported by France and imported by Japan, as predicted by the law of comparative advantage.

Note that none of these businesspeople needed to know anything about the theory of comparative advantage. They merely looked at the price differences in the two markets and made their business decisions based on the desire to obtain supplies at the lowest possible cost. Yet they benefit from comparative advantage because prices set in a free market reflect a country's comparative advantage.

Relative Factor Endowments

The theory of comparative advantage begs a broader question: What determines the products for which a country will have a comparative advantage? To answer this question, two Swedish economists, Eli Heckscher and Bertil Ohlin, developed the **theory of relative factor endowments**, now often referred to as the **Heckscher-Ohlin theory**. These economists made two basic observations:

1. *Factor endowments (or types of resources) vary among countries.* For example, Argentina has much fertile land, Saudi Arabia has large crude oil reserves, and China has a large pool of unskilled labor.

2. *Goods differ according to the types of factors that are used to produce them.* For example, wheat requires fertile land, oil production requires crude oil reserves, and clothing requires unskilled labor.

From these observations Heckscher and Ohlin developed their theory: *A country will have a comparative advantage in producing products that intensively use resources (factors of production) it has in abundance.* Thus Argentina has a comparative advantage in wheat growing because of its abundance of fertile land; Saudi Arabia has a comparative advantage in oil production because of its abundance of crude oil reserves; and China has a comparative advantage in clothing manufacture because of its abundance of unskilled labor.

The Heckscher-Ohlin theory suggests a country should export those goods that intensively use those factors of production that are relatively abundant in the country. The theory was tested empirically after World War II by economist Wassily Leontief using input-output analysis, a mathematical technique for measuring the interrelationships among the sectors of an economy. Leontief believed the United States was a capital-abundant and labor-scarce economy. Therefore, according to the Heckscher-Ohlin theory, he reasoned that the United States should export capital-intensive goods, such as bulk chemicals and steel, and import labor-intensive goods, such as clothing and footwear.

Leontief used his input-output model of the U.S. economy to estimate the quantities of labor and capital needed to produce "bundles" of U.S. exports and imports worth $1 million in 1947 (see Figure 5.3). (Each bundle was a weighted average of all U.S. exports or imports in 1947.) He determined that in 1947 U.S. factories utilized $2.551 million of capital and 182.3 person-years of labor, or $13,993 of capital per person-year of labor, to produce a bundle of exports worth $1 million. He also calculated that $3.093 million of capital and 170.0 person-years of labor, or $18,194 of capital per person-year of labor, were used to produce a bundle of U.S. imports worth $1 million in that year. Thus U.S. imports were more capital intensive than U.S. exports. Imports required $4,201 ($18,194 – $13,993) more in capital per person-year of labor to produce than exports did.

These results were not consistent with the predictions of the Heckscher-Ohlin theory: U.S. imports were nearly 30 percent more capital intensive than were U.S. exports. The economics profession was distraught. The Heckscher-Ohlin theory made such intuitive sense, yet Leontief's findings were the reverse of what was expected. Thus was born the **Leontief paradox**.

During the past 40 years numerous economists have repeated Leontief's initial study in an attempt to resolve the paradox. The first such study was performed by

FIGURE 5.3

U.S. Imports and Exports, 1947: The Leontief Paradox

Leontief himself. He thought trade flows may have been distorted in 1947 because much of the world economy was still reeling from World War II. Using 1951 data he found that U.S. imports were 6 percent more capital intensive than U.S. exports were. Although this figure was less than that in his original study, it still disagreed with the predictions of the Heckscher-Ohlin theory.

Some scholars argue that measurement problems flaw Leontief's work. Leontief assumed there are two homogeneous factors of production: labor and capital. Yet other factors of production exist, most notably land, human capital, and technology—none of which were included in Leontief's analysis. Failure to include these factors may have caused him to mismeasure the labor intensity of U.S. exports and imports. Many U.S. exports are intensive in either land (such as agricultural goods) or human knowledge (such as computers, aircraft, and services). Consider the products sold by one of the leading U.S. exporters, Boeing. Leontief's approach measures the physical capital (the plants, property, and equipment) and the physical labor used to construct Boeing aircraft but fails to gauge adequately the role of human capital and technology in the firm's operations. Yet human capital (the well-educated engineers who design the aircraft and highly skilled machinists who assemble it) and technology (the sophisticated management techniques that control the world's largest assembly lines) are more important to Boeing's success than mere physical capital and physical labor. Leontief's failure to measure the role that these other factors of production play in determining international trade patterns may account for his paradoxical results.

> Scandinavia's domestic environment—high consumer income, vibrant technological base, and unpopulated northern regions that make stringing telephone wire expensive—have contributed to the growth of its wireless communication industry. Ericsson and Nokia reign atop this growing industry, marketing their sophisticated equipment to customers around the world, including these young Swedes enjoying a warm Stockholm summer afternoon.

MODERN FIRM-BASED TRADE THEORIES

Since World War II, international business research has focused on the role of the firm rather than the country in promoting international trade. Firm-based theories have developed for several reasons: (1) the growing importance of MNCs in the postwar international economy; (2) the inability of the country-based theories to explain and predict the existence and growth of intraindustry trade (defined in the next section); and (3) the failure of Leontief and other researchers to empirically validate the country-based Heckscher-Ohlin theory. Unlike country-based theories, firm-based theories incorporate factors such as quality, technology, brand names, and customer loyalty into explanations of trade flows. Because firms, not countries, are the agents for international trade, the newer theories explore the firm's role in promoting exports and imports.

Country Similarity Theory

Country-based theories, such as the theory of comparative advantage, do a good job of explaining interindustry trade among countries. **Interindustry trade** is the exchange of goods produced by one industry in country A for goods produced by a different industry in country B, such as the exchange of French wines for Japanese clock radios. Yet much international trade consists of **intraindustry trade**, that is, trade between two countries of goods produced by the same industry. For example, Japan exports Toyotas to Germany, while Germany exports BMWs to Japan.

Intraindustry trade accounts for approximately 40 percent of world trade, and it is not predicted by country-based theories.

In 1961 Swedish economist Steffan Linder sought to explain the phenomenon of intraindustry trade. Linder hypothesized that international trade in manufactured goods results from similarities of preferences among consumers in countries that are at the same stage of economic development. In his view firms initially manufacture goods to serve the firms' domestic market. As they explore exporting opportunities, they discover that the most promising foreign markets are in countries where consumer preferences resemble those of their own domestic market. The Japanese market, for example, provides BMW with well-off, prestige- and performance-seeking automobile buyers similar to the ones who purchase its cars in Germany. The German market provides Toyota with quality-conscious and value-oriented customers similar to those found in its home market. As each company targets the other's home market, intraindustry trade arises. Linder's **country similarity theory** suggests that most trade in manufactured goods should be between countries with similar per capita incomes and that intraindustry trade in manufactured goods should be common. This theory is particularly useful in explaining trade in differentiated goods such as automobiles, expensive electronics equipment, and personal care products, for which brand names and product reputations play an important role in consumer decision making.

Product Life Cycle Theory

Product life cycle theory, which originated in the marketing field to describe the evolution of marketing strategies as a product matures, is a second firm-based theory of international trade (and, as we will see, of international investment). As developed in the 1960s by Raymond Vernon of the Harvard Business School, international product life cycle theory traces the roles of innovation, market expansion, comparative advantage, and strategic responses of global rivals in international production, trade, and investment decisions. According to Vernon's theory and as illustrated in Figure 5.4, the international product life cycle consists of three stages called new product, maturing product, and standardized product.

In stage 1, the *new product stage*, a firm develops and introduces an innovative product, such as a photocopier or a personal computer, in response to a perceived need in the domestic market. Because the product is new, the innovating firm is uncertain whether a profitable market for the product exists. The firm's marketing executives must closely monitor customer reactions to ensure the new product satisfies consumer needs. Quick market feedback is important, so the product is likely to be initially produced in the country where its research and development occurred, typically a developed country like Japan, Germany, or the United States. Further, because the market size also is uncertain, the firm usually will minimize its investment in manufacturing capacity for the product. Most output initially is sold in the domestic market, and export sales are limited.

For example, during the early days of the personal computer industry the small producers that populated the industry had their hands full trying to meet the burgeoning demand for their product. Apple Computer typified this problem. Founded on April Fool's Day in 1976, its initial assembly plant was located in cofounder Steve Jobs's garage. The first large order for its homemade computers—50 units from a local computer hobbyist store—almost bankrupted the firm because it lacked the financing to buy the necessary parts.[5] Apple survived because of the nurturing environment in which it was born, California's Silicon Valley. Home to major electronics firms such as Hewlett-Packard, Intel, and National Semiconductor, Silicon Valley was full of electrical engineers who could design and build Apple's products and venture capitalists who were seeking the "next Xerox." It was the perfect locale for Apple's sales to grow from zero in 1976 to $7.8 million in 1978 and $6.1 billion in 1999.

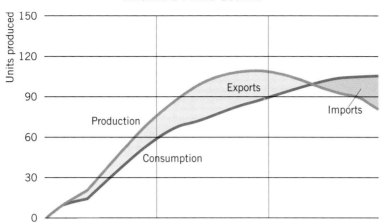

INNOVATING FIRM'S COUNTRY

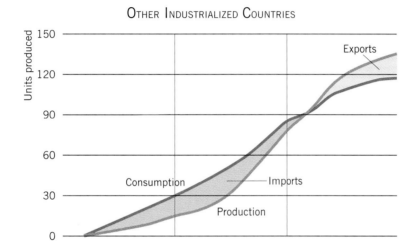

OTHER INDUSTRIALIZED COUNTRIES

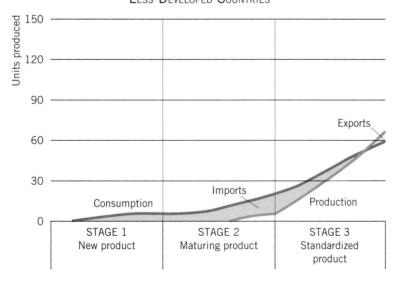

LESS-DEVELOPED COUNTRIES

FIGURE 5.4

The International Product Life Cycle

Source: Raymond Vernon/Louis T. Wells, Jr., *The Economic Environment of International Business*, 5th ed., © 1991, p. 85. Adapted by permission of Prentice Hall, Upper Saddle River, NJ.

In stage 2, the *maturing product stage*, demand for the product expands dramatically as consumers recognize its value. The innovating firm builds new factories to expand its capacity and satisfy domestic and foreign demand for the product. Domestic and foreign competitors begin to emerge, lured by the prospect of lucrative earnings. In the case of Apple, the firm introduced a hand-assembled version of its second model, the Apple II, at a San Francisco computer fair in the spring of 1977. Within three years Apple had sold 130,000 units and expanded its production facilities beyond Jobs's garage. To serve domestic and foreign customers, Apple IIs were manufactured in California and Texas and distributed from warehouses in the United States and the Netherlands.

In stage 3, the *standardized product stage*, the market for the product stabilizes. The product becomes more of a commodity, and firms are pressured to lower their manufacturing costs as much as possible by shifting production to facilities in countries with low labor costs. As a result, the product begins to be imported into the innovating firm's home market (by either the firm or its competitors). In some cases imports may result in the complete elimination of domestic production.

The personal computer industry has entered the standardized product stage. In the U.S. market low-priced brand-name imports from new producers such as South Korea's Hyundai and Samsung have threatened the more established U.S. manufacturers. Taiwanese manufacturers such as Tatung, Mitac International, First International, and TECO Information Systems—none of them household names in the United States—annually export to the United States millions of personal computers, many of which are produced under contract for foreign distributors. To meet the challenge of these new competitors and price its products more competitively, Apple simplified its product line, expanded its use of industry standard parts, outsourced manufacture of many components, and streamlined its warehousing operations.[6] Despite these efforts, domestic and foreign competitors continue to eat away at Apple's market share and profit margins, and the company has been relegated to a niche player in the industry it pioneered.

According to the international product life cycle theory, domestic production begins in stage 1, peaks in stage 2, and slumps in stage 3. Exports by the innovating firm's country also begin in stage 1 and peak in stage 2. By stage 3, however, the innovating firm's country becomes a net importer of the product. Foreign competition begins to emerge toward the end of stage 1, as firms in other industrialized countries recognize the product's market potential. In stage 2 foreign competitors expand their productive capacity, thus servicing an increasing portion of their home markets and perhaps becoming net exporters. However, as competition intensifies in stage 2, the innovating firm and its domestic and foreign rivals seek to lower their production costs by shifting production to low-cost sites in less developed countries. Eventually, in stage 3, the less developed countries may become net exporters of the product.

Global Strategic Rivalry Theory

More recent explanations of the pattern of international trade, developed in the 1980s by such economists as Paul Krugman[7] and Kelvin Lancaster,[8] examine the impact on trade flows of global strategic rivalry between MNCs. According to this view, firms struggle to develop some sustainable competitive advantage, which they can then exploit to dominate the global marketplace. Like Linder's approach, global strategic rivalry theory predicts that intraindustry trade will be commonplace. However, it focuses on strategic decisions firms adopt as they compete internationally. These decisions affect both international trade and international investment. Companies like Caterpillar and Komatsu, Unilever and Procter & Gamble, and Toyota and Ford continually play cat-and-mouse games with one another on a global basis as they attempt to leverage their own strengths and neutralize those of their rivals. "Venturing Abroad" depicts one such struggle, that between Kodak and Fuji.

VENTURING *Abroad*
AN OLYMPIC-SIZED RIVALRY

As visitors poured into Nagano, Japan, during the 1998 winter Olympics, among the first things they saw were two billboards. The first, featuring the familiar gold tones of Eastman Kodak, the official film of the 1998 winter games, announced "Honored to Be Part of the Olympics." The second, sponsored by Kodak's chief rival, proclaimed "Fuji Film: It Captures the Moment of Truth."

Kodak and Fuji are bitter rivals around the globe. Kodak's share of the world film market is an estimated 39 percent, while Fuji's is 37 percent. Kodak owns the lion's share of the $2.7 billion U.S. film market, while Fuji enjoys similar dominance in the $2.0 billion Japanese market. In the late 1990s, however, Fuji intensified its assault on the U.S. market. It launched a pricing war there, cutting the price of its multiple-roll packs of film by as much as 50 percent. Fuji's attack was successful, taking several points of market share away from Kodak and forcing Kodak to cut its own prices and lay off thousands of employees. Global strategic rivalry theory suggests the wisdom of Fuji's offensive. The price war in the U.S. market did far more damage to Kodak's bottom line than to Fuji's. By forcing Kodak to hemorrhage red ink to stop its loss of U.S. market share, Fuji hoped to weaken Kodak's ability to compete with it elsewhere.

Kodak did not throw in the towel and surrender. Rather, it vigorously counterattacked Fuji in the Japanese market. Kodak's status as an official Olympic sponsor was a key element of its strategy. For two years prior to the games, it built its presence in the Nagano market to ensure that the 1.2 million people who visited the Olympics were able to buy film in Kodak's gold boxes rather than Fuji's green ones. To bypass distributors loyal to Fuji, Kodak trucked film into Nagano and subsidized a local entrepreneur to open a Kodak store right next to Nagano's leading Fuji dealer. Kodak installed its own film processing lab in Nagano to meet the needs of Olympic photographers and visitors. It flooded the town with Olympic-themed outdoor advertisements, outfitted local buses with photos of its products, and slashed its prices. Special promotions offering Olympic pins for purchasers of Kodak film provided further enticements for local Fuji-loyal shutterbugs to try Kodak film. Through these efforts Kodak increased its share of the Nagano market to 20 percent, double its share of the Japanese market as a whole. In response Fuji was forced to cut its own prices in the area, something it rarely does in the Japanese market.

Ironically, Kodak has been an official sponsor of every Olympics since 1896, except one: the 1984 summer games in Los Angeles. At those games Fuji was the official sponsor. Many industry experts trace Fuji's success in the U.S. market to its sponsorship of the 1984 summer games, which gave it instant visibility in the huge U.S. market and doubled its U.S. market share in the space of four years. Kodak obviously hopes that lightning will strike twice and that it too can use the Olympic Games to boost its long-term profits and market share in the home market of its chief rival.

Sources: "Kodak and U.S. Government Team Up for New Drive on Japan's Film Market," *Wall Street Journal*, February 4, 1998, p. A4; "A Film War Breaks Out in Nagano," *Wall Street Journal*, February 3, 1998, p. B1; "A Dark Moment for Kodak," *Business Week*, August 4, 1997, p. 30.

Firms competing in the global marketplace have numerous ways of obtaining a sustainable competitive advantage. The more popular ones are owning intellectual property rights, investing in research and development, achieving economies of scale or scope, and exploiting the experience curve. We discuss each of these options next.

Owning Intellectual Property Rights. A firm that owns an **intellectual property right**—a trademark, brand name, patent, or copyright—often gains advantages over its competitors. For example, in early 2000 Germany's EM.TV & Merchandising AG paid $680 million for the Jim Henson Co. Through this purchase EM.TV acquired such children's series as *The Muppet Show*, *Muppet Babies*, and *Fraggle Rock* plus the licensing rights to such characters as Miss Piggy and her beloved Kermit the Frog. The acquisition gave EM.TV new avenues for expanding its family-oriented broadcasting and licensing businesses beyond its European base. Similarly, owning prestigious brand names enables Ireland's Waterford Wedgewood Company and France's Louis Vuitton to charge premium prices for their upscale products. And Coca-Cola and PepsiCo compete for customers worldwide on the basis of their trademarks and brand names.

Investing in Research and Development.   Research and development (R&D) is a major component of the total cost of high-technology products. For example, Airbus plans to spend $12 billion to develop its new superjumbo jet, the A380. Firms in the computer, pharmaceutical, and semiconductor industries also spend large amounts on R&D to maintain their competitiveness. Because of such large "entry" costs, other firms often hesitate to compete against established firms. Thus the firm that acts first often gains a **first-mover advantage**.

However, knowledge does not have a nationality. Firms that invest up front and secure the first-mover advantage have the opportunity to dominate the world market for goods that are intensive in R&D. According to the global strategic rivalry theory, trade flows may be determined by which firms make the necessary R&D expenditures. Why is the European Union a large exporter of commercial aircraft? Because Airbus is one of the few firms willing to spend the large sums of money required to develop new aircraft and because it just happens to be headquartered in Europe.

Firms with large domestic markets may have an advantage over their foreign rivals in high-technology markets because these firms often are able to obtain quicker and richer feedback from customers. With this feedback the firms can fine-tune their R&D efforts, enabling the firms to better meet the needs of their domestic customers. This knowledge can then be utilized to serve foreign customers. For example, U.S. agricultural chemical producers such as Monsanto and Eli Lilly have an advantage over Japanese rivals in developing soybean pesticides because the U.S. market for such pesticides is large while the Japanese market is small. Knowledge gained in the U.S. pesticide market can be readily transferred to meet the needs of Japanese farmers.

Achieving Economies of Scale or Scope.   Economies of scale or scope offer firms another opportunity to obtain a sustainable competitive advantage in international markets. **Economies of scale** occur when a product's average costs decrease as the number of units produced increases. **Economies of scope** occur when a firm's average costs decrease as the number of different products it sells increases. Firms that are able to achieve economies of scale or scope enjoy low average costs, which give the firms a competitive advantage over their global rivals. Both of these economies are particularly important for e-retailers. Amazon.com, for example, has spent enormous sums developing and maintaining its Web site and building its customer base. Because many of these costs are fixed, the company's average costs per sale decline as the company expands its sales. In its quest to capture the volume-driven economies of scale, Amazon.com has been expanding its operations into the international marketplace. Moreover, the marginal cost of adding an additional product line to its Web site is relatively small. Accordingly, the company has expanded from books to compact discs to videos to auctions in order to capture such economies of scope.

Exploiting the Experience Curve.   Another source of firm-specific advantages in international trade is exploitation of the experience curve. For certain types of products production costs decline as the firm gains more experience in manufacturing the product. Experience curves may be so significant that they govern global competition within an industry. For example, in semiconductor chip production, unit cost reductions of 25 to 30 percent with each doubling of a firm's cumulative chip production are not uncommon.[9] Any firm attempting to be a low-cost producer of so-called commodity chips—such as 64 MB memory chips—can achieve that goal only if it moves further along the experience curve than its rivals do. Both U.S. and Asian chip manufacturers have often priced their new products below current production costs to capture the sales necessary to generate the production experience that will in turn enable the manufacturers to lower future production costs. Because of their technological leadership in manufacturing and their aggressive, price-cutting strategies, Asian semiconductor manufacturers such as NEC and Samsung dominate the production of low-cost, standardized semiconductor chips.[10] Similarly, innovative U.S. semiconductor firms such as Intel and Advanced Micro Devices utilize the experience curve to maintain leadership in the production of higher-priced, proprietary chips, such as the Pentium III and Athlon chips that form the brains of newer microcomputers.

Porter's National Competitive Advantage

Harvard Business School professor Michael Porter's **theory of national competitive advantage** is the newest addition to international trade theory. Porter believes that success in international trade comes from the interaction of four country- and firm-specific elements: factor conditions; demand conditions; related and supporting industries; and firm strategy, structure, and rivalry. Porter represents these four elements as the four corners of a diamond, as shown in Figure 5.5.

Factor Conditions. A country's endowment of factors of production affects its ability to compete internationally. Although factor endowments were the center-piece of the Hecksher-Ohlin theory, Porter goes beyond the basic factors—land, labor, capital—considered by the classical trade theorists to include more advanced factors such as the educational level of the workforce and the quality of the country's infrastructure. His work stresses the role of factor creation through training, research, and innovation.

Demand Conditions. The existence of a large, sophisticated domestic consumer base often stimulates the development and distribution of innovative products as firms struggle for dominance in their domestic market. In meeting their domestic customers' needs, however, firms continually develop and fine-tune products that also can be marketed internationally. Thus pioneering firms can stay ahead of their international competitors as well. For example, Japanese consumer electronics producers maintain a competitive edge internationally because of the willingness of Japan's large, well-off middle class to buy the latest electronic creations of Sony, Toshiba, and Matsushita. After being fine-tuned in the domestic market, new models of Japanese camcorders, big screen TVs, and VCRs are sold to eager European and North American consumers. A similar phenomenon is occurring in the Internet market, where the rapid adoption of the Internet by North

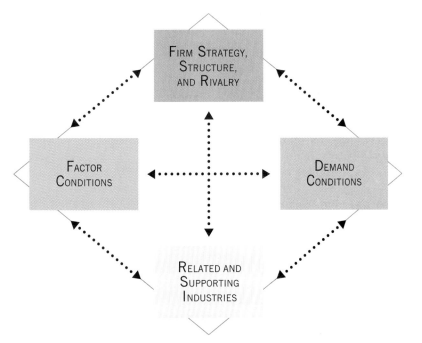

FIGURE 5.5

Porter's Diamond of National Competitive Advantage

Source: Reprinted by permission of *Harvard Business Review.* An exhibit from "The Competitive Advantage of Nations" by Michael E. Porter, March/April 1990. Copyright © 1990 by the President and Fellows of Harvard College; all rights reserved.

American consumers and companies has created a fertile climate for new companies such as eBay and iVillage to develop and tailor new products to meet the needs of this market.

Related and Supporting Industries.   The emergence of an industry often stimulates the development of local suppliers eager to meet that industry's production, marketing, and distribution needs. An industry located close to its suppliers will enjoy better communication and the exchange of cost-saving ideas and inventions with those suppliers. Competition among these input suppliers leads to lower prices, higher-quality products, and technological innovations in the input market, in turn reinforcing the industry's competitive advantage in world markets. For example, as we noted earlier, Apple's path-breaking personal computer was first made in Steve Jobs's California garage in the mid-1970s. As demand for personal computers exploded, supplier firms located in the Silicon Valley to be closer to Apple and other personal computer manufacturers. The local availability of sophisticated software, disk drive, and computer chip suppliers strengthened the competitive advantage of California personal computer manufacturers in world markets.

Firm Strategy, Structure, and Rivalry.   The domestic environment in which firms compete shapes their ability to compete in international markets. To survive, firms facing vigorous competition domestically must continuously strive to reduce costs, boost product quality, raise productivity, and develop innovative products. Firms that have been tested in this way often develop the skills needed to succeed internationally. Further, many of the investments they made to succeed in the domestic market (for example, in R&D, quality control, brand image, and employee training) are transferable to international markets at low cost. Such firms have an edge as they expand abroad. Thus, according to Porter's theory, the international success of Japanese automakers and consumer electronics goods manufacturers and of U.S. personal computer manufacturers is aided by intense domestic competition in these firms' home countries.

Porter holds that national policies may also affect firms' international strategies and opportunities in more subtle ways. Consider the German automobile market. German labor costs are very high, so German automakers find it difficult to compete internationally on the basis of price. However, as most auto enthusiasts know, there are no speed limits on Germany's famed autobahns. So German automakers such as Daimler-Benz, Porsche, and BMW have chosen to compete on the basis of quality and high performance by engineering chassis, engines, brakes, and suspensions that can withstand the stresses of high-speed driving. Consequently, these firms dominate the world market for high-performance automobiles. "Wiring the World" provides another illustration of this phenomenon: Nokia's rise to global prominence resulting from the geography of its home country, Finland.

Porter's theory is a hybrid: It blends the traditional country-based theories that emphasize factor endowments with the firm-based theories that focus on the actions of individual firms. Countries (or their governments) play a critical role in creating an environment that can aid or harm the ability of firms to compete internationally, but firms are the actors that actually participate in international trade. Some firms succeed internationally; others do not. Porsche, Daimler-Benz, and BMW successfully grasped the opportunity presented by Germany's decision to allow unlimited speeds on its highways and captured the high-performance niche of the worldwide automobile industry. Conversely, Volkswagen and Opel chose to focus on the broader middle segment of the German automobile market, ultimately limiting their international options.

In summary no single theory of international trade explains all trade flows among countries. The classical country-based theories are useful in explaining interindustry trade of homogeneous, undifferentiated products, such as agricultural goods, raw materials, and processed goods like steel and aluminum. The firm-based theories are more helpful in understanding intraindustry trade of heteroge-

Wiring the World

NOKIA'S INCREDIBLE TRANSFORMATION

Nokia Corporation is a study in contrasts. Compared to most contemporary high-technology telecommunications companies, it is ancient—it was founded in 1865. By other measures, however, it is not only one of the world's newest but also one of the most vibrant and exciting big companies.

Nokia was formed by Fredrik Idestam, a Finnish engineer. Its early success is consistent with the theory of comparative advantage. Idestam's young company set up shop on the Nokia River in Finland (hence the firm's name) to manufacture pulp and paper using the area's lush forests as raw material. Nokia flourished in anonymity for about a hundred years, focusing almost exclusively on its domestic market.

During the 1960s the firm's management decided to start expanding regionally. In 1967, with the government's encouragement, Nokia took over two state-owned firms, Finnish Rubber Works and Finnish Cable Works. In 1981 Nokia's destiny was altered dramatically by one seminal event: Because it had done so well with the rubber and cable operations, the Finnish government offered to sell Nokia 51 percent of the state-owned Finnish Telecommunications Company.

Because Nokia had already been developing competencies in digital technologies, it quickly seized this opportunity and pushed aggressively into a variety of telecommunications businesses. For example, Nokia created Europe's first digital telephone network in

1982. A series of other acquisitions and partnerships propelled Nokia to the number one position in the global market for mobile telephones.

At face value it might seem that larger industrial countries like the United States, Germany, and Japan should be leading the way in this market. Conditions in Finland, however, provide a unique catalyst for Nokia's success. Many parts of the Finnish landscape are heavily forested, and vast regions of the country are very sparsely populated. Creating, maintaining, and updating land-based wired communication networks can be very slow and extremely expensive, making wireless digital systems a relative bargain. Thus conditions were near perfect for an astute, forward-looking company like Nokia to strike gold.

Nokia has not been content to rest on its laurels. To the contrary, the company is moving aggressively to expand its technological prowess to new markets, such as providing reliable and affordable Web content to cellular telephones. Nokia was first out of the gate in this area and quickly established its own innovation, WAP (an acronym for wireless application protocol), as the likely standard that others will have little choice but to license for their own use.

Sources: *Hoover's Handbook of World Business 2000* (Austin, Texas: Hoover's Business Press, 2000), pp. 410–411; "It Takes a Cell Phone," *Wall Street Journal*, June 25, 1999, pp. B1, B4.

neous, differentiated goods, such as Sony televisions and Caterpillar bulldozers, many of which are sold on the basis of their brand names and reputations. Further, in many ways, Porter's theory synthesizes the features of the existing country-based and firm-based theories.

AN OVERVIEW OF INTERNATIONAL INVESTMENT ❮

Trade is the most obvious but not the only form of international business. Another major form is international investment, whereby residents of one country supply capital to a second country. Sometimes trade and investment are substitutes for each other. For example, Honda's plants in the United States act as a substitute for international trade because they allow Honda to export fewer cars and parts from its Japanese plants to the United States, thereby reducing international trade. At other times international trade and investment may be complementary. For example, to reduce production costs, Compaq Computer, headquartered in Houston, Texas, operates two factories in Scotland's "Silicon Glen"—the region between

Glasgow and Edinburgh where 10 percent of the world's personal computers are produced.[11] U.S.-bound exports from Compaq's Scottish factories illustrate the complementary relationship between international trade and investment.

Types of International Investments

International investment, as discussed in Chapter 1, is divided into two categories: portfolio investment and foreign direct investment (FDI). The distinction between the two rests on the question of control: Does the investor seek an active management role in the firm or merely a return from a passive investment?

Portfolio investments represent passive holdings of securities such as foreign stocks, bonds, or other financial assets, none of which entail active management or control of the securities' issuer by the investor. Modern finance theory suggests that foreign portfolio investments will be motivated by attempts to seek an attractive rate of return as well as the reduction of risk that can come from geographically diversifying one's investment portfolio. Sophisticated money managers in New York, London, Frankfurt, Tokyo, and other financial centers are well aware of the advantages of international diversification. For example, in 1999 private U.S. citizens purchased $98 billion worth of foreign securities, bringing their total holdings of such securities to $2.6 trillion. Foreign private investors purchased $304 billion worth of U.S. corporate, federal, state, and local securities, raising their total holdings of such securities to $3.7 trillion.[12]

Foreign direct investment (FDI) is acquisition of foreign assets for the purpose of controlling them. U.S. government statisticians define FDI as "ownership or control of 10 percent or more of an enterprise's voting securities . . . or the equivalent interest in an unincorporated business."[13] FDI may take many forms, including purchase of existing assets in a foreign country, new investment in property, plant, and equipment, and participation in a joint venture with a local partner. Perhaps the most historically significant FDI in the United States was the $24 that Dutch explorer Peter Minuet paid local Native Americans for Manhattan Island.[14] The result: New York City, one of the world's leading financial and commercial centers.

The Growth of Foreign Direct Investment

The growth of foreign direct investment during the past 30 years has been phenomenal. As Table 5.4(a) indicates, in 1967 the total stock (or cumulative value) of FDI made by countries worldwide was slightly over $112 billion. Current worldwide FDI is about $3.5 trillion. As you might expect, most FDI comes from developed countries, which have consistently accounted for over 90 percent of all direct investments in foreign countries, as the first highlighted line in Table 5.4(a) indicates. If, in the 1990s, the Four Tigers (Hong Kong, Singapore, South Korea, and Taiwan) are included among the developed countries, then the enlarged group accounts for over 97 percent of FDI between 1967 and 1997.

During this period, however, significant shifts in the source of FDI have occurred. As shown in the second highlighted line in Table 5.4(a), the United States has become a less important source of FDI. FDI by U.S. firms has continued to increase in absolute terms but has shrunk in relative terms. The United States accounted for over half the stock of FDI in 1967 but only 25.6 percent in 1997. The importance of Japan and Germany as sources of FDI has increased dramatically during the same period, as shown by the third and fourth highlighted lines in Table 5.4(a). Note from the first two highlighted lines in Table 5.4(b) that the share of FDI *received* by the developed countries increased from 1967 to 1990, as did that of the United States. Although the shares of both the developed countries and the United States fell from 1990 to 1997, this occurred primarily because of the large influx of FDI into China seeking access to the world's most populous market. These data reflect a shift toward FDI motivated by penetration of large consumer markets and

TABLE 5.4

Destination and Source of FDI, 1967–1997 (billions of U.S. dollars)

a. Source of FDI by major home countries and regions

COUNTRIES/REGIONS	1967 Value	1967 Percent of total	1980 Value	1980 Percent of total	1990 Value	1990 Percent of total	1997 Value	1997 Percent of total
Developed market economies	109.3	97.3	507.5	98.8	1629.8	95.6	3192.5	90.1
United States	56.6	50.4	220.2	42.9	435.2	25.5	907.5	25.6
United Kingdom	15.8	14.1	80.4	15.7	229.3	13.5	413.2	11.7
Japan	1.5	1.3	18.8	3.7	201.4	11.8	284.6	8.0
Germany	3.0	2.7	43.1	8.4	151.6	8.9	326.0	9.2
Switzerland	2.5	2.2	21.5	4.2	65.7	3.9	156.7	4.4
Netherlands	11.0	9.8	42.1	8.2	109.0	6.4	213.2	6.0
Canada	3.7	3.3	22.6	4.4	84.8	5.0	137.7	3.9
France	6.0	5.3	23.6	4.6	110.1	6.5	226.8	6.4
Italy	2.1	1.9	7.3	1.4	56.1	3.3	125.1	3.5
Sweden	1.7	1.5	5.6	1.1	49.5	2.9	74.8	2.1
Other developed	5.4	4.8	22.3	4.3	137.1	8.0	326.9	9.2
Developing countries	3.0	2.7	6.2	1.2	74.7	4.4	348.9	9.9
Four Tigers*	NA	NA	1.0	0.2	38.1	2.2	233.1	6.6
Total	112.3	100.0	513.7	100.0	1704.5	100.0	3541.4	100.0

b. Destination of FDI by major host countries and regions

COUNTRIES/REGIONS	1967 Value	1967 Percent of total	1980 Value	1980 Percent of total	1990 Value	1990 Percent of total	1997 Value	1997 Percent of total
Developed market economies	73.2	69.4	373.5	77.5	1377.6	79.3	2349.4	68.0
United States	9.9	9.4	83.0	17.2	394.9	22.7	720.8	20.9
Canada	NA	NA	54.2	11.2	113.1	6.5	137.1	4.0
Western Europe	31.4	29.8	200.3	41.6	766.2	44.1	1276.4	36.9
European Union	NA	NA	185.0	38.4	719.8	41.5	1195.6	34.6
United Kingdom	7.9	7.5	63.0	13.1	203.9	11.7	274.4	7.9
France	NA	NA	22.6	4.7	86.8	5.0	174.2	5.0
Germany	3.6	3.4	36.6	7.6	111.2	6.4	137.7	4.0
Spain	NA	NA	5.1	1.1	65.2	3.8	110.6	3.2
Japan	0.6	0.6	3.3	0.7	9.9	0.6	33.2	1.0
Australia	NA	NA	13.2	2.7	74.3	4.3	126.3	3.7
Developing countries	32.3	30.6	108.3	22.5	358.7	20.7	1106.1	32.0
Africa	5.6	5.3	20.8	4.3	37.5	2.2	65.2	1.9
Latin America and Caribbean	18.5	17.5	48.0	10.0	124.0	7.1	375.4	10.9
Asia	8.3	7.9	38.0	7.9	192.7	11.1	593.7	17.2
Four Tigers*	NA	NA	11.5	2.4	57.4	3.3	137.6	4.0
China	negl.	negl.	negl.	negl.	18.6	1.1	217.3	6.3
Total	105.5	100.0	481.8	100.0	1736.3	100.0	3455.5	100.0

*Singapore, Taiwan, South Korea, and Hong Kong
NA = not available.
Sources: World Bank, *World Investment Report 1999*; John H. Dunning, *Multinational Enterprises and the Global Economy*. Wokingham, England: Addison-Wesley Publishers Ltd., 1993. Reprinted with permission.

away from FDI designed to exploit natural resources. Finally, although FDI by Japan has increased (see Table 5.4[a]), Japan's role as a destination country has remained about the same (Table 5.4[b]).

Foreign Direct Investment and the United States

We can gain additional insights into FDI by looking at individual countries. Consider the stock of FDI in the United States, which totaled $987 billion (measured at historical cost) at the end of 1999 (see Table 5.5[a]). The United Kingdom was the most important source of this FDI, accounting for $183.1 billion, or 19 percent, of the total. The countries listed by name in Table 5.5(a) account for 88 percent of total FDI in the United States.

The stock of FDI by U.S. residents in foreign countries totaled $1.1 trillion at the end of 1999 (see Table 5.5[b]). Most of this FDI was in other developed countries, particularly the United Kingdom ($213.1 billion) and Canada ($111.7 billion). The countries listed by name in Table 5.5(b) account for 62 percent of total FDI from the United States.

Looking at Table 5.5, you may wonder why Bermuda, the Bahamas, and other small Caribbean islands are so important. They serve as offshore financial centers, which we will discuss in Chapter 7. Many U.S. companies set up finance subsidiaries in such centers to take advantage of low taxes and business friendly regu-

TABLE 5.5

Patterns of FDI for the United States, end of 1999 (billions of dollars)

a. Sources of FDI in the United States	
United Kingdom	183.1
Japan	148.5
Netherlands	130.7
Germany	111.1
Canada	79.7
France	77.6
Switzerland	55.3
Luxembourg	54.9
Bermuda, the Bahamas, and other Caribbean islands	31.8
Other European countries	73.1
All other countries	40.5
Total	986.7
b. Destinations of FDI from the United States	
United Kingdom	213.1
Canada	111.7
Netherlands	106.4
Bermuda, the Bahamas, and other Caribbean islands	77.0
Germany	49.6
Japan	47.8
Switzerland	51.2
France	40.0
Other European countries	121.4
All other countries	314.4
Total	1,132.6

Source: Survey of Current Business, July 2000, pp. 67 and 69.

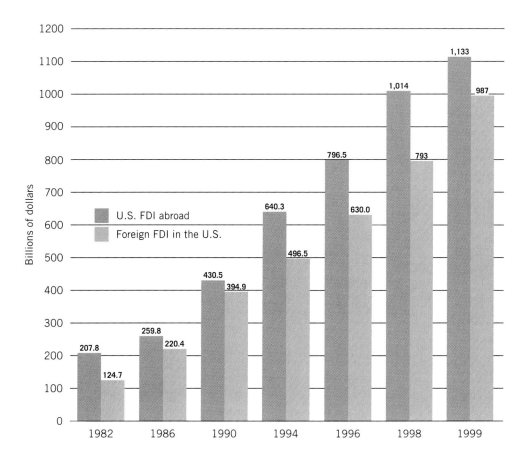

FIGURE 5.6

Outward and Inward U.S. FDI, 1982–1999

Source: *Survey of Current Business,* July 2000, pp. 67 and 69.

lations. Similarly, many financial services companies from other countries establish such subsidiaries as the legal owners of their U.S. operations.

During the past decade outward FDI has remained larger than inward FDI for the United States (see Figure 5.6), but both categories have more than doubled in size. Although inward and outward flows of FDI are not perfectly matched, the pattern is clear: Most FDI is made by and destined for the most prosperous countries. In the next section we discuss how this pattern suggests the crucial role MNCs play in FDI.

INTERNATIONAL INVESTMENT THEORIES ‹

Why does FDI occur? A sophomore taking his or her first finance course might answer with the obvious: Average rates of return are higher in foreign markets. Yet given the pattern of FDI between countries that we just discussed, this answer is not satisfactory. Canada and the United Kingdom are both major sources of FDI *in* the United States and important destinations for FDI *from* the United States. Average rates of return in Canada and the United Kingdom cannot be simultaneously below that of the United States (which would justify inward U.S. FDI) and above that of the United States (which would justify outward U.S. FDI). The same pattern of two-way investment occurs on an industry basis. By the end of 1999, for example, U.S. firms had invested $4.2 billion in the chemical industry in Belgium, while Belgian firms had invested $3.2 billion in the U.S. chemical industry. This pattern cannot be explained by national or industry differences in rates of return. We must search for another explanation for FDI.

Ownership Advantages

More powerful explanations for FDI focus on the role of the firm. Initially researchers explored how firm ownership of competitive advantages affected FDI. The **ownership advantage theory** suggests that a firm owning a valuable asset that creates a competitive advantage domestically can use that advantage to penetrate foreign markets through FDI. The asset could be, for example, a superior technology, a well-known brand name, or economies of scale. This theory is consistent with the observed patterns of international and intraindustry FDI discussed earlier in this chapter. Caterpillar, for example, built factories in Asia, Europe, Australia, South America, and North America to exploit proprietary technologies and its brand name. Its chief rival, Komatsu, constructed plants in Asia, Europe, and the United States for the same reason.

Internalization Theory

The ownership advantage theory only partly explains why FDI occurs. It does not explain why a firm would choose to enter a foreign market via FDI rather than exploit its ownership advantages internationally through other means, such as exporting its products, franchising a brand name, or licensing technology to foreign firms. For example, McDonald's has successfully internationalized by franchising its fast-food operations outside the United States, while Boeing has relied on exporting to serve its foreign customers.

Internalization theory addresses this question. In doing so, it relies heavily on the concept of transaction costs. **Transaction costs** are the costs of entering into a transaction, that is, those connected to negotiating, monitoring, and enforcing a contract. A firm must decide whether it is better to own and operate its own factory overseas or to contract with a foreign firm to do this through a franchise, licensing, or supply agreement. **Internalization theory** suggests that FDI is more likely to occur—that is, international production will be *internalized* within the firm—when the costs of negotiating, monitoring, and enforcing a contract with a second firm are high. For example, Toyota's primary competitive advantages are its reputation for high quality and its sophisticated manufacturing techniques, neither of which are easily conveyed by contract. As a result, Toyota has chosen to maintain ownership of its overseas automobile assembly plants.

Conversely, internalization theory holds that when transaction costs are low, firms are more likely to contract with outsiders and internationalize by licensing their brand names or franchising their business operations. For example, McDonald's is the premier expert in the United States in devising easily enforceable franchising agreements. Because McDonald's is so successful in reducing transaction costs between itself and its franchisees, it has continued to rely on franchising for its international operations.

Dunning's Eclectic Theory

Although internalization theory addresses why firms choose FDI as the mode for entering international markets, the theory ignores the question of why production, by either the company or a contractor, should be located abroad. In other words, is there a location advantage to producing abroad? This issue was incorporated by John Dunning in his **eclectic theory**, which combines ownership advantage, location advantage, and internalization advantage to form a unified theory of FDI. This theory recognizes that FDI reflects both *international* business activity and business activity *internal* to the firm. According to Dunning, FDI will occur when three conditions are satisfied:

1. *Ownership advantage.* The firm must own some unique competitive advantage that overcomes the disadvantages of competing with foreign firms on their home turfs. This advantage may be a brand name, ownership of proprietary technology, the benefits of economies of scale, and so on. Caterpillar enjoys all three of these advantages in competing in Brazil against local firms.

2. *Location advantage.* Undertaking the business activity must be more profitable in a foreign location than undertaking it in a domestic location. For example, Caterpillar produces bulldozers in Brazil to enjoy lower labor costs and avoid high tariff walls on goods exported from its U.S. factories.

3. *Internalization advantage.* The firm must benefit more from controlling the foreign business activity than from hiring an independent local company to provide the service. Control is advantageous, for example, when monitoring and enforcing the contractual performance of the local company is expensive, when the local company may misappropriate proprietary technology, or when the firm's reputation and brand name could be jeopardized by poor behavior by the local company. All of these factors are important to Caterpillar.

FACTORS INFLUENCING FOREIGN DIRECT INVESTMENT ❬

Given the complexity of the global economy and the diversity of opportunities that firms face in different countries, it is not surprising that numerous factors may influence a firm's decision to undertake FDI. These can be classified as supply factors, demand factors, and political factors (see Table 5.6).

Supply Factors

FDI may be motivated by a firm's efforts to control its own costs. Some of the most important supply factors that may influence a firm's decision to undertake FDI are production costs, logistics, availability of natural resources, and access to key technology.

Production Costs.   Firms often undertake FDI to lower production costs. Foreign locations may be more attractive than domestic sites because of lower land prices, tax rates, or commercial real estate rents or because of better availability and lower cost of skilled or unskilled labor. For example, Novolabs, a small German software company, has shifted much of its programming to Novosibirsk, Russia. Novolabs was able to hire high-quality, imaginative programmers in that Siberian city at one-third the salaries it was paying at its headquarters in Dusseldorf.[15] Similarly, GumSung Plastics, a small family-owned Korean firm, invested $8 million in a factory in Mexicali, Mexico, to produce plastic casings for TVs and computer monitors. By so doing, the company reduced its labor costs by two-thirds.[16]

Logistics.   If transportation costs are significant, a firm may choose to produce in the foreign market rather than export from domestic factories. For example, Heineken has utilized FDI extensively as part of its internationalization strategy because its products are primarily water. Brewing its beverages close to where its foreign consumers live is cheaper for Heineken than transporting the beverages long distances from the company's Dutch breweries. International businesses also often make host-country investments to reduce distribution costs. For example, Citrovita, a Brazilian producer of orange juice concentrate, operates a storage and distribution terminal at the Port of Antwerp rather than ship to European grocery

SUPPLY FACTORS	DEMAND FACTORS	POLITICAL FACTORS
Production costs	Customer access	Avoidance of trade barriers
Logistics	Marketing advantages	Economic development incentives
Resource availability	Exploitation of competitive advantages	
Access to technology	Customer mobility	

TABLE 5.6

Factors Affecting the FDI Decision

chains directly from Brazil. Citrovita can take advantage of low ocean shipping rates to transport its goods in bulk from Brazil to the Belgian port. The company then uses the Antwerp facility to repackage and distribute concentrate to its customers in France, Germany, and the Benelux countries.

Availability of Natural Resources.   Firms may utilize FDI to access natural resources that are critical to their operations. For example, because of the decrease in oil production in the United States, many U.S.-based oil companies have been forced to make significant investments worldwide to obtain new oil reserves. Often international businesses negotiate with host governments to obtain access to raw materials in return for FDI. For example, Manila's Ayala Corporation built tuna canneries on the northern Indonesian island of Sulawesi; this was part of a deal with the Indonesian government to allow Philippine tuna boats based in the southern Philippine island of Mindanao to fish in Indonesia's territorial waters (see Map 5.1). This deal has benefited both countries: Over 8,000 people in the Philippines and Indonesia are now employed in nine canneries and on 600 fishing vessels, part of an operation that annually exports $34 million worth of tuna to North American and European consumers.[17]

Access to Key Technology.   Another motive for FDI is to gain access to technology. Firms may find it more advantageous to acquire ownership interests in an existing firm than to assemble an in-house group of research scientists to develop or reproduce an emerging technology. For example, many Swiss pharmaceutical manufacturers have invested in small U.S. biogenetics companies as an inexpensive means of obtaining cutting-edge biotechnology. Similarly, Taiwan's Acer Inc., a manufacturer of personal computers and workstations, paid $100 million in the 1990s for a pair of Silicon Valley computer companies in hopes of leveraging their technology and existing distribution networks to boost Acer's share of the U.S. personal computer market.[18]

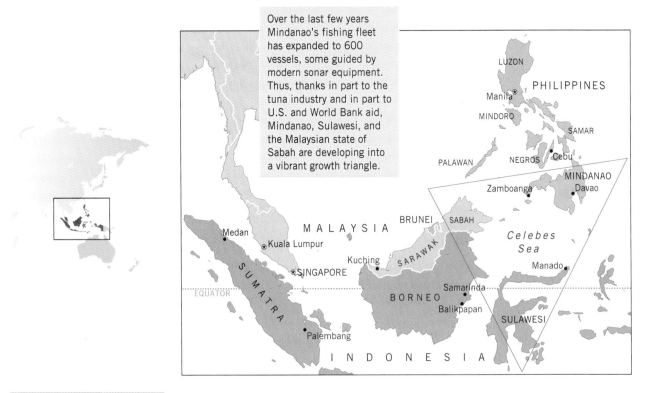

Over the last few years Mindanao's fishing fleet has expanded to 600 vessels, some guided by modern sonar equipment. Thus, thanks in part to the tuna industry and in part to U.S. and World Bank aid, Mindanao, Sulawesi, and the Malaysian state of Sabah are developing into a vibrant growth triangle.

MAP 5.1   **The Tuna Industry in Indonesia and the Philippines**

Demand Factors

Firms also may engage in FDI to expand the market for their products. The demand factors that encourage FDI include customer access, marketing advantages, exploitation of competitive advantages, and customer mobility.

Customer Access.   Many types of international business require firms to have a physical presence in the market. For example, fast-food restaurants and retailers must provide convenient access to their outlets for competitive reasons. KFC cannot provide its freshly prepared fried chicken to Japanese customers from its restaurants in the United States; it must locate outlets in Japan to do so. Similarly, IKEA's success in broadening its customer base beyond its home market in Sweden is due to its opening a large number of new stores worldwide.

Marketing Advantages.   FDI may generate several types of marketing advantages. The physical presence of a factory may enhance the visibility of a foreign firm's products in the host market. The foreign firm also gains from "buy local" attitudes of host country consumers. For example, through ads in such magazines as *Time* and *Sports Illustrated*, Toyota has publicized the beneficial impact of its U.S. factories and input purchases on the U.S. economy. Firms may also engage in FDI to improve their customer service. Taiwan's Delta Products, which makes battery packs for laptop computers, was concerned that it could not respond quickly and flexibly enough from its factories in China and Thailand to meet the changing needs of its U.S. customers. As one of its executives noted, if you "build in the Far East, you're too far away. You can't do a last-moment modification while the product is on the ocean." Accordingly, Delta shifted some of its production to a Mexican factory just across the border from Nogales, Arizona, to better serve its U.S. customers.[19]

Exploitation of Competitive Advantages.   FDI may be a firm's best means to exploit a competitive advantage that it already enjoys. An owner of a valuable trademark, brand name, or technology may choose to operate in foreign countries rather than export to them. Often this decision depends on the product's nature. For example, Pari Mutuel Urbain (PMU) operates 7,000 off-track betting facilities in Europe. It developed an ingenious network of computers, on-site terminals, and satellite communications to make it France's seventh largest service company with annual revenues of $6 billion. PMU's success in harnessing modern communications technology to meet the needs of horse-racing fans has boosted its French business by 25 percent and enabled it to expand its off-track betting operations into Switzerland and Monaco.[20]

Customer Mobility.   A firm's FDI also may be motivated by FDI of its customers or clients. If one of a firm's existing customers builds a foreign factory, the firm may decide to locate a new facility of its own nearby, thus enabling it to continue to supply its customer promptly and attentively. Equally important, establishing a new facility reduces the possibility that a competitor in the host country will step in and steal the customer. For example, Japanese parts suppliers to the major Japanese automakers have responded to the construction of Japanese-owned automobile assembly plants in the United States by building their own U.S. factories, warehouses, and research facilities. Their need to locate facilities in the United States is magnified by the automakers' use of just-in-time (JIT) inventory management techniques; JIT minimizes the amount of parts inventory held at an assembly plant, putting a parts-supply facility located in Japan at a severe disadvantage. Likewise, after Samsung decided to construct and operate an electronics factory in northeast England, six of its Korean parts suppliers also established factories in the vicinity.[21]

Political Factors

Political factors may also enter into a firm's decision to undertake FDI. Firms may invest in a foreign country to avoid trade barriers by the host country or to take advantage of economic development incentives offered by the host government.

Avoidance of Trade Barriers.   Firms often build foreign facilities to avoid trade barriers. For example, in the late 1990s the Fuji Photo Film Company invested $200 million in its Greenwood, South Carolina, factory complex to begin manufacturing film for sale in the United States. Previously, the company supplied film to its U.S. customers from its factories in the Netherlands and Japan. By producing in the United States rather than exporting to it, Fuji avoided a 3.7 percent tariff on film imposed by the United States and deflected claims by Kodak that Fuji was unfairly "dumping" Japanese-made film in the U.S. market (dumping is explained in Chapter 8).[22]

Economic Development Incentives.   Most democratically elected governments—local, state, and national—are vitally concerned with promoting the economic welfare of their citizens, many of whom are, of course, voters. Many governments offer incentives to firms to induce them to locate new facilities in the governments' jurisdictions. Governmental incentives that can be an important catalyst for FDI include reduced utility rates, employee training programs, infrastructure additions (such as new roads and railroad spurs), and tax reductions or tax holidays. Often MNCs benefit from bidding wars among communities eager to attract the companies and the jobs they bring. Siemens, for example, invested $380 million to construct and operate a memory chip factory near Oporto, Portugal, as a result of economic development incentives granted by Portugal and the European Union; the incentives cover approximately 40 percent of Siemens's investment and training costs. When fully operational, the factory will create 750 jobs and 150 million DRAM memory chips annually.[23] Likewise, Alabama provided Daimler-Benz with $253 million in incentives to capture that firm's first U.S. plant.

CHAPTER REVIEW

Summary

International trade is an important form of international business—over $6.9 trillion of goods and services were traded between residents of different countries in 1999. Most of this trade involved the wealthy Quad countries. International trade affects domestic economies both directly and indirectly. Exports stimulate additional demand for products, thus generating income and employment gains. Imports lower consumer prices and pressure domestic firms to become more efficient and productive.

Because of trade's importance to businesses and governments worldwide, scholars have offered numerous explanations for its existence. The earliest theories, such as absolute advantage, comparative advantage, and relative factor endowments, relied on characteristics of countries to explain patterns of exports and imports. These country-based theories help explain trade in undifferentiated goods such as wheat, sugar, and steel.

Coincident with the rise of MNCs, post–World War II research focused on firm-based explanations for international trade. Country similarity, product life cycle, and global strategic rivalry theories focus on the firm as the agent for generating trade and investment decisions. These firm-based theories help explain intraindustry trade and trade in differentiated goods such as automobiles, personal care products, and consumer electronics goods.

International investment is the second major way in which firms participate in international business. International investments fall into two categories: portfolio investments and FDI. FDI has risen in importance as MNCs have increased in size and number.

Dunning's eclectic theory suggests that FDI will occur when three conditions are met: (1) the firm possesses a competitive advantage that allows it to overcome the disadvantage of competing on the foreign firm's home turf, (2) the foreign location is superior to a domestic location, and (3) the firm finds it cheaper (because of high transaction costs) to produce the product itself rather than hire a foreign firm to do so.

Numerous factors can influence a firm's decision to undertake FDI. Some FDI may be undertaken to reduce the firm's costs. Such supply factors include production costs, logistics, availability of natural resources, and access to key technology. The decision to engage in FDI may be affected by such demand factors as developing access to new customers, obtaining marketing advantages through local production, exploiting competitive advantages, and maintaining nearness to customers as they internationalize their operations. Political considerations may also play a role in FDI. Often firms use FDI to avoid host country trade barriers or to capture economic development incentives offered by host country governments.

Review Questions

1. What is international trade? Why does it occur?
2. How do the theories of absolute advantage and comparative advantage differ?
3. Why are Leontief's findings called a paradox?
4. How useful are country-based theories in explaining international trade?
5. How do interindustry and intraindustry trade differ?
6. Explain the impact of the product life cycle on international trade and international investment.
7. What are the primary sources of the competitive advantages firms use to compete in international markets?
8. What are the four elements of Porter's diamond of national competitive advantage?
9. How do portfolio investments and FDI differ?
10. What are the three parts of Dunning's eclectic theory?
11. How do political factors influence international trade and investment?

Questions for Discussion

1. In our example of France trading wine to Japan for clock radios, we arbitrarily assumed the countries would trade at a price ratio of 1 bottle of wine for 2 clock radios. Over what range of prices can trade occur between the two countries? (*Hint:* In the absence of trade what is the price of clock radios in terms of wine in France? In Japan?) Does your answer differ if you use Table 5.2 instead of Table 5.1?

2. In the public debate over ratification of the North American Free Trade Agreement, Ross Perot said he heard a "giant sucking sound" of U.S. jobs headed south because of low wage rates in Mexico. Using the theory of comparative advantage, discuss whether Perot's fears are valid.

3. Why is intraindustry trade not predicted by country-based theories of trade?

4. Siemens decided to build a new semiconductor plant in Oporto, Portugal.
   a. What factors do you think Siemens considered in selecting Portugal as the site for the factory? What about Oporto in particular?
   b. Who benefits and who loses from the new plant in Portugal?
   c. Is the firm's decision to build the new plant consistent with Dunning's eclectic theory?

BUILDING GLOBAL SKILLS

The U.S. market for computers is dominated by domestic firms such as IBM, Apple, Compaq, and Dell. The U.S. market for consumer electronics is dominated by Japanese firms and brands such as Sony, JVC, Panasonic, Mitsubishi, and Toshiba. However, the U.S. automobile market includes both strong domestic firms like Ford and General Motors and formidable Japanese competitors like Toyota and Honda.

Your instructor will divide the class into groups of four or five and assign each group one of the three industries just noted. To begin, discuss within your group your individual views why different patterns exist for these industries.

Next, analyze the industry assigned to your group from the standpoint of each country-based and firm-based theory of international trade discussed in this chapter. Try to agree on which theory is the best predictor and which is the worst predictor of reality for your specific industry.

Now reconvene as a class. Each group should select a spokesperson. Each spokesperson should indicate the industry that the person's group discussed and identify the best and worst theories selected. Note the points on which the groups who analyzed the same industries agree.

Finally, separate again into your small groups and discuss the areas of common disagreements. Also discuss the following questions:

1. Do some theories work better than others for different industries? Why?

2. What other industries can you think of that fit one of the three patterns noted in the opening paragraph?

3. Do the same theories work as well in making predictions for those industries?

4. Based on what you know about the Japanese market, decide whether the same pattern of competitiveness that exists in the United States for the computer, consumer electronics, and automobile industries also holds true for the Japanese market. Why or why not?

WORKING WITH THE WEB: BUILDING GLOBAL INTERNET SKILLS

Export Data Web Sites: The Good, the Bad, and the Ugly

Information about trade and investment flows between countries is often of great use to market researchers. For example, a Canadian maker of machine tools who wishes to export to South America can gain insights into that market by examining the volume of machine tools imported to the region. Another firm may specialize in outfitting new factories and have an existing customer base among Canadian, U.S., and U.K. auto parts firms. Accordingly, this firm needs to carefully monitor foreign investments made by auto parts firms from these three countries.

Numerous Web sites, some of which can be accessed at this book's Web site, provide information about international trade and investment. Some of these Web sites present highly aggregated data about trade and investment flows between countries. Some provide industry-level data. Others, quite frankly, are pretty useless.

The assignment: Pick an industry and a product, such as automotive parts/mufflers or agriculture/cotton. Locate five Web sites that contain data about trade or foreign investment in the industry and the product that you selected. Which Web sites would be the most useful to businesses? Which ones would be of little use? Defend your answers.

WE INVITE YOU TO VISIT THIS BOOK'S COMPANION WEB SITE AT www.prenhall.com/griffin

IN THE NEWS

Click on "Industries" from the homepage of the *Financial Times* (*www.ft.com*), and select an industry from those listed. Read the news stories presented for this industry. How important is the international market to the companies discussed in these stories? How significant is FDI? What insights do these stories offer regarding the nature of competition in the industry you chose?

CLOSING CASE

Home Field Disadvantage

A case study in why Europeans lose to American rivals.

BY WILLIAM ECHIKSON

Vacation rentals were going to be Peter Ingelbrecht's road to riches. After having trouble finding a house for a holiday on Spain's Costa del Sol . . . , the 35-year-old Belgian consultant teamed up with friend Laurent Coppieters to found Rent-a-Holiday—an online booking agency for villas and apartments. "I wanted to create something like in Silicon Valley," Ingelbrecht says. But across the globe, Microsoft Corp. alumni Greg Slyngstad and Steve Murch were dreaming of a similar path to fortune. They had spent a combined 14 years at the software giant. "Microsoft was getting so big," Slyngstad says. "I wanted to create something on my own." In October 1997, nine months after the Belgians started their company, Slyngstad and Murch founded VacationSpot.com, aiming to serve the same villa and home rental market worldwide.

The ensuing competition crystallizes the obstacles facing European Internet entrepreneurs. Rent-a-Holiday succeeded in signing up as many real estate agents as its transatlantic competitor. But the Europeans found it harder than the Americans to raise money and recruit staff. They had more trouble gaining precious exposure on portals such as Yahoo! And they were unable to charge the same premiums for ad space as the Americans.

The denouement was inevitable: In an all-stock deal . . . , VacationSpot.com bought Rent-a-Holiday for an undisclosed sum. While the founders of Rent-a-Holiday made some errors that led to the buyout, their story also reveals systemic problems that need to be redressed if Europe wants to be a serious contender in e-commerce.

No Proof

What hobbled the Europeans? Their difficulties started with finance. Soon after Ingelbrecht returned from his Spanish holiday, he and Coppieters pitched their business plan to local venture capitalists. Both had strong resumes: Coppieters had a degree from Belgium's prestigious Solvay Business School, and Ingelbrecht graduated from Stanford University Graduate School of Business. But Belgian financiers rebuffed their overtures. "They wanted to see proven assets and a proven cash flow," recalls Coppieters. "If we had that, we wouldn't have needed them." In the end, the two put together $400,000 of their own savings and family money. Three months later, in June 1997, a Belgian venture capitalist finally agreed to chip in $850,000.

By contrast, the American entrepreneurs were deluged with financial options. "These tremendous executives with great experience at Microsoft walked into my office with an interesting idea," says Jay Hoag, a managing partner at Technology Crossover Ventures, backer of such successes as Real Networks and CNET. "Of course we were interested." After sifting through a half-dozen offers, Slyngstad and

Murch took $5 million from Technology Crossover and $4 million from other investors. "It's heaven for entrepreneurs now in America," says Slyngstad.

Hiring good staff proved to be another bugaboo in Europe, where many rising stars still prefer established companies to start-ups. "Success for most of my friends still means working for an IBM or Procter & Gamble and making your way up the ladder until you are 55 years old with a big office and a big cigar," says Ingelbrecht. When he told friends he was quitting his job to start a Net company, they were shocked.

Even mid-level employees were tough to find. Although Western Europe suffers from 10 percent unemployment, technical staff such as Web designers are rare. International Data Corp. says 320,000 such jobs are unfilled in Europe. "There may be a lot of jobless here, but not in computer fields," says Coppieters.

The Americans faced no such difficulties. "MBAs were fighting to join up with us," says Slyngstad. Within a few months, VacationSpot.com had hired 45 employees—three times the number the Europeans could attract. Slyngstad didn't have to offer huge salaries, either. Stock options sufficed.

Dream Homes

And then there's strategy. The Europeans focused on signing up real estate agents and expanding their listings to an impressive 9,000 rental properties. Visitors to the site would find their vacation dream house, jot down the details, and get in touch via e-mail or phone. Rent-a-Holiday made money by charging real estate agents a flat fee for listings.

The Americans attacked a larger target. Like the Europeans, they began by signing up real estate agents. But since Internet penetration is much higher in the U.S. than Europe, VacationSpot could charge twice the price per listing. At the same time, Slyngstad began building a full-service site that would allow customers to book a holiday villa online. Instead of just taking a fee from agents, the company charges a commission on each rental.

Attracting traffic is key to success on the Net, and here, too, the Americans had an advantage because portals are much less developed in Europe. Rent-a-Holiday did strike a deal with portal Lycos Inc. But VacationSpot.com became a preferred supplier to Yahoo!, Microsoft Expedia, Preview Travel, Travelocity, and others. "We underestimated both the importance and cost" of such agreements, admits Ingelbrecht. After a year, VacationSpot was getting five times more hits than Rent-a-Holiday.

The Europeans faced other mounting pressures. Their investors wanted to see a profit. The Americans' backers weren't in such a rush. "We wanted VacationSpot.com to become a dominant player in the long run, not make money in the short term," says venture capitalist Hoag.

The Americans did have one major weakness: few European listings. "We needed better coverage there," Slyngstad says. Building a European presence from the ground up would have been too slow to please investors, so Slyngstad called Brussels. . . .

Ingelbrecht and Coppieters saw the logic of selling out. They would gain VacationSpot's superior financing and technology and be able to offer their staff its stock-option plan. The Belgians flew to Seattle . . . , but the talks broke down over price. The Americans

offered the Europeans less than 20 percent of the combined company in an all-stock takeover. VacationSpot had five times Rent-a-Holiday's traffic so Slyngstad and Murch argued this was fair. But Rent-a-Holiday had nearly as many listings as VacationSpot, so the Europeans thought the split should be closer to equal.

The Americans didn't give up. They upped their offer, and . . . the deal was done. The Europeans ended up with a little more than 20 percent of the new company. Slyngstad remains as chief operating officer. VacationSpot.com will be the single brand name. Ingelbrecht and Coppieters become joint directors of European operations.

Rather than feel defeated, the two Belgian entrepreneurs are optimistic. Rent-a-Holiday was years away from going public in Europe's underdeveloped Internet capital markets. But VacationSpot plans an initial public offering. . . . "We get to share an American valuation," Ingelbrecht says with a smile. Indeed. He and Coppieters walked away with a fistful of stock and options, although they decline to provide details. As it turns out, vacation rentals over the Web may still prove to be their road to riches. But the message for other European entrepreneurs is sobering: Competing with U.S. start-ups—even with a head start—is likely to be an uphill, uneven fight.

U.S. To European Entrepreneurs: Take a Lesson

U.S. based Internet startup VacationSpot.com fared better than its European competition, Rent-a-Holiday. Here's why:

- **Forget about early profits.** American investors concentrated on building market share. European investors wanted to see an early payback. Now, U.S. startups have better market positions.

- **Do not neglect distribution.** Americans spend heavily on deals with portals such as Yahoo! to generate traffic. The Europeans focused instead on building up their site with listings of rental homes.

- **Recruit top flight staff.** The Americans attracted experienced managers by offering stock options. The Europeans had trouble recruiting staff because their stock options were taxed.

- **Go up the value chain.** While the Europeans depended on advertising and listing revenues, the Americans poured money into building a full-service site that could process online orders. Now they are ahead of the game in e-commerce.

Case Questions

1. Porter's theory of national competitive advantage argues that characteristics of individual nations shape the ability of firms to compete. What advantages did the American entrepreneurs gain from their American location? Did they suffer any disadvantages?

2. Did the European entrepreneurs gain from their European location? What disadvantages did they suffer?

3. What can European policy makers do to improve opportunities available to dot-com start-up companies? What can U.S. policy makers do to encourage the growth of such companies?

Source: "Home Field Disadvantage," *Business Week E. Biz*, December 13, 1999, pp. EB72ff. Reprinted with permission.

Will the Stars Shine on Astra Again?

PT Astra International is one of the oldest and largest conglomerates in Southeast Asia, employing at its peak 125,000 people. For many years the company thrived as Indonesia's dominant automobile assembler, producing about 400,000 vehicles a year. Other Astra subsidiaries build and sell tractors, operate coal mines, run plantations (tea, cocoa, and rubber), and offer financial services (banking, leasing, and insurance). Astra benefited from the phenomenal growth of Indonesia's economy during the 1980s and much of the 1990s, when the country's annual growth in per capita gross domestic product (GDP) averaged 4 percent, more than triple the world's average during that time span. High tariff walls and government procurement policies that favored domestically produced goods shielded many of Astra's factories from foreign competitors.

> "Astra's automobile **sales shrank** by almost **90 percent** within the year."

This producer's paradise came to an abrupt end in the late 1990s. One set of problems arose from the "crony capitalism" that characterized Indonesia during the 32-year rule of President Suharto (1966 to 1998). Crony capitalism refers to the common practice in some countries of government agencies favoring businesses with close ties to high-ranking government officials. In 1996 the Suharto govern-

6

The International Monetary System and the Balance of Payments

After studying this chapter, you should be able to:

> Discuss the role of the international monetary system in promoting international trade and investment.

> Explain the evolution and functioning of the gold standard.

> Summarize the role of the World Bank Group and the International Monetary Fund in the post-World War II international monetary system established at Bretton Woods.

> Explain the evolution of the flexible exchange rate system.

> Describe the function and structure of the balance of payments accounting system.

> Differentiate among the various definitions of a balance of payments surplus and deficit.

ment launched its "national car" program, granting favorable tax treatment to cars built in Indonesia using Indonesian-made parts. Only one company initially qualified for these tax preferences—a company controlled by Suharto's son Tommy. To avoid losing the Indonesian market to this upstart, Astra's managers borrowed $800 million from foreign bankers to expand its production of auto parts, allowing it to qualify for the preferential tax treatment as well. This task was essentially completed by the end of 1997. But Astra's timing was lousy. The Asian currency crisis erupted that year, leading to a devaluation of Indonesia's currency, the rupiah. At one point the rupiah lost 74 percent of its value in the foreign exchange market. (For a complete explanation of the Asian currency crisis, see Chapter 7's closing case.) Astra's bank borrowings threatened to crush the company because most of these new loans were denominated in foreign currencies like the U.S. dollar and the Japanese yen. Because of the rupiah's loss of value, Astra would need to generate many more rupiah in profits than it had planned on to obtain the dollars and yen needed to repay the interest and principal on its loans. Unfortunately, the Asian currency crisis traumatized Indonesia's banks, real estate industry, and stock market. As a result of the government-ordered restructuring of

Indonesia's banking industry, 39 percent of Astra's stock fell into the hands of the Indonesian Bank Restructuring Agency (IBRA). Furthermore, as Indonesia's economy imploded, many companies laid off employees, and the demand for automobiles—Astra's main product—collapsed. Astra's automobile sales shrank by almost 90 percent within the year. To make matters worse, as a condition for extending $18 billion in emergency loans, the International Monetary Fund (IMF) demanded that Indonesia dismantle the trade barriers that the country constructed to encourage domestic industry. The impact was painful: Thai-made automobiles became available in the Indonesian market at prices 30 percent less than Astra's costs.

Into this mess stepped Rini Soewandi. Although relatively young—only 40 at the time of her appointment as Astra's president in June 1998—she understood the company and its problems. Soewandi recognized that Astra would have to restructure itself if it were to survive the cataclysmic changes in its operating environment. Her first action was to slash the company's workforce by 20 percent. She then went to work cleaning up Astra's balance sheet, spending many long and tense hours renegotiating the company's debt with its 70 bankers. To free up cash, she sold off nonstrategic assets like Astra Microtronics Technology, reaping $90 million on that sale alone.

Soewandi faced even more thorny challenges in reforming the company's culture. When Astra's autos were protected from foreign competition by Indonesia's high tariffs, Astra could easily sell every car it produced. The concept of customer service was a bitter joke. "Go wait in line" was the most common retort to most customers' questions. Soewandi beefed up sales force training and encouraged the Astra sales staff to go door-to-door to uncover potential buyers. Even more important changes were made in the executive suite. Soewandi introduced new compensation programs that linked pay with performance. Under her direction Astra became the first company in Indonesia to introduce stock options to compensate and motivate managers. Soewandi also targeted conflicts of interest—many senior executives had owned stock in companies that supplied parts to Astra—by strengthening the powers of internal auditors and by imposing a new corporate code of ethics that frowned on such financial ties.

Soewandi's initiatives paid off, and Astra's damaged operations and balance sheet slowly began to mend. Unfortunately for her, Astra's fate became entwined in a complex loan negotiation between Indonesia's government and the IMF. As a condition for offering additional aid, the IMF demanded that the Indonesian government sell off assets held by various state holding companies. Ironically, as a result of Soewandi's efforts, Astra was one of the more desirable companies in the IBRA's $81 billion portfolio. The IBRA announced it would sell its stake in Astra to foreign investors. Soewandi fought this decision, arguing that Astra was well on the road to recovery and deserved a chance to remain independent. Fearing the wrath of the IMF more than that of Soewandi, the IBRA squeezed her out of office and proceeded with the stock sale in March 2000. The winning bidder may have gotten a real bargain. It paid only $506 million (3,700 rupiah per share) for its 39 percent stake in Astra, whereas experts believe the stock's price could rise to 5,800 rupiah per share within several years as Indonesia's economy recovers from the recession brought on by the currency crisis and as Soewandi's reforms take root within Astra.

As its managers learned the hard way, even a domestically oriented company like PT Astra International must be attuned to changes in the global economy. Astra's crisis was not homegrown. Events outside the country's borders triggered a crisis in the international monetary system, which led to the collapse of the Indonesian economy and decimated the value of its currency. These circumstances caused the domestic market for Astra's products to dry up and its debt burden to balloon to unsustainable levels. Officials of multilateral organizations like the IMF were then able to dictate economic reforms to the government, reforms that caused a controlling interest in the company to be sold to foreign investors. The lesson of Astra's travails is clear. Managers—even those focused on the domestic marketplace—ignore the workings of the international monetary system and the international institutions that monitor it at their own peril.

The international monetary system exists because most countries have their own currencies. A means of exchanging these currencies is needed if business is to be conducted across national boundaries. The **international monetary system** establishes the rules by which countries value and exchange their currencies. It also provides a mechanism for correcting imbalances between a country's international payments and its receipts. Further, the cost of converting foreign money into a firm's home currency—a variable critical to the profitability of international operations—depends on the smooth functioning of the international monetary system.

International businesspeople also monitor the international monetary system's accounting system, the balance of payments. The **balance of payments (BOP) accounting system** records international transactions and supplies vital information about the health of a national economy and likely changes in its fiscal and monetary policies. BOP statistics can be used to detect signs of trouble that could eventually lead to governmental trade restrictions, higher interest rates, accelerated inflation, reduced aggregate demand, or general changes in the cost of doing business in any given country.

HISTORY OF THE INTERNATIONAL MONETARY SYSTEM ‹

Today's international monetary system can trace its roots to the ancient allure of gold and silver, both of which served as media of exchange in early trade between tribes and in later trade between city-states. Silver, for example, was used in trade among India, Babylon, and Phoenicia as early as the seventh century B.C.[1] As the modern nation-states of Europe took form in the sixteenth and seventeenth centuries, their coins were traded on the basis of their relative gold and silver content.

The Gold Standard

Ancient reliance on gold coins as an international medium of exchange led to the adoption of an international monetary system known as the gold standard. Under the **gold standard** countries agree to buy or sell their paper currencies in exchange for gold on the request of any individual or firm and, in contrast to mercantilism's hoarding of gold, to allow the free export of gold bullion and coins. In 1821 the United Kingdom became the first country to adopt the gold standard. During the nineteenth century most other important trading countries—including Russia, Austria-Hungary, France, Germany, and the United States—did the same.

The gold standard effectively created a fixed exchange rate system. An **exchange rate** is the price of one currency in terms of a second currency. Under a **fixed exchange rate system** the price of a given currency does not change relative to each other currency. The gold standard created a fixed exchange rate system because each country tied, or **pegged**, the value of its currency to gold. The United Kingdom, for example, pledged to buy or sell an ounce of gold for 4.247 pounds sterling, thereby establishing the pound's **par value**, or official price in terms of gold. The United States agreed to buy or sell an ounce of gold for a par value of $20.67. The two currencies could be freely exchanged for the stated amount of gold, making £4.247 = 1 ounce of gold = $20.67. This implied a fixed exchange rate between the pound and the dollar of £1 = $4.867, or $20.67/£4.247.

As long as firms had faith in a country's pledge to exchange its currency for gold at the promised rate when requested to do so, many actually preferred to be paid in currency. Transacting in gold was expensive. Suppose Jardine Matheson, a Hong Kong trading company, sold £100,000 worth of tea to Twining & Company, a

London distributor of fine teas. If it wanted to be paid in gold by Twining & Company upon delivery of the tea, Jardine Matheson had to bear the costs of loading the gold into the cargo hold of a ship, guarding it against theft, transporting it, and insuring it against possible disasters. Moreover, because of the slowness of sailing ships, Jardine Matheson would be unable to earn interest on the £100,000 payment while the gold was in transit from London to Hong Kong. However, if Jardine Matheson were willing to be paid in British pounds, Twining could draft a check to Jardine Matheson and give it to the firm's London agent. The London agent could then either immediately deposit the check in Jardine Matheson's interest-bearing London bank account or transfer the funds via telegraph to the firm's account at its Hong Kong bank.

From 1821 until the end of World War I in 1918, the most important currency in international commerce was the British pound sterling, a reflection of the United Kingdom's emergence from the Napoleonic Wars as Europe's dominant economic and military power. Most firms worldwide were willing to accept either gold or British pounds in settlement of transactions. As a result, the international monetary system during this period is often called a **sterling-based gold standard**. The pound's role in world commerce was reinforced by the expansion of the British Empire. The Union Jack flew over so many lands (see Map 6.1)—for example, present-day Canada, Australia, New Zealand, Hong Kong, Singapore, India, Pakistan, Bangladesh, Kenya, Zimbabwe, South Africa, Gibraltar, Bermuda, and Belize—that the claim was made that "the sun never sets on the British Empire." In each British colony British banks established branches and used the pound sterling to settle international transactions among themselves. Because of the international trust in British currency, London became a dominant international financial center in the nineteenth century, a position it still holds. The international reputations and competitive strengths of such British firms as Barclays Bank, Thomas Cook, and Lloyd's of London stem from the role of the pound sterling in the nineteenth-century gold standard.

The Collapse of the Gold Standard

During World War I the sterling-based gold standard unraveled. With the outbreak of war, normal commercial transactions between the Allies (France, Russia, and the United Kingdom) and the Central Powers (Austria-Hungary, Germany, and the Ottoman Empire) ceased. The economic pressures of war caused country after country to suspend their pledges to buy or sell gold at their currencies' par values. After the war, conferences at Brussels (1920) and Genoa (1922) yielded general agreements among the major economic powers to return to the prewar gold standard. Most countries, including the United States, the United Kingdom, and France, readopted the gold standard in the 1920s despite the high levels of inflation, unemployment, and political instability that were wracking Europe.

The resuscitation of the gold standard proved to be short lived, however. The standard was doomed by economic stresses triggered by the worldwide Great Depression. The Bank of England, the United Kingdom's central bank, was unable to honor its pledge to maintain the value of the pound. On September 21, 1931, it allowed the pound to **float**, meaning that the pound's value would be determined by the forces of supply and demand and the Bank of England would no longer redeem British paper currency for gold at par value.

After the United Kingdom abandoned the gold standard, a "sterling area" emerged as some countries, primarily members of the British Commonwealth, pegged their currencies to the pound and relied on sterling balances held in London as their international reserves.[2] Other countries tied the value of their currencies to the U.S. dollar or the French franc. The harmony of the international monetary system degenerated further as some countries—including the United States, France,

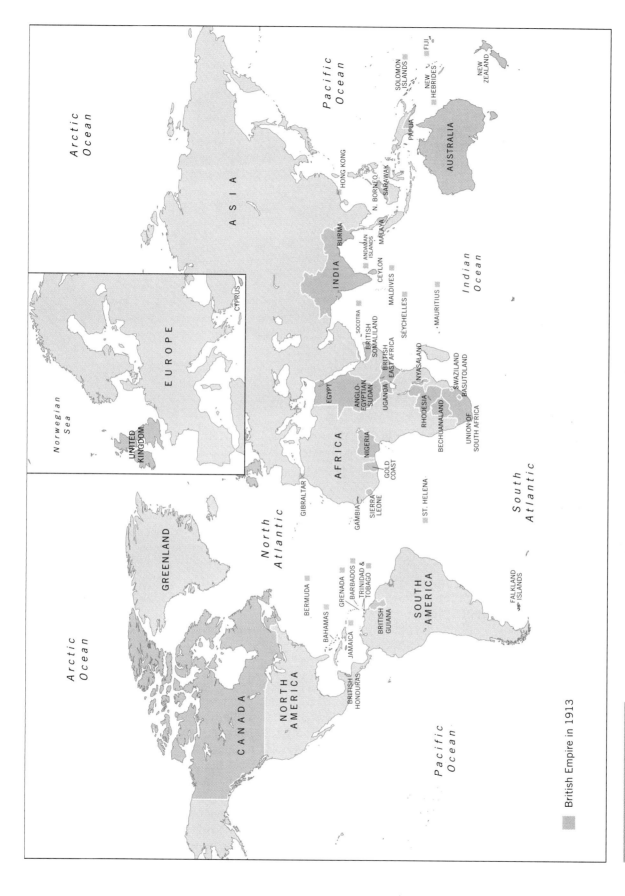

Arctic Ocean

Pacific Ocean

A S I A

HONG KONG

N. BORNEO
SARAWAK

BURMA

MALAYA

PAPUA

SOLOMON
ISLANDS

NEW
HEBRIDES

FIJI

NEW
ZEALAND

AUSTRALIA

ANDAMAN
ISLANDS

INDIA

CEYLON

Indian Ocean

MALDIVES

SEYCHELLES

MAURITIUS

CYPRUS

EUROPE

SOCOTRA

BRITISH
SOMALILAND

BRITISH
EAST AFRICA

NYASALAND

SWAZILAND
BASUTOLAND

Norwegian Sea

EGYPT

ANGLO-
EGYPTIAN
SUDAN

UGANDA

RHODESIA

UNITED
KINGDOM

AFRICA

NIGERIA

BECHUANALAND

UNION OF
SOUTH AFRICA

GIBRALTAR

GOLD
COAST

GAMBIA

SIERRA
LEONE

ST. HELENA

South Atlantic

North Atlantic

GREENLAND

BERMUDA

GRENADA
BARBADOS
TRINIDAD &
TOBAGO

BAHAMAS

JAMAICA

BRITISH
GUIANA

SOUTH
AMERICA

FALKLAND
ISLANDS

BRITISH
HONDURAS

CANADA

NORTH
AMERICA

Arctic Ocean

Pacific Ocean

British Empire in 1913

MAP 6.1 **The British Empire in 1913**

FIGURE 6.1

Down the Tube: The Contraction of World Trade, 1929–1933

Note: Total imports of 75 countries (monthly values, millions of dollars).

Source: Charlies Kindleberger, *The World in Depression*, Berkeley: University of California Press, 1986, p. 170.

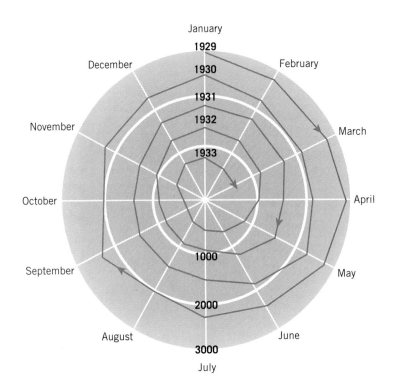

the United Kingdom, Belgium, Latvia, the Netherlands, Switzerland, and Italy—engaged in a series of competitive devaluations of their currencies. By deliberately and artificially lowering (devaluing) the official value of its currency, each nation hoped to make its own goods cheaper in world markets, thereby stimulating its exports and reducing its imports. Any such gains were offset, however, when other countries also devalued their currencies. (If two countries each devalue their currency by 20 percent, neither gains an advantage because each currency's value relative to the other remains the same.) Most countries also raised the tariffs they imposed on imported goods in the hope of protecting domestic jobs in import-competing industries. Yet as more and more countries adopted these **beggar-thy-neighbor policies**, international trade contracted (see Figure 6.1), hurting employment in each country's export industries. More ominously, this international economic conflict was soon replaced by international military conflict—the outbreak of World War II in 1939.

The Bretton Woods Era

Many politicians and historians believe the breakdown of the international monetary system and international trade after World War I created economic conditions that helped bring about World War II. Inflation, unemployment, and the costs of rebuilding war-torn economies created political instability that enabled fascist and communist dictators (Hitler, Mussolini, and Stalin) to seize control of their respective governments. Determined not to repeat the mistakes that had caused World War II, Western diplomats desired to create a postwar economic environment that would promote worldwide peace and prosperity. In 1944 representatives of 44 countries met at a resort in Bretton Woods, New Hampshire, with that objective in mind. The Bretton Woods conferees agreed to renew the gold standard on a greatly modified basis. They also agreed to the creation of two new international organizations that would assist in rebuilding the world economy and the international monetary system: the International Bank for Reconstruction and Development and the International Monetary Fund.

The International Bank for Reconstruction and Development

The **International Bank for Reconstruction and Development (IBRD)** is the official name of the **World Bank**. Established in 1945, the World Bank's initial goal was to help finance reconstruction of the war-torn European economies. With the assistance of the Marshall Plan, the World Bank accomplished this task by the mid-1950s. The bank then adopted a new mission—to build the economies of the world's developing countries.

As its mission has expanded over time, the World Bank has created three affiliated organizations:

1. The International Development Association
2. The International Finance Corporation
3. The Multilateral Investment Guarantee Agency

Together with the World Bank, these constitute the **World Bank Group** (see Figure 6.2). The World Bank, which currently has $117 billion in loans outstanding, is owned by its 182 member countries. In reaching its decisions, the World Bank uses a weighted voting system that reflects the economic power and contributions of its members. The United States currently controls the largest bloc of votes (17 percent), followed by Japan (8 percent), Germany (5 percent), the United Kingdom (4 percent), France (4 percent), and six countries with 3 percent each: Canada, China, India, Italy, Russia, and Saudi Arabia. From time to time the voting weights are reassessed as economic power shifts or as new members join the World Bank. To finance its lending operations, the World Bank borrows money in its own name from international capital markets. Interest earned on existing loans it has made provides it with additional lending power. New lending by the World Bank averaged $18 billion per year from 1995 to 1999.

According to its charter, the World Bank may lend only for "productive purposes" that will stimulate economic growth within the recipient country. An example of such a loan is the $100 million provided to Kazakhstan in 1999 to rehabilitate and modernize its national highways. The World Bank cannot finance a trade deficit, but it can finance an infrastructure project, such as a new railroad or harbor facility, that will bolster a country's economy. It may lend only to national governments or for projects that are guaranteed by a national government, and its loans may not be tied to the purchase of goods or services from any country. Most important, the

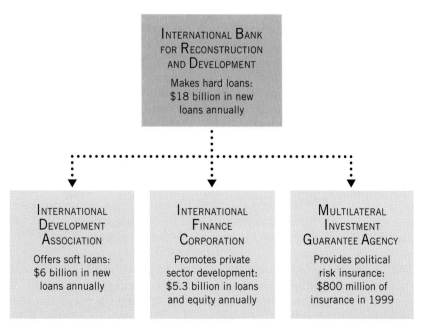

FIGURE 6.2

Organization of the World Bank Group

World Bank must follow a **hard loan policy**; that is, it may make a loan only if there is a reasonable expectation that the loan will be repaid.

The hard loan policy was severely criticized in the 1950s by poorer countries, who complained it hindered their ability to obtain World Bank loans. In response, the World Bank established the **International Development Association (IDA)** in 1960. The IDA offers **soft loans**, loans that bear some significant risk of not being repaid. IDA loans carry no interest rate, although the IDA collects a small service charge (currently 0.75 percent) from borrowers. The loans also have long maturities (normally 35 to 40 years), and borrowers are often granted a 10-year grace period before they need to begin repaying their loans. The IDA's lending efforts focus on the least-developed countries. A typical loan is the $45 million provided Bangladesh in 1999 to repair damage to its bridges and waterways after a devastating flood hit that country the year before. The IDA obtains resources from the initial subscriptions its members make when joining it, from transferred World Bank profits, and from periodic replenishments contributed by richer countries. From 1995 to 1999, IDA disbursements averaged $6 billion per year.

The two other affiliates of the World Bank Group have narrower missions. The **International Finance Corporation (IFC)**, created in 1956, is charged with promoting the development of the private sector in developing countries. Acting like an investment banker, the IFC, in collaboration with private investors, provides debt and equity capital for promising commercial activities. For example, in 1999 the IFC provided Senegal's Ciments du Sahel S.A. $4.7 million in equity and $13.5 million in loans to help it build a $90-million cement plant to serve the construction industry in Senegal's capital city, Dakar, and the regional market. In total the IFC provided $5.3 billion of financing to supplement $13.3 billion of capital raised from other sources for private-sector projects in 1999.

The other World Bank affiliate, the **Multilateral Investment Guarantee Agency (MIGA)**, was set up in 1988 to overcome private-sector reluctance to invest in developing countries because of perceived political riskiness—a topic covered in Chapter 3. MIGA encourages direct investment in developing countries by offering private investors insurance against noncommercial risks. For example, in 1999 MIGA issued Avon Cycles Ltd, an Indian bicycle manufacturer, $710,000 of political risk insurance to protect its investment in a newly privatized bicycle manufacturing plant in Dar-es-Salaam, Tanzania, against war and civil disturbance. Similarly, MIGA issued Turkey's Efes Sinai Yatirim Ve Tircaret $27.6 million in political risk insurance to protect its investment in two Coca-Cola bottling companies it was establishing in the Kyrgyz Republic and Kazakhstan with local joint venture partners. As a result of this insurance, Efes was protected against losses due to expropriation, war, or other civil disturbances. In 1999 MIGA underwrote about $800 million of political risk insurance.

Paralleling the efforts of the World Bank are the **regional development banks**, such as the African Development Bank, the Asian Development Bank, and the Inter-American Development Bank. These organizations promote the economic development of the poorer countries in their respective regions. The most recently created regional development bank is the European Bank for Reconstruction and Development. It was established by the Western countries to assist in the reconstruction of Central Europe and Eastern Europe after the regions' communist regimes collapsed. The regional development banks and the World Bank often work together on development projects. For example, the Asian Development Bank, in conjunction with the World Bank and several other agencies, recently helped fund and insure a hydroelectric power plant near Kathmandu, Nepal, which when operational will supply 25 percent of Nepal's electrical power.

The International Monetary Fund. The Bretton Woods attendees believed that the deterioration of international trade during the years after World War I was attributable in part to the competitive exchange rate devaluations that plagued international commerce. To ensure that the post-World War II monetary system would promote international commerce, the Bretton Woods Agreement called for the creation of the **International Monetary Fund (IMF)** to oversee the functioning of the international monetary system. Article I of the IMF's Articles of Agreement lays out the organization's objectives:

1. To promote international monetary cooperation

2. To facilitate the expansion and balanced growth of international trade

3. To promote exchange stability, to maintain orderly exchange arrangements among members, and to avoid competitive exchange depreciation

4. To assist in the establishment of a multilateral system of payments

5. To give confidence to members by making the general resources of the IMF temporarily available to them and to correct maladjustments in their balances of payments

6. To shorten the duration and lessen the degree of disequilibrium in the international balances of payments of members

Membership in the IMF is available to any country willing to agree to its rules and regulations. As of April 2001, 183 countries were members. To join, a country must pay a deposit, called a **quota**, partly in gold and partly in the country's own currency. The quota's size primarily reflects the global importance of the country's economy, although political considerations may also have some effect. The size of a quota is important for several reasons:

1. A country's quota determines its voting power within the IMF. Currently the United States controls 17 percent of the votes in the IMF. Germany and Japan each control the next largest blocs (6 percent), followed by France (5 percent), the United Kingdom (5 percent), and Saudi Arabia (3 percent).

2. A country's quota serves as part of its official reserves (we discuss official reserves later in the chapter).

3. The quota determines the country's borrowing power from the IMF. Each IMF member has an unconditional right to borrow up to 25 percent of its quota from the IMF. IMF policy allows additional borrowings contingent on the member country's agreeing to IMF-imposed restrictions—called **IMF conditionality**—on its economic policies. For example, in return for an IMF loan of $21 billion, South Korea agreed in December 1997 to undertake major economic reforms, including permitting foreign banks to take over their Korean counterparts, closing insolvent merchant banks, reducing government favoritism toward the larger chaebol, and lowering tariffs on many goods. That same year the IMF consented to lend Indonesia $10 billion after that country pledged to scrap state monopolies controlling certain foodstuffs, reform its banking industry, and cut trade barriers directed against imported goods.[3] As noted in the opening case, the IMF also pressured Indonesia's government to liquidate its holdings in various companies, which led to the sale of PT Astra International to a Singapore consortium. Local politicians and interest groups often bitterly protest the IMF's conditionality requirements, arguing that foreigners, working through the IMF, are taking advantage of the country's short-term problems to extract changes favorable to the foreigners. At times, the situation can turn uglier. For example, in 1998 Indonesia was wracked by rioting after prices and unemployment soared as a result of the austerity measures demanded by the IMF, and long-time President Suharto was forced to resign his office.

A Dollar-Based Gold Standard.   The IMF and the World Bank provided the institutional framework for the post-World War II international monetary system. The Bretton Woods participants also addressed the problem of how the system would function in practice. All countries agreed to peg the value of their currencies

When the IMF and the World Bank held their annual conferences in Prague in September 2000, thousands of demonstrators marched in the streets. The protestors believe these institutions should devote more resources to helping the world's poor and protecting the environment.

to gold. For example, the par value of the U.S. dollar was established at $35 per ounce of gold. However, only the United States pledged to redeem its currency for gold at the request of a foreign central bank. Thus the U.S. dollar became the keystone of the Bretton Woods system. Why this central role for the U.S. dollar? During the early postwar years only the U.S. and Canadian dollars were **convertible currencies**, that is, ones that could be freely exchanged for other currencies without legal restrictions. Countries had faith in the U.S. economy and so were willing to accept U.S. dollars to settle their transactions. As the British pound sterling had been in the nineteenth century, the U.S. dollar became the preferred vehicle for settling most international transactions. The effect of the Bretton Woods conference was thus to establish a U.S. dollar-based gold standard.

Because each country established a par value for its currency, the Bretton Woods Agreement resulted in a fixed exchange rate system. (Figure 6.3 shows the structure of exchange rates at the end of the Bretton Woods era.) Under the agreement each country pledged to maintain the value of its currency within ±1 percent of its par value. If the market value of its currency fell outside that range, a country was obligated to intervene in the foreign-exchange market to bring the value back within ±1 percent of par value. This stability in exchange rates benefited international businesses because the Bretton Woods system *generally* provided an assurance that the value of each currency would remain stable.

Note the use of the qualifier *generally*. Under extraordinary circumstances the Bretton Woods Agreement allowed a country to adjust its currency's par value. Accordingly, the Bretton Woods system is often described as using an **adjustable peg** because currencies were pegged to gold but the pegs themselves could be altered under certain conditions. For example, under the system the British pound's par value was first set at $2.80. (Technically, the par value was pegged to an ounce of gold, which then could be translated into dollars at a rate of $35.00 per ounce. Most businesspeople ignored this technicality and focused on the implicit par value of a currency in terms of the U.S. dollar.) Thus the Bank of England was obligated to keep the pound's value between $2.772 and $2.828 (±1 percent of $2.80). Suppose pessimism about the British economy caused the pound's market price to fall to $2.76. The Bank of England would be required to defend the value of the pound by selling some of its gold or U.S.-dollar holdings to buy pounds. This move would increase the demand for pounds, and the market price would return to within the legal range—from $2.772 to $2.828.

This arrangement worked well as long as pessimism about a country's economy was temporary, but if a country suffered from structural macroeconomic problems, major difficulties could arise. For example, in the late 1960s, Labour governments striving for social justice dominated British politics, and British unions secured higher wages, better working conditions, and protective work rules. At the same time, however, British productivity decreased relative to that of its major international competitors, and the pound's value weakened. The Bank of England had to intervene continually in the foreign-currency market, selling gold and foreign currencies to support the pound. In so doing, however, the Bank's holdings of official reserves, which were needed to back up the country's Bretton Woods pledge, began to dwindle. International currency traders began to fear the Bank would run out of reserves. As that fear mounted, inter-

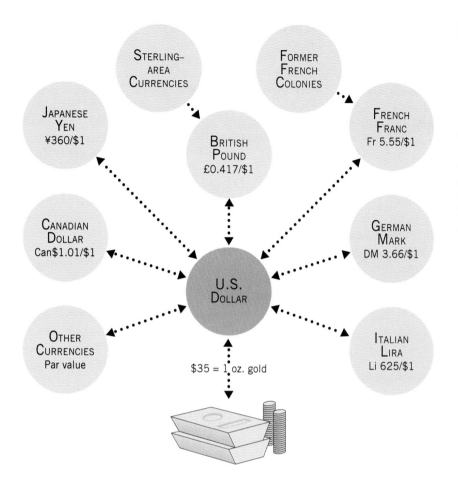

FIGURE 6.3

Role of the U.S. Dollar in the Bretton Woods System

Note: Par values as of December 31, 1970.

Source: Reproduced from Franklin R. Root, *International Trade and Investment*, 5th ed., with the permission of South-Western College Publishing. Copyright 1984 by South-Western College Publishing. All rights reserved.

national banks, currency traders, and other market participants became unwilling to hold British pounds in their inventory of foreign currencies. They began dumping pounds on the market as soon as they received them. A vicious cycle developed: As the Bank of England continued to drain its official reserves to support the pound, the fears of the currency-market participants that the Bank would run out of reserves were worsened.

The situation resembles a run on a bank. Banks never have enough cash on hand to honor all their liabilities. However, as long as everyone trusts that their bank will give them their money if they need it, no one worries. If people lose that trust and withdraw more of their money than the bank has on hand, the bank could be in trouble. The Bretton Woods system was particularly susceptible to speculative "runs on the bank" because there was little risk in betting against a currency in times of doubt. For example, speculators distrustful of the Bank of England's ability to honor the U.K.'s Bretton Woods pledge could convert their pounds into dollars. If they guessed right and the pound were devalued, they could make a quick financial killing. If they guessed wrong and the Bank of England maintained the pound's par value, the speculators could always reconvert their dollar holdings back into pounds with little penalty.

The United Kingdom faced this type of bank run in November 1967. The Bank of England could not counter the flood of pounds dumped on the market by speculators and was forced to devalue the pound by 14.3 percent (from $2.80 to $2.40 per pound). France faced a similar run in 1969 and had to devalue the franc. These devaluations tested the international business community's faith in the Bretton Woods system. But the system faced its true Waterloo when the dollar came under attack in the early 1970s.

The End of the Bretton Woods System

These runs on the British and French central banks were a precursor to a run on the most important bank in the Bretton Woods system—the U.S. Federal Reserve Bank. Ironically, the reliance of the Bretton Woods system on the dollar ultimately led to the system's undoing. Because the supply of gold did not expand in the short run, the only source of the liquidity needed to expand international trade was the U.S. dollar. Under the Bretton Woods system the expansion of international liquidity depended on foreigners' willingness to continually increase their holdings of dollars. Foreigners were perfectly happy to hold dollars as long as they trusted the integrity of the U.S. currency, and during the 1950s and 1960s the number of dollars held by foreigners rose steadily.

As foreign dollar holdings increased, however, people began to question the ability of the United States to live up to its Bretton Woods obligation. This led to the **Triffin paradox**, named after the Belgian-born Yale University economist Robert Triffin, who first identified the problem. The paradox arose because foreigners needed to increase their holdings of dollars to finance expansion of international trade, but the more dollars they owned, the less faith they had in the ability of the United States to redeem those dollars for gold. The less faith foreigners had in the United States, the more they wanted to rid themselves of dollars and get gold in return. If they did this, however, international trade and the international monetary system might collapse because the United States did not have enough gold to redeem all the dollars held by foreigners.

As a means of injecting more liquidity into the international monetary system while reducing the demands placed on the dollar as a reserve currency, IMF members agreed in 1967 to create **special drawing rights (SDRs)**. IMF members can use SDRs to settle official transactions at the IMF. Thus SDRs are sometimes called "paper gold." As of April 2001, approximately 18.4 billion SDRs, representing about 1.2 percent of the world's total reserves, were held by IMF members. An SDR's value is currently calculated daily as a weighted average of the market value of four major currencies—U.S. dollar, euro, Japanese yen, and British pound sterling—with the weights revised every five years. As of April 2001, the SDR was worth $1.26 in U.S. dollars.

Although SDRs did provide new liquidity for the international monetary system, they did not reduce the fundamental problem of the glut of dollars held by foreigners. By mid-1971 the Bretton Woods system was tottering, the victim of fears about the dollar's instability. During the first seven months of 1971 the United States was forced to sell one-third of its gold reserves to maintain the dollar's value. It became clear to the marketplace that the United States did not have sufficient gold on hand to meet the demands of those who still wanted to exchange their dollars for gold. In a dramatic address on August 15, 1971, President Richard M. Nixon announced that the United States would no longer redeem gold at $35 per ounce. The Bretton Woods system was ended. In effect the bank was closing its doors.

After Nixon's speech most currencies began to float, their values being determined by supply and demand in the foreign-exchange market. The value of the U.S. dollar fell relative to most of the world's major currencies. The nations of the world, however, were not yet ready to abandon the fixed exchange rate system. At the **Smithsonian Conference**, held in Washington, D.C. in December 1971, central bank representatives from the Group of Ten (see Table 6.1) agreed to restore the fixed exchange rate system but with restructured rates of exchange between the major trading currencies. The U.S. dollar was devalued to $38 per ounce but remained inconvertible into gold, and the par values of strong currencies such as the yen were revalued upward. Currencies were allowed to fluctuate around their new par values by ±2.25 percent, which replaced the narrower ±1.00 percent range authorized by the Bretton Woods Agreement.

	GROUP OF FIVE	GROUP OF SEVEN	GROUP OF TEN*	PERCENTAGE OF WORLD GDP
	United States	United States	United States	28.8
	Japan	Japan	Japan	14.5
	Germany	Germany	Germany	6.9
	France	France	France	4.7
	United Kingdom	United Kingdom	United Kingdom	4.5
		Italy	Italy	3.8
		Canada	Canada	2.0
			Netherlands	1.3
			Switzerland	.9
			Belgium	.8
			Sweden	.7
Cumulative Percentage of World GDP	59.4	65.2	68.9	

TABLE 6.1

The Groups of Five, Seven, and Ten

*The Group of Ten has 11 members.

Performance of the International Monetary System Since 1971

Free-market forces disputed the new set of par values established by the Smithsonian conferees. Speculators, believing the dollar and the pound were over-valued, sold both and hoarded currencies they believed were undervalued, such as the Swiss franc and the German mark. The Bank of England was unable to maintain the pound's value within the ±2.25 percent band and in June 1972 had to allow the pound to float downward. Switzerland let the Swiss franc float upward in early 1973. The United States devalued the dollar by 10 percent in February 1973. By March 1973 the central banks (see Table 6.2 for a list of the most important of today's central banks) conceded they could not successfully resist free-market forces and so established a flexible exchange rate system. Under a **flexible** (or **floating) exchange rate system**, supply and demand for a currency determine its price in the world market. Since 1973, exchange rates among many currencies have been established *primarily* by the interaction of supply and demand. We use the qualifier *primarily* because central banks sometimes try to affect exchange rates by buying or selling currencies on the foreign-exchange market. Thus the current arrangements are often called a **managed float** (or, more poetically, a **dirty float**) because exchange rates are not determined purely by private-sector market forces. "Bringing the World into Focus" discusses other differences between fixed and flexible exchange rates.

COUNTRY	BANK
Canada	Bank of Canada
European Union (12 members using the euro)	European Central Bank
Japan	Bank of Japan
United Kingdom	Bank of England
United States	Federal Reserve Bank

TABLE 6.2

Key Central Banks

Bringing the World into FOCUS

FIXED VERSUS FLEXIBLE EXCHANGE RATES

One important difference between fixed and flexible exchange rate systems is the way they reach equilibrium. Under the fixed exchange rate system, such as the gold standard (1821 to 1914) and the Bretton Woods system (1945 to 1971), each country pledges to maintain the value of its currency against some standard, such as gold or another currency. If the value of the country's currency falls below par value, the country's central bank boosts the currency's price by buying it in the foreign-exchange market, selling off its gold reserves or stock of convertible currencies in the process. If the currency's value rises above par value, the central bank sells the currency in the foreign-exchange market, acquiring additional gold or foreign currency in the process. Long-run equilibrium is supposed to occur through the deflationary or inflationary impact of changes in the country's money supply attributable to the central bank's actions in the foreign-exchange market.

Although this automatic adjustment process worked reasonably well under the nineteenth-century gold standard, it did not work well under the Bretton Woods system. In practice, the adjustment process under the Bretton Woods system was asym-

metric. A country with a BOP surplus did not need to do anything, provided it was willing to accumulate foreign exchange or gold. A country suffering a BOP deficit saw a continuing decrease in its official reserves. It had to cure its BOP problems well before it ran out of reserves. If the country did nothing, other countries (and investors), seeing its reserves dwindling, would begin to distrust the country's ability to honor its pledge to maintain its currency's par value. These foreigners would rush to sell their holdings of the currency, thereby worsening the drain on the country's reserves. Ultimately the government would have to renege on its promise to convert at the fixed rate and would resort to devaluing its currency. This is what happened to the United Kingdom in 1967, France in 1969, and the United States in 1971.

Conversely, under a flexible exchange rate system, the exchange rate is determined by the forces of supply and demand for each currency. Assuming a country's central bank is willing to live with the outcome of these market forces, its official reserves need not be depleted because consumers and investors are determining the currency's value through their self-interested transactions.

The new flexible exchange rate system was legitimized by an international conference held in Jamaica in January 1976. According to the resulting **Jamaica Agreement**, each country was free to adopt whatever exchange rate system best met its own requirements. The United States adopted a floating exchange rate. Other countries adopted a fixed exchange rate by pegging their currencies to the dollar, the French franc, or some other currency.

Of particular note is the strategy adopted by European Union (EU) members in the belief that flexible exchange rates would hinder their ability to create an integrated European economy. In 1979 EU members created the **European Monetary System (EMS)** to manage currency relationships among themselves. Most EMS members chose to participate in the EU's **exchange rate mechanism (ERM)**. ERM participants pledged to maintain fixed exchange rates among their currencies within a narrow range of ±2.25 percent of par value and a floating rate against the U.S. dollar and other currencies. The exchange rate mechanism facilitated the creation of the EU's single currency, the euro, in 1999, a topic we will cover more thoroughly in Chapter 9.

Map 6.2 shows the current status of the world's exchange rate arrangements. The current international monetary system is an amalgam of fixed and flexible exchange rates. For example, as just discussed, most members of the EU have adopted a common currency, while other countries have voluntarily adopted a fixed exchange rate against the U.S. dollar, the French franc, or some other currency. Still other countries, such as Canada, Japan, the United Kingdom, and the United States, have cho-

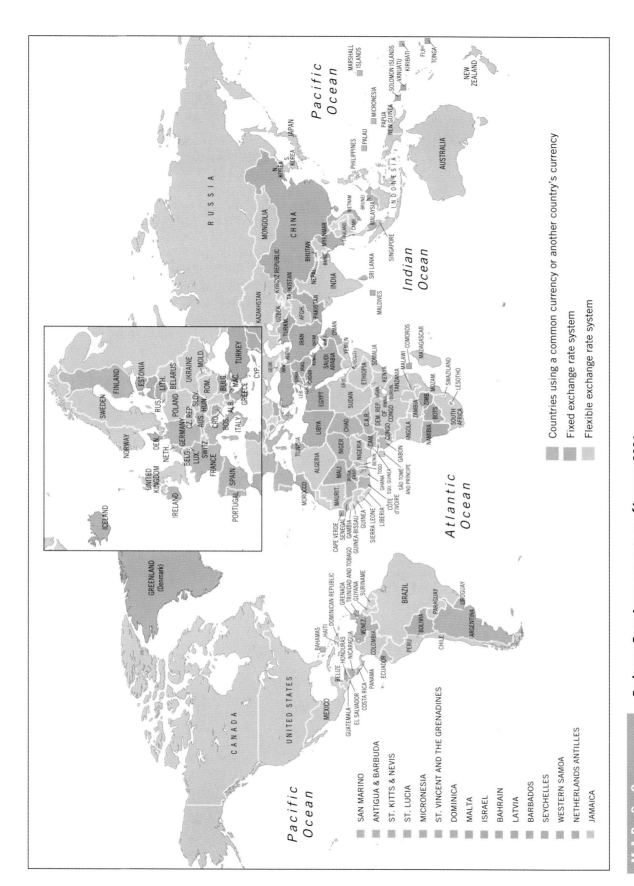

MAP 6.2   **Exchange Rate Arrangements as of January 2001**

Source: IMF, *International Financial Statistics*, March 2001, pp. 2–3. Reprinted with permission.

Countries using a common currency or another country's currency

Fixed exchange rate system

Flexible exchange rate system

SAN MARINO
ANTIGUA & BARBUDA
ST. KITTS & NEVIS
ST. LUCIA
MICRONESIA
ST. VINCENT AND THE GRENADINES
DOMINICA
MALTA
ISRAEL
BAHRAIN
LATVIA
BARBADOS
SEYCHELLES
WESTERN SAMOA
NETHERLANDS ANTILLES
JAMAICA

sen to let their currencies float. Accordingly, under the current international monetary system, currencies of one country grouping float against the currencies of other country groupings. For example, the U.S. dollar and currencies fixed to the U.S. dollar float against the euro and currencies fixed to it. The U.S. dollar and the euro in turn float against numerous independently floating currencies, such as the Canadian dollar, the Australian dollar, the British pound, and the Swiss franc.

Other Post-World War II Conferences.   The international monetary system that has grown out of the Jamaica Agreement has not pleased all the world's central banks all the time. Since 1976, the central banks have met numerous times to iron out policy conflicts among themselves. For example, U.S. complaints that an overvalued dollar was hurting the competitiveness of U.S. exports and allowing cheap imports to damage U.S. industries prompted finance ministers of the Group of Five (see Table 6.1) to meet in September 1985 at the Plaza Hotel in New York City. The meeting led to the **Plaza Accord**, in which the central banks agreed to let the dollar's value fall on currency markets—and fall it did. From its peak in February 1985 the dollar plummeted almost 46 percent against the deutsche mark and 41 percent against the yen by the beginning of 1987. Fearing that continued devaluation of the dollar would disrupt world trade, finance ministers from the Group of Five met again, this time at the Louvre in Paris in February 1987. The **Louvre Accord** signaled the commitment of these five countries to stabilizing the dollar's value. However, the foreign-exchange market was once again thrown into turmoil in 1990, this time by the onset of the Persian Gulf hostilities. The values of key currencies continued to fluctuate through the end of the century. Figure 6.4 shows changes in the dollar's value against the yen and the mark since the collapse of the Bretton Woods system.

These fluctuations in currency values are of great importance to international businesses. When the value of their domestic currency increases in the foreign-exchange market, firms find it harder to export their goods, more difficult to protect their domestic markets from the threat of foreign imports, and more advantageous to shift their production from domestic factories to foreign factories. A decrease in the domestic currency's value has the opposite effect. Savvy international businesspeople are mindful of the impact of these currency fluctuations on their business opportunities. Recall from the discussion of the Caterpillar-Komatsu rivalry in Chapter 5 that the strong dollar caused Caterpillar problems during the early 1980s, and the weak dollar (and strong yen) caused Komatsu problems during the late 1980s and early 1990s. The dollar's rise since mid-1995 has eased Komatsu's concerns but raised Caterpillar's.

FIGURE 6.4

Exchange Rates of the Dollar Versus the Yen and the Deutsche Mark, 1960–1999

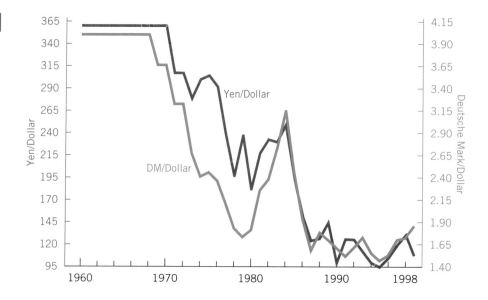

Bringing the World into FOCUS

SHOULD BRETTON WOODS BE RESTORED?

International policy makers have debated the value of reconstructing the Bretton Woods system. Proponents of the system believe fixed exchange rates offer international businesses several advantages. Exchange rates are not subject to wide daily, weekly, and monthly fluctuations. The riskiness of international trade transactions is thus reduced, and firms have greater assurance of stability in the values of foreign currencies. Also, fixed exchange rates are an important anti-inflationary tool because the loss of official reserves forces a country to counteract inflationary tendencies in its economy. Bretton Woods proponents also are distressed because the wild swings in the values of key currencies that occur in flexible exchange rate systems can disrupt sound international investment decision making.

Advocates of flexible exchange rates look at the other side of the coin. If balance of payments (BOP) equilibrium can be reached through changes in exchange rates, then domestic policy makers are free to focus on domestic economic concerns without worrying about the BOP consequences of their actions. Flexible exchange rates also reduce the need for international coordination of domestic economic policies and allow each country to follow its own economic destiny. For example, if Mexico's monetary authorities choose more inflationary, growth-oriented economic policies than those adopted by its major trading partners, changes in exchange rates will bring about BOP equilibrium. Flexible exchange rates can absorb the impact of damaging external economic events, such as occurred during the two oil embargoes in the 1970s. Proponents of flexible exchange rates also suggest that fixed exchange rate systems are not invulnerable to disorderly changes in currency values and cite the depreciation of the pound in 1967, the French franc in 1969, and the U.S. dollar in 1971. Similarly, they point out the chaos and hardships created by the 1997-1998 collapse of the fixed exchange rate systems used by Thailand, Indonesia, and other Southeast Asian countries.

Currency fluctuations also affect international investment opportunities. For example, the appreciation of the mark against the dollar after 1985 made it more difficult for Bayerische Motoren Werke to sustain its sales of BMWs in the United States. The company's solution was to build an automobile assembly plant near Spartanburg, South Carolina, a move designed to lower the company's production costs and raise its visibility in the North American market. The mark's fall against the dollar since 1995 has eroded some of the cost advantages to BMW of its South Carolina plant. As "Bringing the World into Focus" suggests, the problems caused by these exchange rate fluctuations have motivated some experts to call for a restoration of the Bretton Woods system.

The International Debt Crisis. The flexible exchange rate system instituted in 1973 was immediately put to a severe test. In response to the Israeli victory in the Arab-Israeli War of 1973, Arab nations imposed an embargo on oil shipments to countries such as the United States and the Netherlands, which had supported the Israeli cause. As a result, the Organization of Petroleum Exporting Countries (OPEC) succeeded in quadrupling world oil prices from $3 a barrel in October 1973 to $12 a barrel by March 1974. This rapid increase in oil prices caused inflationary pressures in oil-importing countries. For example, in the United States inflation rose from 6.1 percent in 1973 to 11.1 percent in 1974. In 1974 alone $60 billion in wealth was transferred from oil-importing countries to oil-exporting countries. The new international monetary arrangements absorbed some of the shock caused by this upheaval in the oil market, as exchange rates adjusted to account for changes in the value of each country's oil exports or imports. The currencies of the oil exporters strengthened, while those of the oil importers weakened.

This enormous transfer of wealth raised certain economic concerns. The higher oil prices acted as a tax on the economies of the oil-importing countries. Some economists feared that worldwide depression would develop as consumer demand fell in the richer countries. Other economists worried that because trade in oil was denominated in dollars, international liquidity would dry up as dollars piled up in Arab bank accounts. Neither of these fears was realized. Many of the oil-exporting countries went on spending sprees, using their new wealth to improve their infrastructures or to invest in new facilities (such as petroleum refineries) to produce wealth for future generations. The unspent petrodollars were deposited in banks in international money centers such as London and New York City. The international banking community then recycled these petrodollars through its international lending activities to help revive the economies damaged by rising oil prices.

Unfortunately, the international banks were too aggressive in recycling these dollars. Many countries borrowed more than they could repay. Mexico, for example, borrowed $90 billion, while Brazil took on $67 billion in new loans. The financial positions of these borrowers became precarious after the oil shock of 1978-1979, which was triggered by the toppling from power of the Shah of Iran. The price of oil skyrocketed from $13 a barrel in 1978 to over $30 a barrel in 1980, triggering another round of worldwide inflation. Interest rates on these loans rose, as most carried a floating interest rate, further burdening the heavily indebted nations. The international debt crisis formally began when Mexico declared in August 1982 that it could not service its external debts. Mexico requested a rescheduling of its debts, a moratorium on repayment of principal, and a loan from the IMF to help it through its debt crisis. Mexico was soon joined by Brazil and Argentina. In total more than 40 countries in Asia, Africa, and Latin America sought relief from their external debts. Negotiations among the debtor countries, creditor countries, private banks, and international organizations continued through the rest of the 1980s.

Various approaches were used to resolve the crisis. The 1985 **Baker Plan** (named after then U.S. Treasury Secretary James Baker) stressed the importance of debt rescheduling, tight IMF-imposed controls over domestic monetary and fiscal policies, and continued lending to debtor countries in hopes that economic growth would allow them to repay their creditors. In Mexico's case the IMF agreed to provide a loan package only if private foreign banks holding Mexican debt agreed to reschedule their loans and provide Mexico with additional financing. However, the debtor nations made little progress in repaying their loans. Debtors and creditors alike agreed that a new approach was needed. The 1989 **Brady Plan** (named after the Bush administration's treasury secretary, Nicholas Brady) focused on the need to reduce the debts of the troubled countries by writing off parts of the debts or by providing the countries with funds to buy back their loan notes at below face value.

The international debt crisis receded during the 1990s as the debt-servicing requirements of debtor countries were made more manageable via a combination of IMF loans, debt rescheduling, and changes in governmental economic policies (see the discussion of economic reforms in Mexico, Argentina, and Brazil in Chapter 2). The impact of the crisis cannot be overstated. Many experts consider the 1980s the "lost decade" for economic development in Latin America.

The most recent crisis facing the international monetary system erupted in July 1997, when Thailand, which had pegged its currency to a dollar-dominated basket of currencies, was forced to unpeg its currency, the baht, after investors began to distrust the abilities of Thai borrowers to repay their foreign loans and of the Thai government to maintain the baht's value. Not wanting to hold a currency likely to be devalued, foreign and domestic investors converted their bahts to dollars and other currencies. The Thai central bank spent much of its official reserves desperately trying to maintain the pegged value of the baht. After Thailand was forced to abandon the peg on July 2, the baht promptly fell 20 percent in value. As investors realized that other countries in the region shared Thailand's overdependence on foreign short-term capital, their currencies also came under attack and their stock markets

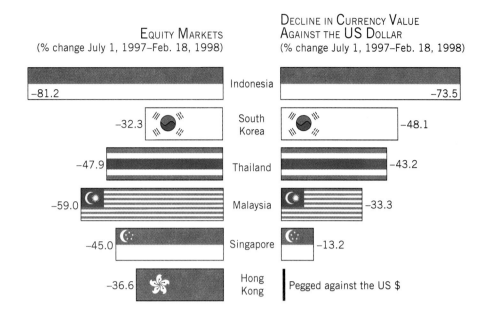

EQUITY MARKETS
(% change July 1, 1997–Feb. 18, 1998)

DECLINE IN CURRENCY VALUE
AGAINST THE US DOLLAR
(% change July 1, 1997–Feb. 18, 1998)

	Equity Markets	Decline in Currency Value
Indonesia	−81.2	−73.5
South Korea	−32.3	−48.1
Thailand	−47.9	−43.2
Malaysia	−59.0	−33.3
Singapore	−45.0	−13.2
Hong Kong	−36.6	Pegged against the US $

FIGURE 6.5

The Asian Contagion

Source: Gerard Baker, "U.S. Looks to G7 Backing on Asia Crisis," *Financial Times*, February 20, 1998, p. 4. Reprinted with permission.

were devastated. Indonesia was hit the worst by the so-called Asian contagion, as our earlier discussion of PT Astra International indicated and as Figure 6.5 shows. Aftershocks of the crisis spread to Latin America and Russia, and the Russian government effectively defaulted on its foreign debts. All told, the IMF and the Quad countries pledged over $100 billion in loans to help restore these countries to economic health. The closing case of Chapter 7 and the "Point-Counterpoint" that follows that chapter discuss this crisis in more detail.

These crises did not come as a surprise to the analysts who had been monitoring the affected countries' balance of payments accounts for danger signs. The BOP accounting system provided clear warning of the deteriorating performance of the countries in crisis and the increasing riskiness of their overextended external debt positions. A careful reading of BOP statistics could have protected international bankers from bad investments and risky loans. Because the BOP accounting system provides such valuable economic intelligence information, the next section discusses it in detail.

THE BALANCE OF PAYMENTS ACCOUNTING SYSTEM ‹

Each year countries purchase trillions of dollars of goods, services, and assets from each other. The BOP accounting system is a double-entry bookkeeping system designed to measure and record all economic transactions between residents of one country and residents of all other countries during a particular time period. It helps policy makers understand the performance of each country's economy in international markets. It also signals fundamental changes in the competitiveness of countries and assists policy makers in designing appropriate public policies to respond to these changes.

International businesspeople need to pay close attention to countries' BOP statistics for several reasons, including the following:

1. BOP statistics help identify emerging markets for goods and services.

2. BOP statistics can warn of possible new policies that may alter a country's business climate, thereby affecting the profitability of a firm's operations in that country. For example, sharp rises in a country's imports may signal an overheated economy and portend a tightening of the domestic money supply. In this case attentive businesspeople will shrink their inventories in anticipation of a reduction in customer demand.

3. BOP statistics can indicate reductions in a country's foreign-exchange reserves, which may mean that the country's currency will depreciate in the future, as occurred in Thailand in 1997. Exporters to such a country may find that domestic producers will become more price competitive.

4. As was true in the international debt crisis, BOP statistics can signal increased riskiness of lending to particular countries.

Four important aspects of the BOP accounting system need to be highlighted:

1. The BOP accounting system records international transactions made during some time period, for example, a year.

2. It records only economic transactions, those that involve something of monetary value.

3. It records transactions between residents of one country and residents of all other countries. Residents can be individuals, businesses, government agencies, or nonprofit organizations, but defining residency is sometimes tricky. Persons temporarily located in a country—tourists, students, and military or diplomatic personnel—are still considered residents of their home country for BOP purposes. Businesses are considered residents of the country in which they are incorporated. Firms often conduct international business by locating either a branch or a subsidiary in a foreign country. A branch, which by definition is an unincorporated operation and thus not legally distinct from its parent corporation, is a resident of the parent's home country. A subsidiary, which by definition is a separately incorporated operation, is a resident of the country in which it is incorporated. In most cases the subsidiary is incorporated in the host country to take advantage of legally being a resident of the country in which it is operating.

4. The BOP accounting system is a double-entry system. Each transaction produces a credit entry and a debit entry of equal size. In most international business dealings the first entry in a BOP transaction involves the purchase or sale of something—a good, a service, or an asset. The second entry records the payment or receipt of payment for the thing bought or sold. Figuring out which is the BOP debit entry and which is the BOP credit entry is not a skill that most people are born with. Many experts compare a BOP accounting statement to a statement of sources and uses of funds. Debit entries reflect uses of funds; credit entries measure sources of funds. Under this framework, buying things creates debits, and selling things produces credits.

The Major Components of the Balance of Payments Accounting System

The BOP accounting system can be divided conceptually into four major accounts. The first two accounts—the current account and the capital account—record purchases of goods, services, and assets by the private and public sectors. The official reserves account reflects the impact of central bank intervention in the foreign-exchange market. The last account—errors and omissions—captures mistakes made in recording BOP transactions.

Current Account.   The **current account** records four types of transactions among residents of different countries:

1. Exports and imports of goods (or merchandise)

2. Exports and imports of services

3. Investment income

4. Gifts

Table 6.3 summarizes debit and credit entries for transactions involving the current account.

	DEBIT	CREDIT
Goods	Buy	Sell
Services	Buy	Sell
Dividends and interest (investment income)	Pay	Receive
Gifts	Give	Receive

TABLE 6.3

BOP Entries, Current Account

For example, to Germany the sale of a Mercedes-Benz automobile to a doctor in Marseilles is a **merchandise export**, and the purchase by a German resident of Dom Perignon champagne from France is a **merchandise import.** (The British use the term **trade in visibles** to refer to merchandise trade.) The difference between a country's exports and imports of goods is called the **balance on merchandise trade**. For example, the United States, which has been importing more goods than it has been exporting, has a *merchandise trade deficit*; Japan, which has been exporting more goods than it has been importing, has a *merchandise trade surplus.*

The services account records sales and purchases of such services as transportation, tourism, medical care, telecommunications, advertising, financial services, and education. The sale of a service to a resident of another country is a **service export**, and the purchase by a resident of a service from another country is a **service import**. (The British use the term **trade in invisibles** to denote trade in services.) For example, for Germany a German student spending a year studying at the Sorbonne in Paris is an import of services, and the telephone call home that an Italian tourist makes during the Oktoberfest in Munich represents a service export. The difference between a country's exports of services and its imports of services is called the **balance on services trade**.

The third type of transaction recorded in the current account is investment income. Income German residents earn from their foreign investments is viewed as an **export of the services of capital** by Germany. This income takes the form of either interest and dividends earned by German residents on their investments in foreign stocks, bonds, and deposit accounts or profits that are repatriated back to Germany from incorporated subsidiaries in other countries that are owned by German firms. Of course, foreigners also make investments in Germany. Income earned by foreigners from their investments in Germany is viewed as an **import of the services of capital** by Germany. This income includes interest and dividends paid by firms in Germany on stocks, bonds, and deposit accounts owned by foreign residents, as well as profits that are repatriated by foreign-owned incorporated subsidiaries in Germany back to their corporate parents.

The fourth type of transaction in the current account is **unilateral transfers**, or gifts between residents of one country and another. Unilateral transfers include private and public gifts. For example, Pakistani-born residents of Kuwait who send part of their earnings back home to their relatives are engaging in private unilateral transfers. In contrast, governmental aid from the United Kingdom used for a flood control project in Bangladesh is a public unilateral transfer. In both cases, the recipients need not provide any compensation to the donors.

The **current account balance** measures the net balance resulting from merchandise trade, service trade, investment income, and unilateral transfers. It is closely scrutinized by government officials and policy makers because it broadly reflects the country's current competitiveness in international markets.

Capital Account. The second major account in the BOP accounting system is the **capital account**, which records capital transactions—purchases and sales of assets—between residents of one country and those of other countries. Capital account transactions (summarized in Table 6.4) can be divided into two categories: foreign direct investment (FDI) and portfolio investment.

TABLE 6.4

Capital Account Transactions

	MATURITY	MOTIVATION	TYPICAL INVESTMENTS
Portfolio (short-term)	One year or less	Investment income or facilitation of international commerce	Checking account balances Time deposits Commercial paper Bank loans
Portfolio (long-term)	More than one year	Investment income	Government bills, notes, and bonds Corporate stocks and bonds
Foreign direct investment	Indeterminate	Active control of organization (own at least 10 percent of voting stock)	Foreign subsidiaries Foreign factories International joint ventures

FDI is any investment made for purpose of controlling the organization in which the investment is made, typically through ownership of significant blocks of common stock with voting privileges. Under U.S. BOP accounting standards control is defined as ownership of at least 10 percent of a company's voting stock. A portfolio investment is any investment made for purposes other than control. Portfolio investments are divided into two subcategories: short-term investments and long-term investments. **Short-term portfolio investments** are financial instruments with maturities of one year or less. Included in this category are commercial paper; checking accounts, time deposits, and certificates of deposit held by residents of a country in foreign banks or by foreigners in domestic banks; trade receivables and deposits from international commercial customers; and banks' short-term international lending activities, such as commercial loans. **Long-term portfolio investments** are stocks, bonds, and other financial instruments issued by private and public organizations that have maturities greater than one year and that are held for purposes other than control. For example, when IBM invests excess cash balances overnight in a Paris bank to earn a higher interest rate than it could earn in New York, it is making a short-term portfolio investment. When the California Public Employers Retirement System Pension Fund buys stock in British Airways, it is making a long-term portfolio investment. When British Airways purchases 23 percent of the common stock of USAir, it is making an FDI.

Current account transactions invariably affect the short-term component of the capital account. Why? As noted earlier in the chapter, the first entry in the double-entry BOP accounting system records the purchase or sale of something—a good, a service, or an asset. The second entry typically records the payment or receipt of payment for the thing bought or sold. In most cases this second entry reflects a change in someone's checking account balance, which in the BOP accounting system is a short-term capital account transaction. ("Building Global Skills" at the end of this chapter walks you through this linkage between the current account and the capital account in more detail.)

> Renault's purchase of Samsung Motors in 2000 improved its access to Korea's automobile market. This foreign direct investment is recorded in the French balance of payments as a debit to the capital account.

Capital inflows are credits in the BOP accounting system. They can occur in two ways:

1. *Foreign ownership of assets in a country increases.* An example of a capital inflow into the United States is the purchase of Lycos, a U.S. Web portal company, by Terra Networks SA, a Spanish dot-com company, for $8.5 billion in late 2000.[4] A capital inflow also occurs if a foreign firm deposits a check in a U.S. bank. In this case, the asset being purchased is a claim on a U.S. bank, which of course is all that a checking account balance represents.

2. *Ownership of foreign assets by a country's residents declines.* When K-Mart and a U.S. partner sold K-Mart's Canadian operations to Zeller's (a division of Canada's Hudson's Bay Company) for $168 million in the late 1990s, the United States experienced a capital inflow. Similarly, when IBM pays a Japanese disk drive supplier with a check drawn on IBM's account at a Tokyo bank, IBM's Japanese checking account balance declines and the United States experiences a capital inflow because IBM is partially liquidating its ownership of foreign assets.

Capital outflows are debits in the BOP accounting system. They also can occur in two ways:

1. *Ownership of foreign assets by a country's residents increases.* Ford's £1.5 billion purchase of the British firm Jaguar Motor Company represented a capital outflow from the United States. A U.S. capital outflow also occurs when Delta Air Lines deposits a check from a London businessperson into an account it holds in an English bank.

2. *Foreign ownership of assets in a country declines.* A German mutual fund that sells 100,000 shares of GM common stock from its portfolio to a U.S. resident causes a capital outflow from the United States. A U.S. capital outflow also occurs if Japan Air Lines writes a check drawn on its account at an Hawaiian bank to pay its fuel supplier at Honolulu Airport. In both cases foreigners are liquidating a portion of their U.S. assets.

Table 6.5 summarizes the impact of various capital account transactions on the BOP accounting system.

	DEBT (OUTFLOW)	CREDIT (INFLOW)
Portfolio (short term)	Receiving a payment from a foreigner	Making a payment to a foreigner
	Buying a short-term foreign asset	Selling a domestic short-term asset to a foreigner
	Buying back a short-term domestic asset from its foreign owner	Selling a short-term foreign asset acquired previously
Portfolio (long-term)	Buying a long-term foreign asset (not for purposes of control)	Selling a domestic long-term asset to a foreigner (not for purposes of control)
	Buying back a long-term domestic asset from its foreign owner (not for purposes of control)	Selling a long-term foreign asset acquired previously (not for purposes of control)
Foreign direct investment	Buying a foreign asset for purposes of control	Selling a domestic asset to a foreigner for purposes of control
	Buying back from its foreign owner a domestic asset previously acquired for purposes of control	Selling a foreign asset previously acquired for purposes of control

TABLE 6.5

BOP Entries, Capital Account

Official Reserves Account.   The third major account in the BOP accounting system, the **official reserves account**, records the level of official reserve~ held by a national government. These reserves are used to intervene in the exchange market and in transactions with other central banks. Official comprise four types of assets:

1. Gold
2. Convertible currencies
3. SDRs
4. Reserve positions at the IMF

Official gold holdings are measured using a par value established by treasury or finance ministry. Convertible currencies are currencies tha exchangeable in world currency markets. The convertible currencies monly used as official reserves are the U.S. dollar, the euro and associa cies, and the yen. The last two types of reserves—SDRs and reserve po: tas minus IMF borrowings) at the IMF—were discussed earlier in this (

Errors and Omissions.   The last account in the BOP accounting s errors and omissions account. One truism of the BOP accounting sy the BOP must balance. In theory the following equality should be obs

$$\text{Current Account} + \text{Capital Account} + \text{Official Reserves Account} = 0$$

However, this equality is never achieved in practice because of measurement errors. The **errors and omissions** account is used to make the BOP balance in accordance with the following equation:

$$\text{Current Account} + \text{Capital Account} + \text{Official Reserves Account}$$
$$+ \text{Errors and Omissions} = 0$$

The errors and omissions account can be quite large. In 1999, for example, the U.S. errors and omissions account totaled $11.6 billion. In 1998 it was $69.7 billion. Experts suspect that a large portion of the errors and omissions account balance is due to underreporting of capital account transactions. Such innovations as instantaneous, round-the-clock foreign-exchange trading, sophisticated monetary swaps and hedges, and international money market funds have made it difficult for government statisticians to keep up with the growing volume of legal short-term money flowing between countries in search of the highest interest rate.

Sometimes, errors and omissions are due to deliberate actions by individuals who are engaged in illegal activities such as drug smuggling, money laundering, or evasion of currency and investment controls imposed by their home governments. Politically stable countries, such as the United States, are often the destination of **flight capital**, money sent abroad by foreign residents seeking a safe haven for their assets, hidden from the sticky fingers of their home governments. Given the often illegal nature of flight capital, persons sending it to the United States often try to avoid any official recognition of their transactions, making it difficult for government BOP statisticians to record such transactions. Residents of other countries who distrust the stability of their own currency may also choose to use a stronger currency, such as the dollar or the yen, to transact their business or keep their savings, as "Venturing Abroad" suggests. In 1999 alone some $22 billion of U.S. currency flowed overseas, as concerns about the Y2K problem, exchange rate fluctuations, and financial instability increased the desire of foreigners to hold U.S. currency.[5]

Some errors may crop up in the current account as well. Statistics for merchandise imports are generally thought to be reasonably accurate because most countries' customs services scrutinize imports to ensure that all appropriate taxes are collected. This scrutiny generates paper trails that facilitate the collection of accurate statistics. However, few countries tax exports, so customs services have less incentive to assess the accuracy of statistics concerning merchandise exports.

Abroad

BEN FRANKLIN, WORLD TRAVELER

ell-known American outside the borders of the
eorge W. Bush?... Madonna?... Gwyneth
rgument can be made for Ben Franklin, whose
.S. $100 bill. Economists and accountants at the
ve Bank (FRB) have been trying for years to esti-
U.S. currency is held by foreigners. Their best
he $515 billion in U.S. currency in circulation in
, or 49 percent, is held by foreigners. Most of this
ency is in $100 bills; U.S. consumers prefer to uti-
mination bills.
n the total number of dollars held overseas is rather
based on a mixture of sophisticated economic
mer surveys, and educated guesswork. A 1995 FRB
survey of U.S. households could account for only 3 percent of the
$100 bills printed by the U.S. government, yet the number of such
bills in circulation has increased by $143 billion since 1990. FRB
staffers also know that the Los Angeles and New York City branches
of the FRB distribute enormous numbers of $100 bills relative to the
other branches. From 1990 to 1996 these two branches accounted
for 84 percent of the new $100 bills placed in circulation. Experts
believe that most of this currency flows to citizens of countries
where economic and/or political unrest is high. Russia, other former
Soviet Republics, the Middle East, and Latin America appear to be
particularly important destinations for U.S. $100 bills.

Another contributing factor is the increasing "dollarization" of
Latin America. On New Year's Day 2001 El Salvador made the U.S.

dollar legal tender there. El Salvador's Central Reserve Bank purchased $450 million worth of U.S. currency to implement this
change. Ecuador adopted a similar policy in mid-2000, and
Guatemala has taken steps to dollarize its economy as well.

These foreign holdings of U.S. paper currency provide an
important benefit to the U.S. Treasury and ultimately to the U.S.
taxpayer because they effectively serve as an interest-free loan.
Normally, to fund the U.S. debt, the U.S. Treasury must float loans
in the form of bonds, notes, and bills. Currency holdings substitute for such loans and reduce the amount the treasury must borrow. If 30-year treasury bonds bear an interest rate of 6.5 percent,
then the U.S taxpayer saves $16.3 billion (6.5 percent times $251
billion) in interest payments annually as a result of foreign holdings of U.S. currency. This is one of the benefits American citizens
receive as a result of the country's economic and political stability.
Other countries—in particular, Germany—also benefit from large
holdings of their paper currencies by residents of other countries.
Many experts believe that many foreigners will also hold euros
once that currency becomes available in 2002.

Sources: "Dollar's Share of World Reserves Grows," *Wall Street Journal*,
September 10, 1997, p. A2; *Survey of Current Business*, July 2000, p. 51; "Russia
Counts Cost of Change as US Set to Issue New $100 Bill," *Financial Times*,
January 16, 1996, p. 20; "Where's the Buck? Dollars Make the World Go
Around," Fed Says," *Houston Chronicle*, October 13, 1995, p. 2C; "El Salvador
Switching to U.S. Dollar," *Houston Chronicle*, December 30, 2000, p. 1C.

Statistics for trade in services also may contain inaccuracies. Many service trade
statistics are generated by surveys. For example, U.S. tourism exports are measured by surveying foreign tourists on how many days they spent in the United
States and how many dollars they spent per day. If tourists underestimate their
daily spending, then U.S. service exports are underestimated. To help you gain a
better understanding of the BOP accounts, we next review the international transactions of the United States in 1999.

The U.S. Balance of Payments in 1999

The first component of the current account is merchandise (goods) exports and
imports. As shown in Table 6.6, U.S. merchandise exports totaled $684.3 billion in
1999. Figure 6.6(a) presents a more detailed picture of the leading U.S. exports.
Automobiles and auto parts were the largest component of U.S. merchandise
exports, generating $75.8 billion in sales. Of U.S. automobile exports 60 percent
were to Canada, a reflection of the integrated nature of North American automobile
production that resulted from the 1965 Auto Pact between the United States and
Canada. (Canada—meaning primarily GM, Ford, and Chrysler plants that are
located in Canada—exported $63.9 billion in automobiles and auto parts to the

U.S. BOP, 1999 (in billions of dollars)

Current Account		
Goods		
Exports	+$684.3	
Imports	−1,029.9	
Balance on Merchandise Trade	−345.6	
Services		
Exports	+271.9	
Imports	−191.3	
Balance on Services Trade	+80.6	
Investment Income		
Received	276.2	
Paid	−294.7	
Balance on Investment Income	−18.5	
Unilateral Transfers (net)	−48.0	
(− means outward gifts greater than inward)		
Balance on Current Account		−331.5
Capital Account		
Portfolio, Short-Term (Net Outflow)	−28.4	
Portfolio, Long-Term		
New Foreign Investment in U.S.	+343.6	
New U.S. Investment Abroad	−128.6	
Foreign Direct Investment		
New FDI in U.S.	+275.5	
New U.S. FDI Abroad	−150.9	
Balance on Capital Account		+311.2
Official Reserves Account		+8.7
Errors and Omissions		+11.6
Net Balance		0

United States.) The six industries shown in Figure 6.6(a) accounted for 43 percent of U.S. merchandise exports in 1999.

From Table 6.6, you can see that U.S. merchandise imports totaled $1,029.9 billion in 1999. From Figure 6.6(b) you can see that the leading import was automobiles and auto parts, at $179.4 billion, or 17 percent of imports. Six industries accounted for $466.5 billion, or 45 percent of total U.S. merchandise imports.

The second component of the current account is trade in services. U.S. exports of services totaled $271.9 billion in 1999, with travel and tourism being the largest portion ($94.7 billion). U.S. service imports equaled $191.3, with travel and tourism again being the largest portion ($80.8 billion). The United States had a positive balance on services trade of $80.6 billion (see Table 6.6).

Figure 6.7 shows exports and imports for the major trading partners of the United States and includes trade in both goods and services. From this figure you can see that the United States tends to import more goods from its major trading partners than it exports to them; you can also see that the United States tends to export more services to its trading partners than it imports from them.

The third component of the current account is investment income (see Table 6.6). In 1999 U.S. residents received $276.2 billion from foreign investments and

a. Leading U.S. merchandise exports, 1999

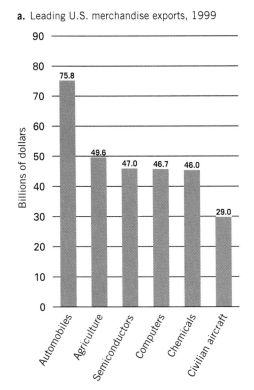

b. Leading U.S. merchandise imports, 1999

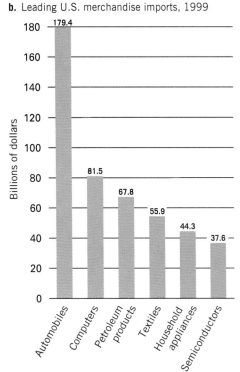

FIGURE 6.6

Leading U.S. Merchandise Exports and Imports, 1999

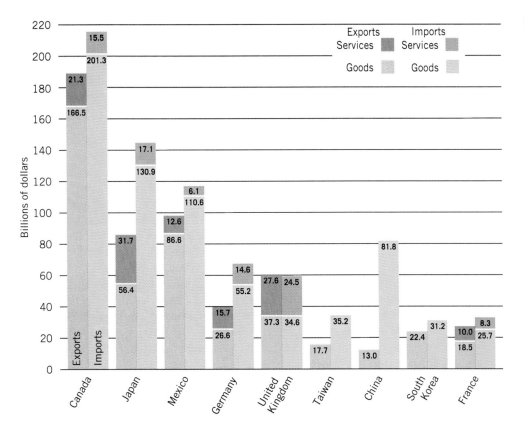

FIGURE 6.7

Trade Between the United States and Its Major Trading Partners, 1999

Note: Data on services exports and imports are not available for Taiwan, China, and South Korea.

> As a condition for joining the World Trade Organization, China agreed to reduce its trade barriers against foreign goods. Here Florida's Agriculture Commissioner hands a ceremonial "first grapefruit" to a Beijing shopper at a media event heralding the initial shipment of U.S. citrus fruit. U.S. agricultural exports reached almost $50 billion in 1999.

paid out $294.7 billion to foreigners for a net negative balance on investment income of $18.5 billion. The United States had a net deficit of $48 billion in the fourth component of the current account, unilateral transfers. Summing up the four components yielded a 1999 current account deficit of $331.5 billion.

The capital account is the second major BOP account (see Table 6.6). In 1999 new U.S. FDI abroad (outflows) totaled $150.9 billion, while new FDI in the United States (inflows) totaled $275.5 billion. New U.S. long-term international portfolio investments were $128.6 billion in 1999, while new foreign long-term portfolio investments in the United States were $343.6 billion. There was also a net outflow of short-term portfolio investment from the United States, totaling $28.4 billion. The capital account balance was $311.2 billion in 1999, as foreigners bought more U.S. assets than U.S. residents bought foreign assets.

U.S. official reserves account transactions were $8.7 billion. If the BOP statistical data net were perfect, the current account balance plus the capital account balance plus the official reserves account balance should equal zero. Any discrepancy is put into the errors and omissions account. In 1999 there was a discrepancy of $11.6 billion. Therefore, for the U.S. BOP in 1999 the following equation applies:

Current Account		Capital Account		Changes in Official Reserves		Errors and Omissions		
(−$331.5 billion)	+	(+$311.2 billion)	+	(+$8.7 billion)	+	(+$11.6 billion)	=	0

Defining Balance of Payments Surpluses and Deficits

Every month the federal government reports the performance of U.S. firms in international markets when it releases the monthly BOP statistics. In most months during the past decade, newscasters have solemnly reported on the evening news that the U.S. BOP is in deficit.

What do the newscasters mean? We just said that the BOP always balances (equals zero), so how can there be a BOP deficit? In reality when knowledgeable people (or even newscasters) talk about a BOP surplus or deficit, they are referring only to a subset of the BOP accounts. Most newscasters are in fact reporting on the balance on trade in goods and services. When a country exports more goods and services than it imports, it has a trade surplus. When it imports more goods and services than it exports, it has a trade deficit.

Because the balance on trade in goods and services is readily understandable and quickly available to the news media, it receives the most public attention. However, other balances also exist, such as the balance on services, the balance on merchandise trade, and the current account balance. Another closely watched BOP balance is the **official settlements balance**. The official settlements balance reflects changes in a country's official reserves; essentially, it records the net impact of the central bank's interventions in the foreign-exchange market in support of the local currency.

Which of these BOP balances is *the* balance of payments? That is really a trick question. There is no single measure of a country's global economic performance. Rather, as in the parable of the blind men touching the elephant, each balance presents a different perspective on the nation's position in the international economy.

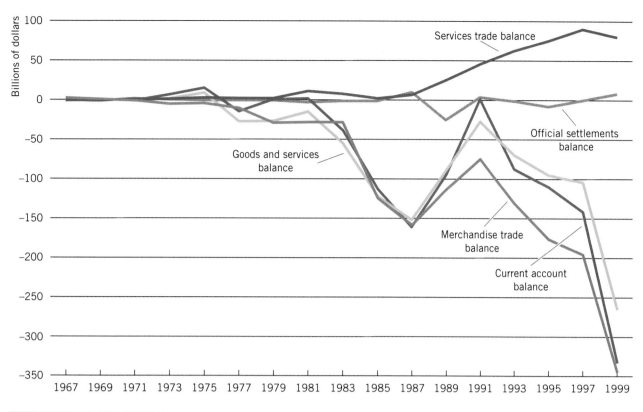

FIGURE 6.8   **The U.S. BOP According to Various Reporting Measures**

Which BOP concept to use depends on the issue confronting the international businessperson or government policy maker. The balance on merchandise trade reflects the competitiveness of a country's manufacturing sector. The balance on services reflects the service sector's global competitiveness. Although the balance on merchandise trade often receives more publicity, the balance on services is growing in importance because of the expansion of the service sector in many national economies. The balance on goods and services reflects the combined international competitiveness of a country's manufacturing and service sectors. The current account balance shows the combined performance of the manufacturing and service sectors and also reflects the generosity of the country's residents (unilateral transfers) as well as income generated by past investments. The official settlements balance reflects the net quantity demanded and supplied of the country's currency by all market participants, other than the country's central bank.[6] Figure 6.8 shows the U.S. balance of payments for the past decade according to these various measures.

CHAPTER REVIEW

Summary

In their normal commercial activities international businesses often deal with currencies other than those of their home countries. For international commerce to thrive, some system for exchanging and valuing different currencies, preferably at low cost, must exist. The international monetary system accomplishes this by establishing the rules for valuing and exchanging different currencies.

The economic growth of the nineteenth century is attributable in part to the success of the gold standard in providing a stable, reliable international monetary system based on fixed exchange rates.

However, the gold standard broke down during World War I and could not be satisfactorily revived in the years between the two world wars.

The Bretton Woods Agreement of 1944 structured the post-World War II international monetary system. In addition to creating the International Bank for Reconstruction and Development (the World Bank) and the IMF, the agreement reinstituted a fixed exchange rate system, with the U.S. dollar playing a key role in international transactions. However, as the number of dollars held by foreigners increased, the marketplace began to distrust the ability of the United States to redeem its currency at $35 per ounce of gold as required by the agreement. After fending off waves of speculation against the dollar, the United States abandoned the Bretton Woods Agreement in August 1971.

Since then, the international monetary system has relied on a combination of fixed and flexible exchange rate systems. Some countries have allowed their currencies to float; others, such as the EU members, have attempted to maintain fixed exchange rates among their currencies. The system has proven responsive to major shocks to the world economy, such as the shift of wealth from oil-consuming to oil-producing countries after the 1973-1974 oil embargo, the 1980s international debt crisis, and the 1997-1998 Asian currency crisis.

The BOP accounting system, which is used to record international transactions, is important to international businesspeople. The BOP system provides economic intelligence data about the international competitiveness of a country's industries, likely changes in its fiscal and monetary policies, and its ability to repay its international debts.

The BOP accounting system comprises four accounts. The current account reflects exports and imports of goods, exports and imports of services, investment income, and gifts. The capital account records capital transactions among countries and includes FDI and portfolio investments. Portfolio investments in turn can be divided into long-term and short-term investments. The official reserves account is a record of changes in a country's official reserves, which include central bank holdings of gold, convertible currencies, SDRs, and reserves at the IMF. The errors and omissions account captures statistical discrepancies that often result from transactions that participants want to hide from government officials.

There are numerous ways to measure a balance of payments surplus or deficit. Each presents a different perspective on a country's global economic performance. The balance on merchandise trade measures the difference between a country's exports and imports of goods. The balance on services is growing in importance because of the rapid expansion of the service sector in many economies. The balance on goods and services measures a country's trade in goods and services. The current account balance reflects both trade in goods and trade in services, as well as net investment income and gifts. The official settlements balance shows changes in a country's official reserves.

Review Questions

1. What is the function of the international monetary system?
2. Why is the gold standard a type of fixed exchange rate system?
3. What were the key accomplishments of the Bretton Woods conference?
4. Why was the IFC established by the World Bank?
5. Why are quotas important to IMF members?
6. Why did the Bretton Woods system collapse in 1971?
7. Describe the differences between a fixed exchange rate system and a flexible exchange rate system.
8. List the four major accounts of the BOP accounting system and their components.
9. What factors cause measurement errors in the BOP accounts?
10. Differentiate among the different types of balance of payments surpluses and deficits.

Questions for Discussion

1. What parallels exist between the role of the British pound in the nineteenth-century international monetary system and that of the U.S. dollar since 1945?
2. Did the key role that the dollar played in the Bretton Woods system benefit or hurt the United States?
3. Under what conditions might a country devalue its currency today?
4. Are there any circumstances under which a country might want to increase its currency's value?
5. Can international businesses operate more easily in a fixed exchange rate system or in a flexible exchange rate system?
6. What connections exist between the current account and the capital account?

BUILDING GLOBAL SKILLS

This exercise explains how U.S. governmental statisticians account for international transactions. You may want to refer to Tables 6.3 and 6.5 and to the definitions of capital inflows and capital outflows on page 175.

Example 1

Suppose Wal-Mart imports $1 million worth of VCRs from the Sony Corporation of Japan. The debit entry is a merchandise import of $1 million. The import of the Japanese goods means the United States will observe an outflow (or a use) of foreign exchange.

Here is the tough part. What is the offsetting credit entry? The answer is a capital inflow affecting the short-term portfolio account. Recall that a capital inflow occurs because of either an increase in foreign-owned U.S. assets or a decrease in U.S.-owned foreign assets. If Wal-Mart pays Sony with a $1-million check that Sony deposits in its U.S. bank, foreign ownership of assets in the United States increases, which is a short-term capital inflow. If Wal-Mart pays Sony in yen by drawing down a Wal-Mart checking account balance at a Tokyo bank, a decrease of U.S.-owned assets in foreign countries occurs, which is also a short-term capital inflow. Either way, a short-term capital inflow occurs because the VCRs are being exchanged for a change in a checking account balance.

What if Wal-Mart pays Sony with a $1-million check, but Sony wants yen? Sony will take the check to its U.S. bank and ask the bank to convert the $1-million check to yen. The U.S. bank can accommodate Sony in one of two ways:

1. Give Sony yen that the U.S. bank already owns—this represents a decrease in U.S.-owned foreign assets.

2. Pass along the check to a Japanese bank that keeps the $1 million but gives Sony the equivalent in yen—this represents an increase in U.S. assets owned by foreigners (the Japanese bank).

In either case, a capital inflow occurs. Thus Wal-Mart's purchase of the VCRs from Sony enters the U.S. BOP accounts as follows:

	DEBIT	CREDIT
Merchandise imports account	$1 million	
Short-term portfolio account		$1 million

The merchandise import account is debited to reflect a use of funds. The payment itself is credited because effectively a foreigner has purchased a U.S. asset (either an increase in foreign claims on the United States or a decrease in U.S. claims on foreigners). Note the linkage between the current account and the capital account.

Example 2

A Kosovar restaurant owner in Los Angeles who escaped her homeland during the Serbian-Kosovo civil war in 1999 smuggles $1,000 in cash back to her relatives in Serbia. The U.S. BOP accounts *should* record this transaction as follows:

	DEBIT	CREDIT
Unilateral transfer account	$1,000	
Short-term portfolio account		$1,000

The transaction involves a unilateral transfer because the $1,000 is a gift. Because the gift is being given by a U.S. resident, it is a debit. The capital account is credited because foreigners have increased their claims on the United States. (A country's currency reflects a claim on its goods, services, and assets.) Had the restaurant owners sent a $1,000 stereo system instead of cash, the credit entry would have been a merchandise export.

Note the use of the qualifier *should* in the previous paragraph. If U.S. governmental statisticians were omniscient, the transaction would be recorded as just explained. However, if the restaurant owner wished to hide her transaction from the government, it is unlikely U.S. statisticians would ever learn of it. When you consider the widespread usage of the dollar in countries suffering political turmoil, it is not surprising that the errors and omissions account is as large as it is.

Example 3

Mitsubishi buys 51 percent of Rockefeller Center for $846 million from a Rockefeller family trust. This transaction will be recorded in the U.S. BOP accounts as follows:

	DEBIT	CREDIT
Foreign direct investment account		$846 million
Short-term portfolio account	$846 million	

In this transaction two assets are being exchanged. Japan is buying a long-term asset—Rockefeller Center—for purposes of control, and the United States is buying a short-term asset called an "increase of claims on foreigners or a decrease of foreign claims on the United States." The U.S. BOP is credited with a long-term FDI capital inflow of $846 million because foreign ownership of U.S. assets (for purposes of control) has increased. However, the actual payment of the $846 million is debited as a short-term capital outflow: Either Japanese-owned checking account balances in the United States declined by $846 million or U.S.-owned checking account balances in Japan rose by $846 million.

Unlike Examples 1 and 2, this transaction does not involve a current account entry and a capital account entry. Both the debit entry and the credit entry affect the capital account. However, a balance in someone's checking account is affected by this transaction, as was the case in Example 1.

Do the following exercises on your own. How will the following transactions be recorded in the U.S. BOP accounts?

1. A Swiss entrepreneur seeking to sell souvenirs at the 2002 winter Olympics in Salt Lake City, Utah, pays Delta, a U.S. airline, $1,400 for a Zurich-Salt Lake City round-trip ticket.

2. The Swiss entrepreneur instead pays Swissair (a Swiss airline) $1,400 for a Zurich-Salt Lake City round-trip ticket.

3. Ford Motor Company (U.S.) pays $2.5 billion for the Jaguar Motor Co. (U.K.).

4. The U.S. government gives Rwanda $500 million worth of food to feed starving refugees.

WORKING WITH THE WEB: BUILDING GLOBAL INTERNET SKILLS

Doing Business with the World Bank

The Web site of the World Bank provides a variety of information about the bank's mission, its policies, and how and where it is spending its moneys. Because the bank lends billions of dollars a year, its Web site is a treasure trove of marketing leads for a wide variety of companies that sell goods and services needed by the bank's clients.

Assignment: You are currently employed by WaterPure, a company that manufactures water treatment machinery and hydroelectric generating technology. Most of its sales are to large, publicly owned water treatment facilities and public power authorities. WaterPure is currently examining whether it should place a sales office in Africa to take advantage of the political and economic reforms adopted by many African countries. Because the World Bank finances many infrastructure projects in Africa, you are assigned the task of determining whether the bank is likely to fund any water treatment or hydroelectric projects there in the near future. Such information is contained in the World Bank's annual report, which is accessible from its Web site. If you recommend that WaterPure should place an office in Africa, in what city should it be placed? (The book's Web site provides a link to the World Bank's Web site.)

WE INVITE YOU TO VISIT THIS BOOK'S COMPANION WEB SITE AT www.prenhall.com/griffin

IN THE NEWS

From the homepage of the *Financial Times* (*www.ft.com*) search for current articles on "balance of payments." Read four or five of these articles, and then write a brief, one-paragraph summary of each. What significance do the events discussed in these articles have for international businesspeople? Do the articles suggest that certain firms, industries, or countries will benefit as a result of what is happening? Do the articles raise fears that a particular country faces tough economic times?

CLOSING CASE

Recent U.S. BOP Performance: Is the Sky Falling?

During much of the past decade the U.S. BOP performance could be characterized as follows:

- The U.S. current account recorded large annual deficits.
- The U.S. capital account recorded large annual surpluses of roughly the same magnitude as the current account deficits.
- Changes in the official reserves account were small relative to the magnitude of the current account deficits.

Two scenarios can be developed from the facts just cited:

1. The sky is falling. U.S. industries are uncompetitive in international markets (as indicated by the first fact), and foreigners are taking over the country by buying up valuable U.S. assets and transforming the country into the largest debtor in international history (as indicated by the second fact).

2. Everything is wonderful. Foreigners are so enthralled with the future prospects of the U.S. market, which is a showcase of economic democracy, that they are eagerly investing in the U.S. economy (the second fact). The only way they can do so, however, is by running a current account surplus with the United States (the first fact).

Needless to say, these two scenarios conflict, *even though both are consistent with the data*. They reflect a policy war that is occurring between protectionists and free traders, between Rust Belt firms and Sunbelt firms, between liberals and conservatives, and between export-oriented firms and firms threatened by foreign imports.

People who believe the sky is falling argue that the United States must reduce its balance of trade deficit. They argue that U.S. firms are increasingly uncompetitive in global markets and must be strengthened via aggressive government policies, such as those calling for worker-training programs, increased investment in infrastructure, and tax credits for R&D and investment expenditures. These people assert that U.S. firms are victimized by the unfair trade practices of foreign firms and governments. They propose stiffer tariffs and quotas on imported goods and believe that the federal government should do more to promote U.S. exports and restrict foreign ownership of U.S. assets.

People who believe everything is wonderful say the best policy is to continue to make the United States an attractive economy in which to invest. By keeping tax rates low and governmental regulation modest, the United States will attract foreign capital. U.S. industries, consumers, and workers will then benefit from increased capital investment and the enhancements in productivity that will ensue from this investment. U.S. consumers will benefit from the availability of low-priced, high-quality imported goods and services. Moreover, U.S. firms will become "leaner and meaner" as they respond to foreign competitors.

A variant of this "everything is wonderful" argument has been offered by Nobel laureate Milton Friedman, the provocative free-market advocate from the University of Chicago. Friedman argues that Japanese workers have been busily producing VCRs, Toyota Camrys, and Sony Walkmans in return for dollar bills from U.S. consumers. If the Japanese are happy voluntarily exchanging their goods for pieces of paper (that is, dollar bills), and U.S. citizens are happy voluntarily exchanging pieces of paper for goods, why should anyone worry?

As you ponder these divergent perspectives, recognize that they have developed because of two very different views of what represents a BOP deficit. The "sky is falling" crowd is focusing on the balance on merchandise trade and assessing whether U.S. firms are able to sell as many goods to foreigners as foreigners buy from U.S. firms. The "everything is wonderful" folks are focusing on voluntary transactions in the marketplace. In their view, if U.S. citizens find that being net buyers of foreign goods is in their self-interest and foreigners find that being net buyers of U.S. assets is in their self-interest, then what is the problem?

Because BOP statistics affect the ongoing domestic political battle over international trade policy, they are important to virtually every U.S. firm. Export-oriented firms and workers benefit from the free-trade policies promoted by the "everything is wonderful" crowd, as do communities that benefit from jobs created by inward FDI. Firms and workers threatened by imported goods or by the output of new domestic factories built by foreign competitors are more likely to support the "sky is falling" view.

Case Questions

1. What is more important to an economy—exports or foreign capital inflows?
2. What is the connection between the U.S. current account deficit and capital account surplus?
3. Which of the following groups are likely to endorse the "sky is falling" view of the U.S. BOP?
   • Import-threatened firms such as textile producers
   • Textile workers
   • A cash-starved California biotechnology company
   • Merrill Lynch
   • Boeing Aircraft, one of the country's largest exporters
   • Consumers

CHAPTER

Dollar Makes Canada a Land of the Spree

Love brought them here, but the cheap Canadian dollar kept them from leaving.

Joseph Carte and Annette Lovejoy drove for two days from their home in Cottageville, West Virginia, to Niagara Falls, New York, to get married, but the prices they found on a brief tour on the Canadian side of the Niagara River persuaded them to tie the knot here. The clincher was the exchange rate they received for their American dollars at a local bank. "We gave them $300," the new bride exulted, "and they gave us $432 back."

> "**Love** brought them here, but the **cheap** Canadian dollar kept them from leaving."

The Canadian dollar, nicknamed the loonie (for the bird on the back of the dollar coin), has been on a two-year descent that some people say is a little bit crazy.

The decline has prompted a bargain-hunting boom by Americans. They are saving money by boarding flights to the Caribbean from Canada, placing mail orders in Canada, buying vacation homes in Canada, and even sending their children to college in Canada.

Of course, not all things Canadian are bargains. Certain products—notably gasoline and alcohol—remain far cheaper in the United States because of higher Canadian taxes. And other goods are routinely priced to reflect currency values; a book, for example, might be stamped "US$27.50/$45.00 CAN."

7

Foreign Exchange and International Financial Markets

After studying this chapter, you should be able to:

> Describe how demand and supply determine the price of foreign exchange.

> Discuss the role of international banks in the foreign-exchange market.

> Assess the different ways firms can use the spot and forward markets to settle international transactions.

> Summarize the role of arbitrage in the foreign-exchange market.

> Discuss the important aspects of the international capital market.

But whenever a currency is strong, there are good prices to be had in markets away from home, and the U.S. dollar is king around the world these days. The hegemony is making it cheaper for Americans to honeymoon in Paris or to vacation in Brazil. But Canada is closer to home, so it gets more than its share of American visitors out to get the biggest bang for their bucks.

Americans made a record 43.9 million visits to Canada in 1998, up 8.4 percent from the previous record of 40.5 million in 1997, when the Canadian dollar began its dive, according to the Canadian government. The American visitors threw their money around, too, spending a record $8.6 billion in 1998, up 24 percent from $6.9 billion in 1997, in United States dollars. And travel industry executives say the numbers have almost certainly risen during 1999.

American companies are also getting in on the action, spending $12.7 billion (United States) on acquisitions in Canada during 1998, up 70 percent from $7.5 billion in 1997 and nearly three times the $4.4 billion in 1994, according to KPMG Corporate Finance of Toronto.

"In a way, we're kind of another Mexico," said Ross H. Chafe, the president of Flags Unlimited in Barrie, Ontario. Last year, Aberdeen Fabrics of Aberdeen, North Carolina, bought a controlling stake in the company, which makes a half-million Canadian flags a year. "It was relatively cheap for them to invest in Canada," Mr. Chafe said, "and the dollar allows us to compete very well in the American market."

But this is also a game for weekend warriors, not just big players. During 1998 about 20,000 Americans who live near the Canadian border drove to Canadian airports to fly to places like Jamaica, Cancun, and Las Vegas on package tours sold by **Signature Vacations** of Toronto, according to Chris C. Robinson, the company's national marketing director. That's twice as many as in 1996.

Americans don't even have to leave home to take advantage of the favorable exchange rate. Motorcycle riders, for example, can log onto the Internet to order oil filters, luggage, and other accessories sent by mail from Wolf BMW in Ailsa Craig, Ontario, halfway between Detroit and Toronto.

"The mail-order business is something we got going about a year and a half ago in response to the Canadian dollar being so weak" said Christine C. McQueen, a co-owner of Wolf BMW. "We sell quite a bit of stuff across the border."

American students are flocking to college in Canada, also because the price is right. Michael Reed, 18, of New Haven, New York, plans to attend the University of Toronto, a prestigious Canadian school where a partial scholarship will winnow down the costs to $8,000 a year.

Americans are also buying vacation retreats in Canada. Keith D. Hodson of Stevensville, Montana, a manager for **Para-Chem**, an adhesives maker, just bought a third home, a two-bedroom condominium 16 floors above downtown Vancouver in a building called the Venice. The price was 280,000 loonies— only $188,000 in American money. The exchange rate "just makes it a much better buy." Mr. Hodson said.

As American tourists throw money around across the border, the ever-polite Canadians are holding their noses as they pocket the cash.

Robin N. Rootes, 23, a waitress in Vancouver, says the big tips she receives from American customers more than make up for their sometimes arrogant attitudes. "They come over and spend and say they can spend as much as they want," Rootes said. "Yes, they are demanding, and yes, they are high-maintenance." But, compared with the natives, they tend to leave more loonies and toonies (the nickname for Canada's $2 coins) on the table.

"Quite honestly, we're going to make money off of them," she said.

The weak dollar is good news for Canadian exporters, too, because their goods cost less in American dollars. As a result, Canada's trade surplus with the United States widened by 7.7 percent in 1998, to $16.65 billion.

The losers, of course, are Canadian consumers, who have to pay more for American imports and can only dream about the bargain-hunting trips they once made south of the border. Maxinne Cheng, who manages a store in Vancouver's tourist district, said she missed her trips to Seattle, three hours away by car, where she used to shop.

"There has been an exact switch," Cheng said. "Five years ago, we would go down to Seattle to get good deals. Now the Americans come here for shopping."

The latest figures from the Canadian government shows that day trips by Canadians to the United States dropped 11 percent during 1998, to 31.9 million, the lowest level in more than a decade and about half the 60 million in 1991.

As the effects of the powerful American dollar reverberate across Canada, Canadian nationalists are fuming about economic imperialism. "There has been a fire sale of Canadian assets and an influx of foreign capital," said Peter S. Bleyer, executive director of the Council of Canadians, a nonprofit advocacy group in Ottawa. "It is about taking existing economic assets out of the hands of Canadians."

He fears that in times of trouble, American companies will let their hearts overrule their wallets and close factories in Canada before laying off employees at home.[1]

One factor that obviously distinguishes international business from domestic business is the use of more than one currency in commercial transactions. If Marks and Spencer, one of the United Kingdom's leading department stores, purchases kitchen appliances from a British supplier, that is a domestic transaction that will be completed entirely in pounds. However, if Marks and Spencer chooses to purchase the appliances from Iowa-based Maytag Corporation, this international transaction will require some mechanism for exchanging pounds (Mark and Spencer's home currency), and U.S. dollars (Maytag's home currency). The foreign-exchange market exists to facilitate this conversion of currencies, thereby allowing firms to conduct trade more efficiently across national boundaries. The foreign-exchange market also facilitates international investment and capital flows. Firms can shop for low-cost financing in capital markets around the world and then use the foreign-exchange market to convert the foreign funds they obtain into whatever currency they require.

THE ECONOMICS OF FOREIGN EXCHANGE ❮

Foreign exchange is a commodity that consists of currencies issued by countries other than one's own. Like the prices of other commodities, the price of foreign exchange—given a flexible exchange rate system—is set by demand and supply in the marketplace. And, as the opening case indicates, changes in exchange rates affect where people vacation, where firms invest, and even where students go to college.

Let us look more closely at what this means by using the market between U.S. dollars and Japanese yen as an example. Figure 7.1 presents the demand curve for Japanese yen. Economists call this demand curve a *derived demand* curve because the demand for yen is derived from foreigners' desire to acquire Japanese goods, services, and assets. To buy Japanese goods, foreigners first need to buy Japanese yen. Like other demand curves, it is downward sloping, so as the price of yen falls, the quantity of yen demanded increases. This is shown as a movement from point *A* to point *B* on the demand curve.

Figure 7.2 presents the supply curve for yen. Underlying the supply curve for yen is the desire by the Japanese to acquire foreign goods, services, and assets. To buy foreign products, Japanese need to obtain foreign currencies, which they do by selling yen and using the proceeds to buy the foreign currencies. Selling yen has the effect of supplying yen to the foreign-exchange market. As with other goods, as the price of yen rises, the quantity supplied also rises; you can see this when you

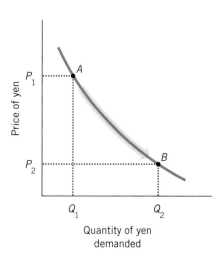

FOREIGNERS' DEMAND FOR YEN

FIGURE 7.1

The Demand for Japanese Yen Is Derived from Foreigners' Demand for Japanese Products

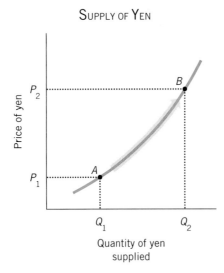

FIGURE 7.2

The Supply of Yen Is Derived from Japanese Demand for Foreign Products

SUPPLY OF YEN

move from point *A* to point *B* along the supply curve in Figure 7.2. The supply curve for yen thus behaves like most other supply curves: People offer more yen for sale as the price of yen rises.[2]

Figure 7.3 depicts the determination of equilibrium price of yen. Points along the vertical axis show the price of yen in dollars—how many dollars one must pay for each yen purchased. Points along the horizontal axis show the quantity of yen. As in other markets, the intersection of the supply curve (S) and the demand curve (D) yields the market-clearing, equilibrium price ($.009/yen in this case) and the equilibrium quantity demanded and supplied (200 million yen). Recall from Chapter 6 that this equilibrium price is called the *exchange rate*, the price of one country's currency in terms of another country's currency.

Although Figure 7.3 illustrates the dollar-yen foreign-exchange market, a similar figure could be drawn for every possible pair of currencies in the world, each of which would constitute a separate market, with the equilibrium prices of the currencies determined by the supply of and demand for them. Foreign-exchange rates are published daily in most major newspapers worldwide. For example, Figure 7.4 presents rates for February 21, 2001, published in the *Wall Street Journal*. These rates are quoted in two ways. A **direct exchange rate** (or **direct quote**) is the price of the foreign currency in terms of the home currency. For example, from the perspective of a U.S. resident, the direct exchange rate between the U.S. dollar and the

FIGURE 7.3

The Market for Yen

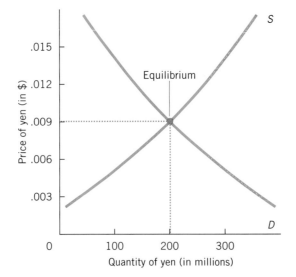

CURRENCY TRADING

EXCHANGE RATES

Wednesday, February 21, 2001

The New York foreign exchange mid-range rates below apply to trading among banks in amounts of $1 million and more, as quoted at 4 p.m. Eastern time by Reuters and other sources. Retail transactions provide fewer units of foreign currency per dollar. Rates for the 12 Euro currency countries are derived from the latest dollar-euro rate using the exchange ratios set 1/1/99.

COUNTRY	U.S. $ Equiv. Wed	Tue	Currency per U.S. $ Wed	Tue
Argentina (Peso)	1.0001	1.0001	.9999	.9999
Australia (Dollar)........	.5244	.5235	1.9071	1.9104
Austria (Schilling).......	.06608	.06630	15.134	15.084
Bahrain (Dinar).........	2.6525	2.6525	.3770	.3770
Belgium (Franc)	.0225	.0226	44.3661	44.2202
Brazil (Real)	.4903	.4983	2.0395	2.0070
Britain (Pound)	1.4429	1.4472	.6930	.6910
1-month forward	1.4428	1.4470	.6931	.6911
3-months forward	1.4419	1.4462	.6935	.6915
6-months forward	1.4404	1.4448	.6943	.6921
Canada (Dollar)	.6509	.6493	1.5363	1.5401
1-month forward	.6510	.6494	1.5360	1.5398
3-months forward	.6512	.6496	1.5357	1.5394
6-months forward	.6514	.6499	1.5352	1.5388
Chile (Peso)	.001764	.001778	566.75	562.38
China (Renminbi)	.1208	.1208	8.2772	8.2767
Colombia (Peso)	.0004441	.0004436	2251.75	2254.25
Czech. Rep. (Koruna) ...	....	....	....	....
Commercial rate	.02618	.02637	38.198	37.928
Denmark (Krone).......	.1219	.1221	8.2058	8.1868
Ecuador (US Dollar)-e...	1.0000	1.0000	1.0000	1.0000
Finland (Markka)	.1529	.1534	6.5392	6.5177
France (Franc)	.1386	.1391	7.2143	7.1905
1-month forward	.1387	.1391	7.2106	7.1868
3-months forward	.1388	.1393	7.2056	7.1810
6-months forward	.1389	.1394	7.1987	7.1729
Germany (Mark)........	.4649	.4664	2.1510	2.1440
1-month forward	.4651	.4667	2.1499	2.1428
3-months forward	.4654	.4670	2.1485	2.1411
6-months forward	.4659	.4676	2.1464	2.1387
Greece (Drachma)......	.002668	.002677	374.76	373.57
Hong Kong (Dollar)	.1282	.1282	7.8000	7.7998
Hungary (Forint)........	.003417	.003435	292.66	291.14
India (Rupee)..........	.02146	.02147	46.595	46.580
Indonesia (Rupiah)	.0001039	.0001035	9620.50	9660.00
Ireland (Punt)	1.1545	1.1583	.8662	.8633
Israel (Shekel)	.2425	.2426	4.1230	4.1220
Italy (Lira)	.0004696	.0004711	2129.52	2122.52
Japan (Yen)............	.008579	.008644	116.57	115.69
1-month forward	.008613	.008679	116.10	115.23
3-months forward	.008684	.008750	115.16	114.29
6-months forward	.008788	.008855	113.79	112.93
Jordan (Dinar)	1.4065	1.4065	.7110	.7110
Kuwait (Dinar)	3.2605	3.2595	.3067	.3068
Lebanon (Pound)	.0006606	.0006604	1514.00	1514.25
Malaysia (Ringgit)-b	.2632	.2632	3.8000	3.8000
Malta (Lira)..........	2.2462	2.2507	.4452	.4443
Mexico (Peso)	....	....	....	....
Floating rate	.1027	.1032	9.7350	9.6930
Netherlands (Guilder) ...	.4126	.4140	2.4237	2.4157
New Zealand (Dollar)...	.4291	.4293	2.3305	2.3294
Norway (Krone)........	.1105	.1111	9.0477	9.0031
Pakistan (Rupee)	.01669	.01692	59.900	59.100
Peru (new Sol).........	.2835	.2836	3.5278	3.5255
Philippines (Peso)	.02077	.02096	48.150	47.700
Poland (Zloty)-d	.2406	.2441	4.1560	4.0975
Portugal (Escudo)	.004535	.004550	220.49	219.77
Russia (Ruble)-a	.03486	.03484	28.688	28.702
Saudi Arabia (Riyal)	.2666	.2666	3.7507	3.7507
Singapore (Dollar).....	.5732	.5743	1.7445	1.7413
Slovak Rep. (Koruna)...	.02079	.02088	48.090	47.882
South Africa (Rand)	.1280	.1292	7.8125	7.7425
South Korea (Won)	.0008071	.0008110	1239.00	1233.00
Spain (Peseta).........	.005465	.005483	182.99	182.39
Sweden (Krona)	.1009	.1015	9.9070	9.8542
Switzerland (Franc)	.5929	.5942	1.6885	1.6829
1-month forward	.5939	.5951	1.6839	1.6803
3-months forward	.5956	.5969	1.6791	1.6753
6-months forward	.5979	.5994	1.6724	1.6683
Taiwan (Dollar)	.03101	.03101	32.250	32.250
Thailand (Baht)	.02330	.02339	42.925	42.755
Turkey (Lira)	.00000145	.00000145	687550.00	687550.00
United Arab (Dirham)...	.2723	.2723	3.6730	3.6730
Uruguay (New Peso) ...	....	....	....	....
Financial	.07921	.07936	12.625	12.601
Venezuela (Bolivar)	.001420	.001421	704.26	703.76
SDR	1.2890	1.2868	.7758	.7771
ECU	.9093	.9123	1.0997	1.0961

Special Drawing Rights (SDR) are based on exchange rates for the U.S., German, British, French, and Japanese currencies. Source: International Monetary Fund.

a-Russian Central Bank rate. b-Government rate. d-Floating rate: trading band suspended on 4/11/00. e-Adopted U.S. dollar as of 9/11/00. Foreign Exchange rates are available from Readers' Reference Service (413) 592-3600.

FIGURE 7.4

Direct and Indirect Exchange Rates

Source: *Wall Street Journal*, February 22, 2001, p. C18. Reprinted by permission of the *Wall Street Journal*, © 2001 Dow Jones & Company, Inc. All Rights Reserved Worldwide.

yen (¥) on Wednesday, February 21, was $.008579/¥1. An **indirect exchange rate** (or **indirect quote**) is the price of the home currency in terms of the foreign currency. From the U.S. resident's perspective, the indirect exchange rate on Wednesday, February 21, was ¥116.57/$1. Mathematically, the direct exchange rate and the indirect exchange rate are reciprocals of one another. By tradition—and sometimes for convenience—certain exchange rates are typically quoted on a direct basis and others on an indirect basis. For example, common U.S. practice is to quote British pounds on a direct basis but Japanese yen, German marks, and French francs on an indirect basis.

If you get confused about which is the direct rate and which is the indirect rate, just remember that you normally buy things using the direct rate. If you go to the store to buy bread, it is typically priced using the direct rate: A loaf of bread costs $1.29. The indirect rate would be .775 loaves of bread per dollar. "Venturing Abroad" provides additional hints for understanding the foreign exchange market.

THE STRUCTURE OF THE FOREIGN-EXCHANGE MARKET ‹

The foreign-exchange market comprises buyers and sellers of currencies issued by the world's countries. Anyone who owns money denominated in one currency and wants to convert that money to a second currency participates in the foreign-exchange market. Pakistani tourists exchanging rupees for British pounds at London's Heathrow Airport utilize the foreign-exchange market, as does Toyota

Not everyone reading this book is a finance major. Some readers may have difficulty with the concept of using money to buy money and what is meant by a currency's value rising or falling. If you are having trouble with this, here is a simple trick. In Figure 7.3 replace the currency that is being bought and sold with the phrase "loaf of bread" (or the name of any other tangible good). If you do this, then the vertical axis is the price in dollars of one unit of bread and the horizontal axis is the quantity of bread sold—a standard supply and demand graph that you encountered in your basic economics course. Nothing has changed in the supply and demand graph except the label. Think about this until you feel comfortable with the notion that yen are merely a good like bread or widgets.

As you read the rest of the book, if you get confused about what is up and what is down when we say a currency is rising or falling in value, you can use the same trick. For example, suppose on Monday the British pound is worth $1.73 and on Tuesday it is worth $1.74. From Monday to Tuesday the pound rose in value, while the dollar fell in value. If that is obvious to you, fine. If it is not, substitute loaf of bread for pound. A statement about this example would then read, "On Monday a loaf of bread is worth $1.73, and on Tuesday a loaf of bread is worth $1.74." The conclusion is that a loaf of bread has gone up in value because more dollars are needed to buy it on Tuesday. Conversely, you can say the dollar has gone down in value because each dollar on Tuesday buys less bread.

when it exports automobiles to Canada from its factories in Japan, and the British government when it arranges a multimillion-pound loan to rebuild the monsoon-ravaged economy of Bangladesh. So too do all those Americans shopping, honeymooning, investing, and studying in Canada who were portrayed in the opening case. The worldwide volume of foreign-exchange trading is estimated at $1.5 trillion *per day*. Foreign exchange is being traded somewhere in the world every minute of the day (see Map 7.1). The largest foreign-exchange market is in London, followed by New York, Tokyo, and Singapore. These four locations account for 65 percent of global foreign-exchange trading. As Figure 7.5 indicates, approximately 87 percent of the transactions involve the U.S. dollar, a dominance stemming from the dollar's role in the Bretton Woods system. Because the dollar is used to facilitate most currency exchange, it is known as the primary **transaction currency** for the foreign-exchange market.

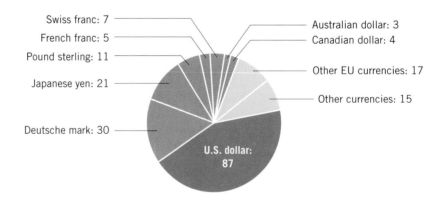

FIGURE 7.5   **Currencies Involved in Foreign-Exchange Market Transactions**

Percentage share of foreign-exchange transactions involving selected currencies. Because there are two currencies involved in each transaction, the percentages add up to 200 percent.

Source: Bank for International Settlements, *Central Bank Survey of Foreign Exchange and Derivatives Market Activity* (Basle, May 1999), p. 9.

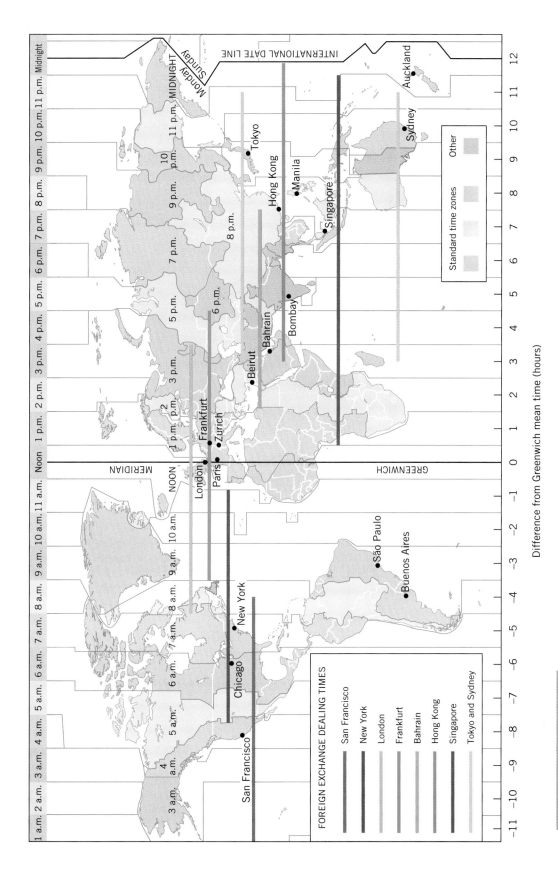

MAP 7.1   **A Day of Foreign-Exchange Trading**

Traditionally, the trading day begins in Auckland, New Zealand, which lies just west of the international date line. As the earth rotates, foreign-exchange markets open in other cities, including Sydney, Tokyo, Hong Kong, Singapore, Bahrain, Frankfurt, Zurich, Paris, London, New York, Chicago, and San Francisco.

Difference from Greenwich mean time (hours)

FOREIGN EXCHANGE DEALING TIMES

San Francisco
New York
London
Frankfurt
Bahrain
Hong Kong
Singapore
Tokyo and Sydney

Standard time zones

Other

› This Tokyo foreign-exchange dealer is an important link in the $1.5 trillion per day global foreign-exchange market. Tokyo is the third largest center for foreign-exchange trading, trailing only London and New York.

The Role of Banks

The foreign-exchange departments of large international banks such as Chase Manhattan, Barclays, and Deutsche Bank in major financial centers such as New York, London, and Frankfurt play a dominant role in the foreign-exchange market. These banks stand ready to buy or sell the major traded currencies. They profit from the foreign-exchange market in several ways. Much of their profits come from the spread between the bid and ask prices for foreign exchange. For example, if Chase Manhattan buys 10 million Swiss francs from one customer at a price of SwFr 1.649/$1 and sells those Swiss francs to a second customer at SwFr 1.648/$1, Chase makes $3,679.38. (Get out your calculator and do the arithmetic! Chase buys the Swiss francs for 10,000,000 ÷ 1.649, or $6,064,281.38, and sells them for 10,000,000 ÷ 1.648, or $6,067,961.17, thereby earning a profit of $3679.78.) Sometimes international banks act as speculators, betting that they can guess which direction exchange rates are headed. Such speculation can be enormously profitable, although it is always risky. And, as discussed later in this chapter, banks also may act as arbitrageurs in the foreign-exchange market.

International banks are key players in the wholesale market for foreign exchange, dealing for their own accounts or on behalf of large commercial customers. Interbank transactions, typically involving at least $1 million (or the foreign-currency equivalent), account for the vast majority of foreign-exchange transactions. Banks may rely on the assistance of independent foreign-exchange brokers, who provide current information about the prices of different foreign currencies and who facilitate transactions by linking buyers and sellers of foreign exchange. Using computers, telephones, e-mail, and fax machines, banks and brokers in one market are in constant contact with their counterparts in other markets to seek the best currency prices. Online currency trading is a growing component of this market, as "Wiring the World" indicates.

International banks also play a key role in the retail market for foreign exchange, dealing with individual customers who want to buy or sell foreign currencies in large or small amounts. Typically, the price paid by retail customers for foreign exchange is the prevailing wholesale exchange rate plus a premium. The size of the premium is in turn a function of the size of the transaction and the importance of the customer to the bank. For example, a Danish music store chain that needs $100,000 to pay for 20,000 compact discs of Celine Dion's or U2's latest release will pay a higher premium for its foreign currency than will General Motors when it needs £20 million to repay British investors. And, of course, foreign tourists cashing in a traveler's check for local currency at a bank or exchange office pay an even higher premium.

The clients of the foreign-exchange departments of banks fall into several categories:

- *Commercial customers* engage in foreign-exchange transactions as part of their normal commercial activities, such as exporting or importing goods and services, paying or receiving dividends and interest from foreign sources, and purchasing or selling foreign assets and investments. Some commercial customers may also use the market to hedge, or reduce, their risks due to potential unfavorable changes in foreign-exchange rates for monies to be paid or received in the future.

THE BIGGEST ONLINE MARKET

The foreign-exchange market is the world's biggest single market—some $1.5 trillion a day in volume. It is no surprise that this market is moving online, for electronic trading should lower the cost of completing foreign-exchange (FX) transactions. Within a few years online sales of foreign exchange may dwarf the sales of any other product sold on the Internet. Most of the major international banks have begun to provide Internet-based selling of foreign exchange to their corporate and institutional clients. For example, Chase Manhattan, Deutsche Bank, Citigroup, and UBS offer such services to their retail customers. Deutsche Bank believes that 90 percent of its retail (i.e., noninterbank) FX transactions will move to the Internet by 2003. Furthermore, banks are aggressively seeking out online niche markets. Barclays Bank and discount stockbroker Charles Schwab Corp. have teamed up to create a customized FX service that allows smaller investors to obtain the foreign exchange they need to purchase foreign stocks and bonds.

Although this retail market has attracted much publicity, the big opportunities lie in the enormous interbank market, which establishes the wholesale prices for FX. Several banks have tried to establish their own individual online trading platforms. However, these go-it-alone approaches are likely to lose out to multibank services like FXall.com, a joint venture founded and controlled by seven of the largest players in the foreign-exchange market—Bank of America, Goldman Sachs, Credit Suisse First Boston, J. P. Morgan, Morgan Stanley Dean Witter, UBS Warburg, and HSBC. FXall.com's chairman, Paul Kimball, believes that the multibank approach will prove victorious, arguing that most currency traders will prefer to go to one Web site rather than surf numerous single-vendor sites. However, even FXall.com's future is not secure, considering the fact that Citigroup, Chase Manhattan, and Deutsche Bank have announced plans for their own multivendor online currency exchange, tentatively called Atriax.

Sources: "Foreign Exchange Banks Charge into Online Battle," *Financial Times*, August 15, 2000, p. 19; "Banks Move Towards Online Currency Trading," *Financial Times*, June 7, 2000, p. 20; "Deutsche Bank, Chase Manhattan Join Move Toward Online Currency Dealing," *Wall Street Journal*, April 3, 2000, p. A43D.

- *Speculators* deliberately assume exchange rate risks by acquiring positions in a currency, hoping that they can correctly predict changes in the currency's market value. Foreign-exchange speculation can be very lucrative if one guesses correctly, but it is also extremely risky.

- *Arbitrageurs* attempt to exploit small differences in the price of a currency between markets. They seek to obtain riskless profits by simultaneously buying the currency in the lower-priced market and selling it in the higher-priced market.

Countries' central banks and treasury departments are also major players in the foreign-exchange market. As discussed in Chapter 6, under the gold standard and the Bretton Woods system, a country's central bank was required to intervene in the foreign-exchange market to ensure that the market value of the country's currency approximated the currency's par value. Countries that have chosen to peg their currencies to that of another country must do the same. And, of course, central banks of countries that allow their currencies to float are free to intervene in the foreign-exchange market to influence the market values of their currencies if they so desire.

Active markets exist for relatively few pairs of currency other than those involving the U.S. dollar, the euro and associated currencies, the British pound, and the Japanese yen. Suppose a Swedish knitting mill needs New Zealand dollars to pay for 100,000 pounds of merino wool. The foreign-exchange market between the Swedish krona and the New Zealand dollar is very small—in fact, no active market exists for the direct exchange of these two currencies. Usually, the U.S. dollar would be used as an intermediary currency to facilitate this transaction. The knitting mill's Swedish banker would obtain the necessary New Zealand dollars by first selling Swedish krona to obtain U.S. dollars and then selling the U.S. dollars to obtain New Zealand dollars. Such transactions are routine for international banks.

Domestic laws may constrain the ability to trade a currency in the foreign-exchange market. Currencies that are freely tradable are called **convertible currencies**. Also called **hard currencies**, these include the various European Union (EU) currencies, the Canadian dollar, the Swiss franc, the Japanese yen, and the U.S. dollar. Currencies that are not freely tradable because of domestic laws or the unwillingness of foreigners to hold them are called **inconvertible currencies**, or **soft currencies**. The currencies of many developing countries fall in the soft category.

Spot and Forward Markets

Many international business transactions involve payments to be made in the future. Such transactions include lending activities and purchases on credit. Because changes in currency values are common, such international transactions would appear to be risky in the post-Bretton Woods era. How can a firm know for sure the future value of a foreign currency? Fortunately, in addition to its geographical dimension, the foreign-exchange market also has a time dimension. Currencies can be bought and sold for immediate delivery or for delivery at some point in the future. The **spot market** consists of foreign-exchange transactions that are to be consummated immediately. ("Immediately" is normally defined as two days after the trade date because of the time historically needed for payment to clear the international banking system.) Spot transactions account for 40 percent of all foreign-exchange transactions.

The **forward market** consists of foreign-exchange transactions that are to occur sometime in the future. Prices are often published for foreign exchange that will be delivered 30 days, 90 days, and 180 days in the future. For example, the following *Wall Street Journal* excerpt indicates that on Wednesday, February 21, 2001, the spot price of the British pound was $1.4429, while the forward price for pounds for delivery in 30 days was $1.4428 and for delivery in 180 days was $1.4404.

	U.S. $ EQUIV.		CURRENCY PER U.S. $	
	Wed.	Tues.	Wed.	Tues.
Britain (Pound)	1.4429	1.4472	.6930	.6910
30-Day Forward	1.4428	1.4470	.6931	.6911
90-Day Forward	1.4419	1.4462	.6935	.6915
180-Day Forward	1.4404	1.4448	.6943	.6921

Many users of the forward market engage in swap transactions. A **swap transaction** is a transaction in which the same currency is bought and sold simultaneously, but delivery is made at two different points in time. For example, in a typical "spot against forward" swap, a U.S. manufacturer borrowing £10 million from a British bank for 30 days will sell the £10 million in the spot market to obtain U.S. dollars and simultaneously buy £10 million (plus the number of pounds it owes in interest payments) in the 30-day forward market to repay its pound-denominated loan.

Normally an international business that wants to buy or sell foreign exchange on a spot or forward basis will contract with an international bank to do so. The bank will charge the firm the prevailing wholesale rate for the currency, plus a small premium for its services. Because of the bank's extensive involvement in the foreign-exchange market, it is typically willing and able to customize the spot, forward, or swap contract to meet the customer's specific needs. For example, if DaimlerChrysler expects to receive 10.7 million francs from Swiss customers in 42 days, its bank will usually agree to enter into a forward contract to buy those Swiss francs from DaimlerChrysler with delivery in 42 days.

The foreign-exchange market has developed two other mechanisms to allow firms to obtain foreign exchange in the future. Neither, however, provides the flexibility in amount and in timing that international banks offer. The first mechanism is the **currency future**. Publicly traded on many exchanges worldwide, a currency future is a contract that resembles a forward contract. However, unlike the forward contract, the currency future is for a standard amount (for example, ¥12.5 million or SwFr 125,000) on a standard delivery date (for example, the third Wednesday of the contract's maturity month). As with a forward contract, a firm signing a currency-future contract must complete the transaction by buying or selling the specified amount of foreign currency at the specified price and time. This obligation is usually not troublesome, however; a firm wanting to be released from a currency-future obligation can simply make an offsetting transaction. In practice, 98 percent of currency futures are settled in this manner. Currency futures represent only 1 percent of the foreign-exchange market.

The second mechanism, the **currency option**, allows, but does not require, a firm to buy or sell a specified amount of a foreign currency at a specified price at any time up to a specified date. A **call option** grants the right to *buy* the foreign currency in question; a **put option** grants the right to *sell* the foreign currency. Currency options are publicly traded on organized exchanges worldwide. For example, put and call options are available for Canadian dollars on the Chicago Mercantile Exchange (in contract sizes of Can$100,000) and on the Philadelphia Exchange (in contract sizes of Can$50,000). Figure 7.6 lists some of the options available on the Chicago Mercantile Exchange on February 21, 2001. Because of the inflexibility of publicly traded options, international bankers often are willing to write currency options customized as to amount and time for their commercial clients. Currency options account for 5 percent of foreign-exchange market activity.

FIGURE 7.6

Foreign-Exchange Options on the Chicago Mercantile Exchange

Source: *Wall Street Journal*, February 22, 2001, p. C14. Reprinted by permission of the *Wall Street Journal*, © 2001 Dow Jones & Company, Inc. All Rights Reserved Worldwide.

JAPANESE YEN
12,500,000 yen; cents per 100 yen

Strike Price	Calls-Settle Mar	Calls-Settle Apr	Calls-Settle May	Puts-Settle Mar	Puts-Settle Apr	Puts-Settle May
8500	1.47	....	....	0.41	0.60	....
8550	1.13	....	....	0.57	0.73	....
8600	0.84	....	....	0.78	0.89	....
8650	0.60	....	....	1.04	....	....
8700	0.43	1.39	....	1.37	....	....
8750	0.30	....	....	1.74	....	....

Est vol 3,423 Tue 640 calls 433 puts
Op int Tue 43,901 calls 40,244 puts

CANADIAN DOLLAR
100,000 Can.$, cents per Can.$;

Strike Price	Calls-Settle Mar	Calls-Settle Apr	Calls-Settle May	Puts-Settle Mar	Puts-Settle Apr	Puts-Settle May
6400	1.16	....	....	0.08	....	....
6450	0.73	....	....	0.15	....	....
6500	0.39	....	....	0.31	....	....
6550	0.19	....	....	0.61	0.78	....
6600	0.10	....	....	1.02	....	....
6650	0.06	....	....	1.48	....	....

Est vol 510 Tue 119 calls 134 puts
Op int Tue 16,257 calls 3,825 puts

BRITISH POUND
62,500 pounds; cents per pound;

Strike Price	Calls-Settle Mar	Calls-Settle Apr	Calls-Settle May	Puts-Settle Mar	Puts-Settle Apr	Puts-Settle May
1420	2.64	....	....	0.38	1.00	....
1430	1.90	....	....	0.64	1.36	....
1440	1.28	1.92	....	1.02	1.80	....
1450	0.80	1.50	....	1.54	....	....
1460	0.48	1.12	....	2.22	....	....
1470	0.30	0.80	....	3.04	....	....

Est vol 822 Tue 688 calls 278 puts
Op int Tue 7,683 calls 5,933 puts

SWISS FRANC
125,000 francs; cents per franc;

Strike Price	Calls-Settle Mar	Calls-Settle Apr	Calls-Settle May	Puts-Settle Mar	Puts-Settle Apr	Puts-Settle May
5850	....	....	....	0.30	....	....
5900	0.79	....	....	0.48	0.76	....
5950	0.54	....	....	0.73	....	....
6000	0.36	0.85	....	1.05	....	....
6050	0.25	....	....	1.44	....	....
6100	0.16	....	....	1.85	....	....

Est vol 254 Tue 76 calls 410 puts
Op int Tue 7,277 calls 5,870 puts

The forward market, currency options, and currency futures facilitate international trade and investment by allowing firms to hedge, or reduce, the foreign-exchange risks inherent in international transactions. Suppose Toys 'R' Us wants to purchase Sony PlayStation 2 game players for ¥140 million for delivery 90 days in the future, with payment due at delivery. Rather than having to buy yen today and hold them for 90 days, Toys 'R' Us can simply go to its bank and contract to buy the ¥140 million for delivery in 90 days. The firm's bank will in turn charge Toys 'R' Us for those yen based on the yen's current price in the 90-day forward wholesale market. Toys 'R' Us could also protect itself from increases in the yen's price by purchasing a currency future or a currency option. (We discuss the advantages and disadvantages of these different hedging techniques more thoroughly in Chapter 18.)

The forward price of a foreign currency often differs from its spot price. If the forward price (using a direct quote) is less than the spot price, the currency is selling at a **forward discount**. If the forward price is higher than the spot price, the currency is selling at a **forward premium**. For example, as Figure 7.4 indicates, the *Wall Street Journal* reported that the spot price of the British pound on February 21, 2001, was $1.4429. On the same day the 90-day forward price was $1.4419, indicating that the pound was selling at a forward discount. The annualized forward premium or discount on the pound can be calculated by using the following formula:

$$\text{Annualized forward premium or discount} = \frac{P_f - P_s}{P_s} \times n$$

where, using our example,

$$P_f = \text{90-day forward price} = \$1.4419$$
$$P_s = \text{spot price} = \$1.4429$$
$$n = \text{the number of periods in a year} = 4$$

(Because the example calls for a 90-day forward rate, n equals 4; there are four 90-day periods in a year.) Thus

$$\text{Annualized forward premium or discount} = \frac{\$1.4419 - \$1.4429}{\$1.4429} \times 4$$

$$= -0.00277 = -0.28\%$$

Because the equation results in a small negative number, the pound is selling at a slight forward discount. Had the forward price of the pound been higher than the spot price (using the direct quote), the sign of the equation would have been positive and the formula would have yielded the annualized forward premium for the pound.

The forward price represents the marketplace's aggregate prediction of the spot price of the exchange rate in the future. Thus the forward price helps international businesspeople forecast future changes in exchange rates. These changes can affect the price of imported components as well as the competitiveness and profitability of the firm's exports. If a currency is selling at a forward discount, the foreign-exchange market believes the currency will depreciate over time. Firms may want to reduce their holdings of assets or increase their liabilities denominated in such a currency. The currencies of countries suffering balance of payment (BOP) trade deficits or high inflation rates often sell at a forward discount. Conversely, if a currency is selling at a forward premium, the foreign-exchange market believes the currency will appreciate over time. Firms may want to increase their holdings of assets and reduce their liabilities denominated in such a currency. The currencies of countries enjoying BOP trade surpluses or low inflation rates often sell at a forward premium. Thus the difference between the spot and forward prices of a country's currency often signals the market's expectations regarding that country's economic policies and prospects.

Arbitrage and the Currency Market

Another important component of the foreign-exchange market is arbitrage activities. **Arbitrage** is the riskless purchase of a product in one market for immediate resale in a second market in order to profit from a price discrepancy. We explore two types of arbitrage activities that affect the foreign-exchange market: arbitrage of goods and arbitrage of money.

Arbitrage of Goods—Purchasing Power Parity.   Underlying the arbitrage of goods is a very simple notion: If the price of a good differs between two markets, people will tend to buy the good in the market offering the lower price, the "cheap" market, and resell it in the market offering the higher price, the "expensive" market. Under the *law of one price* such arbitrage activities will continue until the price of the good is identical in both markets (excluding transactions costs, transportation costs, taxes, and so on). This notion induced purchasing agents for Galeries Lafayette to buy clock radios in Japan and export them to France in the example in Chapter 5 and U.S. honeymooners, shoppers, and investors to purchase Canadian goods, services, and assets in the chapter's opening case.

The arbitrage of goods across national boundaries is represented by the theory of **purchasing power parity (PPP)**. This theory states that the prices of tradable goods, when expressed in a common currency, will tend to equalize across countries as a result of exchange rate changes. PPP occurs because the process of buying goods in the cheap market and reselling them in the expensive market affects the demand for, and thus the price of, the foreign currency, as well as the market price of the good itself in the two product markets in question. For example, assume the exchange rate between U.S. and Canadian dollars is US$0.80 = Can$1. Suppose Levi's jeans sell for US$24 in the United States and Can$30 in Canada. PPP would exist in this case. At the existing exchange rate

$$\frac{US\$0.80}{Can\$1} \times Can\$30 = US\$24$$

Thus the Levi's jeans are the same price in both markets (expressed in either U.S. or Canadian dollars), and neither U.S. nor Canadian residents would have any reason to cross their shared border to purchase the jeans in the other country.

Now suppose Canadian firms decide to increase their investments in Mexico as a result of opportunities created by the North American Free Trade Agreement. As Canadians sell their dollars to buy Mexican pesos, they increase the supply of Canadian dollars in the foreign-exchange market, causing the value of the Canadian dollar to fall. Suppose the new exchange rate between U.S. and Canadian dollars is US$0.60 = Can$1. PPP would no longer exist. At this new exchange rate U.S. residents could cross the border, exchange US$18 for Can$30, and buy their Levi's in Canada, thereby saving themselves US$6.

This arbitrage process affects three markets: the foreign-exchange market between U.S. and Canadian dollars; the market for Levi's in the United States; and the market for Levi's in Canada. First, by buying their jeans in Canada, U.S. residents increase the supply of U.S. dollars in the foreign-exchange market, thereby raising the value of the Canadian dollar relative to the U.S. dollar. Second, the behavior of the U.S. residents reduces the demand for Levi's in the United States, lowering their price there. Third, the actions of the U.S. residents increase the demand for Levi's in Canada, thereby raising their price there. This arbitrage behavior will continue until the law of one price is met—the price of Levi's jeans, stated in either Canadian dollars or U.S. dollars, is the same in both countries. This will occur through some combination of changes in the exchange rate and changes in the two product markets.

Does this really happen? Obviously, teenagers from Miami, Florida, do not fly to Calgary, Alberta, just to save US$6 on a pair of jeans. However, for residents of Sault Ste. Marie, Ontario, and Sault Ste. Marie, Michigan, Calais, Maine, and St. Stephen,

› The prices these Mexican shoppers pay for foreign-made goods are affected by fluctuations in the value of the peso in the foreign-exchange market.

New Brunswick, or Seattle, Washington, and Vancouver, British Columbia, the border is but a short trip away, making arbitrage-driven cross-border shopping feasible. Spring break skiers and snowboarders may chose Whistler Mountain over Crested Butte or Tremblant over Killington, depending on the exchange rate between Canadian and U.S. dollars. And as the opening case indicated, Internet shopping facilitates cross-border arbitrage as well, benefiting firms like Ontario-based Wolf BMW.

Of course, the Canadian-U.S. exchange rate is determined by much more than the relative price of jeans in the two countries, border trade between cities like the two Sault Ste. Maries, spring break skiers, or bikers seeking cheaper oil filters. Nonetheless, if PPP does not exist in the two countries for jeans (or any other tradable good), people will buy the good in the cheap market and transport it to the expensive market, thereby affecting prices in the two product markets, as well as supply and demand in the foreign-exchange market. That is why the PPP theory states that prices of tradable goods will *tend* to equalize.

International economists use PPP to help them compare standards of living across countries. Consider, for example, Japan and the United States. Converting Japan's 1999 per capita income measured in yen into U.S. dollars using the average 1999 exchange rate between the yen and the dollar would yield $32,230. U.S. per capita income for 1999 was $31,915. These figures suggest that the average Japanese citizen enjoys a higher income than the average U.S. citizen. However, this comparison fails to take into account differences in price levels between the two countries. After adjusting for purchasing power, Japan's per capita income falls to $24,041, indicating that the average Japanese is worse off than the average American. Because of such distortions due to price levels, international businesspeople who use international income data to make decisions, such as which market to enter or how to position a product, must pay close attention to whether the data are reported with or without PPP adjustments.

Foreign-exchange analysts also use the PPP theory to forecast long-term changes in exchange rates. The analysts believe that broad purchasing power imbalances between countries signal possible changes in exchange rates. As a quick and dirty way of assessing misalignments in exchange rates, the British business weekly *The Economist* periodically reports the prices of McDonald's Big Macs around the world; see "Bringing the World into Focus." As the article suggests, even the prices of Big Macs may signal whether currencies are overvalued or undervalued in the foreign-exchange market.

Arbitrage of Money. Although we do not want to diminish the long-run importance of the arbitrage of goods, its impact on the foreign-exchange market is dwarfed by that of the short-term arbitrage of money. Much of the $1.5 trillion in daily trading of foreign exchange stems from financial arbitrage. Professional traders employed by money market banks and other financial organizations seek to profit from small differences in the price of foreign exchange in different markets. Although not all the volume in currency markets reflects arbitrage activities, the importance of financial activities relative to real activities (purchases of goods and services) in foreign-exchange markets is indicated by the ratio of daily foreign-currency trading ($1.5 trillion) to daily international trade ($17 billion).

Whenever the foreign-exchange market is not in equilibrium, professional traders can profit through arbitraging money. Numerous forms of foreign-exchange arbitrage are possible, but we discuss three common examples: two-point, three-point, and covered interest.

Two-point arbitrage, also called **geographic arbitrage**, involves profiting from price differences in two geographically distinct markets. Suppose £1 is trading for $2.00 in New York City and $1.80 in London. A profitable arbitrage opportunity is available. A foreign-exchange trader at Chase Manhattan could take $1.80 and use it to buy £1 in London's foreign-exchange market. The trader could then take the pound and sell it for $2.00 in New York's foreign-exchange market. Through this two-point, or geographic, arbitrage, the trader at Chase Manhattan transforms $1.80 into $2.00 at no risk whatsoever.

Of course, currency traders at other banks will also note the opportunity for quick profits. As arbitrageurs sell dollars and buy pounds in London, the dollar falls in value relative to the pound in the London market. As arbitrageurs sell pounds and buy dollars in New York, the pound falls in value relative to the dollar in that market. This process will continue until the pound-dollar exchange rate is identical in both markets. Only when there is no possibility of profitable arbitrage will the foreign-exchange market be in equilibrium.

We add one caveat: If the costs of making an arbitrage transaction were large, there could be differences in the exchange rates in the two markets that reflected the size of the transaction costs. However, for major currencies foreign exchange is sold in large amounts by very large, well-known international banks. Accordingly, transaction costs are extremely small, and two-point arbitrage generally will cause exchange rates between any two major currencies to be identical in all markets.

Consider another example. Suppose that £1 can buy $2 in New York, Tokyo, and London, $1 can buy ¥120 in those three markets, and £1 can buy ¥200 in all three. Because the exchange rate between each pair of currencies is the same in each country, no possibility of profitable two-point arbitrage exists. However, profitable **three-point arbitrage** opportunities exist. Three-point arbitrage is the buying and selling of three different currencies to make a riskless profit. Figure 7.7 shows how this can work:

Step 1: Convert £1 into $2.

Step 2: Convert the $2 into ¥240.

Step 3: Convert the ¥240 into £1.2.

Through these three steps, £1 has been converted into £1.2, for a riskless profit of £0.2.

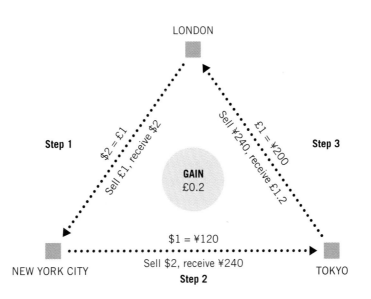

FIGURE 7.7

Three-Point Arbitrage

Bringing the World into FOCUS

BIG MAC CURRENCIES

Some people read tea leaves to predict the future. We prefer hamburgers.

It is that time of the year when *The Economist* munches its way around the globe in order to update our Big Mac index. We first launched this 14 years ago as a lighthearted guide to whether currencies are at their "correct" exchange rate. It is not intended as a precise predictor of exchange rates, but a tool to make economic theory more digestible.

Burgernomics is based on the theory of purchasing-power parity, the notion that a dollar should buy the same amount in all countries. Thus in the long run, the exchange rate between two currencies should move towards the rate that equalises the prices of an identical basket of goods and services in each country. Our "basket" is a McDonald's Big Mac, which is produced in about 120 countries. The Big Mac PPP is the exchange rate that would mean hamburgers cost the same in America as abroad. Comparing actual exchange rates with PPPs indicates whether a currency is under- or overvalued.

The first column of the table shows local-currency prices of a Big Mac; the second converts them into dollars. The average price of a Big Mac (including tax) in four American cities is $2.51. The cheapest burger among the countries in the table is once again in Malaysia ($1.19); at the other extreme the most expensive is $3.58 in Israel. This is another way of saying that the Malaysian ringgit is the most undervalued currency (by 53%), and the Israeli shekel the most overvalued (by 43%).

The third column calculates Big Mac PPPs. For instance, dividing the Japanese price by the American one gives a dollar PPP of ¥117. On April 25th the actual rate was ¥106, implying that the yen is 11% overvalued against the dollar.

Despite a single currency, the price of a Big Mac varies considerably within the euro area—from a bargain $2.09 in Spain to a beefy $3.12 in Finland. The average price (weighted by GDPs) in the 11 countries is €2.56, or $2.37 at current exchange rates. The euro's Big Mac PPP against the dollar is €1 = $0.98, which sug-gests that the euro is 5% undervalued—considerably less than many market commentators claim.

The most undervalued of all the rich-world currencies is the Australian dollar, currently 38% below McParity. In contrast, most of the West European currencies outside the euro—notably, sterling, the Danish krone and the Swiss franc—are hugely overvalued, by 20–40%.

Most emerging market currencies are undervalued against the dollar on a Big Mac PPP basis. Besides the Israeli shekel, the other main exception is the South Korean won which, as a result of currency appreciation, is now 8% overvalued against the dollar. In early 1998, at the height of the Asian crisis, it was 31% undervalued.

Adjustment back to PPP does not always come about through a shift in exchange rates, but sometimes through price changes. In 1994, for instance., Argentina's peso was 60% overvalued against the dollar; today it is spot on McParity—not because the peso has fallen (it is fixed against the dollar), but because the price of a Big Mac has tumbled in Argentina.

Some readers beef that our Big Mac index does not cut the mustard. They are right that hamburgers are a flawed measure of PPP, because local prices may be distorted by trade barriers on beef, sales taxes or big differences in the cost of non-traded inputs such as rents. Thus, whereas Big Mac PPPs can be a handy guide to the cost of living in countries, they may not be a reliable guide to future exchange-rate movements. Yet, curiously, several academic studies have concluded that the Big Mac index is surprisingly accurate in tracking exchange rates over the longer term.

Indeed, the Big Mac has had several forecasting successes. When the euro was launched at the start of 1999, most forecasters predicted that it would rise. But the euro has instead tumbled—exactly as the Big Mac index had signalled. At the start of 1999, euro burgers were much dearer than American ones. Burgernomics is far from perfect, but our mouths are where our money is.

The Golden-Arches Standard

	BIG MAC PRICES		IMPLIED PPP* OF THE DOLLAR	ACTUAL $ EXCHANGE RATE 25/04/00	UNDER (−)/OVER (+) VALUATION AGAINST THE DOLLAR, %
	in local currency	in dollars			
United States†	$2.51	2.51	—	—	—
Argentina	Peso2.50	2.50	1.00	1.00	0
Australia	A$2.59	1.54	1.03	1.68	−38
Brazil	Real2.95	1.65	1.18	1.79	−34
Britain	£1.90	3.00	1.32‡	1.58‡	+20
Canada	C$2.85	1.94	1.14	1.47	−23
Chile	Peso1,260	2.45	502	514	−2
China	Yuan9.90	1.20	3.94	8.28	−52
Czech Rep	Koruna54.37	1.39	21.7	39.1	−45
Denmark	DKr24.75	3.08	9.86	8.04	+23
Euro area	€2.56	2.37	0.98§	0.93§	−5
France	FFr18.50	2.62	7.37	7.07	+4
Germany	DM4.99	2.37	1.99	2.11	−6
Italy	Lire4,500	2.16	1,793	2,088	−14
Spain	Pta375	2.09	149	179	−17
Hong Kong	HK$10.20	1.31	4.06	7.79	−48
Hungary	Forint339	1.21	135	279	−52
Indonesia	Rupiah14,500	1.83	5,777	7,945	−27
Israel	Shekel14.5	3.58	5.78	4.05	+43
Japan	¥294	2.78	117	106	+11
Malaysia	M$4.52	1.19	1.80	3.80	−53
Mexico	Peso20.90	2.22	8.33	9.41	−11
New Zealand	NZ$3.40	1.69	1.35	2.01	−33
Poland	Zloty5.50	1.28	2.19	4.30	−49
Russia	Rouble39.50	1.39	15.7	28.5	−45
Singapore	S$3.20	1.88	1.27	1.70	−25
South Africa	Rand9.00	1.34	3.59	6.72	−47
South Korea	Won3,000	2.71	1,195	1,108	+8
Sweden	SKr24.00	2.71	9.56	8.84	+8
Switzerland	SFr5.90	3.48	2.35	1.70	+39
Taiwan	NT$70.00	2.29	27.9	30.6	−9
Thailand	Baht55.00	1.45	21.9	38.0	−42

*Purchasing-power parity: local price divided by price in United States.
†Average of New York, Chicago, San Francisco and Atlanta.
‡Dollars per pound.
§Dollars per euro.
Source: McDonald's: *The Economist*.

Professional currency traders can make profits through three-point arbitrage whenever the cost of buying a currency directly (such as using pounds to buy yen) differs from the cross rate of exchange. The **cross rate** is an exchange rate between two currencies calculated through the use of a third currency (such as using pounds to buy dollars and then using the dollars to buy yen). Because of the depth and liquidity of dollar-denominated currency markets, the U.S. dollar is the primary third currency used in calculating cross rates. In the earlier example the direct quote between pounds and yen is £1/¥200, while the cross rate is

$$\frac{£1}{\$2} \times \frac{\$1}{¥120} = \frac{£1}{¥240}$$

The difference between these two rates offers arbitrage profits to foreign-exchange market professionals. The market for the three currencies will be in equilibrium only when arbitrage profits do not exist, which occurs when the direct quote and the cross rate for each possible pair of the three currencies are equal.

The real significance of three-point arbitrage is that it links together individual foreign-exchange markets. Changes in the pound/dollar market will affect both the yen/pound market and the dollar/yen market because of the direct quote-cross rate equilibrium relationship. These changes will in turn affect other markets, such as the dollar/euro market, the yen/euro market, and the pound/euro market. Because of three-point arbitrage, changes in any one foreign-exchange market can affect prices in all other foreign-exchange markets.

The third form of arbitrage we discuss is covered-interest arbitrage. **Covered-interest arbitrage** is arbitrage that occurs when the difference between two countries' interest rates is not equal to the forward discount/premium on their currencies. In practice, it is the most important form of arbitrage in the foreign-exchange market. It occurs because international bankers, insurance companies, and corporate treasurers are continually scanning money markets worldwide to obtain the best returns on their short-term excess cash balances and the lowest rates on short-term loans. In doing so, however, they often want to protect, or *cover* (hence the term *covered-interest arbitrage*), themselves from exchange rate risks.

A simple example demonstrates how covered-interest arbitrage works. Suppose the annual interest rate for 90-day deposits is 12 percent in London and 8 percent in New York. New York investors will be eager to earn the higher returns available in London. To do so, they must convert their dollars to pounds today in order to invest in London. However, the New York investors ultimately want dollars, not pounds, so they must reconvert the pounds back to dollars at the end of 90 days. But what if the pound's value were to fall during that period? The extra interest the New Yorkers will earn in London might then be wiped out by losses suffered when they exchange pounds for dollars in 90 days.

The New York investors can capture the higher London interest rates but avoid exchange rate dangers by covering in the forward market their exposure to potential drops in the pound's value. Suppose they have $1 million to invest, the spot pound is selling for $1.60, and the 90-day forward pound is selling for $1.59. They have two choices:

1. They can invest their money in New York at 8 percent interest.

2. They can convert their dollars into pounds today, invest in London at 12 percent interest, and in 90 days liquidate their London investment and convert it back to dollars.

If the New York investors choose the first option and invest their funds in the New York money market for 90 days at 8 percent annual interest (or 2 percent for 90 days), at the end of the 90 days their investment will be

$$\$1,000,000 \times 1.02 = \$1,020,000$$

Or they can invest their money in London for 90 days. To do so, they first convert their $1,000,000 into £625,000 at the spot rate of $1.60/£1. At the 12 percent annual interest rate available in London (or 3 percent for 90 days), their investment will grow in 90 days to

$$£625,000 \times 1.03 = £643,750$$

If they want to avoid exposure to exchange rate fluctuations, they can sell the £643,750 today in the 90-day forward market at the current 90-day forward rate of $1.59/£1, which, at the end of 90 days, yields

$$£643,750 \times \$1.59/£1 = \$1,023,562.50$$

The New Yorkers thus earn more money by investing in London than they would at home ($23,562.50 versus $20,000). Covered-interest arbitrage allows them to capture the higher interest rate in London while covering themselves from exchange rate fluctuations by using the forward market. So short-term investment money, seeking the higher covered return, will flow from New York to London.

What happens in the two lending markets and the foreign-exchange market when such arbitrage occurs? When funds are transferred from New York to London, interest rates will rise in New York because the supply of lendable money in New York decreases. Interest rates will fall in London because the supply of lendable money increases there. In the spot market the demand for pounds increases, thereby raising the spot price of pounds. In the 90-day forward market the supply of pounds increases, thereby lowering the forward price of pounds. Lendable funds will continue to flow from New York to London until the return on the covered investment is the same in London as it is in New York. Only then will all possibilities for profitable covered-interest arbitrage be exhausted.

Returns to international investors will be equal—and arbitrage-driven, short-term international capital flows will end—when the interest rate difference between the two markets equals the 90-day forward discount on the pound. Said another way, covered-interest arbitrage will end if the gains investors capture from the higher interest rates in the London market are just offset by the exchange rate losses they suffer from the conversion of their dollars to pounds today and reconversion of their pounds back to dollars in 90 days. (Note that the pound's forward discount measures in percentage terms the exchange rate loss on this "spot against forward" swap transaction.)

The short-term capital flows that result from covered-interest arbitrage are so important to the foreign-exchange market that, in practice, the short-term interest rate differential between two countries determines the forward discount or forward premium on their currencies.

This last statement raises another question: Why should interest rates vary among countries in the first place? Addressing this question in 1930, Yale economist Irving Fisher demonstrated that a country's nominal interest rate reflects the real interest rate plus expected inflation in that country. National differences in expected inflation rates thus yield differences in nominal interest rates among countries, a phenomenon known as the **international Fisher effect**. Because of the international Fisher effect and covered-interest arbitrage, an increase in a country's expected inflation rate implies higher interest rates in that country. This in turn will lead to either a shrinking of the forward premium or a widening of the forward discount on the country's currency in the foreign-exchange market. Because of this linkage between inflation and expected changes in exchange rates, international businesspeople and foreign-currency traders carefully monitor countries' inflation trends. The connection between inflation and exchange rates also affects the international monetary system. For example, a fixed exchange rate system functions poorly if inflation rates vary widely among countries participating in the system.

In summary arbitrage activities are important for several reasons. Arbitrage constitutes a major portion of the $1.5 trillion in currencies traded globally each working day. It affects the supply and demand for each of the major trading currencies. It also ties together the foreign-exchange markets, thereby overcoming differences in geography (two-point arbitrage), currency type (three-point arbitrage), and time (covered-interest arbitrage). Arbitrage truly makes the foreign-exchange market global.

❯ THE INTERNATIONAL CAPITAL MARKET

Not only are international banks important in the functioning of the foreign-exchange market and arbitrage transactions, but they also play a critical role in financing the operations of international businesses, acting as both commercial bankers and investment bankers. As commercial bankers, they finance exports and imports, accept deposits, provide working capital loans, and offer sophisticated cash management services for their clients. As investment bankers, they may underwrite or syndicate local, foreign, or multinational loans and broker, facilitate, or even finance mergers and joint ventures between foreign and domestic firms.

Major International Banks

The international banking system is centered in large money market banks headquartered in the world's financial centers—Japan, the United States, the United Kingdom, Germany, and France. These banks are involved in international commerce on a global scale (see Table 7.1).

International banking takes many forms. Originally, most international banking was done through reciprocal correspondent relationships among banks located in different countries. A **correspondent relationship** is an agent relationship whereby one bank acts as a correspondent, or agent, for another bank in the first bank's home country and vice versa. For example, a U.S. bank could be the correspondent for a Danish bank in the United States, while the Danish bank could be the U.S. bank's correspondent in Denmark. Services performed by correspondent banks include paying or collecting foreign funds, providing credit information, and honoring letters of credit. To facilitate these transactions, each bank maintains accounts at the other bank denominated in the local currency.

As the larger banks have internationalized their operations, they have increasingly provided their own overseas operations, rather than utilizing correspondent banks, to improve their ability to compete internationally. A bank that has its own foreign operations is better able to access new sources of deposits and profitable lending opportunities. Equally important, as its domestic clients internationalize, the bank can better meet those clients' international banking needs. Thus it retains the international business of its domestic clients and reduces the risk that some other international bank will steal them away.

An overseas banking operation can be established in several ways. If it is separately incorporated from the parent, it is called a **subsidiary bank**; if it is not separately incorporated, it is called a **branch bank**. Sometimes an international bank may choose to create an **affiliated bank**, an overseas operation in which it takes part ownership in conjunction with a local or foreign partner.

Commercial Banking Services.   International banks and their overseas operations are important providers of international commercial banking services. Exporters and tourists utilize such banking services when they exchange their home currency or traveler's checks for local currency. Although the physical exchange of one country's paper currency for another's is part of international banking operations, a far more important part entails financing and facilitating everyday commercial transactions. For example, when Hallmark orders $10 million

TABLE 7.1

The World's 25 Largest Banks

RANK		COMPANY (COUNTRY)	1999 ASSETS ($ MILLIONS)
1999	1998		
1	1	Deutsche Bank (Germany)	$955,579
2	4	Bank of Tokyo-Mitsubishi (Japan)	726,286
3	3	Citigroup (U.S.)	716,937
4	19/25	BNP Paribas (France)	703,091
5	5	Bank of America (U.S.)	632,574
6	2	UBS (Switzerland)	616,798
7	8	HSBC Holdings (U.K./Hong Kong)	601,847
8	6	Fuji Bank (Japan)	561,345
9	10	Bayerische Hypo Bank (Germany)	559,860
10	11	Sumitomo Bank (Japan)	519,153
11	13	Dai-Ichi Kangyo Bank (Japan)	503,203
12	12	ING Group (Netherlands)	495,968
13	16	Sakura Bank (Japan)	474,474
14	17	Dresdner Bank (Germany)	460,139
15	7	ABN Amro (Netherlands)	459,574
16	15	Sanwa Bank (Japan)	453,454
17	9	Credit Suisse (Switzerland)	452,143
18	20	Commerzbank (Germany)	427,896
19	18	Industrial Bank of Japan (Japan)	415,482
20	22	Barclays (U.K.)	412,412
21	14	Societe Generale de France (France)	409,410
22	21	Chase Manhattan (U.S.)	406,105
23	44/68	Gruppo Intesa (Italy)	305,538
24	27	Tokai Bank (Japan)	295,921
25	26	Abbey National (U.K.)	292,561

Source: Wall Street Journal, September 25, 2000, p. R25.

worth of Hello Kitty merchandise from its Japanese manufacturer, with payment due in 90 days, Hallmark may require any of the following banking services:

- Short-term financing of the purchase
- International electronic funds transfer
- Forward purchases of Japanese yen
- Advice about proper documentation for importing and paying for the goods

The international department of the firm's bank will provide any or all of these services as part of its normal commercial banking operations.

Investment Banking Services.   In addition to commercial banking services, most international banks provide investment banking services. Investment banking services are also furnished by large securities firms like Nomura, Salomon Smith Barney, Goldman Sachs, and Merrill Lynch. Corporate clients hire investment bankers to package and locate long-term debt and equity funding and to arrange mergers and acquisitions of domestic and foreign firms. Competition has forced investment bankers to globalize their operations to secure capital for their clients at the lowest possible cost.

The Eurocurrency Market

Another important facet of the international financial system is the Eurocurrency market. Originally called the Eurodollar market, the Eurocurrency market originated in the early 1950s when the communist-controlled governments of Central Europe and Eastern Europe needed dollars to finance their international trade but feared the U.S. government would confiscate or block their holdings of dollars in U.S. banks for political reasons. The communist governments solved this problem by using European banks that were willing to maintain dollar accounts for them. Thus Eurodollars—U.S. dollars deposited in European bank accounts—were born. As other banks worldwide, particularly in Canada and Japan, began offering dollar-denominated deposit accounts, the term **Eurodollar** evolved to mean U.S. dollars deposited in any bank account outside the United States. As other currencies became stronger in the post-World War II era—particularly the yen, the pound, and the deutsche mark—the Eurocurrency market broadened to include Euroyen, Europounds, and other currencies. Today a **Eurocurrency** is defined as a currency on deposit outside its country of issue. Some $6 trillion worth of Eurocurrencies are on deposit in banks worldwide; roughly two-thirds of these deposits are in the form of Eurodollars.[3]

The Euroloan market has grown up with the Eurocurrency market. The Euroloan market is extremely competitive, and lenders operate on razor-thin margins. Euroloans are often quoted on the basis of the **London Interbank Offer Rate (LIBOR)**, the interest rate that London banks charge each other for short-term Eurocurrency loans. The Euroloan market is often the low-cost source of loans for large, creditworthy borrowers, such as governments and large multinational corporations (MNCs), for three reasons. First, Euroloans are free of costly government banking regulations, such as reserve requirements, that are designed to control the domestic money supply but that drive up lending costs. Second, Euroloans involve large transactions, so the average cost of making the loans is lower. Third, because only the most creditworthy borrowers use the Euroloan market, the risk premium that lenders charge also is lower.

During the 1970s U.S. banks complained that reserve requirements and other expensive regulations imposed by the Federal Reserve Board prevented them from competing with European and Asian banks in issuing dollar-denominated international loans. These loans account for 60 percent of the Euroloan market. Foreign banks lending in Eurodollars were not subject to the regulations. To counter this problem, the Federal Reserve Board in 1981 authorized the creation of international banking facilities. An **international banking facility (IBF)** is an entity of a U.S. bank that is legally distinct from the bank's domestic operations and that may offer only international banking services. IBFs do not need to observe the numerous U.S. domestic banking regulations. Of course, the Federal Reserve Board has issued various regulations to ensure IBFs do not engage in domestic banking services. For example, IBFs may accept deposits from or make loans to only non-U.S. residents. Nonetheless, IBFs enable U.S. banks to compete with other international bankers on a more equal footing in the critical Euroloan market.

The International Bond Market

The international bond market represents a major source of debt financing for the world's governments, international organizations, and larger firms. This market has traditionally consisted of two types of bonds: foreign bonds and Eurobonds. **Foreign bonds** are bonds issued by a resident of country A but sold to residents of country B and denominated in the currency of country B. For example, the Nestlé Corporation, a Swiss resident, might issue a foreign bond denominated in yen and sold primarily to residents of Japan. A **Eurobond** is a bond issued in the currency of country A but sold to residents of other countries. For example, American Airlines could borrow $500 million to finance new aircraft purchases by selling

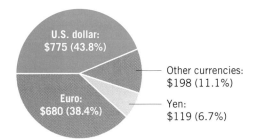

FIGURE 7.8

International Bond Issues, 1999, by Currency (in billions of U.S. Dollars)

Source: Bank for International Settlements, "International Banking and Financial Market Developments" (Basle, August 2000), p. 23.

Eurobonds denominated in dollars to residents of Denmark and Germany. The U.S. dollar and the EU's euro are the dominant currencies in the international bond market (see Figure 7.8).

As the global capital market has evolved, the international bond market has grown increasingly sophisticated. Syndicates of investment banks, securities firms, and commercial banks put together complex packages of international bonds to serve the borrowing needs of large, creditworthy borrowers, such as major MNCs, national governments, and international organizations. The global bond is one such innovative financial instrument. A **global bond** is a large, liquid financial asset that can be traded anywhere at any time. Its use was pioneered by the World Bank, which simultaneously sold $1.5 billion of U.S.-dollar denominated global bonds in North America, Europe, and Japan and succeeded in lowering its interest costs on the bond issue by about 0.225 percentage points. Although 0.225 percentage points may not seem much, multiplying that amount by $1.5 billion reveals that the bank reduced its annual financing costs by $3,375,000. Attracted by the World Bank's success, many other large organizations, such as Matsushita Electric, the Province of Ontario, Citicorp, and Household Finance, have also issued global bonds.

Other innovative opportunities exist in the bond market. For example, at the borrower's option, bond interest may be paid in one currency and the principal paid in another currency. Or the borrower may secure a lower interest rate by offering inflation protection that pegs the principal repayment to the value of gold or special drawing rights.

Like the Euroloan market, the international bond market is highly competitive, and borrowers are often able to obtain funds on very favorable terms. Large transaction sizes, creditworthy borrowers, and freedom from costly regulations imposed on domestic capital markets all lower the interest rates charged on such loans.

Global Equity Markets

The growing importance of multinational operations and improvements in telecommunications technology have also made equity markets more global. Start-up companies are no longer restricted to raising new equity solely from domestic sources. For example, Swiss pharmaceutical firms are a major source of equity capital for new U.S. biotechnology firms. Established firms also tap into the global equity market. When expanding into a foreign market, a firm may choose to raise capital for its foreign subsidiary in the foreign market. For example, the Walt Disney Company initially sold

› The enormous growth potential of international e-commerce has attracted the attention of investors worldwide, such as these Hong Kong residents seeking to buy shares in the Web portal firm tom.com.

51 percent of its Disneyland Paris project to French investors. Numerous MNCs also cross-list their common stocks on multiple stock exchanges. British Airways, for example, is listed on both the London Stock Exchange and the New York Stock Exchange, thereby enabling both European and American investors to purchase its shares conveniently. Another innovation is the development of country funds. A **country fund** is a mutual fund that specializes in investing in a given country's firms.

The globalization of equity markets has been facilitated by the globalization of the financial services industry. Most major financial services firms, such as Merrill Lynch, Daiwa Securities, and Deutsche Bank, have expanded operations from their domestic bases into the major international financial centers. These financial services firms are eager to raise capital, provide investment advice, offer stock market analyses, and put together financing deals for clients anywhere around the world.

Offshore Financial Centers

Offshore financial centers focus on offering banking and other financial services to nonresident customers. Many of these centers are located on island states, such as the Bahamas, Bahrain, the Cayman Islands, Bermuda, the Netherlands Antilles, and Singapore. Luxembourg and Switzerland, although not islands, are also important "offshore" financial centers.

MNCs often use offshore financial centers to obtain low-cost Eurocurrency loans. Many MNCs locate financing subsidiaries in these centers to take advantage of the benefits they offer: political stability, a regulatory climate that facilitates international capital transactions, excellent communications links to other major financial centers, and availability of legal, accounting, financial, and other expertise needed to package large loans. The efficiency of offshore financial centers in attracting deposits and then lending these funds to customers worldwide is an important factor in the growing globalization of the capital market.[4]

CHAPTER REVIEW

Summary

A currency's price in the foreign-exchange market is determined by the interaction of the demand for and supply of the currency. Underlying demand for a particular currency is the desire of foreigners to buy goods, services, and assets of the issuing country. Underlying the supply is the desire of residents to purchase goods, services, and assets owned by foreigners.

Major international banks in financial centers such as London, Frankfurt, Tokyo, and New York City play a critical role in the functioning of the foreign-exchange market. Key players in the wholesale market, these banks account for the vast majority of foreign-exchange transactions. In serving their clients' needs, the banks are also an important component of the retail market. They assist commercial customers, speculators, and arbitrageurs in acquiring foreign currency on both the spot and forward markets.

An important feature of the foreign-exchange market is its time dimension. International businesses may buy currency in the spot market for immediate delivery or in the forward market for future delivery. The forward market, currency futures, and currency options enable firms to protect themselves from unfavorable future exchange rate movements.

Arbitrage activities affect the demand for and supply of foreign exchange. The theory of purchasing power parity says the prices of tradable goods will tend to equalize among countries. Arbitrage of foreign exchange itself is even more important. Two-point arbitrage implies that the exchange rate between two currencies will be the same in all geographic markets. Three-point arbitrage links individual foreign-exchange markets together. Covered-interest arbitrage causes geographic differences in interest rates to equal differences between spot and forward exchange rates.

The international capital market is growing in sophistication as a result of technological advances in telecommunications and computers. Major international banks still utilize their traditional correspondent relationships with other banks but also are increasingly engaged in overseas bank operations themselves. The Eurocurrency market allows banks of any country to conduct lending operations in whatever currencies their clients require. MNCs now commonly raise capital, both debt and equity, on a global basis, wherever its cost is lowest.

Review Questions

1. What determines the demand for any given currency in the foreign-exchange market?
2. What determines the supply of any given currency in the foreign-exchange market?
3. How are prices established in the foreign-exchange market?
4. What is the role of international banks in the foreign-exchange market?
5. Explain the different techniques firms can use to protect themselves from future changes in exchange rates.
6. Discuss the major types of arbitrage activities that affect the foreign-exchange market.
7. Describe the various forms a bank's overseas operations may take.
8. What are Eurocurrencies?
9. What are the major characteristics of offshore financial centers?

Questions for Discussion

1. Suppose the Federal Reserve Board unexpectedly raises interest rates in the United States. How will this action affect the foreign-exchange market?
2. How important are communications and computing technologies to the smooth functioning of the foreign-exchange market? If the technological advances of the past four decades were eliminated—for example, no PCs or satellite telecommunications—how would the foreign-exchange market be affected?
3. Do you expect the U.S. dollar to maintain its position as the dominant currency in the foreign-exchange market once the euro is fully established? Why or why not?
4. Suppose the spot pound and the 90-day forward pound are both selling for $1.65, while U.S. interest rates are 10 percent and British interest rates are 6 percent. Using the covered-interest arbitrage theory, describe what will happen to the spot price of the pound, the 90-day forward price of the pound, interest rates in the United States, and interest rates in the United Kingdom when arbitrageurs enter this market.
5. How important is the creation of international banking facilities to the international competitiveness of the U.S. banking industry?
6. What would be the impact on world trade and investment if there were only one currency?

BUILDING GLOBAL SKILLS

Please refer to Figure 7.4 to answer the following questions:

1. What is the spot rate for the British pound on Wednesday in terms of the U.S. dollar? (Or, stated differently, how many dollars does a pound cost? Or, from the U.S. perspective, what is the direct quote on pounds?)
2. What is the spot price for the dollar on Wednesday in terms of the Swiss franc? (Or, from the U.S. perspective, what is the indirect rate on Swiss francs?)
3. Calculate the cross rate of exchange between the British pound and the Swiss franc.
4. Calculate the annualized forward premium or discount on 180-day yen.
5. If you are planning to go to Japan this summer, should you buy your yen today? Why or why not?
6. According to the covered-interest arbitrage theory, is the United States or Japan expected to have higher interest rates?
7. According to the covered-interest arbitrage theory, what is the expected difference between interest rates in the United States and Japan?
8. According to the international Fisher effect, is expected inflation higher in Japan or the United States?
9. Did the value of the Canadian dollar rise or fall between Tuesday and Wednesday?

WORKING WITH THE WEB: BUILDING GLOBAL INTERNET SKILLS

What Will the Zloty Be Worth in a Year?

You are the head of marketing for a small U.S. producer of innovative, high-quality computer-controlled machine tools called Machine Solutions. Machine Solutions has bid on a contract to supply four stamping machines over the next 12 months to one of Poland's leading and fastest growing auto parts manufacturers. The bidding is likely to be extremely competitive. Winning this contract is important to Machine Solutions for several reasons. First, it gains the company access to the growing auto parts industry in Central Europe and Eastern Europe. Second, the Polish company has been experiencing rapid growth and is likely to need additional stamping machines in the future. Third, the contract will increase Machine Solutions' annual sales by 25 percent. Fourth, because Machine Solutions was started only two years ago, it is experiencing growing pains and cash flow problems.

Machine Solutions offers to sell the Polish company four machines at $1 million each, payable on delivery. In accord with the

Polish company's request, Machine Solutions agrees to deliver two machines in 90 days, one in 180 days, and the last one a year from now. After you submit your bid, the purchasing manager of the Polish company says the firm is extremely interested in your offer, but Machine Solutions can win the contract only if it agrees to invoice the Polish company in its home currency, zlotys. Because Machine Solutions is being asked to accept the foreign-exchange risk in the transaction, the purchasing manager says there may be some "wiggle room" on the price. However, the manager will buy from other companies if the price in zlotys is too high.

You present this news to Machine Solutions' other executives. The firm's treasurer hits the roof, arguing that he knows nothing about zlotniks or whatever the money is called, and is afraid that changes in the value of the currency will rob the sale of its profits. You respond that this sale is vital to Machine Solutions' future health, allowing it to get its foot in the door at a growing company in a growing market. After listening to the argument, the CEO tells you to rework the proposed contract, agreeing to accept zlotys in payment but to protect Machine Solutions from foreign-exchange risk.

Your first thought is to go to the *Wall Street Journal* and look up the price of Polish zlotys in the spot and forward market. Unfortunately, the *Journal* only publishes a spot price for the zloty. Accordingly, you either have to find someone who will quote you a forward rate for the zloty or develop some means of forecasting what the zloty will be worth in 90 days, 180 days, and a year from now, when the machines are to be paid for. You know that the value of the zloty over this period will be influenced by a variety of factors, such as interest rates, inflation rates, balance of payments performance, the stability of Poland's economic and political policies, and other factors. You are also aware that many banks and consulting firms scrutinize such markets for their clients.

Here is your task: Determine the prices in zlotys that Machine Solutions should propose to charge for the four stamping machines as they are delivered over the course of the year. You can use whatever criteria you wish to establish these prices, but you must defend how you arrived at them. The textbook's Web site provides hot-links to some useful sources of information, although of course you are free to use other sources as you see fit.

WE INVITE YOU TO VISIT THIS BOOK'S COMPANION WEB SITE AT www.prenhall.com/griffin

IN THE NEWS

Go to the "Currency" section of the "Markets" page of the *Financial Times* Web site (*www.ft.com*). Read the current articles on what is happening in the foreign-exchange market. Based on your readings, which currencies do you expect to rise in value? To fall in value? How will these currency changes affect the ability of firms from your home country to export their goods? Will these changes have any impact on the willingness of foreign firms to invest in your home country?

CLOSING CASE

A Bad Case of Bahtulism

On February 3, 1997, Goldman Sachs & Co., the large New York-based international investment banking house, announced that it feared that Thailand's currency, the baht, might be devalued during the following six months. Goldman Sachs' warnings followed on the heels of reports that Thailand's government had suffered a budget deficit and that foreign investors were withdrawing some of their short-term investments from the country in fear of a devaluation. Goldman Sachs executives were also concerned about the impact of the rising value of the U.S. dollar on the international competitiveness of Thailand's exports. The country's central bank, the Bank of Thailand, relied on a variant of a

fixed exchange rate system in which the bank pegged the value of the baht to a bundle of currencies, with the U.S. dollar comprising about 80 percent of the bundle. Because of the fixed relationship between the baht and the U.S. dollar, the dollar's rise in value from its nadir in summer 1995 meant that Thai exports were becoming increasingly expensive relative to goods produced in other locales.

However, the Bank of Thailand felt confident that it could maintain the baht's value in the foreign-exchange market. To counteract the short-term capital outflows, the bank raised interest rates, making Thai investments more attractive to foreign investors. If that proved inadequate, the bank pledged to spend its $38.7 billion in foreign-currency reserves to support the baht's value.

Unfortunately, that is not how it turned out. Goldman Sachs' February warning proved accurate. Foreign-currency speculators sold their baht, believing that the Thai government would be forced to devalue the currency because of the increasing uncompetitiveness of Thai exports and the long-term domestic economic damage that would be caused by high interest rates. The Bank of Thailand spent almost $10 billion of its foreign-currency reserves defending the fixed value of the baht before throwing in the towel. On July 2, 1997, the bank unpegged the baht, which promptly fell 20 percent on the foreign-exchange market, rewarding all those speculators who believed such an action was inevitable. The devaluation "baht-ered" the domestic economy. Secure in the belief—false, as it turned out—that the Bank of Thailand would maintain a fixed rate with the U.S. dollar, many Thai companies had borrowed dollars to fund their domestic capital needs. This had seemed to be a reasonable approach because interest rates on dollar-denominated loans secured in the international lending market were lower than the interest rates charged for locally procured baht-denominated loans. Some had even used the borrowed dollars to relend in the domestic capital market. Unfortunately, these dollar-denominated loans became much more expensive due to the devaluation—more baht would be needed to pay each dollar of interest and principal—creating cash flow problems for the borrowers and raising the likelihood that they might default on their loans and declare bankruptcy. Thai financial services firms were particularly vulnerable because many of them had funded property speculators who had trouble meeting payments as commercial real estate prices in Bangkok and other Thai cities tumbled. Even the profits of otherwise healthy companies like Siam Cement were wiped out due to the difficulty of servicing their foreign debts.

The currency crisis also hurt foreign MNCs doing business in Thailand. Goodyear's subsidiary in Thailand, for example, was hit with a double whammy. First, its primary customer, the Thai new-car market, was in free fall due to the devaluation-created economic crisis. Second, its profit margins shrank significantly, for although it sells its tires for baht, many of its costs are denominated in dollars. The company estimated its costs increased by 20 percent as a result of the baht's devaluation.

Thailand's problems soon spread to its neighbors. The so-called bahtulism epidemic (or "Asian contagion") infected neighboring countries such as Indonesia, Malaysia, and the Philippines, all of which compete with Thailand for foreign direct investment from international businesses looking to build factories to tap the region's abundant hard-working, low-cost labor supply. With the devaluation of the baht, Thai exports suddenly became 20 percent cheaper, making Indonesian, Malaysian, and Philippine exports relatively more expensive. Speculators turned their attention to these countries, believing that they too would have to devalue their currencies to remain competitive with Thailand. By early September 1997 the baht had devalued 26 percent relative to its value against the dollar a year earlier, the Indonesian rupiah had devalued 21 percent, the Malaysian ringgit 14 percent, and the Philippine peso 13 percent. The epidemic then spread eastward, wracking the South Korean economy. The Korean won plummeted, as bankers realized that many Korean firms were threatened by overborrowing and devaluation-induced price cutting by regional rivals.

The currency crisis affected more than the foreign-exchange market. Area stock markets were hit hard as well because investors feared that the burden of paying back dollar-denominated debt with the depreciated local currencies would hurt the earnings of regional corporations. By early September 1997 the average Thai stock lost 60 percent of its dollar value, the average Philippine stock lost 45 percent, the average Malaysian stock 40 percent, and the average Indonesian stock 30 percent relative to their values a year earlier. Even foreign stocks were hurt by the crisis. The prices of so-called global consumer stocks such as Coca-Cola, Gillette, and Whirlpool fell as investors realized that a slowdown in the growth of these emerging Southeast Asian markets would cost the companies sales.

As fear of a worldwide recession arose, the International Monetary Fund (IMF) and the governments of the Quad countries hurriedly assembled financial aid packages to help Thailand, Malaysia, Indonesia, the Philippines, and South Korea. Over $100 billion was pledged to restore these countries to economic health and to end the spread of the Asian contagion. The IMF's actions proved successful, and most Southeast Asian economies are now on the upswing. Despite its success, the IMF's aid package has proven to be quite controversial, as the "Point-Counterpoint" following this chapter suggests. Critics around the world are demanding reforms in the way the IMF should address such crises in the future.[5]

Case Questions

1. How can a central bank use its currency reserves to support the value of its country's currency in the foreign-exchange market?
2. Would Thailand have been better off using a flexible exchange rate system instead of the fixed system it did use?
3. If you were a manager of an international business in Thailand in February 1997, what could you have done to protect your company against the possibility of a devaluation of the baht?
4. According to an old saying, "It's an ill wind that blows no good." Can you think of anyone who benefited from Thailand's currency crisis?
5. What impact do you think the Asian contagion had on other emerging economies, such as those in Latin America or in Eastern Europe?

Should the IMF Bail Out Asia?

Yes, IMF aid is critical to restoring the economic health of the regional and global economies.

International Monetary Fund (IMF) aid to Asia can be justified solely on humanitarian grounds. For example, when Thailand shuttered 56 of its 58 investment banks as a result of its currency crisis, 20,000 white-collar employees were put out of work. Without international assistance other Thai firms would have followed suit, and the Thai people would have faced economic disaster. The IMF's actions also can be justified on more pragmatic grounds. In today's global economy economic troubles in one country are quickly transmitted to others. Thailand's problems triggered similar crises in Indonesia, Malaysia, the Philippines, and South Korea. Their crises in turn threaten to damage economies around the world.

Stock markets in London, Frankfurt, and New York weakened as investors realized that recession in Indonesia, the Philippines, and other far-off lands would reduce demand for North American and European products. Communities in Brazil, France, and Mexico were devastated when Korean *chaebol* announced the cancellation or delay of new factories that had promised to bring jobs and prosperity to their citizens. By getting the battered Asian economies back on their feet, the IMF is ensuring that not only will Asian jobs be saved but also jobs in the other five inhabited continents.

In the long run the IMF's intervention often improves the productivity of the recipient countries and the lives of their citizens. Conditions imposed by the IMF (so-called IMF conditionality) lead to necessary economic and political reforms. Consider the problem of crony capitalism, typified by companies owned by the family of former Indonesian President Suharto. These companies benefited from a variety of tax and tariff concessions, subsidized loans, and preferential treatment from Suharto's ministers. As part of Indonesia's agreement with the IMF, Suharto was forced to revoke these privileges. Their elimination will make the Indonesian economy more productive and give businesses not connected to the Suharto family a chance to thrive. Similarly, Korea has been required to impose more control over the borrowing and investment policies of the *chaebol*, relax its import regulations, and permit foreign entry into Korea's financial services markets. These reforms will boost the efficiency of the Korean economy and bolster opportunities for other firms, domestic and foreign alike, to compete for the Korean market.

Critics like to point out that the IMF's actions bail out bad bankers and corrupt governments. Even if that is true, does it make any sense to let their mistakes drag down the entire global economy? A little IMF money, well spent and with appropriate conditions attached, is the best means available to restore these countries as productive members of the global economy.

Thomas Balino (left), head of three-man IMF advance guard, talks to South Korean Choi Yon-Chong, vice president of Bank of Korea, at the bank. Balino and his team came to work out the terms of a multibillion dollar bailout loan to extricate South Korea from its financial crisis.

No, IMF aid rewards governments, banks, and businesses for making bad decisions.

IMF bailouts undermine the efficiency of the global economy. If investors know the IMF will bail them out if their investments go sour, they are more likely to invest in risky projects. If their investments prove successful, they will not share their profits with the taxpayers who fund the IMF. Why then should these taxpayers share their losses?

International competition also is disrupted by IMF bailouts. Consider Idaho's Micron Technology, a memory chip manufacturer. Micron's profitability has been harmed by competition from Korean rivals like Samsung, LG, and Hyundai, who Micron believes have senselessly expanded their chip-making capacity, fueled by cheap loans from Korean banks, Output from their factories has caused the market price of 16 MB DRAM chips to fall by 94 percent in the space of two years. If IMF funds—supplied by taxpayers around the world like Micron—are used by the Korean government to help these firms, then Micron is effectively subsidizing its foreign rivals for their mistakes and helping them get back on their feet so they can better compete against Micron in the future. Needless to say, Micron objects to such a policy.

The mere existence of the IMF encourages governments to ignore economic problems when they first arise. Instead of taking quick action that creates some short-term pain, they prefer to maintain monetary and spending policies in hopes that the problem will go away. But delaying the day of reckoning inevitably worsens the situation. Delay has an important political benefit to the government, however. When the IMF steps in and imposes conditions on the country, its leaders can blame the IMF for the ensuing hardships its people must inevitably suffer.

The IMF's bailout of Asia may cost the world's taxpayers over $100 billion. And what is the result of this philanthropy? International bankers who made risky loans will get their money back. Government officials who lined their pockets or spent money their countries did not have will not have to pay for their sins. Who is left holding the bag? Taxpayers from the contributing countries and the average citizen of the receiving countries, who inevitably will suffer a decline in their standards of living.

Indonesian students protest outside the U.S. Embassy in Jakarta, Indonesia, against what they say were U.S. attempts to delay foreign loans to Indonesia. About 50 students participated in a peaceful protest where they accused the United States of conspiring to stall the disbursement of aid tied to a $43-billion IMF rescue package, prolonging the suffering of the nation's poor during the country's worst economic crisis in decades.

Wrap-up

1. If Indonesia had been unwilling to abandon its policies favoring firms linked to the Suharto family, should the IMF still have assisted the country?

2. If you were the official U.S. delegate to the IMF's board of governors, how would you have responded to Micron's complaint?

3. Some Koreans believe the IMF has taken unfair advantage of Korea's financial problems to force it to make concessions in its trade and foreign direct investment regulations. Do you agree with this complaint? Why or why not?

Sources: "Who Needs the IMF?" *Wall Street Journal*, February 3, 1998, p. A22; "Suharto Family Benefits in Peril from Spirit of Reform," *Financial Times*, January 16, 1998, p. 16; "Fingerprints of Korea's Cash Woes Cover Globe," *Wall Street Journal*, December 15, 1997, p. A16; "Micron Technology Opposes U.S. Role in Korean Bailout," *Wall Street Journal*, December 2, 1997, p. B6.

WELCOME TO GM POLAND

CHAPTER

Desmarais Is Tired of Being Dumped On

At first glance Desmarais & Frère, Ltd. (Desmarais), a Longueuil, Quebec, manufacturer founded in 1951, would appear to be in an enviable position. It employs as many as 400 workers during peak production periods and is Canada's largest producer of photo albums with self-adhesive pages. Its albums retail at $15 to $50 and are sold through mass marketers such as Wal-Mart, Zellers, and Metropolitan. In fact, 10 customers account for 70 percent of Desmarais's annual sales, keeping its marketing costs low. Further, all but one small domestic competitor has fallen by the wayside. Thus Desmarais captured 50 to 90 percent of the Canadian market for these photo albums during the 1970s and 1980s—an enviable market share level in any industry.

"...**plagued** by import **competition** from low-priced photo albums **produced** in Asia."

In truth, however, the firm's situation is not so rosy. For 30 years it has been plagued by import competition from low-priced photo albums produced in Asia. One response Desmarais considered to counter this threat was to focus on quality. Yet its major discount-chain customers pride themselves on providing the lowest possible prices for consumers and are willing to use whatever supplier is cheapest, whether foreign or domestic. Further, the photo albums are typically shrink-wrapped in

Formulation of National Trade Policies

8

OBJECTIVES

After studying this chapter, you should be able to:

> Present the major arguments in favor of and against governmental intervention in international trade.

> Identify the advantages and disadvantages of adopting an industrial policy.

> Analyze the role of domestic politics in formulating a country's international trade policies.

> Describe the major tools countries use to restrict trade.

> Specify the techniques countries use to promote international trade.

> Explain how countries protect themselves against unfair trade practices.

clear plastic, which makes it impossible for a retail customer to compare the quality of different producers' albums. Because albums are bought infrequently by the average consumer, developing brand loyalty among consumers is difficult as well.

Desmarais believed it was being victimized by a practice known as dumping. A firm engages in **dumping** when it sells its products outside its domestic market at prices below those it charges in its domestic market. Fortunately for Desmarais, Canadian law protects Canadian businesses from dumping. In 1975 Desmarais petitioned the Canadian Import Tribunal (CIT), which had jurisdiction over such cases, for relief from the low prices charged by Japanese and Korean photo album manufacturers. The CIT determined that firms from these two countries were indeed dumping their albums in Canada, thereby causing material injury to Desmarais and its smaller Canadian rivals. The CIT then imposed an **antidumping duty**—a tax on the dumped imported goods—on Korean and Japanese photo albums. This duty was equivalent to the difference between the lower price the Asians were charging in the Canadian market and the higher price they were charging in their home markets. In theory the duty would eliminate any price advantage the Asian producers gained from dumping.

However, the new duty did not solve Desmarais's problem because it applied only to Japanese and Korean producers. The production of photo albums simply shifted to other Asian locations, which were not covered by the duty. By 1984 Desmarais's share of the Canadian market had fallen to an all-time low of 50 percent. The foreign competition had hurt the company's profit margins, profits, and financial performance because it could not raise its prices to compensate for increases in its costs. In 1985 it filed a second successful complaint with the CIT against dumping by Hong Kong, South Korea, and the United States. (The United States entered the picture because Korean manufacturers were shipping the photo albums to the United States and then reexporting them from there to Canada.) Desmarais then filed dumping complaints against China in 1986, against Singapore, Malaysia, and Taiwan in 1987, and against Indonesia, Thailand, and the Philippines in 1991.

In all these cases the CIT or its successor, the Canadian International Trade Tribunal (CITT), determined that dumping had occurred. Desmarais's case was reviewed again in 1996, and the CITT found Desmarais still vulnerable to dumping by its foreign competitors. The antidumping duties imposed by the CIT and the CITT were not trivial. For example, as a result of the 1991 complaint (which is still in effect), antidumping duties were imposed ranging from 35.1 percent (on self-adhesive pages) to 78 percent (on photo albums with self-adhesive pages). Yet Desmarais cannot rest easy. For 30 years its home market has been targeted by Asian producers. As soon as the firm obtains relief from the CIT or the CITT, production of photo albums shifts to a country not covered by an antidumping duty. Desmarais has little reason to be optimistic that it will be able to raise its prices to recover its cost increases over the past three decades.[1]

In today's global economy firms must deal with both domestic and foreign competitors. The problem facing Desmarais & Frère, Ltd., exemplifies the plight of domestic manufacturers threatened by competition from low-priced foreign producers. And its reaction typifies that of similar firms: It asked its national government for protection against the foreigners. However, many other firms benefit from international trade, finding foreign markets a rich source of additional customers. Exports generate domestic jobs, so many national governments promote the success of their countries' domestic firms in international markets. In this chapter we discuss the development of national trade policies that protect domestic firms from foreign competition and help promote the country's exports. We also explore the rationale for these policies and the means by which governments implement them.

› RATIONALES FOR TRADE INTERVENTION

Politicians, economists, and businesspeople have been arguing for centuries over government policy toward international trade. Two principal issues have shaped the debate on appropriate trade policies:

1. Whether a national government should intervene to protect the country's domestic firms by taxing foreign goods entering the domestic market or constructing other barriers against imports
2. Whether a national government should directly help the country's domestic firms increase their foreign sales through export subsidies, government-to-government negotiations, and guaranteed loan programs

In North America the trade policy debate has recently focused on the issue of whether the government should promote "free" trade or "fair" trade. **Free trade** implies that the national government exerts minimal influence on the exporting and importing decisions of private firms and individuals. **Fair trade**, sometimes called **managed trade**, suggests that the national government should actively intervene to ensure that domestic firms' exports receive an equitable share of foreign markets and that imports are controlled to minimize losses of domestic jobs and market share in specific industries. Some fair traders also argue that the government should ensure a "level playing field" on which foreign and domestic firms can compete on equal terms. Although sounding reasonable, the "level playing field" argument is often used to justify policies that restrict foreign competition.

The outcome of the debate is critical to international managers. The policies individual countries adopt affect the size and profitability of foreign markets and investments, as well as the degree to which firms are threatened by foreign imports in their domestic markets. Governments worldwide are continually pressured by successful and efficient firms that produce goods for export, as well as by the firms' labor forces and the communities in which their factories are located, to adopt policies supporting freer trade. Companies such as Sony, Volkswagen, and Caterpillar gain increased sales and investment opportunities in foreign markets when international trade barriers are lowered. At the same time governments are petitioned by firms beleaguered by foreign competitors, as well as by these firms' labor forces and the communities in which their factories are located, to raise barriers to imported goods by adopting fair-trade policies. Companies such as Desmarais and French automakers Citroen and Peugeot gain increased sales opportunities in their domestic markets when international trade barriers exist.

The debate also affects consumers in every country, influencing the prices they pay for automobiles, clothing, televisions, and thousands of other goods. Barriers erected by the U.S. government against free trade in textiles and sugar, for example, raise the prices that parents must pay to clothe and feed their children.

> Free trade opens new markets for efficient producers and improves employment opportunities for workers like Karla Valdez, who helps assemble Ford autos in Hermosillo, Mexico.

Industry-Level Arguments

The argument for free trade follows Adam Smith's analysis outlined in Chapter 5: Voluntary exchange makes both parties to the transaction better off and allocates resources to their highest valued use. In Smith's view the welfare of a country and its citizens is best promoted by allowing self-interested individuals, regardless of where they reside, to exchange goods, services, and assets as they see fit. However, many businesspeople, politicians, and policy makers believe that, under certain circumstances, deviations from free trade are appropriate. In this section we review the primary arguments against free trade and for government intervention, and we discuss trade policies that focus on the needs of individual industries. In the next section we explore broader, national-level policies.

The National Defense Argument. National defense has often been used as a reason to support governmental protection of specific industries. Because world events can suddenly turn hostile to a country's interests, the **national defense argument** holds that a country must be self-sufficient in critical raw materials, machinery, and technology or else be vulnerable to foreign threats. For example, the vulnerability of Japan's supply lines was demonstrated by the extensive damage done to its merchant marine fleet by Allied submarines during World War II. After the war Japan banned the importation of rice as a means of promoting domestic self-sufficiency in the country's dietary staple. Similarly, the United States, to retain shipbuilding skills and expertise within the country in case of war, has developed numerous programs to support its domestic shipbuilding industry. For example, all U.S. naval vessels must be built in U.S. shipyards, and ocean transportation between U.S. ports must be conducted by U.S.-built ships. Many of the 120,000 jobs in the U.S. shipbuilding industry would be lost without these federal protections because U.S. shipyards are not competitive with those of Japan, Korea, Norway, Denmark, or Germany. One federal study found that the average bid by U.S. shipyards on commercial contracts was 97 percent higher than the lowest foreign bid.[2]

The national defense argument appeals to the general public, which is concerned that its country will be pushed around by other countries that control critical resources. Many special-interest groups have used this politically appealing argument to protect their industries from foreign competition. For example, the U.S. mohair industry produces wool that was once used in military uniforms. It benefited from federal subsidies after passage of the 1954 National Wool Act, which protected the industry purportedly in the country's strategic interest. Even though the military had long since replaced mohair garments with synthetic ones, the subsidy remained in effect for over 40 years. Other U.S. industries receiving favorable treatment for national defense reasons include steel, electronics, machine tools, and the merchant marine.[3]

The Infant Industry Argument. Alexander Hamilton, the first U.S. secretary of the treasury, articulated the **infant industry argument** in 1791. Hamilton believed that the newly independent country's infant manufacturing sector possessed a comparative advantage that would ultimately allow it to thrive in international markets. However, he feared that the young nation's manufacturers would not survive their infancy and adolescence because of fierce competition from more mature European firms. Hamilton thus fought for the imposition of tariffs on numerous imported manufactured goods to give U.S. firms temporary protection from foreign competition until they could fully establish themselves. His philosophy has been adopted by countries worldwide. Japan, for example, has been particularly effective in nurturing its domestic industries. Since the end of World War II, Japan has developed thriving metal fabrication industries (iron and steel, aluminum, copper, and zinc) despite its lack of significant natural resources. Japan has done this by eliminating tariffs on imports of raw ores and ore concentrates while imposing high tariffs on processed and fabricated metals. For example, in 1970 no tariff was imposed on copper ore imported in Japan, but fabricated copper products bore tariffs as high as 22 percent. As its metal fabrication industry matured, Japan reduced the level of import protection. Today its tariffs on copper products are negligible.[4]

Governmental nurturing of domestic industries that will ultimately have a comparative advantage can be a powerful economic development strategy, as Japan's postwar economic success indicates. However, determining which industries deserve infant industry protection is often done on a political, rather than an economic, basis. Firms, workers, and shareholders are not shy about using the infant industry argument to bolster support for import protection or export subsidies for their industries. Moreover, once an industry is granted protection, it may be reluctant to give the protection up. Many infant industries end up being protected well into their old age.

Maintenance of Existing Jobs. Well-established firms and their workers, particularly in high-wage countries, are often threatened by imports from low-wage countries, as shown in the case of Desmarais. To maintain existing employment levels, firms and workers often petition their governments for relief from foreign competition. Government officials, eager to avoid the human and economic misery inflicted on workers and communities when factories are shut down, tend to lend a sympathetic ear to such pleas. Assistance may come in the form of tariffs, quotas, or other barriers that we discuss in more detail in the next section. The assistance may be temporary, as was the case when Harley-Davidson received tariff protection from Japanese imports for five years in the mid-1980s to allow the firm to revamp its operations and restore its image in the marketplace. Conversely, the assistance may be long lived, as in the case of governmental protection of the U.S. commercial shipbuilding industry, which has extended that industry's life by over 30 years.

Strategic Trade Theory.   When firms and labor union officials plead for government intervention to help them compete internationally, their efforts are usually criticized by economists, who claim that such intervention ultimately harms the economy. The economists base that claim on the theoretical predictions of the classical trade theories—absolute advantage and comparative advantage—discussed in Chapter 5. These trade theories, however, assume that firms operate in perfectly competitive markets of the sort that exist only in economics textbooks. The theories also assume that each country's consumers are able to buy goods and services at the lowest possible prices from the world's most efficient producers. According to the classical theories, any governmental intervention that denies consumers these buying opportunities will make the country as a whole worse off, although it could make certain groups within the society better off.

In the early 1980s, however, new models of international trade—known collectively as **strategic trade theory**—were developed. These models provide a new theoretical justification for government trade intervention, thereby supporting firms' requests for protection. Strategic trade theory makes very different assumptions about the industry environment in which firms operate than do the classical theories. Strategic trade theory applies to those industries capable of supporting only a few firms worldwide, perhaps because of high product development costs or strong experience curve effects. A firm can earn monopoly profits if it can succeed in becoming one of the few firms in such a highly concentrated industry. Strategic trade theory suggests that a national government can make its country better off if it adopts trade policies that improve the competitiveness of its domestic firms in such oligopolistic industries.

For example, consider the potential market for a new nuclear power plant design, one that could safely and cheaply supply electrical energy. Assume that because of economies of scale, the market will be extremely profitable if one—and only one—firm decides to enter it. Further assume that only two firms, France's Framatome and Japan's Mitsubishi, have the engineering talent and financial resources to develop the new plant design and that both are equally capable of successfully completing the project. Figure 8.1 shows the payoff matrix for the two

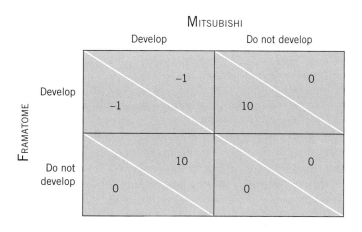

FIGURE 8.1

Payoff Matrix: Profits from Developing a Nuclear Power Plant Design (in billions of dollars)

firms. If Mitsubishi decides to develop the plant design and Framatome decides not to (see the lower left-hand corner), Mitsubishi profits by $10 billion, while Framatome makes nothing. If Framatome decides to develop the plant design and Mitsubishi does not, Framatome profits by $10 billion, while Mitsubishi makes nothing (see the upper right-hand corner). If neither firm chooses to develop the design, they both make nothing (see the lower right-hand corner). If both decide to develop the design, both will lose $1 billion because the market is too small to be profitable for both of them. Neither firm has a strategy that it should follow regardless of what its rival does.

Now suppose the French government learns of the large profits that one of its country's firms could earn if that firm were the sole developer of the new plant design. If France were to offer Framatome a subsidy of $2 billion to develop the new nuclear technology, the payoff matrix would change to that shown in Figure 8.2. Because of the subsidy Framatome's payoff is increased by $2 billion if and only if it develops the technology (see the first row). With the subsidy Framatome will develop the technology regardless of what Mitsubishi does because Framatome makes more money by developing than by not developing. If Mitsubishi chooses to develop, Framatome makes nothing if it does not develop and $1 billion if it does develop. If Mitsubishi does not develop, Framatome makes nothing if it does not develop and $12 billion if it does develop. Thus Framatome will always choose to develop. But if Mitsubishi knows Framatome will always choose to develop, then the best strategy for Mitsubishi is not to develop.

What has the French government accomplished with its $2 billion subsidy?

1. It has induced Framatome to develop the new nuclear power plant technology.

2. It has induced the Japanese firm to stay out of the market.

3. It has succeeded in allowing a French firm to make a $12 billion profit at a cost to French taxpayers of only $2 billion.

By adopting a strategic trade policy in a market where monopoly profits are available, the French government has made French residents as a group better off by $10 billion ($12 billion in profits minus $2 billion in subsidies).

However, strategic trade theory applies only to markets that are incapable of supporting more than a handful of firms on a worldwide basis. (One industry that may meet the requirements of strategic trade theory is the commercial aircraft industry; see "Venturing Abroad.") Most global industries are more competitive than this. A country's wholesale adoption of strategic trade policies to cover a broad group of industries may actually reduce the country's overall international competitiveness because favoring certain industries inevitably hurts others. For example, if the French government chooses to subsidize the nuclear power industry, the demand for and the salaries paid to the mechanical engineers, computer program-

FIGURE 8.2

Payoff Matrix: Profits Resulting from a $2 Billion Subsidy to Framatome (in billions of dollars)

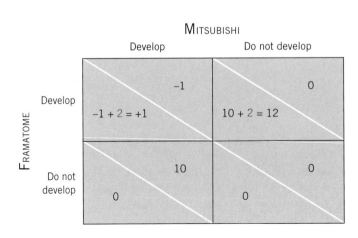

VENTURING *Abroad*

JUMBO BATTLE OVER JUMBO JETS

A real-world example of strategic trade theory dominated the business press in 2000 in reports about Airbus's plans to build a superjumbo jet. Airbus executives hope this aircraft will destroy the lucrative monopoly that the Boeing 747 now holds in the jumbo jet market.

Since its initial commercial flight in 1969, the Boeing 747 has benefited from its status as the world's largest commercial aircraft. Its costs per seat mile are lower than that of any other aircraft available, largely because the 747 can seat as many as 495 people. Although its low costs are attractive on transatlantic and transcontinental routes, they are of particular importance in charter, transpacific, and freighter operations. Boeing's monopoly in the jumbo jet market confers advantages over Airbus in selling smaller aircraft as well. Spare parts can often be used for different models of aircraft produced by the same manufacturer, which sometimes is enough of an advantage to sway an airline to purchase a Boeing product over the comparable one manufactured by Airbus.

Airbus has targeted the 747 for years. Its engineers have drawn up preliminary plans for a 650-seat aircraft, currently labeled the A380, which would dwarf the Boeing product. Airbus believes the A380's costs per seat mile will be 17 percent less than those of the 747. However, R&D costs for the A380 are estimated to run between $12 billion and $16 billion. To help finance these upfront costs, Airbus is seeking $3.5 billion in low-cost loans from the German, French, and British governments. (Airbus's primary investors are four companies from France, Germany, Spain, and the United Kingdom.) Boeing officials believe these loans to Airbus are nothing more than government subsidies and should be barred under international trade law. Moreover, Boeing believes that Airbus officials are vastly overestimating the size of the market. Airbus asserts the market for superjumbo jets will reach 1,500 in the next 20 years, and thus the A380 has a bright future. Boeing claims that the true market is only one-quarter to one-third of that estimate, and thus the A380 will be a financial disaster. Once production starts, however, Boeing fears that the government loans will be forgiven. Worse, the A380 would then

continue in production, dragging down the profitability of Boeing's 747 operations.

The European Union (EU) and the United States have fought over this issue before. The U.S. government has argued that previous European loans to Airbus have been written off as worthless, thereby providing the airframe manufacturer with illegal subsidies. For example, in early 1999 the German Finance Ministry relieved DaimlerChrysler Aerospace AG of an obligation to repay $750 million in loans to design Airbus's A330 and A340 jets. EU officials respond that Boeing's commercial aircraft division has benefited from hidden subsidies from the U.S. Defense Department. EU officials believe that Boeing has been able to develop new aircraft technologies by winning U.S. Defense Department contracts that are limited to U.S. firms. Having acquired that technology from its defense contracts, Boeing then can transfer the technology to its commercial aircraft operations.

A 1992 agreement between the EU and the United States led to a truce in this verbal war. That accord limited the amount of indirect subsidies the United States could grant Boeing through military contracts, while European governments are allowed to provide limited loans to Airbus for development of new aircraft. However, this agreement predates the World Trade Organization (WTO) and the new obligations imposed on members of that organization (see the next chapter for a full discussion of the WTO). As Airbus proceeds with the A380, the U.S. government will undoubtedly file a complaint with the WTO, and the WTO will face its most important and politically tricky challenge to date.

Sources: "Airbus Wins First Order for Super Jumbo from Emirates," *Financial Times*, May 2, 2000, p. 1; "US Critical of UK Aid to Airbus Super Jumbo Project," *Financial Times*, March 14, 2000, p. 1; "UK Backing for Airbus 'Superjumbo,'" *Financial Times*, March 14, 2000, p. 9; "Loan Sparks US Charge of Illegal Subsidy," *Financial Times*, March 14, 2000, p. 9; "U.S. Questions Need for Loans by Britain to British Aerospace," *Wall Street Journal*, March 14, 2000, p A27; "U.S. Delay on Airbus Challenge Concerns Boeing," *Wall Street Journal*, January 24, 2000, p. A3.

mers, and systems analysts needed by the nuclear power industry will rise, thereby reducing the international competitiveness of other French industries requiring such skilled personnel. Further, the benefit of the subsidy could be neutralized if another country adopts a similar strategy. If Japan responded to France's $2 billion subsidy by giving a $3 billion subsidy to Mitsubishi, the payoff matrix would change: Mitsubishi would be encouraged to develop the power plant as well. Any anticipated monopoly profits might be dissipated if the two countries engaged in an all-out subsidy war.

National Trade Policies

The policies just discussed address the needs of individual industries. A national government also may develop trade policies that begin by taking an economy-wide perspective. After assessing the needs of the national economy, the government then adopts industry-by-industry policies to promote the country's overall economic agenda.

Economic Development Programs.   An important policy goal of many governments, particularly those of developing countries, is economic development. International commerce can play a major role in economic development programs. Countries that depend on a single export often choose to diversify their economies to reduce the impact of, say, a bad harvest or falling prices for the dominant export. For example, the West African country of Ghana, which once depended heavily on cocoa, began an industrialization program to protect itself from fluctuations in cocoa prices. Kuwait chose to diversify away from its heavy dependency on oil sales, electing to do so through investment rather than trade. The country used cash from its oil revenues to build up its investment portfolio, a strategy so successful that much of Kuwait's resistance to the 1990 Iraqi invasion was financed by its overseas investments.

As discussed in Chapter 2, some countries, such as Japan, Korea, and Taiwan, based their post-World War II economic development on heavy reliance on exports. According to this **export promotion strategy**, a country encourages firms to compete in foreign markets by harnessing some advantage the country possesses, such as low labor costs. Other countries, such as Australia, Argentina, India, and Brazil, adopted an **import substitution strategy** after World War II; such a strategy encourages the growth of domestic manufacturing industries by erecting high barriers to imported goods. Many multinational corporations (MNCs) responded by locating production facilities within these countries to avoid the costs resulting from the high barriers. In general the export promotion strategy has been more successful than the import substitution strategy, as Chapter 2 indicated.

Industrial Policy.   In many countries the government plays an active role in managing the national economy. Often an important element of this task is determining which industries should receive favorable governmental treatment. Bureaucrats within Japan's Ministry of International Trade and Industry (MITI), for example, identify emerging technologies and products, and through subsidies, public statements, and behind-the-scenes maneuvering, encourage Japanese firms to enter those markets. During the 1950s and 1960s MITI actively diverted scarce credit and foreign exchange from low-value-added, labor-intensive industries such as textiles into high-value-added, capital-intensive heavy industries such as steel and automobiles. During the 1970s and 1980s MITI targeted industries with high growth potential, such as semiconductors, aerospace, biotechnology, and ceramics. The Korean government patterned its economic development strategies after the successful Japanese model.

Because of the postwar economic successes of Japan and Korea, the governments of most other Quad countries face the major issue of whether to adopt **industrial policy**, by which the national government identifies key domestic industries critical to the country's future economic growth and then formulates programs that promote their competitiveness. Ideally, industrial policy assists a country's firms in capturing large shares of important, growing global markets, as MITI has done for Japanese MNCs.

Many experts, however, do not view industrial policy as a panacea for improving the global competitiveness of a country's firms. They argue that government bureaucrats cannot perfectly identify the right industries to favor under such a policy. As an example, they cite France, where postwar industrial policies targeting automobiles, computers, military and commercial aircraft, and telecommunications created some spectacularly unprofitable enterprises that required large government subsidies. These industries became a drag on the French economy rather than a generator of new wealth. Even Japan has not been infallible. During the early 1980s MITI bureaucrats encouraged domestic consumer electronics firms to develop high-definition television (HDTV) that relied on Japan's lead in analog-based TV technology. Although HDTV is viewed as the wave of the future, the technical transmission standards for HDTV adopted by U.S. and European regulators rely on more sophisticated digital technology being developed by Western firms rather than the dated analog technology imposed on Japanese firms by MITI. Consequently, the multibillion-dollar investment of the leading Japanese consumer electronics firms in analog-based HDTV turned out to be a total loss.

Opponents of industrial policy also fear that the choice of industries to receive governmental largesse will depend on the domestic political clout of those industries, rather than on their potential international competitiveness. Instead of selecting future winners in the international marketplace, opponents say, industrial policy will become a more sophisticated-sounding version of pork barrel politics.

At the heart of the industrial policy debate is the question of what is the proper role of government in a market economy. Not surprisingly, in the United States recent Republican administrations have rejected formally adopting an industrial policy, on the grounds that the government should limit its role in the economy.[5] Conversely, the Clinton administration believed that improving the global competitiveness of the country's firms was too important to be left to the private sector. To further this belief, during its first term the Clinton administration designated five emerging technologies that would receive increased federal R&D support: genetics, health care information systems, electronics, automobiles and highway systems, and computer software.[6]

Public Choice Analysis.   Although many arguments favoring governmental trade intervention are couched in terms of national interest, such intervention typically helps some special-interest groups but invariably hurts other domestic interests and the general public. For example, the CIT's decision to impose antidumping duties helped Desmarais and its Quebec workforce. However, it reduced the work available to dockworkers who unload foreign cargos in British Columbia's Port of Vancouver and raised the prices that Canadian consumers had to pay for photo albums.

Why do national governments adopt public policies that hinder international business and hurt their own citizenry overall, even though the policies may benefit small groups within their societies? According to **public choice analysis**, a branch of economics that analyzes public decision making, the special interest will often dominate the general interest on any given issue for a simple reason: Special-interest groups are willing to work harder for the passage of laws favorable to their interests than the general public is willing to work for the defeat of laws unfavorable to its interest. For example, under the 1920 Jones Act, the United States restricts foreign ships from providing transportation services between U.S. ports. This restriction is supported by owners of U.S. oceangoing vessels, who gain increased profits estimated at $630 million per year. However, the Jones Act is also estimated to increase the transportation costs consumers pay by $10.5 billion annually, or $40 per person. Further, like other restrictions on free trade, the Jones Act has had unintended consequences, as Map 8.1 suggests.

Public choice analysis suggests that few consumers will be motivated to learn how the Jones Act impacts them or to write or call their elected officials to save a trivial sum like $40. However, the special interests, such as shipowners and mem-

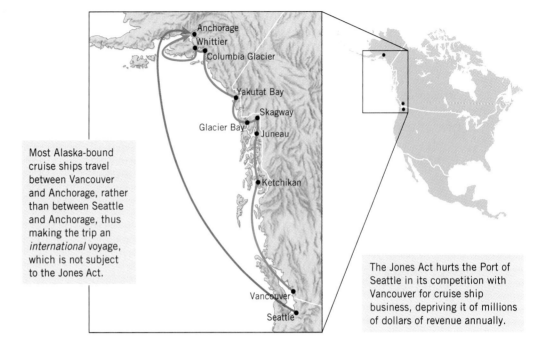

Most Alaska-bound cruise ships travel between Vancouver and Anchorage, rather than between Seattle and Anchorage, thus making the trip an *international* voyage, which is not subject to the Jones Act.

The Jones Act hurts the Port of Seattle in its competition with Vancouver for cruise ship business, depriving it of millions of dollars of revenue annually.

bers of U.S. maritime unions, are motivated to know all the ins and outs of the Jones Act and to protect it from repeal because what they gain makes it worth their while to do so. As a result, members of Congress constantly hear from special-interest groups about the importance of preserving the Jones Act, while the average consumer is silent on the issue.[7] Knowing that they will be harmed by the special-interest groups and will not be rewarded by the general public if they repeal the Jones Act, members of Congress will rationally vote with the special interests on this issue.

According to public choice analysis, domestic trade policies that affect international business stem not from some grandiose vision of a country's international responsibilities but rather from the mundane interaction of politicians trying to get elected. And who elects the politicians? The people in their legislative districts. Hence former Speaker of the House of Representatives Tip O'Neill's brilliant insight: "All politics is local." For example, Japan's unwillingness to open its markets to imported rice stems from the need of Japan's ruling party in parliament to retain the votes of local farmers. The impact of this policy on Texas rice farmers, the Port of Houston, or the world economy is of little concern to the domestic politicians.

Savvy international businesspeople recognize these political realities. Often a foreign firm needs to find domestic political allies to run interference for it. For example, Nissan and Toyota received much criticism for the size of their exports to the U.S. market, so in the 1980s they began building new factories in the United States. The congressional delegations of Indiana, West Virginia, Tennessee, and Kentucky, where these factories are located, can now be expected to support the firms legislatively to protect the jobs of their constituents working for the Japanese firms. Clearly, Toyota and Nissan understand that "all politics is local."

› BARRIERS TO INTERNATIONAL TRADE

We have seen that domestic politics often causes countries to try to protect their domestic firms from foreign competitors by erecting barriers to trade. Such forms of government intervention can be divided into two categories: tariffs and nontariff barriers. Countries have been erecting trade barriers since the creation of the modern nation-state in the sixteenth century in hopes of increasing national income, promoting economic growth, and/or raising their citizens' standard of living. Sometimes, as you just read, national trade policies that benefit special-interest groups are adopted at the expense of the general public or society at large.

Tariffs

A **tariff** is a tax placed on a good that is traded internationally. Some tariffs are levied on goods as they leave the country (an **export tariff**) or as they pass through one country bound for another (a **transit tariff**). Most, however, are collected on imported goods (an **import tariff**). Three forms of import tariffs exist:

1. An **ad valorem tariff** is assessed as a percentage of the market value of the imported good. For example, in Table 8.1 (which is drawn from the existing U.S. tariff code) a 2.1 percent ad valorem tariff is levied against imported pineapples preserved by sugar.

2. A **specific tariff** is assessed as a specific dollar amount per unit of weight or other standard measure. As Table 8.1 shows, imported citrus fruit preserved by sugar bears a specific tariff of 6 cents per kilogram.

3. A **compound tariff** has both an ad valorem component and a specific component. Imported cherries preserved in sugar are levied a 6.4 percent ad valorem tariff and a 9.9 cents per kilogram specific tariff.

In practice most tariffs imposed by developed countries are ad valorem. The tariff applies to the product's value, which is typically the sales price at which the product enters the country. For example, suppose Kmart buys a large shipment of canned pineapples preserved by sugar from a Philippine food processor at $400 a ton. When the pineapples are delivered to the Port of Los Angeles, Kmart will have to pay the U.S. Customs Service a duty of 2.1 percent of $400, or $8.40, for each ton it imports, a cost Kmart will pass on to its customers.

Most countries have adopted a detailed classification scheme for imported goods called the **harmonized tariff schedule (HTS)**. Because of its complexity, the HTS can sometimes be difficult to use. The first problem facing an importer is anticipating what customs officials will decide is the appropriate tariff classification for an imported good. For example, leather ski gloves imported into the United States are

HEADING/ SUBHEADING	STAT. SUFFIX	ARTICLE DESCRIPTION	UNITS OF QUANTITY	RATES OF DUTY
2006.00		Fruit, nuts, fruit peel and other parts of plants, preserved by sugar (drained, glacé or crystallized):		
2006.00.20	00	Cherries	kg	9.9¢/kg + 6.4%
2006.00.30	00	Ginger root	kg	2.4%
2006.00.40	00	Pineapples	kg	2.1%
		Other, including mixtures:		
2006.00.50	00	Mixtures	kg	16%
2006.00.60	00	Citrus fruit; peel of citrus or other fruit	kg	6¢/kg
2006.00.70	00	Other fruit and nuts	kg	8%
2006.00.90	00	Other	kg	16%

TABLE 8.1

A Section of the Harmonized Tariff Schedule of the United States

Source: U.S. International Trade Commission, *Harmonized Tariff Schedule of the United States* (Washington, D.C.: ITC Trade Data Base as of October 12, 2000).

Michele R. Markowitz, Esquire
Sharretts, Paley, Carter & Blauvelt, P.C.
67 Broad Street
New York, New York 10004

Dear Ms. Markowitz:

This letter is in response to your request of July 25, 1995, on behalf of your client, Dan Dee, concerning the classification of items identified as "Reindeer Caps" imported from China. Two sample caps were submitted with your request. . . .

FACTS: The sample articles identified by item nos. X53081 and X53082 are hats/caps composed of plush, knit, man-made fibers. Extending from the top of each cap is a pair of antlers, within which are contained electrical wires and light emitting diodes (LEDs). A textile patch on the front of each cap displays the words "PRESS HERE." When pressed, a switch activates a battery powered module sewn into the interior top of each cap. The device causes the LEDs to flash and produces the sounds of Christmas carols and the words "Merry Christmas" or "Happy New Year." . . . The items are said to be designed, bought, sold, advertised, marketed, and primarily used as festive articles.

ISSUE: Whether the items are classified in heading 9505, HTSUS, as festive articles; in heading 9503, HTSUS, as other toys; or in heading 6505, HTSUS, as hats and other headgear.

LAW AND ANALYSIS:
* * *

In general, merchandise is classifiable in heading 9505, HTSUS, as a festive article when the article, as a whole: 1. Is of nondurable material or, generally, is not purchased because of its extreme worth, or intrinsic value; 2. Functions primarily as a decoration (e.g., its primary function is not utilitarian); and 3. Is traditionally associated or used with a particular festival (e.g., stockings and tree ornaments for Christmas, decorative eggs for Easter).

Although we find the reindeer hats to be made of durable material, they are not likely to be purchased for their extreme worth or value. As is the case with hats in general, these items are both decorative and utilitarian and neither function clearly predominates. In addition to decorating the head in a humorous fashion, the hats are sturdy and warm. . . . Since the hats do not function primarily as decorations, they do not satisfy the second criterion.

Upon examination of the third criterion, we do not find reindeer or reindeer hats to be traditionally associated or used with a particular festival. . . . Reindeer are associated with cold climates and snow-filled regions of the world where they are often domesticated, trained to pull sleds, raced, hunted, eaten, etc. North American reindeer (caribou) are occasionally associated with controversy due to the effects of wolf populations on their numbers. We do not find that the reindeer hats would only be worn during the Christmas/New Year holidays. It is not uncommon to see hats of a similar nature being worn to keep the head warm, get attention, and provoke responses throughout the colder months at ski slopes, skating rinks, sports events, etc.
* * *

We next consider your alternative assertion that the hats are toys. . . . Customs will classify [an item as] a stuffed toy representing an animal or non-human creature . . . if the toy is a reasonably full-figured depiction of the animal's or creature's anatomy that the toy seeks to represent. The representation must be constructed in a sculpted, three dimensional form. Since the reindeer hats represent only the head or part of the head of a reindeer, they are not classifiable as stuffed toy animals.

The American College Dictionary (1970) defines "hat" in pertinent part as "1. a shaped covering for the head, usually with a crown and a brim, worn outdoors." Although this definition comfortably fits the reindeer hats, it does little to indicate whether or not the goods are classifiable as toy hats. . . . As previously noted, the reindeer hats are not only amusing but are also fully functional. Not all merchandise that amuses is properly classified in a toy provision and we find that the play value of the reindeer hats is secondary to their utilitarian purpose. . . .

HOLDING: The "Reindeer Caps," identified by item nos. X53081 and X53082, are properly classified in subheading 6505.90.6090, HTSUSA, textile category 659, the provision for "hats and other headgear, knitted or crocheted, or made up from lace, felt or other textile fabric . . ." The applicable duty rate is 37.7 cents per kilogram plus 13.4 percent ad valorem.

Sincerely,

John Durant
Director, Tariff Appeals Division

FIGURE 8.3   **U.S. Customs Service Letter to Dan Dee, Inc.**

assessed a 5.5 percent ad valorem tariff, but if the gloves are specifically designed for cross-country skiing, then the ad valorem tariff is only 3.5 percent.

An importer's expected profit margin on a transaction can shrink or disappear if a customs official subjects the imported good to a higher tariff rate than the importer expected. To reduce this risk, U.S. importers can request an advance tariff classification on prospective importations by writing the U.S. Customs Service. Figure 8.3 reproduces parts of a letter from the Customs Service in response to such a request from a small importer, Dan Dee, which wants to import "Reindeer Caps" from China. These caps come with a full set of fabric antlers; when the proper button is pushed, lights sewn into the antlers flash, Christmas music plays, and a voice shouts "Merry Christmas." Dan Dee wanted to know whether this item would be classified as a toy, a hat, or a festive article. After pondering the question for four months, customs officials determined that the item was indeed a hat for reasons stated in the letter. Discreet as good civil servants should be, the officials made no comment about the good taste or sobriety of the people who would purchase and wear these caps. Based on this written decision of the Customs Service, Dan Dee can import its goods with full knowledge of their landed cost.

Tariffs historically have been imposed for two reasons:

1. Tariffs raise revenue for the national government. As Figure 8.4 shows, tariff revenues account for a significant portion of government revenues of developing countries such as Lesotho and Sierra Leone. Such countries depend heavily on subsistence agriculture and so find it difficult to collect significant tax revenues from domestic sources. Customs duties, however, are reasonably easy to collect. Further, imported goods tend to be purchased by the wealthier members of society, so heavy reliance on import tariffs adds progressivity to the domestic tax system. Conversely, taxes on international trade form a relatively small percentage of government revenues in more developed countries that have broader tax bases such as Thailand, Egypt, and Mexico. Of course, people try to avoid paying tariffs when they can, as "Bringing the World into Focus" indicates.

2. A tariff acts as a trade barrier. Because tariffs raise the prices paid by domestic consumers for foreign goods, they increase the demand for domestically produced substitute goods.

Tariffs affect both domestic and foreign special-interest groups. For example, suppose the U.S. government imposes a $2,000 specific tariff on imported minivans.

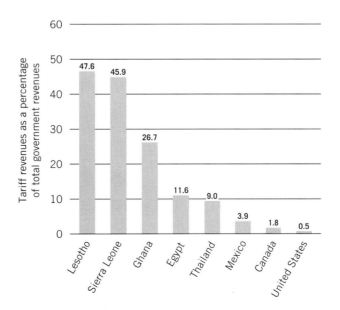

FIGURE 8.4

Tariff Revenues as a Percentage of Total Government Revenues for Selected Countries, 1999

Bringing the World into FOCUS

A LOOPHOLE BIG ENOUGH TO DRIVE THROUGH

Few people like to pay taxes, and Poles are no exception. Polish tariffs on imported automobiles are sky-high: The duty is $1,900 or 33 percent of the vehicle's value—whichever is higher. In addition, Poland levies a 22 percent value-added tax on the vehicles.

However, the tariffs on automobile parts are much lower, so a common sight at border crossings between Germany and Poland is late-model cars, minus their engines, tires, and other easily removable parts, being towed on open trailers. Ten or 15 places back in the customs queue is the vehicle's engine, being transported by a friend of the owner of the chassis up ahead. The remaining parts will be found even further back in the line in a third vehicle. German officials do not care, as long as the vehicles are not stolen. Polish customs officials understand what is going on but are powerless to do anything about it as long as the vehicles are for personal use. Complains one government official, "Sometimes a Pole would tell me he just picked up a body of a new car, as if it fell out of the sky. Can I believe that?"

The Polish customs service can still levy taxes on the automobile parts, but these are about half of the tariffs paid for a fully-assembled vehicle. For many Poles, this is a sufficient savings to go through the hassle of disassembling their newly purchased vehicles on the German side of the border and reassembling them on the Polish side.

Source: "Car Importers Take Apart Customs Regulations," *Financial Times*, June 29/30, 1996, p. 2.

Foreign producers of minivans will be forced to raise their U.S. prices, thereby reducing their U.S. sales. However, foreign-made minivans and U.S.-made minivans are substitute goods. Thus the higher prices of foreign minivans will increase the demand for U.S.-made minivans. This is shown in Figure 8.5 by the shift in the demand for U.S.-made minivans from D to D_1, resulting in more domestic vehicles being sold at higher prices. The $2,000 specific tariff creates both gainers and losers. Gainers include GM, Ford, and Chrysler dealerships selling domestic minivans; suppliers to domestic producers; workers at domestic GM, Ford, and Chrysler minivan assembly plants; and the communities in which domestic minivan factories are located. Domestic consumers are losers because they pay higher prices for both

FIGURE 8.5

Impact of an Import Tariff on Demand for U.S.-Made Minivans

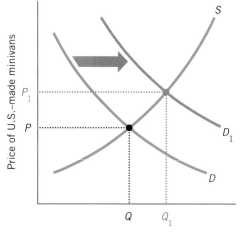

domestic and foreign minivans. Foreign producers also lose, as do people and firms that depend on them, including Toyota and Mazda dealerships in the United States, workers and suppliers in Japan, and communities in Japan in which the minivans are manufactured.

Nontariff Barriers

Nontariff barriers are the second category of governmental controls on international trade. Any government regulation, policy, or procedure other than a tariff that has the effect of impeding international trade may be labeled a **nontariff barrier (NTB)**. In this section we discuss three kinds of NTBs: quotas, numerical export controls, and other nontariff barriers.

Quotas.   Countries may restrain international trade by imposing quotas. A **quota** is a numerical limit on the quantity of a good that may be imported into a country during some time period, such as a year. Quotas have traditionally been used to protect politically powerful industries, such as agriculture, automobiles, and textiles, from the threat of competition, as in the case of Japan's and the Philippines' use of quotas to limit imports of rice. However, as a result of trade agreements such as the Uruguay Round (see Chapter 9), many countries have replaced quotas with tariff rate quotas. A **tariff rate quota** (TRQ) imposes a low tariff rate on a limited amount of imports of a specific good; above that threshold a TRQ imposes a prohibitively high tariff rate on the good. This situation is depicted in Figure 8.6, where the first 100,000 widgets imported into a country are subjected to a low tariff rate, T_L; all widgets after the first 100,000 are subjected to the high tariff rate, T_H. Canada, for example, has substituted a tariff rate quota for its previous quotas on imports of eggs, dairy products, and poultry. Imports of these goods above the threshold may carry tariffs as high as 350 percent. In the short run such high tariffs have the same effect as a quota: They normally limit imports of a good to the threshold level. However, at least in concept, exporters are allowed to increase their sales to the country as long as they are willing to pay the high tariff. And because tariffs are more visible than quotas, most experts believe that converting quotas to tariff rate quotas makes it easier to eliminate this type of trade barrier over time through trade negotiations.

A quota or tariff rate quota helps domestic producers of the good in question but invariably hurts domestic consumers. Consider, for example, the impact on the U.S. market of the tariff rate quota on sugar. The U.S. government effectively

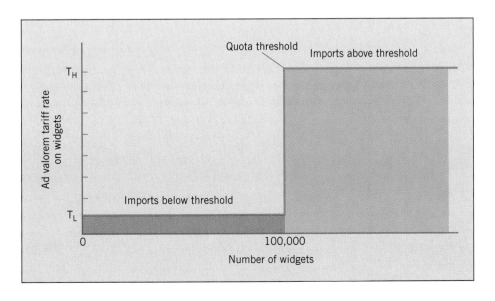

FIGURE 8.6

Tariff Rate Quota on Widgets
A tariff rate quota imposes high tariff rates on imports above the threshold level.

› A complex web of quotas imposed by developed countries restricts the ability of this Chinese factory to sell its cotton internationally.

restricts the amount of foreign sugar that can be imported to about 2 million tons annually by slapping a 17¢ specific tariff on each pound of sugar imported into the United States above that amount. (Domestic producers normally produce about 8 million tons per year.) The price of sugar is higher in the United States than elsewhere in the world because the tariff rate quota prevents more imports from flowing into the U.S. market to equalize the prices. In April 2001, for example, the U.S. price for sugar was 21¢ per pound, while the world price was only 9¢ per pound.

Who gains from the tariff rate quota? Domestic sugar producers, such as sugarcane growers in Louisiana and sugar beet growers in North Dakota, benefit because domestic production is increased and the price that domestic suppliers receive rises. Producers of sugar substitutes, such as Archer Daniels Midland, the largest domestic producer of corn-based fructose sweeteners, and Corn Belt farmers who supply the corn for the fructose sweeteners also gain as manufacturers of sweetened products substitute lower-cost fructose sweeteners for sugar. Losers from the policy include domestic candy manufacturers and soft-drink makers, which must pay higher prices for sugar, as well as U.S. consumers, who pay a higher price—an estimated $1.9 billion a year—for all goods containing sugar. U.S. firms, such as San Francisco's Ghiardelli Chocolate Company (premium chocolates) or Corsicana, Texas's Collin Street Bakery (fruitcakes), that export goods with high sugar content become less competitive in world markets because the sugar quota increases the cost of their ingredients.

Anyone with the right to import sugar into the United States within the 2-million-ton threshold also gains because the holder of such a right can buy sugar at the lower world price and resell it in the United States at the higher U.S. price. For this reason, the U.S. government uses such rights as instruments of foreign policy and foreign aid. Countries that are politically sympathetic to the United States or that the United States is trying to woo often receive generous rights, while countries hostile to the United States find their rights reduced or eliminated. The chapter's closing case, "The Great Quota Hustle," similarly describes the unintended consequences of the U.S. quotas imposed on textile imports.

Numerical Export Controls.   A country also may impose quantitative barriers to trade in the form of numerical limits on the amount of a good it will export. A **voluntary export restraint (VER)** is a promise by a country to limit its exports of a good to another country to a prespecified amount or percentage of the affected market. Often this is done to resolve or avoid trade conflicts with an otherwise friendly trade partner. For example, since 1982 the United States and Canada have been squabbling over whether Canada has been subsidizing its lumber industry by charging low stumpage fees (rights to harvest timber) in government-owned forests. To end the conflict, Canada agreed in 1996 to adopt a VER, limiting its annual exports to the United States of softwood lumber from Alberta, British Columbia, Ontario, and Quebec to 14.7 billion board feet. Canada also pledged to levy a substantial tax on any exports above that level bound for the United States. In return, the United States agreed it would not initiate any investigations of Canadian softwood lumber exports for five years.

Export controls may also be adopted to punish a country's political enemies. An **embargo**—an absolute ban on the exporting (and/or importing) of goods to a particular destination—is adopted by a country or international governmental authority to discipline another country. For example, after Iraq invaded Kuwait in 1990, the United Nations imposed an embargo on trade with Iraq.

Other Nontariff Barriers.   Countries also use various other NTBs to protect themselves from foreign competition. Some NTBs are adopted for legitimate domestic public policy reasons but have the effect of restricting trade. Most NTBs, however, are blatantly protectionist. As we discuss in Chapter 9, international negotiations in the post-World War II era have reduced the use of tariffs and quotas. For this reason nonquantitative NTBs have now become major impediments to the growth of international trade. These NTBs are more difficult to eliminate than tariffs and quotas because they often are embedded in bureaucratic procedures and are not quickly changeable. Among the most common forms of nonquantitative NTBs are the following:

- Product and testing standards
- Restricted access to distribution networks
- Public-sector procurement policies
- Local-purchase requirements
- Regulatory controls
- Currency controls
- Investment controls

We discuss these in the following sections.

Product and Testing Standards. A common form of NTB is a requirement that foreign goods meet a country's product standards or testing standards before the goods can be offered for sale in that country. Foreign firms often claim these standards discriminate against their products. Taiwan, for example, uses more extensive and costly purity testing for imported fruit juices than for domestically produced juices. China requires foreign pesticide and agricultural chemical manufacturers to undergo elaborate testing procedures that may cost as much as $5 million per product, but it imposes no such regulation on domestic manufacturers of these products. Further, manufacturers wishing to export pressure boilers to China must pay for Chinese inspectors to visit the manufacturers' factories and the factories of all their suppliers to ensure that the boilers meet Chinese safety standards, which are not well spelled out. Not only does the average cost of these inspections approach $100,000, but most of the inspectors are linked to research institutes tied to Chinese manufacturers of these goods.[8]

Restricted Access to Distribution Networks. Restricting foreign suppliers' access to the normal channels of distribution may also function as an NTB. Indonesia, for example, for many years allowed retail distribution to be provided only by Indonesian companies or individuals, although that regulation was dropped at the request of the International Monetary Fund in the aftermath of the 1997-98 Asian currency crisis. Taiwan allows only 58 prints of a given movie to be imported into the country and limits the number of theaters that can simultaneously show the same movie to 18. This policy helps protect the local film industry.[9]

Japan has borne the brunt of world criticism over the issue of access to distribution networks. Foreigners' access to Japan's networks is often restricted because of the tight corporate and cultural ties among domestic manufacturers, wholesalers, and retailers. For example, Michigan-based Guardian Industries, one of the world's largest producers of flat glass, has had trouble penetrating the Japanese market despite offering prices 25 percent lower than those of its Japanese competitors. Guardian's problem has been finding Japanese intermediaries to handle its product line. Often Japanese glass fabricators and wholesalers fear retribution from the three large Japanese flat-glass producers, which dominate the domestic market, if they handle a competitor's products.[10]

In several cases Japan's *keiretsu* system has been explicitly blamed for restricting foreigners' access to the Japanese market. For example, AIG, a leading multinational insurance company, has been selling consumer-oriented insurance in the Japanese market since 1946 but still finds it difficult to sell industrial-risk insurance because most major Japanese firms buy such insurance from an insurance company affiliated with their *keiretsu*. Of course, these close corporate ties, while acting as an NTB, may not be discriminatory because they hurt both foreign and domestic newcomers in the Japanese market.

Public-Sector Procurement Policies. Public-sector procurement policies that give preferential treatment to domestic firms are another form of NTB. In the United States, "Buy American" restrictions are common at the federal, state, and local levels. The city of Los Angeles, for example, biased its procurement of mass transit equipment in favor of U.S. producers.[11] The federal government generally requires that international air travel purchased with U.S. government funds occur on U.S. airlines.

Despite its own discriminatory policies, the U.S. government has loudly criticized similar policies in other countries. For example, the United States fought a long battle with the Japanese government over the right of U.S. construction firms to bid on public construction projects in Japan. The U.S. claimed that the Japanese policy of excluding foreign firms from the bidding process unless they had previous construction experience in Japan created a burdensome chicken-or-egg dilemma for U.S. firms.

Public-sector procurement policies are particularly important in countries that have extensive state ownership of industry and in industries in which state ownership is common. If a national government adopts procurement policies that favor local firms, then foreigners are locked out of much of the market. The large size of the state-controlled sector in Brazil, for example, coupled with the country's "Buy Brazilian" policies, deters imports in such industries as computers, computer software, and telecommunications. Bidders for government contracts that meet the criteria for preferential treatment—either Brazilian owned, using Brazilian technology or products, or meeting local content thresholds—are given bidding preferences of up to 12 percent. (That is, a Brazilian bidder will be victorious if its bid is no more than 12 percent above the lowest foreign bid.) Belarus follows a similar procedure, giving its local companies a 20 percent bidding preference for government contracts.[12]

Local-Purchase Requirements. Host governments may hinder foreign firms from exporting to or operating in the host countries by requiring the firms to purchase goods or services from local suppliers. For example, China requires that power plants of less than 600 megawatt capacity use only domestically made equipment. Russia mandates that joint ventures in its oil industry buy at least 70 percent of their equipment domestically. The French government requires local TV services, such as TF1 or Canal Plus, to show French-made films at least 40 percent of the time and European-made films at least 60 percent of the time, thus restricting the market available to non-European films. Such quotas exist in radio broadcasting as well. During prime time at least 40 percent of the songs played on France's 1700 AM and FM stations must be written or sung by French or Francophone artists.[13] Similarly, the European Union (EU) requires that the majority of programming broadcast by European television stations be of European origin. The U.S. government has strongly protested the French and EU requirements, arguing that they are designed to restrict competition from U.S. music, movie, and television producers.[14]

Regulatory Controls. Governments can create NTBs by adopting regulatory controls, such as conducting health and safety inspections, enforcing environmental regulations, requiring firms to obtain licenses before beginning operations or constructing new plants, and charging taxes and fees for public services that affect the ability of international businesses to compete in host markets. For example, Taiwan's National Health Insurance Bureau's reimbursement schedule for pharmaceuticals favors domestically made generic drugs over foreign-produced ones. In India the Central Board of Film Certification controls the importation of foreign films, checking to make sure that their content is deemed appropriate for local audiences. In Turkmenistan all imports of consumer goods must be approved by the State Standards Committee. The slowness of this approval process discourages the import of perishable goods. And U.S. exporters believe that South Korea's food labeling laws, which are controlled by three separate agencies and often change arbitrarily without warning or notification to foreign food producers, are a deliberate attempt to discourage imports of foreign agricultural goods.[15]

Seemingly innocent laws may affect international trade. For example, in the early 1990s Ontario imposed a 10¢ per bottle fee on all beer sold in nonrefillable containers. Although this regulation might appear to be designed to protect the environment, Anheuser-Busch and the Miller Brewing Company believed it was structured to hurt the sales of imported U.S. beers, most of which are sold in recyclable aluminum cans, and increase the sales of Canadian beers, most of which are bottled. Noting that the 10¢ tax did not apply to all beverages sold in aluminum cans (such as soft drinks), the United States retaliated by imposing a 50 percent duty on Canadian exports of beer to the United States, triggering a round of trade negotiations between the two countries.[16]

Currency Controls. Many countries, particularly developing countries and those with centrally planned economies, raise barriers to international trade through currency controls. Exporters of goods are allowed to exchange foreign currency at favorable rates so as to make foreign markets attractive sales outlets for domestic producers. Importers are forced to purchase foreign exchange from the central bank at unfavorable exchange rates, thus raising the domestic prices of foreign goods. Tourists may be offered a separate exchange rate that is designed to extract as much foreign exchange as possible from free-spending foreigners.

Uzbekistan, for example, has suffered from a shortage of foreign exchange since declaring its independence from the Soviet Union in 1991. To address this problem, the government of Uzbekistan controls the disbursement of foreign exchange. In allocating scarce foreign exchange, the government favors firms importing capital goods over those importing consumer goods. Zimbabwe forbids local banks from offering foreign currency-denominated bank accounts, making it more difficult for domestic firms to obtain the foreign exchange needed to pay for imported goods. Syria has adopted a more complicated approach. It utilizes five official and two unofficial exchange rates. The most favorable rate is reserved for repayment of official government loans. Another favorable rate is used for public-sector exports of petroleum and all imports by the government. Less favorable rates are used for Syrian students studying abroad, payment of fees to the government, tourists, capital inflows, and other international transactions. Other countries using dual or multiple exchange rate systems include Cambodia, Guinea-Bissau, Iran, Nigeria, and Zambia.[17]

Investment Controls. Controls on foreign investment and ownership are common, particularly in key industries like broadcasting, utilities, air transportation, defense contracting, and financial services. Such controls often make it difficult for foreign firms to develop an effective presence in such markets. Poland, for example, limits foreign ownership in such industries as broadcasting and fisheries to 49 percent. The Philippines restricts foreign ownership in advertising to 30 percent and public utilities to 40 percent. Indonesia limits foreign ownership of radio and television broadcasting, forestry concessions, and film and video distribution.

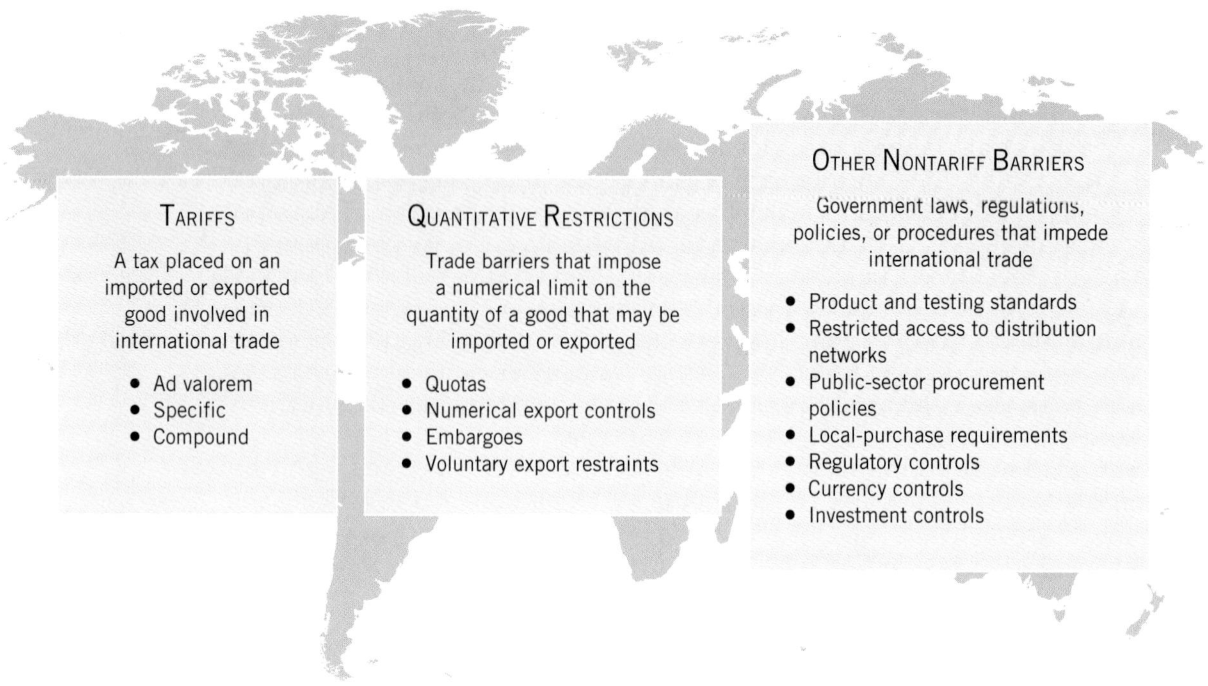

TARIFFS	QUANTITATIVE RESTRICTIONS	OTHER NONTARIFF BARRIERS
A tax placed on an imported or exported good involved in international trade	Trade barriers that impose a numerical limit on the quantity of a good that may be imported or exported	Government laws, regulations, policies, or procedures that impede international trade
• Ad valorem • Specific • Compound	• Quotas • Numerical export controls • Embargoes • Voluntary export restraints	• Product and testing standards • Restricted access to distribution networks • Public-sector procurement policies • Local-purchase requirements • Regulatory controls • Currency controls • Investment controls

FIGURE 8.7   Types of Barriers to International Trade: A Summary

The United States similarly constrains foreign ownership of airlines and broadcast stations.

These NTBs are now more important impediments to international trade than tariffs are. And because they are sometimes imposed for sound domestic policy reasons but affect the competitiveness of foreign firms, NTBs can quickly cause intense international conflicts. International businesses whose operations are affected by NTBs often need the support of their home governments to help resolve these problems. "Building Global Skills" at the end of the chapter will acquaint you with some of the U.S. government agencies that can help such firms. Figure 8.7 summarizes the various forms that trade barriers can take.

❯ PROMOTION OF INTERNATIONAL TRADE

We have just explored some techniques that governments use to restrict foreign business activity. In this section we discuss government policies that promote international business, including subsidies, establishment of foreign trade zones, and export financing programs. Typically, these programs are designed to create jobs in the export sector or to attract investment to economically depressed areas.

Subsidies

Countries often seek to stimulate exports by offering subsidies designed to reduce firms' costs of doing business. Brazil and Kenya, for example, exempt imported inputs that are used to produce goods for export from taxes and tariffs, while India exempts export earnings from income taxes. Australia has adopted similar schemes to encourage automotive, textile, clothing, and footwear exports.[18]

National, state, and local governments often provide economic development incentives—another type of subsidy—to entice firms to locate or expand facilities in their communities to provide jobs and increase local tax bases. These incentives may be in the form of property tax abatements, free land, training of workforces, reduced utility rates, new highway construction, and so on. Competition among different localities can be fierce. For example, in late 2000 Mississippi beat out a host of states competing to attract a new Nissan factory by offering the firm a $295 million incentives package.

Because subsidies reduce the cost of doing business, they may affect international trade by artificially improving a firm's competitiveness in export markets or by helping domestic firms fight off foreign imports. Subsidies, however, can grow so large as to disrupt the normal pattern of international trade. The shipbuilding, wheat, and butter industries are notorious examples of markets where trade is distorted because of the high level of subsidies. The big losers in the subsidy wars are efficient producers in countries that lack large-scale subsidies, such as Australia's wheat industry or New Zealand's dairy industry.

Foreign Trade Zones

A **foreign trade zone (FTZ)** is a geographical area where imported or exported goods receive preferential tariff treatment. An FTZ may be as small as a warehouse or a factory site (such as Caterpillar's diesel engine facility in Mossville, Illinois) or as large as the entire city of Shenzhen, China (which neighbors Hong Kong).[19] FTZs are used by governments worldwide to spur regional economic development. For example, an FTZ has played a key role in the economic development of the small African island nation of Mauritius (see Map 8.2). Through utilization of an FTZ, a firm typically can reduce, delay, or sometimes totally eliminate customs duties. Generally a firm can import a component into an FTZ, process it further, and then export the processed good abroad and avoid paying customs duties on the value of the imported component.

The *maquiladora* system represents another example of the use of FTZs. A **maquiladora** is a factory located in an FTZ in Mexico; most are situated near the

Mauritius, which was once a French naval base, is a tropical island, roughly 10½ times the area of Washington, D.C. For much of its history Mauritius's 1.1 million residents depended on sugarcane, and even today 90 percent of its cultivated land is devoted to this crop.

Mauritius has created a foreign trade zone (FTZ) to diversify its economy and encourage manufacturing. Today the country exports over $1.5 billion worth of textiles, apparel, and other goods to Europe and the United States. Because of the FTZ's success, the country's economy has enjoyed a 4.9 percent annual growth during the 1990s.

MAP 8.2   **Foreign Trade Zone on Mauritius**

U.S. border. These factories import unfinished goods or component parts, further process the goods or parts, and reexport them. The goods produced by *maquiladoras* enjoy preferential customs and tax treatment. Mexico levies no customs duties on unfinished goods imported by a *maquiladora*, provided the goods are reexported after having been further processed in Mexico. Machinery imported into Mexico and used by a *maquiladora* is also exempt from customs duties. U.S. customs duties on *maquiladoras'* exports are applied only to the value of the processing performed in Mexico. Today the *maquiladora* industry is the second largest sector of the Mexican economy (after oil production) and the second largest source of Mexico's foreign exchange earnings. However, as a result of the North American Free Trade Agreement, many tariff advantages once enjoyed only by the *maquiladoras* are now available to factories throughout Mexico. Thus interior cities such as Monterrey and Saltillo have been put on a more even footing with border communities such as Nuevo Laredo and Matamoros in terms of attracting new plants to serve the North American market.

Export Financing Programs

For many big-ticket items such as aircraft, supercomputers, and large construction projects, success or failure in exporting depends on a firm's producing a high-quality product, providing reliable repair service after the sale, and—often the deciding factor—offering an attractive financing package. For example, Boeing competes with Airbus to sell Air Canada 200-seat short-range aircraft. When Air Canada is deciding which firm's aircraft to buy, it carefully weighs price, after-sale technical support, aircraft operating costs, and financing expenses. All other things being equal, the financing terms offered to Air Canada may be critical in its decision of which firm wins the contract.

Because of the importance of the financing package, most major trading countries have created government-owned agencies to assist their domestic firms in arranging financing of export sales, both large and small. The **Export-Import Bank of the United States (Eximbank)** provides financing for U.S. exports through direct loans and loan guarantees; in 1999 it supplied financing for over 2,200 export transactions worth $16.7 billion. Large firms like Boeing are important clients, but the Eximbank also services small U.S. exporters. For example, it guaranteed $7.9 million in bank loans for the family-owned De Francisci Machine Corporation, thereby allowing this small New York manufacturer of food-processing equipment to export noodle-drying and pasta-making equipment to two factories in Poland. Eximbank or its subcontractors also provide routine commercial insurance services for Eximbank-supported exports.[20] Another U.S. government-sponsored organization, the **Overseas Private Investment Corporation (OPIC)**, provides a very different type of insurance—political-risk insurance, a subject covered in Chapter 3. If a foreign country confiscates an insured firm's goods or assets, OPIC will compensate the firm for its losses. Most major trading countries have similar organizations that provide export financing, commercial insurance, and political-risk insurance.

› CONTROLLING UNFAIR TRADE PRACTICES

With governments around the world adopting programs designed to protect domestic industries from imports and other programs to promote their exports, it should not be surprising that competitors often cry foul. In response to these complaints many countries have implemented laws protecting their domestic firms from unfair trade practices.

In the United States complaints from firms affected by alleged unfair trade practices are first investigated by the International Trade Administration (ITA), a division of the U.S. Department of Commerce, which determines whether an unfair trade practice has occurred. The Department of Commerce transfers confirmed cases of unfair trading to the U.S. International Trade Commission (ITC), an independent government agency. If a majority of the six ITC commissioners decide that U.S. producers have suffered "material injury," the ITC will impose duties on the offending imports to counteract the unfair trade practice. The ITC, like Canada's CITT in the case of Desmarais and like similar government agencies worldwide, focuses on two types of unfair trade practices: government subsidies that distort trade and unfair pricing practices.

Countervailing Duties

Most countries protect local firms from foreign competitors that benefit from subsidies granted by their home governments. A **countervailing duty (CVD)** is an ad valorem tariff on an imported good that is imposed by the importing country to counter the impact of foreign subsidies. The CVD is calculated to just offset the advantage the exporter obtains from the subsidy. In this way trade can still be driven by the competitive strengths of individual firms and the laws of comparative advantage, rather than by the level of subsidies governments offer their firms.

> Brazil's Embraer competes with Canada's Bombardier in the regional jet market. The Canadian government believes Brazil has illegally subsidized the sale of Embraer aircraft. The Brazilian government believes Canada has done the same for Bombardier planes.

Not all government subsidies give a foreign firm an unfair advantage in the domestic market. Most countries impose CVDs only when foreign subsidization of a product leads to a distortion of international trade. For example, the U.S. government, in administering its CVD rules, tries to determine whether a particular subsidy is generally available to all industries in a country, in which case CVDs will not be applied, or whether the subsidy is restricted to a specific industry, in which case CVDs may be imposed. If a foreign government grants a tax credit to all employers for training handicapped workers, a CVD will not be applied because the tax credit is available to all the country's firms. If the tax credit is restricted to the footwear industry, however, a CVD may be imposed on imported footwear equal to the value of the tax credit.

CVD complaints are often triggered by some governmental action designed to overcome some other governmental action. For example, the EU's common agricultural policy has had the effect of raising the prices paid to European grain farmers. Unfortunately, the high cost of feed grains raised the costs of European swine producers and made their meat products uncompetitive in world markets. To undo the damage caused to swine producers by high grain prices, the EU agreed to provide an export subsidy for canned hams and other processed meat products. With the aid of this subsidy Danish and Dutch pork processors were able to capture 25 percent of the Canadian canned ham and canned luncheon meat market. As a result, Canadian pork-packing houses successfully petitioned the Canadian International Trade Tribunal to impose a countervailing duty on Danish and Dutch canned pork products.

Antidumping Regulations

Many countries are also concerned about their domestic firms being victimized by discriminatory or predatory pricing practices of foreign firms, such as dumping. Recall from the chapter's opening case that dumping occurs when a firm sells its goods in a foreign market at a price below what it charges in its home market. This type of dumping is a form of international price discrimination.

Another type of dumping involves the firm's selling its goods below cost in the foreign market, in which case the dumping is a form of predatory pricing. The concern with predatory pricing is that a foreign company may lower its prices in the host country, drive host country firms out of the market, and then charge monopoly prices to host country consumers once competitors have been eliminated. Antidumping laws protect local industries from dumping by foreign firms.

Determining whether the first type of dumping—price discrimination—has actually occurred is not always easy. For example, many Western politicians incorrectly accuse Japanese companies of dumping, noting that Japanese goods often retail for higher prices in Tokyo than in New York City. Retail prices, however, are irrelevant in determining whether dumping has occurred. The comparison should be made between the prices charged foreign customers and domestic customers at the factory gate; these prices are often difficult to obtain. The high retail prices in Tokyo might reflect the inefficient Japanese distribution system or high costs of retailing there rather than dumping by the manufacturer.

In the second type of dumping—predatory pricing—defining costs is complicated, particularly when dealing with a large, multidivisional MNC such as Toyota or Nissan. For example, when the ITA is determining the "cost" of a Toyota Sienna minivan, should it measure cost as the marginal cost of producing one more Sienna? Should it include some of Toyota's minivan-related R&D expenses, or should it simply recognize that these R&D costs would have been incurred whether or not the U.S. market existed? Should it include charges for Toyota's corporate overhead? Foreigners' guilt or innocence in dumping cases often turns on the answers to such accounting questions.

Super 301

Another weapon available to the U.S. government to combat unfair trading practices of foreign countries is Section 301—so-called Super 301—of the 1974 Trade Act. **Super 301** requires the U.S. trade representative, a member of the executive branch, to publicly list those countries engaging in the most flagrant unfair trade practices. The U.S. trade representative is then required to negotiate the elimination of the alleged unfair trade practices with the listed countries. If the negotiations are unsuccessful, the executive branch must impose on the recalcitrant offenders appropriate retaliatory restrictions such as tariffs or import quotas.

Super 301 gives U.S. negotiators a big club in their dealings with foreign governments. For example, the U.S. government determined in the early 1990s that U.S. firms were having difficulty obtaining contracts for large-scale construction projects in Japan, despite their success and experience in managing major construction projects around the world. The then U.S. trade representative, Carla Hills, threatened to prohibit Japanese firms from bidding on federally funded construction projects in the United States. The Japanese government agreed to improve the access of U.S. construction firms to major Japanese building projects.[21]

Section 301 technically expired in 1994. However, President Clinton resuscitated it via executive order, and it remains a powerful, though controversial, weapon in the U.S. trade arsenal. The use of Super 301 has not won the United States many friends internationally. Because Super 301 provides relief solely for U.S. firms, EU members have been particularly displeased with it, arguing that it hinders the development of global trade and promotes unilateral, rather than multilateral, attempts to redress problems facing international commerce. Many targets of Super 301 actions are similarly resentful. They believe its use represents bullying by the United States and pandering to those special-interest groups that have the ear of Congress at any point in time.

Should Countries Enforce Their Unfair Trade Practice Laws?

It may be surprising to learn that many economists argue for abolishing unfair trade practice laws. Who, after all, would support promoting unfair trade? Advocates of abolishing unfair trade practice laws generally agree with the objectives of these laws:

- Promote global efficiency by encouraging production in those countries that can produce a good most efficiently
- Ensure that trade occurs on the basis of comparative advantage, not the size of government subsidies
- Protect consumers from predatory behavior

However, abolition advocates assert that in practice these laws do more harm than good. Much of their concerns rest on how the laws are enforced. Foreign firms alleged to have dumped goods in the United States must provide comprehensive documentation of their pricing and cost accounting procedures, in English, using U.S. generally accepted accounting principles. Firms failing to comply with the short deadlines for supplying these documents find themselves at a disadvantage in defending themselves before the International Trade Commission. Moreover, critics of unfair trade practice laws argue that the ITC's costing methodology is flawed and biased toward finding dumping when none exists. New Zealand kiwi fruit was banned from the U.S. market for nearly a decade, for example, on what many experts consider to be flimsy evidence. Indeed, most major trading countries believe that U.S. enforcement of its unfair trade practice laws is based on politics, not the law, and thus the laws serve as a protectionist trade barrier.

Some economists go even further in their disdain for unfair trade practice laws. They believe the laws make no sense, either in theory or in practice, because of the harm they cause consumers. These economists are skeptical of the predatory pricing argument, contending that decades of economic research have failed to find many real-world examples of such behavior. With regard to international price discrimination or government subsidization, the economists argue that if foreigners are kind enough (or dumb enough) to sell their goods to our country below cost, why should we complain?

CHAPTER REVIEW

Summary

Formulating trade policies that advance the economic interests of their citizens is an important task facing most national governments. Although some policy makers suggest that free trade is the most appropriate policy, numerous firms, government bureaucrats, and other interested parties argue for active governmental intervention in international trade.

Some rationales for governmental intervention focus on the specific needs of an industry (national defense, infant industry, maintenance of existing jobs, and strategic trade arguments), while others focus on the country's overall needs (economic development and industrial policy).

Over the centuries governments have developed a variety of trade barriers. Import tariffs raise revenues for the government as well as help domestically produced goods compete with imported goods. Quotas and VERs place a numerical limitation on the amount of a good that can be imported or exported. Other NTBs may also disadvantage foreign products in the market. These barriers include product and testing standards, restricted access to distribution systems, public procurement policies that favor local firms, local-purchase requirements, regulatory powers, and currency and investment controls.

National governments also seek to promote the interests of domestic firms in international trade through other programs. The governments may subsidize local production of goods and services to make them more competitive in international markets. They also may authorize the establishment of FTZs to help domestic firms export goods. Export financing programs have been developed to assist exporters in marketing their goods.

National governments protect local producers from unfair foreign competition by enacting unfair trade laws. CVDs are imposed on foreign products that benefit from government subsidies that distort international trade. Antidumping laws protect domestic producers from being victimized by predatory pricing or price discrimination policies of foreign firms. Super 301 strengthens the bargaining power of U.S. negotiators in international trade conflicts.

Review Questions

1. What is fair trade? Who benefits from it?
2. What is the infant industry argument?
3. What are the different types of tariffs?
4. Why is it useful for an importer to seek out an advance tariff classification from the U.S. Customs Service?
5. Why might a country adopt a VER?
6. What are the major forms of NTBs?
7. What is an FTZ?
8. What is the role of the Eximbank?
9. What is the purpose of a CVD?
10. What are the two definitions of dumping?

Questions for Discussion

1. What are the advantages and disadvantages of an industrial policy?
2. Because of Japan's success in competing in international markets, it has been the target of numerous complaints that it restricts foreign access to its local markets. As Japan reduces its barriers to imported goods, who is likely to gain from lowered barriers? Who is likely to lose from them?
3. Strategic trade theory applies to industries that are composed of only a few firms worldwide. List as many industries as possible that fit this description.
4. Since 1992 Indonesia has imposed high export taxes on the export of raw wood and sawn timber. Why would it do this? (Hint: What is the impact of these export tariffs on the domestic market for wood and timber? Which domestic industries would benefit from this impact?) Who is hurt by these high export taxes?
5. Should we worry if foreigners sell us goods cheaply?

BUILDING GLOBAL SKILLS

In the United States at least 18 separate government agencies have some responsibility for promoting exports of U.S. firms. The International Trade Administration (ITA) coordinates the export development efforts of these federal agencies. The U.S. and Foreign Commercial Service (US&FCS), a branch of the ITA, staffs offices throughout the United States and in foreign countries with international trade experts available to help U.S. firms export their products. These experts can help firms assess their products' export potential, identify the most likely markets for their goods, and locate promising overseas partners and distributors. To promote exports, US&FCS experts also work with 51 District Export Councils, 107 field offices of the Small Business Administration (SBA), the Foreign Agricultural Service (part of the Department of Agriculture), commercial banks, chambers of commerce, and state governments. These groups provide seminars on exporting and information about exporting opportunities in different countries and product lines. A quick listing of these services can be found in the Department of Commerce's accurately titled publication, *A Basic Guide to Exporting,* which provides an informative overview of the exporting process.

Assignment

The U.S. government has so many sources of information available to help first-time exporters that managers are often overwhelmed by deciding where to begin. Put yourself in the shoes of a neophyte exporter who wants to learn about the exporting process. (If you are not reading this book at a U.S. university, answer the questions from the perspective of an exporter in your home country. Begin by identifying the government agency that promotes exports in your country.)

1. Find out which branch office of the US&FCS serves your local market. You can do this by using *A Basic Guide to Exporting* in your library, looking in your local phone book, calling your congressperson's office (the staff there are experts about the federal bureaucracy), asking a local banker, or chatting with local chambers of commerce. Ask the local US&FCS office to send you literature on its activities and a list of its "Country Desk Officers" (experts knowledgeable about the markets in specific countries) and "Industry Desk Officers" (experts knowledgeable about the international markets for individual products).

2. Find out which state agencies in your state are responsible for promotion of exports from local firms. Ask the agencies about their export development programs.

3. Identify the SBA district office in your area. Ask the office how it can help local firms identify promising export markets.

4. Locate private organizations (profit and nonprofit) in your area that provide trade development services. Ask them about the types of services they offer their members and newcomers like yourself.

Much of this information is available on the Internet as well. The textbook's Web site provides links to other Web sites that are useful for this assignment.

WORKING WITH THE WEB:
BUILDING GLOBAL INTERNET SKILLS

Assessing Trade Barriers

The ability of firms to market their products in foreign countries is often affected by trade barriers imposed by individual countries. Your assignment is to pick an industry or product, and report on the barriers to trade or investment that five countries impose on it. Because the members of the EU have common trade policies, only one of the five countries can be an EU member.

Fortunately, there are numerous sources of useful information available in published form and on the Internet. The Office of the U.S. Trade Representative publishes annually an analysis of trade barriers imposed by other nations titled the *National Trade Estimate Report on Foreign Trade Barriers*. This study also provides a detailed description of the evolution of existing trade conflicts between the United States and the rest of the world. The EU provides similar information in its Market Access Sectoral and Trade Barriers Database, which is available on the EU's Web site. The U.S. Customs Service's Web site provides information on tariffs imposed by the United States. Other groups, such as the World Trade Organization and industry trade associations, also publish useful information. The textbook's Web site for Chapter 8 provides links to Web sites you may find useful for this assignment.

WE INVITE YOU TO VISIT THIS BOOK'S
COMPANION WEB SITE AT www.prenhall.com/griffin

IN THE NEWS

1. Use the search feature of the *Financial Times* homepage (*www.ft.com*) to locate recent articles on the topic "trade barriers." Choose an article about a country, firm, or industry that interests you, and use it as a starting point for further research into the particular trade barrier described. What type of barrier is it? Who is imposing it, and why? Who are the winners and losers in the situation?

2. Use the *Financial Times* search feature again to research one of the following: Free trade zone, foreign trade zone, Eximbank, OPIC, *maquiladoras*. Select an article and summarize the means by which trade is being promoted (trade zone, financing, etc.). What country, industry, and/or firm will benefit? Does anyone stand to lose by the support being offered?

CLOSING CASE

The Great Quota Hustle

Lands' End placed an order . . . for 200,000 pairs of cotton chino pants from Thailand. The big Wisconsin-based catalog retailer intended to advertise the trousers in its February 2000 catalog. But trouble brewed. The Thai exporter couldn't come up with the necessary cotton-pants quota to ship the merchandise to the U.S. in 1999, thereby missing the selling season. Lands' End yanked the pages from the catalog after it had gone to press.

Just another loony result of the weird laws that surround the international clothing trade. Says Lands' End Chief Executive David Dyer, "Apparel quotas are very onerous for us." . . .

The quota system . . . now encompasses no fewer than 1,000 different import allotments, covering scores of categories from each of dozens of countries. For this system, U.S. consumers pay tens of billions of dollars a year in higher prices.

And what benefit does the U.S. get from this system? Not even the protectionism that the rules were set up to provide. That's because a wily bunch of manufacturers and middlemen have concocted an elaborate response to the quota system that has factories, workers and textiles being shipped to far corners of the earth in search of loopholes. In the end, you still get your pants. They are quite possibly still being made by the

Chinese workers who would make them in a free global economy. But they cost more, much more, than they would without quotas. Some of this higher cost redounds to the U.S. Treasury in the form of tariffs. But billions of the extra dollars consumers spend are spread abroad. Some of the money is dissipated on the high seas in circuitous boat trips. A lot of it sticks to the fingers of well-connected foreigners who own or control quotas. In the Far East, quota rights are brazenly traded like so many stock options.

David Lee, general manager of Hong Kong's Comey Ltd., chuckles when he recalls his family setting up its cashmere-knitting factories in Madagascar in the early 1990s.... Cashmere hair comes from the soft underbelly of goats raised in the frigid mountains and plains of Mongolia and northern China. Comey, which sells to U.S. firms such as Gap, the Limited, and Calvin Klein, sends the material on a four-to-six-week boat ride from China to its three plants in Madagascar. Why there? Because it has no quota restrictions in the U.S. or European markets, while China has tiny quotas for wool sweaters and therefore punitive quota prices. This year Hong Kong-based Lee, most of whose family has relocated to Madagascar, estimates he will ship 1.2 million cashmere sweaters from there to the U.S. and Europe....

How did the U.S., which considers itself a shining beacon of free trade, come to engage in this tortured kind of protectionism? In 1957 the U.S. apparel industry persuaded legislators to choke off cotton textile imports from Japan. In the early 1960s we began restricting apparel shipments from Hong Kong. And then the quota lists got longer and longer—so many dozen ladies' shorts from country X, so many pajamas from Y, so many brassieres, mittens, socks, even pillowcases and towels. Like a tax system with thousands of rules, the quota system invites, besides the (mostly legal) trading of quotas within a country, a lot of chicanery. The fraudulent labeling of goods as coming from countries with unfilled quotas is rampant in Asia and the Middle East. Catching these "transshipment" bad labels keeps hundreds of U.S. inspectors busy.

But the biggest returns in this game come from playing strictly by the book.

Marjorie Yang ... returned to Hong Kong from the U.S. in 1978 ... to help her Shanghai-born father, Y. L. Yang, run Esquel Group.

Today family-owned Esquel is the world's largest men's cotton shirt maker, with sales of about $500 million and aftertax profits in excess of $50 million, according to Margie Yang, now chairman. Esquel produces about 48 million shirts a year and 5 million pairs of pants, and employs 43,000 workers. Its customers are the cream of the industry, labels like Polo Ralph Lauren, Tommy Hilfiger, Brooks Brothers, Hugo Boss, Nordstrom, Eddie Bauer, Abercrombie & Fitch, and Lands' End.

The Yang's special genius is an understanding of the trade system. When they started the firm in 1978, they were expected, as a new player, to buy Hong Kong quota rights in the market. Instead of doing that they produced in mainland China. In no time they were shipping 12 million garments a year. But then the U.S. and Europe slapped tight quotas on China's textile and apparel exports. So Y. L. acquired a plant in Penang, Malaysia, and built up a large export position in men's and women's shirts. Soon enough, the U.S. slapped quotas on Malaysia.

So the Yangs started production in Sri Lanka and in Mauritius, an island in the middle of the Indian Ocean. "If it weren't for quota, nobody in their right mind would go to Mauritius to ship to the U.S.," says the daughter. "Can you get any further than that? Doesn't it seem ludicrous?"

Esquel farms extra-long staple cotton in western China, and spins the yarn there and in Guangdong, southern China. It loads rolls of fiber and accessories on boats to Malaysia and Mauritius, to be assembled into apparel for the U.S. and Europe. Now, Mauritius is quota-rich, but it's short of labor. So Esquel has imported 2,000 factory workers from China to Mauritius....

This kind of rag-trade ritual is repeated all around the globe. Dubai and Bahrain have generous quotas but no workers, so they import labor from India and Pakistan. Saipan, a U.S. territory, brings in labor from China and the Philippines for its apparel plants. Cambodia has abundant quotas but no management, so it imports middle managers from China. The quota-short Koreans built hundreds of clothing factories in Guatemala, Honduras, and Indonesia: the Taiwanese, strong in synthetic fibers, are heavily invested in Vietnam and China....

American capitalists aren't oblivious to this scheming. Richard Sutton is a second-generation rag trader at New York-based Lollytogs, which supplies garments to Target, Sears, and Mervyn's and sells school uniforms under the Bugle Boy license. Lollytogs, a family-owned outfit with sales of more than $100 million, imports 95% of its garments.

Sutton spends a lot of time on airplanes. "I'm in 15 countries banging on doors mainly because of quotas," he explains. "I had a great run in Oman. I was there 10 years and no one could find it on the map. Then others came in, quotas were slapped on, and little by little prices were bid up to the point where I couldn't beat Kmart prices and make it in Oman." So he moved to Tanzania, Egypt, and Bangladesh. "Bangladesh happens to have fairly decent relations with the U.S.," he explains. "Egypt has unusually high quotas for cotton men's and boy's pants because they have great political ties with the U.S."

Without such sway, a nation will soon lose its opening. "At some point someone in the U.S. says imports from that country have reached a level where it's hurting U.S. industry," Sutton says. "Foreign countries have zero say when and how it will happen."

Does the system anger him? "The more complex it is, the better for me," he responds. Sutton needn't worry that the system will get any simpler, trade pacts or no ...

Keeping up with the rules is part of a big exporter's challenge. The other is enforcing them....

William E. Connor & Associates Ltd. has 27 offices monitoring production in 31 countries.... Connor says that 250 of the 800 staff in his buying operation are technicians who visit garment factories in places like Inner Mongolia, Mauritius, and Sri Lanka to verify the "origin-conferring process." He notes that a decade ago these same technicians would have focused on quality inspection. Today the field presence must physically witness origin-conferring steps such as sweater panels being knitted and shirt components assembled. U.S. Customs frequently conducts country-of-origin audits on the entire manufacturing history of a garment shipment, which requires 1,000 or more pages of documents such as payroll records, bills of lading, electrical bills, and fabric-cutting tickets as evidence.

Your tax money at work: The U.S. government employs "jump teams" to visit overseas factories and peruse invoices, count sewing machines, and watch seamstresses. An American jump team typically includes a U.S. Customs agent and a textile expert. More than 350 factories in Hong Kong, Macau, and Taiwan have been blacklisted by Customs on suspicion of transshipment.

All the while, in offices around the globe, quota brokers are poring over U.S. Customs rules looking for the latest opening. Jimmy Lai, the controversial Hong King publisher, made his first fortune in the rag trade. The U.S. restricted imports of cotton, wool, synthetic fiber, linen, and silk. But Lai discovered that ramie, a coarse vegetable fiber that grows in sugarcane plantations, had no quota in the U.S. So he shipped ramie sweaters to the U.S. Eventually, the U.S. put quotas on ramie, too. . . .

Case Questions

1. What was the original purpose of placing quotas on clothing and textile imports? Are those goals now being met?
2. What is the impact on the U.S. economy of these quotas?
3. Who gains and who loses from the use of these quotas?
4. The quota system is scheduled to be eliminated later in this decade. Will its elimination benefit or harm the U.S. economy? Defend your answer.

Source: "The Great Quota Hustle," by Andrew Tanzer. *Forbes*, March 6, 2000, pp. 119–125. Reproduced with permission.

CHAPTER

Trade and Prosperity: The Case of Mexico

Is trade or aid the best means of promoting economic development? For Mexico the answer is clear: Trade. From 1917 to 1982 Mexico relied on inward-looking economic policies: high tariffs to discourage imports, restrictions on foreign direct investment (FDI) to reduce foreign presence in the economy, government ownership of key industries, and powerful, conservative bureaucracies that strangled entrepreneurship and innovation. Although the Mexican economy grew during this time span, its performance did not match that of export-driven economies like those of Hong Kong or South Korea. The last four presidents of Mexico have reversed these policies, in the process lowering tariffs, encouraging FDI, privatizing state-owned enterprises, and joining the General Agreement on Tariffs and Trade and the World Trade Organization. Under their leadership Mexico signed a series of free trade agreements with the United States and Canada, the European Union (EU), Chile, and five of its other hemispheric neighbors.

"Mexican **entrepreneurs** have been **quick** to spot new **opportunities**."

Although Mexico's treaty with the EU is its newest (the deal was signed in March 2000), Mexico has attracted the attention of many European investors, particularly auto manufacturers. Volkswagen plans to infuse $1 billion into its plant in Puebla, which assembles VW Beetles and Jettas. Under the

International Cooperation Among Nations

terms of the agreement autos made in Mexico can be exported to the EU tariff free starting in 2003, while the tariff on imported parts will be halved (to 4 percent) by 2005. VW officials believe Mexico can serve as a bridge between the huge U.S./Canadian market and that of the EU. Renault and Peugot are planning similar investments, attracted by growth in Mexico's consumer market as well as its benefits as a production platform.

For now, however, the North American Free Trade Agreement (NAFTA) is the big story. Its implementation in 1994 opened up the U.S. and Canadian markets to Mexican firms, allowing the firms to take advantage of Mexico's lower labor costs. Although most newspaper headlines focused on NAFTA's likely impact on big industries like autos or textiles, Mexican entrepreneurs have been quick to spot new opportunities. For example, a $100 million a year dental supply business has sprung up in Mexico as a result of NAFTA, producing labor-intensive products like buccal tubes (the straps that bind braces to teeth), endodontic files (stainless steel corkscrews used in root canals), and dental wax (a gummy paste used as a mold for crowns).

Another booming market is contract manufacturing (particularly in Guadalajara, Mexico's second largest city), which is being driven by the changing economics of the electronics goods market. Many electronics firms are outsourcing their manufacturing because they recognize they cannot methodically erect a facility to build each new product conjured up by their engineers. By the time the factory is ready, the product may be obsolete. Thus high-tech firms turn to contract manufacturers, who know the ins and outs of starting up a production line for the latest electronic gizmo and can ramp production up or down should demand for it soar—or collapse. Contract manufacturers like Flextronics International, Solectron, and SCI Systems have invested over $2 billion in Guadalajara plants to produce goods for companies like Cisco, Ericsson, and Compaq. If the trend continues, Guadalajara will be the single most important source of consumer electronics goods sold in the United States, even though labor costs are higher in Guadalajara than in China or other Asian countries. Closeness to customers, not labor costs, is the key. UPS and Federal Express air freighters can deliver goods made in Guadalajara to Canadian and U.S. customers the next morning. Delivering Asian-made high-tech products is either too slow (a ship takes two weeks) or too expensive (long-distance air freight can be costly).

Mexican service industries are also booming. For example, Servicios Textiles de Baja California sorts, launders, folds, and delivers some 20 tons of linens a week to firms located on both sides of the Mexican-U.S. border. Other companies have located call centers, data-processing facilities, and other customer support services in Mexico. Seagate Technology's Reynosa facility provides after-sales support for its high-tech customers, while America West, The Gap, and U-Haul operate call centers at various border locations. All told, Mexico's service *maquiladoras* export over $1 billion in services a year and employ 50,000 workers.

These opportunities have created dramatic shifts in the Mexican labor market. Since the mid-1980s, Mexican emigration has averaged about 300,000 persons a year. However, the boom in employment growth created by free trade has created pockets of labor scarcity where jobs were once nonexistent. Zaplotanejo (in the western state of Jalisco), for example, traditionally was a "sender" village, which most working-age men left for the better job prospects in the north. Free trade has reversed this exodus, and Zaplotanejo is now populated with garment assembly shops and help wanted signs. If Mexico's gross domestic product (GDP) continues to grow at 4 percent a year, demographers predict that its job growth and labor force growth will equal one another in 2006. When that happens, Mexican emigration will dry to a trickle, and workers no longer will need to be separated from their families for months or years at a time.[1]

In Chapter 8 we explored the ways in which national governments intervene in international trade and investment. When a country adopts restrictions on international commerce, it can benefit at least some of its producers and workers. But other countries may retaliate with similar restrictions, thinking that they too will gain. As restrictions proliferate, international trading opportunities decline, and all countries end up losing. They often then realize that each is better off if they cooperate and agree to forswear trade restrictions. Such policy changes underlie the transformation of the Mexican economy, as we just noted.

International cooperative agreements form a major part of the economic environment in which international businesses operate. To be successful, international businesspeople must be knowledgeable about these agreements and use them to create business opportunities for their firms and counteract competitors' actions. Of particular importance is the growth of regional trading blocs, such as the Mercosur Accord and NAFTA, which are designed to reduce trade barriers among their members. By far the boldest of these regional economic integration efforts is that of the EU, which is trying to replace marks, francs, guilders, and lira with a single currency, the euro.

› THE GENERAL AGREEMENT ON TARIFFS AND TRADE AND THE WORLD TRADE ORGANIZATION

The collapse of the international economy during the Great Depression between World Wars I and II has been partly blamed on countries' imposing prohibitive tariffs, quotas, and other protectionist measures on imported goods. Trading and investment opportunities for international businesses dried up as country after country adopted such "beggar-thy-neighbor" policies. By raising tariff and quota barriers, each nation believed that it could help its own industries and citizens, even though in doing so it might harm the citizens and industries of other countries. For example, in 1930 the United States sought to protect domestic industries from import competition by raising tariffs under the Smoot-Hawley Tariff Act to an average of 53 percent. However, as other countries, such as the United Kingdom, Italy, and France, constructed similarly high tariff walls, none gained a competitive advantage over another, and as international trade declined, all suffered from the contraction of export markets.

To ensure that the post-World War II international peace would not be threatened by such trade wars, representatives of the leading trading nations met in Havana, Cuba, in 1947 to create the International Trade Organization (ITO). The ITO's mission was to promote international trade; however, the organization never came into being because of a controversy over how extensive its powers should be. Instead the ITO's planned mission was taken over by the **General Agreement on Tariffs and Trade (GATT)**, which had been developed as part of the preparations for the Havana conference. From 1947 to 1994 the signatories to the GATT (the GATT was technically an agreement, not an organization) fought to reduce barriers to international trade. The GATT provided a forum for trade ministers to discuss policies and problems of common concern. In January 1995 it was replaced by the World Trade Organization (WTO), which adopted the GATT's mission.

The Role of the General Agreement on Tariffs and Trade

The GATT's goal was to promote a free and competitive international trading environment benefiting efficient producers, an objective supported by many multinational corporations (MNCs). The GATT accomplished this by sponsoring multilateral negotiations to reduce tariffs, quotas, and other nontariff barriers. Because high tariffs were initially the most serious impediment to world trade, the GATT first focused on reducing the general level of tariff protection. It sponsored a series of eight negotiating "rounds," generally named after the location where each round of negotiations began (see Table 9.1), during its lifetime. The cumulative effect of the GATT's eight rounds was a substantial reduction in tariffs. Tariffs imposed by the developed countries fell from an average of over 40 percent in 1948 to approximately 3 percent in 2000. As Figure 9.1 shows, the GATT negotiations led to dramatic growth in world trade over the past 50 years.

ROUND	DATES	NUMBER OF PARTICIPANTS	AVERAGE TARIFF CUT (%)
Geneva	1947	23	35
Annecy	1949	13	NA
Torquay	1950–1951	38	25
Geneva	1956	26	NA
Dillon	1960–1962	45	NA
Kennedy	1964–1967	62	35
Tokyo	1973–1979	99	33
Uruguay	1986–1994	117	36

TABLE 9.1

GATT Negotiating Rounds

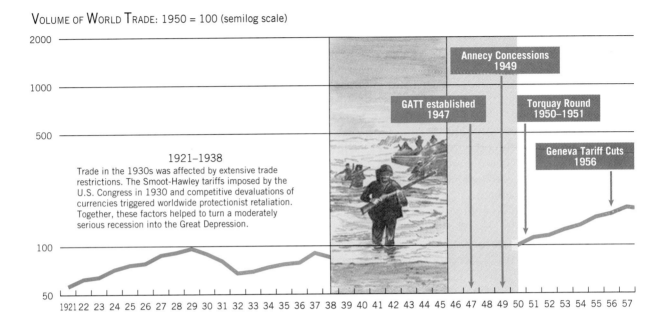

Volume of World Trade: 1950 = 100 (semilog scale)

1921–1938
Trade in the 1930s was affected by extensive trade restrictions. The Smoot-Hawley tariffs imposed by the U.S. Congress in 1930 and competitive devaluations of currencies triggered worldwide protectionist retaliation. Together, these factors helped to turn a moderately serious recession into the Great Depression.

GATT established 1947

Annecy Concessions 1949

Torquay Round 1950–1951

Geneva Tariff Cuts 1956

FIGURE 9.1   **The History of GATT's Effect on World Trade in Goods**

Source: Adapted from *Financial Times*, December 16, 1993, p. 5. Reproduced with permission. Updated using data from the World Trade Organization's Web site, *www.wto.org*

To help international businesses compete in world markets regardless of their nationality, the GATT sought to ensure that international trade was conducted on a nondiscriminatory basis. This was accomplished through use of the **most favored nation (MFN) principle**, which requires that any preferential treatment granted to one country must be extended to all countries. (See "Bringing the World into Focus" for further discussion of MFN.) Under GATT rules all members were required to utilize the MFN principle in dealing with other members. For example, if the United States cut the tariff on imports of British trucks to 20 percent, it also had to reduce its tariffs on imported trucks from all other members to 20 percent. Because of the MFN principle, multilateral, rather than bilateral, trade negotiations were encouraged, thereby strengthening GATT's role.

There are two important exceptions to the MFN principle:

1. To assist poorer countries in their economic development efforts, the GATT permitted members to lower tariffs to developing countries without lowering them for more developed countries. In the U.S. tariff code such reduced rates offered to developing countries are known as the **generalized system of preferences**. Other developed countries have similar exemptions. Obviously, by reducing these tariffs, the generalized system of preferences increases the pressures on domestic firms that are vulnerable to import competition from the developing countries. In contrast, MNCs can reduce their input and production costs by locating factories and assembly facilities in countries benefiting from the generalized system of preferences.

2. The second exemption is for regional arrangements that promote economic integration, such as the EU and NAFTA.

Although GATT's underlying principles were noble, its framers recognized that domestic political pressures often forced countries to retreat from pure free trade policies. The GATT permitted countries to protect their domestic industries on a nondiscriminatory basis, although under GATT rules countries were supposedly restricted to the use of tariffs only. Quotas and other nontariff barriers can often be applied discrim-

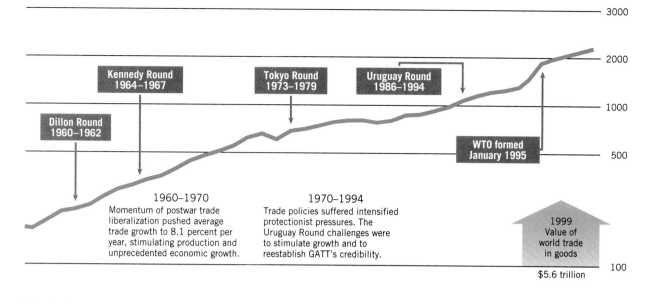

inatorily, and they are less "transparent"—that is, it is often harder to judge their impact on competition. However, there were loopholes in these rules, so many countries adopted quotas and other nontariff barriers yet remained in compliance with the GATT. For example, U.S. quotas restricting imports of peanuts, sugar, and other agricultural products that were granted a "temporary" waiver from GATT rules in 1955 remained in effect for decades. Countries were allowed exemptions to preserve national security or to remedy balance of payments problems. The GATT also permitted countries in certain circumstances to protect themselves against "too much" foreign competition.

The eighth, and final, round of GATT negotiations began in Uruguay in September 1986. Ratified by GATT members in Morocco in March 1994, the **Uruguay Round**

Bringing the World into FOCUS

MOST NATIONS ARE FAVORED

As part of the rules of membership in the GATT and the WTO, each member must grant every other member most favored nation (MFN) status. However, members are also free to grant nonmembers MFN status as well. The United States, for example, grants most favored nation status to nearly all countries. The few countries excluded are those considered diplomatically unfriendly to it. Currently, Afghanistan, Cuba, Laos, and North Korea are among the unfortunate few not qualifying for MFN treatment by the United States. Libya is also excluded; trade between Libya and the United States is currently embargoed because of Libya's sponsorship of terrorist organizations.

The Clinton administration decided to adopt the term "normal trade relations" (NTR) to replace MFN. It had two reasons for doing so. The public reason was that NTR was a more accurate description; if almost all countries receive such treatment, then the practice is "normal" rather than "most favored." There was also a political reason. The administration was in a battle to secure permanent MFN status for China as part of the administration's agreement to allow China to join the WTO. President Clinton judged that it would be easier to sway public opinion and win the vote in Congress if the United States were perceived to be treating China normally, rather than providing it favorable treatment. Hence MFN became NTR.

agreement took effect in 1995. Like its seven predecessors, the Uruguay Round cut tariffs on imported goods—in this case from an average of 4.7 percent to 3 percent. As average tariff rates declined, however, most countries recognized that nontariff barriers had become a more important impediment to the growth of world trade, so the Uruguay Round addressed them as well. For example, the participants made substantial progress in abolishing quotas by encouraging countries to convert existing quotas to tariff rate quotas (see Chapter 8). More important, Uruguay Round participants agreed to create the WTO, established its initial agenda, and granted it more power to attack trade barriers than the GATT had possessed.

The World Trade Organization

The **World Trade Organization (WTO)** came into being on January 1, 1995. Headquartered in Geneva, Switzerland, as of April 2001 the WTO includes 140 member and 32 observer countries. Members are required to open their markets to international trade and to follow the WTO's rules. The WTO has three primary goals:

1. Promote trade flows by encouraging nations to adopt nondiscriminatory, predictable trade policies. (Figure 9.2 details the WTO's principles for the world trading system.)

2. Reduce remaining trade barriers through multilateral negotiations. During the first five years of its existence the WTO has emphasized negotiations focused on specific sectors of the world economy. For example, the WTO sponsored 1996's Information Technology Agreement to eliminate tariffs on such products as computers, software, fax machines, and pagers. Similar agreements covering financial services and telecommunications were signed in 1997.

3. Establish impartial procedures for resolving trade disputes among members.

The WTO was clearly designed to build on and expand the successes of the GATT; indeed, the GATT agreement was incorporated into the WTO agreement. The WTO differs from the GATT in two important dimensions. First, the GATT focused on promoting trade in goods. The WTO's mandate is much broader. It is responsible for trade in goods, trade in services, international intellectual property protec-

---

FIGURE 9.2

The WTO's Principles of the Trading System

Source: "About the WTO,"
http://www.wto.org

WTO's TRADING SYSTEM PRINCIPLES

WITHOUT DISCRIMINATION
Members should not discriminate between their trading partners (all are granted "most favored nation status") nor discriminate between their own and foreign products, services, or nationals (who receive "national treatment").

FREER
Members lower trade barriers through negotiations.

PREDICTABLE
Members agree not to arbitrarily raise trade barriers (including tariffs and nontariff barriers) against foreign companies, investors, and governments.

MORE COMPETITIVE
The WTO discourages "unfair" practices such as export subsidies and dumping products below cost to gain market share.

BENEFICIAL FOR LESS DEVELOPED COUNTRIES
The WTO gives less developed nations more time to adjust, greater flexibility, and special privileges.

tion, and trade-related investment. Second, the WTO's enforcement powers are much stronger than those possessed by the GATT.

Problem Sectors.   Needless to say, the WTO faces a variety of challenges. One is dealing with sectors of the economy that seemingly receive government protection in every country. Two such sectors are agriculture and textiles. Trade in many agricultural products has been distorted by export subsidies, import restrictions, and other trade barriers. The **Cairns Group**, a group of major agricultural exporters led by Argentina, Australia, Brazil, Canada, and Thailand, has pressured the WTO to ensure that the Uruguay Round agreements dealing with agricultural trade are implemented according to schedule. Similarly, trade in textiles has been governed since 1974 by the **Multifibre Agreement**, which created a complex array of quotas and tariffs that affected 65 percent of the annual $250 billion trade in textile and apparel products. The impact of these barriers was the subject of Chapter 8's closing case. Developing countries are monitoring the WTO's dismantling of the Multifibre Agreement to ensure that their goods will have freer access to the markets of developed countries.

› The WTO has attracted protests from activists who believe it should incorporate protection of human rights and the environment into its rules.

The General Agreement on Trade in Services (GATS).   Another challenge facing the WTO is reducing barriers to trade in services. The Uruguay Round developed a set of principles under which such trade should be conducted. For example, government controls on service trade should be administered in a nondiscriminatory fashion. One nondiscriminatory approach is the use of **national treatment**, whereby a country treats foreign firms the same way it treats domestic firms. If, for example, national insurance regulators require domestic firms to maintain reserves equal to 10 percent of their outstanding policies, then the identical requirement should be imposed on foreign firms operating in that country. However, service industries are very diverse, and few concrete agreements regarding specific service industries were included in the Uruguay Round. The WTO members began negotiating a new GATS agreement in 2000.

Agreement on Trade-Related Aspects of Intellectual Property Rights (TRIPS).   Entrepreneurs, artists, and inventors have been hurt by inadequate enforcement by many countries of laws prohibiting illegal usage, copying, or counterfeiting of intellectual property. These problems are particularly widespread in the music, filmed entertainment, and computer software industries. The Uruguay Round agreement substantially strengthened the protection granted to owners of intellectual property rights and developed enforcement and dispute settlement procedures to punish violators. However, because most such owners reside in the developed countries and many violators live in developing countries, the Uruguay Round negotiators agreed to phase in intellectual property protections over a decade. Not all industries were happy with this concession. For example, the Pharmaceutical Manufacturers Association believes the concession grants developing countries carte blanche to continue pirating patented drugs for another ten years.[2]

Trade-Related Investment Measures Agreement (TRIMS).   WTO members are well aware of the relationship between trade and investment: Approximately one-third of the $6.9 billion of annual trade in goods and services is between subsidiaries of a parent organization. However, the developing countries believe FDI can be an important mechanism for promoting economic growth, technology transfer, and industrialization and thus were unwilling to yield much control over it. Accordingly, the TRIMS agreement in the Uruguay Round is but a modest start toward eliminating national regulations on FDI that may distort or restrict trade. The TRIMS agreement affects:

- *Trade-balancing rules:* Countries may not require foreign investors to limit their imports of inputs to an amount equal to their exports of local production.
- *Foreign-exchange access:* Countries may not restrict foreign investors' access to foreign exchange.
- *domestic sales requirements:* Countries may not require the investor to sell a percentage of a factory's output in the local market.[3]

Under certain circumstances, however, developing countries are able to waive these requirements.

Enforcement of WTO Decisions.   The enforcement power of the GATT was notoriously weak. A country found to have violated its GATT obligations by an arbitration panel was in effect asked, "Is it OK if we punish you?" Most countries, as you might expect, answered "no," and there the matter ended. Under WTO rules, a country failing to live up to the agreement—for example, by imposing a nontariff barrier contrary to the WTO agreement—may have a complaint filed against it. If a WTO panel finds the country in violation of the rules, the panel will likely ask the country to eliminate the trade barrier. If the country refuses, the WTO will allow the complaining country to impose trade barriers on the offending country equal to the damage caused by the trade barrier. Furthermore, the offending country is not allowed to counterretaliate by imposing new trade barriers against the complainant.

Although barriers to international trade and investment remain, no one believed they would come tumbling down like the walls of Jericho as soon as the WTO arrived on the scene. Most experts give the WTO high marks for its accomplishments during its first seven years of existence. The WTO's initial actions, such as the sectoral agreements in telecommunications, information technology, and financial services, are laying the foundation for the continued elimination of impediments to international commerce. However, the growing importance of the WTO has also attracted opposition to its actions, as "Bringing the World into Focus" makes clear.

› REGIONAL ECONOMIC INTEGRATION

Regional alliances to promote liberalization of international trade are an important feature of the post-World War II international landscape. Over 100 such agreements are in existence, although not all have had much practical impact. They present international businesses with myriad opportunities and challenges. The past decade in particular has seen a rise in the number and strengthening of trading blocs, as countries seek to integrate their economies more closely in order to open new markets for their firms and lower prices for their consumers.

Forms of Economic Integration

Regional trading blocs differ significantly in form and function. The characteristic of most importance to international businesses is the extent of economic integration among a bloc's members. This is of utmost importance because it affects exporting and investment opportunities available to firms from member and nonmember countries. There are five different forms of regional economic integration: free trade area, customs union, common market, economic union, and political union. We discuss these next in order of ascending degree of economic integration.

Bringing the World into FOCUS

THE WTO MAKES THE HEADLINES

Newspaper headlines in November 1999 heralded stories about thousands of protesters filling the streets of Seattle, Washington. The reason for their protests? Delegates to the World Trade Organization (WTO) were meeting there.

The WTO drew the wrath of a broad coalition of public interest groups. Environmentalists argued that WTO rules needed to be rewritten to incorporate environmental concerns into its decision making. Human rights and working rights advocates maintained that countries should be allowed to require that goods sold within their borders comply with codes of fair conduct. These codes might require that workers be paid a minimum wage, that overtime pay be mandated, or that child labor be forbidden.

Union members were also well represented among the Seattle protesters. Teamster members argued against allowing trucks and drivers from any NAFTA country to transport cargoes between U.S. cities, claiming that highway safety would be jeopardized. Representatives of the United Auto Workers were upset that WTO rules would further the exodus of auto industry jobs from the United States to Mexico and other lower-wage countries. The United Steelworkers claimed that the WTO would promote what the union believed to be illegal dumping of steel and steel products in the United States.

Free Trade Area.   A **free trade area** encourages trade among its members by eliminating trade barriers (tariffs, quotas, and other nontariff barriers [NTBs]) among them. An example of such an arrangement is NAFTA, which reduces tariff and NTBs to trade among Canada, Mexico, and the United States.

Although a free trade area reduces trade barriers among its members, each member is free to establish its own trade policies against nonmembers. As a result, members of free trade areas are often vulnerable to the problem of **trade deflection**, in which nonmembers reroute (or deflect) their exports to the member nation with the lowest external trade barriers. Canada, for example, may use high tariffs or quotas to discourage imports of a given product from nonmembers, while the United States may impose few restrictions on imports of the same good from nonmembers. Taking advantage of the latter's low barriers, nonmembers may deflect their Canada-destined exports by first shipping the good to the United States and then reexporting it from the United States to Canada. In Chapter 8 we noted that Desmarais & Frère, well before NAFTA was signed, was victimized by trade deflection as Korean manufacturers first shipped photo albums to the United States and then reexported them from the United States to Canada to avoid Canada's antidumping duty on Korean photo albums. To prevent trade deflection from destroying their members' trade policies toward nonmembers, most free trade agreements specify **rules of origin**, which detail the conditions under which a good is classified as a member good or a nonmember good. For example, under NAFTA rules of origin, photo albums qualify for preferential treatment as a North American product only if they undergo substantial processing or assembly in Mexico, Canada, or the United States.

Customs Union.   A **customs union** combines the elimination of internal trade barriers among its members with the adoption of common external trade policies toward nonmembers. Because of the uniform treatment of products from nonmember countries, a customs union avoids the trade deflection problem. A firm from a nonmember country pays the same tariff rate on exports to any member of the customs union.

Historically the most important customs union was the Zollverein, created in 1834 by several independent principalities in what is now Germany. The eventual unification of Germany in 1870 was hastened by this customs union, which tightened the economic bonds among the Germanic principalities and facilitated their political union. A more contemporary example of a customs union is the Mercosur Accord, an agreement signed by Argentina, Brazil, Paraguay, and Uruguay to promote trade among themselves.

Common Market. A **common market** is a third step along the path to total economic integration. As in a customs union, members of a common market eliminate internal trade barriers among themselves and adopt a common external trade policy toward nonmembers. A common market goes a step further, however, by eliminating barriers that inhibit the movement of factors of production—labor, capital, and technology—among its members. Workers may move from their homeland and practice their profession or trade in any of the other member nations. Firms may locate production facilities, invest in other businesses, and utilize their technologies anywhere within the common market. Productivity within the common market is expected to rise because factors of production are free to locate where the returns to them are highest. An example of a common market is the European Economic Area, which is an agreement by EU members and several other European countries to promote the free movement of labor, capital, and technology among them.

Economic Union. An **economic union** represents full integration of the economies of two or more countries. In addition to eliminating internal trade barriers, adopting common external trade policies, and abolishing restrictions on the mobility of factors of production among members, an economic union requires its members to coordinate their economic policies (monetary policy, fiscal policy, taxation, and social welfare programs) in order to blend their economies into a single entity. Twelve members of the EU are in the process of creating an economic union among themselves that will feature the use of a single currency by all 12 participants.

Political Union. A **political union** is the complete political as well as economic integration of two or more countries, thereby effectively making them one country. An example of a political union is the integration of the 13 separate colonies operating under the Articles of Confederation into a new country, the United States of America. Figure 9.3 summarizes the five forms of economic integration.

FIGURE 9.3

Forms of Economic Integration

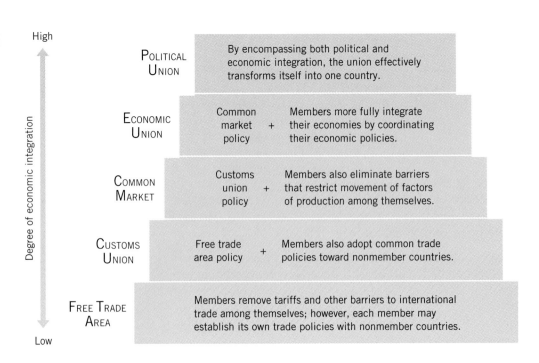

Degree of economic integration — High / Low

POLITICAL UNION — By encompassing both political and economic integration, the union effectively transforms itself into one country.

ECONOMIC UNION — Common market policy + Members more fully integrate their economies by coordinating their economic policies.

COMMON MARKET — Customs union policy + Members also eliminate barriers that restrict movement of factors of production among themselves.

CUSTOMS UNION — Free trade area policy + Members also adopt common trade policies toward nonmember countries.

FREE TRADE AREA — Members remove tariffs and other barriers to international trade among themselves; however, each member may establish its own trade policies with nonmember countries.

The Impact of Economic Integration on Firms

From the viewpoint of an individual firm regional integration is a two-edged sword. Consider elimination of internal trade barriers, a feature common to all five forms of economic integration. Lowering tariffs within the regional trading bloc opens the markets of member countries to all member country firms. Firms can lower their average production and distribution costs by capturing economies of scale as they expand their customer base within the trading bloc. The lower cost structure will also help the firms compete internationally outside the trading bloc. For example, many Canadian manufacturers supported their country's free trade agreements with the United States. They believed that improved access to the large U.S. market would allow longer production runs in Canadian factories, thereby lowering their average costs and making Canadian goods more competitive in international markets inside and outside the free trade area. However, elimination of trade barriers also exposes a firm's home market to competition from firms located in other member countries, thus threatening less efficient firms.

A regional trading bloc may also attract FDI from nonmember countries, as firms outside the bloc seek the benefits of insider status by establishing manufacturing facilities within the bloc. Most non-European MNCs, including General Mills, Toyota, and Samsung, have invested heavily in the EU to take advantage of Europe's increased economic integration. These investments bolster the productivity of European workers and increase the choices available to European consumers but threaten established European firms such as Unilever, Renault, and Siemens.

Typically each form of economic integration confers benefits on the national economy as a whole but often hurts specific sectors and communities within the economy. As a result, negotiating any form of economic integration is not easy. Special-interest groups that feel they will be harmed by an agreement will lobby against it. For example, U.S. and Canadian autoworkers lobbied against NAFTA, fearing that Ford, GM, and Chrysler would shift production to Mexico to take advantage of its lower-cost labor. As a result of such internal political pressures, few economic integration treaties are "pure"; most contain some exemptions to quiet politically powerful domestic special-interest groups.

THE EUROPEAN UNION ‹

The most important regional trading bloc in the world today is the European Union (EU). The EU's 15 member countries, with a combined population of 377 million, compose one of the world's richest markets, with a total GDP of $8.3 trillion, or 27 percent of the world economy. (See Table 9.2 and Map 9.1.)

Like the International Monetary Fund, the World Bank, and the GATT, the creation of the EU was motivated by the desires of war-weary Europeans to promote peace and prosperity through economic and political cooperation. To further this objective, six European nations—France, West Germany, Italy, and the Benelux nations (*Bel*gium, the *Net*herlands, and *Lux*embourg)—signed the **Treaty of Rome** in 1957. The Treaty of Rome established the European Economic Community (EEC) and called for the development of a common market among the six member states.

Over the ensuing five decades the EEC changed its name twice and expanded its membership to 15 countries. During the 1970s the United Kingdom, Denmark, and Ireland joined the EEC, which became commonly referred to as the European Community (EC). During the 1980s Greece, Portugal, and Spain entered the EC, bringing its membership to 12 countries. In 1993 the 12 EC members signed the Treaty of Maastricht; as a result of this agreement, the EC became known as the EU. In 1995 Austria, Finland, and Sweden joined the EU. Today Norway and Switzerland are the only major Western European nations that do not belong to the EU. Although they were invited to join, both declined for domestic political reasons.

TABLE 9.2

The European Union, 1999 Data

MEMBERS	POPULATION (MILLIONS)	GDP (BILLIONS OF U.S. DOLLARS)	PER CAPITA GDP*	DATE OF ENTRY
Original Six				
Belgium	10.2	245.7	$24,200	1957
France	60.8	1,410.3	21,897	1957
Luxembourg	0.4	17.6	38,247	1957
Germany	82.0	2,081.2	22,404	1957
Italy	57.6	1,150.0	20,751	1957
Netherlands	15.8	384.8	23,052	1957
Later Entrants				
Demark	5.3	174.3	24,280	1973
Ireland	3.7	81.9	19,180	1973
United Kingdom	59.1	1,373.6	20,883	1973
Greece	10.5	123.9	14,595	1981
Spain	39.4	562.2	16,730	1986
Portugal	10.0	107.7	15,147	1986
Recent Entrants				
Austria	8.1	208.9	23,808	1995
Finland	5.2	126.1	21,209	1995
Sweden	8.9	226.4	20,829	1995
Total, 15 Members	377.1	8,274.6	20,893	

*GDP per capita adjusted by World Bank for purchasing power parity.
Source: World Bank, *World Development Report,* 1999–2000, and World Bank Web site.

MAP 9.1

The European Union

Governing the European Union

The EU is a unique institution. Its members are sovereign nations that have agreed, sometimes begrudgingly, to cede certain of their powers to the EU. The EU can be characterized both as an "intergovernmental government" because it is a government of national governments and as a "supranational government" because it exercises power above the national level. The EU is governed by four organizations that perform its executive, administrative, legislative, and judicial functions:

- The Council of the European Union (headquartered in Brussels, Belgium)
- The European Commission (also based in Brussels)
- The European Parliament (normally meets in Strasbourg, France)
- The European Court of Justice (sitting in Luxembourg)

Because most of the EU's employees are located in Brussels, many Europeans refer to the EU's government as "Brussels," the same way many Canadians refer to their national government as "Ottawa" or many Americans refer to theirs as "Washington."

The Council of the European Union. The **Council of the European Union** (sometimes called the Council of Ministers) is composed of 15 representatives, each selected directly by and responsible to his or her home government. Which representative a country sends to a Council meeting depends on the Council's agenda. For example, if the Council is dealing with farm policies, each country may send its minister of agriculture. The Council presidency rotates among the members every six months. In Council decisions France, Germany, Italy, and the United Kingdom have 10 votes each; Spain has 8; Belgium, Greece, the Netherlands, and Portugal, 5 each; Austria and Sweden, 4 each; Denmark, Finland, and Ireland, 3 each; and Luxembourg, 2. The allocation of votes is in rough proportion to the population and economic importance of the members.

The Council is the EU's most powerful decision-making body. Each representative pursues the interests of his or her home government. The Council's strong powers reflect the reluctance of the member states to surrender power to Brussels on issues they view as vital to their national interests. As a result, some Council decisions require unanimous approval. On matters perceived to be less threatening to national interests, Council decisions require only a qualified majority (62 out of a total 87 votes) for passage. Effectively, a coalition of two large countries and three smaller countries can block a decision. However, the EU strives to create consensus on all issues and often slows its deliberations to develop compromises amenable to all the members, even when unanimity is not required. As a result, an overwhelming percentage of Council decisions are made unanimously, regardless of the voting rules.

The European Commission. The **European Commission** is composed of 20 people selected for five-year terms. The smaller EU countries each nominate one citizen to serve on the Commission; the larger countries select two. However, once these individuals are in office, their loyalty is to the EU itself, not to their home countries. The Commission's primary mandate is to be the "guardian of the Treaties." The Commission also acts as the EU's administrative branch and manages the EU's $100 billion annual budget. Its functions include the following:

- It proposes legislation to be considered by the Council.
- It implements the provisions of the Treaty of Rome and other EU treaties.
- It protects the EU's interests in political debates, particularly in Council deliberations.
- It has extensive powers in implementing the EU's customs union, the Common Agricultural Policy (CAP), and the completion of the internal market.
- It administers the EU's permanent bureaucracy, which employs about 15,000 people—popularly known as "Eurocrats"—two-thirds of whom work at Commission headquarters in Brussels. (Because the EU has 11 official languages, one-fifth of the Commission's employees are engaged in translation services!)

The European Parliament. The **European Parliament** comprises 626 representatives elected in national elections to serve five-year terms. Seats are allocated in rough proportion to a country's population, but the allocation also reflects political jockeying among members. For example, Germany has 99 seats, while France, Italy, and the United Kingdom are allocated 87 seats each, even though Germany's population is at least 40 percent larger than that of any of the other three countries (refer back to Table 9.2). Of the EU's governing bodies the Parliament was originally the weakest. Initially it had only a consultative role in EU policy making. However, it has used its budgetary powers to enlarge its influence within the EU's governing institutions, and it also gained additional powers under the Maastricht and Amsterdam Treaties, as discussed later in the chapter.

The most telling example of the growing importance of the European Parliament was the mass resignation of all 20 EU Commissioners in March 1999, after a Parliamentary inquiry uncovered fraud, inept management, favoritism, and a lack of accountability in several Commission-administered programs. Because many Europeans are concerned about the lack of accountability in the EU's programs (particularly the British) and the lack of democracy in its decision-making processes (a concern of the Swedes and Danes), the role of the European Parliament is likely to expand and its powers grow over time.

The European Court of Justice. The **European Court of Justice** consists of 15 judges who serve six-year terms. It interprets EU law and ensures that members follow EU regulations and policies. Because national governments carry out the EU's policies, many cases reaching the European Court are referred from national courts asking it to interpret EU law. For example, the Court declared Germany's 450-year-old beer purity law regulating beer additives illegal, ruling that the law unreasonably restricted imports into Germany. Also, as discussed later, its ruling in the *Cassis de Dijon* case smoothed the way for the creation of the common market called for in the Treaty of Rome.

The Legislative Process. The legislative process in the EU has never been simple, although it was once understandable, as captured in the catch phrase "the Commission proposes, the Parliament advises, and the Council disposes." As the Parliament has gained increased powers, the complexity of passing legislation has increased exponentially, as Figure 9.4, which depicts decision making under the **co-decision procedure**, shows. The co-decision procedure is used in such areas as health, consumer policy, and free movement of workers. On issues where the co-decision process is not used, the process is simpler and the Parliament's power is weaker.

Because the EU prefers to develop a strong consensus on issues among its members before it adopts new legislation, transforming a Commission proposal into an EU law and then implementing that law into national legislation often takes years. The complicated governance arrangements of the EU reflect the ongoing struggle between the members' desire to retain their national sovereignty and their wish to create a supranational government with an international political and economic stature equal to those of the United States and Japan. (As "Venturing Abroad" suggests, many MNCs exploit this power struggle to their benefit.) The member countries have granted EU governing bodies power over trade and agricultural policy. The EU and its members share responsibility for formulating transportation policy and environmental policy. Many other areas of responsibility remain with members' governments. The debate over national sovereignty versus supranational government is manifested in another way: Although EU policies are formulated supranationally, they must be implemented by members at a national level.

The Struggle to Create a Common Market

The Treaty of Rome's goal of creating a common market was indeed visionary. Unfortunately, for the first 35 years of the EU's existence, it was nothing more than a cruel mirage. To establish a common market that would permit the free flow of goods, services,

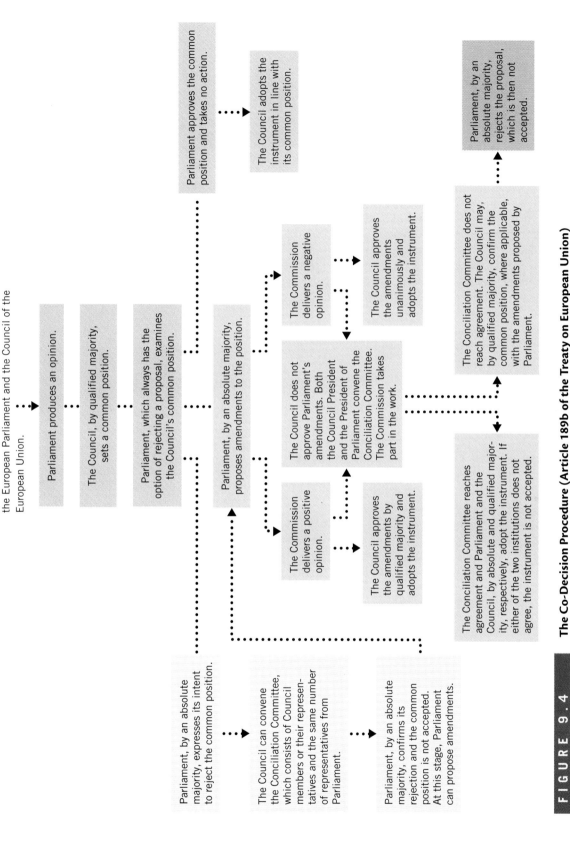

The European Commission offers a proposal to the European Parliament and the Council of the European Union.

Parliament produces an opinion.

The Council, by qualified majority, sets a common position.

Parliament, which always has the option of rejecting a proposal, examines the Council's common position.

Parliament approves the common position and takes no action.

The Council adopts the instrument in line with its common position.

Parliament, by an absolute majority, proposes amendments to the position.

The Commission delivers a positive opinion.

The Commission delivers a negative opinion.

The Council does not approve Parliament's amendments. Both the Council President and the President of Parliament convene the Conciliation Committee. The Commission takes part in the work.

The Council approves the amendments by qualified majority and adopts the instrument.

The Council approves the amendments unanimously and adopts the instrument.

Parliament, by an absolute majority, expresses its intent to reject the common position.

The Council can convene the Conciliation Committee, which consists of Council members or their representatives and the same number of representatives from Parliament.

Parliament, by an absolute majority, confirms its rejection and the common position is not accepted. At this stage, Parliament can propose amendments.

The Conciliation Committee reaches agreement and Parliament and the Council, by absolute and qualified majority, respectively, adopt the instrument. If either of the two institutions does not agree, the instrument is not accepted.

The Conciliation Committee does not reach agreement. The Council may, by qualified majority, confirm the common position, where applicable, with the amendments proposed by Parliament.

Parliament, by an absolute majority, rejects the proposal, which is then not accepted.

F I G U R E 9 . 4   **The Co-Decision Procedure (Article 189b of the Treaty on European Union)**

Source: *The European Union*, Luxembourg: Office for Official Publications of the European Communities, 1997, pp. 24–25.

VENTURING *Abroad* LOBBYING THE EUROPEAN UNION

The government of the European Union (EU) is engaged in many activities that affect international businesses. For example, the EU has decided that at least 50 percent of the programs broadcast on TV stations in its member countries must be European in origin. The effect of this regulation is to shrink the market for movies and TV shows produced in the United States, Mexico, Australia, and other countries. Because of the impact of the EU's decisions on the opening or closing of the enormous European market to international businesses, most countries maintain diplomatic relationships with the EU to ensure the EU does not disregard their economic interests. The United States, for example, maintains a United States Mission to the European Union, led by a senior State Department official with ambassadorial status.

Savvy international businesspeople, however, do not rely solely on their home governments to protect them from adverse EU regulations. The first step is understanding the power relationships within the EU—particularly between the Council of the European Union, which defends national interests, and the European Commission, which promotes the interests of an integrated Europe. Firms threatened by pending EU regulations can adopt two strategies:

1. They may lobby the Commission and its elaborate bureaucracy to adopt regulations more beneficial to their interests. Because the Commission must continually balance the often diverse interests of EU

members, firms can often influence the Commission to add their interests to the long list of other factors that it will consider in proposing legislation to the Council. Also, because of the Commission's commitment to completing the EU's internal market, firms have found that arguments promoting increased European integration are particularly well received by Eurocrats. For example, the Commission dropped proposed franchising regulations after U.S. firms convinced its staff that the pending regulations would hinder European integration.

2. Firms may lobby an ally on the Council. For example, remembering that "all politics is local," Japanese automakers that built assembly plants in the United Kingdom were able to enlist the help of the British representative on the Council—who was interested in preserving jobs in his country—when French and Italian automakers were urging the EU to adopt regulations prejudicial to those U.K. assembly plants.

Sources: James N. Gardner, "Lobbying, European-Style," *Europe*, November 1991 (Number 311), pp. 29–30; "European Bureaucrats Are Writing the Rules Americans Will Live By," *Wall Street Journal*, May 17, 1989, p. A1; "Lobbying Brussels in Anticipation of 1992," *Wall Street Journal*, March 6, 1989, p. A12.

labor, capital, and technology, each EU member had to agree to change thousands of its national laws, product standards, and regulations to ensure that they were compatible with those of other EU members. In practice, the member nations moved cautiously because of political pressures from domestic special-interest groups.

As a result, conflicting national regulations, which affected nearly every good and service purchased by Europeans, hindered trade and the completion of the common market. For example, Spain required that keyboards sold within its borders contain a "tilde" key, an accent mark commonly used in the Spanish language. No other EU country prescribed such a regulation. Italy required pasta to be made of durum wheat, a requirement not decreed by other EU members.

The EU initially relied on a process of **harmonization** to eliminate such conflicts. The EU encouraged member countries to voluntarily adopt common, EU-wide ("harmonized") regulations affecting intra-EU trade in goods and services and movement of resources. The harmonization process moved slowly, however, as domestic political forces within the member states resisted change. For example, to protect the purity of its language, Spain refused to yield on the tilde issue. EU producers spent an estimated $260 billion (in 1988 dollars) annually to comply with different national regulations.[4] These increased costs raised the prices paid by European consumers and reduced the global competitiveness of European manufacturers.

Progress toward eliminating conflicting product standards was so slow that some pessimists believed the EU would disintegrate. However, in 1979 the European Court of Justice heard the now famous *Cassis de Dijon* case. Rewe Zentral AG, a German wholesaler, wished to import Cassis de Dijon, a French liqueur made from black currants, into Germany. However, Cassis de Dijon failed to meet German regulatory standards—its alcohol content was too low. Rewe Zentral sued, arguing that Germany violated its obligations under the Treaty of Rome to promote the free movement of goods. The European Court of Justice found for the German wholesaler. In so doing, the Court created the concept of **mutual recognition**: If one member state determines that a product is appropriate for sale, then all other EU members are also obliged to do so under the provisions of the Treaty of Rome. Because France had determined Cassis de Dijon to be a legitimate liqueur, Germany was obligated to allow its sale as well.

Although the Court's findings contained some loopholes, the implications of the *Cassis de Dijon* case were profound. Adopting the concept of mutual recognition meant that the slow harmonization process could be bypassed, and conflicting product standards would no longer serve as barriers to trade among EU members. The timing of the case was also fortunate: Many European economic and political leaders were becoming increasingly concerned about the competitiveness of European firms in world markets. Their concerns reinvigorated the EU's commitment to completing the common market called for in the Treaty of Rome.

In 1985 the European Commission issued its *White Paper on Completing the Internal Market*. The *White Paper* called for accelerated progress on ending all trade barriers and restrictions on the free movement of goods, services, capital, and labor among members. Accepting the vision of the *White Paper*, the members in February 1986 signed the Single European Act, which took effect on July 1, 1987. The act was intended to help complete the formation of the internal market (the term developed by the Eurocrats to mean common market) by December 31, 1992. Under the Single European Act 279 broad regulatory changes had to be made to complete the internal market. Although not all these changes were completely implemented by the 1992 deadline, most were. Accordingly, most experts agree that by the end of 1992 the Treaty of Rome's goal of creating a common market had been accomplished—and it only took 35 years to do so! However, if you think of the magnitude of the challenge—getting so many governments to cooperate peacefully on such a broad range of activities—perhaps 35 years is a remarkably short period of time.

The benefits of creating the common market are substantial to European firms, economies, and workers. The common market offers firms the opportunity to sell their goods in a large, rich market free from any barriers to trade. However, although firms in EU member countries have gained improved access to a larger market, they also face increased competition in their home markets from other members' firms. This increased competition benefits consumers throughout the EU. Marketing, production, and R&D costs have been reduced because firms generally have to comply with only one, EU-wide set of regulations instead of 15 separate sets of national regulations. Many firms have been able to restructure their European manufacturing operations to capture economies of scale and lower their production costs. For example, Samsung shifted its European color television production, which was previously split between factories in Portugal and Spain, to its plant in Billingham, England. It dedicated its Spanish factory to producing VCRs for the entire EU market and its Portuguese factory to supplying parts for its other European operations. Samsung determined that the economies of scale obtained by this realignment of its operations would lower its manufacturing costs, improve the quality of its products, and create new jobs for European workers.[5] And the EU has been a magnet for new investment from other foreign firms eager to enter the lucrative European market and benefit from its common market. U.S. FDI in the EU has risen from $84 billion in 1985, when the *White Paper* was first issued, to $512 billion in 1999. Similarly, over 500 Japanese companies have established operations in the EU since 1985.

From Common Market to Economic Union

The EU members were justifiably proud of the completion of the internal market in 1992. As the necessary changes were being finalized, the Cold War ended. The Soviet Union dissolved, the countries of Eastern Europe and Central Europe abandoned communism, and the threat of nuclear war diminished. The United States stood alone as the world's remaining superpower. Some European politicians believed that Europe should reassert itself on the world's stage and free itself from geopolitical domination by the United States. Meanwhile, many EU economists were arguing that European firms remained at a competitive disadvantage with regard to their North American and Asian rivals because of the risks and costs associated with doing business in so many different currencies. Addressing these concerns, the EU's Council of Ministers met in the Dutch city of Maastricht in December 1991 to discuss the EU's economic and political future. The result was a new treaty that amended the Treaty of Rome; this new treaty was known formally as the **Treaty on European Union** and informally as the **Maastricht Treaty**. After ratification by the then 12 EU members, the Maastricht Treaty came into force on November 1, 1993.

The Maastricht Treaty rests on three "pillars" designed to further Europe's economic and political integration:

1. A new agreement to create common foreign and defense policies among members

2. A new agreement to cooperate on police, judicial, and public safety matters

3. The old familiar European Community, with new provisions to create an economic and monetary union among member states

After the treaty was implemented, the European Community became commonly known as the European Union in recognition of the increasing integration of Europe. The Maastricht Treaty granted citizens the right to live, work, vote, and run for election anywhere within the EU and strengthened the powers of the EU's legislative body, the European Parliament, in budgetary, trade, cultural, and health matters. The treaty also created a new **cohesion fund**, a means of funneling economic development aid to countries whose per capita GDP is less than 90 percent of the EU average. The initial recipients of cohesion funds included Spain, Portugal, Greece, and Ireland, although Ireland's access to this aid is soon likely to terminate as a result of its booming economy.

Without a doubt the most important aspect of the Maastricht Treaty is the establishment of the **economic and monetary union**. Its major task is to create a single-currency, called the euro, to replace the existing national currencies. Denmark, Sweden, and the United Kingdom chose not to become charter members of the single-currency bloc. Greece did not initially meet the economic criteria necessary to join the single-currency bloc, although it later met the criteria and joined at the beginning of 2001.

The euro came into being on January 1, 1999. On that date the 11 charter participants irrevocably fixed the value of their national currencies to the euro. However, euro coins and bank notes did not become available on that date. During a three-year transition period (1999 to 2001), the euro exists only as a bookkeeping currency to settle transactions among participating EU governments and banking systems. At the beginning of 2002 euro coins and bills will be placed into circulation, allowing ordinary citizens to use euros to transact their daily business. For a few months thereafter euros will co-circulate with francs, lira, pesetas, marks, and so forth. After this transition period expires, the national currencies of the participants will be withdrawn from circulation and no longer be accepted as legal tender.

European financial services firms hope that the euro will become as important in international commerce as the U.S. dollar or the yen. European economists and political leaders believe that creation of the euro will significantly reduce the exchange rate risks and currency conversion costs borne by European MNCs. Prior to the advent of the euro firms conducting cross-border business within Europe were forced to pay fees to bankers typically ranging from 0.4 percent to 2 percent of the transaction amount anytime the firms wished to convert French francs into Belgian francs, Dutch guilders into Austrian schillings, and so on. Moreover, firms bore exchange rate risks in such transactions, as Chapter 7 discussed. Although the foreign-exchange market developed a variety of techniques to reduce (or hedge) this risk, these techniques nonetheless entailed paying fees to bankers or brokers. EU officials believe the creation of the euro will save Europeans $25 to $30 billion annually in currency conversion and hedging costs. Companies expect to capture significant savings, which should flow right to their bottom lines. Germany's Robert Bosch Company estimates that its annual currency conversion costs will fall by $28.5 million due to the single currency, although it also expects that its one-time costs of converting its accounting and financial systems to the euro may run as high as $30 million.[6] The benefits stemming from the creation of the euro are so alluring that many MNCs operating in Europe immediately began to convert their accounting records to euros, and urged their suppliers and customers to invoice and pay them in euros.

Creation of a single currency is not without controversy, however. Its development implies that participating members will lose the ability to control their own domestic money supplies and economic destinies. National governments will then become vulnerable to losing elections because of short-term pocketbook issues. The newly created **European Central Bank** is now responsible for controlling the euro-zone's money supply, interest rates, and inflation. Yet disagreement exists over the European Central Bank's fundamental objective—should it promote employment growth or should it focus on fighting inflation? Some critics of the euro fear that a "one size fits all" monetary policy for the entire euro-zone will create hardships in individual countries whose economies are diverging from those of the rest of the euro-zone. For example, in 2000 Ireland suffered from its highest inflation rate in a decade as a result of the country's booming economy. Irish government officials would have preferred that the European Central Bank aggressively raise interest rates in hopes of cooling down Ireland's economy, but the bank chose to move more deliberately because it had to balance Ireland's needs against those of the other euro-zone economies.

The latest step the EU has taken toward integration is the **Treaty for Europe** (more popularly known as the **Treaty of Amsterdam**), which was signed in 1997. The more important components of the Treaty of Amsterdam include:

- A strong commitment to attack the EU's chronic high levels of unemployment, particularly among younger citizens

- A plan to strengthen the role of the European Parliament by expanding the number of areas that require use of the co-decision procedure

- Establishment of a two-track system, allowing groups of members to proceed with economic and political integration faster than the EU as a whole

〉 EU members adopting the euro as their currency lose control over their monetary policy. This London protestor believes the United Kingdom should continue to use the pound.

Future EU Challenges. The members of the EU have made remarkable progress in implementing the goals of the Treaty of Rome. Political conflicts still remain, of course. One divisive issue is state aid to industry. Under EU rules national governments may not provide subsidies to firms that "distort" competition. Yet many governments are loathe to let domestic firms go bankrupt, especially if local jobs are threatened. This is a particular problem in the airline industry, where privately owned car-

› British Airways and other privately owned EU carriers object to grants of state aid to their publicly owned rivals like Alitalia and Olympic Airlines.

riers like British Airways, Lufthansa, and KLM are outraged by state subsidies to state-owned Alitalia, Iberia, TAP, and Olympic Airlines, with whom the privately owned carriers compete in intra-EU markets. France and the United Kingdom continue to squabble over the EU's Common Agricultural Policy, which disproportionately benefits French farmers to the detriment of British interests and hurts European MNCs by poisoning relationships between the United States and the EU. Other countries, such as Denmark, are concerned about the paucity of democracy within the EU. They believe more power should be given to the EU's only directly elected governing body, the European Parliament.

Perhaps the most important issue, however, is whether, how, and when EU membership should be expanded. The EU members met in Nice, France, in December 2000 to begin negotiating answers to these questions. A dozen countries have applied for membership in the EU. The existing members are divided on many aspects of expansion. Some members believe that the EU should broaden its scope quickly, while others believe the EU should move slowly. Another group believes that the EU will have to curtail the powers of the Council of Ministers, which protects national interests, to accommodate the larger number of members. Others assert that the EU will have to slash its aid to farmers and poorer regions if new—and poorer—countries are added to the EU. At the core of the disagreement is the **"wider vs. deeper"** question. "Wider" proponents argue that the EU should rapidly broaden its membership, even if doing so makes it more difficult for the EU to fully integrate the economies of its members and to develop common foreign and defense policies. "Deeper" proponents believe that the EU should expand more slowly, carefully making sure that each new member is ready to participate in all of the EU's economic and political initiatives. At the heart of the wider vs. deeper controversy are competing visions of the EU: Is the primary mission of the EU to promote trade and investment or to promote the political integration of Europe?

› OTHER REGIONAL TRADING BLOCS

The EU's success in enriching its members through trade promotion has stimulated the development of other regional trading blocs. Every inhabited continent now contains at least one regional trading group. Europe, for example, has many other smaller trading blocs, such as the **European Free Trade Association**. Its members are Iceland, Liechtenstein, Norway, and Switzerland. The first three of these countries have joined with the EU to create a common market known as the **European Economic Area**, which promotes the free movement of goods, services, labor, and capital among its 18 members. Members of the Commonwealth of Independent States have created a free trade area as well. Russia, Belarus, Kazakhstan, and Kyrgyzstan have gone one step further, forming a customs union in 1995.

The North American Free Trade Agreement

Another important example of regional economic integration is NAFTA. Implemented in 1994 to reduce barriers to trade and investment among Canada, Mexico, and the United States, NAFTA builds on the 1988 Canadian-U.S. Free Trade Agreement. Canada and the United States enjoy the world's largest bilateral trading relationship, with two-way trade totaling $405 billion in 1999. The United States is Mexico's largest trading partner, while Mexico is the third largest trading partner of the United States (after Canada and Japan). However, trade between Canada and Mexico, while growing, is rather small.

NAFTA promises an increasing integration of the North American economies. Over a 15-year time span tariff walls will be lowered, NTBs reduced, and investment opportunities increased for firms located in the three countries. However, some industries received special treatment in the agreement. Negotiators from all three countries recognized the political sensitivity of certain issues and industries and chose to compromise on their treatment within NAFTA to ensure the agreement's ratification. For example, because Canada fears being dominated by U.S. media, NAFTA allows Canada to limit foreign investments in its culture industries (publishing, music, television, radio, cable, and film). Similarly, Mexico may restrain foreign investments in its energy sector, while the United States may bar foreign ownership in its airline and broadcasting industries.

U.S. and Canadian negotiators also were concerned that firms from nonmember countries might locate so-called screwdriver plants in Mexico as a means of evading U.S. and Canadian tariffs. A **screwdriver plant** is a factory in which very little transformation of a product is undertaken. Speaking metaphorically, in such factories the only tool workers need is the screwdriver they use to assemble a product. Therefore the negotiators developed detailed rules of origin that defined whether a good was North American in origin and thus qualified for preferential tariff status. In the automobile industry, for example, U.S. and Canadian labor unions worried that European and Asian automakers would exploit the treaty by producing major components elsewhere and then establishing a North American factory merely to assemble motor vehicles, thereby causing the loss of jobs at Canadian and U.S. parts-producing factories. To diminish this problem, NAFTA specifies that for an automobile to qualify as a North American product, 62.5 percent of its value must be produced in Canada, Mexico, or the United States. Similarly, to protect textile industry jobs, clothing and other textile products must use North American-produced fibers to benefit from NAFTA's preferential tariff treatment.

Most experts believe that NAFTA has benefited all three countries, although the gains have been more modest in Canada and the United States than most NAFTA advocates expected. However, the impact on the Mexican economy has been dramatic, as the chapter's opening case indicated.

Expansion of NAFTA to include other countries in the Americas has been endorsed by leaders of the three members. The United States has been unable to proceed, however, because the **fast-track authority** that Congress granted to the president expired during President Clinton's first term in office. Fast-track authority allows the president to negotiate trade treaties with other countries. Although the resultant treaties need the approval of both the House of Representatives and the Senate, the treaties may not be amended by Congress. President Clinton requested that presidential fast-track authority be renewed, but Democratic Congressional leaders were unwilling to grant his request unless the ensuing trade treaties contain language protecting the environment, workers rights, and human rights. Republican legislators believed that environmental policy, workers rights, and human rights should not be linked to trade policy. Accordingly, both Canada and Mexico have negotiated bilateral free trade agreements with Chile, which is the most likely candidate to be the fourth member of NAFTA, while the United States has not yet done so.

Other Free Trade Agreements in the Americas

Many other countries are negotiating or implementing free trade agreements on a bilateral or multilateral basis. For example, Mexico, Venezuela, and Colombia hammered out a trilateral agreement that called for relaxing trade barriers against each other's goods. Mexico has also negotiated free trade pacts with its five Central American neighbors.

The Caribbean Basin Initiative. In 1983 the United States established the Caribbean Basin Initiative to facilitate the economic development of the countries of Central America and the Caribbean Sea. The **Caribbean Basin Initiative (CBI)** overlaps two regional free trade areas: the Central American Common Market and the Caribbean Community and Common Market (their members are listed in Table 9.3 and shown in Map 9.2). The CBI, which acts as a unidirectional free trade agreement, permits duty-free import into the United States of a wide range of goods that originate in Caribbean Basin countries or that have been assembled there from U.S.-produced parts. However, numerous politically sensitive goods, many of

TABLE 9.3

Major Regional Trade Associations

ACRONYM	FULL NAME/MEMBERS
AFTA	ASEAN Free Trade Area Brunei, Cambodia, Indonesia, Laos, Malaysia, Myanmar, Philippines, Singapore, Thailand, Vietnam
ANCOM	Andean Pact Bolivia, Colombia, Ecuador, Peru, Venezuela
APEC	Asia-Pacific Economic Cooperation Australia, Brunei, Canada, Chile, China, Hong Kong, Indonesia, Japan, Malaysia, Mexico, New Zealand, Papua New Guinea, Peru, Philippines, Russia, Singapore, South Korea, Taiwan, Thailand, United States, Vietnam
CACM	Central American Common Market Costa Rica, El Salvador, Guatemala, Honduras, Nicaragua
CARICOM	Caribbean Community and Common Market Antigua and Barbuda, Bahamas, Barbados, Belize, Dominica, Grenada, Guyana, Jamaica, Montserrat, St. Kitts and Nevis, St. Lucia, St. Vincent and the Grenadines, Suriname, Trinidad and Tobago
CEEAC	Economic Community of Central African States Angola, Burundi, Cameroon, Central African Republic, Chad, Democratic Republic of the Congo, Republic of the Congo, Equatorial Guinea, Gabon, Rwanda, Sao Tome and Principe
CER	Australia–New Zealand Closer Economic Trade Relations Agreement Australia, New Zealand
ECOWAS	Economic Community of West African States Benin, Burkina Faso, Cape Verde, Gambia, Ghana, Guinea, Guinea-Bissau, Ivory Coast, Liberia, Mali, Mauritania, Niger, Nigeria, Senegal, Sierra Leone, Togo
EU	European Union Austria, Belgium, Denmark, Finland, France, Germany, Greece, Ireland, Italy, Luxembourg, Netherlands, Portugal, Spain, Sweden, United Kingdom
EFTA	European Free Trade Association Iceland, Liechtenstein, Norway, Switzerland
GCC	Gulf Cooperation Council Bahrain, Kuwait, Oman, Qatar, Saudi Arabia, United Arab Emirates
MERCOSUR	Southern Cone Customs Union Argentina, Brazil, Paraguay, Uruguay; Associate Members: Bolivia, Chile
NAFTA	North American Free Trade Agreement Canada, Mexico, United States
SADC	Southern African Development Community Angola, Botswana, Democratic Republic of the Congo, Lesotho, Malawi, Mauritius, Mozambique, Namibia, Seychelles, South Africa, Swaziland, Tanzania, Zambia, Zimbabwe

ANTIGUA AND BARBUDA

BARBADOS

DOMINICA

GRENADA

MONTSERRAT

ST. KITTS AND NEVIS

ST. LUCIA

ST. VINCENT AND THE GRENADINES

TRINIDAD AND TOBAGO

Andean Pact

CACM

CARICOM

MERCOSUR

MAP 9.2   **Free Trade Agreements in Central and South America and the Caribbean**

which are traditional exports of the area, have been excluded from the CBI, including textiles, canned tuna, luggage, apparel, footwear, petroleum, and petroleum products. Through this pattern of duty-free access to the U.S. market, the United States hopes to stimulate investment by domestic, U.S., and other foreign firms in new industries in the Caribbean Basin countries.

The Mercosur Accord.   In 1991 the governments of Argentina, Brazil, Paraguay, and Uruguay signed the **Mercosur Accord**, an agreement to create a customs union among themselves. They agreed to establish common external tariffs and to cut over four years their internal tariffs on goods that account for 85 percent of intra-Mercosur trade. Full implementation of the customs union began in 1995. Chile and Bolivia later joined Mercosur as associate members, allowing them to participate in the accord's free trade area component. Firms from the six countries have preferential access to a combined market of 237 million people and a total GDP of $1.2 trillion. During Mercosur's first six years trade among its members tripled.

The Mercosur Accord is a direct response to the growth of other regional trading blocs. It is also a key element of the free-market-oriented economic reforms adopted by the Argentinian and Brazilian governments elected in 1989 to revitalize their stagnating economies. By opening up their countries' economies, these governments hope to stimulate new flows of FDI, which will enhance the productivity of their workforces and make their goods more competitive in world markets. As noted by Argentina's then President Carlos Menem, "There aren't many options. Either we work out a joint strategy in line with our development needs, or we will be the objects of outside strategies."[7] To date the Mercosur nations have been a magnet for FDI. Particularly noticeable is the expansion of the area's automotive industry, which has attracted $18 billion in new FDI from the world's leading car manufacturers since Mercosur was founded.[8]

Andean Pact. The **Andean Pact** is a 1969 agreement to promote free trade among five small South American countries—Bolivia, Chile, Colombia, Ecuador, and Peru—to make them more competitive with the continent's larger countries. Venezuela joined the pact in 1973, but Chile dropped out in 1976. During its first 20 years the agreement was not very successful; trade among members totaled only 5 percent of their total trade. Geography played a role in this failure: The Andes mountain range, from which the agreement got its name, makes land transportation of goods between some members costly. More important, most members adopted protectionist, import substitution policies that hindered trade.

In response to the threat posed by the Mercosur Accord, in 1991 the Andean Pact members agreed to reinvigorate their agreement. A year later the members established a customs union that provided for phased elimination of tariffs among themselves on most goods, a common external tariff, and harmonized regulations on capital movements, immigration, and agriculture. However, this liberalization has not gone smoothly. Creation of a common external tariff was stalled by political squabbling over the appropriate tariff level and structure. Peru suspended its membership in the group after judging that the customs union agreement permitted too many loopholes that allowed members to subsidize local firms and erect barriers to imported goods. Despite these setbacks, trade in the region is likely to become freer over time. One indication of this is the pledge by the leaders of every country in the Americas except Cuba to create a Free Trade Area of the Americas by 2005.

Trade Arrangements in the Asia-Pacific Region

Trade groups are also growing in importance in the Asia-Pacific region. One of the longest standing is governed by the Closer Economic Relations Trade Agreement between Australia and New Zealand. More recently the Association of Southeast Asian Nations has initiated a free trade agreement. Members of APEC (Asia-Pacific Economic Cooperation) have begun to reduce trade barriers among themselves as well.

The Australia–New Zealand Agreement. For most of their histories Australia and New Zealand have been trade rivals because they are both commodities producers. As members of the British Commonwealth, both enjoyed preferential access to the U.K. market. After the United Kingdom joined the EU, however, both countries lost their privileged status in the British market. This change was particularly damaging to their agricultural sectors.

The ensuing poor performance by both the New Zealand and Australian economies during the 1970s, and the flow of human capital from the more depressed New Zealand to Australia, led to calls for closer economic ties between the two countries. The **Australia–New Zealand Closer Economic Relations Trade Agreement**, known as **ANZCERTA** or more simply as **CER**, took effect on January 1, 1983. Over time it eliminated tariffs and NTBs between the two countries. The CER also strengthened and fostered links and cooperation in fields as diverse as investment, marketing, the movement of people, tourism, and transport. Although some areas have been excluded from the CER, such as broadcasting, postal services, and air traffic control, most analysts believe the CER has been one of the world's most successful free trade agreements.

Association of Southeast Asian Nations. The Association of Southeast Asian Nations (ASEAN) was established in August 1967 to promote regional political and economic cooperation (see Map 9.3). Its founding members were Brunei, Indonesia, Malaysia, Philippines, Singapore, and Thailand. Cambodia, Laos, Myanmar, and Vietnam joined during the 1990s. These countries are by no means homogeneous: Oil-rich Brunei had a 1999 per capita income of over $15,000, while Vietnam's was only $368.

To promote intra-ASEAN trade, members established the ASEAN Free Trade Area (AFTA), effective January 1, 1993. AFTA members promised to slash their tariffs to 5 percent or less on most manufactured goods by 2003 and on all goods by 2010. As with the Mercosur Accord and the Andean Pact, creation of the ASEAN trading bloc

MAP 9.3

The ASEAN Members
The ASEAN economy has been developing rapidly because its poorer members provide large pools of low-cost labor, receive preferential tariff rates under the U.S. Generalized System of Preferences and those of other WTO members, and have attracted significant Japanese, European, and North American direct investment.

stems from two factors: a decrease in government control of national economies that has stimulated local entrepreneurs and attracted FDI, and a defensive response to the growth of other regional trading blocs such as the EU and NAFTA.

Intra-ASEAN trade currently represents about 20 percent of total trade for the group as a whole, and it is growing quickly. Recent meetings of ASEAN country ministers have addressed trade in services, removal of NTBs, and the creation of an ASEAN Free Investment Area. As with other new trading blocs, firms have reacted quickly to take advantage of opportunities created by AFTA. For example, shortly after the agreement was negotiated, Philippine brewer San Miguel, which controls 90 percent of its home market, purchased Jakarta-based Delta brewery, which controls 40 percent of the Indonesian beer market. By moving rapidly, San Miguel hoped to dominate the entire ASEAN market prior to the fall of tariff rates triggered by AFTA.

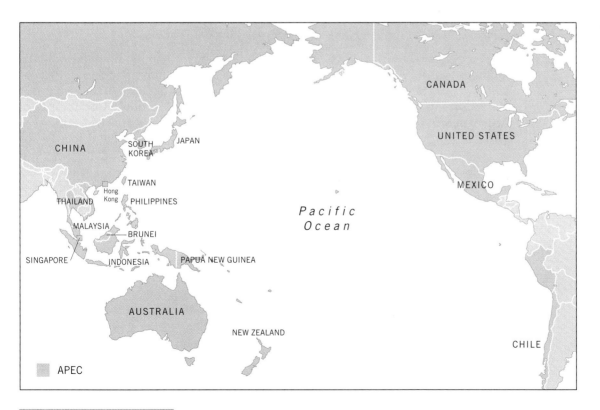

MAP 9.4   **Asia-Pacific Economic Cooperation Initiative (APEC)**

MAP 9.5

**Free Trade Agreements
in Africa**

CEEAC

SADC

ECOWAS

The Asia-Pacific Economic Cooperation Initiative. **Asia-Pacific Economic Cooperation (APEC)** includes 21 countries from both sides of the Pacific Ocean (see Map 9.4). It was founded in 1989 in response to the growing interdependence of the Asia-Pacific economies. In 1999 merchandise exports from APEC members were valued at over $2.4 trillion and represented about 40 percent of total world exports. A 1994 APEC meeting in Indonesia led to a declaration committing members to achieve free trade in goods, services, and investment among members by 2010 for developed economies and by 2020 for developing economies. This objective was furthered at APEC's 1996 meeting in Manila, where many countries made explicit pledges to reduce barriers to Asia-Pacific trade.

African Initiatives. Many African countries have also established regional trading blocs. As shown in Table 9.3 and Map 9.5, the most important of these groups are the **Southern African Development Community (SADC)**, the **Economic Community of Central African States (CEEAC)**, and the **Economic Community of West African States (ECOWAS)**. Although these groups were established during the 1970s and early 1980s, they have not had a major impact on regional trade. This is due to inadequate intraregional transportation facilities and the failure of most domestic governments to create economic and political systems that encourage significant regional trade. Intra-Africa trade to date accounts for less than 7 percent of the continent's total exports.

CHAPTER REVIEW

Summary

Countries have come together to create numerous international agreements and organizations to promote their joint interests in international commerce. One of the most important was the GATT. The goal of this 1947 agreement was to promote global prosperity by reducing international trade barriers. Through a

series of negotiating rounds over 47 years, the GATT significantly reduced the average level of tariffs facing exporters. The most recent series of GATT negotiations, the Uruguay Round, continued the trend of reducing tariffs and NTBs. In 1995 the GATT's mission was taken over by the WTO.

Countries may also band together in various ways to integrate their economies regionally. Free trade areas promote economic integration by abolishing trade barriers among their members. Members of a customs union carry regional economic integration a step further by adopting common external trade barriers as well as abolishing internal barriers to trade. A common market combines the characteristics of a customs union with the elimination of controls on the free movement of labor, capital, and technology among its members. An economic union adds the coordination of economic policies to the features of a common market. A political union involves complete political as well as economic integration of two or more countries.

The most important example of a regional trading bloc is the EU, a market of 377 million consumers and a combined GDP of $8.3 trillion. Spurred by the passage of the Single European Act of 1987, EU members dismantled most of the physical, technical, and fiscal trade barriers among themselves. Under the Maastricht Treaty the EU is attempting to create a common currency and a true economic union, an effort that goes beyond the common market originally envisioned by the 1957 Treaty of Rome.

A second but much newer regional integration effort is occurring in North America. The United States, Mexico, and Canada have instituted NAFTA, which came into effect in January 1994. NAFTA's implementation signals a commitment to tightening the economic bonds among the North American countries.

The development of regional trading blocs in Europe and North America has stimulated efforts to promote regional economic integration on other continents. South America is home to two such agreements, the Mercosur Accord and the Andean Pact. The chances of their future success have been increased by the economic reforms many South American countries have adopted, reforms that have increased the competitiveness of the countries' products in international markets. Australia and New Zealand and the ASEAN countries have similarly created free trade areas to promote regional economic integration. Several regional economic integration agreements negotiated by various African countries have yet to show much promise.

Review Questions

1. What does most favored nation (MFN) mean?
2. Under what conditions can WTO members not use MFN when dealing with one another?
3. How does the WTO differ from the GATT?
4. How do the various forms of economic integration differ?
5. Why do free trade areas develop rules of origin?
6. What was the goal of the Treaty of Rome?
7. Describe the four major organizations governing the EU.
8. What are NAFTA's major provisions?
9. What is the Caribbean Basin Initiative? What is its goal?
10. What efforts have South American countries made to regionally integrate their economies?

Questions for Discussion

1. Consider the opening case. How has Mexico's success affected the Canadian and U.S. economies?
2. How does the WTO affect the operations of large MNCs? Did MNCs benefit from the successful completion of the Uruguay Round?
3. Should international businesses promote or fight the creation of regional trading blocs?
4. What strategies can North American and Asian firms adopt to ensure access to the enormous EU market?
5. Is the abandonment of import substitution policies by South American governments a necessary condition for the success of the Andean Pact and the Mercosur Accord?
6. Of what importance are rules of origin to international businesses?
7. Why does the MFN principle promote multilateral, rather than bilateral, negotiations among WTO members?

BUILDING GLOBAL SKILLS

NAFTA has been lauded by some as creating a major new market opportunity for U.S. businesses; it has been criticized by others because of the potential loss of domestic jobs as firms relocate production to Mexico to take advantage of lower-cost labor. This exercise will help you learn more about the effects of NAFTA on various firms.

Your instructor will divide the class into groups of four to five students each. Working with your group members, identify four products made by firms in each of the three countries that are part of NAFTA. The four products should include two that would seem to benefit from NAFTA and two that would seem to face increased threats from competitors in the two other member countries as a result of NAFTA. For example, identify two Canadian-made products that have considerable market potential in the United States and/or Mexico and two Canadian-made products that would seem to face new competition from U.S. and/or Mexican firms. Each group should identify a total of 12 different products.

Next, work with your group members to determine and assess the appeal of each product in the NAFTA market. Investigate for each the current market share, domestic competitors, foreign competitors, and so forth. Research how well each was doing before and after NAFTA's passage. Discuss how NAFTA has affected and/or may potentially affect each product.

Follow-Up Questions

1. Has NAFTA provided new market opportunities for some of the products you identified? Why or why not?
2. Has NAFTA increased competition from other producers?
3. Have the effects of NAFTA on each product been consistent with what advocates or critics of NAFTA might have predicted?

WORKING WITH THE WEB:
BUILDING GLOBAL INTERNET SKILLS

Evaluating New EU Entrants

The next group of countries to be considered for membership in the EU includes Cyprus, the Czech Republic, Estonia, Hungary, Poland, and Slovenia. Pick one of these countries. What impact would the country's entry into the EU have on the country itself and on the existing EU members? For example, how much would the country pay in taxes to the EU? Would the country receive any cohesion fund payments? Are there any EU programs from which the country would benefit? How many votes would it have in the European Parliament? Is the country likely to abandon its currency and adopt the euro? Do you foresee any problems with the country entering the EU?

Visiting the EU's Web site is a good way to start this assignment. It provides information about how the EU works, the composition and responsibilities of its governing organizations, the EU's policy initiatives, and much more. The textbook's Web site provides links to the EU's Web site and to other Web sites that are useful for this exercise.

WE INVITE YOU TO VISIT THIS BOOK'S COMPANION WEB SITE AT www.prenhall.com/griffin

IN THE NEWS

Use the search feature of the *Financial Times* homepage (*www.ft.com*) to locate recent articles on discussions that are taking place in the United Kingdom and within the British government about whether the British should abandon the pound and adopt the euro as their currency. You might wish to start your search with the topic "euro and the pound." From the United Kingdom's perspective, what are the advantages and disadvantages of the euro? What action on the euro is currently pending in the United Kingdom? What do you think will happen next?

CLOSING CASE

Will Whirlpool Clean Up in Europe?

For years international businesses looked forward to the EU's emergence as a single, integrated market. Among these firms are ones that produce so-called white goods, or appliances such as refrigerators, dishwashers, ovens, washers, and dryers. (In the past kitchen and laundry room appliances mostly came in white, hence the industry's name. Consumer electronics such as radios, televisions, and stereos came in brown, so these consumer durables are called "brown goods". Today's widespread use of color in appliances makes these labels somewhat anachronistic.)

The emergence of a single market in Europe has changed the way white goods manufacturers do business. Previously, they had to customize their products to meet the often conflicting standards of the EU's 15 national governments. Harmonized product standards resulting from the Single European Act allow the manufacturers to standardize their products, thus permitting them to cut product development and production costs. Reduced barriers to intra-EU trade allow them to concentrate production in one factory that can serve markets throughout the EU. Reduced impediments to cross-border advertising make it easier to develop pan-European brands, which in turn reduce marketing and distribution costs. Elimination of physical barriers at border crossing points and of restrictions on trucking competition by national governments leads to productivity gains in logistics and physical distribution management.

One of the most aggressive firms seeking to conquer the new European market is Whirlpool, the world's largest white goods manufacturer. The firm's managers have a clearly defined view of this market:

> Among the truths about the European home-appliance market, there are two whose net effect Whirlpool has a particular interest in: first, consumers in Europe spend up to

twice as many days of household income for appliances as do their U.S. counterparts, creating . . . a consumer "value gap"; second, industry profit margins in the region are traditionally much lower than those of North American manufacturers. The reason for this truth is cultural: historically, the industry was organized to do business in individual, national markets, an approach with inherent cost inefficiencies. Now, however, with barriers to pan-European business disappearing, Whirlpool believes that it can use its unique regional position to deliver greater home-appliance value to customers and, in turn, establish a competitive advantage for itself. A strategy to do so suggests that the opportunity to eliminate costs which do not add to consumers' perceptions of value—and invest some of the savings into product and service characteristics that do add perceived value—will be substantial.[9]

For the past decade Whirlpool's managers have been attacking the European white goods market by translating these words into concrete actions. One key element of the firm's strategy was the purchase of the appliance business of Philips Industries, the large Netherlands-based MNC; this gave Whirlpool control over Philips' European white goods production facilities and distribution systems. Whirlpool has also sought many other operating and marketing economies:

1. It produces and markets three well-established pan-European brands: Bauknecht, a premium upscale product; Whirlpool, for the broad middle segment of the white goods market; and Ignis, its low-price "value" brand aimed at price-sensitive consumers. This comprehensive product strategy allows Whirlpool to fully utilize its European production facilities and distribution systems and market its goods to Europeans at all income levels.

2. It consolidated 13 separate national sales offices for these three product lines into five regional operations in order to cut costs, coordinate pan-European promotional campaigns, and enhance the productivity of its sales force.

3. It centralized Whirlpool Europe's logistics, information technology, and consumer services operations to ease the task of warehousing products and distributing them throughout the EU.

4. It has redeployed its manufacturing capacity to take advantage of the elimination of national trade barriers. For example, it concentrates its production of refrigerators for its European customers in Trento, Italy, and that of automatic washers in Schondorf, Germany, thus allowing it to achieve significant manufacturing economies of scale.

5. It has encouraged technology transfer between its European and North American operations, a task made easier by the centralization of its European operations. For example, Whirlpool Europe now produces a line of clothes dryers that features easier loading and unloading and gentler treatment of clothes, features first developed by Whirlpool's Marion, Ohio, division. Conversely, European engineers are helping Whirlpool's U.S. engineers adapt energy-efficient horizontal-axis washing machines, which are common in Europe, for the North American market in order to meet pending federal energy efficiency standards.

To implement its European strategy, Whirlpool has already spent $2 billion and plans to expend an additional $1 billion over the next five years.

Of course, Whirlpool's EU competitors have not stood still while Whirlpool has invaded their home markets. Germany's Bosch Siemens Hausgeräte, for example, has poured money into R&D to maintain the innovativeness of its appliances. It has dramatically increased the efficiency of its dishwashers, reducing their energy usage by 62 percent and their water usage by 34 percent compared to the machines it made two decades previously. It has also spent $350 million automating its production facilities in Germany and built new factories in Poland, Spain, and the Czech Republic to reduce its dependence on high-cost German labor. Sweden's Electrolux, which vies with Whirlpool for the title of the world's largest white goods manufacturer, purchased the appliance business of AEG Hausgeräte from Daimler-Benz. Already controlling a 20 to 25 percent market share in Europe, Electrolux increased its market share by about 6 percentage points through this acquisition. Electrolux is also aggressively moving to control its costs, by closing 25 factories and reducing its payrolls by 12,000.

Despite this intensified competition, Whirlpool remains optimistic that its European strategy will be successful. It has already established itself as the number 3 white goods manufacturer in Europe, earning $171 million in profits on sales of $2.5 billion in 1999. Moreover, it believes the EU market will become even bigger and more important when as many as a dozen new countries join the EU within the decade.[10]

Case Questions

1. What are the advantages of consolidating production of product lines at single factories in the EU? What are the disadvantages?

2. Should Whirlpool continue to produce and market in Europe its three product lines (Bauknecht, Whirlpool, and Ignis), which span the entire white goods market, or should it focus on one market niche?

3. What benefits will Whirlpool gain by broadening the Whirlpool brand name from a North American brand to a global one?

4. In light of the aggressive responses of Electrolux and Bosch Siemens Hausgeräte, should Whirlpool revise or abandon its European strategy?

5. Do you think it is possible to design and sell the same basic appliance around the world?

The International Monetary System

Background

The World Bank is an international agency created to provide loans for development to countries in need. Along with the International Monetary Fund (IMF), the World Bank is a major player in today's international monetary system.

This video illustrates the importance of the World Bank and the IMF in financial markets and the role these two agencies play in the international monetary system. Futhermore, the video shows how the Bretton Woods Agreement of 1944 created a new era of international transactions.

The World Bank

The World Bank Group consists of several affiliated organizations—the International Bank for Reconstruction and Development (IBRD), the International Development Association (IDA), the International Finance Corporation (IFC), the Multilateral Investment Guarantee Agency (MIGA), and the International Centre for the Settlement of Investment Disputes (ICSID).

The IBRD and the IDA together are the largest provider of development assistance to developing countries and countries in transition, committing approximately $24 billion in new loans each year. Their main focus is to help people in developing countries raise their standard of living through finance for agriculture, schools, health programs, transportation, and other essential needs. The World Bank opened for business on June 25, 1946 and gave its first loan the following year, $250 million to France, to finance postwar construction. Today the World Bank has a lending portfolio of $117 billion.

Questions

1. What was the purpose of the Bretton Woods conference?
2. What is the role of the World Bank in global financial markets?
3. How is the 1944 Bretton Woods Agreement significant today?
4. What is the role of the IMF in the world economy today?

Regulatory Warfare

One of the bitterest battles being fought today involves the struggle between Kodak and Fuji for dominance in the world film market. Both companies are arguing that they are being victimized by unfair trade practices in the other's country. Kodak has moved aggressively to bolster its position by appealing to the U.S. government for relief from what it claims are unfair Japanese practices.

Kodak enjoys a 70 percent share of the U.S. film market; Fuji has a mere 11 percent, and the remaining 19 percent is divided among firms like Polaroid, Japan's Konica, Germany's Agfa-Gavaert, and a handful of private-label brands. The numbers are reversed in Japan, where Fuji owns 67 percent of the market, Kodak 11 percent, and other firms the remainder. The rest of the world is split almost evenly between these three groups: Kodak has 36 percent of the market outside Japan and the United States, Fuji 33 percent, and all other firms 31 percent.

Fuji developed into a powerhouse brand in its home market due to high tariffs—40 percent ad valorem—on imported film that freed it from competition from Kodak and other non-Japanese brands during the early post-World War II period. In 1980, however, these tariffs started being cut and in 1990 were totally eliminated. Ironically, it is the United States that now has the higher tariff on imported film, albeit a modest 3.7 percent tariff.

Kodak believes its poor showing in the Japanese market is due to trade barriers erected by Japan, and not due to any lack of effort or commitment on its part—Kodak has invested some $750 million in Japan. Taking Kodak's side, the U.S. government has complained that Japan's government has promoted exclusive wholesaling arrangements that favor Fuji, hindered the growth of large discount stores that would stock foreign goods, and restricted the use of price competition and price promotions that would allow Kodak to underprice Fuji. Of particular concern is the Japanese film distribution system, which is dominated by four distributors who together control 70 percent of the film market. These four distributors have signed exclusive dealing contracts with Fuji, effectively locking Kodak and other film manufacturers out of these important distribution channels. These distributors are particularly important suppliers to Japan's camera stores and film shops, which market to skilled amateurs and professionals. At such shops profit margins are high because these stores compete primarily on service, not price. Allegedly, Fuji grants these retailers secret rebates based on their sales of its film, further discouraging them from stocking competitive brands. Kodak, Agfa, and other manufacturers like Konica are forced to focus most of their competitive energies at discount outlets where profit margins are lower.

Kodak also filed a complaint before the U.S. Department of Commerce (DOC), claiming that Fuji was dumping film in the U.S. market. Officials at DOC's International Trade Administration and the International Trade Commission agreed with Kodak's charges and levied antidumping duties on Fuji film manufactured at its facilities in Japan and the Netherlands. But this tactic seems to have backfired on Kodak. Fuji expanded its manufacturing complex in Greenwood, South Carolina, allowing it to begin manufacturing film in the United States. By so doing, Fuji avoided the 3.7 percent tariff on imported film. More important, Fuji shortened its supply lines and rendered Kodak's antidumping complaint moot. It can now respond to changing circumstances in the U.S. market more quickly because the film is produced locally, not thousands of miles way.

Fuji has engaged Kodak in a war of words, arguing that the Japanese market is more open than the U.S. market. Japan imposes no tariffs on imported film, and discounters and supermarkets are among the fastest growing segments of Japanese retailing. Fuji points to Agfa's success in capturing 5 percent of the Japanese film market since 1990 by focusing on selling private-label film. Fuji also claims that Kodak uses a variety of techniques in the United States to discourage retailers from selling other brands of film. For example, Kodak offers many retailers a 3 percent rebate if their sales of Kodak film meet the previous year's level. Fuji notes that Kodak has systematically purchased wholesale photofinishers, which allows it to control 70 percent of the U.S. wholesale photofinishing market.

Kodak counters that it has access to only 15 percent of the Japanese market because of the exclusive contracts that the big four distributors have with many Japanese film retailers; conversely, it says that Fuji film is available at retail outlets that generate 65 percent of U.S. film sales. Kodak also notes that the openness of the U.S. market gives Fuji more maneuvering room in the United States than Kodak has in Japan. For example, in August 1996 Fuji bought six photofinishing labs from Wal-Mart, giving its film the inside track at thousands of Wal-Mart and Sam's Club stores.

Kodak then successfully lobbied the U.S. government to file a complaint before the World Trade Organization (WTO). The U.S. government filed over 20,000 pages of documents detailing, it believes, covert measures by the Japanese government to restrict foreign access to the Japanese film market. Unfortunately for Kodak, in December 1997 the WTO ruled in Fuji's favor, rejecting all of the U.S. charges.

Despite its loss, Kodak claimed the millions of dollars it spent preparing the case before the WTO were monies well spent. The Japanese government was forced to rebut Kodak's case point by point rather than dismiss its claims with vague language. In so doing, it made promises to the WTO that, if kept, will help Kodak compete in the Japanese film market. For example, prior to the filing of the case before the WTO, the Japanese government restricted Kodak's ability to gain market share through price discounting, disallowing 2-for-1 offers and other promotional techniques that would encourage loyal Fuji users to try Kodak film. (Such price discounting has been an important means by which Fuji has gained market share in the United States.) In its WTO filings the Japanese government pledged to not stand in the way of price discounting, a decision that Kodak, as the underdog in the Japanese market, believes favors its interests.

In response to the WTO's decision, Kodak and the U.S. government announced a new strategy in February 1998. The Japanese government had asserted in its filing before the WTO that it does not permit anticompetitive behavior, that is encourages the importing of film, and that the Japanese film market is open. The U.S. government plans to monitor the Japanese government to check whether its actions are consistent with these assertions. For example, it will enumerate the number of Japanese retail photo outlets that carry foreign-film brands to see if such brands have reasonable access to Japanese consumers. It will also observe whether the Japanese government imposes restrictions on pricing promotions that Kodak may adopt to woo Japanese customers to purchase its products.

Questions

1. Fuji's success seems to be a good example of the application of the infant industry argument for intervening in free trade. Do you think Fuji would have been able to dominate Japan's film market if Japan had not initially imposed tariffs on photo film?

2. Kodak's strategy seems to be to use the regulatory process to accomplish what it has not been able to do through normal competitive processes. Do you agree with this strategy? Are there dangers to it?

3. Consider Fuji's argument that it does to Kodak in Japan what Kodak does to it in the U.S. market. If true, does this weaken Kodak's case?

4. How significant for Kodak is the Japanese government's pledge to not stand in the way of price competition?

Sources: "Kodak and U.S. Government Team Up for New Drive on Japan's Film Market," *Wall Street Journal*, February 4, 1998, p. A4; Fuji Photo Film Co., Ltd. Annual Report 1997; "WTO Weighs Up Fuji-Kodak Dispute," *Financial Times*, April 18, 1997, p. 9; "Exposed: Kodak's Path to the WTO," *Financial Times*, June 16, 1996, p. 5; "Fuji Invests $100 Million in U.S. Plant," *Wall Street Journal*, February 21, 1996, p. A3; "Kodak Says Fuji Response a Diversionary Tactic," *Business Wire*, July 31, 1995, p. 1; "Kodak Boosts Pressure on Washington to Force Tokyo to Open Photo Market," *Wall Street Journal*, June 1, 1995, p. A4; "Kodak Exposes Fuji's Market Grip," *Financial Times*, June 1, 1995, p. 7.

Nike Inc.: Developing an Effective Public Relations Strategy

It had been almost a decade since the media first alleged that Nike-aligned factories in China and Indonesia were forcing employees to work long hours for low pay under harsh working conditions, and for utilizing physically and verbally abusive managers. At that time, these allegations seemed so absurd to Nike managers, no response was deemed necessary. However, the global media campaign was to gather such momentum that by the mid-1990s it had created a public relations nightmare for the company.

The media began running weekly and even daily accounts describing supposedly harsh factory conditions, low pay, and instances of management abuse. Watchdog groups, including such high-profile groups as the Washington, D.C.-based Campaign for Labor Rights and San Francisco's Global Exchange, accused managers at Nike's subcontracted factories of forcing factory workers to work excessively long hours, in unsatisfactory working conditions, for below average wages. These and other activists groups authored numerous articles outlining several particular incidences of worker abuses throughout Southeast Asia, targeting Nike-aligned facilities specifically. Their articles included stories depicting alleged humiliation and intimidation, and physical abuse of workers (the vast majority of whom were female) by their (male, foreign) managers—in an environment of record profits for Nike and high-profile multimillion dollar endorsement contracts. Watchdog groups accused Nike of worker exploitation through low pay, stating that workers' pay was not only inadequate but was spent mainly on feeding and housing themselves and their families, leaving them no chance to save money. Yet other accusations involved excess levels of toxic fumes in the workplace and forced overtime.

Nike's Response

Nike's initial response was to ignore the problem. One senior executive quoted in 1990 suggested any problems were the responsibility of Nike's subcontractors, not Nike itself: "We don't pay anyone at the factories, and we don't set policy within the factories. It's their business to run."

Nike's next step was to draft a Code of Conduct in 1992, which applied to Nike and its subcontractors. Among other things, the code prohibited child labor; required factories to pay at least the minimum wage, all legally mandated benefits, and overtime; and provide a safe and healthy work environment.

Despite this effort, Nike's critics were not satisfied and continued to denounce Nike's labor policies. To better address these concerns, Nike created its Corporate Responsibility Division, which was put in charge of Nike's community affairs, labor practices, and environmental operations. The new division's first initiative was the MESH (Manufacturing-Environment-Safety-Health) program.

MESH was designed to ensure best practices in human resource management, protection of the environment, and compliance on health and safety policies. Moreover, every Nike subcontracted manufacturing facility was obligated to adhere to Nike's Manufacturing Leadership Standards, which included:

- Nike's stance against fines for disciplinary shortcomings and deposits as a condition of employment

- Protection from discrimination against pregnant workers, to ensure equal opportunity for female workers.

- The strict requirement for all contractors to have a "simple, clear, written and mandatory Personal Protective Equipment (PPE) policy" and all applicable PPE available where appropriate

- The provision of annual leave at the worker's request (accompanied by an encouragement of taking the time off versus working for additional bonus pay)

- Strict monitoring of timekeeping through the use of time clocks and pay documentation through clear payment records, which must accompany a worker's wage

- The compensation of workers during their training period and a fair wage structure

- The agreement of the subcontracted factory to undergo a Pricewaterhouse Coopers Labor Practices Assessment Audit and a Nike SHAPE (Safety-Health-Attitude of Management-Environment) inspection before approval

Nike was committed to ensuring that the principles behind its Corporate Standards programs were applied in reality. When deficiencies were found, Nike and the factory in question worked together on plans of action to bring the factory into compliance. If the factory management team was unwilling or unable to meet Nike's standards, the contractor was "formally fined, put on probation and given specific time lines and target actions to accomplish, or face losing the business," according to a Nike corporate document outlining its policy on enforcement of the Code of Conduct. If that failed, the relationship would be terminated—a move Nike had resorted to only 10 times since 1996, given the adverse impact such a step would have on the workers and their dependents.

However, despite the breadth and scope of Nike's Standards and Practices programs, they were ultimately ineffective in persuading the public that Nike was serious in eradicating poor labor conditions in its subcontracted factories throughout Southeast Asia. Critics relentlessly contended that the Code of Conduct actually meant little, if anything, to the average factory worker and remained highly cynical that the code was making any real impact on the working environment. The deluge of damaging press continued. If anything, perceived shortcomings in Nike's plan to improve conditions had increased the anti-Nike sentiment among watchdog groups and consumers. Nike consistently drew its critics' attention back to the Code of Conduct, as well as its extensive use of independent monitoring.

Nike's Auditing and Independent Monitoring

With a view to improving corporate practices where necessary, Nike commissioned Dartmouth College's Tuck School of Business and former UN Ambassador Andrew Young to visit 15 Nike factories and to report on conditions. The Tuck students reported that "workers earned above the local minimum wage, and with special allowances such as meals, housing and health care, as well as the opportunity to work overtime, the workers were earning more than enough to cover their basic needs."

The Young report, released by Nike in the summer of 1997, was similarly encouraging, and Nike felt that it presented an accurate appraisal of factory conditions. Young's conclusion: "Nike is doing a good job—but can do better." Young went on to say that "though Nike's performance was positive overall, the Code of Conduct is not visible on the factory floors and [is] not well understood by the factory workers." In response, Nike issued each worker a laminated pocket-sized card, printed in the local language, which outlined acceptable corporate labor practices. Nike also launched training programs in factories to ensure the code was well understood by all workers at every level.

Nonetheless, the study was widely criticized by human rights groups as lacking objectivity. One critic was quoted as saying, "Nike has spent millions of dollars buying off major athletes—now it's bought off Andrew Young." Garry Trudeau created a whole series of Doonesbury comic strip ridiculing Nike for its labor practices. It seemed that despite Nike's well-organized and genuine efforts to improve conditions, its actions were misconstrued by its critics' well-oiled anti-Nike machine. According to Nike, there were innumerable examples of how Nike's detractors ignored the larger, far-reaching implications of many issues.

Wages at Nike subcontracted factories, for example, were a hotly debated issue. Nike's position on the issue of wages was that multinational factories had a responsibility to pay competitive wages but not to change the living standards of a nation. Nike consistently reinforced in all its media communications that in each and every developing country, the wage that workers at Nike subcontracted factories received was at least the minimum wage as dictated by the regional governments. Nike further explained that with little or no social security programs, factory jobs were highly valued throughout developing countries in Southeast Asia. For millions of unskilled workers and their families, a factory job was a valuable prize—a chance to send money back to their home to support an entire family and to "retire" after several years with enough money to begin their own business in their village. Nike noted average annual employee turnover in Vietnam was around 1 percent.

Nike also adopted an open-door-policy. Congressional critics were invited to visit Nike factories. Nike announced that it would fly several students from the University of North Carolina—where students were particularly vocal about Nike's labor practices—to inspect overseas working conditions firsthand. Nonetheless, critics remained highly skeptical, accusing Nike of cherry picking those factories that were to be monitored and audited.

By 1998, beyond independent auditing, Nike had taken several other proactive measures to manage its brand image, including:

- Purchasing full-page ads in U.S. major newspapers
- Conducting press conferences and issuing press releases outlining the steps that Nike had taken to ensure compliance around the world with its Code of Conduct
- Posting progress on improving labor conditions on the corporate Web site
- Responding to each inquiry from the media or watchdog groups and trying to openly communicate with them
- Establishing a Web site specifically addressing labor issues

Nonetheless, despite Nike's extensive efforts at informing the public of the improvements in the conditions at its subcontracted factories, Nike's own surveys demonstrated that the company's image continued to be tarnished through a seemingly endless barrage of negative publicity. Several other surveys suggested that consumers' purchasing decisions were not affected by their views of Nike's labor practices. Managers, however, felt that though there was little adverse effect on consumers' brand loyalty at present, there was a danger of erosion of Nike's brand equity among younger consumers if the issue was not dealt with deftly and swiftly.

Moreover, Nike had to compete with highly talented, resourceful, and powerful companies that had not been subjected to negative press to the extent Nike had. Key senior managers believed that if Nike were to remain the world's leading supplier of athletic footwear and apparel, Nike would need to repair its public profile and design an effective and comprehensive public relations strategy. As one noted,

> There is a growing recognition that issues, left unchecked and unanswered, can have a long-term negative connotation. We need to be more aggressive communicating the positive things that Nike has done over the last few years.

The questions that remained was how would Nike and its Corporate Responsibility team accomplish this goal?

Questions

1. What can Nike's Corporate Responsibility team do to improve Nike's public image?
2. Why have Nike's attempts to date to address its critics been unsuccessful?
3. What damage, if any, has been done to Nike? Has Nike reacted appropriately? Has it overreacted? Underreacted?
4. Many of Nike's competitors subcontract production to Asian factories similar to those used by Nike. Why was Nike singled out by human rights and labor rights activists?
5. What responsibility does Nike have to the workers in the factories of its subcontractors? What wage rates should it require them to pay their workers?

Source: Adapted with permission from the Richard Ivey School of Business, University of Western Ontario, Case number 9A99C034, "Nike Inc.: Developing an Effective Public Relations Strategy."

CHAPTER

Global Mickey

Mickey Mouse is every bit as popular around the globe as Coca-Cola's soft drinks and McDonald's burgers. Indeed, the mouse's famed silhouette is no doubt just as recognizable in Brazil, India, Italy, and South Africa as is the shape of a Coke bottle or the golden arches of McDonald's. The Walt Disney Company, however, has done a surprisingly poor job of capitalizing on the global potential for its various products. In 1999, for instance, 80 percent of Disney's $23.4 billion in revenues came from the United States, a country with only 5 percent of the world's population. This contrasts markedly with Coca-Cola and McDonald's, each of which derives about two-thirds of its revenue from other countries.

"Disney continues to struggle in other areas of its international operations."

Perhaps Disney's most public effort at internationalization has been its theme park operations. Its first theme park, Disneyland, opened in Anaheim, California, in 1955 and was soon generating huge profits. The firm's next major theme park development, Walt Disney World, opened near Orlando, Florida, in 1971; it also was a major success. Because the two parks generate enormous profits, Disney has continued to invest in them by building new attractions and on-site hotels and by opening new parks adjacent to the existing ones. For example, the fourth Walt Disney World theme park, the

International Strategic Management

10

OBJECTIVES

After studying this chapter, you should be able to:

> Characterize the challenges of international strategic management.

> Assess the basic strategic alternatives available to firms.

> Distinguish and analyze the components of international strategy.

> Describe the international strategic management process.

> Identify and characterize the levels of international strategies.

Animal Kingdom, opened in 1998, and a new park adjacent to Disneyland, Disney's California Adventure, opened in 2001.

Given the enormous popularity of Disney characters abroad, the firm saw opportunities to expand theme park operations to foreign markets. Its first venture into a foreign market, Tokyo Disneyland, opened in 1984. The Japanese have long been Disney fans, and many Japanese tourists visit Disneyland and Disney World each year. Market research also showed the Japanese enthusiastically supported the idea of a Disney park in Japan. To limit its risk, though, the firm did not invest directly in the park—a decision Disney managers would eventually come to regret. Instead, a Japanese investment group called the Oriental Land Company financed and entirely owns Tokyo Disneyland. Disney oversaw the park's construction and manages it but receives only royalty income from it. Tokyo Disneyland has been an enormous success from the day it opened its gates: It greeted its 100 millionth visitor after only eight years, a milestone that Disneyland took twice as long to reach.

The success of Tokyo Disneyland inspired the firm to seek other foreign-market opportunities. After evaluating potential sites throughout Europe, the firm narrowed its choices to one in France (just outside Paris) and one in Spain (close to Barcelona). The Spanish site held the advantage of a more favorable climate, similar to Florida's. However, the French site, although sub-

International Strategic Management

10

ject to harsher winter weather conditions, was closer to Europe's major population centers. Some 350 million people live within a two-hour plane ride of Paris. After careful consideration of the two locations, Disney chose the French site and made its plans for Euro Disney public in 1988.

This time, though, Disney decided to participate more fully in both the park's ownership and its profits. However, the French government decreed that Disney's ownership in the new venture could be no more than 49 percent, with the remaining 51 percent made available for trade on European stock exchanges. The French government's offer of numerous economic incentives also played a role in Disney's decision. The government sold the land for the park at bargain-basement prices and agreed to extend the Parisian rail system to the park's front door. But as Euro Disney took shape, storm clouds loomed. The cultural elite in Paris lambasted the project as an affront to French cultural traditions. Farmers protested the manner in which the French government condemned their land so that it could be sold to Disney. The firm found itself defending its conservative employee dress codes, regimented training practices, and plans to ban alcohol from park facilities. Amid the controversy Euro Disney opened its doors to the public on April 12, 1992.

Unfortunately, Disney's timing could not have been worse—a recession swept through Europe just as the park was opening. To aggravate matters, the British, Italian, and Spanish central banks devalued their respective currencies, raising the cost for their citizens to vacation in France. Disney was forced to drop its plan to reduce its debt by selling land near the park to local developers. The carrying cost of its debt rose further as French interest rates climbed. Disney also severely misjudged the spending habits of park visitors, who spent 12 percent less on food and souvenirs than expected. Disney planners also presumed hotel guests would stay an average of three days, as they did in Orlando, but Euro Disney visitors typically stayed two days or less. Further, the firm had planned to sell the hotels shortly after the park's opening and use the proceeds to finance expansion in other areas. Unfortunately, the low occupancy rates made the properties less attractive, and Disney found no buyers. At this point Euro Disney seemed to be burning money, and it actually came close to being shut down. Eventually, a complex and costly financial restructuring plan implemented in 1994 barely saved the park, and it has only been within the last few years that Disneyland Paris, as the park was renamed, has begun earning profits.

Fortunately, Disney seems to be getting its act together regarding international theme park operations. For example, in 2001 it opened Tokyo DisneySea adjacent to Tokyo Disneyland. Both attendance and spending have gradually improved at Disneyland Paris, and the new Disney Studios theme park will open there in 2002. Disney's biggest news, though, was its decision to build a new park in Hong Kong. The company gets a 43 percent equity stake in the $3.6 billion project in exchange for an investment of only $314 million. The local government, in turn, will invest over $2.9 billion in low-interest loans, land, and infrastructure improvements for the remaining 57 percent share.

But Disney continues to struggle in other areas of its international operations. For example, there are only 11 million subscribers to the Disney Channel cable television network outside the United States; this contrasts with 54 million foreign subscribers to AOL Time Warner's Cartoon Network. Disney has experienced a $159 million decline in worldwide licensing revenues in recent years. Indeed, things have gotten so bad that the company is overhauling its business and has created a separate unit called Walt Disney International. Its goal? Obviously, to increase international revenues. Company executives have calculated that if they can increase per capita consumer spending on Disney-related products in just five countries—the United Kingdom, Italy, Germany, France, and Japan—to 80 percent of the level in the United States, the firm would generate an additional $2 billion in annual revenues.[1]

To survive in today's global marketplace, a firm must be able to quickly exploit opportunities presented to it anywhere in the world and respond to changes in domestic and foreign markets as they arise. This requires a cogent definition of the firm's corporate mission, a vision for achieving that mission, and an unambiguous understanding of how it intends to compete with other firms. To obtain this understanding, a firm must carefully compare its strengths and weaknesses to those of its worldwide competitors; assess likely political, economic, and social changes among its current and prospective customers; and analyze the impact of new technologies on its ways of doing business.

Disney's decisions to build Tokyo Disneyland, Disneyland Paris, Tokyo DisneySea, Disney Studios Paris, and Hong Kong Disneyland are consistent with its strategy to be a global entertainment firm. So, too, are its efforts to increase worldwide licensing of its characters and expand its audience for the Disney Channel to other countries. The firm stumbled badly, however, in its initial efforts with Disneyland Paris and knows its competitors will continue to fight for market share. European vacationers can enjoy other amusement parks, such as Denmark's Legoland or France's Cipal-Parc Asterix. Mickey Mouse lunch boxes compete for the attention of the world's schoolchildren with lunch boxes featuring England's Paddington Bear, France's Babar the Elephant, and Belgium's Smurfs. And AOL Time Warner's Cartoon Network has been outperforming the mouse for years. Thus Disney's top managers know that they are in a continuous battle for the entertainment dollars (and yen and pounds and euros) of the world's consumers and that it is up to the managers to deploy the firm's resources to achieve desired levels of profitability, growth, and market share.

THE CHALLENGES OF INTERNATIONAL STRATEGIC MANAGEMENT ❮

Disney's managers, like those of other international businesses, utilize strategic management to address these challenges. More specifically, **international strategic management** is a comprehensive and ongoing management planning process aimed at formulating and implementing strategies that enable a firm to compete effectively internationally. The process of developing a particular international strategy is often referred to as **strategic planning**. Strategic planning is usually the responsibility of top-level executives at corporate headquarters and senior managers in domestic and foreign operating subsidiaries. Most larger firms also have a permanent planning staff to provide technical assistance for top managers as they develop strategies. Disney's five-person planning staff, for example, gathered demographic and economic data that the firm's decision makers used to select the original French site for Euro Disney.

International strategic management results in the development of various **international strategies**, which are comprehensive frameworks for achieving a firm's fundamental goals. Conceptually, there are many similarities between developing a strategy for competing in a single country and developing one for competing in multiple countries. In both cases the firm's strategic planners must answer the same fundamental questions:

- What products and/or services does the firm intend to sell?
- Where and how will it make those products or services?
- Where and how will it sell them?
- Where and how will it acquire the necessary resources?
- How does it expect to outperform its competitors?[2]

Developing an international strategy, however, is far more complex than developing a domestic one, as "Venturing Abroad" indicates.[3] Managers developing a

VENTURING *Abroad* — IT MAY NOT BE AS EASY AS IT SEEMS!

Online businesses are all the rage these days. It seems that companies everywhere are rushing to start an e-business or move their existing business onto the Internet. One of the most promising market opportunities for online businesses is international expansion. Its potential is due to the presumed ease of foreign-market entry—low fixed costs, no transportation expenses, and so forth. Online businesses are nevertheless advised to keep several things in mind as they venture abroad.

First, domestic Web site hits might be a good indicator of market potential. Thus if a firm is getting 500 or more hits a day from one particular country, that country might have excellent potential for a local electronic operation. Conversely, only a handful of hits might indicate that the market potential is so small as to be not worth the time. Second, cultural norms should also be considered. For example, it might be perfectly appropriate in some countries to have a Web site image featuring a woman with bare arms or a man smoking a cigar, but in other countries these images might be taboo.

Language issues are also important. Hiring a domestic translator to create foreign-language versions of a Web site might be economical, but the translator might not know regional dialects or other language nuances. Thus experts advise using a local service to at least review language content. Further, although practices such as selling customer lists or asking for personal information in exchange for various incentives might be acceptable in some countries, they may be legally prohibited or strongly discouraged in other countries.

Cross-browser compatibility may also be an issue. Different character sets, for example, can pose real problems when users export a Web site. Credit card usage also varies widely in different countries. Just because a firm is successful selling to customers using Master Card or Visa in one country does not necessarily mean it can use the same technique in another country. Finally, online businesses should not overlook the complications associated with shipping across national boundaries. Selling a product via a Web site to a customer in Asia might be relatively easy, but the seller must still get the goods there, and getting them there may entail myriad shipping expenses and customs regulations.

Source: Omid Rahmat, "'I Ain't No Gringo,'" *NewMedia*, July 1999, pp. 27–36.

strategy for a domestic firm must deal with one national government, one currency, one accounting system, one political system, one legal system, and, usually, a single language and a comparatively homogeneous culture. Conversely, managers responsible for developing a strategy for an international firm must understand and deal with multiple governments, multiple currencies, multiple accounting systems, multiple political systems, multiple legal systems, and a variety of languages and cultures. These and other differences in domestic and international operations and how they affect a firm's strategy are summarized in Table 10.1.

Moreover, managers in an international business must also coordinate the implementation of their firm's strategy among business units located in different parts of the world with different time zones, different cultural contexts, and different economic conditions, as well as monitor and control their performance. Managers usually consider these complexities acceptable trade-offs for the additional opportunities that come with global expansion. Indeed, international businesses have the ability to exploit three sources of competitive advantage unavailable to domestic firms:

- *Global efficiencies*: International firms can improve their efficiency through several means unaccessible to a domestic firm. They can capture *location efficiencies* by locating their facilities anywhere in the world that yields them the lowest production or distribution costs or that best improves the quality of service they offer their customers. Production of athletic shoes, for example, is very labor intensive, and Nike, like many of its competitors, centers its manufacturing in

TABLE 10.1

Differences Between Domestic and International Operations That Affect Strategic Management for U.S. Firms

FACTOR	U.S. OPERATIONS	INTERNATIONAL OPERATIONS
Language	English used almost universally	Use of local language required in many situations
Culture	Relatively homogeneous	Quite diverse, both between countries and within countries
Politics	Stable and relatively unimportant	Often volatile and of decisive importance
Economy	Relatively uniform	Wide variations among countries and among regions within countries
Governmental interference	Minimal and reasonably predictable	Often extensive and subject to rapid change
Labor	Skilled labor available	Skilled labor often scarce, requiring training or redesign of production methods
Financing	Well-developed financial markets	Often poorly developed financial markets; capital flows subject to government control
Market research	Data easy to collect	Sometimes data difficult and expensive to collect
Advertising	Many media available; few restrictions	Media limited; many restrictions; low literacy rates rule out print media in some countries
Money	U.S. dollar used universally	Must change from one currency to another; problems created by changing exchange rates and governmental restrictions
Transportation/ communication	Among the best in the world	Often inadequate
Control	Always a problem, but centralized control will work	A worse problem; must walk a tightrope between overcentralizing and losing control through too much decentralizing
Contracts	Once signed, are binding on both parties even if one party makes a bad deal	Can be voided and renegotiated if one party becomes dissatisfied
Labor relations	Collective bargaining, layoff of workers easy	Layoff of workers often not possible; may have mandatory worker participation in management; workers may seek change through political process rather than collective bargaining

Source: Adapted from R. G. Murdick, R. C. Moor, R. H. Eckhouse, and T. W. Zimmerer, *Business Policy: A Framework for Analysis* (Columbus, Ohio: Grid, 1984), p. 275; as found in Pearce and Robinson, *Strategic Management Formulation, Implementation, and Control*, 5th ed., © 1994 (Burr Ridge, Ill.: Richard D. Irwin, Inc.). Reprinted with permission.

countries where labor costs are especially low.[4] Similarly, by building factories to serve more than one country, international firms may also lower their production costs by capturing *economies of scale*. For example, rather than splitting production of its new sports utility vehicle among several factories, Mercedes-Benz decided to produce this vehicle only at its Alabama assembly plant to benefit from economies of scale in production.[5] Finally, by broadening their product lines in each of the countries they enter, international firms may enjoy *economies of scope*, lowering their production and marketing costs and enhancing their bottom lines. When Nissan first started selling cars in the United States, it introduced a single model and sold the car through dealerships owned by other companies. In relative terms the costs of distributing a single vehicle model in this manner were quite high. Over time, however, as the firm's reputation became established, it gradually introduced other models and today has its own North American sales and distribution network selling a wide range of cars and trucks. As a result, Nissan's distribution costs per vehicle model are much lower than when it first entered the U.S. market.[6]

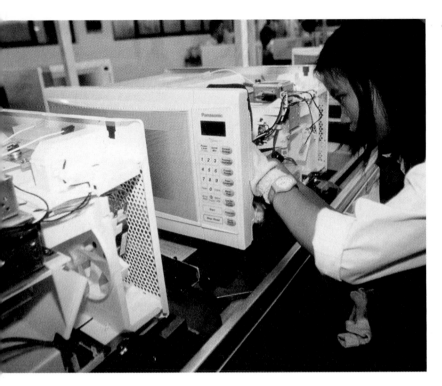

› Capturing global efficiencies is an important component in the formulation of an international firm's strategy. Japanese MNC Matsushita has captured location efficiencies by producing microwaves in Shanghai to take advantage of China's low labor costs. One-third of the world's microwaves are produced in China—some 10 million a year.

- *Multimarket flexibility*: As we discussed in Chapters 3 and 4, there are wide variations in the political, economic, legal, and cultural environments of countries. Moreover, these environments are constantly changing: New laws are passed, new governments are elected, economic policies are changed, new competitors may enter (or leave) the national market, and so on. International businesses thus face the challenge of responding to these multiple diverse and changing environments. Often firms find it beneficial to empower local managers to respond quickly to such changes. However, unlike domestic firms, which operate in and respond to changes in the context of a single domestic environment, international businesses may also respond to a change in one country by implementing a change in another country. Chicken processor Tyson Foods, for example, has benefited over the past decade from the increased demand by health-conscious U.S. consumers for chicken breasts. In producing more chicken breasts, Tyson also produced more chicken legs and thighs, which are considered less desirable by U.S. consumers. Tyson capitalized on its surplus by targeting the Russian market, where dark meat is preferred over light, and the Chinese market, where chicken feet are considered a tasty delicacy. Tyson exports over $250 million worth of chicken thighs and legs to Russia and China.[7] In a variety of ways similar to this, international businesses can exploit and respond to changes in their operating environments better than domestic firms can.

- *Worldwide learning*: The diverse operating environments of multinational corporations (MNCs) may also contribute to organizational learning.[8] Differences in these operating environments may cause the firm to operate differently in one country than another. An astute firm may learn from these differences and transfer this learning to its operations in other countries.[9] For example, McDonald's U.S. managers once believed that its restaurants should be freestanding entities located in suburbs and small towns. A Japanese franchisee convinced McDonald's to allow it to open a restaurant in an inner-city office building. That restaurant's success caused McDonald's executives to rethink their store location criteria. Nontraditional locations—office buildings, Wal-Mart superstores, even airplanes—are now an important source of new growth for the firm. See "Bringing the World into Focus" for another example of this phenomenon.

Unfortunately, it is difficult to exploit these three factors simultaneously. Global efficiencies can be more easily obtained when a single unit of a firm is given worldwide responsibility for the task at hand. BMW's engineering staff at headquarters in Munich, for example, is responsible for the research and design of the company's new automobiles. By focusing its research and development (R&D) efforts at one location, BMW engineers designing new transmissions are better able to coordinate their activities with their counterparts designing new engines. However, centralizing control of its R&D operations also hinders BMW's ability to customize its product to meet the differing needs of customers in different countries. Consider the simple question of whether to include cup holders in its cars. In designing cars to be driven safely at the prevailing high speeds of Germany's autobahn, the company's engineers decided that cup holders were both irrelevant and dangerous. Driving speeds in the United States, however, are much lower, and cup holders are

Bringing the World into FOCUS

"TEACHING AN OLD DOG NEW TRICKS"

General Motors provides a dramatic example of the benefits of worldwide learning. During the 1980s the company was suffering from high production costs, deterioration in the quality of its vehicles, and a loss of market share to its domestic and foreign rivals. In 1984 General Motors entered into a joint venture with Toyota to establish a new company called NUMMI. GM's goal in creating NUMMI was to learn more about how Toyota's lean manufacturing, *kaizen* (continuous improvement), and just-in-time inventory controls systems worked.[10] GM then used this knowledge in developing its newest U.S. automotive division, Saturn. Later, the lessons learned from NUMMI were adopted by

GM's Germany subsidiary, Adam Opel AG, when it built its new factory in the East German town of Eisenach in the early 1990s. Today the Eisenach operation is not only Europe's most efficient auto assembly plant, it is also GM's: Its productivity is double GM's average. GM is now incorporating the lessons learned from its Eisenach/Saturn/NUMMI experiences into three new factories in Argentina, China, and Poland as well as its existing factories in Europe and the Americas.

Source: "GM Is Building Plants in Developing Nations to Woo New Markets," *Wall Street Journal*, August 4, 1997, p. A1.

an important comfort feature in autos sold to U.S. consumers. Lengthy battles were fought between BMW's German engineers and its U.S. marketing managers over this seemingly trivial issue. Only in the mid-1990s did cup holders finally become a standard feature in the firm's automobiles sold in North America.

As this example illustrates, if too much power is centralized in one unit of a firm, the unit may ignore the needs of consumers in other markets. Conversely, multimarket flexibility is enhanced when a firm delegates responsibility to the managers of local subsidiaries. Vesting power in local managers allows each subsidiary to tailor its products, personnel policies, marketing techniques, and other business practices to meet the specific needs and wants of potential customers in each market the firm serves. However, this increased flexibility will reduce the firm's ability to obtain global efficiencies in such areas as production, marketing, and R&D.

Furthermore, the unbridled pursuit of global efficiencies and/or multimarket flexibility may stifle the firm's attempts to promote worldwide learning. Centralizing power in a single unit of the firm to capture global efficiencies may cause the unit to ignore lessons and information acquired by other units of the firm. Moreover, the other units may have little incentive or ability to acquire such information if they know that the "experts" at headquarters will ignore them. Decentralizing power in the hands of local subsidiary managers may create similar problems. A decentralized

❯ GE uses its management councils to encourage the sharing of new techniques and ideas. Its medical-imaging managers may learn new ways of selling goods in China, for example, by listening to the experiences of managers from other GE divisions operating there.

structure may make it difficult to transfer learning from one subsidiary to another. Local subsidiaries may be disposed to automatically reject outside information as not being germane to the local situation. Firms wishing to promote worldwide learning must utilize an organizational structure that promotes knowledge transfer among its subsidiaries and corporate headquarters. The firms must also create incentive structures that motivate managers at headquarters and in subsidiaries to acquire, disseminate, and act upon worldwide learning opportunities.

For example, consider the success of Nokia, headquartered in Helsinki, Finland, which is among the world's leaders in the cellular telephone and telecommunications industries. Nokia, like other telecommunications equipment manufacturers, was struggling to keep pace with rapid shifts in its worldwide markets. Managers in different regions had little idea what their counterparts in other markets were doing, and Nokia factories were grappling with excess inventories of some products and inventory shortages of others. In some instances Nokia factories in one country would shut down for a lack of a critical part that a Nokia factory in another country had in surplus. In response the firm's CEO, Jorma Ollila, established what he called "commando teams" to attack these problems. The teams were charged with improving efficiency throughout the firm. Using a new worldwide information system, Nokia managers now monitor global, regional, and local sales and inventory on a real-time basis. This allows them to make internal transfers of parts and finished goods efficiently. More important, this approach has allowed Nokia to spot market trends and new product developments that arise in one region of the world and transfer this knowledge to improve its competitiveness in other areas and product lines.[11]

General Electric adopted a different approach to facilitate learning transfer among its units. It established 12 management councils, composed of senior executives from different subsidiaries. At the quarterly meetings of these councils each member must present a new idea that other subsidiaries can use in their businesses as well. In this way hard-earned knowledge of new techniques or market opportunities can be quickly spread throughout GE's operations.[12]

› STRATEGIC ALTERNATIVES

MNCs typically adopt one of four strategic alternatives in their attempt to balance the three goals of global efficiencies, multimarket flexibility, and worldwide learning.

The first of these strategic alternatives is the *home replication strategy*. In this approach a firm utilizes the core competency or firm-specific advantage it developed at home as its main competitive weapon in the foreign markets that it enters. That is, the firm takes what it does exceptionally well in its home market and attempts to duplicate that in foreign markets. Mercedes-Benz's home replication strategy, for example, relies on its well-known brand name and its reputation for building well-engineered, luxurious cars capable of traveling safely at very high speeds. It is this market segment that Mercedes-Benz has chosen to exploit internationally, despite the fact that only a very few countries have both the high income levels and the high speed limits appropriate for its products. Yet consumers in Asia, the rest of Europe, and the Americas, attracted by the car's mystique, eagerly buy it, knowing that they too could drive their new car 150 miles per hour, if only the local police would let them.

The *multidomestic strategy* is a second alternative available to international firms.[13] A multidomestic corporation views itself as a collection of relatively independent operating subsidiaries, each of which focuses on a specific domestic market. In addition, each of these subsidiaries is free to customize its products, its marketing campaigns, and its operating techniques to best meet the needs of its local customers. The multidomestic approach is particularly effective when there are clear differences among national markets; when economies of scale for production, distribution, and marketing are low; and when the cost of coordination between the parent corporation and its various foreign subsidiaries is high. Because each subsidiary in a multidomestic corporation must be responsive to the local market, the parent company usually delegates considerable power and authority to managers of its subsidiaries in various host countries. MNCs operating before World War II often adopted this approach because of the difficulties in controlling distant foreign subsidiaries, given the communication and transportation technologies of that time.

The *global strategy* is the third alternative philosophy available for international firms. A global corporation views the world as a single marketplace and has as its primary goal the creation of standardized goods and services that will address the needs of customers worldwide. The global strategy is almost the exact opposite of the multidomestic strategy. Whereas the multidomestic firm believes that its customers in every country are fundamentally different and must be approached from that perspective, a global corporation assumes that customers are fundamentally the same regardless of their nationalities. Thus the global corporation views the world market as a single entity as the corporation develops, produces, and sells its products. It tries to capture economies of scale in production and marketing by concentrating its production activities in a handful of highly efficient factories and then creating global advertising and marketing campaigns to sell the goods produced in those factories. Because the global corporation must coordinate its worldwide production and marketing strategies, it usually concentrates power and decision-making responsibility at a central headquarters.

The home replication strategy and the global strategy share an important similarity: Under either approach a firm conducts business the same way anywhere in the world. There is also an important difference between the two approaches. A firm utilizing the home replication strategy takes its domestic way of doing business and uses that approach in foreign markets as well. In essence a firm using this strategy believes that if its business practices work in its domestic market, then they should also work in foreign markets. Conversely, the starting point for a firm adopting a global strategy has no such home country bias. In fact, the concept of a home market is irrelevant because the global firm thinks of its market as a global one, not one divided into domestic and foreign segments. The global firm tries to figure out the best way to serve all of its customers in the global market and then does so.

A fourth approach available to international firms is the *transnational strategy*. The transnational corporation attempts to combine the benefits of global scale efficiencies, such as those pursued by a global corporation, with the benefits and advantages of local responsiveness, which is the goal of a multidomestic corporation. To do so, the transnational corporation does not automatically centralize or decentralize authority. Rather, it carefully assigns responsibility for various organizational tasks to the unit of the organization best able to achieve the dual goals of efficiency and flexibility.

A transnational corporation may choose to centralize certain management functions and decision making, such as R&D and financial operations, at corporate headquarters. Other management functions, such as human resource management and marketing, may be decentralized, allowing managers of local subsidiaries to customize their business activities to better respond to the local culture and business environment. Microsoft, for example, locates most of its product development efforts in the United States, while responsibility for marketing is delegated to its foreign subsidiaries. Oftentimes transnational corporations locate responsibility for one product line in one country and responsibility for a second product line in another country. To achieve an interdependent network of operations, transnational corporations focus considerable attention on integration and coordination among their various subsidiaries.

Figure 10.1 assesses these four strategic approaches against two criteria: the need for flexibility and responsiveness to local conditions and the need to achieve global efficiencies. Firms must pay particular attention to local conditions when consumer tastes or preferences vary widely across countries; when large differences exist in local laws, economic conditions, and infrastructure; or when host country governments play a major role in the particular industry. Pressures for global efficiencies arise when a firm is selling a standardized commodity with little ability to differentiate its products through features or quality, such as agricultural goods, bulk chemicals, ores, and low-end semiconductor chips. If trade barriers and transportation costs are low, such firms must strive to produce their goods at the lowest possible cost. Conversely, if the product features desired by consumers vary by country or if firms are able to differentiate their products through brand names, after-sales support services, and quality differences, the pressures for global efficiencies are lessened.

The home replication strategy is often adopted by firms when both the pressures for global efficiencies and the need for local responsiveness are low, as the lower left-hand cell in Figure 10.1 shows. Toys 'R' Us, for example, has adopted this approach to internationalizing its operations. It uses the marketing, procurement, and distribution techniques developed in its U.S. retail outlets in its foreign stores as well. The company's managers believe that the firm's path to success internationally is the same as it was domestically: Build large, warehouselike stores, buy in volume, cut prices, and take market share from smaller, high-cost toy retailers. Accordingly, the managers see little reason to adjust the firm's basic domestic strategy as they enter new international markets.

The multidomestic approach is often used when the need to respond to local conditions is high, but the pressures for global efficiencies are low. Many companies selling brand name food products have adopted this approach. Although not unmindful of the benefits of reducing manufacturing costs, such marketing-driven companies as Kraft, Unilever, and Cadbury Schweppes are more concerned with meeting the specific needs of local customers, thereby ensuring that these customers will continue to pay a premium price for the brand name goods the companies sell. Moreover, the companies often rely on local production facilities to ensure that local consumers will readily find fresh, high-quality products on their supermarket shelves.

The global strategy is most appropriate when the pressures for global efficiencies are high but the need for local responsiveness and flexibility is low. In such cases

FIGURE 10.1

Strategic Alternatives for Balancing Pressures for Global Integration and Local Responsiveness

Source: Adapted from Sumantra Ghoshal and Nitin Nohria, "Horses for Courses: Organizational Forms for Multinational Corporations," *Sloan Management Review*, Winter 1993, pp. 27 and 31.

PRESSURES FOR GLOBAL EFFICIENCIES

High

Low

GLOBAL STRATEGY
The firm views the world as a single marketplace and its primary goal is to create standardized goods and services that will address the needs of customers worldwide.

TRANSNATIONAL STRATEGY
The firm attempts to combine the benefits of global scale efficiencies with the benefits of local responsiveness.

HOME REPLICATION STRATEGY
The firm uses the core competency or firm-specific advantage it developed at home as its main competitive weapon in the foreign markets it enters.

MULTIDOMESTIC STRATEGY
The firm views itself as a collection of relatively independent operating subsidiaries, each of which focuses on a specific domestic market.

Low   High

PRESSURES FOR LOCAL RESPONSIVENESS AND FLEXIBILITY

firms can focus on creating standardized goods, marketing campaigns, distribution systems, and so forth. This strategy has been adopted by many Japanese consumer electronics firms such as Sony and Matsushita, which design their products with the world in mind. Aside from minor adaptations for differences in local electrical systems, these firms' stereos, portable disc players, VCRs, and DVD players are sold to consumers throughout the Quad countries with little need for customization. Thus these firms are free to seek global efficiencies by capturing economies of scale in manufacturing and concentrating their production in countries offering low-cost manufacturing facilities.

The transnational strategy is most appropriate when pressures for global efficiencies and local responsiveness are both high. The Ford Motor Company has been attempting to employ this strategy. For example, Ford now has a single manager responsible for global engine and transmission development. Other managers have similar responsibilities for product design and development, production, and marketing. However, each manager is also responsible for ensuring that Ford products are tailored to meet local consumer tastes and preferences. For instance, Ford products sold in the United Kingdom must have their steering wheel mounted on the right side of the passenger compartment. Body styles may also need to be slightly altered in different markets to be more appealing to local customer tastes.

Not addressed to this point has been the issue of worldwide learning. Worldwide learning requires the transfer of information and experiences from the parent to each subsidiary, from each subsidiary to the parent, and among subsidiaries. Neither the home replication, multidomestic, nor global strategy is explicitly designed, however, to accomplish such learning transfer. The home replication strategy is predicated on the parent company transferring the firm's core competencies to its foreign subsidiaries. The multidomestic strategy decentralizes power to the local subsidiaries so they can respond easily to local conditions. The global strategy centralizes decision making so the firm can achieve global integration of its activities.

The transnational strategy would appear to be better able to promote global learning with its mix of centralization and decentralization of functions—a primary reason for adopting the transnational strategy in the first place. Transnational corporations utilize such techniques as matrix organizational designs, project teams, informal management networks, and corporate cultures to help promote transfer of knowledge among their subsidiaries. Such approaches to promote worldwide learning are also available to firms adopting the home replication, multidomestic, and global approaches. However, such firms need to exert a systematic effort to successfully make use of these techniques.

COMPONENTS OF AN INTERNATIONAL STRATEGY ❮

After determining the overall international strategic philosophy of their firm, managers who engage in international strategic planning then need to address the four basic components of strategy development. These components are distinctive competence, scope of operations, resource deployment, and synergy.[14]

Distinctive Competence

Distinctive competence, the first component of international strategy, answers the question "What do we do exceptionally well, especially as compared to our competitors?" A firm's distinctive competence may be cutting-edge technology, efficient distribution networks, superior organizational practices, or well-respected brand names. As our discussion of Dunning's eclectic theory in Chapter 5 suggested, a firm's possession of a distinctive competence (what Dunning called an ownership advantage) is thought by many experts to be a necessary condition for a firm to compete successfully outside its home market. Without a distinctive competence a foreign firm will have difficulty competing with local firms that are presumed to know the local market better. The Disney name, image, and portfolio of characters, for example, are a distinctive competence that allows the firm to succeed in foreign markets. Similarly, the ready availability of software programs compatible with Windows gives Microsoft an advantage in competing with local firms outside the United States.

Whatever its form, this distinctive competence represents an important resource to the firm. A firm often wishes to exploit this advantage by expanding its operations into as many markets as its resources allow. To a large degree the internationalization strategy adopted by a company reflects the interplay between its distinctive competence and the business opportunities available in different countries.[15]

For example, Stuttgart-based Robert Bosch GmbH, the world's largest automotive electronic equipment supplier, was the first company to develop and sell electronic fuel injection and antilock brake systems. This head start resulted in a distinctive competence that other firms have found difficult to match. Bosch still enjoys a 50 percent share of these lucrative markets, selling to automobile manufacturers in all six inhabited continents.[16] Similarly, Frankfurt's Glasbau Hahn constructs glass showcases with self-contained climate controls and fiber optic lighting. Because the showcases are perceived to be the world's best, museums pay Glasbau Hahn as much as $100,000 for a case in which to display priceless art, sculpture, or artifacts. Exploiting its distinctive competence in this specialized market, Glasbau Hahn has built a $12 million international business.[17]

Scope of Operations

The second component, the **scope of operations**, answers the question "Where are we going to conduct business?" Scope may be defined in terms of geographical regions, such as countries, regions within a country, and/or clusters of countries. Alternatively, scope may focus on market or product niches within one or more regions, such as the premium-quality market niche, the low-cost market niche, or other specialized market niches. Because all firms have finite resources and because markets differ in their relative attractiveness for various products, managers must decide which markets are most attractive to their firm. Scope is, of course, tied to the firm's distinctive competence: If the firm possesses a distinctive competence only in certain regions or in specific product lines, then the firm's scope of operations will focus on those areas where it enjoys the distinctive competence.

For example, the geographical scope of Disney's theme park operations consists of the United States, Japan, and France, with Hong Kong to come, while the geographical scope of Disney's movie distribution and merchandise sales operations is more than 100 countries. Other companies have chosen to participate in many lines of business but narrow their geographic focus, such as Grupo Luksics, a family-owned conglomerate with interests in beer, copper, banking, hotels, railroads, telecommunications, and ranching in Chile and neighboring countries. Conversely, Ballantyne, a small ($12 million in annual revenues) Nebraska-based company, is sharply focused, just like its primary product: feature-film projectors, in which the company enjoys a 65 percent share of the U.S. market and a 30 percent market share elsewhere.[18] Similarly, in the semiconductor industry, many firms have chosen to limit their operations to specific product niches. Asian semiconductor manufacturers like Samsung, NEC, and Toshiba dominate the global memory chip market. California-based Intel focuses on producing the microprocessors that power most IBM-compatible personal computers. Texas Instruments specializes in digital signal processors, which convert analog signals into digital signals. Such chips have many uses, from computer modems to stereo systems to cellular phones. Siemens concentrates on chips that have automotive applications, and Philips specializes in the development of multimedia semiconductors, which bridge consumer electronics and computers.[19] Thus strategic planning results in some international businesses choosing to compete in only a few markets, some to compete in many, and others (such as Disney) to vary their operations across the different types of business operations in which they are involved.

Resource Deployment

Resource deployment answers the question "Given that we are going to compete in these markets, how will we allocate our resources to them?" For example, even though Disney will soon have theme park operations in four countries, the firm does not have an equal resource commitment to each market. Disney invested nothing in Tokyo Disneyland, limited its original investment in Disneyland Paris to 49 percent of its equity, and will cap its investment in Hong Kong as well. However, it continues to invest heavily in its U.S. theme park operations and in filmed entertainment.

Resource deployment might be specified along product lines, geographical lines, or both.[20] This part of strategic planning determines relative priorities for a firm's limited resources. Disney could have easily solved Disneyland Paris's financial difficulties without outside assistance. However, additional investment would have taken the firm's commitment far beyond the level it thought viable for its resource deployment goals and perhaps jeopardized its ability to build the Animal Kingdom in Orlando or to purchase Capital Cities/ABC.

Some large MNCs choose to deploy their resources worldwide. For example, Osaka-based Sharp Corporation manufactures its electronic goods in 33 plants in 26 countries. Other firms have opted to focus their production in one country. Boeing, the leading U.S. exporter, concentrates final assembly of commercial aircraft in the Seattle, Washington, region. DaimlerChrysler concentrates production of Mercedes-Benz automobiles in Germany; even though its newest plant is in Alabama, 9 out of 10 Mercedes are still German built.[21] Although these firms buy materials and sell products globally, they have limited most of their production resource deployment to their home countries.

Synergy

The fourth component of international strategy, **synergy**, answers the question "How can different elements of our business benefit each other?" The goal of synergy is to create a situation where the whole is greater than the sum of the parts. Disney has excelled at generating synergy in the United States. People know the Disney characters from television, so they plan vacations to Disney theme parks. At the parks they are bombarded with information about the newest Disney movies, and they buy merchandise featuring Disney characters, which encourage them to watch Disney characters on TV, starting the cycle all over again. However, as noted earlier, the firm has struggled in its efforts to be as effective in global markets.

DEVELOPING INTERNATIONAL STRATEGIES <

Developing international strategies is not a one-dimensional process. Firms generally carry out international strategic management in two broad stages: strategy formulation and strategy implementation. Simply put, strategy formulation is deciding what to do, and strategy implementation is actually doing it.

1. In *strategy formulation* the firm establishes its goals and the strategic plan that will lead to the achievement of those goals. In international strategy formulation

Wiring the World

A REAL (LACK OF) DIFFERENTIATION

Whenever an Internet firm sets up shop in a different country, one of the first questions its managers have to ask is how to differentiate itself from other sites. In an interesting twist one major player in the global arena has gone in the opposite direction—imitation rather than differentiation. The firm is Yahoo! Japan and, so far at least, its strategy is paying off in a big way. As of the end of 2000, Yahoo! Japan's stock has risen 6000 percent since its initial listing in November 1997.

It all started when Masahiro Inoue decided to seek a licensing agreement with Yahoo! to create and maintain a Japanese Web site patterned after the popular Yahoo! site in the United States. In his own words, "I decided to copy everything from the U.S." As a result, Yahoo! Japan looks and works exactly like its U.S. counterpart. Its category headings even follow English alphabetical order, even though they use Japanese characters.

This strategy flies in the face of conventional Japanese wisdom, which suggest that patience and meticulous attention to local tastes are necessary ingredients for success. Yahoo! Japan, meanwhile, has been a smashing success. An estimated 85 percent of Japanese Internet users visit Yahoo! Japan at least once a month, and the firm has an overwhelming market share in a high-growth market—a kind of Internet nirvana often sought but seldom achieved. Indeed, a new lesson seems to be emerging: E-business lessons learned and brands solidified in the United States can work very well for those who execute them in other countries.

Sources: "Yahoo! Japan Learns from Parent's Achievements, Errors, " *Wall Street Journal*, December 11, 2000, p. A28; "For Yahoo Japan, Imitation and Speed Lead to Dominance," *Wall Street Journal*, July 8, 1999, pp. B1, B4.

managers develop, refine, and agree on which markets to enter (or exit) and how best to compete in each. Much of what we discuss in the rest of this chapter and in the next two chapters primarily concerns international strategy formulation. ("Wiring the World" presents an example of how one entrepreneur formulated his firm's strategy.)

2. In *strategy implementation* the firm develops the tactics for achieving the formulated international strategies. Disney's decision to build Disneyland Paris was part of strategy formulation, but deciding which attractions to include, when to open, and what to charge for admission was part of strategy implementation. Strategy implementation is usually achieved via the organization's design, the work of its employees, and its control systems and processes. Chapters 13 through 15 deal primarily with implementation issues.

Although every strategic planning process is in many ways unique, there is nevertheless a set of general steps that managers usually follow as they set about developing their strategies. These steps, shown in Figure 10.2, are discussed next.

Mission Statement

Most organizations begin the international strategic planning process by creating a **mission statement**, which clarifies the organization's purpose, values, and directions. The mission statement is often used as a way of communicating with internal and external constituents and stakeholders about the firm's strategic direction. It may specify such factors as the firm's target customers and markets, principal products or services, geographical domain, core technologies, concerns for survival, plans for growth and profitability, basic philosophy, and desired public

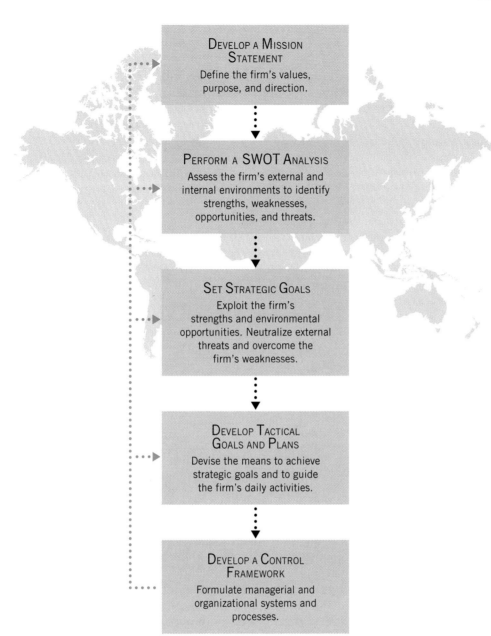

FIGURE 10.2

**Steps in International
Strategy Formulation**

DEVELOP A MISSION STATEMENT
Define the firm's values, purpose, and direction.

PERFORM A SWOT ANALYSIS
Assess the firm's external and internal environments to identify strengths, weaknesses, opportunities, and threats.

SET STRATEGIC GOALS
Exploit the firm's strengths and environmental opportunities. Neutralize external threats and overcome the firm's weaknesses.

DEVELOP TACTICAL GOALS AND PLANS
Devise the means to achieve strategic goals and to guide the firm's daily activities.

DEVELOP A CONTROL FRAMEWORK
Formulate managerial and organizational systems and processes.

image.[22] For example, the mission statement of The Walt Disney Company is "to create shareholder value by continuing to be the world's premier entertainment company from a creative, strategic, and financial standpoint." Hershey Foods' mission statement includes the goal of being the "No. 1 confectionery company in North America." Carpenter Technology specifies its mission to be a "major, profitable, and growing international producer and distributor of specialty alloys, materials, and components." MNCs may have multiple mission statements—one for the overall firm and one for each of its various foreign subsidiaries. Of course, a firm that has multiple mission statements must ensure that they are compatible.

Environmental Scanning and the SWOT Analysis

The second step in developing a strategy is conducting a **SWOT analysis**. SWOT is an acronym for "Strengths, Weaknesses, Opportunities, and Threats." A firm typically initiates its SWOT analysis by performing an **environmental scan**, a systematic collection of data about all elements of the firm's external and internal environments, including markets, regulatory issues, competitors' actions, production costs, and labor productivity.[23]

When members of a planning staff scan the external environment, they try to identify both *opportunities* (the O in SWOT) and *threats* (the T in SWOT) confronting the firm. They obtain data about economic, financial, political, legal, social, and competitive changes in the various markets the firm serves or might want to serve. (Such data are also used for political risk analysis, discussed in Chapter 3, as well as the country market analysis discussed in Chapter 11.) For example, Boeing continuously monitors changes in political and economic forces that affect air travel. During the early 1990s political shifts in China led to more competition in the domestic air travel market. The Chinese government split the giant state-owned carrier CAAC into competing regional carriers and allowed Hong Kong's Cathay Pacific airline to offer air travel within China. Boeing's environmental scanning suggested that a booming demand for air travel would make the Chinese market a particularly appealing opportunity. Accordingly, the firm chose to locate a new sales office in Beijing. The move paid off, and China has become one of Boeing's most important markets.

External environmental scanning also yields data about environmental threats to the firm, such as shrinking markets, increasing competition, the potential for new government regulation, political instability in key markets, and the development of new technologies that could make the firm's manufacturing facilities or product lines obsolete. Threats to Disney include increased competition in the U.S. market from Universal Studios, Six Flags, and other theme parks; potential competition in Europe from theme parks there; French resentment of U.S. intrusion in France; and fluctuating exchange rates. Threats to BMW include changing U.S. automobile fuel efficiency standards, increased competition from Japanese producers in the luxury car market, and high German labor costs. Threats to Federal Express include not only competition in the international express package delivery market from firms such as DHL Worldwide and TNT, but also the rapidly growing usage of e-mail and fax machines to send messages internationally.

In conducting a SWOT analysis, a firm's strategic managers must also assess the firm's internal environment, that is, its *strengths* and *weaknesses* (the S and W in SWOT). Organizational strengths are skills, resources, and other advantages the firm possesses relative to its competitors. Potential strengths, which form the basis of a firm's distinctive competence, might include an abundance of managerial talent, cutting-edge technology, well-known brand names, surplus cash, a good public image, and strong market shares in key countries. Disney's strengths include low corporate debt and the international appeal of its characters. BMW's strengths include its skilled workforce, innovative engineers, and reputation for producing high-quality automobiles.

A firm also needs to acknowledge its organizational weaknesses. These weaknesses reflect deficiencies or shortcomings in skills, resources, or other factors that hinder the firm's competitiveness. They may include poor distribution networks outside the home market, poor labor relations, a lack of skilled international managers, or product development efforts that lag behind those of competitors. Disney's organizational weaknesses regarding Disneyland Paris include high capital costs, negative publicity, and underutilized hotel capacity. BMW's weaknesses include its extremely high domestic labor costs, which make it difficult for it to compete on the basis of price.

One technique for assessing a firm's strengths and weaknesses is the value chain. Developed by Harvard Business School Professor Michael Porter, the **value chain** is a breakdown of the firm into its important activities—production, marketing, human resource management, and so forth—to enable its strategists to identify its competitive advantages and disadvantages. Each primary and support activ-

FIGURE 10.3

Primary activities →

Manufacturing	Marketing & Sales	Service

Company Infrastructure

Information Systems

Human Resources

Research & Development

Sourcing & Logistics

Support activities

The Value Chain

Source: Adapted with the permission of The Free Press, a Division of Simon & Schuster, from *Competitive Advantage: Creating and Sustaining Superior Performance*, by Michael E. Porter, Copyright © 1985 by Michael E. Porter.

ity depicted in Figure 10.3 can be the source of an organizational strength (distinctive competence) or weakness. For example, the quality of Caterpillar's products (Research and Development in the figure) and the strength of its worldwide dealership network (Marketing, Sales, and Service) are among its organizational strengths, but poor labor relations (Human Resources) represent one of its organizational weaknesses.

Managers use information derived from the SWOT analysis to develop specific effective strategies. Effective strategies are those that exploit environmental opportunities and organizational strengths, neutralize environmental threats, and protect or overcome organizational weaknesses. For example, BMW's decision to build automobiles in South Carolina took advantage of its strong brand image in the United States. This decision also neutralized the firm's internal weakness of high German labor costs and its vulnerability to loss of U.S. customers if Germany's currency were to rise in value relative to the U.S. dollar.

Strategic Goals

With the mission statement and SWOT analysis as context, international strategic planning is largely framed by the setting of strategic goals. **Strategic goals** are the major objectives the firm wants to accomplish through pursuing a particular course of action. By definition they should be measurable, feasible, and time limited (answering the questions "How much, how, and by when?"). For example, Disney set strategic goals for Disneyland Paris for projected attendance, revenues, and so on, but as the Scottish poet Robert Burns noted, "the best laid plans of mice and men" often go awry. Part of the park's resultant financial problems arose from the firm's goals not being met. Disney's strategic managers had to revise the firm's strategic plan and goals, taking into account the new information painfully learned from the first years of the park's unprofitable operation.

Tactics

As shown in Figure 10.2, after a SWOT analysis has been performed and strategic goals set, the next step in strategic planning is to develop specific tactical goals and plans, or **tactics**. Tactics usually involve middle managers and focus on the details of implementing the firm's strategic goals. For example, Grand Metropolitan, a huge British food company, and Guinness, a major British spirits maker, merged to create Diageo PLC, one of the world's largest consumer products companies with revenues of $17 billion. The merger agreement reflected strategic decisions by the two companies. After plans for the merger were announced, middle managers in both companies were faced with the challenge of integrating various components of the two original companies into a single new one. Tactical issues such as the integration of the firms' accounting and information systems, human resource procedures involving hiring, compensation, and career paths, and distribution and logistics questions ranging from shipping and transportation to warehousing all had to be addressed and synthesized into one new way of doing business.[24]

Control Framework

The final aspect of strategy formulation is the development of a **control framework**, the set of managerial and organizational processes that keep the firm moving toward its strategic goals. For example, Disneyland Paris had a first-year attendance goal of 12 million visitors. When it became apparent that this goal would not be met, the firm increased its advertising to help boost attendance and temporarily closed one of its hotels to cut costs. Had attendance been running ahead of the goal, the firm might have decreased advertising and extended the theme park's operating hours. Each set of responses stems from the control framework established to keep the firm on course. As shown by Figure 10.2's feedback loops, the control framework can prompt revisions in any of the preceding steps in the strategy formulation process. We discuss control frameworks more fully in Chapter 15.

› LEVELS OF INTERNATIONAL STRATEGY

Given the complexities of international strategic management, many international businesses—especially MNCs—find it useful to develop strategies for three distinct levels within the organization. These levels of international strategy, illustrated in Figure 10.4, are corporate, business, and functional.[25]

Corporate Strategy

Corporate strategy attempts to define the domain of businesses the firm intends to operate. Consider three Japanese electronics firms: Sony competes in the global market for consumer electronics and entertainment but has not broadened its

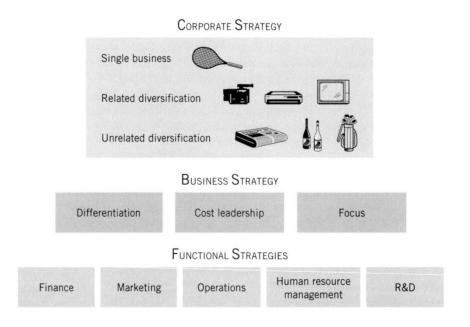

FIGURE 10.4

Three Levels of Strategy for MNCs

CORPORATE STRATEGY

Single business

Related diversification

Unrelated diversification

BUSINESS STRATEGY

Differentiation

Cost leadership

Focus

FUNCTIONAL STRATEGIES

Finance

Marketing

Operations

Human resource management

R&D

scope into home and kitchen appliances. Archrival Matsushita competes in all these industries, while Pioneer Electronic Corporation focuses only on electronic audio and video products. Each firm has answered quite differently the question of what constitutes its business domain. Their divergent answers reflect their differing corporate strengths and weaknesses, as well as their differing assessments of the opportunities and threats produced by the global economic and political environments. A firm might adopt any one of three forms of corporate strategy: a single-business strategy, a related diversification strategy, or an unrelated diversification strategy.

The Single-Business Strategy.   The **single-business strategy** calls for a firm to rely on a single business, product, or service for all its revenue. The most significant advantage of this strategy is that the firm can concentrate all its resources and expertise on that one product or service. However, this strategy also increases the firm's vulnerability to its competition and to changes in the external environment. For example, for a firm producing only VCRs, a new innovation such as the DVD player makes the firm's single product obsolete, and the firm may be unable to develop new products quickly enough to survive. Nonetheless, many MNCs, such as Air Canada, McDonald's, and Dell, have found the single-business strategy a rewarding one.

Related Diversification.   The most common corporate strategy, **related diversification**, calls for the firm to operate in several different but fundamentally related businesses, industries, or markets at the same time. This strategy allows the firm to leverage a distinctive competence in one market to strengthen its competitiveness in other markets. The goal of related diversification and the basic relationship linking various operations are often defined in the firm's mission statement.

Disney uses the related diversification strategy. Each of its operations is linked to the others via Disney characters, the Disney logo, a theme of wholesomeness, and a reputation for providing high-quality family entertainment. Disney movies and TV shows, many of which are broadcast over Disney-owned networks, help sell Disney theme parks, which in turn help sell Disney merchandise. Accor SA, the world's second largest hotel operator, also uses a related diversification strategy. Originally the operator of a chain restaurant, this Paris-based firm began acquiring luxury hotel chains such as Sofitel and budget chains such as Motel 6. To keep its dining rooms and hotel beds full, Accor then branched out into the package tour business and the rental car business. To promote tourism, the firm even opened its own theme park north of Paris, based on the French cartoon character Asterix the Gaul.[26]

Related diversification has several advantages. First, the firm depends less on a single product or service, so it is less vulnerable to competitive or economic threats.[27] For example, if Disney faces increased competition in the theme park business, its movie, television, and licensing divisions can offset potential declines in theme park revenues. Moreover, these related businesses may make it more difficult for an outsider to compete with Disney in the first place. For example, non-Disney animated movies have trouble competing against new animated releases from the Disney Studios. Makers of non-Disney movies must buy advertising at commercial rates, while Disney can inexpensively promote its new releases to families waiting in line at its theme parks and to viewers of shows on ABC or the Disney Channel. Similar problems confront rival theme park operators, who have to contend with the constant exposure that Disney's theme parks receive on network television and the Disney Channel and on T-shirts and caps worn by kids of all ages worldwide.

Second, related diversification may produce economies of scale for a firm. For example, The Limited, Inc., takes advantage of its vast size to buy new clothing lines at favorable prices from Far Eastern manufacturers and then divides the purchases among its Limited, Express, Lerner, and other divisions. Similarly, Disney has created a division it calls Strategic Sourcing. This unit's purpose is to consolidate as much of the firm's global purchasing as possible. For example, the company buys all its packaging materials from one supplier. Consumers who buy merchandise from Disneyland Paris, the Disney Store in Los Angeles, the *Lion King* show in London, a Disney Web site, or the direct-mail Disney catalog will all receive their purchases in the same style box bought from the same manufacturer. The company estimates that within five years it will be saving over $300 million annually from this approach.[28]

Third, related diversification may allow a firm to use technology or expertise developed in one market to enter a second market more cheaply and easily. For example, Pirelli SpA used its expertise in producing rubber products and insulated cables, refined over 100 years ago, to become the world's fifth largest producer of automobile tires. Pirelli has also transferred its knowledge of rubber cables to become a major producer of fiber optic cables. More recently, Casio Computer Company transferred the knowledge it gained in making hand-held electric calculators during the 1970s to the production of inexpensive electronic digital watches, musical synthesizers, and pocket televisions. Such potential synergies are a major advantage of the related diversification strategy.

One potential disadvantage of related diversification is the cost of coordinating the operations of the related divisions. A second is the possibility that all the firm's business units may be affected simultaneously by changes in economic conditions. For example, Accor can create synergies by steering travel customers to its hotels and restaurants. Yet all of Accor's divisions are vulnerable to a downturn in tourism. If another oil crisis erupts or an increase in terrorist actions keeps travelers at home, all Accor businesses will suffer.

Unrelated Diversification. A third corporate strategy international businesses may use is **unrelated diversification**, whereby a firm operates in several unrelated industries and markets. For example, Pearson PLC, a British firm, owns publishing companies, a fledgling restaurant chain, and a television production business.[29] Similarly, General Electric owns such diverse business units as a television network (NBC), a lighting manufacturer, a medical technology firm, an aircraft engine producer, a semiconductor manufacturer, and an investment bank. These operations are unrelated to each other, and there is little reason to anticipate synergy among such diverse operations and businesses.

During the 1960s unrelated diversification was the most popular investment strategy. Many large firms, such as ITT, Gulf and Western, LTV, and Textron, became **conglomerates**, the term used for firms comprising unrelated businesses. The unrelated diversification strategy yields several benefits. First, the corporate parent may be able to raise capital more easily than any of its independent units can separately. The parent can then allocate this capital to the most profitable opportunities available among its subsidiaries. Second, overall riskiness may be reduced because a conglomerate is less subject to business cycle fluctuations. For example, temporary difficulties facing one of its units might be offset by success in another. Third, a conglomerate is less vulnerable to competitive threats because any given threat is likely to affect only a portion of its total operations. Fourth, a conglomerate can more easily shed unprofitable operations because they are independent. It also can buy new operations without worrying about how to integrate them into existing businesses.

Nonetheless, the creation of conglomerates through the unrelated diversification strategy is out of favor today primarily because of the lack of potential synergy across unrelated businesses. Because the businesses are unrelated, no one operation can regularly sustain or enhance the others. For example, GE managers cannot use any of the competitive advantages they may have developed in the lighting business to help offset low ratings at the firm's television network. Further, it is difficult for staff at corporate headquarters to effectively manage diverse businesses because the staff must understand a much wider array of businesses and markets than if operations are related. This complicates the performance monitoring of individual operations. As a result, although some conglomerates such as GE and Textron have thrived, many others have changed their strategy or disappeared altogether. DaimlerChrysler, for example, is considering a reorientation of its business away from unrelated diversification and more toward related diversification. Currently the firm has operations in passenger cars and trucks, commercial vehicles, financial services and information technology, aerospace, rail, diesel engines, and auto electronics. However, DaimlerChrysler is consolidating some of its nonautomotive activities, selling others, and putting more and more emphasis on its automobile operations.[30]

Business Strategy

Whereas corporate strategy deals with the overall organization, business strategy focuses on specific businesses, subsidiaries, or operating units within the firm. Business strategy seeks to answer the question "How should we compete in each market we have chosen to enter?"

Firms that pursue corporate strategies of related diversification or unrelated diversification tend to bundle sets of businesses together into **strategic business units (SBUs)**. In firms that follow the related diversification strategy, the products and services of each SBU are somewhat similar to each other. For example, Disney defines its SBUs as theme parks and resorts, creative content (filmed entertainment, character licensing, Disney Stores), and broadcasting (ABC, the Disney Channel, ESPN). In firms that follow unrelated diversification strategies, products and services of each SBU are dissimilar. Textron, for example, has created four SBUs: aircraft, automotive products, financial services, and industrial products.

By focusing on the competitive environment of each business or SBU, business strategy helps the firm improve its distinctive competence for that business or unit. Once a firm selects a business strategy for an SBU, it typically uses that strategy in all geographical markets the SBU serves. The firm may develop a unique business strategy for each of its SBUs, or it may pursue the same business strategy for all of them. The three basic forms of business strategy are differentiation, overall cost leadership, and focus.[31]

Differentiation.   **Differentiation strategy** is a commonly used business strategy. It attempts to establish and maintain the image (either real or perceived) that the SBU's products or services are fundamentally unique from other products or services in the same market segment. Many international businesses today are attempting to use quality as a differentiating factor. If successful at establishing a high-quality image, they can charge higher prices for their products or services. For example, Rolex sells its timepieces worldwide for premium prices. The firm limits its sales agreements to only a few dealers in any given area, stresses quality and status in its advertising, and seldom discounts its products. Other international firms that use the differentiation strategy effectively include Coca-Cola (soft drinks), Nikon (cameras), Calvin Klein (fashion apparel), and Waterford Wedgewood (fine china and glassware).

Other firms adopt value as their differentiating factor. They compete by charging reasonable prices for quality goods and services. Marks and Spencer has used the value factor to thrive in the department store market in the United Kingdom and on the European continent. Lands' End, a Wisconsin mail-order clothing seller, has also used this differentiation strategy to grow into a billion-dollar company. It has established operations in the United Kingdom, Germany, and Japan. By translating its catalogs into the local language, providing local mailing addresses and telephone numbers, and accepting local currencies, its international operations have come to account for almost 10 percent of its sales. Ironically, this effort puts Marks and Spencer and Lands' End in direct competition with each other, with each stressing the value factor. They may have to switch to differentiation based on distribution mode—catalog versus retail outlet sales.

Overall Cost Leadership. The **overall cost leadership strategy** calls for a firm to focus on achieving highly efficient operating procedures so that its costs are lower than its competitors' costs. This allows the firm to sell its goods or services for lower prices. A successful overall cost leadership strategy may result in lower levels of unit profitability (due to lower prices) but higher total profitability (due to increased sales volume). For example, France's Bic Pen Company makes approximately 3 million pens a day. By concentrating on making those pens as cheaply as possible, the firm is able to sell them for a very low price. Taken together, volume production and a worldwide distribution network have allowed Bic to flourish. Other firms that use this strategy are Timex (watches), Fuji (film), Hyundai (automobiles), the LG Group (consumer electronics), and NEC (semiconductors).

Focus. A **focus strategy** calls for a firm to target specific types of products for certain customer groups or regions. Doing this allows the firm to match the features of specific products to the needs of specific consumer groups. These groups might be characterized by geographical region, ethnicity, purchasing power, tastes in fashion, or any other factor that influences their purchasing patterns. For example, Cadbury Schweppes PLC markets Hires Root Beer only in the United States because root beer does not appeal to people elsewhere. In other countries Cadbury sells other flavors of soft drinks, including Solo (mixed fruit flavored) and Trina (grapefruit flavored), that do not appeal to U.S. consumers. Honda sells Accord station wagons primarily in the United States because U.S. consumers like station wagons more than do consumers in other countries. It concentrates on selling its low-priced Civic in less-developed countries, where consumers have less discretionary income, and emphasizes its faster Prelude in Europe, where speed limits tend to be higher. Sony's business strategy for its consumer electronics SBU focuses on continually upgrading and refining the products through extensive R&D while maintaining its reputation for producing high-quality electronics.

Functional Strategies

Functional strategies attempt to answer the question "How will we manage the functions of finance, marketing, operations, human resources, and R&D in ways consistent with our international corporate and business strategies?" We briefly introduce each common functional strategy here but leave more detailed discussion to later chapters.

International *financial* strategy deals with such issues as the firm's desired capital structure, investment policies, foreign-exchange holdings, risk reduction techniques, debt policies, and working-capital management. Typically, an international business develops a financial strategy for the overall firm as well as for each SBU. We cover international financial strategy more fully in Chapter 18.

International *marketing* strategy concerns the distribution and selling of the firm's products or services. It addresses questions of product mix, advertising, promotion, pricing, and distribution. International marketing strategy is the subject of Chapter 16.

International *operations* strategy deals with the creation of the firm's products or services. It guides decisions on such issues as sourcing, plant location, plant layout and design, technology, and inventory management. We return to international operations management in Chapter 17.

International *human resource* strategy focuses on the people who work for an organization. This strategy guides decisions regarding how the firm will recruit, train, and evaluate employees and what it will pay them, as well as how it will deal with labor relations. International human resource strategy is the subject of Chapter 20.

Finally, a firm's international *R&D* strategy is concerned with the magnitude and direction of the firm's investment in creating new products and developing new technologies.

The next step in formulating international strategy is to determine which foreign markets to enter and which to avoid. The firm's managers must then decide how to enter the chosen markets. These two issues are the subjects of Chapters 11 and 12.

CHAPTER REVIEW

Summary

International strategic management is a comprehensive and ongoing management planning process aimed at formulating and implementing strategies that enable a firm to compete effectively in different markets. Although there are many similarities in developing domestic and international strategies, international firms have three additional sources of competitive advantages unavailable to domestic firms. These are global efficiencies, multimarket flexibility, and worldwide learning.

Firms participating in international business usually adopt one of four strategic alternatives: the home replication strategy, the multidomestic strategy, the global strategy, or the transnational strategy. Each of these strategies has advantages and disadvantages in terms of its ability to help firms be responsive to local circumstances and to achieve the benefits of global efficiencies.

A well-conceived strategy has four essential components:

1. Distinctive competence—what the firm does exceptionally well
2. Scope of operations—the array of markets in which the firm plans to operate
3. Resource deployment—how the firm will distribute its resources across different areas
4. Synergy—the degree to which different operations within the firm can benefit each other

International strategy formulation is the process of creating a firm's international strategies. The process of carrying out these strategies via specific tactics is called international strategy implementation. In international strategy formulation a firm follows three general steps:

1. Develop a mission statement that specifies the firm's values, purpose, and directions.
2. Thoroughly analyze the firm's strengths and weaknesses, as well as the opportunities and threats that exist in its environment.
3. Set strategic goals, outline tactical goals and plans, and develop a control framework.

Most firms develop strategy at three levels:

1. Corporate strategy answers the question "What businesses will we operate?" Basic corporate strategies are single business, related diversification, and unrelated diversification.
2. Business strategy answers the question "How should we compete in each market we have chosen to enter?" Fundamental business strategies are differentiation, overall cost leadership, and focus.
3. Functional strategy deals with how the firm intends to manage the functions of finance, marketing, operations, human resources, and R&D.

Review Questions

1. What is international strategic management?
2. What are the three sources of competitive advantage available to international businesses that are not available to domestic firms?
3. Why is it difficult for firms to exploit these three competitive advantages simultaneously?
4. What are the four basic philosophies that guide strategic management in most MNCs?
5. How do international strategy formulation and international strategy implementation differ?
6. What are the steps in international strategy formulation? Are these likely to vary among firms?
7. Identify the four components of an international strategy.
8. Describe the role and importance of distinctive competence in international strategy formulation.
9. What are the three levels of international strategy? Why is it important to distinguish among the levels?
10. Identify three common approaches to corporate strategy and distinguish among them.

11. Identify three common approaches to business strategy and distinguish among them.
12. What are the basic types of functional strategies most firms use? Is it likely that some firms have different functional strategies?

Questions for Discussion

1. What are the basic differences between a domestic strategy and an international strategy?
2. Should the same managers be involved in both formulating and implementing international strategy, or should each part of the process be handled by different managers? Why?
3. Successful implementation of the global and the transnational approaches requires high levels of coordination and rapid information flows between corporate headquarters and subsidiaries. Accordingly, would you expect to find many companies adopting either of these approaches in the nineteenth century? Prior to World War II? Prior to the advent of personal computers?
4. Study mission statements from several international businesses. How do they differ, and how are they similar?
5. How can a poor SWOT analysis affect strategic planning?
6. Why do relatively few international firms pursue a single-product strategy?

7. How are the components of international strategy (scope of operations, resource deployment, distinctive competence, and synergy) likely to vary across different types of corporate strategy (single business, related diversification, and unrelated diversification)?
8. The scheduled opening for the new Disney Studios theme park adjacent to Disneyland Paris is 2002. Develop a list of at least five ways other units of the Disney corporation can help promote and publicize this park's opening.
9. Is a firm with a corporate strategy of related diversification more or less likely than a firm with a corporate strategy of unrelated diversification to use the same business strategy for all its SBUs? Why or why not?
10. Identify products you use regularly that are made by international firms that use the three different business strategies.
11. Related diversification and unrelated diversification represent extremes of a continuum. Discuss why a firm might want to take a mid-range approach to diversification, as opposed to being purely one or the other.
12. What are some of the issues that a firm might need to address if it decides to change its corporate or business strategy? For example, how would an MNC go about changing from a strategy of related diversification to a strategy of unrelated diversification?

BUILDING GLOBAL SKILLS

Form a group with three or four of your classmates. Your group represents the planning department of a large manufacturer that has been pursuing a domestic corporate strategy of unrelated diversification. Currently, the firm makes four basic products:

1. *All-terrain recreational vehicles*: This product line consists of small two- and three-wheeled recreational vehicles, the most popular of which is a gasoline-powered mountain bike.
2. *Color televisions*: The firm concentrates on high-quality large-screen projection-type televisions.
3. *Luggage*: This line is aimed at the low end of the market and comprises pieces made from inexpensive aluminum frames covered with ballistics material (high-strength, tear-resistant fabric). Backpacks are especially popular.
4. *Writing instruments*: The firm makes a full line of mechanical pens and pencils pitched to the middle-market segment, between low-end products such as Bic and high-end ones such as Montblanc.

Your firm's CEO is contemplating international expansion. However, the CEO also thinks that to raise its profitability, the corporation should begin pursuing a strategy of related diversification.

This may mean selling off some businesses and perhaps buying or starting new ones. The CEO has instructed you to develop alternatives, evaluate those alternatives, and then make recommendations as to how the company should proceed. With this in mind, follow these steps:

1. Characterize the current business strategies the company appears to be following with each of its four existing businesses.
2. Evaluate the extent to which any of the four existing businesses may be related.
3. Using any criteria your group prefers, select one of the existing businesses and assume you will recommend that it be kept and the other three sold.
4. Identify existing competitors for the business you chose to keep, including both domestic and international firms.
5. Identify three other countries where there might be potential for business expansion. Explain why.
6. Think of at least two other businesses that are related to the business you will keep and that might be targets for acquisition.

WORKING WITH THE WEB:
BUILDING GLOBAL INTERNET SKILLS

Assessing the Strategic Content of Web Sites

The chapter notes four different strategic alternatives that a firm might pursue in an effort to globalize. These are the home replication, multidomestic, global, and transnational strategies. The chapter also points out that businesses usually adopt a competitive strategy based on differentiation, cost leadership, or focus.

To start this exercise, locate, visit, and study the Web sites for the following companies (you may find it convenient to go to the textbook's Web site for links to the company Web sites):

- Groupe Danone SA
- BASF AG
- Textron
- Mitsubishi Group
- Tata Enterprises

Based on the information you find, see if you can classify each company in terms of both its strategy for internationalization and the business strategy it seems to use.

Follow-Up Questions

1. How much confidence can you place in your interpretation?
2. What are the advantages and disadvantages to a firm that result from its using a Web site to promote its internationalization and competitive strategies?
3. Might a company use its Web site in ways to deceive its competitors regarding its internationalization and competitive strategies? Are there risks in doing this?

WE INVITE YOU TO VISIT THIS BOOK'S
COMPANION WEB SITE AT www.prenhall.com/griffin

IN THE NEWS

1. On the *Financial Times* Web site (*www.ft.com*) use the "Companies" tab to locate "Companies in the News." Review the list of companies profiled, and select two or three that are familiar to you, making sure they are from different industries. Read the linked article about each firm, and then research the company (on this site or on the company's own homepage) to identify the international strategy that seems to be at play in the news story you read. Does each company's actions as reported in the news story fit well with each company's stated strategy? If not, can you identify reasons why?

2. On the same Web page as in activity 1 find two additional companies, this time in the same industry. Read the linked articles about the two firms, and determine what challenge each firm faces, according to the *Financial Times*. Next, research the two firms, and identify their respective international strategies. Are they identical, similar, or different? Analyze how the two strategies explain each company's actions in the story you read. How does their being in the same industry affect their actions?

CLOSING CASE

The New Conquistador

The South American continent has emerged as one of the world's hottest markets due to economic policy changes initiated in the 1990s. Privatization, deregulation, and regional economic integration have unshackled the imaginations and energies of the continent's entrepreneurs and attracted the attention of foreign investors.

No industry has been more affected by these changes than telecommunications. Once the sleepy preserve of inefficient and overstaffed state-owned enterprises, the industry has become a magnet for new firms and new technologies. One aggressive entrant is Telefonica SA. Telefonica's managers knew all too well the problems of state-owned telecommunications monopolists because Telefonica was just such a firm in its former guise as government-run Telefonica de España. Telefonica de España first obtained its monopoly concession on telephone services in Spain in 1924. Originally privately owned, the company was nationalized in 1945, with the government owning outright 41 percent of the company's shares.

For four decades the company enjoyed the easy life of a monopolist. The seeds of change were planted in 1986, when Spain joined the European Union (EU). Telefonica de España was ill-equipped to handle the explosive growth in telephone service or the chorus of complaints about poor service that followed. Moreover, as part of its single-market initiative, the EU announced that state-sponsored telephone monopolies would be abolished by 1998. Any European telecommunications firm would then be able to provide service anywhere within the EU. Faced with the threat of new entry from European rivals that promised increased competition, lower prices, and smaller profit margins, Telefonica's managers realized they had to transform the company. A leaner and more competitive company emerged as managers trimmed fat, shed unprofitable operations, and pumped up investments in new technologies and facilities. With the EU-directed ending of state telephone monopolies, Telefonica's managers confronted a new strategic problem: Should they change the scope of their operations? Should they erect a fortress in Spain and keep out EU rivals, should they expand into other EU markets, or should they do something else?

In analyzing their strategic choices, Telefonica's managers recognized they had a strong position in Spain and that domestic demand for telephone services would continue in the relatively underserved Spanish market. Thus the company continues to invest in new equipment and technologies there. This approach has worked: Telefonica has over 16 million local fixed-line subscribers and 5 million cellular customers—about three-quarters of that market in Spain.

In assessing their international prospects, Telefonica's managers decided that the company lacked a competitive advantage against European rivals like British Telecom and Deutsche Telekom, who had equal if not better access to the latest technology and managerial talent. That ruled out attacking other EU markets. However, the managers noted that many South American countries were about to privatize their own state-owned telephone monopolies and that investing in these companies made strategic sense. Telefonica did have a competitive advantage vis-à-vis local entrepreneurs in accessing technology, capital, and managerial talent. Moreover, because of linguistic and cultural ties between Spain and South America, Telefonica believed it had a competitive advantage over any of its European rivals who might wish to enter the South American market.

Telefonica de España launched its invasion of the South American market in 1990, when it acquired a minority interest in Compania de Telefonos de Chile and a contract to manage the southern half of Argentina's telephone system. In 1995 it purchased a majority interest in Telefonica del Peru, that country's state-owned monopoly provider of telephone services. A year later it acquired 35 percent of a regional Brazilian telephone company at a state-sponsored auction. Telefonica also acquired interests in Argentina's largest cable company and a digital satellite TV provider. The Spanish government also sold off the last of its ownership position, making Telefonica de España wholly privately owned. In 1998 the company, which had changed its name to Telefonica SA, entered into a strategic alliance with MCI WorldCom and paid $4.9 billion at auction to acquire control of the fixed-line and cellular operations of Telebras, Brazil's former state-owned telephone giant.

All told, Telefonica has invested over $10 billion in South America and now operates more telephone lines there than in Spain. It has followed the same pattern in each country it has entered: Trim excess payrolls ruthlessly and expand capacity aggressively. For example, it laid off half of the 22,000 workers in its Argentine subsidiary while doubling its network there to 4 million lines.

Overall, this strategy seems to be working. During the past decade the company's revenues have grown 15.4 percent a year, net income 3 percent, and stock price 19.2 percent. Telefonica's actions have not lacked criticism, however. Its tactics have been denounced by local skeptics as "conquistador capitalism." After winning the Telebras auction, Telefonica moved quickly to expand service in Brazil's commercial center, São Paulo, while laying off thousands of workers. This strategy of doing more with less backfired, as chaotic disruptions in service led to numerous complaints. In addition, minority shareholders have complained that Telefonica charges its South American subsidiaries exorbitant management fees that reduce the value of minority shareholders' interests. For example, its Argentine subsidiary pays 4.6 percent of its revenues to Telefonica for management services provided by the parent corporation.

Minority shareholders have also protested Telefonica's practice of transferring product lines with high growth potential from the subsidiaries to the parent. For example, Telefonica created Terra Networks SA to consolidate all of its South American Internet operations. Telefonica then sold to the public 30 percent of Terra Networks, retained the other 70 percent, and listed it on stock exchanges in Madrid and the United States, where it last had a total market capitalization of $11.2 billion. As part of this deal, Telefonica transferred the Internet operations of its Chilean subsidiary to Terra Networks for $40 million; minority owners believed that the price should have been double that figure. Minority shareholders in other subsidiaries have made similar complaints. Similarly, Telefonica has been transferring the telemarketing operations of its South American subsidiaries to an umbrella company in Madrid, arguing that the operations would benefit from the economies of scale that a consolidated operation would offer. Investors' concerns about such practices have caused the value of shares in Telefonica's South American subsidiaries to stagnate over the past two years, even as those of Telefonica continue to do well.

Telefonica also faces some operational challenges. Some are of its own doing: It was forced to pay $8 million in refunds in 1999 to São Paulo customers because of poor service. Others it had no control over: It was forced to take a $300 million write-off for currency losses after Brazil devalued its currency in 1998. Moreover, changes in government policies loom. For example, Argentina and Peru began to deregulate their telecommunications industries in 2000, ending their reliance on monopoly provision of telephone service. Also, Telefonica's success has attracted new competitors. In 1999, for example, BellSouth signed up 1 million cellular phone subscribers in São Paulo, capturing nearly 50 percent of that market in only 10 months of operations.[32]

Case Questions

1. Go back in time to 1986. Do a SWOT analysis for Telefonica de España. Does your analysis lead to the same conclusions as Telefonica's managers?

2. How would you characterize the corporate strategy adopted by Telefonica?

3. Minority investors in Telefonica's South American subsidiaries are unhappy with the parent corporation. Suppose you are a senior manager at the parent corporation. How would you handle the problem of the minority investors? What would you recommend to the CEO as to what should be done about them?

4. Many South American countries are in the process of deregulating their telephone industries. How should Telefonica respond to the increased likelihood of new entrants into its formerly protected markets?

CHAPTER

Heineken Brews Up Global Strategy

Heineken NV is the world's second largest beer producer, after Anheuser-Busch and slightly ahead of Miller. These two large U.S. brewers, however, have a relatively small international presence: More than 90 percent of their sales are made to U.S. customers. Heineken sells more beer outside the United States than either of the two U.S. companies. Of its $6.3 billion in 1999 sales, only 15 percent was in its home market of the Netherlands. Not only is Heineken a market leader in every European country, it also sells its products throughout North and South America, Africa, and Asia—170 countries in all.

"...the firm uses the **Internet** to keep distributors **informed** about sales."

Heineken was founded in Amsterdam by Gerald Heineken in 1864. Almost from the start the firm was successful. Within a few years of its founding it was exporting beer to France, Italy, Spain, Germany, and even the Far East. In 1914 Heineken's managers decided to export beer to the United States. Gerald Heineken's son Henri, who was running the firm at the time, sailed to the United States to set up the operation. On the ship he met a young bartender named Leo van Munching. Impressed with van Munching's knowledge of beer, Heineken contracted with him to import and distribute the firm's products in North America under the name Van Munching & Company.

11

Strategies for Analyzing and Entering Foreign Markets

OBJECTIVES

After studying this chapter, you should be able to:

> Discuss how firms analyze foreign markets.

> Outline the process by which firms choose their mode of entry into a foreign market.

> Describe forms of exporting and the types of intermediaries available to assist firms in exporting their goods.

> Identify the basic issues in international licensing, and discuss the advantages and disadvantages of licensing.

> Identify the basic issues in international franchising, and discuss the advantages and disadvantages of franchising.

> Analyze contract manufacturing, management contracts, and turnkey projects as specialized entry modes for international business.

> Characterize the greenfield and acquisition forms of FDI.

Despite the firm's success, Heineken ceased its U.S. operations during Prohibition. After Prohibition's repeal in 1933, the company reestablished those operations, again granting Van Munching & Company of New York exclusive rights to import Heineken products into the United States. After World War II Henri Heineken sent his son, Alfred, to New York to study marketing and advertising under Van Munching. Alfred returned to the Netherlands in 1948 with knowledge he used to help launch Heineken into other foreign markets worldwide.

Heineken has continued to grow steadily. It has breweries in over 50 countries. Some of the largest breweries are in Canada and France; however, the firm also produces in New Guinea, Australia, and Brazil. Its joint venture with a leading Japanese brewer, Kirin, gives it a strong presence in that key market. Heineken bought its largest Dutch competitor, Amstel, in 1968. Anticipating the European Union's (EU's) completion of its common market, Heineken aggressively expanded in Europe during the 1980s. Its goal was to establish the same sort of overwhelming market dominance in Europe that Anheuser-Busch has in the United States. Heineken bought breweries in France, Greece, Ireland, Italy, and Spain to expand its product lines and facilitate distribution throughout Europe. It also bought controlling interests in the Hungarian brewer Komaromi Sorgyar and the Slovak Zlaty Bazont Brewery. Further, to cut its operating costs, it closed 10 of its older breweries and modernized six others. To help manage its complex international distribution system, Heineken invested heavily in new Internet-based technology. The firm uses the Internet to keep distributors informed about sales, promotions, and so forth, and distributors can use the Internet to supply sales figures and place orders.

Interestingly, Heineken has refused to establish a brewery in the United States. Why? Consider a case in point. Several years ago Miller, owner of rights to distribute Lowenbrau in the United States, was selling as much of that Munich-brewed beer in the United States as it could import from Germany. To help keep pace with demand, Miller renegotiated its contract with Lowenbrau and began brewing the beer in Texas under license. Sales soon began to drop, in part because the beer was no longer an import and was perceived to have lost its cachet as an authentic Bavarian beer. To avoid Lowenbrau's mistake and retain its product's image as a true "imported" beer, Heineken continues to ship its beer into the U.S. market even though making it there might be cheaper.

Heineken has recently made one important strategic decision regarding the U.S. market: It bought Van Munching & Company, changed its name to Heineken USA, and now owns its U.S. distribution arm outright. Its being under Heineken's control has helped cut costs and added additional profit to each bottle of beer sold in the United States. Heineken also can now more easily coordinate its U.S. marketing campaigns with its global promotional efforts for its world-famous beer.[1]

Chapter 10 focused on the process by which a firm formulates its international strategy. This chapter discusses the next steps in the implementation of strategy: choosing the markets the firm will enter and the modes of entry it will use to compete in these markets. As the opening case indicates, multinational corporations (MNCs) such as Heineken are free to choose among the world's markets and are not restricted to using a single method for participating in international business. For example, Heineken exports its products to a variety of markets. In other markets it uses licensing agreements with independent firms to promote its business interests. Further, in New Guinea, Australia, and Brazil Heineken-owned subsidiaries produce, distribute, and sell Heineken beer. As we discuss in this chapter, in deciding whether and how to enter a market, a well-managed firm will match its internal strengths and weaknesses to the unique opportunities and needs of that market. Heineken has done this successfully in each of the national markets in which it participates.

› FOREIGN-MARKET ANALYSIS

Regardless of their strategies, most international businesses have the fundamental goals of expanding market share, revenues, and profits. The firms often achieve these goals by entering new markets or by introducing new products into markets in which they already have a presence. A firm's ability to do this effectively hinges on its developing a thorough understanding of a given geographical or product market.[2] To successfully increase market share, revenues and profits, firms must normally follow three steps: (1) assess alternative markets, (2) evaluate the respective costs, benefits, and risks of entering each, and (3) select those that hold the most potential for entry or expansion.

Assessing Alternative Foreign Markets

In assessing alternative foreign markets, a firm must consider a variety of factors, including the current and potential sizes of these markets, the levels of competition the firm will face, the markets' legal and political environments, and sociocultural factors that may affect the firm's operations and performance.[3] Table 11.1 summarizes some of the most critical of these factors.

Information about some of these factors is relatively objective and easy to obtain. For example, a country's currency stability is important to a firm contemplating exporting to or importing from that country or analyzing investment opportunities there. Objective information about this topic can be easily obtained from various published sources in the firm's home country or on the Internet. Other information about foreign markets is much more subjective and may be quite difficult to obtain. For example, information about the honesty of local government officials or about the process of obtaining utility permits may be very hard to acquire in the firm's home country. Obtaining such information often entails visiting the foreign location early in the decision-making process to talk to local experts, such as embassy staff and chamber of commerce officials, or contracting with a consulting firm to obtain the needed data.[4]

TABLE 11.1

Critical Factors in Assessing New Market Opportunities

TOPIC OF APPRAISAL	ITEMS TO BE CONSIDERED
Product-market dimensions	How big is the product market in terms of unit size and sales volume?
Major product-market "differences"	What are the major differences relative to the firm's experience elsewhere in terms of customer profiles, price levels, national purchase patterns, and product technology?
	How will these differences affect the transferability of the firm's capabilities to the new business environment and their effectiveness?
Structural characteristics of the national product market	What links and associations exist between potential customers and established national competitors currently supplying these customers?
	What are the major channels of distribution (discount structure, ties to present producers, levels of distribution separating producers from final customers, links between wholesalers, links between wholesalers and retailers, finance, role of government)?
	What links exist between established producers and their suppliers?
	Do industry concentration and collusive agreements exist?
Competitor analysis	What are major competitor characteristics (size, capacity utilization, strengths and weaknesses, technology, supply sources, preferential market arrangements, and relations with the government)?
	What is competitor performance in terms of market share, sales growth, and profit margins?
Potential target markets	What are the characteristics of major product-market segments?
	Which segments are potential targets upon entry?
Relevant trends (historic and projected)	What changes have occurred in total size of product market (short-, medium-, and long-term)?
	What changes have occurred in competitor performance (market share, sales, and profits)?
	What is the nature of competition (e.g., national or international)?
	What changes have occurred in market structure?
Explanation of change	Why are some firms gaining and others losing?
	Are foreign firms already operating here gaining or losing?
	Is there some general explanation of observed change, for example, product life cycle, change in overall business activity, and shift in nature of demand?
	What is the future outlook?
Success factors	What are the key factors behind success in this business environment, the pressure points that can shift market share from one firm to another?
	How are these different from those we have experienced in other countries?
	How do these success factors relate to our firm?
Strategic options	What elements emerge from the above analysis that point to possible strategies for this country?
	What additional information is required to identify our options more precisely?

Source: Reprinted with the permission of Lexington Books, an imprint of The Free Press, a Division of Simon & Schuster, from *Multinational Corporate Strategy: Planning for World Markets* by James C. Leontiades. Copyright © 1985 by Lexington Books.

Market Potential.   The first step in foreign-market selection is assessing market potential. Many publications, such as those listed in "Building Global Skills" in Chapter 2, provide data about population, gross domestic product (GDP), per capita GDP, public infrastructure, and ownership of such goods as automobiles and televisions. Such data permit firms to conduct a preliminary "quick and dirty" screening of various foreign markets.

The decisions a firm draws from this information often depend on the positioning of the firm's products relative to those of its competitors. A firm producing high-quality products at premium prices will find richer markets attractive but may have more difficulty penetrating a poorer market. Conversely, a firm specializing in low-priced, lower-quality goods may find the poorer market more lucrative than the richer market. For example, consider the market differences between the two Chinas—the Peoples' Republic of China and the Republic of China (Taiwan)—highlighted in Map 11.1. Although China's population dwarfs that of Taiwan, per capita income in Taiwan is quite high and ownership of various consumer durable goods is widespread, while the reverse is the case in China. A firm attempting to sell its products in both of these markets would clearly have a very different set of considerations to address for each.

After assessing market potential, a firm must collect data relevant to the specific product line under consideration. For example, if Pirelli SpA is contemplating

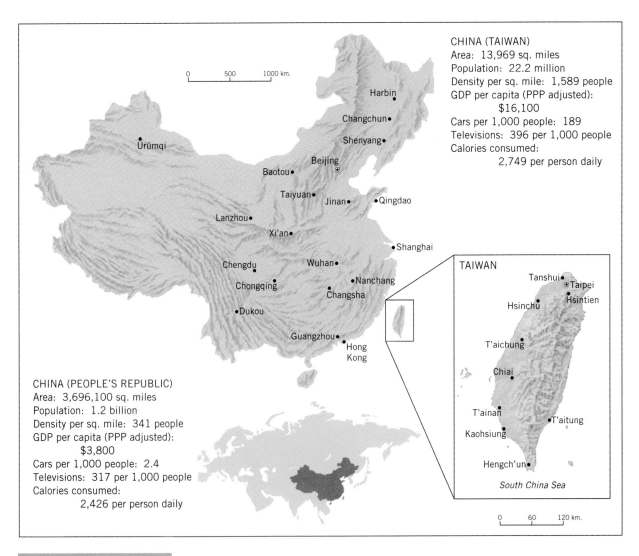

CHINA (TAIWAN)
Area: 13,969 sq. miles
Population: 22.2 million
Density per sq. mile: 1,589 people
GDP per capita (PPP adjusted):
            $16,100
Cars per 1,000 people: 189
Televisions: 396 per 1,000 people
Calories consumed:
            2,749 per person daily

CHINA (PEOPLE'S REPUBLIC)
Area: 3,696,100 sq. miles
Population: 1.2 billion
Density per sq. mile: 341 people
GDP per capita (PPP adjusted):
            $3,800
Cars per 1,000 people: 2.4
Televisions: 317 per 1,000 people
Calories consumed:
            2,426 per person daily

M A P   1 1 . 1   **A Tale of Two Chinas**

exporting tires to Thailand, its strategic managers must collect data about that country's transportation infrastructure, transportation alternatives, gasoline prices, and growth of vehicle ownership. Pirelli would also need data on the average age of motor vehicles and the production of automobiles in Thailand to assess whether it should focus its marketing efforts on the replacement market or the OEM (original equipment manufacturer) market. In some situations a firm may have to resort to using proxy data. For example, Whirlpool, in deciding whether to enter the dishwasher market in South Korea, could examine sales of other household appliances, per capita electricity consumption, or the number of two-income families.

Such data, however, reflect the past, not the future. Firms must also consider the potential for growth in a country's economy by using objective measures. These include changes in per capita income, energy consumption, GDP, and ownership of consumer durables such as private automobiles. Subjective considerations must also be taken into account when assessing potential growth. For example, following the collapse of communist economies in Central Europe and Eastern Europe, many Western firms ignored the data indicating negative economic growth in these countries. Instead, the firms focused on the prospects for future growth as the countries adopted new economic policies and programs. As a result, firms such as Procter & Gamble and Unilever established production facilities, distribution channels, and brand recognition to seize first-mover advantages as these economies recovered from the process of adjusting to capitalism.

Levels of Competition.   Another factor a firm must consider in selecting a foreign market is the level of competition in the market—both the current level and the likely future level. To assess the competitive environment, a firm should identify the number and sizes of companies already competing in the target market, their relative market shares, their pricing and distribution strategies, and their relative strengths and weaknesses, both individually and collectively. The firm must then weigh these factors against actual market conditions and its own competitive position. For example, Kia recently entered the crowded North American automobile market, believing low labor costs at its Korean factories would allow it to charge lower prices than entrenched competitors like GM, Ford, Toyota, and Volkswagen.

Most successful firms continually monitor major markets to exploit opportunities as they become available. This is particularly critical for industries undergoing technological or regulatory changes. The telecommunications industry provides an important example of this phenomenon. Once the home of inefficient, plodding state-owned monopolies, this industry is now the epicenter of converging new technologies—fiber optics, personal pagers, cellular service, satellite networks, and so on. Many of these firms—particularly in Europe and Latin America—have been or are being privatized. Privatization has been coupled with the tumbling of regulatory barriers to entry and innovation, allowing firms to enter new geographic and product markets, as Telefonica has done in Latin America. (See Chapter 10's closing case, "The New Conquistador".)

Legal and Political Environments.   A firm contemplating entry into a particular market also needs to understand the host country's trade policies and its general legal and political environments. A firm may choose to forgo exporting its goods to a country that has high tariffs and other trade restrictions in favor of exporting to one that has fewer or less significant barriers. Conversely, trade policies and/or trade barriers may induce a firm to enter a market via foreign direct investment (FDI). For example, Ford, GM, Audi, and Mercedes-Benz built auto factories in Brazil to avoid that country's high tariffs and to use Brazil as a production platform to access other Mercosur members.[5] Some countries require foreign firms wanting to establish local operations to work with a local joint-venture partner.

Government stability is an important factor in foreign-market assessment. Some less developed countries have been prone to military coups and similar disruptions. Government regulation of pricing and promotional activities may need to be considered. For example, many governments restrict advertising for tobacco and alcohol products, so foreign manufacturers of these products must understand how the restrictions will affect the firms' ability to market their goods in those countries. Care also may need to be taken to avoid offending the political sensibilities of the host nation. For example, consider the political implications of Map 11.1. The leadership of the Peoples' Republic of China refuses to recognize the Republic of China (Taiwan) as an independent nation, viewing Taiwan as a breakaway province. Our labeling of Taiwan in Map 11.1 as the Republic of China might discourage sales of this textbook in the Peoples' Republic; failure to do so might hurt sales in Taiwan.

Sociocultural Influences.   Managers assessing foreign markets must also consider sociocultural influences, which, because of their subjective nature, are often difficult to quantify. To reduce the uncertainty associated with these factors, firms often focus their initial internationalization efforts in countries culturally similar to the firms' home markets.[6] In early 2001, for example, Krispy Kreme, a North Carolina-based purveyor of exquisite doughnuts, announced it would commence internationalizing its sales. Not surprisingly, its initial foreign market is to be Canada.

If the proposed strategy is to produce goods in another country and export them to the market under consideration, the most relevant sociocultural factors are those associated with consumers. Firms that fail to recognize the needs and preferences of host country consumers often run into trouble. For example, Denmark's Bang & Olufsen, a well-known stereo system manufacturer, has floundered in some markets because its designers stress style rather than function. Japanese competitors meanwhile stress function and innovation over style and design. Bang & Olufsen's Danish managers have failed to realize that consumers in markets such as the United States are generally more interested in function than in design and are more willing to pay for new technology than for an interesting appearance.[7]

A firm considering FDI in a factory or distribution center must also evaluate sociocultural factors associated with potential employees.[8] It must understand the motivational basis for work in that country, the norms for working hours and pay, and the role of labor unions. By hiring—and listening to—local managers, foreign firms can often avoid or reduce cultural conflicts.

Evaluating Costs, Benefits, and Risks

The next step in foreign-market assessment is a careful evaluation of the costs, benefits, and risks associated with doing business in a particular foreign market.

Costs.   Two types of costs are relevant at this point: direct and opportunity. Direct costs are those the firm incurs in entering a new foreign market and include costs associated with setting up a business operation (leasing or buying a facility, for example), transferring managers to run it, and shipping equipment and merchandise. The firm also incurs opportunity costs. Because a firm has limited resources, entering one market may preclude or delay its entry into another. The profits it would have earned in that second market are its opportunity costs—the organization has forfeited or delayed its opportunity to earn those profits by choosing to enter another market first. Thus the firm's planners must carefully assess all the alternatives available to it.

Benefits.   Entering a new market presumably offers a firm many potential benefits; otherwise, why do it? Among the most obvious potential benefits are the expected sales and profits from the market. Other possible benefits include lower acquisition and manufacturing costs (if materials and/or labor are cheap); foreclosing of markets to competitors (which limits competitors' ability to earn profits); competitive advantage (which allows the firm to keep ahead of or abreast with its competition); access to new technology; and the opportunity to achieve synergy with other operations.

Risks.   Of course, few benefits are achieved without some degree of risk. Many of the earlier chapters provided overviews of the specific types of risks facing international businesses. Generally, a firm entering a new market incurs the risks of exchange rate fluctuations, additional operating complexity, and direct financial losses due to inaccurate assessment of market potential. In extreme cases a firm also faces the risk of loss through government seizure of property or due to war or terrorism.

The many factors a firm must consider when assessing foreign markets may seem burdensome. Nonetheless, successful international businesses carefully analyze these factors to uncover and exploit any and all opportunities available to them. At best poor market assessments may rob a firm of profitable opportunities. At worst a continued inability to reach the right decisions may threaten the firm's existence.

CHOOSING A MODE OF ENTRY

Having decided which markets to enter, the firm is now faced with another decision: Which mode of entry should it use? Dunning's eclectic theory, discussed in Chapter 5, provides useful insights into the factors that affect the choice among either home country production (exporting), host country production in firm-owned factories (FDI and joint venture), or host country production performed by others (licensing, franchising, and contract manufacturing). Recall that the eclectic theory considers three factors: ownership advantages, location advantages, and internalization advantages.[9] Other factors a firm may consider include the firm's need for control, the availability of resources, and the firm's global strategy. The role of these factors in the entry mode decision is illustrated in Figure 11.1.

Ownership advantages are tangible or intangible resources owned by a firm which grant it a competitive advantage over its industry rivals. The ownership by Toronto-based Inco, Ltd., of rich, nickel-bearing ores has allowed the firm, formerly known as International Nickel, to dominate the production of both primary nickel and nickel-based metal alloys. Although a more intangible resource than a nickel ore mine, the luxury appeal of Dom Perignon champagne and Christian Dior perfumes—both products of France's LVMH Moet Hennessy Louis Vuitton—similarly

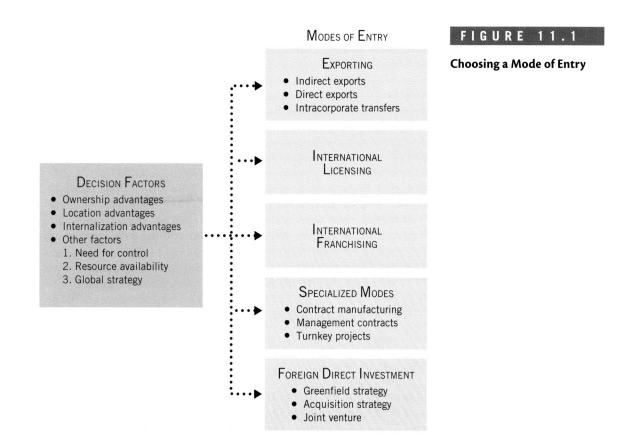

FIGURE 11.1

Choosing a Mode of Entry

grants the Parisian firm a competitive advantage over its rivals in international markets. Assuming that local firms know more about their home turf than foreigners do, a foreign firm contemplating entry into a new market should possess some ownership advantage to overcome the information advantage of local firms. As discussed later in this chapter, the nature of the firm's ownership advantage affects its selection of entry mode. Embedded technology, for example, is often best transferred through an equity mode, whereas firms whose competitive advantage is based on a well-known brand name sometimes enter foreign markets through a licensing or franchising mode. Further, a firm's advantages are primary determinants of bargaining strength; thus advantages can influence the outcome of entry mode negotiations.

Location advantages are those factors that affect the desirability of host country production relative to home country production. Firms routinely compare economic and noneconomic characteristics of the home market with those of the foreign market in determining where to locate production facilities. If home country production is found to be more desirable than host country production, the firm will choose to enter the host country market via exporting. For example, Siam Cement, one of the world's lowest-cost producers, has relied on exports from its modern Thailand factories to serve the Cambodian, Vietnamese, and Laotian markets rather than setting up production facilities in those countries. If host country production is more desirable, however, the firm may invest in foreign facilities or license the use of its technology and brand names to existing host country producers.

The choice between home country and host country production is affected by many factors. Relative wage rates and land acquisition costs in the countries are important, but firms may also consider surplus or unused capacity in existing factories, access to research and development (R&D) facilities, logistical requirements, the needs of customers, and the additional administrative costs of managing a foreign facility. Political risk must also be considered. The presence of civil war, official corruption, or unstable governments will discourage many firms from devoting significant resources to a host country.

Government policies also can have a major influence.[10] High tariff walls discourage exporting and encourage local production, whereas high corporate taxes or government prohibitions against repatriation of profits inhibit FDI. Even government inaction may affect location decisions. McDonald's built a bakery in Cairo in the late 1990s to supply its regional restaurants, in part because of its frustration in dealing with Egyptian customs bureaucrats, who required the company to obtain more than a dozen signatures each time it wished to import hamburger buns into Egypt.[11]

Location advantages may also be culture bound. Turkey has benefited from its geographic, religious, linguistic, and cultural ties to the Central Asian and Caucasus republics of the former Soviet Union (see Map 11.2). MNCs like Siemens, Chase Manhattan, and Goodyear have based their regional headquarters and export operations in Istanbul, viewing it as the ideal jumping-off point for doing business in the entire Eurasian region.[12]

Internalization advantages are those that make it desirable for a firm to produce a good or service itself rather than contracting with another firm to produce the good or service. The level of transaction costs (costs of negotiating, monitoring, and enforcing an agreement) is critical to this decision. If such costs are high, the firm may rely on FDI and joint ventures as entry modes. If the costs are low, the firm may use franchising, licensing, or contract manufacturing. In deciding, the firm must consider both the nature of the ownership advantage it possesses and its ability to ensure productive and harmonious working relations with any local firm with which it does business. Toyota, for example, possesses two important ownership advantages: efficient manufacturing techniques and a reputation for producing high-quality automobiles. Neither asset is readily saleable or transferable to other firms; thus Toyota has used FDI and joint ventures rather than franchising and licensing for its foreign production of automobiles.

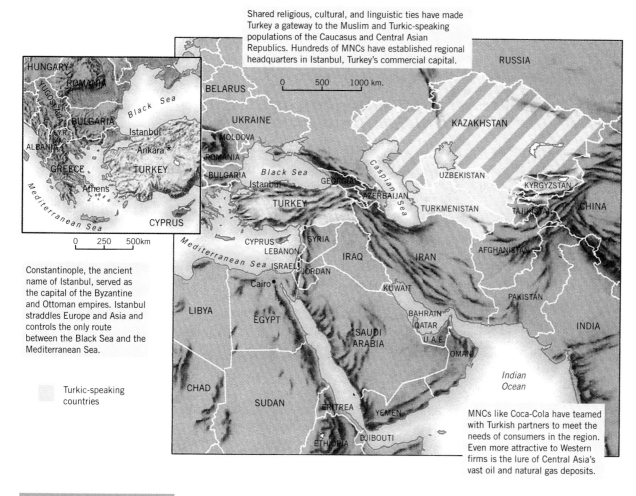

Shared religious, cultural, and linguistic ties have made Turkey a gateway to the Muslim and Turkic-speaking populations of the Caucasus and Central Asian Republics. Hundreds of MNCs have established regional headquarters in Istanbul, Turkey's commercial capital.

Constantinople, the ancient name of Istanbul, served as the capital of the Byzantine and Ottoman empires. Istanbul straddles Europe and Asia and controls the only route between the Black Sea and the Mediterranean Sea.

Turkic-speaking countries

MNCs like Coca-Cola have teamed with Turkish partners to meet the needs of consumers in the region. Even more attractive to Western firms is the lure of Central Asia's vast oil and natural gas deposits.

MAP 11.2

Turkey: The Gateway to the Central Asian Republics and the Caucasus

Source: "Istanbul's Location Gives It a Crucial Role," *Wall Street Journal*, March 27, 1997, p. A10.

Pharmaceutical firms routinely use licensing as their entry mode. In this industry two common ownership advantages are the ownership of a patented drug that has unique medical properties and the ownership of local distribution networks. Obtaining either is expensive; researching, developing, and testing a new wonder drug can cost several hundred million dollars, while distribution networks must be large to be effective. In Japan, for example, a sales force of at least 1,000 employees is necessary to efficiently market prescription drugs.[13] Once a pharmaceutical firm has developed and patented a new drug, it is eager to amortize its R&D costs in both domestic and foreign markets. Many such firms prefer to forgo the expensive and time-consuming process of setting up overseas production facilities and foreign distribution networks. Instead the firms grant existing local companies the right to manufacture and distribute the patented drug in return for royalty payments. For example, Merck licensed Israel's Teva Pharmaceutical Industries to manufacture and market Merck's pharmaceutical products in Israel, saving Merck the expense of establishing its own Israeli sales force. Licensing is also attractive in this industry because the costs of monitoring the sales and product quality of patented drugs sold in the host country by the licensee are relatively low.

Other factors may also affect the choice of entry mode. A firm is likely to consider its need for control and the availability of resources.[14] A firm's lack of experience in a foreign market may cause a certain degree of uncertainty. To reduce this uncertainty, some firms may prefer an initial entry mode that offers them a high degree of control.[15] However, firms short on capital or thin in executive talent may be unable or unwilling to commit themselves to the large capital investments this control entails; these firms may prefer an entry mode that economizes on their financial and managerial commitments, such as licensing. Cash-rich firms may view FDI more favorably, believing that it offers high profit potential and the opportunity to more fully internationalize the training of their young, fast-track managers.

A firm's overall global strategy also may affect the choice of entry mode. Firms such as Ford that seek to exploit economies of scale and synergies between their domestic and international operations may prefer ownership-oriented entry modes. Conversely, firms such as Microsoft and Yahoo!, whose competitive strengths lie in flexibility and quick response to changing market conditions, are more likely to use any and all entry modes warranted by local conditions in a given host country.[16] A firm's choice also may be driven by its need to coordinate its activities across all markets as part of its global strategy. For this reason IBM traditionally has favored ownership-oriented entry modes as part of its globalization strategy.[17]

In short, like most business activities, the choice of entry mode is often a trade-off between the level of risk borne by the firm, the potential rewards to be obtained from a market, the magnitude of the resource commitment necessary to compete effectively, and the level of control the firm seeks. Next we look at each mode of entry in detail.

› EXPORTING TO FOREIGN MARKETS

Perhaps the simplest mode of internationalizing a domestic business is exporting, the most common form of international business activity. Its advantages and disadvantages, and those of the other modes of entry, are summarized in Table 11.2. Recall from Chapter 1 that exporting is the process of sending goods or services from one country to other countries for use or sale there. Merchandise exports in the world economy totaled $5.6 trillion in 1999, or 19 percent of the world's total economic activity. Service exports amounted to $1.3 trillion in 1999.

Exporting offers a firm several advantages. First, the firm can control its financial exposure to the host country market as it deems appropriate. Little or no capital investment may be needed if the firm chooses to hire a company in the host country to distribute its products. In this case the firm's financial exposure is often limited to start-up costs associated with market research, locating and choosing its local distributor, and/or local advertising plus the value of the goods and services involved in any given overseas shipment. Alternatively, the firm may choose to distribute its products itself to better control their marketing. If the firm opts for this approach, it is then able to raise its selling prices because a middleman has been eliminated. However, its investment costs and its financial exposure may rise substantially because the firm will have to equip and operate its own distribution centers, hire its own employees, and market its products.

Second, exporting permits a firm to enter a foreign market gradually, thereby allowing it to assess local conditions and fine-tune its products to meet the idiosyncratic needs of host country consumers. If its exports are well received by foreign consumers, the firm may use this experience as a basis for a more extensive entry into that market. For example, the firm may choose to take over distribution of its product from the host country distributor or to build a factory in the host country to supply its customers there, particularly if it finds it can reduce its production and distribution costs or improve the quality of its customer service. "Venturing Abroad" describes how a British company has started exporting jams to Japan. Its current arrangement is a classic example of the advantages of exporting, but the door is open for changes in the way it operates in Japan as it learns more about that market.

Firms may have proactive or reactive motivations for exporting. *Proactive motivations* are those that *pull* a firm into foreign markets as a result of opportunities avail-

MODE	PRIMARY ADVANTAGES	PRIMARY DISADVANTAGES
Exporting	Relatively low financial exposure Permit gradual market entry Acquire knowledge about local market Avoid restrictions on foreign investment	Vulnerability to tariffs and NTBs Logistical complexities Potential conflicts with distributors
Licensing	Low financial risks Low-cost way to assess market potential Avoid tariffs, NTBs, restrictions on foreign investment Licensee provides knowledge of local markets	Limited market opportunities/profits Dependence on licensee Potential conflicts with licensee Possibility of creating future competitor
Franchising	Low financial risks Low-cost way to assess market potential Avoid tariffs, NTBs, restrictions on foreign investment Maintain more control than with licensing Franchisee provides knowledge of local market	Limits market opportunities/profits Dependence on franchisee Potential conflicts with franchisee May be creating future competitor
Contract manufacturing	Low financial risks Minimize resources devoted to manufacturing Focus firm's resources on other elements of the value chain	Reduced control (may affect quality, delivery schedules, etc.) Reduced learning potential Potential public relations problems—may need to monitor working conditions, etc.
Management contracts	Focus firm's resources on its area of expertise Minimal financial exposure	Potential returns limited by contract May unintentionally transfer proprietary knowledge and techniques to contractee
Turnkey projects	Focus firm's resources on its area of expertise Avoid all long-term operational risks	Financial risks (cost overruns, etc.) Construction risks (delays, problems with suppliers, etc.)
Foreign direct investment	High profit potential Maintain control over operations Acquire knowledge of local market Avoid tariffs and NTBs	High financial and managerial investments Higher exposure to political risk Vulnerability to restrictions on foreign investment Greater managerial complexity

TABLE 11.2

Advantages and Disadvantages of Different Modes of Entry

able there. For example, San Antonio's Pace, Inc., a maker of Tex-Mex food products, began exporting proactively to Mexico in the early 1990s after discovering that Mexican consumers enjoy its picante sauce as much as its U.S. customers do.[18] A firm also may export proactively to exploit a technological advantage or to spread fixed R&D expenses over a wider customer base, thereby allowing the firm to price its products more competitively in both domestic and foreign markets. For example, the break-even price of commercial airliners produced by Airbus and Boeing would skyrocket if these firms limited their sales to either domestic or foreign customers.

Reactive motivations for exporting are those that *push* a firm into foreign markets, often because opportunities are decreasing in the domestic market. Some firms turn to exporting because their production lines are running below capacity

VENTURING *Abroad* — JUMPING ON A JAPANESE JAM DEAL

Managers at Chivers Hartley recently scored a major coup by landing a big order from Jusco, one of Japan's largest retailers. Chivers is a U.K. firm that makes a variety of fruit preserves—jellies, jams, and marmalades. Because its domestic market has matured, Chivers sees exports as an important growth opportunity. The firm currently obtains 15 percent of its revenues from exports, with France, Germany, and Holland its largest foreign markets.

Chivers spent two years cultivating the deal with Jusco. A senior marketing manager from the U.K. company initially established a contact with Jusco, which expressed interest in selling Chivers's products. Jusco executives then visited Chivers's factory near Cambridge, England, and laid out exactly what Chivers would need to do to compete in the Japanese market.

Based on this feedback, Chivers began developing a new product line just for the Japanese market. First, product formulas were altered to include more fruit and less sugar. In addition, Chivers developed blueberry as a flavor because it is popular among Japanese consumers. The firm also switched to smaller jars because Japanese consumers shop more frequently, use jams more sparingly, and have less storage space than British consumers. Chivers also created an exclusive new brand name just for Jusco called Cambridgeshire. The jar labels have a sepia picture of King's College, Cambridge, taking advantage of Japanese respect for British universities.

Chivers was rewarded for its efforts when Jusco placed an order for 2,900 cases and promised to promote the product in 300 of its stores. Chivers and Jusco expect Cambridgeshire to compete with the number one local brand, Blue Flag. Chivers also hopes that this is just the first step toward Japan becoming the firm's fourth largest export market.

Source: "Japanese Jam Deal Set to Boost Preserves Group," *Financial Times*, November 3, 1997, p. 8.

or because they seek higher profit margins in foreign markets in the face of downturns in domestic demand. For example, Space-Lok, Inc., a small California manufacturer of high-stress fasteners for the aerospace industry, began to internationalize its operations only after the U.S. defense budget began to shrink as a result of the Cold War's end. Similarly, Toto Ltd. dominated Japan's porcelain bathroom fixtures market but paid little attention to export markets until the Japanese economy slowed down in the early 1990s. Although Toto has managed to carve out a 15 percent share of the market for imported commodes in such key markets as China, its late start has put it at a disadvantage compared to other foreign competitors like American Standard.[19]

Forms of Exporting

Export activities may take several forms (see Figure 11.2), including indirect exporting, direct exporting, and intracorporate transfers.

Indirect Exporting. **Indirect exporting** occurs when a firm sells its product to a domestic customer, which in turn exports the product in either its original form or a modified form. For example, if Hewlett-Packard (a U.S. firm) buys microchips from Intel (also a U.S. firm) to use in manufacturing computers and then exports those completed computers to Europe, Intel's chips have been indirectly exported. Another example is when a firm sells goods to a domestic wholesaler who then sells them to an overseas firm. A firm also may sell to a foreign firm's local subsidiary, which then transports the first firm's products to the foreign country.

Some indirect exporting activities reflect conscious actions by domestic producers. For example, the Association of Guatemala Coffee Producers sells bags of coffee to passengers boarding international flights in Guatemala City to gain export sales and to build consumer awareness of its product. In most cases, however, indirect exporting activities are not part of a conscious internationalization strategy by

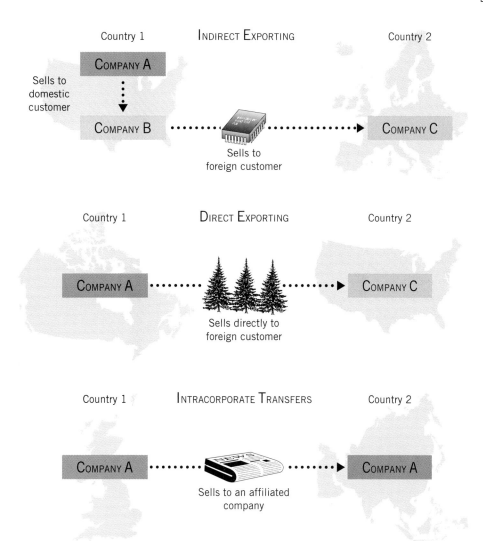

FIGURE 11.2

Forms of Exporting

a firm. Thus they yield the firm little experience in conducting international business. Further, the potential short-term and long-term profits available from indirect exporting are often limited for firms that passively rely on the actions of others.

Direct Exporting.   **Direct exporting** occurs through sales to customers—either distributors or end users—located outside the firm's home country. Research suggests that in one-third of cases, a firm's initial direct exporting to a foreign market is the result of an unsolicited order. However, the firm's subsequent direct exporting typically results from deliberate efforts to expand its business internationally. In such cases the firm actively selects the products it will sell, the foreign markets it will service, and the means by which its products will be distributed in those markets. Through direct exporting activities the firm gains valuable expertise about operating internationally and specific knowledge concerning the individual countries in which it operates. And export success often breeds additional export success. Increasing experience with exporting often prompts a firm to become more aggressive in exploiting new international exporting opportunities.[20] Such experience also often proves useful if the firm later engages in FDI. Baskin-Robbins, for example, followed this deliberate approach in entering the Russian market. It began by shipping ice cream to that country in 1990 from company-owned plants in Canada and Texas. Over a five-year period the company opened 74 retail outlets with Russian partners, carefully observing the likes and dislikes of local consumers. Only after gaining a thorough understanding of the Russian market did

Baskin-Robbins invest $30 million in a new ice cream plant in Moscow, ensuring a constant flow of Jamoca Almond Fudge and (at least) 30 other flavors to please Russian appetites.[21]

Intracorporate Transfers. A third form of export activity is the intracorporate transfer, which has become more important as the sizes of MNCs have increased. An **intracorporate transfer** is the sale of goods by a firm in one country to an affiliated firm in another. For example, when BP Amoco ships crude oil from its storage facilities in Kuwait to its Australian subsidiary, the transaction is counted as a Kuwaiti export and an Australian import, but the revenues for the transaction remain within the same firm.

Intracorporate transfers are an important part of international trade. They account for about 40 percent of all U.S. merchandise exports and imports. Many MNCs constantly engage in such transfers, importing and exporting semifinished products and component parts to lower their production costs. By so doing, they use the productive capacity of both their domestic and foreign factories more efficiently, concentrating production of individual inputs at specific factories and shipping these inputs to other factories as needed. (We discuss these factors more thoroughly in Chapter 17 when we analyze the global sourcing strategies of MNCs.) For example, consider the Ford Crown Victoria automobile. Ford's U.S. assembly plant imports the automobile's fuel tank, windshield, instrument panel, and seats from Ford factories in Mexico; its wheels from a Ford factory in England; its electronic engine control system from a Ford factory in Spain; and its electronic control system for its antilock brakes from a Ford factory in Germany.[22] Ford's intricate meshing of inputs produced at various locations is typical of the behavior of many MNCs.

Such transfers are also common in the service sector. For example, the Dow-Jones Company publishes both Asian and European versions of the *Wall Street Journal* in addition to its U.S. edition. Although some of the stories in each edition are written locally and are intended for local audiences, others are written in one location and printed in all editions of the newspaper. The usage of stories first published by a Dow-Jones subsidiary in one country by Dow-Jones affiliates in other countries is an intracorporate transfer of services.

Additional Considerations

In considering exporting as its entry mode, a firm must consider many other factors besides which form of exporting to use. These factors include government policies, marketing concerns, logistical considerations, and distribution issues.

Government Policies. Export promotion policies, export financing programs, and other forms of home country subsidization encourage exporting as an entry mode. Conversely, host countries may impose tariffs and nontariff barriers (NTBs) on imported goods, thereby discouraging the firm from relying on exports as an entry mode. Similarly, Japan's imposition of voluntary export restraints on Japanese automobiles reduced Japanese exports, but it also encouraged Japanese automakers to construct assembly plants in the United States.

Marketing Concerns. Marketing concerns, such as image, distribution, and responsiveness to the customer, may also affect the decision to export. Often foreign goods have a certain product image or cachet that domestically produced goods cannot duplicate. For example, buyers of Dom Perignon champagne are purchasing, at least in part, the allure of France's finest champagne. This allure would be lost should LVMH Moet Hennessy Louis Vuitton choose to produce the product in Lubbock, Texas, even though Lubbock vineyards yield a regionally acclaimed wine, Llano Estacado. Also, recall Lowenbrau's U.S. marketing disaster, described in the opening case. Produced in Munich, Lowenbrau was a premium product to U.S. consumers; produced in the United States, it was just another beer. Swiss watches, German automobiles, Italian shoes, Cuban cigars, and Scottish wool are among the other product groups whose allure is closely associated with specific countries.

The choice of exporting is also influenced by a firm's need to obtain quick and constant feedback from its customers. Such feedback is less important for standardized products whose designs change slowly, if at all, such as toothbrushes and coffeemakers. On the other hand, producers of goods such as personal computers must continually monitor the marketplace to ensure that they are meeting the rapidly changing needs of their customers. For example, Hyundai shifted its production of personal computers from factories in its Korean homeland to the United States because it needed to be closer to its U.S. customer base.

Logistical Considerations. Logistical considerations also enter into the decision to export. The firm must consider the physical distribution costs of warehousing, packaging, transporting, and distributing its goods, as well as its inventory carrying costs and those of its foreign customers. Typically, such logistical costs will be higher for exported goods than for locally produced goods. But logistical considerations go beyond mere costs. Because exporting means longer supply lines and increased difficulties in communicating with foreign customers, firms choosing to export from domestic factories must ensure that they maintain competitive levels of customer service for their foreign customers.

Distribution Issues. A final issue that may influence a firm's decision to export is distribution. A firm experienced in exporting may choose to establish its own distribution networks in its key markets. For example, Japanese consumer electronics manufacturers like Sony, Minolta, and Hitachi typically rely on wholly owned host country subsidiaries to distribute their products to wholesalers and retailers in the Quad countries. The costs of establishing and operating these distribution networks are offset by two important benefits. First, a firm captures additional revenues by performing the distribution function. Second, the firm maintains control over the distribution process, thereby avoiding the problems that we discuss in the following paragraphs.

However, a firm—particularly a smaller business or one just beginning to export—often lacks the expertise to market its products abroad, so it will seek a local distributor to handle its products in the target market. The selection of this distributor is critical to the firm's success; the distributor must have sufficient expertise and resources (capital, labor, facilities, and local reputation) to successfully market the firm's products. However, the best local distributors are often already handling the products of existing firms. Consequently, a firm must sometimes choose between an experienced local distributor and a less-experienced one that will handle the firm's products exclusively.

The profitability and growth potential of exporting to a foreign market will be affected by the firm's agreement with the local distributor. The local distributor must be compensated for its services, of course. This compensation will reduce the exporter's profit margin. Further, the exporter and its local distributor depend on each other to ensure that a satisfactory business relationship is established and maintained. If the host country distributor inadequately markets, distributes, and/or services the exporter's products, it is the exporter that will suffer lost sales and damaged reputation. For example, Apple's initial share of the Japanese personal computer market was hurt by the performance of a Canon subsidiary hired to market and distribute the firm's products in Japan. Apple took over these tasks and quickly quintupled its market share.[23]

Problems may also arise if the business judgments of the local distributor and the exporter differ. The exporter and the importer may disagree on pricing strategies, with the exporter preferring lower retail prices to stimulate sales and the distributor favoring higher prices to fatten its profit margins. The exporter may want its distributor to market its products more aggressively in hopes of building sales volume; the distributor may believe that the additional sales generated by this strategy will not cover the increased expenses incurred. Thus the importance of selecting a distributor whose goals and business philosophy are compatible with those of the exporter cannot be overstressed.

Export Intermediaries

An exporter may also market and distribute its goods in international markets by using one or more **intermediaries**, third parties that specialize in facilitating imports and exports. These specialists may offer limited services, such as handling only transportation and documentation, or they may perform more extensive roles, including taking ownership of foreign-bound goods and/or assuming total responsibility for marketing and financing exports. Types of intermediaries that offer a broad range of services include the following:

- Export management companies
- Webb-Pomerene associations
- International trading companies

Export Management Company. An **export management company (EMC)** is a firm that acts as its client's export department. Most EMCs are small operations that rely on the services of a handful of professionals. An EMC's staff typically is knowledgeable about the legal, financial, and logistical details of exporting and so frees the exporter from having to develop this expertise in house. The EMC may also provide advice about consumer needs and available distribution channels in the foreign markets the exporter wants to penetrate.

EMCs usually operate in one of two ways:

1. Some act as commission agents for exporters. They handle the details of shipping, clearing customs, and document preparation in return for an agreed-on fee. In such cases the exporter normally invoices the client and provides any necessary financing it may need.

2. Other EMCs take title to the goods. They make money by buying the goods from the exporter and reselling them at a higher price to foreign customers. Such EMCs may offer customer financing and also design and implement advertising and promotional campaigns for the product.

Webb-Pomerene Association. A **Webb-Pomerene association** is a group of U.S. firms that operate within the same industry and that are allowed by law to coordinate their export activities without fear of violating U.S. antitrust laws. First authorized by the Export Trade Act of 1918, a Webb-Pomerene association engages in market research, overseas promotional activities, freight consolidation, contract negotiations, and other services for its members. It may also directly engage in exporting by buying goods domestically from members and selling the goods in foreign markets on the association's behalf. Although such associations were originally designed to allow smaller, related firms to cooperate in promoting exports, most are now dominated by larger firms. In general Webb-Pomerene associations have not played a major role in international business. Fewer than 25 such associations exist today, and they tend to be concentrated in raw materials such as wood pulp, sulfur, and phosphate rock.

International Trading Company. An **international trading company** is a firm directly engaged in importing and exporting a wide variety of goods for its own account. It differs from an EMC in that it participates in both importing and exporting activities. An international trading company provides a full gamut of services, including market research, customs documentation, international transportation, and host country distribution, marketing, and financing. Typically, international trading companies have agents and offices worldwide. The economic intelligence information they glean from these far-flung operations is one of their most potent competitive weapons.

The most important international trading companies in the global marketplace are Japan's *sogo sosha*, which are an integral part of Japan's *keiretsu* system. The *sogo sosha* have prospered for several reasons. Because of their far-flung operations, they continuously obtain information about economic conditions and business opportunities in virtually every corner of the world. As part of a *keiretsu*, a *sogo sosha* enjoys ready access to financing (from the *keiretsu*'s lead bank) and a built-in source of customers (its fellow *keiretsu* members). This customer base reduces the *sogo sosha*'s costs of soliciting clients and builds up its business volume, thereby allowing it to reap economies of scale in its transportation and information-gathering roles. Nonmembers of the *keiretsu* are then attracted to doing business with the *sogo sosha* because of its low cost structure and international expertise. Japan's international trading companies have been so successful that they are among the world's largest service companies. The five largest *sogo soshas* are featured in Table 11.3.

TABLE 11.3

The Five Largest *Sogo Soshas*

RANK	FIRM	1999 SALES ($ MILLIONS)	KEY SUBSIDIARIES AND AFFILIATES
1	Mitsui & Company	188,555	Japan Steel Works, Ltd. (steel manufacturing) Mitsui Construction Company, Ltd. (construction) Mitsukoshi, Ltd. (department stores) Mitsui Mutual Life Insurance Company, Ltd. Onoda Cement Company, Ltd. (construction materials) Sakura Bank
2	Mitsubishi Corporation	117,766	Kirin Brewery (alcoholic beverages) The Mitsubishi Bank, Ltd. Mitsubishi Heavy Industries, Ltd. (construction) Mitsubishi Motor Corporation (automobiles) Nikon Corporation (cameras and video equipment) The Tokyo Marine and Fire Insurance Company
3	Itochu Corporation	109,366	American Isuzu Motors (wholesaling) ATR Wires & Cable Company (steel tire cords) Century 21 Real Estate of Japan, Ltd. (real estate brokerage) Dunhill Group Japan, Inc. (men's clothing and accessories) Mazda Motor of America (wholesaling) Time Warner Entertainment of Japan (25 percent limited partnership) VIDEOSAT, Inc. (satellite transmission of video signals)
4	Sumitomo Group	95,701	Asahi Breweries, Ltd. (alcoholic beverages) NEC Corp. (electronics) Nippon Sheet Glass Company The Sumitomo Bank, Ltd. Sumitomo Cement Company, Ltd. Sumitomo Chemical Company, Ltd. Sumitomo Coal Mining Company, Ltd. Sumitomo Forestry Company, Ltd. Sumitomo Metal Industries, Ltd. Sumitomo Realty & Development Company, Ltd.
5	Marubeni	91,087	Archer Pipe and Tube Company (steel pipe sales) Bactec Corporation (insecticides) Columbia Grain International (grain trading) Fremont Beef Company (meat processing) Kubota Tractor Company (farm equipment) Precision Tools Service, Inc. (machine tools)

Source: "The World's Largest Corporations," *Fortune*, July 24, 2000, p. F-1.

Other Intermediaries. In addition to the intermediaries that provide a broad range of services to international exporters and importers, numerous other types, including the following, offer more specialized services:

- **Manufacturers' agents** solicit domestic orders for foreign manufacturers, usually on a commission basis.
- **Manufacturers' export agents** act as a foreign sales department for domestic manufacturers, selling those firms' goods in foreign markets.
- **Export and import brokers** bring together international buyers and sellers of such standardized commodities as coffee, cocoa, and grains.
- **Freight forwarders** specialize in the physical transportation of goods, arranging customs documentation and obtaining transportation services for their clients.

This list is by no means complete. Indeed, specialists are available to provide virtually every service needed by exporters and importers in international trade.

› INTERNATIONAL LICENSING

Another means of entering a foreign market is **licensing**, in which a firm, called the **licensor**, leases the right to use its intellectual property—technology, work methods, patents, copyrights, brand names, or trademarks—to another firm, called the **licensee**, in return for a fee. This process is illustrated in Figure 11.3. The use of licensing as an entry mode may be affected by host country policies. Firms are advised not to use licensing in countries that offer weak protection for intellectual property because the firms may have difficulty enforcing licensing agreements in the host country's courts. On the other hand, the use of licensing may be encouraged by high tariffs and NTBs, which discourage imports, or by host country restrictions on FDI or repatriation of profits.

Licensing is a popular mode for entering foreign markets because it involves little out-of-pocket cost. A firm has already incurred the costs of developing the intellectual property to be licensed; thus revenues received through a licensing agreement often go straight to the firm's bottom line. Licensing also allows a firm to take advantage of any locational advantages of foreign production without incurring any ownership, managerial, or investment obligations.

Licensing is an important element of the strategies of many international firms. Consider the Nintendo Company. The firm manufactures electronic video game players and game cartridges. It also licenses dozens of firms worldwide to design and, in some cases, to manufacture game cartridges to be used in its game players.

FIGURE 11.3

The Licensing Process

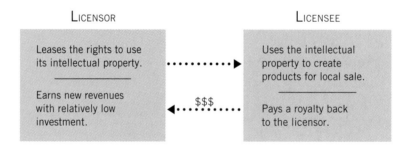

BASIC ISSUES
1. Set the boundaries of the agreement.
2. Establish compensation rates.
3. Agree on the rights, privileges, and constraints conveyed in the agreement.
4. Specify the duration of the agreement.

As part of its licensing arrangements, Nintendo provides game designers with technical specifications for how its game players work. The design firms create the games and then pay Nintendo a fee to manufacture those games. A few firms manufacture the games themselves, but they must still pay a licensing fee to Nintendo. Through licensing Nintendo not only generates new revenues; it also inspires the development of new video games, which in turn stimulate demand for Nintendo game players. Similar arrangements are used by many video game and software firms.[24]

Another firm that relies on a licensing strategy is Cantab Pharmaceuticals PLC, a biotech firm founded in 1989 by a scientist at Cambridge University. Cantab specializes in immunogenics, a branch of medicine that uses genetically engineered vaccines and drugs to repair and rejuvenate the body's immune system to fight such diseases as herpes, genital warts, and cervical cancer. Preferring to focus its energies on developing new immunogenic drugs and lacking the resources to quickly and effectively manufacture and distribute its cutting-edge products on its own, the young British company has chosen to license its technology to pharmaceutical giants like GlaxoSmithKline and Pfizer.[25]

Basic Issues in International Licensing

Nearly every international licensing arrangement is unique because of variations in corporate strategy, the levels of competition, the nature of the product, and the interests of the licensor and licensee. Normally the terms of a licensing agreement are specified in a detailed legal contract, which addresses such issues as specifying the boundaries of the agreement; determining compensation; establishing rights, privileges, and constraints; and specifying the duration of the contract.

Specifying the Agreement's Boundaries. The licensor and licensee must determine which rights and privileges are and are not being conveyed in the agreement. For example, Heineken is exclusively licensed to manufacture and sell Pepsi-Cola in the Netherlands. PepsiCo must either provide Heineken with the formula for its soft drink or supply concentrated cola syrup. Heineken is then allowed to add carbonated water to create the beverage, package it in appropriate containers, and distribute and sell it in the Netherlands. PepsiCo cannot enter into a competing licensing agreement with another firm to sell Pepsi-Cola in the Netherlands; Heineken cannot begin duplicating other products owned by PepsiCo (such as Lay's Potato Chips) without a separate agreement, nor can it alter PepsiCo's formula, market the firm's products as its own, or ship them outside the Netherlands.

Determining Compensation. Compensation is another basic issue that is specified in a licensing agreement. Obviously, the licensor wants to receive as much compensation as possible, while the licensee wants to pay as little as possible. Yet each also wants the agreement to be profitable for the other so that both parties will willingly perform their contractual obligations. The licensee must be careful to ensure that it can reach its target level of profitability after paying licensing fees; the licensor will attempt to establish a rate that allows it to recoup its variable costs of negotiating and enforcing the licensing agreement plus recover at least part of its fixed investment in the intellectual property being licensed. From the licensor's perspective, the license fee, after deducting these variable costs, should also exceed the licensor's opportunity costs—that is, the profits it would have earned had it entered the market via a different entry mode.

Compensation under a licensing agreement is called a **royalty**. The royalty is usually paid to the licensor in the form of a flat fee, a fixed amount per unit sold, or, most commonly, a percentage of the sales of the licensed product or service. Although the royalty amount is often determined by prevailing market forces, royalties of 3 to 5 percent of sales are typical and have long been viewed as reasonable and appropriate. Some licensing agreements also guarantee a minimum royalty payment to ensure that the foreign licensee will take full advantage of the market value of whatever has been licensed, rather than merely acquiring and then shelving it to keep domestic rivals from obtaining it.

Establishing Rights, Privileges, and Constraints.   Other basic issues to be addressed in licensing agreements are the rights and privileges given to the licensee and the constraints imposed on it by the licensor. For example, if a licensee began using inferior materials as a way to boost its profit margin, the image of the licensor's product could be severely damaged. Similarly, if the agreement included the transfer of technology, production processes, or work methods, the licensee might be tempted to sell this information to another firm, thereby harming the licensor. Alternatively, the licensee could simply underreport licensed sales as a means of reducing its licensing fees.

To prevent these practices, licensing agreements usually limit the licensee's freedom to divulge information it has obtained from the licensor to third parties; specify the type and form of records the licensee must keep regarding sales of the licensed products or services; and define standards that will be adhered to regarding product and service quality. To avoid costly litigation, the licensing agreement should also detail how the parties will resolve any disagreements. Many licensing agreements require, for example, that disputes be resolved through the use of a third-party mediator.

Specifying the Agreement's Duration.   The licensor may view the licensing agreement as a short-term strategy designed to obtain knowledge about the foreign market at low cost and with little risk. If sales of its products or services are strong, it may want to enter the market itself after the agreement has ended. Thus the licensor may seek a short-term agreement. However, if the contract's duration is too short, the licensee may be unwilling to invest in necessary consumer research, distribution networks, and/or production facilities, believing it will be unable to amortize its investment over the life of the licensing contract. Normally the licensor wants the licensee to undertake these market development efforts. Accordingly, the greater the investment costs incurred by the licensee, the longer is the likely duration of the licensing agreement. For example, the licensees that built Tokyo Disneyland insisted on a 100-year licensing agreement with The Walt Disney Company before agreeing to invest the millions of dollars necessary to build the park. However, in most cases the term of the licensing agreement is far shorter than this.

Advantages and Disadvantages of International Licensing

Licensing carries relatively low financial risk, provided the licensor fully investigates its market opportunities and the abilities of its licensees. Licensing also allows the licensor to learn more about the sales potential of its products and services in a new market without significant commitment of financial and managerial resources. Licensees benefit through the opportunity to make and sell, with relatively little R&D cost, products and services that have been successful in other international markets. Nintendo game designers, for example, have the relative safety of knowing there are millions of game system units available that will play their games.

However, licensing does have opportunity costs. It limits the market opportunities for both parties. For example, as long as the licensing agreement between PepsiCo and Heineken is in effect, PepsiCo cannot enter the soft-drink market in the Netherlands, and Heineken cannot sell competing soft drinks such as Coca-Cola. Licensor and licensee also depend on each other to maintain product quality and to promote the product's brand image. Improper actions by one party can damage the other party. Further, if the licensee or licensor does not adhere to the agreement, costly and tedious litigation may hurt both parties.

No matter how carefully worded a licensing agreement may be, there is always the risk of problems and misunderstandings. For example, several years ago Oleg Cassini licensed Jovan, a U.S. subsidiary of London's GlaxoSmithKline, to market the Cassini beauty products line in the United States. After signing the agreement, Jovan was approached by Diane Von Furstenberg Cosmetics with a similar proposal but better terms. Jovan subsequently signed a licensing agreement with Von Furstenberg to make and market its products instead of Cassini's. Cassini was left without a licensee in the United States. To complicate things even further, a clause in the contract between Jovan and Cassini prevented Cassini from licensing its name to any other U.S. firm. Cassini sued Jovan for $789 million. The dispute was eventually settled out of court, but it was more than three years beyond Cassini's original target date when the firm finally got its products into the United States.[26]

A final concern is the long-term strategic implications of licensing a firm's technology. Many firms are concerned that sharing their technology will inadvertently create a future competitor. The licensee, by producing under the licensing agreement, may be able to learn the manufacturing secrets of the licensor or develop new production tricks of its own. The licensee can also build an independent reputation for manufacturing quality and service excellence while operating under the contract. Although the licensing agreement may restrict the geographical area in which the licensee can manufacture and sell the product, once the agreement expires, the former licensee may choose to expand its operations into the licensor's existing territory. This is a risk the licensor must take if it chooses to license its product.

INTERNATIONAL FRANCHISING ❮

Still another popular strategy for internationalizing a business is franchising, which is a special form of licensing. **Franchising** allows the franchisor more control over the franchisee and provides for more support from the franchisor to the franchisee than is the case in the licensor-licensee relationship. International franchising is among the fastest growing forms of international business activity today. A franchising agreement allows an independent entrepreneur or organization, called the **franchisee**, to operate a business under the name of another, called the **franchisor**, in return for a fee. The franchisor provides its franchisees with trademarks, operating systems, and well-known product reputations, as well as continuous support services such as advertising, training, reservation services (for hotel operations), and quality assurance programs.

Basic Issues in International Franchising

International franchising is likely to succeed when certain market conditions exist:

- The franchisor has been successful domestically because of unique products and advantageous operating procedures and systems. McDonald's was successful initially because it provided a popular menu that was consistently prepared and service that was quick and efficient.

- The factors that contributed to domestic success are transferable to foreign locations. McDonald's prospered because "American" food is popular in other countries; efficiency and lower prices are valued by consumers worldwide; and foreign visitors to the United States usually seem to want to visit a McDonald's restaurant.

- The franchisor has already achieved considerable success in franchising in its domestic market. For example, there were hundreds of franchised McDonald's restaurants in the United States before the first was built abroad.

- Foreign investors must be interested in entering into franchise agreements. For well-established franchisors like McDonald's, this usually is not a problem.

❯ Franchising is a popular mode for entering foreign markets. Dunkin' Donuts is one of the world's most successful franchisers. CEO Jack Shafer oversees this $2.5-billion company, which is owned by a U.K. food and beverages conglomerate, Allied Domecq.

Like licensing agreements, franchising agreements are spelled out in formal contracts, with terms typically as follows:

- The franchisor receives a fixed payment plus a royalty based on the franchisee's sales for the rights to use the franchisor's name, trademarks, formulas, and operating procedures.

- The franchisee agrees to adhere to the franchisor's requirements for appearance, financial reporting, and operating procedures. However, franchisors are likely to allow some degree of flexibility to meet local customs and tastes. In fact, as with other licensing arrangements, one of the services the franchisee offers the franchisor is knowledge about the local market's culture and customs. For example, McDonald's restaurants sell beer in Germany and Switzerland and wine in France. And, as John Travolta's character pointed out in *Pulp Fiction*, McDonald's franchisee altered the name of the quarter pounder because of France's use of the metric system.

- The franchisor helps the franchisee establish the new business; provides expertise, advertising, and a corporate image; and is usually able to negotiate favorable arrangements with suppliers.

Numerous MNCs rely on franchising to internationalize their operations. Fast-food firms such as McDonald's, Dunkin' Donuts, Baskin-Robbins, Pizza Hut, and KFC have franchised restaurants worldwide. Benetton relies on franchised retail stores to distribute its stylish clothing in over 120 countries. Japan's Bridgestone Corporation franchises both Bridgestone and Firestone tire retail outlets in the United States as well as several other countries. (For a discussion of how the Internet is affecting the franchising business, see "Wiring the World.")

Advantages and Disadvantages of International Franchising

On the plus side franchisees can enter a business that has an established and proven product and operating system, and franchisors can expand internationally with relatively low risk and cost. A franchisor also can obtain critical information about local market customs and cultures from host country entrepreneurs that it otherwise might have difficulty obtaining. It further can learn valuable lessons from franchisees that apply to more than the host country. McDonald's, for example, benefited from this worldwide learning phenomenon (see Chapter 10). Its U.S. managers once believed that the firm's restaurants would be successful only if they were freestanding entities located in suburbs and smaller towns. A Japanese franchisee convinced the firm to allow him to open a restaurant in an inner-city office building. The restaurant quickly became one of the firm's most popular. Because of the insight of its Japanese franchisee, McDonald's now has restaurants in downtown locations in many cities throughout the world.

On the negative side, as with licensing, both parties to a franchising agreement must share the revenues earned at the franchised location. International franchising may also be more complicated than domestic franchising. For example, when McDonald's expanded to Moscow, it had to teach local farmers how to grow potatoes that met its standards. Control is also an issue in international franchising. McDonald's was once forced to revoke the franchise it had awarded a French investor because his stores were not maintained according to McDonald's standards.

Wiring the World

ADVICE FROM AFAR

The Internet is revolutionizing the world's franchising business, as the managers at the Cendant Corporation are quick to acknowledge. Cendant, a $5.4-billion company headquartered in New York City, is one of the world's largest hotel franchisers, controlling such well-known brands as Days Inn, Howard Johnson, Ramada, Super 8, and Travelodge. As part of its obligations to its franchisees, which are located in over 80 countries, Cendant's staff stands ready to answer questions and solve problems quickly using e-mail and the Internet.

Cendant's Parsippany, New Jersey, facility houses its franchise support operations. A typical day there might bring a request from a Days Inn in South Africa for help in transferring a Web page to a compact disk. A quick e-mail can solve that technical problem. A Curacao franchise might need a logo of Travelodge's sleepy bear for a new marketing brochure. The solution: Scan the logo into a file, and zip it across the Internet. Sometimes the inquiries are more urgent. A Mexican franchisee may need advice on how to deal with striking workers who have blockaded the hotel's front door, refusing to let new guests enter the hotel. The e-mailed answer from an experienced former hotel manager: Move guests to a different wing of the hotel, or check them into nearby hotels. Losing revenue is a small price to pay for maintaining the guests' goodwill and avoiding lawsuits.

Of course, Cendant provides other services to its franchisees. It operates an in-house hotel management school in Parsippany for its franchisees. It conducts seminars in Mexico City, Prague, and other cities where its franchisees operate to bring them up to date on the latest hotel management techniques. Cendant's reliance on the Internet, however, allows the company to improve the quality of service it offers its franchisees while lowering the cost of doing so.

Sources: "Exporting Management Savvy," *Wall Street Journal*, October 24, 2000, p. B1; Cendant Corporation Web site.

SPECIALIZED ENTRY MODES FOR INTERNATIONAL BUSINESS ‹

A firm also may use any of several specialized strategies to participate in international business without making long-term investments. Such specialized modes include contract manufacturing, management contracts, and turnkey projects.

Contract Manufacturing

Contract manufacturing is used by firms, both large and small, that outsource some or all of their manufacturing needs to other companies. This strategy reduces the financial and human resources firms need to devote to the physical production of their products. Nike, for example, has chosen to focus its corporate energies on marketing its products and has contracted with numerous factories throughout Southeast Asia to produce its athletic footwear. Mega Toys, a $30-million Los Angeles-based company started by Charlie Woo, an immigrant from Hong Kong, similarly contracts with Chinese plants to produce the firm's inexpensive toys and party favors, allowing Mega Toys to concentrate on marketing its products. By using this approach, international businesses can focus on that part of the value chain where their distinctive competence lies yet benefit from any locational advantages generated by host country production. However, the companies also surrender control over the production process, which can lead to quality problems or other unexpected surprises. Nike, for example, has suffered a string of blows to its public image—including a series of unflattering *Doonesbury* cartoons—because of reports of unsafe and harsh working conditions in Vietnamese factories churning out Nike footwear.[27] (For more information, see pages 277–279.)

> Contract manufacturing involves outsourcing manufacturing activities to other companies. Nike relies on contract manufacturers to produce its goods, such as this one in Indonesia. This strategy allows the firm to concentrate on the marketing function, which is the firm's competitive strength.

Management Contract

A **management contract** is an agreement whereby one firm provides managerial assistance, technical expertise, or specialized services to a second firm for some agreed-on time in return for monetary compensation. For its services the first firm may receive either a flat fee or a percentage of sales. The management contract may also specify performance bonuses based on profitability, sales growth, or quality measures. Management contracts allow firms to earn additional revenues without incurring any investment risks or obligations. A subsidiary of Hilton Hotels, for example, offers hotel management and reservation services to hotels that bear the Hilton logo but that are not company owned. Similarly, major airlines such as Air France, British Airways, and KLM often sell their management expertise to small state-owned airlines headquartered in developing countries.

Turnkey Project

Another specialized strategy for participating in international business is the turnkey project. A **turnkey project** is a contract under which a firm agrees to fully design, construct, and equip a facility and then turn the project over to the purchaser when it is ready for operation. The turnkey contract may be for a fixed price, in which case the firm makes its profit by keeping its costs below the fixed price, or the contract may provide for payment on a cost-plus basis, which shifts the risk of cost overruns from the contractor to the purchaser.

International turnkey contracts often involve large, complex, multiyear projects such as construction of a nuclear power plant, an airport, or an oil refinery. Managing such complex construction projects requires special expertise. As a result, most are administered by large construction firms such as Bechtel, Brown and Root, Hyundai Group, New Zealand's Fletcher Challenge Ltd., and Germany's Friedrich Krupp GmbH. The awarding of lucrative turnkey projects is often based on the availability of home government financing, such as through the Eximbank of the United States, or on political ties between the host and home countries. U.S. construction engineering firms have secured many contracts in Saudi Arabia because of the friendly relations between the two countries, while French construction companies have done well in Francophone Africa.

An increasingly popular variant of the turnkey project is the so-called **B-O-T project**, in which the firm *builds* a facility, *operates* it, and later *transfers* ownership of the project to some other party. Through this approach the contractor profits from operation and ownership of the project for some period of time but bears any financial risks associated with it during this period. For example, the government of Gabon wished to upgrade the quality of electrical service and fresh water delivered to its citizens. Aided by the International Finance Corporation, a branch of the World Bank Group discussed in Chapter 6, Gabon contracted with Ireland's Electricity Supply Board International and France's Compagnie Generale des Eaux to operate Gabon's electrical and water systems for 20 years. The two companies invested $600 million to improve these basic services. After the 20-year contract expires, ownership of these assets will be transferred to the government of Gabon.

> FOREIGN DIRECT INVESTMENT

Exporting, licensing, franchising, and the specialized strategies just discussed all allow a firm to internationalize its business without investing in foreign factories or facilities. However, many firms prefer to enter international markets through ownership and control of assets in host countries. Other firms may first establish themselves in a foreign market through exporting, licensing, franchising, or contract manufacturing. After gaining knowledge of and expertise in operating in the host country, the firms may then want to expand in the market through ownership of production or distribution facilities, as was Baskin-Robbins' strategy in Russia.

Such FDI affords the firm increased control over its international business operations, as well as increased profit potential. Control is particularly important to the firm if:

1. It needs to closely coordinate the activities of its foreign subsidiaries to achieve strategic synergies, as IBM has long done; or

2. It determines that the control is necessary to fully exploit the economic potential of proprietary technology, manufacturing expertise, or some other intellectual property right.

In one study, for example, British subsidiaries of U.S.-headquartered MNCs were found to be more effective and successful competitors in the United Kingdom than a matched set of British-owned firms, primarily because the U.S. parents were able to transfer their technological and managerial expertise to their British affiliates.[28]

> Bagels by Bell, a small Brooklyn baker, exports 120,000 bagels per month to Japan. The owner, Warren Bell, adapted his recipes to meet Japanese tastes, adding blueberries, chocolate chips, and apple-cinnamon to his bagels.

FDI is also beneficial if host country customers prefer dealing with local factories. Many firms and governments participate in programs that favor locally made products—for example, "Buy American" or "Buy Korean"—to promote their local economies. Equally important, many purchasing managers perceive that local production implies more reliable supply, faster service, and better communication with suppliers.

On the other hand, FDI exposes a firm to greater economic and political risks and operating complexity, as well as the potential erosion of the value of its foreign investments if exchange rates change adversely. A firm's decision to engage in FDI may also be influenced by government policies. As noted in Chapter 3, host countries may discourage FDI through direct controls on foreign capital, bans on the acquisition of local companies by foreigners, or restrictions on repatriation of dividends and capital; home countries can promote FDI through such devices as political-risk insurance. Firms using FDI also must meet the standard challenges of managing, operating, and financing their foreign subsidiaries while facing the additional hurdle of doing so in political, legal, and cultural milieus different from their own.

There are three methods for FDI: (1) building new facilities (called the **greenfield strategy**), (2) buying existing assets in a foreign country (called the **acquisition strategy** or the **brownfield strategy**), and (3) participating in a joint venture.

The Greenfield Strategy

The greenfield strategy involves starting a new operation from scratch (the word *greenfield* arises from the image of starting with a virgin green site and then building on it). The firm buys or leases land, constructs new facilities, hires and/or transfers its managers and employees, and then launches the new operation. Fuji's film production factory in South Carolina represents a greenfield investment, as do the Mercedes-Benz' automobile assembly plant in Alabama and Nissan's factory in Sunderland, England.

The greenfield strategy has several advantages:

• The firm can select the site that best meets its needs and construct modern, up-to-date facilities. Local communities often offer economic development incentives to attract such facilities because they will create new jobs; these incentives lower the firm's costs.

- The firm starts with a clean slate. Managers do not have to deal with existing debts, nurse outmoded equipment, or struggle to modify ancient work rules protected by intransigent labor unions. For example, at its new Eisenach factory in former East Germany GM can implement Japanese-style production techniques and labor policies without having to battle workers wedded to the old way of doing things. This is considered a major advantage by GM's managers.

- The firm can acclimate itself to the new national business culture at its own pace, rather than having the instant responsibility of managing a newly acquired, ongoing business. Research indicates that the greater the cultural differences between the home and host countries, the more likely a firm is to build a new factory rather than purchase an existing firm.[29]

However, the greenfield strategy has some disadvantages:

- Successful implementation takes time and patience.
- Often land in the desired location is unavailable or very expensive.
- In building the new factory, the firm must comply with various local and national regulations and oversee the factory's construction.
- The firm must recruit a local workforce and train it to meet the firm's performance standards.
- The firm, by constructing a new facility, may be more strongly perceived as a foreign enterprise.

Disney managers faced several of these difficulties in building Disneyland Paris. Although the French government sold the necessary land to Disney at bargain prices, Disney was not fully prepared to deal with French construction contractors. For example, Disney executives had numerous communications difficulties with a painter who applied 20 different shades of pink to a hotel before the firm approved the color. The park's grand opening was threatened when local contractors demanded an additional $150 million for extra work allegedly requested by Disney. In addition, Disney clashed with its French employees, who resisted the firm's attempt to impose its U.S. work values and grooming standards on them.[30]

The Acquisition Strategy

A second FDI strategy is acquisition of an existing firm conducting business in the host country. Although the actual transaction may be very complex—requiring bankers, lawyers, regulators, and mergers and acquisitions specialists from several countries—the motivation for it is quite simple. By acquiring a going concern, the purchaser quickly obtains control over the acquired firm's factories, employees, technology, brand names, and distribution networks. The acquired firm can continue to generate revenues as the purchaser integrates it into the purchaser's overall international strategy. Further, unlike the greenfield strategy, the acquisition strategy adds no new capacity to the industry. In times of overcapacity this is an obvious benefit.

Sometimes international businesses acquire local firms simply as a means of entering a new market. For example, in the late 1990s Procter & Gamble chose to enter the Mexican tissue products market by purchasing Loreto y Pena Pobre from its owner, Grupo Carso SA. By so doing, Procter & Gamble acquired Loreto's manufacturing facilities, its well-known tissue and toilet paper brand names, and its existing distribution system.[31] Similarly, in 2000 American Eagle Outfitters purchased two youth-oriented Canadian apparel chains, Braemar and Thriftys. Acquiring their 150 outlets allowed the U.S. retailer to enter the Canadian market quickly and broadly.[32]

At other times acquisitions may be undertaken by a firm as a means of implementing a major strategic change. For example, the state-owned Saudi Arabian Oil Co. has tried to reduce its dependence on crude oil production by purchasing "downstream" firms, such as Petron Corporation, the largest petroleum refiner in the

Philippines, and South Korea's Ssangyong Oil Refining Company. Similarly, after its privatization in 1994, Koninklijke PTT Netherland, the Netherlands's formerly state-owned postal and telephone company, determined that it would need to expand internationally if it were to survive in the EU's deregulated market. To improve its competitiveness, it purchased Australia's TNT Ltd., allowing the Dutch company to combine its postal operations with TNT's express package delivery services.[33]

The acquisition strategy does have some disadvantages, however. The acquiring firm assumes all the liabilities—financial, managerial, and otherwise—of the acquired firm. For example, if the acquired firm has poor labor relations, unfunded pension obligations, or hidden environmental cleanup liabilities, the acquiring firm becomes financially responsible for solving the problem. The acquiring firm usually must also spend substantial sums up front. For example, when Matsushita purchased U.S. entertainment conglomerate MCA for $6.6 billion in the early 1990s, it had to pay out this vast sum shortly after the deal was closed. The greenfield strategy, in contrast, may allow a firm to grow slowly and spread its investment over an extended period. An international acquisition may also reveal unexpected local issues that must be subsequently resolved, as "Bringing the World into Focus" suggests.

Joint Ventures

Another form of FDI is the joint venture. **Joint ventures** are created when two or more firms agree to work together and create a jointly owned separate firm to promote their mutual interests. The number of such arrangements is burgeoning as rapid changes in technology, telecommunications, and government policies outstrip the ability of international firms to exploit opportunities on their own. Because of the growing importance of international intercorporate cooperation, as well as the unique set of challenges it offers international firms, we devote Chapter 12 to this subject.

Bringing the World into FOCUS

A BUBBLY BUSINESS

Plantagenet is a large San Francisco-based private equity investment firm. For most of its existence the company invested solely in U.S. businesses. A few years ago, however, it began to cautiously venture into foreign investments. Recently it decided to take on an even bigger challenge—investing in France, a country notoriously cumbersome for U.S. investors.

Plantagenet decided to pay $10 million for a small family-owned champagne maker, Albert LeBrune, which had been passed down from generation to generation since 1840. Things quickly became very complicated, however. At the crux of the problem was a French law requiring that bequeathed assets be split evenly among all siblings. Albert LeBrune was owned by five brothers, so Plantagenet had to reach agreement with all of them—a chore that proved to be very complicated because the brothers could not agree with each other on the details of the transaction.

Eventually everything was ironed out, but in the words of Derek Anderson, Plantagenet's partner in charge of the acquisition, "It was not easy, particularly for a Yankee. Luckily, we have a good French partner. I'm not sure someone riding in on a big white horse with saddlebags overflowing with money would have pulled it off. It takes sensitivity and local knowledge."

Plantagenet is exploring other potential French acquisitions. The firm has also learned a new lesson—to avoid heavy French corporate taxes, it is now doing its deals through a company incorporated in Luxembourg.

Sources: "Champagne Deal Uncorks French Quirks," *USA Today*, March 11, 1999, p. 2B; "Europe Catches Merger Fever," *USA Today*, March 11, 1999, pp. 1B, 2B.

CHAPTER REVIEW

Summary

An important aspect of international strategy formulation is determining which markets to enter. To make this decision, a firm must consider many factors, including market potential, competition, legal and political environments, and sociocultural influences. It also must carefully assess the costs, benefits, and risks associated with each prospective market. Once a firm has decided to expand its international operations and assessed potential foreign markets, it must decide how to enter and compete most effectively in the selected foreign markets. An array of strategic options is available for doing this. Choosing an entry mode involves careful assessment of firm-specific ownership advantages, location advantages, and internalization advantages.

Exporting, the most common initial entry mode, is the process of sending goods or services from one country to other countries for use or sale there. Exporting continues to grow rapidly. There are several forms of exporting, including indirect exporting, direct exporting, and intracorporate transfer. In deciding whether to export, a firm must consider such factors as government policies, marketing concerns, consumer information needs, logistical matters, and distribution issues. Export intermediaries often are used to facilitate exporting. These include export management companies, Webb-Pomerene associations, and international trading companies.

International licensing, another popular entry mode, occurs when one firm leases the right to use its intellectual property to another firm. Basic issues in international licensing include negotiating mutually acceptable terms, determining compensation, defining the rights and privileges of and the constraints imposed on the licensee, and specifying the duration of the agreement.

International franchising also is growing rapidly as an entry mode. International franchising is an arrangement whereby an independent organization or entrepreneur operates a business under the name of another. Several market conditions must exist for a firm to successfully franchise. As with licensing agreements, the terms of a franchising agreement are usually quite detailed and specific.

Three specialized entry modes are contract manufacturing, the management contract, and the turnkey project. Contract manufacturing permits a firm to outsource physical production of its product and focus its energies on some other element of the value chain. A management contract calls for one firm to provide managerial assistance, technical assistance, or specialized services to another firm for a fee. A turnkey project involves one firm agreeing to fully design, construct, and equip a facility for another firm.

The most complex entry mode is FDI. FDI involves the ownership and control of assets in a foreign market. The greenfield strategy for FDI calls for the investing firm to start a totally new enterprise from scratch. In contrast, the acquisition strategy involves buying an existing firm or operation in the foreign market. A third form of FDI is a joint venture, in which ownership and control are shared by two or more firms.

Review Questions

1. What are the steps in conducting a foreign-market analysis?
2. What are some of the basic issues a firm must confront when choosing an entry mode for a new foreign market?
3. What is exporting? Why has it increased so dramatically in recent years?
4. What are the primary advantages and disadvantages of exporting?
5. What are three forms of exporting?
6. What is an export intermediary? What is its role? What are the various types of export intermediaries?
7. What is international licensing? What are its advantages and disadvantages?
8. What is international franchising? What are its advantages and disadvantages?
9. What are three specialized entry modes for international business, and how do they work?
10. What is FDI? What are its three basic forms? What are the relative advantages and disadvantages of each?

Questions for Discussion

1. Is it possible for someone to make a decision about entering a particular foreign market without having visited that market? Why or why not?
2. How difficult or easy is it for managers to gauge the costs, benefits, and risks of a particular foreign market?
3. How does each advantage in Dunning's eclectic theory specifically affect a firm's decision regarding entry mode?
4. Why is exporting the most popular initial entry mode?
5. What specific factors could cause a firm to reject exporting as an entry mode?
6. What conditions must exist for an intracorporate transfer to be cost effective?
7. Your firm is about to begin exporting. In selecting an export intermediary, what characteristics would you look for?
8. Do you think trading companies like Japan's *sogo sosha* will ever become common in the United States? Why or why not?
9. What factors could cause you to reject an offer from a potential licensee to make and market your firm's products in a foreign market?
10. Under what conditions should a firm consider a greenfield strategy for FDI? An acquisition strategy?

BUILDING GLOBAL SKILLS

When Heineken enters a new market, it follows a basic set of steps designed to maximize its potential profits in that market:

1. It often begins to export its beer into that market as a way to boost brand familiarity and image.

2. If sales look promising, it then licenses its brands to a local brewer. Doing this allows Heineken to build its sales further while simultaneously becoming more familiar with local distribution networks.

3. If this relationship also yields promising results, Heineken then either buys partial ownership of the local brewer or forms a new joint venture with the brewer.

The end result is a two-tier arrangement with the more expensive Heineken label at the top end of the market and the lower-priced local brands at the bottom end, all sharing a common brewery, sales force, and distribution network.

After reading and thinking about Heineken's approach, break up into groups of four or five people each and proceed as follows:

1. Identify at least five products or brands you are familiar with that could use the same three-step approach perfected by Heineken for entering foreign markets. Develop a clear rationale to support each example.

2. Identify at least five products or brands that probably could not use Heineken's strategy. Develop a clear rationale to support each example.

3. Randomly list the 10 examples you identified, keeping the rationale for each hidden. Exchange lists with another group. Each group should discuss the list given to it by the other group and classify the various products or brands into one of two categories: "can copy Heineken's approach" or "cannot copy Heineken's approach." Be sure to have some rationale for your decision.

4. Each pair of groups that exchanged lists should form one new group. Compare lists and note areas in which the smaller groups agreed and disagreed on their classifications. Discuss the reasons for any disagreements in classification.

Follow-Up Questions

1. What are the specific factors that enable Heineken to use the approach described and simultaneously make it difficult for some other firms to copy the approach? What types of firms are most and least likely to be able to use this approach?

2. What does this exercise teach you about international business?

WORKING WITH THE WEB: BUILDING GLOBAL INTERNET SKILLS

Assessing Foreign Market Entry Conditions

A variety of useful information about domestic and foreign markets is available on the Internet. Statistics about population, per capita income, consumption of different products, and other relevant information are provided by national governments, international organizations, and private companies. Similarly, information about national laws affecting business activity are available from a variety of sources. For example, the U.S. State Department's *Country Commercial Guides* are posted on its Web site. (Links to its Web site and other sites that may be useful for this assignment are available at the textbook's Web site.)

Now, assume that you own a chain of computer accessory stores, which sell such items as software, speakers, keyboards, antiglare screens, mouse pads, and so forth. Some of your stores are company owned, while others are franchised. You have a total of 300 retail outlets, located in most major U.S. cities, and you see only limited opportunities for future growth in the U.S. market.

You have recently decided to look into the possibility of expanding into foreign countries. Start by making a list of 10 countries that would seem like logical candidates for foreign expansion. Then visit the *Country Commercial Guides* mentioned above and any other relevant sources, and research the 10 countries' business regulations. Rank the countries in order on the basis of apparent ease of entry, and determine which mode of entry would be most appropriate to use in each country.

WE INVITE YOU TO VISIT THIS BOOK'S COMPANION WEB SITE AT www.prenhall.com/griffin

IN THE NEWS

Assume you own a start-up firm that manufactures and sells expensive car audio systems, and you are considering expanding into the global marketplace. Your task is to select a country to enter and a mode of entry to use to enter that country. Justify your decision, listing the advantages you hope to gain and the means by which you will overcome any difficulties.

Use the "Industries" tab on the *Financial Times* homepage (*www.ft.com*) and/or the "Companies" tab to research firms you might compete with. Use their experiences to shape your answer.

You can also use this site to research the specific country or countries where you plan to start your expansion, to find out what benefits you may gain and challenges you may face.

CLOSING CASE

David Versus Goliath

Because U.S. firms got such a big head start in electronic commerce, some experts believed that most European e-businesses would end up playing second fiddle to U.S. enterprises. The dominance of eBay, Inc.—one of the most visible of all dot-com businesses—in the online auction market seemed to validate this hypothesis. However, do not tell that to the German entrepreneurs who started Ricardo.de in 1997 and three years later sold their company to QXL, Britain's largest online auctioneer, for $261 million in QXL stock.

eBay, of course, is a very young firm itself. Started as a cyberspace flea market in 1995, the company adopted its present name in 1997, went public in 1998, and acquired the upscale auction house Butterfield & Butterfield in 1999. eBay currently has 1,600 different categories of products being offered by potential sellers and has about 4 million registered users. Unlike many dot-com businesses, eBay is already quite profitable—it takes a percentage of each sale from every successful auction transaction. Not surprisingly, then, eBay has attracted new competitors. For example, both Amazon.com and Yahoo! have launched auction sites.

Ricardo.de has emerged as one of eBay's most formidable challengers in Europe. The three young German entrepreneurs behind Ricardo.de—Stefan Glaenzer, Christoph Linkwitz, and Stefan Wiskemann—intended to create an online publishing business. However, when they auctioned off a new Mercedes A-Class car on the Internet to promote an online business directory their firm had just published, the overwhelming response quickly diverted their attention in new directions. Wiskemann quipped, "We figured it's better to do e-commerce than write about it."

However, as the firm began its metamorphosis from publisher to auction house, one problem after another arose. First, some potential investors backed off after expressing concerns that Ricardo.de—named after the early nineteenth-century English economist David Ricardo, an early champion of free markets and the author of the theory of comparative advantage discussed in Chapter 5—lacked a clear strategy for differentiating itself from eBay. Moreover, eBay appeared to get the inside track in Germany when it acquired Alando.de, a Berlin-based online auction firm that was already up and running.

Alando.de also had the advantage of being a partner with T-Online, Europe's largest Internet access provider.

Ricardo.de dealt with the first concern when it formalized its strategy. Rather than concentrate on used articles and collectibles, like eBay, Ricardo.de started selling only new merchandise—mostly discontinued or overstocked electronics, appliances, and computers bought at bargain prices from wholesalers and retailers. In addition, Ricardo.de promised to hold regular five-minute "live" auctions with a moderator calling the action, chatting with bidders, and congratulating the winners. Ricardo.de established a new affiliate, ricardoBIZ.com, to provide an electronic trading platform and online marketplace for the motor vehicle, electronics, and garment industries. It purchased a 27-percent stake in Allocation Network, an online specialist in auctioning surplus industrial goods. It also entered into other online alliances with companies dealing in telecommunications and information technology, office articles, and meat wholesaling.

This approach seemed to make a lot of sense to local investors, and they quickly lined up to help launch Ricardo.de's initial public offering (IPO). The optimism surrounding the company, however, began to evaporate almost as soon as it started when two more setbacks occurred. A group of traditional auctioneers filed a lawsuit against Ricardo.de, citing a 100-year-old law that made it illegal to sell new goods at public auction in Germany. Further, on the very eve of the IPO, one of the deal's major underwriters, Westdeutsche Landesbank, backed out because of a dispute with the lead investment banker, Deutsche Bank AG.

As the old adage goes, sometimes it is darkest right before the dawn. Clearly, the founders of Ricardo.de must have felt very grim in mid-1999. But just as the future looked its bleakest for the three young Germans, things started breaking in their favor. First of all, in a surprise move a judge threw out the lawsuit by the auctioneers against Ricardo.de, opening the door for it to proceed with its business plan. Next, eBay inexplicably decided to not renew its exclusive deal with T-Online, and Ricardo.de quickly signed on in eBay's place. Finally, Deutsche Bank agreed to pick up the part of the stock deal that the other bank had abandoned. This series of events spurred new optimism about Ricardo.de's potential, and the price of its shares soared over 500 percent by the end of 1999.

The foundation of Ricardo.de's strategy was to get big quickly. One means of accomplishing this was to build the company through alliances with other online firms. The company also sought to garner free publicity by auctioning attention-getting goods. Ricardo.de auctioned off a tennis racket used by Steffi Graf in her last Grand Slam win on behalf of her favorite charity, the Children for Tomorrow Trust. Even more free publicity was obtained when the company auctioned two dives on a deep-sea submersible to visit the wreckage of the Titanic 3,775 meters below the ocean's surface. As a result of such efforts, Ricardo.de enjoys phenomenal brand awareness in its home market: Some 80 percent of German Internet users recognize the company in e-commerce market surveys.

By the beginning of 2000 Ricardo.de had achieved its initial target of being one of the largest Internet auction channels in Germany. It had signed up 500,000 registered users in Germany alone, putting it right behind eBay's 580,000 figure. It next set its sights on being number one in Europe. Ricardo.de launched operations in Britain in January 2000, bought the top Dutch and Swiss auction sites in February, and expanded into France and Italy in April. In May Ricardo.de's founders were approached by executives from QXL, Britain's largest online auctioneer, to merge their companies, arguing that combining operations would make the two more competitive with eBay. Four months later Ricardo agreed to be acquired by QXL for $261 million in QXL stock—not bad for an upstart company less than three years old!

Case Questions

1. Turn back the clock to 1997. Suppose you were hired by Ricardo.de's founders to map out an entry strategy for the firm. What advice would you have given them? Would you have done anything differently?
2. Why did Ricardo.de strive to grow quickly? Do you agree with this strategy? Should it have grown more slowly?
3. What advantages does eBay possess over upstart competitors like Ricardo.de?
4. What advantages does a combined Ricardo.de-QXL have over eBay?
5. Do you agree with Ricardo.de's decision to be acquired by QXL?

Sources: "QXL Falls from Grace as It Aims at Ricardo," *Financial Times*, August 17, 2000, p. 19; "Europe's Internet Jitters Pressure QXL," *Wall Street Journal*, August 16, 2000, p. A18; "Web Auctioneer QXL Reviews Plan to Buy Germany's Ricardo," *Wall Street Journal*, August 11, 2000, p. A11; Neal E. Boudette, "No Junk, Bitte! German Upstart Takes on eBay," *Wall Street Journal*, March 1, 2000, pp. B1, B4; Malcolm Gladwell, "Clicks & Mortar," *The New Yorker*, December 6, 1999, pp. 106–115; miscellaneous press releases available on Ricardo.de's Web site.

Should Trade in Ivory Be Allowed?

Yes, because trade in ivory promotes healthy elephant herds.

Elephant herds were decimated in the 1970s and early 1980s by poachers armed with automatic weapons. Kenya and Uganda lost 85 percent of their elephants from 1973 to 1987, mostly to poachers. Since 1989, however, the Convention of International Trade in Endangered Species (CITES)—a 152-country organization sponsored by the United Nations—has banned trade in ivory. The CITES ban has worked. But it's obsolete, and continuing the ban will do more harm than good.

Elephant herds are blossoming, particularly in southern Africa. The elephant population in Botswana has increased from 20,000 in 1981 to 106,000 in 1999; Zimbabwe's from 49,000 to 70,000. South Africa and Namibia have had smaller but still significant increases. Countries whose elephants are no longer endangered should be allowed to sell limited amounts of elephant tusks to fund environmental projects. Without economic incentives their commitment to preservation may waiver, particularly as growing human populations put more pressure on Africa's arable lands. Further, authorizing limited sales of ivory will reduce its price and lower the incentives for poaching and smuggling in the first place.

Allowing trade in ivory will ensure the survival of many other species of African flora and fauna. The growth in elephant populations now threatens to overwhelm available habitat. Rangers in South Africa's Kruger National Park have had to relocate 1,600 elephants from the park to other places because overgrazing by the giant mammals was destroying trees and other habitat critical for ecological balance.

South African officials would like to auction off 30 tons of ivory being held in storehouses, most of which was taken from elephants who died of natural causes. The sale will net $5 million, which will be ploughed back into their conservation and protection efforts. Such moneys are critical in a growing nation facing severe budgetary constraints and many competing uses for available government resources.

Zimbabwe's government also has wisely managed its elephant herds. Its CAMPFIRE program provides financial incentives to local communities to protect the herds; these funds are generated primarily by hunters and tourists attracted by the country's abundant wildlife. Controlled sales of ivory would increase the funds available for the CAMPFIRE project.

It is true that restoration of elephant populations has not been as successful in many northern African countries. However, that is no reason for denying southern African countries the right to sell ivory from their herds. Notes a representative of South Africa's Endangered Wildlife Trust, "I can't see why we should bear the burden of mismanagement of elephants in other parts of Africa." Moreover, new scientific methods can determine the source of an individual piece of ivory, so customs officials and environmental officers would be able to determine if it is being sold legally or not.

The elephant populations in southern Africa have grown so large they now threaten the ecological balance. Limited ivory sales will restore the herds to a more proper size and finance other vital environmental projects.

No, continuing the ban is the right policy.

There is little doubt that the CITES ban was necessary. In 1979 Africa had 1.3 million elephants; by 1990 that number had fallen to 600,000. There is also little doubt that the ban has worked well. It has robbed poachers and smugglers of the opportunity to make easy money and reduced the ecological havoc they create. Prior to the ban, for example, 3,500 elephants were killed annually in Kenya; after the ban the number fell to only one a week.

Although it may be true the herds in southern Africa are being restored, that is not the case in all countries. Poaching remains a pressing problem in the north—in Cameroon, the Central African Republic, and Mali, among other countries. Even limited legal trade in ivory will create new opportunities for poachers.

Past experiences demonstrate that any controls short of an outright ban will not work. For example, in 1986 CITES established an ivory quota system. Each tusk was supposed to be marked, with its country of origin duly noted and entered into a data base. Merchants evaded controls on exports of raw ivory by carving each tusk ever so slightly so that it would be classified as "worked ivory," which was free from the export controls. Less than half of the 35 African nations signing the CITES agreement imposed workable controls on the ivory trade. Many countries had difficulties in enforcing quota rules back in 1986. There is every reason to believe they would have equal difficulties today, particularly given the financial difficulties many of them face.

Moreover, smuggling continues today, despite the existing ban on trade in ivory. In April 2000, Japanese police caught a Japanese and a Hong Kong resident trying to smuggle 500 kilograms of ivory into Japan from their base in Singapore. A month later, Chinese customs officers seized 507 kilos of African ivory in Shenzen and arrested two smugglers. If smuggling is rampant despite a total ban on ivory trade, imagine the new heights to which illegal trade would rise if loopholes were created for southern African ivory.

In short, the CITES ban on ivory has been effective, as demonstrated by the fact that the southern African elephant herds are being restored to their pre-crises levels. People who propose to cancel the ban on the ivory trade ought to remember the words of the old adage: If it ain't broke, don't fix it.

Elephants in central Africa remain endangered. Eliminating the ban on ivory sales will encourage poaching and threaten the survival of elephants in Kenya, Mali, and Cameroon.

Wrap-up

1. Should the southern African countries like Botswana, South Africa, and Zimbabwe that have restored their elephant herds be allowed to sell surplus ivory?
2. Will allowing limited ivory exports encourage or discourage poachers?
3. Is permitting ivory exports the best way to encourage countries to protect their elephant herds?

Source: "Ivory Sales Delayed Two Years," *Boston Globe*, April 18, 2000, p. A12; "Treasured Beast That Divides a Continent," *Financial Times*, April 15/16, 2000, p. 9.

CHAPTER

The European Cereal Wars

Kellogg virtually created the market for breakfast cereals in Europe. The maker of such popular brands as Kellogg's Corn Flakes, Rice Krispies, and Frosted Flakes, Kellogg began introducing its products in the United Kingdom in the 1920s and on the Continent in the 1950s. However, Europeans traditionally favored bread, fruit, eggs, and meat for breakfast, so the firm had a tough sell on its hands. Indeed, it has taken decades for Europeans to accept cereals as a viable breakfast choice.

"...**growth** of commercial TV outlets has helped firms increase **demand** through advertising."

During the last several years demand for breakfast cereals in Europe has begun to accelerate as European consumers have become more health-conscious and started looking for breakfast alternatives to eggs and meat. The busy schedules of the increasing number of dual-career families have also spurred demand for prepackaged foods. Another contributing factor has been the emergence of supermarkets in Europe. Traditionally most food products in Europe were sold at small specialty stores, which often were reluctant to stock cereals because they take up so much shelf space. In recent years, however, more full-line supermarkets have opened in Europe, and shelf space is now available for a wider array of products. Finally, the

12 International Strategic Alliances

OBJECTIVES

After studying this chapter, you should be able to:

> Compare joint ventures and other forms of strategic alliances.

> Characterize the benefits of strategic alliances.

> Describe the scope of strategic alliances.

> Discuss the forms of management used for strategic alliances.

> Identify the limitations of strategic alliances.

growth of commercial TV outlets in Europe has helped firms increase demand through advertising. Needless to say, the enormous potential of the European cereal market has attracted the interests of Kellogg's competitors.

One of Kellogg's biggest competitors in the United States is General Mills, which makes Cheerios, Golden Grahams, and other popular brands. General Mills traditionally concentrated on the North American market, but in 1989 its managers decided it was time to enter the European market. However, they also recognized that taking on Kellogg, which controlled 50 percent of the worldwide cereal market and dominated the European market, would be a monumental battle.

After careful consideration General Mills's CEO Bruce Atwater decided the firm could compete most effectively in Europe if it worked with a strategic ally located there. It did not take him long to choose one: Nestlé, the world's largest food-processing firm. Nestlé is a household name in Europe, has a well-established distribution system, and owns manufacturing plants worldwide. One major area in which Nestlé had never succeeded, however, was the cereal market. Thus Atwater reasoned that Nestlé would be a logical partner.

When he approached his counterpart at Nestlé, Atwater was amazed to discover that Nestlé had already been considering approaching General Mills about just such an arrangement. From Nestlé's perspective General Mills could contribute its knowledge of cereal technology, its array of proven cereal products, and its expertise in marketing cereals to consumers, especially children.

Top managers of the two firms met and quickly outlined a plan of attack. Each firm contributed around $80 million to form a new firm called Cereal Partners Worldwide (CPW). General Mills agreed to install its proprietary manufacturing systems in existing Nestlé factories, oversee the production of cereals, and help develop advertising campaigns. Nestlé in turn agreed to use its own corporate name on the products and to handle sales and distribution throughout Europe. The two partners set two major goals for CPW: They wanted CPW to be generating annual sales of $1 billion and to be a strong number two in market share outside North America by the year 2000.

By almost any measure CPW has been a big success. Among its first triumphs was a deal struck with Disneyland Paris to supply breakfast cereals to the restaurants and hotels at the French theme park and to use Disney characters to promote CPW's cereals. The firm quickly established itself as a major player in the European cereal market, where it achieved its goal of being number two in that market with a 12 percent market share. Having solidified its beachhead in Europe, CPW then expanded its operations to Latin America and Asia. It now operates in over 60 countries, delivering a steady and growing stream of earnings for its parents, Nestlé and General Mills.[1]

G lobalization can be a very expensive process, particularly when a firm must perfectly coordinate research and development (R&D), production, distribution, marketing, and financial decisions throughout the world in order to succeed. A firm may discover that it lacks all the necessary internal resources to effectively compete against its rivals internationally. The high costs of researching and developing new products alone may stretch its corporate budget. Thus a firm may seek out partners to share these costs. A firm may develop a new technology but lack a distribution network or production facilities in all the national markets it wants to serve. Accordingly the firm may seek out other firms with skills or advantages that complement its own and negotiate agreements to work together. Such factors motivated General Mills and Nestlé to team up, as the opening case indicated.

❯ INTERNATIONAL CORPORATE COOPERATION

Cooperation between international firms can take many forms, such as cross-licensing of proprietary technology, sharing of production facilities, cofunding of research projects, and marketing of each other's products using existing distribution networks. Such forms of cooperation are known collectively as **strategic alliances**, business arrangements whereby two or more firms choose to cooperate for their mutual benefit. The partners in a strategic alliance may agree to pool R&D activities, marketing expertise, and/or managerial talent. For example, beginning in 1992, Kodak and Fuji—two fierce competitors in the film market—formed a strategic alliance with camera manufacturers Canon, Minolta, and Nikon to develop a new standard for cameras and film, the Advanced Photo System, to make picture taking easier and more goof-proof.[2]

A **joint venture (JV)** is a special type of strategic alliance in which two or more firms join together to create a new business entity that is legally separate and distinct from its parents. Joint ventures normally are established as corporations and are owned by the founding parents in whatever proportions they negotiate. Many are owned equally by the founding firms, although unequal ownership is also common.

A strategic alliance is only one method by which a firm can enter or expand its international operations. As Chapter 11 discussed, other alternatives exist: exporting, licensing, franchising, and foreign direct investment. In each of these alternatives, however, a firm acts alone or hires a second individual or firm—often one further down the distribution chain—to act on its behalf. In contrast, a strategic alliance results from cooperation between two or more firms. Each participant in a strategic alliance is motivated to promote its own self-interest but has determined that cooperation is the best way to achieve its goals.

Some means is required for managing any cooperative agreement. A joint venture, as a separate legal entity, must have its own set of managers and board of directors. It may be managed in any of three ways. First, the founding firms may jointly share management, with each appointing key personnel who report back to officers of the parent. Second, one parent may assume primary responsibility. Third, an independent team of managers may be hired to run the joint venture. The third approach is often preferred because independent managers focus on what is best for the joint venture rather than attempt to placate bosses from the founding firms.[3] Other types of strategic alliances may be managed more informally—for example, by a coordinating committee, composed of employees of each of the partners, which oversees the alliance's progress.

A formal management organization allows a joint venture to be broader in purpose, scope (or range of operations), and duration than other types of strategic alliances. A strategic alliance that is not a joint venture may be formed merely to allow the partners to overcome a particular hurdle that each faces in the short run. A joint venture will be more helpful if the two firms plan a more extensive and long-term relationship. A typical non-joint venture strategic alliance has a narrow purpose and scope, such as marketing a new videophone system in Canada. A joint venture might be formed if firms wanted to cooperate in the design, production, and sale of a broad line of telecommunications equipment in North America. Non-joint venture strategic alliances often are formed for a specific purpose that may have a natural ending. For example, the agreement among the camera manufacturers Canon, Minolta, and Nikon and the film manufacturers Fuji and Kodak to jointly create the Advanced Photo System for cameras and film terminated in 1996, after the new standards were developed. Each participant then marketed the resulting products on its own.[4] However, because joint ventures are separate legal entities, they generally have a longer duration.

> As part of its joint venture with Western oil companies to exploit Arctic Russia's vast oil reserves, Lukoil is building a tanker fleet to haul the oil to Asian and American refineries.

Because of their narrow mission and lack of a formal organizational structure, non-joint venture strategic alliances are relatively less stable than joint ventures. For example, in 1988 United Airlines and British Airways entered into an agreement to form a strategic marketing alliance involving their North American and European routes. At the time United was offering limited service to Europe and was losing market share to archrivals Delta and American Airlines, both of which offered more extensive service to Europe. To solve its problem, United agreed to coordinate its flight schedules with British Airways, thereby making it more convenient for a Europe-bound U.S. traveler to board a domestic United flight and then transfer to a transatlantic British Airways flight. United and British Airways both prominently described the arrangement in their marketing campaigns and in the visits of their marketing reps to U.S. and European travel agencies. Within a year, however, Pan Am's routes to London were placed on the auction block. United quickly purchased those routes from Pan Am and severed relations with its strategic ally. British Airways was of little use to United once United could operate in London on its own. Needing a transatlantic partner, British Airways then entered into a similar strategic alliance with US Air in 1993. Three years later American Airlines and British Airways agreed to form a separate strategic alliance. US Air, believing it would be the odd man out in a three-way alliance, promptly sued British Airways and terminated their alliance.

› BENEFITS OF STRATEGIC ALLIANCES

Firms that enter into strategic alliances usually expect to benefit in one or more ways. As summarized in Figure 12.1, international business may realize four benefits from strategic alliances: ease of market entry, shared risk, shared knowledge and expertise, and synergy and competitive advantage.[5]

Ease of Market Entry

A firm wishing to enter a new market often faces major obstacles, such as entrenched competition or hostile government regulations. Partnering with a local firm often can help the entering firm navigate around such barriers. In other cases economies of scale and scope in marketing and distribution confer benefits on firms that aggressively and quickly enter numerous markets.[6] Yet the costs of speed and boldness are often high and beyond the capabilities of a single firm. A strategic alliance may allow the firm to achieve the benefits of rapid entry while keeping costs down.

For example, Warner Brothers, a movie distribution subsidiary of AOL Time Warner, recently targeted Europe as an important growth market. To speed its entry, Warner Brothers entered into several joint ventures with European movie theater chains. It established a joint venture with Lusomundo, a leading Portuguese media company, to build 20 multiplex theaters in Spain. Warner Brothers also constructed 23 new multiplex theaters in the United Kingdom in partnership with Village Roadshow, an Australian-based company with extensive theater holdings in Europe.[7] A similar meshing of strengths motivated a joint venture between Cigna, the U.S. insurance giant, and Banco Excel Economico, one of Brazil's largest privately owned banks, to sell personal insurance in Brazil. Cigna provides expertise in selling life, accident, and credit insurance to consumers, while Banco Excel supplies its knowledge of the Brazilian financial service industry, as well as access to its existing retail customer base. Each partner contributed half the $19 million invested in the new company, Excel Cigna Seguradora.[8]

FIGURE 12.1

Benefits of Strategic Alliances

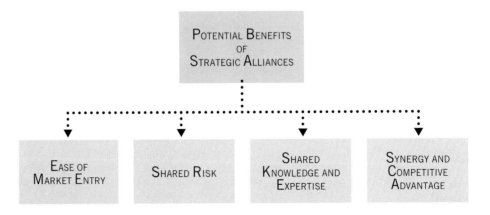

Regulations imposed by national governments also influence the formation of joint ventures. Many countries are so concerned about the influence of foreign firms on their economies that they require multinational corporations (MNCs) to work with a local partner if they want to operate in the countries.[9] For example, the government of Namibia, an African nation, requires foreign investors operating fishing fleets off its coast to work with local partners (see Map 12.1). At other times governments strongly encourage foreign companies to participate in joint ventures in order to promote other policy goals. A case in point is China, which has been concerned about the disappearance of local brands from store shelves because many Chinese consumers prefer Western products to often shoddy goods produced by state-owned factories. Recognizing the importance of local brands, Coca-Cola established a joint venture with a local company to create a noncarbonated line of drinks, Heaven and Earth, which is tailored to Chinese tastes.[10]

Shared Risk

Today's major industries are so competitive that no firm has a guarantee of success when it enters a new market or develops a new product. Strategic alliances can be used to either reduce or control an individual firm's risks. For example, Boeing established a strategic alliance with several Japanese firms to reduce its financial risk in the development and production of the Boeing 777. Researching, designing, and safety testing a new aircraft model costs billions of dollars, much of which must be spent before the manufacturer can establish how well the airplane will be received in the marketplace. Even though Boeing has enjoyed much success as a manufacturer of commercial aircraft, it wanted to reduce its financial exposure on the 777 project. Thus it collaborated with three Japanese partners— Fuji, Mitsubishi, and Kawasaki—agreeing to let them build 20 percent of the 777 airframe. Boeing, the controlling partner in the alliance, also hoped its allies would help sell the new aircraft to large Japanese customers such as Japan Air Lines and All Nippon Airways.

Also consider the strategic alliance involving Kodak and Fuji and three Japanese camera firms. At face value it might seem odd for Kodak to agree to collaborate with Fuji, Kodak's biggest competitor, to develop a new film that both will make and sell. Closer scrutiny, however, suggests that the arrangement reduces Kodak's risks considerably. Kodak managers realized that if they developed the film alone, Fuji would aggressively fight the innovation in the marketplace, and Kodak would have to work hard to gain consumer acceptance of its new standard for film. Still worse,

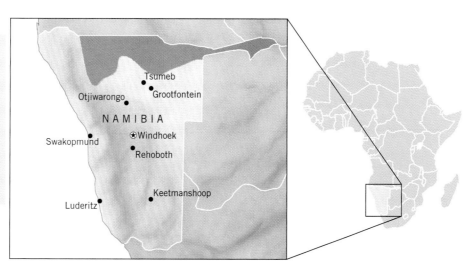

Namibia's government has promoted development of the country's fishing industry by requiring foreign investors who wish to fish its waters to join with local partners in establishing onshore fish-processing plants. As a result, joint ventures have created jobs, both onshore and offshore, for some 10,000 Namibians.

Desert and desert shrub

Wooded savanna

MAP 12.1   **Namibia and Joint Ventures**

Fuji might have decided to develop its own new film standard, thereby jeopardizing Kodak's R&D investment should the Japanese-dominated camera-manufacturing industry adopt Fuji's approach rather than Kodak's. Mindful of the financial losses incurred by Sony when VHS rather than Betamax became the standard format for VCRs, Kodak chose to include Fuji in the deal. Through this strategic alliance Kodak reduced its risks. It also can compete on a playing field of its own choosing, free to harness its marketing clout, distribution networks, and formidable brand name against the efforts of its rivals.

Shared risk is an especially important consideration when a firm is entering a market that has just opened up or that is characterized by much uncertainty and instability. "Venturing Abroad" discusses how one international business, Otis Elevator, uses joint ventures to slash its risks in such situations.

Shared Knowledge and Expertise

Still another common reason for strategic alliances is the potential for a firm to gain knowledge and expertise that it lacks. The firm may want to learn more about how to produce something, how to acquire certain resources, how to deal with local governments' regulations, or how to manage in a different environment—information that a partner often can offer.[11] The firm then can use the newly acquired information for other purposes.

One of the more successful joint ventures in the United States has been that between Toyota and GM. In 1982 GM closed an old automobile manufacturing plant in Fremont, California, because it was inefficient. In 1984 Toyota agreed to reopen the plant and manage it through a joint venture called Nummi (New United Motor Manufacturing, Inc.). Although Nummi is owned equally by the two partners, Toyota manages the facility and makes automobiles for both. Each firm entered into the deal primarily to acquire knowledge. Toyota wanted to learn more about how to deal with labor and parts suppliers in the U.S. market; GM wanted to observe Japanese management practices firsthand.[12] Toyota used its newly acquired information when it opened its own manufacturing plant in Georgetown, Kentucky, in 1988. GM used lessons learned from Nummi in developing and operating its newest automotive division, Saturn, and in organizing its new assembly plant in Eisenach, Germany. As a result, productivity in the German plant is double that of GM's plants in the United States.

Synergy and Competitive Advantage

Firms also may enter into strategic alliances to attain synergy and competitive advantage. These related advantages reflect combinations of the other advantages discussed in this section: The idea is that through some combination of market entry, risk sharing, and learning potential, each collaborating firm will be able to achieve more and to compete more effectively than if it had attempted to enter a new market or industry alone.

For example, creating a favorable brand image in consumers' minds is an expensive, time-consuming process, as is creating efficient distribution networks and obtaining the necessary clout with retailers to capture shelf space for one's products. These factors led PepsiCo, the world's second largest soft-drink firm, to establish a joint venture with Thomas J. Lipton Co., a division of Unilever, to produce and market ready-to-drink teas in the United States. Lipton, which has a 50 percent share of the $400-million worldwide market for ready-to-drink teas, provided the joint venture with manufacturing expertise and brand recognition in teas. PepsiCo supplied its extensive and experienced U.S. distribution network.[13] Similarly, Siemens and Motorola established a joint venture in the mid-1990s to produce 64-megabyte and 256-megabyte DRAM computer chips. Motorola teamed with Siemens in part to help finance the new $1.5-billion factory the partners agreed to build, while Siemens sought to benefit from Motorola's manufacturing

VENTURING *Abroad*

Entering a new market is always a risky proposition, but when a firm is the first foreigner to enter, its risks are even greater. That is why many foreign firms who try to be first often look for a local partner for help. A good case in point is Otis Elevator.

A division of United Technologies, Otis has a strategy of trying to be the first foreign elevator manufacturer to enter emerging markets. For example, the firm entered China in 1984. The morning after the Berlin Wall fell, Otis executives began negotiating with prospective local partners in Central Europe and Eastern Europe. More recently, it was among the very first U.S. companies to announce plans to enter Vietnam when President Clinton lifted the trade embargo with that country.

Otis always looks for one or more local partners to ease its entry and reduce its risks. For example, the firm currently has five different joint ventures in China (see Map 12.2). Total investments by Otis in China now exceed $70 million, and the firm has about 25 percent of the market. Otis's sales in China are about $260 million and growing at a rapid pace. Its Vietnam deal involved two local partners, and expectations for sales and profits there are running high.

Otis sees local partners as an important mechanism for reducing its risks. These partners know the local landscape and can help the company avoid problems. They also aid the marketing of Otis's products. For example, Otis won the lucrative contract to provide 158 escalators for the Shanghai metro system thanks in part to Otis's Chinese partners. On the other hand, Otis often has to work hard to get its partners "up to speed." It took Otis three years to get its first Chinese partner to phase out its antiquated product line and replace it with newer Otis equipment. Convincing the partner about the benefits of customer service took even longer. To instill the service-oriented spirit vital to its success, Otis now spends over $2 million a year training its 5,000 Chinese managers and employees.

Otis's strategy seems to be a sound one. Providing its local partner with cutting-edge technology, equipment, and training often yields high returns. Yet often low-tech solutions are equally as valuable. For example, the simple act of providing its new Russian workforce with vans boosted productivity; previously these workers often transported spare parts by carrying them on the Moscow subway. Otis now services over 118,000 elevators throughout Russia and Ukraine. All told, 88 percent of Otis's revenues are earned outside the United States. Perhaps more important, the company is perfectly positioned to benefit from the elevated growth prospects of many large emerging markets.

Sources: "The Pioneers," *Wall Street Journal*, September 26, 1996, pp. R1, R14; "Overseas, Otis and Its Parent Get In on the Ground Floor," *Wall Street Journal*, April 21, 1995, p. A6.

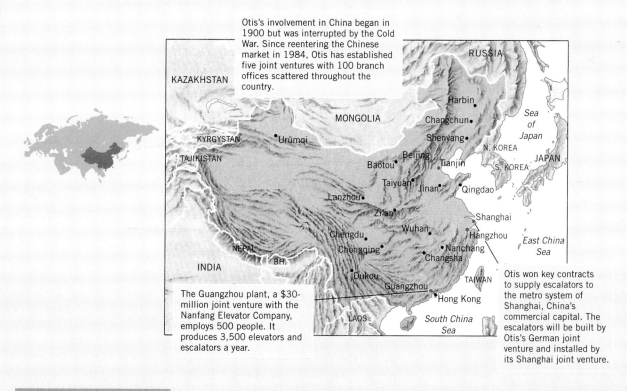

Otis's involvement in China began in 1900 but was interrupted by the Cold War. Since reentering the Chinese market in 1984, Otis has established five joint ventures with 100 branch offices scattered throughout the country.

The Guangzhou plant, a $30-million joint venture with the Nanfang Elevator Company, employs 500 people. It produces 3,500 elevators and escalators a year.

Otis won key contracts to supply escalators to the metro system of Shanghai, China's commercial capital. The escalators will be built by Otis's German joint venture and installed by its Shanghai joint venture.

MAP 12.2   **Otis Elevators' Joint Ventures in China (Shown in Red)**

SEA LAUNCH:
A MATCH MADE IN THE HEAVENS

One company whose goal is out of this world is Sea Launch, a joint venture formed in 1994 by Ukraine's PO Yuzhmash, Norway's Kvaerner Group, Russia's RSC Energia, and Boeing. Its goal is to capture the lion's share of the $6.6-billion-a-year market launching satellites into space. One advantage the company has is the offshore location of its launch site in the Pacific near the equator, which is perfect for efficiently putting its clients' satellites into geosynchronous orbit. Another advantage is the expertise of its owners. Yuzhmash was one of the Soviet Union's premier missile design and fabrication companies. It made the SS-4 missiles that triggered the Cuban missile crisis in 1992 and the SS-18 which could deliver 10 nuclear warheads. With the end of the Cold War, however, there was little demand for ballistic missiles, so Yuzhmash was eager to transform its technological expertise to civilian use. Energia contributes its knowledge of booster engines, which it built for Soviet rocketry

forces. Kvaerner, an offshore drilling specialist, constructed the offshore launch platform and provides the expertise for transporting the rockets to the launch site. Boeing builds the satellite payload compartment and serves as overall manager of the joint venture.

Happy to see the energies of these companies directed at building rockets aimed at the skies rather than at each other, the World Bank has provided $200 million to finance Sea Launch's start-up. The company already has launched four satellites and has 18 more lined up for clients like Hughes Electronics, Loral Space & Communications Ltd., and PanAmSat Corp. Given the booming market for telecommunications services worldwide, Sea Launch's partners believe the sky's the limit.

Source: "Old Soviet Missile Factory Takes New Aim," *Wall Street Journal*, October 23, 2000, p. C15.

expertise and to improve its access to the U.S. market, which typically accounts for 40 percent of the worldwide market for DRAM memory chips.[14] "Wiring the World" provides another example of this phenomenon.

› SCOPE OF STRATEGIC ALLIANCES

The scope of cooperation among firms may vary significantly, as Figure. 12.2 illustrates. For example, it may consist of a comprehensive alliance, in which the partners participate in all facets of conducting business, ranging from product design to manufacturing to marketing, or it may consist of a more narrowly defined alliance that focuses on only one element of the business, such as R&D. The degree of collaboration will depend on the basic goals of each partner.

Comprehensive Alliances

Comprehensive alliances arise when the participating firms agree to perform together multiple stages of the process by which goods or services are brought to the market: R&D, design, production, marketing, and distribution. Because of the broad scope of such alliances, the firms must establish procedures for meshing such functional areas as finance, production, and marketing for the alliance to succeed. Yet integrating the different operating procedures of the parents over a broad range of functional activities is difficult in the absence of a formal organizational structure. As a result, most comprehensive alliances are organized as joint ventures. As an independent entity, the joint venture can adopt operating procedures that suit its specific needs, rather than attempt to accommodate the often

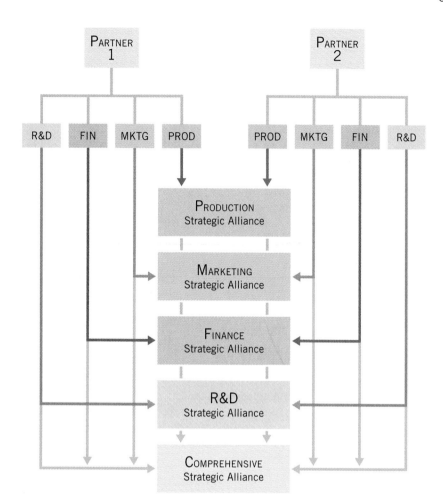

FIGURE 12.2

The Scope of Strategic Alliances

incompatible procedures of the parents, as might be the case with another type of strategic alliance.

Moreover, by fully integrating their efforts, participating firms in a comprehensive alliance are able to achieve greater synergy through sheer size and total resources. For example, General Mills still would have had a major uphill battle in the European cereal market if its joint venture with Nestlé had covered only a single function such as marketing. A complete meshing of each firm's relative strengths (General Mills's cereal-making expertise and Nestlé's European distribution network and name recognition) resulted in a business unit that has emerged as a formidable competitor for Kellogg.

Functional Alliances

Strategic alliances also may be narrow in scope, involving only a single functional area of the business. In such cases integrating the needs of the parent firms is less complex. Thus functionally based alliances often do not take the form of a joint venture, although joint ventures are still the more common form of organization. Types of functional alliances include production alliances, marketing alliances, financial alliances, and R&D alliances.

Production Alliances.   A **production alliance** is a functional alliance in which two or more firms each manufacture products or provide services in a shared or common facility. A production alliance may utilize a facility one partner already owns. For example, as we discussed earlier, the Nummi joint venture between

Toyota and GM is housed in a former GM assembly plant in California, which the company had closed down. Alternatively, the partners may choose to build a new plant, as was the case in a $500-million joint venture Chrysler and BMW formed to build 1.4-liter four-cylinder engines in South America in the late 1990s. Both companies believed they needed to develop this size engine if they were to compete effectively in South America and in the emerging countries of Asia. Each company determined independently that to capture economies of scale, an efficient engine factory would need to produce 400,000 engines annually, yet each believed it could sell only half that number of cars powered by a 1.4-liter engine. Creation of the joint venture readily solved their problem, and, as an added bonus, allowed them better access to the rapidly growing Mercosur countries.[15]

Marketing Alliances.   A **marketing alliance** is a functional alliance in which two or more firms share marketing services or expertise. In most cases one partner introduces its products or services into a market in which the other partner already has a presence. The established firm helps the newcomer by promoting, advertising, and/or distributing its products or services. The established firm may negotiate a fixed price for its assistance or may share in a percentage of the newcomer's sales or profits. Alternatively, the firms may agree to market each others' products on a reciprocal basis. For example, U.S. toy maker Mattel and its Japanese rival Bandai established a strategic marketing alliance in 1999. Bandai agreed to distribute Mattel products like Barbie dolls, Hot Wheels, and Fisher Price toys in Japan, while Mattel agreed to market Bandai's Power Rangers and Digimon in Latin America, where Mattel's distribution network is strong but Bandai's nonexistent.[16] However, when forming a marketing alliance, partners must take care to ensure that their expectations and needs are mutually understood. As "Bringing the World into Focus" indicates, failure to reach such an understanding can reduce the success of the alliance.

Financial Alliances.   A **financial alliance** is a functional alliance of firms that want to reduce the financial risks associated with a project. Partners may share equally in contributing financial resources to the project, or one partner may contribute the bulk of the financing while the other partner (or partners) provides special expertise or makes other kinds of contributions to partially offset its lack of financial investment. The strategic alliance between Boeing and its three Japanese partners was created primarily for financial purposes—Boeing wanted the other firms to help cover R&D and manufacturing costs. Those firms, in turn, saw a chance to gain valuable experience in commercial aircraft manufacturing as well as profits. Similarly, Twentieth Century Fox and Paramount Pictures were financial allies in producing *Titanic*, the most successful movie in history.

Research and Development Alliances.   Rapid technological change in high-technology industries and the skyrocketing cost of staying abreast of that change have prompted an increase in functional alliances that focuses on R&D. In an **R&D alliance** the partners agree to undertake joint research to develop new products or services. An example of a typical R&D alliance is the one formed in 2000 among Intel, Micron Technology, Samsung, Hyundai, NEC, and Siemens to develop the next generation of DRAM chips.[17] Similarly, Bayer AG formed R&D alliances with smaller biotechnology companies like Millenium Pharmaceuticals and Morphosys to strengthen their joint search for new miracle drugs.[18]

Such alliances usually are not formed as joint ventures because scientific knowledge can be transmitted among partners through private research conferences, the exchange of scientific papers, and laboratory visits. Moreover, forming a separate legal organization and staffing it with teams of researchers drawn from the partners' staffs might disrupt ongoing scientific work in each partner's laboratory. Instead each partner may simply agree to cross-license whatever new technology is developed in its labs, thereby allowing its partner (or partners) to use its patents at

Bringing the World into FOCUS

CULTURE CLASH AT GM AND TOYOTA

It seemed like a marketing marriage made in heaven, at least for General Motors. Long constrained in its ability to sell its cars in Japan, GM negotiated a deal with Toyota wherein the Japanese firm would market the GM Chevrolet Cavalier under a Toyota nameplate in its domestic market. The deal has fallen on hard times, however, in part due to cultural clashes between the firms at both the corporate and the national levels.

Both parties knew going in that the GM car would have to be modified to fit the Japanese market. Major changes included moving the steering wheel from the left side of the car to the right side and redesigning the front fenders to cover the tires (a legal requirement in Japan).

Problems surfaced when Toyota began to mandate additional changes beyond the scope of the original agreement. For example, the gas pedal needed to be moved forward to accommodate shorter drivers, and the hand brake and steering wheel had to be covered in leather to meet local consumer tastes. Toyota also found major quality problems with the GM cars, requiring rework on 80 to 90 percent of them.

From its perspective GM sees things a bit differently. For example, it argued that too much luxury was being added, driving up the price unnecessarily and making its cars less competitive with Japanese-produced vehicles. Also, GM charged that defects were being overstated by Toyota. GM managers came to believe that their Japanese counterparts were simply looking for problems to reinforce their perceptions about lower quality in U.S. products. Thus, although the marketing venture is still in place, it has proven so far to be a big disappointment for both partners.

Sources: "Is Cavalier Japanese for Edsel?" *Business Week*, June 24, 1996, p. 39; "Shaking Up an Old Giant," *Forbes*, May 20, 1996, pp. 68–80.

will. Each partner then has equal access to all technology developed by the alliance, an arrangement that guarantees the partners will not fall behind each other in the technological race. Partners also are freed from legal disputes among themselves over ownership and validity of patents. For example, the alliance among Kodak, Fuji, and the three Japanese camera makers focused solely on R&D. Both Kodak and Fuji are licensed to make the new film they developed; the three camera makers are free to market the cameras to use it.

Because of the importance of high-tech industries to the world economy, many countries are supporting the efforts of R&D consortia as part of their industrial policies. An **R&D consortium** is a confederation of organizations that band together to research and develop new products and processes for world markets. It represents a special case of strategic alliance in that governmental support plays a major role in its formation and continued operation. Japanese firms have successfully practiced this type of arrangement for many years. For example, over two decades ago the Japanese government, Nippon Telephone and Telegraph, Mitsubishi, Matsushita, and three other Japanese firms agreed to work together to create new types of high-capacity memory chips. They were so successful that they now dominate this market. The most successful R&D consortium in the United States is SEMATECH, which was founded in 1987 to conduct research in and promote the global competitiveness of the U.S. semiconductor industry. Similarly, the European Union has developed a wide array of joint research efforts with clever acronyms—such as ESPRIT, RACE, BRITE, EURAM, JOULE, and SCIENCE—to ensure that its firms can compete against U.S. and Japanese firms in high-tech markets.

› IMPLEMENTATION OF STRATEGIC ALLIANCES

The decision to form a strategic alliance should develop from a firm's strategic planning process, discussed in Chapter 10. Having made this decision, the firm's managers must then address several significant issues, which set the stage for how the alliance will be managed. Some of the most critical of these issues are the selection of partners, the form of ownership, and joint management considerations.

Selection of Partners

The success of any cooperative undertaking depends on choosing the appropriate partner(s). Research suggests that strategic alliances are more likely to be successful if the skills and resources of the partners are complementary—each must bring to the alliance some organizational strength the other lacks.[19] A firm contemplating a strategic alliance should consider at least four factors in selecting a partner (or partners): (1) compatibility, (2) the nature of the potential partner's products or services, (3) the relative safeness of the alliance, and (4) the learning potential of the alliance.

Compatibility. The firm should select a compatible partner it can trust and with which it can work effectively. Without mutual trust a strategic alliance is unlikely to succeed. But incompatibilities in corporate operating philosophies also may doom an alliance. For example, an alliance between General Electric Corporation (a U.K. firm unrelated to the U.S. firm of the same name) and the German firm Siemens failed because of incompatible management styles. The former firm is run by financial experts and the latter by engineers. General Electric Corporation's financial managers continually worried about bottom-line issues, short-term profitability, and related financial considerations. Siemens's managers cared little about financial issues and paid more attention to innovation, design, and product development.[20] In contrast, a key ingredient in CPW's success is the high level of compatibility between General Mills and Nestlé.

Nature of a Potential Partner's Products or Services. Another factor to consider is the nature of a potential partner's products or services. It is often hard to cooperate with a firm in one market while doing battle with the same firm in a second market. Under such circumstances each partner may be unwilling to reveal all its expertise to the other partner for fear that the partner will use the knowledge against the firm in another market.

Most experts believe a firm should ally itself with a partner whose products or services are complementary to but not directly competitive with its own. The joint venture between General Mills and Nestlé is an example of this principle in action: Both are food-processing firms, but Nestlé does not make cereal, the product on which it is collaborating with General Mills. Similarly, PepsiCo and Lipton complement but do not compete with one another, thus raising the likelihood of success for their joint venture to market ready-to-drink tea in the United States.

› Anglo-American, a giant South African mining company, formed a joint venture with the government of Zambia to exploit that country's copper reserves.

Sometimes, however, a firm may receive a rude surprise. For example, JVC, a subsidiary of the Japanese firm Matsushita, wanted to enter the European VCR market. It formed a 50/50 joint venture with a small German firm. The new venture had only limited success because the German firm lacked the necessary marketing expertise to help JVC gain a foothold. Thomson SA, a large French electronics firm, bought out the German firm and learned the tricks of producing VCRs from JVC. JVC was unconcerned about the potential transfer of its technology to Thomson because JVC's worldwide sales totaled over 5 million VCRs compared to a mere 800,000 units for its European joint venture. Unfortunately for JVC, Thomson later acquired General Electric's consumer electronics business. That purchase boosted Thomson's VCR sales to 5 million a year—making the technology it gained through the joint venture with JVC a very valuable commodity indeed.[21]

The Relative Safeness of the Alliance. Given the complexities and potential costs of failed agreements, managers should gather as much information as possible about a potential partner before entering into a strategic alliance. For example, managers should assess the success or failure of previous strategic alliances formed by the potential partner. Also, it often makes sense to analyze the prospective deal from the other firm's side. What does the potential partner hope to gain from the arrangement? What are the partner's strengths and weaknesses? How will the partner contribute to the venture? Does the proposed arrangement meet its strategic goals? The probability of success rises if the deal makes good business sense for both parties.[22]

For example, Corning, Inc., created a joint venture—Asahi Video Products Company—by integrating its television glass production with the operations of Asahi Glass, a producer of large television bulbs. Corning believed this joint venture would be a sound one for several reasons:

- Asahi Glass's expertise in large television bulb technology complemented Corning's strength in other bulb sizes.
- The joint venture would benefit from Asahi Glass's ongoing business connections with the increasing number of Japanese television manufacturers that were establishing North American facilities.
- The combined strengths of the two firms would help both keep abreast of technological innovations in the video display industry.
- Asahi Glass would benefit from Corning's technology and marketing clout in the U.S. market.
- Corning had successfully operated another joint venture with Asahi Glass since 1965.

In fact, Corning is so good at developing joint ventures that almost half its profits are generated by joint ventures with PPG, Dow Chemical, Samsung, Siemens, Ciba-Geigy, IBM, and, of course, Asahi Glass.

The Learning Potential of the Alliance. Before establishing a strategic alliance, partners should also assess the potential to learn from each other. Areas of learning can range from the very specific, such as how to manage inventory more efficiently or how to train employees more effectively, to the very general, such as how to modify corporate culture or how to manage more strategically. At the same time, each partner should carefully assess the value of its own information and not provide the other partner with information that will result in competitive disadvantage for itself should the alliance dissolve—a point we revisit in the next section.

Form of Ownership

Another issue in establishing a strategic alliance is the exact form of ownership to be used. A joint venture almost always takes the form of a corporation, usually incorporated in the country where it will be doing business. In some instances it may be incorporated in a different country, such as one that offers tax or legal advantages. The Bahamas, for example, is sometimes seen as a favorable tax haven for the incorporation of joint ventures.

The corporate form enables the partners to arrange a beneficial tax structure, implement novel ownership arrangements, and better protect their other assets. This form also allows the joint venture to create its own identity. Of course, if either or both of the partners have favorable reputations, the new corporation may choose to rely on those, perhaps by including the partners' names as part of its name.

A new corporation also provides a neutral setting in which the partners can do business. The potential for conflict may be reduced if the interaction between the partners occurs outside their own facilities or organizations. It also may be reduced if the corporation does not rely on employees identified with either partner and instead hires its own executives and workforce whose first loyalty is to the joint venture. For example, a joint venture formed by Corning and Genentech was not performing as well as expected. Corning soon discovered one source of the difficulties: Managers contributed by Genentech to the joint venture were actually on leave from Genentech. To ensure that these managers' loyalties were not divided between Genentech and the joint venture, Corning requested that they resign from Genentech. Once they did, the performance of the joint venture improved rapidly.[23]

In isolated cases incorporating a joint venture may not be possible or desirable. For example, local restrictions on corporations may be so stringent or burdensome that incorporating is not optimal. The partners in these cases usually choose to operate under a limited partnership arrangement. In a limited partnership one firm is the managing partner and assumes full financial responsibility for the venture, regardless of the amount of its own investment. The other partner (or partners) has liability limited to its own investment. Obviously, such arrangements are riskier for the managing partner.

Public-Private Venture.   A special form of joint venture, a **public-private venture**, is one that involves a partnership between a privately owned firm and a government. Such an arrangement may be created under any of several circumstances:

1. When the government of a country controls a resource it wants developed, it may enlist the assistance of a firm that has expertise related to the resource. For example, South American countries have used several foreign lumber firms, such as Weyerhaeuser, to assist in the development of the countries' forests and surrounding lands. A similar pattern exists in the discovery, exploration, and development of oil fields. National governments that control access to and ownership of oil fields may lack the technical expertise to drill for and manage the extraction of crude oil reserves. International oil firms, on the other hand, possess the requisite knowledge and expertise but may lack the necessary drilling rights. A common result is a joint venture in which the government grants drilling rights, and the private oil firms provide capital and expertise. For example, in the late 1990s the government of the Ivory Coast formed a venture with Canada's Ranger Oil Ltd. and Gulf Canada to explore and develop prospective oil fields in the African country's coastal waters.[24]

2. A firm may pursue a public-private venture if a particular country does not allow wholly owned foreign operations. If the firm cannot locate a suitable local partner, the firm may invite the government itself to participate in a joint venture, or the government may request an ownership share. Public-private ventures are typical in the oil industry. In assessing the opportunities and drawbacks of such a venture, a firm should consider the various aspects of the political and legal environments it will be facing. Foremost among these aspects is the stability of the government. In a politically unstable country the

current government may be replaced with another, and the firm may face serious challenges. At best the venture will be considered less important by the new government because of the venture's association with the old government. At worst the firm's investment may be completely wiped out, its assets seized, and its operation shut down. However, if negotiations are handled properly and if the local government is relatively stable, public-private ventures can be quite beneficial. The government may act benignly and allow the firm to run the joint venture. The government also may use its position to protect its own investment—and therefore that of its partner—by restricting competing business activity.

3. A firm entering a country with a centrally planned economy may have no choice but to enlist governmental support because such a government often limits the freedom of both domestic and foreign firms. In this case the firm should ensure that it thoroughly understands the expectations and commitments of the host country's government. These concerns are most obvious in China. Because of the vast size and growth prospects of the Chinese market, many firms are interested in investment opportunities there, and joint ventures with state-owned firms have been the most common mode of entry for MNCs. Many Western firms have prospered through such arrangements. For example, Shanghai Bell, Alcatel's joint venture with the Ministry of Post and Telecommunications, has captured more than half the market for switching equipment in the booming Chinese telecommunications market, much to the chagrin of Alcatel's traditional rivals, Siemens and Lucent Technologies.

   However, other Western firms have had their share of troubles with these arrangements, prompting a bitter joke among expatriates in China: "What qualities should you look for in a joint venture partner?" "One who never comes to the office." For example, Unilever's joint venture partner in Shanghai continued to sell its own brand of detergent, White Cat, in competition with the Unilever product, Omo, produced by the joint venture. The partner also copied Omo's formula and packaged the detergent in a box that copycatted Omo's. Similarly, Daimler-Benz signed an agreement in 1995 to establish a joint venture with state-owned Nanfang South China Motor Corporation to build minivans. Two years later, nothing had been done as the two partners bickered over a variety of issues. Nanfang, for example, wanted to assemble the minivans at two plant sites, while Daimler-Benz officials fought for a single plant to capture economies of scale.[25]

Joint Management Considerations

Further issues and questions are associated with how a strategic alliance will be managed. In general there are three means that may be used to jointly manage a strategic alliance (see Fig. 12.3): shared management agreements, assigned arrangements, and delegated arrangements.

Under a **shared management agreement** each partner fully and actively participates in managing the alliance. The partners run the alliance, and their managers regularly pass on instructions and details to the alliance's managers. The alliance managers have limited authority of their own and must defer most decisions to managers from the parent firms. This type of agreement requires a high level of coordination and near-perfect agreement between the participating partners. Thus it is the most difficult to maintain and the one most prone to conflict among the partners. An example of a joint venture operating under a shared management agreement is one formed by Coca-Cola and France's Groupe Danone to distribute Coke's Minute Maid orange juice in Europe and Latin America. This joint venture combines Danone's distribution network and production facilities (Danone supplies between 15 and 30 percent of the dairy products

FIGURE 12.3

Managing Strategic Alliances

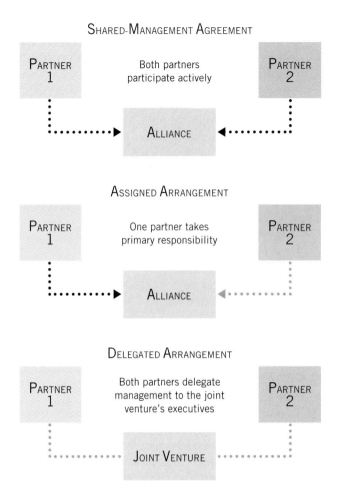

SHARED-MANAGEMENT AGREEMENT

PARTNER 1 — Both partners participate actively — PARTNER 2 → ALLIANCE ←

ASSIGNED ARRANGEMENT

PARTNER 1 — One partner takes primary responsibility — PARTNER 2 → ALLIANCE ←

DELEGATED ARRANGEMENT

PARTNER 1 — Both partners delegate management to the joint venture's executives — PARTNER 2 — JOINT VENTURE

sold by supermarkets in Europe and Latin America) with the Minute Maid brand name. The joint venture operates under a shared management arrangement: Each company supplies three members of the joint venture's board of directors. Danone is responsible for the joint venture's operations, while Coke controls its marketing and finance.[26]

Under an **assigned arrangement** one partner assumes primary responsibility for the operations of the strategic alliance. For example, GM has a 67-percent stake in a joint venture with Raba, a Hungarian truck, engine, and tractor manufacturer and has assumed management control over the venture's operations.[27] Boeing controls the overall operations of its strategic alliance with Fuji, Mitsubishi, and Kawasaki for the design and production of Boeing's 777 commercial aircraft. Under an assigned arrangement management of the alliance is greatly simplified because the dominant partner has the power to set its own agenda for the new unit, break ties among decision makers, and even overrule its partner(s). Of course, these actions may create conflict, but they keep the alliance from becoming paralyzed, which may happen if equal partners cannot agree on a decision.

Under a **delegated arrangement**, which is reserved for joint ventures, the partners agree not to get involved in ongoing operations and delegate management control to the executives of the joint venture itself. These executives may be specifically hired to run the new operation or may be transferred from the participating firms. They are responsible for the day-to-day decision making and management of the venture and for implementing its strategy. Thus they have real power and the autonomy to make significant decisions and are much less accountable to managers in the partner firms. For example, both American Motors and the Beijing Automotive Works contributed experienced managers to the operation of Beijing Jeep so that its management team could learn both modern automobile assembly operations and operating conditions in China. Moreover, these managers were given responsibility for the joint venture's operations.

PITFALLS OF STRATEGIC ALLIANCES ‹

Regardless of the care and deliberation a firm puts into constructing a strategic alliance, it still must consider limitations and pitfalls. Figure 12.4 summarizes five fundamental sources of problems that often threaten the viability of strategic alliances: (1) incompatibility of partners, (2) access to information, (3) conflicts over distributing earnings, (4) loss of autonomy, and (5) changing circumstances.

Incompatibility of Partners

Incompatibility among the partners of a strategic alliance is a primary cause of the failure of such arrangements. At times incompatibility can lead to outright conflict, although typically it merely leads to poor performance of the alliance. We noted earlier in the chapter the example of the conflict between Siemens's engineering-oriented management and General Electric Corporation's financially oriented management. Incompatibility can stem from differences in corporate culture, national culture, goals and objectives, or virtually any other fundamental dimension linking the two partners.

In many cases compatibility problems can be anticipated if the partners carefully discuss and analyze the reasons why each is entering into the alliance in the first place. A useful starting point may be a meeting between top managers of the two partners to discuss their mutual interests, goals, and beliefs about strategy. How the managers are able to work together during such a meeting may be a critical clue to their ability to cooperate in a strategic alliance. Obviously, if the partners cannot agree on basic issues—such as how much decision-making power to delegate to the alliance's business unit, what the alliance's strategy should be, how it is to be organized, or how it should be staffed—compromise will probably be difficult to achieve, and the alliance is unlikely to succeed. For example, a marketing alliance between AT&T and Italy's Olivetti announced with great fanfare in the mid-1990s quickly failed after the firms could not reach agreement on a marketing strategy, what they wanted the alliance to accomplish, and how they planned to work together.

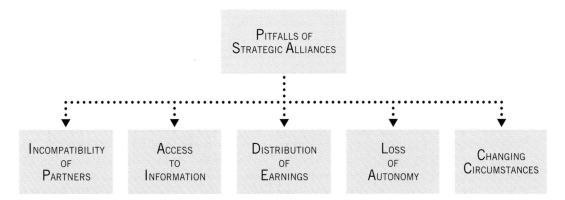

FIGURE 12.4   **Pitfalls of Strategic Alliances**

> Beijing Jeep, a joint venture between American Motors Company (now part of DaimlerChrysler) and municipally owned Beijing Auto Works, has lost money because of conflicts between the partners. AMC believes the factory is overstaffed, whereas its Chinese partner wishes to preserve assembly line jobs.

Access to Information

Limited access to information is another drawback of many strategic alliances. For a collaboration to work effectively, one partner (or both) may have to provide the other with information it would prefer to keep secret. It is often difficult to identify such needs ahead of time; thus a firm may enter into an agreement not anticipating having to share certain information. When the reality of the situation becomes apparent, the firm may have to be forthcoming with the information or else compromise the effectiveness of the collaboration.[28]

For example, Unisys, a U.S. computer firm, negotiated a joint venture with Hitachi, a Japanese electronics firm. Only after the venture was well underway did Unisys realize that it would have to provide Hitachi with most of the technical specifications Unisys used to build computers. Although Unisys managers reluctantly gave Hitachi the information, they feared they were compromising their own firm's competitiveness. An alliance between Ford and Mazda to collaborate on the design of the new Ford Escort almost stalled when Mazda officials would not allow their Ford counterparts to visit Mazda's research laboratory. After several weeks of arguing, a compromise was eventually reached whereby Ford engineers could enter the facility but only for a limited time.

Conflicts over Distributing Earnings

An obvious limitation of strategic alliances relates to the distribution of earnings. Because the partners share risks and costs, they also share profits. For example, General Mills and Nestlé split the profits from their European joint venture on a 50/50 basis. This aspect of collaborative arrangements is known ahead of time and is virtually always negotiated as part of the original agreement.

However, there are other financial considerations beyond the basic distribution of earnings that can cause disagreement. The partners also must agree on the proportion of the joint earnings that will be distributed to themselves as opposed to being reinvested in the business, the accounting procedures that will be used to calculate earnings or profits, and the way transfer pricing will be handled. For example, in the mid-1990s Rubbermaid ended its joint venture to manufacture and distribute rubber and plastic houseware products throughout Europe, North Africa, and the Middle East because its local partner, the Dutch chemical company DSM Group NV, resisted reinvesting profits to develop new products to expand the joint venture's sales as Rubbermaid preferred.[29]

Loss of Autonomy

Another pitfall of a strategic alliance is the potential loss of autonomy. Just as firms share risks and profits, they also share control, thereby limiting what each can do. Most attempts to introduce new products or services, change the way the alliance does business, or introduce any other significant organizational change first must be discussed and negotiated. For example, as part of its contract with General Mills, Nestlé had to agree that if the joint venture were ever terminated, Nestlé could not enter the North American cereal market for at least 10 years.

At the extreme a strategic alliance even may be the first step toward a takeover. In the early 1980s the Japanese firm Fujitsu negotiated a strategic alliance with International Computers, Ltd. (ICL), a British computer firm. After nine years of working together, Fujitsu bought 80 percent of ICL. One survey of 150 terminated strategic alliances found that over three-fourths ended because a Japanese firm had taken over its non-Japanese partner.[30] In other cases partners may accuse each other of opportunistic behavior, that is, trying to take unfair advantage of each other. For example, a joint venture between The Walt Disney Company and Sky Television, a British pay-TV channel operator, broke down after Sky accused Disney of deliberately delaying the supply of promised programming. Disney in turn accused Sky of proceeding too hastily and without consulting Disney.[31]

Changing Circumstances

Changing circumstances also may affect the viability of a strategic alliance. The economic conditions that motivated the cooperative arrangement may no longer exist, or technological advances may have rendered the agreement obsolete. For example, in the mid-1990s Ford Motor Co. and Volkswagen disbanded their 1987 joint venture, Autolatina, which was the biggest car manufacturer in South America at the time. When Autolatina was established, the economies of Brazil and its main regional trading partners were being battered by inflation and the debt crisis of the 1980s. Both companies thought they could best weather these economic storms by combining their South American operations. However, economic reforms in Brazil and Argentina and the reduction in trade barriers due to the Mercosur Accord and the Uruguay Round boosted the demand for cars in the region. Ford executives increasingly viewed Autolatina as an impediment to implementation of Ford's new globalization strategy. Because Volkswagen executives also believed they could do better if they were free of their partnership, the joint venture was terminated by mutual consent.[32]

CHAPTER REVIEW

Summary

Strategic alliances, in which two or more firms agree to cooperate for their mutual benefit, are becoming increasingly popular in international business. A joint venture, a common type of strategic alliance, involves two or more firms joining together to create a new entity that is legally separate and distinct from its parents.

Strategic alliances offer several benefits to firms that use them. First, the alliances facilitate market entry. Second, they allow the partners to share risks. Third, they make it easier for each partner to gain new knowledge and expertise from the other partner(s). Finally, they foster synergy and competitive advantage among the partners.

The scope of strategic alliances can vary significantly. Comprehensive alliances involve a full array of business activities and operations. Functional alliances involving only one aspect of a business, such as production, marketing, finance, or R&D, are also common.

The decision to form a strategic alliance needs to be based on a number of different considerations. Selecting a partner is critically important and must take into account compatibility, the nature of the potential partner's products or services, the relative safety of the alliance, and the learning potential of the alliance. Selecting a form of organization is also very important to the success of the alliance. A special form of strategic alliance involves public and private partners. The management structure of the strategic alliance also must be given careful consideration.

Partners in a strategic alliance must be aware of several pitfalls that can undermine the success of their cooperative arrangement. These include incompatibility of the partners, access to information, conflicts over distributing earnings, loss of autonomy, and changing circumstances.

Review Questions

1. What are the basic differences between a joint venture and other types of strategic alliances?
2. Why have strategic alliances grown in popularity in recent years?
3. What are the basic benefits partners are likely to gain from their strategic alliance? Briefly explain each.

4. What are the basic characteristics of a comprehensive alliance? What form is it likely to take?

5. What are the four common types of functional alliances? Briefly explain each.

6. What is an R&D consortium?

7. What factors should be considered in selecting a strategic-alliance partner?

8. What are the three basic ways of managing a strategic alliance?

9. Under what circumstances might a strategic alliance be undertaken by public and private partners?

10. What are the potential pitfalls of strategic alliances?

Questions for Discussion

1. What are the relative advantages and disadvantages of joint ventures compared to other types of strategic alliances?

2. Assume you are a manager for a large international firm, which has decided to enlist a foreign partner in a strategic alliance and has asked you to be involved in the collaboration. What effects, if any, might the decision to structure the collaboration as a joint venture have on you personally and on your career?

3. What factors could conceivably cause a sharp decline in the number of new strategic alliances formed?

4. Could a firm conceivably undertake too many strategic alliances at one time? Why or why not?

5. Can you think of any foreign products you use that may have been marketed in this country as a result of a strategic alliance? What are they?

6. What are some of the issues involved in a firm trying to learn from a strategic alliance partner without giving out too much valuable information of its own?

7. Why would a firm decide to enter a new market on its own rather than using a strategic alliance?

8. What are some of the similarities and differences between forming a strategic alliance with a firm from your home country and forming one with a firm from a foreign country?

9. The joint venture between General Mills and Nestlé was worked out in only 23 days. Most experts, however, argue that a firm should spend a long time getting to know a prospective partner before proceeding with an alliance. What factors might account for CPW being an exception to this general rule?

10. Otis Elevator has sought to obtain first-mover advantages by quickly entering emerging markets with the help of local partners. This strategy has proven very successful for Otis. Should all firms adopt this strategy? Under what conditions is this strategy most likely to be successful?

BUILDING GLOBAL SKILLS

Break into small groups of four to five people. Assume your group is the executive committee (that is, the top managers) of Resteaze, Inc. Resteaze is a large manufacturer of mattresses, box springs, and water beds. The publicly traded firm is among the largest in the U.S. bedding market. It operates 15 factories, employs over 5,000 people, and last year generated $20 million in profits on sales of $380 million. Resteaze products are sold through department stores, furniture stores, and specialty shops and have the reputation of being of good quality and medium priced.

Your committee is thinking about entering the European bedding market. You know little about the European market, so you are thinking about forming a joint venture. Your committee has identified three possible candidates for such an arrangement.

One candidate is Bedrest. Bedrest is a French firm that makes bedding. Unfortunately, Bedrest products have a poor reputation in Europe, and most of its sales stem from the fact that its products are exceptionally cheap. However, there are possibilities for growth in Eastern Europe. The consultant who recommended Bedrest suggests that your higher-quality products would mesh well with Bedrest's cheaper ones. Bedrest is known to be having financial difficulties because of declining sales. However, the consultant thinks the firm will soon turn things around.

A second candidate is Home Furnishings, Inc., a German firm that manufactures high-quality furniture. Its line of bedroom furniture (headboards, dressers, chests, etc.) is among the most popular in Europe. The firm is known to be interested in entering the U.S. furniture market. Home Furnishings is a privately owned company and is assumed to have a strong financial position. Because of its prices, however, the firm is not expected to be able to compete effectively in Eastern Europe.

Finally, Pacific Enterprises, Inc., is a huge Japanese conglomerate that is just now entering the European market. The firm does not have any current operations in Europe but has enormous financial reserves to put behind any new undertaking it might decide to pursue. Its major product lines are machine tools, auto replacement parts, communications equipment, and consumer electronics.

Your task is to assess the relative advantages and disadvantages of each of these prospective partners for Resteaze. The European market is important to you, this is your first venture abroad, and you want the highest probability for success. After assessing each candidate, rank the three in order of their relative attractiveness to your firm.

Follow-Up Questions

1. How straightforward or ambiguous was the task of evaluating and ranking the three alternatives?

2. Determine and discuss the degree of agreement or disagreement among the various groups in the class.

WORKING WITH THE WEB:
BUILDING GLOBAL INTERNET SKILLS

Implementing Strategic Alliances

This exercise will give you Internet experience in learning more about foreign government regulation of strategic alliances and sources of information regarding potential strategic partners. As a first step, read the exercise scenario that follows.

Exercise Scenario

You are the marketing manager for a medium-size computer company. Your firm buys components from other suppliers, assembles computers using those components, and then markets the computers directly to small businesses using print advertising, telephone sales, and direct mail. One of the keys to your firm's success is that the company has developed its own software packages. The software works with existing products like those marketed by Microsoft but provides extra applications for small businesses, independent contractors, professional specialists like lawyers and doctors, and so forth.

Your CEO wants to begin a slow expansion into foreign markets. To minimize language difficulties; she believes that the best place to start is the United Kingdom, Canada, or Australia. The CEO's idea is to locate an existing computer company in one of those countries and discuss with its owners the idea of a strategic alliance. Your firm would modify its software for the foreign market and provide the software to your partner in exchange for the partner agreeing to help you sell your computers in that market.

With this information as context, do the following:

1. Use the Internet to learn as much as possible about government regulations in each of the three countries that (a) may affect your business and (b) may affect the relative attractiveness of each market.

2. From the information you gathered on the Internet, select a market for entry.

3. Use the Internet again to find one or more potential strategic partners in the country you have chosen to enter.

WE INVITE YOU TO VISIT THIS BOOK'S
COMPANION WEB SITE AT www.prenhall.com/griffin

IN THE NEWS

1. Ford and General Motors are both hoping to improve their position in the Asian car market by means of strategic alliances, among other strategies. Use the search feature on the *Financial Times* homepage (*www.ft.com*) to locate recent articles about either company's efforts to form or manage strategic alliances in Asia. What does the U.S. firm bring to the partnership? What do the Asian firms bring? What role will each firm play in the alliance?

2. The United States and Yugoslavia are moving to renew diplomatic relations. From the *Financial Times* homepage launch a search on the word "Yugoslavia." Read several recent articles about the country's economic growth and prospects. You can also use the "News" tab to access "Country Surveys" for more information about Yugoslavia. Based on the information you gather, what kinds of U.S. companies might be looking for strategic partners in Yugoslavia in the near future and which markets might they want to serve? What difficulties will the companies face, and what advantages might they gain? How can a U.S. company looking for strategic partners best present itself to Yugoslavian firms?

CLOSING CASE

Sri Lanka Keeps Victoria's Secret

Dian Gomes strides through the factory he runs on the tropical island of Sri Lanka, introducing some of his managers. Among them: a recently recruited investment banker, a mathematician with a doctorate from Yale, and a physicist who measured the electromagnetic field generated by honeybees.

"And now they're making panties," giggles Mr. Gomes, managing director of Slimline Ltd., a leading supplier to Victoria's Secret. Slimline, a Sri Lankan-U.S.-British venture, produces much of the lingerie that turned on millions of men during ... Victoria's Secret Internet fashion show. Something else turns on Mr. Gomes. "I don't think any other apparel factory has so much brainpower," he says.

Slimline's total work force of about 1,400 includes 70 university graduates, some with advance degrees. In a region rife with exploited labor and primitive work conditions, Slimline uses first-rate technology in an ergonomically advance environment. Slimline's machinists, virtually all women, stitch in the relative comfort of air conditioning. They use pneumatic sewing machines instead of manual models, and sit on contoured, upholstered office chairs rather than stools.

In the factory's management wing a batch of new hires, including the honeybee specialist, are installing a $4-million computer system. Slimline is the first Sri Lankan company of any kind to buy such a sophisticated system to monitor production and distribution and to handle electronic commerce that puts the factory in direct contact with U.S. retailers.

Slimline is the child of two high-powered Western suppliers and a local family-run firm. It is one-third-owned by **Courtaulds Textiles** PLC of London, which supplies Marks & Spencer. The U.S. partner is Mast Industries Inc., the Andover, Massachusetts, sourcing division of **Limited** Inc. (which also is majority owner of the company that operates Victoria's Secret). Mast is the largest U.S. investor in Sri Lanka and has more joint ventures here—36, employing some 16,000 people—than in any other country. Sri Lanka is now Mast's top hub for making lingerie.

Slimline's Sri Lankan partner is MAS Holdings Ltd., MAS is a family-owned outfit that has built one of the country's biggest businesses in less than a decade. In part it has done so by wooing professionals, such as Mr. Gomes, an accountant who was looking for new challenges when MAS's chairman approached him in 1990 with what seemed to be an ambitious goal: to quadruple sales to $24 million in six years.

"I started sweating," recalls Mr. Gomes, who is 41 years old. "I had never seen a garment machine." Yet the company achieved its target in three years and has grown from two factories to 11, with sales of $150 million in 1998. (MAS won't disclose profit figures.)

Slimline, founded in 1993, is Sri Lanka's largest apparel exporter, churning out 500,000 pieces of sportswear and baby clothes and 1.5 million panties a month. Matching bras are made nearby at Bodyline Ltd., owned by MAS, Mast, and a German partner.

After falling into the garment business, Mr. Gomes is gleefully bringing other unlikely converts along. Slimline's controller, Sanjay Senanayake, says his parents thought he was "mad" to quit a respected Sri Lankan bank for an obscure garment factory. "The bank wasn't a total meritocracy. Here, I feel there is potential," says the 32-year-old.

Given a free hand by his bosses, Mr. Gomes has introduced a smorgasbord of business practices absorbed on study stints abroad, "This is one thing we learned from the Japanese," he says, pointing to a tidy, color-coded inventory board off the shop floor. Another is the *kaizen* method of working in clusters rather than in one production line.

Mr. Gomes has adapted team-building concepts picked up during executive-training stints at Harvard and Wharton business schools, even producing an in-house motivational film set to the Byrds' 1960s hit, "Turn! Turn! Turn!" He reinforces teamwork with an egalitarian structure that is uncommon locally. All employees wear name tags with their first names; managers work regular shifts in quality control; and a new gym, decked out with exercise machines and a full-time trainer, is open to executives and seamstresses alike. "You have to make this place fun to work at," says Mr. Gomes.

But shop-floor work at Slimline isn't a lark. International benchmarks spur Slimline's workers toward faster, more efficient output. In one team a seamstress rushes to stitch hems on Marks & Spencer infant body suits in her allotted 18 seconds. Each suit should take four minutes to complete, and the team aims to make 200 every hour. In a separate unit a woman named Kumari says she earned a 1,500-rupee ($35) bonus last month, on top of her salary of 2,900 rupees, because she and her teammates produced at 120 percent efficiency.

"The pressure is no problem," she says, smiling at Mr. Gomes.

Work and safety conditions at Slimline are among the best in Sri Lanka. A state-of-the-art machine cuts most of the fabric, and where it's done manually, workers wear protective metal-mesh gloves that cost $170 a pair—too much of a splurge for many garment makers. Indeed, says Mr. Gomes, some rivals have chided MAS for air-conditioning its factories.

Mr. Gomes also hopes to set standards in labor relations. Slimline salaries start about 7 percent higher than the minimum wage.... Employees, though, aren't unionized—a sore point for international labor groups. Still, annual raises usually well exceed inflation, and a management-employee council hears gripes. One recent worker victory: Slimline agreed to subsidize new public bus routes to make commuting easier.

"We feel this is our company," says Indrani, a 26-year-old workers' representative who was first impressed by Mr. Gomes's willingness to have tea with employees. Mr. Gomes, noting that Slimline is Indrani's first job, plays down the compliment. "She would appreciate me even more if she had worked somewhere else," he says.

Case Questions

1. Slimline Ltd. is a joint venture among three companies—a local Sri Lankan firm, a British firm, and a U.S. firm. What are the benefits of this joint venture to each of these companies? Why did

each choose to form a joint venture rather than operate its own wholly owned subsidiary?

2. From the perspective of each of the partners, are there any potential pitfalls to joining this joint venture?

3. Although many human rights advocates are critical of the working conditions found in many textile factories, Slimline appears to have gone out of its way to provide its workers with first-rate working conditions. Why do you think Slimline has done this? Do you agree with this approach?

Source: Adapted from Jonathan Karp, "Sri Lanka Keeps Victoria's Secret," *Wall Street Journal*, July 13, 1999, pp. B1, B4.

CHAPTER

Unilever Matches Strategy and Structure

Unilever is not exactly a household word. Hence, it may come as a surprise to learn that Unilever is the world's second largest packaged consumer goods company; with $45 billion in annual sales it trails only U.S. giant Procter & Gamble in this industry. Among its best-known brand names are Lipton, Dove, Helene Curtis, Vaseline, and Q-tips. Unilever's major product groups include margarine and oils, frozen foods, drinks, and personal-care products. Unilever is also the world's largest ice cream maker.

The firm's ownership and management structure are unique. Unilever is jointly headquartered in London and Rotterdam. It is operated by two different holding companies, one based in each of these two cities. The holding companies have separate stock listings but identical boards of directors; a single management team runs the entire enterprise. Over the years Unilever occasionally has set up other businesses to support its consumer products operations. For example, the firm established a chemical unit to process the oils it uses to make margarine. At the time managers believed this route provided them with a predictable and controllable source of materials. Fragrances and food flavorings operations were created for the same reason. In similar fashion Unilever often has grown by

> "...allowing Unilever to focus all of its **attention** on **competing** with Procter & Gamble."

Organization Design for International Business

After studying this chapter, you should be able to:

> Define and discuss the nature of international organization design.

> Identify and describe the initial impacts of international business activity on organization design.

> Identify and describe five advanced forms of international organization design and discuss hybrid global designs.

> Identify and describe related issues in global organization design.

> Discuss the role of corporate culture in international business.

> Describe the management of change in international business.

acquiring other consumer products businesses, many of which had supporting operations as well.

Unilever eventually evolved to the point where it was structured around five basic business groups: food products, personal-care products, soap/laundry products, cosmetics/perfume/hair products, and specialty chemicals. As the company continued to expand, however, this arrangement grew increasingly unwieldy. The methods and operations used to package, distribute, and promote the products and brands in the four consumer products groups were all very similar. Managers could be transferred across businesses easily, and knowledge about local market conditions in different countries was freely exchanged.

The specialty chemical group, however, was an altogether different story. Because it had no consumer products, only indirect linkages existed between its operations and those in the consumer products groups. For example, in some markets the chemical companies made chemicals that were then "sold" to Unilever's consumer products businesses. These businesses in turn used the chemicals to create their consumer products for resale around the world. By 1997 Unilever's board of directors had grown concerned about the firm's seeming inability to gain market share from Procter & Gamble. In market after market Procter & Gamble brands had the largest share, and Unilever was a solid but consistent second. A new CEO, Niall FitzGerald, was hired to remedy this situation and to improve Unilever's financial performance.

After carefully studying Unilever's operations, FitzGerald concluded that the firm's specialty chemical businesses were part of the problem. For one thing, they did not meet the firm's profitability targets. For another, some of the chemicals they were making actually could be bought on the open market for the same—and sometimes lower—prices. Finally, the firm had higher administrative costs due to the lack of synergy between its dissimilar units (chemical and consumer products).

As a result of these conclusions, Unilever executives decided to sell the specialty chemical units. The sale would eliminate inefficiencies created by the firm's structure. It also would generate cash that could be used to reduce debt and to finance new acquisitions in Unilever's core business areas. FitzGerald argued that the new structure would allow Unilever to focus all its attention on competing with Procter & Gamble and other firms in the consumer products markets. Accordingly, in 1997 Unilever negotiated the sale of its specialty chemical group to Britain's Imperial Chemical Industries PLC for a price of approximately $8 billion.

Part of the proceeds from this sale were used to acquire Ben & Jerry's Homemade Inc., a quirky ice cream maker, and SlimFast Foods Company, a leading diet products firm. However, managers soon realized that selling the chemicals business and buying new food products businesses were not really addressing Unilever's fundamental problems, which were its slow decision making and weak control of worldwide marketing strategies. As a result, in 2000 FitzGerald announced another major restructuring of Unilever, reorganizing it into two units rather than four. One unit would be responsible for all food products and the other for all home and personal-care products. Each unit was then assigned its own chief executive responsible for all its global operations.[1]

Unilever's efforts to sell its specialty chemical operations represent an important strategic decision. The underlying basis for that decision was the firm's organization design. Developed over time in somewhat piecemeal fashion, the firm's design came to represent a burden in the marketplace and a barrier to effective competition. Thus the new CEO decided to change the firm's design to improve the organization's ability to compete in international markets.

In this chapter we describe the various organization designs that international businesses use to achieve their strategic goals. Because these designs typically evolve along a well-defined path as firms become more international, we first discuss the initial forms of organization design firms use as they begin to internationalize their operations.[2] We then analyze the more advanced forms of organization design that firms adopt as they broaden their participation in international business to become true multinational corporations (MNCs). Next we discuss several related issues in global organization design. We conclude by describing two other aspects of organization design: corporate culture and change.

› THE NATURE OF INTERNATIONAL ORGANIZATION DESIGN

Organization design (sometimes called *organization structure*) is the overall pattern of structural components and configurations used to manage the total organization. Organization design is the basic vehicle through which strategy is ultimately implemented and through which the work of the organization is actually accomplished.

A firm cannot function unless its various structural components are appropriately assembled.[3] Through its design the firm does four things. First, it allocates organizational resources. Second, it assigns tasks to its employees. Third, it informs those employees about the firm's rules, procedures, and expectations about the employees' job performances. Fourth, it collects and transmits information necessary for problem solving and decision making.[4] This last task is particularly important for large MNCs, which must manage sharing vast amounts of information between corporate headquarters and subsidiaries and staff spread worldwide.

Early studies of organization design sought to identify the single best design that all organizations should use. The pioneering work of the German sociologist Max Weber, for example, described a so-called **bureaucratic design**, which was based on rational rules, regulations, and standard operating procedures.[5] Later research, however, suggested there was no one best way to design an organization. Eventually, stimulated by British researchers Joan Woodward, Tom Burns, G. M. Stalker, Derek Pugh, and David Hickson, managers came to learn there are many different ways to effectively design organizations.[6] Certain key elements determine the appropriate design for any given organization, including the firm's size, strategy, technology, and environment, as well as the cultures of the countries in which the firm operates. Various theories and research suggest that the appropriate form of organization design for any particular company is contingent on one or more of these factors.[7]

For example, often a firm that sells brand-name consumer goods customized for markets in different host countries will structure itself geographically so that regional managers knowledgeable about the idiosyncratic needs of local customers will be empowered with appropriate decision-making authority. Procter & Gamble is an example of a firm that used this approach for many years. In contrast, a firm that seeks manufacturing efficiencies may organize itself along product lines to utilize its lowest-cost production facilities, regardless of their geographical location. Black & Decker has done this.

However, an organization's structure is not created and then left alone; organization design is an ongoing process. Indeed, managers change the design of their firms almost continually. For example, shortly after Unilever sold off its specialty chemical operations, it combined the U.S. operations of its Cheesebrough-Pond's, Helene Curtis, and Lever Brothers affiliates to form a new subsidiary, Unilever Home & Personal Care USA. By so doing, Unilever believed it could achieve economies of scale and scope in marketing and distributing its products in the U.S. market. One study found that most firms and divisions of large firms make moderate design changes about once a year and one or more major design changes every four to five years.[8] These changes often result from changes in a firm's strategy because an important characteristic of a successful firm is its ability to match its strategy with a compatible organization design, as Unilever has sought to do.[9]

INITIAL IMPACTS OF INTERNATIONAL ACTIVITY ON ORGANIZATION DESIGN

As a domestic firm expands internationally, it will change its organization design to accommodate its increased international activities. To see how this happens, we will start by considering a domestic firm that has no international sales. This is not an unreasonable starting point. Many entrepreneurs, particularly in larger economies such as those of the United States, Japan, and Germany, start new firms in response to some perceived need in the local market; they give little immediate thought to the international marketplace. Also, many small, domestically oriented firms enter international markets passively through indirect exporting, as discussed in Chapter 11. Such a firm may sell its product to a domestic customer, and that customer then incorporates the product into a good that it distributes in foreign markets. Alternatively, a domestic customer may purchase the firm's product for one of the customer's foreign subsidiaries, or a domestic purchasing agent of a foreign wholesaler may order the firm's product. Because such indirect exporting occurs as a routine part of the firm's domestic business, the firm's organization design need not change at all.

The Corollary Approach

Now assume that the hypothetical firm just described begins to engage in direct exporting on a modest level. Its initial response to international sales and orders is the **corollary approach**, whereby the firm delegates responsibility for processing such orders to individuals within an existing department, such as finance or marketing. Under this approach the firm continues to use its existing domestic organization design. This approach is typical of a firm that has only a very small level of international activity.

For example, Texas-based O.I. International produces highly specialized equipment to analyze and monitor oil-drilling activities. In its early years O.I. had little need to think internationally because oil-drilling activity in Texas and elsewhere in the United States was booming. However, as oil field activity slowed in the United States, O.I. needed new sources of revenue. One day CEO John Huey was reading a trade magazine and noticed an announcement of an industrial exhibition in Japan. He quickly made arrangements to attend the show to promote O.I. products. During the show he contracted with JASKO International, a Japanese equipment firm, to distribute O.I. products in Pacific Asia. Because initial sales were relatively small, and because Huey had negotiated the agreement himself, he initially handled sales to JASKO through his own office. There was certainly no need to overhaul the firm's structure to deal with this level of international involvement.

The Export Department

As a firm's export sales become more significant, its next step usually is to create a separate export department. The export department takes responsibility for overseeing international operations, marketing products, processing orders, working with foreign distributors, and arranging financing when necessary. Initially, the head of the export department may report to a senior marketing or finance executive. As exports grow in importance, however, the export department may achieve equality on the organization chart with finance, marketing, human resources, and the other functional areas of the firm. O.I., for example, eventually created a small export department—comprising one manager and an assistant—to handle its exports to Japan. Figure 13.1 illustrates how an export department fits into a typical small firm.

The International Division

When selling to foreign customers is not fundamentally different from selling to domestic ones, the export department may get by with knowing only a little about foreign markets. However, as international activities increase, firms often find that an export department no longer serves their needs. Once a firm begins to station employees abroad or establish foreign subsidiaries to produce, distribute, and/or market its products, managerial responsibilities, coordination complexities, and information requirements all swell beyond the export department's capabilities and expertise. Familiarity with foreign markets becomes more important and new methods for organizing may be required.

Firms respond to the challenges of controlling their burgeoning international business by changing their organization design through the creation of an international division that specializes in managing foreign operations. The international

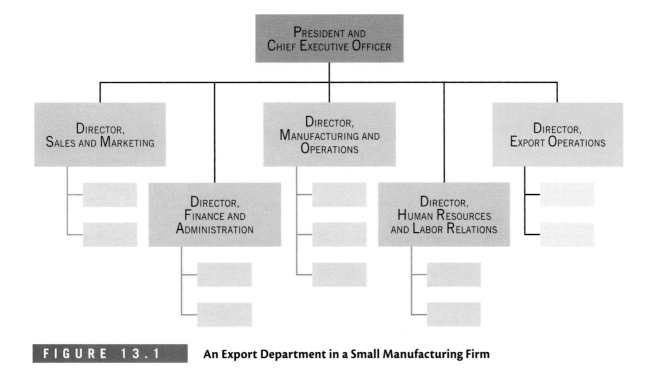

FIGURE 13.1   An Export Department in a Small Manufacturing Firm

division allows a firm to concentrate resources and create specialized programs targeted on international business activity while simultaneously keeping that activity segregated from the firm's ongoing domestic activities.

Brazil's Banco Excel Economico SA, the oldest private bank in Latin America, uses the international division approach. As Figure 13.2 shows, Banco Excel Economico's organization design emphasizes the bank's product lines—corporate finance and nonfinancial investments, retail banking, and corporate banking. The international banking division has equal status with each of these product groups

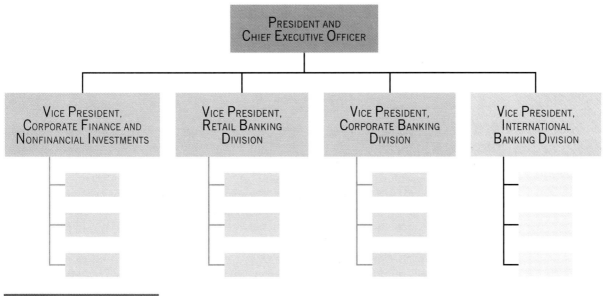

FIGURE 13.2   Banco Excel Economico S.A.'s International Division Design

Wiring the World

E-COMMERCE AND THE WORLD OF PUBLISHING

Germany's Bertelsmann AG is the world's largest book publisher and second largest music distributor, as well as the European market leader in television and magazines. Now the company is using its vast content empire to launch an aggressive expansion into cyberspace. Bertelsmann's CEO, Thomas Middelhoff, got an early start in e-commerce by buying a stake in America Online (AOL) and arranging to deliver content through an AOL partnership. He tried to negotiate a merger with AOL, but Steve Case, AOL's CEO, chose rival media group Time Warner for his merger partner. So Middelhoff retained the content partnership but divested his holdings in AOL Europe and AOL Australia to rethink Bertelsmann's online activities.

After evaluating Bertelsmann's existing Internet businesses, Middelhoff decided that the company's future should be linked to online sales of media content rather than Internet access. As a result of this decision, he sold off Bertelsmann's Internet service provider units and pursued an alliance to participate in a European portal for wireless Internet users. Next, he created a new division, the Bertelsmann E-Commerce Group, as an umbrella for five Internet-related units: the e-commerce unit, covering the company's stake in online book retailer Barnesandnoble.com and its European counterpart, bol.com; the m-commerce unit, covering wireless Web and communications activities; the b-commerce unit, covering broadband and other television activities; BECG Ventures, providing venture capital to new technologies; and the strategic alliances unit, covering partnerships with AOL and other Internet companies.

Finally, Middelhoff addressed the critical management issue of coordination. Traditionally, Bertelsmann's divisions had been given a great deal of independence to encourage initiative and innovation. Realizing that Bertelsmann's plans for online growth required closer coordination, Middelhoff created the new position of chief creative officer, charged with identifying internal opportunities for synergy among the diverse global businesses.

Sources: "Bertelsmann Creates Global E-Commerce Group," *Publishers Weekly*, June 19, 2000, p. 17; "Bertelsmann: Under E-Construction," *The Economist*, June 10, 2000, pp. 69–70; Deborah Cole, "Powerhouse Cyber Services Make 'Net Gain," *Variety*, May 29, 2000, p. 50.

on the organization chart. International division managers are responsible for operating the bank's international branches and foreign-exchange operations and for providing corporate banking and corporate financial services to meet the needs of foreign customers, as well as the international needs of domestic customers. Similarly, "Wiring the World" describes how Bertelsmann AG set up a separate division to facilitate its international e-commerce initiatives.

› GLOBAL ORGANIZATION DESIGNS

As a firm evolves from being domestically oriented with international operations to becoming a true multinational corporation with global aspirations, it typically abandons the international division approach. In place of that division it usually creates a global organization design to achieve synergies among its far-flung operations and to implement its organizational strategy.[10] For example, until recently Aetna maintained a separate division for its small but growing international operations. Because international revenues more than doubled between 1996 and 1999, however, the firm announced plans to eliminate the international division and integrate Aetna's global initiatives into its existing structure. Executives at the firm indicated that their new structure would make it easier to transfer knowledge and technology between international markets.[11] Indeed, the global design adopted by any firm must deal with the need to integrate three types of knowledge to compete effectively internationally:[12]

- *Area knowledge*: Managers must understand the cultural, commercial, social, and economic conditions in each host country market in which the firm does business.

- *Product knowledge*: Managers must comprehend such factors as technological trends, customer needs, and competitive forces affecting the goods the firm produces and sells.

- *Functional knowledge*: Managers must have access to coworkers with expertise in basic business functions such as production, marketing, finance, accounting, human resource management, and information technology.

The five most common forms of global organization design are product, area, functional, customer, and matrix. As we will discuss, each form allows the firm to emphasize one type of knowledge, yet perhaps each also makes it more difficult to incorporate the other types of knowledge into the firm's decision-making processes. Accordingly, the global design the MNC chooses will reflect the relative importance of each of the three types of knowledge in the firm's operations, as well as its need for coordination among its units, the source of its firm-specific advantages, and its managerial philosophy about its position in the world economy.[13]

MNCs typically adopt one of three managerial philosophies that guide their approach to such functions as organization design and marketing. The **ethnocentric approach** is used by firms that operate internationally the same way they do domestically. The **polycentric approach** is used by firms that customize their operations for each foreign market they serve. The **geocentric approach** is used by firms that analyze the needs of their customers worldwide and then adopt standardized operations for all markets they serve. (We discuss these concepts more fully in Chapter 16.)

Global Product Design

The most common form of organization design adopted by MNCs is the global product design. The **global product design** assigns worldwide responsibility for specific products or product groups to separate operating divisions within a firm. This design works best when the firm has diverse product lines or when its product lines are sold in diverse markets, thereby rendering the need for coordination between product lines relatively unimportant. If the products are related, the organization of the firm takes on what is often called an **M-form design**; if the products are unrelated, the design is called an **H-form design**. The M in M-form stands for "multidivisional"—the various divisions of the firm are usually self-contained operations with interrelated activities. The H in H-form stands for "holding," as in "holding company"—the various unrelated businesses function with autonomy and little interdependence. After selling its specialty chemicals group, Unilever became an M-form business because the businesses it chose to retain were all somewhat related to one another.

> The Danone Group uses a global product design. Employees of its dairy products division have the enviable task of taste testing Danone's famous yogurt.

Shougang Corp., one of the largest and oldest state-owned companies in China, provides an example of an H-form organization using a global product design. For over 20 years Shougang has been pursuing a strategy of unrelated diversification, which in turn has resulted in the organization design shown in Figure. 13.3.

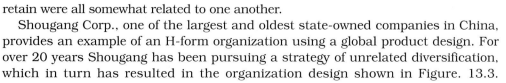

FIGURE 13.3

Shougang Corp.'s Global Product Design

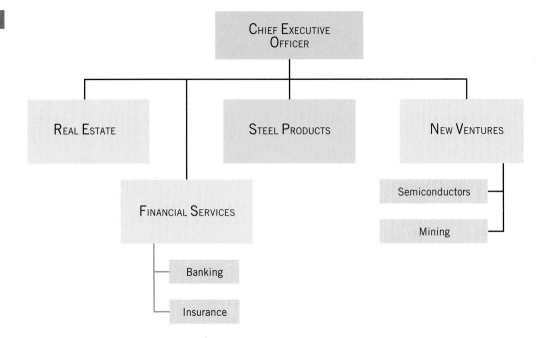

Shougang's core business is the production of various steel products, and steel remains a central product group within the company. Shougang also has several operations in various financial markets and groups these together in its financial products group. Examples include Canadian Eastern Life Assurance and Huaxia Bank. Another product group consists of various real estate projects and developments. Finally, its new ventures group includes such businesses as a semiconductor joint venture with Japan's NEC and a mining operation.[14]

Pennsylvania's Harsco Corporation also is organized according to its major product groups—industrial services and building products, engineered products, and defense. Each group is responsible for managing domestic and international production, marketing, and distribution for its individual product lines.

The global product design has several advantages:

1. Because a division focuses on a single product or product group, the division managers gain expertise in all aspects of the product or products, better enabling them to compete globally. In Harsco's case one of the firm's competitive advantages lies in its specialized knowledge of how to convert steel mill waste into useful products. Using the global product design, Harsco can focus this expertise within its industrial services and building products group, which then uses the knowledge to compete internationally for contracts with steel mills.

2. The global product design facilitates efficiencies in production because managers are free to manufacture the product wherever manufacturing costs are the lowest.

3. It allows managers to coordinate production at their various facilities, shifting output from factory to factory as global demand or cost conditions fluctuate.

4. Because managers have extensive product knowledge, they are better able to incorporate new technologies into their product(s) and respond quickly and flexibly to technological changes that affect their market.

5. The global product design facilitates global marketing of the product. The firm gains flexibility in introducing, promoting, and distributing each product or product group. Rather than being tied to one marketing plan that encompasses the whole firm, individual product line managers may pursue their own plans.

6. Because the global product design forces managers to think globally, it facilitates geocentric corporate philosophies. This is a useful mind-set as firms work to develop greater international skills internally.[15]

The global product design also has disadvantages:

1. It may encourage expensive duplication because each product group needs its own functional-area skills such as marketing, finance, and information management, and sometimes even its own physical facilities for production, distribution, and research and development (R&D).

2. Each product group must develop its own knowledge about the cultural, legal, and political environments of the various regional and national markets in which it operates.

3. Coordination and corporate learning across product groups becomes more difficult. If such coordination is an important part of the firm's international strategy, a different global design, such as the global area design, may be preferable.

Thus businesses must carefully consider the relative advantages and disadvantages of using the global product design when deciding the best form of organization design for their particular circumstances.

Global Area Design

The **global area design** organizes the firm's activities around specific areas or regions of the world. This approach is particularly useful for firms with a polycentric or multidomestic corporate philosophy.[16] A global area design is most likely to be used by a firm whose products are not readily transferable across regions. Bertelsmann AG, described earlier, uses this design for most of its businesses. For instance, because of language differences and cultural preferences,

VENTURING *Abroad*   FLYING SOLO IN CHINA

When most foreign firms doing business in China first set up shop in that country, they used a local partner. Such partners were generally required by Chinese law, and they theoretically served an important role in helping foreign managers better navigate the Chinese bureaucratic maze. For instance, since 1979 U.S. companies have signed over 30,000 contracts to do business in China, and virtually all those contracts included one or more local partners.

In 2000, however, observers began to notice some changes. China was hoping to be admitted into the World Trade Organization and wanted to put forward as business friendly a face as possible. As a result, China began to ease its requirements for local business partners in selected industries. (Telecommunications firms, automakers, and energy companies still require local partners.)

Foreign firms quickly began to take advantage of the new rules. Many had found, for instance, that their local partners were serving little purpose and were instead a drain on assets. Others may have benefited from the local partner but had subsequently learned what they needed to know about doing business in China and were prepared to work alone.

As a result, two things have been happening. First, many foreign firms partnering with local firms have been buying out their joint venture partners. Second, foreign firms have been steering their new investments into wholly owned subsidiaries and businesses. Procter & Gamble, Kimberly-Clark, Dow Chemical, and Delphi Automotive are among the businesses moving aggressively in these new directions. In general firms that are taking this approach are setting up their Chinese operations as separate business units. This allows the firms to focus on the needs of local consumers and maintain a concentrated focus on the evolving Chinese marketplace.

Sources: "More U.S. Firms Expected to Fly Solo in China," *USA Today*, April 10, 2000, p. 1B; Jim Rohwer, "China's Coming Telecom Battle," *Fortune*, November 27, 2000, pp. 209–214.

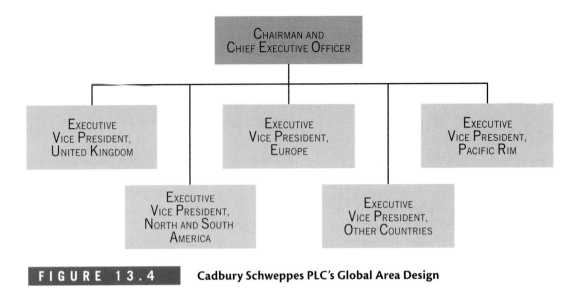

FIGURE 13.4   Cadbury Schweppes PLC's Global Area Design

a Bertelsmann magazine published in the United States cannot be exported in large quantities for sale in Germany or Japan. Thus the firm has separate headquarters in each country in which it operates. The U.S. headquarters, for example, oversees publication of books under the mastheads of Bantam, Dell, and Doubleday and of magazines such as *Parents* and *YM* and records music under such labels as Arista and RCA. Similarly, the firm's German operation publishes books under the label Bertelsmann Club, publishes magazines such as *Der Spiegel*, and records music under the label BMG Ariola. "Venturing Abroad" discusses how many firms doing business in China also are using the global area design.

As shown in Figure 13.4, Cadbury Schweppes PLC, a British soft-drink and candy firm, also uses the global area design. Cadbury owns such brand names as Canada Dry, Hires, Holland House, Cadbury Chocolate, and Beechnut. The firm has five basic divisions, each representing a different area of the world—the United Kingdom, Other Europe, the Pacific Rim, North and South America, and Other Countries. Managers in each area division handle distribution, promotion, advertising, and other functions for all Cadbury Schweppes products in their particular markets.

The global area design is particularly useful for a firm whose strategy is marketing-driven rather than predicated on manufacturing efficiencies or technological innovation or for a firm whose competitive strength lies in the reputation of its brand name products. Both conditions apply to Cadbury Schweppes. Further, the geographical focus of this design allows a firm to develop expertise about the local market. Area managers can freely adapt the firm's products to meet local needs and can quickly respond to changes in the local marketplace. They also can tailor the product mix they offer within a given area. For example, Cadbury managers do not sell all the firm's products in all areas but instead promote only those that match local tastes and preferences.

The global area design does have disadvantages, however:

1. By focusing on the needs of the area market, the firm may sacrifice cost efficiencies that might be gained through global production.

2. Diffusion of technology is slowed because innovations generated in one area division may not be adopted by all the others. Thus this design may not be suitable for product lines undergoing rapid technological change.

3. The global area design results in duplication of resources because each area division must have its own functional specialists, product experts, and, in many cases, production facilities.

4. It makes coordination across areas expensive and discourages global product planning.

Global Functional Design

The **global functional design** calls for a firm to create departments or divisions that have worldwide responsibility for the common organizational functions—finance, operations, marketing, R&D, and human resources management. This design is used by MNCs that have relatively narrow or similar product lines. It results in what is often called a **U-form organization**, where the U stands for "unity." An example of the global functional design is that used by British Airways, shown in Figure 13.5. This firm is essentially a single-business firm—it provides air transport services—and has company-wide functional operations dedicated to marketing and operations, public affairs, engineering, corporate finance, human resources, and other basic functions.

The global functional design offers several advantages:

1. The firm can easily transfer expertise within each functional area. For example, Exxon Mobil uses the global functional design, so production skills learned by Exxon Mobil's crews operating in the Gulf of Mexico can be used by its offshore operations in Malaysia's Jerneh field, and new catalytic cracking technology tested at its Baton Rouge, Louisiana, refinery can be adopted by its refineries in Singapore and Trecate, Italy.

2. Managers can maintain highly centralized control over functional operations. For example, the head of Exxon Mobil's refinery division can rapidly adjust the production runs or product mix of refineries to meet changes in worldwide demand, thereby achieving efficient usage of these very expensive corporate resources.

3. The global functional design focuses attention on the key functions of the firm. For example, managers can easily isolate a problem in marketing and distinguish it from activities in other functional areas.

Despite these advantages, this design is inappropriate for many businesses. In particular, it has three major shortcomings:

1. The global functional design is practical only when the firm has relatively few products or customers.

2. Coordination between divisions can be a major problem. For example, the manufacturing division and the marketing division may become so differentiated from each other that each may start pursuing its own goals to the detriment of the firm as a whole.

3. There may be duplication of resources among managers. For example, the finance, marketing, and operations managers may each hire an expert on Japanese regulation, when a single expert could have served all three functional areas just as effectively.

Because of these problems, the global functional design has limited applicability. It is used by many firms engaged in extracting and processing natural resources, such as the mining and energy industries, because in their case the ability to transfer technical expertise is important. Firms that need to impose uniform standards on all their operations also may adopt this approach. For example, to ensure safety, British Airways standardizes its maintenance and flight procedures regardless of whether a flight originates in London, Hong Kong, or Sydney.

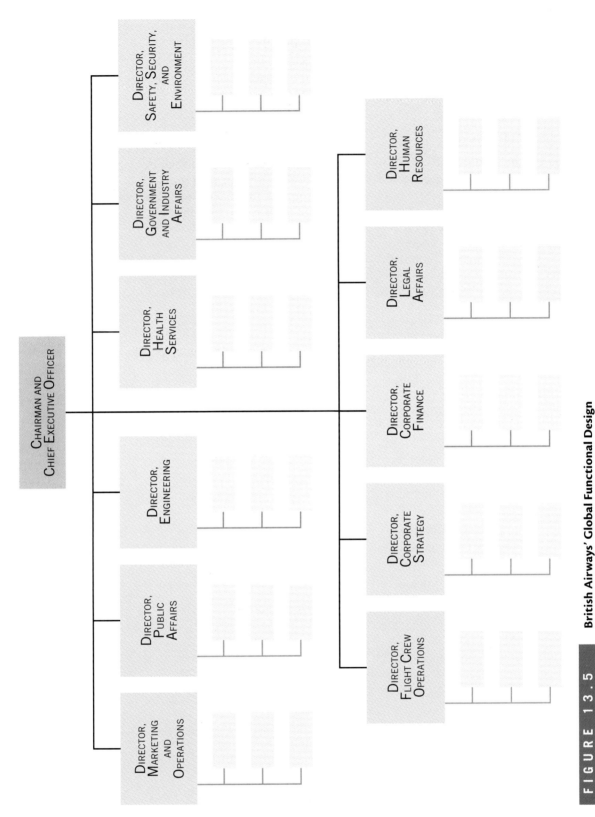

FIGURE 13.5 British Airways' Global Functional Design

Global Customer Design

The **global customer design** is used when a firm serves different customers or customer groups, each with specific needs calling for special expertise or attention. For example, Kodak has adopted a global customer design, as is shown in Figure 13.6. Its Commercial Business Group focuses on selling high-quality film to studios in Hollywood, London, Munich, Hong Kong, Toronto, and other centers for filmed entertainment, as well as film and supplies to the medical community and other commercial customers. Its Consumer Business Group sells to professional and amateur photographers, while its New Business Group targets emerging markets and new technologies of relevance to leading-edge customers around the world.[17]

Japan's Bridgestone Corporation, the world's third largest tire manufacturer, uses the global customer design in selling tires worldwide under its brand names Bridgestone and Firestone. One division deals with automobile manufacturers such as Ford, Nissan, and BMW, which buy tires as original equipment for new automobiles. Another deals with individual consumers and markets tires through the firm's network of automotive retail outlets. Still another division markets tires to agricultural users through firms such as Deere and Case. (A fourth division oversees manufacturing and technology).[18]

This design is useful when the various customer groups targeted by a firm are so diverse as to require totally distinct marketing approaches. For example, selling four replacement tires to an individual is a completely different task from selling 4 million tires to an automaker. The global customer approach allows the firm to meet the specific needs of each customer segment and track how well the firm's products or services are doing among those segments. On the other hand, the global customer design may lead to a significant duplication of resources if each

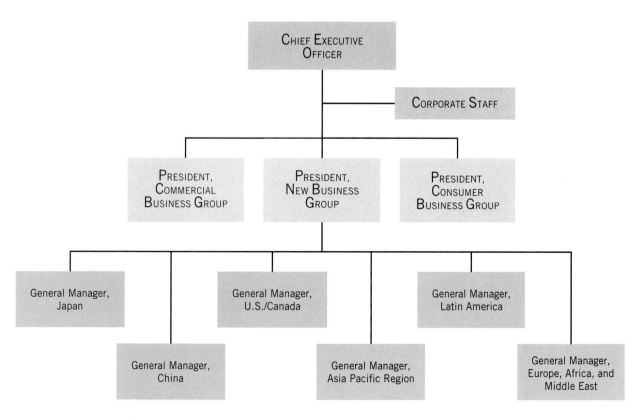

FIGURE 13.6   Eastman Kodak's Global Customer Design

customer group needs its own area and functional specialists. Coordination between the different divisions is also difficult because each is concerned with a fundamentally different market.

Global Matrix Design

The most complex form of international organization design is the global matrix design.[19] A **global matrix design** is the result of superimposing one form of organization design on top of an existing, different form. The resulting design is usually quite fluid, with new matrix dimensions being created, downscaled, and eliminated as needed. For example, the global matrix design shown in Figure 13.7 was created by superimposing a global product design (shown down the side) on an existing global functional design (shown across the top). Using a global matrix design, a firm can form specific product groups comprising members from existing functional departments. These product groups can then plan, design, develop, produce, and market new products with appropriate input from each functional area. In this way the firm can draw on both the functional and the product expertise of its employees. After a given product development task is completed, the product group may be dissolved; its members will then move on to new assignments. Of course, other matrix arrangements are possible. For example, an area design could be overlaid on a functional design, thereby allowing area specialists to coordinate activities with functional experts.

An advantage of the global matrix design is that it helps bring together the functional, area, and product expertise of the firm into teams that develop new products

FIGURE 13.7

A Global Matrix Design

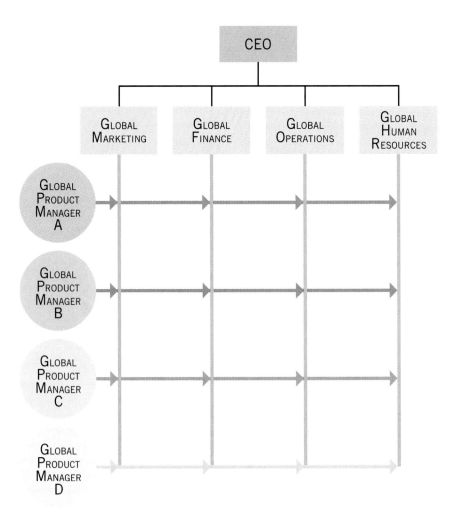

or respond to new challenges in the global marketplace. For example, Texas Instruments (TI) often uses a global matrix design for new product development, although its underlying organization design is based on function. At any one time TI has several product development groups in operation. Within any given country in which the firm operates, the groups draw members from relevant functional groups and work toward creating new products or new uses for existing ones. If and when such breakthroughs are achieved, matrix-based product groups are used to transfer the new technology throughout the rest of the firm. After the task assigned to the product group is completed (for example, after the new product has been launched), the group may be dissolved.

The global matrix design thus promotes organizational flexibility. It allows firms to take advantage of functional, area, customer, and product organization designs as needed while simultaneously minimizing the disadvantages of each. Members of a product development team can be added or dropped from the team as the firm's needs change. The global matrix design also promotes coordination and communication among managers from different divisions.

The global matrix design has disadvantages, however:

1. It is not appropriate for a firm that has few products and that operates in relatively stable markets.

2. It often puts employees in the position of being accountable to more than one manager. For example, at any given time an employee may be a member of his or her functional, area, or product group as well as of two or three product development groups. As a result, the individual may have split loyalties—caught between competing sets of demands and pressures as the area manager to whom the employee reports wants one thing and the product line manager wants another.

3. The global matrix design creates a paradox regarding authority. On the one hand, part of the design's purpose is to put decision-making authority in the hands of those managers most able to use it quickly. On the other hand, because reporting relationships are so complex and vague, getting approval for major decisions may actually take longer.

4. The global matrix design tends to promote compromises, or decisions based on the relative political clout of the managers involved.[20]

Hybrid Global Designs

Each global form of international organization design described in this section represents an ideal. Most firms create a hybrid design that best suits their purposes, as dictated in part by the firms' size, strategy, technology, environment, and culture. Most MNCs are likely to blend elements of all the designs discussed. A firm may use a global product design as its overall approach, but it may have more of a functional orientation or area focus in some of its product groups than in others. In fact, if it were possible to compare the designs used by the world's 500 largest MNCs, no two would look exactly the same. A firm's managers start with the basic prototypes, merge them, throw out bits and pieces, and create new elements unique to their firm as they respond to changes in the organization's strategy and competitive environment.

Figure 13.8 illustrates how Nissan Motor Corporation uses a hybrid design to structure its U.S. operations. At the top level of the firm Nissan has some managers dedicated to products (such as the vice president and general manager for the Infiniti division) and others dedicated to functions (such as the vice president and chief financial officer). The marketing function for Nissan automobiles is broken down by product, with specific units responsible for sedans, sports cars, and trucks and utility vehicles. Both the Infiniti and Nissan divisions also have regional general managers organized by area. In similar fashion all large international firms mix and match forms of organization in different areas and at different levels to

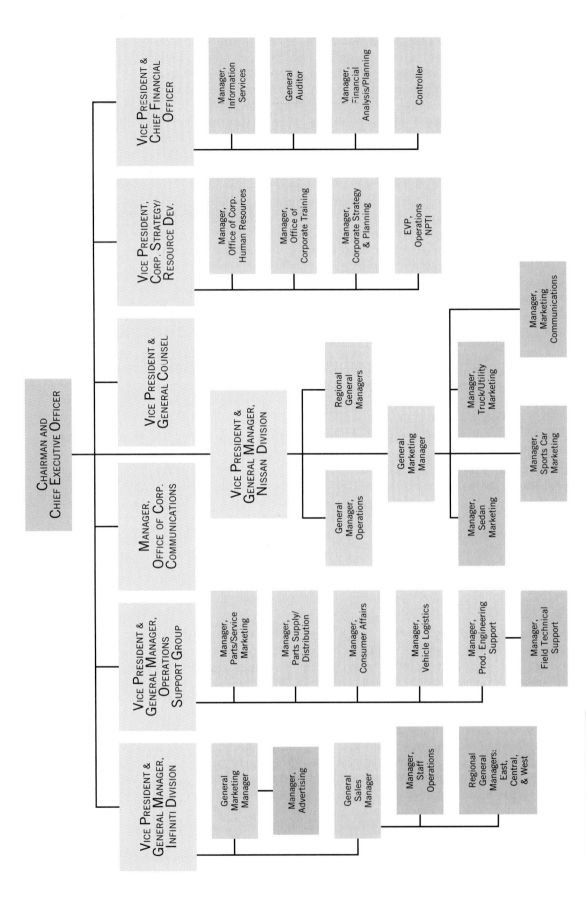

FIGURE 13.8 Nissan USA's Hybrid Design

create hybrid organization designs that their managers believe best serve the firm's needs. For example, although Ford Motor Company essentially uses a functional design to maintain centralized thinking about design and production, the firm also is working to increase its area focus by giving brand and regional units more autonomy in global markets.[21]

RELATED ISSUES IN GLOBAL ORGANIZATION DESIGN ‹

In addition to the fundamental issues of organization design we have addressed, MNCs face a number of related organizational issues that must be carefully managed.

Centralization Versus Decentralization

When designing its organization, an MNC must make a particularly critical decision that determines the level of autonomy, power, and control it wants to grant its subsidiaries. Suppose it chooses to decentralize decision making by allowing individual subsidiaries great discretion over strategy, finance, production, and marketing decisions, thereby letting those decisions be made by managers closest to the market. These managers may then focus only on the subsidiary's needs rather than on the firm's overall needs. An MNC can remedy this deficiency by tightly centralizing decision-making authority at corporate headquarters. Decisions made by the corporate staff can then take into account the firm's overall needs. However, these decisions often hinder the ability of subsidiary managers to quickly and effectively respond to changes in their local market conditions. Because both centralization and decentralization offer attractive benefits to the MNC, most firms constantly tinker with a blend of the two to achieve the best outcome in terms of overall strategy.[22] For example, "Bringing the World into Focus" discusses how Coca-Cola is currently reversing a move toward centralization in favor of a more decentralized approach.

Despite Coca-Cola's move toward decentralization, there seems to be a trend among some MNCs toward greater centralization. Although the need to address local factors in different markets is best handled by decentralizing control to local managers, some managers believe it is more important to address the specific needs of different customer groups across many markets, a task best handled via centralization. For example, Europcar International SA, Europe's largest car rental firm, used to be very decentralized. High-ranking local managers in the nine countries it served held great authority and ran their local operations with virtual autonomy. However, the firm's new CEO decided that business customers, tourists, and local individual renters each represented a clear market segment whose needs could better be handled via centralization. He thus fired the country managers—replacing them with lower-level managers—and centralized operations at headquarters.

Advancements in electronic communications also have made it easier for firms to centralize more of their operations. For example, workers at Sun Microsystems who want to change their employee benefits can log onto the corporate Web site and fill out forms electronically from anywhere. This allows Sun to maintain a single centralized benefits coordination unit, rather than have many such units attached to its subsidiaries around the world.[23]

› When Renault purchased a controlling interest in Nissan, the French automaker chose to operate Nissan as a stand-alone, decentralized subsidiary. It installed one of its most experienced managers, Carlos Ghosn (shown here at a Tokyo auto show), as Nissan's CEO.

Bringing the World into FOCUS

COCA-COLA—STILL "THE ONE"?

For as long as most people can remember, Coca-Cola has clearly been "the one," as its popular advertising slogan once proclaimed in dozens of languages around the globe. Although Coke has been a staple around the world for decades, about 10 years ago, under the leadership of first Roberto Goizueta and then Douglas Ivester, the firm embarked on an even more aggressive international expansion campaign.

During the 1990s Coca-Cola spent more than $100 million on two new bottling plants in Russia. It installed literally thousands of new vending machines in Japan, ultimately reaching a total of 1 million machines in that country alone. It made similar major investments in China, India, Venezuela, Austria, Italy, and Poland. Yet at the same time, Coca-Cola managers believed they could best manage their increasingly global empire from the firm's corporate headquarters in Atlanta.

In 1999 and 2000, however, major problems began to surface. Among other things the firm had to admit it would not be able to meet the lofty growth goals established in the late 1990s. The company also acknowledged that it had overinvested in several key foreign markets. For instance, the new Russian plants sit idle and are being used only as distribution centers. Moreover, a por-

tion of the investment in new vending machines in Japan had to be written off. These failures led Coca-Cola's board of directors to install a new CEO, Douglas Daft, who is scaling back just about everywhere.

At the same time, though, the firm is acknowledging that it had tried to retain too much decision-making power in Atlanta. To remedy this problem, Daft has created a new mantra inside Coke: "Think locally and act locally." He is encouraging local managers at far-flung locations to start making more of their own decisions. For example, many now can set their own pricing and tailor their advertising campaigns to local market conditions, decisions and activities that previously were handled by corporate executives in Atlanta. Coke distributors also are being given more freedom to introduce their own new brands tailored to meet local tastes. All in all, Coke is trying to reverse its current skid by moving away from a tightly controlled centralized model to a more locally oriented decentralized approach to doing business.

Sources: "Doug Daft Isn't Sugarcoating Things," *Business Week*, February 7, 2000, pp. 36–37; *Hoover's Handbook of American Business 2001* (Austin: Hoover's Business Press, 2001), pp. 390–391.

Role of Subsidiary Boards of Directors

An MNC typically incorporates each of its subsidiaries in the subsidiary's country of operation. This is done to limit the subsidiary's liability and to allow it to attain legal status as a local citizen. Most countries require each corporation, including a wholly owned subsidiary of a foreign MNC, to have a board of directors.[24] The board is elected by corporate shareholders (which is the MNC), is responsible to those shareholders for the effective management of the subsidiary (which is owned by the MNC), and oversees the activities of top-level managers (who are hired by the MNC). The issue facing most MNCs is whether to view the creation of a subsidiary board of directors as a pro forma exercise and therefore give the board little real authority or to empower the board with substantial decision-making authority.[25]

Empowering the subsidiary's board has a primary advantage of promoting decentralization. Foreign subsidiaries may need the authority to act quickly and decisively without having to always seek the parent's approval. Also, if the MNC decentralizes authority to local levels, an active board provides a clear accountability and reporting link back to corporate headquarters. Some MNCs also have found that appointing prominent local citizens to the subsidiary's board is helpful in conducting business in a foreign country. These members can help the subsidiary integrate itself into the local business community and can be an effective source of information for both parent and subsidiary about local business and political conditions. For example, prominent local business officials on the board of Apple's Japanese subsidiary were key to the firm's success in the Japanese market in the early 1990s. They enhanced the credibility of Apple's products in a market where corporate connections and status are an important marketing tool, while their appointment demonstrated Apple's long-term commitment to the Japanese market.

A subsidiary board also can help monitor the subsidiary's ethical and social responsibility practices. A potential disadvantage of empowering a subsidiary's board is that the subsidiary may become too independent as its board assumes too much authority and thereby fails to maintain the desired level of accountability to the parent.

In general a subsidiary board is most useful when the subsidiary has a great deal of autonomy, its own self-contained management structure, and a business identity separate from the parent's. Active subsidiary boards are particularly useful in H-form organizations because a holding company's subsidiaries are typically run independently of one another. For example, Nestlé's U.S. subsidiary, Carnation, meets each of the three criteria noted above. Not surprisingly, therefore, Carnation also has a very active board of directors. Honda, Matsushita, Hewlett-Packard, and Dow also empower their local boards of directors to make decisions and respond to local conditions.

Coordination in the Global Organization

Finally, as part of creating an effective design for itself, an international firm must address its coordination needs. In this sense **coordination** is the process of linking and integrating functions and activities of different groups, units, or divisions. Coordination needs vary as a function of interdependence among the firm's divisions and functions. In other words the higher the level of interdependence among divisions and functions, the more coordination is necessary among them. There are three levels of interdependence:

1. Organizations that have less need for coordination have *pooled interdependence*; that is, each division or activity functions with relatively little dependence on the others because each does its own work, and its results are pooled with the others' at the corporate level. Examples are H-form organizations and firms that use the global product design.

2. Firms with moderate coordination needs are characterized by *sequential interdependence*; that is, each division or activity is dependent on only some of the others because work flows between divisions in a one-way or sequential fashion. Examples are M-form organizations and firms that use global area or customer designs.

3. The highest coordination needs are found in organizations that have *reciprocal interdependence*; that is, each division or activity is dependent on all other divisions or activities because work flows back and forth between divisions in a reciprocal fashion. Examples are U-form organizations and firms that use global functional and matrix designs.

MNCs use any of several strategies to achieve and manage their desired level of coordination. The organizational hierarchy itself is one way to manage interdependence and promote coordination. An organization design that clearly specifies all reporting relationships and directions of influence facilitates coordination because each manager knows how to channel communications, decision making, and so on. Rules and procedures also facilitate coordination. For example, a standard operating procedure that requires the reporting of monthly and quarterly revenue, cost, and profit data to headquarters allows corporate staff to coordinate the firm's cash flows and to quickly identify troublesome markets.

MNCs also may adopt somewhat more temporary or ad hoc coordination techniques.[26] Using employees in liaison roles is one such technique. For example, suppose two divisions of an MNC are collaborating on an activity or function. Each may designate a specific manager as its liaison with the other. If any manager in one unit has information or questions that involve the other unit, they are channeled through the liaison to the appropriate person or unit. Toyota, for example, frequently uses this technique for managing relatively small-scale joint efforts.

When the magnitude of the collaboration is significant, task forces may be used for coordination. In such cases each participating unit or division assigns one or more representatives to serve on the task force. The assignment may be either full time or part time. Ford and Mazda, for example, used a task force when they collaborated on the design of the new Ford Focus. Each firm designated members of its design, engineering, operations, and finance departments to serve on the task force. Employees of the two firms rotated on and off the task force depending on its needs and on the automobile's stage of development. When the final design was complete and the automobile was put into production, the task force was dissolved.

Task forces also may be used to resolve intraorganizational conflicts or to build commitment to new projects. For example, in the early days of the personal computer industry, Toshiba had to decide which operating system its personal computers would use. To the managers of its U.S. affiliate, Toshiba America, there was only one choice: IBM compatible. However, the firm's Japanese engineers and marketing staff resisted this choice. So Toshiba created a task force composed of Toshiba America managers, Japanese R&D staff, and Japanese marketers, who, with the aid of a consulting firm, interviewed computer users, distributors, and dealers. In the end the task force decided that Toshiba's personal computers should be IBM compatible. Although this decision was obvious to the U.S. managers, the task force was still invaluable because it resulted in the Japanese employees being fully committed to the IBM-compatible operating system.[27]

Many international firms also rely heavily on informal coordination mechanisms. Informal management networks can be especially effective. An **informal management network** is simply a group of managers from different parts of the world who are connected to one another in some way. These connections often form as a result of personal contact, mutual acquaintances, and interaction achieved via travel, training programs, joint meetings, task force experiences, and so on. Informal management networks can be very powerful for short-circuiting bureaucracy that may delay communication and decision making. They also can be effective for getting things done more quickly and more effectively than if normal and routine procedures were always followed.[28]

❯ CORPORATE CULTURE IN INTERNATIONAL BUSINESS

Although the structural components of an organization design can be objectively specified and drawn in an organizational chart, there are informal elements of an organization that are subjective and amorphous. This informal organization, which also plays a critical role in coordination, is called the corporate culture. **Corporate culture** is the set of shared values that defines for its members what the organization stands for, how it functions, and what it considers important. Most managers agree that it is important to develop a clearly defined and consistent culture to help guide the behavior of managers. Such a culture not only helps managers make sense of the organization and facilitates their understanding of their own jobs but also contributes to overall competitiveness.[29]

Creating such a culture is difficult for any organization. Success in doing so is considerably more important for an MNC, however, than for a purely domestic firm. Each unit within the MNC will naturally have its own culture. This unit culture will be partially defined by the national culture in which the unit functions. At the same time, however, there needs to be an overall corporate culture that permeates the entire organization. At Sony, for example, the firm's Japanese units have one culture, while its U.S. units have another culture. Each culture was developed from the context of the national culture of the units, but there is also the overall culture—what the firm calls "Sony's Way"—that permeates the entire firm.

Creating the Corporate Culture in International Business

The creation of a corporate culture for an MNC usually starts with the firm's mission statement. As discussed in Chapter 10, the mission statement spells out the firm's values, goals, and basic operating philosophy. Managers throughout the firm must accept and enact the corporate culture if it is to become a reality. Contributing to the development of a strong and accepted corporate culture are symbols (such as the corporate logo), heroes (usually successful and distinctive managers), legends (including stories about past successes and failures that get passed from manager to manager), and shared experiences (such as working together toward shared goals). Sony's former chairman, Akio Morita, was one of the firm's founders, and his personal values and beliefs still permeate the entire organization. He is given credit for much of the firm's success and is revered by many of the firm's employees. Because of his integrity, loyalty to his employees, and exemplary managerial acumen, Morita's influence is indelibly felt throughout the firm.

Many MNCs have found that changing their corporate culture is an important element in improving their global competitiveness. For example, when Helmut Maucher became CEO of Nestlé, he soon decided that the firm was too bureaucratic and not sufficiently interested in innovation. Maucher is a tough-minded executive who abhors bureaucracy. He hates to read reports and thinks most firms spend too much time processing paperwork instead of carrying out their business. He adopted the slogan "Let's have more pepper and less paper" to let people know he wanted them to spend less time on paperwork and more time communicating, stimulating innovation, and generating new ideas. He repeatedly used this slogan in conversations and meetings with Nestlé managers worldwide. As a result, it gradually became embedded in the firm's corporate culture.

Of course, there is no one best culture toward which international firms should aspire. For example, TI, Honda, and BMW each have a distinctive corporate culture that helps everyone understand how the firm functions. TI has what its managers call a "shirtsleeve" culture in which people "roll up their sleeves" and work hard; there are few status differences among TI's managers. Honda, on the other hand, has a culture that stresses teamwork and togetherness. All Honda employees understand that they are to take responsibility for doing whatever is necessary to enhance quality. BMW's culture centers around technology and performance. The firm and its managers always have focused on applying technology as efficiently and effectively as possible. As a result, BMW managers put a premium on technological innovation and refinement. The firm also considers its German operations to be superior to its operations in other countries, and so it tends to concentrate its highest-profile and highest-profit activities in its German factories.

Managing the Corporate Culture in International Business

Given the amorphous nature of corporate culture, managers may question the extent to which they can affect or manage it in a rational manner. Effectively managing the corporate culture requires consistency and communication. Managers should take every opportunity to communicate the firm's culture to others so as to keep it in the forefront of decision making and other activities. Frequent contact and interaction between managers and other employees are also useful for transmitting and reinforcing the corporate culture. Still another way to spread the culture throughout the organization is to transfer key managers to different units so the managers can continue to diffuse what they know about the culture into those units.

When corporate culture is not properly managed, the firm is likely to stumble and its effectiveness diminish. For example, Bond Corporation Holdings, Inc., once a high-flying Australian conglomerate, was forced into liquidation, in part because of its disjointed and vague culture. During the 1980s Bond amassed a collection of businesses ranging from breweries to newspapers to banks to resorts. Some units thought cost control was paramount; others thought they were supposed to expand aggressively with little regard for the bottom line; still others believed their mandate was to earn profits regardless of the methods employed. Thus the firm followed diverse approaches and had a poorly articulated corporate vision. The Bond empire crumbled, in large part because its managers failed to develop a strong, clearly defined culture.

In contrast, Merrill Lynch works hard at spreading its corporate culture to its new operations as it expands around the world. The financial services firm wants to be known for doing business in a straightforward and honest way with few of the elaborate trappings used by many other Wall Street brokerage firms. Whenever Merrill Lynch opens a branch in another country, it hires local managers to run it. Those managers, however, are first brought to the firm's U.S. training center to learn the Merrill Lynch system, including not only operating procedures but the company's values and culture as well. Moreover, each office contains a sign in the local language reflecting Merrill Lynch's philosophy: "Integrity: No one's personal bottom line is more important than the reputation of the firm."[30]

❯ MANAGING CHANGE IN INTERNATIONAL BUSINESS

Another critical facet of organization design in international firms is change management. In this context **organization change** is any significant modification or alteration in a firm's strategy, organization design, technology, and/or employees. The process of internationalizing a firm's design, discussed earlier in the chapter, is an important example of organization change. Because the international environment in which a firm operates is never static, managing change in ways that enhance the firm's productivity and profitability is a continual challenge confronting international managers. Managing change is both complex and important, so international executives must understand the reasons for change, the varieties of change they may confront, and how to implement change most effectively.[31]

Reasons for Change in International Business

Change in a firm may be necessitated by any number of factors.[32] Among the most significant forces for organization change are changes in the environment in which the firm operates. As new markets open or existing markets shrink, for example, the firm must develop appropriate responses. Consider the completion of the European Union's (EU's) internal market in 1992. Literally thousands of firms changed their strategies for doing business in that market.[33] Some rearranged production among their existing factories, hoping to benefit from economies of scale. Unilever, for example, restructured its detergent product line by replacing autonomous, nearly independent national operations with a new subsidiary, Lever Europe, which was charged with treating Europe as one big market. Other firms bought out their competitors to broaden their presence within the EU. Air France prepared for the EU's deregulation of air services by purchasing Air Inter, the leading provider of internal air services in France. Firms headquartered outside the EU, such as Samsung, Toshiba, Whirlpool, and Procter & Gamble, increased their direct investments in that area. As non-EU firms increased their presence, firms within the EU were forced to respond. For example, entrenched European automakers such as Fiat, BMW, and Ford of Europe have had to improve their productivity and quality in the face of increased competition from non-EU firms such as Toyota, Nissan, and Mitsubishi.

Organization change also can result from changes in technology. New technology may redefine work roles and reporting relationships among employees. For example, the spread of personal computers in the workplace reduced the need for mainframe computers, altered the role of corporate Management Information Systems staff, and offered customer service employees far more information than their counterparts possessed two decades ago, thereby raising their stature as well as their educational requirements. Advances in telecommunications technology also have affected organization design. U.S. computer firms, for example, have established joint ventures in Ireland and India to supply software, which is then transported electronically via satellite to program developers in the United States.

Changes in cultural values and mores also can prompt organization change. For example, decreased consumption of tobacco products in the United States has caused makers of such products to diversify into other products. Philip

> Technological innovations often create the need for organization change. For example, the rapid growth of India's software industry has caused many Indian high-tech firms to change their compensation programs and forge alliances with foreign rivals. Many have changed their organization design as well.

Morris purchased General Foods in 1985 and Kraft in 1988. It then aggressively attacked the European market, acquiring chocolate and coffee marketer Jacob Suchard as well as the leading cigarette company in former East Germany. However, Philip Morris had to admit to at least one failure: It could not get French consumers to buy Kraft Velveeta cheese.[34]

Types of Change in International Business

Change in a firm can take many forms. One significant change occurs when a firm alters its corporate strategy, which results when an international firm moves among the single-product, related diversification, and unrelated diversification strategies discussed in Chapter 10. A firm that enters a new market is undertaking strategic change, as is a firm that adopts a new entry mode such as foreign direct investment or a joint venture. Even more dramatic strategic changes include acquiring or being acquired by another firm.

As such changes in corporate strategy develop, compensating changes in organization design are often necessary to implement the new strategy successfully.[35] Design changes may alter the way the firm is configured, the way it delegates authority to its subsidiaries abroad, its degree of required coordination, and its internal reporting relationships. Market conditions also may prompt changes in organization design.

A final type of organization change involves a firm's employees. A firm sometimes wants to change the attitudes of its employees—for example, enhance their morale or improve their job satisfaction. A firm also may find it useful to improve its employees' ability or performance levels. For example, Collins & Aikman implemented a systematic program of improving its employees' reading and math skills to ensure they can efficiently operate the firm's increasingly sophisticated textile machinery.

In other cases a firm effects employee change via transfers, promotions, terminations, or the hiring of more qualified people. For example, several years ago the board of directors of Beecham Group PLC (now GlaxoSmithKline) wanted a CEO who had a strong commitment to and understanding of global competitiveness. However, the firm did not think any current Beecham executive had those qualities, so it hired an experienced U.S. manager, Robert P. Bauman, who had demonstrated his abilities in several previous positions.[36] Similarly, when GM became concerned that its automobiles' old-fashioned appearance was endangering the firm's short-term profitability and long-term viability, it transferred the chief designer at its German subsidiary to Detroit to head its worldwide design programs.

CHAPTER REVIEW

Summary

Organization design is the overall pattern of structural components and configurations used to manage the total organization. Early attempts to identify the one best way to design organizations included the bureaucratic design. However, managers now realize that the most appropriate design of an organization depends on its situation. Managers today also realize that organization design is an evolutionary process.

When a firm first begins to operate internationally, it usually must change its design in one or more ways. Such change may involve following the corollary approach, then establishing an export department, and then creating an international division.

After a firm has established a significant international presence, it will usually develop a global organization design. The most common approaches to global organization design are the global product design, the global area design, the global functional design, the global customer design, and the global matrix design. Each of these approaches has unique advantages and disadvantages, and one approach may be more suitable for some firms than for others. Indeed, many firms actually use a hybrid global design best suited to their needs.

MNCs also must make other decisions related to organization design. Particularly important are those regarding centralization versus decentralization, the role of subsidiary boards of directors, and which coordination mechanisms to use. Informal management networks are especially powerful mechanisms for coordination.

Whereas a firm's design is relatively formal and objective, its culture is more informal and subjective. Corporate culture is the set of values that defines for members what the firm stands for, how it functions, and what it considers important. Culture is shaped by such things as the firm's mission statement, symbols, heroes, legends, past successes and failures, and shared experiences. A strong, clearly defined, and well-managed culture can be a major contributor to the firm's success.

Organization change is any significant modification or alteration in a firm's strategy, organization design, technology, and/or employees. Most firms find they must change regularly for various reasons. The key is to keep change properly focused on specific objectives and in line with other aspects of the firm.

Review Questions

1. What is organization design?
2. What are some of the initial impacts of international activity on organization design?

3. What is the global product design? What are its strengths and weaknesses?
4. What is the global area design? What are its strengths and weaknesses?
5. What is the global functional design? What are its strengths and weaknesses?
6. What is the global customer design? What are its strengths and weaknesses?
7. What is the global matrix design? What are its strengths and weaknesses?
8. What are three issues related to organization design that MNCs face?
9. What is corporate culture? Why is it important in international business?
10. What is organization change? Why do managers of international firms need to understand organization change?

Questions for Discussion

1. Why does a firm's organization design depend on the firm's situation? Why is the design evolutionary?
2. If a new organization starts out with a global perspective, will it necessarily experience any of the initial impacts of international activity on organization design? Why or why not?
3. Do managers of international firms need to approach organization design differently from their counterparts in domestic firms? Why or why not?
4. How do the global product, area, functional, and customer approaches to organization design differ? How are they similar?
5. Why is a global matrix design almost always transitional in nature?
6. Why do international firms need to develop a unique organization design rather than simply model themselves after other firms?
7. Why is coordination important in international business?
8. Can a strong corporate culture be bad? If not, why? If so, give an example.
9. How are national culture and corporate culture likely to be related?
10. Under what circumstances might a firm need to change the global design it is using to a different global design?

BUILDING GLOBAL SKILLS

Form small groups of three or four students each. Assume that your group is the board of directors of a large firm, Unipro Incorporated, which for many years followed a single-product strategy. It manufactured small jet aircraft and sold them worldwide. Its products are market leaders in North America, Asia, and Europe and also sell well in South America and Africa. Because of the single-product strategy, Unipro set up a global functional organization design, which it still uses.

The board has been concerned about the firm's dependence on a single product, so several years ago it decided to diversify the firm. Over four years the firm has bought several other businesses:

- General Chemical (based in England; almost 90 percent of its revenues come from Europe)
- Total Software (based in Canada; most of its revenues come from North America and Europe)
- Pleasure Park (an amusement park in Japan)

- Fundamental Foods (a large food-processing firm with strong operations in the United States, Europe, and Japan)

Now that Unipro's diversification strategy has been fully implemented, the board (your group) sees that it needs to change the firm's organization design to better fit the new business mix. Based solely on the information you have, sketch a new organization design for the firm. When you are finished, draw your organization design on the blackboard. Be prepared to defend your design.

Follow-Up Questions

1. How is your group's organization design similar to and different from those of other groups?
2. What do you see as the biggest advantages and disadvantages of your group's organization design?
3. What additional information would have made it easier for you to develop a new organization design for Unipro?

WORKING WITH THE WEB: BUILDING GLOBAL INTERNET SKILLS

Matching Intranets and Organization Design

Most larger companies today make use of what they call an "intranet." An intranet is similar to the Internet but is specific to a single company. Various Web pages are developed for different divisions, functions, and operations within the company, and users move through the system using a browser such as Netscape. There also is a security screen around most intranets—usually called a *firewall*—that keeps unauthorized users from accessing the system. The system itself is used for communication and coordination among people in the organization.

On a sheet of paper draw a 2 × 5 matrix. Label each of the "5" cells to correspond to the five basic global organization designs (exclude the hybrid design). Label the "2" cells "centralized" and "decentralized." Inside each cell note one or two especially important criteria for the effective use of an intranet for that particular situation.

For example, an intranet for a centralized/global product design might require local product managers frequently to report and share information with authorities at corporate headquarters. Likewise, an intranet for a decentralized/global matrix design might need to focus more on multiple-directional communication capabilities.

After you have completed filling in your matrix, form small groups with three or four of your classmates. Compare and contrast the criteria you each developed individually, and then develop a group matrix.

Questions for Discussion

1. What are the similarities and differences that need to be kept in mind when developing intranet and Internet Web sites?
2. What role might an intranet play in an international company beyond communication and coordination, as addressed in this exercise?

WE INVITE YOU TO VISIT THIS BOOK'S COMPANION WEB SITE AT www.prenhall.com/griffin

IN THE NEWS

Corporate culture, the set of shared values that defines for its members what the organization is about, is difficult to create and to sustain. When an international company undergoes the kind of rapid change so frequent in most markets and industries today, retaining the best or most desired elements of the company's culture can become quite a challenge. The problem is even more complex when the company maintains different cultures in different countries.

From the homepage of the *Financial Times* (*www.ft.com*), select the "Company" tab at the top, and review the alphabetical list of companies currently in the news. Scan the descriptions of the articles, and select one or two that discuss companies that are changing their names, restructuring, introducing new products, consolidating divisions or creating new ones, making acquisitions or being acquired, or opening new stores or offices in new markets. Read the articles and do further research on the companies if necessary so you can report on how the actions or events outlined in the articles will affect the company's corporate culture.

CLOSING CASE

Procter & Gamble Remakes (and Remakes) Itself

For decades Procter & Gamble has been one of the preeminent marketing companies in the world. Popular P&G brands such as Tide laundry detergent, Crisco shortening, Ivory soap, Crest toothpaste, and Pampers disposable diapers long ruled their respective markets. P&G seemed like an unstoppable juggernaut as its flagship products and brands became increasingly entrenched as icons around the world. Indeed, as discussed at the beginning of this chapter, the firm's biggest global competitor, Unilever, has been frustrated in its attempts to gain significant market share against P&G.

One key to P&G's heritage of success has been a finely tuned set of procedures for developing new products, getting them to market, and then promoting them with relentless efficiency. All told, the firm sells more than 300 brands in 140 countries. There is at least one P&G product tucked away in virtually every kitchen cabinet or under every bathroom sink in North America. Indeed, P&G executives were so bullish in 1997 that they promised investors the firm would double its annual revenues from that year's $35 billion to a stunning $70 billion by the year 2006. When that goal was announced, Wall Street analysts responded by encouraging investors to buy P&G stock, and the business press lauded the company for its aggressive and forward-looking leadership. Almost before the ink had dried, however, observers began to identify chinks in the P&G armor, and within a short time the firm's growth seemed to grind to a halt.

How could such a well-oiled marketing machine lose its momentum so quickly? As it turned out, P&G's problems had started years before they became apparent. In a nutshell what had been a major advantage for the firm had become a major liability—it had stopped innovating and was taking far too long to make changes and get new products to market. For example, whereas competitors like Unilever and Colgate were busily creating new products and nimbly getting them in the hands of consumers, P&G stuck with its tried-and-true approach of reformulating existing products and relaunching them as "improved."

Tide, for instance, has undergone more than 60 product upgrades since its initial launch. Although these upgrades have helped keep the product at the forefront of its market, they also have kept P&G from being too concerned about developing new products. Because the firm had enjoyed such a long period of sustained dominance, its culture acquired a pervasive and unerring adherence to precedent. Managers had come to believe they had to do things the way they always had been done, and individuals were criticized or even fired when they tried something new or different.

Looking back over the last decade, P&G's decline becomes more apparent. Its Ivory soap lost its market leadership position in 1991 to Unilever's Dove and today has less than 5 percent of the market. Pampers disposable diapers experienced a 50 percent drop in market share and lost the market leadership position to Kimberly-Clark's Huggies in 1993. Crest toothpaste, perhaps P&G's most entrenched product, was overtaken by a new Colgate toothpaste in 1998. While Crest was still focusing on preventing cavities—its hallmark since being introduced in 1955—Colgate and other competitors had started stressing not only cavity prevention but fighting tartar, plaque, bad breath, and gingivitis. Because of these and other setbacks, P&G's hopes of reaching its lofty revenues goal seem increasingly remote.

To combat the onset of decline, P&G decided it needed some major changes at the top and in early 1999 appointed Durk Jager, a senior executive from the Netherlands, as CEO. Jager thought he knew what the problems were and went right to work. One of his major initiatives was a series of internal changes designed to promote faster innovation. Perhaps his biggest change was an overhaul of the firm's global organization design. Specifically, in a program he dubbed "Organization 2005," Jager quickly transformed P&G into seven global business divisions organized around products or product groups, each intended to run essentially as an independent multinational corporation. Previously, the firm had operated under a global area design, with operations organized around individual countries or clusters of countries.

Jager promised to have the overhaul completed by 2005 and predicted that P&G would be running smoothly again and pulling away from its rivals by that date. His goal was to hasten decision making and make the firm much more responsive to competitors' actions and changing consumer tastes than it had been in the past. Unfortunately for Jager, he tried to do too much too quickly, especially given P&G's long history of near-insular stability. Managers complained they did not know who was responsible for what, and some P&G units in different countries realized they were starting to compete against each other. Less than 18 months after his appointment Jager was forced out and replaced by A. G. Lafley, who at the time was running P&G's global beauty care unit and all of P&G's North American operations.

Almost immediately, Lafley announced that Jager's plans for reorganizing the company would be halted. In general, Lafley agreed with his predecessor's decision but thought it had been implemented too quickly and with too little involvement from other managers. As a result, people had resisted the change, resulting in a loss of morale, the defection of several valuable executives, and a degree of chaos throughout the company. Lafley worked diligently to calm things down. He also began to undo some of the structural changes imposed by Jager. Lafley acknowledged that the firm's old structure was not really suited to global competition but also suggested that Organization 2005 was too radical a change. The final result, Lafley suggested, would look more like a global matrix structure, with the global product design being superimposed on top of the old area design, rather than replacing that design altogether.

Case Questions

1. Describe Procter & Gamble's organization designs prior to Dirk Jager's changes, his vision for Organization 2005, and A. G. Lafley's revised approach.
2. Discuss the role of corporate culture in Dirk Jager's plans and his subsequent ouster as CEO.
3. From the standpoint of organization change, what might Jager have done differently to be more successful?

Sources: "Rallying the Troops at P&G," *Wall Street Journal*, August 31, 2000, pp. B1, B4; "Reformer Jager Was Too Much for P&G; So What Will Work?" *Wall Street Journal*, June 9, 2000, pp. A1, A10; "Impatient P&G Ousts Jager," *USA Today*, June 9, 2000, pp. 1B, 2B; "P&G: How New and Improved?" *Business Week*, June 21, 1999, p. 36.

CHAPTER

A Leadership Firestorm at Firestone

Even though its name sounds decidedly Western, Bridgestone Corporation, one of the world's largest tire manufacturers, is a Japanese company through and through. To boost its market share globally and in the vital U.S. market, in 1988 Bridgestone purchased Firestone, a major U.S. tire company. At the time Bridgestone's Japanese leaders persuaded Firestone's CEO, John Nevin, to stay on and run the operation. Nevin's leadership style was blunt and straightforward, with little time wasted on subtleties. He also was wired into the local Nashville community where Firestone is headquartered. For instance, he was active in local civic organizations, served on several local boards, and regularly played golf with other movers and shakers. Senior managers at Bridgestone felt that his local contacts were very important and would add continuing value to the firm.

Nevin and his new bosses soon realized, however, that his leadership style did not fit the profile of what Japanese leaders are expected to do. His brash and often confrontational mannerisms quickly wore thin with his new colleagues because in Japan leaders are expected to be polite and reserved. Even though both sides seemed to make an honest effort to adjust, Nevin left the firm by mutual agreement in 1989 and was replaced by a Japanese executive from the home office. In 1993 this individual was rotated back

> "...in Japan **leaders** are expected to be **polite** and **reserved**."

Managing Behavior and Interpersonal Relations

14

After studying this chapter, you should be able to:

> Identify and discuss the basic perspectives on individual differences in different cultures.

> Evaluate basic views of employee motivation in international business.

> Identify basic views of managerial leadership in international business.

> Discuss the nature of managerial decision making in international business.

> Describe group dynamics and discuss how teams are managed across cultures.

to Japan and the position was assumed by Masatoshi Ono, a quiet and reserved Japanese executive who had been groomed by Bridgestone for a senior management position. Indeed, Ono was the prototypic Japanese executive—he kept to himself, made few contacts, and spent most of his time secluded in the home Bridgestone purchased on his behalf in an exclusive Nashville neighborhood.

For the rest of the decade Ono's quiet and reserved style worked wonders at Firestone. The firm began to gradually increase its market share year in and year out, primarily by becoming the major supplier to another increasingly popular business, Ford Motor Company. By the end of the 1990s Bridgestone/Firestone had become the third largest tire company in the world, trailing only Goodyear and Michelin.

In 2000, however, disaster struck. Reports began to surface that many Firestone tires had a fundamental manufacturing defect, which could cause the tires to come apart under certain high-speed road conditions. The problem was especially acute for the Firestone Wilderness tires, which came as standard equipment on the Ford Explorer, the world's most popular sports utility vehicle. Within a matter of weeks Firestone and Ford were collaborating on one of the largest product recall programs in history.

Fixing the tire problem was only the beginning. Almost as soon as the recall started, reports began to surface that managers at Firestone apparently had known about the manufacturing problem for years but had chosen to do nothing about it. These allegations prompted a firestorm of outrage and recriminations; the press severely criticized the firm, consumer groups howled in outrage, and there was even a Congressional investigation. Throughout the ordeal Ono remained stoic. He never appeared to get angry, depressed, or frustrated. He also did not apologize for the company's actions or accept any corporate responsibility for what had happened (other than recalling and replacing the defective tires). Jacques Nasser, his counterpart at Ford, took a decidedly different approach—he assumed personal responsibility for Ford's part of the recall, met regularly with the media, and was always careful to outline what Ford was doing to head off future problems.

Ono's behavior was in keeping with Japanese norms. Leaders in Japan are expected to remain calm, stay behind the scenes, and maintain a low profile. U.S. observers, however, only saw indifference and a lack of involvement, and for these Ono was roundly criticized. Finally, in October 2000 he took a step that is common in Japan but rare in the United States—he resigned from his position, symbolically accepting responsibility for his company's mistakes. He quietly left Nashville and few people even knew about it.

Bridgestone meanwhile had begun to recognize the magnitude of the public relations nightmare facing Firestone. Rather than dispatch another senior Japanese leader (who likely would have fallen prey to the same criticisms that had bedeviled Ono), the firm appointed a senior American-born Firestone executive, John Lampe, to take over. Lampe, who better understood what the U.S. public expected of a corporation in crisis, immediately held a news conference in which he apologized on behalf of the company and pledged to get the problems fixed as soon as possible.[1]

The story of Bridgestone's leaders illustrates two very important messages for managers but especially those who work in international businesses. First, as we detailed more fully in Chapter 4, culture can be a powerful determinant of human behavior. In Japan, for example, cultural norms prescribe very explicit behaviors on the part of managers. The norms in the United States, however, are quite different. Thus leaders from either country need to understand the differences, especially when they are being sent to the other country to work.

Second, people differ in terms of their personalities, goals, and motives and in the way they perceive and interpret their environments. They also differ in terms of their values, emotions, and priorities and in what they want from their work. They differ in the way they respond to various types of supervision, rewards, feedback, and work settings, and they exhibit different levels of job satisfaction, commitment, absenteeism, turnover, and stress. People also behave differently when they are put into groups. Take a group of five people with a well-developed and understood set of behavioral profiles. Remove one member, add another, and the behavior of each member shifts, even if only a little.[2]

Managers who operate in a domestic firm must understand and contend with a complex set of behavioral and interpersonal processes. Managers in a multinational firm have the additional challenge of managing people with diverse frames of reference and perspectives on work and organizations. International managers who develop insights into dealing with people from different cultural backgrounds will be far ahead of those who do not.

In Chapter 4 we discussed national culture and its implications for firms with international operations. We now look more closely at the actual behaviors of managers and employees in different cultures and how those behavioral differences affect the conduct of international business. We start by discussing the nature of individual differences in different cultures. Then we introduce and discuss four aspects of behavior that are especially important for international businesses: motivation, leadership, decision making, and groups and cross-cultural teams.

INDIVIDUAL BEHAVIOR IN INTERNATIONAL BUSINESS ❮

Individual behavior in organizations is strongly influenced by a variety of individual differences—specific dimensions or characteristics of a person which influence that person.[3] Most patterns of individual differences are in turn based on personality. Other important dimensions that relate to individual behavior are attitudes, perception, creativity, and stress.

Personality Differences Across Cultures

Personality is the relatively stable set of psychological attributes that distinguishes one person from another.[4] A long-standing debate among psychologists—often referred to as the question of "nature versus nurture"—is the extent to which personality attributes are biologically inherited (the "nature" argument) or shaped by the social and cultural environment in which people are raised (the "nurture" argument). In reality both biological factors and environmental factors play important roles in determining personalities.[5] Although the details of this debate are beyond the scope of our discussion, international managers should recognize the limitations of sweeping generalizations about people's behavior based on their cultural backgrounds and acknowledge that individual differences also exist within any given cultural group. That is, although culture may lead to certain behavioral tendencies, as outlined in Chapter 4, individual behavior within any given culture also can vary significantly.

The "Big Five" Personality Traits.   Psychologists have identified literally thousands of personality traits and dimensions that differentiate one person from another. In recent years, however, researchers have identified five fundamental personality traits that are especially relevant to organizations. Because these five traits, illustrated in Figure 14.1, are so important and because they are currently

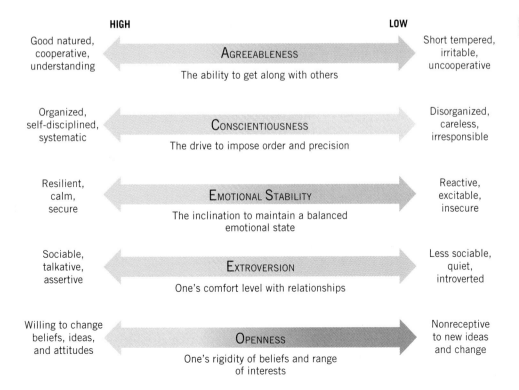

FIGURE 14.1

The "Big Five" Personality Traits

the subject of so much attention, they are commonly referred to as the **"big five" personality traits**.[6]

Agreeableness refers to a person's ability to get along with others. Agreeableness causes some people to be gentle, cooperative, understanding, and good natured in their dealings with others; its absence results in people who are irritable, short tempered, and uncooperative toward other people. **Conscientiousness** refers to the order and precision a person imposes on activities. This trait measures whether one is organized, systematic, responsible, and self-disciplined or whether one is disorganized, careless, and irresponsible. The third of the "big five" personality dimensions is **emotional stability**, which causes some individuals to be poised, calm, resilient, and secure; people who have less emotional stability are excitable, insecure, reactive, and subject to extreme mood swings. **Extroversion**, a person's comfort level with relationships, indicates that some people are sociable, talkative, and assertive, whereas others are less sociable and more introverted. Finally, **openness** measures a person's rigidity of beliefs and range of interests. This trait results in some people being willing to listen to new ideas and to change their own ideas, beliefs, and attitudes as a result of new information; people who are less open are less receptive to new ideas and less willing to change their minds.

A growing body of research has emerged on the big-five framework in the United States. In general this work focuses on using one or more of the five traits to predict performance in various kinds of jobs. Recently this research has been extended to other countries. Researchers have found that in the European Union (EU), as in the United States, conscientiousness and emotional stability appear to be reasonable predictors of performance across a variety of job criteria and occupational groups. That is, Europeans with high conscientiousness and emotional stability are likely to perform at a higher level than Europeans with low conscientiousness and less emotional stability. Similarly, extroversion is a useful predictor of managerial performance in China and among certain occupational groups in the EU, most notably managers in sales and marketing. Openness and agreeableness predict performance across more occupational types but only for certain performance criteria, most notably training proficiency.[7] Thus, when selecting individuals for job assignments in different countries, managers should take advantage of any valid and reliable personality measures that might help with their choices, but they also should be sure to not overgeneralize the validity and reliability of such measures across cultures.

Other Personality Traits at Work. Besides the "big five," there are several other personality traits that influence behavior in organizations. Among the most important are locus of control, self-efficacy, authoritarianism, and self-esteem.

Locus of control is the extent to which people believe that their behavior has a real effect on what happens to them.[8] Some people trust that if they work hard they will succeed. They also may believe that people who fail do so because they lack ability or motivation. People who maintain that individuals are in control of their lives are said to have an *internal locus of control*. Other people think that fate, chance, luck, or other people's behavior determines what happens to them. For example, employees who fail to get promotions may attribute that failure to politically motivated bosses or just bad luck rather than to their own lack of skills or poor performance record. People who think that forces beyond their control dictate what happens to them are said to have an *external locus of control*.

Although not yet demonstrated by research, it seems reasonable to suggest that people from relatively individualistic and power-tolerant cultures are more likely to have an internal locus of control, whereas people from relatively collectivistic and power-respecting cultures are more likely to have an external locus of control. Similarly, an external locus of control is likely to be prevalent among Moslems, whereas an internal locus of control is more consistent with Protestantism. A study of a sampling of people in New Zealand and Singapore found them to be relatively internal in their orientation, as are many people in the United States.[9] It also seems likely, however, that locus of control will vary significantly across cultures.

Self-efficacy is a related but subtly different personality characteristic. Self-efficacy indicates people's beliefs about their ability to perform a task.[10] People with high self-efficacy believe they can perform well on a specific task, while people with low self-efficacy tend to doubt their ability to perform the task. Although self-assessments of ability contribute to self-efficacy, so too does an individual's personality. Some people simply have more self-confidence than others. This belief in their ability to perform a task effectively results in their being more self-assured and more able to focus their attention on performance. In one recent study the self-efficacy of senior managers was found to be positively related to the performance of international joint ventures. In other words, joint venture managers who had confidence in their abilities to meet the goals and objectives of the business were more likely to do so than were managers who had lower confidence in their abilities.[11]

Another important personality characteristic is **authoritarianism**, the extent to which an individual believes that power and status differences are appropriate within hierarchical social systems like business organizations.[12] For example, an individual who is highly authoritarian may accept directives or orders from someone with more authority purely because that person is "the boss." On the other hand, a person who is not highly authoritarian is more likely to question things, express disagreement with the boss, and even refuse to carry out orders if they are objectionable. A highly authoritarian manager may be relatively autocratic and demanding, and highly authoritarian subordinates will be more likely to accept this behavior from their leader. On the other hand, a less authoritarian manager may allow subordinates a bigger role in making decisions, and less authoritarian subordinates will respond positively to this behavior. This trait is obviously quite similar to the concept of power orientation discussed in Chapter 4.

Self-esteem is the extent to which people believe they are worthwhile and deserving individuals. People with high self-esteem are more likely to seek higher-status jobs, be more confident in their ability to achieve higher levels of performance, and derive greater intrinsic satisfaction from their accomplishments. In contrast, people with less self-esteem may be more content to remain in lower-level jobs, be less confident in their abilities, and focus more on extrinsic rewards.

Among the major personality dimensions, self-esteem is the one that has been most widely studied in other countries. Although more research is clearly needed, the published evidence does suggest that self-esteem is an important personality trait in most Western European countries, throughout North America and South America, and in Australia. However, self-esteem has not been found to exist as a separate personality trait among people in Africa and the Middle East. Self-esteem has not yet been studied in most Asian countries. In societies where self-esteem does emerge as a meaningful personality trait, people with high levels of self-esteem seem to be more motivated and to perform at a higher level than people with lower levels of self-esteem.[13]

Attitudes Across Cultures

Another dimension of individuals within organizations is their attitudes. **Attitudes** are complexes of beliefs and feelings that people have about specific ideas, situations, or other people. Although some attitudes are deeply rooted and long lasting, others can be formed or changed quickly. For example, attitudes toward political parties or major social issues, such as pollution control or abortion, evolve over an extended period of time. Attitudes about a new restaurant, however, may be formed immediately after eating there for the first time.

Attitudes are important because they provide a way for most people to express their feelings. Statements by employees that they are underpaid reflect their feelings about their pay. Similarly, when managers endorse a new advertising cam-

Wiring the World

PRIVACY AT WORK IN RUSSIA

One of the biggest workplace issues today is an employee's right to privacy (or lack thereof) at work, a topic fueled by the dramatic growth in electronic communication. For example, some employees claim they have the right to send and receive personal e-mail and to "surf the net" at work as long as these activities do not interfere with their work. Some employers argue they have the right to restrict or prohibit such activities, especially when employees are using company-owned equipment. Moreover, today's software makes it increasingly easier for management to monitor the actions of everyone in the organization.

This same issue has surfaced in Russia and made one local man a true folk hero. For years it has been standard practice for the government to eavesdrop on private e-mail correspondence. Indeed, a 1995 law gives the Russian government carte blanche to read private e-mail and postal correspondence as well as to listen in on telephone calls. Nail Murzakhanov, a small local Internet provider, decided enough was enough.

Under the law Internet service providers and telephone operators must install a device that reroutes traffic through the headquarters of local law enforcement agencies. These agencies claim they need such access to combat Russia's growing crime problems. Murzakhanov refused to obey the law because he thought individual privacy was of greater importance. So far the government has backed down from its threats to force him to comply, and other Internet providers in Russia are following his lead. Clearly, Murzakhanov's informal leadership in this area is helping effect significant social change.

Sources: "A High-Tech Folk Hero Challenges Russia's Right to Snoop," *Wall Street Journal*, November 27, 2000, p. A28; "Bosses and Workers Face Internet Dilemma—Highly Sophisticated Software Creates Combustible Issue Between Managers and Staff," *Wall Street Journal Europe*, October 26, 1999, p. 4; "Now the Boss Knows Where You're Clicking," *Wall Street Journal*, October 21, 2000, p. B1.

paign, they are expressing their feelings about the organization's marketing efforts. In recent times attitudes toward workplace privacy have become especially important in light of the increased use of e-mail, the Internet, and other forms of electronic communication. As discussed in "Wiring the World," the issue is not strictly a North American phenomenon.

Job Satisfaction. One especially important attitude in most organizations is job satisfaction. **Job satisfaction** or **dissatisfaction** is an attitude that reflects the extent to which individuals are gratified by or fulfilled in their work. Extensive research has indicated that personal factors such as an individual's needs and aspirations determine job satisfaction, along with group and organizational factors such as relationships with coworkers and supervisors and working conditions, work policies, and compensation.[14] A satisfied employee also tends to be absent less often, to make positive contributions, and to stay with the organization. In contrast, a dissatisfied employee may be absent more often, may experience stress that disrupts coworkers, and may be continually looking for another job. However, high levels of job satisfaction do not necessarily lead to higher levels of performance.

Research has shown, at least in some settings, that expatriates who are dissatisfied with their jobs and foreign assignments are more likely to leave their employers than are more satisfied managers.[15] One survey measured job satisfaction among 8,300 workers in 106 factories in Japan and the United States. Contrary to what many people believe, this survey found that Japanese workers in general are less satisfied with their jobs than are their counterparts in the United States.[16] Some of the more interesting results of this study are summarized in Table 14.1.

JOB SATISFACTION QUESTION	JAPANESE MEAN	U.S. MEAN
All in all, how satisfied would you say you are with your job? (0 = not at all, 4 = very)	2.12*	2.95
If a good friend of yours told you that he or she was interested in working at a job like yours at this company, what would you say? (0 = would advise against it, 1 = would have second thoughts, 2 = would recommend it)	0.91	1.52
Knowing what you know now, if you had to decide all over again whether to take the job you now have, what would you decide? (0 = would not take job again, 1 = would have some second thoughts, 2 = would take job again)	0.84	1.61
How much does your job measure up to the kind of job you wanted when you first took it? (0 = not what I wanted, 1 = somewhat, 2 = what I wanted)	0.43	1.20

TABLE 14.1

Job Satisfaction Differences Between Japanese and U.S. Workers

*The differences in average response to each question are statistically significant, which means that the differences between U.S. and Japanese responses are large enough that they do not appear to be chance results.
Source: Adapted from J. R. Lincoln, "Employee work attitudes and management practice in the U.S. and Japan: Evidence from a large comparative survey," Copyright © 1989 by the Regents of the University of California. Reprinted from the *California Management Review*, Fall 1989, p. 91 by permission of the Regents.

Another survey found that managers in the former U.S.S.R. are relatively dissatisfied with their jobs, especially in terms of their autonomy to make important decisions.[17] Still another study suggests that Vietnamese workers are relatively satisfied with their jobs, with younger workers (those born since 1975) especially satisfied.[18]

Organizational Commitment. Another important job-related attitude is **organizational commitment**, which reflects an individual's identification with and loyalty to the organization. One comparative study of Western, Asian, and local employees working in Saudi Arabia found that the expatriate Asians reported higher levels of organizational commitment than did the Westerners and local Saudis.[19] Another study found that U.S. production workers reported higher levels of organizational commitment than did Japanese workers.[20] A more recent study looked at the organizational commitment among U.S. expatriates in four Asian and four European countries. The study found that the expatriates retained high levels of commitment to their parent company if they had a long service history with the company, received extensive pretransfer training, and adjusted easily to the foreign culture after transfer. Expatriates with shorter service histories, and who had less pretransfer training and a more difficult adjustment period, actually developed stronger levels of commitment toward the *foreign* affiliate.[21] These findings seem reasonable: The first group of employees had made major personal investments in the parent organization and, because of the ease of their transfer, had less need to invest themselves emotionally in their new assignments. The second group had less attachment to their domestic employers but needed to make larger personal investments in their new assignments to overcome the difficulties they were encountering. Similar "bonding" is observed among people who undergo stressful situations together, such as basic training in the military, initiation week in a fraternity or sorority, or the "ropes" course commonly used by many corporate trainers.

Perception Across Cultures

One important determinant of an attitude is the individual's perception of the object about which the attitude is formed. **Perception** is the set of processes by which an individual becomes aware of and interprets information about the environment. Perception starts when we see, hear, touch, smell, or taste something. Each individual, however, interprets that awareness through filtering processes that are unique to that person. For example, two people supporting different teams can watch the same play on a soccer or rugby field and "see" very different realities. An individual's cultural background obviously plays a role in shaping how the person's filtering mechanisms work.

Stereotyping is one common perceptual process that affects international business. *Stereotyping* occurs when we make inferences about someone because of one or more characteristics the person possesses. For example, some people in the United States hold stereotypes that Japanese managers work all the time, that Swiss managers are well organized, and that French managers are elitist. Some people in those countries stereotype U.S. managers as greedy. Although such stereotypes may sometimes be useful as cultural generalizations, all managers should be aware that each individual is unique and may or may not fit preconceived impressions. To demonstrate some of the pitfalls of stereotyping, "Bringing the World into Focus" describes a variety of stereotypes held by some Chinese about Americans.[22]

Aside from stereotyping, perception can affect international business in many other ways. For example, as described in Chapter 3, international managers must assess political and other forms of risk in foreign markets. However, there may be differences across cultures as to how risk is perceived. As illustrated in one recent study, managers from six Latin American countries perceived common business risks (such as political, commercial, and exchange rate risks) very differently from one another.[23] For example, managers in Costa Rica saw risk as a definable and manageable part of the environment, whereas managers from Guatemala saw risk as an abstract force that was determined almost by chance.

Similarly, a study of Japanese expatriates and British locals working together in Japanese-owned banks in London found that the two groups perceived each other in very different ways.[24] The Japanese expatriates saw their British coworkers as being most interested in protecting their jobs and maintaining their income, whereas the British locals saw the Japanese as being most interested in profit and group harmony. Another study found that senior executives in the United States, the United Kingdom, Germany, and Austria perceived ethical situations very differently from one another.[25] Clearly, international managers must consider the role of perception as they conduct business in different countries.

Stress Across Cultures

Another important element of behavior in organizations is stress. **Stress** is an individual's response to a strong stimulus.[26] This stimulus is called a **stressor**. We should note that stress is not all bad. In the absence of stress we may experience lethargy and stagnation. An optimal level of stress can result in motivation and excitement; too much stress, however, can have negative consequences.

It is also important to understand that stress can be caused by "good" as well as "bad" things. Excessive pressure, unreasonable demands on our time, and bad

❯ The Asian currency crisis wreaked economic havoc on Asian economies. It also acted as an important stressor for employees throughout the region, including this Malaysian stock trader.

Bringing the World into FOCUS

THE U.S. IS CROWDED WITH LIARS WHO PREFER PETS TO KIDS

More than 90 percent of Americans lie frequently. Some Americans so love guns that they sleep with them. Others are habitually sadomasochistic. And when they die, many Americans leave their estates to their pets, not their children.

That, at least, is a view of Americans Chinese can glean from reading the country's state-controlled press. While Beijing is ratcheting up a campaign against the Western media for biased reporting of China, Chinese media aren't entirely innocent when it comes to screwy depictions of the other side of the Pacific. Just as some Western reports about China may paint a distorted view of China, some of China's portrayals of the U.S. speak volumes about the misperceptions that color the two countries' ties.

Consider these recent findings from the Chinese press:

- The *Beijing Youth Daily* reported that three out of 10 people killed by police in the U.S. threw themselves in the line of fire to commit suicide.

- Many Americans are addicted to lying. A state newspaper reported a survey showing that 79 percent of Americans admit to giving fake names and phone numbers to strangers on airplanes; 91 percent often lie; and 20 percent say they can't get through a day without lying. People lie most about weight, age, money, and hair color, the newspaper said.

- "Survival of the fittest" best describes relations between employers and employees in the U.S., and there is no need to curry favor, as bosses never want lasting relations with staff, the *Sichuan Workers' News* told readers.

- One newspaper asserted that Americans like to leave inheritances to their pets, instead of their children. After all, a third newspaper found incidents of mothers abusing or even killing their children occur often. "No doubt, the world that American children live in is full of darkness, violence, and cruelty."

Qian Ning, son of China's Foreign Minister Qian Qichen and author of a best-selling book about Chinese studying in the U.S., says he only learned that "the U.S. is very normal—American masses are like [China's] masses, its farmers are . . . down-to-earth like [our] farmers, and its businessmen are more savvy, like [our] businessmen"—after living in the U.S. for six years. Growing up in China and reading its newspapers, he recalls, "I had gotten the impression that the U.S. was a very strange country."

The negative tone of many news stories on the U.S. also may reflect the attitude of Chinese leaders, who often use the state-run news outlets to push their own propaganda. When Sino-U.S. ties plunged to new lows in 1995 and 1996, the official Chinese media were filled with stories about how the U.S. dominated other nations. During the 1996 summer Olympics in Atlanta, Beijing ordered Chinese reporters to play down U.S. medal wins and positive aspects of U.S. life in their articles.

But with relations now on the upswing and after two decades of economic reforms, Chinese media coverage of the U.S. increasingly consists of a confusing mixture of begrudging admiration, outright stereotyping and—as with media everywhere—a healthy dose of titillation.

Despite the Chinese media's odd depictions of the U.S., many Chinese still retain a glowing—indeed, overly rosy—impression of life in America. Many believe the U.S. government is a bully and U.S. crime rates are frighteningly high, but they also cherish the U.S. as a land of opportunity.

news can all cause stress. However, receiving a bonus and then having to decide what to do with the money can also be stressful. So too can receiving a promotion, gaining recognition, and similar positive events.

There are two different perspectives on stress that are especially relevant for international managers. One is managing stress resulting from international assignments, which is covered in Chapter 20. The other is recognizing that people in different cultures may experience different forms of stress and then handle the stress in different ways. For example, in one study that looked at stress patterns across 10 countries, Swedish executives experienced the least stress. Executives from the United States, the United Kingdom, and the former West Germany reported relatively moderate stress; they also reported they were managing the stress effectively. Managers from Japan, Brazil, Egypt, Singapore, South Africa, and Nigeria reported they were experiencing very high levels of stress and/or were having difficulties managing stress.[27] Another study reported managers in Germany do a better job of maintaining a healthy balance between work and non-work activities than do managers in the United Kingdom.[28]

› MOTIVATION IN INTERNATIONAL BUSINESS

All international businesses face the challenge of motivating their workforces to reduce costs, develop new products, enhance product quality, and improve customer service. **Motivation** is the overall set of forces that causes people to choose certain behaviors from a set of available behaviors. Yet the factors that influence an individual's behavior at work differ across cultures. An appreciation of these individual differences is an important first step in understanding how managers can better motivate their employees to promote the organization's goals.

Needs and Values Across Cultures

The starting point in understanding motivation is to consider needs and values. **Needs** are what an individual must have or wants to have. **Values** are what people believe to be important. Not surprisingly, most people have a large number of needs and values. Primary needs are things that people require to survive, such as food, water, and shelter. Thus primary needs are instinctive and physiologically based. Secondary needs are more psychological in character and are learned from the environment and culture in which an individual lives. Examples of secondary needs include the needs for achievement, autonomy, power, order, affiliation, and understanding. Secondary needs often manifest themselves in organizational settings. For example, if people are to be satisfied with their jobs, the rewards provided by the organization must be consistent with their needs. Offering a nice office and job security may not be sufficient if an individual is primarily seeking income and promotion opportunities. Values, meanwhile, are learned and developed as a person grows and matures. These values are influenced by one's family, peers, experiences, and culture.

Motivational Processes Across Cultures

Most modern theoretical approaches to motivation fall into one of three categories. *Need-based models of motivation* are those that attempt to identify the specific need or set of needs that results in motivated behavior. *Process-based models of motivation* focus more on the conscious thought processes people use to select one behavior from among several. The *reinforcement model* deals with how people assess the consequences of their behavioral choices and how that assessment goes into their future choice of behaviors. This model incorporates the roles of rewards and punishment in maintaining or altering existing behavioral patterns.

Need-Based Models Across Cultures

Hofstede's work, discussed in Chapter 4, provides some useful insights into how need-based models of motivation are likely to vary across cultures.[29] Common needs incorporated into most models of motivation include the needs for security, for being part of a social network, and for having opportunities to grow and develop. By relating these need categories to four of Hofstede's dimensions—social orientation, power orientation, uncertainty orientation, and goal orientation—we can draw several inferences about differences in motivation across cultures.

For example, managers and employees in countries that are individualistic may be most strongly motivated by individually based needs and rewards. Opportunities to demonstrate personal competencies and to receive recognition and rewards as a result may be particularly attractive to such people. In contrast, people from collectivistic cultures may be more strongly motivated by group-based needs and rewards. Indeed, such people may be uncomfortable in situations in which they are singled out for rewards apart from the group with which they work.

Conflicts easily can arise when an international firm's mechanisms for motivating workers clash with cultural attitudes. For example, many U.S. managers working for Japanese multinational corporations (MNCs) have difficulty with the seniority-based, group-performance-oriented compensation systems of their employers. Similarly, Michigan autoworkers resisted the attempts by Mazda officials to get the workers to "voluntarily" wear Mazda baseball caps as part of their work uniforms.[30] American-born athletes playing professional baseball in Japan, who are accustomed to the "star system" that accords them status, prestige, and special privileges, often are shocked by the team-based approach in Japan, which discourages attention to individuals.

Power-respecting individuals are those who accept their boss's right to direct their efforts purely on the basis of organizational legitimacy. As a consequence of this power respect, they may be motivated by the possibility of gaining their boss's approval and acceptance. Thus they may willingly and unquestioningly accept and attempt to carry out directives and mandates. In contrast, power-tolerant people attach less legitimacy to hierarchical rank. Thus they may be less motivated by gaining their boss's approval than by opportunities for pay raises and promotions.

Managers and employees in uncertainty-avoiding cultures may be highly motivated by opportunities to maintain or increase their perceived levels of job security and job stability. Any effort to reduce or eliminate that security or stability may be met with resistance. In contrast, people in uncertainty-accepting cultures may be less motivated by security needs and less inclined to seek job security or stability as a condition of employment. They also may be more motivated by change and by new challenges and opportunities for personal growth and development. For example, recent studies comparing U.S. and German workers revealed substantial differences in their preferences regarding job values. Job security and shorter work hours were valued more highly by the German workers than the U.S. workers. Income, opportunities for promotion, and the importance of one's work were valued more highly by the U.S. workers than by their German counterparts.[31]

Finally, people from more aggressive goal behavior cultures are more likely to be motivated by money and other material rewards. They may pursue behavioral choices they perceive as having the highest probability of financial payoff. They also may be disinclined to work toward rewards whose primary attraction is mere comfort or personal satisfaction. In contrast, workers in passive goal behavior cultures may be more motivated by needs and rewards that can potentially enhance the quality of their lives. They may be less interested in behavioral choices whose primary appeal is a higher financial payoff. For example, Swedish firms provide generous vacations and fringe benefits, whereas many firms operating in China, where wage rates are low by world standards, provide workers with housing, medical care, and other support services.

› Many German employees, such as this Siemens assembly line worker, prefer more job security and a shorter work week than their U.S. counterparts.

Various studies have tested specific motivation theories in different cultural settings. The theory receiving the most attention has been Abraham Maslow's hierarchy of five basic needs: physiological, security, social, self-esteem, and self-actualization.[32] International research on Maslow's hierarchy provides two different insights. First, managers in many different countries, including the United States, Mexico, Japan, and Canada, usually agree that all the needs included in Maslow's hierarchy are important to them. Second, the relative importance and preference ordering of the needs vary considerably by country.[33] For example, managers in less developed countries such as Liberia and India place a higher priority on satisfying self-esteem and security needs than do managers from more developed countries.[34]

Results from research based on another motivation theory, David McClelland's learned needs framework, have been slightly more consistent. In particular, the need for achievement (to grow, learn, and accomplish important things) has been shown to exist in many different countries. McClelland also has demonstrated that the need for achievement can be taught to people in different cultures.[35] However, given the role of Hofstede's cultural differences, it follows that McClelland's needs are not likely to be constant across cultures. In particular, individualistic, uncertainty-accepting, power-tolerant, and aggressive goal behavior cultures seem more likely to foster and promote the needs for achievement and power (to control resources) than the need for affiliation (to be part of a social network). In contrast, collectivistic, uncertainty-avoiding, power-respecting, and passive goal behavior cultures may promote the need for affiliation more than the needs for achievement and power.[36]

Frederick Herzberg's two-factor theory is another popular need-based theory of motivation.[37] This theory suggests that one set of factors affects dissatisfaction and another set affects satisfaction. It too has been tested cross-culturally with varied results. For example, research has found different patterns of factors when comparing U.S. managers with managers from New Zealand and Panama.[38] Results from U.S. employees suggested that supervision contributed to dissatisfaction but not to satisfaction. However, supervision did contribute to employees' satisfaction in New Zealand. Unfortunately, Herzberg's theory often fails to yield consistent results even within a single culture. Thus, even though the theory is well known and popular among managers, managers should be particularly cautious in attempting to apply it in different cultural contexts.

Process-Based Models Across Cultures

In contrast to need-based theories, expectancy theory takes a process view of motivation.[39] The theory suggests people are motivated to behave in certain ways to the extent they perceive such behaviors will lead to outcomes they find personally attractive. The theory acknowledges that different people have different needs—one person may need money, another recognition, another social satisfaction, and still another prestige. However, all will be willing to improve their performance if they believe the result will be fulfillment of the need they find most important.

Relatively little research has explicitly tested expectancy theory in countries other than the United States. It does seem logical, however, that the basic framework of the theory should have wide applicability. Regardless of where people work, they are likely to work toward goals they think are important. However, cultural factors will partially determine both the nature of those work goals and people's perceptions of how they should most fruitfully pursue them.

One particularly complex factor that is likely to affect the expectancy process is the cultural dimension of social orientation. The expectancy theory is essentially a model of individual decisions regarding individual behavioral choices targeted at individual outcomes. Thus it may be less able to explain behavior in collectivistic cultures, but otherwise it may be one of the most likely candidates for a culturally unbiased explanation of motivated behavior. For example, expectancy theory helps explain the success Sony has enjoyed. People who go to work for Sony know they will be able to pursue diverse opportunities and will be kept informed about what is happening in the firm. People who see these conditions as especially important will be most strongly motivated to work for Sony.

The Reinforcement Model Across Cultures

Like expectancy theory, the reinforcement model has undergone relatively few tests in different cultures. This model says behavior that results in a positive outcome (reinforcement) will likely be repeated under the same circumstances in the future. Behavioral choice that results in negative consequences (punishment) will result in a different choice under the same circumstances in the future. Because this model makes no attempt to specify what people will find reinforcing or punishing, it may also be generalizable to different cultures.

Like expectancy theory, the reinforcement model may have exceptions. In Muslim cultures, for example, people tend to believe that the consequences they experience are the will of God rather than a function of their own behavior. Thus reinforcement and punishment are likely to have less effect on their future behavioral decisions. Aside from relatively narrow exceptions such as this, the reinforcement model, like expectancy theory, warrants careful attention from international managers, provided they understand that what constitutes reward and punishment will vary across cultures.

LEADERSHIP IN INTERNATIONAL BUSINESS ‹

Another important behavioral and interpersonal consideration in international business is leadership. **Leadership** is the use of noncoercive influence to shape the goals of a group or organization, to motivate behavior toward reaching those goals, and to help determine the group or organizational culture.[40]

Some people mistakenly equate management and leadership, but as Table 14.2 demonstrates, there are clear and substantive differences between these two important processes. Management tends to rely on formal power and authority and to focus on administration and decision making. Leadership, in contrast, relies more on personal power and focuses more on motivation and communication. Leadership has been widely studied by organizational scientists for decades. Early studies attempted to identify physical traits or universal behaviors that most clearly distinguished leaders from nonleaders. More recently, attention has focused on matching leadership with situations. Although some studies still focus on traits, most leadership models suggest that appropriate leader behavior depends on situational factors.[41]

Contemporary leadership theories recognize that leaders cannot succeed by always using the same set of behaviors in all circumstances. Instead, leaders must carefully assess the situation in which they find themselves and then tailor one or more behaviors to fit that situation. Common situational factors that affect appropriate leader behavior include individual differences among subordinates; characteristics of the group, the organization, and the leader; and subordinates' desire to participate.[42]

Clearly, cultural factors will affect appropriate leader behavior, and the way in which managers spend their workday will vary among cultures.[43] Figure 14.2 summarizes some interesting findings from an early international study of leadership. Managers were asked to indicate the extent to which they agreed with the statement "It is important for a manager to have at hand precise answers to most of the questions that subordinates may raise about their work." As shown in the figure, about three-quarters of the managers in Japan and Indonesia agreed with this statement, whereas a much smaller percentage of managers in Sweden, the Netherlands, and the United States agreed with the statement. In general, agreement would suggest that managers and leaders are perceived as experts who should know all the answers. Those who disagree with the statement believe that managers and leaders are supposed to be problem solvers who may not know the answer to a question but can figure it out or know how to find the answer. In the United States, therefore, a manager who failed to refer a subordinate to a more

TABLE 14.2

Differences Between Leadership and Management

ACTIVITY	MANAGEMENT	LEADERSHIP
Creating an agenda	Planning and budgeting. Establishing detailed steps and timetables for achieving needed results; allocating the resources necessary to make those needed results happen	Establishing direction. Developing a vision of the future, often the distant future, and strategies for producing the changes needed to achieve that vision.
Developing a human network for achieving the agenda	Organizing and staffing. Establishing some structure for accomplishing plan requirements, staffing that structure with individuals, delegating responsibility and authority for carrying out the plan, providing policies and procedures to help guide people, and creating methods or systems to monitor implementation	Aligning people. Communicating the direction by words and deeds to all those whose cooperation may be needed to influence the creation of teams and coalitions that understand the vision and strategies and accept their validity
Executing plans	Controlling and problem solving. Monitoring results vs. plan in some detail, identifying deviations, and then planning and organizing to solve these problems	Motivating and inspiring. Energizing people to overcome major political, bureaucratic, and resource barriers to change by satisfying very basic, but often unfulfilled, human needs
Outcomes	Produces a degree of predictability and order and has the potential to consistently produce major results expected by various stakeholders (e.g., for customers, always being on time; for stockholders, always being on budget)	Produces change, often to a dramatic degree, and has the potential to produce extremely useful change (e.g., new products that customers want, new approaches to labor relations that help make a firm more competitive)

Source: Reprinted with permission of The Free Press, a Division of Simon & Schuster Inc., from *A Force for Change: How Leadership Differs from Management*, by John P. Kotter. Copyright © 1990 by John P. Kotter, Inc.

knowledgeable authority would be seen as arrogant. In Indonesia a manager who referred a subordinate to someone else for answers would likely be seen as incompetent.

Several implications for leaders in international settings can be drawn from the cultural factors identified in Hofstede's work. In individualistic cultures leaders may need to focus their behavior on individual employees rather than the group. In contrast, in a collectivistic culture leader behaviors will need to focus on the group rather than on individual group members. In a group-oriented culture such as that of Japan an effective leader must guide subordinates while preserving group harmony. At Sony, for example, managers are expected to allow their employees to transfer at will to more interesting job settings because such transfers are believed to be in the firm's overall best interests. The Japanese management system focuses on consensus-building efforts to ensure that leaders and subordinates reach a common decision. Leaders would destroy group harmony if they dictatorially commanded their subordinates to implement the leaders' decisions. One problem that may develop, however, is that junior managers may attempt to anticipate their boss's preferred strategy and then offer it as their own. A leader confronted with such a strong tendency toward conformity must seek ways to encourage creative solutions from subordinates to new problems as they arise. Japanese managers may thus distance themselves from pending decisions, thereby encouraging subordinates to discuss a variety of options among themselves. Only then will the man-

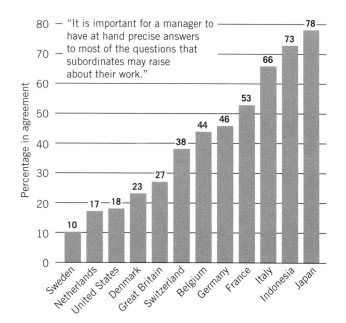

FIGURE 14.2

The Role of Managers Varies Across Cultures

Source: Reprinted from *International Studies of Management and Organization.* Vol. XIII, No. 1–2, Spring–Summer 1983, by permission of M. E. Sharpe, Inc., Armonk, N.Y. 10504.

agers lead by dropping subtle hints regarding what they see as the correct solution to an issue.[44]

Power orientation carries even more direct implications for situational leadership. In power-respecting cultures employees may expect leaders to take charge, to make decisions, and to direct the employees' efforts. Leaders therefore may need to concentrate on performance-oriented behaviors (direct, structured, and goal-oriented behaviors), avoid employee-oriented behaviors (caring, concern, and interpersonally oriented behaviors), and make little attempt to foster participation. However, if power tolerance is the more pervasive cultural value, a leader should spend less time on performance-oriented behaviors. In such situations, employee-oriented behaviors and more employee participation may result in higher levels of effectiveness.

Attempts at blurring the distinctions between managers and workers may not be well received in more authoritarian, hierarchical societies. For example, one U.S. firm exported the "company picnic" concept to its Spanish subsidiary, complete with company executives serving food to the Spanish employees. However, this informality was not well received by the employees, who were embarrassed at being served by their "superiors."[45]

Uncertainty orientation also is an important situational factor to consider. Where uncertainty avoidance is the rule, employees will have a strong desire for structure and direction. Thus performance-oriented behaviors are likely to be more successful, whereas employee-oriented behaviors and attempts to use participation may be less so. For example, German managers tend to be autocratic and task oriented, making decisions with reference to existing corporate rules and procedures. Having determined departmental objectives, the managers then confidently delegate tasks to subordinates, whom they expect to competently carry out the tasks necessary to achieve the objective.[46]

In contrast, employees more prone toward uncertainty acceptance may respond more favorably to opportunities for participation. They may even prefer participative behaviors on the part of their leaders. However, performance-oriented leadership may be undesirable or unnecessary, while employee-oriented leadership may have little impact. That is, employees may have such a strong desire to participate and be involved in their work that they see performance-oriented or employee-oriented behaviors from their supervisor as being redundant with or even negating their own opportunities for participation.

Finally, differences in goal orientation will affect leader behavior. Recall that people in aggressive goal behavior cultures tend to value money and other material rewards. If performance-oriented leadership or higher levels of participation are perceived by followers to result in higher rewards, those behaviors will be more acceptable. In contrast, outcomes enhancing quality of life are more desirable in passive goal behavior cultures. To the extent that employee-oriented leader behaviors may cause followers to feel more satisfied with their work and the organization, such behaviors may be more effective in these settings.

Cultural factors are among the most difficult and complex to assess and understand. They also may be among the most critical in determining leader effectiveness. It is important that leaders attempt to match their behaviors with the context—the people they are leading and the organization in which they are functioning.[47] For example, one study analyzed the productivity of U.S. and Mexican factories owned by the same MNC. Cultural differences clearly exist between the two countries. Mexico ranks high on power respect relative to the United States. U.S. residents are far more individualistic than residents of Mexico, while the family is more highly valued in Mexico than in the United States. Mexican cultural values translate into the paternalistic, authoritarian management style adopted by managers of the MNC's Mexican facilities. Managers of its U.S. facilities, however, adopted less paternalistic and more participative styles in managing their employees. By allowing management styles to adapt to national culture, the MNC enjoyed equally high levels of productivity from both facilities.[48]

› DECISION MAKING IN INTERNATIONAL BUSINESS

Another area of international business in which cultural differences exist is decision making. **Decision making** is the process of choosing one alternative from a set of alternatives in order to promote the decision maker's objectives.

Models of Decision Making

There are two different views of how managers go about making decisions, as illustrated in Figure 14.3. The *normative model of decision making* suggests that managers apply logic and rationality in making the best decisions. In contrast, the *descriptive model of decision making* argues that behavioral processes limit a manager's ability to always be logical and rational.[49]

The normative model suggests that decision making starts when managers recognize that a problem exists and a decision has to be made. For example, a Shell refinery manager recently noticed that turnover among a certain group of workers had increased substantially. After recognizing that a problem exists, managers must then identify potential alternatives for addressing the problem. To continue our example, the Shell manager determined that turnover can be caused by low wages, poor working conditions, or poor supervision, so her alternatives included raising wages, improving working conditions, or changing the group's supervisor.

The third step in the normative model is to evaluate each alternative in light of the original problem. The Shell manager knew the group's wages were comparable to the wages of other workers in the refinery. She also realized that the group's work area recently had been refurbished, so she assumed working conditions were not a problem. In addition, she discovered that a new supervisor recently had been appointed for the group. Using this information, the manager proceeded to the fourth step in the normative process, selecting the best alternative. She felt the problem was due to poor supervision, so she looked more closely at that part of the situation.

After scrutinizing the new supervisor's records, the manager saw that the supervisor had been promoted during a very hectic period and had not gone through the refinery's normal supervisory training program. The fifth step of the normative model suggests that the chosen alternative be implemented, so the

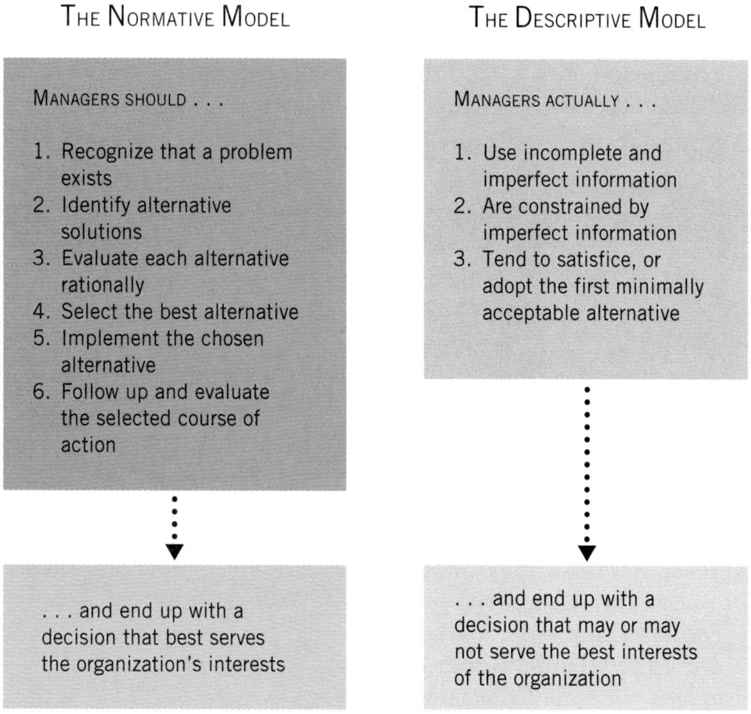

THE NORMATIVE MODEL

MANAGERS SHOULD . . .

1. Recognize that a problem exists
2. Identify alternative solutions
3. Evaluate each alternative rationally
4. Select the best alternative
5. Implement the chosen alternative
6. Follow up and evaluate the selected course of action

. . . and end up with a decision that best serves the organization's interests

THE DESCRIPTIVE MODEL

MANAGERS ACTUALLY . . .

1. Use incomplete and imperfect information
2. Are constrained by imperfect information
3. Tend to satisfice, or adopt the first minimally acceptable alternative

. . . and end up with a decision that may or may not serve the best interests of the organization

FIGURE 14.3

Models of the Decision-Making Process

manager arranged for the new supervisor to complete his training. After six months turnover in the group dropped significantly, and the manager was certain from this follow-up and evaluation that her chosen course of action had been the correct one.

The descriptive model acknowledges that the foregoing is perhaps how managers should make their decisions. However, the model also notes that in reality managers are affected by two important behavioral processes. The first is called bounded rationality. *Bounded rationality* suggests that decision makers are constrained in their ability to be objective and rational by limitations of the human mind. Thus they often use incomplete and imperfect information. Notice that the Shell manager did not consult with the members of the group to find out why turnover had increased. Had she done so, she might have gained additional information. The other behavioral process is called satisficing. *Satisficing* suggests that managers sometimes adopt the first minimally acceptable alternative they identify, when a further search might suggest an even better alternative. For example, because the supervisor had an opportunity to gain some experience, he might have been able to improve his skills with an abbreviated or accelerated training program rather than going through the full program.

The Normative Model Across Cultures

We can draw several possible implications from applying our basic understanding of the normative and descriptive models to decision making in other cultures.[50] To explore these implications, we first walk through the steps in the normative model.

Step 1: Problem Recognition.   People from different cultures are likely to recognize and define problem situations in very different ways. In individualistic cultures problems are likely to be defined in terms of individual scenarios and consequences. In collectivistic cultures the focus will be more on group-related issues and situations. In an uncertainty-accepting culture managers are more likely to take risks in solving problems and making decisions. In uncertainty-avoiding cultures, managers may be much more cautious and strive to reduce uncertainty as much as possible before making a decision. As a result, they may fall back on company policies and rules to provide a course of action ("We can't do that because it's against company policy").

Step 2: Identifying Alternatives.   The processes through which alternatives are identified also will vary across cultures. In power respecting cultures managers may be much less willing to consider an alternative that potentially threatens the hierarchy—for example, that a suggestion from a subordinate might be valid or that a problem might exist at a higher level in the organization. In power-tolerant cultures such hierarchical issues are more likely to be considered possible remedies to organizational problems.

In collectivistic societies the desire for group harmony and conflict avoidance may be so strong that decision making is approached in unique ways. For example, the Japanese concern for maintaining group harmony has given rise to the *ringi* system for identifying alternatives and making decisions. The **ringi system** provides that decisions cannot be made unilaterally; doing that would be too individualistic and therefore destructive of group harmony. To encourage creative solutions, a manager may draw up a document, called the *ringisho*, which defines the problem and sets out a proposed solution. The Japanese corporate belief is that those who implement a solution should be those most affected by the problem because they understand the problem and are motivated to solve it. Thus most *ringisho* originate from middle managers.

Although the *ringisho* originates from an individual, it is soon subsumed by the group. The document is circulated to all members of the originator's work group, as well as to other groups affected by it. As the *ringisho* passes through the workplace, it may be accepted, rejected, or modified. Only a document that is approved by all its reviewers is passed to a more senior manager for approval or disapproval. Before a *ringisho* reaches this stage, however, any senior manager worth his salt will have already dropped hints if he had objections to any parts of it. Appropriate changes then would have been incorporated into the document by some subordinate before the *ringisho* arrived at the senior manager's desk. Through the *ringi* system, creativity, innovation, and group harmony are all promoted.[51]

In contrast, the German business structure is both strongly hierarchical and compartmentalized. Decision making tends to be slow and drawn out, designed to build consensus within a department of a firm. Data are painstakingly gathered, then communicated to the appropriate employees within the hierarchy. However, information often does not flow easily between departments, and a decision, once reached, may be difficult to change. Also, established operating procedures are followed carefully. These factors substantially reduce the firm's flexibility and responsiveness to rapidly changing conditions. The resulting inflexibility often hinders the performance of foreign subsidiaries of German MNCs, which have difficulty getting the home office to acknowledge that their operating conditions may differ from those in Germany.[52]

Step 3: Evaluating Alternatives.   Evaluating alternatives also can be affected by cultural phenomena. For example, an alternative that results in financial gain may be more attractive in an aggressive goal behavior culture than in a passive goal behavior culture, which may prefer an alternative that results in improved quality of work life. Uncertainty avoidance also will be a consideration; alternatives with varying levels of associated uncertainty may be perceived to be more or less attractive.

Evaluating alternatives is further complicated in countries where people tend to avoid taking responsibility for making decisions. China's economic policies, for example, have changed so quickly and drastically over the past five decades that bureaucrats supporting today's economic policies may find themselves in political difficulties tomorrow. A Chinese proverb, "The tall tree gets broken off in the wind," suggests the tendency of many Chinese officials to avoid association with any decision that could haunt them later. Group decision making reduces the potential blame an individual bureaucrat may suffer.[53]

Step 4: Selecting the Best Alternative.   Cultural factors can affect the actual selection of an alternative. In an individualistic culture, for example, a manager may be prone to select an alternative that has the most positive impact on the manager personally; in a collectivistic culture the impact of the alternative on the total group will carry more weight. Not surprisingly, a manager trained in one culture will often use the same techniques when operating in a different culture, even though they may be ineffective there. In one recent study comparing U.S. managers operating in the United States with U.S. managers operating in Hong Kong, the managerial behaviors of the two groups were found to be the same. These behaviors included managerial supportiveness of subordinates, problem solving, openness of communication, disciplining of subordinates, and so on. However, although these behaviors positively affected company performance in the United States, they had no effect on company performance in Hong Kong.[54]

Cultural differences in problem solving and decision making may be particularly troublesome for partners in a joint venture because the partners must develop mutually acceptable decisions. U.S. managers often deliberately use conflict (in the form of devil's advocate or dialectical inquiry techniques) as a means of improving the decision-making process. Managers from more consensus-oriented societies, such as Japan, find this disharmonious approach very distasteful and unproductive.[55]

Step 5: Implementation.   In a power-respecting culture implementation may be mandated by a manager at the top of the organization and accepted without question by others. In a power-tolerant culture participation may be more crucial to ensure acceptance. In an uncertainty-avoiding culture managers may need to carefully plan every step of the implementation before proceeding so that everyone knows what to expect. In an uncertainty-accepting culture managers may be more willing to start implementation before all the final details have been arranged.

Step 6: Follow-Up and Evaluation.   Follow-up and evaluation also have cultural implications, most notably regarding power orientation. In a power-respecting culture a manager may be unwilling to find fault with an alternative suggested by a higher-level manager. Also, too much credit may be given to a higher-level manager purely on the basis of the manager's position in the hierarchy. In a power-tolerant culture responsibility, blame, and credit are more likely to be accurately attributed.

The Descriptive Model Across Cultures

The behavioral processes of bounded rationality and satisficing are more difficult to relate to cultural differences. Few research efforts have specifically explored these phenomena in different cultures, and their very nature makes it hard to draw reasonable generalizations. It is likely that bounded rationality and satisficing do have some impact on business decisions made in different cultures and therefore need to be understood by managers, but more research needs to be conducted on their precise influence. In particular, all managers need to understand the potential limitations of applying different modes of decision making in different cultural settings. For example, a few years ago the Japanese owners of the Dunes Hotel and Casino in Las Vegas tried to implement a variety of Japanese management practices in the casino operation. One was decision making by consensus. The owners quickly recognized that this practice was far too slow for the intensely competitive, fast-changing casino industry.[56]

> The Dunes Hotel and Casino is owned by a group of Japanese investors. A few years ago, they tried to implement the methodical, consensus-oriented approach to decision making that works so well in Japan. They soon discovered, however, that their U.S. workers found this approach ineffective for the dynamic and fluid environment in which they worked.

› GROUPS AND TEAMS IN INTERNATIONAL BUSINESS

Other important behavioral processes that international managers should understand are those associated with groups and teams. Regardless of whether a firm is a small domestic company or a large MNC, much of its work is accomplished by people working together as a team, task force, committee, or operating group.

The Nature of Group Dynamics

Firms use groups frequently because, in theory, people working together as a group can accomplish more than they can working individually. Although organizations use many different kinds of groups, teams are especially popular today. Indeed, many managers now refer to all their groups as teams. Technically, a *group* is any collection of people working together to accomplish a common purpose, whereas a *team* is a specific type of group that assumes responsibility for its own work. Because teams are so ubiquitous today and the term is so common among managers, we will use this term in our discussion.

A mature team in a firm generally has certain characteristics:

1. It develops a well-defined role structure; each member has a part to play on the team, accepts that part, and makes a worthwhile contribution.

2. It establishes norms for its members. Norms are standards of behavior, such as how people should dress, when team meetings or activities will begin, the consequences of being absent, how much each member should produce, and so on.

3. It is cohesive. That is, team members identify more and more strongly with the team, and each member respects, values, and works well with the others.

4. Some teams identify informal leaders among their members—individuals whom the team accords special status and who can lead and direct the team without benefit of formal authority.

A team can potentially reach maximum effectiveness if its role structure promotes efficiency, its norms reinforce high performance, it truly is cohesive, and its informal leaders support the firm's goals. Sony's computer development group took on all these characteristics, which no doubt helped contribute to the group's ability to reach its goal ahead of schedule. However, if a team's role structure is inefficient, its performance norms are low, it is not cohesive, and/or its informal leaders do not support the firm's goals, then the team may become very ineffective from the firm's standpoint.

Managing Cross-Cultural Teams

The composition of a team plays a major role in the dynamics that emerge from it. A relatively homogeneous team generally has less conflict, better communication, less creativity, more uniform norms, higher cohesiveness, and clear informal leadership. A more heterogeneous team often has more conflict, poorer communication, more creativity, less uniform norms, a lower level of cohesiveness, and more ambiguous informal leadership.

Managers charged with building teams in different cultures need to assess the nature of the task to be performed and, as much as possible, match the composition of the team to the type of task. For example, if the task is relatively routine and straightforward, a homogeneous team may be more effective. Similarities in knowledge, background, values, and beliefs can make the work go more smoothly and efficiently. If the task is nonroutine, complex, and/or ambiguous, a heterogeneous team may be more effective because of members' diverse backgrounds, experiences, knowledge, and values. "Venturing Abroad" illustrates what can happen when these issues are ignored.

Other cultural factors also may play a role in team dynamics. In an individualistic culture establishing shared norms and cohesiveness may be somewhat difficult,

VENTURING *Abroad*

MIXING A
MATCHING
NEW JOINT VE

Because work teams have become so ubiquitous in management today, it follows that many new joint ventures and other alliances will have work teams as a critical component. Managers need to pay careful attention to the culturally based differences that can exist among people in such settings and how those differences can facilitate or hinder the new venture.

Consider the experiences that three multinational firms had a few years ago when they decided to "venture abroad" together. It all started when IBM, Siemens, and Toshiba entered into a new joint venture to work together in developing an advanced type of computer chip. Each firm identified a set of research scientists for the project, and the total group of around 100 people assembled for work at an IBM facility in East Fishkill, a small Hudson River Valley town in New York. The idea was that the best and brightest minds from three diverse companies would bring such an array of knowledge, insight, and creativity to the project that it was bound to succeed.

Unfortunately, things did not start out well, and it took much longer than expected for the firms to figure out how to work together. The biggest reasons cited for the early difficulties related to the cultural differences and barriers that existed among the group members. For example, the Japanese scientists were accustomed to working in one big room where everyone could interact with everyone else and where it was easy to overhear what others were saying. The IBM facility, however, had small, cramped offices that could only hold a few people at a time. The Germans were unhappy because most of their offices lacked windows—they claimed that back home no one would be asked to work in a windowless office.

Interpersonal styles also caused conflict at times. the U.S. and Japanese scientists criticized their German colleagues for planning and organizing too much, whereas the Japanese were criticized for their unwillingness to make clear decisions. The German and Japanese scientists felt that their U.S. hosts did not spend enough time socializing with them after work. There also were problems with employee privacy and workplace rights. The office doors at the IBM facility had small windows that visitors could use to see whether or not the occupant was busy before knocking. Both the Germans and the Japanese saw this as an invasion of their privacy and often hung their coats over the windows. They also objected to IBM's strict no-smoking policy, which mandated that people go outside to smoke, regardless of weather conditions.

Because of these problems, the group's initial progress (or lack of it) was discouraging. Managers felt that a big part of the problem was that they did not adequately train the group members before transferring them to the project and that better cultural training in particular would have been useful. Fortunately for the joint venture, the group members eventually started to socialize and train themselves in how to overcome the cultural differences. Indeed, after the early rough spots the new venture finally took off, and the new chip was developed only a few months behind schedule.

Sources: "Siemens Climbs Back," *Business Week*, June 5, 2000, pp. 79–82; "Computer Chip Project Brings Rivals Together, but the Cultures Clash," *Wall Street Journal*, May 3, 1994, pp. A1, A8; *Hoover's Handbook of American Business 2001* (Austin: Hoover's Business Press, 2001), pp. 780–781; *Hoover's Handbook of World Business 2001* (Austin: Hoover's Business Press, 2001), pp. 548–549, 620–621.

whereas in a collectivistic culture team cohesiveness may emerge naturally. In a power-respecting culture team members should probably be from the same level of the organization because members from lower levels may be intimidated and subservient to those from higher levels. In a power-tolerant culture variation in organizational level may be less of a problem. Uncertainty avoidance and team dynamics also may interact as a function of task. If a task is vague, ambiguous, or unstructured, an uncertainty-avoiding group may be unable to function effectively; in contrast, an uncertainty-accepting group may actually thrive. Finally, teams in an aggressive goal behavior culture may work together more effectively if their goal has financial implications, whereas teams in a passive goal behavior culture may be more motivated to work toward attitudinal or quality-of-work outcomes.[57]

Matching business behavior with the cultural values of the workforce is a key ingredient to promoting organizational performance. Much of the competitive strength of Japanese firms, for example, is due to their incorporation of Japanese cultural norms into the workplace. Japanese culture emphasizes the importance of group harmony and respect for superiors. "Silent leaders," those who guide rather than command subordinates and who preserve group harmony, are more admired than are authoritarian managers. The *ringi* system ensures that new approaches are granted group approval before being implemented. The traditional lifetime employment practices that some major Japanese firms use promote employee loyalty to the organization. All these features are reinforced by careful selection of new employees. Only those persons who are willing to subordinate their individual goals to the needs of the group are hired. This corporate philosophy carries over to foreign operations of Japanese MNCs. For example, many U.S. newspapers have reported on the extraordinary amounts of testing and interviewing that such firms operating in North America do before hiring an employee.

CHAPTER REVIEW

Summary

Behavioral and interpersonal processes are vitally important in any organization. Both their importance and their complexity are magnified in international firms. Individual differences provide the cornerstone for understanding behavioral patterns in different cultures. Personality traits, attitudes, perceptions, and stress are important individual differences that international managers should understand.

Motivation is the overall set of forces that causes people to choose certain behaviors from a set of available behaviors. Need-based, process-based, and reinforcement models of motivation each explain different aspects of motivation. Although none of these models is generalizable to all cultures, each can provide insights into motivation in similar cultures.

Leadership is the use of noncoercive influence to shape the goals of a group or organization, to motivate behavior toward reaching those goals, and to help determine the group or organizational culture. People from different cultures react in different ways to each type of leadership behavior. These different reactions are determined partially by cultural dimensions and partially by the individuals themselves.

Decision making is the process of choosing an alternative from a set of alternatives designed to promote the decision maker's objectives. People from different cultures approach each step in the decision-making process differently. Again, variation along cultural dimensions is a significant determinant of variations in decision-making processes.

Groups and teams are part of all organizations. A team's role structure, cohesiveness, norms, and informal leadership contribute to its success or failure. Culture plays a major role in determining the team's degree of heterogeneity or homogeneity, which in turn helps determine its overall level of effectiveness.

Review Questions

1. Define personality and explain how personality differences affect individual behavior.
2. Explain how attitudes vary across cultures.
3. Discuss the basic perceptual process and note how it differs across cultures.
4. Explain how attitudes and perception can affect each other.
5. Discuss stress and how it varies across cultures.
6. Identify some of the basic issues managers must confront when attempting to motivate employees in different cultures.
7. How do needs and values differ in different cultures?
8. Summarize the steps in the normative model of decision making and relate each to international business.
9. Why are teams so important? What are the basic implications of teams for an international business?

Questions for Discussion

1. Which do you think is a more powerful determinant of human behavior—cultural factors or individual differences?
2. Think of two or three personality traits that you believe are especially strong in your culture and two or three that are especially weak. Relate these to Hofstede's cultural dimensions.
3. Assume you have just been transferred by your company to a new facility in a foreign location. Which of your own personal dimensions do you think will be most effective in helping you deal with this new situation? Does your answer depend on which country you are sent to?
4. How might perception affect motivation in different cultures?
5. How might organizations in different cultures go about trying to enhance leadership capabilities?
6. Do you think it will ever be possible to develop a motivation framework that is applicable in all cultures? Why or why not?
7. How do motivation and leadership affect corporate culture?
8. What advice would you give a Japanese, an Australian, and an Italian manager just transferred to the United States?
9. Assume you are leading a team composed of representatives from British, Mexican, Brazilian, and Egyptian subsidiaries of your firm. The team must make a number of major decisions.
   a. What guidelines might you develop for yourself for leading the team through its decision-making process?
   b. What steps might you take to enhance the team's cohesiveness? How successful do you think such an effort would be?

BUILDING GLOBAL SKILLS

Select a country in which you have some interest and about which you can readily find information (for example, Japan as opposed to Bhutan). Go to your library and learn as much as you can about the behavior of people from the country you selected. Concentrate on such culturally based social phenomena as the following:

- The meaning people from the country attach to a few common English words
- The meaning they attach to common gestures
- How they interpret basic colors
- The basic rules of business etiquette they follow
- Their preferences regarding personal space
- How the country is characterized along Hofstede's dimensions

Team up with a classmate who chose a different country. Each of you should pick a product or commodity that is produced in the country you studied (such as stereos, bananas, oil, or machine parts).

Attempt to negotiate a contract for selling your product or commodity to the other. As you negotiate, play the role of someone from the country you studied as authentically as possible. For example, if people from that culture are offended by a certain gesture, and your counterpart happens to make that gesture while negotiating, act offended!

Spend approximately 15 minutes negotiating. Then spend another 15 minutes discussing with your classmate how the cultural background each of you adopted affected (or could have affected) the negotiation process.

Follow-Up Questions

1. How easy or difficult is it to model the behavior of someone from another country?
2. What other forms of advance preparation might a manager need to undertake before negotiating with someone from another country?

WORKING WITH THE WEB: BUILDING GLOBAL INTERNET SKILLS

Preparing for an International Expansion

Assume you are a senior human resource manager with a large food products firm. Your company has recently decided to increase its international activities and is aggressively seeking new market opportunities abroad. As a first step, your firm is exploring joint venture or strategic alliance partnerships in Sweden, Denmark, Italy, Indonesia, and Japan.

One of your responsibilities will be to train your firm's managers as they prepare to relocate to foreign settings to represent your firm in the partnerships being negotiated. You know that each set of managers destined for specific locations will need specialized language training. You are less sure, however, about the leadership and cultural training you need to develop. That is, you are unsure whether each set of managers will need unique training, whether they can go

through common training together, or if there is some optimal combination of training for certain sets of managers together.

Use the Internet to learn as much as you can about individual behavior and interpersonal relations in the countries your firm is considering. Specifically, see if you can locate useful information about individual differences, motivation, leadership, decision-making, and group processes in these countries. Next, using the information you have located, make a tentative decision about the number of leadership and cultural training programs you will need to develop and whether sets of managers destined for certain countries can be combined or need to be trained separately. Finally, form small groups with two or three of your classmates and compare notes. How similar or dissimilar are the training strategies you each developed? Why did these similarities and differences emerge?

WE INVITE YOU TO VISIT THIS BOOK'S COMPANION WEB SITE AT www.prenhall.com/griffin

IN THE NEWS

Stress is a fact of life. Individuals react to stress differently both within and across cultures, and those who are living and working outside their home cultures are particularly vulnerable to the effects of stress. Demands at work can be complicated by the adjustments necessary to create a whole new life in unfamiliar circumstances.

Using the homepage of the *Financial Times* (www.ft.com) as a starting point (click on "FT Expat" at the left of the page and check under "Health"), find out what you can about stress among expatriate workers. You may need to widen your search to report on best practices for such challenges as selecting workers for overseas assignments, training them, offering support to their families, keeping in touch with them while they are away, and integrating them back into the home office when their assignment is over. Remember to focus on ways expatriates can deal with and reduce stress.

CLOSING CASE

adidas-Salomon Runs To Catch Up

Many people think of adidas as a second-tier athletic shoe company. These observers often are surprised to learn that the German apparel company once dominated the athletic sportswear business. A long series of missteps and mistakes, however, caused the firm to lose its dominant position in the industry to U.S. upstarts Nike and Reebok. Only in the last few years has adidas begun to turn itself around and to show signs of life.

adidas was founded in 1948 by Adi Dassler, a Bavarian shoe designer. For years the firm dominated the athletic shoe market. For example, when U.S. discus thrower Al Oerter won the first of his four Olympic gold medals in 1956, he was wearing adidas shoes. Basketball Hall of Famer Kareem Abdul-Jabbar, who played first for UCLA and then the Los Angeles Lakers of the NBA, wore adidas shoes throughout his career.

Trials and tribulations, however, sometimes come with success. The first big problem for adidas arose when Adi Dassler's brother, Rudolf, grew frustrated playing second fiddle to Adi and left to form his own company, Puma. Adi's son, Horst, also left adidas and started his own company as well. Horst and Adi eventually reconciled, and Horst took over the management of adidas when Adi retired in 1985. Although the family travails had taken a toll on the company's performance, Horst did seem to understand the problems facing the firm and had a vision for straightening them out. However, when Horst died two years later, there was no one in line to run the firm.

Horst Dassler's two sisters, who inherited ownership of the firm, sold adidas to a French financier named Bernard Tapie in 1989 for $320 million. By this time, however, the firm was going downhill fast. Its share of the U.S. athletic shoe market had dropped from an amazingly strong 70 percent to an amazingly weak 2 percent. This drop was due in part to new competition from Nike and Reebok but also in part to neglect and mismanagement.

Tapie promised to inject $100 million of new money into the firm but never carried through. He was so involved in left-wing politics in his native France that he paid little attention to the firm and ignored its growing losses. Tapie was indicted in a soccer-fixing scandal while serving as France's Urban Affairs Minister and sentenced to 18 months in jail. He eventually declared bankruptcy. adidas, meanwhile, was taken over by its creditors in 1993. At the time the company was losing $100 million a year.

The creditors knew they needed an astute manager, a strong leader, and an extraordinary turnaround artist if adidas was to regain its competitiveness. Fortunately for them, they found all three in a single person—Robert Louis-Dreyfuss, another French financier. At the time Louis-Dreyfuss was 42, had pocketed $10 million from previous turnarounds, and was restlessly retired. He quickly jumped at the opportunity to take on another interesting challenge.

Louis-Dreyfuss began to appreciate the size of his task on his first day at work when he saw that he was required to approve a salesperson's expense account for $300. He subsequently identified many of the problems as resulting from an old-line rigid bureaucracy based on rank, title, and status and a belief in slow, calculated decision making. He quickly realized that these were perhaps not the best traits for competing in the fast-moving athletic footwear market where the hottest style one month may be a loser the next, particularly among urban teenagers who represent the most profitable niche in this market.

Within a matter of weeks Louis-Dreyfuss had fired the firm's entire top management team—all German—and set in motion plans for streamlining the company. He brought in a French friend to head up sales, a Swede to run marketing, and an Australian as finance director. He also changed the firm's official language to English.

Next up was manufacturing. Louis-Dreyfuss shut down the firm's high-cost factories in Germany, Austria, and France, moving production to Asian countries with lower labor costs. At the same time he began to invest heavily in marketing and advertising. Under previous management teams marketing was cut regularly as a way of slashing costs. Louis-Dreyfuss knew that more—not less—marketing was necessary if adidas was to get back on track. Following the model established by Nike, adidas is now rapidly signing up big-name athletes to wear and endorse its shoes.

Louis-Dreyfuss also stressed that decision making was going to occur much faster than before. A good example of his imprint came when the New York Yankees let it be known they were looking to make a deal with an athletic shoe company. While Nike and Reebok were slowly and methodically calculating and reviewing the financial details of making such an arrangement with the best-known baseball team in the world, adidas put together a package very quickly and won the contract.

Under Louis-Dreyfuss's leadership adidas has again become a force with which to be reckoned. Its market share is growing, and more and more adidas shoes are showing up on the basketball courts and soccer fields of the world. Nike is still growing, primarily due to its expansion into sportswear and other athletic equipment. adidas, however, is gaining ground on Reebok, which holds second place in the athletic shoe market, and has both Reebok and Nike taking an occasional look over their shoulders to see who is gaining on them.

In 1997 Louis-Dreyfuss decided that adidas had sufficiently reestablished itself in the athletic apparel market that he could afford to look for other avenues for growth. He also wanted to move into new areas where adidas did not compete with Nike and Reebok. After looking around a bit, he found just what he wanted—Salomon, a French firm that was a market leader in snow ski equipment and in golf equipment with its Taylor Made Golf subsidiary. He quickly put together a deal, bought the firm for $1.4 billion, and changed the name of the company to adidas-Salomon AG. Among other things this acquisition gave the firm an opportunity for market growth and expansion without having to go head-to-head in additional marketing battles with Nike and Reebok. So far, at least, the new combined firm seems to be running downhill on nicely packed powder![58]

Case Questions

1. What role has leadership played in both the decline and recovery of adidas-Salomon?
2. Contrast adidas-Salomon's former and current approaches to decision making to what you now know about the normal German approach.
3. How do you think adidas-Salomon's current success is affecting the motivation of its employees?

CHAPTER

Daimler and Chrysler: A Dream Partnership?

Several years ago executives at Daimler-Benz, a large German manufacturer, embarked on a new grand strategy of diversification. Their goal was to create an organization that relied less on its motor vehicle business and instead generated revenues across a variety of product groups and businesses. To facilitate the implementation of this strategy, they created a new organization design for the company, one closely resembling a holding company comprised of several independent divisions. The firm's core business, Mercedes-Benz, was set up as a near-autonomous entity run by its own CEO. This was done in part because Mercedes-Benz was contributing about two-thirds of the firm's revenues.

> **"Executives at Daimler-Benz and Chrysler called the deal 'a marriage of equals.'"**

The other subsidiaries created were Debis (Daimler-Benz Interservices), which included computing and communication, financial, insurance, trading, and marketing services; AEG, which included automation, rail systems, domestic appliances, electrotechnical systems and components, microelectronics, and office and communication systems businesses; and Deutsche Aerospace, which consisted of aircraft, space systems, defense systems, and propulsion systems businesses and related activities.

15

Controlling the International Business

Each subsidiary, like Mercedes-Benz, was given its own CEO who was made responsible and accountable for that subsidiary's performance.

Unfortunately, this strategy failed to produce the results that company executives had envisioned. Indeed, the new organization design proved to be so unwieldy that the firm's performance actually began to decline rather than improve. Profits from Mercedes-Benz had to be used to cover losses in other Daimler-Benz businesses, costs were going up throughout the firm, and productivity was suffering. Finally, Jurgen Schrempp, a senior Daimler-Benz executive, was appointed CEO of the company in 1994 and given a mandate to clean things up.

As a starting point, Schrempp spent several months studying every aspect of the company. Though he previously had headed up one of Daimler-Benz's business units, he did not have a complete understanding of the entire company. However, it soon became apparent to him how problems should be corrected. Specifically, he decided to fold Mercedes-Benz back into the core of the business, renew the firm's commitment to the automobile industry, look for opportunities to lower costs, and shed some of the corporation's poorer performing business units.

As a start, Schrempp eliminated 40,000 jobs at Daimler-Benz and sold 12 unprofitable businesses in 1995. He also centralized decision-making power for virtually all significant decisions in the hands of his senior executive team. The CEO position at Mercedes-Benz also was eliminated and replaced with a president. This president in turn was given less power and autonomy than had been enjoyed by the previous leader. Then in May 1998 Schrempp orchestrated his boldest move of all when he announced a merger with U.S-based Chrysler Corporation.

Executives at Daimler-Benz and Chrysler called the deal a "marriage of equals." To reinforce this idea, Schrempp also indicated that he and Chrysler's CEO, Robert Eaton, would serve as cochairs for at least three years. In reality, however, rather than a merger the deal was more accurately an acquisition, with Daimler-Benz owning 58 percent of the new company and retaining most of the senior management positions. The new enterprise was dubbed DaimlerChrysler and instantaneously became the third largest automaker in the world.

Investors and other analysts hailed the deal as a dream partnership and a perfect match. For example, Daimler engineers could teach Chrysler about quality and technology, and Chrysler could give the Germans lessons in efficiency and speed to market. Daimler's well-developed distribution network could boost Chrysler's expansion in Europe, and Chrysler could help Mercedes-Benz with logistics and other support in the United States. Their products were almost perfectly complementary, with Mercedes-Benz having the cachet of expensive, finely engineered, and high-performance passenger cars, and Chrysler providing a nice mix of lower-priced cars and minivans plus the valuable Jeep brand name for its sports utility vehicles. Finally, DaimlerChrysler also would have more combined muscle to attack emerging markets in Asia and South America. All in all, the union seemed to be a corporate marriage made in heaven.[1]

The partnership between Daimler-Benz and Chrysler promised to create a new enterprise based on global synergies and efficiencies and to boost the firm's productivity around the world. However, to successfully blend the two separate companies into one and to then capitalize on the potential benefits of the merger, managers would have to effectively engage in another crucial management function, control. For an international firm control can be focused on activities within a given market, within several markets, or across the entire organization. **Control** is the process of monitoring and regulating activities in a firm so that some targeted measure of performance is achieved or maintained. The control process begins with the establishment of a goal or other performance target (for example, meeting sales goals or cost limits). Managers then monitor progress toward meeting that goal or target and take appropriate actions to keep the firm on track. Control activities may focus on direct financial performance (such as the profit margin achieved by an individual manager, business unit, or foreign subsidiary) or on some other aspect of performance (such as cutting labor costs, improving quality, or reducing parts inventories).[2]

For example, suppose the European purchasing manager of a Canadian manufacturing firm has an annual travel budget of $48,000. Based on previous experience, the manager expects travel costs to be spread evenly throughout the year, or around $4,000 per month. So travel expenses of $3,900 in January lead her to assume that costs are about where they should be. However, if her February travel expenses are $7,000, she may need to cut back in March or, if she feels more travel is needed, request an increase in her travel budget from headquarters. The manager is controlling travel costs by monitoring monthly expenses to keep them within an expected range and then taking action if they fall too far outside that range.

In this chapter we introduce the three basic levels in international firms at which control systems may be used: strategic, organizational, and operational. We also discuss some methods by which control can be more effectively managed. Then we describe three important aspects of international management that are in fact forms of control systems: the management of productivity, quality, and information.

LEVELS OF CONTROL IN INTERNATIONAL BUSINESS ‹

As illustrated in Figure 15.1, there are three main levels at which control can be implemented and managed in an international business. These three key levels of control are the strategic, organizational, and operations levels. Although each is important on its own merits, the three levels also are important collectively as an organizing framework for managers to use in approaching international control from a comprehensive and integrated perspective.

Strategic Control

Strategic control is intended to monitor both how well an international business formulates strategy and how well it goes about implementing that strategy.[3] Thus strategic control focuses on how well the firm defines and maintains its desired strategic alignment with the firm's environment and how effectively the firm is set-

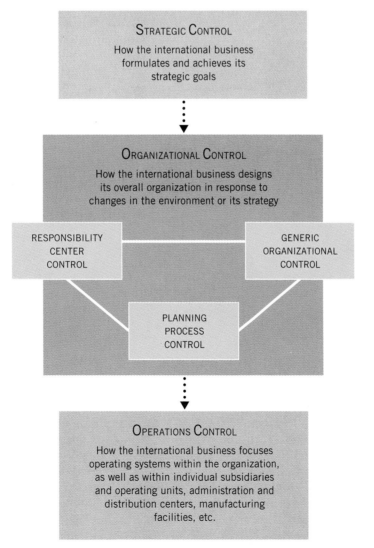

FIGURE 15.1

Levels of International Control

ting and achieving its strategic goals. For example, Daimler's merger with Chrysler represented a logical and attractive acquisition. It seemed clear that the firms could learn from each other, that their existing product lines and organizational strengths complemented one another, and that the combined firm would be able to compete more effectively in global markets with other behemoths such as General Motors, Ford, and Toyota.

Strategic control also plays a major role in the decisions firms make about foreign-market entry and expansion. This is especially true when the market holds both considerable potential and considerable uncertainty and risk. For example, in the wake of India's overtures for foreign direct investment, many firms are expanding their operations in that country. Hindustan Lever, Unilever's Indian subsidiary, has increased its capacity for soap and detergent manufacturing and launched new food-processing operations as well. These steps represent a strategic commitment by the firm to the Indian market. As this strategy is implemented, strategic control systems will be used to ensure a smooth process. If opportunities in the Indian market continue to unfold, Unilever no doubt will continue to expand there. However, if uncertainty and risk become too great, the firm may become cautious, perhaps even reversing its expansion in India.

Often the most critical aspect of strategic control is control of an international firm's financial resources. Money is the driving force of any organization, whether that money is in the form of profits or of cash flow to ensure that ongoing expenses can be covered. Moreover, if a firm has surplus revenues, managers must ensure that those funds are invested wisely to maximize their payoff for the firm and its shareholders. Thus it is extremely important that an international firm develop and maintain effective accounting systems. Such systems should allow managers to fully monitor and understand where the firm's revenues are coming from in every market in which the firm operates, to track and evaluate all its costs and expenses, and to see how its parts contribute to its overall profitability.[4]

Poor financial control can cripple a firm's ability to compete globally. For example, Mantrust, an Indonesian firm, bought Van Camp Seafood, packager of Chicken of the Sea tuna, for $300 million. Most of that money was borrowed from Indonesian banks. Mantrust's owner was unskilled at managing debt, and the firm had difficulties making its loan payments. Both Mantrust and Van Camp struggled for years until Mantrust sold Van Camp to Tri-Union Seafood, a limited partnership owned by investors in the United States and Thailand.

Financial control is generally a separate area of strategic control in an international firm. Most firms create one or more special managerial positions to handle financial control. Such a position is usually called **controller**. Large international firms often have a corporate controller responsible for the financial resources of the entire organization. Each division within the firm is likely to have a divisional controller who is based in a country where the division operates and who oversees local financial control. Divisional controllers usually are responsible both to the heads of their respective divisions and to the corporate controller. These control relationships are managed primarily through budgets and financial forecasts.

A special concern of an international controller is managing the inventory of various currencies needed to run the firm's subsidiaries and to pay its vendors.[5] For

⟩ Zhang Yue, the founder and CEO of China's Broad Air Conditioning, built his $192-million company by incorporating management techniques pioneered by Japanese firms. The firm's air conditioning systems command a 20 percent price premium over those sold by competitors because of Broad's high quality and energy efficiency.

example, Coca-Cola has to manage its holdings of over 150 currencies as part of its daily operations. Each foreign subsidiary of an international firm needs to maintain a certain amount of local currency for the subsidiary's domestic operations. Each also needs access to the currency of the parent corporation's home country to remit dividend payments, reimburse the parent for the use of intellectual property, and pay for other intracorporate transactions. The subsidiary further must be able to obtain other currencies to pay suppliers of imported raw materials and component parts as their invoices are received.

Given the possibility of exchange rate fluctuations, as discussed in Chapter 7, the controller needs to oversee the firm's holdings of diverse currencies to avoid losses if exchange rates change. Many multinational corporations (MNCs) centralize the management of exchange rate risk at the corporate level. However, others, such as the Royal Dutch/Shell Group, allow their foreign affiliates to use both domestic and international financial and commodity markets to protect the affiliates' costs and prices against exchange rate fluctuations. Firms that decentralize this task need to maintain adequate financial controls on their subsidiaries or face financial disaster. For example, a few years ago Shell's Japanese affiliate, Showa Shell Seikiyu KK, engaged in widespread speculative trading in foreign-currency markets, a practice forbidden by Shell. That is, rather than trying to hedge against exchange rate fluctuations, the Japanese affiliate was trying to earn profits through exchange rate fluctuations. Knowledge of this speculative trading was brought to light only when the Japanese affiliate reported a loss of over $1 billion. Clearly, Shell's internal controls had broken down and failed to detect the speculative activities. As a result, corporate officials implemented new procedures and tighter controls to better manage the firm's financial resources.

Managers in international firms must have access to the information they need to engage in strategic control. Information networks and systems should be designed to provide as much relevant, current, and accurate information as possible to managers so they can make informed decisions. Failure to do so can lead to expensive mistakes. For example, the Mitsui Construction Company was seeking a site in London on which to build a new office complex. Rather than gather their own information on potential sites, Mitsui managers relied on a British consulting firm. The consultants convinced Mitsui to bid on the site of an old building, indicating that the property would sell for no more than $250 million and that the old building could be cheaply demolished. After Mitsui bought the property, it discovered that its bid of $255 million was $90 million more than the next highest bid. Even worse, a few days later the British government declared the building a historic site, so it could not be demolished. Clearly, Mitsui had acted on inaccurate and misleading information.

Another type of strategic control that is increasingly important to international firms is control of joint ventures and other strategic alliances.[6] As we discussed in Chapter 12, strategic alliances, particularly joint ventures, are being used more often by and becoming more important to international firms. It follows that strategic control systems also must account for the performances of such alliances. By definition a joint venture or other strategic alliance is operated as a relatively autonomous enterprise; therefore, most partners agree to develop an independent control system for each alliance in which they participate. The financial control of these alliances then becomes an ingredient in the overall strategic control system for each partner's firm. That is, the alliance maintains its own independent control systems, but the results are communicated not only to the managers of the alliance but also to each partner.

Organizational Control

Organizational control focuses on the design of the organization itself. As discussed in Chapter 13, there are many different forms of organization design that an international firm can use. However, selecting and implementing a particular design does not necessarily end the organization design process. For example, as a firm's environment or strategy changes, managers may need to alter the firm's design to better enable the firm to function in the new circumstances. Adding new product lines, entering a new market, or opening a new factory—all can dictate the need for a change in design.

International firms generally use one or more of three types of organizational control systems: responsibility center control, generic organizational control, and planning process control.[7] The first two types are based on the **locus of authority**, where the power to make various decisions resides within the organization. If it is appropriate for individual subsidiaries to call the shots in an MNC, then many of their controls logically can be decentralized. In other cases it may be more appropriate for headquarters or some other centralized location to maintain more direct control over various decisions. The third type of control system is based on the planning process.

Responsibility Center Control. The most common type of organizational control system is a decentralized one called **responsibility center control**. Using this system, the firm first identifies fundamental responsibility centers within the organization. Strategic business units are frequently defined as responsibility centers, as are geographical regions or product groups. Once the centers are identified, the firm then evaluates each on the basis of how effectively it meets its strategic goals. Thus a unique control system is developed for each responsibility center. These systems are tailored to meet local accounting and reporting requirements, the local competitive environment, and other circumstances.

Nestlé uses responsibility center control for each of its units, such as Poland Springs, Alcon Labs, and Nestlé-Rowntree (see Map 15.1). These subsidiaries regularly provide financial performance data to corporate headquarters. Managers at Poland Springs, for example, file quarterly reports to Nestlé headquarters in Switzerland so that headquarters can keep abreast of how well its U.S. subsidiary is doing. By keeping each subsidiary defined as a separate and distinct unit and allowing each to use the control system that best fits its own competitive environment, corporate managers in Switzerland can see how each unit is performing within the context of its own market. Each report must contain certain basic information, such as sales and profits, but each also has unique entries that best reflect the individual subsidiary and its market.

Generic Organizational Control. A firm may prefer to use **generic organizational control** across its entire organization; that is, the control systems used are the same for each unit or operation, and the locus of authority generally resides at the firm's headquarters. Generic organizational control most commonly is used by international firms that pursue similar strategies in each market in which they compete. Because there is no strategic variation between markets, responsibility center control would be inappropriate. The firm is able to apply the same centralized decision making and control standards to the strategic performance of each unit or operation. Moreover, international firms that use the same strategy in every market often have relatively stable and predictable operations; therefore, the organizational control system the firms use also can be relatively stable and straightforward. For example, United Distillers PLC markets its line of bourbon products in the United States, Japan, and throughout Europe. Because the product line is essentially the same in every market and the characteristics of its consumers vary little across markets, the firm uses the same control methods for each market. Similarly, Starbucks achieved its initial success in the United States by practicing rigid quality control throughout every aspect of its operations. As the firm is expanding internationally—for example, it is currently opening stores in Canada, Japan, Singapore, and across Europe—it is using exactly the same control standards and methods it has been using in the United States for 30 years.[8]

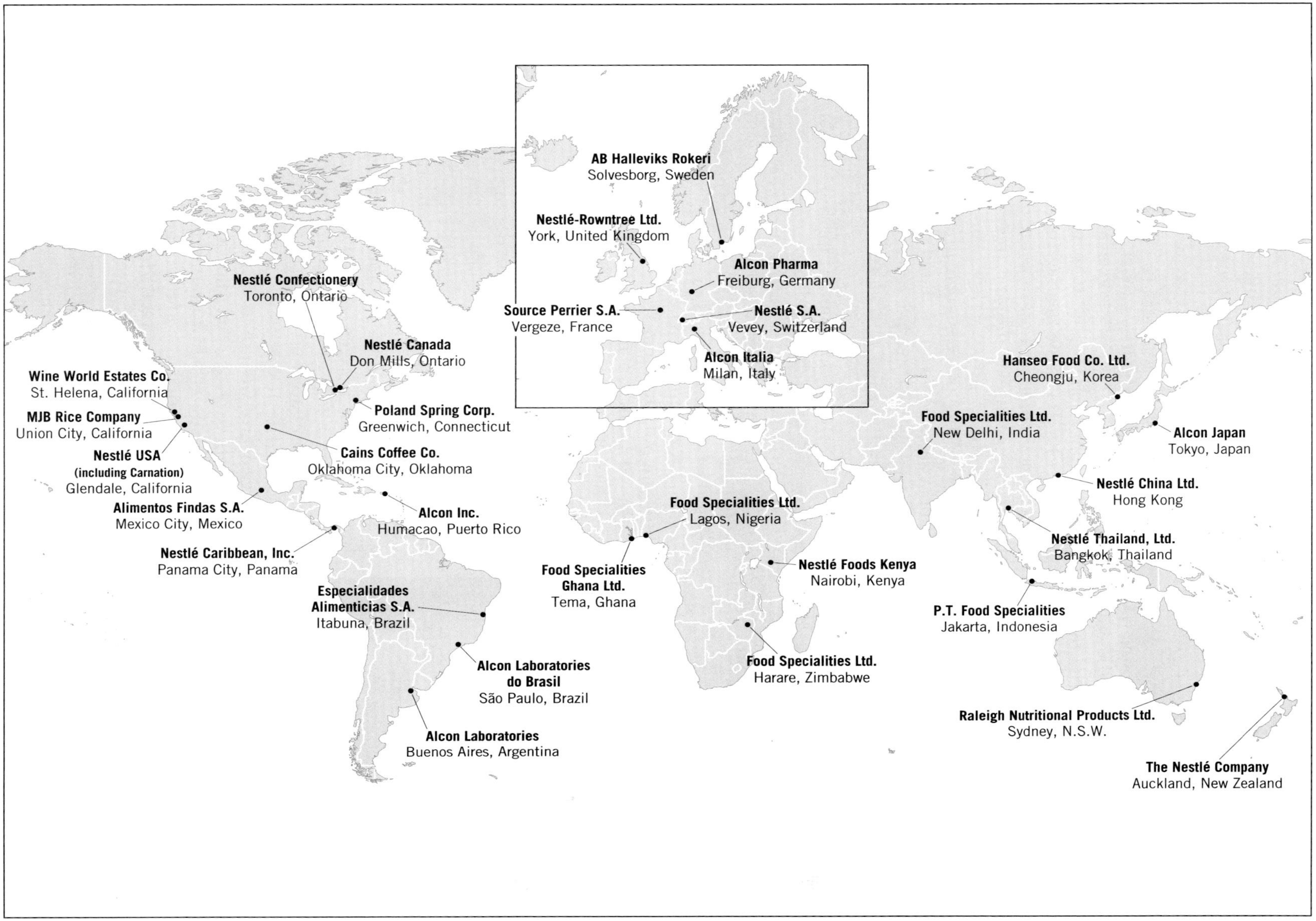

MAP 15.1 **A Sampling of Nestlé's Global Holdings, Subsidiaries, and Affiliates**

Alcon Japan
Tokyo, Japan

Nestlé China Ltd.
Hong Kong

Nestlé Thailand, Ltd.
Bangkok, Thailand

Hanseo Food Co. Ltd.
Cheongju, Korea

Food Specialities Ltd.
New Delhi, India

P.T. Food Specialities
Jakarta, Indonesia

Raleigh Nutritional Products Ltd.
Sydney, N.S.W.

The Nestlé Company
Auckland, New Zealand

Nestlé Foods Kenya
Nairobi, Kenya

Food Specialities Ltd.
Harare, Zimbabwe

Food Specialities Ltd.
Lagos, Nigeria

Food Specialities Ghana Ltd.
Tema, Ghana

AB Halleviks Rokeri
Solvesborg, Sweden

Alcon Pharma
Freiburg, Germany

Nestlé S.A.
Vevey, Switzerland

Alcon Italia
Milan, Italy

Nestlé-Rowntree Ltd.
York, United Kingdom

Source Perrier S.A.
Vergeze, France

Nestlé Canada
Don Mills, Ontario

Poland Spring Corp.
Greenwich, Connecticut

Cains Coffee Co.
Oklahoma City, Oklahoma

Alcon Inc.
Humacao, Puerto Rico

Nestlé Confectionery
Toronto, Ontario

Especialidades
Alimenticias S.A.
Itabuna, Brazil

Alcon Laboratories
do Brasil
São Paulo, Brazil

Alcon Laboratories
Buenos Aires, Argentina

Wine World Estates Co.
St. Helena, California

MJB Rice Company
Union City, California

Nestlé USA
(including Carnation)
Glendale, California

Alimentos Findas S.A.
Mexico City, Mexico

Nestlé Caribbean, Inc.
Panama City, Panama

427

Planning Process Control.   A third type of organizational control, which could be used in combination with either responsibility center control or generic organizational control, focuses on the strategic planning process itself rather than on outcomes. **Planning process control** calls for a firm to concentrate its organizational control system on the actual mechanics and processes the firm uses to develop strategic plans. This approach is based on the assumption that if the firm controls its strategies, desired outcomes are more likely to result. Each business unit may then concentrate more on implementing its strategy, rather than worrying as much about the outcomes of that strategy.

Nortel Networks uses this approach for part of its organizational control process. Whenever a unit fails to meet its goals, the head of that unit meets with the firm's executive committee. The meeting focuses on how the original goals were set and why they were not met. Throughout the meeting the emphasis is on the process that was followed that led to the unsuccessful outcome. The goal, therefore, is to correct shortcomings in the actual process each unit uses. For example, a unit might have based its unmet sales goals on outdated market research data because there were insufficient funds for new market research. Planning process control would focus not on correcting the sales shortfall but on enabling more accurate forecasting in the future.

❯ Operations control is an important element of America Online's success. Operating and maintaining these racks of modems efficiently and effectively is critical to retaining the loyalty of the millions of subscribers to the firm's Internet services.

There are clear and important linkages between strategic control and organizational control in an international firm. When a firm adopts a centralized form of organization design, strategic control is facilitated as a logical and complementary extension of that design. When a firm uses a decentralized design, strategic control is not as logically connected with that design.[9] A decentralized design gives foreign affiliates more autonomy and freedom while making it more difficult for the parent to maintain adequate control. The challenge facing managers of the parent is to foster the autonomy and freedom that accompany a decentralized design while simultaneously maintaining effective parent control of operating subsidiaries.

For a large international firm organizational control must be addressed at multiple levels. At the highest level the appropriate form of organization design must be maintained for the entire firm. At a lower level the appropriate form of organization design must be maintained for each subsidiary or operating unit. The firm also must ensure that these designs mesh with each other. Consider, for example, France's Cap Gemini S.A., the world's third largest computer services firm. Cap Gemini uses organizational control as an overarching framework for managing its entire array of control systems scattered across the globe. The firm's founder and CEO, Serge Kampf, has structured Cap Gemini as a holding company. This structure allows each subsidiary in the various countries in which the firm operates to create a unique design that works most effectively in the particular country. Each subsidiary is run by a top manager who reports directly to Kampf and who is responsible for maintaining effective control within the unit while still being accountable to the parent corporation. Thus Kampf can maintain tight control over all the firm's operations by isolating group performance, growth, and costs within clearly defined operating units. Each unit manager also is instructed to create a control network within the unit so that the manager can report to Kampf on any aspect of the business at any time.[10] In 2000, however, Cap Gemini purchased the consulting business of Ernst & Young. As a result, Kampf will have to restructure the firm's organizational controls to accommodate its expanded operations.

Operations Control

The third level of control in an international firm is operations control. **Operations control** focuses specifically on operating processes and systems within both the firm and its subsidiaries and operating units. Thus a firm needs an operations control system within each business unit and within each country or market in which the firm operates. The firm also may need an operations control system for each of its manufacturing facilities, distribution centers, administrative centers, and so on.

Strategic control often involves time periods of several years, while organizational control may deal with periods of a few years or months. Operations control, however, involves relatively short periods of time, dealing with components of performance that need to be assessed on a regular—perhaps even daily or hourly—basis. An operations control system is also likely to be much more specific and focused than strategic and organizational control systems.

For example, a manufacturing firm may monitor daily output, scrappage, and worker productivity within a given manufacturing facility, while a retail outlet may measure daily sales. A firm that wants to increase the productivity of its workforce or enhance the quality of its products or services primarily will use operations control to pursue these goals. Operations control usually focuses on the lower levels of a firm, such as first-line managers and operating employees.

Consider Aldi, a German grocery chain. Although people in the United States are used to sprawling, full-line supermarkets that carry everything from apples to zippers, typical European grocery stores tend to be smaller and less service oriented, to carry fewer product lines, and to charge higher prices. Aldi has prospered in Europe through an elaborate operations control system that relies heavily on cost control and efficiency. Aldi stores do not advertise or even list their numbers in telephone directories. Products are not unpacked and put on shelves but instead are sold directly from crates and boxes. The no-frills stores are also usually located in low-rent districts. Customers bring their own sacks (or pay Aldi 5¢ each for sacks), bag their own purchases, and rent shopping carts for 25¢ (refunded if the customer returns the cart to the storage rack). Aldi does not accept checks or coupons and provides little customer service, but this austere approach allows the firm to charge rock-bottom prices. Aldi has effectively transferred its control methods to its U.S. operation. The result? Aldi's net profit margins and sales per square foot in the United States are about double the industry norm. With 549 stores operating in 21 states, Aldi has become one of the country's most profitable grocery chains.

MANAGING THE CONTROL FUNCTION IN INTERNATIONAL BUSINESS ‹

Given the obvious complexities in control, it should come as no surprise that international firms must address a variety of issues in managing the control function. To effectively manage control, managers in such firms need to understand how to establish control systems, what the essential techniques for control are, why some people resist control, and what managers can do to overcome this resistance.

Establishing International Control Systems

As illustrated in Figure 15.2, control systems in international business are established through four basic steps: (1) Set control standards for performance, (2) measure actual performance, (3) compare performance against standards, and (4) respond to deviations. There obviously will be differences in specificity, time frame, and sophistication, but these steps are applicable to any area and any level of control.

FIGURE 15.2

Steps in International Control

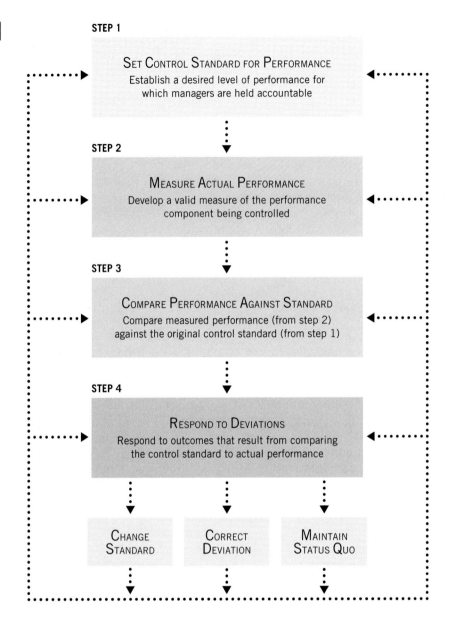

Set Control Standards for Performance. The first step in establishing an international control system is to define relevant control standards. A **control standard** in this context is a target, or a desired level of the performance component the firm is attempting to control. Control standards need to be objective and consistent with the firm's goals. Suppose a firm is about to open its first manufacturing facility in Thailand. It might set the following four control standards for the plant:

1. Productivity and quality in the new plant will exceed the levels in the firm's existing plants.

2. After an initial break-in period 90 percent of all management positions in the plant will be filled by local managers.

3. The plant will obtain at least 80 percent of its resources from local suppliers.

4. The plant will produce and sell 100,000 units per month.

These control standards help provide a road map for managers involved in opening and running the new plant. Managers can readily see that sales, productivity, and quality are critical and that the firm expects them to hire and buy locally.

Where did these standards come from? The firm set them on the basis of its objectives for the new plant, its experience with similar operations, and its overall goals.[11] The second and third goals may have resulted from a conscious strategy of reducing political risk or the parent firm's desire to be a good corporate citizen in each country in which it operates.

Measure Actual Performance.   The second step in creating an international control system is to develop a valid measure of the performance component being controlled. Some elements of performance are relatively easy and straightforward to measure; examples are actual output, worker productivity, product quality, unit sales, materials waste, travel expenses, hiring practices, and employee turnover. Considerably more difficult are measuring the effectiveness of an advertising campaign to improve a firm's public image, measuring ethical managerial conduct, and measuring employee attitudes and motivation. For the firm introducing a new product in a foreign market, performance may be based on the actual number of units sold. For the new plant in Thailand used as an example earlier, performance would be assessed in terms of sales, productivity, quality, and hiring and purchasing practices.

Compare Performance Against Standards.   The third step in establishing an international control system is to compare measured performance (obtained in step 2) against the original control standards (defined in step 1). Again, when control standards are straightforward and objective and performance is relatively easy to assess, this comparison is easy. For example, comparing actual sales of 80,437 units against a target sales level of 100,000 is simple. Likewise, comparing the actual hiring of 20 Thai managers against a target of hiring 19 Thai managers is also straightforward. When control standards and performance measures are less concrete, however, comparing one against the other is considerably more complicated. Suppose a manager established a control standard of "significantly increasing market share" and now finds that market share has increased by 4 percent. Is this significant? Obviously, this comparison is ambiguous and difficult to interpret. Managers are advised to use specific and objective standards and performance measures whenever possible.

Responding to Deviations.   The fourth and final step in establishing an international control system is responding to deviations observed in step 3. One of three different outcomes can result when comparing a control standard and actual performance: the control standard has been met, it has not been met, or it has been exceeded. For example, if the standard is sales of 100,000 units, actual sales of 99,980 units probably means the standard has been met, whereas sales of only 62,300 units means it has not been met. Actual sales of 140,329 units clearly surpasses the standard.

Depending on the circumstances, managers have many alternative responses to these outcomes. If a standard has not been met and a manager believes it is because of performance deficiencies by employees accountable for the performance, the manager may mandate higher performance, increase incentives to perform at a higher level, or discipline or even terminate those employees. Of course, the actual course taken depends on the nature of the standard versus performance expectations, the context within which the failure has occurred, and myriad other factors.

Sometimes standards are not met for unforeseen reasons, such as unexpected competition, an unexpected labor strike, unpredictable raw material shortages, or local political upheavals. On the other hand, the original control standard may have been set too high to begin with, in which case it may be possible to adjust the standard downward or to make additional allowances.

Finally, actual performance occasionally exceeds the control standard. Again, there may be multiple explanations: Managers and employees may have expended

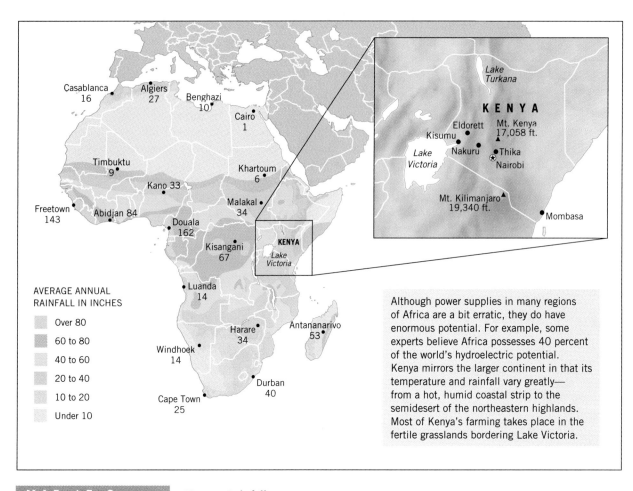

Although power supplies in many regions of Africa are a bit erratic, they do have enormous potential. For example, some experts believe Africa possesses 40 percent of the world's hydroelectric potential. Kenya mirrors the larger continent in that its temperature and rainfall vary greatly—from a hot, humid coastal strip to the semidesert of the northeastern highlands. Most of Kenya's farming takes place in the fertile grasslands bordering Lake Victoria.

MAP 15.2   **Kenyan Rainfall**

extra effort, the original standard may have been too low, or competitors may have bungled their own opportunities. In this case managers may need to provide additional rewards or bonuses, adjust their control standards upward, or aggressively seize new opportunities.

Kenya Power & Lighting (KP&L) often finds it must react to deviations between control standards and actual performance in its distribution of electric power throughout Kenya. Businesses and municipalities in Kenya are more heavily dependent on hydroelectric power than are those in most other countries. Whenever Kenya experiences inadequate rain or prolonged dry spells (see Map 15.2), KP&L's water-powered electric plants have to ration electricity. Twice in the last 15 years, the government-run utility has been forced to enact nationwide rationing to ensure adequate power. It also has used smaller-scale rationing on numerous other occasions. During each rationing period continued supplies of electricity were guaranteed to hospitals and security installations, whereas big businesses were required to cut energy consumption by 30 percent, and homeowners were subjected to two-hour blackout periods each day. As soon as energy supplies reached an acceptable limit, rationing was phased out.

Essential Control Techniques

Because of the complexities of both the international environment and international firms themselves, those firms rely on a wide variety of different control techniques. We do not describe them all but introduce a few of the most impor-

VENTURING *Abroad* | EFFECTIVE CONTROL AT SIEBEL SYSTEMS

Control is paying off for Siebel Systems, a fast-growing U.S. company that rings up $1.6 billion in annual sales of sophisticated enterprise software to corporations such as British Telecom, Cap Gemini, and Sun Microsystems. Siebel's software helps corporate customers better manage sales and other critical functions, allowing more effective monitoring and control of activities and results. The firm currently earns about 60 percent of its revenues from the U.S. customers but is rapidly expanding into foreign markets.

Tom Siebel, the founder and CEO, is a strong believer in control. He enforces standards for almost everything in the organization, from employee performance to customer service to service response. This helps him maintain control over operations, finances, structure, and strategy covering 5,200-plus employees in 100 offices worldwide.

Siebel needs peak performance day in and day out to fuel the company's torrid rate of growth, which is more than 117 percent a year. So every six months the company ranks the employees in each department. Those who fall in the lowest 5 percent are terminated, whereas top performers are rewarded. Still, Siebel's turnover is lower than that of other high-tech firms. This control process will help Siebel maintain high performance while doubling its global workforce to more than 10,000 and adding 2 million square feet of office space in the coming years.

Operations are another area where Siebel exerts strict control. Too often, software companies announce plans to introduce updated or new programs, then miss the launch date by months or even years. Not Siebel. Customers know the company can be depended on to release updated versions of its software every spring. They also know they can get speedy, knowledgeable help if they have problems installing or operating some of the complex programs Siebel sells. The CEO and his management team set an example for all employees by spending considerable time working with customers. Tom Seibel, for example, devotes about 60 per-

cent of his working day meeting with customers, learning about their problems, offering advice, and showing how his firm's products can provide solutions.

Unlike many high-tech firms, Siebel has an unwritten dress code mandating professional business wear at work. Male employees are expected to appear in suits and ties; female employees are expected to wear skirts and jackets or pantsuits. This dress code supports the air of professionalism that pervades the entire company. Every Siebel office is decorated in the same way, with blue carpeting and off-white walls, gray desktops, and maple furniture. Every desk is neat, with no empty soda cans or pizza cartons (eating at the desk is forbidden). In another departure from Silicon Valley norms, Siebel does not allow the on-site basketball games and beer blasts that are so common in many high-tech firms. In short Siebel is all business, an approach that impresses customers and adds, in a small way, to Siebel's ability to compete against Oracle, PeopleSoft, Baan, and other rivals.

As CEO, Siebel holds tight rein on his company, but lately he has begun sharing some control with other top executives. Until recently he was the only manager who could sign off on expenses over $10,000; now two senior managers have been given the authority to approve expenses up to $50,000, with higher amounts going to Siebel's desk for review and approval. He also has appointed a chief operating officer to oversee day-to-day issues in marketing and sales, engineering, and services. Still, he expects managers and employees to move quickly when he asks questions or requests action. After Siebel met with a customer one Friday, he promised a complete proposal by Monday—impossible for many companies but a normal reaction time for the people at Siebel.

Sources: Melanie Warner, "Confessions of a Control Freak," *Fortune*, September 4, 2000, pp. 130–140; *Hoover's Handbook of Emerging Companies 2001* (Austin: Hoover's Business Press, 2001), p. 120.

tant ones. "Venturing Abroad" also highlights several control techniques and related issues.

Accounting Systems. Accounting is a comprehensive system for collecting, analyzing, and communicating data about a firm's financial resources. Accounting procedures are heavily regulated and must follow prescribed methods dictated by national governments. Because of these regulations, investors, government agencies, and other organizational stakeholders within a given country can better compare the financial performance of different organizations, have a common understanding of what various kinds of information mean, and place reasonable trust in the accuracy and meaning of that information.

International firms face more difficulties in establishing their accounting procedures than do purely domestic firms. International businesses must develop accounting systems to control and monitor the performance of the overall firm and each division, operating unit, or subsidiary. These systems enable managers to keep abreast of the financial performance of every part of the firm. Dickson Poon, a Hong Kong investor, uses accounting systems to maintain tight financial control over poor-performing retailers that he buys and then revitalizes. For example, he bought the struggling Harvey Nichol's department store in London a few years ago, implemented a stronger accounting system (along with other changes, of course), and turned the store into a moneymaker. More recently, he purchased the bankrupt Barneys New York chain in the United States, and he is using the same strategy to return that retailer to profitability.[12]

Problems can arise when the accounting standards or procedures of the countries in which a firm operates are incompatible with each other, as is frequently the case. Each subsidiary must maintain its accounting records in accordance with local procedures and denominate its accounts in the local currency to satisfy local government regulations and meet the needs of local managers. Yet to meet the needs of investors, regulators, and tax collectors in the parent's home country, the parent needs the local accounting records of each subsidiary translated into the parent's currency using accounting procedures dictated by the parent's home country. The parent further must decide whether it will evaluate the performance of its subsidiaries and the subsidiaries' managers using the local accounting system, the parent's home country accounting system, or some combination of the two. We discuss international accounting in more detail in Chapter 19.

Procedures.   Firms also use various procedures to maintain effective control. Policies, standard operating procedures, rules, and regulations all help managers carry out the control function. For example, as part of a manufacturing firm's political agreement with its host country, the firm may establish a policy that at least 75 percent of the raw materials it buys must be obtained from local suppliers. This policy guides plant managers in making purchasing decisions and allocations. A firm also could have a rule that each employee transferred to a foreign unit must attain basic proficiency in the local language within six months. This rule would serve as an ongoing and easily referenced measure of what is expected.

Firms often alter their procedures in the face of adversity. For example, during the recent crisis involving the Firestone/Ford recall of defective tires, both firms had to deviate from their established procedures in order to satisfy both their customers and government regulators. Firestone replaced tires at no cost instead of prorating costs based on tread wear. Ford replaced many Firestone tires with more expensive Michelin tires at no extra cost. At times both firms even refused to sell new tires to unaffected customers to maintain a sufficient inventory for the recall program.

Performance Ratios.   International firms also use various performance ratios to maintain control. A **performance ratio** is a numerical index of performance that the firm wants to maintain. A common performance ratio used by many firms is inventory turnover. Holding excessive inventory is dysfunctional because the inventory ties up resources that could otherwise be used for different purposes and because the longer materials sit in inventory, the more prone they are to damage and loss. Based on a firm's unique circumstances, it may decide it does not want anything to sit in inventory for more than 30 days. That is, the firm wants to turn over its inventory 12 times a year, and the performance ratio for inventory management is therefore 12. For example, Laura Ashley uses inventory turnover ratios to more effectively manage its stock of garments and household design accessories. Turnover ratios are likely to differ among different types of retailers and among different countries depending on the amount of floor space, the sophistication of inventory management systems, and the reliability of suppliers. For example, because rents are so high in Tokyo, convenience stores like 7–11 have little room for storage. They must maintain high inventory turnover ratios to remain profitable. Often vendors resupply the 7–11s four or five times a day to ensure that goods are available for customers. Sophisticated electronic linkages allow the stores to communicate their inventory needs to suppliers on a real-time basis.

British Airways also uses performance ratios to maintain control of its airline operations. One key ratio for an airline is the percentage of seats filled on its flights. If this ratio falls below a set minimum, the firm looks into alternative ways to generate passenger demand, such as discounts or additional promotional activity. Another ratio of interest to British Airways is the percentage of its flights that arrive and depart on time. If this ratio slips too much, managers try to identify and eliminate the reasons for delays.

Behavioral Aspects of International Control

Regardless of how well formulated and implemented a control system may be, managers must understand that human behavior plays a fundamental role in how well control works. Essential to this understanding is being aware that some people resist control. Also essential is recognizing that resistance can be minimized. Although resistance to control is likely to exist within most cultures, its magnitude will vary across cultures.

Resistance to Control.   People in international firms may resist control for various reasons. One potential reason is overcontrol, whereby the firm tries to exert more control over individuals than they think is appropriate.[13] By definition control regulates and constrains behavior; most people accept this within what they perceive to be reasonable limits (with the limits being partially determined by the cultural context). However, if attempts to control behavior begin to exceed those perceived limits, people may balk and begin to resist. For example, when Disney first opened Disneyland Paris, it attempted to apply the same grooming standards for its employees there that it uses in the United States, banning beards and mandating trimmed hair. French employees saw this as overcontrol. They complained about the standards, vented their grievances in the media, and occasionally ignored the standards altogether. The resistance grew to the point where Disney eventually backed off and developed standards that were more acceptable to its European employees.

People also may resist control because it may be inappropriately focused; that is, the firm inadvertently may be trying to control the wrong things. For example, if a firm places so much emphasis on lowering costs that quality is compromised and employee morale suffers, employees may become indignant and attempt to circumvent the control system. Whistler Radar, a U.S. firm, encountered this problem in its assembly of radar detectors. Its control system focused on quality control only at the end of the assembly process. When managers discovered that 100 of the firm's 250 employees were doing nothing more than reworking defective units assembled by the other 150, the managers realized that control should have been focused on quality throughout the assembly process.

Finally, people may resist control because control increases their accountability. In the absence of an effective control system employees may be able to get by with substandard performance because managers do not understand what the employees are doing relative to what they should be doing. For example, if a foreign-branch manager has to submit financial performance data only annually, the manager may not do as good a job on a day-to-day basis as the firm would like. If the firm were to request performance reports more frequently, it could increase the manager's accountability. At the same time, if the firm demands too much reporting, it becomes prone to overcontrol. Thus it is important to strike a balance between appropriate and acceptable levels of accountability without edging over into overcontrol.

People from different cultures will respond in different ways to control. Using the framework discussed in Chapter 4, for example, individuals from power-tolerant cultures may be more likely to resist control because they are inclined to discount power relationships within their organization. Conversely, people from power-accepting cultures may perceive control as a normal part of organizations. Uncertainty acceptance also will be important. People who want to avoid uncertainty may accept more control than will people who do not mind uncertainty.

Overcoming Resistance to Control.   Although there are no guaranteed methods for eliminating resistance to control, there are a few that can help minimize it. The appropriate method, as well as its likely effectiveness, will vary by culture.

For many cultures—particularly power tolerant ones—an important method is to promote participation. Involving employees who are going to be affected by control in its planning and implementation will enable them to better understand the goal of the control system, how and why the system works, and how their jobs fit into the system. As a result, the employees may be less prone to resist it.

Another method to reduce resistance that works well in most cultures is to create a control system that has a clear appropriate focus and that creates reasonable accountability without overcontrolling. GlaxoSmithKline, the U.K.'s largest pharmaceutical firm and the world's second largest, uses this method. The firm is very receptive to allowing scientists to explore ideas and possibilities for new prescription drugs, thereby motivating those scientists to pursue ideas and creating an atmosphere of creativity and innovation. At the same time Glaxo managers carefully monitor the progress of new product development. If costs start becoming excessive or if development begins to lag too far behind the competition, managers may choose to curtail a given project. Employees see this as a viable strategy because it gives them the opportunity to pursue their scientific interests while simultaneously keeping costs in check.[14]

A firm also may overcome resistance to control by providing a diagnostic mechanism for addressing unacceptable deviations. Suppose a plant manager reports productivity levels far below those expected by headquarters. Top managers should avoid jumping to a potentially wrong conclusion, such as simply assuming the manager has done a poor job and reprimanding the manager, or worse. Instead they first should learn why the poor performance occurred. For example, it may have resulted from the corporate purchasing manager's having bought inferior materials for the plant.

Again, it is important to account for cultural factors when planning how to deal with resistance to control. People from power-accepting cultures, for example, may be reluctant to actively participate in planning and implementing control because they view such activities as the domain of management.

Finally, behavioral aspects of control can be approached and managed from a cultural perspective. A firm may attempt to replace behaviors resulting from national culture with those more consistent with the firm's corporate culture. Being careful to hire people with values, experiences, work habits, and goals that are consistent with the firm's can go a long way toward this goal. Managers of Japanese-owned automobile factories in the United States, for example, spend thousands of dollars per worker selecting U.S. employees who will be receptive to the Japanese way of working. Further refinements in behavior can be expedited through training and management development programs designed to help impart the firm's cultural values and business methods.

› CONTROLLING PRODUCTIVITY IN INTERNATIONAL BUSINESS

A key consideration in the control systems of many international firms is productivity. Productivity is distinct from control, yet the two also are closely related in that the ultimate aim of most control systems is to ensure high levels of productivity. An understanding of productivity allows a better grasp of all the means of attaining it. Thus in this section we define productivity, examine productivity around the world, and discuss how firms manage productivity.

At its simplest level **productivity** is an economic measure of efficiency that summarizes the value of outputs relative to the value of the inputs used to create the outputs.[15] Productivity is important for various reasons. For one thing, it helps determine a firm's overall success and contributes to its long-term survival. For another, productivity contributes directly to the overall standard of living within a particular country. If the firms within a country are especially productive, the country's citizens will have more products and services to consume. Moreover, the firm's goods and services can be exported to other countries, thereby bringing additional revenues back into the country of origin. Each of these factors positively impacts gross domestic product and thus benefits the whole country.

Productivity can be measured in many ways. **Overall productivity** (also called **total factor productivity**) is determined by dividing total outputs by total inputs. This summary index, however, is often of little direct value to managers, who are likely to be more interested in productivity relative to specific outputs and/or specific inputs. For example, **labor productivity**, a measure of how efficiently a firm is using its workforce, is determined by dividing output by direct labor (either hours or dollars). Comparing labor productivity for different subsidiaries may help managers identify problems before they become excessively costly. For example, because it was previously a monopoly, Japan's Nippon Telegraph & Telephone (NTT) did not worry too much about labor productivity. However, it has had to take a closer look at this measure of its performance once its industry underwent deregulation. As it turns out, NTT's labor productivity is only about one-third that of AT&T's. As a result of this comparison, managers at NTT are seeking ways to boost their labor productivity.[16]

Productivity Around the World

Although calculating productivity is relatively easy, finding the data to use in the calculations is another matter altogether. Few firms divulge their productivity statistics, and countries often report their data in such different terms that comparisons are difficult. Nevertheless, there is good evidence regarding productivity in the United States, Japan, Germany, and most other Quad countries. Among these countries clear differences exist between absolute levels of productivity and productivity growth rates. In absolute terms the United States is the world's most productive major economy. But although U.S. workers are more productive than their foreign counterparts, U.S. productivity growth has fluctuated. Throughout the 1980s productivity growth rates were greater in both Germany and Japan than in the United States. More recently, productivity growth in the United States has begun to accelerate again, whereas productivity growth in Japan has stalled, due at least in part to that country's economic recession. Germany's productivity growth also slowed due to the difficulties of integrating the previously independent economies and political systems of East Germany and West Germany.

Managing Productivity

Regardless of where a firm operates, one of its fundamental goals must be to continue to monitor and control its productivity. There are several general strategies a firm can pursue in its efforts to maintain and/or boost productivity. Three approaches in particular often help firms become more productive: (1) Spend more on research and development (R&D), (2) improve operations, and (3) increase employee involvement.

Spend More on R&D. The starting point in improving productivity is often to invest more heavily in R&D. Through R&D firms identify new products, new uses for existing products, and new methods for making products. Each of these outcomes in turn contributes directly to higher productivity. U.S. firms spend more on R&D than do their foreign competitors, but the gap is narrowing as more foreign firms increasingly invest in R&D. Moreover, U.S. firms have a long and painful history of achieving significant scientific breakthroughs but then being ineffective in getting them to market.[17]

Improve Operations.   Another important way to increase productivity is to improve operations. This is where control comes in; a firm seeking to increase productivity needs to examine how it does things and then look for ways to do them more efficiently. Replacing outmoded equipment, automating selected tasks, training workers to be more efficient, and simplifying manufacturing processes are all ways to improve operations and boost productivity. Japanese manufacturers have been especially successful at increasing productivity through improved operations. Just-in-time manufacturing and inventory control techniques, consistent investments in technology, and a concentration on efficiency have paid big dividends for many Japanese firms. U.S. firms also are paying more attention to operations. For example, General Electric once required three weeks to fill an order for a custom-made industrial circuit breaker box. Further, the firm had six plants making the boxes. Through improved operations—more efficient manufacturing methods and product simplification, among other improvements—the firm now fills such an order in only three days and makes all its circuit breaker boxes in a single facility.

Boliviana de Energia Electrica SA, known in the United States as Bolivia Power, has worked continuously for years to improve its operations. As one of the few foreign-owned utility firms in Latin America (it is a subsidiary of a British utility), Bolivia Power repeatedly escaped attempts at nationalization by demonstrating that it produces electricity more efficiently as a privately owned firm than it could if it were state owned. Its managers have consistently sought ways to be more efficient, cut costs, and boost output. For example, they have always stressed the value of using the newest technology. By continuing to invest in new equipment and machinery, they have consistently increased productivity. This strategy and their attention to other areas of operations have streamlined the firm's operations to the point that it is among the world's most productive utility firms.[18] "Wiring the World" also illustrates how firms are using electronic purchasing as a way to improve operations and thus boost their productivity.

Increase Employee Involvement.   Finally, productivity can be improved by increasing employee involvement, particularly in power-tolerant cultures. The idea is that if managers give employees more say in how they do their jobs, those employees will become more motivated to work and more committed to the firm's goals. Further, because they are the ones actually doing the jobs, the employees probably have more insights than anyone else into how to do the jobs better.[19] Increased involvement is generally operationalized through the use of self-managed teams. Groups of workers are formed into teams, each of which has considerable autonomy over how it does its job. Self-managed teams were pioneered in Sweden and the United Kingdom, refined in Japan, and are now used extensively worldwide.[20]

For example, Lufthansa currently uses employee participation in its efforts to cut costs. The firm's overhead had grown out of control, and it needed to be reduced for the firm to remain competitive. Lufthansa wanted to cut its payroll in Germany but was stymied because of two strong national unions. So the firm enlisted the assistance of the unions to meet its cost-cutting goals. Representatives from the firm and both unions now meet regularly to devise ways to trim payroll costs without resorting to massive layoffs. So far the cuts have focused on reducing work rules and eliminating jobs through attrition and early retirement.

Wiring the World

E-PURCHASING TO IMPROVE OPERATIONS

Buying from other businesses is big business. Every year companies buy more than $7 trillion worth of parts, supplies, and services from suppliers around the world. Not so long ago, purchasing agents and other buyers had to hunt through mountains of supplier catalogs and make dozens of phone calls to track down stock numbers and quotes before writing purchase orders. Now, by using technology to tighten control of the purchasing function, a company can take much of the time and the hassle out of the process of acquiring inputs—and expand its scope to scour the globe for the lowest prices or the quickest delivery times.

On the CheMatch.com Web site, for example, buyers can see current market prices and availability for chemicals such as benzene and book orders online with a few keystrokes. On the Petrocosm Marketplace site buyers for energy companies can instantly compare competitive prices on drilling machinery and other supplies, then place orders online with hundreds of suppliers from dozens of different countries. On FreeMarkets.com buyers can arrange reverse auctions in which suppliers bid for the right to provide a particular input.

The savings can be enormous. John Deere's e-purchasing initiative is expected to shave 5 percent off the firm's annual cost of parts and supplies. Over the course of five years the farm equipment manufacturer will save a total of $1 billion, giving its bottom line a healthy boost. Moreover, Deere is achieving these impressive results while reducing the size of its purchasing department by 25 percent. IBM now uses the Web to buy 90 percent of its supplies, streamlining control of its procurement budget. Online reverse auctions have helped the Naval Supply Systems Command save 22 percent on bunk units purchased for U.S. Navy ships. Tighter control, increased efficiency, and lower costs—the combination makes e-purchasing an attractive technique for businesses of any size.

Sources: "E-Purchasing Saves Businesses Billions," *USA Today*, February 7, 2000, pp. 1B, 2B; "The E-Numbers Game," *Time*, April 17, 2000, p. 66.

CONTROLLING QUALITY IN INTERNATIONAL BUSINESS ‹

Control also helps firms maintain and enhance the quality of their products and/or services. Indeed, quality has become such a significant competitive issue in most industries that control strategies invariably have quality as a central focus. The American Society for Quality Control has defined **quality** as the totality of features and characteristics of a product or service that bear on its ability to satisfy stated or implied needs.[21] The International Organization for Standardization (ISO) has been working to develop and refine an international set of quality guidelines. These guidelines, called collectively ISO 9000, provide the basis for a quality certification that is becoming increasingly important in international business. Indeed, major companies in more than 50 countries, including the United States and all European Union members, have agreed to adopt ISO 9000 guidelines as they are developed.[22]

Quality is of vital importance for several reasons. First, many firms today compete on the basis of quality.[23] Firms whose products or services have a poor reputation for quality are unlikely to succeed. For example, Daewoo, Samsung, and the LG Group, three Korean firms, have had some difficulty competing in Europe because their products are not perceived by Europeans as being of the same quality as those made by European firms. As we explain in Chapters 16 and 17, such country-of-origin factors play a major role in the marketing and location decisions of international firms. The South Korean *chaebols* are attempting to overcome this shortcoming by opening plants in Europe, establishing strategic alliances with European firms, and working to meet ISO 9000 guidelines and standards.

Second, quality is important because it is directly linked with productivity. Higher quality means increased productivity because of fewer defects, fewer resources devoted to reworking defective products, and fewer resources devoted to quality control itself. Recall, for example, how Whistler Radar, by improving its product quality, also improved the productivity of its workers. Higher quality also serves to lower the costs associated with customer returns and warranty service.

Finally, higher quality helps firms develop and maintain customer loyalty. Customers who buy products and services that fulfill quality expectations are more likely to buy again from the same firm.

Quality consists of eight dimensions:[24]

1. **Performance** comprises the product's primary operating characteristics, such as an automobile's ability to transport its driver.

2. **Features** include supplementary characteristics, such as power windows on an automobile.

3. **Reliability** refers to the dependability of a product, such as the probability that an automobile will start.

4. **Conformance** is how well the product meets normal standards.

5. **Durability** refers to the product's expected life span.

6. **Serviceability** refers to how fast and easily the product can be repaired.

7. **Aesthetics** refers to how the product looks, feels, tastes, and/or smells.

8. **Perceived** quality is the level of quality as seen by the customer. Perceived quality can be viewed in terms of price and expectations. For example, Sony manufactures and sells a variety of color televisions ranging in price from $200 to well over $10,000. For $200 a customer might expect a fairly reliable, small-screen television with basic features and good picture clarity. For $10,000 the same customer is likely to expect an extremely reliable, big-screen television with numerous features and exceptional picture clarity. It is difficult to compare the quality of the two televisions without understanding the price and expectations for each. That is, the two televisions may be of equal perceived quality based on actual quality adjusted for price and expectations.

Quality Around the World

As with productivity, measuring quality may seem to be a reasonably straightforward task, but obtaining valid and reliable data is not as easy as might be imagined. Nevertheless, two studies provide insights into quality in different countries. One study surveyed perceptions of managers; the other focused on consumers' perceptions.

Managerial Perceptions of International Quality. A major study of managers' perceptions of international quality was conducted by Ernst & Young and the American Quality Foundation.[25] This study involved teams of executives from more than 500 firms in the automotive, banking, computer, and health care industries in Canada, Germany, Japan, and the United States. Table 15.1 summarizes the study's major findings.

Two findings are particularly noteworthy. First, the Japanese firms that were studied indicated they do not use work teams nearly as much as many people think, but *overall* more of their employees participated in decision making. This suggests that Japanese firms have done a better job of institutionalizing participation throughout their organizations, whereas firms in other countries still tend to use structural dimensions like work teams to achieve participation. Second, the Japanese are far ahead of the rest of the world in using process simplification (finding easier and simpler ways of doing things) and cycle time reduction (doing things faster). These practices are a part of improving operations, which was identified

TABLE 15.1

Management Perceptions of International Quality

1. Japanese firms do not organize the majority of their workforce into teams that focus on quality programs, but they do have the highest rate of employee participation in regularly scheduled meetings about quality.

2. Firms in Canada, Germany, and the United States expect to increase their involvement of employees in quality-related teams. Firms in Japan expect little change in their use of quality teams.

3. More than half the firms in all four countries evaluate the business consequences of quality performance at least monthly. However, almost 20 percent of the U.S. firms review quality less than annually or not at all.

4. Although quality performance was used only on a limited basis in the past, its use as a criterion for compensating senior management is expected to increase substantially in all four countries; in the United States, more than half the firms plan to use this measure.

5. About 40 percent of firms in Canada, Japan, and the United States place primary importance on customer satisfaction in strategic planning; 22 percent of German firms do so.

6. German and Japanese firms are far ahead of Canadian and U.S. firms in incorporating customer expectations into the design of new products and services.

7. Japanese firms use technology twice as much as U.S. firms in meeting customer expectations. Although firms in all four countries expect to substantially increase the use of technology in meeting customer expectations, Japanese firms will still lead the others.

8. German firms rarely place primary emphasis on competitors in the strategic planning process; however, almost one-third of Japanese and U.S. firms do. In Canada, only one-fourth do.

9. Japan dramatically leads the other countries in the routine use of process simplification and cycle time reduction. About half of Japanese firms use both of these practices more than 90 percent of the time.

10. About 20 percent of Canadian and U.S. firms always or almost always use process simplification techniques or process cycle time analyses to improve business processes; only 6 percent of German firms do so.

Source: Data from the Ernst & Young and American Quality Foundation study of managerial perceptions of international quality among U.S., Japanese, Canadian, and German executives. Adapted from Karen Bemowski, "The International Quality Study," *Quality Progress* (November 1991), pp. 33–37.

earlier in this chapter as a method for boosting productivity. German firms use these practices far less than U.S. and Canadian firms.

Consumers' Perceptions of International Quality. The consumer quality survey was conducted by the Gallup organization and the American Society for Quality Control.[26] The survey results are based on interviews with 1,008 U.S. consumers, 1,446 Japanese consumers, and 1,000 German consumers. Each consumer was asked various questions about the meaning of quality and was asked to evaluate the quality of various products from each of the three countries. Table 15.2 summarizes some of the survey's findings.

One clear finding is that domestic consumers in each country generally perceive the quality of products from their own country to be superior to the quality of products from the other two countries. Indeed, "TVs and VCRs" and "personal computers" were the only categories in which consumers picked products from another country (Japan) as being of higher quality than those made domestically.

Beyond these basic findings the survey also revealed other interesting patterns. For one thing, Japanese and German consumers generally believe U.S. workers are not committed to quality. For another, U.S. firms have a better reputation abroad for services and soft goods than they do for hard goods. Although U.S. firms do lag in quality, they are seen as the world's style leader—consumers in both Japan and Germany agreed that products made or introduced by U.S. firms tend to be more visually appealing than those made in their own countries. Finally, consumers in

TABLE 15.2

Consumer Perceptions of International Quality

	PERCENTAGE OF RESPONDENTS CHOOSING EACH COUNTRY		
	U.S. Consumers	Japanese Consumers	German Consumers
Best-quality autos			
United States	41	1	2
Japan	36	71	18
Germany	18	23	78
Don't know	5	5	2
Best-quality personal computers			
United States	48	12	14
Japan	39	80	45
Germany	1	1	33
Don't know	12	7	8
Best-quality TV's and VCR's			
United States	28	2	2
Japan	66	91	59
Germany	1	1	37
Don't know	5	6	2
Best-quality clothing			
United States	89	17	7
Japan	3	75	3
Germany	2	2	87
Don't know	6	6	3
Best-quality cosmetics			
United States	81	21	23
Japan	2	68	4
Germany	2	3	67
Don't know	15	8	6
Best-quality financial services			
United States	79	21	12
Japan	8	63	7
Germany	2	4	75
Don't know	11	12	6
Best-quality health care services			
United States	75	23	8
Japan	6	52	4
Germany	9	12	84
Don't know	10	13	4
Number of interviews	**1,008**	**1,446**	**1,000**

Source: From "Looking for Quality in a World Marketplace," 1991 ASQC/Gallup survey. © 1991 American Society for Quality Control. Reprinted with permission.

all three countries indicated they are willing to pay higher prices for higher-quality products and services.

Total Quality Management

Because of the increasing importance of quality, firms worldwide are putting more and more emphasis on improving the quality of their products and services. Many of these firms call their efforts total quality management. **Total quality management (TQM)** is an integrated effort to systematically and continuously improve the quality of an organization's products and/or services.

Components of TQM. TQM programs vary by firm and must be adapted to fit each firm's unique circumstances. As shown in Figure 15.3, TQM must start with a strategic commitment to quality. This means the quality initiative must start at the top of the firm, and top managers must be willing to commit the resources necessary to achieve continuous improvement. Firms that only pay lip service to quality and try to fool employees and customers into believing they care about it are almost certain to fail.[27]

With a strong strategic commitment as a foundation TQM programs rely on four operational components to implement quality improvement. Employee involvement almost always is cited as a critical requirement in quality improvement. All employees must participate in helping to accomplish the firm's quality-related objectives. Materials also must be scrutinized. Firms often can improve the quality of their products by requiring higher-quality parts and materials from their suppliers and procuring inputs only from suppliers whose commitment to quality matches their own. The firm also must be willing to invest in new technology to become more efficient and to achieve higher-quality manufacturing processes. Finally, the firm must be willing to adopt new and improved methods of getting work done.

Quality Improvement Tools. Firms using TQM have a variety of tools and techniques from which they can draw, including statistical process control and benchmarking. **Statistical process control** is a family of mathematically based tools for monitoring and controlling quality. Its basic purposes are to define the target level of quality, specify an acceptable range of deviation, and then ensure that product quality is hitting the target. For example, Source Perrier SA uses statistical process control to monitor its bottling operations. Managers there have determined that a large bottle of Perrier water should contain 23 fluid ounces. Of course, regardless of how careful managers are, few bottles will have exactly 23 ounces—some will have a bit more, some a bit less. However, if too many bottles are filled with either too much or too little, adjustments must be made. An acceptable range for this situation might be an actual content of between 22.8 and 23.2 ounces, with a target of 99.9 percent of all bottles having content within this range.

FIGURE 15.3

The Essential Components of Total Quality Management

Samples of finished products are taken, and their actual content measured. As long as 99.9 percent of all samples have between 22.8 and 23.2 ounces, production continues. However, if only 97 percent of one sample falls within the acceptable range, managers may stop production and adjust their bottling equipment.

Another important TQM technique is benchmarking. **Benchmarking** is the process of legally and ethically studying how other firms do something in a high-quality way and then either imitating or improving on their methods. The managerial quality perception study summarized earlier in the chapter found that 31 percent of all U.S. firms engage in regular benchmarking; only 7 percent never use benchmarking. Japanese and German firms also engage in benchmarking but not to the same extent as U.S. firms.

Xerox started the benchmarking movement in the United States as a result of competitive pressures from foreign rivals. Canon, a Japanese firm, once introduced a mid-sized copier that sold for less than $10,000. Xerox was sure Canon was selling it below cost to gain market share. To learn more about what was going on, Xerox sent a team of managers to Japan to work with Fuji-Xerox, a joint venture a Xerox affiliate had established with Fuji to make copiers in Asia. While there, the managers bought a Canon copier and took it apart. To their surprise they found the Canon copier to be of higher quality and lower cost than the copiers Xerox was making. By imitating Canon's materials and methods, Xerox was able to begin making its own higher-quality and lower-cost equipment.

❭ CONTROLLING INFORMATION IN INTERNATIONAL BUSINESS

A final and increasingly important aspect of control in international business involves information. **Information** is data in a form that is of value to a manager in making decisions and performing related tasks.

❭ A renewed commitment to product quality and customer service has paid off for IMSA, one of Mexico's largest steel producers. Use of enterprise resource planning software has improved its on-time delivery performance and reduced its work-in-process inventory.

The Role of Information

Information is vitally important to any firm. Managers use it in every phase of their work because it is necessary to the decision-making process. Obtaining accurate and timely information is of particular importance to international firms. Managers use information to better understand their firm's environment—its customers, competitors, and suppliers; the government policies that affect its hiring, producing, and financing decisions; and virtually every other element of its environment. "Bringing the World into Focus" highlights some of the language and cultural issues yet to be surmounted in using the Internet as an information resource and an advertising medium in other countries.

Managers also use information to help them decide how to respond to the environment. Meetings, reports, data summaries, telephone calls, and electronic mail messages are all used as managers set strategic goals and map out strategic plans. Information is also critical to implementing those strategic plans. For example, top managers must communicate their goals and expectations to managers of their foreign operations. Information is needed continually as managers make decisions daily and provide feedback to others in the firm about the consequences of those decisions. Finally, information is an important part of the control process itself as managers monitor

Bringing the World into FOCUS

LANGUAGE SNAFUS AND THE INTERNET

Can translation technology help businesses bring their World Wide Web pages to the world? That's what Vladimir Bogdanov, president of Allmusic.com, needed to do when he purchased software to translate his site's text from English into six languages for a global audience interested in music and musicians. Unfortunately, the translations were far from polished; Bogdanov says international readers actually laughed at the quirky wording. He quickly arranged for traditional translation services, choosing the human touch over the electronic approach.

Numerous Web sites offer free, instant translation services for people who want to communicate messages in other languages. At the AltaVista Babel Fish site, for example, users simply choose the languages being translated to and from, then type in the words, phrases, or sentences to be translated. At a click of the mouse the site prepares a literal translation. Because translations are basically word for word, single words or phrases often translate more smoothly than sentences.

Even Web sites such as Multicity.com, which specializes in translating conversations to support chat and instant messaging functions in several European languages, have difficulty with the meaning of idioms and slang terms. As a result, chatters fare better when they avoid slang and follow standard grammatical conventions instead. Users seeking to translate just one or two words can find the foreign-language equivalents on Allwords.com and, at a click, hear the correct pronunciations.

People who communicate online in languages other than English sometimes face the problem of writing words in a different alphabet or character set, such as Cyrillic or Hindi. WordWalla.com comes to the rescue with an online keyboard that shows the correct characters for the chosen language. Of course, users must be familiar with the language to operate this system.

Researchers are working on artificial intelligence systems capable of identifying and translating the subtle nuances of more sophisticated messages without human intervention. For now, however, many companies are turning to professional translators rather than risk simplistic or laughable electronic translations.

Source: "Tongue-Tied," *Forbes*, September 11, 2000, p. 80.

and assess how well they are meeting goals and executing plans. No manager likes to be taken by surprise. Having ready access to information that can be used to gauge ongoing performance and actual accomplishments is an important part of a manager's ability to function effectively.[28]

The importance of information management depends on the type of strategy and organization design the firm uses. If a firm is using related diversification, it is very important that various parts of the firm be able to communicate with other parts so the firm can most effectively capitalize on the potential synergies of this strategy. If the firm is highly centralized, information systems are vital for top managers so they can maintain the control they seek from using this particular design. On the other hand, if a firm is using unrelated diversification, its information systems needs will be quite different. For example, communication among the various businesses within the firm will be far less important. Finally, if the firm is using a decentralized form of organization design, its top managers will need and expect somewhat less information reporting by managers of various divisions and units.

Managing Information

The nature of international business adds considerable complexity to information and its role in a firm. In a domestic firm information is almost certain to be in a common language, within the same legal context (the same accounting standards, financial reporting requirements, and so on will apply), and stored, manipulated, and accessible through common computer software and hardware configurations.

In an international firm information is likely to be in different languages and subject to different legal contexts. For example, foreign partners and foreign governments may constrain the flow of information into and/or out of their countries. Moreover, computer software and hardware configurations are not always compatible. Thus managing information is not only very important for an international firm; it also is more complex than for a domestic firm.

Firms increasingly are working to develop integrated information systems to more effectively manage their information. An **information system** is a methodology created by a firm to gather, assemble, and provide data in a form or forms useful to managers. Most information systems are computerized, although they do not necessarily have to be—routing slips, files, and file storage systems can effectively manage information in small firms. Larger firms today almost always use computerized systems to manage their information. For example, managers at Laura Ashley, a British fashion and home furnishings chain, use a computerized information system to help the firm manage its information more effectively. Each sale is electronically recorded and used by managers to make decisions about reordering hot-selling merchandise.

To the extent possible international firms would like to use information systems to link their operations, so their managers in any part of the world can access information and communicate with counterparts from any of the firm's operations. The sheer size of this undertaking, however, along with computer software and hardware limitations, makes it difficult for firms to achieve true global integration of their information systems. Thus most firms develop information subsystems for specific functional operations or divisions.

Texas Instruments is farther along the path toward a truly global system than most firms are. One of its subsidiaries, Tiris (Texas Instruments Registration and Identification Systems), is headquartered in the United Kingdom; its product development units are in Germany and the Netherlands, and its manufacturing facilities are in Japan and Malaysia. Managers and engineers at each facility communicate with each other over an integrated computer-based information system that enables them to function as if they were across the hall from each other rather than thousands of miles apart. For example, a manager in England might respond to a new customer order by sending a request electronically to a designer in Germany to make a small modification in a part to meet the customer's specifications. After the modification is made, the design specifications and order information can be sent electronically to Japan where the products will be manufactured. The original manager in England receives verification that the parts have been made and shipped and can call the customer with the news. At any time during the entire process any manager or designer can electronically monitor what is being done with the order and where it will be sent next. This approach helps Texas Instruments compete internationally by enabling it to reduce its costs and meet differing needs of customers in different countries.

CHAPTER REVIEW

Summary

Control is the process of monitoring and regulating activities of a firm so that a targeted component of performance is achieved or maintained. For an MNC control must be managed both at the corporate level and within each subsidiary.

Most MNCs usually address control at three levels. Strategic control monitors how well an international firm formulates strategy and then goes about trying to implement it. Financial control is an especially important area of strategic control in international business. Poor financial control can cripple a firm's ability to compete globally. Most

MNCs have a corporate controller as well as controllers within each subsidiary. Organizational control involves the design of the firm. Three basic forms of organizational control are responsibility center control, generic strategic control, and planning process control. Operations control focuses specifically on operating procedures and systems within the firm.

When international firms establish control systems, they first set control standards, then measure actual performance. Next they compare performance against the standards and respond to deviations. Essential control techniques include accounting systems, procedures, and performance ratios. International managers also need to understand behavioral aspects of control, such as why people resist control and how to overcome that resistance. Cultural factors are an important ingredient in addressing behavioral aspects of control.

Productivity is an economic measure of efficiency that summarizes the value of outputs relative to the value of inputs used to create the outputs. Productivity can be assessed at a variety of levels and in many different forms. U.S. workers are the world's most productive, but Japan and Germany have had greater productivity growth rates until recently. Experts agree that a firm can improve productivity by spending more on R&D, improving operations, and increasing employee involvement.

Quality is the total set of features and characteristics of a product or service that bears on its ability to satisfy stated or implied needs. Quality has become a critical factor in both domestic and global competition. Most domestic consumers in the Quad countries see products made in their own country as being of high quality. To improve quality, many firms are relying on TQM. TQM starts with a strategic commitment and is based on employee involvement, high-quality materials, up-to-date technology, and effective methods. Quality improvement tools include statistical process control and benchmarking.

Information is data in a form that is of value to a manager. It plays a major role in international business. Managers use information to understand their environment and to make decisions. Information is also an important element in effective control. Managing information in an international firm is complex, and many firms use sophisticated electronic information systems to do so more effectively.

Review Questions

1. What are the three levels of control in international business?
2. Why is financial control so important?
3. What are three types of organizational control? Describe them.
4. What is the basic difference between responsibility center control and generic strategic control?
5. What is the basic focus of organizational control in international business?
6. What are the four basic steps in establishing an international control system?
7. Identify and discuss several essential control techniques.
8. Why is it important for organizations to control productivity?
9. What is quality? Why is it an important area of control for international firms?
10. How do firms manage information as part of control?

Questions for Discussion

1. Why is control an important management function in international business?
2. Do you think the three common types of international organizational control are mutually exclusive? Why or why not?
3. What are the advantages and disadvantages of each type of international organizational control?
4. Which form of control system would you most and least prefer for your own work? Why?
5. Which control techniques are most likely to be tailored to international settings? Which can be merely extensions of domestic operations?
6. What role does ethics play in control?
7. Why is it more common for developing countries to report dramatic increases in productivity, whereas more developed countries usually report much smaller increases?
8. List 10 products you use for which quality is important in your purchasing decision. Which countries, if any, have reputations (good or bad) for each of these particular products?
9. Which of the findings in Table 15.1 do you think are most expected? Which are least expected?
10. What types of information are particularly important to an international firm?

BUILDING GLOBAL SKILLS

This exercise is to help you learn more about control in international business. To begin, read the following introduction about your firm and your role in it. Then complete the small-group exercise that follows.

Wahner, Inc., is a moderately large international holding company with subsidiaries in eight countries. Until recently the firm was managed by its founder, Pete Wahner, who got his start by using his inheritance to buy an importing firm. Over the years Wahner bought and

sold various businesses until he accumulated the current set of subsidiaries. In total, Wahner, Inc., consists of 15 subsidiaries operating around the world. Wahner died of cancer two years ago, and the firm has been run by his former assistant, Thomas Henderson. Wahner's heirs have become concerned that the firm is not being effectively managed and that Henderson may not have the skills necessary to manage a complex international business. An audit of the firm revealed several significant problems, and your consulting firm has been hired to straighten things out. After four weeks of learning the business, you have developed the following impressions:

- A French subsidiary that exports wine has been operating at a loss for three years. Because the firm was required to report revenues only annually, no one paid much attention to what was happening until recently. You now see that the losses are escalating.

- An Australian subsidiary that makes beer containers has been steadily losing market share because of deteriorating product quality. Three of its largest customers recently took their business to other suppliers.

- A manager at an Argentinean subsidiary has allegedly been stealing money from the firm, although this allegation is only in the form of a confidential report submitted by two of his subordinates. These subordinates are known to be trustworthy, however, and you believe the allegations are true.

- A German subsidiary has been enormously profitable but has several million surplus marks sitting idly in checking accounts. These funds are not drawing interest and have been accumulating for at least three years.

- Two subsidiaries in the United States, as well as one in Mexico and one in Egypt, have been performing effectively. Each is making a good profit and seems to be effectively managed.

- The audits of the remaining seven subsidiaries have not yet been completed, but a preliminary report suggests that there are few major problems in any of them. All of these subsidiaries are based in Canada and report to a single executive vice president, Nancy Gleason. Gleason is currently considering leaving Wahner for the top position in another firm.

Your task is to develop a control framework for getting Wahner, Inc., back on track. Working in small groups, do the following:

1. Develop preliminary ideas as to why and how the current state of affairs has emerged.

2. Outline control-related issues that need to be addressed.

3. Determine how you will go about establishing control at Wahner.

WORKING WITH THE WEB: BUILDING GLOBAL INTERNET SKILLS

Quality Certification

Quality is becoming an increasingly important aspect of international competition. Many organizations and governments are assisting firms in their quest to improve the quality of their products and customer service.

Suppose an important customer of your company has decided that it wishes to purchase inputs only from companies that are ISO certified. The manager of your group has no idea what the customer is talking about and assigns you the task of learning about the ISO

certification process. He also asks you to report back on how your company can use quality certification as a marketing tool.

To begin with, explore the Web site of the ISO to find out what it does and how it operates. You also should do a search for other organizations that help firms improve their commitment to quality and for consultants who can guide a firm through the ISO's procedures. Then write a brief memo to your boss reporting what you have learned. (The textbook's Web site provides links to some Web sites that may be useful for this assignment.)

WE INVITE YOU TO VISIT THIS BOOK'S COMPANION WEB SITE AT www.prenhall.com/griffin

IN THE NEWS

Productivity is a control tool, in that it measures the value of outputs in relation to the value of inputs used to create them. It can be assessed on a national level, as well as on a firm-by-firm basis.

However we measure it, productivity can generally be increased by a strong investment in research and development as well as efficient operations and thoughtful employee input.

Use the *Financial Times* homepage (*www.ft.com*) to research productivity and the way it is measured in today's economy. You can select either two or three different countries, or two or three different companies in the same industry but in different countries if possible.

Find out as much as you can about your subjects' productivity levels now and in the recent past, and projected levels for the future. What measures are used to assess productivity? Are they the same for all your subjects? If not, how do they differ, and how

does that affect the data they report? What contributes to productivity, and what changes are being considered to those inputs (more R&D, streamlined operations, etc.)? What do you think the effect will be?

Finally, how much similarity can you find between the countries or firms you surveyed? What accounts for any differences?

CLOSING CASE

Daimler and Chrysler: A Nightmare Partnership!

As recounted in the chapter's opening case, the merger between Daimler-Benz and Chrysler to create DaimlerChrysler seemed like a perfect partnership. By 2000, however, investors and observers alike were calling it more like a marriage made in hell rather than one made in heaven. None of the anticipated advantages had been achieved, and innumerable problems had the firm so mired down that by the end of 2000 its market value was lower than it had been for either Daimler or Chrysler before the merger. In early 2001 DaimlerChrysler announced it would reduce Chrysler's payrolls by 26,000, about 20 percent of its workforce. How did such a dream partnership end up as a nightmare? Several different factors can be identified.

One notable factor was the major differences between the cultures and operating procedures that existed at Daimler and Chrysler. Chrysler had been one of the world's most profitable automobile makers by being nimble and responsive—decisions were made quickly, there were few long meetings to slow things down, and management reports were kept to a minimum. Just the opposite circumstances existed at Daimler-Benz. Most major decisions were made in marathon meetings that sometimes went on for days, and most operations were driven by lengthy and detailed management reports. Reconciling the two systems proved to be harder than expected, and most meetings seemed to end in shouting matches.

Another problem was that Chrysler was not in as good a condition as observers thought at the time of the merger. Although it was selling lots of automobiles and sports utility vehicles and racking up big profits, its product lines were also growing stale. Some of its most popular products, such as the Jeep Grand Cherokee, needed major redesign and others, such as its best-selling line of minivans, were gradually losing market share to aggressive competitors such as Toyota and Honda. Although some new models were introduced, most notably the funky PT Cruiser, Chrysler had few other new products in the pipeline. Finally, Chrysler was so intent on improving product quality that it was adding about $2,000 in costs to many of its top sellers for improvements that many consumers did not want and that could not be seen, such as more sound-proofing material and stronger braking systems.

The new firm also seemed to have trouble curbing its spending. For example, shortly after the merger was announced, Daimler wanted to start using Chrysler's U.S. distributors to transport parts and equipment to Mercedes dealers. However, the dealers did not want Chrysler or Dodge vans on their premises, so at considerable

expense all of Chrysler's vans were repainted and a new discreet DaimlerChrysler logo affixed.

Similarly, during the implementation of the merger there were repeated clashes over travel expenses. Chrysler executives were accustomed to flying coach and staying in Holiday Inns; Daimler executives flew first class and stayed in expensive suites. One Chrysler executive estimated that during the first year of the merger, senior executives of the combined firm spent over $5 million on rooms and meals just for meetings in New York City, meetings that served little or no purpose. At some meetings every executive in attendance got a $500-per-night suite at the Waldorf-Astoria or St. Regis, even though many of the executives were not spending the night in the city.

Morale was—and continues to be—a problem. Although originally billed as a merger of equals, everyone quickly saw that Daimler was actually overwhelming Chrysler. Most senior Chrysler executives were systematically replaced by German executives from the parent company, and Chrysler procedures and policies were routinely replaced with those already in place at Daimler. As a result, turnover among key people is high, shareholders have sued the firm because they feel they were misled about the original merger, and UAW labor leaders in the United States and Canada are threatening to strike if the company attempts to lower their wages or reduce their benefits, something the firm has been hinting about.

DaimlerChrysler executives also are being criticized for not giving the merger time to be properly implemented before undertaking new ventures. For example, shortly after the two firms started being combined, the firm announced it was considering buying Nissan, Japan's second largest automaker. After extended negotiations, however, the firm backed off and instead invested heavily in two other auto companies, Mitsubishi and Hyundai. So far these deals also have been a bust as both firms have been losing money.

So where does the deal stand now? Jurgen Schrempp and his Daimler executives remain optimistic that things eventually will get back on track. He predicts that when Chrysler's product redesign and manufacturing retooling are finished at the end of 2001, Chrysler will again take off. He believes the integration of the two firms has overcome its initial problems and the new DaimlerChrysler is on the road to growth and profitability. He also claims that the firm's Asian investments will begin to soon pay off. Investors and critics, however, are getting restless, and some wonder how much more rope the firm's board of directors can give Schrempp—and what he will end up doing with it.

Case Questions

1. Identify the basic control issues at DaimlerChrysler from all three levels.
2. How do you think the control function should be organized and managed at DaimlerChrysler?
3. Describe how behavioral issues may have played a role in DaimlerChrysler's problems.
4. Identify several productivity and quality issues at DaimlerChrysler.
5. What role might information technology play at improving the situation at DaimlerChrysler?

Sources: Bill Vlasic and Bradley A. Stertz, "Taken for a Ride," *Business Week*, June 5, 2000, pp. 84–92; "The Merger That Can't Get in Gear," *Business Week*, July 31, 2000, pp. 46–47; "Purging Chrysler," *Time*, December 4, 2000, pp. 58–60; "For Two Car Giants, a Megamerger Isn't the Road to Riches," *Wall Street Journal*, October 27, 2000, pp. A1, A8; "DaimlerChrysler Hit by More Lawsuits, Labor Unrest," *USA Today*, November 30, 2000, p. 3B; "Chrysler's Rescue Team," *Business Week*, January 15, 2001, pp. 48–50.

A Strategic Partnership Aids Teva's March into Foreign Markets

Background

While spending his college summers in the 1980s as a boatman on the Colorado River, Mark Thatcher fell in love with white-water recreational sports. Determined to avoid a 9-to-5 job, he soon saw an opportunity to fill the need for a well-made water sandal that would appeal to fellow water sports enthusiasts. And so, the Teva sandal was born. Thatcher literally took his first samples on the road, working out of an old pickup truck to market them at outfitters along the rivers of Arizona, New Mexico, Utah, and Wyoming. National success came quickly, with international success not far behind.

Teva

Today there are more than 60 different Teva styles, in categories like casual, precision sport, wilderness, and utility. With their patented strapping system they are designed for men, women, and children, and the company markets them as comfortable and stylish yet hardy enough for outdoor uses such as kayaking and sailing.

Now based in Flagstaff, Arizona, Teva (the name means "nature" in Hebrew) is still a privately owned firm with which Thatcher is closely associated. It makes its products in Costa Rica, Mexico, China, the United States, and other countries under exclusive license to Deckers Outdoor Corporation. Teva sells its sandals through Decker's wholesale arm, which distributes them to many sporting goods and specialty outdoor gear shops.

In 1996 Teva launched its own Web site and realized the great potential of the Internet in both building its brand and serving customer needs. Customers from all over the world can browse styles, check product information, and purchase sandals directly from the company. Making the full range of products available has been one of the biggest challenges the company has faced from its Internet presence. Not every retailer carries all Teva styles in all sizes, so the Web site (http://www.teva.com/) has to go above and beyond traditional retail offerings.

Deckers

Still a big factor in Teva's international success, however, is the international production and marketing savvy of Deckers, which has exclusive rights to manufacture, distribute, and sell Teva products. Deckers handles all the domestic and international negotiations, contracts, and agreements concerning new plant locations, raw materials purchasing, and sales to distributors at home and abroad. If Teva needs a new manufacturing plant overseas to increase capacity, Deckers will research sites, select a location, and negotiate all of the relevant government regulations, laws, restrictions, and customs until it can get all parties to agree. If Teva needs new sources of raw materials, Deckers investigates suppliers' ability to deliver high-quality materials on time and at a reasonable cost, and negotiates the contracts for Teva. When wholesalers are ready to place their orders, Deckers assures them of receiving the styles and quantities they want, when the want them.

In all of these tasks Deckers must deal with a myriad of government regulations and cultural norms in each of the countries in which it operates. Language differences, exchange rate fluctuations, and even ethical issues can all come into play.

Questions

1. If Deckers outsources its manufacturing to other companies overseas, what are some of the challenges it might face in ensuring that these companies adhere to high standards in their employment practices? Does Teva have any responsibility to monitor Deckers's decisions on plant locations and labor practices, or is that Deckers's sole responsibility?

2. What are the major challenges Deckers is likely to face in interacting with different governments abroad? How can it develop the expertise it needs to be successful in widely different manufacturing environments?

3. Should Teva continue to let Deckers take care of all its global efforts? What are the pros and cons of letting Deckers handle so much?

4. How can international firms acquire expertise in their dealings with the governments of other countries? For example, what public and private agencies in your own country would you consult before starting an international venture? What questions would you need to ask?

Sources: Scott Walters, "Taking the Trade Online," *Arizona Daily Sun*, September 26, 1999, p. 19; "Mark Thatcher," *The Pine* (NAU alumni magazine), Winter 1999, p. 9, Teva Sports Sandals and Deckers Outdoor Corp.

PART-CLOSING CASES

Ben & Jerry's—Japan

On an autumn evening in Tokyo in 1997, Perry Odak, Angelo Pezzani, Bruce Bowman, and Riv Hight gratefully accepted the hot steaming *oshibori* towels their kimono-bedecked waitress quietly offered. It had been just over nine months since Odak had committed to resolving the conundrum of whether to introduce Ben & Jerry's ice cream to the Japanese market and, if so, how. The next morning would be their last chance to hammer out the details for a market entry through Seven-Eleven's 7,000 stores in Japan or to give the go-ahead to Ken Yamada, a prospective licensee who would manage the Japanese market for Ben & Jerry's. Any delay in reaching a decision would mean missing the summer 1998 ice cream season, but with Japan's economy continuing to contract, perhaps passing on the Japanese market would not be a bad idea.

Perry Odak was just entering his eleventh month as CEO of the famous ice cream company named for its offbeat founders. He knew the Seven-Eleven deal could represent a sudden boost in the company's flagging sales of the past several years. He also knew that a company with the tremendous brand recognition Ben & Jerry's enjoyed needed to approach new market opportunities from a strategic, not an opportunistic, perspective.

The Market for Superpremium Ice Cream in Japan

Starting in 1994, Ben & Jerry's began making inquiries about opportunities in Japan, the second largest ice cream market in the world, with annual sales of approximately $4.5 billion. Although the market was big, it was also daunting. Japan was known to have a highly complex distribution system; its barriers to foreign products were high; and the distance for shipping a frozen product from America was immense. Ben & Jerry's would be a late entrant, more than 10 years behind Haagen-Dazs in gaining a foothold in the market. In addition, there were at least six Japanese ice cream manufacturers selling a superpremium product.

Despite the challenges of entering Japan, that market had several compelling features. It was arguably the most affluent country in the world, and Japanese consumers were known for demanding high quality products with great varieties of styles and flavors (which practically defined Ben & Jerry's).

Though Haagen-Dazs's financial figures were not published, market intelligence suggested the ice cream maker had Japanese sales of about $300 million. Haagen-Dazs had managed to capture nearly half the superpremium market in Japan. On the one hand, Haagen-Dazs would be a formidable competitor that would likely guard its market share. On the other hand, there would be no apparent need for Ben & Jerry's to teach the local market about superpremium ice cream. The market seemed to welcome imported ice cream, and expectations of falling tariffs on dairy products suggested new opportunities for ice cream imports from abroad. Although prices were attractive in Japan, about $6 per pint, it was unclear how much of that would go into the pockets of the manufacturer versus various distributors.

Jerry Greenfield, one of Ben & Jerry's founders, was interested enough to visit Japan on a market research tour in early 1996. The purpose was to see just how Ben & Jerry's might gain distribution if the company were to enter the Japanese market.

Greenfield met with a high-level team of Seven-Eleven executives, including Masahiko Iida, the senior managing director. Iida expressed interest in selling Ben & Jerry's ice cream, suggesting that Ben & Jerry's could sell directly to Seven-Eleven, avoiding some of the distribution costs that are typical of the usual multi-layer distribution system in Japan. However, a major American beverage distributor in Japan warned it would be the kiss of death to enter the market through some kind of exclusive arrangement with a huge convenience-store chain like Seven-Eleven. The balance of power would be overwhelmingly in the retailer's favor.

Another possibility emerged in the form of Ken Yamada, a well-recommended third-generation Japanese-American who was already running Domino's Pizza franchise in Japan. Greenfield learned Yamada was interested in acting as a licensee for Ben & Jerry's in Japan overseeing marketing and distribution of its products there.

A Fresh Look at the Japanese Options

Perry Odak assumed leadership of Ben & Jerry's in January 1997. Odak had the board's agreement that the company's sales (and especially profits) must grow and that non-U.S. markets were the most likely key to that growth.

In February 1997 Odak added a business-related detour to a scheduled trip to Thailand with his wife. He stopped by Tokyo for a courtesy call to Mr. Iida. After about 10 minutes of pleasantries at this introductory meeting at the Seven-Eleven headquarters in Tokyo, Iida asked Odak point blank: "Is there anyone at Ben & Jerry's who can make a marketing decision? We'd like to sell your product but don't know how to proceed or with whom." Rather taken aback at this surprisingly direct inquiry, Odak replied that he could indeed make a decision, and he resolved to sort through the Japanese options and get back to Iida in short order.

Back in Burlington, Odak installed Angelo Pezzani as the new international director for Ben & Jerry's Homemade. Going over the options with Pezzani, it appeared that partnering with Yamada was still the strongest option for entering Japan, but the Seven-Eleven option had not yet been well developed for consideration. Yamada represented considerable strength with his Domino's success and with the fact that Domino's already offered ice cream cups as part of its delivery service in Japan. A possible drawback was his insistence on having exclusive rights to the entire Japanese market, with full control of all branding and marketing efforts there.

Pezzani and Odak decided to continue negotiations with Yamada, keeping that option alive, and to simultaneously let Iida know they wanted to explore options with Seven-Eleven. They journeyed to Japan in April to meet with Iida and hash out the many details that would be involved if Ben & Jerry's were to enter the Japanese market through Seven-Eleven. Odak arrived with more questions than answers, but he was determined that any product Ben & Jerry's might sell in Japan would be manufactured in Vermont, where the company had considerable excess capacity. Also, the costs of labor and raw dairy products were higher in Japan than the United States, so the 23.3 percent tariff and cost of shipping seemed not to be prohibitive. As a result of the Uruguay Round of the General Agreement on Tariffs and Trade, the tariff would be reduced to 21 percent in the year 2000. The introductory meeting went well, but they had not yet addressed any of the difficult issues except to establish that it would be possible to export the product from Vermont to Japan.

Wrestling with the Details of the Seven-Eleven Option

Although Ben & Jerry's management was leaning toward an entry into Japan, it was not a foregone conclusion. The entry would require a commitment of capital and managerial attention. As the product would be exported from the United States, there would be the risk of negative exchange rate movements that could make exports to Japan unprofitable. Commodity risk was also a serious concern in that the price of milk could rise in the United States, hurting Ben & Jerry's relative to competitors producing ice cream in Japan.

Assuming an entry into the Japanese market was desirable, there were a number of apparent options for gaining distribution there, making it necessary to seriously consider the pros and cons of entering by way of Seven-Eleven. The most obvious pro was immediate placement in the freezer compartments of over 7,000 convenience stores in that country.

On the negative side, if the product was introduced to the market through a convenience store and it was just one of many brands there, would it be able to build its own brand capital in Japan like Haagen-Dazs had? Would the product essentially become a store brand? Would committing to one huge retail chain be a case of putting too many eggs in one basket? A falling out between Ben & Jerry's and Seven-Eleven Japan could leave the ice cream maker with nothing in Japan.

While weighing the pros and cons of the business arrangement, there were also production issues which Ben & Jerry's had to consider. Seven-Eleven insisted the ice cream be packaged only in personal cups (120 ml) and not the 473-ml (1 pint) size that Ben & Jerry's currently packed. The main argument for the small cups was that ice cream is seldom consumed as a family dessert in Japan but rather is consumed as a snack item. A secondary argument was that, for sanitation purposes, customers liked their own individual servings. Designing a production system that would accommodate small cups the company had never packed before would require $2 million of new equipment. The sizes of some of the chunks would have to be reduced for them to not overwhelm the small cups. Seven-Eleven might be expected to request other product changes as well. Japanese buyers were known for being particularly demanding in their specifications.

Ben & Jerry's had long been shipping ice cream to the West Coast and to Europe in freezer containers. Shipments to Japan were feasible, though the Seven-Eleven approach to just-in-time inventory procedures would make delivery reliability especially key, and, of course, costs would have to be minimized. Logistics research indicated it would likely take at least three weeks shipping time from the plant in Vermont to the warehouse in Japan. Because of the Japanese label needed in Japan, production would have to carefully match the orders from Seven-Eleven. The product could not be shifted to another customer nor could another customer's product be shifted to Japan.

The Approaching Deadline for a Summer 1998 Japanese Launch

Odak and his staff had made steady progress narrowing and developing their Japanese options during the summer of 1997. If they were to enter the Japanese market for the summer 1998 season, though, they would have to commit to one plan or another no later than autumn 1997. Two distinct entry options had emerged.

The Yamada option was largely the same as it had been at the beginning of the year. His proposal was to have full control of marketing and sales for Ben & Jerry's in Japan. He would position the brand, devise and orchestrate the initial launch, and take care of marketing and distribution well into the future. He would earn a royalty on all sales in the market. By giving Yamada full control of the Japanese market, Ben & Jerry's would have instant expertise in an otherwise unfamiliar market, as well as relief from having to address the many issues involved in putting together an entry strategy and in ongoing market management. Yamada knew frozen foods, and he had an entrepreneurial spirit and marketing savvy, evidenced by his success in launching and building up the Domino's pizza chain in Japan. Giving up control of a potentially major market, though, could

not be taken lightly. Because Yamada would invest his time in developing a marketing plan only after reaching agreement with Ben & Jerry's, there was no specific plan available for consideration. Even if there were, Yamada would retain the right to change it. For the near term, however, Yamada would expect to add selected flavors of Ben & Jerry's ice cream cups to the Domino's delivery menu, providing an opportunity to collect market data based on customer response.

The Seven-Eleven option would leave Ben & Jerry's in control of whatever market development it might want to pursue beyond supplying Seven-Eleven in Japan. Although Seven-Eleven would provide an instant entry to the market, the company would not be in a position to help Ben & Jerry's develop other distribution channels in Japan. The retailer thought it could sell at least six cups per day at each store, which would be the minimum to justify continuing to stock Ben & Jerry's. Looking at the size of Seven-Eleven's ice cream freezer cases suggested this would require approximately 10 percent of Seven-Eleven's cup ice cream sales to be Ben & Jerry's products. Ben & Jerry's was as yet unknown in Japan, and it did not have the budget for a marketing campaign there. Sales would have to rely primarily on promotional efforts by Seven-Eleven, but the company was making no specific commitment for such efforts.

Another option was increasingly compelling—that of holding off on any entry into Japan. Japan's economy was continuing to languish, with increasing talk that it could be years before recovery. A financial crisis that had commenced with a devaluation of Thailand's currency in July 1997 seemed to be spreading across Asia. If the pending Asian crisis hit an already weakened Japanese economy, the economics of exporting ice cream from Vermont to Japan could become infeasible. Though the value of the yen had recently fallen to 125 yen to the dollar, Ben & Jerry's could still sell the product at the plant gate at an acceptable profit with room for both shipping expense and satisfactory margins for Seven-Eleven and its franchisees. If the rate went as high as 160 yen to the dollar, then the price in Japan would have to be raised to a level that might seriously cut into demand, especially relative to Haagen-Dazs, which had manufacturing facilities in Japan.

It would be a long evening meal as Odak, Pezzani, Bowman, and Hight gave their final thoughts to the decision before them. Not only had Odak promised Iida he would make a decision, but Yamada needed an answer to his proposal as well. In any event Ben & Jerry's had to proceed with one plan or another if it were going to have any Japanese sales in its 1998 income statement.

Questions

1. Analyze the Japanese ice cream market. What does Ben & Jerry's have to do to succeed there?
2. Discuss the advantages and disadvantages of relying on Seven-Eleven to distribute Ben & Jerry's in the Japanese market.
3. Discuss the advantages and disadvantages of distributing Ben & Jerry's products through a licensing agreement with Ken Yamada.
4. Some Ben & Jerry's managers believe the company should delay entering the Japanese market because of Japan's short-term economic problems. Do you agree? Defend your answer.

Source: Adapted from "Ben & Jerry's—Japan," Richard Ivey School of Business, University of Western Ontario, Case (A) 2000-02-02. Reproduced with permission of Richard Ivey School of Business.

Reinventing Nissan

During the 1980s it was hard to pick up a copy of *Business Week*, *Fortune*, or *Forbes* that did not feature some article extolling the virtues of Japanese management techniques and the Japanese way of doing business. Many Western commentators urged U.S. and European firms to adopt such Japanese corporate policies as lifetime employment, group-oriented compensation, and reliance on tight customer-supplier networks like those found in the *keiretsu* system. Among the most admired of these firms were Japan's premier automakers—Toyota, Nissan, and Honda.

The 1990s, however, were disastrous for many Japanese firms. The collapse of Japan's so-called bubble economy at the end of the 1980s condemned Japan to a decade of slow growth, stagnant stock markets, and loss of confidence. Among Japan's corporate elite, Nissan perhaps suffered the greatest fall of all. Although Nissan had prospered during the 1980s, the 1990s were far less kind. Expansion of its domestic auto-making capacity during the 1980s left Nissan with far too many factories and workers, and it was forced to battle for market share in the crowded Japanese domestic market by keeping its prices low. (Japan has more domestic automobile manufacturers—11—than any other country.) The company suffered from excess capacity in its European operations as well. And the high value of the yen during the first half of the 1990s made it difficult for the company to export its way out of its difficulties. The Asian currency crisis of 1997–98 dried up that region's demand for the company's products in the waning years of the twentieth century. Confronted with these diverse challenges, the company eked out a small profit in 1991 but lost money in 1992 and 1993.

To restore the company to profitability, Nissan's executives announced a major cost-cutting program in 1994. As one part of this program, Nissan pledged to slash the number of suppliers the firm would buy from in the future. It hoped this would result in better prices for auto parts by increasing the size of its orders to individual suppliers. Nissan also decided to trim its workforce and to reduce the number of parts used in the company's cars, thereby simplifying its procurement operations and reducing its inventory costs. Unfortunately, these efforts did not work, in part because the program's targets were not met. As a result, Nissan continued to lose money in 1994 and 1995. Although the company earned a modest profit in 1996, its profits turned negative once again in 1997. Profit performance for 1998 and 1999 was no better.

Unable to overcome its mounting problems, Nissan suffered the ultimate humiliation for a Japanese company: It was taken over by a foreigner. In May 1999 France's Renault SA purchased 37 percent of Nissan's common stock for $5.4 billion, effectively transferring control of Japan's second largest auto manufacturer to the French firm. Renault empowered one of its most highly respected executives, Carlos Ghosn, to clean up the mess at Nissan. Ghosn first spent five months carefully reviewing Nissan's operations. In October 1999 the Brazilian-born Ghosn announced a "revival plan" for the company designed to reduce Nissan's annual costs by nearly $10 billion. To reach this goal, five Nissan factories in Japan would have to be shuttered and 21,000 jobs eliminated. About 16,000 of the job cuts would occur in Nissan's domestic operations. Mindful of Japan's distaste for layoffs and Japanese labor laws that make firing employees expensive,

the employment reductions were to be implemented via attrition, which averages about 2,000 domestic employees per year.

Other options, such as voluntary retirement programs, were initially shelved due to opposition from Nissan's union leaders, although the options have not been permanently ruled out. Further cost reductions were to be implemented by eliminating regional offices in such cities as New York and Washington and cutting the number of different vehicle models produced and marketed by Nissan. To ensure that no one misunderstood the importance of cost cutting to revive the company, Ghosn announced that "No one in purchasing, engineering, or administration will receive a pay raise until they [show] what their contribution is to this [cost cutting]."[1]

Ghosn recognized the need to hack away at Nissan's mountain of debt—some 2.4 trillion yen (in early 2001, 117 yen were worth 1 U.S. dollar)—and set a target of halving it by 2002. Ghosn also sought to streamline Nissan's dealership networks in Japan and North America. In Japan, for example, Nissan owns about half of its distributorships. Unfortunately, many of its distributors act like employees, rather than entrepreneurs, an attitude that Ghosn hopes to change by trimming company-owned outlets.

Review of the firm's marketing operations unearthed another set of problems. Ghosn quickly recognized that Nissan's product image differed from country to country, making it hard to launch cost-effective cross-border advertising campaigns. Far worse, he discovered that Nissan suffered from a "brand deficiency," causing consumers to value rivals' vehicles over those produced by Nissan. In the United States, for example, comparable cars sold by Honda, Toyota, Chrysler, and Ford might sell for $1,000 more than Nissan's product. To sharpen its brand identity and develop a uniform global image for its products, Nissan contracted with TBWA Worldwide to handle all of its advertising throughout the world—an account worth an estimated $1.1 billion in annual billings.

Perhaps the most controversial of Ghosn's initiatives dealt with parts procurement. He estimated that Nissan's parts procurement costs were 10 percent higher than those of Renault. Ghosn believed that by combining, centralizing, and globalizing Renault's and Nissan's parts procurement, these costs could be cut by 20 percent. To accomplish this, however, Ghosn needed to overcome a key element of the Japanese environment—the *keiretsu* system. The *keiretsu* system, in which members of a *keiretsu* group own shares in each other, has been a mainstay of the Japanese economy since World War II. The system is designed to build trust and promote stable, long-term cooperative relationships among suppliers and customers. Under this system Nissan funneled orders for parts and components to *keiretsu* affiliates, many of which were partially owned by Nissan. Ghosn's criticism of the *keiretsu* system was blunt. He believed that Nissan's purchase of parts and components from *keiretsu* affiliates promoted inefficiency and mediocrity. Because they were guaranteed business from Nissan, Ghosn felt that many of Nissan's *keiretsu* members failed to continue to innovate and cut costs:

> About sixty percent of our costs are in the suppliers. You have to have suppliers that are innovative. You want suppliers offering products to many customers so there is a flow of information about best standards. That won't happen with *keiretsu* companies.[2]

Accordingly, Ghosn announced he would liquidate Nissan's holdings in all but four of its 1,394 *keiretsu* partners. In a separate but related announcement he also said Nissan would halve the number of its suppliers to about 600. Instead of purchasing the same part from several suppliers, Nissan would now concentrate its purchases among a smaller number of suppliers, allowing them to achieve economies of scale and reduce their costs. Offering a carrot and a stick, he announced that suppliers cutting their prices to Nissan by 20 percent would get more of Nissan's business. Those failing to do so, however, risked losing Nissan as a customer. Not surprisingly, these tough measures were not embraced by everyone. For example, the then prime minister of Japan, Keizo Obuchi, promptly denounced Ghosn's plan, fearing job losses in the tens of thousands as Nissan cut back parts purchases from inefficient affiliates and suppliers.

Perhaps an even bigger challenge to Ghosn was to change Nissan's corporate culture. He learned that too many Nissan executives were focused on protecting their turf than on promoting the company's objectives. Moreover, he discovered to his horror that communication among divisions was nonexistent:

> Country [organizations] were not talking to each other, people were not talking to each other ... This company is very territorial, very divisional; this goes deep into the history and tradition of Nissan. There is nothing that upsets me more than turfism.[3]

Ghosn knew he needed to redirect the company's managers, refocusing their efforts on improving profits and enhancing customer satisfaction. To implement this objective, he created a network of multinational, cross-functional teams to reexamine and reinvigorate each of the firm's activities, from research and development to purchasing to manufacturing to distribution. These teams were also charged with spreading the restructuring gospel and tearing down the walls that have divided Nissan's operating divisions. Further down the line Ghosn plans to implement American-style compensation schemes, such as stock options and bonuses based on profitability and performance, for managerial and nonmanagerial employees alike. If implemented, compensation will no longer be based merely on seniority, as it traditionally has been in Japan. And to drive home the point that Nissan could no longer operate as it did in the past, he made English Nissan's official language.

Not all of Nissan's critics are convinced that Ghosn's strategy will work. One skeptic noted that many of the senior managers surrounding Ghosn are the same ones who were in charge of Nissan's operations while it hemorrhaged red ink during the 1990s. Others

believe that any outsider—even a Brazilian from a French company—lacks the understanding of the Japanese business culture and the credibility necessary to motivate domestic managers and workers.

Questions

1. What benefits will Nissan gain if its procurement of parts is combined with Renault's parts procurement on a global basis? Are there any costs to this change? What problems does Nissan create if it abandons the *keiretsu* system for purchasing parts? In what ways might the Internet facilitate this change?
2. Suppose natural attrition fails to allow Nissan to reach its goal of reducing its workforce by 21,000 people. If this occurs, what would you advise Carlos Ghosn to do? Should he abandon the planned job cuts? Or should he begin to fire workers and risk violating one of Japan's strongest cultural norms?
3. Given Japan's culture, will the introduction of performance-based compensation schemes create any problems for Nissan in Japan? If so, what is the nature of these problems? Do you have any suggestions for overcoming these problems?
4. Do you agree with the criticism that any foreign executive who tries to turn around a Japanese company is doomed to failure because of a lack of understanding of the Japanese business culture? Or do you think that being an outsider helps in this situation?
5. Prime Minister Obuchi's comments send a clear signal that Japanese politicians will resist any restructuring of Nissan's operations that lead to significant losses of domestic jobs. How important is this political threat to Ghosn's plans? What advice would you give to Ghosn to overcome or address Obuchi's concerns?

Sources: "Nissan Sizes Up TBWA for $1 Bil Global Ad Prize," *Advertising Age*, December 6, 1999, pp. 1ff; "Remaking Nissan," *Business Week*, November 15, 1999, pp. 70ff; "The Circle Is Broken," *Financial Times*, November 9, 1999, p. 18; "'Le Cost-Killer' Makes His Move," *Financial Times*, November 9, 1999, p. 15; "Nissan's Ambitious Restructuring Plan Delivers a Blow to Japan's Longstanding System of Corporate Families," *Wall Street Journal*, October 20, 1999, p. A20; "Nissan's Cost Cutter Shows How He Got His Nickname," *Financial Times*, October 19, 1999, p. 20; "Nissan Outlines Restructuring to Get into the Black," *Wall Street Journal*, October 19, 1999, p. A18; "Nissan's Ghosn Faces Obstacles in Carrying out 'Revival Plan'," *Wall Street Journal*, October 18, 1999, p. A37; "'Killer' to Make Unkindest Cut," *Financial Times*, October 18, 1999, p. 14; "Can Japan Keep 11 Carmakers?" *Financial Times*, July 22, 1998, p. 13; "Nissan Finds the Road Is Rough Despite Cost Cutting," *Wall Street Journal*, April 4, 1994, p. B4; "The World's Top Automakers Change Lanes," *Fortune*, October 4, 1993, p. 73ff.

CHAPTER

Wal-Mart Courts European Shoppers

When you are the biggest retailer in your home market—with $165 billion in sales—international expansion is the key to continued growth, as Wal-Mart's executives were quick to note. The company's initial internationalization efforts in the early 1990s focused on Mexico and Canada. At the end of the decade Wal-Mart trained its sights on a much more lucrative and complex target, Europe.

"Wal-Mart adapted its products to better appeal to German customers."

In 1999 Wal-Mart entered the United Kingdom by buying the Asda retailing chain, which operates more than 230 stores. The purchase meshed well with Wal-Mart's business strategy because the firms were alike in stressing aggressive growth and low prices. Soon after the acquisition Wal-Mart announced it would build six new Asda outlets, super-size six more, and establish a dozen new facilities to cut distribution costs. Wal-Mart's goal was to expand the breadth of its British operations, allowing it to replicate the efficient, low-cost logistics system that forms the basis of its competitive advantage in the United States.

The new management team also began tightening the screws on Asda's competition by cutting prices further, highlighting selection, and promoting friendly service. Wal-Mart has touched off price wars in food products and other categories, sending competitors scrambling to meet or beat its price

International
Marketing

tags. Because other British retailers are accustomed to higher profit margins, the Wal-Mart formula of low-markup pricing has put pressure on rival chains such as Tesco, Safeway, and Sainsbury and given smaller stores even bigger headaches. So far the strategy seems to be paying off: In 1999 Asda earned about $715 million on sales of $13 billion.

Wal-Mart adopted an acquisition strategy to attack the German market as well. In 1997 it acquired the 21-store Wertkauf chain; a year later it gobbled up Spar Handels AG and its 74 stores. Wal-Mart hung an American flag outside each store to herald the change in management and symbolize its superior service and selection. Because German rivals have much narrower merchandise selection than Wal-Mart, shoppers initially gawked at the huge quantities of food items, from fresh fruits and vegetables to specialty meats and cheeses, in Wal-Mart outlets in Dortmund and other cities. As in the United States, the Wal-Mart stores in Germany also carry toys, clothing, appliances, and assorted products for household and personal use. Customer service is as much a draw as selection because service in German stores is much less friendly and personalized. Wal-Mart's friendly greeters, with "smiley faces" pinned to their vests, are a vivid symbol that the U.S. company believes the customer comes first.

Wal-Mart's next step was to commence a massive renovation project to enlarge and modernize each outlet, with wider aisles, brighter lights, and more accessible shelving loaded with merchandise—all of which are helping to boost sales. German shoppers also are pleased at not having to bag their own purchases or pay for the plastic bags at Wal-Mart, as they do at many German stores. Moreover, German consumers have benefited from the company's low pricing policies.

Wal-Mart also has adapted some of its products to better appeal to German consumers. The company eliminated aloe vera scents and printed tape on its house brand diapers after German parents rejected such frivolities. It also replaced the English setter on the packaging of Ol' Roy dog food with a terrier after learning that terriers are popular in Germany, whereas setters are not.

Wal-Mart has run into a few rough spots in its attempts to crack the German market. The company's "Always low prices" policy has upset German regulators who fear that price-cutting may force mom-and-pop retailers out of business. The German Cartel Office has warned the company to raise its prices on loss leaders like flour, cooking oil, and butter, which it had been selling below cost. Also, many experts believe Wal-Mart will need to expand more rapidly—either by building new stores or acquiring additional existing retailers—to achieve the critical mass needed to implement efficiently its trademark high-volume, low-cost distribution system. Although Wal-Mart has great hopes for its German initiatives, they have yet to pay off: Analysts estimate Wal-Mart lost between $120 and $150 million in Germany in 1999.[1]

Wal-Mart has achieved a dominant position among U.S. retailers with its aggressive and innovative marketing policies, which stress low prices, good selection, friendly service, and efficient distribution. It is now seeking to transfer this same formula to Europe. As we will discuss throughout this chapter, marketing is a key ingredient in the success of any international business. Yet marketing also can be a significant stumbling block for the misinformed manager.

Marketing is "the process of planning and executing the conception, pricing, promotion, and distribution of ideas, goods, and services to create exchanges that satisfy individual and organizational objectives."[2] **International marketing** is the extension of these activities across national boundaries. Firms expanding into new markets in foreign countries must deal with different political, cultural, and legal systems, as well as unfamiliar economic conditions, advertising media, and distribution channels. For example, an international firm accustomed to promoting its products on television will have to alter its approach when entering a less developed market in which relatively few people have televisions. Advertising regulations also vary by country. French law, for example, discourages advertisements that disparage competing products; comparative advertisements must contain at least two significant, objective, and verifiable differences between products.[3] New Zealand regulators may ban ads for a variety of reasons. A Nike ad featured a coach telling his players to "visualize your opponent as your worst enemy," who then gets tackled by the team; the ad was banned by the regulators for being too violent. Similarly, a Coca-Cola ad featuring aboriginal dancers was banned for being "culturally insensitive."[4]

In addition to dealing with national differences, international marketing managers confront two tasks their domestic counterparts do not face: capturing synergies among various national markets and coordinating marketing activities in those markets. Synergies are important because they provide opportunities for additional revenues and for growth and cross-fertilization. Coordination is important because it can help lower marketing costs and create a unified marketing effort.

INTERNATIONAL MARKETING MANAGEMENT ‹

An international firm's marketing activities often are organized as a separate and self-contained function within the firm. Yet that function both affects and is affected by virtually every other organizational activity, as shown in Figure 16.1. These interrelationships make international marketing management a critical component of international business success. International marketing management encompasses a firm's efforts to ensure that its international marketing activities mesh with the firm's corporate strategy, business strategy, and other functional strategies.

International Marketing and Business Strategies

A key challenge for a firm's marketing managers is to adopt an international marketing strategy that supports the firm's overall business strategy.[5] As we discussed in Chapter 10, business strategy can take one of three forms: differentiation, cost leadership, or focus.

A differentiation strategy requires marketing managers to develop products as well as pricing, promotional, and distribution tactics that differentiate the firm's products or services from those of its competitors in the eyes of customers. Differentiation can be based on perceived quality, fashion, reliability, or other salient characteristics, as the marketing managers of such products as Rolex watches, BMW automobiles, and Montblanc pens successfully have shown. Assuming the differentiation can be communicated adequately to customers, the firm will be able to charge higher prices for its product or insulate itself from price competition from lesser brands. For example, Rolex, which has successfully implemented a differentiation strategy, does not need to cut the price for its diamond-encrusted $15,000 watches whenever Kmart features Timex quartz watches for $39.95 on a blue light special.

Alternatively, a firm may adopt an international business strategy that stresses its overall cost leadership. Cost leadership can be pursued and achieved through systematic reductions in production and manufacturing costs, reductions in sales costs, the acceptance of lower profit margins, the use of less expensive materials and component parts, or other means. Marketing managers for a firm adopting this strategy will concentrate their promotional efforts on advertising the low price of the product and will utilize channels of distribution that allow the firm to keep the retail price low—for example, by selling through discounters rather than through fashionable boutiques. Texas Instruments calculators, Hyundai automobiles, and Bic pens all are marketed using a cost leadership strategy. And Timex's cost leadership approach has allowed it to thrive in the large market for low-price watches.

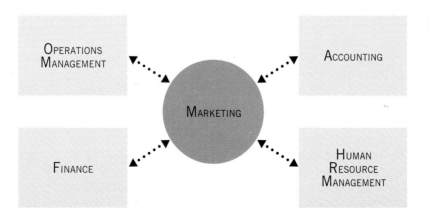

FIGURE 16.1

International Marketing as an Integrated Functional Area

Wiring the World

PRETTY GARLIC

John Huang, the managing director of a small exporting company in Shenzhen, China, sells but one product: garlic. He recently faced an interesting challenge: how to convince the world's food-processing companies to order his garlic, despite his lack of a marketing budget.

Huang's solution was to use the Internet to build worldwide recognition of his company and its simple product line. He designed an attractive Web site—*www.prettygarlic.com*—that provides much of the information a prospective buyer of garlic needs—prices, ordering information, payment terms, shipping arrangements, and packaging details. The Web site also provides information of use to garlic retailers, such as the plant's health benefits. It is probably the only site on the Internet that features color photos showcasing the different sizes and types of garlic. Although most Web surfers have no need to see a photo of a 5.5-centimeter pure-white Pizhou garlic, buyers for the world's food processors and grocery chains do. Half of Huang's orders are generated by the Internet, and the company now ships 15,000 tons of garlic a year. Needless to say, the Internet has provided a perfect means for Huang to reach his small but focused target market.

Source: "The Web @ Work," *Wall Street Journal*, August 7, 2000, p. B4; *www.prettygarlic.com* Web site.

A firm also may adopt a focus strategy. In this case marketing managers will concentrate their efforts on particular segments of the consumer market or on particular areas or regions within a market. International marketing managers will need to concentrate on getting the appropriate message regarding the firm's products or services to the various selected target markets. For example, the Swiss watchmaker Ste. Suisse Microelectronique et d'Horlogerie SA (SMH), which manufactures the popular Swatch watches, focuses its marketing efforts on selling this inexpensive line of watches to young, fashion-oriented consumers in Europe, North America, and Asia. "Wiring the World" demonstrates how one Chinese entrepreneur used the Internet as a key element in implementing his focus strategy.

A critical element for a firm's success is the congruency of its international marketing efforts with its overall business strategy. Timex, Rolex, and SMH—all watchmakers—have chosen different strategies, yet all are successful internationally because they match their international marketing efforts to their business strategies. Timex's cost leadership strategy implies that the firm must seek out low-cost suppliers globally and sell its watches in discount stores such as Wal-Mart and Target, rather than in fashionable department stores such as Saks Fifth Avenue and Harrod's. Rolex's differentiation strategy, based on the firm's carefully nurtured worldwide image, might collapse if Rolex distributed its watches through armies of street vendors stationed in front of subway stations throughout the world, rather than through a handful of chic and expensive horologists located on the most fashionable avenues of the world's most glamorous cities. Similarly, SMH does not advertise Swatch watches to the upper-class, middle-aged audiences of *Town and Country* and *Architectural Digest* or to the predominantly male readership of *Field and Stream* and *Popular Electronics*. It does advertise its wares in the U.S., Chinese, and French editions of *Elle*, which are read by demographically similar young, trendy female audiences—the target of its focus strategy.

Having adopted an overall international business strategy, a firm must assess where it wants to do business. Decisions about whether to enter a particular foreign market are derived from and must be consistent with the firm's overall business strategy. For example, the steady economic growth of such low-to-middle-income countries as Costa Rica, Namibia, Poland, and Turkey offers exciting new business opportunities for Timex but not necessarily for Rolex.

Because of budget and resource limitations, international firms must carefully assess countries and rank them according to their potential for the firms' products. Influencing this ranking may be factors such as culture, levels of competition, channels of distribution, and availability of infrastructure. Depending on the nature of the product and other circumstances, a firm may choose to enter simultaneously all markets that meet certain acceptability criteria. For example, consumer goods marketers like Nike and Coca-Cola often introduce new products broadly throughout North America or Europe to maximize the impact of their mass media advertising campaigns. Alternatively, a firm may choose to enter markets one by one, in an order based on their potential to the firm. Caterpillar, for example, uses this approach because its marketing strategy is based on the painstaking development of strong local dealerships, not glitzy TV campaigns highlighting the endorsements of the latest music and sports stars.

The Marketing Mix

After an international firm has decided to enter a particular foreign market, further marketing decisions must be made.[6] In particular, international marketing managers must address four issues:

1. How to develop the firm's product(s)
2. How to price those products
3. How to sell those products
4. How to distribute those products to the firm's customers

These elements are collectively known as the **marketing mix** and colloquially referred to as the *four Ps of marketing:* product, pricing, promotion, and place (or distribution). The role of the four Ps in international marketing is illustrated in Figure 16.2.

International marketing-mix issues and decisions parallel those of domestic marketing in many ways, although they are more complex. The array of variables international marketing managers must consider is far broader, and the interrelationships among those variables far more intricate, than is the case for domestic marketing managers. Before we discuss these complexities, however, we need to focus on another important issue in international marketing—the extent to which an international firm should standardize its marketing mix in all the countries it enters.

Standardization Versus Customization

A firm's marketers usually choose from three basic approaches in deciding whether to standardize or customize their firm's marketing mix:

1. Should the firm adopt an *ethnocentric approach*, that is, simply market its goods internationally the same way it does domestically?
2. Should it adopt a *polycentric approach*, that is, customize the marketing mix to meet the specific needs of each foreign market it serves?
3. Should it adopt a *geocentric approach*, that is, analyze the needs of customers worldwide and then adopt a standardized marketing mix for all the markets it serves?[7]

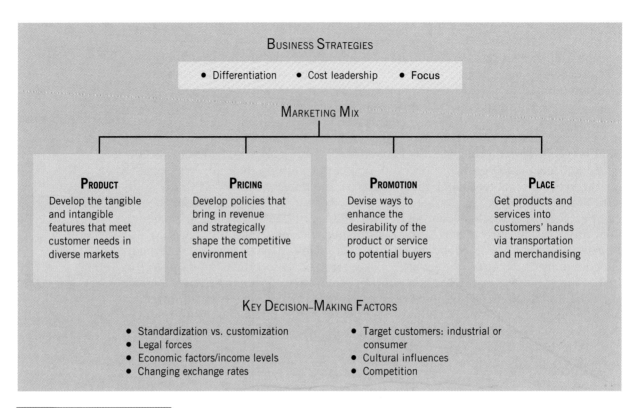

BUSINESS STRATEGIES

• Differentiation   • Cost leadership   • Focus

MARKETING MIX

PRODUCT

Develop the tangible and intangible features that meet customer needs in diverse markets

PRICING

Develop policies that bring in revenue and strategically shape the competitive environment

PROMOTION

Devise ways to enhance the desirability of the product or service to potential buyers

PLACE

Get products and services into customers' hands via transportation and merchandising

KEY DECISION–MAKING FACTORS

• Standardization vs. customization
• Legal forces
• Economic factors/income levels
• Changing exchange rates

• Target customers: industrial or consumer
• Cultural influences
• Competition

FIGURE 16.2   **The Elements of the Marketing Mix for International Firms**

The **ethnocentric approach** is relatively easy to adopt. The firm simply markets its goods in international markets using the same marketing mix it uses domestically, thereby avoiding the expense of developing new marketing techniques to serve foreign customers. When some firms first internationalize, they adopt this approach, believing that a marketing mix that worked at home should be as successful abroad. For example, when Lands' End targeted the German mail-order market in the mid-1990s—which on a per capita basis is the largest in the world—it deliberately replicated its U.S. marketing strategy. Stressing its "down home" roots, the company trumpets to its U.S. consumers its location next to a rural Wisconsin cornfield, the friendliness of its operators and production staff, and its generous return policy—consumers can return all Lands' End products, even if they are used or worn out, with no questions asked. When it entered the German market, Lands' End established its local headquarters in an old schoolhouse in the tiny, picturesque village of Mettlach on the Saar River. The company spent months training its telephone operators to ensure they would meet its standards for friendly, helpful service. It also transplanted its "no questions asked" return service, much to the consternation of its German competitors, whose policy was to accept returns only if the goods were flawed or inaccurately described in their catalogs and then only if the goods were unused and in good condition.[8] The ethnocentric approach may not be desirable, however, if the firm loses sales because it fails to take into account the idiosyncratic needs of its foreign customers. Should this be the case, successful firms will modify their marketing mixes to meet local conditions and needs after the firms learn more about the local market.

The **polycentric approach** is far more costly because international marketers attempt to customize the firm's marketing mix in each market the firm enters in order to meet the idiosyncratic needs of customers in that market. Customization may increase the firm's revenues if its marketers are successful in this task. Firms that adopt this approach believe customers will be more willing to buy and more willing to pay a higher price for a product that exactly meets their needs than a product that does not. Often international firms that view themselves as multidomestic adopt this approach.

The **geocentric approach** calls for standardization of the marketing mix, allowing the firm to provide essentially the same product or service in different markets and to use essentially the same marketing approach to sell that product or service globally. Coca-Cola was one of the first international businesses to adopt this approach. It sells its popular soft drink worldwide and uses essentially the same packaging, product, and advertising themes everywhere. Indeed, the contoured shape of a Coca-Cola bottle is one of the world's most widely recognized images.

Note that both the ethnocentric and the geocentric approaches argue for standardization of the marketing mix. As we saw in Chapter 10, a firm using the ethnocentric approach standardizes on the basis of what the firm does in its home country. A firm using the geocentric approach starts with no such home country bias. Instead, the geocentric approach considers the needs of all the firm's customers around the world and then standardizes on that basis.

Standardization became a popular buzzword during the 1980s, as proponents such as Kenichi Ohmae (then managing director of McKinsey & Company's Tokyo office) argued that customers in the Triad were becoming increasingly alike, with similar incomes, educational achievements, lifestyles, and aspirations, so that expensive customization of the marketing mix by country was less necessary.[9] Similarly, Harvard Business School marketing guru Theodore Levitt believes that standardization of a firm's products and other elements of its marketing mix creates huge economies of scale in production, distribution, and promotion. By transforming these cost savings into reduced prices worldwide, Levitt argues, a firm that adopts standardization can outperform its international competitors.[10]

The trade-offs between standardization and customization are clear. Standardization allows a firm to achieve manufacturing, distribution, and promotional efficiencies and to maintain simpler and more streamlined operations.[11] However, the firm may suffer lost sales if its products fail to meet the unique needs of customers in a given market. Customization allows a firm to tailor its products to meet the needs of customers in each market, although the firm may sacrifice cost efficiencies by so doing. In essence, standardization focuses on the cost side of the profit equation; by driving down costs, the firm's profits are enhanced. Customization focuses on the revenue side of the profit equation; by attending to the unique customer needs in each market, the firm is able to charge higher prices and sell more goods in each market. In practice, most firms avoid the extremes of either approach.[12] Many successful firms have adopted a strategy of "think globally, act locally" to gain the economies of scale of a global marketing mix while retaining the ability to meet the needs of customers in different national markets. Even Coca-Cola, a pioneer in the use of global marketing, has begun to encourage more localized thinking within its global marketing framework.

The home appliance market provides a useful example of this strategy. U.S. kitchens tend to be large and spacious, and consumers prefer large stoves, refrigerators, and dishwashers. The smaller kitchens of Europe and Japan dictate the use of much smaller appliances. Further, within Europe there are marked differences in power supply characteristics and in consumer preferences for various design features and alternatives. Thus appliance manufacturers must develop

› Whirlpool designed its World Washer to meet the needs of these Brazilian shoppers, as well as the growing middle class in other emerging economies like India and Mexico.

specific and unique product lines for each country in which the firms do business. Whirlpool has tried to reduce some of the costs of customization by designing its products to meet the needs of market niches that cross national boundaries. For example, Whirlpool designers have developed a World Washer, a small, stripped-down automatic washing machine targeted to meet the needs of the emerging middle classes in such countries as Brazil, Mexico, and India. Whirlpool, however, stands ready to customize even the World Washer when needed. It modified the agitators of World Washers sold in India to ensure the machines would not shred or tangle the delicate saris traditionally worn by Indian women.[13]

The degree of standardization or customization a firm adopts depends on many factors, including product type, the cultural differences between the home country and the host countries, and the host countries' legal systems. The firm may adopt one approach for one element of the marketing mix and another for a second element. Often firms standardize product designs to capture manufacturing economies of scale but customize advertisements and the channels of distribution to meet specific local market needs. The degree of standardization also may be influenced by the firm's perception of the global marketplace, which is similar to the conundrum "Is the glass half full or half empty?" A firm tilting toward standardization assumes consumers around the world are basically similar but then adjusts for differences among them. A firm tilting toward customization assumes consumers are different but then adjusts for similarities among them.

An international firm also must consider its own organizational structure. Standardization implies that power and control should be centralized, often at the firm's headquarters, whereas customization suggests that headquarters must delegate considerable decision-making power to local managers. Thus a strongly centralized firm (see Chapter 13) can more easily standardize its international marketing mix than can a decentralized firm. Often international firms address these organizational issues by adopting a two-step process:

1. The decision to standardize some elements of the marketing mix, such as product design, brand name, packaging, and product positioning, is made centrally.

2. Then local managers are called on to critique the global marketing program and to develop plans to implement customized elements of the marketing mix, such as promotion and distribution.[14]

Table 16.1 summarizes some factors that may lead a firm to adopt standardization or customization for all or part of its international marketing efforts.

› PRODUCT POLICY

The first P of the international marketing mix is the product itself. Here, **product** comprises both the set of tangible factors that the consumer can see or touch (the physical product and its packaging) and numerous intangible factors

STANDARDIZED INTERNATIONAL MARKETING	
Advantages	**Disadvantages**
1. Reduces marketing costs	1. Ignores different conditions of product use
2. Facilitates centralized control of marketing	2. Ignores local legal differences
3. Promotes efficiency in R&D	3. Ignores differences in buyer behavior patterns
4. Results in economies of scale in production	4. Inhibits local marketing initiatives
5. Reflects the trend toward a single global marketplace	5. Ignores other differences in individual markets

CUSTOMIZED INTERNATIONAL MARKETING	
Advantages	**Disadvantages**
1. Reflects different conditions of product use	1. Increases marketing costs
2. Acknowledges local legal differences	2. Inhibits centralized control of marketing
3. Accounts for differences in buyer behavior patterns	3. Creates inefficiency in R&D
4. Promotes local marketing initiatives	4. Reduces economies of scale in production
5. Accounts for other differences in individual markets	5. Ignores the trend toward a single global marketplace

TABLE 16.1

Advantages and Disadvantages of Standardized and Customized International Marketing

such as image, installation, warranties, and credit terms. Critical to a firm's ability to compete internationally is its success in developing products with tangible and intangible features that meet the wants and needs of customers in diverse national markets.[15] For example, Toyota's success in selling its automobiles in Europe, Asia, and the Americas reflects its product-related achievements in designing and producing mechanically reliable vehicles, offering competitive warranties, building a solid brand name for its products, providing spare parts and repair manuals, and furnishing financing to its dealers and retail customers.

Standardized Products or Customized Products?

A key product policy decision facing international marketers is the extent to which their firms' products should be standardized across markets or customized within individual markets. For example, Toyota, like many international firms, has adopted a blend of customization and standardization. It has standardized its corporate commitment to building high-quality, mechanically reliable automobiles and to maintaining the prestige of the Toyota brand name. Yet it customizes its products and product mix to meet the needs of local markets. For example, it sells right-hand-drive motor vehicles in Japan, Australia, and the United Kingdom and left-hand-drive vehicles in the Americas and continental Europe. It also adjusts its warranties from country to country based on the warranties offered by its competitors. The name under which it sells a product also may vary by country. The automobile sold as a Lexus Sports Coupe in the United States is sold as a Toyota Soarer in Japan. Toyota will even adjust the products it sells in order to meet local market conditions. For example, its initial entry into the U.S. minivan market suffered from poor handling and a lack of power and therefore failed to make a dent in Chrysler's dominance of this market. The firm corrected these problems in its Previa van, which it rushed to the U.S. market. However, because Chrysler's sales in Asian markets were limited and of little threat, Toyota continued to sell its original van model for several years in those markets.

Sometimes firms learn they have customized their products not by design but by accident. For example, in the late 1980s Unilever discovered to its horror that for no apparent reason it was using 85 different recipes for its chicken soups and 15 different cone shapes for its Cornetto ice creams in Europe. Once the problem was detected, Unilever quickly standardized its ice cream cone design and slashed the number of chicken soup flavors it offered European customers, thereby reducing its production and inventory costs and simplifying its distribution requirements.[16]

The extent to which products should be customized to meet local needs varies according to several factors. One is the nature of the product's target customers—are they industrial users or are they individual consumers? Although some industrial products are customized and some consumer products are standardized, generally speaking, industrial products are more likely to be standardized than consumer products. For example, Caterpillar's bulldozers and front-end loaders are sold throughout the world with only minor modifications to meet local operating and regulatory requirements. Products sold as commodities also are typically standardized across different markets; examples include agricultural products, petroleum, 16MB computer memory chips, and chemicals. A general rule of thumb is that the closer to the body a product is consumed, the more likely it will need to be customized. For example, to boost its sales in Japan, Eddie Bauer altered the styles of clothing it sells there, adding to its store shelves stretchy shirts and straight-legged pants that the Japanese prefer.[17] The Big Boy burger chain added pork omelettes and fried rice to its menus in Thailand to attract local consumers.[18]

Legal Forces

The laws and regulations of host countries also may affect the product policies adopted by international firms. For example, countries often impose detailed labeling requirements and health standards on consumer products that firms, both foreign and domestic, must follow strictly. International firms must adjust the packaging and even the products themselves to meet these consumer protection regulations. For example, Grupo Modelo SA, the brewer of Corona beer, had to reduce the nitrosamine levels of the beer it sells in Germany, Austria, and Switzerland to meet those countries' health standards.[19] Countries also may regulate the design of consumer products to simplify purchase and replacement decisions. For example, Saudi Arabia requires electrical connecting cords on consumer appliances to be 2 meters long. GE suffered the embarrassment (and a loss of profits) of having its goods turned back at a Saudi port when an inspector determined GE's connecting cords were only 2 yards long.[20] Widely varying technical standards adopted by countries for such products as electrical appliances and broadcasting and telecommunications equipment also force firms to customize their products. For example, the electrical plugs of home appliances sold in Europe must be modified on a country-by-country basis to fit the array of electrical outlets found there. Laws designed for an earlier age also create numerous problems for online marketers, as "Wiring the World" indicates.

Cultural Influences

International firms often must adapt their products to meet the cultural needs of local markets. One typical adaptation is to change the labeling on the product's package into the primary language of the host country. However, in some cases a

E-MARKETING:
BEWARE THE REGULATORS

The Internet offers marketers the opportunity to develop new ways of doing business. Unfortunately, these new approaches may conflict with laws designed for an earlier age. For example, Primus Online, a German e-retailer of consumer electronics, discovered an innovative use for the Internet's ability to obtain, process, and disseminate information to consumers nearly instantaneously. Like many discounters, Primus orders goods in bulk from its suppliers. The more goods it purchases, the lower the prices it gets from its suppliers. Primus's marketing insight was to pass along these savings to its customers in real time: As Primus gets more orders for a given good, it lowers the price of the good to its customers, thereby generating more demand for the good. German law, however, discourages price discounting. It generally restricts discounts to no more than 3 percent from the advertised price.

Philips and Sony used this law to prevent Primus Online from discounting the televisions, VCRs, and stereo systems it buys from them.

French courts banned the use of the Internet by Nart, an online auction company, to auction expensive art. Such auctions are reserved for a state-controlled group of auctioneers. Nart tried to utilize the Internet to crack this monopoly by having its New York subsidiary advertise and operate the online auctions. Through this approach Nart also believed it could avoid paying commissions and France's value-added tax. French courts ruled, however, that because the auctions were advertised in France, the art works were displayed in France, and Nart's headquarters was located in France, Nart was subject to French law.

foreign language may be used to connote quality or fashion. For example, after the collapse of communism, Procter & Gamble added German words to the labels of detergents sold in the Czech Republic. Market researchers had determined that products in packages labeled in English or German were viewed by Czechs as being of higher quality than products in packages labeled in Czech.[21] Often the ingredients of food products are modified to better please local palates. Gerber, for example, customizes its baby food to meet the requirements of the local culture. The company found that Polish mothers refused to purchase its mashed bananas for their infants because the fruit was viewed as an expensive luxury. Instead, Polish mothers favor such Gerber delicacies as Vegetable and Rabbit Meat to help nurture their infants; Japanese mothers choose Gerber's Freeze Dried Sardines and Rice for their children.[22] Pepsi's Frito-Lay division also has modified its snack foods to better meet the needs of foreign consumers, offering, for example, paprika-flavored chips to Poles and Hungarians and shrimp-flavored chips to Koreans. Its food scientists also are busily working on a squid-peanut snack food Frito-Lay believes will be very successful among Southeast Asians. Presumably for cultural reasons, neither Gerber nor Frito-Lay has yet made plans to market these items in North America.

Culture may affect product policy in other ways. For example, foreign automobile makers have learned that Japanese consumers are extremely quality conscious. For many Japanese consumers an automobile is more a status symbol than a mode of transportation—the average car in Japan is driven only 5,000 miles per year, about one-third the U.S. average. Thus the way the car looks is often more important than the way it drives. A Japanese customer may reject a car if the paint underneath the hood is uneven or the gas tank cover fits

468 > Chapter 16   International Marketing

loosely.[24] Many German consumers are very environment conscious. As a result, firms often must redesign products they sell in Germany to allow for easier disposal and recycling. And Mattel's Japanese subsidiary makes its Barbie dolls more Japanese in appearance. This move boosted the annual sales of Barbie dolls in Japan by 2 million units.[25]

At other times culture may force changes in a foreign product. For example, although U.S. films are very popular in Asia, HBO often has to edit its movies before they can be broadcast in Asia's culturally conservative countries. HBO could not show *Schindler's List* or *Amistad* in Malaysia because both films contained brief nudity, and their director, Steven Spielberg, refuses to allow others to cut scenes from his movies. And given the prevailing policies of regulators in Singapore, it is unlikely that HBO's *Sex in the City* will ever be televised there.[26]

Economic Factors

A country's level of economic development may affect the desired attributes of a product. Consumers in richer countries often favor products loaded with extra performance features; more price-sensitive consumers in poorer countries typically opt for stripped-down versions of the same products. Sometimes a firm may have to adjust package size or design to meet local conditions. For example, firms selling toothpaste or shampoo in poorer countries often package their goods in single-use sizes to make the products more affordable to local citizens. The quality of a country's infrastructure also may affect the customization decision; thus manufacturers may reinforce the suspension systems of motor vehicles sold in countries where road maintenance is poor. The availability and cost of repair services also can affect product design. For example, most automobiles sold in North America use electronic fuel injectors rather than carburetors. In poorer countries the reverse is true, primarily because of maintenance considerations. Maintaining fuel injectors requires sophisticated electronic testing equipment backed up by highly trained technicians; any mechanic can tune up a carburetor.

Brand Names

One element international firms often like to standardize is the brand name of a product. A firm that does this can reduce its packaging, design, and advertising production costs. It also can capture spillovers of its advertising messages from one market to the next. For example, Avon's entry into the China market was made easier by the fact that millions of consumers had seen its products advertised on Hong Kong television.[27] Mars, Inc., sought to capture the benefits of standardization by dropping its successful local brand names for the Marathon bar in the British market and the Raider chocolate biscuit on the Continent in favor of the more universally known Snickers and Twix brands.[28] However, sometimes legal or cultural factors force a firm to alter the brand names under which it sells its products. For example, Grupo Modelo SA markets Corona beer in Spain as Coronita because a Spanish vineyard owns the Corona brand name.[29] Coca-Cola calls its low-calorie soft drink Diet Coke in weight-conscious North America but Coca-Cola Light in other markets.

> PRICING ISSUES AND DECISIONS

The second P of the international marketing mix is pricing. Developing effective prices and pricing policies is a critical determinant of any firm's success.[30] Pricing policies directly affect the size of the revenues earned by a firm. The policies also serve as an important strategic weapon by allowing the firm to shape the competitive environment in which it does business. For example, Toys 'R' Us has achieved success in Germany, Japan, the United States, and other countries by selling low-priced toys in low-cost warehouselike settings. Its low prices have placed enormous pressure on its competitors to slash their costs, alter their distribution systems, and shrink their profit margins. The firm's aggressive pricing strategy has effectively forced its competitors to fight the battle for Asian, European, and North American consumers on terms dictated by Toys 'R' Us. As the opening case suggests, Wal-Mart is doing much the same in Europe.

Both domestic and international firms must strive to develop pricing strategies that will produce profitable operations, but the task facing an international firm is more complex than that facing a purely domestic firm. To begin with, a firm's costs of doing business vary widely by country. Differences in transportation charges and tariffs cause the landed price of goods to vary by country. Differences in distribution practices also affect the final price the end customer pays. For example, intense competition among distributors in the United States minimizes the margin between retail prices and manufacturers' prices. In contrast, Japan's inefficient multilayered distribution system, which relies on a chain of distributors to get goods into the hands of consumers, often inflates the prices Japanese consumers pay for goods.

Exchange rate fluctuations also can create pricing problems. If an exporter's home currency rises in value, the exporter must choose between maintaining its prices in the home currency (which makes its goods more expensive in the importing country) and maintaining its prices in the host currency (which cuts its profit margins by lowering the amount of home country currency it receives for each unit sold).

International firms must consider these factors in developing their pricing policies for each national market the firms serve. They must decide whether they want to apply consistent prices across all those markets or customize prices to meet the needs of each. In reaching this decision, the firms must remember that competition, culture, distribution channels, income levels, legal requirements, and exchange rate stability may vary widely by country.

Pricing Policies

International firms generally adopt one of three pricing policies:[31]

1. Standard price policy
2. Two-tiered pricing
3. Market pricing

An international firm following a geocentric approach to international marketing will adopt a **standard price policy**, whereby the firm charges the same price for its products and services regardless of where they are sold or the nationality of the customer. Firms that sell goods which are easily tradable and transportable often adopt this pricing approach out of necessity. For example, if a firm manufacturing DRAM memory chips charged different customers vastly different prices, some of its favored customers might begin to resell the chips to less favored customers—an easy task, given the small size and high value of the chips. Similarly, firms that sell commodity goods in competitive markets often use this pricing policy. For example, producers of crude oil, such as Aramco, Kuwait Oil, and Pemex, sell their products to any and all customers at prices determined by supply and demand in the world crude oil market. Other commodities produced and traded worldwide, such as coal and agricultural goods, also are sold at competitive prices with suitable adjustments for quality differentials and transportation costs and little regard to the purchaser's nationality.

An international firm that follows an ethnocentric marketing approach will use a **two-tiered pricing policy**, whereby the firm sets one price for all its domestic sales and a second price for all its international sales. A firm that adopts a two-tiered pricing policy commonly allocates to domestic sales all accounting charges associated with research and development, administrative overhead, capital depreciation, and so on. The firm then can establish a uniform foreign sales price without having to worry about covering these costs. Indeed, the only costs that need to be covered by the foreign sales price are the marginal costs associated with foreign sales, such as the product's unit manufacturing costs, shipping costs, tariffs, and foreign distribution costs.

Two-tiered pricing often is used by domestic firms just beginning to internationalize. In the short run charging foreign customers a price that covers only marginal costs may be an appropriate approach for such firms. However, the strong ethnocentric bias of two-tiered pricing suggests it is not a suitable long-run pricing strategy. A firm that views foreign customers as marginal—rather than integral—to its business is unlikely to develop the international skills, expertise, and outlook necessary to compete successfully in the international marketplace.

Firms that adopt a two-tiered pricing policy also are vulnerable to charges of dumping. Recall from Chapter 8 that dumping is the selling of a firm's products in a foreign market for a price lower than that charged in the firm's domestic market—an outcome that easily can result from a two-tiered pricing system. Most major trading countries have issued regulations intended to protect domestic firms from dumping by foreign competitors. For example, in the mid-1990s Toyota and Mazda were charged with dumping minivans in the U.S. market. Although the Japanese automakers were not penalized in this case, both subsequently raised their minivan prices to avoid future dumping complaints.

Market Pricing

An international firm that follows a polycentric approach to international marketing will use a **market pricing policy**. Market pricing is the most complex of the three pricing policies and the one most commonly adopted. A firm utilizing market pricing customizes its prices on a market-by-market basis to maximize its profits in each market.

As you may remember from your microeconomics class, the profit-maximizing output (the quantity the firm must produce to maximize its profit) occurs at the intersection of the firm's marginal revenue curve and its marginal cost curve. The profit-maximizing price is found by reading across from the point on the firm's demand curve where the profit-maximizing output occurs. In Figure 16.3(a) the intersection of the marginal revenue curve (*MR*) and the marginal cost curve (*MC*) occurs at Q, which is the profit-maximizing output. If you read straight up from Q until you reach the demand curve (*D*), then move left to the y-axis, you find the profit-maximizing price, *P*, the maximum price at which quantity Q of the good can be sold. With market pricing the firm calculates and charges the profit-maximizing price in each market it serves. Figure 16.3(b) shows two markets in which a firm has identical demand and marginal revenue curves but faces different marginal cost curves. The firm faces higher marginal costs in country 1 (MC_1) than in country 2 (MC_2). Accordingly, its profit-maximizing price in country 1 (P_1) is higher than that in country 2 (P_2).

Two conditions must be met if a firm is to successfully practice market pricing:

1. The firm must face different demand and/or cost conditions in the countries in which it sells its products. This condition usually is met because taxes, tariffs, standards of living, levels of competition, infrastructure costs and availability, and numerous other factors vary by country.

2. The firm must be able to prevent arbitrage, a concept discussed in Chapter 7. The firm's market pricing policy will unravel if customers are able to buy the firm's products in a low-price country and resell them profitably in a high-price

a. Finding the profit-maximizing price

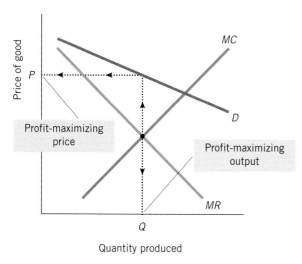

b. Finding the profit-maximizing price for two markets

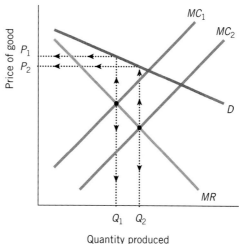

FIGURE 16.3   **Determining the Profit-Maximizing Price**

country. Because of tariffs, transportation costs, and other transaction costs, arbitrage is usually not a problem if country-to-country price variations are small. If prices vary widely by country, however, arbitrage can upset the firm's market pricing strategy.

Assuming these conditions are met, the advantages of this polycentric approach are obvious. The firm can set higher prices where markets will tolerate them and lower prices where necessary to remain competitive. It also can directly allocate relevant local costs against local sales within each foreign market, thereby allowing corporate strategists and planners to better allocate the firm's resources across markets. Such flexibility comes with a cost, however. To capture the benefits of market pricing, local managers must closely monitor sales and competitive conditions within their markets so that appropriate and timely adjustments can be made. Also, corporate headquarters must be willing to delegate authority to local managers to allow them to adjust prices within their markets.

A market pricing policy, however, can expose a firm to complaints about dumping (as discussed earlier) as well as to three other risks: (1) damage to its brand name, (2) development of a gray market for its products, and (3) consumer resentment against discriminatory prices.

The firm needs to ensure that the prices it charges in one market do not damage the brand image it has carefully nurtured in other markets. For example, suppose Seagram encouraged its North American and European brand managers to market Chivas Regal as a premium scotch whiskey sold at a premium price but allowed its Japanese brand managers to peddle Chivas Regal as a nonprestigious brand sold at rock-bottom prices. Because of its marketing approach in Japan, Seagram would risk deterioration of Chivas Regal's premium brand image in North America and Europe. Thus any international firm that sells brand name products and adopts market pricing should review the prices charged by local managers to ensure that the integrity of its brand names and its market images is maintained across all of its markets.

A firm that follows a market pricing policy also risks the development of gray markets for its products as a result of arbitrage. A **gray market** is a market that results when products are imported into a country legally but outside the normal channels of distribution authorized by the manufacturer. (This phenomenon also is known as **parallel importing**.) A gray market may develop when the price in one market is sufficiently lower than the price the firm charges in another market that entrepreneurs can buy the good in the lower-price market and resell it profitably in the higher-price market. Thus the firm that has large price differences among markets is vulnerable to having these differentials undercut by gray markets. Gray markets frequently arise when firms fail to adjust local prices after major fluctuations in exchange rates. Coca-Cola, for example, faced such a problem in the mid-1990s after the yen strengthened relative to the U.S. dollar. Japanese discounters were able to purchase and import Coke made in the United States for 27 percent less than the price of Coke made in Japan, thereby disrupting the firm's pricing strategy in both countries.[32] Merck had a similar problem when the British pound rose relative to other European Union (EU) currencies. The company was forced to cut the prices in the United Kingdom of many of its drugs, such as the recently developed AIDS drug Crixivan, because of parallel importing from other EU countries.[33] Products commonly influenced by gray markets include big-ticket items such as automobiles, cameras, computers, ski equipment, and watches. Gray markets also are more prevalent in free-market economies, where fewer government regulations make it easier for gray markets to emerge. One recent estimate suggests gray-market sales in the United States approach $130 billion each year.[34] Many multinational corporations (MNCs) have attempted to eliminate or control gray markets through legal action, but few have had much success.

Gray-market sales undermine a firm's market pricing policy and often lower the firm's profits. Gray-market sales also cause friction between the firm and its distributors, who lose sales but often are stuck with the costs of either providing customer support and honoring product guarantees on gray-market goods or explaining to unhappy customers why they will not do so. For example, Charles of the Ritz reports that over 10,000 retailers sell its Opium perfume, although the firm has authorized only 1,300 to do so. The prices its authorized dealers charge are continually being undercut by the prices offered by gray-market sellers, thereby making it difficult for the authorized dealers to adhere to the firm's suggested pricing schedule. Charles of the Ritz has sought to smooth over the resulting friction by helping its authorized dealers compete with the gray marketers through additional advertising allowances and special price reductions. This practice, however, harms the firm's profit margins.

A third danger lies in consumer resentment. Consumers in the high-priced country may feel they are being gouged by such pricing policies. Estee Lauder, for example, charges $40 for Clinique facial soap in Tokyo; the same soap sells for only $10 in the United States. J. Crew charges Japanese customers $130 for wool sweaters that sell for $48 in the United States. Japanese newspapers and television stations have highlighted this issue, claiming that foreign companies take advantage of Japanese consumers. Although spokespersons from various companies have argued that the price differences are due to the high cost of doing business in Japan, the ill will engendered by the controversy has not helped the companies' sales.[35]

❯ PROMOTION ISSUES AND DECISIONS

Promotion, the third P of international marketing mix, encompasses all efforts by an international firm to enhance the desirability of its products among potential buyers. Although many promotional activities are specifically targeted at buyers, successful firms recognize they also must communicate with their distributors and the general public to ensure favorable sentiment toward the firms themselves and their products. Because promotion relies on communication with audiences in the host country, it is the most culture bound of the four Ps. Thus a firm must take special care to ensure that the message host country audiences receive is in fact the message the firm intended to send. International marketing managers must therefore effectively blend and utilize the four elements of the **promotion mix**—advertising, personal selling, sales promotion, and public relations—to motivate potential customers to buy their firms' products.

Advertising

For most international firms, especially those selling consumer products and services, advertising is the most important element in the promotion mix. As a firm develops its advertising strategy, it must consider three factors:

1. The message it wants to convey
2. The media available for conveying the message
3. The extent to which the firm wants to globalize its advertising effort

At the same time the firm must take into account relevant cultural, linguistic, and legal constraints found in various national markets.

Message.   The **message** of an advertisement is the facts or impressions the advertiser wants to convey to potential customers. An automaker may want to convey a message of value (low price), reliability (quality), and/or style (image and prestige). The choice of message is an important reflection of the way the firm sees its products and services and the way it wants them to be seen by customers. Coca-Cola, for example, believes its products help consumers enjoy life, and its advertising messages consistently stress this theme worldwide. Products that are used for different purposes in different areas will need to be marketed differently. For example, in the United States motorcycles are seen primarily as recreational products, but in many other countries they are seen mainly as a means of transportation. Thus Honda's and Kawasaki's ads in the United States stress the fun and excitement of riding. In poorer countries they stress the reliability and functionalism of motorcycles as a mode of inexpensive transportation.[36]

A product's country of origin often serves as an important part of the advertising message.[37] For example, among fashion-conscious teenagers and young adults in Europe and Japan, U.S. goods often are viewed as being very trendy. Thus Harley-Davidson, Gibson guitars, Stetson hats, and the National Basketball Association, among others, highlight the U.S. origins of their products. Japanese products often

› International firms planning advertising campaigns must be attuned to how consumers in different countries will use their products. For example, in the United States, Honda markets its motorcycles as sports and recreation equipment because that is how they are most often used. But in other countries, motorcycles are a basic form of transportation, and Honda must use a different advertising message there.

are perceived to be of high quality, so international marketers stress the Japanese origin of such products as Toyota automobiles and Sony electronics goods.

Medium. The **medium** is the communication channel used by the advertiser to convey a message. A firm's international marketing manager must alter the media used to convey its message from market to market based on availability, legal restrictions, standards of living, literacy rates, the cultural homogeneity of the national market, and other factors. In bilingual or multilingual countries such as Belgium, Switzerland, and Canada, international firms must adjust their mix of media outlets to reach each of the country's cultural groups. For example, Swissair communicates to its French-speaking Swiss audience by advertising in French-language newspapers and to its German-speaking Swiss audience via ads in German-language newspapers.

A country's level of economic development also may affect the media firms use. In many less developed countries television ownership may be limited and literacy rates low. This eliminates television, newspapers, and magazines as useful advertising media but raises the importance of radio. Some firms have developed innovative solutions to communicate with potential consumers. For example, Colgate-Palmolive wished to increase its sales in rural India. Unfortunately, only one-third of rural Indians own television sets, and more than half are illiterate. To reach these customers, the company's marketers outfitted "video vans" to tour the rural countryside. After showing rural villagers a half-hour infomercial extolling the virtues of the company's oral hygiene products, sales representatives handed out samples of Colgate toothpaste and toothbrushes. This technique has proved successful, doubling toothpaste consumption in rural areas during the past decade.[38] "Bringing the World into Focus" illustrates another

Bringing the World into FOCUS

SAILING FOR SALES

For many years advertising in Egypt usually took one of two forms: dancing women pitching products on static-filled television ads or poor-quality billboards haphazardly thrown up along highways. However, the desire to catch the attention of the 68 million residents of this North African country recently has led international advertisers to search for newer media.

The advertising medium that has attracted the most attention has been the felucca. Feluccas are sailboats that travel up and down the Nile; they have provided transportation and recreation since the days of the pharaohs. Companies use feluccas to transport merchandise, and families frequently rent them for an evening's gathering. Tourists also queue up for rides.

Feluccas are propelled by large, triangular white sails on which Coca-Cola recently decided to place its ads. The firm signed a two-year deal with one of Egypt's largest felucca operators for

27,000 Egyptian pounds (around $8,000) plus new sails. At first Coca-Cola wanted to use red sails to better display its trademark. But because felucca sails have always been white, the firm had to resort to white sails emblazoned with Coke's red logo.

Perrier quickly followed Coke's lead and now has its own advertising agreement with another large felucca operator. Egypt's recently privatized Al Ahram Beverages Co. of Cairo chose to use feluccas to promote its products as well. Still, it is sometimes hard to shape tradition. Even though the Coca-Cola-sponsored feluccas come equipped with complimentary Coke beverages, most Egyptians instead opt for their traditional favorite—apple juice!

Source: "Advertising Breezes Along the Nile River with Signs for Sails," *Wall Street Journal*, July 18, 1997, pp. A1, A11.

unusual but innovative approach to developing advertising media customized for the local market.

Legal restrictions also may prompt the use of certain media. Most national governments limit the number of TV stations as well as the amount of broadcast time sold to advertisers. Countries often outlaw the use of certain media for advertising products that may be harmful to their societies. For example, South Korea, Malaysia, Hong Kong, China, and Singapore ban cigarette advertising on television. South Korea has broadened the ban to magazines read primarily by women and by persons under the age of 20; Hong Kong has extended it to radio; China to radio, newspapers, and magazines; and Singapore to all other media.[39] As in the United States, however, this ban has prompted tobacco firms to sponsor athletic events and to purchase display ads at stadiums that will be picked up by TV cameras.[40] Legal restrictions on the advertising of alcoholic products also are common throughout the world.

Global Versus Local Advertising.   A firm also must decide whether advertising for its product or service can be the same everywhere or must be tailored to each local market the firm serves.[41] Some products, such as Coca-Cola soft drinks, Bic pens, Levi jeans, and McDonald's hamburgers, have almost universal appeal. Such companies frequently advertise globally, utilizing the same advertising campaign in all of the markets they serve. For example, in the late 1990s Coca-Cola introduced a series of ads shown globally that featured its "Always Coca-Cola" slogan.[42]

Sometimes international businesses may choose to make subtle adaptations to meet the needs of the local market. Unilever applied this approach to an advertising campaign for Dove soap. The company's TV commercials were identical in each market, but the actors were not. On the same stage and set, U.S., Italian, German, French, and Australian models were filmed in succession, each stating in her own language, "Dove has one-quarter cleansing cream."[43] Nestlé used a single theme in promoting Kit Kat candy to its European customers—"Have a break, have a Kit Kat"—but changed the backgrounds to better appeal to customers across national markets.

Other firms have opted for a regionalization strategy. IBM, for example, began advertising its PCs in European markets by creating a pan-European advertising campaign. Instead of customizing its ads by country, IBM featured the same text and visual images in all its European ads, altering only the language used for its broadcast and print ads. IBM determined that this approach saved $22 to $30 million in creative and production expenses (of a total advertising budget of $150 million). However, maintaining uniformity of the product's image was of paramount concern. The campaign was designed specifically to ensure that IBM's European clients, regardless of the country in which they were located, received the same message about its product.[44] Similarly, Levi Strauss used the same TV ad to sell its 501 jeans in six European markets. Because each of its commercials costs about $500,000 to shoot, Levi Strauss would have spent about $3 million on six ads and thus saved $2.5 million in production costs alone by choosing this regional strategy.[45]

Whether to choose a standardized or a specialized advertising campaign also is a function of the message the firm wants to convey. Standardized advertisements tend to contain less concrete information than do more specialized advertisements.

› This Warsaw ad is representative of Coca-Cola's bold and splashy advertising in Central Europe. As a result of such initiatives, Coca-Cola derives a majority of its revenues from markets outside the United States.

Ads for products such as candy and soft drinks often can be standardized because the ads stress the warm, emotional aspects of consuming the good, whereas ads for products such as credit cards, automobiles, and airline services tend to be customized to meet the needs of local consumers.[46]

Personal Selling

The second element of the promotion mix is **personal selling**—making sales on the basis of personal contacts. The use of sales representatives, who call on potential customers and attempt to sell them a firm's products or services, is the most common approach to personal selling.[47] Because of the close contact between the salesperson and the potential customer, sellers are likely to rely on host country nationals to serve as their representatives. A firm just starting international operations often will subcontract personal selling to local sales organizations that handle product lines from several firms. As the firm grows and develops a sales base in new markets, it may establish its own sales force. Colgate-Palmolive, for example, made very effective use of personal selling to gain market share in Central Europe. The firm opened a sales office in Warsaw after the Iron Curtain fell and used it to develop a well-trained professional sales staff. That staff has made Colgate-Palmolive the consumer products market leader in Poland.[48]

The importance of personal selling as an element of the promotion mix differs for industrial products and for consumer products. For industrial products (such as complex machinery, electronic equipment, and customized computer software) customers often need technical information about product characteristics, usage, maintenance requirements, and availability of after-sales support. Well-trained sales representatives often are better able to convey information about the intricacies of such products to customers than are print or broadcast media. For consumer products personal selling normally is confined to selling to wholesalers and to retail chains. Most consumer products firms find that advertising, particularly in print and broadcast media, is a more efficient means of communicating with consumers than is personal selling. However, personal selling can be used to market some goods. Avon and Amway, for example, have successfully exported to the Asian and European markets the personal selling techniques they developed in the United States. Similarly, American International Group (AIG) carefully built its 5,000-person sales force in Shanghai over a four-year period; today AIG enjoys a 90 percent share of the life insurance market in that city.[49]

In Amway's case personal selling and the ethnic ties of its existing distributors have played a critical role in the firm's internationalization strategy. When Amway decided to enter the Philippines in 1997, it encouraged distributors of Philippine heritage from the United States, New Zealand, and Australia to act as ambassadors, recruiting new distributors there. Because the ambassadors receive a percentage of the sales generated by the persons they recruit, over 100 existing distributors eagerly traveled to the Philippines at their own expense to develop Amway's sales force. The company has used a similar approach to break into the Korean and Chinese markets.[50]

Personal selling has several advantages for an international firm:

- Firms that hire local sales representatives can be reasonably confident that those individuals understand the local culture, norms, and customs. For example, a native of India selling products in that country will be better informed about local conditions than will someone sent from Spain to sell products in India.

- Personal selling promotes close, personal contact with customers. Customers see real people and come to associate that personal contact with the firm.

- Personal selling makes it easier for the firm to obtain valuable market information. Knowledgeable local sales representatives are an excellent source of information that can be used to develop new products and/or improve existing products for the local market.

On the other hand, personal selling is a relatively high-cost strategy. Each sales representative must be adequately compensated even though each may reach relatively few customers. An industrial products sales representative, for example, may need a full day or more to see just one potential customer. After a sale is closed, the sales representative may still find it necessary to spend large blocks of time with the customer explaining how things work and trying to generate new business. Most larger international firms also find it necessary to establish regional sales offices staffed by sales managers and other support personnel, which add more sales-related costs.

Sales Promotion

Sales promotion comprises specialized marketing efforts such as coupons, in-store promotions, sampling, direct mail campaigns, cooperative advertising, and trade fair attendance. Sales promotion activities focused on wholesalers and retailers are designed to increase the number and commitment of these intermediaries working with the firm. Many international firms participate in international trade shows such as the Paris Air Show or the Tokyo Auto Mart to generate interest among existing and potential distributors for the firms' products. Participation in international trade shows often is recommended as a first step for firms wanting to internationalize their sales. The U.S. Department of Commerce often will help small U.S. firms participate in overseas trade shows as part of its export promotion efforts. Agencies with a similar mission exist in the governments of most major trading nations. Firms also may develop cooperative advertising campaigns or provide advertising allowances to encourage retailers to promote the firms' products.

Sales promotion activities may be narrowly targeted to consumers and/or offered for only a short time before being dropped or replaced with more permanent efforts. This flexible nature of sales promotions makes them ideal for a marketing campaign tailored to fit local customs and circumstances. For example, British American Tobacco, Philip Morris, and R.J. Reynolds competed in the Taiwanese market by handing out free cigarettes, a practice not utilized in the U.S. market. Philip Morris and R.J. Reynolds built market share by offering Korean consumers free cigarette lighters and desk diaries emblazoned with the firms' logos in return for cigarette purchases.[51] U.S. airlines have effectively used direct mail to lure international travelers away from foreign airlines. By carefully analyzing the travel habits of members of their frequent-flyer programs, carriers like American and Continental can target their mailings (and customize incentives, such as awarding bonus frequent-flyer miles) to those customers who are most likely to respond to such lures.

Public Relations

Public relations consists of efforts aimed at enhancing a firm's reputation and image with the general public, as opposed to touting the specific advantages of an individual product or service. The consequence of effective public relations is a general belief that the firm is a good "corporate citizen," that it is reputable, and that it can be trusted.

Savvy international firms recognize that money spent on public relations is money well spent because it earns them political allies and makes it easier to communicate the firms' needs to the general public. They also recognize that, as "foreigners," they often are appealing political targets; thus the firms attempt to reduce their exposure to political attacks. Toyota provides a case in point. The company received large financial incentives from the state of Kentucky to build its first wholly owned U.S. auto assembly plant in Georgetown. During the first few years it operated that plant, Toyota received a fair amount of criticism for its lack of community concern—Japanese firms, unlike their U.S. counterparts, do not have a tradition of corporate philanthropy. The firm eventually realized it had to adapt its corporate attitudes to local customs if it wanted to maintain the goodwill of local politicians. Toyota subsequently became a model corporate citizen, providing grants to local charities, funding college scholarships to graduating high school students, and sponsoring local youth sports teams.

The impact of good public relations is hard to quantify, but over time an international firm's positive image and reputation are likely to benefit the firm in a host country. Consumers are more likely to resist "buy local" pitches when the foreign firm also is perceived to be a good guy. Good public relations also can help the firm when it has to negotiate with a host country government for a zoning permit or an operating license or when it encounters a crisis or unfavorable publicity. For example, Toshiba found itself in deep trouble in 1986 when a Toshiba subsidiary was discovered to have been illegally selling to the Soviet Union advanced technology designed to make the detection of nuclear submarines harder. Normally, few citizens would be aware of the importance of such a breach of security. Unfortunately for Toshiba, one of the best-selling novels of the 1980s, Tom Clancy's *The Hunt for Red October*, had educated U.S. readers about the technological nature of submarine warfare. Fortunately for Toshiba, the firm had been a good corporate citizen in the United States. Relying on the goodwill it had previously fostered with local government officials, community leaders, and its workforce, Toshiba was able to avoid trade sanctions that would have jeopardized its stature in the United States. This example offers a clear lesson: An international firm cannot rely on goodwill to bail it out of a crisis if the firm has no goodwill with important stakeholders to begin with.

› DISTRIBUTION ISSUES AND DECISIONS

The fourth P of the international marketing mix is place—more commonly referred to as distribution. **Distribution** is the process of getting products and services from the firm into the hands of customers. (As we discuss in Chapter 17, distribution is also one component of international logistics management.) An international firm faces two important sets of distribution issues:

1. Physically transporting its goods and services from where they are created to the various markets in which they are to be sold
2. Selecting the means by which to merchandise its goods in the markets it wants to serve

International Distribution

The most obvious issue an international firm's distribution managers must address is the selection of a mode (or modes) of transportation for shipping the firm's goods from their point of origin to their destination. This choice entails a clear trade-off between time and money, as Table 16.2 indicates. Faster modes of transportation, such as air freight and motor carrier, are more expensive than slower modes, such as ocean shipping, railroad, pipeline, and barge. However, the transportation mode selected affects the firm's inventory costs and customer service levels, as well as the product's useful shelf life, exposure to damage, and packaging requirements. International air freight, for example, scores high on each of these dimensions, whereas ocean shipping ranks very low.

TRANSPORTATION MODE	ADVANTAGES	DISADVANTAGES	SAMPLE PRODUCTS
Train	Safe Reliable Inexpensive	Limited to rail routes Slow	Automobiles Grains
Airplane	Safe Reliable	Expensive Limited access	Jewelry Medicine
Truck	Versatile Inexpensive	Small size	Consumer goods
Ship	Inexpensive Good for large products	Slow Indirect	Automobiles Furniture
Electronic media	Fast	Unusable for many products	Information

TABLE 16.2

Advantages and Disadvantages of Different Modes of Transportation for Exports

Consider the impact of transportation mode on the firm's inventory expenses and the level of customer service. If the firm relies on slower modes of transportation, it can maintain a given level of inventory at the point of sale only by maintaining higher levels of inventory in transit. If the firm selects unreliable modes that make it difficult to predict when shipments will actually arrive, the firm will have to increase buffer stocks in its inventory to avoid stock-outs that will lead to disappointed customers. Slower modes of transportation also increase the firm's **international order cycle time**—the time between the placement of an order and its receipt by the customer—for any given level of inventories. Longer order cycle times lower the firm's customer service levels and may induce its customers to seek alternative supply sources.

The product's shelf life affects the selection of transportation mode. Goods that are highly perishable because of physical or cultural forces—such as cut flowers or fashionable dresses—are typically shipped by air freight because of their short shelf life. Less perishable products, such as coal, crude oil, or men's socks, are shipped using less expensive modes. In some cases the transportation mode may affect the product's packaging requirements. For example, goods sent on long ocean voyages may need special packaging to protect them from humidity and damage due to rough seas; the firm could avoid the extra costs of packaging if it chose a faster mode such as air freight. Of course, a simple solution is sometimes available: When Calpis, a Colorado-based agricultural goods processor, entered the Japanese orange juice market, the firm switched its packaging from glass bottles to cans to reduce breakage.[52]

Channels of Distribution

An international firm's marketing managers also must determine which distribution channels to use to merchandise the firm's products in each national market it serves. Figure 16.4 shows the basic channel options used by most international manufacturing firms. Note that a distribution channel can consist of as many as four basic parts:

1. The manufacturer that creates the product or service
2. A wholesaler that buys products and services from the manufacturer and then resells them to retailers
3. The retailer, which buys from wholesalers and then sells to customers
4. The actual customer, who buys the product or service for final consumption

Import agents (discussed in Chapter 11) also may be used as intermediaries, especially by smaller firms.

FIGURE 16.4

Distribution Channel Options

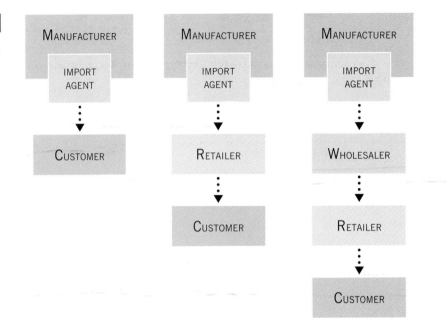

One important factor illustrated by Figure 16.4 is **channel length**, the number of stages in the distribution channel. A firm that sells directly to its customers, which then pay the business directly, bypasses wholesalers and retailers and therefore has a very short distribution channel. This approach is called **direct sales** because the firm is dealing directly with its final consumer. Dell Computer started out as a direct-sales business, taking customer orders over toll-free, 24-hour telephone lines. The advantage of this approach is that the firm maintains control over retail distribution of its products and retains any retailing profits it earns. Unfortunately, the firm also bears the costs and risks of retailing its products.

A slightly longer channel of distribution involves selling to retailers, which then market and sell the products to customers. This is easiest to do when retailers in a given market are heavily concentrated. When there are relatively few large retailers, selling directly to each is easier for manufacturers; when a larger number of smaller retailers are present, selling to each is more complex. For example, huge supermarkets with vast selections of foods and toiletries exist throughout the United States. In Europe, however, many consumers still buy food from small neighborhood stores, and few of these carry toiletries. A consumer products firm therefore will have to use very different approaches to distributing its products in the two markets. For example, in the United States Procter & Gamble (P&G) may sell directly to Kroger or Safeway, which will routinely stock several hundred tubes of toothpaste of various sizes on its shelves and store cartons of inventory in its warehouses. A European retailer, however, may have retail space for only a few tubes and little storage space for backup inventory, thereby making it more difficult for P&G to sell directly to such outlets.

The longest distribution channel involves the use of wholesalers. Wholesalers are separate businesses that buy from manufacturers and then resell to retailers or, in some cases, to other wholesalers. For example, small farmers cannot easily sell their produce to large grocery chains because those chains find it inefficient to deal with large numbers of small suppliers. Instead, farmers sell their produce to wholesalers, which then sell it to grocery stores; thus the grocery stores must deal with only a few large suppliers. Similarly, in markets with little retail concentration, a consumer products firm like P&G generally finds it easier to sell to a few wholesalers rather than attempt to deal with a huge number of small retailers. The use of wholesalers makes it easier to market in countries with little retail concentration and also allows the firm to maintain a smaller sales staff. On the other hand, profit margins tend to be smaller because there are more businesses involved, each of which expects to make a profit. Rather than keeping all the profits for itself, as in the case of direct sales, a firm must share them with wholesalers and retailers.

The challenge for international marketing managers is to find the optimal distribution channel to match the firm's unique competitive strengths and weaknesses with the requirements of each national market it serves. In practice, as with other elements of international marketing, most international firms develop a flexible distribution strategy—they may use a short channel in some markets and a longer channel in others.

The firm's distribution strategy also may be an important component of its promotion strategy. For example, SMH manufactures not only relatively inexpensive Swatch watches but also high-priced watches such as Omega and Tissot. It distributes its expensive watches through exclusive jewelry stores and its Swatch watches through department stores like Macy's and Dillard's.[53] Toyota adopted different distribution strategies for its luxury cars in the United States and Japan. In the United States it named the model Lexus and set up an independent dealership network to strengthen the prestige of that brand name. In Japan, where the firm has less need to bolster its image, the same model is sold under the Toyota name through existing Toyota dealerships. And Unilever has developed a unique approach for distributing and promoting its products in rural Tanzania. Its brigade of pedaling peddlers journeys into the countryside each morning on bicycles to hawk small packets of the company's soaps, toothpaste, and laundry powders.[54]

As noted in Chapter 11, some international firms, particularly producers of more specialized products, may hire a sales or import agent to distribute their goods. For example, the National Football League contracted with Japan Marketing Services to promote NFL-licensed goods in Japan. Annual Japanese sales of T-shirts, sweatshirts, and other clothing bearing the names of U.S. football teams exceed $50 million.[55] Many governments, as part of their efforts to stimulate exports, have developed programs to help firms locate suitable international import agents. For example, the U.S. and Foreign Commercial Service, a branch of the U.S. Department of Commerce, provides lists of foreign firms that have expressed a willingness to distribute given products in their market areas. These data can be obtained by contacting local offices of the U.S. and Foreign Commercial Service or through the National Trade Data Bank.

Firms should exercise caution when selecting a foreign distributor. The distributor is the firm as far as local customers are concerned, so a poor distributor jeopardizes the firm's reputation and performance in that market, often for a very long time. Further, local laws may make it difficult for a firm to terminate the distributor. In Saudi Arabia, for example, a foreign firm must hire a local national to represent it, and firing that agent is virtually impossible without the agent's consent.

Finding an appropriate distributor is a particular challenge in China, where many distributors are state owned with little knowledge or incentive to market foreign consumer products appropriately. For example, the primary distributors of Wrigley gum are controlled by the China National Cereal & Oils Import & Export Corporation, a state-owned trading company. Its managers believe it is a waste of time to deliver goods to smaller wholesalers and retail outlets, preferring that these smaller customers come to its warehouses. Although this tactic may lower China National's transportation costs, it makes it more costly for small wholesalers and retailers to stock Wrigley's gum, which drives down Wrigley's sales.[56] Firms like Amway and Avon, however, have been very successful in China because their sales force, relying on in-home parties and door-to-door sales, bypasses such distributor-created bottlenecks.[57]

Some international firms attempt to transfer to international markets the distribution systems developed in their home countries. McDonald's, for example, gained its status as the leading food service company in the United States by taking great care in selecting its franchisees and by nurturing their enterprises to the mutual benefit of both the franchisees and McDonald's. The firm has followed a similar distribution strategy to capture fast-food dollars in Europe, Asia, Australia, Africa, and Central and South America. Similarly, Coca-Cola utilizes a network of subsidiaries and bottlers (in some of which Coca-Cola has an equity stake) to market its soft drinks in virtually every country—a distribution strategy identical to that used by the firm in its home market.

At other times a firm may adapt its distribution practices to match local customs. In Russia, for example, many goods are sold at street-side kiosks; Pepsi-Cola and Coca-Cola are sold at hundreds of these stands in Moscow alone.[58] Local laws also affect distribution strategies. For many years the ability of foreigners to establish distribution systems was limited in India, Mexico, and China. As a result, most MNCs established joint ventures with local firms in order to distribute their products in those countries. Also, the complexities of Japan's culture and the complicated nature of its distribution networks have prompted many Western firms to seek joint-venture partners to help the firms penetrate the Japanese market. KFC, for example, teamed up with Mitsubishi to create a joint venture to market KFC's products in Japan. Mitsubishi contributed chicken (one of its subsidiaries is a major chicken producer), distribution networks, and an understanding of the cultural nuances of dealing with Japanese consumers. KFC contributed its brand name, an American image that appealed to fashion-conscious Japanese, and its technology and trade secrets—including, of course, the secret spices that make its product so finger-lickin' good.

CHAPTER REVIEW

Summary

International marketing is the process of planning and executing the conception, pricing, promotion, and distribution of ideas, goods, and services across national boundaries to create exchanges that satisfy individual and organizational objectives.

International marketing management is a critical organizational operation that should be integrated with other basic functions such as operations and human resource management. International marketing is generally based on one of three business strategies: differentiation, cost leadership, or focus. Determining the firm's marketing mix involves making decisions about product, pricing, promotion, and place (distribution). A related basic issue that marketing managers must address is the extent to which the marketing mix will be standardized or customized for different markets. A variety of factors must be considered in making this decision.

Product policy focuses on the tangible and intangible factors that characterize the product itself. Standardization versus customization is again a consideration. Industrial products and consumer products usually require different types of product policies. Legal, cultural, and economic forces also affect product policy and must be carefully evaluated.

Pricing issues and decisions constitute the second element of the marketing mix. The three basic pricing philosophies are standard pricing, two-tiered pricing, and market pricing. Market pricing, the most widely used and complex policy, involves setting different prices for each market. Basic economic analyses are used to arrive at the prices. Concerns related to gray markets, dumping, and potential consumer resentment must be addressed by firms that use this approach. Otherwise, serious problems may result.

Promotion issues and decisions generally concern the use of advertising and other forms of promotion. The promotion mix is a blend of advertising, personal selling, sales promotion, and public relations. Each of these elements is usually carefully tailored for the market in which it will be used and implemented accordingly.

Finally, international marketing managers also must plan for distribution—getting products and services from the firm to customers. International distribution may involve a variety of transportation modes, each with its own unique set of advantages and disadvantages. A firm must also develop appropriate distribution channels, which may involve wholesalers and retailers in addition to the firm and its customers. Effective distribution can have a significant impact on a firm's profitability.

Review Questions

1. What is international marketing?
2. What is the marketing mix?
3. What are the basic factors involved in deciding whether to use standardization or customization?
4. How do legal, cultural, and economic factors influence product policy?
5. Why are brand names an important marketing tool for international business?
6. What are the three basic pricing policies?
7. What are the problems that a firm using market pricing might encounter?
8. What are the four elements of the international promotion mix?
9. What are some of the fundamental issues that must be addressed in international advertising?
10. What is a distribution channel? What options does an international firm have in developing its channels?

Questions for Discussion

1. What are the similarities and differences between domestic and international marketing?
2. Are the four Ps of international marketing of equal importance to all firms? What factors might cause some to be more or less important than others?
3. Identify several products you think could be marketed in a variety of foreign markets with little customization. Identify other products that clearly would require customization.
4. How do legal, cultural, and economic factors in your home country affect product policy for foreign firms?
5. What are the pros and cons of trying to use a single brand name in different markets, as opposed to creating unique brand names for various markets?
6. What are the advantages and disadvantages of each pricing policy? Why do most international firms use market pricing?
7. The ethnocentric approach and the geocentric approach both suggest standardization of the marketing mix. What is the difference between these two approaches, if both lead to standardization?
8. What are some basic differences you might expect to see in TV ads broadcast in France, Japan, Saudi Arabia, and the United States?
9. Why is the public relations function important to an international firm?
10. What are the advantages and disadvantages of short versus long channels of distribution?

BUILDING GLOBAL SKILLS

Ajax Alarms is a medium-sized U.S. firm that sells alarm clocks. It subcontracts the production of its clocks to a Korean firm, which manufactures them based on Ajax designs and specifications and then ships the clocks directly to the Ajax warehouse in Kansas. Ajax markets and distributes the clocks throughout the United States and Canada. The clocks themselves are brightly colored novelty items. For example, one of the firm's biggest sellers is a plastic rooster that crows in the morning. Last year Ajax reported profits of $5 million on total revenues of slightly more than $50 million.

Ajax managers have determined that the firm has few growth opportunities in the United States and Canada and so must enter new markets if it is to continue to expand. The managers have decided to start by selling in Mexico. They have hired you, an internationally famous marketing consultant, to advise them.

Your assignment is to outline a marketing plan for Ajax. Ajax wants you to consider product policy, pricing, promotion, and distribution issues. In developing your marketing plan, be sure to consider the factors discussed in this chapter, including standardization versus customization, legal forces, cultural influences, economic factors, and brand name questions. Note specific areas where you can make recommendations to your client. For example, if you believe a certain advertising medium will be beneficial to Ajax, make that recommendation (be sure to provide some rationale or justification). If you feel you lack sufficient information to make a recommendation in some area, identify the factors that must be addressed by Ajax in that particular area. For example, if you cannot recommend a pricing policy, describe the information Ajax needs to acquire and evaluate when making that decision.

WORKING WITH THE WEB: BUILDING GLOBAL INTERNET SKILLS

Web Marketing

There is great variance in how MNCs use their Web sites. Visit the sites of 10 MNCs. What is the underlying theme and purpose of each of these Web sites? Use the information you obtain from the sites to develop a description of each corporation's products and policies, pricing strategies, promotion strategies, and distribution strategies.

Assess which of the Web sites best promotes the corporation's marketing message. Defend your assessment.

If a corporation you have selected operates Web sites in multiple countries, determine if there are any differences in the information it presents among these countries. If there are differences, assess why they exist. Does the firm appear to be using a standardized or customized strategy for its international marketing?

WE INVITE YOU TO VISIT THIS BOOK'S COMPANION WEB SITE AT www.prenhall.com/griffin

IN THE NEWS

1. Sony is known worldwide for developing innovative consumer electronic products, such as the Betamax and the Walkman. Use the homepage of the *Financial Times* (*www.ft.com*) to research the newest electronic gizmos produced by the company. What can you find out about the marketing mix Sony has chosen to use for the products? Does Sony plan to standardize or customize its marketing efforts? Do you think Sony will change the marketing mix as these products mature?

2. Less than 1 percent of the world's 360 million Internet users live in Africa. Use the search feature of the *Financial Times* homepage to find out what challenges e-businesses face in trying to create an African market for their products and services. What marketing strategies best suit this purpose? Based on what you find out, do you agree with those who believe the Internet "will fundamentally transform Africa?"

CLOSING CASE

Pillsbury Presses Flour Power in India

By Miriam Jordan

The Pillsbury Doughboy has landed in India to pitch a product that he had just about abandoned in America: plain old flour.

Pillsbury, the Diageo PLC unit behind the pudgy character, has a raft of higher-margin products such as microwave pizzas in other parts of the world but discovered that in this tradition-bound market, it needs to push the basics.

Even so, selling packaged flour in India is almost revolutionary because most Indian housewives still buy raw wheat in bulk, clean it by hand, store it in huge metal hampers, and , every week, carry some to a neighborhood mill, or *chakki*, where it is ground between two stones.

To help reach those housewives, the Doughboy himself has gotten a makeover. In TV spots, he presses his palms together and bows in the traditional Indian greeting. He speaks six regional languages.

Pillsbury is onto a potentially huge business. India consumes about 69 million tons of wheat a year, second only to China. (The U.S. consumes about 26 million tons.) Much of India's wheat ends up as *roti*, a flat bread prepared on a griddle that accompanies almost every meal. In a nation where people traditionally eat with their hands, *roti* is the spoon. But less than 1 percent of all whole-wheat flour, or *atta*, is sold prepackaged. India's climatic extremes and deplorable roads make it difficult to maintain freshness from mill to warehouse, let alone on store shelves.

Then there are the standards of the Indian housewife, who is determined to serve only the softest, freshest *roti* to her family. "Packaged flour sticks to your stomach and is bad for the intestines," says Poonam Jain, a New Delhi housewife.

Pillsbury knows that ultimately it won't make fistfuls of dough from packaged flour. Its aim is to establish its flour business and then introduce new products to carry its customers up to more lucrative products.

That payoff may take a decade or two. "As a food company, we have to be where the mouths are," says Robert Hancock, marketing director for Europe and Eurasia. "We'll get our rewards later."

Starting a flour operation meant turning back the clock for Pillsbury. Though it was born as a U.S. flour-milling company 130 years ago, the Diageo unit all but exited from that business in the early 1990s to focus on products such as frozen baked goods and ice cream. The food giant thought of introducing high-value products when it first explored India. But it quickly learned that most Indians don't have enough disposable income for such fare. Many lack refrigerators and ovens, too.

Pillsbury is betting that flour will generate sales volumes to compensate for the razor-thin profit margins. "We wanted a product with huge and widespread mainstream appeal," Mr. Hancock says.

Pitching packaged flour meant overcoming thousands of years of tradition. "I'd never met women so intimately involved with the food they prepare," recalls Bill Barrier, who led a Pillsbury team that spent 18 months trying to decode Indian wheat and consumers.

Marketing managers climbed into the attics where housewives store their wheat and accompanied them to their tiny neighborhood flour mills. "Anywhere else, flour is flour," says Samir Behl, vice president of marketing for Pillsbury International. "In India, the color, aroma, feel between the fingers, and mouth feel are all crucial."

Pillsbury had hoped to establish contracts with existing mills, but inspectors found hygiene and safety at some to be appalling. Pillsbury scouts visited 40 plants, where they encountered mice, rotting wheat, and treacherous machinery. They often left coated in fine flour dust, whose presence is a severe fire hazard. In fact, when the electricity went out during a visit to one mill, Pillsbury executives were dumbfounded to see one worker light a match in the dark.

Pillsbury eventually found two mills capable of the required standards. But even then, their rollout was delayed by several months because the company rejected 40 percent of the wheat delivered to the mills after the 1998 harvest.

Many focus groups and lab tests later, Pillsbury came up with its packaged wheat blend, Pillsbury Chakki Fresh Atta. Godrej-Pillsbury Ltd., its joint venture here, launched the flour in southern and western India last year. The blue package, which features the Doughboy hoisting a *roti*, has become the market leader in Bombay, India's largest city, eclipsing the more established Kissan Annapurna brand from the Anglo-Dutch company Unilever PLC.

"People said [prepacked flour] wouldn't taste the same, but my husband and I don't find any difference," says Shivani Zaveri, a Bombay housewife who was introduced to Pillsbury by a friend who works and so has less time to cook.

Responding to consumers' biggest concern, Pillsbury pitches the flour with a promise that *rotis* made from it will stay soft "for six hours." Jigna Shah of Bombay, who makes 60 *rotis* a day and had tried rival packaged brands, is sold. She uses Pillsbury Chakki Fresh Atta to make *rotis* for her husband's lunch box "that don't dry up around the edges or get rigid."

The company declines to say what ingredients keep the flour tasting fresh, though it says there are no artificial preservatives. The packaging is made of a robust plastic laminate that costs about two and a half times as much as the paper wrappers typical in the U.S.

It's too early to declare the Doughboy's foray into India a success. The market is still minuscule, and gains will depend largely on how quickly Indian housewives embrace convenience. Several local companies familiar with Indian tastes have launched branded flour in recent years, only to flounder.

The value of the packaged-flour market in India is $7.14 million. It has expanded by about 45 percent a year since 1997, according to industry estimates, even though flour made the traditional way costs about 30 percent less.

To undermine its U.S. rival, Unilever has offered freebies to consumers, such as a free 1-kilogram packet of flour with every 5-kilogram packet, and a free sample of Surf detergent with every flour pack. Pillsbury has fought back with such promotions as a free sample of sunflower oil with every 5-kilogram package of flour. It has also been paying grocers to display a standing cardboard Doughboy with its product in a visible spot in shops. That's a novelty in this market, where most people buy their staples at small, crammed grocers, which have no room for promotional displays.

Unilever, which went nationwide in January 1998, predicts that its sales by volume will double this year to about 100,000 tons. Pillsbury anticipates production of about 50,000 tons in 1999. That's only a drop in the bucket, given that 30 million tons of wheat are consumed as *rotis* each year.

Case Questions

1. Identify and describe the roles of product policy, pricing, promotion, and distribution in Pillsbury's marketing of flour in India.
2. Did Pillsbury customize or standardize each of the four Ps?
3. What mode of entry did Pillsbury use to enter the Indian market? Why did it choose this mode?
4. Using Dunning's eclectic theory, how would you characterize Pillsbury's ownership advantage? Its location advantage? Its internalization advantage?

Source: "Pillsbury Presses Flour Power in India," *Wall Street Journal*, May 5, 1999, p. B1. Reprinted with permission of the *Wall Street Journal*. © 1999 Dow Jones and Company, Inc. All rights reserved worldwide.

CHAPTER

Coloring the World

Benetton Group SpA, the trendy Italian clothing chain, has grown from a one-knitter operation to a multinational clothing empire. It started in 1955 near Venice, Italy, when Luciano Benetton convinced his sister, Giuliana, to let him sell the brightly colored sweaters she knit. The low-priced, stylish sweaters sold quickly. Their popularity convinced Luciano to sell his accordion and his younger brother's bicycle to buy his sister a knitting machine so she could knit even faster. Over the next few years Luciano and Giuliana worked together managing their rapidly growing operation. The Benetton family eventually built a new factory near Venice and set up operations as a full-line apparel maker.

> "The **starting** point in the Benetton system is **information technology.**"

The first Benetton retail store opened in a fashionable ski resort in the Italian Alps in 1968. Other stores quickly followed in the leading fashion capitals of Europe. When the Iron Curtain fell, Benetton was among the first Western European retailers to set up shop in Central Europe and Eastern Europe. It now has hundreds of stores throughout the former communist bloc, as well as stores in such far-flung locations as Turkey, Japan, and Egypt. Benetton is opening stores in China at a frantic pace, launching 500 outlets there in 2000. In total, Benetton distributes its goods through 7,000 outlets in

17

International Operations Management

OBJECTIVES

After studying this chapter, you should be able to:

⟩ Describe the nature of international operations management.

⟩ Analyze the supply chain management and vertical integration decisions facing international production managers.

⟩ Identify and discuss the basic location decisions in international production management.

⟩ Discuss the basic issues in international logistics and materials management.

⟩ Identify and discuss the basic issues in international service operations.

some 120 countries. Almost all Benetton outlets are independently owned; Benetton licenses its name to these shop owners, who in turn must carry only Benetton goods. Although Benetton provides advertising and marketing support for its licensees, the shop owners provide the capital necessary to acquire their stores, fixtures, and inventory.

Benetton's greatest problem has been cracking the U.S. market, where fashion is more faddish than in Europe, and retail competition from such rivals as The Gap and The Limited is more fierce. Although there were almost 1,000 Benetton stores in the United States in the mid-1980s, today that number is considerably less. Benetton is estimated to have lost some $20 to $25 million in the U.S. market between 1996 and 1998 but returned to profitability in 1999. In Europe, though, Benetton has remained a leading force in the fashion industry. Using the profits supplied by its clothing goods empire, the Benetton Group has expanded into a variety of other areas, including sporting goods, venture capital, and Formula 1 racing.

What are the keys to Benetton's success? Italian styling and reasonable prices are certainly two of the main ones. Reliance on licensees to distribute its apparel has cut Benetton's capital costs and allowed it to benefit from the licensees' superior knowledge of the needs and habits of local customers.

However, it is Benetton's operations management that has enabled the firm to stay a world-class competitor in the fashion industry. Benetton has a commitment to achieving quality and meeting customer needs through its manufacturing and distribution systems. Design and production are centralized in Italy so the firm can maintain tight control over manufacturing costs, quality, and related considerations.

The starting point in the Benetton system is information technology. Each retail transaction in a Benetton store is electronically coded and transmitted to a central information-processing center in Italy. Managers there constantly can track which products are selling where. In particular they can track three vital pieces of information that are critical to success in any retailing operation: absolute sales levels, sales trends and patterns, and inventory distributions. This information also can be analyzed for individual stores, for clusters of stores in a given city or region, by country, or on a global basis.

Managers use this sales information to plan and adjust production activity. Whenever a new sweater or other garment is designed, its creators try to plan for possible variations and alterations. For example, a new shirt will be designed so it can be produced with short, mid-length, or full-length sleeves and with or without a collar. Early production runs and shipments will include all six possible styles. A portion of those runs also will be devoted to making shirt bodies without sleeves or collars. As sales figures begin to arrive, managers very quickly can tailor production adjustments to these inventoried shirt bodies to finish them out according to customer demand. If shirts with mid-length sleeves and a collar sell much faster than other variations, more of this type of shirt can be finished quickly and shipped to stores. The same approach also is used for colors. If blue shirts sell twice as quickly as red ones, managers easily can tilt production toward finishing more blue shirts and fewer red shirts.

Bar codes and scanners are used throughout Benetton factories and warehouses. Using fully networked computer workstations, managers can plan and initiate production runs based on style and color demand. Partially completed products are pulled from shelves by robots and placed on final production lines. As those products are finished out, bar codes are attached, and the products are automatically wrapped, packaged, and shipped to those stores that need inventory replenishment. Through the use of this sophisticated system Benetton can fill an order from any of its 7,000 stores spread throughout the globe in 13 to 27 days.[1]

Benetton has flourished for various reasons. Among them are its ability to track demand for each of its various products and then to take the appropriate steps to satisfy that demand promptly and efficiently. By centralizing its design and manufacturing systems in its home country of Italy, Benetton is able to maintain tight control over those and related functions. By building flexibility into design, production, and distribution, the firm is able to get new inventory to its stores around the world much faster than most of its competitors. The basis for planning and implementing these activities is operations management.

Some firms, such as Shell, Exxon Mobil, and BP Amoco, are concerned with physically transforming natural resources into various products through complex refining processes. Others, such as Compaq, Sony, and Philips, purchase completed component parts from suppliers and then assemble the parts into electronics products. Still others, such as Air France and JAL, use a global travel network to provide transportation services to people. Regardless of a firm's product, however, the goal of its international operations managers is to design, create, and distribute goods or services that meet the needs and wants of customers worldwide—and to do so profitably.

THE NATURE OF INTERNATIONAL OPERATIONS MANAGEMENT ❮

Operations management is the set of activities an organization uses to transform different kinds of inputs (materials, labor, and so on) into final goods and services.[2] **International operations management** refers to the transformation-related activities of an international firm. Figure 17.1 illustrates the international operations management process. As shown, a firm's strategic context provides a necessary backdrop against which it develops and then manages its operations functions. Flowing directly from the strategic context is the question of standardized versus customized production. The positioning of a firm along this continuum in turn helps dictate the appropriate strategies and tactics for other parts of the operations management process. The next part of international operations management is the activities and processes connected with the acquisition of the resources the firm needs to produce the goods or services it intends to sell. Location decisions—where to build factories and other facilities—are also important. Finally, international operations managers are concerned with logistics and materials management—the efficient movement of materials into, within, and out of the firm. We use this framework to organize this chapter's discussion of international operations management.

Operations management is closely linked with both quality and productivity. Chapter 15 described how product quality and productivity have become two key elements in international competitiveness. A firm's operations management system largely determines how inputs are transformed into goods or services. Properly designed and managed operating systems and procedures play a major role in determining product quality and productivity. For example, Benetton is able to squeeze extra measures of productivity from its distribution centers because of its highly efficient and flexible design. Conversely, poorly designed operating systems are a major cause of poor quality and lower productivity. They promote inefficiency

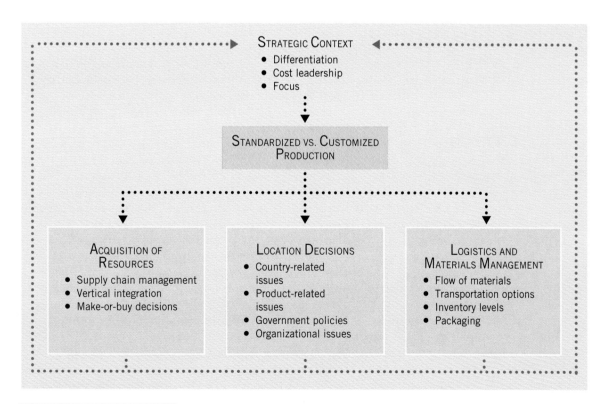

FIGURE 17.1   **The International Operations Management Process**

and can contribute in various ways to higher costs and suboptimal profit performance, as "Bringing the World into Focus" indicates.

Successful firms recognize that to survive they must continually adapt and respond to changes in their environments. These include technological advancements, regional and/or local changes in consumer tastes and preferences, shifting pricing levels, and the actions of competitors in a constantly changing global arena. An operations management system that is properly designed can help managers respond more effectively to these changes. For example, automakers used to shut down for an entire month when they changed equipment to produce a new model or make of automobile. Today the most efficient automakers can enact that same shift in a matter of hours, thereby losing only a small amount of production time. This capability in turn makes it easier and less costly for them to change models or shift production from a low-profit line to a high-profit line. And as already noted,

Bringing the World into FOCUS

"WHERE'S THE FACTORY? THIS IS A WAREHOUSE."

Porsche may be a car enthusiast's dream, but in the early 1990s it was a production manager's nightmare. In 1991 it took 120 hours of very expensive German labor to build a single Porsche 911. In contrast, Japanese automakers routinely use less than 30 hours of labor to build their high-quality vehicles. The rising value of the mark and the growing Japanese share of the high end of the auto market were threatening the very existence of the company. By 1993 it was near death—not because its cars weren't any good; they were just too expensive to build.

In desperation the company's chairman, Wendelin Wiedeking, swallowed his pride and called in a team of Japanese auto consultants. On entering Porsche's main assembly plant for the first time and observing bins full of parts reaching to the ceiling, the Japanese consultants asked, "Where's the factory? This is a warehouse." The first task the consultants tackled was controlling Porsche's inventory. To send the message things had to change, they insisted that Wiedeking himself take a circular saw and decapitate the 10-foot-tall shelves, crammed with parts, that circled the assembly line.

The consultants also were appalled to learn that Porsche obtained its parts from 950 separate suppliers. Keeping track of shipments from this flock of vendors and ensuring the shipments' quality overburdened the purchasing staff. Thirty percent of the parts shipments were in error, and one-fifth were delivered at least three days late. Worse, the rate of defective parts was too high, so Porsche spent too much time and energy rebuilding cars to ensure they met the company's exacting standards. By reorganizing the parts operation—cutting the number of suppliers by two-

thirds, working with suppliers to improve product quality, designing parts to ease the assembly process, and requiring just-in-time deliveries—Porsche has been able to cut the hours needed to build its autos.

To further improve productivity, the company intensified its investment in equipment, spending $150 million on new tools. It also intensified its investment in people, from an appalling 12 minutes of annual training per employee in 1993 to 45 to 50 hours per employee in 2000, to ensure all workers understood the company's commitment to quality and efficiency. The company also took an important symbolic step, changing the award for the best employee idea of the year: Instead of a Harley-Davidson motorcycle, the winning employee gets a year's use of a Porsche 911.

These efforts have started to pay off. For instance, it now takes less than 70 hours to build a Porsche 911, and the company has returned to profitability after several years of losses. The newest Porsche, the hot-selling Boxster, requires only 45 hours of labor to build, thanks to these changes in the company's production techniques. More importantly, Porsche can price the Boxster profitably for a little over $40,000, roughly half of what it was forced to charge for a 911. Porsche also is planning to introduce a supercharged version of the Boxster in 2001 and a sports utility vehicle (a joint venture with Volkswagen) in 2002.

Sources: *Hoover's Handbook of World Business 2001* (Austin: Hoover's Business Press, 2001), pp. 458–459; "Porche Calls 911, Boxster Japanese to the Rescue," *USA Today*, April 8, 1997, p. 1B; "Porsche's Designs Not Limited to Cars, "*Houston Chronicle*, January 2, 2001, p. 2B.

Benetton uses its operating systems to make timely adjustments to sales patterns and consumer preferences. The result is a competitive advantage over many of the firm's rivals around the world.

The Strategic Context of International Operations Management

The central role of operations management is to create the potential for achieving superior value for the firm. That is, operations management is a value-added activity intended to create or add new value to the organization's inputs in ways that directly impact outputs. If operations management can take $2 worth of inputs to create $10 worth of goods or services, it has created considerable value. However, if it requires $9 worth of inputs to create the same $10 worth of goods or services, it has created relatively little value.

Figure 17.1 indicates that international operations management must be aligned closely with a firm's business strategy. Indeed, the business strategy set by top managers at the firm's corporate and regional levels will affect all facets of the planning and implementing of operations management activities, such as supply chain management strategies, location decisions, facilities design, and logistics management.[3] For a company pursuing a differentiation strategy, the operations management function must be able to create goods or services that are clearly different from those of the company's competitors. For a firm like Porsche that wants to compete on the basis of product performance and status, costs will be less important than product quality and design. As a result, production facilities may need to be located where there is a skilled labor force, even if the cost of employing that labor is relatively high.[4] For example, despite its problems discussed in "Bringing the World into Focus," Porsche never considered shifting its production from Stuttgart to a lower-labor-cost locale because its highly skilled workforce is vital to producing its high-quality cars. Moreover, although it recognized that its parts operation needed revamping, the company never considered using lower-quality parts. Rather, it continued to procure only parts capable of meeting the quality expectations of its status-conscious buyers and of performing durably and safely at autobahn speeds.

Conversely, for a firm following a cost leadership strategy, the operations management function must be able to shave the costs of creating goods or services to the absolute minimum so the firm can lower its prices while still earning an acceptable level of profits. In this case cost and price issues are central, whereas quality may be less critical. As a result, locating production facilities where labor costs are especially low may be highly appropriate. Hong Kong's Roly International Holdings, for example, annually sells over $200 million worth of low-priced home decorations, such as Christmas tree lights and plaster bird baths, churned out by its factories in China. Its goods are shipped via slow but low-cost cargo ships to be distributed by discounters such as Wal-Mart and Walgreens.[5]

Another factor affecting the firm's choices is the extent to which it uses standardized or customized production processes and technologies. On the one hand, if the firm uses standardized production processes and technologies in every market where it does business, then its operations systems can—and almost certainly should be—globally integrated. Such firms may choose to adopt global product designs, for example, to capture more easily global efficiencies generated by their operations. On the other hand, if a firm uses a unique operations system in each market where it does business, such global integration is not only unnecessary but also likely to be impossible. Often such firms adopt a global area design to promote responsiveness of their operations managers to local conditions.

For example, Toyota uses a standardized operations management strategy in that it makes the same cars using the same manufacturing processes around the world. Thus it can share technology between plants and freely ship component parts between factories in different countries. Conversely, Nestlé tailors its mix of products, as well as their ingredients and packaging, across markets. So although there may be some sharing of production technology, Nestlé tends to operate each production facility as more of a self-contained unit.

Complexities of International Operations Management

International operations management presents one of the most complex and challenging set of tasks managers face today. The basic complexities inherent in operations management stem from the production problem itself—where and how to produce various goods and services. Operations managers typically must decide important and complex issues in three areas:

1. *Resources*: Managers must decide where and how to obtain the resources the firm needs to produce its products. Key decisions relate to supply chain management and vertical integration.

2. *Location*: Managers must decide where to build administrative facilities, sales offices, and plants, how to design them, and so on.

3. *Logistics*: Managers must decide on modes of transportation and methods of inventory control.

All firms, whether domestic or international, must address these issues. However, resolving them is far more complicated for international firms. A domestic manufacturer may deal with only local suppliers, be subject to one set of government regulations, compete in a relatively homogeneous market, have access to an integrated transportation network, and ship its goods relatively short distances. An international manufacturer, in contrast, is likely to deal with suppliers from different countries and confront different government regulations wherever it does business, as well as very heterogeneous markets, disparate transportation facilities and networks, and relatively long shipping distances. International operations managers must choose the countries in which to locate production facilities, taking into account factors such as costs, tax laws, resource availability, and marketing considerations. They also must consider potential exchange rate movements and noneconomic factors such as government regulations, political risk, and predictability of a country's legal system. Further, they must consider the impact of facilities' locations on the firm's ability to respond to changes in customer tastes and preferences. Finally, they must factor in logistical problems. Just as long supply lines doomed Napoleon's invasion of Russia, locating factories far from one's suppliers may impede timely access to resources and materials.

❭ PRODUCTION MANAGEMENT

Although some similarities exist between creating goods and creating services for international markets, there also are major fundamental differences. Operations management decisions, processes, and issues that involve the creation of tangible goods are called **production management**, and those involving the creation of intangible services are called **service operations management**. This section focuses on production management; service operations management is addressed later in the chapter.

Manufacturing is the creation of goods by transforming raw materials and component parts in combination with capital, labor, and technology. Some examples of manufacturing activities are Sony's production of stereo equipment, BMW's production of automobiles, and Bridgestone's production of tires. BMW, for example, takes thousands of component parts, ranging from sheet metal to engine parts to upholstery to rubber molding, and combines them to make different types of automobiles.

Most successful manufacturers use many sophisticated techniques to produce high-quality goods efficiently. These techniques are best covered in more advanced and specialized production management courses, so we focus here on three important dimensions of international production management: international supply chain management, international facilities location, and international logistics.

Supply Chain Management and Vertical Integration

Because the production of most manufactured goods requires a variety of raw materials, parts, and other resources, the first issue an international production manager faces is deciding how to acquire those inputs.[6] **Supply chain management** is the set of processes and steps a firm uses to acquire the various resources it needs to create its own product (other common terms for this activity include *sourcing* and *procuring*). Supply chain management clearly affects product cost, product quality, and internal demands for capital. Because of these impacts, most international firms approach supply chain management as a strategic issue to be carefully planned and implemented by top management.[7]

The first step in developing a supply chain management strategy is to determine the appropriate degree of vertical integration. **Vertical integration** is the extent to which a firm either provides its own resources or obtains them from other sources. At one extreme, firms that practice relatively high levels of vertical integration are engaged in every step of the operations management process as goods are developed, transformed, packaged, and sold to customers. Various units within the firm can be seen as suppliers to other units within the firm, which can be viewed as the customers of the supplying units. At the other extreme, firms that have little vertical integration are involved in only one step or just a few steps in the production chain. They may buy their inputs and component parts from other suppliers, perform one operation or transformation, and then sell their outputs to other firms or consumers.[8]

BP Amoco is an excellent example of a vertically integrated international business. One unit of the firm is engaged in the worldwide exploration for natural gas and crude oil. After oil is discovered, another unit is responsible for its extraction. The oil then is transported through company-owned pipelines and on company-owned tanker ships to company-owned refineries. Those refineries transform the crude oil into gasoline, processed petroleum, and other petroleum-based fuels. Next, the fuel is transported by company-owned trucks to company-owned service stations and convenience stores, where it is sold to individual consumers. Thus BP Amoco's exploration and extraction business supplies its pipeline business, which supplies its refinery business, which supplies its retailing business. Although the firm occasionally uses third-party suppliers and may sometimes sell its products to other firms, it primarily seeks to maintain an unbroken and efficient chain of vertically integrated operations from the beginning of the production process to the final sale of the product to individual consumers.[9]

In contrast, Heineken NV, the world's second largest beer producer, practices relatively little vertical integration. The firm buys the grains and other inputs it needs to brew beer from local farmers and agricultural cooperatives. From various container suppliers it buys the bottles, labels, and cartons it uses to package its beers. After brewing and bottling its beers, Heineken sells them to distributors, which subsequently resell them to retailers, which in turn resell them to consumers.

The extent of a firm's vertical integration is the result of a series of supply chain management decisions made by production managers.[10] In deciding how to acquire the components necessary to manufacture a firm's products, its production man-

› Acer, a leading Taiwanese computer manufacturer, has chosen to vertically integrate its operations. These workers at an Acer-owned factory in Fujian, China, produce components that will be used at another Acer factory assembling personal computers.

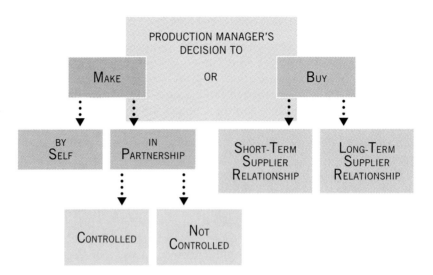

agers have two choices: The firm can make the inputs itself, or it can buy them from outside suppliers. This choice is called the **make-or-buy decision**. The basic make-or-buy options available to an international firm are shown in Figure 17.2. Note in particular that the make-or-buy decision carries with it other decisions as well. For example, a decision to buy rather than make dictates the need to choose between long-term and short-term supplier relationships. A decision to make rather than buy leaves open the option of making by self or making in partnership with others. If partnership is the choice, yet another decision relates to the degree of control the firm wants to have.

The make-or-buy decision can be influenced by a firm's size, scope of operations, and technological expertise and by the nature of its product. For example, because larger firms are better able to benefit from economies of scale in the production of inputs, larger automakers such as GM and Fiat are more likely to make their parts themselves, whereas smaller automakers such as Saab or BMW are more likely to buy parts from outside suppliers. Components embodying relatively new technologies, such as satellite navigation systems and hands-free cellular telephones, are more likely to be purchased from outside suppliers, whereas more standardized components, such as conventional braking systems and AM/FM automotive radios, are more likely to be produced in-house. At other times the make-or-buy decision will depend on existing investments in technology and manufacturing facilities. For example, personal computer manufacturers such as Dell and IBM must decide whether they want to make or buy microprocessors, memory chips, disk drives, motherboards, and power supplies. Because of its extensive manufacturing expertise with mainframe computers, IBM is more likely to make a PC component in-house, whereas Dell is more likely to rely heavily on outside suppliers.

All else being equal, a firm will choose to make or buy simply on the basis of whether it can obtain the resource cheaper by making it internally or by buying it from an external supplier. "All else being equal" seldom occurs, however, so strategic issues also must be considered. Figure 17.3 highlights the need to balance competitive advantage against strategic vulnerability when resolving the make-or-buy decision. For example, if a high potential for competitive advantage exists along with a high degree of strategic vulnerability, the firm is likely to maintain strategic control by producing internally. However, if the potential for competitive advantage and the degree of strategic vulnerability are both low, the firm will need less control and therefore will be more likely to buy "off the shelf." Finally, when intermediate potential for competitive advantage and moderate degree of strategic vulnerability call for moderate control, special ventures or contract arrangements may be most appropriate.

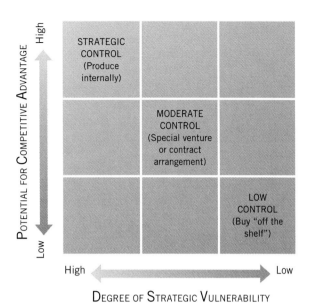

FIGURE 17.3

Competitive Advantage Versus Strategic Vulnerability in the Make-or-Buy Decision

Source: Reprinted from "Strategic Outsourcing" by James Brian Quinn and Frederick G. Hilmer, *Sloan Management Review*, Summer 1994, p. 48, by permission of the publisher. Copyright 1994 by the Sloan Management Review Association. All rights reserved.

In addition to these strategic considerations, other factors may play a role with respect to the make-or-buy decision. In particular, international firms typically must make trade-offs between costs and control, risk, investment, and flexibility.[11]

Control.   Making a component has the advantage of increasing the firm's control over product quality, delivery schedules, design changes, and costs. A firm that buys from external suppliers may become overly dependent on those suppliers. If a given supplier goes out of business, raises its prices, or produces poor-quality materials, the firm will lose its source of inputs, see its costs increase, or experience its own quality-related problems.

Another issue of control relates to the ability to enforce contracts with outside suppliers. Enforcing contracts with foreign suppliers may be difficult or costly because of differences in national legal systems. For example, if laws protecting intellectual property of foreigners are weak in a certain country, entertainment firms such as Sony Records and BMG may be unwilling to license firms in that country to duplicate their CDs and videotapes. When such considerations are important, a firm may prefer to make rather than buy necessary inputs. One strength of the Japanese *keiretsu* system, for example, is its ability to reduce the problem of enforcing contracts between a firm and its suppliers. Cross-ownership of shares among *keiretsu* members, which strengthens trust among members, increases their willingness to enter into long-term contracts and to share intellectual property with each other.[12] "Venturing Abroad" provides another illustration of the importance of good supplier relations.

By making rather than buying, the firm also may be able to develop new business opportunities. BP Amoco, for example, has a chemical division that relies in part on petroleum-based ingredients for the production of certain chemical products. This chemical unit has a relatively dependable and cooperative "built-in" supplier for its petroleum needs. This arrangement allows the unit to more effectively address future price, availability, and delivery schedule questions as it develops its strategic and operational plans.

Risk.   Buying a component from an external supplier has the advantage of reducing the firm's financial and operating risks. BP Amoco, for example, has risk associated with its drilling platforms, pipelines, and every other stage in its production chain. If the firm simply bought crude oil from other firms, it would not have to worry about equipment failure or injuries on drilling platforms because those risks would be assumed by the supplier. The firm also would not have to worry about earning an adequate rate of return on those assets. Equally important,

VENTURING *Abroad*

SUPPLIERS: FRIEND OR FOE?

Relations between manufacturers and their suppliers can be vitally important to each. Manufacturers depend on their suppliers to provide them with high-quality parts and supplies on a timely basis, whereas suppliers depend on their manufacturing customers for revenue. However, the nature of this relationship often varies between countries. Consider, for example, two examples from the auto industry, one in the United States and the other in Japan.

When Ford recently redesigned and reengineered its popular Taurus automobile, the firm intended to copy the Japanese approach to managing supplier relations. Ford wanted its suppliers to make substantive commitments to delivering parts at low costs and to work with the company toward their mutual best interests. However, senior Ford managers in charge of the Taurus project had a fundamental distrust of suppliers, viewing them as antagonists rather than as partners. This attitude in turn crept into many different areas of how Ford treated its suppliers. The result was strained relations and each party sticking strictly to what it was contractually bound to do—and being unwilling to do anything more.

In contrast, Toyota has thrived in the Japanese *keiretsu* system. The level of trust created by Toyota's cooperative relationships with its suppliers has helped it become the world's most efficient automobile manufacturer and to respond quickly to unexpected challenges. For example, in 1997 a fire destroyed the factory of Aisin Seiki Co., the sole supplier to Toyota of a brake valve used in many of its cars. Because Toyota, like most Japanese manufacturers, uses a just-in-time inventory system, it had only four hours' worth of parts on hand. Its other suppliers quickly recognized that Toyota, as well as their own companies, would suffer immeasurably if the auto giant were shut down too long.

Consequently, these suppliers went to heroic efforts to get Toyota back up and running. For example, one supplier prevailed on one of its own suppliers, a sewing machine maker, to retool itself to make some of the brake valves. All told, 36 suppliers and more than 150 additional subcontractors had over 50 separate lines making the brake valves for Toyota within a matter of days. As a result, rather than being out of commission for the several weeks experts originally predicted, Toyota was up and running again in less than five days.

Sources: J. H. Dyer and K. Nobeoka, "Creating and Managing a High-Performance Knowledge-Sharing Network: The Toyota Case," *Strategic Management Journal*, March 2000, pp. 345–368; "A Case Study of Model Changeovers in the Toyota Production System," *Organization Science*, January–February 1999, pp. 52–60; "Toyota's Fast Rebound After Fire at Supplier Shows Why It Is Tough," *Wall Street Journal*, May 8, 1997, pp. A1, A6; "Toyota Factories in Japan Grind to a Halt," *Wall Street Journal*, February 4, 1997, p. A14.

the firm that buys rather than makes can reduce its political risk in a host country. For example, BP Amoco runs the risk that politicians elected on anti-British or antiforeigner platforms in the United States, Nigeria, Colombia, or elsewhere may someday expropriate its refineries. Indeed, this did happen in 1951, when Iran's rulers seized a major BP operation in that country.

Investments in Facilities, Technology, and People. Buying from others lowers the firm's level of investment. By not having to build a new factory or learn a new technology, a firm can free up capital for other productive uses. Benetton, for example, primarily uses licensees to retail its goods, allowing the firm to concentrate on what it does best, manufacturing. Honda provides another example of this approach. As production at Honda's U.S. manufacturing plant in Ohio grew, the firm needed an increased supply of mirrors for its cars. It convinced a local supplier, Donnelly Corp., to build a new factory to assemble mirrors for its automobiles. Thus Honda obtained a convenient and dependable supplier without having to invest its own money in building a mirror factory.[13] Of course, by buying rather than making the mirrors, Honda surrendered the profits of mirror manufacturing to Donnelly.

Buying from others also reduces a firm's training costs and expertise requirements. By contracting with Donnelly, Honda avoided having to develop expertise in designing, manufacturing, and marketing automobile mirrors. BP Amoco, in contrast, needs a wide range of expertise and talent among the ranks of its managers to take full advantage of its highly vertically integrated global operations.

Flexibility.   A firm that buys rather than makes retains the flexibility to change suppliers as circumstances dictate. This is particularly helpful in cases in which technology is evolving rapidly or delivered costs can change as a result of inflation or exchange rate fluctuations. Most personal computer manufacturers, for example, have chosen to buy disk drives, CD-ROM units, and microprocessors from outside suppliers. By so doing, they avoid the risk of product obsolescence and the large research and development expenditures needed to stay on the cutting edge of each of the technologies embedded in the component parts of personal computers. Similarly, Dallas's Peerless Manufacturing buys components from numerous European subcontractors that produce filters and separators. Peerless can shift its sourcing around the Continent depending on currency fluctuations and flows of orders from its customers.[14]

Of course, sometimes a firm must make trade-offs that reduce flexibility. In the case of Honda and Donnelly, Donnelly was concerned it would be at Honda's mercy once it invested in the new mirror factory. To induce Donnelly to agree to build the new factory, the automaker had to assure Donnelly managers that the firm would get all of Honda's mirror business for at least 10 years. By so doing, Honda reduced its capital investment but sacrificed the flexibility of changing suppliers during the 10-year period. This example also illustrates a major trend in buyer-supplier relationships. Not long ago, managers assumed it was useful to use a variety of suppliers to avoid becoming too dependent on a single one. A drawback of this approach, however, is the complexity associated with dealing with a large network of suppliers, especially if that network is global. More recently, some firms have come to realize that by engaging in exclusive or semi-exclusive long-term relationships with fewer suppliers, the firms can better benefit from these suppliers' experience and product knowledge. In the automobile industry many manufacturers are relying on so-called first-tier suppliers such as Johnson Controls or Magna International to work with the automakers' engineers to design component systems, such as seating systems or dashboard assemblies, for new vehicles. For example, in designing its LH models, Chrysler (now a part of DaimlerChrysler) worked closely with its first-tier suppliers, enabling it to cut its design staff by two-thirds and its expected development time by 28 percent. Its suppliers offered nearly 4,000 manufacturing and design suggestions, saving Chrysler an extra $156 million.[15] Companies also are saving additional moneys by relying on first-tier suppliers to manage and monitor the acquisition of parts and subassemblies from second-tier suppliers.

Location Decisions

An international firm that chooses to make rather than buy inputs faces another decision: Where should it locate its production facilities? In reaching a location decision, the firm must consider country-related issues, product-related issues, government policies, and organizational issues.

Country-Related Issues.   Several features of countries can influence the decision about where to locate an international facility. Chief among these are resource availability and cost, infrastructure, and country-of-origin marketing effects.

Resource availability and cost constitute a primary determinant of whether an individual country is a suitable location for a facility. As suggested by the classical trade theories and the Heckscher-Ohlin theory (see Chapter 5), countries that enjoy large, low-cost endowments of a factor of production will attract firms needing that factor of production. For example, China has attracted toy, footwear, and textile manufacturers eager to take advantage of its vast army of low-cost labor. BP Amoco has little choice but to situate drilling platforms where crude oil reserves are located.

Infrastructure also affects the location of production facilities. Most facilities require at least some minimal level of infrastructural support. To build a facility requires construction materials and equipment as well as materials suppliers and

› Customers are willing to pay premium prices for Rolls-Royce automobiles partly because of their careful construction by British craftsmen. Would the cars maintain their luxury appeal if their production were moved out of England?

construction contractors. More important, electrical, water, transportation, telephone, and other services are necessary to utilize the facility productively. In addition, access to medical care, education, adequate housing, entertainment, and other related services are almost certain to be important for the employees and managers who will work at the facility as well as for their families.

Country-of-origin effects also may play a role in locating a facility. Certain countries have "brand images" that affect product marketing. For example, Japan has a reputation for manufacturing high-quality products, whereas Italy often is credited with stylishly designed products. In one interesting experiment a researcher found that consumer preference for Timex watches fell by only 6 percent when interviewees were told the watches were made in Pakistan rather than Germany. However, when consumers were confronted with an unfamiliar brand called Tempomax, their willingness to buy the watches fell by 74 percent when they were told the watches were made in Pakistan instead of Germany. All else being equal, it obviously is easier to sell watches made in Germany than ones made in Pakistan to consumers in industrialized countries, particularly if the product is not backed by a strong brand name. Firms must take into account these country-of-origin effects in deciding where to site a production facility. A firm interested in marketing its product as high quality might choose to locate in Japan or Germany rather than in Pakistan or Indonesia, whereas a firm competing on the basis of low costs and prices might make the opposite choice.

Product-Related Issues. Product-related characteristics also may influence the location decision. Among the more important of these are the product's value-to-weight ratio, the required production technology, and the importance of customer feedback.[16]

The product's value-to-weight ratio affects the importance of transportation costs in the product's delivered price. Goods with low value-to-weight ratios, such as iron ore, cement, coal, bulk chemicals, and raw sugar and other agricultural goods, tend to be produced in multiple locations to minimize transportation costs. Conversely, goods with high value-to-weight ratios, such as microprocessors or diamonds, can be produced in a single location or handful of locations without loss of competitiveness. For example, transportation costs are a trivial part of the cost of producing and distributing Intel's various kinds of computer chips, so Intel is free to locate the chips' production on the basis of nontransportation factors.

The production technology used to manufacture the good also may affect facility location. A firm must compare its expected product sales with the efficient size of a facility in the industry. If a firm's sales are large relative to an efficient-sized facility, the firm is likely to operate many facilities in various locations. If its sales are small relative to an efficient-sized facility, the firm probably will utilize only one plant. For example, the minimum efficient size of a petroleum refinery is about 200,000 barrels per day. Thus BP Amoco, which can produce up to 5 million barrels per day, has chosen to operate 17 refineries located in such countries as the United Kingdom, Spain, and Colombia.

The relative importance of customer feedback also may influence the location decision. Products for which firms desire quick customer feedback often are produced close to the point of final sale. For example, a general rule of thumb in the U.S. apparel industry is that, all else being equal, the more fashionable the item, the more likely it will be produced near or in the United States so the manufacturer can respond quickly to market trends. At the beginning of each selling season women's sportswear buyers for Macy's, Nordstrom's, and Sak's Fifth Avenue carefully monitor which new items are hot sellers. The buyers quickly reorder the hot items and mercilessly dump goods that fashion-conscious shoppers ignore. Because the selling season for such goods may last only two or three months—and no one can predict with certainty what the fashion fanatics will buy—apparel manufacturers in the United States are better able to respond to the sportswear buyers' demands than are producers in Taiwan or Indonesia. Conversely, low-fashion items are more likely to be produced outside the United States to take advantage of lower production costs. For example, J.C. Penney can predict with reasonable certainty how many athletic socks and white cotton briefs it will sell each summer. If for some reason it overestimates summer sales of these items, it can continue to sell them in the fall. Accordingly, Penney's menswear buyers often enter into long-term contracts with Asian knitting mills. In this case cost is a more important variable than speed or flexibility of delivery.

Government Policies.   Government policies also may play a role in the location decision. Especially important are the stability of the political process, national trade policies, economic development incentives, and the existence of foreign trade zones.

The stability of the political process within a country can clearly affect the desirability of locating a factory there. Firms like to know what the rules of the game are so they can make knowledgeable investment, production, and staffing decisions. A government that alters fiscal, monetary, and regulatory policies seemingly on whim and without consulting the business community raises the risk and uncertainty of operating in that country. Unforeseen changes in taxation policy, exchange rates, inflation, and labor laws are particularly troublesome to international firms.

National trade policies also may affect the location decision. To serve its customers, a firm may be forced to locate a facility within a country that has high tariff walls and other trade barriers. For example, Toyota, Nissan, and Mazda built factories in the United States to evade a voluntary export restraint imposed by the Japanese government to limit the exports of Japanese-built automobiles to the United States. Similarly, Compaq Computer located a personal computer manufacturing facility in São Paulo to avoid Brazilian import taxes.[17]

Economic development incentives may influence the location decision. Communities eager to create jobs and add to the local tax base often seek to attract new factories by offering international firms inexpensive land, highway improvements, job-training programs, and discounted water and electric rates. For example, the government of France sold The Walt Disney Company suburban land on which to build Disneyland Paris at a greatly discounted rate. Similarly, Jackson, Mississippi, outbid dozens of North American cities for a new $800-million Nissan assembly plant in late 2000, offering the firm a $295-million package of incentives.[18]

An international firm also may choose a site based on the existence of a foreign trade zone (FTZ). As discussed in Chapter 8, an FTZ is a specially designated and controlled geographical area in which imported or exported goods receive preferential tariff treatment. A country may establish FTZs near its major ports of entry and/or major production centers. It then allows international firms to import products into those zones duty free for specified purposes, sometimes with express limitations; for example, there may be limitations on the types and value of products allowed and on the kind of work that may be performed.

A firm may decide to locate in a particular area because the existence of an FTZ gives the firm greater flexibility regarding importing or exporting and creates avenues for lowering costs.[19] For example, the Port of Houston operates a large FTZ used primarily for storage by non-U.S. automakers. Toyota and Nissan can ship all their automobiles bound for sale in the southern part of North America to Houston, where they are stored without any payment of import tariffs being required. Only when specific automobiles are removed from the zone and shipped to dealerships must the manufacturers pay the duty. However, some automobiles eventually are shipped to Mexico or various Caribbean countries. The firms then pay only whatever duty those countries levy and avoid paying U.S. duties altogether.

Costs can be lowered through the creative use of FTZs. A firm may be able to import component parts, supplement them with other component parts obtained locally, and assemble them all into finished goods. The duty paid on the imported components incorporated into the products assembled in the FTZ may be lower than the duty imposed on imported components in general. For this reason most automobiles produced in the United States are assembled in FTZs. Further, some duties are calculated on the basis of the good's total weight, including packaging. So a firm may lower its duties by bringing goods into the FTZ in lightweight, inexpensive packaging, and then, after duties have been paid, repackaging them with heavier, more substantial materials obtained locally.

Organizational Issues. An international firm's business strategy and its organizational structure also may affect the location decision. Inventory management policies are important considerations as well.

A firm's business strategy may affect its location decisions in various ways. A firm that adopts a cost leadership strategy must seek out low-cost locations, whereas a firm that focuses on product quality must locate facilities in areas that have adequate skilled labor and managerial talent. A firm may choose to concentrate production geographically to better meet organizational goals. Benetton does this with its Italian production facilities so as to better control product design and quality. Similarly, Boeing has concentrated its final aircraft assembly operations in the Seattle area to take advantage of the skilled machinist and engineering talent in the area. Other firms find that strategic goals can be better met by dispersing facilities in various foreign locations. Most electronics firms take this approach. For example, Intel has manufacturing plants in Ireland, Puerto Rico, Israel, Malaysia, and the Philippines to take advantage of the relatively low-cost resources available in each of these markets. Further, shipping the firm's computer chips to distant markets from those manufacturing facilities is relatively easy and inexpensive. Multiple production facilities also protect a firm against exchange rate fluctuations. FMC, for example, often shifts orders for its food-packaging machinery from plants in Chicago to plants in Italy or vice versa, depending on the relative values of the dollar and the euro.

A firm's organizational structure also influences the location of its factories. For example, as noted in Chapter 13, adoption of a global area structure decentralizes authority to area managers. These managers, seeking to maintain control over their area, are likely to favor siting factories within their area to produce goods sold within the area. For example, Ford once was structured as three area groups: North America, Europe, and Asia Pacific. The firm exported few automobiles from these regions; rather, each area focused on producing automobiles to meet the needs of consumers in its area. Ford later abandoned this organizational structure, believing it hindered Ford's ability to truly globalize its automobile production. Conversely, a firm having a global product structure will locate factories anywhere in the world to meet the firm's cost and quality performance goals.

A firm's inventory management policies are affected by plant location decisions. Inventory management is a complex task all operations managers must confront. They must balance the costs of maintaining inventory against the costs of running out of materials and/or finished goods. The costs of maintaining inventory include those associated with storage (operating a warehouse, for example), spoilage and loss (some stored inventory gets ruined, damaged, or stolen), and opportunity costs (an investment in inventory cannot be put to other business uses).

Factory location affects the level of inventory that firms must hold because of the distances and transit times involved in shipping goods. For example, if Wal-Mart purchases private-label televisions for its U.S. stores from a Taiwanese factory, Wal-Mart's inventory levels will be higher than if it purchases the televisions from a

Mexican factory. Compaq Computer has chosen to locate its primary assembly plants in Houston, Scotland, Singapore, and Brazil to improve service to its North American, European, Asian, and South American customers, respectively, while cutting overall inventory levels.

Factory location becomes particularly critical when the popular just-in-time (JIT) inventory management system is adopted. With this approach a firm's suppliers deliver their products directly to the firm's manufacturing center, usually in frequent small shipments, just as they are needed for production. The JIT system requires careful coordination between a firm and its internal and external suppliers. Often parts suppliers locate their facilities near the factories of their major customers to meet the JIT requirements of their customers. For example, many car-part makers, such as Toyota Machine Works, TRW Steering Systems, Eagle-Picher, and Orbseal, have located in Wales or the West Midlands region of England to better serve major customers like Jaguar and Range Rover.[20] Parts manufacturers also have gravitated to the midwestern United States, Ontario, Brazil, Thailand, and other areas where auto assembly plants are clustered.

International Logistics and Materials Management

Regardless of the location of an international firm's factories, its operations management must address issues of international logistics. **International logistics** is the management of the flow of materials, parts, supplies, and other resources from suppliers to the firm; the flow of materials, parts, supplies, and other resources within and between units of the firm itself; and the flow of finished products, services, and goods from the firm to customers.

The first two sets of activities usually are called **materials management**, and the third set often is called physical distribution, or, more simply, distribution.[21] Recall that we discussed distribution issues in Chapter 16 because they often are managed as part of the firm's marketing function. Thus our focus here is on the materials management area of logistics. The role of logistics is particularly important for firms that have developed integrated, but geographically dispersed, manufacturing and distribution networks where parts may be made in one country for assembly in a second country for sale in a third country.[22] "Venturing Abroad" describes how several firms are benefiting from the growing demand for international logistics services.

Three basic factors differentiate domestic and international materials management functions. The first is simply the distance involved in shipping. Shipments within even the largest countries seldom travel more than a couple of thousand miles, and many shipments travel much less. For example, the road distance between New York City and Los Angeles is around 2,800 miles, but the distances between New York and Warsaw, Tokyo, and Sydney are 4,300 miles, 6,700 miles, and 9,900 miles, respectively.[23] Thus assembling component parts in Kansas City, Chicago, and St. Louis and then shipping them to Cincinnati for final assembly is much easier than assembling component parts in San Diego, Montreal, and Cairo and then shipping them to Singapore for final assembly.

The second basic difference between domestic and international materials management functions is the sheer number of transport modes that are likely to be involved. Shipments within the same country often use only a single mode of transportation, such as truck or rail. However, shipments that cross national boundaries, and especially shipments traveling great distances, almost certainly involve multiple modes of transportation.[24] For example, a shipment bound from Kansas City to Berlin may use truck, rail, ship, and then rail and truck again.

Third, the regulatory context for international materials management is much more complex than for domestic materials management. Most countries regulate many aspects of their internal transportation systems—price, safety, packaging, and so on. Shipments that cross through several countries are subject to the regulations of each of those countries. Although various economic trade agreements, such as the North American Free Trade Agreement, have sought to streamline

VENTURING *Abroad* — THE BOOMING MARKET IN LOGISTICS SERVICES

As firms globalize, logistics becomes more important and more sophisticated. This in turn has created new market opportunities for logistics experts. To most people, for example, Caterpillar is a leading earth-moving equipment manufacturer. However, as the opening case in Chapter 5 indicated, Caterpillar has achieved this lofty position because of the quality of service it provides its customers. Construction sites may be shut down if a part breaks on a vital piece of equipment. To minimize downtime and keep its customers happy, Caterpillar has developed one of the world's best parts distribution systems. It normally is capable of getting any of the 550,000 spare parts that go into Caterpillar products to any customer within hours. (In contrast, a typical automobile manufacturer only has to deal with a piddling 70,000 spare parts.) Having developed this expertise, Caterpillar has been only too happy to solve other companies' distribution problems by handling their spare parts operations. Caterpillar is estimated to generate an additional $200 to $300 million in revenue annually by providing logistical services for other companies.

Another emerging logistical market is "one-stop" shipping, in which a customer contracts with one transportation company to handle all of its shipments from door to door. Roadway Express, for example, provides such services. Roadway will pick up merchandise at the client's factory gate, transport the goods to their foreign port of entry, clear customs, and arrange transportation to the foreign customer. Not only does this arrangement save the client money and hassle, but if a transportation problem arises, the customer knows who to call: Roadway. Of course, Roadway, like many of its competitors, has invested heavily in the latest information technology so it can track the whereabouts of any shipment instantaneously. By shifting the transportation responsibilities to an expert like Roadway, the clients can focus on what they do best.

Sources: "A Moving Story of Spare Parts," *Financial Times*, August 29, 1997, p. 7; "More Firms Rely on 'One-Stop' Shopping," *Wall Street Journal*, April 29, 1997; "Sharpening the Claws," *Forbes*, July 26, 1999, pp. 102–105.

international shipping guidelines and procedures, transporting goods across national boundaries is still complex and often involves much red tape.

Seemingly simple logistics and materials management issues often become much more complex in an international context. Packaging issues, which might at first glance seem minor, are in reality a significant consideration in managing international logistics. Packaging protects the goods in transit, helps make the goods easier to handle, and facilitates delivery and/or sale of finished goods at their final destination. International shipping complicates packaging decisions, however, because of the use of multiple modes of transportation as well as the variation in conditions that will be encountered.[25]

Consider the problems confronted by a firm that wants to ship a large quantity of delicate electronics equipment from a plant in California, where the equipment was produced, to a facility in Saudi Arabia, where the equipment will be used. During the course of shipment the equipment likely will be on trucks, railcars, and a ship. These transport settings will have variations in humidity, temperature, and amount of dust. Moreover, each time the equipment is loaded and unloaded, it will be handled with varying degrees of roughness or delicacy. Thus the equipment must be packaged to handle everything it will encounter during its travels.

The weight of the packaging itself also is a consideration, especially for finished goods en route to customers. As noted earlier in the chapter, weight sometimes determines the amount of import duty, so firms frequently repackage goods after shipment. Sometimes customers even go so far as to specify precise total weights, including packaging, they will accept, and may require that packaging meet certain preset specifications.

Logistical considerations may play a critical role in the decision of where to locate a factory. Production costs may be lower in a domestic factory than in a foreign factory. However, the firm also must consider the materials management costs of warehousing, packaging, transporting, and distributing its goods, as well as its inventory carrying costs and those of its foreign customers. Typically, such logistical costs will be higher for exported goods than for locally produced goods. There also are logistical considerations besides costs. Because of longer supply lines and increased difficulties in communicating with foreign customers, a firm that chooses to export from domestic factories must ensure that it maintains competitive levels of service for its foreign customers.

Needless to say, the ongoing globalization of the world's economy has magnified the importance of international logistics. Globalization would be much less extensive and much slower to develop had it not been for rapid changes in information technology (IT). Although the development of personal computers, fax machines, electronic mail, cell phones, the Internet, and the like are widely known, less visible IT breakthroughs such as satellite communications, electronic data interchange, and bar coding have been equally significant. By integrating such technological changes into their logistical operations, firms are able to increase their productivity and enhance customer satisfaction. Firms such as Benetton that have aggressively and innovatively harnessed these new information technologies have improved the efficiency of their overall operations as well as their logistical operations. Cost savings can be huge. Volkswagen, for example, believes it can trim its overall operating costs by 1 percent using electronic data interchange for all of its internal and external transactions.

IT also has promoted a reconceptualization of the logistics process and a rethinking of the supplier-customer relationship. By harnessing IT, firms are able to analyze how to promote the efficiency and productivity of the entire supply chain, rather than just their particular component of it. For example, Kay-Bee Toy Stores' IT system monitors sales at its 1,300 retail outlets and inventory levels at the company's distribution centers. When store inventories of a hot item like the Sony PlayStation 2 run low, replacements can automatically be sent from the company's distribution centers; when inventory runs low at the distribution centers, new orders can be placed with the manufacturers. By using IT creatively, Kay-Bee and other companies not only enhance their own productivity but also raise the satisfaction of their customers. IT has other advantages as well. Investments in IT can act as substitutes for investments in inventory and warehousing capacity, reducing capital costs and improving rates of return on assets. Moreover, IT helps firms monitor their progress toward attainment of their strategic goals.

INTERNATIONAL SERVICE OPERATIONS ‹

The service sector has emerged in recent years as an increasingly important part of many national economies, especially those of developed countries. For example, the service sector accounts for almost three-fourths of the U.S. gross domestic product and is the source of most new U.S. jobs.[26] It therefore should come as no surprise that services are becoming a more integral part of international trade and of the global economy. An **international service business** is a firm that transforms resources into an intangible output that creates utility for its customers. Examples of international services are British Airways' transporting of passengers from London to New Delhi; PricewaterhouseCooper's assistance with the accounting and auditing functions of firms such as BP Amoco, Baxter, and IBM; and Dai-Ichi Kangyo Bank's handling of international corporate business accounts.

Characteristics of International Services

Services have several unique characteristics that create special challenges for firms that want to sell services in the international marketplace. In particular, services often are intangible, are not storable, require customer participation, and may be linked with tangible goods.

Services are intangible. A consumer who goes to a store and buys a Sony Walkman has a tangible product, one that can be held, manipulated, used, stored, damaged, and/or returned. A consumer who goes to an accountant to obtain finan-

> Trade in international services is a growing component of the world's economy. This California shopper enjoys the convenience of an ATM machine installed by CIBC World Markets of Canada at her local Safeway supermarket.

cial advice leaves with intangible knowledge that cannot be held or seen. (The pieces of paper or electronic documents sometimes associated with services—tax statements, insurance policies, and so on—although tangible themselves, are actually just symbols or representations of the service product itself.) Because of this intangibility, assessing a service's value or quality often is more difficult than assessing the value or quality of a good.

Services generally are not storable. Often they cannot be created ahead of time and inventoried or saved for future usage. A service call to repair a broken washing machine can occur only when the technician is physically transported to the site of the broken appliance—and is wasted if no one is home to unlock the door. An empty airline seat, an unused table in a restaurant, an unsold newspaper—all lose their economic value as soon as their associated window of opportunity closes, that is, after the plane takes off, the restaurant kitchen closes, and the next day's newspaper is printed. The high degree of perishability of services makes capacity planning a critical problem for all service providers. **Capacity planning** is deciding how many customers a firm will be able to serve at a given time. Failure to provide sufficient capacity often means permanently lost sales, whereas provision of too much capacity raises the firm's costs and lowers its profits.

Services often require customer participation. International services such as tourism cannot occur without the physical presence of the customer. Because of customer involvement in the delivery of the service, many service providers need to customize the product to meet the purchaser's needs. Thomas Cook, for example, can sell more bus tours in London if it provides Spanish-speaking guides for its Mexican, Venezuelan, and Argentinean clients and Japanese-speaking guides for its Japanese customers. Further, an identical service can be perceived quite differently by each of its customers, thereby creating strategic and marketing problems. The London bus tour, for example, may be viewed with great excitement by Japanese honeymooners on their first trip outside of Osaka but with boredom by a harried Toshiba executive who has visited the city many times.

Many services are tied to the purchase of other products. Many firms offer **product-support services**—assistance with operating, maintaining, and/or repairing products for customers. Such services may be critical to the sale of the related product. For example, Swedish appliance maker AB Electrolux manufactures vacuum cleaners, refrigerators, washing machines, and other appliances under such names as Eureka, Frigidaire, Tappan, and Weed Eater. The firm also has service operations set up to repair those products for consumers who buy them, to provide replacement parts, and so on. The firm's ability to sell its appliances would be harmed substantially if it did not offer these related services. Moreover, not only must it offer the services at its corporate home in Stockholm, Sweden; if AB Electrolux wants to compete in the U.S., Canadian, and British markets, it must provide repair and parts distribution services there as well.

The Role of Government in International Services Trade

An important dimension of the international services market is the role of government. Many governments seek to protect local professionals and to ensure that domestic standards and credentials are upheld by restricting the ability of foreigners to practice such professions as law, accounting, and medicine. Government regulations often stipulate which firms are allowed to enter service markets and the prices they may charge. For instance, in the United States foreign banks and insurance firms are heavily regulated and must follow the directives of numerous state and federal regulatory agencies. In many countries telecommunications, transportation, and utility firms typically need governmental permission to serve individual markets. For example, airline routes between the United States and France are spelled out by a bilateral agreement between those two countries. Air France can fly passengers from Paris to Dallas and from Paris to New York, but it cannot board passengers in New York and fly them to Dallas. U.S. carriers are given similar rights to routes between U.S. and French cities.

The past decade has seen a reduction in domestic and international regulation of many service industries. Continued reductions in barriers to service trade is a high priority of the World Trade Organization. Deregulation and reduced trade barriers have created opportunities for firms in industries such as banking and telecommunications and spurred them to aggressively seek new domestic markets and expand their operations to foreign markets, as we discussed in Chapter 10's closing case, *The New Conquistador*. These changes have also triggered numerous strategic alliances, cross-border investments, and new start-up companies in every corner of the globe.

Managing Service Operations

The actual management of international service operations involves a number of basic issues, including capacity planning, location planning, facilities design and layout, and operations scheduling.

Recall that capacity planning is deciding how many customers the firm will be able to serve at one time. Because of the close customer involvement in the purchase of services, capacity planning affects the quality of the services provided to customers. For example, McDonald's first restaurant in Russia was considerably larger than many of its other restaurants in order to accommodate an anticipated higher level of sales volume. Despite this larger size, customer waiting times at the Moscow restaurant are much longer than those in the United States. The lack of restaurant alternatives makes Muscovites more willing to stand in long lines for their "Big Mek." In contrast, if customers had to wait a half-hour to be served in Boulder, Columbus, or even Paris, McDonald's would lose much of its business.

As with production management, location planning is important for international service operations. By definition most service providers must be close to the customers they plan to serve (exceptions might be information providers that rely on electronic communication). Indeed, most international service operations involve setting up branch offices in each foreign market and then staffing each office with locals.

International service facilities also must be carefully designed so the proper look and layout are established. At times firms operating internationally may highlight their foreign identity or blend their home country heritage with the local culture. At Disneyland Paris, for example, signs are in both English and French. At other times firms may chose to downplay their foreign identity. Most American donut dunkers, for example, are unaware that Dunkin' Donuts is owned by a British conglomerate, Allied Domecq PLC.

Finally, international service firms must schedule their operations to best meet the customers' needs. For example, airlines transporting passengers from the United States to Europe generally depart late in the evening. Doing this gives passengers the opportunity to spend some of the day working before they depart, and they arrive in the early morning the next day. In contrast, westbound flights usually leave Europe in mid-morning and arrive in the United States late that same afternoon. This scheduling provides an optimal arrangement because it factors in customer preferences, time zones, jet lag, and aircraft utilization and maintenance requirements.

CHAPTER REVIEW

Summary

International operations management is the set of activities used by an international firm to transform resources into goods or services. Effective operations management is a key ingredient in any firm's success. A firm's business strategy provides the major direction it will take regarding its operations management activities.

Production management refers to the creation of tangible goods. One of the first decisions production managers must make concerns supply chain management and vertical integration. Supply chain management, also called sourcing or procuring, encompasses the set of processes and steps used in acquiring resources and materials. Vertical integration refers to the extent to which a firm either provides its own resources or obtains them externally.

A key decision is whether to make or buy inputs. Several options exist. Production managers attempting to select from among them must consider strategic issues as well as risks, flexibility, investments in facilities, and questions of control.

Location decisions are also of paramount importance to effective international operations management. Country-related considerations include resource availability and costs, infrastructure, and country-of-origin marketing effects. Product-related issues are the value-to-weight ratio, production technology, and the importance of customer feedback. Governmental factors that must be considered include stability of the political process, tariffs and other trade barriers, economic development incentives, and the existence of FTZs. Finally, organizational issues include the firm's strategy, its structure, and its inventory management policies.

International logistics and materials management are also a basic part of production management. Several factors differentiate international from domestic materials management, including shipping distance, transportation modes, and the regulatory context. Packaging, weight, and factory location also must be considered. Technological changes in information technology are revolutionizing logistics and redefining relationships between suppliers and end users.

Service operations management is concerned with the creation of intangible products. The service sector is an increasingly important part of the global economy. International services are generally characterized as being intangible, not storable, requiring customer participation, and linked with tangible goods. The basic issues involved in managing service operations include capacity planning, location planning, design and layout, and operations scheduling.

Review Questions

1. What is international operations management and how is it accomplished?
2. Why is effective operations management important for an international firm?
3. How does a firm's corporate strategy affect its operations management?
4. How do production management and service operations management differ?
5. What is supply chain management? What is vertical integration?
6. What factors must a firm consider when addressing the make-or-buy decision?
7. What basic set of factors must a firm consider when selecting a location for a production facility?
8. How do materials management and physical distribution differ?
9. What basic factors must be addressed when managing international service operations?

Questions for Discussion

1. How does international operations management relate to international marketing (discussed in Chapter 16)?
2. How are a firm's strategy and operations management interrelated?
3. What constraints do operations impose on strategic options?
4. How do each of the basic business strategies (differentiation, cost leadership, and focus) relate to operations management?
5. In the mid-1990s Jaguar, the producer of expensive motor cars, threatened to shut down its British factory and produce its cars in Portugal. If it were cheaper to produce Jaguars in Portugal, would you advise the company to shift its production there? Can you think of any reason why it should not make such a move? (P.S.: As it turned out, the British government agreed to provide Jaguar with some economic development incentives if it would modernize its existing factory, and Jaguar kept its British factory open.)
6. What are the basic similarities and differences between production management and service operations management?
7. What are the advantages and disadvantages of being vertically integrated?
8. What are the steps a manager might follow in selecting a site for a new factory?
9. Why are services most closely associated with developed, industrialized economies?

BUILDING GLOBAL SKILLS

Begin by reading the following, which is adapted from a *Harvard Business Review* case study titled "The Plant Location Puzzle."[27]

Ann Reardon made her way across the crowded trade show floor, deep in thought and oblivious to the noisy activity all around her. As CEO of The Eldora Company (EDC) for the previous 13 years, she had led her organization through a period of extraordinary success. While larger bicycle makers had moved their manufacturing operations overseas to take advantage of lower labor costs, Eldora had stuck with a domestic manufacturing strategy, keeping its plant on the same campus as its corporate offices in Boulder, Colorado. Ann felt that her strategy of keeping all the parts of the company in the same location, while unconventional, had contributed greatly to cooperation among various departments and, ultimately, to the company's growth: EDC had become the largest and most profitable bicycle company in the United States. Yet her manufacturing vice president, Sean Andrews, was now urging her to build a plant in China.

"Look at the number of companies here," he had said that morning, as they helped several EDC staffers stack brochures on the exhibit table and position the company's latest models around the perimeter of their area. "There are too many players in this market," he had said. "I've been saying this for two months now, and you know the forecasters' numbers back me up. But if they weren't enough to convince you, just look around. The industry is reaching the saturation point here in the States. We have to break into Asia." . . .

Ann thought about what Sean had said about the U.S. market. In 1999 EDC's sales and earnings had hit record levels. The company produced almost 30 percent of the bicycles sold in the United States. But U.S. mass-market bicycle sales were growing by only 2 percent per year, while the Asian market for those same bikes was nearly doubling on an annual basis. And Eldora could not competitively serve those markets from its U.S. manufacturing facility. Two of the largest bike manufacturers in the world, located in rapidly growing Asian markets, enjoyed a significant labor and distribution cost advantage. . . .

One of the reasons the company had been so successful was that Boulder, Colorado, was a bicyclists' mecca. Eldora employees at all levels shared a genuine love of bicycling and eagerly pursued knowledge of the industry's latest trends and styles. Someone was always suggesting a better way to position the hand brakes or a new toe grip that allowed for better traction and easier dismounts. And Eldora never had a shortage of people willing to test out the latest prototypes.

Another reason was that all marketing staff, engineers, designers, and manufacturing personnel worked on one campus, within a 10 minute walk of one another. Ann had bet big on that strategy, and it had paid off. Communication was easy, and changes in styles, production plans, and the like could be made quickly and efficiently. Mountain bikes, for example, had gone from 0 percent to more than 50 percent of the market volume since 1991, and Eldora had met the increased demand with ease. And when orders for cross-bikes—mountain/road bike hybrids that had enjoyed a spurt of popularity—began to fall off, Eldora had been able to adjust its production run with minimal disruption. . . .

Ann's satisfaction was quickly tempered with thoughts of foreign sales performance. Between 1990 and 1997 EDC's foreign sales had grown at an annual rate of over 40 percent. But during the previous two years, they had been flat.

Sean appeared at Ann's side, jolting her out of her thoughts and into the reality of her surroundings. "Dale just finished up the first round of retailers' meetings," he said. "We'd like to get some lunch back over at the hotel and talk about our options." Dale Stewart was Eldora's marketing vice president. His views of what was best for the company often differed from Sean's, but the two had an amiable working relationship and enjoyed frequent spirited verbal sparring matches. . . .

Over sandwiches, Sean made his case. "Our primary markets in North America and Western Europe represent less than a quarter of the worldwide demand. Of the 200 million bicycles made in the world last year, 40 million were sold in China, 30 million in India, and 9 million in Japan. Historically, bikes sold in Asia's developing markets were low-end products used as primary modes of transportation. But the economic picture is changing fast. There's a growing middle class. Suddenly people have disposable income. Many consumers there are now seeking higher quality and trendier styles. Mountain bikes with suspension are in. And cross-bikes are still holding their own. In fact, the demand in those markets for the product categories we produce has been doubling annually, and the growth rates seem sustainable.

"If we're going to compete in Asia, though, we need a local plant. My staff has evaluated many locations there. We've looked at wage rates, proximity to markets, and materials costs, and we feel that China is our best bet. We'd like to open a plant there as soon as possible, and start building our position."

Dale jumped in. "Two of our largest competitors, one from China, one from Taiwan, have been filling the demand so far," he said. "In 1995, 97 percent of the volume produced by these companies was for export. In 2001 they are projecting that 45 percent of their production will be for local markets. We can't compete with them from here. About 20 percent of our product cost is labor, and the hourly wages of the manufacturing workforce in these countries are between 5 percent and 15 percent of ours. It also costs us an additional 20 percent in transportation and duties to get our bicycles to these markets."

He glanced at Sean quickly and continued. "But here's where I disagree with Sean. I think we need a short-term solution. These companies have a big lead on us, and the more I think about it, the more I believe we need to put a direct sales operation in Asia first."

"Dale, you're crazy," Sean said, pouring himself some ice water from the pitcher on the table. "What good would an Asian sales operation do without a manufacturing plant? I know we source components in Asia now, but we could save another 10 percent on those parts if we were located there. Then we would really be bringing Eldora to Asia. If we want to compete there, we have to play from our greatest strength—quality. If we did it your way, you wouldn't be selling Eldora bikes. You'd just be selling some product with our label on it. You wouldn't get the quality. You wouldn't build the same kind of reputation we have here. It wouldn't really be Eldora. Over the long term, it couldn't work."

"We're building bicycles, not rocket ships," Dale countered. "There are lots of companies in Asia that could provide us with a product very quickly if we gave them our designs and helped them with their production process. We could outsource production in the short term, until we made more permanent arrangements." He turned to Ann. "We could even outsource the product permanently, despite what Sean says. What do we know about building and running a plant in China? All I know is we're losing potential share even as we sit here. The trading companies aren't giving our products the attention they deserve, and they also aren't giving us the information we need on the features that consumers in those markets want. A sales operation would help us learn the market even as we're entering it. Setting up a plant first would take too long. We need to be over there now, and opening a sales operation is the quickest way."

Ann cut in. "Dale has a good point, Sean," she said. "We've been successful here in large part because our entire operation is in Boulder, on one site. We've had complete control over our own flexible manufacturing operation, and that's been a key factor in our ability to meet rapid change in the local market. How would we address the challenges inherent in manufacturing in a facility halfway around the world? Would you consider moving there? And for how long?

"Also, think about our other options. If the biggest issue keeping us out of these markets right now is cost, then both of you are ignoring a few obvious alternatives. Right now, only our frame-building operation is automated. We could cut labor costs significantly by automating more processes. And why are you so bent on China? Frankly, when I was there last month touring facilities, a lot of what I saw worried me. You know, that day I was supposed to tour a production facility, there was a power failure. Judging by the reactions of the personnel in the plant the next day, these outages are common. The roads to the facility are in very poor condition. And wastewater and cleaning solvents are regularly dumped untreated into the waterways. We could operate differently if we located there, but what impact would that have on costs?

"Taiwan has a better developed infrastructure than China. What about making that our Asian base? And I've heard that Singapore offers attractive tax arrangements to new manufacturing operations. Then there's Mexico. It's closer to home, and aside from distribution costs, the wage rates are similar to Asia's, and many of the other risks would be minimized. You both feel strongly about this, I know, but this isn't a decision we can make based on enthusiasm." . . .

Walking back to the convention center with Dale and Sean, Ann realized that she wasn't just frustrated because she didn't know which course EDC should pursue. She was concerned that she really didn't know which aspects of the decision were important and which were irrelevant. Should she establish a division in China? If so, which functions should she start with? Manufacturing? Marketing? And what about engineering? Or should she consider a different location? Would China's low labor costs offset problems caused by poor infrastructure?

Growth had always been vitally important to Eldora, both in creating value to shareholders and in providing a work environment that could attract and retain the most talented people. Now it appeared that Ann would have to choose between continued growth and a domestic-only manufacturing strategy that had served her well.

Now that you have read the case study, you are ready to participate in the exercise related to it. First, make sure you completely understand the details of the case. Next, form groups of six people each. One person should adopt the role of Ann Reardon, one the role of Sean Andrews, and one the role of Dale Stewart. The other three group members will constitute the board of directors of The Eldora Company. If the number of people in the class does not divide evenly by six, the board of directors can be increased in size. Ann, Sean, and Dale should each summarize for the board—in two minutes or less—the basic issues each sees regarding the firm's potential entry into the Asian market.

The board of directors then should use its own understanding of the background material (in the case itself) to discuss and debate whether to build a new plant in Asia. Your instructor will then ask each group to summarize its deliberations and report on its final decision.

Follow-Up Questions

1. How similar or different were the reports from each group?
2. Why do you think this pattern of similarities or differences occurred?

WORKING WITH THE WEB:
BUILDING GLOBAL INTERNET SKILLS

Obtaining International Logistic Service

Assume you are the marketing manager of a small valve manufacturer trying to export to Egypt for the first time. Make a list of the logistical issues you are likely to face in exporting to Egypt. Now check out the Web sites of providers of international logistics services. (Chapter 17's section of the textbook's Web site provides links to some Web sites you may find helpful). Which of these Web sites is the most useful to you? What information provided on these Web sites is of the most value to you? What information is missing? Based on the information contained in its Web site, which company would you call first? Why? Would your answers change if you were an experienced exporter?

IN THE NEWS

Location decisions present important challenges to international operations managers. These managers must answer questions about economic feasibility, legal and political conditions, availability of resources, language or cultural barriers, transportation problems, and the like. What goes into a real-world location decision?

From the *Financial Times* homepage (*www.ft.com*), click the companies tab. Use "Companies in the News" to locate an article about a company that has recently made a location decision, and read the article carefully. If you need to do further research to answer the following questions, try a search engine you like or locate the company's Web site.

What strategy motivated the company to make the location decision (expansion, relocation, etc.)? What did it hope to gain by making the decision that it did—what additional resources or technologies were available, what costs were saved, and so forth? How successful was the company's decision in achieving those goals, or, if it is too recent to tell, how will the company know when it has achieved its goal?

CLOSING CASE

Creating a Global Market for Auto Parts

A market is a mechanism for exchange between the buyers and sellers of a particular good or service. In earlier times markets were actual physical settings where buyers and sellers would gather. Although such market settings still are used for things like fish, fruits and vegetables, and antiques and collectibles, many commercial markets today are fundamentally different in that buyers and sellers are not at the same place—they arrange their exchange via mail orders, telephones, fax machines, and so forth. The growth of the Internet and World Wide Web also is serving to transform some markets to make it even easier for buyers and sellers to transact their business at a distance.

A good example of this trend is the recently announced partnership among some of the world's largest automobile manufacturers. It all started when various individual automakers began to create their own global purchasing Web sites. Ford, for instance, had announced plans for and was actively creating a site it called Auto-Xchange. The company intended to post all of its global procurement needs on the site, while also requesting that its suppliers post availability and prices for the parts and equipment the suppliers had to offer. Hence, Ford was viewing the site as the focal point for its entire supply chain management function.

Concerns began to arise, however, when it quickly became apparent that other major automobile manufacturers were planning to do the same thing. Major suppliers to the auto industry, meanwhile, began to realize they might soon be facing an unwieldy array of separate Web sites for each car company, potentially driving their own costs up. So a coalition of the largest suppliers approached Ford and General Motors with a novel proposal—why not team up and create a single site both firms could use?

Ford and GM executives quickly saw the wisdom of this idea and then convinced DaimlerChrysler to join them. Their plan is to create a single Web site that will serve as a marketplace for all interested automobile manufacturers, suppliers, and dealers—essentially creating a global virtual market for all firms in the industry. Almost immediately, France's Renault and Japan's Nissan, which is controlled by Renault, indicated they would join. Toyota also indicated strong interest and is likely to join the alliance soon. In addition, both Ford and GM indicated they would encourage their foreign affiliates and strategic partners to join as well.

Experts believe the impact of this global electronic market will be tremendous. For example, it currently costs GM about $100 in ordering costs to buy parts or supplies the traditional way—with paper, using the telephone, and so forth. Under the new system GM estimates that its ordering costs will drop to less than $10. Clearly, the automakers will realize substantial cost savings. These cost savings in turn will allow the automakers to lower prices and/or realize higher profits per unit sold.

The suppliers also will benefit in various ways. Besides having more information about what different companies need, the suppliers will be able to buy and sell among themselves. For instance, one steel company might have a surplus of a particular grade or quality of steel and can use the network to offer to sell its surplus to other steel companies. Moreover, the Web site will make it easier for suppliers to keep informed about what prices their competitors are charging.

Once complete, developers envision a seamless system on which suppliers can routinely post the products and equipment they are offering; automobile companies can post their short-term and long-term parts and equipment needs; and both buyers and suppliers can efficiently and quickly conduct online auctions. Indeed, the site developers believe it will be so powerful that the auto companies who own it soon will be able to establish the site as an independent business sold to investors through an initial public offering, raising billions of new capital for themselves.[28]

Case Questions

1. Identify and discuss the strategic operations management issues in this case.
2. What are the implications of this form of business-to-business market mechanism for supply chain management?
3. Identify other industries in which this same form of exchange might be applicable.
4. Would this approach work for a service industry? If not, why? If so, what would be the similarities and differences between a manufacturing and a service exchange?

Should International Businesses Promote Human and Worker Rights?

When businesses set up operations in foreign countries, they should have the same regard for their workers as they have at home. These IBM workers in Brazil, for example, have safety equipment and procedures comparable to those used by IBM workers around the world.

International businesses have a moral obligation to protect human and worker rights.

It is a common business practice today for firms to move their manufacturing facilities to countries in which production costs are low or to subcontract production to local firms in those countries. Unfortunately, the reasons for the low production costs may be inadequate wages, unsafe or unhealthy working conditions, and disregard for worker rights. For example, 200 people died in a 1993 fire in a Thai toy factory that lacked basic safety precautions such as fire extinguishers and sprinkler systems.

Businesses that set up shop in foreign countries have an obligation to make the proper treatment of local employees a high priority. Just because a multinational corporation (MNC) might be able to get away with paying substandard wages and providing poor working conditions by no means suggests that it should do so. Indeed, today's international businesses have a social obligation to improve the quality of life for their employees and those of their subcontractors worldwide.

To do so makes good business sense for several reasons. First, it is simply good public relations. Firms that allow their foreign workers to be treated poorly fare badly themselves when their practices receive media attention. For example, in recent years the reputations of Nike, Wal-Mart, and TV personality Kathie Lee Gifford have been damaged as a result of such publicity.

Second, human rights advocates argue that to treat employees poorly violates human rights. This simple premise becomes even more persuasive when it is augmented with stories and examples detailing such abhorrent practices as using what amounts to slave labor and physically abusing workers.

Third, international businesses can make a difference in the world by practicing more humanitarian human resource management policies. Levi Strauss is an excellent example of a firm that has taken to heart the importance of treating its foreign workers with dignity and providing them with the proper rewards and working conditions. This firm mandates that all its foreign plants, including those of its subcontractors, must maintain safety and health practices comparable to those in the United States. For example, drinking water purity and bathroom conditions must meet U.S. standards.

Sources: "Levi Tries to Make Sure Contract Plants in Asia Treat Workers Well," *Wall Street Journal*, July 28, 1994, pp. A1, A6; "Levi's Law," *Far Eastern Economic Review*, April 14, 1994, p. 60; Tim Smith, "The Power of Business for Human Rights," *Business & Society Review* (Winter 1994), pp. 36–38.

Such objectives, while noble, are often counterproductive.

Often the only comparative advantage that developing countries have in the international marketplace is low wage rates. International businesses locating in these countries should be allowed to exploit fully these countries' low-cost production opportunities as long as they adhere to local customs, norms, and laws.

If foreign MNCs were required to pay above-market wages or to provide working conditions equal to those in developed countries, the economic development of poorer countries might be crippled. If an international giant moves into a low-cost region and pays higher-than-normal wages, workers will no longer be willing to work for the prevailing wage rate. Thus costs for local businesses increase. In addition, requiring foreign firms to pay above-market wages and benefits will discourage them from locating in developing countries. Such countries need to lure more foreign capital and technology, not drive it away.

Some government officials in developing countries believe the sentiments expressed by worker rights advocates in richer countries are thinly disguised attempts at protectionism. In their view public pressure to force Western retailers to buy goods only from factories that pay wages and offer working conditions equivalent to those in the Quad countries acts as a nontariff barrier (NTB) against goods from developing countries.

These officials also often resent these pressures as a form of cultural imperialism by Westerners who have little first-hand knowledge of the often harsh economic alternatives facing workers in developing countries. When Levi Strauss recently discovered that one of its Bangladeshi factories was employing young children, it demanded that the factory's practices be changed. The manager pointed out that most of the children were their families' only source of income and to deprive them of a job would bring hardship on entire families. In some regions of Southeast Asia the situation is far worse: Children who are unable to obtain jobs are often sold into prostitution by their families. Critics argue that given these alternatives, foreign MNCs should stick to providing jobs for developing countries and leave the social engineering to local governments.

Requiring foreign-owned factories located in developing countries to provide wages and working conditions equivalent to those in Quad countries will discourage FDI. Job opportunities created by these investments are vital to the economic development of less developed economies.

Wrap-up

1. What ethical responsibilities do MNCs have to their workers in developing countries? Do their ethical responsibilities differ for workers employed at a firm-owned factory and workers employed at a subcontractor's factory?

2. Do you agree that attempts to impose Western-style wage rates and working conditions in factories in developing countries constitute an NTB? Why or why not?

CHAPTER

KLM's Worldwide Financial Management

KLM Royal Dutch Airlines lives or dies in the international market. It has virtually no domestic market because the physical size of the Netherlands does not lend itself to extensive airline travel: The country is smaller than West Virginia, and its two major cities, Amsterdam and Rotterdam, are only 40 miles apart. As the world's seventh largest airline, KLM competes head-to-head against other major international carriers, including American, United, Delta, British Airways, Lufthansa, Air France, Japan Air Lines, Qantas, and Singapore Airlines.

"KLM receives from its customers a **rainbow** of **currencies.**"

The foundation of KLM's global success is its reputation for providing high-quality service. It has lured passengers of all nationalities to its flights, particularly highly valued business travelers, who are willing to pay a premium for safe and reliable service. Only 40 percent of KLM's business is done within the friendly turf of Europe. Asian operations account for 17 percent of its traffic, and the critical transatlantic market for over 26 percent.

A truly international carrier, KLM flies to more than 150 cities on six continents. But its international success brings a major financial challenge—managing its holdings of the 80 or so currencies it uses in the normal conduct of business. KLM receives from its customers a rainbow of currencies, including francs (Belgian, French, and Swiss), crowns (Czech, Danish, Norwegian, Slovak, and Swedish), dollars

18

International Financial Management

(Australian, Canadian, Hong Kong, New Zealand, and U.S.), as well as yen, pounds, and of course Dutch guilders. It also must pay in local currency for local services—landing fees, ground-handling services, travel agent commissions, and so on—in each country in which it does business. When the euro becomes available in 2002, KLM will of course transact in that currency as well.

Managing the firm's revenues, expenses, assets, and liabilities, all denominated in various foreign currencies, is a major task for KLM's financial officers. To pay local expenses, they must maintain local-currency cash balances in each country. They also must search worldwide for sources of low-cost capital to modernize the firm's aircraft fleet and thereby maintain its reputation for high-quality service. In addition, they must protect KLM from exchange rate fluctuations, which will change the value in its home currency—guilders through the end of 2001, euros thereafter—that it receives for its services and the costs it incurs for aircraft, fuel, flight services, and ground handling. These officers must thoroughly understand how the contemporary international monetary system operates. They must monitor changes in the foreign-exchange market, be knowledgeable about potential shifts in government economic policies in their major markets, and constantly shop for the best credit terms in such capital markets as Amsterdam, London, Frankfurt, New York, and Tokyo.[1]

In most business transactions the receipt of goods by the buyer and the receipt of payment by the seller in a form the seller can use immediately do not coincide. Even when a customer pays for goods with a check, the seller will not have access to the funds until the check clears. Until then, the seller risks having the check returned because of insufficient funds. Thus some type of financing and some degree of trust between buyer and seller are necessary to allow business transactions to occur.

Although these problems affect both domestic and international businesses, the problems of financing and credit checking are far greater for international transactions. Differences in laws, customs, financial practices, and currency convertibility among countries mean that an international firm must know the practices both of its home country and of each country in which it does business—or else hire experts who do. A firm also must acquire specific credit information about the foreign firms with which it wants to deal. On top of these problems is that of transacting in a foreign currency—a problem either the buyer or the seller must face. Financial officers of international businesses like KLM are well aware of the challenges created by using different currencies. How international businesses address these myriad problems is the subject of this chapter.

❯ FINANCIAL ISSUES IN INTERNATIONAL TRADE

We begin by considering the problems associated with financing international trade. In any business transaction the buyer and the seller must negotiate and reach agreement on such basic issues as price, quantity, and delivery date. However, when the transaction involves a buyer and a seller from two countries, several other issues arise:

- Which currency to use for the transaction
- When and how to check credit
- Which form of payment to use
- How to arrange financing

Choice of Currency

One problem unique to international business is choosing the currency to use to settle a transaction. Exporters and importers usually have clear—and conflicting—preferences as to which currency to use. The exporter typically prefers payment in its home currency so it can know the exact amount it will receive from the importer. The importer generally prefers to pay in its home currency so it can know the exact amount it must pay the exporter. Sometimes an exporter and an importer may elect to use a third currency. For example, if both parties are based in countries with relatively weak or volatile local currencies, they may prefer to deal in a more stable currency such as the Japanese yen or the U.S. dollar. By some estimates over 70 percent of the exports of less developed countries and 85 percent of the exports of Latin American countries are invoiced using the U.S. dollar. In some industries one currency is customarily used to settle commercial transactions. For instance, in the oil industry the U.S. dollar serves this function. Among the major exporting countries the most common practice is for the exporter to invoice foreign customers using its home currency. However, smaller exporting countries may choose to use the currency of a major trading partner; 91 percent of Thailand's exports are invoiced in U.S. dollars, for example.

Credit Checking

Another critical financial issue in international trade concerns the reliability and trustworthiness of the buyer. If an importer is a financially healthy and reliable company and one with whom an exporter has had previous satisfactory business relations, the exporter may choose to simplify the payment process by extending credit to the importer. However, if the importer is financially troubled or known to be a poor credit risk, the exporter may demand a form of payment that reduces its risk.

In commercial transactions it is wise to check customers' credit ratings. For most domestic business transactions firms have simple and inexpensive mechanisms for doing this. In North America, for example, firms may ask for credit references or contact established sources of credit information such as Dun & Bradstreet. Similar sources are available in other countries; however, many first-time exporters are unaware of them. Fortunately, an exporter's domestic banker often can obtain credit information on foreign customers through the bank's foreign banking operations or through its correspondent bank in a customer's country. Most national government agencies in charge of export promotion also offer credit-checking services. For example, the International Trade Administration, a branch of the U.S. Department of Commerce, provides financial information about foreign firms for a fee. Numerous commercial credit-reporting services also are available. Country desk officers of the U.S. and Foreign Commercial Service are available to steer new exporters to these services.

The firm that ignores the credit-checking process may run into serious payment problems. For example, one small U.S. manufacturer exported $127,000 worth of fan blades to a new customer in Africa. However, it failed to first contact any of the customer's credit references. Frustrated by the subsequent lack of payment, the manufacturer turned the account over to a collection agency, which discovered that the supposed customer had vanished and its credit references were nonexistent.[2]

Implicit in this discussion is an important lesson that many successful international businesspeople have learned the hard way. Because the physical and cultural gaps between the exporter and the importer are often large, finding partners, customers, and distributors with whom to build long-term, trusting relationships is invaluable to any international business.

Method of Payment

Parties to the international transaction normally negotiate a method of payment based on the exporter's assessment of the importer's creditworthiness and the norms of their industry. Many forms of payment have evolved over the centuries, including payment in advance, open account, documentary collection, letters of credit, credit cards, and countertrade. As with most aspects of finance, each form involves different degrees of risk and cost.

Payment in Advance.   From the exporter's perspective the safest method of payment in international trade is payment in advance: The exporter receives the importer's money prior to shipping the goods. Using this method, the exporter reduces its risk and receives payment quickly, which may be important if its working capital balance is low. Exporters prefer payments in advance to be made by wire transfer, which allows immediate use of the funds. Payment by ordinary check may take four to six weeks to clear the banking systems of the two countries involved, depending on the size and sophistication of their financial services sectors.

From the importer's perspective payment in advance is very undesirable. The importer must give up the use of its cash prior to its receipt of the goods and bears the risk that the exporter will fail to deliver the goods in accordance with the sales contract. For these reasons exporters that insist on payment in advance are vulnerable to losing sales to competitors willing to offer more attractive payment terms. Nonetheless, payment in advance may be the preferred form if the importer is a poor credit risk.

Open Account.   From the importer's perspective the safest form of payment is the **open account**, whereby goods are shipped by the exporter and received by the importer prior to payment. The exporter then bills the importer for the goods, stipulating the amount, form, and time at which payment is expected. Open accounts also can be used as a marketing tool because they offer potential buyers short-term financing. Use of an open account enables the importer to avoid the fees charged by banks for alternative means of payment such as letters of credit or documentary collection, which will be discussed shortly. An open account has the further advantage of requiring less paperwork than these other forms of payment.

From the exporter's perspective an open account may be undesirable for several reasons. First, the exporter must rely primarily on the importer's reputation for paying promptly. Second, because the transaction does not involve a financial intermediary like a bank, the exporter cannot fall back on such an intermediary's expertise if a dispute arises with the importer. Third, the exporter may pay a price for the advantage of doing less paperwork: If the importer refuses to pay, the lack of documentation can hamper the exporter's pursuit of a claim in the courts of the importer's home country. Finally, the exporter must tie up working capital to finance foreign accounts receivable. Borrowing working capital collateralized by foreign receivables is often expensive because it may be difficult for domestically oriented lenders to evaluate the riskiness of a firm's portfolio of foreign receivables. Such borrowing is not impossible, however. Numerous firms engage in a specialized international lending activity called **factoring**, in which they buy foreign accounts receivable at a discount from face value. The size of the fees these firms charge (in the form of the discount from face value of the receivables) reflect both the time value of money and the factor's assessment of the portfolio's riskiness.

As a result, an open account is best suited for dealing with well-established, long-term customers or larger firms with impeccable credit ratings and reputations for timely payment of their bills. For example, U.S. video film distributors that deal with Blockbuster Video in the United States on an open account basis might offer the same arrangement to Citivision PLC, Blockbuster's subsidiary in the United Kingdom, particularly if Blockbuster pledged to honor Citivision's trade obligations. Similarly, foreign subsidiaries owned by a common parent corporation often deal with each other on an open account basis because the risk of default in such circumstances is minimal. About 40 percent of U.S. international trade involves transactions between subsidiaries of a parent firm.[3]

Payment in advance and an open account share a basic similarity. Both shift the cash flow burden and risk of default to one party in the transaction: to the buyer in the case of payment in advance and to the seller in the case of an open account.

Documentary Collection.   To get around the cash flow and risk problems caused by the use of payment in advance and open accounts, international businesses and banks have developed several other methods to finance transactions. One is **documentary collection**, whereby commercial banks serve as agents to facilitate the payment process. To initiate this method of payment, the exporter draws up a document called a **draft** (often called a *bill of exchange* outside the United States), in which payment is demanded from the buyer at a specified time. After the exporter ships its goods, it submits to its local banker the draft and appropriate shipping documents, such as the packing list and the bill of lading.[4] The **bill of lading** plays two important roles in documentary collection: It serves both as a contract for transportation between the exporter and the carrier and as a title to the goods in question. Acting on the exporter's instructions, the exporter's bank then contacts its correspondent bank in the importer's country (or one of its own branches there, if it has any). The latter bank is authorized to release the bill of lading, thereby transferring title of the goods, when the importer honors the terms of the exporter's draft.[5] This process is shown in Figure 18.1.

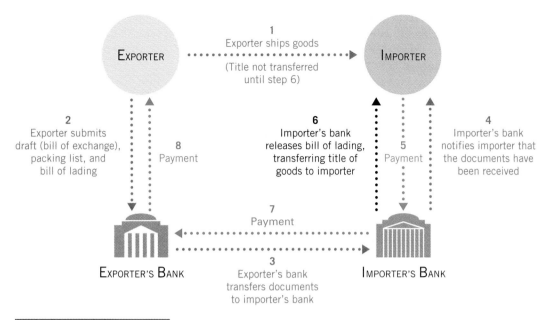

FIGURE 18.1   **Using a Sight Draft**

Note: In the case of a time draft, the importer makes a promise to pay, not the actual payment, in step 5.

Source: Based on *Dynamics of Trade Finance*, Chase Manhattan Bank, 1989, p. 42.

There are two major forms of drafts:

1. A **sight draft** requires payment upon the transfer of title to the goods from the exporter to the importer. When the bank in the importer's country receives the bill of lading and the sight draft from the exporter's bank, it notifies the importer, which then pays the draft. On payment the bank gives the bill of lading to the importer, which then can take title to the goods.

2. A **time draft** extends credit to the importer by requiring payment at some specified time, such as 30 or 60 days, after the importer receives the goods. (A variant of the time draft, the **date draft**, specifies a particular date on which payment will be made.)

To obtain title to the goods when a time draft is used, the importer must write "accepted" on the draft, thereby incurring a legal obligation to pay the draft when it comes due. An accepted time draft is called a **trade acceptance**, which under the laws of most countries is a legally enforceable and negotiable debt instrument. For a fee the importer's bank also may accept a time draft, thereby adding its own obligation to pay the draft to the importer's obligation. In this case the time draft becomes a **banker's acceptance**.

The exporter may hold either a trade acceptance or a banker's acceptance until it comes due. However, banks and other commercial lenders often are willing to buy acceptances at a discount, thereby allowing the exporter to receive immediate cash. Some acceptances are sold **without recourse**, meaning the buyer of the acceptance is stuck with the loss if the importer does not pay. Others are sold **with recourse**, meaning the exporter will have to reimburse the buyer of the acceptance in the case of nonpayment by the importer. Exporters planning to sell their accepted time drafts must balance the prices they will receive for the drafts against the additional banking fees they must pay (in the case of banker's acceptances) and the degree of risk they are willing to bear (in the case of acceptances sold with recourse). Because of their greater riskiness, acceptances sold without recourse are sold at bigger discounts from face value than acceptances sold with recourse. Similarly, because banker's acceptances are guaranteed by the bank as well as by the importer, they are less risky and usually are discounted less than trade acceptances are.

For an exporter payment through documentary collection has several advantages over the use of open accounts. First, the bank fees for documentary collection are quite reasonable because the banks act as agents rather than risk takers (except in the case of a banker's acceptance). Second, a trade acceptance or a banker's acceptance is an enforceable debt instrument under the laws of most countries, thereby solidifying the exporter's legal position if the importer defaults on its promise to pay. Third, using banks simplifies the collection process for the exporter and substitutes the banks' superior expertise in effecting international payments for the exporter's presumably inferior knowledge. Further, because the collection agent is a local bank, and the importer does not want to jeopardize its business reputation with a local lender, the importer is more likely to pay a time draft promptly than an invoice sent under an open account. Finally, because of the enforceability of acceptances in courts of law, arranging financing for foreign accounts receivable is easier and less expensive when documentary collection is used than when open accounts are used.

With documentary collection the exporter still bears some risks, however. Suppose local business conditions change or the importer finds a cheaper supply source. In such a case an importer may simply refuse the shipment and decline to accept the draft, perhaps under a false pretext that the shipment was late or the goods improperly packed. The importer's default on the sales contract places the exporter in the unenviable position of having its goods piled up on a foreign loading dock (and running up storage fees known as *demurrage*) while receiving no payment for them. Alternatively, the importer may default on the time draft when it comes due. The exporter may have legal remedies in either case, but pursuing them is often costly in terms of time, energy, and money.

Letters of Credit. To avoid such difficulties, exporters often request payment using a **letter of credit**, a document that is issued by a bank and contains its promise to pay the exporter on receiving proof that the exporter has fulfilled all requirements specified in the document. Because of the bank's pledge, the exporter bears less risk by using a letter of credit than by relying on documentary collection. However, cautious bankers are unlikely to issue a letter of credit unless they fully expect the importer to reimburse them. Thus using a letter of credit has the additional advantage that the exporter benefits from the bank's knowledge of the importer's creditworthiness, the requirements of the importer's home country customs service, and any restrictions the importer's home country government imposes on currency movements.

Usually, an importer applies to its local bank—in most cases, one with which it has an ongoing relationship—for a letter of credit. The bank then assesses the importer's creditworthiness, examines the proposed transaction, determines whether it wants collateral, and, assuming everything is in order, issues the letter of credit. The bank typically charges the importer a small commission for this service. The letter of credit details the conditions under which the importer's bank will pay the exporter for the goods. The conditions imposed by the issuing bank reflect normal sound business practices. Most letters of credit require the exporter to supply an invoice, appropriate customs documents, a bill of lading, a packing list, and proof of insurance. Depending on the product involved, the importer's bank may demand additional documentation before funding the letter, such as the following:

- *Export licenses* are issued by an agency of the exporter's home country. They may be required for politically sensitive goods, such as nuclear fuels, or for high-technology goods that may have military uses.

- *Certificates of product origin* confirm that the goods being shipped were produced in the exporting country. They may be required by the importing country so it can assess tariffs and enforce quotas.

- *Inspection certificates* may be needed to provide assurance the products have been inspected and they conform to relevant standards. For example, imported foodstuffs often must meet rigorous standards regarding pesticide residues, cleanliness, sanitation, and storage.

After issuing the letter of credit, the importer's bank sends it and the accompanying documents to the exporter's bank, which advises the exporter of the terms of the instrument, thereby creating an **advised letter of credit**. "Venturing Abroad" provides more information about the process of issuing an advised letter of credit. The exporter also can request its bank to add its own guarantee of payment to the letter of credit, thereby creating a **confirmed letter of credit**. This type of instrument is particularly appropriate when the exporter is concerned about political risk. If the importer's home country government later imposes currency controls or otherwise blocks payment by the importer's bank, the exporter can look to the confirming bank for payment.

Another type of letter of credit is the **irrevocable letter of credit**, which cannot be altered without the written consent of both the importer and the exporter. A bank also may issue a **revocable letter of credit**, which the bank may alter at any time and for any reason. An irrevocable letter of credit offers the exporter more protection

VENTURING *Abroad*

WHAT YOUR ADVISING FEES BUY

As an exporter, you may wonder now and again what your advising fee pays for. In addition to the obvious fax and courier expenses, there are a variety of services the advising bank performs before a letter of credit (L/C) is fully advised to you.

Advising banks have a responsibility to use reasonable care to check that any credit or amendment they advise to a beneficiary is authentic. Because of the large amounts of money involved, the letter of credit system has become a target for organized crime. To protect beneficiaries from fraud, advising banks check the validity of each credit and amendment through various private verification procedures. No credit is advised without some form of electronic test or authentication of signatures.

Banks are also required to review letters of credit and amendments for "boycott status." Commonly, L/Cs issued by Middle East banks carry stipulations relating to trade or commerce with Israel. Sometimes, under the Export Administration Act, these provisions are illegal and/or reportable to the government. Under the regulations, it is the responsibility of the advising bank to report boycott provisions in a letter of credit to the U.S. Department of Commerce or Treasury. This pertains not only to Mideast credits but credits worldwide.

The government also maintains a "Specially Designated Nationals" (SDN) list. This list contains names of businesses and individuals around the world who have forfeited their rights to export from or import to the United States. Companies or individuals on the SDN list are there because of their failure to comply with U.S. law. Each beneficiary and applicant on every credit is checked to make sure none is on the SDN list. This, too, is the advising bank's responsibility.

Another important function of the advising bank is to review credits for their workability. Surprisingly, many letters of credit are issued with conflicting stipulations, incorrect terms, and even expired availability dates. While the advising bank reviews the L/C for its "workability," it is important to remember that such review is from a banker's perspective and a bank's perspective on an L/C's "workability" may differ from that of an exporter. Exporters should also review the L/C for its "workability" from their perspective.

Finally, your advising fee pays for good, old-fashioned service. Often, exporters need clarification concerning the documentary requirements of the L/C, payment terms, or stipulations. A good advising bank will be ready, willing, and able to assist you with these and other questions.

than a revocable letter of credit. However, amending such an instrument can be cumbersome, expensive, and time consuming.

Banks that issue, advise on, and/or confirm letters of credit charge for their services. Therefore, international firms must determine which of these services they really need in order to avoid paying unnecessary fees.

When goods arc sold under a letter of credit, payment does not depend on meeting the terms of the sales contract between the buyer and seller. Rather, the bank issuing the letter of credit will make payment only when the terms of that letter have been fulfilled. Thus the exporter must carefully analyze the letter's terms before agreeing to them, to be sure they are compatible with the sales contract.

Surprisingly, it is this feature of letters of credit—that they are paid when their terms are met, not when the sales contract is fulfilled—that makes them so useful in international trade. Once the exporter meets the letter's terms, the importer's bank is obligated to pay the exporter even if the importer refuses the shipment or fails to pay for the goods. Such difficulties become the problem of the importer's bank, not the exporter. However, the likelihood of such difficulties arising are reduced because the importer is unlikely to jeopardize its business reputation or credit lines with its bank. Figure 18.2 shows how a letter of credit is used in a typical international transaction.

Although the issuing bank will not pay the exporter until all the terms of the letter of credit have been met, the exporter often can sell the letter prior to the expected payment date to its bank or another commercial lender at a discount from the face value. The discount will reflect the time value of money, the risk the buyer of the instrument bears if the issuing bank defaults on the transaction, and the buyer's administrative costs. Because confirmed and irrevocable letters of credit reduce the risk of secondary buyers, such letters sell for higher prices (or lower discounts from face value) than do letters of credit without these features. Thus an exporter planning to sell a letter of credit prior to delivery must trade off the incon-

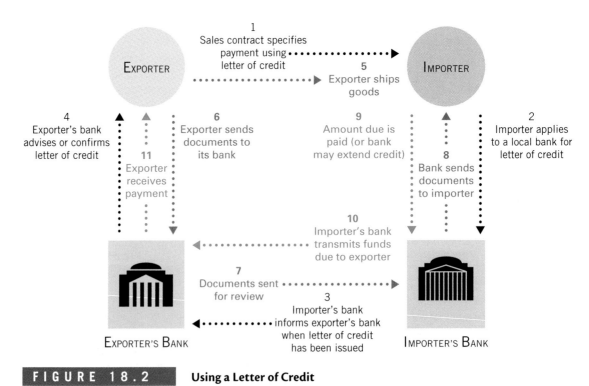

FIGURE 18.2   **Using a Letter of Credit**

Source: Based on *Dynamics of Trade Finance*, Chase Manhattan Bank, 1989, pp. 62–63.

venience or higher fees paid for these less risky types against the higher prices it will receive from secondary buyers of them.

Credit Cards.   For small international transactions, particularly those between international merchants and foreign retail customers, credit cards such as American Express, VISA, and MasterCard may be used. A firm may tap into the well-established credit card network to facilitate international transactions, subject to the normal limitations of these cards. The credit card companies collect transaction fees (usually 2 to 4 percent) from the merchant and in return assume the costs of collecting the funds from the customer and any risks of nonpayment. The companies typically charge an additional 1 to 3 percent for converting currencies. However, they offer exporters and importers none of the help banks do in dealing with the paperwork and documentation requirements of international trade.

Countertrade.   An additional method used for payment in international transactions is countertrade. **Countertrade** occurs when a firm accepts something other than money as payment for its goods or services. Forms of countertrade include barter, counterpurchase, buy-back, and offset purchase.

The simplest form of countertrade is **barter**, in which each party simultaneously swaps its products for the products of the other. For example, in the late 1990s the State Trading Corporation of India agreed to exchange wheat and other grains to Turkmenistan in return for cotton. Similarly, Azerbaijan agreed to import 100,000 tons of wheat from Romania, following a poor harvest in Azerbaijan and a bumper crop in Romania. Payment by Azerbaijan was in the form of crude oil.

A more sophisticated form of countertrade is **counterpurchase**, whereby one firm sells its products to another at one point in time and is compensated in the form of the other's products at some future time. Counterpurchase is the most common form of countertrade. It is sometimes called **parallel barter** as it disconnects the timing of contract performance by the participating parties. In this way one part of the transaction can go ahead even if the second requires more time. Boeing, for example, has used counterpurchase to sell aircraft to Saudi Arabia in return for oil, and to India in return for coffee, rice, castor oil, and other goods.

Another variant of countertrade involves **buy-back**, or compensation arrangements whereby one firm sells capital goods to a second firm and is compensated in the form of output generated as a result of their use. For example, Japan's Fukusuke Corporation sold 10 knitting machines and raw materials to Chinatex, a Shanghai-based clothing manufacturer, in exchange for 1 million pairs of underwear to be produced on the knitting machines.[6] Similarly, Internationale Vine of Latvia agreed to buy equipment for producing apple juice concentrate from PKL of Switzerland and to pay for the equipment with output from the machinery. Because it links payment with output from the purchased goods, a buy-back is particularly useful when the buyer of the goods needs to ensure the exporter will provide necessary after-sale services such as equipment repairs or instructions on how to use the equipment.[7]

Another important type of countertrade involves **offset purchases**, whereby part of an exported good is produced in the importing country. Offset arrangements are particularly important in sales to foreign governments of expensive military equipment such as fighter jets or tanks. General Dynamics, for instance, sold several hundred F-16 military jets to Belgium, Denmark, Norway, and the Netherlands by agreeing to allow those countries to offset the cost of the jets through coproduction agreements. As part of the deal, the countries were allowed to produce 40 percent of the value of the aircraft they purchased from General Dynamics. The firm sweetened the deal by authorizing the European countries to coproduce 10 percent of all F-16s sold to the U.S. military and 15 percent of any F-16s sold to other countries.

Balancing export sales and counterpurchase obligations on a deal-by-deal basis is often cumbersome. To facilitate countertrade, firms may agree to establish **clearinghouse accounts**, in which the exporting firm incurs a counterpurchase obligation of an equivalent value, which is recorded in its clearinghouse account. When the exporting firm eventually buys goods from its partner, its clearinghouse obligation is reduced. Thus a firm does not need to balance any single countertrade transaction, although it must honor its cumulative set of obligations by the time its clearinghouse account expires.

Sometimes firms enter into countertrade agreements to expand their international sales, without having experience in or desire to engage in countertrade. In this case countertrade agreements often permit the use of **switching arrangements**, whereby countertrade obligations are transferred from one firm to another. A variety of consulting firms, many headquartered in either London (because of access to capital markets) or Vienna (because of access to the former communist countries), is available to provide financing, marketing, and legal services needed by international businesses engaging in switching arrangements.[8] Japan's *soga sosha* (large trading companies discussed in Chapter 2) are particularly skillful in the use of switching arrangements and clearinghouse accounts because of the *soga sosha*'s extensive worldwide operations. A *soga sosha* might assist in the sale of Mitsubishi trucks in Ghana, taking payment in cocoa, which then can be sold to *keiretsu*-linked food processors back in Japan or to independent candy makers anywhere in the world.[9]

Some firms specialize in exploiting countertrade opportunities by constructing complicated multiple-market trades as part of the firms' normal business. Consider, for example, Marc Rich & Co., which did over $3 billion in business annually in the former Soviet Union. Soon after the Soviet Union broke up in the early 1990s, the firm engineered a complicated deal among several cash-poor countries that began with its buying 70,000 tons of Brazilian raw sugar on the open market (see Map 18.1). It then hired a Ukrainian firm to refine the sugar and paid the refinery with part of the sugar. Next, it swapped the rest of the refined sugar to oil refineries in Siberia, which needed the sugar for their workers, in return for gasoline. It then swapped 130,000 tons of gasoline to Mongolia in return for 35,000 tons of copper concentrate. The copper concentrate was shipped to copper refineries in Kazakhstan, which received payment in kind. The refined copper then was sold on the world market. At that point, Marc Rich—after several months of efforts—was able to extract its profits on these countertrades in the form of hard currency.[10]

Informed estimates suggest countertrade accounts for 15 to 20 percent of world trade, although some published reports claim the proportion approaches 40 percent.[11] Countertrade is of particular importance to countries that lack a convertible

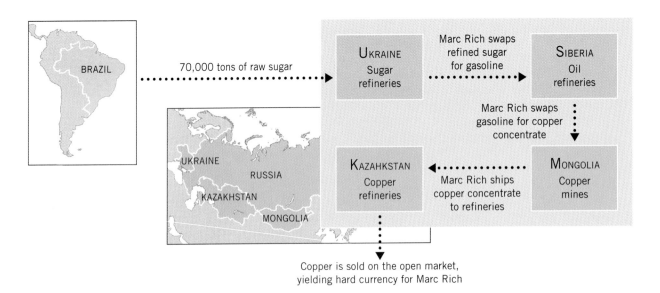

MAP 18.1   **Countertrade by Marc Rich**

currency and is often used as a means of reducing the drain on scarce holdings of convertible foreign currencies. The former Soviet Union, for example, was a major countertrade user. Often goods were traded between the Soviet Union and its former allies using clearinghouse accounts. The former communist countries also engaged in countertrade with capitalist countries.

Table 18.1 summarizes the benefits and costs of the various methods of payment. Techniques that reduce risk for the exporter generally are more expensive. Thus the exporter must decide how much risk it is willing to bear. In dealing with a new and unknown customer, an exporter may choose a safer but more expensive means of securing payment. In dealing with well-established clients, less expensive but riskier payment methods may be acceptable.

TABLE 18.1

Payment Methods for International Trade

METHOD	TIMING OF PAYMENT	TIMING OF DELIVERY OF GOODS	RISK(S) FOR EXPORTER	RISK(S) FOR IMPORTER	AVAILABILITY OF FINANCING FOR EXPORTER	CONDITION(S) FAVORING USE
Payment in advance	Prior to delivery of goods	After payment, when goods arrive in importer's country	None	Exporter may fail to deliver goods	N/A	Exporter has strong bargaining power; importer unknown to exporter
Open account	According to credit terms offered by exporter	When goods arrive in importer's country	Importer may fail to pay account balance	None	Yes, by factoring of accounts receivable	Exporter has complete trust in importer; exporter and importer are part of the same corporate family
Documentary collection	At delivery if sight draft is used; at specified later time if time draft is used	Upon payment if sight draft is used; upon acceptance if time draft is used	Importer may default or fail to accept draft	None	Yes, by discounting draft from its face value	Exporter trusts importer to pay as specified; when risk of default is low
Letter of credit	After terms of letter are fulfilled	According to terms of sales contract and letter of credit	Issuing bank may default; documents may not be prepared correctly	Exporter may honor terms of letter of credit but not terms of sales contract	Yes, by discounting letter from its face value	Exporter lacks knowledge of importer; importer has good credit with local bank
Credit card	According to normal credit card company procedures	When goods arrive in importer's country	None	Exporter fails to deliver goods	N/A	Transaction size is small
Countertrade	When exporter sells countertraded goods	When goods arrive in importer's country	Exporter may not be able to sell countertraded goods	None	No	Importer lacks convertible currency; importer or exporter wants access to foreign distribution network

Financing Trade

Financing terms are often important in closing an international sale. In most industries standard financing arrangements exist, and an international firm must be ready to offer those terms to its foreign customers. Depending on the product, industry practice may be to offer the buyer 30 to 180 days to pay after receipt of an invoice. For the sale of complex products such as commercial aircraft, which will be delivered several years in the future, the payment terms may be much more complicated. They may include down payments, penalty payments for cancellation or late delivery, inflation clauses, and concessionary interest rates for long-term financing. Outside of the Quad countries, capital markets are often not well developed, and local lenders may charge extremely high interest rates, especially to smaller borrowers. Thus exporters with access to low-cost capital can gain a competitive advantage by offering financing to foreign customers who lack access to cheaper financing. Of course, by acting as a lender, the exporter increases the risk of not being paid for its goods. Before deciding to extend credit, the exporter must examine the trade-off between the benefits of increased sales and the higher risks of default.

As noted earlier in this chapter, banks and other commercial lenders often are willing to finance accounts receivable of exporters by purchasing letters of credit or time drafts or factoring open accounts at a discount from face value. Many developed countries supplement the services of these commercial lenders with government-supported financing programs to promote exports. For example, the Export-Import Bank of the United States (Eximbank) offers a working capital guarantee loan program to encourage U.S. exports. Under this program commercial loans made to finance exportable inventory and foreign accounts receivable will be reimbursed 90 percent if the importer defaults on its obligations. Eximbank has made a special effort to serve the needs of small businesses; it approves over $2 billion of support annually for exports by U.S. small businesses. For example, Ormat, Inc., a small Nevada producer of geothermal power generation equipment, beat out Japanese and Italian competitors for a $33.5 million contract with the National Power Corporation of the Philippines, thanks to Eximbank financing.[12] Eximbank also offers medium-term loan guarantees (up to seven years' duration) and long-term guarantees (over 10 years' duration) for telecommunications, electrical generation, and transportation infrastructure projects. However, as "Bringing the World into Focus" indicates, Eximbank financing often is subject to political considerations and sometimes is unavailable to U.S. exporters.

Bringing the World into FOCUS

THE THREE GORGES DAM: IT'S NOT A FEAST FOR U.S. FIRMS

One of the largest and most expensive construction projects in the history of the world is under way in central China. Chinese engineers are busily directing the construction of the 607-foot-high, 1.3-mile-long Three Gorges Dam on the Yangtze River near the village of Sandouping, 3,000 miles from where the river starts at an altitude of 21,700 feet in the Tibetan Plateau and almost 1,000 miles from where it empties into the East China Sea at Shanghai. When the construction work is finished—estimated completion time is the year 2009—the $17-billion Three Gorges Dam will become the world's largest source of hydroelectric power and reduce the likelihood of devastating floods that have claimed 300,000 lives in the past hundred years. Its 18,200-megawatt capacity—the equivalent of 18 nuclear power plants—will dwarf the 12,600-megawatt production of the second largest dam, the Itaipu Dam (on the Parana River between Brazil and Paraguay). Chinese planners believe the dam is critical to providing the electricity needed to power China's economic growth in the new millennium.

Foreign environmentalists, however, are appalled by the project. They argue that the 370-mile-long lake created by the Three Gorges Dam will flood thousands of sites of archaeological value, including 30 Stone Age sites dating back 50,000 years, force 2 million people from their homes, clog the river with sediment, and threaten endangered species such as the Chinese river dolphin. The environmentalists have successfully pressured the World Bank to refuse to provide financing for the dam because of its environmental cost.

U.S. environmentalists have waged a similar lobbying campaign and have convinced the U.S. Export-Import Bank (Eximbank) not to provide export guarantees or working capital loans for U.S. firms seeking Three Gorges contracts. However, as Kermit the Frog once noted, it's not easy being green. Although the U.S. government has chosen not to provide such loans, other countries continue to provide export financing for the massive project. For example, a consortium of three European manufacturers (Siemens, GEC Alsthom, and Asea Brown Boveri Ltd.) won a $740-million contract to supply the dam's power generators; U.S. companies dropped out of the bidding because the Eximbank's decision left them uncompetitive against the European consortium. Because European governments continue to supply export financing for the project, U.S. critics of the Eximbank's policy argue that it does more to promote the profitability of European companies and hurt jobs in the United States than it does to protect the environment.

Sources: "Europe Inc. Muscles Aside the U.S. and Japan in Asia," *Wall Street Journal,* October 2, 1997, p. A15; "China's Three Gorges," *National Geographic,* vol. 192, no. 3, September 1997, pp. 2–33.

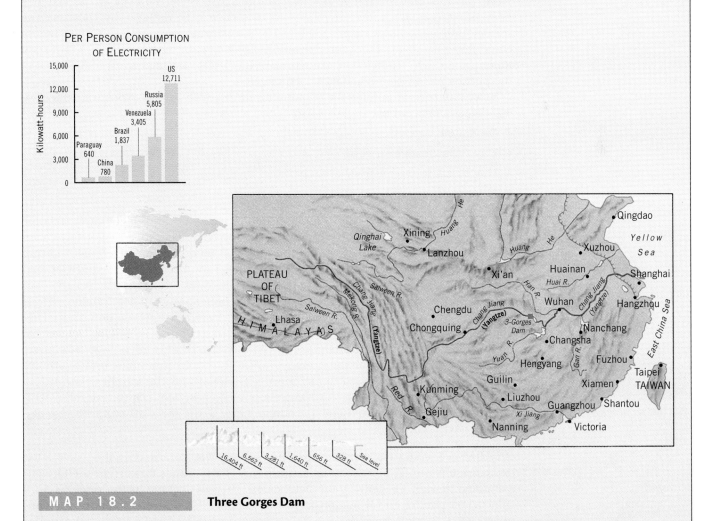

MAP 18.2 **Three Gorges Dam**

› *MANAGING FOREIGN-EXCHANGE RISK*

By using contracts denominated in a foreign currency, KLM and other firms that conduct international trade are exposed to the risk that exchange rate fluctuations may affect the firms adversely. Experts have identified three types of foreign exchange exposure confronting international firms: transaction, translation, and economic.

Transaction Exposure

A firm faces **transaction exposure** when the financial benefits and costs of an international transaction can be affected by exchange rate movements that occur after the firm is legally obligated to complete the transaction. Many typical international business transactions denominated in a foreign currency can lead to transaction exposure, including the following:

- Purchase of goods, services, or assets
- Sales of goods, services, or assets
- Extension of credit
- Borrowing of money

For example, suppose that Saks Fifth Avenue, in order to meet its Christmas needs, agrees on April 10 to buy 5 million Swiss francs' worth of Rolex watches from Rolex's Swiss manufacturer, payable on delivery on October 10. Saks now faces the risk that exchange rate fluctuations will raise the cost of the watches denominated in its home currency—in this case U.S. dollars—by the time the transaction is completed on October 10. (Of course, exchange rate movements could *lower* its costs.) Saks could avoid this risk by contracting in dollars, but then Rolex would face transaction exposure. In most international transactions one of the parties has to bear transaction exposure.

Saks has several options for responding to this transaction exposure, which we will discuss next. In particular it can

- Go naked
- Buy Swiss francs forward
- Buy Swiss franc currency options
- Acquire an offsetting asset

Go Naked. Saks can ignore the transaction exposure and deliberately assume the foreign-exchange risk by choosing to buy the necessary Swiss francs on October 10 when it needs to pay for the watches. By doing so, Saks is betting that the U.S. dollar will rise in value relative to the franc between April and October. This approach has several advantages. First, Saks does not have to tie up any capital in April for the transaction because its only obligation is to pay 5 million Swiss francs on October 10. Second, Saks can benefit from any appreciation of the U.S. dollar versus the Swiss franc. If this happens, Saks can pay its bill on October 10 using fewer dollars than it otherwise would have used. This advantage, of course, can turn sour if the dollar falls relative to the franc. In this unfortunate circumstance Saks would be forced to pay more U.S. dollars for the watches than it had anticipated. By going naked, however, Saks avoids paying fees to any intermediaries, an expense it would incur if it adopted any of the three other strategies, discussed next.

Buy Swiss Francs Forward. Saks has several ways of avoiding the transaction exposure if it wants. For example, it could buy Swiss francs forward in the foreign-exchange market for delivery on October 10, thereby locking in the price in April that it will pay for the 5 million francs in October. This strategy has two advantages. First, Saks guarantees the dollar price it will pay for the imported watches and protects itself from declines in the value of the dollar. Second, it ties up none of its capital until it receives the goods because its only agreement is to buy the currency on October 10 and pay Rolex the 5 million francs on delivery of the watches. On the other hand, with this strategy Saks will miss the opportunity to benefit from any appreciation of the U.S. dollar relative to the Swiss franc. It also will bear some transaction costs in the form of fees and markups charged by the bank through which Saks buys the forward Swiss francs.

A variant of this approach is for Saks to purchase Swiss franc currency futures, as discussed in Chapter 7. Whether the firm chooses to buy currency futures or use the forward market depends on the price of francs in these two markets as well as the relative transaction costs of using the two markets.

Buy Swiss Franc Currency Options.   Alternatively, Saks could acquire a currency options contract allowing it to buy 5 million Swiss francs in October. As discussed in Chapter 7, the purchase of an options contract gives the buyer the opportunity, but not the obligation, to buy a certain currency at a given price in the future. By buying an option, Saks can guarantee it will pay no more for its francs than the price stated in its options contract. When payment for the watches is due in October, Saks can exercise the option if the U.S. dollar has declined in value relative to the franc or let the option expire if the U.S. dollar has increased in value— hence the advantage of an options contract over a forward contract or a futures contract.

Saks is equally protected against depreciation of the dollar by all three types of foreign-exchange transactions; however, it can benefit from an appreciation of the U.S. dollar with an options contract (by letting it expire unused) but not with a forward or a futures contract. The options contract's disadvantage is that it is more expensive than other hedging techniques. Options typically cost from 3.0 to 5.5 percent of the transaction's total value. Accordingly, some multinational corporations (MNCs) prefer currency options to currency futures or forward contracts when hedging their transactions risk because of the "heads I win, tails I don't lose" feature of options. Other MNCs find options too expensive relative to their expected benefit.[13]

Acquire an Offsetting Asset.   Another option for Saks is to neutralize its liability of 5 million Swiss francs pending on October 10 by acquiring an offsetting asset of equivalent size denominated in Swiss francs. For example, suppose the interest rate in April on a six-month certificate of deposit (CD) in Switzerland is 8 percent annually (4 percent for six months). By purchasing a six-month CD in April from a Swiss bank such as Credit Suisse for 4,807,692 francs, Saks will receive 5 million francs (4,807,692 × 1.04) in October when its payment obligation to Rolex comes due. By matching its assets denominated in francs with its liabilities denominated in francs, Saks will suffer no net transaction exposure. The disadvantage of this approach is that Saks has to tie up some of its capital in a Swiss bank until October. Saks will earn interest on the Swiss CD, but it may have been able to earn a higher rate of return if it utilized its capital elsewhere.

Of course, if Saks (or a member of its corporate family) already had an existing franc-denominated CD or receivable due in October, Saks could have used that asset to offset its pending franc-denominated liability to Rolex. Suppose, for example, Saks had licensed a Swiss T-shirt manufacturer to use the Saks logo on its shirts. If Saks expected to receive 5 million Swiss francs in royalties in October from the licensing deal, it could have offset those funds against its October liability to Rolex in order to neutralize its transaction exposure, rather than buying the Swiss CD. If the licensing deal were to yield only 2 million Swiss francs instead of 5 million, Saks could still pair up the two transactions. To eliminate its exposure totally, Saks would then need to cover its *net* transaction exposure of 3 million francs using one of the means just discussed.

STRATEGY	BENEFIT(S)	COST(S)
Go naked	No capital outlay; potential for capital gain if home currency rises in value	Potential for capital loss if home currency falls in value
Buy forward currency	Elimination of transaction exposure; flexibility in size and timing of contract	Fees to banks; lost opportunity for capital gain if home currency rises in value
Buy currency future	Elimination of transaction exposure; ease and relative inexpensiveness of futures contract	Small brokerage fee; inflexibility in size and timing of contract; lost opportunity for capital gain if home currency rises in value
Buy currency option	Elimination of transaction exposure; potential for capital gain if home currency rises in value	Premium paid up front for option because of its "heads I win, tails I don't lose" nature; inflexibility in size and timing of option
Acquire offsetting asset	Elimination of transaction exposure	Effort or expense of arranging offsetting transaction; lost opportunity for capital gain if home currency rises in value

Table 18.2 summarizes the benefits and costs of these different techniques available to manage transaction exposure. Unfortunately, in many developing markets these techniques are unavailable or very expensive to utilize. As a result, many companies operating in such economies choose to go naked. A recent survey conducted by Goldman Sachs of large Indonesian companies with large foreign debts suggested that half of them went naked (i.e., did not hedge these debts), and most of the rest hedged only a small portion of their foreign debts. No doubt the cost of hedging played an important role in their behavior. Consider the case of one Indonesian company that did hedge, Indo-Rama Synthetics. In 1997, just before the Asian currency crisis struck, it borrowed $175 million from a consortium of foreign lenders, payable over a five-year period, to finance an expansion of its operations. Indo-Rama paid a premium of about 10 percent of the face value of the loan to lock in an exchange rate of 2,650 rupiah per dollar for its loan repayments. In hindsight this turned out to be a very fortunate move because within a year the rupiah had fallen in value by over 80 percent against the dollar. Many of Indo-Rama's compatriots, such as Astra International (discussed in Chapter 6), were not so farsighted—or perhaps were unwilling at the time to pay the 10 percent premium to lock in a forward rate for repayment of their debts. There is little doubt that the 1997–98 Asian currency crisis was worsened by the failure of many Asian firms to manage their transaction exposure effectively.[14]

Translation Exposure

As part of reporting its operating results to its shareholders, a firm must integrate the financial statements of its subsidiaries into a set of consolidated financial statements. Problems can arise, however, when the financial statements of a foreign subsidiary are denominated in a foreign currency rather than the firm's home currency. **Translation exposure** is the impact on the firm's consolidated financial statements of fluctuations in exchange rates that change the value of foreign subsidiaries as measured in the parent's currency. If exchange rates were fixed, translation exposure would not exist. (Because translation exposure develops from the need to consolidate financial statements into a common currency, it is often called *accounting exposure*.)

The intricacies of international accounting are covered in Chapter 19, so here we present only a simple example of translation exposure. Suppose GM transfers $15 million to Barclays Bank to open an account for a new British distribution subsidiary, General Motors Import & Distribution Company Ltd., so the subsidiary can begin operations. Further assume that the exchange rate on the day of the transfer is £1 = $1.50. Thus the subsidiary's sole asset is a bank account containing £10 million. If the value of the dollar were to rise to £1 = $1.45, the subsidiary still would have £10 million. However, when GM's accountants prepare the firm's consolidated financial statements, its investment in the British subsidiary would be worth only $14,500,000 (10 million pounds × $1.45). GM thus would suffer a translation loss of $500,000 ($15,000,000 – $14,500,000).

Financial officers can reduce their firm's translation exposure through the use of a balance sheet hedge. A **balance sheet hedge** is created when an international firm matches its assets denominated in a given currency with its liabilities denominated in that same currency. This balancing occurs on a currency-by-currency basis, not on a subsidiary-by-subsidiary basis. For example, Georgia-based AFLAC Inc. is the largest foreign provider of life insurance in Japan. To protect its $1.7-billion investment in Japan from translation exposure, the company utilizes a two-pronged balance sheet hedge. Its Japanese insurance subsidiary owns $1.4 billion of U.S. dollar-denominated securities, reducing the subsidiary's net exposure to changes in the yen-dollar exchange rate to $300 million. To finance its other operations, the parent company borrowed $300 million worth of yen from Japanese banks. Through these transactions AFLAC effectively eliminated its translation exposure to changes in the yen.[15] Procter & Gamble and Owens-Corning follow a similar strategy to reduce their translation exposure.[16]

A controversy exists among financial experts over whether or not firms should protect themselves from translation exposure. Some experts believe managers should ignore translation exposure and instead focus on reducing transaction exposure, arguing that transaction exposure can produce true cash losses to the firm, whereas translation exposure produces only paper, or accounting, losses. This, for example, is the approach used by General Motors.[17] Other experts disagree, stating translation exposure should not be ignored. For instance, firms forced to take write-downs of the value of their foreign subsidiaries may trigger default clauses in their loan contracts if their debt-to-equity ratios rise too high. Further, in AFLAC's case its Japanese operations are so large relative to the rest of the company—over 80 percent of its premium income is generated there—that the company feels compelled to manage its translation exposure.

› Political uncertainty can affect transaction exposure. Many foreign corporations reduced their holdings of Indonesian rupiah in 1998 as protests against the Suharto government spread throughout the country.

Economic Exposure

The third type of foreign-exchange exposure is **economic exposure**, the impact on the value of a firm's operations of unanticipated exchange rate changes. From a strategic perspective the threat of economic exposure deserves close attention from the firm's highest policy makers because it affects virtually every area of operations, including global production, marketing, and financial planning. Unanticipated exchange rate fluctuations may affect a firm's overall sales and profitability in numerous markets. In early 2000, for example, the value of the yen rose in world currency markets. Japanese companies faced the unhappy choice of either raising their local currency prices in their export markets and seeing their market shares erode *or* holding the line on the prices they charged their foreign customers and seeing their profit margins cut.

Long-term investments in property, plant, and equipment are particularly vulnerable to economic exposure, even if they are located in a firm's home country. Honda, for example, faced a double whammy at the beginning of 2000: The yen was rising relative to the U.S. dollar, and the British pound was rising relative to the euro. Each one-yen rise in the yen-dollar exchange rate cost Honda approximately $163 million in profits. To make matters worse, much of Honda's European production was centered in the United Kingdom, making it difficult to sell cars profitably to the 12 euro-zone countries. Honda announced it would reduce sourcing of components from British companies and increase sourcing from euro-zone companies to benefit from the depressed value of the euro. Honda also launched a $500-million program to enhance manufacturing flexibility, increasing the firm's ability to produce different vehicle models on a single assembly line. Such flexibility would allow Honda to shift production of a model from one plant to another in response to demand changes and exchange rate movements.[18] Sony similarly has tried to cut its economic exposure to exchange rate fluctuations by localizing its manufacturing, research and development, and parts procurement to better match its revenue flows and cost flows by country.[19]

As these examples suggest, an important element of managing economic exposure is analyzing likely changes in exchange rates. (Map 18.3 shows exchange rate changes versus the dollar over a five-year period ending in January 2001.) A wide variety of exchange rate experts and expertise is available to assist international businesses in this task. These range from private consultants to the staffs of international banks to the published forecasts of international organizations such as the World Bank and the International Monetary Fund. Exchange rate experts scrutinize many of the factors discussed in Chapter 7. The theory of purchasing power parity, for example, provides guidance regarding long-term trends in exchange rates between countries. In the short term forward exchange rates have been found to be unbiased predictors of future spot rates. Because of the importance of interest arbitrage in establishing equilibrium exchange rates, experts also may forecast countries' monetary policies to predict future currency values. Balance of payments performance also is useful because it provides insights into whether a country's industries are remaining competitive in world markets and whether foreigners' short-term claims on a country are increasing. Prospects for inflation also are carefully assessed because inflation can affect a county's export prospects, demand for imports, and future interest rates.

> MANAGEMENT OF WORKING CAPITAL

Managing foreign-exchange exposure is related to another task that financial officers of international businesses perform—managing working capital, or cash, balances. This task is more complicated for MNCs than for purely domestic firms. An MNC's financial officers must consider the firm's working capital position for each of its foreign subsidiaries and in each currency in which the subsidiaries do business, as well as for the firm as a whole. KLM, for example, normally uses 80 currencies in its operations, and its financial officers must monitor its holdings of each of these currencies. In the process they must balance three corporate financial goals:

1. Minimizing working capital balances
2. Minimizing currency conversion costs
3. Minimizing foreign-exchange risk

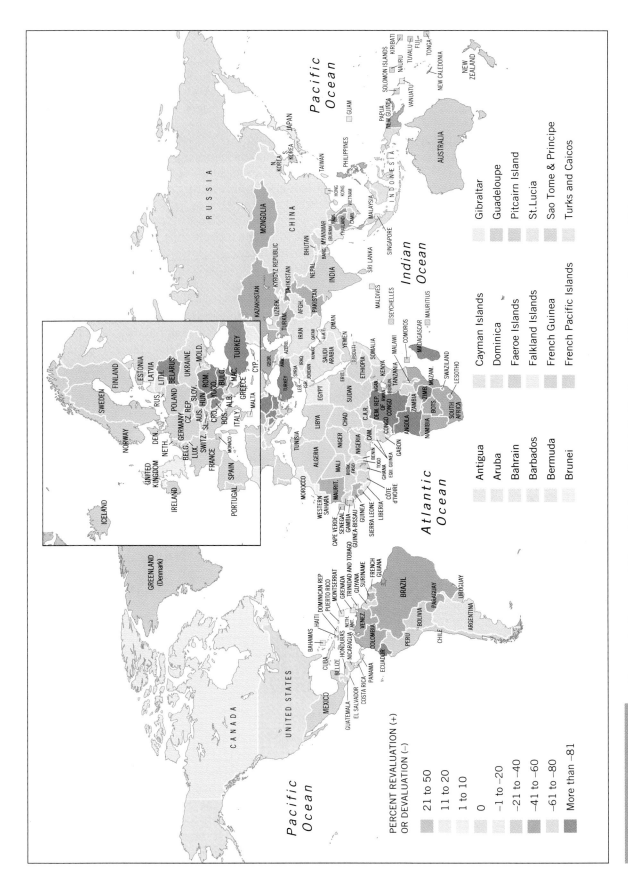

MAP 18.3 Changes in Currency Values Relative to the U.S. Dollar, January 2001 versus January 1996.

PERCENT REVALUATION (+)
OR DEVALUATION (−)

21 to 50
11 to 20
1 to 10
0
−1 to −20
−21 to −40
−41 to −60
−61 to −80
More than −81

Antigua
Aruba
Bahrain
Barbados
Bermuda
Brunei

Cayman Islands
Dominica
Faeroe Islands
Falkland Islands
French Guinea
French Pacific Islands

Gibraltar
Guadeloupe
Pitcairn Island
St.Lucia
Sao Tome & Principe
Turks and Caicos

531

Minimizing Working Capital Balances

Financial officers seek to minimize the firm's working capital balances. Both domestic and international firms must hold working capital for two reasons: to facilitate day-to-day transactions and to cover the firm against unexpected demands for cash. (Note that the term cash refers here to actual cash, checking account balances, and highly liquid marketable securities that normally carry low yields.) Obviously, a firm does not want to run out of cash on hand. Failure to have sufficient cash to pay workers or suppliers can lead, at a minimum, to expensive emergency borrowings or, in the worst case, to an embarrassing loss of reputation that may cause suppliers and lenders to cut off future lines of credit. However, the rate of return on working capital is extremely low, and financial officers prefer to capture higher rates of return, if possible, by investing surplus funds in some other form than cash. Thus they need to balance the firm's needs for cash against the opportunity cost of holding the firm's financial assets in such low-yielding forms.

One technique MNCs can use to minimize their company-wide cash holdings is **centralized cash management**. A centralized cash manager, typically a member of the MNC's corporate treasury staff, coordinates the MNC's worldwide cash flows. Each of the MNC's subsidiaries sends to the centralized cash manager a daily cash report and an analysis of the subsidiary's expected cash balances and needs over the short run, which may range from a week to a month depending on the parent corporation's operating requirements. These reports then are assembled by the centralized cash manager's staff, who uses them to reduce the precautionary balances held by the corporation as a whole and to plan short-term investment and borrowing strategies for the MNC. Instead of each subsidiary holding precautionary, "just in case" cash balances, the staff may direct each subsidiary to send cash in excess of its operational needs to a central corporate bank account. The centralized cash manager will pool these funds, funneling them to subsidiaries when and if emergencies arise. The unexpected need for additional cash by one subsidiary often will be offset by an unexpected excess of cash generated by a second. Thus the central cash manager is able to reduce the precautionary cash balances held by the firm as a whole and thereby reduce the amount of the firm's assets tied up in such a low-yielding form.

Further, the expertise of the centralized cash manager's staff can be used to seek out the best short-term investment opportunities available for the firm's excess cash holdings and to monitor expected changes in the values of foreign currencies. By transferring these tasks from the subsidiaries to the parent corporation, this approach also reduces the number of highly trained, high-salaried financial specialists the corporate family needs. It is more efficient and cost effective to concentrate such financial information gathering and decision making in one unit of the corporation, rather than compelling each subsidiary to develop such expertise in house. (For an innovative solution to working capital problems facing smaller businesses, see "Wiring the World.")

Minimizing Currency Conversion Costs

International businesses face another complication. Their foreign subsidiaries may continually buy and sell parts and finished goods among themselves. For example, Samsung, Korea's largest *chaebol*, has major assembly plants as well as company-owned parts suppliers and distribution companies throughout the world. The constant transfer of parts and finished goods among Samsung subsidiaries generates a blizzard of invoices and a constant need to transfer funds among the subsidiaries' bank accounts. Cumulative bank charges for transferring these funds and converting the currencies involved can be high. For large transactions involving two major currencies, currency conversion fees and expenses may average 0.3 percent of the value of the transaction. For smaller-sized transactions or for transactions involving minor currencies with narrow markets, such fees and expenses can easily be three or four times higher.

COLEFAX AND FOWLER'S CASH FLOW SOLUTION

Smaller businesses also are faced with the task of managing working capital and currency conversion costs. For example, U.K.-based Colefax and Fowler sells its high-priced, trendy wallpaper and fabric to upscale customers and distributors throughout Europe. However, the company's average invoice is only £96, and the bank charges that its French and German customers pay for converting their local currencies into pounds typically total £15 per transaction. In the past these customers often would seek to reduce their currency conversion costs by accumulating their invoices until their total reached some minimum amount. The typical customer paid an average of 86 days after receiving an invoice. This behavior played havoc with Colefax and Fowler's cash flow and increased the size of the working capital loans it needed.

Wanting to improve its cash flow but afraid of losing customers, the firm sought advice from a British financial services consulting firm. That firm recommended that Colefax and Fowler establish bank accounts in each country in which it did significant business. Its customers then could save conversion costs by writing checks denominated in their local currency for deposit in Colefax and Fowler's local accounts.

However, Colefax and Fowler ultimately wants pounds, not French francs, deutsche marks, or euros. So it hired a Dutch firm, EDM, which specializes in handling large numbers of small payments for firms such as the publishers of *Newsweek* and *National Geographic*. EDM contracts with European banks to provide it with daily information about payments made to its clients' accounts. EDM then faxes this account information to its clients so they can credit their customers' accounts. In the case of Colefax and Fowler once local bank balances reach an agreed-on level, EDM instructs the local banks to transfer funds to Colefax and Fowler's British bank account. Although the British firm now bears the currency conversion costs, the new system encourages its customers to buy more goods more often. Moreover, by speeding up the payment process, Colefax and Fowler has saved an estimated £45,000 annually in interest charges on its working capital loans. This savings more than pays for EDM's services.

Source: "Small Cheques, Big Problems," *Financial Times*, June 21, 1994, p. 12.

Let us consider Samsung's operations in just three countries: Mexico, the United Kingdom, and South Korea. As depicted in Figure 18.3, the gross trade among the firm's subsidiaries in the three countries is $21 million (=1 + 3 + 6 + 4 + 5 + 2). (We have denominated their trade in a common currency (U.S. dollars) for simplicity.) If the costs of converting currencies total 0.5 percent of the transactions' value, Samsung would pay 0.5 percent times $21 million, or $105,000, to convert the currencies necessary to settle these transactions among its subsidiaries.

This cost can be cut considerably, however, if the subsidiaries engage in **bilateral netting**, in which two subsidiaries net out their mutual invoices. Consider Samsung's Mexican and British subsidiaries. Rather than have the Mexican subsidiary convert $1 million worth of pesos into pounds and the British subsidiary convert $3 million worth of pounds into pesos, it makes more sense for them to net out the difference. In this case the British subsidiary simply should pay the Mexican subsidiary $2 million in pesos, making them even. In similar fashion the South Korean subsidiary can pay the British subsidiary $2 million worth of pounds ($6 million – $4 million = $2 million), and the Mexican subsidiary can pay the Korean subsidiary $3 million worth of Korean won ($5 million – $2 million = $3 million). By engaging in bilateral netting, Samsung reduces its currency conversion costs to $35,000 (0.5 percent × $7 million).

Currency conversion costs can be reduced further if Samsung engages in **multilateral netting**, which is done among three or more business units. As shown in

FIGURE 18.3

Payment Flows Without Netting

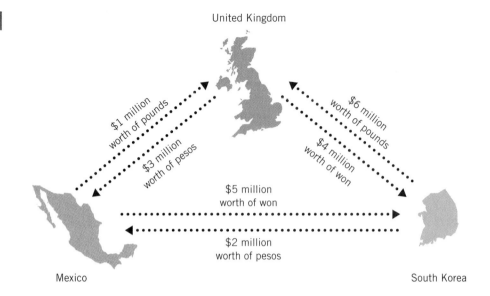

Table 18.3, the British subsidiary owes the equivalent of $7 million to the other two subsidiaries but also is owed $7 million by them. The South Korean subsidiary is owed $9 million but owes $8 million, for a net receipt of $1 million. The Mexican subsidiary is owed $5 million but owes $6 million, for a net debt of $1 million. When accompanied by the appropriate bookkeeping entries, all transactions among the three subsidiaries can be settled by the Mexican subsidiary transferring $1 million worth of won to the South Korean subsidiary. Because only $1 million is being converted physically in the foreign-exchange market and transferred through the banking system, Samsung's conversion costs shrink to $5,000 (0.5 percent × $1 million) as a result of the multilateral netting operation.

In concept multilateral netting differs little from what children do on the playground all the time: "David owes Karen a quarter, but Karen owes LaTisha twenty cents, so David owes LaTisha twenty cents and Karen five cents, and Karen doesn't owe anyone anything." To complicate matters, however, some countries impose restrictions on netting operations to support their local banking industries, which benefit from the fees charged for currency exchange. MNCs wanting to engage in netting operations often have to work around such government-imposed barriers.

Minimizing Foreign-Exchange Risk

Financial officers also typically adjust the mix of currencies that comprise the firm's working capital to minimize foreign-exchange risk. Often firms use a **leads and lags strategy** to try to increase their net holdings of currencies that are

TABLE 18.3

Multilateral Netting in Action (all quantities in millions of U.S. dollar equivalents)

		PAYMENTS OWED BY				
		South Korean Subsidiary	Mexican Subsidiary	British Subsidiary	TOTAL RECEIPTS	NET TRANSFER
	South Korean subsidiary	—	5	4	9	+1
RECEIPTS DUE TO	Mexican subsidiary	2	—	3	5	−1
	British subsidiary	6	1	—	7	0
	TOTAL PAYMENTS	8	6	7	21	

expected to rise in value and to decrease their net holdings of currencies that are expected to fall in value. For example, if the Thai baht were expected to decline in value, the financial officers would try to minimize the MNC's baht-denominated liquid assets, perhaps by demanding quicker (or *leading*) payment on baht-denominated accounts receivable or by reducing baht-denominated bank balances. The officers also would try to increase the firm's baht-denominated short-term liabilities, perhaps by slowing (or *lagging*) payment on baht-denominated accounts payable or by increasing short-term borrowing from Thai banks. Conversely, if the Mexican peso were expected to rise in value, the financial officers would try to maximize the firm's net holdings of pesos through reverse techniques.

Avon adopted these tactics as the Asian currency crisis worsened in late 1997. It bought most of the raw materials needed by its Asian factories locally; the working capital needs of these factories were supplied by local banks with the loans repayable in the local currency. Avon thus increased its liabilities denominated in weakened currencies like the Indonesian rupiah, the Malaysian ringgit, and the Philippine peso. Its Asian subsidiaries were required to repatriate their earnings to headquarters on a weekly basis rather than on the monthly basis they had used previously. In this way Avon minimized its holdings of these vulnerable currencies.[20]

In summary, an MNC's financial officers face a complex task. They must ensure each subsidiary maintains sufficient cash balances to meet expected ordinary day-to-day cash outflows, as well as an appropriate level of precautionary balances to respond quickly to sudden, unexpected increases in cash outflow. They also must balance each subsidiary's expected and unexpected demands for cash against the opportunity cost of holding the firm's financial assets in such low-yielding forms, while simultaneously controlling working capital-related currency conversion costs and foreign-exchange risk. Typically, such tasks are performed by a single unit of the firm, such as the treasury department of the parent corporation. For example, Tate & Lyle, a large British food processor, has followed this approach. Its centralized treasury provides cash management, in-house banking, currency conversion, and foreign-exchange risk management services for all of the company's far-flung subsidiaries. Its centralized treasury handles over $6 billion of intracorporate cash flows a year.[21]

INTERNATIONAL CAPITAL BUDGETING ‹

Another task financial officers of any business face is capital budgeting. Firms have limited funds for investment and often a seemingly endless set of projects from which to choose. Financial officers must establish mechanisms for developing, screening, and selecting projects in which the firm will make significant new investments. Numerous approaches for evaluating investment projects are available, but the most commonly used methods include net present value, internal rate of return, and payback period.

Net Present Value

The net present value approach is based on a basic precept of finance theory that a dollar today is worth more than a dollar in the future. To calculate the net present value of a project, a firm's financial officers estimate the cash flows the project will generate in each time period and then discount them back to the present. For many projects the cash flow in the early years will be negative because the firm must outlay cash for the initial investment and be prepared to suffer start-up operating losses in the first year or two. In later years, of course, the firm expects cash flows to be positive. Financial officers must decide which interest rate, called the *rate of discount*, to use in the calculation, based on the firm's cost of capital. For example, if the firm's cost of capital is 10 percent, then financial officers will use an annual interest rate of 10 percent to discount the cash flows generated by the project through time in order to calculate the present value. The firm will undertake only projects that generate a positive net present value.

› Before investing $500 million in this Chilean copper mine, the financial officers of Vancouver's Placer Dome Inc. carefully analyzed the risks and rewards of the project.

The net present value approach can be used for both domestic and international projects. However, several additional factors must be considered when determining whether to undertake an international project. These factors are risk adjustment, currency selection, and choice of perspective for the calculations.

Risk Adjustment. Because a foreign project may be riskier than a domestic project, international businesses may adjust either the discount rate upward or the expected cash flows downward to account for a higher level of risk. The amount of risk adjustment should reflect the degree of riskiness of operating in the country in question. For example, little if any risk adjustment is needed for Germany because of its political stability, well-respected court system, and superb infrastructure. In contrast, religious conflict in Algeria and civil war in Afghanistan warrant the use of much larger risk adjustments for potential investments in those countries.

Choice of Currency. The determination of the currency in which the project should be evaluated depends on the nature of the investment. If the project is an integral part of the business of an overseas subsidiary, use of the foreign currency is appropriate. For example, GM's German subsidiary Adam Opel AG invested millions of deutsche marks to build a new factory in Eisenach, Germany, in the early 1990s. Constructing the plant was central to Opel's overall business plan, and the subsidiary's financial officers thus made the net present value calculation in deutsche marks. For foreign projects that are more properly viewed as integrated parts of a firm's global procurement strategy, translation into the home country currency may make sense. For example, Houston-based Compaq Computer allocates production between its U.S. and foreign factories as part of an overall strategy of global reduction of production costs. If Compaq invests £10 million to expand the output of its Scottish production facilities, it should calculate the project's net present value in U.S. dollars instead of pounds. To do this, it must estimate revenues and costs for the project and then convert them into dollars. It also must account for any expected changes in the exchange rate between the dollar and the pound over the life of the project.

Whose Perspective: Parent's or Project's? Another factor is determining whether the cash flows that contribute to the net present value of the capital investment should be evaluated from the perspective of the parent or that of the individual project. In practice, some international businesses analyze the cash flows of the individual project, others focus on the project's impact on the parent, and others do both.[22]

The cash flows to the parent can differ from those to the project for several reasons. MNCs often impose arbitrary accounting charges on the revenues of their operating units for the units' use of corporate trademarks or to cover general corporate overhead. These arbitrary charges may reduce the *perceived* cash flows generated by the project but not the *real* cash flows returned to the parent. For example, suppose that when the corporate parent's accountants are calculating a subsidiary's profitability, they routinely assess a 5 percent fee against revenues for general corporate and administrative expenses. This technique may be a reasonable mechanism for allocating general corporate expenses across all the firm's operations. The 5 percent charge, however, does not represent a true drain on the cash flow generated by the subsidiary. Thus the charge should be ignored in the calculation of the net present value to the parent of a project the subsidiary proposes. Similarly, fees assessed against the subsidiary for the use of corporate trademarks, brand names, or patents should not be considered in the net present value calculation because the parent firm incurs no additional costs regardless of whether the subsidiary undertakes the project.

Financial officers also must consider any governmental restrictions on currency movements that would affect the firm's ability to repatriate profits when it wants. A project proposed by a foreign subsidiary may be enormously profitable, but if the profits can never be repatriated to the parent, the project may not be desirable from the perspective of the parent and its shareholders. The importance of currency controls in determining the attractiveness of a project also may be a function of the parent's overall strategy. For example, PepsiCo has made a long-term commitment to the Ukrainian soft-drink market. Any current Ukrainian restrictions on profit repatriation are of little concern to PepsiCo and its shareholders because the firm expects to increase its investments in the country in the short and medium term. However, PepsiCo's shareholders would be concerned if the firm were never allowed to repatriate profits from its Ukrainian operations.

Internal Rate of Return

A second approach commonly used for evaluating investment projects is to calculate the internal rate of return. With this approach financial officers first estimate the cash flows generated by each project under consideration in each time period, as in the net present value analysis. They then calculate the interest rate—called the *internal rate of return*—that makes the net present value of the project just equal to zero. As with the net present value approach, the financial officers must adjust their calculations for any accounting charges that have no cash flow implications (intracorporate licensing fees, overhead charges for general corporate and administrative expenses, and so on). They then compare the project's internal rate of return with the **hurdle rate**—the minimum rate of return the firm finds acceptable for its capital investments. The hurdle rate may vary by country to account for differences in risk. The firm will undertake only projects for which the internal rate of return is higher than the hurdle rate.

Payback Period

A third approach for assessing and selecting projects is to calculate a project's **payback period**—the number of years it will take the firm to recover, or pay back, the original cash investment from the project's earnings. Vancouver's Placer Dome, Inc., often uses a payback approach to evaluate mining investments, such as a proposed $500-million investment in a Chilean copper mine as part of a joint venture with Finland's Outokumpu OY. After determining this project's payback period would be less than five years, Placer decided to proceed with the deal.

The payback period technique has the virtue of simplicity: All one needs is simple arithmetic to calculate the payback period. This approach ignores, however, the profits generated by the investment in the longer run. A project that earns large early profits but whose later profits diminish steadily over time may be selected over a project that suffers initial start-up losses but makes large continuous profits after that.

Because of its simplicity, many firms use the payback period technique for a quick-and-dirty screening of projects and then follow with a more sophisticated method for further analysis of those projects that pass the preliminary screening.[23] A firm may choose different payback criteria for international projects than for domestic ones. Here too adjustments must be made to eliminate intracorporate charges that have no real effect on corporate cash flows.

SOURCES OF INTERNATIONAL INVESTMENT CAPITAL ‹

Firms use capital budgeting techniques to allocate their financial resources toward those domestic and international projects that promise the highest rates of return. Having identified such profitable opportunities, firms must secure sufficient capital to fund them, from either internal or external sources. In doing so, an international business wants to minimize the worldwide cost of its capital, while also minimizing its foreign-exchange risk, political risk, and global tax burden.[24]

Internal Sources of Investment Capital

One source of investment capital for international businesses is the cash flows generated internally (for example, profits from operations and noncash expenses such as depreciation and amortization) by the parent firm and its various subsidiaries. The amount from such sources is significant: In 1999 foreign subsidiaries of U.S.-owned firms earned $118.8 billion, and U.S. subsidiaries of foreign-owned parents earned $56.1 billion.[25] Internal cash flows thus represent an important source of capital for funding subsidiaries' investment projects.

Subject to legal constraints, the parent firm may use the cash flow generated by any subsidiary to fund the investment projects of any member of the corporate family. The corporate parent may access the cash flow directly via the subsidiary's dividend payments to the parent. The parent then can channel those funds to another subsidiary through either a loan or additional equity investments in that subsidiary. Alternatively, one subsidiary can lend funds directly to a second subsidiary. Figure 18.4 summarizes the various internal sources of capital available to the parent and its subsidiaries.

Two legal constraints may affect the parent's ability to shift funds among its subsidiaries. First, if the subsidiary is not wholly owned by the parent, the parent must respect the rights of the subsidiary's other shareholders. Any intracorporate transfers of funds must be done on a fair-market basis. This ensures the parent does not siphon off the subsidiary's profits through self-dealing, thereby harming the other shareholders' interests. If the subsidiary is wholly owned, transfers of funds are not a problem. Second, some countries impose restrictions on the repatriation of profits, thus blocking intracorporate transfers of funds. However, a parent may find that although it cannot shift funds in the form of dividends to itself, it can shift funds in the form of loans to other subsidiaries. Alternatively, the parent may be able to recapture funds from the subsidiary by charging licensing fees for the use of the parent's brand names, trademarks, copyrights, or patents or by imposing fees for general corporate or administrative services. Such payments are not trivial. In 1999 foreign subsidiaries paid their U.S.-owned parents $36.5 billion in royalties and licensing fees, and U.S. subsidiaries paid their foreign-owned parents $13.3 billion for the same purpose.[26] (Please note that we do not mean to imply that any of these fees were paid to evade host country restrictions on currency movements.)

A parent corporation also may shift funds between its operating units by adjusting the transfer prices paid for goods and services in intracorporate transactions between a subsidiary and other branches of the corporate family. Suppose sub-

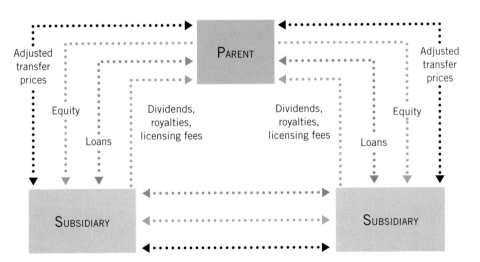

FIGURE 18.4

Internal Sources of Capital for International Businesses

sidiary B operates in a country that restricts profit repatriation, whereas subsidiary A does not. By raising the price charged by subsidiary A for a good purchased by subsidiary B, the MNC can transfer funds from B to A. (Chapter 19 discusses the income tax implications of these pricing policies and the pitfalls awaiting firms that aggressively manipulate transfer prices.) Firms must be aware that transfer-pricing policies are least controversial when used between two wholly owned subsidiaries. Otherwise, the parent may be placing itself in the position of either defrauding the outside investors (in the case of subsidiary B) or enriching them (in the case of subsidiary A) at the expense of its own shareholders.

Although such intracorporate transfers of funds may theoretically benefit the entire firm, they can create serious problems at the subsidiary and managerial levels. From the parent's perspective shifting cash flows from subsidiary to parent may be beneficial. However, it may cause operational problems and increased expenses for the subsidiary. The parent may consider it wise policy to siphon off the subsidiary's working capital and reduce its reported profitability by inflating royalty fees, administrative charges, or other transfer prices. Yet such approaches may result in a misleading picture of the subsidiary's performance in the marketplace. If the parent rewards managerial performance without making adjustments for these financial manipulations, morale among the subsidiary's managers may plummet, to the detriment of the parent.

External Sources of Investment Capital

When raising external financing for their investment projects, international businesses may choose from a rich source of debt and equity alternatives. Investment bankers, such as Goldman Sachs, and securities firms, such as Merrill Lynch and Nomura, can help firms acquire capital from external sources. For example, if a firm wants to increase its equity base, such an intermediary can place the firm's stock with investors in the home country, in the host country, or in other countries. To facilitate the raising of equity internationally, many MNCs list their common stock on stock markets in several different countries. For example, KLM shares are listed on the New York, Amsterdam, Brussels, and Frankfurt stock exchanges. Sony's stock is listed on the New York, Pacific, Chicago, Toronto, London, Paris, Frankfurt, Dusseldorf, Brussels, Antwerp, Vienna, and Swiss stock exchanges, as well as on five Japanese stock exchanges. Through multiple foreign listings international businesses assure foreign investors they can easily dispose of their shares should the need arise.

International firms also have many opportunities to borrow funds internationally on either a short-term or a long-term basis. They may shop for the best credit terms in their home country market, in the host country market, or in other markets. For example, consider New Jersey's Baltek Corporation, which annually produces $30 million worth of balsa wood products at its factory in Ecuador. Baltek relied on local Ecuadorian banks to finance its expansion into shrimp farming in the Gulf of Guayaquil. The firm found those banks more eager for its business than U.S. banks were—an example of the advantages of being a big fish in a small pond.[27] Larger MNCs may rely on syndicated short- and medium-term loans in which a consortium of international banks and pension fund managers join together to provide the capital. Often these syndicated loans use Eurocurrencies because the absence of expensive central bank regulations reduces the cost of Eurocurrency-based loans. MNCs also may secure longer-term loans in the form of home country bonds, foreign bonds, and Eurobonds, as discussed in Chapter 7.

Securities firms and investment banks are continually developing innovative financing techniques to reduce the costs of borrowing for their MNC clients or to exploit gaps in national financial regulations.[28] For example, an MNC may issue dual-currency bonds, whereby it borrows money and pays interest in one currency but repays the principal in a second currency. Alternatively, bonds may be denominated as a basket of several currencies or be redeemable in gold. Some firms get very creative. For instance, in the early 1990s The Walt Disney Company issued

$400 million in Eurobonds that had a different twist: Their interest rate depended on the success of 13 Disney movies. Investors were guaranteed at least a 3 percent rate, with a possible return of 13.5 percent. Comparable quality bonds were yielding only 7 to 8 percent. Eager investors snapped up the bonds, betting that *The Muppet Christmas Carol* and other Disney movies would be box office hits.[29] Pleased with its ability to shift some movie-making risks to the bondholders through low minimum interest rates, several years later Disney offered a similar note linked to a new set of motion pictures.[30]

A particularly important facet of the international capital market is the **swap market**, in which two firms can exchange their financial obligations. Swaps are undertaken to change the cost and nature of a firm's interest obligations or to change the currency in which its debt is denominated. For example, suppose firm A has a fixed-rate obligation but prefers a floating-rate one, whereas firm B has a floating-rate obligation and wants a fixed-rate one. The two firms can swap their obligations. As noted by John Grout, a financial officer at Cadbury Schweppes, "The advantage of the swap market is that it allows you to adjust exposure profiles without having to undo the underlying transactions."[31] Often an international bank will facilitate such swaps by acting as a broker or by undertaking half of a swap for its own account.

MNCs also often engage in currency swaps to shift their interest and payment obligations from a less preferred currency to a more preferred one. An MNC may consider its net obligations in one currency to be too large or may expect exchange rate fluctuations to adversely affect its loan repayment costs. A swap may be arranged between two firms that have differing currency preferences. International banks play a key role in the currency swap market. Because they continually monitor foreign-exchange markets as well as their net currency exposures, they usually can accommodate any MNC's currency swap needs. Most international banks engage in currency swaps with corporate clients on an ongoing basis.

CHAPTER REVIEW

Summary

International firms face financial management challenges that are far more complex than those confronting purely domestic firms. Conflicts may arise between exporters and importers over the currency to use in invoicing international transactions. Exporting firms often find it difficult to check the creditworthiness of their foreign customers. Also, obtaining payment for goods from foreign customers may be more difficult because of greater geographical distances, differing legal systems, and unfamiliar business customs. Fortunately, many methods of payment have been developed over the centuries, including payment in advance, open accounts, letters of credit, documentary collection, credit cards, and countertrade.

International firms must strive to minimize the impact of exchange rate fluctuations on the firms' operations. Three main types of exchange rate exposure exist. Transaction exposure refers to the impact of exchange rate fluctuations on the profitability of a business transaction denominated in a foreign currency. Translation exposure reflects the impact of exchange rate fluctuations on the book value of foreign operations in a firm's accounting records. Economic exposure is the impact unanticipated exchange rate movements have on the value of the firm's operations.

Management of working capital balances presents international businesses with unique challenges. A firm and each of its operating subsidiaries must have sufficient cash to facilitate day-to-day operations and to meet unexpected demands for cash. Also, the firm must monitor its holdings of each currency in which it and its subsidiaries do business. MNCs often use centralized cash management and currency netting operations to control their working capital balances, reduce currency conversion costs, and minimize their exposure to adverse changes in exchange rates.

Financial officers of international firms must adjust capital budgeting techniques to meet the unique requirements of international business. Standard investment evaluation techniques, such as net present value, internal rate of return, and payback period analysis, must be changed to account for differences in risk, government restrictions on currency movements, and various payments between the parent firm and its foreign subsidiaries that do not affect net cash flows generated by an investment project.

Finally, financial officers must look worldwide for low-cost sources of capital. Ongoing operations of the parent firm and its foreign subsidiaries are often an important internal source of investment capital. Well-developed international debt and equity markets can provide external sources of such capital. Also, international businesses often use the swap market to reduce their exposure to adverse changes in currency values or interest rates.

Review Questions

1. What special problems arise in financing and arranging payment for international transactions?
2. What are the major methods of payment used for international transactions?
3. What are the different types of letters of credit?
4. How do a time draft and a sight draft differ? How do a trade acceptance and a banker's acceptance differ?
5. How do the various types of countertrade arrangements differ from each other?
6. What techniques are available to reduce transaction exposure? Discuss each.
7. What is translation exposure? What effect does a balance sheet hedge have on translation exposure?
8. Why do MNCs engage in currency netting operations?
9. What capital budgeting techniques are available to international businesses?
10. What is the difference between an interest rate swap and a currency swap?

Questions for Discussion

1. What are the advantages and disadvantages of each method of payment for international transactions from the exporter's perspective?
2. Which type of letter of credit is most preferable from the exporter's point of view?
3. Why do firms use countertrade? What problems do they face when they do?
4. How does capital budgeting for international projects differ from that for domestic projects?
5. "Bringing the World into Focus" on page 525 noted that some U.S. companies are losing contracts to supply the Three Gorges Dam to European competitors because of the lack of support from the U.S. Export-Import Bank. Should the Eximbank change its policy to aid U.S. exporters? Or should the Eximbank maintain its pro-environment stance?
6. The government of Colefax and Fowler's home country, the United Kingdom, has chosen not to be a charter participant in the European Union's (EU's) single-currency scheme (see "Wiring the World," p. 533). Will this put Colefax and Fowler at a disadvantage in competing for business in other EU countries? If so, is there anything the company can do to reduce its disadvantage?

BUILDING GLOBAL SKILLS

Consider Belgian Lace Products (BLP), a hypothetical table linens manufacturer. BLP consists of a parent corporation, a wholly owned manufacturing subsidiary in Belgium, and four wholly owned distribution subsidiaries in Belgium, the United Kingdom, Japan, and the United States. Its manufacturing subsidiary buys inputs from various suppliers, manufactures high-quality lace napkins and tablecloths, and sells the output to the four BLP-owned distribution subsidiaries. The four distribution subsidiaries in turn sell the products to retail customers in the subsidiaries' marketing areas. The distribution subsidiaries buy certain inputs, such as labor, warehouse space, electricity, and computers, from outside suppliers as well.

The following summarizes typical monthly transactions for each of the BLP operating units (note that the symbol for the euro is €):

Manufacturing Subsidiary

Sales to Belgian distribution subsidiary: €15,000
Sales to British distribution subsidiary: €12,500
Sales to Japanese distribution subsidiary: €17,500
Sales to U.S. distribution subsidiary: €11,250
Costs of inputs purchased from Belgian suppliers: €7,500
Costs of inputs purchased from British suppliers: £25,000
Costs of inputs purchased from Japanese suppliers: ¥3,000,000
Costs of inputs purchased from U.S. suppliers: $5,000

Belgian Distribution Subsidiary

Sales to retail customers: €50,000
Payments to BLP manufacturing subsidiary: €15,000
Payments to external suppliers: €750 and £10,000

British Distribution Subsidiary

Sales to retail customers: £75,000
Payments to BLP manufacturing subsidiary: €12,500
Payments to external suppliers: £5,000, €1,000, and $9,000

Japanese Distribution Subsidiary

Sales to retail customers: ¥5,000,000
Payments to BLP manufacturing subsidiary: €17,500
Payments to external suppliers: ¥3,000,000 and $8,000

U.S. Distribution Subsidiary

Sales to retail customers: $40,000
Payments to BLP manufacturing subsidiary: €11,250
Payments to external suppliers: $10,000 and ¥300,000

Exchange Rates

€1.33 = £1
€1 = $1.00
€1 = ¥120

Use the above information to answer the following questions:

1. Calculate the profitability of each of BLP's five subsidiaries. (Because BLP is Belgian, perform the calculations in terms of euros, which Belgium will use as its national currency beginning in 2002.) Are any of the subsidiaries unprofitable? On the basis of the information provided, would you recommend shutting down an unprofitable subsidiary? Why or why not?
2. Suppose it costs each subsidiary 1 percent of the transaction amount each time it converts its home currency into another

currency to pay its suppliers. Develop a strategy by which BLP as a corporation can reduce its total currency conversion costs. Suppose your strategy costs BLP 400 euros per month to implement. Should the firm still adopt your approach?

3. If the United Kingdom decided to join the EU's single-currency bloc and use the euro, what effect would this have on BLP? What effect would it have on the benefits and costs of the strategy you developed to reduce BLP's currency conversion costs?

WORKING WITH THE WEB: BUILDING GLOBAL INTERNET SKILLS

Export Financing and the Internet

The promotion of exports is important to the economic health of most countries. However, many small businesses ignore export opportunities because the businesses do not understand how they will be paid for their goods: Letters of credit, time drafts, bills of lading, and the like all seem very confusing. If bankers can allay these fears and encourage small businesses to export, the bankers stand to gain substantial revenues from providing trade financing to these new exporters.

Suppose you are on the marketing staff of a regional bank that has decided to target the small-business trade-financing market. One component of the bank's strategy is to develop a Web site explaining to small businesses how the bank can help them export their goods and get paid for their exports. You have been assigned to the team that will develop the bank's Web site and have been given two specific tasks. First, you have been asked to assess what information inexperienced exporters need about trade financing. Second, you have been asked to surf other banks' Web sites and report back to the team which ones do an effective job of providing useful and understandable information to new exporters. After you have concluded these tasks, write a brief memo reporting your findings to the members of your team. Feel free to attach examples of effective Web sites to your memo.

The textbook's Web site provides linkages to several Web sites that may be helpful for this assignment.

 WE INVITE YOU TO VISIT THIS BOOK'S COMPANION WEB SITE AT www.prenhall.com/griffin

IN THE NEWS

Managing exchange rate risk is an important task facing a firm's chief financial officer. Visit the *Financial Times*' Web site, *www.ft.com*, and search for articles dealing with exchange rate risk, hedging, and treasury management. How are recent changes in the financial and foreign-exchange markets affecting the actions of chief financial officers? Do the challenges vary depending on what the firm's home country is?

CLOSING CASE

Janssen Pharmaceutica Cures Its Currency Ills

Janssen Pharmaceutica, started by Dr. Paul Janssen in 1953, is one of the most innovative and successful firms in the pharmaceutical industry. A subsidiary of Johnson & Johnson since 1961, Janssen Pharmaceutica today employs 12,000 people worldwide. About 3,300 work in or near Beerse, the Belgian city where the firm was born and is headquartered.

Janssen's competitive strength lies in new drug development. Since 1970 only one firm in the world ranked higher than Janssen in the number of new drugs developed to cure humankind's ills. The Janssen-developed drugs Risperdal, Propulsid, and Itrizole, for example, combat such diverse medical problems as schizophrenia, nighttime heartburn, and fungal infections.

Janssen is also an important innovator in an area very different from pharmaceuticals: management of corporate treasury operations. Like many European firms, Janssen has production facilities and sales operations throughout Western Europe, the Americas, and Asia. It also purchases inputs and services from a wide variety of suppliers outside Belgium. Before 1984 handling the numerous incoming and outgoing cross-border invoices generated by its operations was very expensive. Much working capital was tied up as each of the firm's 32 far-flung subsidiaries maintained balances in their checking accounts sufficient to handle day-to-day operating needs and to protect against unexpected demands for cash. Further, every time a Janssen subsidiary paid an invoice denominated in a foreign currency, it paid currency conversion charges that averaged 0.5 percent of the amount in question.

In 1983 Belgium sought to improve the international competitiveness of its firms by authorizing the creation of so-called *coordination centers* to reduce the costs of corporate treasury activities. To qualify to establish a coordination center, a company had to have affiliates in at least four countries, to have sales of at least $300 million, and to employ a minimum of 10 employees in its Belgian coordination center. Concomitant changes in Belgian tax laws reduced the corporate income tax burdens on coordination centers to near zero. By 1999 over 400 coordination centers had been established in Belgium, employing more than 8,000 highly trained professionals. The coordination centers have increased demand in Belgium for such corporate support services as accounting, auditing, legal research, and investment banking. Users resemble a who's who of international commerce, including such firms as IBM, BP Amoco, Monsanto, ABB Asea Brown Boveri, and Cable & Wireless PLC. About 30 percent of the coordination centers are owned by U.S. MNCs, 15 percent by Belgian MNCs, and 46 percent by European MNCs headquartered outside of Belgium.

Janssen Pharmaceutica moved quickly to take advantage of the Belgian law by establishing a coordination center in June 1984. This center, a separately incorporated and wholly owned subsidiary of Janssen, provides a variety of financial services for the firm and its subsidiaries. Initially the coordination center focused on **treasury management**—the management of financial flows and of the currency and interest-rate risks associated with these flows. This mission involved three objectives:

1. Identify short- and medium-term financial risks on a worldwide basis.
2. Quantify such risks and recommend appropriate responses to Janssen's executives.
3. Manage and control these financial exposures on a worldwide basis subject to J&J's corporate rules and procedures (which encourage hedging but discourage speculation).

The center's treasury management activities include acting as a centralized cash manager and performing currency netting operations for the Janssen group of companies, thereby lowering the levels of cash balances held by the group and reducing the group's aggregate currency conversion costs. As Janssen has learned to use the center more efficiently, the center's duties have expanded. It now performs all currency and interest rate exposure management and hedging activities for the Janssen group.

The coordination center also has taken over the bank management function. To benefit the whole group, the center established checking accounts in the various countries in which Janssen does business. Suppose Janssen's Swiss subsidiary buys printer cartridges from a British office supply wholesaler. The invoice (denominated in

British pounds) received by the Swiss subsidiary will be sent to the coordination center, which will pay the invoice from its account at a British bank. By dealing with the banking system of only one country, Janssen can predict more reliably when checks will be debited or credited to its accounts. More important, however, this technique reduces currency conversion costs for the group as a whole. The Swiss subsidiary, by shifting the responsibility for obtaining pounds to the coordination center, avoids the cost of converting Swiss francs into British pounds. The coordination center often can obtain the necessary pounds to pay British suppliers without converting any currencies. It does this by depositing pound-denominated revenues received by other Janssen subsidiaries into the coordination center's British bank account. This netting of payments and receipts on a corporate basis substantially reduces the need to convert currencies. The cumulative savings of currency conversion fees on hundreds of thousands of incoming and outgoing invoices amount to millions of Belgian francs each year.

The managers of each Janssen subsidiary of course want credit for the revenues their subsidiary generates. Thus at the end of the monthly accounting period, the coordination center nets out payments and receipts in all the currencies in which the subsidiary does business. The center then sends each subsidiary either a *single* check or a *single* invoice, denominated in its local currency, that reflects the subsidiary's net position. Only 35 employees perform this monthly miracle for the Janssen group, although, as you can imagine, they work with an extremely sophisticated computer and telecommunications network.

In addition, the coordination center acts as an internal bank for the Janssen group. Its specialists interact continuously with the banking community worldwide, seeking the highest short-term interest rates for the group's excess cash balances. The center often can locate sources of low-cost loans for the Janssen subsidiaries. If a subsidiary needs to borrow money, the coordination center offers to match the best local terms available to that subsidiary. The center uses a standardized loan document and so can offer 24-hour turnaround time on loan approvals. It also allocates to the borrowing subsidiary any tax benefits generated by the transaction.

As Janssen's coordination center honed its treasury management, bank management, and lending skills, J&J's corporate managers recognized that Janssen's expertise could be used to benefit the rest of the corporate family. Today Janssen's coordination center provides financial services for the entire J&J family, with one significant change. When it served only the Janssen group, the center focused on managing exchange rate risk in terms of the Belgian franc. However, because J&J is a U.S. firm, the center now manages exchange rate risk in terms of the U.S. dollar.[32]

Case Questions

1. In essence, to qualify for the tax breaks offered to a Belgian coordination center, a firm must be an MNC. Why would Belgium limit these tax breaks to multinationals? Are Belgian authorities happy that Janssen's coordination center is benefiting all of J&J's worldwide operations?
2. What are the advantages of having the Janssen coordination center act for J&J worldwide? Are there any disadvantages?
3. Can you think of any other strategies for reducing currency conversion costs that could be used by firms operating in Europe?

CHAPTER

Mr. Anchovy Was Wrong

A famous Monty Python sketch involves the career dilemma of a Mr. Anchovy, a London-based chartered accountant who finds his chosen profession, "Dull. Dull. My God it's dull, it's so desperately dull and tedious and stuffy and boring and des-per-ate-ly dull." He decides he wants to become a lion tamer, but because of the sheltered life he has led, he has confused anteaters with lions. Upon learning the difference, he decides not to rush into a new career as a lion tamer.

That may or may not be an accurate description of the life of an average English accountant in 1969,

"What do you do for fun in Ulan Bator? . . . hunt wolves on the Mongolian steppe"

when this comedy sketch was first shown on British television. It certainly is not an accurate description of the market for international accounting services today, which is anything but dull. If you are doubtful, just ask Iain Gerrard, a 33-year-old Arthur Andersen partner in Perth, Australia. As a result of a World Bank contract won by his firm, for the past three years he has been helping Erdenet, the biggest company in Mongolia, to modernize its accounting system. This task is critical to the Mongolian economy because Erdenet accounts for 65 percent of the country's exports. And what do you do for fun in Ulan Bator, where the company is headquartered? In winter Gerrard likes to go hunt-

544

International Accounting and Taxation

O B J E C T I V E S

After studying this chapter, you should be able to:

❯ Discuss the various factors that influence the accounting systems countries adopt.

❯ Describe the impact these national accounting differences have on international firms.

❯ Analyze the benefits to international firms of harmonizing differences in national accounting systems.

❯ Describe the accounting procedures used by U.S. firms engaged in international business.

❯ Identify the major international taxation issues affecting international businesses.

❯ Discuss the taxation of foreign income by the U.S. government.

❯ Assess the techniques available to resolve tax conflicts among countries.

ing wolves on the frozen Mongolian steppe, an activity he never dreamed of as a boy growing up in sunny Western Australia.

The accounting industry is dominated by five firms prowling the global marketplace, devouring local competitors, and fighting for the lion's share of one of the fastest growing international service markets. These firms, collectively referred to as the Big Five, together provide accounting, auditing, and consulting services for the vast majority of the world's largest multinational corporations (MNCs). All of the Big Five have enjoyed double-digit growth rates in recent years.

The biggest of the Big Five is PricewaterhouseCoopers, whose 9,000 partners and 160,000 employees generated $17.3 billion in accounting, auditing, and consulting revenues in 1999. PricewaterhouseCooper emerged from a 1998 merger between accounting giants Price Waterhouse and Coopers & Lybrand. Coopers & Lybrand in turn was the product of a 1957 merger among Cooper Brothers & Co. of the United Kingdom, McDonald, Currie and Co. of Canada, and Lybrand, Ross Bros. & Montgomery of the United States.

Megamergers are nothing new in this industry. KPMG Peat Marwick, the second largest of the Big Five (1999 revenues of $12.2 billion), was formed by the 1987 merger of U.S.-based Peat Marwick Mitchell and European-based

Klynveld Main Goerdeler (KMG). Deloitte Touche Tohmatsu was created by the 1989 merger of Deloitte Haskins & Sells with Touche Ross & Company and its Japanese affiliate, Tohmatsu & Co. Similarly, Ernst & Young resulted from the 1989 merger of Ernst & Whinney and Arthur Young. Ernst & Whinney itself was the result of a merger between a U.S. and a U.K. accounting firm shortly after the end of World War II.

This trend toward consolidation can be explained in part by the growth of international business. As their clients have globalized, accounting firms have felt compelled to expand their operations to meet their clients' needs—as well as to retain their business. To navigate among the various accounting regulations and tax laws of the nations in which its MNC clients do business, an accounting firm must be able to offer advice to its clients based on the operating needs of each of their foreign subsidiaries and of the parents themselves. The most effective way of providing this service is to have an office in each country in which the clients do business. By merging with existing accounting firms, the Big Five have gained quick access to many domestic markets as well as to the existing client bases of the acquired firms.

The Big Five are well positioned to continue benefiting from the increase in international business activity. Their clients' international activities are booming, so their international accounting needs also are skyrocketing. That does not mean, however, that managers of the Big Five can afford to relax. They face the daunting challenge of managing their explosive growth, maintaining the quality of services they offer their clients, and nurturing and keeping their employees happy. For example, attitudes toward compensation vary considerably among business cultures; the Big Five must keep group-oriented Japanese partners happy while simultaneously satisfying "what's in it for me" U.S. partners, a problem we noted in Chapter 4. With the boom in international trade and investment, and the resultant need of MNCs to understand the complexities and differences in the accounting standards among countries, these accounting giants face a rosy future in spite of these challenges.

The goal of an accounting system is to identify, measure, and communicate "economic information to permit informed judgments and decisions by users of the information."[1] These users are numerous. The accounting system provides operational information to line managers and financial performance data to top executives to help them make marketing, financial, and strategic decisions. Investors use information about a firm's performance to determine whether to purchase its stock and debt instruments. The government uses this information to assess the firm's tax burdens and to regulate the issuance of its securities.

Accounting has been called the "language of business." Unfortunately for international firms, it is far from being a lingua franca. The accounting tasks of international businesses are much more complex than those of domestic firms. The accounting system of a purely domestic firm must meet the professional and regulatory standards of its home country. An MNC and its subsidiaries, however, must meet the sometimes contradictory standards of all the countries in which they operate. To effectively manage and control their operations, local managers need accounting information prepared according to local accounting concepts and denominated in the local currency. However, for corporate officers to assess a foreign subsidiary's performance and value, the subsidiary's accounting records must be translated into the parent's home currency using accounting concepts and procedures detailed by the parent. Investors around the world, seeking the highest possible returns on their capital, must be able to interpret the firm's track record, even though the firm may be using a currency and an accounting system different from their own. The firm also will have to pay taxes to the countries in which it does business based on the accounting statements it develops in these countries. Further, when a parent corporation attempts to integrate the accounting records of its subsidiaries to create consolidated financial statements, additional complexities arise because of changes in the value of the host and home currencies over time.

This chapter discusses how international businesses deal with national differences in accounting and taxation systems. It first examines the causes of these differences and describes countries' attempts to reduce them. It goes on to describe how accountants of international businesses treat international business transactions in the firms' income statements and balance sheets. Finally, it discusses the impact of national taxation policies on international business and the strategies international firms adopt to reduce their global tax burdens.

NATIONAL DIFFERENCES IN ACCOUNTING <

An international business must develop an accounting system that provides both the internal information required by its managers to run the firm and the external information needed by shareholders, lenders, and government officials in the countries in which the firm operates. Yet as you will see, differences in national accounting philosophies and practices make such a task easier said than done.

The Roots of Differences

A country's accounting standards and practices reflect the influence of legal, cultural, political, and economic factors, as Figure 19.1 indicates.[2] Because these factors vary by country, the underlying goals and philosophy of national accounting systems also vary dramatically.

Consider first the difference between common law and code law countries. In common law countries such as the United Kingdom and the United States, accounting procedures normally evolve via decisions of independent standards-setting boards, such as the U.K.'s Accounting Standards Board or the U.S. Financial Accounting Standards Board (FASB). Each board works in consultation with professional accounting groups, such as the U.K.'s various Institutes of Chartered Accountants or the American Institute of Certified Public Accountants. Accountants in common law countries typically follow so-called generally accepted accounting principles (GAAP) that provide a "true and fair" view of a firm's performance based on the standards agreed on by these professional boards.

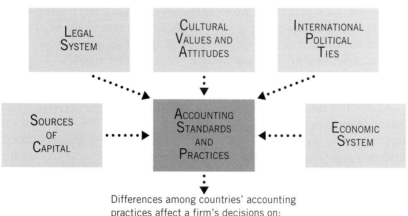

FIGURE 19.1

Influences on a Country's Accounting System

Operating within the boundaries of these principles, accountants have leeway to exercise their professional discretion in reporting a true and fair depiction of a firm's performance.

Conversely, countries relying on code law are likely to codify their national accounting procedures and standards.[3] In these countries accounting practices are determined by the law, not by the collective wisdom of professional accounting groups like the FASB.[4] For example, France's code law system and long tradition of strong central government control over the economy are reflected in its imposition on French firms of a national uniform chart of accounts—the *Plan Comptable Général*. This accounting system, which dates to 1673, creates accounting records designed to serve as proof in legal procedures. To facilitate this legal role, all corporate accounting records must be officially registered with the government. Similarly, German accounting practices adhere strictly to requirements laid down by law or court decisions.

A country's legal system also influences enforcement of accounting practices. Most developed countries rely on both private and public enforcement of business behavior, although the public/private mixture varies by country. Because French and German accounting procedures are laid down by law, the government plays a major role in monitoring accounting practices in those countries. In contrast, the U.S. system relies to a greater extent on private litigation to enforce the accuracy and honesty of firms' accounting practices. Any attempt to mislead private investors or creditors in the United States is likely to prompt a lawsuit; U.S. firms and their accountants have shelled out hundreds of millions of dollars settling such claims. Thus U.S. firms (and their accountants) are motivated to provide accurate information in their public accounting statements because of this threat of private litigation; French and German firms, in contrast, are more concerned about meeting governmental standards. Indeed, French accountants are legally compelled to report to French prosecutors any criminal acts the accountants uncover when auditing a company's books.

A country's accounting system also may reflect its national culture. The detailed accounting procedures laid down by the French government mirror France's statist tradition. Larger French firms also must publish a "social balance sheet" detailing their treatment and compensation of their workforces. Strong anti-inflation biases are embedded in German accounting procedures, a reaction to the tragic hyperinflation of the early 1920s that wiped out much of the wealth of the German middle class and helped Adolf Hitler rise to the chancellorship in 1932.

International political ties are also important determinants of a country's accounting procedures. Most members of the British Commonwealth have adopted the accounting principles and procedures of the United Kingdom, whereas former colonies of France and the Netherlands have adopted those of their colonial rulers. Similarly, the accounting procedures of the Philippines follow those of the United States, which controlled that country from 1898 to 1946.

A country's economic system also influences its accounting practices. In a centrally planned economy the accounting system is driven by the need to provide output-oriented information to the state planners. Such accounting systems focus on documenting how state funds are used and whether state-mandated production quotas are being met.[5] In market-oriented systems, on the other hand, managers and investors require profit- and cost-oriented information.

Capital markets also may affect national accounting standards. U.S. firms historically have raised capital by relying on public investors. U.S. accounting standards therefore emphasize the provision of accurate and useful information to help outsiders—private shareholders and bondholders—make appropriate investment decisions. As part of this goal, publicly owned firms must satisfy all the disclosure regulations of the Securities and Exchange Commission (SEC). In Germany the dominant role of a few large banks in providing capital results in accounting practices that focus on the needs of creditors, for example, by tending to undervalue assets and overvalue liabilities. This conservative approach is favored by the lending banks. The public capital market has been much less important in Germany than in the United States, and German accounting practices provide less information to public investors than do U.S. methods.[6] For example, a German corporation does not need to consolidate the accounts of its subsidiaries if the subsidiaries' activities differ substantially from the parent's or if consolidation would be too expensive for the parent. This lack of consolidation makes it difficult for private investors to assess such a firm's overall performance. It creates no problem for the firm's bankers, however, who often sit on its board of directors and who in their role as lenders have access to all its financial information.

The situation is similar in Japan. Most publicly traded Japanese firms are members of a *keiretsu*. They have relatively few public shareholders because of the pervasive cross-ownership of shares among *keiretsu* members and the extensive share ownership by banks and other financial institutions. Most Japanese firms also have large debt-to-equity ratios by Western standards. Thus Japanese accounting standards are geared toward meeting the needs of a firm's lenders and *keiretsu* partners, both of which already have privileged access to the firm's financial records, rather than the needs of outside investors.

Differences in Accounting Practices

Political, cultural, legal, and economic forces affect each country's philosophy and attitude toward its accounting system. They also affect the way a country's accountants treat different accounting issues. These different treatments in turn impact a firm's reported profits, the value of its assets, its tax bill, and its decision to begin or continue operating in a country. International businesses that rely on foreign accounting records but fail to recognize these differences may make expensive, perhaps fatal, strategic errors and operating mistakes. Let us look at some of the more important national accounting differences that affect international business.

Valuation and Revaluation of Assets.   Most countries' accounting systems begin with the assumption that a firm's assets should be valued on an historical cost basis. That is, an asset is carried on the firm's books according to the asset's original cost, less depreciation. Because of inflation, however, the market value of an asset is often higher than its historical cost. The resolution of this problem differs among national accounting systems. Dutch firms are permitted to raise the value of such assets on their balance sheets to reflect the assets' true replacement value. British accountants may exercise their professional discretion and value assets on an historical cost basis, a current cost basis, or a mixture of the two. Australia, an inheritor of British accounting philosophy, similarly grants a firm's accountants a great degree of professional discretion. Australian firms may alter the value of long-term assets on their balance sheets to take into account inflation or improved economic conditions. In the United States and Japan, however, such upward revaluations are illegal. These differences in asset revaluation procedures suggest the need for caution when comparing the strength of balance sheets of firms from different countries.

Valuation of Inventories.   Every introductory accounting course discusses the two principle methods for valuing inventories: LIFO (last in, first out) and FIFO (first in, first out). In times of inflation LIFO tends to raise the firm's reported costs of goods sold, lower the book value of its inventories, and reduce its reported profits (and, presumably, its taxes) more than FIFO does, whereas FIFO produces a clearer estimate of the value of the firm's existing inventories than does LIFO. Thus in comparing the performance of two firms, one needs to know which technique they use to value their inventories. There are significant international differences in the use of the two methods. U.S., Japanese, and Canadian firms may use either approach. In Australia LIFO cannot be used, whereas in New Zealand LIFO is allowed, but FIFO is generally used. Firms in Brazil and the United Kingdom normally use only FIFO.[7]

Dealing with the Tax Authorities. A firm's accounting records form the basis for assessing its income tax burden. In Germany accounting procedures are detailed explicitly in the German Commercial Code and follow the requirements of German tax laws. A German firm's taxable income is measured by the contents of the firm's financial records. Normally no distinction is made between financial statements reported to shareholders and financial statements reported to German tax authorities. The United States follows a very different approach. U.S. firms commonly report two different sets of financial statements—one to the Internal Revenue Service (IRS) and one to shareholders. Such conduct is authorized by U.S. law and allows firms to take advantage of special tax code provisions to reduce their taxable income. For example, U.S. firms often use accelerated depreciation for tax purposes but not for financial-reporting purposes. A German firm normally does not have this option. If it wants to use accelerated depreciation for tax-reporting purposes (to reduce its current-year taxes), the firm also must use accelerated depreciation in reporting to its shareholders (which reduces its reported income).

Forced to choose between higher taxes and lower reported income, most German firms opt for the latter. Managers and investors need to recognize that the reported profits of German firms are thus biased downward. The inflexibility of Germany's accounting system seems to put German firms at a disadvantage in raising capital. However, German firms typically obtain most of their capital from large financial intermediaries like banks and insurance firms. These inside investors have access to more detailed information about the firm's performance than is available in its public financial statements published in its annual report.

Tax laws also play a major role in French accounting practices, which follow well-defined procedures detailed by the French government in the national uniform chart of accounts. As in the German system, no deductions for tax purposes may be taken unless they have been entered into the firm's annual accounting records. Because of the dominance of tax law in accounting judgments, French firms are likely to bias their reported earnings and net assets downward to reduce their tax burdens.

Use of Accounting Reserves. Another important difference in national accounting systems is in the use of **accounting reserves**, which are accounts created in a firm's financial reports to record foreseeable future expenses that might affect its operations. An office supplies wholesaler, for example, might establish a reserve account for bad debts and for returned merchandise, knowing that when it ships merchandise, some retailers will ship the goods back and some will fail to pay their bills. The use of accounting reserves by U.S. firms is carefully monitored and limited by the IRS and the SEC. The IRS dislikes accounting reserves because charges to them reduce a firm's taxable income. The SEC fears that firms might manipulate their accounting reserves to provide misleading pictures of their financial performance.

In contrast to the restrictive U.S. system, the German Commercial Code liberally permits German firms to establish accounting reserves for various potential future expenses, such as deferred maintenance, future repairs, or exposure to international risks. Because these reserves reduce reported income on which taxes are based, most German firms use them aggressively. In the mid-1990s, for example, Deutsche Bank admitted that its hidden reserves amounted to over $14 billion.[8]

The use of such reserves hampers outside investors' ability to assess German firms' performance. Often these firms use reserve accounts to smooth out fluctuations in their earning flows by adding large sums to their reserves in good years and dipping into their reserves in poor years. Because of their use of accounting reserves, the reported earnings of German firms often fluctuate less than those of comparable U.S. firms, giving the misleading appearance that the former are less risky than the latter. These accounting differences complicate investors' decision making regarding how to diversify their portfolios internationally to reduce overall investments risk.

Other Differences.   Many other differences exist in the way countries treat accounting issues. The following are a few examples:

- *Capitalization of financial leases*: U.S., British, and Canadian firms must capitalize financial leases, whereas French and Swiss firms may do so but are not required to do so.

- *Preparation of consolidated financial statements*: Consolidation of financial statements is mandatory for U.S. and British firms, whereas German firms may exclude consolidating subsidiaries if their activities differ substantially from the parent's or if consolidation would be too expensive for the parent.

- *Capitalization of research and development (R&D) expenses*: Most countries permit firms to capitalize R&D expenses, but this practice is forbidden in the United States except in limited circumstances.

- *Treatment of goodwill*: A firm that acquires a second firm often pays more than the book value of the acquired firm's stock. The excess payment is called **goodwill**. In the Netherlands firms typically amortize goodwill over a five-year period, although they may write it off instantaneously or over a period of up to 10 years. U.K. firms also are allowed to choose between immediately writing off goodwill or capitalizing it on their balance sheets and amortizing it over a period of time. French firms may amortize goodwill over five to 20 years. Japan, however, severely limits firms' ability to write off goodwill.

Table 19.1 summarizes important accounting differences among selected countries.

Impact on Capital Markets

The various national differences in accounting practices would be little more than a curiosity were it not for international businesspeople's need for information to make decisions. These differences can distort the measured performance of firms incorporated in different countries. As already noted, the earnings of German and French firms often are understated because of the congruency between financial reporting and tax reporting. The price-to-earnings ratios of Japanese firms are frequently higher than those of U.S. firms, primarily because Japanese accounting practices often substantially reduce reported profits. For example, Japanese firms report depreciation expenses on an accelerated basis to their shareholders and are allowed to create generous reserve funds for future pension liabilities. The overall impact of these accounting differences is clear: Comparing the financial reports of firms from different countries is exceedingly complex, making it more difficult for international investors to assess the performance of the world's businesses.

These differences can affect the global capital market in other ways. The New York Stock Exchange (NYSE), for example, is concerned about SEC-mandated accounting rules that must be followed by publicly traded corporations under the SEC's jurisdiction. Those rules emphasize full and comprehensive disclosure of a firm's financial performance information, and the NYSE fears that the rules discourage foreign firms from listing on the exchange, thereby threatening the exchange's global competitiveness.[9] Consider the Netherlands-based firm Philips

TABLE 19.1

Summary of International Accounting Differences

	UNITED STATES	JAPAN	UNITED KINGDOM	FRANCE	GERMANY	NETHERLANDS	SWITZERLAND	CANADA	ITALY	BRAZIL
Capitalization of research and development costs	Not allowed	Allowed in certain circumstances	Allowed in certain circumstances	Allowed in certain circumstances	Not allowed	Allowed in certain circumstances	Allowed in certain circumstances	Allowed in certain circumstances	Allowed in certain circumstances	Allowed
Fixed asset revaluations stated at amount in excess of cost	Not allowed	Not allowed	Allowed	Allowed	Not allowed	Allowed in certain circumstances	Allowed in certain circumstances	Not allowed	Required in certain circumstances	Allowed
Inventory valuation using LIFO	Allowed	Allowed	Allowed but rarely done	Allowed	Allowed in certain circumstances	Allowed	Allowed	Allowed	Allowed	Allowed but rarely done
Finance leases capitalized	Required	Allowed in certain circumstances	Required	Allowed	Allowed in certain circumstances	Required	Allowed	Required	Not Allowed	Allowed in certain circumstances
Pension expense accrued during period of service	Required	Allowed	Required	Allowed	Required	Required	Allowed	Required	Allowed	Allowed
Book and tax-timing differences presented on the balance sheet as deferred tax	Required	Allowed in certain circumstances	Required in certain circumstances	Required	Allowed in certain circumstances	Required	Allowed	Required	Generally required	Required
Current rate method used for foreign-currency translation	Required for foreign operations whose functional currency is other than the reporting currency	Generally required	Required	Required for self-sustaining foreign operations	Allowed	Required for self-sustaining foreign operations	Allowed	Required for self-sustaining foreign operations	Required	Required
Pooling method used for mergers	Required in certain circumstances	Allowed	Required in certain circumstances	Not allowed	Allowed in certain circumstances	Allowed but rarely done	Allowed but rarely done	Allowed in rare circumstances	Allowed in rare circumstances	Allowed but rarely done
Equity method used for 20–50 percent ownership	Required	Required	Required	Required	Required	Required	Allowed in certain circumstances	Required	Allowed	Required

Source: From Fredrick D. S. Choi, *International Accounting and Finance Handbook*, 2nd ed. Copyright © 1997 John Wiley & Sons, Inc. Reprinted by permission of John Wiley & Sons, Inc.

NV. Under Dutch accounting standards Philips assesses its assets on a current-value basis. To list its stock on the NYSE, Philips must undergo the expense of revaluing its assets on an historical cost basis to meet SEC requirements.[10]

The information-laden accounting practices used by U.S. firms do offer them certain advantages, however. Many foreign bankers believe that the United States is the easiest foreign locale in which to lend because of U.S. public disclosure policies. Those policies result in reliable numbers for assessing the riskiness of potential loans. In contrast, the German accounting system, which allows firms to lump together various cost categories and establish a variety of reserves, is much less helpful for a potential foreign lender. As one investment manager has noted, "The poor quality of financial information available from many German companies makes it difficult for investors to buy a stock with confidence, since valuations cannot be clearly established."[11] In 1999, for example, Volkswagen was the poorest performer of the blue-chip stocks in the DAX 30 index (Germany's equivalent of the Dow Jones Industrial Average), in part because of its poor financial communication and disclosure policies. Noted one European analyst, "Volkswagen's results [are] a black box." In hopes of improving its standing with institutional investors, in early 2000 Volkswagen announced it would adopt either U.S. GAAP or the International Accounting Standards, an alternative transparent approach to financial reporting.[12]

Similarly, some experts believe the economic problems of Southeast Asian companies triggered by the region's 1997–98 currency crisis was worsened by the lack of transparency in their accounting statements. When times were good in the region, investors seemingly overlooked the lack of information contained in financial reports and assumed the best about the companies' prospects; when the region's economy plunged into trouble after Thailand devalued the baht, investors assumed the worst, driving stock prices down even more. Not surprisingly, because of the information needs of institutional investors, a clear trend has emerged among MNCs to make their financial statements more transparent to better access public capital markets.

Impact of Accounting Procedures on Corporate Financial Controls

National differences in accounting procedures also complicate an MNC's ability to manage its foreign operations. An MNC's subsidiaries must provide the parent's senior executive officers with timely and uniform financial information prepared on a comparable basis to facilitate assessment of the subsidiaries' performances. Accordingly, the parent typically dictates to the subsidiaries the form and procedures to be used for financial reports submitted to it. Coca-Cola, for example, has developed for its subsidiaries an easy-to-use, standardized accounting manual that incorporates U.S. GAAP.[13]

Senior executives of an MNC also must determine whether to use the parent's or the subsidiary's currency in assessing the performances of foreign subsidiaries and their managers. The choice may seem obvious: Translate each subsidiary's financial reports into the parent's currency, thereby allowing easy comparisons by the parent. However, the use of financial reports denominated in the parent's currency may induce the subsidiary's managers to focus their energies on beating the foreign-exchange market rather than on managing the local operations. In practice, there is no uniform answer to the question of which currency to use for performance evaluation: some MNCs choose the host currency and others the home currency, but most appear to use both.[14]

Accounting in Centrally Planned Economies

The goals of centrally planned economies (CPE) differ from those of market economies. Not surprisingly, their accounting systems are also different and offer special challenges to international businesses operating in those countries. CPEs'

〉 China has had to undertake many reforms as its economy moves from communism to capitalism, including reforming its accounting procedures. Previously the accounting records of this state-owned motorcycle company met the needs of state planners. Now they must meet the needs of a market economy.

accounting systems are designed to provide information about an enterprise's aggregate production. This information then is passed from the enterprise to the central planners so they can monitor the enterprise's success in fulfilling its performance goals in the economy's central plan and make mid-plan adjustments as needed.

International businesses must approach financial statements developed in CPEs with great caution. General Electric (GE), for instance, ran into several accounting problems in its purchase of the Hungarian lighting firm Tungsram in the early 1990s. Tungsram was not required by Hungarian law to consolidate its transactions with those of its 17 foreign sales subsidiaries. Because the bonuses of Tungsram's managers were tied to its sales revenues, the firm routinely shipped goods to the subsidiaries even though they might not be able to sell the goods. By so doing, Tungsram was able to declare increased sales and profits on its accounting statements, and managers were allowed to claim their bonuses. Had Tungsram been forced to consolidate its accounts, these sales to subsidiaries would have been recorded as increased inventory levels instead. In one case GE discovered that Tungsram's French and German subsidiaries were warehousing $3 million worth of an obsolete automobile headlight that had not been marketed for over a decade.[15] Had GE recognized these accounting differences up front, it might have either paid substantially less for Tungsram or walked away from the deal.

CPEs' accounting systems are of little use to international businesses trying to meet their own internal managerial and reporting requirements. These systems focus on recording production information needed by central planners but ignore "trivialities" such as revenues, costs, and profits that may be incompatible with Marxist ideology. China's old accounting system, for example, ignored bad debts and obsolete inventory but required foreign-currency transactions to be recorded at the official exchange rate, which often deviated substantially from market rates.[16] Fortunately, because these and other troublesome accounting procedures were perceived to be impediments to China's economic modernization, China's Ministry of Finance has undertaken significant reforms of the country's accounting procedures since 1993 to make them more compatible with the needs of external users.[17]

〉 EFFORTS AT HARMONIZATION

Differences in accounting systems are confusing and costly to international businesses. Incompatibilities in these systems make it more difficult for firms to monitor their foreign operations and for investors to comprehend the relative performance of firms based in different countries. To help solve such problems, many accounting professionals and national regulatory bodies are attempting to harmonize the various national accounting practices. One of the most important of these efforts was the creation of the **International Accounting Standards Committee (IASC)** in 1973. IASC founding members were drawn from the professional accounting societies of the leading trading nations, including the United States, Germany, Japan, the United Kingdom, the Netherlands, Canada, Australia,

Mexico, and Ireland. Today the IASC membership consists of 153 professional societies from 112 countries. The IASC has issued a series of International Accounting Standards designed to harmonize national treatment of various accounting issues within its member countries. Among its most important goals is the promotion of comparability of financial statements across countries by establishing standards for inventory valuation, depreciation, deferred income taxes, and other matters. However, the IASC lacks enforcement powers. National governments often ignore its accounting standards if they disagree with them. The United States and Canada, for example, although supportive of IASC's efforts, continue to impose stricter accounting rules for company shares listed on their stock exchanges.

The European Union (EU) has undertaken a separate initiative to harmonize the accounting systems of its member states as part of its drive to complete the formation of its internal market. By so doing, the EU hopes to reduce the total accounting costs of European MNCs. In addition, as national accounting standards of the EU member states become more similar, investors will find it easier to assess the performance of those countries' firms. The EU's Fourth Directive mandates that each member require its firms to adopt certain accounting practices and to ensure that financial statements provide a "true and fair view" of operations. The Seventh Directive requires firms to publish consolidated financial statements. Each directive, however, allows members a fair amount of discretion in establishing their national accounting standards. For example, inventories may be valued using LIFO, FIFO, actual cost, or weighted cost approaches. Similarly, consolidation is not required if a subsidiary's operations are immaterial to the parent, if the subsidiary's operations are substantially dissimilar from the parent's, or if consolidation would be expensive to perform. Other groups, such as the World Trade Organization (WTO) and IOSCO (an international organization of national securities commissions), also have lobbied for the adoption of international accounting standards.

These harmonization efforts have their critics, however. The costs of harmonization are significant. Accountants, firms, and government officials must incur retooling costs if they abandon existing national accounting standards.[18] National pride also has affected the process. One EU official has proclaimed, "It would not be acceptable for Europe to delegate the setting of accounting standards to the U.S."[19] For its part the U.S. Securities and Exchange Commission has shown little willingness to relax its accounting standards. Some analysts believe that harmonization may affect international competition among accountants. For example, the IASC's standards have a strong bias toward British and U.S. accounting procedures. To the extent that the IASC's standards are adopted worldwide, these countries' accounting firms are favored in the international market for accounting services. As a result, other countries are resisting the universal adoption of IASC-endorsed procedures. France, for example, is aggressively promoting the rules developed by its own standards board, the Conseil National de la Comptabilité. So far this board's standards have been adopted by Bulgaria and Romania, thereby giving French accounting firms the inside track in selling accounting services in those countries.[20]

Nonetheless, there seems to be continual, albeit slow, progress toward harmonization. Much of this progress seems to be driven by the need of MNCs to access the global capital market: As globalization of the world's economies increases, the capital requirements of international firms also grow. To compete successfully with their foreign rivals, MNCs must seek to acquire inputs—including capital—at the lowest possible cost. Change has been particularly noticeable among German firms. Major German MNCs like Daimler-Benz, Veba, Schering, Hoechst, Deutsche Bank, and Bayer have adopted the more transparent accounting procedures of IASC and/or the U.S. GAAP to improve their access to the global capital market and lower their cost of acquiring new capital.[21]

❯ ACCOUNTING FOR INTERNATIONAL BUSINESS ACTIVITIES

Besides the challenges posed by differences in national accounting systems, most international firms also must deal with two types of specific accounting problems that routinely develop when business is conducted internationally:

1. Accounting for transactions denominated in foreign currencies
2. Reporting the operating results of foreign subsidiaries in the firm's consolidated financial statements

Because of the collapse of the Bretton Woods system in 1971, both problems have become increasingly important to international businesses. Under the Bretton Woods fixed exchange rate system the accounting problems raised by international business activities denominated in foreign currencies tended to be minor. In the post-Bretton Woods era, however, currency values can change dramatically. Since 1971, accounting for the impact of exchange rate changes on the value of international transactions and on the firm's consolidated financial statements has become a significant issue for international businesses.

Accounting for Transactions in Foreign Currencies

Chapter 18 introduced the concept of transaction exposure, which is the effect of exchange rate fluctuations on the economic benefits and costs of an international transaction. Firms confront the problem of accounting for transactions in foreign currency whenever they agree to pay or receive payment in a foreign currency in settlement of a purchase or sale of goods, services, or assets. Under the existing flexible exchange rate system it is very likely that the exchange rate will change between the time a firm enters into an international transaction and the time it receives payment or pays for the goods, services, or assets in question. In accordance with FASB Statement 52, issued in 1981, U.S. firms must account for such international transactions by using the **two-transaction approach** in their financial statements.[22]

For example, Microsoft Corporation, the Seattle-based computer software giant, faces this problem when it ships copies of Windows 2000, Office 97, or Microsoft Excel to a British computer store chain and agrees to accept £30,000 in payment in 90 days. If £1 is worth $1.60 when the contract is signed, making the transaction worth $48,000 (£30,000 × $1.60), Microsoft, by following FASB Statement 52, will account for the transaction as follows:

	DEBIT	CREDIT
Accounts Receivable	$48,000	
Sales Revenues		$48,000

Suppose that in 90 days, when Microsoft receives a check for £30,000, the value of the British pound has dropped to $1.50. In terms of its home currency Microsoft has received only $45,000 rather than the $48,000 it expected. The actual receipt of the moneys is accounted for as follows:

	DEBIT	CREDIT
Cash	$45,000	
Foreign-Exchange Loss	3,000	
Accounts Receivable		$48,000

This accounting procedure highlights any foreign-exchange loss or gain resulting from the sale or purchase. Ultimately, the firm's net income is affected by both the primary transaction and any foreign-exchange gains or losses. However, the two-transaction approach has the benefit of separating out information about the success of the firm's core activities—selling its products—from its success in managing its exposure to fluctuations in foreign-currency values. In the example Microsoft's managers would realize they need to improve management of their transaction exposure to such fluctuations, perhaps by engaging in hedging operations through the use of the forward market or currency futures (discussed in Chapter 18).

Because the two-transaction approach distinguishes between the firm's core activities and its management of transaction exposure, the approach is of particular value to stock market analysts, who are often wary of firms that expose themselves to excessive foreign-exchange risk. For example, in the early 1990s Dell Computer lost 10 percent of its market value when it reported $38 million in currency exchange losses, an amount equal to roughly one-quarter of its annual profits at that time. Stock market analysts believed the size of the losses meant Dell was engaging in foreign-currency speculation, rather than merely hedging foreign-currency earnings from its export sales. Dell denied the allegations.[23]

Foreign-Currency Translation

A second type of international accounting problem confronts an MNC when it reports the results of its foreign subsidiaries' operations to its home country shareholders and tax officials. Because its foreign subsidiaries will normally conduct their business using their local currency, the firm must convert its subsidiaries' financial reports into its home currency. The process of transforming a subsidiary's reported operations denominated in a foreign currency into the parent's home currency is called **translation**, which leads to the problem of translation exposure discussed in Chapter 18. For most MNCs the translation process is intertwined with the need to create consolidated financial statements. **Consolidated financial statements** report the combined operations of a parent and its subsidiaries in a single set of accounting statements denominated in a single currency.

Translating financial reports from one currency into another requires the use of an appropriate exchange rate to convert from the first currency to the second. Because the business activities captured in accounting records occur at different times, a question arises as to which exchange rate to use. Should the firm use the exchange rate on the date the transaction occurred (the historical rate), the rate on the date the financial statement is prepared (the current rate), a weighted average over time, or some other rate? For U.S. firms FASB Statement 52 details the exchange rates and accounting procedures firms are to use in translating and then consolidating subsidiaries' financial statements denominated in a foreign currency.

The treatment of foreign investments under FASB Statement 52 depends on the size of the parent's ownership stake in the foreign firm, as summarized in Table 19.2. A U.S. firm that has a portfolio investment in a foreign firm (less than 10 percent ownership) must use the **cost method**. With this method the investment is recorded in the U.S. firm's accounting records at cost using the historical exchange rate—the exchange rate at the time the foreign shares were acquired. Any dividends the U.S. firm receives from its portfolio investment are to be reported in its income statement using the exchange rate in effect on the day it received the dividend. This is the approach Ford uses to account for its 9.4 percent ownership of Korea's Kia Motors.

OWNERSHIP STAKE	METHOD USED
Less than 10 percent	Cost method
Between 10 and 50 percent	Equity method
More than 50 percent	Consolidation method

TABLE 19.2

Parent's Ownership Stake and Accounting Treatment of Its Foreign Investments

A U.S. firm that owns between 10 and 50 percent of a foreign firm's stock must use the **equity method** to value its ownership stake. For example, Ford's 33 percent ownership stake in Mazda is entered into Ford's consolidated financial statements using this approach. The equity method calls for the U.S. firm to record its initial investment in the foreign firm at cost using the historical exchange rate. However, when the foreign firm earns profits or suffers losses, the value of the investment carried on the U.S. firm's consolidated financial statements is adjusted to reflect those profits or losses using the exchange rate prevailing when they were reported. Any dividends issued by the foreign firm reduce the value of the U.S. firm's investment in the foreign firm. This adjustment also is made using the exchange rate in effect on the day when the dividends were paid.

The most complicated accounting issues arise when a U.S. firm purchases more than 50 percent ownership of a foreign firm, such as Ford's purchase of all the stock of Volvo in 1999. In such cases the U.S. firm must use the **consolidation method**. This method calls for the accounting records of the two firms to be consolidated when the U.S. firm reports its operating results to its shareholders and the SEC. Because the foreign subsidiary uses the accounting rules prescribed by its national government or national professional association, the subsidiary's financial statements must first be restated using U.S. GAAP. The next step is to determine the **functional currency** of the subsidiary, defined as the currency of the principal economic environment in which the subsidiary operates. For example, the functional currency of GM's German subsidiary, Adam Opel AG, is the deutsche mark because Opel produces most of its parts in Germany, assembles its vehicles in Germany, and sells most of its output in Germany. (When Germany switches to using the euro as legal tender in 2002, it will become Adam Opel's functional currency.) In contrast, Compaq Computer's production facilities in Scotland and Singapore are integrated into the firm's worldwide sourcing program. Thus the functional currency of those two subsidiaries is their parent's currency, the U.S. dollar.

The U.S. firm will use one of two methods for translating a subsidiary's financial statements into the U.S. dollar (the parent's home currency), depending on the subsidiary's functional currency:

1. The **current rate method** is used if the subsidiary's functional currency is the host country's currency. This method assumes the foreign subsidiary is a stand-alone operation. Any gains or losses arising from translation thus reflect the impact of exchange rate changes, not the subsidiary's operational performance.

2. The **temporal method** is used if the subsidiary's functional currency is the U.S. dollar. This method assumes the foreign subsidiary's operations are integrated into the parent's. Thus its profitability should be evaluated in terms of the parent's currency.

These two approaches differ mainly in how they treat translation losses and gains. Under the temporal method translation losses and gains appear on the firm's income statement; under the current rate method they appear as an adjustment to shareholders' equity. In some cases a firm may use both approaches because of differences in the functional currencies of various subsidiaries. For example, Federal-Mogul, a $6.5 billion Detroit-based producer of motor vehicle parts, uses the temporal method to translate the results of its Brazilian and Argentinean subsidiaries, whose functional currency is the U.S. dollar. It uses the current rate method to translate the results of its British and German subsidiaries, whose functional currencies are the pound and the deutsche mark, respectively. The temporal method is less commonly used and more complicated than is needed for an introduction to international accounting, so we focus on the current rate method for illustrative purposes.

	IN FUNCTIONAL CURRENCY (JAPANESE YEN)	IN HOME CURRENCY (U.S. DOLLARS)
Revenues	350,000,000	3,500,000
Expenses		
Cost of goods sold	210,000,000	2,100,000
General and administrative	45,500,000	455,000
Depreciation	42,000,000	420,000
Income before Taxes	52,500,000	525,000
Income Taxes	24,500,000	245,000
Net Income after Taxes	28,000,000	280,000

TABLE 19.3

Translation of Income Statement of Japanese Subsidiary of U.S. Firm Using the Current Rate Method for the Quarter Ending March 31, 2002

Applying the Current Rate Method to Income Statements.   According to FASB Statement 52, a firm adopting the current rate method to translate a subsidiary's income statement uses either the exchange rate on the day a transaction occurred or a weighted average of exchange rates during the period covered by the income statement. For simplicity's sake firms often use the latter approach. Dividends, however, are translated using the exchange rate in effect on the day they are paid. Table 19.3 presents a simple example of the translation of an income statement of a Japanese subsidiary of a U.S. parent. The subsidiary's functional currency is the Japanese yen, and the average exchange rate between the yen and the U.S. dollar during the three months the statement covers is assumed to be ¥100 = $1.

Applying the Current Rate Method to Balance Sheets.   The foreign subsidiary's balance sheet also must be translated. Under the current rate method the assets and liabilities shown on the subsidiary's balance sheet are translated using the exchange rate in effect on the date for which the balance sheet was prepared (March 31, 2002, for the example in Table 19.4). Equity accounts (common stock and retained earnings) generally are treated on an historical basis. Because two or more different exchange rates are being used, the subsidiary's assets are not likely to equal the sum of its liabilities and shareholders' equity when the assets, liabilities, and shareholders' equity are translated. To reconcile this discrepancy, the firm makes an accounting entry known as the **cumulative translation adjustment** (see Table 19.4), which makes the firm's assets equal the sum of its liabilities and shareholders' equity, an equality necessary to make the balance sheet balance. When a parent consolidates the subsidiary's balance sheet into its own, the cumulative translation adjustment is entered as an adjustment to the parent's shareholders' equity.

Using the cumulative translation adjustment significantly benefits both the firm and its shareholders. Under the current rate method the cumulative translation adjustment is made directly to shareholders' equity rather than first flowing through the firm's income statement. Thus translation gains and losses do not affect the firm's reported net income. Companies are able to avoid the temptation of engaging in expensive efforts to dampen fluctuations in reported earnings resulting from translation gains or losses, a temptation to which many firms succumbed under the FASB accounting requirement that preceded Statement 52.[24] Instead, the current rate method more properly focuses investors' attention on the impact of exchange rate changes on the home currency value of the firm's equity in its foreign subsidiaries.

	IN JAPANESE YEN	EXCHANGE RATE (¥/U.S. DOLLAR)	IN U.S. DOLLARS
ASSETS			
Cash	105,000,000	100	1,050,000
Accounts Receivable	70,000,000	100	700,000
Inventories	70,000,000	100	700,000
Plant and Equipment	140,000,000	100	1,400,000
Total	385,000,000		3,850,000
LIABILITIES AND SHAREHOLDERS' EQUITY			
Current Liabilities	87,500,000	100	875,000
Notes Payable	122,500,000	100	1,225,000
Common Stock	50,000,000	125	400,000
Retained Earnings	125,000,000	115	1,086,957
Cumulative Translation Adjustment*			263,043
Total	385,000,000		3,850,000

*Needed to make assets = liabilities + shareholders' equity when denominated in U.S. dollars.

› INTERNATIONAL TAXATION ISSUES

A close relationship often exists between national accounting procedures and national taxation policies. A country's tax code affects a variety of business behaviors as firms seek to maximize their after-tax profitability. A country may use its tax code not only to raise revenue but also to stimulate certain activities, such as the hiring of persons with physical disabilities or an increase in firms' R&D expenditures. Location, production, and hiring decisions may all be influenced by the structure and level of taxes.

Like domestic firms, international firms seek to maximize their after-tax income. However, they also are challenged to meet the tax requirements (which unfortunately often are in conflict) of all the countries in which they operate. International businesses typically must navigate a careful path between taking advantage of tax incentives and sidestepping punitive taxes.

Transfer Pricing

Two common means international businesses adopt to reduce their overall tax burden are transfer pricing and tax havens. **Transfer pricing** refers to the prices one branch or subsidiary of a parent charges a second branch or subsidiary for goods or services. Transfer pricing is important to international business for several reasons. Intracorporate transfers of goods, technology, and other resources are common between subsidiaries located in different countries. By one estimate intracorporate shipments account for 40 percent of U.S. international trade in goods. Transfer prices also affect an MNC's ability to monitor the performance of individual corporate units and to reward (or punish) managers responsible for a unit's performance. Further, transfer prices affect the taxes an MNC pays both to its home country and to the various host countries in which it operates.

In practice, transfer prices are calculated in one of two ways:

1. Market-based method
2. Nonmarket-based methods

Market-Based Transfer Prices. The market-based method utilizes prices determined in the open market to transfer goods between units of the same corporate parent. Suppose Hyundai wants to export memory chips from South Korea for use in assembling personal computers at one of its U.S. subsidiaries. It can establish the transfer price for the memory chips between its U.S. and Korean subsidiaries by using the open market price for such chips.

This market-based approach has two main benefits. First, it reduces conflict between the two units over the appropriate price. The higher the price charged in the intracorporate transfer, the better the selling subsidiary's performance appears and the poorer the buying subsidiary's performance appears. To the extent that the parent allocates managerial bonuses or investment capital to its subsidiaries on the basis of profitability, the unit managers have incentives to squabble over the transfer price because they care about how the MNC's accounting system reports their unit's performance. From the parent's perspective, however, such arguments waste firm resources. Once the firm's accounting records are consolidated, its overall before-tax profits will remain the same regardless of whether the transfer price overstates unit A's profitability and understates unit B's, or vice versa. Assuming both subsidiaries recognize the basic equity of the market-based price, such intracorporate conflict will be reduced.

Second, the market-based approach promotes the MNC's overall profitability by encouraging the efficiency of the selling unit. If the price the unit can charge for intracorporate sales is limited to the market price, its managers know the unit's profitability depends on their ability to control its costs. Moreover, they recognize that if they successfully produce the product in question more cheaply than their international competitors can, the parent's market-based transfer pricing will acknowledge their efforts in full. Motivated by the prospects of bonuses and lucrative promotions, unit managers have every incentive to improve the efficiency and profitability of their operations.

Nonmarket-Based Transfer Prices. Transfer prices also may be established using nonmarket-based methods. Prices may be set by negotiations between the buying and selling units or on the basis of cost-based rules of thumb, such as production costs plus a fixed markup. Some services of the corporate parent may be assessed as a percentage of the subsidiary's sales, such as charges for general corporate overhead or for the right to use technology or intellectual property owned by the parent.

MNCs commonly use nonmarket-based prices partly because, for some goods and services, no real market exists outside the firm. For example, the sole market for an engine produced in a Ford factory in Spain may consist of Ford automobile assembly plants in Belgium, Germany, and the United Kingdom. Because no external market exists for this engine, Ford may establish a transfer price for the engine based on production costs plus an allowance for overhead and profit. Similarly, Toyota's ability to design and develop new automobile models is not a service that is bought and sold in the open market. Yet Toyota may want to charge its North American, British, and Australian subsidiaries an appropriate fee for the use of its research, design, and development services.

The use of nonmarket-based prices has both disadvantages and advantages. One disadvantage is that managers of the buying and selling units may waste time and energy arguing over the appropriate transfer price because it will affect their reported profits even though it will have no overall impact on the parent's consolidated before-tax income. Nonmarket-based transfer prices also may reduce the selling unit's efficiency. A transfer price based on the seller's costs plus some markup may reduce the seller's incentive to keep its costs low because it can pass along any cost increases to other members of the corporate family through the nonmarket-based price.

However, strategic use of nonmarket-based transfer prices may benefit an international business, as Table 19.5 shows. Creative rearranging of intracorporate prices may allow the parent to lower its overall tax bill. For example, an MNC can lessen the burden of an ad valorem import tariff by reducing the price the selling unit charges the buying unit, thereby lowering the basis on which the tariff is calculated. Further, such pricing may enable a firm to slash its total income taxes. Suppose an MNC operates in two countries, one with high corporate income tax rates and the second with low rates. The firm can raise the transfer prices charged to the subsidiary in the high-tax country and lower those charged to the subsidiary in the low-tax country. Doing this will reduce the profitability of the first subsidiary, as measured by its accounting records, while increasing the profitability of the second. The net effect is to shift the location of the MNC's profits from the high-tax country (which would tax them more) to the low-tax country (which taxes them less), thereby reducing the firm's overall tax burden. Ireland, for example, has effectively exempted exports of manufactured goods from Irish corporate taxation to give MNCs an incentive to locate factories in that country. Yet this tax break also encourages MNCs to manipulate the transfer prices charged by their Irish factories so as to increase the profits reported by those factories and lower the profits reported by their non-Irish subsidiaries.[25]

Clever structuring of transfer prices can even allow a firm to evade host country restrictions on repatriation of profits. Suppose, for example, that a host country blocks repatriation by forbidding dividend payments from the subsidiary to the parent. The parent can evade this restriction by raising the transfer prices it charges the subsidiary for goods and services produced by other units of the corporate family or by charging fees for general corporate services. By means of this technique cash will flow from the subsidiary to other parts of the firm in the form of payments for goods or services, rather than through the forbidden dividend payments. The net effect is the same, however: Funds (in some form) are repatriated from the host country.

A firm's transfer prices often reflect a trade-off between tax consequences and legal constraints imposed by countries in which the firm operates. Numerous stud-

TABLE 19.5

Strategic Use of Nonmarket-Based Transfer Prices

GOAL	TECHNIQUE	EFFECT
Decrease tariff paid on components imported from a subsidiary	Lower transfer price charged by the subsidiary	Lowering the price on which an ad valorem tariff is based decreases total amount of import tariff
Decrease overall corporate income tax	Raise transfer prices paid by subsidiaries in high-tax countries and/or lower transfer prices charged by those subsidiaries; lower transfer prices paid by subsidiaries in low-tax countries and/or raise transfer prices charged by those subsidiaries	Reported profits of subsidiaries in high-tax countries decrease, and reported profits of subsidiaries in low-tax countries increase; total corporate tax burden decreases
Repatriate profits from a subsidiary located in a host country that blocks repatriation	Raise transfer prices paid by the subsidiary; lower transfer prices charged by the subsidiary	Cash flows from the subsidiary to other units, circumventing restriction on repatriation

ies conducted by researchers indicate that MNCs routinely engage in tax-shifting behavior through transfer pricing and other devices.[26]

Government agencies, such as the IRS, are well aware of these opportunities to play accounting games. As a result, both home and host countries scrutinize the transfer-pricing policies of MNCs operating within their borders to ensure the firms do not evade their tax obligations and the governments receive their "fair share" of taxes from the firms. A common approach is to use an **arm's length test** whereby government officials attempt to determine the price that two unrelated firms operating at arm's length would have agreed on. In many cases, however, an appropriate arm's length price is difficult to establish, leading to conflict between international businesses and tax authorities. For example, in 1999 the U.K.'s Inland Revenue agency launched a study of whether IBM inappropriately raised the 8 percent royalty rate paid by its British subsidiary to the U.S. parent to 12 percent for a five-year period beginning in 1991. The effect of the increased royalty rate was to shift $260 million of profits from its U.K. operations to its U.S. operations, thus reducing the taxes IBM owed the British government.[27] Of course, determining the appropriate arm's length price for a unique asset like IBM's trademarks and technology is not simple. Should Inland Revenue determine that IBM owes the country additional taxes, no doubt IBM would fight the decision. Such conflicts are rarely resolved easily or quickly.

Tax Havens

A second device international businesses use to reduce their tax burdens is to locate their activities in **tax havens**, countries that impose little or no corporate income taxes. For a relatively small fee an MNC may set up a wholly owned subsidiary in a tax haven. By manipulating payments such as transfer prices, dividends, interest, royalties, and capital gains between its various subsidiaries, an MNC may divert income from subsidiaries in high-tax countries to the subsidiary operating in the tax haven. By booking its profits in the tax haven subsidiary, the MNC escapes the clutches of revenue agents in other countries. For example, an MNC may give ownership of its trademarks to a subsidiary located in the Cayman Islands. That subsidiary then can charge each of the corporation's operating subsidiaries a fee for the use of the trademarks. The fees paid by the operating subsidiaries reduce their profitability and thus the corporate income taxes they must pay to their host governments. The government of the Cayman Islands, however, imposes no income tax on the trademark licensing fees earned by the subsidiary located there—or on income, profits, capital gains, or dividends. Thus the MNC reduces its overall income tax burden. "Venturing Abroad" explores some of the ethical issues surrounding the use of tax havens and transfer prices to reduce corporate tax burdens.

> Like many countries in the Caribbean, The Bahamas has flourished because of its status as a tax haven. Financial services account for 20 percent of the Bahamian economy.

Several other smaller countries, including Liechtenstein, Luxembourg, and the Netherlands Antilles, also have gone into the business of being tax havens. To attract MNCs, a tax haven must not only refrain from imposing income taxes but also provide a stable political and business climate, an efficient court system,

VENTURING *Abroad*

THE ETHICS OF TAX HAVENS AND TRANSFER PRICING

MNCs can save millions of dollars in income and other taxes through the use of tax havens and transfer prices. For example, by manipulating transfer prices, an MNC can shift profits from high-tax countries to low-tax countries. But is such behavior ethical?

Skillful utilization of tax havens and transfer prices obviously benefits the MNC and its shareholders. However, such techniques reduce the revenues available to the home or host country government to solve important social problems such as poverty, homelessness, and drug addiction. An MNC's failure to pay its "fair share" of taxes in the countries in which it operates means that either the resources needed to solve these problems will be unavailable or that other taxpayers will be forced to pick up the tab. Because an MNC benefits from various services the local governments provide, such as transportation infrastructure, educational facilities, and police protection, many people claim it is unethical for the MNC to shirk paying for its share of these services.

Others argue that as long as an MNC is engaging in tax avoidance, its use of transfer prices and tax havens to reduce its tax burden is ethical. (Experts distinguish between *tax avoidance*, whereby a firm uses legal tax code loopholes to minimize its tax burden, and *tax evasion*, whereby a firm engages in illegal activities to lessen its tax payments.) Many accountants argue that an MNC's officers are bound by their fiduciary duties to their shareholders to take advantage of tax avoidance opportunities provided by various national tax codes. Indeed, from this perspective a manager's failure to do so could be viewed as unethical.

and sophisticated banking and communications industries. In return, the tax haven is able to capture franchising and incorporation fees and generate numerous lucrative professional jobs far beyond what an economy of its size normally could.

Being a tax haven can create a thriving economy. For example, foreign-owned firms outnumber the 32,000 residents of the Cayman Islands. The Cayman Islands' success as a tax haven reflects the high-quality services it provides to international businesses; an MNC can create and incorporate a Cayman Islands subsidiary within 24 hours if needed. The firms create demand for highly paid professionals such as accountants, bankers, and lawyers. As a result, the Cayman Islands is a major world banking and finance center. It is now home to some 500 banks with total assets of $600 billion and over 2,200 investment funds managing over $200 billion of assets.[28] From the Cayman Islands' perspective the tax-haven sector of the local economy represents the ultimate "clean" industry so beloved by economic development officials. However, the existence of tax havens creates numerous headaches for the taxing authorities of other countries, as explained in the next section.

› TAXATION OF FOREIGN INCOME BY THE UNITED STATES

The tax treatment of foreign income varies by country, although some basic similarities exist among many developed countries. As an example, let us review U.S. tax treatment of foreign income from three common sources: exports, foreign branches, and foreign subsidiaries.

Taxation of Exports

Ordinarily the U.S. tax code treats the profits associated with the export of goods and services the same as domestically generated income. Such exports are not trivial: In 1999 U.S. firms exported $684 billion of goods and $272 billion of services. However, to encourage firms to increase their export activities, the U.S. tax code allowed firms to establish **foreign sales corporations (FSC)**. The tax code required that an FSC engage in significant overseas activities, such as marketing, order processing, distribution, invoicing, and financing export sales. If a firm fully complied with all the provisions for establishing an FSC, the firm could significantly reduce its U.S. federal income taxes on its exporting activities.[29] In early 2000, however, the WTO, acting on a complaint filed by the EU, determined that the tax breaks offered FSCs violated its rules against unfair subsidization of exports. The United States is in the process of adjusting its tax code to bring it in compliance with the WTO's rules.

Taxation of Foreign Branch Income

A foreign branch is an unincorporated unit of a corporation. It operates in a foreign country, but because legally it is identical to the parent, the branch's income is treated as if it were the parent's. Thus any earnings of a foreign branch of a U.S. corporation create taxable income for the parent, regardless of whether or not the earnings are repatriated to the parent.

Taxation of Foreign Subsidiary Income

Subsidiaries incorporated in a foreign country are legally distinct from the home country parent corporation. In general, for U.S. tax purposes, a U.S. parent corporation does not need to include the earnings of its foreign subsidiaries in calculating its taxable income, as long as those earnings are reinvested in the foreign subsidiaries. The **deferral rule** in the U.S. tax code states such earnings will be taxed only when they are remitted to the parent in the form of dividends, thus allowing the parent to defer paying U.S. taxes on foreign subsidiaries' reinvested earnings. For example, the deferral rule saved Caterpillar an estimated $22 million in 1999 U.S. federal corporate income taxes.

The deferral rule is intended to stimulate international business activity by U.S. firms. In Caterpillar's case approximately half its sales are outside the United States, and the deferral rule has helped it penetrate key markets in Europe and Asia. However, one important exception to the deferral rule ensures that U.S. firms do not establish shell corporations in tax havens that do little but provide the parent with the ability to defer U.S. taxes. U.S. tax law requires a parent corporation to determine whether each of its foreign subsidiaries is a controlled foreign corporation. A **controlled foreign corporation (CFC)** is a foreign corporation in which U.S. shareholders—each of which holds at least 10 percent of the firm's shares—together own a majority of its stock. This definition may seem strange, but it is designed to focus on foreign firms that are controlled by a single U.S. firm or a group of U.S. firms acting in concert, rather than foreign firms owned by many small U.S. investors. For example, Ford's wholly owned Volvo subsidiary is a CFC, but its 33 percent share of Mazda, which is primarily owned by Japanese investors, is not.

According to the U.S. tax code, the income of CFCs is divided into two types: active income and passive income (also called Subpart F income). **Active income** is income generated by traditional business operations such as production, marketing, and distribution. **Subpart F income**, or **passive income**, is generated by passive activities such as the collection of dividends, interest, royalties, and licensing fees—the type of activities typically performed by subsidiaries incorporated in tax havens. U.S. firms may defer active income earned by CFCs they control. In calculating their U.S. taxes, however, they generally may not defer Subpart F income. In the absence of this restriction U.S. firms could escape federal corporate income taxes on earnings generated by their intellectual property and investment portfolios. The firms could do this by establishing subsidiaries in tax havens and transferring to those subsidiaries legal title to the firms' trademarks, patents, brand names, and investment portfolios. The U.S. government, by treating active and passive earnings of foreign subsidiaries differently, is walking a fine line between stimulating U.S. firms' international business activities and limiting the firms' ability to avoid U.S. taxes through the creation of subsidiaries in tax havens.

> RESOLVING INTERNATIONAL TAX CONFLICTS

Across countries differences exist in tax rates as well as in the definition of what is to be taxed. International businesses must answer to the tax authorities of each country in which the firms operate. Often national tax authorities may be in conflict or may cumulatively impose extremely burdensome levels of taxation on international firms. As a result, resolving international tax conflicts is very important to international businesspeople.

Tax Credits

The earnings of foreign subsidiaries often are taxed by the host country government. If the same earnings also are taxed by the home country government, this dual taxation may become too burdensome for the firm and discourage it from participating in the international marketplace. The home country may reduce the burden of this dual taxation of foreign subsidiary income by granting a tax credit to the parent corporation for income taxes paid to the host country. This tax credit reduces the level of home country taxes the MNC must pay.

The U.S. tax code allows U.S. firms to reduce their federal corporate income taxes by the amount of foreign income taxes paid by the firms' foreign branches or subsidiaries, subject to certain limitations. The foreign income tax credit cannot be larger than the foreign operation's U.S. tax burden. However, under certain circumstances firms may carry excess tax credits backward or forward for a limited number of years. Many common destinations for U.S. foreign direct investment impose higher corporate taxes than the United States does, so the foreign income tax credit offers U.S. MNCs only partial relief from high foreign taxes. Further, the tax credit may be taken only for income taxes, not for other forms of taxes such as value-added taxes or sales taxes. Although these concepts are simple in principle, many provisions of the U.S. tax code dealing with foreign tax credits are far more complicated in practice. International firms generally hire professionals knowledgeable about the intricacies of the tax code's treatment of foreign tax credits.

Tax Treaties

To promote international commerce, many countries sign treaties that address taxation issues affecting international business. For example, the United States has signed over 55 tax treaties with foreign nations. Although the details vary, many of these treaties contain provisions for reducing withholding taxes imposed on firms' foreign branches and subsidiaries. Sometimes these treaties reduce the overall tax burden imposed on foreign income earned by home country firms or completely exempt interest and royalty payments from taxation. Typically, such preferences are granted on a reciprocal basis: Country A provides country B's firms with favorable treatment only if country B treats country A's firms the same way.[30]

"Bashing" of Foreign Firms

Another source of international tax conflict involves the "bashing" of foreign firms by domestic politicians who believe such firms manipulate transfer prices or otherwise structure relationships between the parent corporation and the local subsidiary to avoid paying their "fair share" of taxes (see "Bringing the World into Focus"). For example, Japan's National Tax Administration (NTA) aggressively

Bringing the World into FOCUS

PITY THE POOR TAX COLLECTOR

The United States has attempted to boost its tax take from foreign firms by eliminating a tax loophole called "earnings stripping." In the U.S. tax code firms normally are allowed to deduct interest payments in calculating their tax bills but must pay taxes on any dividends they earn. To take advantage of these provisions, many foreign MNCs provided capital to their U.S. subsidiaries in the form of loans from the parent corporation to the subsidiary rather than in the form of equity investment. Earnings generated by the subsidiary then could be repatriated back to the parent in the form of interest payments untaxed by the U.S. government. Earnings were thereby "stripped" from the income taxes that would otherwise have been paid to the U.S. government.

To eliminate this practice, in 1989 the U.S. tax code was revised to limit the deductability of interest payments made by a U.S. subsidiary to its foreign-owned parent to 50 percent of the subsidiary's taxable income. Foreign MNCs promptly changed their strategy. Instead of the parent corporation providing loans directly to the U.S. subsidiary, the parent corporation arranged and guaranteed bank loans for its U.S. subsidiary. Although this approach was more expensive than the parent lending the funds directly, many foreign MNCs found it a better alternative than paying taxes to the U.S. government.

To counteract this approach, the U.S. tax code was changed in 1994 so that bank loans to the U.S. subsidiary guaranteed by the parent corporation would be treated as loans from the parent. With this new law the IRS thought it had at last outsmarted the foreign companies. However, the primary result to date is that they have developed even more creative means of avoiding U.S. taxes. Some U.S. subsidiaries have sold their assets and leased them back, thereby replacing bank loans with lease payments. Others have issued bonds convertible into the common stock of the foreign parent corporation, which has the effect of the parent guaranteeing the loan in substance but not in law.

Source: "Foreign Firms Fume, Seek Loopholes as U.S. Attempts to Collect More Taxes," *Wall Street Journal*, June 14, 1994, p. A10.

audits the transfer-pricing policies of foreign firms. In the late 1990s it filed claims against 50 foreign firms, alleging underpayment of $492 million in Japanese taxes due to improperly calculated transfer prices. MNCs such as Novartis, Roche, Goodyear, and Coca-Cola have been hit with such claims; most of these cases are as yet unresolved. However, the NTA's actions have created a boom in business for accounting firms: Arthur Andersen alone has quadrupled the number of transfer-pricing specialists employed in its Tokyo office during the past decade.[31]

The IRS similarly has targeted foreign firms after a study indicated that only 28 percent of foreign-owned firms operating in the United States paid any U.S. income tax. Yet it is unclear to what extent foreign firms are engaging in illegal tax evasion, as opposed to the legal use of tax code loopholes to avoid taxes. For example, in the late 1980s and early 1990s the IRS stepped up its enforcement of U.S. transfer-pricing rules. However, because of exemptions in the tax code, it obtained only 26.5 percent of the amount it originally sought. In two significant cases the IRS filed against Merck & Co. and Nestlé during this period, U.S. courts held that the firms were properly following the requirements of the U.S. tax code. To avoid costly and lengthy litigation, many MNCs, such as Matsushita Electric Industrial Co., have chosen to enter into **advance pricing agreements** with the IRS, in which both sides agree in advance to the transfer prices the company will charge for intracorporate transactions. Nonetheless, some U.S. politicians have proposed requiring foreign firms to pay some minimum level of income taxes based on the profitability of their U.S. competitors. So far, Treasury Department officials have opposed such proposals, arguing such taxes would violate existing tax treaties. U.S.-based MNCs also have fought such proposals, believing that unfair treatment of foreign firms by the United States would invite retaliation by foreign governments against foreign subsidiaries of U.S. firms.

CHAPTER REVIEW

Summary

The accounting tasks international businesses confront are more complex than those faced by purely domestic firms. An international firm must meet the accounting requirements of both its home country and all the countries in which it operates. Unfortunately, significant philosophical and operational differences exist in the accounting standards and procedures of the world's countries.

To reduce the costs that different national accounting systems impose on international businesses and international investors, several efforts are underway to harmonize the accounting systems of the major trading nations. The IASC has played an important role in such efforts, as has the EU.

Firms engaged in international business typically face two specific accounting challenges: accounting for transactions in foreign currencies and translating the reported operations of foreign subsidiaries into the currency of the parent firm for purposes of consolidation. FASB Statement 52 details the procedures U.S. corporations use to account for such international transactions.

International businesses also are challenged in dealing with various countries' taxation policies. MNCs try to maximize their after-tax profitability by taking advantage of tax breaks and avoiding punitive taxes. They may manipulate transfer prices to shift reported profits from high-tax countries to low-tax countries. A few smaller countries have built strong local economies by providing tax havens to attract MNCs through the elimination of corporate income taxes and the creation of favorable business climates.

Like many countries, the United States offers favorable tax incentives to encourage its firms to participate in international business. The U.S. tax code allowed firms to establish foreign sales corporations to reduce the taxes the firms pay on exports, although these provisions were recently found to be contrary to WTO rules. Under certain conditions U.S. firms also may defer paying U.S. income taxes on income generated by the firms' foreign subsidiaries. However, foreign branches of U.S. firms enjoy no such tax benefits.

Because of the revenue needs of governments, international businesses often find themselves in conflict with foreign governments. To reduce firms' tax burdens, many home governments offer their firms credits for taxes paid to foreign governments. They also negotiate tax treaties to both reduce firms' tax burdens and promote international commerce. Foreign firms, however, often are the target of "bashing" by domestic politicians who rightly or wrongly believe those firms are not paying their fair share of domestic taxes.

Review Questions

1. What factors influence the accounting procedures a country adopts?
2. How do German firms use accounting reserves?
3. What problems do Western firms and investors face in analyzing the performance of firms in centrally planned economies?
4. What is the impact of differing accounting standards on the international capital market?
5. Which organizations are promoting the harmonization of national accounting standards?
6. What is the two-transaction approach?
7. How do firms establish prices for goods sold by one subsidiary to another?
8. How do U.S. MNCs benefit from the deferral rule?
9. Why are the IRS rules regarding CFCs so complicated? What kind of behavior is the IRS trying to prevent?
10. What mechanisms have national governments adopted to lessen the burden of foreign governments' taxes on home country MNCs?

Questions for Discussion

1. The Big Five have globalized primarily through mergers. What advantages does this growth strategy offer these firms? What are the disadvantages of using mergers to globalize?
2. What impact would harmonization of national accounting standards have on international businesses?
3. What are the benefits of the two-transaction approach to international businesses and international investors?
4. How can an international firm use transfer pricing to increase its after-tax income?
5. The U.S. tax code distinguishes between active and passive income in permitting the deferral of foreign subsidiaries' income. Why has it made this distinction? Why is the distinction important? If tax havens were eliminated, would the tax code need to continue to distinguish between active and passive income?
6. Is the use of transfer pricing to reduce a firm's taxes ethical? Why or why not?
7. Are U.S. firms at a competitive disadvantage because they cannot use accounting reserves as German firms do?

BUILDING GLOBAL SKILLS

International accounting is complex. As this chapter has shown, a firm's international activities affect its financial statements in many ways. To gain a better appreciation of this impact, obtain the most recent annual report of a publicly traded corporation that engages in international business. Most major firms listed on the NYSE, the American Stock Exchange, or NASDAQ are happy to provide you with their most recent annual report if you write or phone their investor relations department. Your local library or members of your family also may be able to provide you with a report. Some firms also provide access to their annual reports at their corporate Web sites.

Next, answer the following questions regarding the firm you selected. (You may not be able to answer all of them. Some firms provide highly detailed information about their foreign operations, whereas others provide very little.)

1. How large is the firm's cumulative translation adjustment in absolute terms? How large is the adjustment relative to shareholders' equity?
2. Did the firm benefit from any special tax breaks on its international business activities? If so, by how much?
3. What percentage of the firm's assets are located in foreign countries? What percentage of its profits come from its foreign operations?
4. How much taxes did the firm pay to foreign countries?
5. How important is exporting to the firm?
6. Did the firm enjoy or suffer any foreign-currency transactions gains or losses? Did it engage in any hedging activities to protect itself from exchange rate changes?

WORKING WITH THE WEB: BUILDING GLOBAL INTERNET SKILLS

Hunting for Low Taxes

Mountain Sports, Inc., is a small U.S. manufacturer of snowboards. It markets its line of high-priced, high-tech snowboards to ski shops throughout the Rocky Mountains and New England. Recently it has decided to expand into the European market, which it believes holds far greater opportunities than the increasingly crowded U.S. market. Its business plan predicts it will sell $6 million in snowboards annually in Europe. To implement this initiative, Mountain Sports plans to establish a small, 10-person sales office somewhere in the Alps. The company estimates it will pay each of its 10 salespersons approximately $60,000. After deducting salaries, rent, travel expenses, and the cost of the snowboards themselves, Mountain Sports expects to gross $1 million in profits in Europe before paying taxes of any kind.

Mountain Sports has decided to locate its European sales office in Austria, Switzerland, or Italy, depending on which country's tax laws are most favorable. To help Mountain Sports make this decision, you are assigned the task of obtaining information about each country's tax laws. In particular, Mountain Sports is concerned about the payroll taxes and income taxes it will have to pay for its European sales office. It also is unsure whether it should operate the office as a branch or as a subsidiary (i.e., should it incorporate the European sales office, thereby making it a subsidiary?). Accordingly, you need to collect information on the various taxes levied on payrolls and on corporate income in these three countries. You also need to determine if there are any advantages to operating as a subsidiary rather than a branch. After obtaining this information, write a brief memo detailing what you have discovered, and provide a recommendation to the CEO of Mountain Sports regarding which country the sales office should be located in and whether it should be incorporated or not. Make sure you justify your recommendation.

Fortunately, some accounting firms and other organizations provide on their Web sites summary information of the tax codes of the world's nations. The textbook's Web site provides linkages to these and other Web sites that may be of help for this assignment.

WE INVITE YOU TO VISIT THIS BOOK'S COMPANION WEB SITE AT www.prenhall.com/griffin

IN THE NEWS

International businesses face highly complex accounting issues because accounting rules and practices differ from country to country, and an MNC must meet the standards of every country in which it operates.

Use the homepage of the *Financial Times* (*www.ft.com*) to research the International Accounting Standards Committee. You also can check the committee's Web site at *www.iasc.org.uk/*, where you will find a students section that may be helpful. Write a brief report summarizing the purpose of this organization and listing the status of its current projects. Are specific industries affected by any of these projects, and if so, which ones and how?

CLOSING CASE

The Aramco Advantage

Between the years 1979 and 1981 Saudi Arabia had a major disagreement with the other members of the Organization of Petroleum Exporting Countries (OPEC) about the appropriate price to charge for a barrel of crude oil. So-called OPEC hawks wanted to keep the price of oil high. Saudi Arabia, fearful that high prices would encourage other countries to explore for new, low-cost oil fields and stimulate consumers to conserve on energy usage, believed the most profitable long-run strategy was to keep prices low. The Saudis' actions resulted in the creation of the "Aramco advantage" and the world's largest tax refund involving transfer pricing.

Aramco is a consortium of four U.S. oil companies—Chevron, Exxon, Mobil, and Texaco—that originally controlled the Saudi oil fields. (Exxon and Mobil have subsequently merged.) After its oil reserves were expropriated by the Saudi government in the 1970s, Aramco continued to play a major role in marketing Saudi oil. The Aramco advantage began in January 1979 when Ahmed Zaki Yamani, the Saudi oil minister, wrote a letter to Aramco forbidding it to sell Saudi oil for more than the price set by Yamani's ministry. This price was well below the world market price for crude oil. The Aramco partners, not wishing to displease the Saudi government, dutifully complied with Yamani's request. They sold the crude oil to their foreign refineries at Yamani's price and then refined the oil into gasoline, diesel fuel, and other petroleum products. Yamani's directive, however, covered only the price of crude oil. Each company was free to sell the refined products at their market prices, which the four companies did. Because they were buying the crude oil at less than the market price, the refining operations of the Aramco partners were soon making money hand over fist. (In case you are wondering, Yamani was not ignorant of the impact of his letter. He had numerous political reasons for his actions.)

The impact of the Aramco advantage was enormous. Exxon's refineries earned an additional $4.5 billion from 1979 to 1981, and Texaco's refineries netted an estimated $1.8 billion. Because these profits were earned by the companies' foreign refinery subsidiaries, the profits could be sheltered from U.S. taxation thanks to the deferral rule—or so the companies thought. The U.S. Internal Revenue Service (IRS) had a different view, arguing that it was the marketing activities of the two companies that were responsible for the profits, not the refining operations. Accordingly, the IRS claimed that $4.5 billion in income should be transferred to Exxon (the parent corporation) from its foreign refineries and that Texaco should make a similar shift of $1.8 billion. Having done so, the companies then should be required to pay U.S. corporate income taxes on these earnings.

Not surprisingly, the companies resisted the IRS's interpretation. They said they were following the explicit instructions of the minister of a sovereign, friendly nation. Because of Yamani's directive, Texaco and Exxon asserted that the parent companies were unable to directly benefit from lower crude oil prices because the companies were forbidden to resell the oil at the market price. Rather, they noted that the Aramco advantage could be captured only by someone operating further down in the production-distribution chain. As things turned out, it was the next link in the chain—the foreign refineries owned by the individual Aramco partners—that garnered the Aramco advantage. Exxon and Texaco also pointed out that the United States had been putting great diplomatic pressure on the Saudis to lower the price of crude oil and that U.S. officials were well aware that the result of this policy would be increased refining profits.

Texaco's case was the first to complete its long journey through the U.S. judicial system. The U.S. Tax Court agreed with Texaco's interpretation. The court found that the $1.8 billion in additional profits generated by the Aramco advantage were earned by Texaco's foreign refining subsidiaries and not subject to U.S. corporate income taxes unless and until the profits were repatriated back to the parent corporation in the form of dividends. A federal appeals court upheld the verdict of the Tax Court, and in April 1997 the U.S. Supreme Court refused to hear the IRS's appeal of the appeals court decision. Texaco's tax refund was estimated to be $700 million.[32]

Case Questions

1. Which unit of Texaco really "earned" the Aramco advantage? Aramco itself? Texaco's foreign refineries? Texaco's marketing operations? Or the parent corporation?

2. Had Aramco sold the crude oil to Texaco's U.S. refineries, would Texaco have been able to avoid U.S. taxation on the Aramco advantage?

3. Because Minister Yamani created the Aramco advantage partly in response to U.S. diplomatic pressure, should Exxon and Texaco have been required to sell their allotment of Saudi crude oil to their domestic refineries?

4. The IRS lawyers argued that the appeals court ruling amounted to a "blueprint for the evasion of U.S. taxes. [It] ... creates substantial tax incentives for United States corporations to encourage or to endure the adoption of profitable foreign 'legal restrictions' that 'require' such corporations to avoid United States taxation." Do you agree with the IRS position? Or is it just being a crybaby because it lost?

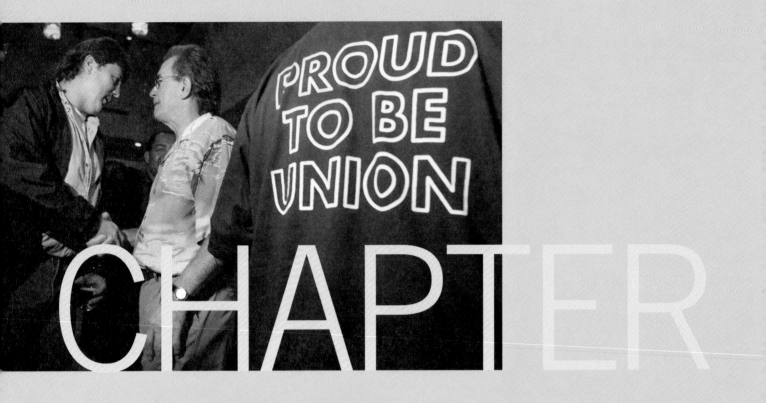

CHAPTER

Training for the World

When an international business opens a new office, manufacturing plant, or other facility in a foreign country, one of its most important tasks is staffing that new facility with managers and operating employees. To do this, the firm must decide how many employees it needs for the new facility, what skills they must have, where they will be hired, how much they will be paid, and many other issues. Most firms think they do a pretty good job in this area. However, when it comes to staffing a foreign operation, Japanese companies are among the most careful and thorough in the world.

Consider how Toyota approached the staffing of its first automobile assembly plant in the United States. In Japan automakers and other manufacturers have set up special training programs in high schools. Students who are not likely to go to college can enter training and apprenticeship programs financed by these businesses. Toyota managers believe it takes a special kind of employee to succeed in their firm. The firm wants to hire only people who will conform to the Japanese emphasis on teamwork, corporate loyalty, and versatility along the production line. In Japan prospective employees have been trained and screened along these dimensions while in high school. In the United States such programs are

> "Toyota managers **believe** it takes **a special kind** of employee to succeed."

International Human Resource Management and Labor Relations

20

After studying this chapter, you should be able to:

❯ Describe the nature of human resource management in international business.

❯ Detail how firms recruit and select managers for international assignments.

❯ Explain how international businesses train and develop expatriate managers.

❯ Discuss how international firms conduct performance appraisals and determine compensation for their expatriate managers.

❯ Analyze retention and turnover issues in international business.

❯ Explain basic human resource issues involving nonmanagerial employees.

❯ Describe labor relations in international business.

rare, so Toyota goes to what some observers see as extraordinary lengths to select its U.S. employees.

When Toyota was opening its first wholly owned U.S. plant in Kentucky, it received over 100,000 applications for 2,700 production jobs and 300 office jobs. Over half of these applicants were rejected immediately because they lacked the minimum education or experience Toyota deemed necessary. Other applicants were eliminated early in the screening process because they lacked one or more other essential qualifications.

The thousands of applicants still under consideration were invited to participate in an exhaustive battery of tests. Applicants for even the lowest-level jobs in the plant were tested for over 14 hours. The initial tests covered such areas as manual dexterity, job skills, and technical knowledge. Worker attitudes toward unionization also were assessed during this phase of testing because Toyota did not want its plant to be unionized by the United Auto Workers, the collective bargaining agent for U.S. automakers.

Those applicants who passed the first level of tests were invited back to participate in an organizational simulation exercise. Although many firms use an organizational simulation when hiring managers, Toyota uses it for all prospective employees. Results from the simulation eliminated still other applicants from the pool, while those who remained were invited back for still more testing. This third wave of testing involved performing mock production line jobs on a simulated conveyor belt under the observation of trained supervisors. Only one of every 20 applicants made it through this test and was invited back yet again, this time for an interview.

The interview was conducted by a panel of officials and representatives from each department in the plant. These interviewers were trained to determine how well the applicant would fit into both the overall Toyota culture and the interviewers' specific departments. Finally, applicants who were favorably evaluated by the interviewers were asked to take a physical exam and a drug test. If they passed both, then—and only then—were they deemed to have met Toyota's standards.

By the time the selection process is completed and Toyota actually hires a person, it has spent over $13,000 on testing and evaluating that individual. Moreover, it has spent thousands of additional dollars eliminating others at earlier stages. Even though Toyota's original U.S. plant has been open for a decade, the firm is just as selective now as in earlier times. The firm allows 24 people a day to sign up for its assessment center evaluation (many more apply each day). About one in a hundred eventually gets a job, although the entire evaluation process and time spent on the waiting list can stretch to two years before the individual actually starts working. Toyota has extended and refined its thorough selection approach into its newest U.S. plants as well. For example, applicants for jobs at the firm's Indiana truck plant and West Virginia engine plant undergo the same rigorous assessment as applicants at the Kentucky factory.

Other foreign automobile companies setting up shop in the United States also recognize that employees are critical to their success. When Mercedes-Benz began hiring people for its factory in Alabama, 45,000 applications were received for 1,500 jobs. Like Toyota, Mercedes established a grueling and comprehensive system to identify just the workers it wanted. Other Japanese auto manufacturers also invest heavily in selecting employees for their U.S. operations. Each puts a slightly different twist on the process, however. Mazda uses more tests relating to job skills, whereas Mitsubishi puts more emphasis on group exercises and simulations. Honda emphasizes tests much less but subjects each applicant to a minimum of three interviews. Nissan takes yet another approach. Applicants who meet its preliminary screening criteria must go through 40 hours of nonpaid preemployment training. After that training is complete, their ability to meet Nissan's performance standards is assessed on a simulated assembly line. Those who meet the minimum acceptable standards may then be eligible for employment with the firm.[1]

At its most basic level any organization—from a small neighborhood convenience store to the largest multinational corporation (MNC)—is nothing more than a collection of jobs, clusters of jobs, and interconnections among those jobs. The people who fill the jobs are a vital ingredient in determining how effectively the organization will be able to meet its goals, remain competitive, and satisfy its constituents. Toyota's care in selecting its U.S. workforce shows that it understands that its employees are among its most important assets.

❯ THE NATURE OF HUMAN RESOURCE MANAGEMENT

Human resource management (HRM) is the set of activities directed at attracting, developing, and maintaining the effective workforce necessary to achieve a firm's objectives. HRM includes recruiting and selecting nonmanagers and managers, providing training and development, appraising performance, and providing compensation and benefits. HR managers, regardless of whether they work for a purely domestic firm or an international one, must develop procedures and policies for accomplishing these tasks.

International HR managers, however, face challenges beyond those confronting their counterparts in purely domestic companies.[2] Specifically, differences in cultures, levels of economic development, and legal systems among the countries in which a firm operates may force it to customize its hiring, firing, training, and compensation programs on a country-by-country basis. Particularly troublesome problems develop when conflicts arise between the culture and laws of the home country and those of the host country. For example, prohibitions against gender discrimination in U.S. equal employment opportunity laws conflict with Saudi Arabian custom and law regarding the role of women. Such conflicts cause problems for U.S. MNCs that want to ensure their female executives receive overseas assignments equivalent to those given to their male colleagues.[3]

The international firm also must determine where various employees should come from—the home country, the host country, or third countries. The optimal mix of employees may differ according to the location of the firm's operations. A firm is likely to hire more employees from its home country to work in production facilities there than to work in foreign facilities. Local laws also must be considered because they may limit or constrain hiring practices. For example, immigration laws may limit the number of work visas granted to foreigners, or employment regulations may mandate the hiring of local citizens as a requirement for doing business in a country.

International businesses also face more complex training and development challenges. For example, HR managers must provide cross-cultural training for corporate executives chosen for overseas assignments. Similarly, training systems for production workers in host countries must be adjusted to reflect the education offered by local school systems. For example, because of the tradition of employment as a lifetime commitment, Toyota, like other large Japanese corporations, goes to great lengths to hire just the right people to work in its factories and offices. As the chapter opener revealed, it has nurtured partnerships with local public school systems in Japan to help train and select future employees. However, Toyota cannot rely on this approach in each country in which it does business because local school systems often are not prepared to operate such training partnerships with individual firms. The German secondary school system provides extensive vocational training for its students, but that training is less firm specific. The United States, on the other hand, emphasizes general education and provides only modest vocational training opportunities through its public schools. Moreover, many countries have labor pools that, when measured along any dimension, are uneducated and unskilled. Toyota thus has adjusted its selection, recruitment, and training practices to meet the requirements of the countries in which it does business.

Finally, because working conditions and the cost of living may vary dramatically by country, international HR managers often must tailor compensation systems to meet the needs of the host country's labor market. They must take into account variations in local laws, which may require the payment of a minimum wage or may mandate certain benefits, such as annual bonuses or health care coverage. These managers also must determine how to compensate executives on overseas assignments, who potentially face higher costs of living, reductions in the quality of their lifestyle, and unhappiness or stress due to separation from friends and relatives.

Strategic Significance of HRM

As with marketing, operations, finance, and accounting, the firm's managers must design an HRM strategy that promotes the company's overall corporate and business strategies. The cultural nuances inherent in international business heighten

FIGURE 20.1

The International Human Resource Management Process

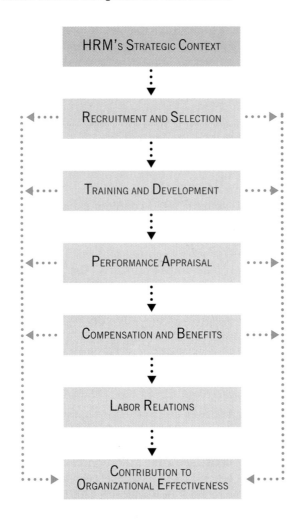

the complexities of developing an effective human resource strategy. The basic elements of the international HRM process are shown in Figure 20.1, which provides the framework around which this chapter is organized. The starting point is recognizing and appreciating HRM's strategic position within the firm and the interconnection between overall firm strategy and HRM strategy. For example, suppose a firm decides to adopt a cost leadership strategy and subsequently identifies the opportunity to undercut competing firms by aggressively pricing its products in new international markets. In implementing this strategy, the firm could decide to purchase more inputs from outside suppliers, or it could shift production to a country with low-cost labor, such as Indonesia or Malaysia. This production location decision could result in less need for home country workers and more need for workers at the foreign facility. The firm's HR managers thus would have to develop severance packages and provide outplacement services for released workers in the home country as well as select, recruit, and train the new workers in the foreign country. Over time the firm's HR managers would have to adjust their HR practices to meet the conditions in the host country, which are likely to differ from those in the home country.

The decision to shift production overseas has other HR consequences. HR managers have to select key managerial personnel to oversee the transfer of the firm's technology, operating policies, and proprietary skills to its new overseas factories. Regardless of the skills or abilities of the selected international managers, few of them will be able to walk into a foreign operation and know exactly how to do things from the first day they arrive. Thus HR managers must provide them with training to help them function more effectively in a new culture.

HR managers also must be prepared to define performance effectiveness and assess how well each international manager is doing relative to that definition. Moreover, international managers must be compensated for their work. Further, companies invest a lot in their international managers, so HR managers must carefully assess how effectively their firm manages retention and turnover.

INTERNATIONAL MANAGERIAL STAFFING NEEDS ❮

The staffing issues confronting international HR managers can be divided into two broad categories. One of these is recruiting, training, and retaining managerial and executive employees. The other is recruiting, training, and retaining nonmanagerial employees, such as blue-collar production workers and white-collar office staff. For managerial employees strategic and developmental issues are of primary importance. For nonmanagerial workers differences in cultural, political, and legal conditions among countries may be of greater significance.

Scope of Internationalization

We begin by focusing on recruiting, training, and retaining managers. The size of this task depends on the scope of the firm's international involvement. Obviously, a firm's needs in the beginning stages of internationalization, such as in indirect exporting, are far less complex and comprehensive than those confronting an MNC with extensive investments in numerous countries. Consider the evolution of organizational structure discussed in Chapter 13:

1. *Export department*: A firm's initial foray into international business usually involves small-scale exporting using output from existing domestic production facilities. Its international activities are administered by an export department, whose manager reports to an existing company executive such as the vice president of marketing. The manager is likely to be a citizen of the home country and may or may not have special training in overseas marketing and financing. As export sales increase, however, the firm quickly recognizes it must increase its staff's expertise, so it hires specialists in export documentation, international trade financing, and overseas distribution and marketing. These specialists often are recruited from international banks, international freight forwarders, or export management companies.

2. *International division*: As its international operations grow in importance, a firm often creates a separate international division to administer all of its international activities. Typically, a firm's international division is housed at corporate headquarters in its home country and is headed by a home country citizen to facilitate communication and coordination between the domestic and international operations. The heads of the firm's foreign subsidiaries in turn report to the vice president of the international division. These foreign subsidiaries' managers (including their presidents as well as heads of functional departments such as finance, marketing, and production) may be either home country or host country citizens. Use of a home country manager facilitates communication and coordination with corporate headquarters because of shared cultural and educational backgrounds.[4] Use of a host country manager often improves the subsidiary's ability to adjust to changes in local economic and political conditions. As we discuss later in this chapter, cost considerations also play a major role in the choice between home country and host country managers.

3. *Global organization*: A firm further along in the internationalization process often adopts a global organization form. (Chapter 13 discussed the global product, global functional, global area, and global customer forms.) Because of the complexity of its operations, a global organization must assemble a team of

managers that have the expertise to produce, finance, and market its products worldwide while simultaneously coordinating its activities to achieve global production, financing, and marketing economies and synergies. To operate successfully, a global firm needs a team of managers that collectively possess expertise in and knowledge of the following:

- The firm's *product line*: Product managers must be aware of such factors as the latest manufacturing techniques, research and development opportunities, and competitors' strategies.

- The *functional skills* (accounting, logistics, marketing, manufacturing management, and so on) necessary to ensure global competitiveness: Functional specialists strive to capture global economies of scale and synergies in a firm's financial, marketing, and production activities.

- The *individual country markets* in which the firm does business: Country managers must understand such factors as local laws, culture, competitors, distribution systems, and advertising media. These managers play a key role in meeting the needs of local customers, ensuring compliance with host country rules and regulations, and enlarging the firm's market share and profitability in the host country.

- The *firm's global strategy*: High-level executives at corporate headquarters must formulate a global strategy for the firm and then control and coordinate the activities of the firm's product, functional, and country managers to ensure its strategy is successfully implemented.

Centralization Versus Decentralization of Control

An international business's HRM needs also are affected by whether the firm wants decision making to be centralized at corporate headquarters or delegated (decentralized) to operating subsidiaries. Firms that use a centralized approach often favor employing home country managers; firms that follow a decentralized decision-making philosophy are more likely to employ host country managers.

Certain organizational approaches and forms affect the choice of centralization or decentralization. Firms that view themselves as multi*domestic* rather than multi*national* are likely to favor decentralization of decision making. The global area form facilitates delegating responsibility to managers of the firm's foreign subsidiaries. Conversely, the international division form favors centralizing decision making at corporate headquarters.

Recall from Chapter 13 that most international businesses operate somewhere along the continuum from pure centralization to pure decentralization. In managing human resources, most adopt an overall HRM strategy at the corporate headquarters level but delegate many day-to-day HR issues to local and regional offices. Doing this allows each foreign operation to meet its own needs and to more effectively deal with local conditions, cultures, and HR practices.

Staffing Philosophy

The extent of the firm's internationalization and its degree of centralization or decentralization affects (and is affected by) its philosophy regarding the nationality of its international managers. Firms can hire from three groups: parent country nationals, host country nationals, and third-country nationals.

Parent country nationals (PCNs) are residents of the international business's home country. Use of PCNs in an MNC's foreign operations provides many advantages to the firm. Because PCNs typically share a common culture and educational background with corporate headquarters staff, they facilitate communication and coordination with corporate headquarters. If the firm's global strategy involves exploiting new technologies or business techniques that were developed in the home market, PCNs often are best able to graft those innovations to a host country setting. For example, Toyota sent a team of executives from Japan to oversee the start-up of its U.S. operations. It wanted to ensure that its manufacturing techniques and corporate commitment to quality were successfully transplanted to Kentucky and the other U.S. plants it subsequently opened. Mercedes followed a similar staffing strategy when it started its Alabama plant.

However, using PCNs has several disadvantages. PCNs typically lack knowledge of the host country's laws, culture, economic conditions, social structure, and political processes. Although PCNs can be trained to overcome these knowledge gaps, such training is expensive (particularly when the opportunity cost of the manager's time is considered) and is not a perfect substitute for having been born and raised in the host country. Further, PCNs are often expensive to relocate and maintain in the host country. Finally, many host countries restrict the number of foreign employees who can be transferred in and/or mandate that a certain percentage of an international firm's payroll must be paid to employees from the host country. Thus an international business may not have total freedom to hire whomever it wants for international assignments. Because of these factors, PCNs are most likely to be used in upper-level and/or technical positions in host countries.

Host country nationals (HCNs) are residents of the host country. HCNs are commonly used by international businesses to fill middle-level and lower-level jobs, but they also often appear in managerial and professional positions. Experienced MNCs such as Intel, Canadian Imperial Bank of Commerce, IBM, Seagrams, and Nortel Networks often hire HCNs instead of transferring home country employees to work in professional positions in the firms' foreign operations. Many smaller firms setting up operations abroad hire HCNs because the firms do not have enough managerial talent at home to send someone on a foreign assignment.[5]

Using HCNs offers two primary advantages. First, HCNs already understand the local laws, culture, and economic conditions. Second, the firm avoids the expenses associated with expatriate managers, such as relocation costs, supplemental wages paid for foreign service, and private schooling for children. However, using HCNs can have disadvantages. HCNs may be unfamiliar with the firm's business culture and practices, thus limiting the effectiveness of the HCNs. As noted earlier in this chapter, Toyota used Japanese executives to shepherd the development of its U.S. operations to ensure its new employees understood the firm's emphasis on producing quality automobiles.

Accenture (formerly Andersen Consulting), the world's largest consulting firm, has developed an innovative approach to training HCNs in its corporate culture. All of Accenture's entry-level consultants, who staff offices in 78 countries, must undergo an intensive three-week education program at the firm's Center for Professional Education in St. Charles, Illinois. The newly recruited professionals learn about the Accenture way of doing business and solving clients' problems. By providing its multinational recruits with common training, the firm transmits its corporate culture throughout its international empire and promotes intracorporate networking of the new employees that transcends national boundaries.

Finally, an international firm may hire **third-country nationals (TCNs)**, who are not citizens of the firm's home country or of the host country. Like PCNs, TCNs are

〉 IBM relies on host country nationals to staff its sales and support center in Dublin, Ireland. This approach works well for IBM because these employees are very familiar with local laws, culture, and economic conditions. Moreover, IBM is spared the costs of relocating large numbers of expatriates to Ireland.

most likely to be used in upper-level and/or technical positions. TCNs and PCNs collectively are known as **expatriates**, or people working and residing in countries other than their native country. In the past TCNs were likely to be used when they had special expertise that was not available to the firm through any other channel. Today they are consciously being employed by some firms to promote a global outlook throughout their operations. Firms such as Nestlé and Philips NV rely heavily on TCNs because they believe those managers bring broader perspectives and experiences to the firms' host country operations. Further, some firms are recruiting more TCNs to serve on their boards of directors to help bring a more global orientation to the boards.

Most international firms develop a systematic strategy for choosing among HCNs, PCNs, and TCNs for various positions. Some firms rely on the **ethnocentric staffing model**, whereby they primarily use PCNs to staff higher-level foreign positions. This approach is based on the assumption that home office perspectives should take precedence over local perspectives and that expatriate PCNs will be most effective in representing the views of the home office in the foreign operation. Other international firms follow a **polycentric staffing model**; that is, they emphasize the use of HCNs in the belief that HCNs know the local market best. Finally, the **geocentric staffing model** puts PCNs, HCNs, and TCNs on an equal footing. Firms that adopt this approach want to hire the best person available, regardless of where that individual comes from.[6]

National culture often affects the staffing model chosen by a firm. European MNCs are more likely than U.S. or Japanese MNCs to adopt the geocentric approach. This approach is encouraged by the European Union (EU) to improve the mobility of workers and managers throughout its member countries. Japanese firms favor the ethnocentric staffing model, partly because their consensus-oriented approach to decision making is facilitated by employing Japanese managers in key roles in the firms' foreign subsidiaries. Japanese firms sometimes rely too heavily on this model, to their own disadvantage. Although they usually hire HCNs for lower-level positions, the firms are reluctant to use non-Japanese managers in higher-level positions. When the firms do hire an HCN as a local manager, they have been accused of being too quick to send in a troubleshooter from the home office at the first sign of a problem. Further, the non-Japanese managers often face a glass ceiling because the top positions in the firms are reserved for Japanese managers. Thus the ethnocentric policy often results in the loss of the best HCN managers, who seek more challenge and responsibility by shifting to non-Japanese employers.

› RECRUITMENT AND SELECTION

A firm's scope of internationalization, level of centralization, and staffing philosophy help determine the skills and abilities its international managers need. As shown in Figure. 20.2, these skills and abilities fall into two general categories: those needed to do the job and those needed to work in a foreign location.

The firm first must define the actual business skills necessary to do the job. For example, a firm that has an assembly plant in a foreign market needs a plant manager who understands the technical aspects of what is to be manufactured, what manufacturing processes will be utilized, and so on. The firm's marketing managers must be knowledgeable about advertising media availability, distribution channels, market competition, and local consumers' demographic characteristics.

The firm next must determine the skills and abilities a manager must have to work and function effectively in the foreign location. These include the manager's ability to adapt to cultural change, ability to speak the local language, overall physical and emotional health, levels of independence and self-reliance, and appropriate levels of experience and education. Obviously, an HCN can meet these require-

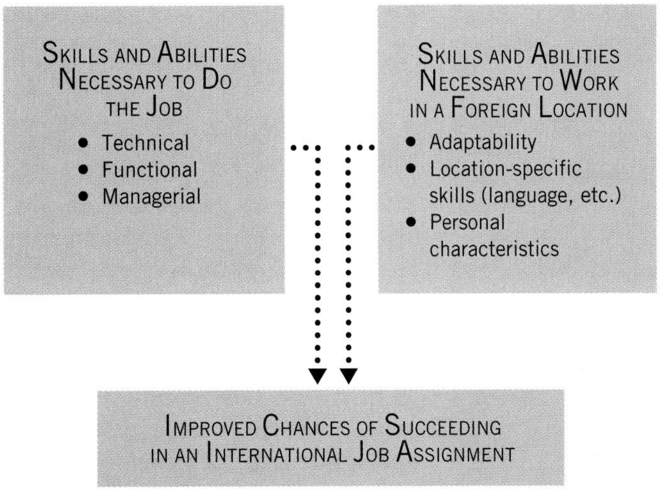

FIGURE 20.2

Necessary Skills and Abilities for International Managers

ments far easier than a PCN or TCN can. Firms relying on the ethnocentric or geocentric staffing models thus must devote more resources to selecting and training PCNs and TCNs for foreign assignments than do firms that rely on the polycentric model. "Wiring the World" discusses some of the recruiting issues facing businesses in high-technology businesses today.

Wiring the World

THE GLOBAL TALENT HUNT

Finding the best employees is never an easy task. In today's burgeoning high-technology age finding good technical employees is a bit akin to looking for the proverbial needle in a haystack. One recent survey reported 190,000 unfilled programming and computer-related jobs in the United States alone. Little wonder, then, that the best firms in high-technology markets are casting a global net in their search for good help.

Electronic Data Systems, a Dallas-based computer services company, currently recruits programmers on three continents for its Texas operations. Accenture, although not a high-technology firm per se, nevertheless needs to hire thousands of technical employees a year to support its management consulting operation. It recently added technical schools in Budapest and Manila to its growing list of recruiting sources. Texas Instruments looks to employees who have been cut loose from their employers in other countries.

Brazil, India, and Russia have become increasingly popular sources of computer talent. Skilled programmers in Brazil may be earning the equivalent of $30,000 a year. By relocating to the United States, they often can more than double their salary. In addition, many U.S. firms cover relocation expenses and give for-

eign programmers a bonus after they work for three years. Even at this salary these programmers often are seen as bargains—a U.S. citizen with the same skills would probably command a salary of as much as $80,000.

There are also other countries where quality technical employees are available and who may be interested in relocating. Some firms have had success in luring employees from Colombia, the Philippines, and South Africa. Even this approach can be difficult. For example, many of the best technical employees in South Africa learn their skills from trade schools that offer excellent training but no diplomas. This lack of a formal degree makes it more difficult for them to obtain immigration papers into countries like the United States.

Sources: Lawrence A. West, Jr., and Walter A. Bogumil, Jr., "Foreign Knowledge Workers as a Strategic Staffing Option," *Academy of Management Executive*, November 2000, pp. 71–84; "Forget the Huddled Masses: Send Nerds," *Business Week*, July 21, 1997, pp. 110–116; "A U.S. Recruiter Goes Far Afield to Bring in Techies," *Wall Street Journal*, January 8, 1998, pp. A1, A2.

› Renault has relied on Brazilian-born Carlos Ghosn to spearhead its restructuring of Nissan. Renault owns a controlling 37 percent share of Nissan's stock. Highly skilled global executives like Ghosn are often a key ingredient to an international firm's success.

Recruitment of Managers

Once the international business determines the skills and abilities an international manager must have, it next must develop a pool of qualified applicants for the job and then recruit and select the best candidate.

Recruitment of Experienced Managers.   International businesses recruit experienced managers through a variety of channels. A common source of recruits is within the firm itself—among employees already working for the firm in the host country or those who, although currently employed in the home country, might be prepared for an international assignment in the host country. The latter group may include both managers who have never held an international assignment and managers who have already completed previous international assignments. For example, when Kal Kan's Canadian subsidiary entered the animal-food market in Poland, the firm relied on a team of Polish-born Canadian executives to start up the new operation. Other companies are dipping into their pool of retired executives to fill short-term international assignments. Whirlpool rehired one of its retired senior engineers to help expand its Shanghai washing machine factory, and Quaker Oats sent a team of five retired employees to oversee the start-up of a cereal plant in that same city. Retired employees often are eager to take on such tasks. For example, Verizon has a pool of 725 former employees willing to tackle short-term foreign assignments.[7]

An international business also may attempt to identify prospective managers who work for other firms. These may be home country managers who are deemed to be qualified for an international assignment or managers already working in an international assignment for another firm. For higher-level positions firms often rely on so-called headhunters to help them locate prospective candidates. **Headhunters** are recruiting firms that actively seek qualified managers and other professionals for possible placement in positions in other organizations. In many parts of the world, including Japan, switching employers has long been frowned on; until recently, headhunting in Europe was considered unethical. Both of these views are changing, however. More firms are finding they can even entice highly qualified Japanese employees away from Japanese firms.

A firm may sometimes find it useful to relocate its facilities to be closer to a pool of qualified employees. For example, when Upjohn and Pharmacia (U.S. and Swedish pharmaceutical firms, respectively) merged in the mid-1990s, they initially selected London for their new corporate headquarters. It quickly became apparent there was not an adequate pool of managerial and technical talent available locally to staff the enterprise. Because London is among the world's most expensive cities, transferring in managers from other locations was not cost effective. Thus the firm subsequently moved its headquarters to New Jersey, where many other drug companies are located. Managers reasoned this would place them closer to a large talent pool of managers with pharmaceutical industry experience and therefore make recruiting a bit easier.[8]

One trend seems clear: As a result of the globalization of business, the market for executive talent also is becoming globalized. For example, fewer than half of the 150 highest-level executives at Imperial Chemical Industries PLC, Britain's largest chemical manufacturer, are British nationals. Firms increasingly value performance more than nationality. Nomura Securities, Japan's largest stock brokerage firm, typifies this trend. Concerned about losses in its global market share, the firm turned to a seasoned U.S. securities executive, Max Chapman, to reinvigorate its global operations, which are headquartered in London.

Recruitment of Younger Managers.   It is uncommon for large MNCs to hire new college graduates for immediate foreign assignments. Some firms, however, will hire new graduates they ultimately intend to send abroad and, in the short term, give the graduates domestic assignments. Particularly attractive are graduates with foreign-language skills, international travel experience, and a major in international business or a related field. A few firms have started taking a longer-term view of developing international managerial talent. Coca-Cola, for example, has developed an innovative strategy for recruiting managers for future international assignments. It actively seeks foreign students who are studying at U.S. colleges and universities and who intend to return to their home countries after receiving their degrees. The firm recruits and hires the best of these graduates and puts them through a one-year training program. The new managers then return home as Coca-Cola employees and take assignments in the firm's operations in their home countries.

Colgate-Palmolive has mounted perhaps the most aggressive effort of this sort. Each year this firm selects about 15 new recruits (from an applicant pool of 15,000) to participate in its fast-track globalization program, which provides quick lessons in competing in the global marketplace. Colgate reaps several benefits from this program. It is able to hire excellent young talent because college graduates from around the world seek one of the coveted slots. By exposing management trainees and entry-level managers to a new culture, the firm can forcefully show its young talent the problems inherent in self-referencing one's culture in international markets. For example, a Dutch trainee brought to the United States was shocked by the huge assortment of goods in a typical U.S. supermarket. That visit created a vivid impression of the high level of competitiveness of the U.S. market and forced the trainee to recognize that marketing strategies that might work in the Netherlands could be dismal failures in the United States. A U.S. trainee sent by Colgate to a Romanian store had a similar experience. When the trainee asked Romanian shoppers which brands of soap they preferred—a perfectly logical question to market researchers in the United States—she was surprised by the response: The Romanian shoppers, accustomed to scarcity, bought whatever soap was available.[9]

Selection of Managers

After the pool of prospective managers has been identified, HR managers must decide which persons from that pool are the best qualified for the assignment. The most promising candidates share the following characteristics:

- Managerial competence (technical and leadership skills, knowledge of the corporate culture)
- Appropriate training (formal education, knowledge of the host market and its culture and language)
- Adaptability to new situations (ability to deal simultaneously with adjusting to a new work and job environment, adjusting to working with HCNs, and adjusting to a new national culture)

The importance of the selection process cannot be overstated when dealing with expatriate managers. The costs to a firm of expatriate failure are extremely high. **Expatriate failure** is the early return of an expatriate manager to the home country because of an inability to perform in the overseas assignment. Experts suggest these costs range from $40,000 to as much as $250,000 (these figures include the expatriate's original training, moving expenses, and lost managerial productivity but do not include the decreased performance of the foreign subsidiary itself). Expatriate failure occurs far too often. Failure rates of 20 to 50 percent are common for many U.S. firms, and rates appear to be much higher for them than for European and Japanese firms.[10]

› With the growth of dual career families, new international assignments often create problems for the trailing spouse. Fortunately for this Montreal family, when Sophie Bouchard was transferred to London to head up European sales for TMP Worldwide, an executive recruiting firm, TMP was able to locate a challenging job for her husband.

The primary cause of expatriate failure is the inability of the managers and/or their spouse and family to adjust to the new locale. As a result, international HR managers increasingly are evaluating the nontechnical aspects of a candidate's suitability for a foreign assignment. Assessing certain skills and abilities is relatively easy. For example, measuring a prospect's language proficiency is a straightforward undertaking. Assessing a person's cultural adaptability is more difficult and must be accomplished through a variety of means. Most firms use a combination of tests (such as personality and aptitude tests) and interviews in their selection process. Assessment centers, which offer programs of exercises, tests, and interviews that last several days, are also useful because they provide an in-depth look at a set of prospective candidates under the same circumstances.

Another important consideration is the prospect's motivation for and interest in the foreign assignment.[11] Some managers are attracted to foreign assignments, perhaps because they relish the thought of living abroad or because they see the experience as being useful in their future career plans. Others balk at the thought of uprooting their family and moving to a foreign environment, particularly one that is culturally distant from their own. As previously noted, failure of the family to adjust to the new culture is a prominent cause of expatriate failure. Thus most firms also consider the family's motivation for and interest in the foreign assignment. The manager's job performance often will deteriorate if the manager has to soothe an unhappy spouse cut off from friends and family and frustrated by dealing with a new culture. Clearly a foreign relocation is far more disruptive to the family than a domestic relocation. Dependent children may face problems integrating into a new school culture—particularly if they do not speak the local language—and may find that material covered in the courses at their new school is well ahead (or well behind) that at their home school.[12] In addition, there is the dual-career problem. Trailing spouses may find it difficult to take leave from their current position, thereby forcing a disruption in their career advancement. Still worse, labor laws in the new country may make it difficult or impossible for the spouse to obtain employment there legally.

Because of the risk of expatriate failure, firms often devote considerable resources to selection and training.[13] AT&T, for example, prides itself on doing an especially thorough job of selecting managers for foreign assignments. The firm has long used personality tests and interviews as part of its selection process. It now also uses psychologists to help assess prospects and is investing more into learning about family considerations. In addition, the prospects complete a self-assessment checklist designed to help them probe their motivations for seeking a foreign transfer. Table 20.1 summarizes sample questions the firm uses to screen potential expatriates and their spouses. AT&T reports that this exercise increases managers' self-awareness. As a result, more managers now remove themselves from consideration for foreign assignments.

Some international businesses are concerned with not only how well a prospective manager will adapt to the foreign culture but also how well the person will fit into that culture.[14] For example, for years some U.S. firms hesitated to send women managers on foreign assignments to some countries, such as Japan,

Would your spouse be interrupting a career to accompany you on an international assignment? If so, how do you think this will affect your spouse and your relationship with each other?

Do you enjoy the challenge of making your own way in new situations?

Securing a job upon reentry will be primarily your responsibility. How do you feel about networking and being your own advocate?

How able are you in initiating new social contacts?

Can you imagine living without television?

How important is it for you to spend significant amounts of time with people of your own ethnic, racial, religious, and national background?

As you look at your personal history, can you isolate any episodes that indicates a real interest in learning about other peoples and cultures?

Has it been your habit to vacation in foreign countries?

Do you enjoy sampling foreign cuisines?

What is your tolerance for waiting for repairs?

TABLE 20.1

AT&T's Questionnaire for Screening Overseas Transferees

Source: Consultants for International Living. From "As Costs of Overseas Assignments Climb, Firms Select Expatriates More Carefully," *Wall Street Journal,* January 9, 1992, p. B1. Reprinted by permission of the *Wall Street Journal,* © 1992 Dow Jones & Company, Inc. All Rights Reserved Worldwide.

because the firms assumed the women would not be accepted in a culture that frowned on women working outside the home. However, research indicates that this fear may be overstated. Host country citizens react primarily to these executives' foreignness, rather than their gender.

Expatriation and Repatriation Issues

PCNs on long-term foreign assignments face great acculturation challenges. Working in and coping with a foreign culture can lead to **culture shock**, a psychological phenomenon that may lead to feelings of fear, helplessness, irritability, and disorientation. New expatriates may experience a sense of loss regarding their old cultural environment as well as confusion, rejection, self-doubt, and decreased self-esteem from working in a new and unfamiliar cultural setting.[15] Acculturation, as shown in Figure 20.3, typically proceeds through four phases.[16]

Culture shock reduces an expatriate's effectiveness and productivity, so international businesses have developed various strategies to mitigate its effects. One simple solution is to provide expatriates (and their families) with predeparture language and cultural training, so they can better understand and anticipate the cultural adjustments they must undergo. In addition to straightforward training, firms also might make initial foreign assignments relatively brief and make sure the expatriates understand the role each assignment plays in their overall career prospects.

Interestingly, international businesses should pay almost as much attention to **repatriation**—bringing a manager back home after a foreign assignment has been completed—as they do to expatriation. If managers and their families have been successfully expatriated, they become comfortable with living and working in the foreign culture. Returning home can be almost as traumatic to them as was the original move abroad. One reason for the difficulty of repatriation is that people tend to assume nothing has changed at home. They look forward to getting back to their friends, familiar surroundings, and daily routines. Yet their friends may have moved or developed new social circles, and their coworkers may have been transferred to other jobs. Some expatriates who have returned to the United States have even been denied credit because they have not had a domestic financial history for several years![17]

FIGURE 20.3

Phases in Acculturation

HONEYMOON
For the first few days or months the new culture seems exotic and stimulating. Excitement of working in new environment makes employee overestimate the ease of adjusting.

DISILLUSIONMENT
Differences between new and old environments are blown out of proportion. As employee and family face challenges of everyday living, differences become magnified. Many transplanted employees remain stuck in this phase.

ADAPTATION
With time employee begins to understand patterns of new culture, gains language competence, and adjusts to everyday living.

BICULTURALISM
Anxiety has ended as transplanted employee gains confidence in ability to function productively in new culture.

Repatriated managers also have to cope with change and uncertainty at work. The firm may not be sure what their job is going to entail. Further, they may have been running the show at the foreign operation and enjoying considerable authority. Back home, however, the managers are likely to have much less authority and to be on a par with many other managers reporting to more senior managers. Also, repatriated managers and their families may have enjoyed a higher social status in the host country than they will enjoy after returning home. Thus readjustment problems may be severe and need the attention of both the managers and the firm.

The repatriation problem can be expensive for a firm. By some estimates one-quarter of all repatriated employees leave their employer within a year after returning home. The average U.S. expatriate costs the employer about $300,000 per year and stays three to four years on an overseas assignment; thus each repatriated executive who leaves the firm represents a million-dollar investment walking out the door.

The bottom line is that expatriation and repatriation problems can be reduced if international businesses systematically provide organizational career development programs for their expatriate managers.[18] Recent research indicates that the likelihood of managers being successful at an overseas assignment increases if the managers:

- Can freely choose whether to accept or reject the expatriate assignment
- Have been given a realistic preview of the new job and assignment
- Have been given a realistic expectation of what their repatriation assignment will be

- Have a mentor back home who will guard their interests and provide corporate and social support during the assignment
- See a clear link between the expatriate assignment and their long-term career path

Of these five elements the last is the most critical in determining expatriate success.

TRAINING AND DEVELOPMENT ‹

The international firm's HR managers also must provide training and development for its home and host country managers to help them perform more effectively. **Training** is instruction directed at enhancing specific job-related skills and abilities. For example, training programs might be designed to help employees learn to speak a foreign language, to use new equipment, or to implement new manufacturing procedures. Special acculturation training is important for employees who are given international assignments. **Development** is general education concerned with preparing managers for new assignments and/or higher-level positions. For example, a development program could be aimed at helping managers improve their ability to make decisions or to motivate subordinates to work harder.

Assessing Training Needs

Before a firm can undertake a meaningful training or development program, it must assess its exact training and development needs. This assessment involves determining the difference between what managers and employees can do and what the firm feels they need to be able to do. For example, suppose a firm that does business in Latin America wants its employees to be able to speak Spanish fluently. If most of its employees are fluent in Spanish, its language-training needs may be minimal, but if relatively few employees are fluent, extensive training may be called for. The assessment of training needs is an extremely important element of international HRM. Firms that underestimate training needs can encounter serious difficulties. Indeed, lack of knowledge about foreign customers and markets is a major barrier to successful entry into such markets, as Figure 20.4 shows.

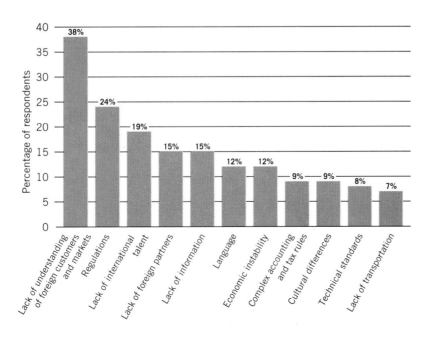

FIGURE 20.4

Barriers to Entering Foreign Markets

Source: "From Cross-Cultural Training Helps in Leap Abroad," *Houston Chronicle*, September 25, 1994, p. 1E. Reprinted with permission. Data: Ernst & Young survey.

A firm just moving into international markets has different training and development needs from those of an established global firm. The newly internationalizing firm is likely to have few, if any, experienced international managers. Thus its training and development needs will be substantial. In contrast, a global firm has a cadre of trained and experienced managers with international backgrounds, skills, and abilities. Yet even then, organization change may necessitate training. For instance, when Jaguar took over a plant in England that had formerly been making Ford Escorts, managers found a workforce that was dispirited and unwilling to accept responsibility for making decisions. All employees were thus sent to several training workshops intended to both enhance their technical skills and to empower them to make key decisions for themselves.[19]

Basic Training Methods and Procedures

The first issue an international business must consider as it plans its training and development efforts is whether to rely on standardized programs or to develop its own customized programs. Certain kinds of training can be readily obtained in common retail outlets—for example, self-paced language training on cassette tapes or CDs. Prudential Insurance even offers packaged training programs for families of expatriates, a good idea in light of the importance of family problems in causing expatriate failure. One advantage of standardized programs is that they tend to be less expensive than customized ones. On the other hand, a standardized program may not precisely fit the firm's needs.

As a result, most training and development programs often are customized to a firm's particular needs. Larger MNCs often have training and development departments that develop customized programs for the unique needs of individual managers and/or business units. Training and development activities may take place in regular classroom settings within the firm, on actual job sites, or off premises in a conference center or hotel. Customized programs are more costly than standardized programs; however, they ensure that employees get the precise information deemed necessary. Regardless of whether training and development programs are standardized or customized, most use a variety of methods as instructional vehicles. Lectures and assigned readings are common, as are videotaped and Web-based instruction.

Role-playing and other forms of experiential exercises are useful for helping people better understand other cultures. Motorola uses a workplace simulation to help prepare its managers for foreign assignments.[20] Case studies also are used, although not as frequently as other methods. Training materials often must be altered to fit different cultural contexts. For example, a consultant hired to make training videos for Bally of Switzerland initially assumed he could use the same basic video for each of Bally's regional offices, with only minor script modifications. As the project progressed, however, he found that so many language and cultural differences affected the video that he essentially had to reshoot it for each office.

The trainers themselves also may need to adapt how they do things. One professional trainer reported difficulties in using her normal style when running a training program in Thailand. She preferred to be informal and to involve the participants through role-playing and other forms of interaction. She found, however, that Thai managers were uncomfortable with her informality and resisted the role-playing approach. She eventually had to adopt a more formal style and use a straightforward lecture approach to get her points across.[21]

Developing Younger International Managers

The increasing globalization of business has prompted most MNCs to recognize the importance of internationalizing their managers earlier in their careers. Until the late 1980s most U.S. MNCs delayed giving their managers significant overseas assignments until they had spent 7 to 10 years with the firm. Today many of these MNCs are beginning to recognize that they need to develop the international awareness and competence of their managers earlier and to systematically integrate international assignments into individual career plans. For example, GE provides language and cross-cultural training to its professional staff even though they may not be scheduled for overseas postings. Such training is important because these employees, even if they never leave their home countries, are likely to work with GE employees from other countries and to deal with visiting executives from GE's foreign partners, suppliers, and customers. Such training also helps the employees gain a better understanding of the firm's international markets. Other firms, such as American Express and Johnson & Johnson, occasionally post managers to overseas assignments after only 18 to 20 months on the job. PepsiCo and Raychem are bringing young managers from the firms' foreign operations to the United States to enrich the managers' understanding of their firms' cultures and technologies.

U.S. firms are not the only ones integrating international assignments into career development plans for younger managers. Honda's U.S. manufacturing subsidiary has been sending U.S. managers to Tokyo for multiyear assignments so they can learn more about the firm's successful manufacturing and operating philosophies. Samsung regularly sends its executives abroad for various assignments. One of its more interesting strategies is to send younger managers to certain foreign locations for as long as a year with no specific job responsibilities. The managers are supposed to spend their time learning the local language and becoming familiar with the culture. The idea is that if they are transferred back to that same location in the future—when they are in a higher-level position—they will be able to function more effectively. Even though the program costs Samsung about $80,000 per person per year, executives believe the firm will quickly recoup its investment.

PERFORMANCE APPRAISAL AND COMPENSATION ‹

Another important part of international HRM consists of conducting performance appraisals and determining compensation and benefits. Whereas recruitment, selection, and training and development tend to focus on preassignment issues, performance appraisal and compensation involve ongoing issues that continue to have an effect well past the initial international assignment.

Assessing Performance in International Business

Performance appraisal is the process of assessing how effectively people are performing their jobs. The purposes of performance appraisal are to provide feedback to individuals on how well they are doing; to provide a basis for rewarding top performers; to identify areas in which additional training and development may be needed; and to identify problem areas that may call for a change in assignment.

Performance appraisals of an international business's top managers must be based on the firm's clear understanding of its goals for its foreign operations. A successful subsidiary in a mature and stable foreign market will have different goals than will a start-up operation in a growing but unstable market. Thus a firm assigning two new managers to head up these different subsidiaries must understand that it cannot expect the same outcome from each of them. Similarly, managers of foreign subsidiaries that serve as cost centers must be judged by different standards from those used for managers of profit centers.

In assessing a manager's actual performance, the firm may consider sales, profit margin, market share growth, or any other measures or indicators it deems important. If a subsidiary has been having problems, performance may be more appropriately assessed in terms of how well the manager has helped to solve those problems. For example, reducing net losses or halting a decline in market share might be considered good performance, at least in the short term.

Expected and actual performance must be compared, and differences must be addressed. This step needs to have a strong diagnostic component: Why and how has the manager's performance been acceptable or unacceptable? Are any problems attributable to the manager's lack of skills? Are some problems attributable to unforeseen circumstances? Is the home office accountable for some of the problems that may have arisen, perhaps because the manager was inadequately trained?

Circumstances will dictate how frequently performance appraisals occur. In a domestic firm they may occur as often as every quarter. Geographical factors, however, can limit the frequency with which international performance appraisals can occur. Generally, international managers are expected to submit reports on performance-based results to headquarters regularly. As long as these reports fall within acceptable parameters, the firm is likely to conduct a formal performance appraisal perhaps on an annual basis. However, if standard reports reveal a problem, performance appraisals may be done more often in an effort to get things back on track.

Determining Compensation in International Business

Another important issue in international HRM is determining managerial compensation. To remain competitive, firms must provide prevailing compensation packages for their managers in a given market. These packages include salary and nonsalary items and are determined by labor market forces such as the supply and demand of managerial talent, occupational status, professional licensing requirements, standards of living, government regulations, tax codes, and similar factors. For example, in Germany employers customarily reimburse their executives for car expenses. In Japan the executive may actually get a car plus expenses. Japanese executives also receive generous entertainment allowances and an allowance for business gifts. Similarly, British companies typically provide company cars to managers. In the United States firms offer managers health care benefits because such benefits are free from income taxes.

Compensating Expatriate Managers.   A more complex set of compensation issues apply to expatriate managers. Most international businesses find it necessary to provide these managers with differential compensation to make up for dramatic differences in currency valuation, standards of living, lifestyle norms, and so on.[22] When managers are on short-term assignments abroad, their home country salaries normally continue unchanged. (Of course, the managers are reimbursed for short-term living expenses such as for hotel rooms, meals, and transportation.) If foreign assignments are indefinite or longer term, compensation is routinely adjusted to allow the managers to maintain their home country standard of living. This adjustment is particularly important if a manager is transferred from a low-cost location to a high-cost location or from a country with a high standard of living to one with a lower standard of living. Table 20.2 summarizes cost-of-living differences for a number of international business centers.

The starting point in differential compensation is a **cost-of-living allowance**. This allowance is intended to offset differences in the cost of living in the home and host countries. The premise is that a manager who accepts a foreign assignment is entitled to the same standard of living the manager enjoyed at home. If the cost of living in the foreign country is higher than that at home, the manager's existing base pay will result in a lower standard of living, and the firm will supplement the base pay to offset this difference. Of course, if the cost of living in the foreign location is lower than at home, no such allowance is needed.

Sometimes firms find they must supplement base pay to get a manager to accept an assignment in a relatively unattractive location. Although it may not be difficult to find people willing to move to England or Japan, it may be much more difficult to entice people to move to Colombia, Somalia, or Afghanistan. Called either a **hardship premium** or a **foreign-service premium**, this supplement is essentially an inducement to the individual to accept the international assignment. As discussed in "Venturing Abroad," some settings for foreign assignments are so troublesome that new businesses have sprung up to provide safety and security.

LOCATION	ANNUAL COST OF LIVING	INDEX
Seoul, Korea	US$155,485	272.3
Tokyo, Japan	US$155,296	271.9
Moscow, Russia	US$113,883	199.4
London, England	US$97,262	170.3
Geneva, Switzerland	US$74,176	129.9
Mexico City, Mexico	US$71,071	124.5
Los Angeles, California	US$63,921	111.9
Rome, Italy	US$61,310	107.4
Sydney, Australia	US$60,181	105.4
Atlanta, Georgia	US$57,107	100.0
Munich, Germany	US$55,516	97.2
Helsinki, Finland	US$55,334	96.9
Melbourne, Australia	US$49,342	86.4
Montreal, Canada	US$48,780	85.4
Barcelona, Spain	US$45,103	79.0

TABLE 20.2

Annual Cost of Living in Selected Locations Worldwide, 2000

The table is for a U.S. family of two with a base salary of $75,000. Total annual costs are based on a combination of housing, transportation, and goods & services. The total also includes a certain amount set aside for investments and savings. Taxes are not included because actual taxes will vary greatly depending upon the tax planning techniques used.

Housing costs are based on home or apartment rental and include utilities and renters insurance.

Transportation costs include both public commutation and private vehicle ownership and operating costs.

Goods & services include the total amounts paid (including sales tax) for food-at-home, food-away-from-home, tobacco & alcohol, household operations, clothing, domestic services, medical care, and recreation.

Source: Runzheimer International.

VENTURING Abroad

SEEING OPPORTUNITY IN SECURITY

The safety and security of employees posted to foreign assignments are a continuing concern for multinational enterprises. In some locations, such as Colombia, local criminals specialize in kidnapping foreigners and/or their families and then demanding the payment of a ransom. Executives are common targets because of the presumption that their employers will pay large sums to secure their release. Other trouble spots are worrisome because of political instability. Recent problems of this type have arisen in Sierra Leone, Indonesia, and the Middle East.

Entrepreneurs sometimes see opportunities in such situations. For instance, local businesses in many unstable and/or hazardous areas often provide personal security services, sell bulletproof glass for car and apartment windows, and offer information about unsafe areas. When problems do arise, local entrepreneurs often are involved in negotiations and investigations.

A particularly successful new enterprise is Air Partner, a British company that specializes in evacuating people when trouble erupts unexpectedly. The founder of Air Partner, Alan Marler, learned that although most MNCs have thoughtful plans for getting their employees out of foreign settings when a problem arises, these plans often go awry because an airplane is not available. Thus Marler maintains reliable access to aircraft and has a long list of international clients who will pay to get their employees out on a moment's notice.

Air Partner has successfully evacuated MNC employees out of tough spots in Chechnya, Kuwait, Saudi Arabia, Albania, the West Indies, and Indonesia. For example, during political unrest in 1999 the firm safely pulled 250 Western executives and their families out of Indonesia. The price? Some firms pay a retainer of $60,000 a year to Air Partner to help as needed. Others pay a flat price of $15,000 per person for its evacuation services.

Source: "Flight to Safety," *Forbes*, May 29, 2000, pp. 166–168.

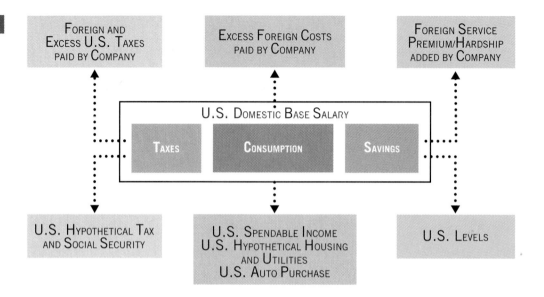

FIGURE 20.5

An Expatriate Balance Sheet

Finally, many international businesses also find they must set up a tax equalization system. A **tax equalization system** is a means of ensuring that the expatriate's after-tax income in the host country is similar to what the person's after-tax income would be in the home country. Each country has unique tax laws that apply to the earnings of its own citizens, to earnings within its borders by foreign citizens, and/or to earnings in another country by its own citizens. The most common tax equalization system has the firm's own accounting department handling the taxes of its expatriates. An accountant from the firm determines what a manager's taxes will be where the manager is living and what they would be at home on the same income and then makes the appropriate adjustment to equalize the two.

Figure 20.5 shows how one major oil company creates compensation packages for its expatriate managers. The blocks in the center reflect an individual's U.S. base compensation prior to being posted to an international assignment. After an assignment has been made, the blocks above and below are used to calculate appropriate adjustments to the employee's compensation. For example, suppose a U.S. executive being transferred abroad currently earns $100,000, of which $25,000 is paid in taxes, $10,000 is saved, and the remaining $65,000 consumed. Further suppose that the executive currently spends $2,000 a month on housing (mortgage plus utilities). The firm will adjust the executive's total compensation to make it as equal as possible to that currently earned in the United States. Assume that housing and utilities in the host country cost about 20 percent more than in the United States, and other consumables cost about 10 percent more. Thus the firm will pay the executive a supplemental housing allowance that is equal to what the executive currently pays times 20 percent, or a total of $400 a month. The remaining part of the executive's consumption spending will be increased by 10 percent. Similar adjustments will be made to the other components of Figure 20.5.

Benefits Packages for Expatriate Managers.   International businesses must provide not only salary adjustments but also special forms of benefits for their expatriate managers in addition to standard benefits such as health insurance and vacation allowances. Special benefits include housing, education, medical treatment, travel to the home country, and club memberships.

A common special benefit involves housing. Like other components of living costs, housing expenses vary in different areas. Duplicating the level of housing the executive enjoyed in the home country may be expensive, so housing often is treated as a separate benefit. If a manager is going on permanent or long-term assignment, the firm may buy the manager's existing home at fair-market value.

The firm also may help the manager buy a house in the host country if housing costs or interest rates are substantially different from those at home.

If the expatriate manager has a family, the firm may need to provide job location assistance for the spouse and help cover education costs for the children. For example, the children may need to attend private school, which the firm would pay for. Schooling represents a particularly important problem for Japanese expatriate managers, whose children may not do well in the national entrance exams for the most prestigious Japanese universities if their Japanese reading and writing skills atrophy as a result of living abroad. Thus many Japanese firms pay for their expatriates' children to attend private schools that help students cram for those exams.

Medical benefits also may need to be adjusted. For example, some people consider Malaysian health care facilities inadequate. Thus managers on assignment there often request that their employer send them to Singapore whenever they need medical attention.

Most international businesses provide expatriates with a travel allowance for trips to the home country for personal reasons, such as to visit other family members or to celebrate holidays. Managers and their families may be allowed one or two trips home per year at company expense. If a manager's family remains at home during a short-term assignment, the manager may be given more frequent opportunities to travel home.

In some cultures belonging to a certain club or participating in a particular activity is a necessary part of the business world. In Japan, for example, many business transactions occur during a round of golf. To be effective in Japan, a foreign manager may need to join a golf club. Memberships in such clubs, however, cost thousands of dollars, and a single round of golf may cost 10 times or more what it costs elsewhere. Because such activities are a normal part of doing business, firms often provide managers transferred to Japan with these benefits.

Equity in Compensation. Thus far our discussion of compensating expatriate managers has not addressed the issue of equity between the compensation granted expatriate managers and that given to HCNs in similar positions. Often the compensation package offered the expatriate manager is much more lucrative than that offered an HCN occupying an equivalent position of power and responsibility. The equity issue becomes even more complicated when dealing with TCNs. For example, if a U.S. international oil firm transfers a Venezuelan executive to its Peruvian operations, should the Venezuelan be paid according to Peruvian, Venezuelan, or U.S. standards?

Unfortunately there is no simple solution to this problem, and MNCs use a variety of approaches in grappling with it. Hewlett-Packard pays expatriates on short-term assignments according to home country standards and those on long-term assignments according to host country standards. Minnesota Mining & Manufacturing (3M) compares the compensation package it offers in the expatriate's home country with what it normally pays HCNs and then gives the expatriate the higher pay package. Phillips Petroleum pegs a TCN's salary to that of the person's home country but offers housing allowances, educational benefits, and home leaves based on costs in the host country.

RETENTION AND TURNOVER ‹

Another important element of international HRM focuses on retention and turnover. **Retention** is the extent to which a firm is able to retain valued employees. **Turnover**, essentially the opposite, is the rate at which people leave a firm.

People choose to leave a firm for any number of reasons—for example, dissatisfaction with their current pay or promotion opportunities or receipt of a better offer to work elsewhere. Turnover is often a result of job transitions such as those associated with expatriation and repatriation: A worker contemplating changing work locations also may consider changing employers. Turnover is a particular problem in international business because of the high cost of developing managers' international business skills. Managers with strong reputations for having those skills are in high demand. As noted earlier, some firms even rely on headhunters to help them locate prospective managers currently working for other firms. For exactly the same reason—a scarcity of skilled, experienced managers—keeping successful managers should be a high priority for any international business. One way to control managerial turnover is to develop strategies designed to reduce expatriate failure and repatriate failure. These may include providing career development counseling or cross-cultural training to ease the stress of relocation.

A firm also may have to provide special inducements or incentives to its most valuable international managers. They may receive higher salaries or be given a greater say in choosing their assignments. The firm also may make stronger guarantees to them regarding the time frame of their assignments. For example, a firm may want to hire a particularly skillful TCN to run its operation in Italy. Because of the costs and other problems associated with relocation, the individual may consider the assignment only if the firm guarantees the assignment will last for a minimum of, say, five years.

Another important element of turnover management is the exit interview. An **exit interview** is an interview with an employee who is leaving a firm. Its purpose is to find out as much as possible about why the person decided to leave. Given the distances involved in international business, however, firms may be reluctant to do exit interviews. Yet the potential value of the information gleaned is high: Managers can use it to reduce future employee losses. Thus firms should give careful consideration to using such interviews as part of their strategy for reducing turnover.

› HUMAN RESOURCE ISSUES FOR NONMANAGERIAL EMPLOYEES

Next, we shift the focus of our discussion of HR issues to nonmanagerial employees in host countries. The standard HRM tasks associated with nonmanagerial employees—recruitment, selection, training, compensation, and so on—are strongly influenced by local laws, culture, and economic conditions. To prosper in the host country environment, HR managers must not fall prey to their own self-referencing criteria. They must be willing to do things the way the locals want, not the way things are done at home. In short, "When in Rome, do as the Romans do." Thus many MNCs hire HCNs to staff their HR operations, so the local knowledge of the HCNs can be incorporated into the policies and procedures of the HR department.

Recruitment and Selection

In international firms' foreign operations nonmanagerial employees, such as blue-collar production workers and white-collar office workers, are typically HCNs. In most cases there are economic reasons for this decision: HCNs are usually cheaper to employ than are PCNs or TCNs. HCNs also are used because local laws often promote the hiring of locals. Immigration and visa laws, for example, typically restrict jobs to citizens and legal residents of the country. A few exceptions to this rule exist. Construction firms in rich countries like Saudi Arabia and Kuwait often use Bangladeshi or Pakistani labor because local citizens dislike the working conditions. Oil firms and airlines often employ PCNs and TCNs for high-skilled jobs such as drilling supervisor and pilot.

Nonetheless, an international business must develop and implement a plan for recruiting and selecting its employees in a host country market.[23] This plan should include assessments of the firm's human resources needs, sources of labor, labor force skills and talents, and training requirements, and also should account for special circumstances that exist in the local labor market. The chapter opening, for example, detailed how Toyota goes about recruiting and selecting U.S. employees for its U.S. production facilities.

When firms are hiring PCNs for foreign assignments, the firms must adhere to their home country's hiring regulations, laws, and norms. When hiring HCNs, the firms must be aware of those regulations, laws, and norms within the host country. For example, in the United States laws and regulations prohibit a firm from discriminating against someone on the basis of gender, race, age, religion, and other characteristics. Toyota had to ensure that during its selection of its U.S. employees, it did not violate any of those laws and regulations. Because of these restrictions, the selection process in the United States emphasizes job relatedness. Job-related criteria such as skills, abilities, and education can be used to hire employees; nonjob-related criteria such as gender or age cannot. In some countries characteristics such as gender, religion, and skin color are commonly used in hiring decisions. For example, firms in Israel and Northern Ireland often discriminate on the basis of religion, and those in Saudi Arabia discriminate on the basis of gender.

Training and Development

HR managers also must assess the training and development needs of the host country's workforces to help them perform their jobs more effectively. The training and development needs of local workforces depend on several factors. An important one is the location of the foreign operation. In highly industrialized markets firms usually find a nucleus of capable workers who may need only a bit of firm-specific training. In an area that is relatively underdeveloped, training needs will be much greater. For example, when Hilton began operating hotels in Eastern Europe, it found that waiters, hotel clerks, and other customer service employees lacked the basic skills necessary to provide high-quality service to guests. These employees were so accustomed to working in a planned economy, where there was little or no need to worry about customer satisfaction, that they had difficulty recognizing why they needed to change their workplace behavior. Hilton had to invest much more in training new employees there than it had anticipated.

Training also is a critical element if an international business wants to take full advantage of locating production abroad. In recent years MNCs have shown a marked tendency to move facilities to certain areas, such as Honduras, Malaysia, and Indonesia, to capitalize on inexpensive labor. But often the productivity of this labor is low, unless the firm is willing to invest in workforce training. In Malaysia, for example, only one-third of adults have more than a sixth-grade education; thus training costs there can be quite high. The owner of Quality Coils, Inc., a U.S. maker of electromagnetic coils, closed the firm's plant in Connecticut and opened a plant in Ciudad Juarez, Mexico, because hourly wage rates there were one-third the wage rates in Connecticut. The owner soon discovered, however, that productivity was also only one-third of what it had been in Connecticut. This, combined with higher absenteeism and the personal costs of running a facility in Mexico, prompted the owner to move the operation back to Connecticut.[24]

Japan is the world leader in training and development. On average its workers receive more annual training on a regular basis than workers in any other country. Workers in Germany, South Korea, Singapore, and France also usually receive more annual training than their U.S. counterparts. On the other hand, firms in Hong Kong are reputed to do a relatively poor job of training and development. Firms in the United States have begun to recognize the importance of training and development and are closing the gap.

Compensation and Performance Appraisal

Compensation and performance appraisal practices for nonmanagerial employees also differ dramatically among countries, depending on local laws, customs, and cultures. Individualistic cultures such as that of the United States focus on assessing the individual's performance and then compensating the person accordingly. More group-oriented cultures such as Japan's emphasize training and motivating the group and place less emphasis on individual performance appraisal and compensation. The HR manager at each foreign operation must develop and implement a performance appraisal and reporting system most appropriate for that setting, given the nature of the work being performed and the cultural context. For example, although U.S. workers often appreciate feedback from the appraisal system—thereby allowing them to do better in the future—German workers are often resentful of feedback, believing it requires them to admit failures and shortcomings.[25]

Compensation practices also reflect local laws, culture, and economic conditions. Prevailing wage rates vary among countries, which has caused many labor-intensive industries to migrate to countries such as Malaysia, Indonesia, and Guatemala. To attract workers, HR managers must ensure their firms' wage scales are consistent with local norms.

Compensation packages entail incentive payments and benefit programs in addition to wages. International business researchers have found that the mix among wages, benefits, and incentive payments varies as a function of national culture. For example, wages on average accounted for 85 percent of the total compensation package for workers in 41 manufacturing industries in four Asian countries. However, wages amounted to only 56 percent of the total compensation package for workers in those same industries in five "Latin European" countries. By adjusting the composition of the compensation package to meet local norms, HR managers ensure their workers (and the firm) get the maximum value from each compensation dollar spent.[26] Local laws also affect an international firm's compensation policies. For example, Mexican law requires employers to provide paid maternity leave, a Christmas bonus of 15 days' pay, and at least three months' severance pay for dismissed workers. "Bringing the World into Focus" discusses how one firm stubbed its toe when it tried to export its compensation plan abroad.

Bringing the World into FOCUS

NOT EVERYTHING CAN BE EXPORTED!

Lincoln Electric, a Cleveland, Ohio, firm, has a world-renowned incentive system for its hourly workers. Base compensation is tied directly to individual productivity. Workers are paid a specified dollar amount for each acceptable unit they produce. Further, at the end of the year, each employee is evaluated in terms of dependability, ideas, quality of output, and quantity of output. The results of this evaluation result in additional compensation in the form of a bonus—often equal to or greater than the worker's regular earnings. The plan has worked well at Lincoln for over 70 years, and the firm is often written up for its highly motivated workforce.

Not surprisingly, then, when Lincoln decided to expand into international markets, it also attempted to use the same incentive system in other countries. The firm was shocked to discover that its well-oiled incentive system either did not work or else resulted in more harm than good in such settings as Venezuela, Brazil, Mexico, and Japan. Why? Management had simply failed to account for cultural differences that played key roles in the kinds of rewards employees wanted and what they did and did not expect from their employer. Almost as quickly as it had implemented its U.S.-developed incentive system in foreign plants, Lincoln had to backtrack and change it to a reward system that was more compatible with local business practices and the expectations of its local workforce.

Sources: "Paying Workers to Meet Goals Spreads, but Gauging Performance Proves Tough," *Wall Street Journal*, September 10, 1996, pp. B1, B8; Donald Hastings, "Lincoln Electric's Harsh Lessons from International Expansion," *Harvard Business Review*, May–June 1999, pp. 162–178.

A final component of international HRM is labor relations. Because of their complexity and importance, labor relations often are handled as a separate organizational function, apart from human resource management.

Comparative Labor Relations

Labor relations in a host country often reflect its laws, culture, social structure, and economic conditions. For example, membership in U.S. labor unions has been steadily declining in recent years and today constitutes less than 15 percent of the country's total workforce. Labor relations in the United States are heavily regulated by various laws, and both the actions of management toward labor and the actions of labor toward management are heavily restricted. Further, the formal labor agreement negotiated between a firm and a union is a binding contract enforceable in a court of law. Because of the heavy regulation, most negotiations are relatively formal and mechanical, with both parties relying on the letter of law.

A different situation exists in many other countries. In some countries union membership is very high and continues to grow. Over half the world's workforce outside the United States belongs to labor unions. In Europe labor unions are much more important than in the United States. Labor unions in many European countries are aligned with political parties, and their fortunes ebb and flow as a function of which party currently controls the government. Throughout most of Europe temporary work stoppages are frequently used by unions in a bid for public backing for their demands. For example, the transport workers' union in Paris often calls for daily work stoppages that result in the city's buses, subways, and railroads being totally shut down. The union hopes the inconvenienced public will call on elected officials to do whatever it takes to avoid such disruptions in the future. Foreign firms that try to alter prevailing host country labor relations may be buying trouble. For example, Toys 'R' Us's unwillingness to adopt the standard collective bargaining agreement used by most Swedish retailers led to a three-month strike against the firm and denunciations by labor leaders who branded the firm "an anti-union interloper bent on breaking established traditions in Sweden," which was not the public image the firm was trying to create.[27]

In contrast, labor relations in Japan tend to be cordial. Labor unions usually are created and run by businesses themselves. Unions and management tend to work cooperatively toward their mutual best interests. The Japanese culture discourages confrontation and hostility, and these norms carry over into labor relations. Disputes are normally resolved cordially and through mutual agreement. In the rare event that a third-party mediator is necessary, there is seldom any hard feelings or hostility after a decision has been rendered. Thus strikes are relatively rare in Japan.

Collective Bargaining

Collective bargaining is the process used to make agreements between management and labor unions. As already noted, collective bargaining in the United States is highly regulated. Aside from passing the laws that regulate the process, however, government plays a relatively passive role in establishing labor agreements. Union and management representatives meet and negotiate a contract. That contract governs their collective working relationship until the contract expires, when a new one is negotiated. Bargaining normally takes place on a firm-by-firm and union-by-union basis. For example, United Air Lines must bargain with a pilots' union, a flight attendants' union, a mechanics' union, and so on, one at a time. Further, each of these unions negotiates individually with each airline whose employees it represents.

In many other countries the government is much more active in collective bargaining. In some European countries collective bargaining is undertaken by representatives of several firms and unions, along with government officials. The outcome is an umbrella agreement that applies to entire industries and collections of related labor unions. In Japan collective bargaining also usually involves government officials but is done on a firm-by-firm basis. A government official serves more as an observer, recording what transpires and answering any questions that arise during the negotiation.

Union Influence and Codetermination

Union influence can be manifested in various ways, including membership, strikes, and public relations. In Europe much of the influence of labor unions arises from the premise of **industrial democracy**—the belief that workers should have a voice in how businesses are run. In some countries, most notably Germany, union influence extends far beyond traditional boundaries of labor-management relations. The approach taken in Germany is called **codetermination** and provides for cooperation between management and labor in running the business.

Codetermination is the result of a 1947 German law that required firms in the coal and steel industries to allow unions to have input into how the firms were run. The law has been amended several times, and today it applies to all German firms with 2,000 or more employees. The law requires all covered firms to establish a supervisory board. Half the seats on this board are elected by the firm's owners (much like the board of directors of a U.S. corporation); the other half are appointed or elected by labor. Of the labor seats one-third are union officials and two-thirds are elected by the workforce. One seat elected by labor must be occupied by a managerial employee, so management essentially controls a potential tie-breaking vote. The supervisory board oversees another board called the board of managers. This board, composed of the firm's top managers, actually runs the business on a day-to-day basis.

The German model represents the most extreme level of industrial democracy. However, other countries, including Sweden, the Netherlands, Norway, Luxembourg, Denmark, and France, take similar approaches in requiring some form of labor representation in running businesses. In contrast, Italy, Ireland, the United Kingdom, Spain, Greece, and Portugal have little or no mandated labor participation. However, the EU has been attempting to standardize labor practices, employment regulations, and benefits packages throughout its member states. The ongoing implementation of its **social charter** (sometimes called the **social policy**) focuses on such concerns as maternity leave, job training, and superannuation (pension) benefits. One motivation for the social charter is to reduce the potential loss of jobs from richer countries, such as Germany or Belgium, to countries with lower wages and poorer benefit programs, such as Portugal, Greece, and Spain. Worker participation reform also is spreading into Pacific Asia. For example, workers in Singapore recently have been given a considerably stronger voice in how businesses are operated.[28] Even though Japanese workers do not have a particularly strong voice in the management of their firms, they traditionally have enjoyed an abundance of personal power and control over how they perform their own jobs.

CHAPTER REVIEW

Summary

Human resource management is the set of activities directed at attracting, developing, and maintaining the effective workforce necessary to achieve a firm's objectives. Because the HR function is central to a firm's success, top managers should adopt a strategic perspective on it.

International human resource needs are partially dictated by a firm's degree of internationalization. The relative degree of centralization versus decentralization of control also plays an important role. A basic staffing philosophy should be developed and followed.

Recruitment and selection are important elements of international HRM. Some firms choose to recruit experienced managers for foreign assignments, whereas others hire younger, and more likely inexperienced, managers. Various avenues may be used for either approach to recruiting. The selection of managers for foreign assignments usually involves consideration of both business and international skills. Managers and firms must address a variety of expatriation and repatriation issues.

Training and development also are important aspects of international HRM. The two principal components of this activity are the assessment of training needs and the selection of basic training methods and procedures.

A firm also must assess the performance of its international managers and determine their compensation. Compensation for expatriate managers usually includes a cost-of-living adjustment as well as special benefits.

Given the high cost of training and development of expatriates, firms need to focus special attention on managing retention and turnover. Each part of international HRM also must be addressed for the firm's nonmanagerial employees.

Labor relations pose an especially complex task for HR managers and often are handled by a special department. One key aspect of labor relations is collective bargaining, or negotiating agreements with unions. Germany's practice of codetermination represents one interesting variation on labor relations.

Review Questions

1. What is human resource management?
2. Along what dimensions does domestic HRM differ from international HRM?
3. How does the degree of centralization or decentralization affect international staffing?
4. What are the basic issues involved in recruiting and selecting managers for foreign assignments?
5. What issues are at the core of expatriation and repatriation problems?

6. How does a firm go about assessing its training needs?
7. Why is performance appraisal important for international firms?
8. What special compensation and benefits issues arise in international HRM?
9. How does international HRM for nonmanagerial employees differ from that for managerial employees?
10. What is codetermination?

Questions for Discussion

1. How does HRM relate to other functional areas such as marketing, finance, and operations management?
2. Why and how does the scope of a firm's internationalization affect its HRM practices?
3. How are the different approaches to recruiting and selecting managers for foreign assignments similar and dissimilar?
4. Which are easier to assess, business skills or international skills? Why?
5. If you were being assigned to a foreign position, what specific training requests would you make of your employer?
6. Do you agree or disagree with the idea that some international assignments require special compensation?
7. How easy or difficult do you think it is to handle the equity issue in international compensation?
8. What does the high cost of replacing an international manager suggest regarding staffing philosophy?
9. Which do you think is easier, HRM for managerial employees or HRM for nonmanagerial employees? Why?
10. Do you think codetermination would work in the United States? Why or why not?
11. Given Korea's current financial difficulties, would you recommend that Samsung end its program of sending young managers on foreign assignments early in their careers?

BUILDING GLOBAL SKILLS

Assume you are the top HR manager for a large international firm. The head of your company's operation in Japan has just resigned unexpectedly to take a job with another firm. You must decide on a replacement as quickly as possible. You have developed the following list of potential candidates for the job:

- *Jack Henderson:* Henderson is a senior vice president based in your Chicago headquarters. Jack has a long and distinguished career with your firm, is well regarded by everyone, and plans to retire in three years. He has never worked outside the United States but is strongly and visibly lobbying for the job in Japan. Because you and your spouse socialize with Jack and his wife outside of work, you know she does not want to move from Chicago.

- *Takeo Takahashi:* Takahashi is the number two manager in your Japanese operation, although he has served in that role for only three months. He was born and raised in Japan. After attending

college in the United States, he returned to Japan and went to work for your firm. Takeo is considered an emerging star in the company but is also relatively young and inexperienced. Your CEO prefers to appoint someone for the Japanese job with at least 15 years of company experience, and Takeo has only eight years of experience. He was being groomed to eventually take over the operation, but the just-departed top executive had been expected to serve until he reached retirement age in another seven years.

- *Jane Yamaguichi:* Yamaguichi is a Hawaiian-born manager currently heading up a major division for your company in the United States. She was a dual economics and Asian studies major at the University of Hawaii. For the last several years she has been studying the Japanese market and has become a true expert on that country. She enjoys traveling and spends as much time in Asia as possible. You know she would be very interested in this job if it were offered, although you are concerned that her husband and two high-school-age children may not share her enthusiasm about living in Japan. In addition, you worry that if she is not offered a new challenge soon, she might start looking for another position.

- *Jacques Moine:* Moine is your most experienced international manager. Originally from France, Jacques has held senior management positions in your firm's operations in Germany, Spain, Canada, Argentina, and Mexico. Moine appears to be quite satis-

fied with his current posting in Mexico. Because that operation is both stable and very efficient, it likely could be run by someone with less experience.

Working alone, carefully consider the strengths and weaknesses of each of the four leading candidates for the job. Select the individual you think is the best candidate.

Then form small groups of four or five students. Share with each other your individual choices for the job in Japan, along with the reasons for making those choices.

WORKING WITH THE WEB: BUILDING GLOBAL INTERNET SKILLS

Researching Expatriate Assignments

Assume you are a Boston-based manager for a growing international business. Your firm is among the leaders in its industry and has recently decided to emphasize its foreign operations even more. You have worked for the firm for 10 years, and it is well known you have been designated for fast-track consideration for top management. You have an MBA from a leading university program and currently earn $150,000 per year. You have two school-age children—one loves to play soccer and one excels in swimming—and your spouse has a thriving medical practice. Neither you nor your spouse has ever lived outside the United States.

Your boss has just told you the firm would like you to get some international experience. An appropriate position for you has opened up in the company's London office, and the firm would like you to take it. Your boss implies that a refusal to relocate would be a serious blow to your career with the firm. Your boss asks you to make a proposal regarding the compensation package you would require to accept this London assignment.

You have made the following list of issues and questions related to your move and your compensation package:

1. What are housing costs in London compared to those in Boston?
2. What are transportation options and costs in London relative to those in Boston?
3. What is the overall cost of living in London compared to that in Boston?
4. What career options exist in London for your spouse?
5. What schooling options exist in London for your children? How much will the schools cost?
6. What are average transportation costs between Boston and London? (You have a big family and anticipate many trips back and forth.)
7. What athletic options exist in London for your children?
8. What are the tax implications of this move for you?

Use the Internet to learn as much as you can about each of these questions.

WE INVITE YOU TO VISIT THIS BOOK'S COMPANION WEB SITE AT www.prenhall.com/griffin

IN THE NEWS

Recruitment is a major task of international human resource managers. Shortage of skilled workers in some industries and in some locations can put pressure on managers to find and retain top-notch employees for key positions.

Use the search feature on the homepage of the *Financial Times* (*www.ft.com*) to locate recent articles on the topic of recruitment. Select at least two articles about multinational firms that are looking to hire workers, and make the following analysis for each. Then compare the two firms and try to explain any differences between their recruitment needs and strategies (different industries, different goals, etc.)

What positions are the firms trying to fill? How many people do they each need? Where are they looking, and what criteria are they using? Are they facing any particular difficulties in hiring, and if so how are they trying to overcome them? What incentives are they able to offer, such as salary, benefits, status, location, and so forth?

CLOSING CASE

"You Americans Work Too Hard"

Andreas Drauschke and Angie Clark work comparable jobs for comparable pay at department stores in Berlin and suburban Washington, D.C. But there is no comparison when it comes to the hours they put in.

Mr. Drauschke's job calls for a 37-hour week with six weeks' annual leave. His store closes for the weekend at 2 P.M. on Saturday afternoon and stays open one evening each week—a new service in Germany that Mr. Drauschke detests. "I can't understand that people go shopping at night in America," says the 29-year-old, who supervises the auto, motorcycle, and bicycle division at Karstadt, Germany's largest department store chain. "Logically speaking, why should someone need to buy a bicycle at 8:30 P.M.?"

Mrs. Clark works at least 44 hours a week, including evening shifts and frequent Saturdays and Sundays. She often brings paperwork home with her, spends her days off scouting the competition, and never takes more than a week off at a time. "If I took any more, I'd feel like I was losing control," says the senior merchandising manager at J.C. Penney in Springfield, Virginia.

The 50-year-old Mrs. Clark was born in Germany but feels like an alien when she visits her native land. "Germans put leisure first and work second," she says. "In America it's the other way around."

While Americans often marvel at German industriousness, a comparison of actual workloads explodes such national stereotypes. In manufacturing, for instance, the weekly U.S. average is 37.7 hours and rising; in Germany it is 30 hours and has fallen steadily over recent decades. All German workers are guaranteed by law a minimum of five weeks' annual holiday.

A day spent at a German and an American department store also shows a wide gulf in the two countries' work ethic, at least as measured by attitudes toward time. The Germans fiercely resist any incursions on their leisure hours, while many J.C. Penney employees work second jobs and rack up 60 hours a week.

But long and irregular hours come at a price. Staff turnover at the German store is negligible; at J.C. Penney it is 40 percent a year. Germans serve apprenticeships of two to three years and know their wares inside out. Workers at J.C. Penney receive training of two to three days. And it is economic necessity, more than any devotion to work for its own sake, that appears to motivate most of the American employees.

"First it's need and then it's greed," says Sylvia Johnson, who sells full time at J.C. Penney and works another 15 to 20 hours a week doing data entry at a computer firm. The two jobs helped her put one child through medical school and another through college. Now 51, Mrs. Johnson says she doesn't need to work so hard—but still does.

"My husband and I have a comfortable home and three cars," she says. "But I guess you always feel like you want something more as a reward for all the hard work you've done."

Mr. Drauschke, the German supervisor, has a much different view: Work hard when you're on the job and get out as fast as you can. A passionate gardener with a wife and young child, he comes in 20 minutes earlier than the rest of his staff but otherwise has no interest in working beyond the 37 hours his contract mandates, even if it means more money. "Free time can't be paid for," he says.

The desire to keep hours short is an obsession in Germany—and a constant mission of its powerful unions. When Germany introduced Thursday-night shopping in 1989, retail workers went on strike. And Mr. Drauschke finds it hard to staff the extra two hours on Thursday evening, even though the late shift is rewarded with an hour less overall on the job. "My wife is opposed to my coming home late," one worker tells him when asked if he will work until 8:30 on a coming Thursday.

Mr. Drauschke, like other Germans, also finds the American habit of taking a second job inconceivable. "I already get home at 7. When should I work?" he asks. As for vacations, it is illegal—yes, illegal—for Germans to work at other jobs during holidays, a time that "is strictly for recovering," Mr. Drauschke explains. He adds, "If we had conditions like in America, you would have to think hard if you wanted to go on in this line of work."

At J.C. Penney, the workday of the merchandising manager Mrs. Clark begins at 8 A.M. when she rides a service elevator to her windowless office off a stock room. Though the store doesn't open until 10 A.M., she feels she needs the extra time to check floor displays and schedules. Most of the sales staff clock in at about 9 A.M. to set up registers and restock shelves—a sharp contrast to Karstadt, where salespeople come in just moments before the shop opens.[29]

Case Questions

1. How does HRM in the United States differ from HRM in Germany?
2. What do you see as the basic advantages and disadvantages of each system?
3. If you were the top HRM executive for an international department store chain with stores in both Germany and the United States, what basic issues would you need to address regarding corporate HR policies?
4. Are the issues more or less acute in the retailing industry versus other industries?
5. Under which system would you prefer to work?

McDonald's Manages Cash Registers Amid Constant Currency Fluctuations

Background

From modest beginnings as a simple hamburger chain that opened in Illinois in 1954, McDonald's has grown to consist of 27,000 restaurants around the world. Almost 1,800 new stores were added in 1999, with approximately 90 percent of them outside the United States. The company has opened its 3,000th restaurant in Japan, its 1,000th in Germany, and its 1,000th in the United Kingdom. McDonald's accounts for nearly half of all the globally branded fast-food restaurants outside of the United States but achieves nearly two-thirds of the total sales in its industry. Management attributes this huge market share to the power of its brand.

McDonald's has always been a franchising company and remains committed to franchising as its primary way of doing business both at home and abroad. About 80 percent of its restaurants worldwide are owned and operated by franchisees.

McDonald's

Every day McDonald's serves more than 43 million people in 27,000 restaurants in 120 countries. That adds up to more then 15 billion customer visits each year.

The company's efforts to increase market share, profitability, and customer satisfaction have produced a compound annual total return to shareholders of 21 percent over the past 10 years. For the fiscal year that ended December 31, 2000, total revenues rose 7 percent to more than $14 billion, with net income of nearly $2 billion.

In 2000 weak foreign currencies negatively affected translated sales and revenues from abroad. McDonald's tries to lessen its exposures, when possible, by financing in local currencies, hedging certain foreign-denominated cash flows, and by purchasing goods and services in local currencies. The primary currencies negatively affecting reported results for the year were the euro, the British pound, and the Australian dollar. Latin American revenue continued to be affected by difficult economic conditions, stemming from the major devaluation in Brazil in January 1999.

Questions

1. What are the special accounting problems an international firm like McDonald's encounters when it operates abroad? How do its accountants create a composite picture of company performance from disparate sources of financial information?
2. How does a company like McDonald's benefit from having operations in so many different parts of the world?
3. Do you think the idea of a single currency like the euro offers an advantage or a disadvantage to an international firm? Why?
4. How can issues of taxation affect an international business like McDonald's?

Carvel Ice Cream—Developing the Beijing Market

Thomas Carvel founded Carvel Corporation (Carvel) in 1934 in Hartsdale, New York, after he converted his mobile ice cream truck into a permanent roadside location. By the mid-1990s Carvel owned and operated over 300 retail stores and had granted franchise rights to over 600 others. It had also established over 4,500 "wholesale" accounts throughout the United States.

In 1994 Carvel established Carvel Asia Limited to act as holding company for the ice cream maker's operational investments in Asia, starting in Beijing. To this end Carvel Asia Limited teamed up with China's Ministry of Agriculture to create Beijing Carvel Food Company Limited (Beijing Carvel), a joint venture equally owned by both parties. The company had experienced losses every year since its inception; however, its financial performance had steadily improved.

The Beijing Market

Steven Wang, a fluently bilingual American-born Chinese, joined Carvel Asia Limited in September 1997 with a mandate to increase Beijing Carvel's sales, particularly in the ice cream cakes category. In summarizing the task before him, Wang stated:

The challenge is to develop a complete marketing program for a product that is relatively new to most Chinese. Therefore, much of what we need to do involves basic education—we need to ensure that our customers and distribution partners understand who we are, what we are about, and what benefits our products provide. At the same time, we have been given a very limited advertising and promotion budget, so whatever actions we take must be cost-effective. Once we put a proven program together in Beijing, we will transfer out learning to other parts of the country.

Wang identified several attributes that needed to be factored into the development of his marketing program. One factor was that China's consumption of dairy products was among the lowest in the world. Wang attributed this to China's poor infrastructure, which prevented sanitary and cost-effective distribution, and a high incidence of lactose intolerance among Chinese. There were encouraging signs, however, that dairy products were becoming much more commonplace in China. Wang had learned that, over the previous decade, overall dairy product consumption had tripled in China and that ice cream was the most popular dairy product consumed. In addition, Chinese health-care professionals had become more vocal in advocating much greater consumption of dairy products in order to achieve improved health.

Wang concluded that there were three customer segments that held the greatest promise for increased sales, namely, middle and upper class Chinese professionals, an emerging generation of so-called "little emperors," and expatriate residents. Wang noted:

> In Beijing our most important customer segment so far has been middle and upper income working professionals who provide us with about 70 percent of our cake sales. But there is still some conservatism within this segment which prevents them from making purchases that are viewed as risky. I think that is one of the reasons why our 8-inch Classic cake is our best seller. Another reason is that the Classic cakes allow our customers to customize their messages on top of the cake—this is something that is very culture driven in China.

Wang believed another lucrative segment was children and young teenagers. He reasoned:

> Back in 1980 the government imposed the "one-child policy" as a means of curtailing the country's exploding population. As a consequence, an entire generation of so-called Little Emperors emerged. Since most of these children have no brothers or sisters, they are continuously spoiled by their parents and two sets of grandparents. These Little Emperors are used to getting almost anything they want. Beijing alone has 1.5 million children between the ages of five and 12.

Wang's task was to get them and their parents more interested in Carvel ice cream cakes.

To date about 10 percent of Beijing Carvel's annual sales came from Beijing's 100,000-strong expatriate community. These were mainly foreign business and embassy employees (and their families) who were living and working in Beijing. In targeting this segment, Wang had mixed feelings. Virtually all North Americans and most Europeans living in Beijing had an excellent command of English, which meant that Beijing Carvel could avoid the cost and effort of translating a total marketing program into Chinese. Moreover, this same group was familiar with ice cream products in general and ice cream cakes in particular. Therefore, comparatively little effort needed to be done to adapt a Western-style marketing program to Beijing because many expatriates understood Beijing Carvel's products and their benefits, and Carvel largely understood the purchasing habits and criteria of these consumers. However, Wang was concerned that too much effort dedicated to attracting expatriate customers would detract from Beijing Carvel's ability to reach a much wider audience.

Improving Beijing Carvel's Performance

As Wang began to develop a marketing program for Beijing Carvel's ice cream cakes, he realized he had several options to analyze before making his final decisions.

Products and Prices

Several decisions had to be made concerning the types of products to focus on selling and their corresponding prices. One option was to expand the number of products offered. Wang believed two products Carvel had marketed in the United States might also suit the Beijing market. The first was the "Little Love," a smaller (6-inch round, 600-gram) Classic cake which retailed in the United States for $7.99. Wang believed the Little Loves had a potentially wide appeal because their lower price would reduce the "purchase risk" felt by hesitant customers. The nature of the product might also appeal to mothers who were interested in satisfying the wishes of their Little Emperors.

The other product Wang believed had potential in the Beijing market was the small, single-slice "Piece of Cake." The rationale underlying their sale was to reduce "purchase risk." Given the smaller incomes in China, Wang believed a "Piece of Cake" might appeal to Beijingers who were still unfamiliar with the ice cream cake concept. Such a product offering would also distinguish Beijing Carvel from its main competitors because they offered no similar product—one that could be easily consumed in store. Also, by providing consumers with what it called a "saleable sample," the company hoped to induce more purchases of its larger cakes.

In terms of current menu items Wang was unsure whether or not he should adjust Beijing Carvel's cake prices because of the effect it might have on Carvel's image relative to its competitors. This was an especially important consideration given that the company's cake prices were already lower than both Baskin-Robbins and Haagen-Dazs.

One possible pricing option was to extract greater cost reductions from the manufacturing process and pass these savings on to the consumer. This could be done by reducing the quality of the ice cream by whipping more air into it during production. Wang estimated he could lower his variable costs by 5 percent by doing so. He also recognized the possibility that this could compromise Carvel's image for quality in the market. Therefore, he knew he would require head office approval before proceeding.

Distribution

In exploring his distribution options, Wang needed to determine, first, how he could improve sales in Beijing Carvel's existing retail and wholesale locations; second, whether or not he should target the growth of specific channels more than others; and third, whether or not he should exit certain locations. The difficulty he faced in making these decisions stemmed from the wide variability in performance among all distribution channel types, wherein no clear pattern of success had yet been established.

In terms of Beijing Carvel's retail stores only four were viewed as "full service" because they alone offered all Carvel product lines and each could accommodate 15 to 20 customers. The remaining six stores were scaled-down outlets which served only hard ice cream and cakes and had little or no available seating. Their average monthly sales ranged from about $2,000 to $15,000. In terms of investment the stores' return on investment ranged from −25 to 60 percent.

In terms of wholesale outlets Beijing Carvel had established sales accounts with various food merchants, which were categorized as follows: 25 in high-end supermarkets, 25 in local supermarkets, 40 in bakeries, and 60 in restaurants and bars. In developing these accounts, Beijing Carvel focused mainly on growing its ice cream cake business, although a limited selection of hard ice cream and novelties was available at certain locations. Eight sales account representatives were responsible for prospecting new accounts and servicing existing accounts. Their duties included educating vendors about the products, as well as demonstrating appropriate placement and presentation. All cakes sold to the wholesalers were priced at a 30 percent discount off Beijing Carvel's retail prices and were displayed in self-contained freezers leased from Beijing Carvel.

The high-end supermarkets serviced by Beijing Carvel were all joint venture companies involving well-known foreign retailers such as Carrefour (from France), Makro (from Holland), and Park 'n' Shop (from Hong Kong). These stores offered the widest range of food and specialty cooking items in Beijing and catered mainly to the expatriate community and the growing number of upper-income Chinese. Despite their strong association with discounting in the West, the cost of many imported food items offered at these stores was out of reach for most Chinese. However, several locally owned supermarket chains had emerged in recent years that catered to the larger (and rapidly growing) middle class in Beijing. Unlike the high-end supermarkets, items in these stores catered to local tastes and were offered at more moderate prices.

Beijing Carvel believed bakeries were a natural point of distribution for ice cream cakes because many consumers frequented these stores for flour-based cakes and other items. One concern that Wang had about developing bakery accounts was related to the average prices for flour-based cakes, which were often 15 to 30 percent less than Beijing Carvel's cakes.

Beijing Carvel's rationale for developing wholesale accounts in bars and restaurants was related to the emergence of Beijing's middle and upper classes and the corresponding explosion in the number of new eating and drinking establishments throughout the city in recent years. The Chinese tradition of conducting business in a social atmosphere also meant that many of Beijing's high-income individuals spent a great deal of time entertaining existing and potential business partners.

Wang was not pleased with the "quality" of many of the wholesale accounts that had been recruited prior to his arrival. Wang suggested:

> Much of the problem is related to the fact that the eight sales reps are compensated by the number of accounts they develop, not the quality of accounts developed. What we need now is radical surgery to ensure that the accounts we have are worth the time and effort required to supervise them. This may mean slashing our nonperforming accounts and reassigning our freezers to other locations.

Advertising

Wang knew that his advertising budget was only $20,000 for the upcoming year. This meant that media such as television and radio were not tenable options. Therefore, Wang needed to rely on various print media to convey what he believed was the most important message he wanted to deliver, specifically "Who we are, what we are about, and the benefits of our products." Wang identified three feasible print media: a newspaper ad, a flyer, and a coupon book.

Beijing Shoppers Guide was a twice-weekly consumer newspaper that targeted the city's emerging upper-middle and upper classes. Each edition had a circulation of 250,000 and cost readers 12¢. Advertising costs were $1,250 per edition for a 4-square-inch placement. Many companies used this space to introduce and describe their products, as well as offer a cut-out, returnable coupon. These coupons typically offered a 12 percent discount off the retail price because the number eight was considered lucky in China, and therefore 88 was seen as doubly lucky. Wang believed that if he were to use this print medium, he would need to offer more than the standard 12 percent discount in order to induce purchase.

The advertising leaflet Wang envisioned would be a dual-language, full-size (about 8.5 inches × 11 inches), double-sided glossy leaflet, which could fold into thirds. One side would present pictures and prices of Beijing Carvel's main menu items, with an emphasis on cakes. The other side would display a miniature map of Beijing indicating the address and phone numbers of the company's retail locations, as well as a discount coupon. Initial costs were estimated to be 5¢ per sheet for a minimum of 2,000 prints. If 5,000 or more copies were ordered, the cost would be reduced to 3¢ per sheet. Wang believed the most effective points of distribution would be outside several new shopping centers, which were key destinations for Beijing's emerging consumer classes. He felt the most appropriate people to distribute the leaflets would be company employees, dressed in full Carvel uniform.

The Beijing chapter of the Asian Hospitality Association (AHA) offered an entertainment coupon book which profiled about 175 mid- to up-scale restaurants, eateries, bars, and recreation establishments. The book was revised annually and sold to about 10,000 local "members," virtually all of whom were in the upper-income segment, for $16 per copy at the start of each year. Members received an AHA membership card which they could then use as many times as they wished throughout the year at any of the participating advertisers' establishments. The discount Wang had in mind was to offer AHA members a 12 percent discount off all cake sales. The cost for participating advertisers was $500 for a half-page placement (3 inches high × 4 inches wide). Wang was confident that, because he knew the publication's manager, he could purchase a standard placement in exchange for $300 worth of Beijing Carvel coupons.

The Days Ahead

In looking at the task before him, Steven Wang realized he needed to make a series of sound decisions before his ice cream cake marketing program was complete. This included resolving questions about who to target, what products to focus on, and what prices to charge for those products. He also needed to resolve what points of distribution would best increase Beijing Carvel's cake sales and how to support these sales through various print media options. The difficulty of these decisions was compounded by the fact that ice cream cakes were new to most Chinese and were derived from a relatively unpopular food group. Furthermore, the information he had at his disposal to help him make his decisions was, at times, unreliable. "But," as Wang determined, "this is not an excuse to avoid making these decisions."

Questions

1. Carvel's new Beijing manager, Steven Wang, has not yet formulated his pricing and product policies. What advice would you give him? Should Wang reduce Carvel's prices, perhaps by reducing product quality?

2. Do you agree with Wang's deemphasizing sales to Beijing's expatriate community?

3. What changes would you make as to how Carvel distributes its products in Beijing? Should it emphasize sales through Carvel retail outlets? Should it shift to bakeries or wholesalers? Defend your answer.

4. Carvel's advertising budget is extremely limited. Where should Carvel advertise?

Source: Adapted from "Carvel Ice Cream—Developing the Beijing Market" (case 1999-07-17) with permission from the Richard Ivey School of Business, the University of Western Ontario.

Target Micronics in China: Disarray in Finance

Introduction

In March 1994 Kim Knight, Target Micronics China's director of finance, received the results of the company's internal audit for the Greater China Region. Much to her dismay, finance had been rated "unsatisfactory." This was but one more piece of bad news for the Hong Kong-based headquarters of Target Micronics' China operations. The office was chronically understaffed, turnover rates were in double digits each month, and morale was dismal. On top of it all, the office was also trying to accommodate the rapid growth and growing complexity of operations in the Greater China Region. Knight now had to begin to formulate a plan for correcting the problems that underlay the "unsatisfactory" rating before the external auditors visited in December. She wondered what she would do.

Target Micronics and China

Target Micronics is a significant player in the Canadian microelectronics industry and one of the leading providers of integrated circuits in the world. Incorporated in 1968, the company pioneered the use of microelectronic circuits for use in the automotive industry. Target Micronics' success had long been due to an aggressive but focused global strategy. The company's 1994 sales topped $2.8 billion, and 32 percent of revenues were generated outside North America from operations in more than 40 countries worldwide.

Target Micronics first entered the Greater China Region—comprised of China, Hong King, Taiwan, and Korea—in 1978, primarily to promote the sale of its product in this region. The region's headquarters, located in Hong Kong, housed the sales, marketing, finance, and operations functions.

Target Micronics enjoyed its first success in China in 1983 when a government-operated appliance manufacturer began to use Target Micronics microelectronic components. In 1988 a joint venture, Zhejiang-Micronics, was established to manufacture integrated circuits in China. By 1991 the joint venture fabrication facility was producing 20,000 units per month, providing chips for a wide range of uses throughout the country.

In 1993 Target Micronics became one of five international microelectronic companies chosen by the Chinese State Planning Commission to supply integrated circuits to China. As part of the deal, Target Micronics committed $20 million in investment over the next five years to work on several joint technology initiatives. Target Micronics expanded its presence in the area with the opening of a Beijing office. Between 1992 and 1994 Target Micronics's business in the region grew nearly 300 percent. Not only did sales explode during this period, but the product range involved also expanded significantly. Further, Target Micronics began to enter into an increasing number of joint ventures with private-sector customers in the region. All these factors created pressure for the finance group in the Greater China Region.

Stresses on the Finance Function

As the head of finance in the Greater China Region, Kim Knight reported to the regional chairman with "dotted line" accountability to the vice president of finance, global business, in the United States, who in turn reported to Target Micronics' chief financial officer. Knight's finance group had responsibility for the basic accounting that accompanied Target Micronics' sales in the region—keeping track of accounts payable and receivable as well as managing cash flow. It also managed the financing of sales to the region. Initially, most Chinese purchases were financed through loans granted by the Economic Development Corporation of Canada. The resulting transactions were relatively simple to process. However, by 1993 the Chinese ministries with which Target Micronics dealt began to demand lower interest rates and to negotiate buybacks of their higher-interest debt. This made transactions much more complicated.

In 1993 Knight's finance office took over responsibility for the financial accounting function for both Taiwanese and Korean operations. As well, the office supported the relocation of Target Micronics regional business staff from Tokyo to Hong Kong. Further, Target Micronics began to enter into a number of joint ventures with private-sector Chinese customers. In each instance the finance department would have to design the financing package and determine under what conditions the deal could earn money. Exacerbating the increasingly complex workload the finance department faced was the inflow of expatriate managers to the region (both to Hong Kong and to Beijing), each of whom required the attention of the department for details such as cash advances, the payment of expenses, and the setting up of payroll.

By early 1994 the system which had been designed to handle $10 million in business was stretched to the extreme, handling in excess of $80 million in business in addition to the myriad other accounting and payroll duties now assigned to it. In the last year alone revenues had more than doubled, from $41 million to $84 million. Moreover, the relatively simple transactions of the past had been replaced by much more complicated dealings. The current staff were simply not equipped to cope. Not only were there not enough of them, but most employees did not have the requisite level of skill to deal with the more complex transactions now confronting the finance group.

Symptoms of the Problem

Perhaps the most severe problem Knight faced after the skills shortage was the rampant turnover of her staff. In 1993 the annual turnover rate was nearly 30 percent, and 1994 looked as if the rate would surpass 40 percent. Knight found it increasingly difficult to hire replacements. The Hong Kong job market was incredibly dynamic and attractive to job seekers. Much to Knight's chagrin, the April 30, 1994 *South China Morning Post* contained 55 pages of employment advertisements with no fewer than 189 positions of interest to her people. As a result, through much of 1994, Target Micronics' Greater China Region finance function was operating with seven of 21 staff positions unfilled.

Several things contributed to the sky-high levels of turnover. Normal hours worked by people in the finance group were 8:30 A.M. until 9:00 or 10:00 P.M., with five-hour days on Saturdays and Sundays. The Hong Kong norm, in contrast, was around 40 hours per week with no weekend work. Working around the clock was not uncommon during month-end closing deadlines. The 1993 year-end was especially bad, as staff worked through the Christmas to New Year's period without a break, often putting in 16-hour days. One staff member did not even go home for three days because the one-hour commute she faced was too long. Instead, she stayed nearby at a colleague's apartment, getting three or four hours sleep before heading back to the office.

Pay was also a problem. As it was, Target Micronics paid salaries that were in the mid-market range for Hong Kong. When the significant amount of unpaid overtime was factored in, salaries became distinctly uncompetitive. The problem was exacerbated by Target Micronics' corporate policy of holding salary increases to no more than 10 percent for 1994. In Hong Kong, however, 10 percent was below inflation and below the average salary increase of 15 percent being paid by local companies. Pay was also individually oriented, despite the need for teamwork in much of the finance function.

Tied to the compensation problem was the issue of titling at Target Micronics. Titles within the company were based on the North American system. In Hong Kong, and Asia more generally, however, titles were very important to people and were used by many employers as an inexpensive perquisite. Thus employees within Target Micronics generally had less prestigious titles than did their peers in other companies. People left Target Micronics in some cases because they were the only one of their classmates not to have achieved a particular title level.

The titling issue was further linked to the issue of career progression within the company. Opportunities for career advancement were an important factor in retaining people. In Hong Kong people were very willing to actively manage their own careers. Hong Kong employees would ask directly about their career opportunities, and if not satisfied that these opportunities were adequate, would move on to where they perceived them to be better. Target Micronics was perceived by many employees in the finance area to be making no investment in training and development for its promising employees.

The bottom line of all these issues was that turnover was unacceptably high. People left Target Micronics' Hong Kong finance operation citing poor pay, the need to follow a spouse, the desire for a more prestigious job title, and the desire for more career opportunities. When people left, they were often replaced by temporary employees, who in turn would leave in rapid succession. Systems fell into disuse, mistakes were rampant, and processes degenerated.

Moreover, because of this chronic understaffing, managers found themselves having to abdicate their managerial responsibilities to help out in the trenches, processing daily transactions. Knight's predecessor was unable to help, as he was occupied full time as a key member of the team negotiating a new fabrication joint venture. As a result of this lack of leadership, staff training was put on hold, plan-

ning ceased, and no strategic overhaul of the system could be done. Managers could not be counted on to resolve staff problems. Consequently, the level of frustration and subsequent turnover among the finance staff grew, as they foresaw no improvement in the near future and found the status quo unbearable.

By early 1994 the finance function was in disarray. The internal audit stated that

> changes to business processes and basic financial support systems could not adequately keep pace with the rapidly increasing change and complexity in the business environment. Another contributing factor is the high staff turnover at both professional and clerical levels due to a highly competitive labor market.

Two major areas were highlighted as requiring immediate attention. First, account reconciliation and analysis were found wanting. Numerous balance sheet accounts had not been reconciled or adjusted recently and supporting documentation was not found to tie into the amounts reflected on the balance sheet. Second, many processes required significant reengineering and streamlining to be effective in the new environment. Most financial processes were designed for a much smaller volume of much simpler transactions and were no longer adequate for current needs. Several processes were highlighted as needing streamlining. Among them were accounting for cash in transit and employee expense vouchers; payment processes for supplier invoices, and a process to strengthen the collection of accounts receivable. Receivables collection was especially problematic, as collection times stretched often twice past their due dates. It was predicted that cutting collection times in half would generate $750,000 in additional cash flow. Finally, the report also highlighted a potential security breach in that only one clerk prepared checks, did the banking, reconciled the bank statements, and created the journal entries, thus weakening internal controls and exposing the company and the clerk to charges of misappropriation.

These major problems were accompanied by a host of other minor incidents. The contract ledger (a subledger) could not be reconciled with the general ledger. Linkages among various systems were nonexistent, so that data across systems could not be reconciled. This created a huge opportunity for human error in the management of each system. In addition, far too many checks were being done manually. Overdrafts on Target Micronics' accounts became commonplace. Employees had to wait months for expense reimbursements. Incoming checks were often just shoved into a drawer and not deposited in the bank. Vendors were becoming increasingly frustrated with late or nonpayment of invoices. The overall result was a significant deterioration in customer and supplier relationships.

Knight's Dilemma

In the wake of the unsatisfactory internal audit, noting the finance department's major weaknesses in finance process and systems, Knight found herself caught between a rock and a hard place. On the one hand, she obviously needed to create and implement a new system. To do so required people with the right skills and experience to design, implement, and operate it. But until such a system was in place, to create order out of the chaos that currently existed, Knight had no hope of recruiting or retaining people who had those necessary skills or experience. She needed to think long and hard about how she was going to do this. Yet she didn't have much time. The external audit was scheduled for December—only nine months away.

Questions

1. Diagnose the problems facing the Target Micronics Greater China finance office. Why did these problems arise?
2. Put yourself in the shoes of Kim Knight, the manager of this office. What could she have done differently? What would you recommend she do prior to the arrival of the external auditors in nine months?
3. Put yourself in the shoes of her boss, the regional chairman for Target Micronics' Greater China operations. What should the regional chairman do?
4. Put yourself in the shoes of the chief financial officer of the parent company. What should the CFO do?

Source: Adapted from "Target Micronics in China: Disarray in Finance" (case 2000-07-27) with permission of the Richard Ivey School of Business, the University of Western Ontario.

ENDNOTES

Chapter 1

1. "Sydney Already Feeling the Heat," *USA Today*, February 15, 2000, pp. 1C, 2C; "How the Olympics Were Bought," *Time*, January 25, 1999; "GM to Spend Up to $1 Billion on Olympics Through 2008 in Pact with USOC, NBC," *Wall Street Journal*, July 29, 1997, p. B5; "Greek Leaders See Winning Olympic Bid as an Endorsement of Market Reforms," *Wall Street Journal*, September 8, 1997; "NBC Wraps Up the Olympics Through 2008," *Wall Street Journal*, December 13, 1995, p. B1; "Japan's Nagano, Site of 1998 Games, Faces Problems of Olympic Proportions," *Wall Street Journal*, March 15, 1994, p. A14; "Olympics Strategy Has Its Rewards," *USA Today*, February 21, 1994, pp. 1B, 2B; "Going for the Gold, Merchandisers and Retailers Promote the Olympics Two Years in Advance," *Wall Street Journal*, December 7, 1993, pp. B1, B16; "Let the Bidding Begin for the TV Rights to '96 Olympics, and Watch It Heat Up," *Wall Street Journal*, August 7, 1992, p. B1; "The Olympics: Brought to You by . . . ," *USA Today*, July 21, 1992, pp. 1B, 2B; "NBC's Olympic Gamble," *Newsweek*, January 13, 1992, p. 44.
2. *Survey of Current Business* (Washington, D.C.: U.S. Department of Commerce), June 2000, pp. D-59 and D-61.
3. Simcha Ronen, *Comparative and Multinational Management* (New York: John Wiley & Sons, 1986).
4. S. D. Chapman, "British-Based Investment Groups Before 1914," *Economic History Review*, vol. 38 (1985), pp. 230–235.
5. John H. Dunning, *Multinational Enterprises and the Global Economy* (Wokingham, England: Addison-Wesley Publishing Company, 1993), p. 3.
6. Ibid., pp. 106ff.
7. "Compaq at the 'Crossroads,'" *Business Week*, July 22, 1996, pp. 70–71.
8. "The Internet Economy: The World's Next Growth Engine," *Business Week*, October 4, 1999, pp. 72–77.
9. "E-purchasing Saves Businesses Billions," *USA Today*, February 7, 2000, pp. 1B, 2B.

Chapter 2

1. "Entrepreneurs Find Belarus Is Tough Going," *Wall Street Journal*, June 1, 1998, p. A4; "Ad Agencies Are Stumbling in East Europe," *Wall Street Journal*, May 10, 1996, p. B1; "Ukraine's Bureaucrats Stymie U.S. Firms," *Wall Street Journal*, November 4, 1996, p. A14.
2. This chapter reports population, GDP, and per capita GDP data for the world's countries. Most of the data are taken from the World Bank's World Development Report 1999/2000 or from the World Bank's Web site.
3. "Czech Republic Is Free, Fun to Visit and Rich, but Only Superficially," *Wall Street Journal*, July 15, 1997, p. A1; "Czech's Economic Success Loses Edge," *Wall Street Journal*, May 28, 1997, p. A12; "Bohemia's Fading Rhapsody," *The Economist*, May 31, 1997, p. 65.
4. "Booming Economy in Poland Brings Jobs, Wealth and Apathy," *Wall Street Journal*, November 25, 1996, p. A1.
5. "Hungary Begins to Reach Steady Growth," *Wall Street Journal*, July 16, 1997, p. A17; "Bohemia's Fading Rhapsody," *The Economist*, May 31, 1997, p. 65; "Hungary's Privatization Czar Is Unloaded," *Wall Street Journal*, October 21, 1996, p. A19.
6. "Soaring Indian Tech Salaries Reflect the Country's Brain Drain," *Wall Street Journal*, August 21, 2000, p. A13; "Software Boosts India's Fortunes," *Financial Times*, July 3, 2000, p. 1; "India's Plans to Plug the Brain Drain," *Financial Times*, April 24, 2000, p. 16; "India Wired," *Business Week*, March 6, 2000, pp. 82ff; "Investment in India's Software Sector Doubles," *Financial Times*, February 7, 2000, p. 3; "India Software Capital Praised for Its Growth," *Financial Times*, January 20, 2000, p. 7; "New Corporate Gurus Tap India's Brainpower to Galvanize Economy," *Wall Street Journal*, September 27, 1999, p. A1; "Silicon Subcontinent," *Financial Times*, March 15, 1999, p. 14.

Chapter 3

1. "China Looks to Linux as a Way Not to Get Locked Into Windows," *Wall Street Journal*, April 25, 2000, p. A11; "China Creates Office to Regulate News On Internet Sites," *Wall Street Journal*, April 24, 2000, p. A21; "State Control Gains Upper Hand Among China Websites," *Financial Times*, April 18, 2000, p. 7; "Beijing Set to Step Up Curbs on Internet," *Financial Times*, March 22, 2000, p. 6; "China Reverses Harsh Internet Rules, Easing Threat to Trade," *Wall Street Journal*, March 13, 2000, p. A21; "China Restricts News Further Over Internet," *Wall Street Journal*, February 22, 2000, p. A26; "Microsoft Is Test Case for Chinese Rules," *Wall Street Journal*, February 17, 2000, p. A13; "Internet Firms Seek to Sway Lawmakers to See Benefits in Wider China Trade," *Wall Street Journal*, February 15, 2000, p. A6; "China Cracks Down on Internet Chat," *Houston Chronicle*, January 27, 2000, p. A15; "Government Shadow Over China's 'Web' Grows," *Wall Street Journal*, January 26, 2000, p. A17; "Internet Phone Service Catches On with Millions in China," *Wall Street Journal*, December 21, 1999, p. A14; "E-Business Is Tapping China's Online Wonderlust," *Wall Street Journal*, October 27, 1999, p. A13; "Intel Becomes Cautious on China, Deferring Decision on Net Center," *Wall Street Journal*, October 26, 2000, p. A21.
2. "Portugal's Overburdened Justice System in the Dock," *Financial Times*, February 12, 1999, p. 3; "India's Laws a Mixed Blessing for Investors," *Wall Street Journal*, July 11, 1997, p. A10.
3. "Court Ruling on Islamic Banking Poses a Challenge for Pakistan Interests," *Financial Times*, January 4, 2000, p. 2; "Court Orders Islamabad to Ban Interest," *Financial Times*, December 24/25, 1999, p. 4; "Pakistani Court Rules That Interest Is Illegal," *Houston Chronicle*, December 24, 1999, p. 2C.
4. "Mining Executives Woo Rebels with Billion-Dollar Mineral Deals," *Houston Chronicle*, April 17, 1997, p. A20; "As Zaire's War Wages, Foreign Businesses Scramble for Inroads," *Wall Street Journal*, April 14, 1997, p. A1.
5. "U.S. Appetite for Mexican Food Grows, Cooking Up Hotter Sales for Exporters," *Wall Street Journal*, February 5, 1992, p. A6.

6. "U.S. Plans to Indict McDonnell Douglas for Alleged Violation of Export Laws," *Wall Street Journal*, October 11, 1999, p. A4.

7. George Graham, "Pilkington Bows to U.S. Pressure on Process Licensing," *Financial Times*, May 27, 1994, p. 1; George Graham, "Washington's New Anti-Trust Vigor," *Financial Times*, May 27, 1994, p. 6.

8. Thomas M. Burton, "Baxter Agreed to Cut-Rate Shipments of Supplies to Syria, U.S. Probe Finds," *Wall Street Journal*, December 22, 1992, p. A3; "How Baxter Got Off the Arab Blacklist and How It Got Nailed," *Wall Street Journal*, March 23, 1993, p. A1.

9. "Keeping the Lid on Helms-Burton," *Financial Times*, July 31, 1997, p. 4; "Stet Avoids Helms-Burton Sanctions," *Financial Times*, July 24, 1997, p. 1; "Property Issue Harks Back to Old Cuba," *Houston Chronicle*, October 3, 1996, p. 1C.

10. "With Boom Gone Bust, Spain's Social Agenda Still Haunts Economy," *Wall Street Journal*, June 13, 1994, p. A1.

11. Richard Schaffer, Beverley Earle, and Filiberto Agusti, *International Business Law and Its Environment* (St. Paul, Minn.: West Publishing, 1990), p. 196.

12. Ibid., pp. 196–197.

13. "Commercial Law Plan in Francophone Africa," *Financial Times*, May 13, 1999, p. 9.

14. Op cit., pp. 429–430.

15. Business Software Alliance, *1999 Global Software Piracy Report*; "Video Pirates Rush Out 'Phantom Menace'," *Wall Street Journal*, May 28, 1999, p. B1.

16. Masaaki Kotabe, "A Comparative Study of U.S. and Japanese Patent Systems," *Journal of International Business Studies*, vol. 23, no. 1 (First Quarter 1992), p. 150.

17. "Patent Suit Shows Small U.S. Firms' Fears," *Wall Street Journal*, June 5, 1996, p. A10.

18. "Trademark Piracy at Home and Abroad," *Wall Street Journal*, May 7, 1991, p. A20.

19. "Fujitsu Backed in Patent Dispute," *Financial Times*, September 11, 1997, p. 8.

20. Overseas Private Investment Corporation, *1999 Annual Report*, p. 17.

21. Schaffer, Earle, and Agusti, op. cit., pp. 410–421.

22. "Regulatory Surprises in Ukraine Lead Motorola to Pull Investment," *Wall Street Journal*, March 28, 1997, p. A12; "Ukraine's Bureaucrats Stymie U.S. Firms," *Wall Street Journal*, November 4, 1996, p. A14.

23. "IBM to Close Two-Year-Old Venture in Russia, Citing Onerous Taxes for Step," *Wall Street Journal*, February 29, 1996, p. A10.

24. "Foreigners Learn to Play by Russia's Rules," *Wall Street Journal*, August 14, 1997, p. A10; "Some Russian Officials Consider Bribery Just a Part of Job," *Houston Chronicle*, August 2, 1997, p. A30.

25. "Ukraine's Women Love These Two Firms," *Wall Street Journal*, February 6, 1992, p. A10.

26. "Oil Firms Eye Caspian Area," *Houston Chronicle*, November 28, 1997, p.1C; "Unocal to Route Turkmenistan Pipeline Though Afghanistan," *Houston Chronicle*, November 11, 1997, p. 4C; "Older Oil City Enjoys New Boom," *Houston Chronicle*, October 7, 1997, p. 1C; "Texaco, Mobil Expect Deals with Kazakhstan," *Wall Street Journal*, October 3, 1997, p. A6; "China's Rebellious Province," *The Economist*, August 23, 1997, p. 29; "Superpowers Circle Caspian," *Financial Times*, August 8, 1997, p. 4; "Resourceful Competitors," *Wall Street Journal*, July 28, 1997, p. A18; "Oil Companies Rush into the Caucasus to Tap the Caspian," *Wall Street Journal*, April 25, 1997, p. A1; "The Combustible Caspian," *The Economist*, January 11, 1997, p. 45.

Chapter 4

1. "Education System Fosters Creativity," *Financial Times*, May 11, 2000, p. VII; "Throw the Rule-Book Out of the Window," *Financial Times*, May 11, 2000, p. 14; "Singapore Trains Old Workers to Be Fit for the New Economy," *Financial Times*, March 31, 2000, p. 6; "How a Software Titan Missed the Internet Revolution," *Wall Street Journal*, January 18, 2000, p. B1; "Internet Start-Ups Revolutionize Korean Economy," *Wall Street Journal*, December 28, 1999, p. A8; "Newcomers to the Game," *Financial Times*, September 29, 1999, p. VI.

2. "Edging Towards the Information Age," *Business Week*, January 31, 2000, p. 90.

3. "The Overseas Chinese: A Driving Force," *The Economist*, July 18, 1992, pp. 21–24.

4. Nancy Adler, *International Dimensions of Organizational Behavior*, 3rd ed. (Cincinnati: South-Western College Publishing, 1997), pp. 15–16.

5. Vern Terpstra and Kenneth David, *The Cultural Environment of International Business* (Cincinnati: South-Western College Publishing, 1985), p. 20.

6. John R. Schermerhorn, Jr., "Language Effects in Cross-Cultural Management Research: An Empirical Study and a Word of Caution," *Proceedings of the Academy of Management*, 1987, p. 103.

7. John C. Condon and Fathi Yousef, *An Introduction to Intercultural Communication* (New York: Bobbs-Merrill, 1975), p. 174; Jon P. Alston, *The American Samurai: Blending American and Japanese Business Practices* (New York: Walter de Gruyter, 1986), p. 325.

8. Adler, op. cit., p. 16.

9. "Going Global," *Wall Street Journal*, October 16, 1992, p. R20.

10. "Spanish Firms Discover Latin American Business as New World of Profit," *Wall Street Journal*, May 23, 1996, p. A1.

11. Trenholme J. Griffin and W. Russell Daggatt, *The Global Negotiator* (New York: Harper Business, 1990), p. 40; "Mother of all Tongues," *Financial Times*, April 4/April 5, 1998, p. 25.

12. "Some Firms Resume Manufacturing in U.S. After Foreign Fiascoes," *Wall Street Journal*, October 14, 1986, pp. 1, 27.

13. Terpstra and David, op. cit., p. 37.

14. Alston, op. cit., p. 331.

15. Henry W. Lane and Joseph J. DiStefano, *International Management Behavior* (Boston; PWS-Kent Publishing, 1992), p. 214.

16. Ibid., p. 3.

17. Gary P. Ferraro, *The Cultural Dimension of International Business* (Upper Saddle River, N.J.: Prentice Hall, 1990), p. 82.

18. Ferraro, op. cit., p. 76.

19. "For Japanese, Silent Negotiation Is Golden," *Houston Chronicle*, December 14, 1992, p. 2B.

20. Alston, op. cit., pp. 305–306.

21. Gavin Kennedy, *Doing Business Abroad* (New York: Simon and Schuster, 1985), p. 92.

22. Hall and Hall, *Hidden Differences*, p. 109.

23. Marlene L. Rossman, *The International Businesswoman* (New York: Praeger Publishers, 1986), p. 40.

24. Jon P. Alston, "Wa, Guanxi, and Inhwa: Managerial Principles in Japan, China, and Korea," *Business Horizons*, March –April 1989, pp. 26–31.

25. "The Reincarnation of Caste," *The Economist*, June 8, 1991, pp. 21–23.

26. Ferraro, op. cit., p. 99.

27. Kennedy, op. cit., pp. 97–98.

28. "Miyazawa, Making Waves, Seeks to Cut the Clout of Tokyo University's Alumni," *Wall Street Journal*, March 5, 1992, p. A12.

29. "The Reincarnation of Caste," *The Economist*, op. cit.

30. Edward T. Hall, *Beyond Culture* (Garden City, N.Y.: Anchor Press, 1976).

31. Edward T. Hall and Mildred Reed Hall, *Understanding Cultural Differences* (Yarmouth, Me.: Intercultural Press, 1990), pp. 72–73.

32. Edward T. Hall and Mildred Reed Hall, *Hidden Differences* (Garden City, N.Y.: Doubleday, 1987), pp. 9–10.

33. Bruce Kogut and Harbir Singh, "The Effect of National Culture on the Choice of Entry Mode," *Journal of International Business Studies*, Fall 1988, pp. 411–432.

34. Geert Hofstede, *Culture's Consequences: International Differences in Work Related Values* (Beverly Hills, Calif: Sage, 1980).

35. We have taken the liberty of changing some of the labels Hofstede applied to each of the dimensions. The terms we have chosen are more descriptive, simpler, and more self-evident in their meaning.

36. Ferraro, op. cit., p. 157.

37. Adler, op. cit., pp. 45–46; Andre Laurent, "The Cultural Diversity of Western Conceptions of Management," *International Studies of Management and Organization*, Vol. XIII, No. 1–2 (Spring–Summer 1983), pp. 75–96.

38. Ferraro, op. cit., p. 162.

39. "Crash Near London Points to Korean Air Poor Safety Record," *Financial Times*, December 24, 1999, p. 2; "Pilot Error Is Cited in Korea Air Crash; FAA Is Criticized on Foreign Oversight," *Wall Street Journal*, November 3, 1999, p. A6; "Korean Air Confronts Dismal Safety Record Rooted in Its Culture," *Wall Street Journal*, July 7, 1999, p. A1; "Korean Air to Hire More Foreign Pilots," *Wall Street Journal*, April 15, 1999, p. A14.

40. B. Bass and L. Eldridge, "Accelerated Managers' Objectives in Twelve Countries," *Industrial Relations*, vol. 12 (1973), pp. 158–171.

41. Susan C. Schneider, "National Versus Corporate Culture: Implications for Human Resource Management," *Human Resource Management*, vol. 27, no. 2 (Summer 1988), pp. 231–246.

42. Kathleen K. Reardon, "It's the Thought That Counts," *Harvard Business Review*, September–October 1984, pp. 136–141.

43. Stephen Kobrin, *International Expertise in American Business* (New York: Institute of International Education, 1984), p. 38.

44. "Firms Grapple with Language," *Wall Street Journal*, November 7, 1989, pp. B1, B10.

Chapter 5

1. Caterpillar Inc., 1990 *Annual Report*, p. 15.

2. Caterpillar Inc., 1999 *Annual Report*; "Caterpillar, UAW Face Renewed Hurdles," *Wall Street Journal*, February 24, 1998, p. A2; Ronald Henkoff, "This Cat Is Acting Like a Tiger," *Fortune*, December 19, 1988, pp. 69ff; "Cat vs. Labor: Hardhats, Anyone?" *Business Week*, August 26, 1991, p. 48; "Union and Company Waging 'Holy War,'" *Bryan–College Station Eagle*, August 7, 1994, p. C1; *Hoover's Handbook of American Business 2000* (Austin, Texas: Hoover's Business Press, 2000), pp. 332–333.

3. Arthur M. Schlesinger, *The Colonial Merchants and the American Revolution 1763–1776* (New York: Facsimile Library, 1939), pp. 16–20.

4. David Ricardo, *The Principles of Political Economy and Taxation* (Homewood: Irwin, 1963). (Ricardo's book was first published in 1817.)

5. Michael Moritz, *The Little Kingdom: The Private Story of Apple Computer* (New York: William Morrow, 1984).

6. Apple Computer 10-K filing, December 22, 1999.

7. P. Krugman, "Intraindustry Specialization and the Gains from Trade," *Journal of Political Economy*, vol. 89 (October 1981), pp. 959–973.

8. K. Lancaster, "Intra-Industry Trade Under Perfect Monopolistic Competition," *Journal of International Economics*, vol. 10 (May 1980), pp. 151–175.

9. Andrew R. Dick, "Learning by Doing and Dumping in the Semiconductor Industry," *Journal of Law and Economics*, vol. 34, no. 1 (April 1991), p. 134.

10. Fred Warshofsky, *The Chip War* (New York: Scribner's 1989), pp. 131–132.

11. "Scotland Becomes High-Tech Giant," *Houston Chronicle*, May 11, 1992, p. 4B.

12. The FDI statistics for this section are taken from the *Survey of Current Business*, July 2000, pp. 46ff.

13. A. Quijana, "A Guide to BEA Statistics on Foreign Direct Investment in the United States," *Survey of Current Business*, February 1990, pp. 29–37.

14. Grant T. Hammond, *Countertrade, Offsets and Barter in International Political Economy* (St. Martin's Press: New York, 1990), p. 3.

15. "Siberian City Sees Its Future in Software," *Financial Times*, February 23, 2000, p. 2.

16. "Asian Investment Floods into Mexican Border Region," *Wall Street Journal*, September 6, 1996, p. A10.

17. Rigoberto Tiglao, "Growth Zones," *Far Eastern Economic Review*, February 10, 1994, pp. 40ff.

18. "Acer Is Still Searching for the Password to the U.S.," *Business Week*, May 18, 1992, p. 129.

19. "Asian Investment Floods into Mexican Border Region," *Wall Street Journal*, September 6, 1996, p. A10.

20. Peter Mikelbank, "I've Got the Cheval Right Here," *Sports Illustrated*, November 11, 1991, pp. 9–10.

21. "Samsung Attracts Six Korean Suppliers," *Financial Times*, April 24, 1996, p. 9.
22. "Fuji, Challenging Kodak, to Make Film in U.S.," *Wall Street Journal*, May 8, 1997, p. A3.
23. "Portugal Wins Siemens' Chip Plant Project," *Financial Times*, May 30, 1996, p. 5.

Chapter 6

1. Del Mar, *A History of Money in Ancient Countries* (New York: Burt Franklin, 1968; originally published in 1885), p. 71.
2. Cohen, op. cit., p. 68.
3. "South Korea Reaches Accord with IMF over Terms of Bailout," *Wall Street Journal*, December 1, 1997, p. A15; "Group Offers Indonesia Loans of Up to $40 Billion," *Houston Chronicle*, November 1, 1997, p. 1C.
4. "Freeserve Shares Drop to New Low," *Financial Times*, November 14, 2000, p. 18.
5. *Survey of Current Business*, April 2000, p. 173.
6. "Basic Truths," *The Economist*, August 24, 1991, p. 68.

Chapter 7

1. Adapted from "Dollar Makes Canada a Land of the Spree," by Robyn Meredith, *New York Times*, August 1, 1999.
2. To simplify the exposition, we assumed the foreign-exchange supply curve is upward sloping like most supply curves. Unfortunately, foreign-exchange supply curves may bend backward, a complication that can be left for graduate students in economics and finance to deal with.
3. Paul R. Krugman and Maurice Obstfeld, *International Economics*, 3rd ed. (New York: HarperCollins, 1994), pp. 642ff.
4. Eiteman, Stonehill, and Moffett, op. cit., p. 281.
5. "Goodyear's Thai Subsidiary Sees Bad Year," *Wall Street Journal*, September 5, 1997, p. A9; "The Real Lesson from Asia," *Financial Times*, September 2, 1997, p. 15; "Asia's Endangered Tigers," *Financial Times*, August 30/August 31, 1997, p. 6; "Thais Count Cost of Baht Defence," *Financial Times*, August 29, 1997, p. 5; "The IMF: Immune from (Frequent) Failure," *Wall Street Journal*, August 25, 1997, p. A18; "Thais Face Slow Economic Climb," *USA Today*, August 12, 1997, p. 4B; "Southeast Asia Seems Still on Track to Grow Despite Currency Slide," *Wall Street Journal*, August 5, 1997, p. A1; "Economic Troubles in Thailand Stoke Betting Against the Baht," *Wall Street Journal*, February 10, 1997, p. A14.

Chapter 8

1. Information for this case was obtained from various decisions of the Canadian Import Tribunal and the Canadian International Trade Tribunal, including: "Photo Albums Originating in or Exported from Singapore, Malaysia, and Taiwan," Inquiry No. CIT-5-87; CITT Review No. RR-89-012; CITT Inquiry No. NQ-90-003; and CITT review dated September 16, 1997 in RR-94-0062.
2. U. S. International Trade Commission, *Shipbuilding Trade Reform Act of 1992: Likely Economic Effects of Enactment*, USITC Publication 2495 (June 1992), Washington, D.C. The U.S. ship-

building industry is so uncompetitive in world markets that from 1960 to 1994 the industry exported no commercial ocean-going vessels (p. 6).
3. "The Trough," *The Economist*, June 27, 1992, p. 22.
4. Edward J. Lincoln, *Japan's Unequal Trade* (Washington, D. C.: The Brookings Institution, 1990), p. 112.
5. Krugman and Obstfeld, op. cit., Chapter 11.
6. "U.S. Picks Areas of Technology It Wants to Back," *Wall Street Journal*, April 26, 1994, p. A4.
7. "Torpedo Shipping Protectionism," *Wall Street Journal*, November 26, 1991, p. A14.
8. "China Hinders Its Own Bid for WTO, Adding Trade Barriers as Old Ones Fall," *Wall Street Journal*, May 20, 1997, p. A15; Office of the U.S. Trade Representative, *National Trade Estimate Report on Foreign Trade Barriers 1997*, p. 351.
9. Ibid., p. 393.
10. "Japan Glass Market Proves Hard to Crack," *Wall Street Journal*, August 7, 1991, p. A4.
11. "Los Angeles Proposal Gives Preference to Local Bids," *Wall Street Journal*, February 7, 1992, p. A7.
12. Office of the U.S. Trade Representative, *National Trade Estimate Report on Foreign Trade Barriers 1997*, pp. 23–24 and 273.
13. Office of the U.S. Trade Representative, *National Trade Estimate Report on Foreign Trade Barriers 1997*, p. 101.
14. "U.S. Criticizes EC's TV-Content Stance, Seeks Arbitration," *Wall Street Journal*, October 11, 1989, p. A15.
15. Office of the U.S. Trade Representative, *National Trade Estimate Report on Foreign Trade Barriers 1997*, pp. 159, 237, 275, and 351.
16. "Beer Blast," *Wall Street Journal*, August 4, 1992, p. A14.
17. International Monetary Fund, *Exchange Arrangements and Exchange Restrictions Annual Report 1997*. Washington, D.C.: IMF, 1997.
18. Office of the U.S. Trade Representative, *National Trade Estimate Report on Foreign Trade Barriers 1997*, pp. 17, 24, 161, and 230.
19. Committee on Ways and Means, *Operation of the Foreign Trade Zones Program of the United States and Its Implications for the U.S. Economy and U.S. International Trade*, October 1989, Serial 101-56, pp. 281 and 326.
20. Export-Import Bank of the United States, *1997 Annual Report* (Washington, D.C.: Eximbank, 1998); *1992 Annual Report* (Washington, D.C.: Eximbank, 1993); *1994 Annual Report* (Washington, D.C.: Eximbank, 1995).
21. "U.S., Japan Failing in Talks to Expand Construction Trade," *Wall Street Journal*, May 24, 1991, p. A8.

Chapter 9

1. "The World's New Tiger on the Export Scene Isn't Asian; It's Mexico," *Wall Street Journal*, May 9, 2000, p. A1; "A New Market for Mexico's Work Force," *Wall Street Journal*, April 14, 2000, p. A15; "Mexico, EU Sign Free-Trade Agreement," *Wall Street Journal*, March 24, 2000, p. A15; "How a Need for Speed Turned Guadalajara into a High-Tech Hub," *Wall Street Journal*, March 2, 2000, p. A1; "Mexico's Next Big Export: Your Teeth," *Wall Street Journal*, March 14, 2000, p. B6; "First Came Assembly; Now, Services Soar," *Wall Street Journal*, February 28, 2000, p. A1;

"European Carmakers Converge on Mexican Gateway to the US," *Financial Times*, January 5, 2000, p. 5.

2. John Maggs and Keith M. Rockwell, "Hollywood Scuffle: US Concession Stuns Experts," *Journal of Commerce*, December 16, 1993.

3. United Nations Conference on Trade and Development, *The Outcome of the Uruguay Round: An Initial Assessment (Supporting Papers to the Trade and Development Report, 1994)*. New York: United Nations, 1994, p. 143.

4. *Consumer Policy in the Single Market* (Luxembourg: Office for Official Publications of the European Communities, 1991), pp. 7–8.

5. "Daewoo, Samsung, and Goldstar: Made in Europe?" *Business Week*, August 24, 1992, p. 43.

6. "Emu 'Boost for Bosch,'" *Financial Times*, July 8, 1997, p. 2; The European Commission, *Economic and Monetary Union* (Luxembourg: Office for Official Publications of the European Communities, 1996), p. 13.

7. In an address to the Brazilian Congress, as reported by the *Houston Chronicle*, November 6, 1989, p. B1.

8. "Latin Auto Sales Drive Investment," *Houston Chronicle*, May 15, 1997, p. 1C.

9. Whirlpool Corporation, *1993 Annual Report*, p. 15.

10. Whirlpool *1999 Annual Report*; "Whirlpool Expected Easy Going in Europe, and It Got a Big Shock," *Wall Street Journal*, April 10, 1998, p. A1. "Whirlpool Net Doubled in 4th Quarter; Gains in Europe, Revamping Are Cited," *Wall Street Journal*, February 4, 1998, p. A6; "Despite Setbacks, Whirlpool Pursues Overseas Markets," *Wall Street Journal*, December 9, 1997, p. B4; "Rough and Tumble Industry," *Financial Times*, July 2, 1997, p. 13; "Whirlpool to Build Washing Machines with European, Fuel-Efficient Design," *Wall Street Journal*, August 19, 1994; Rahul Jabob, "The Big Rise," *Fortune*, May 30, 1994, pp. 74–90; "If You Can't Stand the Heat, Upgrade the Kitchen," *Business Week*, April 25, 1994, "A Chance to Clean Up in European White Goods," *Financial Times*, December 13, 1993, p. 23; Maytag, *1993 Annual Report*.

Chapter 10

1. "Mickey Stumbles at the Border," *Forbes*, June 12, 2000, p. 58; "Euro Disney's Sales Climb 17%," *Wall Street Journal*, January 22, 1998, p. A15; "Euro Disney—Oui or Non?" *Travel & Leisure*, August 1992, pp. 80–115; "An American in Paris," *Business Week*, March 12, 1990, pp. 60–64; "Fans Like Euro Disney but Its Parent's Goofs Weigh the Park Down," *Wall Street Journal*, March 10, 1994, p. A1; "Walt Disney Prepares to Share the Pain," *Financial Times*, March 15, 1994, p. 25; "Euro Disney Rescue Package Wins Approval," *Wall Street Journal*, March 15, 1994, p. A3; "How Disney Snared a Princely Sum," *Business Week*, June 20, 1994, pp. 61–62; "Euro Disney's Prince Charming?" *Business Week*, June 13, 1994, p. 42.

2. See Charles W. L. Hill and Gareth R. Jones, *Strategic Management: An Analytical Approach*, 5th ed. (Boston: Houghton Mifflin, 2001), for an overview of strategy and strategic management. See also Bjorn Lovas and Sumantra Ghoshal, "Strategy as Guided Evolution," *Strategic Management Journal*, vol. 21, no. 9, 2000, pp. 875–896.

3. Howard Thomas, Timothy Pollock, and Philip Gorman, "Global Strategic Analyses: Frameworks and Approaches," *Academy of Management Executive*, vol. 13, no. 1, 1999, pp. 70ff.

4. Kasra Ferdows, "Making the Most of Foreign Factories," *Harvard Business Review*, March–April 1997, pp. 73–88.

5. "Mercedes Bends Rules," *USA Today*, July 16, 1997, pp. B1, B2.

6. "Nissan's Slow U-Turn," *Business Week*, May 12, 1997, pp. 54–55.

7. "Russia Bans U.S. Chicken Shipments, Inspiring Fears of Tough Trade Battle," *Wall Street Journal*, February 23, 1996, p. A2.

8. Anil K. Gupta and Vijay Govindarajan, "Knowledge Flows Within Multinational Corporations," *Strategic Management Journal*, vol. 21, no. 4, 2000, pp. 473–496.

9. Christopher A. Bartlett and Sumantra Ghoshal, *Transnational Management*, 2nd ed. (Chicago, Illinois: Richard D. Irwin, 1995), pp. 237–242. See also Tatiana Kostova, "Transnational Transfer of Strategic Organizational Practices: A contextual perspective, *Academy of Management Review*, vol. 24, no. 2, 1999, pp. 308–324.

10. For recent details, see Jeffrey H. Dyer and Kentaro Nobeoka, "Creating and Managing a High-Performance Knowledge-Sharing Network: The Toyota Case," *Strategic Management Journal*, vol. 21, 2000, pp. 345–367.

11. "At Nokia, a Comeback—And Then Some," *Business Week*, December 2, 1996, p. 106.

12. "Conglomerate Plays to Its Strength," *Financial Times*, November 23, 1999, p. 11.

13. Bartlett and Ghoshal label this strategy the *multinational strategy*. We have altered their terminology to avoid confusion with other uses of the term multinational.

14. See Hill and Jones, *Strategic Management*.

15. Bruce Kogut, "Designing Global Strategies: Comparative and Competitive Value-Added Chains," *Sloan Management Review* (Summer 1985), pp. 15–28.

16. *Hoover's Handbook of World Business 2000* (Austin, Texas: Hoover's Business Press, 2000), pp. 494–495.

17. "Think Small," *Business Week*, November 4, 1991, p. 58.

18. "Producer of Feature-Film Projectors Reels in Fat Profit as Cinemas Expand," *Wall Street Journal*, October 22, 1996, p. B5; "Chile's Luksics: Battle-Tested and on the Prowl," *Wall Street Journal*, December 1, 1995, p. A10.

19. Stephen Kreider Yoder, "Intel, Backing Its Bets with Big Chips, Wins," *Wall Street Journal*, September 24, 1992, p. B1; Michiyo Nakamoto, "Looking for Smaller World to Conquer," *Financial Times*, September 2, 1992.

20. Olav Sorenson, "Letting the Market Work for You: An Evolutionary Perspective on Product Strategy," *Strategic Management Journal*, vol. 21, 2000, pp. 577–592.

21. "European Auto Makers Show Signs of Bouncing Back," *Wall Street Journal*, September 15, 1994, p. B4.

22. John A. Pearce II and Fred David, "Corporate Mission Statements: The Bottom Line," *The Academy of Management Executive*, May 1987, pp. 109–115.

23. See Anil Gupta and Vijay Govindarajan, "Knowledge Flows Within Multinational Corporations," *Strategic Management Journal*, vol. 21, 2000, pp. 473–496.

24. "Grand Met, Guinness to Form Liquor Colossus," *Wall Street Journal*, May 13, 1997, pp. B1, B8.

25. Hill and Jones, op. cit.

26. "Accor SA, Europe's Biggest Hotel Firm, Takes on a New Look Under a New CEO," *Wall Street Journal*, January 30, 1998, p. B6A.

27. For example, see J. Michael Geringer, Stephen Tallman, and David M. Olsen, "Product and International Diversification Among Japanese Multinational Firms," *Strategic Management Journal*, vol. 21, no. 1, 2000, pp. 51–80.

28. *The Walt Disney Company Annual Report 1999.*

29. *Hoover's Handbook of World Business 2000*, op. cit., pp. 434–435.

30. "DaimlerChrysler's Focus May Be Narrowing," *Wall Street Journal*, October 18, 1999, pp. A37, A39.

31. C. Campbell-Hunt, "What Have We Learned About Generic Competitive Strategy? A Meta-Analysis," *Strategic Management Journal*, vol. 21, no. 2, 2000, pp. 127–154.

32. "Telefonica Posts 43% Jump in Earnings," *Wall Street Journal*, November 19, 1999, p. A18; "Spain's Telefonica Jolts Latin America with Tough Tactics," *Wall Street Journal*, November 18, 1999, p. A1; *Hoover's Handbook of World Business 1999*, pp. 572ff.

Chapter 11

1. Heineken 1999 Annual Report; "Replacing Inventory with Information," *Forbes*, March 24, 1997, pp. 54–58; "Heineken Finds Strong Global Brew," *Financial Times*, February 7, 1996, p. 16; "Heineken's Battle to Stay Top Bottle," *Business Week*, August 1, 1994, pp. 60–62; Gary Hoover, Alta Campbell, Alan Chai, and Patrick J. Spain (eds.), *Hoovers's Handbook of World Business 1994* (Austin, Tex.: Reference Press, 1993), p. 250; Brett Duval Fromson, "Cheers to Heineken," *Fortune*, November 19, 1990, p. 172.

2. Anoop Madhok, "Cost, Value, and Foreign Market Entry Mode: The Transaction and the Firm," *Strategic Management Journal*, vol. 18, 1997, p. 37.

3. See George S. Yip and George A. Coundouriotis, "Diagnosing Global Strategy Potential: The World Chocolate Confectionery Industry," *Planning Review*, January–February 1991, pp. 4–14, for an example of how this can be done.

4. William H. Davidson, "The Role of Global Scanning in Business Planning," *Organizational Dynamics*, Winter 1991, pp. 4–16.

5. "Ford Plans $800m Brazil Plant," *Financial Times*, October 3, 1997, p. 6; "GM Plans to Develop Car in Brazil," *Financial Times*, June 3, 1997, p. 5.

6. M. Krishna Erramilli, "The Experience Factor in Foreign Market Entry Behavior of Service Firms," *Journal of International Business Studies*, vol. 22, no. 3 (Third Quarter 1991), pp. 479–501.

7. "A Beautiful Face Is Not Enough," *Forbes*, May 13, 1991, pp. 105–106.

8. Susan C. Schneider and Arnoud De Mayer, "Interpreting and Responding to Strategic Issues: The Impact of National Culture," *Strategic Management Journal*, vol. 12 (1991), pp. 307–320.

9. John H. Dunning, "Trade, Location of Economic Activity and the MNE: A Search for an Eclectic Approach," in Bertil Ohlin et al., eds., *The International Allocation of Economic Activity* (London: Macmillan, 1977); Alan M. Rugman, "A New Theory of the Multinational Enterprise: Internationalization versus Internalization," *Columbia Journal of World Business*, 1980, pp. 23–29.

10. Jean J. Boddewyn, "Political Aspects of MNE Theory," *Journal of International Business Studies*, vol. 19, no. 1 (1988), pp. 341–363; Thomas L. Brewer, "Effects of Government Policies on Foreign Direct Investment as a Strategic Choice of Firms: An Expansion of Internalization Theory," *The International Trade Journal*, vol. 7, no. 1 (Fall 1992), pp. 111–129.

11. "Egypt Suddenly Is a Magnet for Investors," *Wall Street Journal*, April 10, 1997, p. A6.

12. "Istanbul's Locations Again Makes It Crucial to the Entire Region," *Wall Street Journal*, March 27, 1997, p. A1.

13. Kenichi Ohmae, "The Global Logic of Strategic Alliances," *Harvard Business Review*, March–April 1989, p. 151.

14. John M. Stopford and Louis T. Wells, *Managing the Multinational Enterprise: Organization of the Firm and Ownership of the Subsidiaries* (New York: Basic Books, 1972).

15. M. Krishna Erramilli, "The Experience Factor in Foreign Market Entry Behavior of Service Firms," *The Journal of International Business Studies*, vol. 22, no. 3 (Third Quarter 1991), pp. 479–504.

16. Bruce Kogut, "Designing Global Strategies: Profiting from Operational Flexibility," *Sloan Management Review*, Fall 1985, pp. 27–38; Edward W. Desmond, "Byting Japan," *Time*, October 5, 1992, pp. 68–69.

17. W. Chan Kim and Peter Hwang, "Global Strategy and Multinationals' Entry Mode Choice," *Journal of International Business Studies*, vol. 23, no. 1 (First Quarter 1992), pp. 29–54; see also Sumantra Ghoshal, "Global Strategy: An Organizing Framework," *Strategic Management Journal*, vol. 8 (1987), pp. 425–440.

18. "Latin Links," *Wall Street Journal*, September 24, 1992, p. R6.

19. "Top Toilet Makers from U.S. and Japan Vie for Chinese Market," *Wall Street Journal*, December 19, 1996, p. A1.

20. Geir Grispsud, "The Determinants of Export Decisions and Attitudes to a Distant Market: Norwegian Fishery Exports to Japan," *The Journal of International Business Studies*, vol. 21, no. 3 (Third Quarter 1990), pp. 469–494.

21. "Baskin-Robbins to Open Plant in Moscow," *Bryan College Station Eagle*, August 14, 1995, p. A1.

22. Alex Taylor III, "Do You Know Where Your Car Was Made?" *Fortune*, June 17, 1991, pp. 52–56.

23. Desmond, op. cit.

24. "Nintendo to Ease Restrictions on U.S. Game Designers," *Wall Street Journal*, October 22, 1991, pp. B1, B4.

25. "Cantab Bounces Back with a Fierce Immune Response," *Wall Street Journal*, March 31, 1997, p. B4.

26. "Oleg Cassini, Inc., Sues Firm over Licensing," *Wall Street Journal*, March 28, 1984, p. 5.

27. "Unsafe Conditions at Nike Factory in Vietnam Revealed in '96 Audit," *Houston Chronicle*, November 10, 1997, p. 18A.

28. J. H. Dunning, *American Investment in British Manufacturing Industry* (London: George Allen and Unwin, 1958).

29. Bruce Kogut and Harbir Singh, "The Effect of National Culture on the Choice of Entry Mode," *Journal of International Business Studies*, vol. 19 (Fall 1988), pp. 411–432.

30. "Disney's Rough Ride in France," *Fortune*, March 23, 1992, p. 14.

31. "Carso Unit Provides Entry to Mexican Tissue Market," *Wall Street Journal*, July 22, 1997, p. A13.

32. "American Eagle Works at Keeping Its Performance Aloft," *Wall Street Journal*, November 28, 2000, p. B2.

33. "KPN Grows to Challenge Delivery Giants," *Wall Street Journal*, December 17, 1996, p. A14.

Chapter 12

1. "Breakfast Cereals: The International Market," *Euromonitor International*, June 9, 2000; "General Mills Reports Record Earnings of 78 Cents Per Share for Fiscal 1997 Third Quarter," *PR Newswire*, March 12, 1997; "Cereal Partners Venture Shakes Up Kellogg's" *Eurofood*, July 1995, p. 24; Christopher Knowlton, "Europe Cooks Up a Cereal Brawl," *Fortune*, June 3, 1992, pp. 175–179; "Cafe au Lait, a Croissant—and Trix," *Business Week*, August 24, 1992, pp. 50–52.

2. "For Kodak's Advantix, Double Exposure as Company Relaunches Camera System," *Wall Street Journal*, April 23, 1997, p. B1; "Camera System Is Developed but Not Delivered," *Wall Street Journal*, August 7, 1996, p. B1; "Kodak Joins Fuji, Others for Project," *USA Today*, March 26, 1992, p. B1.

3. Peter J. Killing, "How to Make a Global Joint Venture Work," *Harvard Business Review* (May–June 1982), pp. 120–127.

4. "Camera System Is Developed but Not Delivered," op. cit.

5. David Lei and John W. Slocum, Jr., "Global Strategic Alliances: Payoffs and Pitfalls," *Organizational Dynamics* (Winter 1991), pp. 44–62.

6. Michael E. Porter, *Competitive Strategy* (New York: Free Press, 1980), p. 275.

7. "Time Warner to Attack Spain's Cinema Market," *Financial Times*, April 8, 1997, p. 19.

8. "Cigna Enters Retail Alliance in Brazil," *Financial Times*, March 21, 1997, p. 18.

9. Farok J. Contractor, "Ownership Pattern of U.S. Joint Ventures Abroad and the Liberalization of Foreign Government Regulations in the 1980s: Evidence from the Benchmark Surveys," *Journal of International Business Studies*, vol. 21, no. 1 (First Quarter 1990), pp. 55–73.

10. "Chinese Government Struggles to Rejuvenate National Brands," *Wall Street Journal*, June 24, 1996, p. B1.

11. Bruce Kogut, "Joint Ventures: Theoretical and Empirical Perspectives," *Strategic Management Journal*, vol. 9 (1988), pp. 319–332; Andrew C. Inkpen and Paul W. Beamish, "Knowledge, Bargaining Power, and the Instability of International Joint Ventures," *Academy of Management Review*, vol. 22, no. 1 (1997), pp. 177–202.

12. Jeremy Main, "Making a Global Alliance Work," *Fortune*, December 17, 1990, pp. 121–126.

13. "PepsiCo Planning Tea-Drink Venture with Unilever Unit," *Wall Street Journal*, December 4, 1991, p. B8.

14. "Siemens, Motorola Plan U.S. Chip Plant," *Wall Street Journal*, October 26, 1995, p. A18.

15. "Chrysler and BMW Team Up to Build Small-Engine Plant in South America," *Wall Street Journal*, October 2, 1996, p. A4.

16. "Mattel Forms an Alliance with Bandai of Japan," *Wall Street Journal*, July 22, 1999, p. A20.

17. "Big Chip Makers Join to Develop New DRAM Technology," *Wall Street Journal*, January 18, 2000, p. A21.

18. "Bayer Forms Research Partnership for Antibodies with Morphosys," *Wall Street Journal*, December 23, 1999, p. A14.

19. J. Michael Geringer, "Strategic Determinants of Partner Selection Criteria in International Joint Ventures," *Journal of International Business Studies*, vol. 22, no. 1 (First Quarter 1991), pp. 41–62; Kathryn R. Harringan, *Strategies for Joint Venture Success* (Lexington, Mass.: Lexington, 1985); Keith D. Brouthers, Lance Eliot Brouthers, and Timothy J. Wilkinson, "Strategic Alliances: Choose Your Partners," *Long Range Planning*, vol. 28, no. 3 (1995), pp. 18–25.

20. Main, op. cit.

21. Joseph E. Pattison, "Global Joint Ventures," *Overseas Business* (Winter 1990), pp. 24–29.

22. Stephen J. Kohn, "The Benefits and Pitfalls of Joint Ventures," *The Bankers Magazine* (May/June 1990), pp. 12–18.

23. Joseph E. Pattison, "Global Joint Ventures," *Overseas Business* (Winter 1990), pp. 24–29.

24. "Ivory Coast Oil Exploration Pact Signed," *Houston Chronicle*, December 28, 1997, p. 4E.

25. "Daimler-Benz May Pull Out of Venture to Build Cars with Chinese Company," *Wall Street Journal*, May 23, 1997, p. A8; "Going It Alone," *The Economist*, April 19, 1997, pp. 54–55; "Ford Hopes Small Investment in China Will Pay Off Big," *Wall Street Journal*, November 9, 1995, p. B3.

26. "Coke in Venture with France's Danone to Distribute Orange Juice Overseas," *Wall Street Journal*, September 25, 1996, p. B8.

27. Nicholas Denton, "GM Puts Further DM100m into Its Hungary Venture," *Financial Times*, November 6, 1991, p. 7.

28. Karen J. Hladik and Lawrence H. Linden, "Is an International Joint Venture in R&D for You?" *Research Technology Management* (July–August 1989), pp. 11–13.

29. "Rubbermaid Ends Venture in Europe, Signalling Desire to Call Its Own Shots," *Wall Street Journal*, June 1, 1994, p. A4.

30. Main, op. cit.

31. "Murdoch Firm Sues Disney, Alleges Violation of Pact for Pay TV in Britain," *Wall Street Journal*, May 17, 1989, p. B6.

32. "Bruised in Brazil: Ford Slips as Market Booms," *Wall Street Journal*, December 13, 1996, p. A10.

Chapter 13

1. "Unilever Refashions Itself into Two Units," *Wall Street Journal*, August 7, 2000, p. A11; "Unilever to Sell Specialty-Chemical Unit to ICI of the U.K. for About $8 Billion," *Wall Street Journal*, May 7, 1997, pp. A3, A12; "Unilever Sells Off Four Chemical Units," *USA Today*, May 8, 1997, p. 3B; *Hoover's Handbook of World Business 2001* (Austin, Texas: Hoover's Business Press, 2001) pp. 626–627.

2. J. M. Stopford and L. T. Wells, *Managing the Multinational Enterprise* (New York: Basic Books, 1972).

3. Alfred Chandler, Jr., *Strategy and Structure* (Cambridge, Mass.: MIT Press, 1962).

4. Gareth Jones, *Organizational Theory*, 3rd ed. (Upper Saddle River, NJ: Prentice Hall, 2001). See also Monique Forte, James J. Hoffman, Bruce T. Lamont, and Erich N. Brockmann, "Organizational Form and Environment: An Analysis of Between-Form and Within-Form Responses to Environmental Change," *Strategic Management Journal*, 2000, vol. 21, no. 7, pp. 753–773.

5. Max Weber, *Theory of Social and Economic Organizations*, translated by T. Parsons (New York: Free Press, 1947).

6. See John Woodward, *Industrial Organization: Theory and Practice* (London: Oxford University Press, 1965); Tom Burns and G. M. Stalker, *The Management of Innovation* (London: Tavistock, 1961); Derek S. Pugh and David J. Hickson, *Organization Structure in Its Context: The Aston Program* (Lexington, Mass.: D. C. Heath, 1976).

7. See Jones, op. cit., for a review.

8. John P. Kotter and Leonard A. Schlesinger, "Choosing Strategies for Change," *Harvard Business Review*, March–April 1979, pp. 106–119.

9. Chandler, op. cit.

10. Anant K. Sundaram and J. Stewart Black, "The Environment and Internal Organization of Multinational Enterprises," *Academy of Management Review*, 1992, vol. 17, no. 4, pp. 729–757.

11. "Aetna to Merge Global, U.S. Divisions," *Wall Street Journal*, January 10, 1999, pp. A3, A20.

12. Anil K. Gupta and Vijay Govindarajan, "Knowledge Flows Within Multinational Corporations," *Strategic Management Journal*, 2000, vol. 21, no. 4, pp. 473–496.

13. Kendall Roth, David M. Schweiger, and Allen J. Morrison, "Global Strategy Implementation at the Business Unit Level: Operational Capabilities and Administrative Mechanisms," *The Journal of International Business Studies*, 1991, vol. 22, no. 3, pp. 369–402.

14. "Dinosaur Rescue," *Business Week*, October 20, 1997, pp. 52–53. See also J. Michael Geringer, Stephen Tallman, and David M. Olsen, "Product and International Diversification Among Japanese Multinational Firms," *Strategic Management Journal*, 2000, vol. 21, no. 1, pp. 51–80.

15. See Tarun Khana and Krishna Palepu, "The Right Way to Restructure Conglomerates in Emerging Markets," *Harvard Business Review*, July–August 1999, pp. 125–134.

16. Christopher A. Bartlett, "Organizing for Worldwide Effectiveness: The Transnational Solution," *California Management Review*, Fall 1988, pp. 54–74.

17. Eastman Kodak Company Web site (details posted October 23, 2000).

18. "Bridgestone Consolidates 16 Tire Units into Four to Provide Better Oversight," *Wall Street Journal*, October 19, 2000, p. A6.

19. Christopher A. Bartlett and Sumantra Ghospal, "Matrix Management: Not a Structure, a Frame of Mind," *Harvard Business Review*, July–August 1990, pp. 138–145.

20. Lawton R. Burns and Douglas R. Wholey, "Adoption and Abandonment of Matrix Management Programs: Effects of Organizational Characteristics and Interorganizational Networks," *Academy of Management Journal*, 1993, vol. 36, no. 1, pp. 105–138.

21. "Nasser: Ford Be Nimble," *Business Week*, September 27, 1999, pp. 42–43.

22. C. K. Prahalad and Jan P. Oosterveld, "Transforming Internal Governance: The Challenge for Multinationals," *Sloan Management Review*, Spring 1999, pp. 31–41.

23. "Building a New Home," *Wall Street Journal*, September 26, 1997, p. 1B.

24. See Steen Thomsen and Torben Pedersen, "Ownership Structure and Economic Performance in the Largest European Companies," *Strategic Management Journal*, 2000, vol. 21, no. 6, pp. 689–705, for a recent discussion of these issues.

25. S. Watson O'Donnell, "Managing Foreign Subsidiaries: Agents of Headquarters, or an Interdependent Network?" *Strategic Management Journal*, 2000, vol. 21, no. 5, pp. 525–548.

26. Jon I. Martinez and J. Carlos Jarillo, "The Evolution of Research on Coordination Mechanisms in Multinational Corporations," *The Journal of International Business Studies*, 1989, vol. 20, pp. 489–514.

27. John Rehfeld, "What Working for a Japanese Company Taught Me," *Harvard Business Review*, November–December 1990, pp. 167–176.

28. Sumantra Ghoshal and Christopher A. Bartlett, "The Multinational Corporation as an Interorganizational Network," *Academy of Management Review*, 1990, vol. 15, no. 4, pp. 603–625.

29. Jay Barney, "Organizational Culture: Can It Be a Source of Sustained Competitive Advantage?" *Academy of Management Review*, 1986, vol. 10, no. 2, pp. 656–665.

30. "Merrillizing the World," *Forbes*, February 10, 1997, pp. 146–151.

31. Richard Whittington, Andrew Pettigrew, Simon Peck, Evelyn Fenton, and Martin Conyon, "Change and Complementarities in the New Competitive Landscape," *Organization Science*, 1999, vol. 10, no. 5, pp. 583–600.

32. Rosabeth Moss Kanter, "Transcending Business Boundaries—12,000 World Managers View Change," *Harvard Business Review*, May–June 1991, pp. 151–164.

33. See Marie-Laure Djelic and Antti Ainamo, "The Coevolution of New Organizational Forms in the Fashion Industry: A Historical and Comparative Study of France, Italy, and the United States," *Organization Science*, 1999, vol. 10, no. 5, pp. 622–637, for one example.

34. Patricia Sellars, "Can He Keep Philip Morris Growing?" *Fortune*, April 6, 1992, pp. 86–92.

35. William G. Egelhoff, *Organizing the Multinational Enterprise* (Cambridge, Mass.: Ballinger, 1988).

36. "Beecham's Chief Imports American Ways," *Wall Street Journal*, October 27, 1988, p. B9.

Chapter 14

1. "Ono Leaves No Tracks in Nashville," *USA Today*, October 11, 2000, p. 3B; "New Firestone CEO Faces Huge Challenges," *USA Today*, October 11, 2000, p. 3B; "Bridgestone Consolidates 16 Tire Units into Four to Provide Better Oversight," *Wall Street Journal*, October 19, 2000, p. A6.

2. For a review of behavioral processes in organizations, see Gregory Moorhead and Ricky W. Griffin, *Organizational Behavior*, 6th ed. (Boston: Houghton Mifflin, 2001).

3. Ibid.

4. Lawrence Pervin, "Personality," in Mark Rosenzweig and Lyman Porter, eds., *Annual Review of Psychology*, vol. 36 (Palo Alto, Calif.: Annual Reviews, 1985), pp. 83–114.

5. Jennifer George, "The Role of Personality in Organizational Life: Issues and Evidence," *Journal of Management*, vol. 18 (1992), pp. 185–213.

6. L. R. Goldberg, "An Alternative 'Description of Personality': The Big Five Factor Structure," *Journal of Personality and Social Psychology*, vol. 59 (1990), pp. 1216–1229; M. R. Barrick and M. K. Mount, "The Big Five Personality Dimensions and Job Performance," *Personal Psychology*, vol. 44 (1991), pp. 1–26.

7. Jesus F. Salgado, "The Five Factor Model of Personality and Job Performance in the European Community," *Journal of Applied Psychology*, vol. 82, no. 1 (1997), pp. 30–43.

8. J. B. Rotter, "Generalized Expectancies for Internal vs. External Control of Reinforcement," *Psychological Monographs*, vol. 80 (1966), pp. 1–28; Bert De Brabander and Christopher Boone, "Sex Differences in Perceived Locus of Control," *The Journal of Social Psychology*, vol. 130 (1990), pp. 271–276.

9 Colleen Ward and Antony Kennedy, "Locus of Control, Mood Disturbance, and Social Difficulties During Cross-Cultural Transitions," *International Journal of Intercultural Relations*, vol. 16 (1992), pp. 175–194.

10. Marilyn E. Gist and Terence R. Mitchell, "Self-Efficacy: A Theoretical Analysis of Its Determinants and Malleability," *Academy of Management Review* (April 1992), pp. 183–211.

11. J. Michael Geringer and Colette A. Frayne, "Self-Efficacy, Outcome Expectancy and Performance of International Joint Venture General Managers," *Canadian Journal of Administrative Sciences*, vol. 10, no. 4 (1993), pp. 322–333.

12. T. W. Adorno, E. Frenkel-Brunswick, D. J. Levinson, and R. N. Sanford, *The Authoritarian Personality* (New York: Harper & Row, 1950).

13. Michael Harris Bond and Peter B. Smith, "Cross-Cultural Social and Organizational Psychology," in Janet Spence, ed., *Annual Review of Psychology*, vol. 47 (Palo Alto, Calif.: Annual Reviews, 1996), pp. 205–235.

14. Patricia C. Smith, L. M. Kendall, and Charles Hulin, *The Measurement of Satisfaction in Work and Behavior* (Chicago: Rand-McNally, 1969).

15. Meg G. Birdseye and John S. Hill, "Individual, Organizational/Work and Environmental Influences on Expatriate Turnover Tendencies: An Empirical Study," *Journal of International Business Studies* (Fourth Quarter 1995), pp. 787–813.

16. James R. Lincoln, "Employee Work Attitudes and Management Practice in the U.S. and Japan: Evidence from a Large Comparative Study," *California Management Review* (Fall 1989), pp. 89–106.

17. Daniel J. McCarthy and Sheila M. Puffer, "Perestroika at the Plant Level—Managers's Job Attitudes and Views of Decision-Making in the Former USSR," *The Columbia Journal of World Business* (Spring 1992), pp. 86–99.

18. Thang Van Nguyen and Nancy Napier, "Work Attitudes in Vietnam," *Academy of Management Executive*, 2000, vol. 14, no. 4, pp. 142–143.

19. Abdul Rahim A. Al-Meer, "Organizational Commitment: A Comparison of Westerners, Asians, and Saudis," *International Studies of Management and Organization*, vol. 19, no. 2 (1989), pp. 74–84.

20. Janet Near, "Organizational Commitment Among Japanese and U.S. Workers," *Organization Studies*, vol. 10, no. 3 (1989), pp. 281–300.

21. Hal B. Gregersen and J. Stewart Black, "Antecedents to Commitment to a Parent Company and a Foreign Operation," *Academy of Management Journal*, vol. 35, no. 1 (1992), pp. 65–90.

22. See also Joyce S. Osland and Allan Bird, "Beyond Sophisticated Stereotyping: Cultural Sensemaking in Context," *Academy of Management Executive*, vol. 14, no. 1 (2000), pp. 65–74.

23. Kent D. Miller, "Industry and Country Effects on Managers' Perceptions of Environmental Uncertainties," *Journal of International Business Studies* (Fourth Quarter 1993), pp. 693–714.

24. Satoko Watanabe and Ryozo Yamaguchi, "Intercultural Perceptions at the Workplace: The Case of the British Subsidiaries of Japanese Firms," *Human Relations*, vol. 48, no. 5 (1995), pp. 581–607.

25. Bodo B. Schlegelmilch and Diana C. Robertson, "The Influence of Country and Industry on Ethical Perceptions of Senior Executives in the U.S. and Europe," *Journal of International Business Studies* (Fourth Quarter 1995) pp. 859–881.

26. For a recent overview of the stress literature, see Frank Landy, James Campbell Quick, and Stanislav Kasl, "Work, Stress, and Well-Being," *International Journal of Stress Management*, vol. 1, no. 1 (1994), pp. 33–73.

27. "Executive Stress: A Ten-Country Comparison," *Chicago Tribune*, March 31, 1988.

28. Bruce D. Kirkcaldy and Cary L. Cooper, "Stress Differences Among German and U.K. Managers," *Human Relations*, vol. 46, no. 5 (1993), pp. 669–680.

29. Geert Hofstede, "Motivation, Leadership, and Organization: Do American Theories Apply Abroad?" *Organizational Dynamics* (Summer 1980), pp. 42–63.

30. Joseph J. Fucini and Suzy Fucini, *Working for the Japanese: Inside Mazda's American Auto Plant* (New York: Free Press, 1990).

31. Charles Weaver and Michael Landeck, "Cross-National Differences in Job Values: A Segmented Comparative Analysis of United States and West German Workers" (Laredo State University, 1991), mimeo.

32. Abraham Maslow, "A Theory of Human Motivation," *Psychological Review* (July 1943), pp. 370–396.

33. Nancy Adler, *International Dimensions of Organizational Behavior*, 3rd ed. (Cincinnati: South-Western, 1997), pp. 130–138.

34. P. Howell, J. Strauss, and P. F. Sorenson, "Research Note: Cultural and Situational Determinants of Job Satisfaction Among Management in Liberia," *Journal of Management Studies* (May 1975), pp. 225–227.

35. David McClelland, *The Achieving Society* (Princeton, N.J.: Van Nostrand, 1961).

36. Adler, op. cit.

37. Frederick Herzberg, Bernard Mausner, and Barbara Snyderman, *The Motivation to Work* (New York: Wiley, 1959).

38. G. H. Hines, "Achievement, Motivation, Occupations and Labor Turnover in New Zealand," *Journal of Applied Psychology*, vol. 58, no. 3 (1973), pp. 313–317.

39. Victor Vroom, *Work and Motivation* (New York: Wiley, 1964).

40. Gary Yukl, *Leadership in Organizations*, 2nd ed. (Englewood Cliffs, N.J.: Prentice Hall, 1989).

41. David A. Ralston, David J. Gustafson, Fanny M. Cheung, and Robert H. Terpstra, "Differences in Managerial Values: A Study of U.S., Hong Kong, and PRC Managers," *Journal of International Business Studies* (Second Quarter 1993), pp. 249–275.

42. See Joseph A. Petrick, Robert F. Scherer, James D. Brodzinski, John F. Quinn, and M. Fall Ainina, "Global Leadership Skills and Reputational Capital: Intangible Resources for Sustainable Competitive Advantage," *Academy of Management Executive*, vol. 13, no. 1 (1999), pp. 58–69.

43. Robert H. Doktor, "Asian and American CEOs: A Comparative Study," *Organizational Dynamics*, vol. 18, no. 3 (1990), pp. 46–56.

44. Jon P. Alston, *The American Samurai* (New York: Walter de Gruyter, 1986), pp. 103–113.

45. "The Spanish-American Business Wars," *Worldwide P & I Planning* (May–June 1971), pp. 30–40.

46. Arvin Parkhe, "Interfirm Diversity, Organizational Learning, and Longevity in Global Strategic Alliances," *Journal of International Business Studies*, vol. 22, no. 4 (Fourth Quarter 1991), pp. 592–593; Edward T. Hall and Mildred Reed Hall, *Understanding Cultural Differences* (Yarmouth, Maine: Intercultural Press, 1990), pp. 55–62.

47. For example, see Manfred F. R. Kets de Vries, "Leadership Style and Organizational Practices in Russia," *Organizational Dynamics*, vol. 28, no. 4 (2000), pp. 67–81.

48. Tom Morris and Cynthia M. Pavett, "Management Style and Productivity in Two Cultures," *Journal of International Business Studies*, vol. 23, no. 1 (First Quarter 1992), pp. 169–179.

49. Herbert A. Simon, *Administrative Behavior*, 3rd ed. (New York: Free Press, 1976).

50. Adler, op. cit.

51. Alston, op. cit., pp. 181–186.

52. Hall and Hall, op. cit., pp. 33–84.

53. Lawrence C. Wolken, "Doing Business in China," *Texas A&M Business Forum* (Fall 1987), pp. 39–42.

54. J. Stewart Black and Lyman W. Porter, "Managerial Behaviors and Job Performance: A Successful Manager in Los Angeles May Not Succeed in Hong Kong," *Journal of International Business Studies*, vol. 22, no. 1 (First Quarter 1991), pp. 99–113.

55. Parkhe, op. cit., pp. 579–601.

56. Ricks, op. cit.

57. See Chantell E. Nicholls, Henry W. Lane, and Mauricio Brehm Brechu, "Taking Self-Managed Teams to Mexico," *Academy of Management Executive*, vol. 13, no. 3 (2000), pp. 15–25.

58. *Hoover's Handbook of World Business 2001* (Austin: Hoover's Business Press, 2001), pp. 70–71; Charles Wallace, "Adidas—Back in the Game," *Fortune*, August 1997, pp. 176–182; *Hoover's Handbook of American Business 2001* (Austin: Hoover's Business Press, 2001), pp. 1044–1045, 1220–1221; "Adidas Is Dropping the Other Shoe," *International Herald Tribune*, March 20, 1998, pp. 15, 18.

Chapter 15

1. Alex Taylor III, "The Germans Take Charge," *Fortune*, January 11, 1999, pp. 92–96; *Hoover's Handbook of World Business 2001* (Austin: Hoover's Business Press, 2001), pp. 204–205.

2. For example, see Arnoldo C. Hax and Dean L. Wilde II, "The Delta Model: Adaptive Management for a Changing World," *Sloan Management Review*, Winter 1999, pp. 11–28.

3. David Asch, "Strategic Control: A Problem Looking for a Solution," *Long Range Planning* (February 1992), pp. 120–132.

4. John K. Shank and Joseph Fisher, "Target Costing as a Strategic Tool," *Sloan Management Review*, Fall, 1999, pp. 73–82.

5. Lane Daley, James Jiambalvo, Gary Sundem, and Yasumasa Kondon, "Attitudes Toward Financial Control Systems in the United States and Japan," *Journal of International Business Studies* (Fall 1985), pp. 91–110.

6. Hans Mjoen and Stephen Tallman, "Control and Performance in International Joint Ventures," *Organization Science* (May–June 1997), pp. 257–268.

7. Asch, op. cit., pp. 120–132.

8. "Now, Starbucks Uses Its Bean," *Business Week*, February 14, 2000, pp. 92–93; Vijay Vishwanath and David Harding, "The Starbucks Effect," *Harvard Business Review*, March–April 2000, pp. 17–18.

9. Michael Goold, "Strategic Control in the Decentralized Firm," *Sloan Management Review* (Winter 1991), pp. 69–81.

10. *Hoover's Handbook of World Business 2001* (Austin: Hoover's Business Press, 2001), pp. 168–169.

11. Robert S. Kaplan and David P. Norton, "The Balanced Scoreboard—Measures That Drive Performance," *Harvard Business Review* (January–February 1992), pp. 71–79.

12. "Luxury's Mandarin," *Newsweek*, August 25, 1997, p. 43.

13. See Mark Gimein, "CEOs Who Manage Too Much," *Fortune*, September 4, 2000, pp. 234–242.

14. "Why to Kill New Product Ideas," *Fortune*, December 14, 1992, pp. 91–94; Mark Keil and Ramiro Montealegre, "Cutting Your Losses: Extricating Your Organization When a Big Project Goes Awry," *Sloan Management Review*, Spring 2000, pp. 55–68.

15. John W. Kendrick, *Understanding Productivity: An Introduction to the Dynamics of Productivity* (Baltimore: Johns Hopkins, 1977).

16. "This Gorilla Wants to Dance," *Forbes*, September 22, 1997, pp. 97–102.

17. Gene Bylinsky, "Look Who's Doing R&D," *Fortune*, November 27, 2000, pp. 232[B]–232[F].

18. "Stiff Upper Lip," *Forbes*, February 15, 1993, pp. 54–56.

19. See Rob Cross and Lloyd Baird, "Technology Is Not Enough: Improving Performance by Building Organizational Memory," *Sloan Management Review*, Spring 2000, pp. 69–78.

20. Brian Dumaine, "Who Needs a Boss?" *Fortune*, May 7, 1990, pp. 52–60; Brian Dumaine, "The Trouble with Teams," *Fortune*, September 5, 1994, pp. 86–92.

21. Ross Johnson and William O. Winchell, *Management and Quality* (Milwaukee: American Society for Quality Control, 1989).

22. Ronald Henkoff, "The Hot New Seal of Quality," *Fortune*, June 28, 1993, pp. 116–120.

23. See Sandra Vandermerwe, "How Increasing Value to Customers Improves Business Results," *Sloan Management Review*, Fall 2000, pp. 27–38.

24. David A. Garvin, "Competing on the Eight Dimensions of Quality," *Harvard Business Review* (November–December 1987), pp. 101–109.

25. Karen Bemowski, "The International Quality Study," *Quality Progress* (November 1991), pp. 33–37; Stephen L. Yearout, "The International Quality Study Reveals Which Countries Lead the Race for Total Quality," *The Journal of European Quality* (March/April 1992), pp. 27–30.

26. *Looking for Quality in a World Marketplace* (Milwaukee: American Society for Quality Control, 1991).

27. Marshall Sashkin and Kenneth J. Kiser, *Putting Total Quality Management to Work* (San Francisco: Berrett-Koehler, 1993).

28. Donald A. Marchand, William J. Kettinger, and John D. Rollins, "Information Orientation: People, Technology, and the Bottom Line," *Sloan Management Review*, Summer 2000, pp. 69–80.

Part Three Closing Cases

1. "Remaking Nissan," *Business Week*, November 15, 1999, p. 71.

2. "The Circle Is Broken," *Financial Times*, November 9, 1999, p. 18.

3. "'Le Cost-Killer' Makes His Move," *Financial Times*, November 9, 1999, p. 15.

Chapter 16

1. "Wal-Mart Plans Major Expansion in Germany," *Wall Street Journal*, July 20, 2000, p. A21; Steven Komarow, "Wal-Mart Takes Slow Road in Germany," *USA Today*, May 9, 2000, p. 3B; Kerry Capell and Heidi Dawley, "Wal-Mart's Not-So-Secret British Weapon," *Business Week*, January 24, 2000, http://www.business-week.com/2000/00_04/b3665095.htm (July 10, 2000); "Britain's Ailing Sainsbury Faces Stark Choice," *Wall Street Journal*, October 25, 1999, p. A44; "As Wal-Mart Invades Europe, Rivals Rush to Match Its Formula," *Wall Street Journal*, October 6, 1999, p. A1.

2. From "AMA Board Approves New Marketing Definition," *Marketing News*, March 31, 1985, p. 1.

3. "France Retreats from 'Knocking' Adverts," *Financial Times*, August 14, 1995, p. 3.

4. "New Zealand Bans Reebok, Other Ads It Deems Politically Incorrect for TV," *Wall Street Journal*, July 25, 1995, p. A12.

5. David Lei, "Strategies for Global Competition," *Long Range Planning*, vol. 22, no. 1 (1989), pp. 102–109. See also Yoram Wind and Susan Douglas, "International Portfolio Analysis and Strategy: The Challenge of the 1980s," *Journal of International Business Studies* (Fall 1981), pp. 69–82.

6. Nicholas Papadopoulos and Louise A. Heslop (Eds.), *Product-Country Images—Impact and Role in International Marketing* (New York: International Business Press, 1993).

7. For an overview see David McCutcheon, Amitabh Raturi, and Jack Meredith, "The Customization-Responsiveness Squeeze," *Sloan Management Review* (Winter 1994), pp. 89–100.

8. "U.S. Catalog Firms Go After Europeans," *Wall Street Journal*, January 6, 1998, p. A15.

9. Kenichi Ohmae, "The Triad World View," *Journal of Business Strategy*, vol. 7, no. 4 (Spring 1987), pp. 8–19.

10. Theodore Levitt, "The Globalization of Markets," *Harvard Business Review* (May–June 1983), pp. 92–102.

11. Aysegul Ozsomer, Muzzafer Bodur, and S. Tamer Cavusgil, "Marketing Standardisation by Multinationals in an Emerging Market," *European Journal of Marketing*, vol. 25, no. 12 (1991), pp. 50–63.

12. John A. Quelch and Edward J. Hoff, "Customizing Global Marketing," *Harvard Business Review* (May–June 1986), pp. 59–68.

13. "The Right Way to Go Global: An Interview with Whirlpool CEO David Whitwam," *Harvard Business Review* (March–April 1994), pp. 134–145; "A Little Washing Machine That Won't Shred a Sari," *Business Week*, June 3, 1991, p. 100.

14. Quelch and Hoff, op. cit.

15. Judie Lannon, "Developing Brand Strategies Across Borders," *Marketing and Research Today* (August 1991), pp. 160–167.

16. Guy de Jonquieres, "Just One Cornetto," *Financial Times*, October 28, 1991.

17. "U.S. Superstores Find Japanese Are a Hard Sell," *Wall Street Journal*, February 14, 2000, p. B1.

18. "Big Boy's Adventures in Thailand," *Wall Street Journal*, April 12, 2000, p. B1.

19. "Mexico's Corona Brew Wins Back Cachet Lost During the Late '80s," *Wall Street Journal*, January 19, 1993, p. B6.

20. "U.S. Firms Are Letting Saudi Market Slip," *Wall Street Journal*, January 20, 1994, p. A10.

21. "Eastern Europe Poses Obstacles for Ads," *Wall Street Journal*, July 30, 1992, p. B6.

22. "It's Goo, Goo, Goo, Goo Vibrations at the Gerber Lab," *Wall Street Journal*, December 4, 1996, p. A1.

23. "Pepsi Mounts Effort to Make Potato Chips International Snack," *Wall Street Journal*, November 30, 1995, p. B10.

24. "Adapting a U.S. Car to Japanese Tastes," *Wall Street Journal*, June 26, 1995, p. B1.

25. Philip Kotler, "Global Standardization—Courting Danger," *The Journal of Consumer Marketing*, vol. 3, no. 2 (Spring 1986), p. 14.

26. "Asia Proves Unexpectedly Tough Terrain for HBO, Cinemax Channels," *Wall Street Journal*, August 23, 2000, p. B1.

27. "U.S. Companies in China Find Patience, Persistence and Salesmanship Pay Off," *Wall Street Journal*, April 3, 1992, p. B1.

28. "In Pursuit of the Elusive Euroconsumer," *Wall Street Journal*, April 23, 1992, p. B1.

29. "Mexico's Corona Brew Wins Back Cachet," op. cit.

30. Clive Sims, Adam Phillips, and Trevor Richards, "Developing a Global Pricing Strategy," *Marketing and Research Today* (March 1992), pp. 3–14.

31. William Pride and O. C. Ferrell, *Marketing*, 9th ed. (Boston: Houghton Mifflin, 1995).

32. "Coca-Cola Faces a Price War," *Wall Street Journal*, July 7, 1994, p. A1; "Cola Price War Breaks Out in Japan," *Financial Times*, July 14, 1994, p. 1.

33. "Merck Cuts Price of AIDS Drug," *Financial Times*, March 20, 1997, p. 8.

34. "Copyrights Can't Stop Gray Markets," *Houston Chronicle*, March 10, 1998, p. 1C.

35. "Luxury Prices for U.S. Goods No Longer Pass Muster in Japan," *Wall Street Journal*, February 8, 1996, p. B1.

36. "World Marketing: Going Global or Acting Local? Five Expert Viewpoints," *Journal of Consumer Marketing* (Spring 1986), pp. 5–26.

37. Martin S. Roth and Jean B. Romeo, "Matching Product Category and Country Image Perceptions: A Framework for Managing Country-of-Origin Effects," *Journal of International Business Studies*, vol. 23, no. 3 (Third Quarter 1992), pp. 477–498; John R. Darling and Van R. Wood, "A Longitudinal Study Comparing Perceptions of U.S. and Japanese Consumer Products in a Third/Neutral Country: Finland 1975 to 1985," *Journal of International Business Studies*, vol. 21, no. 3 (Third Quarter 1990), pp. 427–450.

38. "In Rural India, Video Vans Sell Toothpaste and Shampoo," *Wall Street Journal*, January 10, 1996, p. B1.

39. "U.S. Cigarette Firms Are Battling Taiwan's Bid to Stiffen Ad Curbs Like Other Asian Nations," *Wall Street Journal*, May 5, 1992, p. C25.

40. General Accounting Office, *Advertising and Promoting U.S. Cigarettes in Selected Asian Countries*, Report GAO/GGD-93-38 (December 1992), p. 38f.

41. Barbara Mueller, "Multinational Advertising: Factors Influencing the Standardised vs. Specialised Approach," *International Marketing Review*, vol. 8, no. 1 (1991), pp. 7–18.

42. "Coke Global Image Ads," *Wall Street Journal*, April 29, 1997, p. B15

43. "Global Ad Campaigns, After Many Missteps, Finally Pay Dividends," *Wall Street Journal*, August 27, 1992, p. A1.

44. "IBM Strives for a Single Image in Its European Ad Campaign," *Wall Street Journal*, April 16, 1991, p. B12.

45. "A Universal Message," *Financial Times*, May 27, 1993.

46. Barbara Mueller, "An Analysis of Information Content in Standardized vs. Specialized Multinational Advertisements," *Journal of International Business Studies*, vol. 22, no. 1 (First Quarter 1991), pp. 23–40.

47. For a review of the issues involved, see Sudhir H. Kale and John W. Barnes, "Understanding the Domain of Cross-National Buyer-Seller Interactions," *Journal of International Business Studies*, vol. 23, no. 1 (First Quarter 1992), pp. 101–132.

48. "Colgate-Palmolive Is Really Cleaning Up in Poland," *Business Week*, March 15, 1993, pp. 54–56.

49. "AIG Reshapes China's Insurance Industry," *Wall Street Journal*, February 9, 1996, p. A8.

50. "Amway Grows Abroad, Sending 'Ambassadors' to Spread the Word," *Wall Street Journal*, May 14, 1997, p. A1.

51. General Accounting Office, *Advertising and Promoting U.S. Cigarettes in Selected Asian Countries*, op. cit., pp. 37ff.

52. Ashley Blaker, "For Global Assistance, Dyal a Marketer," *San Antonio Business Journal*, August 7, 1989, p. 8.

53. "SMH Leads a Revival of Swiss Watchmaking Industry," *Wall Street Journal*, January 20, 1992, p. B4.

54. "Bicycle Brigade Takes Unilever to the People," *Financial Times*, August 17, 2000, p. 8.

55. Jean Downey, "Touchdown!" *Business Tokyo*, March 1992, p. 34.

56. "Doublemint in China: Distribution Isn't Double the Fun," *Wall Street Journal*, December 5, 1995, p. B1.

57. "Cosmetic Makers Offer World's Women an All-American Look with Local Twists," *Wall Street Journal*, May 8, 1995, p. B1.

58. "Coca-Cola to Open Plant in Moscow," *Wall Street Journal*, January 17, 1992, p. A3.

Chapter 17

1. *Hoover's Handbook of World Business 2001* (Austin: Hoover's Business, 2001), pp. 122–123; "Cross-Belt Sortation Maximizes Distribution Center Efficiency," *Modern Materials Handling*, January 1998, pp. 59–60; "Benetton Ad Models Are Dressed to Kill Sales," *Wall Street Journal*, March 20, 2000, p. A34.

2. See Anil Lhurana, "Managing Complex Production Processes," *Sloan Management Review*, Winter 1999, pp. 85–98.

3. Robert H. Hayes and Gary P. Pisano, "Beyond World-Class: The New Manufacturing Strategy," *Harvard Business Review*, January–February 1994, pp. 77–87.

4. Michael McGrath and Richard Hoole, "Manufacturing's New Economies of Scale," *Harvard Business Review*, May–June 1992, pp. 94–103.

5. "Roly's Products Deck the Halls in U.S., Asia," *Wall Street Journal*, December 27, 1996, p. A3B.

6. Masaaki Kotabe and Janet Y. Murray, "Linking Product and Process Innovations and Modes of International Sourcing in Global Competition: A Case of Foreign Manufacturing Firms," *Journal of International Business Studies* (Third Quarter, 1990), pp. 383–408.

7. James Brian Quinn and Frederick G. Hilmer, "Strategic Outsourcing," *Sloan Management Review*, Summer 1994, pp. 43–55; James Brian Quinn, "Outsourcing Innovation: The New Engine of Growth," *Sloan Management Review*, Summer 2000, pp. 13–28.

8. Stephen J. Kobrin, "An Empirical Analysis of the Determinants of Global Integration," *Strategic Management Journal*, vol. 12 (1991), pp. 17–31.

9. Peter Siddall, Keith Willey, and Jorge Tavares, "Building a Transnational Organization for British Petroleum," *Long Range Planning*, vol. 25, no. 1 (1992), pp. 18–26.

10. Welch and Nayak, op. cit.

11. See Paul S. Adler, Barbara Goldoftas, and David I. Levine, "Flexibility Versus Efficiency," *Organization Science*, 1999, vol. 10, no. 1, pp. 43–52.

12. Jeffrey K. Liker and Yen-Chun Wu, "Japanese Automakers, U.S. Suppliers and Supply Chain Superiority," *Sloan Management Review*, Fall 2000, pp. 81–93.

13. "An Efficiency Guru Refits Honda to Fight Auto Giants," *Wall Street Journal*, September 15, 1999, pp. B1, B4.

14. "U.S. Companies Move to Limit Currency Risk," *Wall Street Journal*, August 3, 1993, p. A10.

15. Lorraine Eden, Kaye G. Husbands, and Maureen Appel Molot, "Shocks and Responses: Canadian Auto Parts Suppliers Adjust to Free Trade and Lean Production," mimeo, 1997.

16. Andrew D. Bartmess, "The Plant Location Puzzle," *Harvard Business Review* (March–April 1994), pp. 20–22.

17. Dwight Silverman, "Compaq Plans to Build $15 Million Brazil Plant," *Houston Chronicle*, March 23, 1994, p. 1B.

18. "Nissan to Say 'We're Back' with New Mississippi Plant," *Houston Chronicle*, November 9, 2000, p. 3C.

19. Patriya S. Tansuhaj and George C. Jackson, "Foreign Trade Zones: A Comparative Analysis of Users and Non-Users," *Journal of Business Logistics*, vol. 10, no. 1 (1989), pp. 15–30.

20. "The Supplier Moves Next Door," *Financial Times*, July 24, 1997, p. IV.

21. David Arnold, "Seven Rules of International Distribution," *Harvard Business Review*, November–December 2000, pp. 131–137.

22. Stanley E. Fawcett, Linda L. Stanley, and Sheldon R. Smith, "Developing a Logistics Capability to Improve the Performance of International Operations," *Journal of Business Logistics*, vol. 18, no. 2 (1997), p. 102.

23. Walter Zinn and Robert E. Grosse, "Barriers to Globalization: Is Global Distribution Possible?" *The International Journal of Logistics Management*, vol. 1 (1990), pp. 13–18.

24. Adam J. Fein and Sandy D. Jap, "Manage Consolidation in the Distribution Channel," *Sloan Management Review*, March 29, 1999, pp. A1, A8.

25. Clyde E. Witt, "Packaging: From the Plant Floor to the Global Customer," *Material Handling Engineer* (October 1992), pp. 3–31.

26. Richard B. Chase and Warren J. Erikson, "The Service Factory," *The Academy of Management Executive* (August 1988), pp. 191–196.

27. Reprinted by permission of *Harvard Business Review*. An excerpt from "The Plant Location Puzzle" by Andrew D. Bartmess, March/April 1994. Copyright © 1994 by the President and Fellows of Harvard College; all rights reserved.

28. "Three Carmakers Create Link," *USA Today*, February 28, 2000, p. 8B; "Big Three Car Makers Plan Net Exchange," *Wall Street Journal*, February 28, 2000, pp. A3, A16; Shawn Tully, "The B2B Tool That Really *Is* Changing the World," *Fortune*, March 20, 2000, pp. 132–145.

Chapter 18

1. KLM *Annual Reports* for 1999/2000, 1996/97, and 1993/94; U.S. Department of Transportation, *U.S. International Air Passenger and Freight Statistics Calendar Year 1995; Fortune*, August 22, 1994, p. 190.

2. "Small Firms Hit Foreign Obstacles in Billing Overseas," *Wall Street Journal*, December 8, 1992, p. B2.

3. *Survey of Current Business*, February 1997, p. 24.

4. Richard Schaffer, Beverly Earle, and Filiberto Agusti, *International Business Law and Its Environment* (St. Paul, Minn.: West Publishing, 1990), pp. 154–155.

5. Chase Manhattan Bank, *Dynamics of Trade Finance* (New York: Chase Manhattan, 1984), pp. 41–58; Steve Murphy, *Complete Export Guide Manual* (Manhattan Beach, Calif.: Tran Publishing House, 1980).

6. Pompiliu Verzariu, *Countertrade Practices in East Europe, the Soviet Union and China: An Introductory Guide to Business* (Washington, D. C.: Department of Commerce, International Trade Administration, November 1984), pp. 98, 101.

7. Rolf Mirus and Bernard Yeung, "Economic Incentives for Countertrade," *The Journal of International Business Studies* (Fall 1986), pp. 27–39.

8. Grant T. Hammond, *Countertrade, Offsets and Barter in International Political Economy* (New York: St. Martin's, 1990), p. 75.

9. Max Eli, *Japan Inc.* (Chicago: Probus Publishing, 1999), pp. 101–104.

10. "Marc Rich & Co. Does Big Deals at Big Risk in Former U.S.S.R.," *Wall Street Journal*, May 15, 1993, p. A1.

11. Hammond, op. cit., p. 11.

12. Export-Import Bank of the United States, *1991 Annual Report*, p. 7.

13. "Foreign Currency Trades Slow at Merc as Firms Back Away," *Wall Street Journal*, October 20, 1992, p. C1.

14. "What Made the Indonesian Currency Plummet," *Wall Street Journal*, December 30, 1997, p. A4.

15. AFLAC Incorporated, *1996 Annual Report*, p. 44.

16. The Procter & Gamble Company, *1996 Annual Report*, p. 37; Owens Corning, *1996 Annual Report*, p. 42.

17. General Motors, *1996 Annual Report*, p. 70.

18. "Honda Threat to Boost Euro Components," *Financial Times*, June 6, 2000, p. 21; "Smooth Route to Sales Success May End Up Backfiring." *Financial Times*, June 6, 2000, p. 21.

19. *Sony Annual Report Year Ended March 31, 1996*, p. 31.

20. "How U.S. Firm Copes with Asia Crisis," *Wall Street Journal*, December 26, 1997, p. A2.

21. "Centralisation Lessens the Risk," *Financial Times*, April 18, 1997, p. III.

22. Marjorie Stanley and Stanley Block, "An Empirical Study of Management and Financial Variables Influencing Capital Budgeting Decisions for Multinational Corporations in the 1980s," *Management International Review*, vol. 23, no. 3 (1983), pp. 61–71.

23. U. Rao Cherukuri, "Capital Budgeting in India," in S. Kerry Cooper, Ed., *Southwest Review of International Business Research* (1992), pp. 194–204.

24. Eiteman, Stonehill, and Moffett, op. cit., p. 416.

25. *Survey of Current Business*, July 2000, p. 89.

26. Ibid.

27. "When It's Smart to Use Foreign Banks," *International Business* (January 1992), pp. 17–18.

28. Gunter Dufey and Ian H. Giddy, "Innovation in the International Financial Market," *The Journal of International Business Studies* (Fall 1981), pp. 33–51.

29. "A Eurobond Issue Tied to Film Results," *Wall Street Journal*, October 12, 1992, p. C17.

30. "Walt Disney to Sell Notes Tied to Films' Results, with Initial Yield Linked to U.S. 7-Year Issue," *Wall Street Journal*, February 17, 1994, p. C20.

31. "Vital Tool in Minimizing Costs," *Financial Times*, November 11, 1992, p. III.

32. Johnson & Johnson, 1999 and 1996 Annual Reports; lectures and personal interviews, staff of Janssen International N.V., May 25,

1994; "Visa Plans Small Payments Cross-Border Service," *Financial Times*, July 12, 1993, p. 1; "One Euro Currency Saves on Accounting but Not on Worries," *Wall Street Journal*, December 9, 1991, p. A9; "Belgium Steps Up Its Efforts to Keep Attracting Multinational Companies," *Wall Street Journal*, January 19, 1996, p. A9.

Chapter 19

1. American Accounting Association, *A Statement of Basic Accounting Theory* (Evanston, Ill.: AAA, 1966), p. 1.

2. Much of the discussion in this section is taken from Frederick D. S. Choi, Carol Ann Frost, and Gary K. Meek, *International Accounting*, 3rd ed. (Upper Saddle River, N.J.: Prentice Hall, 1999), Chapters 2 and 3, and from reports of the Working Group on Accounting Standards, Organisation for Economic Cooperation and Development, published in 1987: "Accounting Standards Harmonization, No. 2: Consolidation Policies in OECD Nations" and "Accounting Standards Harmonization, No. 3: The Relationship Between Taxation and Financial Reporting," Frederick D. S. Choi (ed.), *International Accounting and Finance Handbook* (New York: John Wiley & Sons, 1997).

3. Stephen B. Salter and Timothy D. Doupnik, "The Relationship Between Legal Systems and Accounting Practices," In Kenneth S. Most (ed.), *Advances in International Accounting*, vol. 5 (Greenwich, Conn.: JAI Press, 1992).

4. Hanns-Martin W. Schoenfeld, "International Accounting: Development, Issues, and Future Directions." *Journal of International Business Studies* (Fall 1981), pp. 83–100.

5. "Chinese Practitioners Ready for Their Great Leap Forward," *Financial Times*, August 13, 1993, p. 20.

6. Timothy S. Doupnik, "Recent Innovations in German Accounting Practice," in Kenneth S. Most (ed.), *Advances in International Accounting*, vol. 5 (Greenwich, Conn.: JAI Press, 1992).

7. Robert Bloom, Jayne Fuglister, and Jeffrey Kantor, "Toward Internationalization of Upper-Level Financial Accounting Courses," in Kenneth S. Most (ed.), *Advances in International Accounting*, vol. 5 (Greenwich, Conn.: JAI Press, 1992), pp. 239–253; Frederick D. S. Choi and Richard Levich, *The Capital Market Effects of International Accounting Diversity* (Homewood, Ill.: Dow Jones-Irwin, 1990), pp. 115–117.

8. "Deutsche Bank Says Net Jumped 24% in 1995, Discloses Big Hidden Reserves," *Wall Street Journal*, March 29, 1996, p. A8.

9. "Big Board Chief Renews His Pitch on Foreign Stocks," *Wall Street Journal*, January 7, 1992, p. A2.

10. S. J. Gray, J. C. Shaw, and L. B. McSweeney, "Accounting Standards and Multinational Corporations," *Journal of International Business Studies* (Spring/Summer 1981), pp. 121–136.

11. "Daimler-Benz Gears Up for a Drive on the Freeway," *Financial Times*, April 30, 1993.

12. "VW Plans to Switch Accounting Standards," *Financial Times*, February 21, 2000, p. 17; "Volkswagen Reluctantly Changes Lanes," *Financial Times*, February 21, 2000, p. 21.

13. Andrew L. Nodar, "Coca-Cola Writes an Accounting Procedures Manual," *Management Accounting*, vol. 68 (October 1986), pp. 52–53.

14. Istemi S. Demirag, "Assessing Foreign Subsidiary Performance: The Currency Choice of U.K. MNCs," *Journal of International Business Studies*, vol. 19, no. 2 (Summer 1988), pp. 257–275.

15. Shawn Tully, "GE in Hungary: Let There Be Light," *Fortune*, October 22, 1990, p. 142.

16. "Chinese Practitioners Ready for Their Great Leap Forward," *Financial Times*, August 13, 1993, p. 20.

17. Lee H. Radebaugh and Sidney J. Gray, *International Accounting and Multinational Enterprises* (New York: John Wiley & Sons, Inc., 1997), pp. 111–112.

18. Stephen B. Salter, *Classification of Financial Reporting Systems and a Test of Their Environmental Determinants*, unpublished Ph.D. dissertation, University of South Carolina (1991), p. 5.

19. "Language Lessons for Accountants," *Financial Times*, July 11, 1995, p. 4.

20. "France Girds Itself for an International Market," *Financial Times*, June 28, 1991, p. 13.

21. "German Conglomerate Adopts U.S. System of Filing Accounts," *Financial Times*, March 28, 1996, p. 11; "Bonn Signals Softer Line on Accounting," *Financial Times*, May 22, 1995, p. 2; "German Firms Shift to More-Open Accounting," *Wall Street Journal*, March 15, 1995, p. C1.

22. Financial Accounting Standards Board, *Statement of Financial Accounting Standards No. 52: Foreign Currency Translation* (Stamford, Conn.: FASB, December 1981).

23. "Dell Computer at War with Analyst Critical of Its Currency Trades," *Wall Street Journal*, November 30, 1992, p. A1; "Dell Computer Shares Drop by 9.8% on Analyst's Currency-Trading Report," *Wall Street Journal*, November 11, 1992, p. A5.

24. Robert G. Ruland and Timothy S. Doupnik, "Foreign Currency Translation and the Behavior of Exchange Rates," *Journal of International Business Studies*, vol. 19, no. 3 (Fall 1988), p. 462.

25. J. C. Stewart, "Transfer Pricing: Some Empirical Evidence from Ireland," *Journal of Economic Studies*, vol. 16, no. 3, pp. 40–56.

26. David Harris, Randall Morck, Joel Slemrod, and Bernard Yeung, "Income Shifting in U.S. Multinational Corporations," University of Michigan, mimeo, 1991; James R. Hines and Eric Rice, "Fiscal Paradise: Foreign Tax Havens and American Business," N.B.E.R. Working Paper #3477 (Cambridge, Mass., 1990); James Wheeler, "An Academic Look at Transfer Pricing in a Global Economy," *Tax Notes*, July 4, 1988.

27. "IBM Probed Over Payments Of U.K. Taxes," *Wall Street Journal*, August 6, 1999, p. A3.

28. "Generation of Huge Changes," *Financial Times*, February 2, 2000, p. III.

29. Bruce W. Reynolds and Alan R. Levenson, "Setting Up a Foreign Sales Corporation Can Cut Your Tax Bill," *Journal of European Business* (July/August 1992), pp. 59–64; Mark A. Goldstein and Arthur I. Aronoff, "Foreign Sales Corporations: Tax Incentives for U.S. Exporters," *Business Credit* (April 1991), pp. 20–23.

30. Choi and Mueller, op. cit., p. 554.

31. "Japan's Tax Man Leans on Foreign Firms," *Wall Street Journal*, November 25, 1996, p. A13.

32. "Court Blocks Challenge of Big Tax Refund for Texaco," *New York Times*, April 22, 1997, p. C1; "Texaco Wins Billion-Dollar Tax Battle," *Houston Chronicle*, April 22, 1997, p. 1C.

Chapter 20

1. *Hoover's Handbook of World Business 2001* (Austin: Hoover's Business Press, 2001), pp. 624–625; Justin Martin, "Mercedes: Made in Alabama," *Fortune*, July 7, 1997, pp. 150–158; "Toyota Devises Grueling Workout for Job Seekers," *USA Today*, August 11, 1997, p. 3B.

2. Angelo S. DeNisi and Ricky W. Griffin, *Human Resource Management* (Boston: Houghton Mifflin, 2001), chapter 4, pp. 102–134.

3. "To Get Shipped Abroad, Women Must Overcome Prejudice at Home," *Wall Street Journal*, June 29, 1999, p. B1.

4. Nakiye Boyacigiller, "The Role of Expatriates in the Management of Interdependence, Complexity, and Risk in Multinational Corporations," *Journal of International Business Studies*, vol. 21, no. 3 (Third Quarter 1990), pp. 357–382.

5. Gretchen M. Spreitzer, Morgan W. McCall, Jr., and Joan D. Mahoney, "Early Identification of International Executive Potential," *Journal of Applied Psychology*, vol. 82, no. 1 (1997), pp. 6–29.

6. See DeNisi and Griffin, *Human Resource Management*.

7. "Companies Send Intrepid Retirees to Work Abroad," *Wall Street Journal*, March 2, 1998, p. B1.

8. "Pharmacia to Move Headquarters to U.S. East Coast," *Wall Street Journal*, October 14, 1997, p. B14.

9. "Younger Managers Learn Global Skills," *Wall Street Journal*, March 31, 1992, p. B1.

10. See J. Stewart Black and Hal B. Gregersen, "The Right Way to Manage Expats," *Harvard Business Review*, March–April 1999, pp. 52–62.

11. See Paula M. Caligiuri, "The Big Five Personality Characteristics as Predictors of Expatriate's Desire to Terminate the Assignment," *Personnel Psychology*, 2000, vol. 53, no. 1, pp. 67–78.

12. "To Smooth a Transfer Abroad, a New Focus on Kids," *Wall Street Journal*, January 26, 1999, pp. B1, B14.

13. Andrea C. Poe, "Destination Everywhere," *HRMagazine*, October 2000, pp. 67–77.

14. Ann Marie Ryan, Lynn McFarland, Helen Baron, and Ron Page, "An International Look at Selection Practices: Nation and Culture as Explanations for Variability in Practice," *Personnel Psychology*, 1999, vol. 52, no. 2, pp. 58–70.

15. Joel D. Nicholson, Lee P. Stepina, and Wayne Hochwarter, "Psychological Aspects of Expatriate Effectiveness," in Ben B. Shaw and John E. Beck (guest editors), Gerald R. Ferris and Kendrith M. Rowland (eds.), *Research in Personnel and Human Resources Management* (Supplement 2: International Human Resources Management) (Greenwich, Conn.: JAI Press, 1990), pp. 127–145.

16. Gary P. Ferraro, *The Cultural Dimension of International Business* (Upper Saddle River, N.J.: Prentice Hall, 1990), pp. 143–144.

17. "Before Going Overseas, Smart Managers Plan Their Homecoming," *Wall Street Journal*, September 28, 1999, p. B1; "Expatriates Find Long Stints Abroad Can Close Doors to Credit at Home," *Wall Street Journal*, May 17, 1993, pp. B1, B6.

18. Juan I Sanchez, Paul E. Spector, and Cary L. Cooper, "Adapting to a Boundaryless World: A Developmental Expatriate Model," *Academy of Management Executive*, May 2000, pp. 96–105.

19. "New Plant Gets Jaguar in Gear," *USA Today*, November 27, 2000, p. 4B.

20. "Distractions Make Global Manager a Difficult Role," *Wall Street Journal*, November 21, 1999, p. B1, B18.

21. Michael J. Marquardt and Dean W. Engel, "HRD Competencies for a Shrinking World," *Training & Development* (May 1993), pp. 59–60.

22. Shirley Fung, "How Should We Pay Them?" *Across the Board*, June 1999, pp. 37–41.

23. Lawrence A. West, Jr., and Walter A. Bogumil, Jr., "Foreign Knowledge Workers as a Strategic Staffing Option," *Academy of Management Executive*, November 2000, pp. 71–84.

24. "Some U.S. Companies Find Mexican Workers Not So Cheap After All," *Wall Street Journal*, September 15, 1993, pp. A1, A16.

25. Christopher Lorenz, "Learning to Live with a Cultural Mix," *Financial Times*, April 23, 1993, p. 18.

26. Anthony M. Townsend, K. Dow Scott, and Steven E. Markham, "An Examination of Country and Culture-Based Differences in Compensation Practices," *Journal of International Business Studies*, vol. 21, no. 4 (Fourth Quarter 1990), pp. 667–678.

27. "Bitter Swedish Dispute Set to End," *Financial Times*, May 30, 1995, p. 3.

28. Cheng Soo May, "Worker Participation in Private Companies in Singapore," in Albert Nedd (guest editor), Gerald R. Ferris and Kendrith M. Rowland (eds.), *Research in Personnel and Human Resources Management* (Supplement 1: International Human Resources Management) (Greenwich, Conn.: JAI Press, 1989), pp. 97–120.

29. Daniel Benjamin and Tony Horwitz, "German View: 'You Americans Work Too Hard—and for What?'," *Wall Street Journal*, July 14, 1994, pp. B5–B6. Reprinted by permission of the *Wall Street Journal*, © 1994 Dow Jones & Company, Inc. All Rights Reserved Worldwide.

Glossary

The number in parentheses following each definition gives the page on which the term is introduced.

absolute advantage, theory of: theory stating that trade between nations occurs when one nation is absolutely more productive than other nations in the production of a good; according to Adam Smith, nations should export those goods for which they possess an absolute advantage and import goods for which other nations possess an absolute advantage (125)

accounting reserves: reserves created by firms for foreseeable future expenses (550)

acculturation: process of understanding and learning how to operate in a new culture (112)

acquisition strategy: form of foreign direct investment involving the purchase of existing assets in a foreign country (333)

active income: income generated by active business operations such as production, marketing, and distribution (565)

ad valorem tariff: tax assessed as a percentage of the market value of an imported good (227)

advance pricing agreement: an agreement between an international business and the U.S. Internal Revenue Service establishing in advance the transfer prices the company will charge for intracorporate transactions (567)

adjustable peg: feature of the Bretton Woods system by which a country had a limited right to adjust the value of its currency in terms of gold (162)

advised letter of credit: letter of credit in which the seller's bank advises the seller about the creditworthiness of the bank issuing the letter of credit (519)

affiliated bank: partly owned, separately incorporated overseas banking operation of a home country bank (206)

aggressive goal behavior: behavior based on the cultural belief that material possessions, money, and assertiveness underlie motivation and reflect the goals that a person should pursue (110)

agreeableness: a "big five" personality trait referring to a person's ability to get along with others (398)

Aktiengesellschaft (AG): a form of corporate organization in Germany; a typical AG is a large, publicly held firm with limited liability; the firm must have a management board and a board of directors (8)

Andean Pact: customs union composed of Bolivia, Colombia, Ecuador, Peru, and Venezuela (270)

antidumping duty: tax on imported goods designed to protect domestic firms from sales of imported goods at less than their cost of production or at prices less than they sell for in their home markets (217)

arbitrage: riskless purchase of a product in one market for immediate resale in a second market in order to profit from price differences between the markets (199)

arbitration: dispute resolution technique in which both parties agree to submit their cases to a private individual or body for resolution (68)

arm's length test: test imposed by the Internal Revenue Service to determine the appropriateness of transfer prices; reflects the price that one independent company would charge a second for a good or service (563)

Asia-Pacific Economic Cooperation (APEC): a group of countries on both sides of the Pacific working to promote trade among themselves through the reduction or elimination of trade barriers (272)

assigned arrangement: management arrangement in which one partner in a strategic alliance assumes primary responsibility for the operations of the alliance (358)

attitudes: complexes of beliefs and feelings a person has about specific ideas, situations, or other people (399)

Australia–New Zealand Closer Economic Relations Trade Agreement (ANZCERTA or CER): an agreement between Australia and New Zealand intended to eliminate trade barriers between the two countries (270)

authoritarianism: personality trait determining the extent to which an individual believes that power and status differences are appropriate within hierarchical social systems like organizations (399)

backtranslation: technique used to check for translation errors; after one person translates a document from language A to language B, a second person translates the document from B back to A to check if the intended message is actually being sent (92)

Baker Plan: plan developed in 1985 by U.S. Treasury Secretary James Baker to solve the international debt crisis; stressed debt rescheduling, tight controls over domestic monetary and fiscal policies, and continued loans to debtor nations (170)

balance of payments (BOP) accounting system: accounting system that records commercial transactions between the residents of one country and residents of other countries (155)

balance on merchandise trade: difference between a country's merchandise exports and imports (173)

balance on services trade: difference between a country's service exports and imports (173)

balance sheet hedge: technique for eliminating translation exposure in which a firm matches its assets and liabilities denominated in a given currency on a consolidated basis (529)

banker's acceptance: time draft that has been endorsed by a bank, signifying the bank's promise to guarantee payment at the designated time (517)

barter: form of countertrade involving simultaneous exchange of goods or services between two parties (521)

beggar-thy-neighbor policies: domestic economic policies that ignore the economic damage done to other countries (158)

benchmarking: process of legally and ethically studying how other firms do something in a high-quality way and then either imitating or improving on their methods (444)

besloten vennootschap (BV): term used in the Netherlands to refer to a privately held, limited liability firm (8)

"big five" personality traits: popular personality model based on five dominant traits—agreeableness, conscientiousness, emotional stability, extroversion, and openness (398)

bilateral netting: netting of transactions between two business units (533)

bill of lading: international trade document that serves (1) as a contract between the exporter and the transporter and (2) as a title to the exported goods (516)

B-O-T project: variant of a turnkey project for market entry in which a firm builds a facility, operates it, and then later transfers ownership of the project to some other party (332)

Brady Plan: plan developed in 1989 by U.S. Treasury Secretary Nicholas Brady to solve the international debt crisis; involves writing off a portion of the debtor nations' debts or repurchase of their debts at less than face value (170)

branch bank: overseas banking operation of a home country bank that is not separately incorporated (206)

brownfield strategy: see acquisition strategy

bureaucratic design: model of organization design based on rational rules, regulations, and standard operation procedures (369)

bureaucratic law: legal system based on interpretations, actions, and decisions of government employees (61)

buy-back: form of countertrade in which a firm is compensated in the form of goods produced by equipment or technology that it has sold to another firm (521)

Cairns Group: group of major agricultural exporting nations, led by Argentina, Australia, and Canada, that lobbies for reductions in agricultural subsidies (253)

call option: publicly traded contract granting the owner the right, but not the obligation, to buy a specific amount of foreign currency at a specified price at a stated future date (197)

capacity planning: deciding how many customers a firm will be able to serve at a given time (504)

capital account: BOP account that records capital transactions between res-

idents of one country and those of other countries (173)

Caribbean Basin Initiative (CBI): program developed by the United States to spur the economic development of countries in the Caribbean Basin; allows duty-free importation of selected goods into the United States from these countries (268)

centralized cash management: system controlled by a parent corporation that coordinates worldwide cash flows of its subsidiaries and pools their cash reserves (532)

centrally planned economy (CPE): economy in which government planners determine price and production levels for individual firms (76)

chaebol: any of the large business conglomerates that dominate the Korean economy (42)

channel length: number of stages in a distribution channel (480)

civil law: law based on detailed codification of permissible and nonpermissible activities; world's most common form of legal system (61)

clearinghouse accounts: accounting system used to facilitate international countertrade; a firm must balance its overall countertrade transactions but need not balance any single countertrade transaction (521)

co-decision procedure: procedure that shares decision-making power between the European Parliament and the Council of the European Union (260)

codetermination: German system that provides for cooperation between management and labor in running a business (598)

cohesion fund: means of funneling economic development aid to countries whose per capita GDP is less than 90 percent of the EU average (264)

collective bargaining: process used to make agreements between management and labor unions (597)

collectivism: cultural belief that the group comes first (104)

comity, principle of: principle of international law that one country will honor and enforce within its own territory the judgments and decisions of foreign courts (68)

common law: law that forms the foundation of the legal system in Anglo-American countries; based on cumula-

tive findings of judges in individual cases (60)

common market: form of regional economic integration that combines features of a customs union with elimination of barriers inhibiting the movement of factors of production among members (256)

Commonwealth of Independent States: organization formed by 12 former Soviet republics to promote free trade and discuss issues of common concern (35)

comparative advantage, theory of: theory stating that trade between countries occurs when one country is relatively more productive than others in the production of a good (126)

compound tariff: tax that combines elements of an ad valorem tariff and a specific tariff (227)

comprehensive alliance: strategic alliance in which participants agree to perform together multiple stages of the process by which goods or services are brought to market (350)

confirmed letter of credit: letter of credit in which the seller's bank adds its promise to pay should the issuing bank fail to pay the seller (519)

confiscation: involuntary transfer of property, with little or no compensation, from a privately owned firm to the host government (64)

conglomerate: firm that uses a strategy of unrelated diversification (300)

conscientiousness: a "big five" personality trait referring to the order and precision a person imposes on activities (398)

consolidated financial statement: a financial statement combining the accounting records of a parent corporation and all its subsidiaries into a single set of statements denominated in a single currency (557)

consolidation method: technique used to consolidate accounting records of subsidiaries in which the parent company's ownership stake is more than 50 percent (558)

contract manufacturing: process of outsourcing manufacturing to other firms to reduce the amount of a firm's financial and human resources devoted to the physical production of its products (331)

control: process of monitoring and regulating activities in a firm so that targeted measures of performance are achieved or maintained (422)

control framework: managerial and organizational processes used to keep a firm on target toward its strategic goals (298)

control standard: desired level of a performance component a firm is attempting to control (430)

controlled foreign corporation (CFC): foreign corporation in which certain U.S. shareholders (each of which must own at least 10 percent of the foreign corporation's stock) cumulatively own at least 50 percent of the foreign corporation's stock (565)

controller: managerial position in an organization given specific responsibility for financial control (424)

convertible currencies: currencies that are freely traded and accepted in international commerce; also called hard currencies (162, 196)

coordination: process of linking and integrating functions and activities of different groups, units, or divisions (385)

core competency: a distinctive strength or advantage of a firm which allows it to compete effectively with its rivals (12)

corollary approach: approach whereby a firm delegates responsibility for processing international sales orders to individuals within an existing department, such as finance or marketing (370)

corporate culture: set of shared values that defines for its members what the organization stands for (386)

correspondent relationship: agency relationship whereby a bank in country A acts as an agent for a bank from country B, providing banking services in country A for both the B bank and its clients; typically done on a reciprocal basis (206)

cost-of-living allowance: compensation for managers on international assignment designed to offset differences in living costs (590)

cost method: technique used to consolidate accounting records of subsidiaries in which the parent company's ownership stake is less than 10 percent (557)

Council of the European Union: main decision-making body of the EU; composed of 15 members, who represent the interests of their home governments in Council deliberations (259)

counterpurchase: form of countertrade in which one firm sells its products to another at one point in time and is compensated in the form of the other's products at some future time (521)

countertrade: form of payment in which a seller accepts something other than money in compensation (521)

countervailing duty (CVD): ad valorem tariff placed on imported goods to offset subsidies granted by foreign governments (239)

country fund: mutual fund that specializes in investing in stocks and bonds issued by firms in a specific country (210)

country similarity theory: theory stating that international trade in manufactured goods will occur between countries with similar income levels and at similar stages of economic development (132)

covered-interest arbitrage: arbitrage that exploits geographic differences in interest rates and differences in exchange rates over time (204)

cross-cultural literacy: ability to understand and operate in more than one culture (111)

cross rate: exchange rate between two currencies, A and B, derived by using currency A to buy currency C and then using currency C to buy currency B (204)

cultural cluster: group of countries that share many cultural similarities (101)

cultural convergence: convergence of two or more cultures (111)

culture: collection of values, beliefs, behaviors, customs, and attitudes that distinguish and define a society (85)

culture shock: psychological phenomenon arising from being in a different culture; may lead to feelings of fear, helplessness, irritability, and disorientation (585)

cumulative translation adjustment: account created to balance any difference between a subsidiary's assets and its liabilities and stockholder's equity when the current rate method is used to value its balance sheet (559)

currency future: publicly traded contract involving the sale or purchase of a specific amount of foreign currency at a specified price with delivery at a stated future date (197)

currency option: publicly traded contract giving the owner the right, but not the obligation, to sell or buy a specific amount of foreign currency at a specified price at a stated future date (see also call option; put option) (197)

current account: BOP account that records exports and imports of goods, exports and imports of services, investment income, and gifts (172)

current account balance: net balance resulting from merchandise exports and imports, service exports and imports, investment income, and unilateral transfers (173)

current rate method: approach used to consolidate the financial statements of a foreign subsidiary when the subsidiary's functional currency is the subsidiary's home currency (558)

customs union: form of regional economic integration that combines features of a free trade area with common trade policies toward nonmember countries (255)

date draft: draft that requires payment at some specified date (517)

decision making: process of choosing one alternative from among a set of alternatives to promote the decision maker's objectives (410)

deferral rule: rule permitting U.S. companies to defer paying U.S. income taxes on profits earned by their foreign subsidiaries (565)

delegated arrangement: management arrangement in which partners in a strategic alliance play little or no management role, delegating responsibility to the executives of the alliance itself (358)

development: general education aimed at preparing managers for new assignments and/or higher-level positions (587)

differentiation strategy: business-level strategy that emphasizes the distinctiveness of products or services (301)

direct exchange rate: price of a foreign currency in terms of the home currency; also called a direct quote (190)

direct exporting: product sales to customers, either distributors or end users, located outside the firm's home country (321)

direct quote: see direct exchange rate

direct sales: selling products to final consumers (480)

dirty float: see managed float

distinctive competence: component of strategy that answers the question "What do we do exceptionally well, especially as compared to our competitors?" (291)

distribution: process of getting a firm's products and services to its customers (478)

documentary collection: form of payment in which goods are released to the buyer only after the buyer pays for them or signs a document binding the buyer to pay for them (516)

draft: document demanding payment from the buyer (516)

dual use: products that may be used for both civilian and military purposes (63)

dumping: sale of imported goods either (1) at prices below what a company charges in its home market or (2) at prices below cost (217)

eclectic theory: theory that foreign direct investment occurs because of location advantages, ownership advantages, and internalization advantages (144)

economic and monetary union (EMU): goal established by the Maastricht Treaty to create a single currency for the EU, thereby eliminating exchange rate risks and the costs of converting currencies for intra-EU trade (264)

Economic Community of Central African States (CEEAC): organization promoting regional economic cooperation created by Central African countries (272)

Economic Community of West African States (ECOWAS): organization promoting regional economic cooperation created by 16 West African countries (272)

economic exposure: impact on the value of a firm's operations of unanticipated exchange rate changes (529)

economic union: form of regional economic integration that combines features of a common market with coordination of economic policies among its members (256)

economies of scale: condition that occurs when average costs of production decline as the number of units produced increases (136)

economies of scope: condition that occurs when a firm's average costs decline as the number of different products it sells increases (136)

embargo: ban on the exporting and/or importing of goods to a particular country (63, 233)

emotional stability: a "big five" personality trait defining a person's poise, calmness, and resilience (398)

environmental scanning: the systematic collection of data about all elements of a firm's external and internal environments (295)

equity method: technique used to consolidate accounting records of subsidiaries in which the parent's ownership stake is between 10 and 50 percent (558)

errors and omissions: BOP account that results from measurement errors; equals the negative of the sum of the current account, the capital account, and the official reserves account (176)

ethnocentric approach: managerial approach in which a firm operates internationally the same way it does domestically (373, 462)

ethnocentric staffing model: approach that primarily uses PCNs to staff upper-level foreign positions (580)

Eurobonds: bonds denominated in one country's currency but sold to residents of other countries (208)

Eurocurrency: currency on deposit in banks outside its country of issue (208)

Eurodollars: U.S. dollars deposited in banks outside the borders of the United States (208)

European Central Bank: the central bank responsible for controlling monetary policy for all EU countries adopting the euro as their currency (265)

European Commission: 20-person group that acts as the EU's administrative branch of government and proposes all EU legislation (259)

European Court of Justice: 15-member court charged with interpreting EU law; also interprets whether the national laws of the 15 EU members are consistent with EU laws and regulations (260)

European Economic Area: common market created by the EU and Iceland, Liechtenstein, and Norway (266)

European Free Trade Association: trading bloc in Europe that works closely with the EU to promote intra-European trade; current members are Iceland, Liechtenstein, Norway, and Switzerland (266)

European Monetary System (EMS): system based on 1979 agreement among members of the European Union to manage currency relationships among themselves (166)

European Parliament: legislature with 626 members elected from districts in member countries that has a consultative role in EU decision making (260)

exchange rate: price of one currency in terms of a second currency (155)

exchange rate mechanism (ERM): agreement among European Union members to maintain fixed exchange rates among themselves within a narrow band (166)

exit interview: interview with an employee who is leaving the organization (594)

expatriate failure: early return of an expatriate manager to his or her home country because of an inability to perform in the overseas assignment (583)

expatriates: collective name for parent country nationals (PCNs) and third-country nationals (TCNs) (580)

export and import brokers: agents who bring together international buyers and sellers of standardized commodities such as coffee, cocoa, and grains (326)

Export-Import Bank of the United States (Eximbank): U.S. government agency that promotes U.S. exports by offering direct loans and loan guarantees (238)

export management company (EMC): firm that acts as its clients' export department (324)

export of the services of capital: income that a country's residents earn from their foreign investments (173)

export promotion: economic development strategy based on building a vibrant manufacturing sector by stimulating exports, often by harnessing some advantage the country possesses, such as low labor costs (48, 224)

export promotion strategy: see export promotion

export tariff: tax levied on goods as they leave the country (227)

exporting: selling products made in one's own country for use or resale in other countries (8)

expropriation: involuntary transfer of property, with compensation, from a privately owned firm to a host country government (64)

extraterritoriality: application of a country's laws to activities occurring outside its borders (63)

extroversion: a "big five" personality trait defining a person's comfort level with relationships, resulting in some people being sociable, talkative, and assertive, and others being less sociable and more introverted (398)

factoring: specialized international lending activity in which firms buy foreign accounts receivable at a discount from face value (516)

fair trade: trade between nations that takes place under active government intervention to ensure that the companies of each nation receive their fair share of the economic benefits of trade; also called managed trade (219)

fast-track authority: authority delegated by the U.S. Congress to the president allowing him/her to negotiate trade treaties with other countries; after treaty is negotiated, Congress may accept or reject it but cannot amend or change it (267)

financial alliance: strategic alliance in which two or more firms work together to reduce the financial risks associated with a project (352)

first-mover advantage: competitive advantage gained by the first firm to enter a market, develop a product, introduce a technology, and so forth (136)

fixed exchange rate system: international monetary system in which each government promises to maintain the price of its currency in terms of other currencies (155)

flexible (or floating) exchange rate system: system in which exchange rates are determined by supply and demand (165)

flight capital: money sent out of politically or economically unstable countries by investors seeking a safe haven for their assets (29, 176)

float: to allow a currency's value to be determined by forces of supply and demand (156)

focus strategy: business-level strategy targeting specific types of products for certain customer groups or regions (302)

foreign bonds: bonds issued by residents of one country to residents of a second country and denominated in the second country's currency (208)

Foreign Corrupt Practices Act (FCPA): U.S. law enacted in 1977 prohibiting U.S. firms, their employees, and agents acting on their behalf from paying or offering to pay foreign government officials to influence official actions or policies or to gain or retain business (65)

foreign direct investment (FDI): acquisition of foreign assets for the purpose of controlling them; under U.S. regulations FDI occurs when an investor owns at least 10 percent of the voting stock of a foreign company (9, 140)

foreign exchange: currencies issued by countries other than one's own (189)

foreign sales corporation (FSC): subsidiary of a U.S. MNC that enjoys substantial income tax savings from profits earned from exporting activities (565)

foreign service premium: see hardship premium

Foreign Sovereign Immunities Act of 1976: U.S. law that limits the ability of U.S. citizens to sue foreign governments in U.S. courts (68)

foreign trade zone (FTZ): geographical area in which imported or exported goods receive preferential tariff treatment (237)

forum shopping: attempt to seek a court system or judge that will be most sympathetic to an attorney's client (67)

forward discount: difference between the forward and the spot price of a currency expressed as an annualized percentage (assumes the forward price is less than the spot price) (see also forward premium) (198)

forward market: market for foreign exchange involving delivery of currency at some point in the future (196)

forward premium: difference between the forward and the spot price of a currency expressed as an annualized percentage (assumes the forward price is more than the spot price) (see also forward discount) (198)

franchisee: independent entrepreneur or organization that operates a business under the name of another (329)

franchising: special form of licensing allowing the licensor more control over the licensee while also providing more support from the licensor to the licensee (11, 329)

franchisor: firm that allows an independent entrepreneur or organization to operate a business under its name (329)

free trade: trade between nations that is unrestricted by governmental actions (218)

free trade area: regional trading bloc that encourages trade by eliminating trade barriers among its members (255)

freight forwarders: agents who specialize in the physical transportation of goods, arranging customs documentation and obtaining transportation services for their clients (326)

functional currency: currency of the principal economic environment in which a subsidiary operates (558)

General Agreement on Tariffs and Trade (GATT): international agreement that sponsors negotiations to promote world trade (249)

generalized system of preferences: system of reduced tariff rates offered on goods exported from developing countries (250)

generic organizational control: form of organizational control based on centralized generic controls across the entire organization (426)

geocentric approach: management approach in which a firm analyzes the needs of its customers worldwide and then adopts standardized operating practices for all markets it serves (373, 463)

geocentric staffing model: approach using a mix of PCNs, HCNs, and TCNs to staff upper-level foreign positions (580)

geographic arbitrage: see two-point arbitrage

Gesellschaft mit beschränkter Haftung (GmbH): a form of corporate organization in Germany; a typical GmbH is a small, privately held company (8)

global area design: form of organization design that centers a firm's activities around specific areas or regions of the world (375)

global bonds: large, liquid bond issues designed to be traded in numerous capital markets (209)

global customer design: form of organization design centered around different customers or customer groups, each requiring special expertise or attention (379)

global functional design: form of organization design based on departments or divisions having worldwide responsibility for a single organizational function such as finance, operations, or marketing; also called U-form organization (377)

global matrix design: complex form of international organization design created by superimposing one form of design on top of an existing different form (380)

global product design: form of organization design that assigns worldwide responsibility for specific products or product groups to separate operating divisions within a firm (373)

goal orientation: cultural beliefs about motivation and the different goals toward which people work (110)

gold standard: international monetary system based on the willingness of countries to buy or sell their paper currencies for gold at a fixed rate (155)

goodwill: payment in excess of the book value of a firm's stock (551)

gray market: market created when products are imported into a country legally but outside the normal channels of distribution authorized by the manufacturer (472)

greenfield investment: form of investment in which the firm designs and builds a new factory from scratch, starting with nothing but a "green field" (101)

greenfield strategy: form of foreign direct investment that involves building new facilities (333)

gross domestic product (GDP): measure of market value of goods and services produced in a country (27)

hard currencies: currencies that are freely tradable; also called convertible currencies (196)

hard loan policy: World Bank lending policy requiring that loans be made only if they are likely to be repaid (160)

hardship premium: supplemental compensation to induce managers to accept relatively unattractive international assignments; also called foreign service premium (590)

harmonization: voluntary adoption of common regulations, policies, and procedures by members of a regional trading bloc to promote internal trade (262)

harmonized tariff schedule (HTS): classification scheme used by many nations to determine tariffs on imported goods (227)

headhunters: recruiting firms that actively seek qualified managers and other professionals for possible placement in positions in other organizations (582)

Heckscher-Ohlin theory: see relative factor endowments, theory of

H-form design: form of organization design in which products are unrelated to each other (373)

high-context culture: culture in which the context in which a discussion is held is equally as important as the actual words that are spoken in conveying the speaker's message to the listener (100)

home country: country in which a firm's headquarters is located (9)

host country: country other than a firm's home country in which it operates (9)

host country nationals (HCNs): employees who are citizens of the host country where an international business operates (579)

human resource management (HRM): set of activities directed at attracting, developing, and maintaining the effective workforce necessary to achieve a firm's objectives (574)

hurdle rate: minimum rate of return a firm finds acceptable for its capital investments (537)

IMF conditionality: restrictions placed on economic policies of countries receiving IMF loans (161)

import of the services of capital: payments that a country's residents make on capital supplied by foreigners (173)

import substitution policy: economic development strategy that relies on the stimulation of domestic manufacturing firms by erecting barriers to imported goods (48, 224)

import tariff: tax levied on goods as they enter a country (227)

importing: buying products made in other countries for use or resale in one's own country (8)

Inc.: abbreviation for incorporated, meaning that the liability of the company's owners is limited to the extent of their investments if the company fails or encounters financial or legal difficulties (8)

inconvertible currencies: currencies that are not freely traded because of legal restrictions imposed by the issuing country or that are not generally accepted by foreigners in settlement of international transactions; also called soft currencies (196)

indirect exchange rate: price of the home currency in terms of the foreign currency; also called indirect quote (191)

indirect exporting: sales of a firm's products to a domestic customer, which in turn exports the product, in either its original form or a modified form (320)

indirect quote: see indirect exchange rate

individualism: cultural belief that the person comes first (104)

industrial democracy: system based on the belief that workers should have a voice in how businesses are run (598)

industrial policy: economic development strategy in which a national government identifies key domestic industries critical to the country's economic future and then formulates policies that promote the international competitiveness of these industries (224)

infant industry argument: argument in favor of governmental intervention in trade: a nation should protect fledgling industries for which the nation will ultimately possess a comparative advantage (220)

informal management network: group of managers from different parts of the world who are connected to one another in some way (386)

information: data in a form that is of value to a manager (444)

information system: methodology created by a firm to gather, assemble, and provide data in a form or forms useful to managers (446)

intellectual property rights: intangible property rights that include patents, copyrights, trademarks, brand names, and trade secrets (135)

interindustry trade: international trade involving the exchange of goods produced in one industry in one country for goods produced in another industry in a different country (131)

intermediaries: third parties that specialize in facilitating imports and exports (324)

internalization advantages: factors that affect the desirability of a firm's producing a good or service itself rather than relying on other firms to control production (316)

internalization theory: theory stating that foreign direct investment occurs because of the high costs of entering into production or procurement contracts with foreign firms (144)

International Accounting Standards Committee (IASC): international organization whose mission is to harmonize the national accounting standards used by various nations (554)

International Bank for Reconstruction and Development (IBRD): official name of the World Bank, which was established by the Bretton Woods agreement to reconstruct the war-torn economies of Western Europe and whose mission changed in the 1950s to aid the development of less developed countries (159)

international banking facility (IBF): entity of a U.S. bank that is exempted from domestic banking regulations as long as it provides only international banking services (208)

international business: business that engages in cross-border commercial transactions with individuals, private firms, and/or public-sector organizations; term is also used to refer to cross-border transactions (5, 11)

International Development Association (IDA): World Bank affiliate that specializes in loans to less developed countries (160)

International Finance Corporation (IFC): World Bank affiliate whose mission is the development of the private sector in developing countries (160)

international Fisher effect: observation that differences in nominal interest rates among countries are due to differences in their expected inflation rates (205)

international investments: capital supplied by residents of one country to residents of another (9)

international logistics: management functions associated with the international flow of materials, parts, supplies, and finished products from suppliers to the firm, between units of the firm itself, and from the firm to customers (501)

international marketing: extension of marketing activities across national boundaries; see also marketing (458)

International Monetary Fund (IMF): agency created by the Bretton Woods Agreement to promote international monetary cooperation after World War II (161)

international monetary system: system by which countries value and exchange their currencies (155)

international operations management: transformation-related activities of an international firm (489)

international order cycle time: time between placement of an order and its receipt by the customer (479)

international service business: firm that transforms resources into an intangible output that creates utility for its customers (503)

international strategic management: comprehensive and ongoing management planning process aimed at formulating and implementing strategies that enable a firm to compete effectively internationally (283)

international strategies: comprehensive frameworks for achieving a firm's fundamental goals (283)

international trade: voluntary exchange of goods, services, or assets between a person or organization located in one country and a person or organization located in another country (123)

international trading company: firm directly engaged in importing and exporting a wide variety of goods for its own account (324)

intracorporate transfer: selling of goods by a firm in one country to an affiliated firm in another country (322)

intraindustry trade: trade between two countries involving the exchange of goods produced by the same industry (131)

invoicing currency: currency in which an international transaction is invoiced (29)

irrevocable letter of credit: letter of credit that cannot be changed without the consent of the buyer, the seller, and the issuing bank (519)

Jamaica Agreement: agreement among central bankers made in 1976, allowing each country to adopt whatever exchange rate system it wished (166)

job satisfaction/dissatisfaction: an attitude that reflects the extent to which an individual is gratified by or fulfilled in his or her work (400)

joint venture (JV): special form of strategic alliance created when two or more firms agree to work together and jointly own a separate firm to promote their mutual interests (335, 344)

just-in-time (JIT) systems: systems in which suppliers are expected to deliver necessary inputs just as they are needed (7)

kabushiki kaisha (KK): in Japan term used to represent all limited-liability companies (8)

keiretsu: family of Japanese companies, often centered around a large bank or trading company, having extensive cross-ownership of shares and interacting with one another as suppliers or customers (38)

Kommanditgesellschaft auf Aktien (KGaA): a form of corporate organization in Germany; a typical KGaA is primarily owned by partners with limited liability, although at least one shareholder must have unlimited liability (8)

labor productivity: measure determined by dividing output by direct labor hours or costs; used to assess how efficiently an organization is using its workforce (437)

leadership: use of noncoercive influence to shape the goals of a group or organization, to motivate behavior toward reaching those goals, and to help determine the group or organizational culture (407)

leads and lags strategy: money management technique in which an MNC attempts to increase its holding of currencies and assets denominated in currencies that are expected to rise in value and to decrease its holdings of currencies and assets denominated in currencies that are expected to fall in value (534)

Leontief paradox: empirical finding that U.S. exports are more labor intensive than U.S. imports, which is contrary to the predictions of the theory of relative factor endowments (130)

letter of credit: document issued by a bank promising to pay the seller if all conditions specified in the letter of credit are met (518)

licensee: firm that buys the rights to use the intellectual property of another firm (326)

licensing: transaction in which a firm (called the licensor) sells the rights to use its intellectual property to another firm (called a licensee) in return for a fee (11, 326)

licensor: firm that sells the rights to use its intellectual property to another firm (326)

lingua franca: common language (90)

location advantages: factors that affect the desirability of host country production relative to home country production (316)

locus of authority: where the power to make various decisions resides within the organization (426)

locus of control: personality trait determining the extent to which people believe that their behavior has a real affect on what happens to them (398)

London Interbank Offer Rate (LIBOR): interest rate that London banks charge each other for short-term Eurocurrency loans (208)

long-term portfolio investments: portfolio investments with maturities of more than one year (174)

Louvre Accord: agreement made in 1987 among central bankers to stabilize the value of the U.S. dollar (168)

low-context culture: culture in which the words being spoken explicitly convey the speaker's message to the listener (100)

Ltd.: abbreviation used in the United Kingdom to indicate a privately held, limited-liability company (8)

Maastricht Treaty: common name given to the Treaty on European Union (264)

macropolitical risk: political risk that affects all firms operating within a country (72)

make-or-buy decision: decision for an organization to either make its own inputs or buy them from outside suppliers (494)

managed float: flexible exchange system in which government intervention plays a major role in determining exchange rates; also called a dirty float (165)

managed trade: see fair trade

management contract: agreement whereby one firm provides managerial assistance, technical expertise, or specialized services to a second firm for some agreed-on time in return for a fee (11, 332)

manufacturers' agents: agents who solicit domestic orders for foreign manufacturers, usually on a commission basis (326)

manufacturers' export agents: agents who act as an export department for domestic manufacturers, selling those firms' goods in foreign markets (326)

maquiladoras: Mexican factories, mostly located along the U.S.-Mexico border, that receive preferential tariff treatment (237)

marketing: process of planning and executing the conception, pricing, promotion, and distribution of ideas, goods, and services to create exchanges that satisfy individual and organizational objectives (458)

marketing alliance: strategic alliance in which two or more firms share marketing services or expertise (352)

marketing mix: how a firm chooses to address product development, pricing, promotion, and distribution (461)

market pricing policy: pricing policy under which prices are set on a market-by-market basis (470)

market socialism: form of socialism that allows significant private ownership of resources (37)

materials management: part of logistics management concerned with the flow of materials into the firm from suppliers and between units of the firm itself (501)

medium: communication channel used by an advertiser to convey a message (474)

message: facts or impressions an advertiser wishes to convey to potential customers (473)

mercantilism: economic philosophy based on the belief that a nation's wealth is measured by its holdings of gold and silver (124)

merchandise export: sale of a good to a resident of a foreign country (173)

merchandise exports and imports: trade involving tangible products (9)

merchandise import: purchase of a good from a resident of a foreign country (173)

Mercosur Accord: customs union composed of Argentina, Brazil, Paraguay, and Uruguay; Bolivia and Chile are associate members (269)

M-form design: form of organization design in which products are related in some way (373)

micropolitical risk: political risk that affects only specific firms or a specific industry operating within a country (72)

mission statement: definition of a firm's values, purpose, and directions (294)

most favored nation (MFN) principle: principle that any preferential treatment granted to one country must be extended to all countries (250)

motivation: overall set of forces that cause people to choose certain behaviors from a set of available behaviors (404)

Multifibre Agreement: commodity agreement among exporting and importing countries of textiles and apparel to control trade in those goods (253)

Multilateral Investment Guarantee Agency (MIGA): World Bank affiliate that offers political risk insurance to investors in developing countries (74, 160)

multilateral netting: netting of transactions between three or more business units (533)

multinational corporation (MNC): incorporated firm that has extensive involvement in international business, engages in foreign direct investment, and owns or controls value-adding activities in more than one country (11)

multinational enterprise (MNE): business that may or may not be incorporated and has extensive involvement in international business (11)

multinational organization (MNO): any organization—business or not-for-profit—with extensive international involvement (11)

mutual recognition: legal concept created by the European Court of Justice; this concept implies that if one EU member determines that a product is valid for sale within its borders, then other EU members must also recognize its validity and allow it to be sold within their borders (263)

naamloze vennootschap (NV): term used in the Netherlands to refer to a publicly held, limited-liability firm (8)

national competitive advantage, theory of: theory stating that success in international trade is based on the interaction of four elements: factor conditions, demand conditions, related and supporting industries, and firm strategy, structure, and rivalry (137)

national defense argument: argument in favor of governmental intervention in trade holding that a nation should be self-sufficient in critical raw materials, machinery, and technology (219)

national treatment: imposing the same standards, regulations, and so forth on foreign firms that are imposed on domestic firms (253)

nationalization: transfer of property from a privately owned firm to the government (64)

needs: the things an individual must have or wants to have (404)

neomercantilists: modern supporters of mercantilism, who hold that a country should erect barriers to trade to protect its industries from foreign competition; also called protectionists (125)

Newly Independent States (NIS): term used to refer collectively to the 15 independent countries created as a result of the breakup of the Soviet Union (35)

nontariff barrier (NTB): any governmental regulation, policy, or procedure other than a tariff that has the effect of impeding international trade (231)

official reserves account: BOP account that records changes in official reserves owned by a central bank (176)

official settlements balance: BOP balance that measures changes in a country's official reserves (180)

offset purchases: form of countertrade in which a portion of the exported good is produced in the importing country (521)

open account: type of payment in which the seller ships goods to the buyer prior to payment; seller relies on the promise of the buyer that payment will be forthcoming (516)

openness: a "big five" personality trait referring to a person's rigidity of beliefs and range of interests (398)

operations control: level of control that focuses on operating processes and systems within both the organization and its subsidiaries and operating units (429)

operations management: set of activities used by an organization to transform different kinds of resource inputs into final goods and services (489)

opportunity cost: value of what is given up to get the good or service in question (126)

organizational commitment: an attitude reflecting an individual's identification with and loyalty to the organization (401)

organizational control: level of control that focuses on the design of the organization itself (425)

organization change: any significant modification or alteration in a firm's strategy, organization design, technology, and/or employees (388)

organization design: overall pattern of structural components and configurations used to manage the total organization; also called organization structure (368)

Organization for Economic Cooperation and Development (OECD): organization whose 30 members are among the world's richest countries and consist of Canada, Mexico, the United States, Japan, Australia, New Zealand, South Korea, and 23 Western European countries (27)

organization structure: see organization design

overall cost leadership strategy: business-level strategy that emphasizes low costs (302)

overall productivity: productivity measure determined by dividing total outputs by total inputs; also called total factor productivity (437)

Overseas Private Investment Corporation (OPIC): U.S. government agency that promotes U.S. international business activities by providing political risk insurance (74, 238)

ownership advantages: resources owned by a firm that grant it a competitive advantage over its industry rivals (315)

ownership advantage theory: theory stating that foreign direct investment occurs because of ownership of valuable assets that confer monopolistic advantages in foreign markets (143)

paper gold: see special drawing rights

par value: official price of a currency in terms of gold (155)

parallel barter: see counterpurchase

parallel importing: market that results from products being imported into a country legally but outside the normal channels of distribution authorized by a manufacturer (synonymous with grey market) (472)

parent country nationals (PCNs): employees who are citizens of an international business's home country and are transferred to one of its foreign operations (578)

passive goal behavior: behavior based on the cultural belief that social relationships, quality of life, and concern for others are the basis of motivation and reflect the goals that a person should pursue (110)

passive income: see Subpart F income

payback period: number of years it takes a project to repay a firm's initial investment in that project (537)

pegged: tied to, as in "The gold standard created a fixed exchange rate system because each country pegged the value of its currency to gold" (155)

per capita income: average income per person in a country (27)

perception: the set of processes by which an individual becomes aware of and interprets information about the environment (402)

performance appraisal: process of assessing how effectively a person is performing his or her job (589)

performance ratio: control technique based on a numerical index of performance that the firm wants to maintain (434)

personal selling: making sales on the basis of personal contacts (476)

personality: the relatively stable set of psychological attributes that distinguish one person from another (397)

planning process control: form of organizational control that focuses on the actual mechanics and processes a firm uses to develop strategic plans (428)

Plaza Accord: agreement made in 1985 among central bankers to allow the U.S. dollar to fall in value (168)

PLC: abbreviation used in the United Kingdom to indicate a publicly held, limited-liability company (8)

political risk: change in the political environment that may adversely affect the value of a firm (72)

political risk assessment: systematic analysis of the political risks that a firm faces when operating in a foreign country (72)

political union: complete political as well as economic integration of two or more countries (256)

polycentric approach: management approach in which a firm customizes its operations for each foreign market it serves (373, 463)

polycentric staffing model: approach primarily using HCNs to staff upper-level foreign positions (580)

portfolio investments: passive holdings of stock, bonds, or other financial assets that do not entail active management or control of the securities' issuer by the investor (10, 140)

power orientation: cultural beliefs about the appropriateness of power and authority in hierarchies such as business organizations (106)

power respect: cultural belief that the use of power and authority is acceptable simply on the basis of position in a hierarchy (106)

power tolerance: cultural belief that the use of power and authority is not acceptable simply on the basis of position in a hierarchy (106)

principle of comity: see comity, principle of

privatization: sale of publicly owned property to private investors (65)

product: international marketing mix component that comprises both tangible factors that the consumer can see or touch and numerous intangible factors (464)

product-support services: assistance a firm provides for customers regarding the operation, maintenance, and/or repair of its products (504)

production alliance: strategic alliance in which two or more firms each manufacture products or provide services in a shared or common facility (351)

production management: international operations management decisions and processes involving the creation of tangible goods (492)

productivity: economic measure of efficiency that summarizes the value of outputs relative to the value of inputs used to create them (437)

promotion: set of all efforts by an international firm to enhance the desirability of its products among potential buyers (472)

promotion mix: mix of advertising, personal selling, sales promotion, and public relations used by a firm to market its products (473)

protectionists: see neomercantilists

Protestant ethic: belief that hard work, frugality, and achievement are means of glorifying God (96)

public choice analysis: branch of economics that analyzes public decision making (225)

public-private venture: joint venture involving a partnership between a privately owned foreign firm and a government (356)

public relations: efforts aimed at enhancing a firm's reputation and image (477)

purchasing power parity (PPP): theory stating that the prices of tradable goods, when expressed in a common currency, will tend to equalize across countries as a result of exchange rate changes (199)

put option: publicly traded contract granting the owner the right, but not the obligation, to sell a specific amount of foreign currency at a specified price at a stated future date (197)

Quad: economic grouping of countries, consisting of Canada, the European Union, Japan, and the United States (26)

quality: totality of features and characteristics of a product or service that bear on its ability to satisfy stated or implied needs (439)

quota: deposit paid by a member nation when joining the International Monetary Fund (161)

quota: numerical limit on the quantity of a good that may be imported into a country (231)

R&D alliance: strategic alliance in which two or more firms agree to undertake joint research to develop new products or services (352)

R&D consortium: confederation of organizations that band together to research and develop new products and processes for world markets (353)

reexporting: process of importation of a good into a country for immediate exportation, with little or no transformation of the good (43)

regional development banks: banks whose mission is to promote economic development of poorer nations within the region they serve (160)

related diversification: corporate-level strategy in which the firm operates in several different but related businesses, industries, or markets at the same time (299)

relative factor endowments, theory of: theory stating that a country will have a comparative advantage in producing goods that intensively use factors of production it has in abundance; also called Heckscher-Ohlin theory (129)

religious law: law based on officially established rules governing the faith and practice of a particular religion (61)

repatriate: to return to a home country (66)

repatriation: moving a manager back home after a foreign assignment has been completed (585)

resource deployment: component of strategy that answers the question "Given that we are going to compete in these markets, how will we allocate our resources to them?" (293)

responsibility center control: form of organizational control based on decentralized responsibility centers (426)

retention: extent to which a firm is able to retain its employees (593)

revocable letter of credit: letter of credit that can be changed by the bank without the consent of the buyer and the seller (519)

ringi system: Japanese approach to ensuring that decisions are made collectively, rather than by an individual (412)

royalty: compensation paid by a licensee to a licensor (327)

rules of origin: rules to determine which goods will benefit from reduced trade barriers in regional trading blocs (255)

sales promotion: specialized marketing efforts using such techniques as coupons and sampling (477)

sanctions: government-imposed restraints against commerce with a foreign country (63)

scope of operations: component of strategy that answers the question "Where are we going to conduct business?" (292)

screwdriver plant: domestic factory that assembles imported parts in which little value is added to the parts (267)

self-efficacy: personality trait determining a person's beliefs about his or her capabilities to perform a task (399)

self-esteem: personality trait determining the extent to which a person believes that he or she is a worthwhile and deserving individual (399)

self-reference criterion: unconscious use of one's own culture to assess and understand a new culture (111)

service export: sale of a service to a resident of a foreign country (173)

service exports and imports: trade involving intangible products (9)

service import: purchase of a service from a resident of a foreign country (173)

service operations management: international operations management decisions and processes involving the creation of intangible services (492)

shared management agreement: management arrangement in which each partner in a strategic alliance fully and actively participates in managing the alliance (357)

short-term portfolio investments: portfolio investments with maturities of one year or less (174)

sight draft: draft that requires payment upon transfer of the goods to the buyer (517)

single-business strategy: corporate-level strategy that calls for a firm to rely on a single business, product, or service for all its revenue (299)

Smithsonian Conference: meeting held in Washington, D.C., in December 1971, during which central bank representatives from the Group of Ten agreed to restore the fixed exchange rate system but with restructured rates of exchange between the major trading currencies (164)

social charter: EU policy promoting common job-related benefits and working conditions throughout the EU; also called social policy (598)

social mobility: ability of individuals to move from one stratum of society to another (88)

social orientation: cultural beliefs about the relative importance of the individual and the groups to which an individual belongs (104)

social policy: see social charter

social stratification: organization of society into hierarchies based on birth, occupation, wealth, educational achievements, and/or other characteristics (86)

società per azioni (SpA): a form of corporate organization in Italy in which owners of the firm enjoy limited liability (8)

soft currencies: see inconvertible currencies

soft loans: loans made by the World Bank Group that bear significant risk of not being repaid (160)

sogo sosha: large Japanese trading company (38)

Southern African Development Community (SADC): free trade area created by twelve Southern African countries (272)

special drawing rights (SDRs): credits granted by the IMF that can be used to settle transactions among central banks; also called paper gold (164)

specific tariff: tax assessed as a specific dollar amount per unit of weight or other standard measure (227)

spot market: market for foreign exchange involving immediate delivery of the currency in question (196)

standard price policy: pricing policy under which a firm charges the same price for its products and services regardless of where they are sold (469)

statistical process control: family of mathematically based tools for monitoring and controlling quality (443)

statutory laws: laws enacted by legislative action (60)

sterling-based gold standard: gold standard in which the British pound is commonly used as an alternative means of settlement of transactions (156)

strategic alliance: business arrangement in which two or more firms choose to cooperate for their mutual benefit (344)

strategic business units (SBUs): "bundles" of businesses created by a firm using a corporate strategy of either related or unrelated diversification (301)

strategic control: process of monitoring how well an international business formulates and implements its strategies (423)

strategic goals: major objectives a firm wants to accomplish through the pursuit of a particular course of action (297)

strategic planning: process of developing a particular international strategy (283)

strategic trade theory: theory addressing the optimal policies through which a government may benefit its country by aiding domestic firms in monopolistic or highly oligopolistic industries (221)

stress: an individual's response to a strong stimulus (402)

stressor: a stimulus that results in stress (402)

Subpart F income: income earned from financial transactions, such as dividends, interest, and royalties; also called passive income (565)

subsidiary bank: separately incorporated overseas banking operation (206)

Super 301: section of U.S. trade law that requires the U.S. trade representative to publicly identify countries that flagrantly engage in unfair trade practices (240)

supply chain management: set of processes and steps a firm uses to acquire raw materials, parts, and other resources it needs to create its own products (493)

swap market: facet of international capital market in which two firms can exchange financial obligations (540)

swap transaction: transaction involving the simultaneous purchase and sale of a foreign currency with delivery at two different points in time (196)

switching arrangements: agreement under which firms may transfer their countertrade obligations to a third party (522)

SWOT analysis: analysis of a firm and its environment to determine its strengths, weaknesses, opportunities, and threats (295)

synergy: component of strategy that answers the question "How can different elements of our business benefit each other?" (293)

tactics: methods used by middle managers to implement strategic plans (297)

tariff: tax placed on a good involved in international trade (227)

tariff rate quota: a type of quota that imposes a low tariff rate on a limited amount of imports of a specific good into the country but then subjects all imports above that threshold to a prohibitively high tariff (231)

tax equalization system: system for ensuring that an expatriate's after-tax income in the host country is compara-

ble to what the person's after-tax income would be in the home country (592)

tax havens: countries that charge low, often zero, taxes on corporate incomes and that offer an attractive business climate (563)

technology transfer: the transmittal of technology from one country to another (69)

temporal method: approach used to consolidate the financial statements of a foreign subsidiary whose functional currency is the U.S. dollar (558)

theocracy: country whose legal system is based on religious law (61)

theory of absolute advantage: see absolute advantage, theory of

theory of comparative advantage: see comparative advantage, theory of

theory of national competitive advantage: see national competitive advantage, theory of

theory of purchasing power parity: see purchasing power parity (PPP)

theory of relative factor endowments: see relative factor endowments, theory of

third-country nationals (TCNs): employees of an international business who are not citizens of the firm's home or host country (579)

three-point arbitrage: arbitrage based on exploiting differences between the direct rate of exchange between two currencies and their cross rate of exchange using a third currency (201)

time draft: draft that requires payment at some specified time after the transfer of goods to the buyer (517)

time orientation: cultural beliefs regarding long-term versus short-term outlooks on work, life, and other aspects of society (111)

total factor productivity: see overall productivity

total quality management (TQM): integrated effort to systematically and continuously improve the quality of an organization's products and/or services (443)

trade: voluntary exchange of goods, services, or assets between one person or organization and another (123)

trade acceptance: time draft that has been signed by the buyer signifying a promise to honor the payment terms (517)

trade deflection: rerouting of exported goods to the member of a free trade area with the lowest barriers to imports from nonmember countries (255)

trade in invisibles: British term denoting trade in services (173)

trade in visibles: British term referring to merchandise trade (173)

training: instruction directed at enhancing job-related skills and abilities (587)

transaction costs: costs of negotiating, monitoring, and enforcing a contract (144)

transaction currency: currency in which an international transaction is denominated (192)

transaction exposure: financial risks that occur because the financial benefits and costs of an international transaction may be affected by exchange rate movements occurring after the firm is legally obligated to the transaction (526)

transfer pricing: prices that one branch or subsidiary of a parent firm charges for goods, services, or property sold to a second branch or subsidiary of the same parent firm (560)

transit tariff: tax levied on goods as they pass through one country bound for another (227)

translation: process of transforming the accounting statements of a foreign subsidiary into the home country's currency using the home country's accounting procedures (557)

translation exposure: impact on a firm's consolidated financial statements of fluctuations in foreign exchange rates that change the value of foreign subsidiaries as measured in the parent's currency (528)

treasury management: management of financial flows and their associated currency and interest-rate risks (543)

Treaty for Europe: see Treaty of Amsterdam

Treaty of Amsterdam: 1997 treaty furthering integration among EU members (265)

Treaty of Rome: treaty signed in 1957 that established the European Economic Community; its original six signatories have expanded to 15 over time (257)

Treaty on European Union: treaty signed in 1992 that came into force on November 1, 1993, furthering economic and political integration of the EC's members; important provisions include the creation of an economic and monetary union, a cohesion fund, a pledge to cooperate on foreign and defense policies, and the renaming of the EC as the European Union; commonly known as the Maastricht Treaty (264)

Triad: grouping of countries that dominate the world economy, consisting of the European Union, Japan, and the United States (26)

Triffin paradox: paradox that resulted from reliance on the U.S. dollar as the primary source of liquidity in the Bretton Woods system; for trade to grow, foreigners needed to hold more dollars; the more dollars they held, however, the less faith they had in the U.S. dollar, thereby undermining the Bretton Woods system (164)

turnkey project: contract under which a firm agrees to fully design, construct, and equip a facility and then turn the project over to the purchaser when it is ready for operation (332)

turnover: rate at which people leave an organization (593)

two-point arbitrage: riskless purchase of a product in one geographic market for immediate resale in a second geographic market to profit from price differences between the markets; also called geographic arbitrage (201)

two-tiered pricing policy: pricing policy under which a firm sets one price for all its domestic sales and a second price for all its international sales (469)

two-transaction approach: approach used by U.S. firms to account on their income statements for transactions denominated in foreign currencies (556)

U-form organization: form of organization design based on global functional design (377)

uncertainty acceptance: cultural belief that uncertainty and ambiguity are stimulating and present new opportunities (108)

uncertainty avoidance: cultural belief that uncertainty and ambiguity are unpleasant and should be avoided (108)

uncertainty orientation: cultural beliefs about uncertainty and ambiguity (108)

unilateral transfers: gifts made by residents of one country to residents of another country (173)

unrelated diversification: corporate-level strategy that calls for a firm to operate in several unrelated businesses, industries, or markets (300)

Uruguay Round: GATT negotiations (1986–1994) that created the World Trade Organization, slashed tariff rates, and strengthened enforcement of intellectual property rights (251)

value chain: technique for assessing a firm's strengths and weaknesses by identifying its most important activities (296)

values: the things that people believe to be important (404)

vertical integration: extent to which a firm either provides its own resources or obtains them from other sources (493)

voluntary export restraint (VER): promise by a country to limit its exports of a good to another country (232)

Webb-Pomerene association: group of U.S. firms that operate within the same industry and that are allowed by law to coordinate their export activities without fear of violating U.S. antitrust laws (324)

"wider vs. deeper": debate among EU members, with those arguing for "wider" wanting to expand membership as a first priority and those arguing for "deeper" wanting to more thoroughly integrate existing members as a first priority (266)

with recourse: term signifying that should a trade acceptance or banker's acceptance sold by an exporter to an investor fail to be paid, the exporter will reimburse the investor; the exporter retains the risk of default by the signer of the acceptance (517)

without recourse: term signifying that should a trade acceptance or banker's acceptance sold by an exporter to an investor fail to be paid, the exporter is not obligated to reimburse the investor; the investor retains the risk of default by the signer of the acceptance (517)

World Bank: see International Bank for Reconstruction and Development

World Bank Group: organization consisting of the World Bank and its affiliated organizations, the International Development Agency, the International Finance Corporation, and the Multilateral Investment Guarantee Agency (159)

World Trade Organization (WTO): successor organization to the GATT founded in 1995; created by the Uruguay Round negotiations (252)

Photo Credits

Company Index

Subject Index

Your personal guide to the content-rich, free online resources for Griffin/Pustay

INTERNATIONAL BUSINESS, THIRD EDITION!

Featuring one-click access to all of the **new** resources created by our award-winning team of educators, myPHLIP provides a **personalized view** of the great new resources available:

NEW **myPHLIP pages**—Your personal access page unites all your Prentice Hall myPHLIP texts.

NEW **Notes**—Add personal notes to our resources for personal reminders and references.

NEW **Messages**—Instructors can send messages to individual students or to all students linked to your course.

NEW **Student Resources**—Instructors can add premium PHLIP resources for students to view and download (such as our PowerPoints and spreadsheets).

NEW **Syllabus**—New and improved online syllabus tools help instructors add personal syllabi to our site in minutes.

NEW **Business Headlines**—Provide links to articles in today's business news!

NEW **Search**—Search all PHLIP resources for relevant articles and exercises.

NEW **Instructor's Manual**—myPHLIP Instructor's Manual provides tips and suggestions from our PHLIP faculty for integrating PHLIP resources into your course.

NEW **Online Learning Solutions**—In Blackboard, WebCT, and Pearson CourseCompass (free with new text purchase). Standard courses include traditional online course features:

- Online Testing
- Course Management and Page Tracking
- Syllabus and Calendar Functions
- Course Information

- Multiple-Section Chat Rooms
- Bulletin Board Conferencing
- Gradebook
- E-mail Capability